Library of Congress Cataloging-in-Publication Data

Jenkins, Dennis R.
X-15 : extending the frontiers of flight / Dennis R. Jenkins.
p. cm.
Includes bibliographical references and index.
ISBN 978-0-16-079285-4
1. X-15 (Rocket aircraft)--History. 2. Aerodynamics, Hypersonic--Research--United States--History. I. Title.
TL789.8.U6X5532 2007
629.133'38--dc22

2007042448

ISBN 978-0-16-079285-4

For sale by the Superintendent of Documents, U.S. Government Printing Office
Internet: bookstore.gpo.gov Phone: toll free (866) 512-1800; DC area (202) 512-1800
Fax: (202) 512-2104 Mail: Stop IDCC, Washington, DC 20402-0001

ISBN 978-0-16-079285-4

X-15: Extending the Frontiers Of Flight

Dennis R. Jenkins

SP-2007-562

X-15 ready for flight on the flight line. (NASA)

FOREWORD: WILLIAM H. DANA

The X-15 was an airplane of accelerations. When an X-15 pilot looks back on his X-15 flights, it is the accelerations he remembers. The first of these sensations was the acceleration due to B-52 lift, which held the X-15 at launch altitude and prevented it from falling to Earth. When the X-15 pilot hit the launch switch, the B-52 lift was no longer accessible to the X-15. The X-15 fell at the acceleration due to Earth's gravity, which the pilot recognized as "free fall" or "zero g." Only when the pilot started the engine and put some "g" on the X-15 was this sensation of falling relieved.

The next impression encountered on the X-15 flight came as the engine lit, just a few seconds after launch. A 33,000-pound airplane was accelerated by a 57,000-lbf engine, resulting in a chest-to-back acceleration of almost 2 g. Then, as the propellant burned away and the atmosphere thinned with increasing altitude, the chest-to-back acceleration increased and the drag caused by the atmosphere lessened. For a standard altitude mission (250,000 feet), the weight and thrust were closer to 15,000 pounds and 60,000-lbf at shutdown, resulting in almost 4-g chest-to-back acceleration. The human body is not stressed for 4 g chest to back, and by shutdown the boost was starting to get a little painful. Milt Thompson once observed that the X-15 was the only aircraft he had ever flown where he was glad when the engine quit.

On a mission to high altitude (above 250,000 feet), the pilot did not regain any sensible air with which to execute a pullout until about 180,000 feet, and could not pull 1 g of lift until 130,000 feet. Flying a constant angle of attack on reentry, the pilot allowed g to build up to 5, and then maintained 5 g until the aircraft was level at about 80,000 feet. There was a deceleration from Mach 5 at 80,000 feet to about Mach 1 over the landing runway, and the pilot determined the magnitude of the deceleration by the use of speed brakes. This ended the high-g portion of the flight, except for one pilot who elected to start his traffic pattern at 50,000 feet and Mach 2, and flew a 360-degree overhead pattern from that starting point.

Flight to high altitude represented about two-thirds of the 199 X-15 flights. Flights to high speed or high dynamic pressure accounted for the other third, and those flights remained well within the atmosphere for the entire mission. The pilot of a high-speed flight got a small taste of chest-to-back acceleration during the boost (thrust was still greater than drag, but not by such a large margin as on the high-altitude flights). The deceleration after burnout was a new sensation. This condition was high drag and zero thrust, and it had the pilot hanging in his shoulder straps, with perspiration dripping off the tip of his nose onto the inside of his face plate.

Milt Thompson collected anecdotes about the X-15 that remain astonishing to this day. Milt noted that at Mach 5, a simple 20-degree heading change required 5 g of normal acceleration for 10 seconds. Milt also pointed out that on a speed flight, the (unmodified) X-15-1 accelerated from Mach 5 to Mach 6 in six seconds. These were eye-opening numbers at the time of the X-15 program.

Those of us in the program at flight 190 thought that the X-15 would continue indefinitely. Then, on flight 191, Major Michael J. Adams experienced electrical irregularities that made the inertial flight instruments unreliable and may have disoriented him. In any case, at peak altitude (266,000 feet), the X-15 began a yaw to the right. It reentered the atmosphere, yawed crosswise to the flight path, and went into a high-speed spin. It eventually came out of the spin but broke up during the reentry, killing the pilot.

The loss of the airplane and pilot was the death knell for the entire program. Program management decided not to fly the X-15A-2 again, and to fly X-15-1 only for calendar year 1968. The X-15 flew its last flight on 24 October of that year, and then faded into aeronautical history.

William H. Dana
Test Pilot, Dryden Flight Research Center
Pilot, last X-15 flight

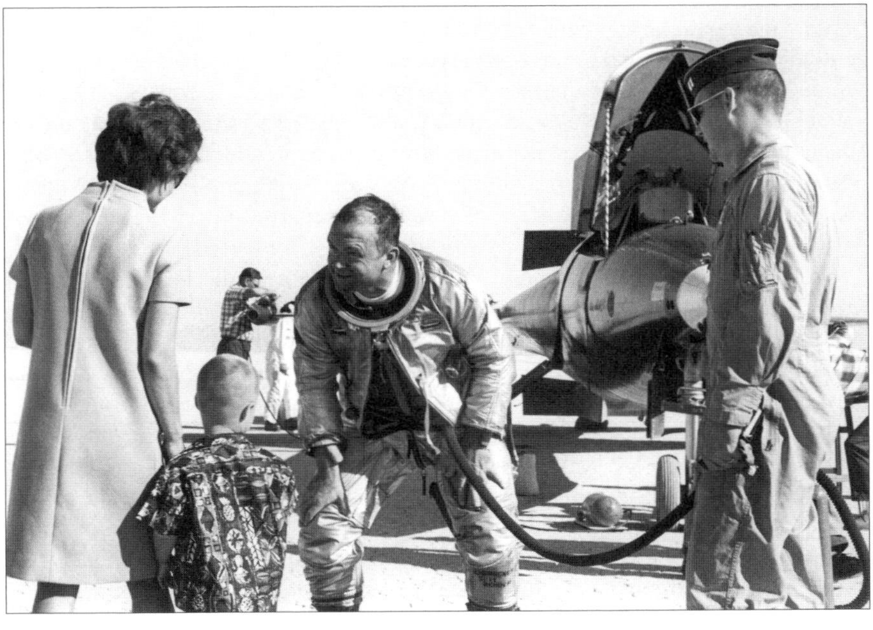

Bill Dana greets his family after the last flight of the X-15 program on 24 October 1968. (NASA)

PREFACE: ROCKETS OVER THE HIGH DESERT

Neil Armstrong, among others, has called the X-15 "the most successful research airplane in history." That might be stretching a point, but it was certainly the most successful of the high-speed X-planes. Given the major advances in materials and computer technology made in the 40 years since the flight program ended, it is unlikely that many of the actual hardware lessons are still applicable. Having said that, the lessons learned from hypersonic modeling and pilot-in-the-loop simulation, and the insight gained by being able to evaluate actual X-15 flight test results against wind-tunnel and theoretical predictions greatly expanded the confidence of researchers during the 1970s and 1980s.[1]

It would not have surprised anybody involved that the actual X-15 technology did not find further application. Researchers such as John Becker and Norris Dow, and engineers like Harrison Storms and Charlie Feltz never intended the design to represent anything other than a convenient platform to acquire aero-thermo data. Becker once opined that proceeding with a general research configuration rather than a prototype of a vehicle designed to achieve a specific mission was critical to the ultimate success of the X-15. Had the prototype route been taken, Becker believed, "we would have picked the wrong mission, the wrong structure, the wrong aerodynamic shapes, and the wrong propulsion." They are good words of advice.[2]

In fact, the decision to pursue a pure research shape was somewhat controversial at the beginning. Kelly Johnson, for one, believed the vehicle should be adaptable as a strategic reconnaissance aircraft. Indeed, several of the proposals for the X-15 sought to design a vehicle with some future application. Nevertheless, the original Langley concept of a vehicle optimized to collect the desired data as safely as possible ultimately won. As Harley Soulé told Harrison Storms, "You have a little airplane and a big engine with a large thrust margin. We want to go to 250,000 feet altitude and Mach 6. We want to study aerodynamic heating. We do not want to worry about aerodynamic stability and control, or the airplane breaking up. So, if you make any errors, make them on the strong side. You should have enough thrust to do the job." North American succeeded brilliantly.[3]

It had taken 44 years to go from Kitty Hawk to Chuck Yeager's first supersonic flight in the X-1. Six more years were required before Scott Crossfield got to Mach 2 in the D-558-2 Skyrocket. A remarkably short three years had passed when Mel Apt coaxed the X-2 above Mach 3, before tumbling out of control to his death. There progress stalled, awaiting the arrival of the three small black airplanes that would more than double the speed and altitude milestones.

The X-15 flight program began slowly, mostly because the XLR99 was not ready. This undoubtedly worked in the program's favor since it forced the engineers and pilots to gain experience with the airplane and its systems prior to

1 The Armstrong quote is in the foreword to Milton O. Thompson, *At the Edge of Space: the X-15 Flight Program* (Washington, DC: Smithsonian Institution Press, 1992), p. xii.

2 John V. Becker, "The X-15 Program in Retrospect," 3rd Eugen Sänger Memorial Lecture, Bonn, Germany, 5 December 1968, pp. 1-2

3 Harrison A. Storms, "X-15 Hardware Design Challenges," a paper in the *Proceedings of the X-15 30th Anniversary Celebration*, Dryden Flight Research Facility, Edwards, California, 8 June 1989, NASA CP-3105, p. 27.

pushing the envelope too far. The first 20 months took the X-15 from Crossfield's glide flight to essentially duplicating the performance of the X-2: Mach 3.5 and 136,500 feet. Then the XLR99s arrived and things got serious. Six days after the last flight with the interim XLR11s, Bob White took X-15-2 past Mach 4, the first time a piloted aircraft had flown that fast. Mach 5 fell, also to Bob White, four months later. Mach 6, again to White, took six more months. Once the X-15 began flying with the ultimate engine, it took only 15 flights to double the maximum Mach number achieved by the X-2.

Altitude was a similar story. Iven Kincheloe was the first person to fly above 100,000 feet, in the X-2 on 7 September 1956. Thirteen flights with the big engine allowed Bob White to fly above 200,000 feet for the first time. Three months later, he broke 300,000 feet. Once it began flying with the ultimate engine, the X-15 took only 19 months to double the maximum altitude achieved by the X-2. These were stunning achievements.

It is interesting to note that although the X-15 is generally considered a Mach 6 aircraft, only two of the three airplanes ever flew that fast, and then only four times. On the other hand, 108 other flights exceeded Mach 5, accumulating 1 hour, 25 minutes, and 33 seconds of hypersonic flight. At the other end of the spectrum, just two flights were not supersonic (one of these was the first glide flight), and only 14 others did not exceed Mach 2. It was a fast airplane. Similarly, there were only four flights above 300,000 feet (all by X-15-3), but only the initial glide flight was below 40,000 feet.[4]

Despite appearances, however, the program was not about setting records.[5] The actual speed and altitude achieved by the program was not the ultimate test, and the fact that the basic airplane never achieved its advertised 6,600 feet per second velocity was of little consequence. What interested the researchers was the environment in which the airplane flew. They wanted to study dynamic pressures, heating rates, and total temperatures. More specifically, the goals were to:

1. Verify existing (1954) theory and wind-tunnel techniques
2. Study aircraft structures and stability and control under high (2,000 psf) dynamic pressures
3. Study aircraft structures under high (1,200°F) heating
4. Investigate stability and control problems associated with high-altitude boost and reentry
5. Investigate the biomedical effects of both weightless and high-g flight

The X-15 achieved all of these design goals, although Project Mercury and other manned space efforts quickly eclipsed the airplane's contribution to

4 In the 3rd Eugen Sänger Memorial Lecture in 1968, John Becker stated that 109 flights exceeded Mach 5. A reevaluation of the flight data shows that only 108 actually did. See Becker, "The X-15 Program in Retrospect," p. 3 for Becker's original numbers.

5 Despite all that is written, the program held very few "official" records, mainly because it seldom invited the FAI out to witness the flights. In fact, it appears that the 314,750-foot altitude record set by Bob White is the only official record ever set by the program.

weightless research. The program ultimately achieved a velocity of 6,629 fps (with X-15A-2), 354,200 feet altitude, 1,350°F, and dynamic pressures over 2,200 psf.[6]

With 40 years of hindsight, it is apparent that the most important lessons to be learned from the X-15 concern not the hardware, but the culture. The world was different during the 1950s, certainly within the government-contracting environment. The military and NACA initiated and funded the X-15 program without congressional approval or oversight, although this was not an effort to hide the program or circumvent the appropriations process. The military services had contingency funds available to use as they saw fit. They ultimately needed to explain to Congress and the White House how they spent the funds, but there was little second-guessing from the politicians. This allowed the program to ramp up quickly and absorb the significant cost overruns that would come. Following its likely origin in February 1954, the Air Force awarded the X-15 development contract in September 1955 and North American rolled out the first airplane in October 1958. The maiden glide flight was in June 1959, just over five years from a gleam in John Becker's eye to Scott Crossfield soaring over the high desert. It could not happen today.

There is a story in the main text about a meeting Harrison Storms attended at Edwards, and some important words of wisdom: "[T]here is a very fine line between stopping progress and being reckless. That the necessary ingredient in this situation of solving a sticky problem is attitude and approach. The answer, in my opinion, is what I refer to as 'thoughtful courage.' If you don't have that, you will very easily fall into the habit of 'fearful safety' and end up with a very long and tedious-type solution at the hands of some committee. This can very well end up giving a test program a disease commonly referred to as 'cancelitis,' which results in little or no progress."[7]

Storms must have had a crystal ball. In today's environment, the system will not allow programs to have problems. If the Air Force and NASA were trying to develop the X-15 today, Congress would cancel it long before the first flight. A series of configuration changes and production problems added weight and lowered the expected performance before the airplane flew. The XLR99 engine was tremendously behind schedule, so much so that the program selected interim engines just to allow the airplane to begin flying. Ultimately, however, the airplane and the engine were hugely successful. Compare this to how the X-33 program reacted to issues with its composite propellant tanks.

When Crossfield finally released from the carrier aircraft on the initial glide flight in X-15-1, his landing was less than ideal. In today's world, the program would have stood down to work out this issue and assess the risk. In 1959 North

6 Ronald G. Boston, "Outline of the X-15's Contributions to Aerospace Technology," 21 November 1977. Unpublished preliminary version of the typescript available in the NASA Dryden History Office. For those interested in Boston's original paper, the easiest place to find a copy is in the *Hypersonic Revolution*, republished by the Air Force History and Museums program. It constitutes the last section in the X-15 chapter; Letter, William H. Dana, Chief, Flight Crew Branch, DFRC, to Lee Saegesser NASA History Office, transmitting a copy of the SETP paper for the file. A slightly rewritten (more politically correct) version of the paper was later published as *The X-15 Airplane—Lessons Learned* (American Institute of Aeronautics and Astronautics, a paper prepared for the 31st Aerospace Sciences Meeting, Reno Nevada, AIAA-93-0309, 11-14 January 1993). Boston listed 1,300°F as the maximum temperature, but Bill Dana reported 1,350°F in his SETP and AIAA papers. Boston also listed the max-q as 2,000 psf, but in reality it was 2,202 psf on Flight 1-66-111.

7 Storms, "X-15 Hardware Design Challenges," pp. 32-33

American made some adjustments and launched Crossfield again three months later. It was a short-lived reprieve. Less than 60 days later, Crossfield broke the back of X-15-2 during a hard landing that followed an in-flight abort. Instead of canceling the program, the X-15 went back to the factory for repair. Three months later Crossfield was flying again.

During the initial ground-testing of the ultimate XLR99 engine in X-15-3 at Edwards, an explosion destroyed the airplane. Nobody was seriously hurt and North American subsequently rebuilt the airplane with an advanced flight control system intended for the stillborn X-20 Dyna-Soar. The program was flying two months later using X-15-1 and the rebuilt X-15-3 went on to become the high-altitude workhorse.

It was the same across the board. When Jack McKay made his emergency landing at Mud Lake that essentially destroyed X-15-2, the Air Force did not cancel the program. Five weeks later Bob White made a Mach 5.65 flight in X-15-3; McKay was his NASA-1. North American rebuilt X-15-2 and the airplane began flying again 18 months later. Jack McKay went on to fly 22 more X-15 flights, although the lingering effects of his injuries shortened his lifetime considerably.

In each case the program quickly analyzed the cause of the failure, instituted appropriate changes, and moved on. Always cautious, never reckless. No prolonged down times. No thought of cancellation. It would not happen that way today. One of the risks when extending any frontier is that you do not understand all the risks.

Paul Bikle, the director of the Flight Research Center, had long warned that the flight program should end when it achieved the design speed and altitude. However, the X-15s provided an ideal platform for follow-on experiments that had little or nothing to do with the design aero-thermo research mission. The temptation was too great, and NASA extended the flight program several years. Bikle knew that eventually the odds would catch up with the program. The day they did, Mike Adams was at the controls of X-15-3, and the consequences were as bad as anything Bikle could have imagined. The crash killed Mike Adams and destroyed X-15-3. Even so, the program made sure it learned from the accident and was flying again less than four months later. This time, however, it would not be for long. Eight more flights were conducted before the program ended when funding expired at the end of 1968.

John Becker, arguably the father of the X-15, once stated that the project came along at "the most propitious of all possible times for its promotion and approval." At the time, it was not considered necessary to have a defined operational program in order to conduct basic research. There were no "glamorous and expensive" manned space projects to compete for funding, and the general feeling within the nation was one of trying to go faster, higher, or further. In today's environment, as in 1968 when Becker made his comment, it is highly unlikely that a program such as the X-15 could gain approval.[8]

Dill Hunley, a former DFRC historian, once opined that "This situation should give pause to those who fund aerospace projects solely on the basis of their presumably predictable outcomes and their expected cost effectiveness. Without

8 Becker, "The X-15 Program in Retrospect," pp. 1-2

the X-15's pioneering work, it is quite possible that the manned space program would have been slowed, conceivably with disastrous consequences for national prestige." It is certain that the development of the Space Shuttle would have carried a far greater risk if not for the lessons learned from the development and flight-testing of the X-15. Fifty years later, the X-15 experience still provides the bulk of the available hypersonic data available to aircraft designers.[9]

Perhaps we have not learned well enough.

Dennis R. Jenkins
Cape Canaveral, Florida

9 J. D. Hunley, "The Significance of the X-15," 1999, unpublished. Typescript available at the DFRC History Office.

ACKNOWLEDGMENTS

Robert S. Houston, a historian at the Air Force Wright Air Development Center, wrote the most frequently quoted X-15 history in 1959. This narrative, unsurprisingly, centered on the early Air Force involvement in the program, and concentrated mostly—as is normal for Air Force histories—on the program management aspects rather than the technology. Dr. Richard P. Hallion, later the chief historian for the U.S. Air Force, updated Houston's history in 1987 as part of volume II of *The Hypersonic Revolution*, a collection of papers published by the Aeronautical Systems Office at Wright-Patterson AFB. Hallion added coverage of the last nine years of the program, drawing mainly from his own *On the Frontier: Flight Research at Dryden, 1946-1981* (Washington, DC: NASA, 1984) and "Outline of the X-15's Contributions to Aerospace Technology," written in 1977 by Ronald G. Boston. These historians did an excellent job, but unfortunately their work received comparatively limited distribution.

I began this history by using these earlier works as a basis, checking the sources, expanding upon them as appropriate, and adding a NACA/NASA and Navy perspective. Amazingly, almost all of the original source documentation still existed in one archive or another, allowing an evaluation of the tone and inflection of some of the earliest material. Although it is largely a new work, anybody who is intimately familiar with the earlier histories will recognize some passages—the original historians did a remarkably thorough job.

Many people assisted in the preparation of this work, and all gave generously and freely, well beyond any reasonable expectation an author might have. Foremost were Betty J. Love, Tony Landis at Dryden, and Dr. Roger D. Launius at the National Air and Space Museum. The surviving X-15 pilots—Neil A. Armstrong, A. Scott Crossfield, William H. Dana, Brigadier General Joe H. Engle (USAF, Retired), Colonel William J. "Pete" Knight (USAF, Retired), and Major General Robert M. White (USAF, Retired)—contributed immensely, and several of them read the manuscript multiple times to ensure that nothing significant was missed or misrepresented. John V. Becker and Charles H. Feltz spent many hours explaining things I probably should have already known, greatly improving the manuscript. Then there are the flight planners—Johnny G. Armstrong,[10] Richard E. Day, and Robert G. Hoey. I would have missed many subtleties without the patient tutoring from these engineers, all of whom read and commented on several versions of this manuscript and continued my education well past my two engineering degrees.

There was correspondence with many individuals who had been involved with the program: William P. Albrecht, Colonel John E. "Jack" Allavie (USAF, Retired), Colonel Clarence E. "Bud" Anderson (USAF, Retired), Bill Arnold (RMD/Thiokol, Retired), Colonel Charles C. Bock, Jr., (USAF, Retired), Jerry Brandt, Richard J. Harer, Gerald M. Truszynski, and Alvin S. White. In addition,

10 Officially, Johnny Armstrong (who is now the chief engineer in the Hypersonic Flight Test Team) maintains the AFFTC Hypersonic Flight Test Team Project Files and is, fortunately, something of a pack rat. However, to everybody at Edwards and Dryden, this wonderful collection is simply the Armstrong Memorial Library.

Jack Bassick at the David Clark Company, Stephen J. Garber and Colin A. Fries at the NASA History Office, Michael J. Lombardi at the Boeing Company Archives, Air Force Chief Historian Dr. Richard P. Hallion, Dr. James H. Young and Cheryl Gumm at the AFFTC History Office, and John D. "Jack" Weber at the AFMC History Office all provided excellent support. Friends and fellow authors Gerald H. Balzer, Robert E. Bradley, Benjamin F. Guenther, Scott Lowther, Mike Machat, Michael Moore, Terry Panopalis, and Mick Roth also assisted.

Others who contributed include Lynn Albaugh at Ames, Jack Beilman, Rodney K. Bogue at DFRC, Anita Borger at Ames, John W. Boyd at Ames, Russell Castonguay at the JPL archives, Erik M. Conway at Langley and NASM, Mark L. Evans at the Naval Historical Center, Dr. Michael H. Gorn at the DFRC History Office, Matt Graham at DFRC, Fred W. Haise, Jr., Wesley B. Henry at the Air Force Museum, T.A. Heppenheimer, James B. Hill at the John Fitzgerald Kennedy Library, Dr. J. D. "Dill" Hunley at the DFRC History Office, Kenneth W. Iliff (DFRC, Retired), Bob James (DFRC, Retired), Jack Kittrell (DFRC, Retired), Christian Ledet, F. Robert van der Linden at the National Air and Space Museum, Marilyn Meade at the University of Wisconsin, Roger E. Moore, Claude S. Morse at the AEDC, Karen Moze at Ames, Doug Nelson at the AFFTC Museum, Anne-Laure Perret at the Fédération Aéronautique Internationale (FAI), Colonel Bruce A. Peterson (USMCR, Retired), Charles E. Rogers at the AFFTC, Mary F. Shafer (DFRC, Retired), Bonita S. Smith at GRC, Colonel Donald M. Sorlie (USAF, Retired), and Henry Spencer.

It all would never have seen the light of day had it not been for Tony Springer of the Aeronautics Research Mission Directorate at NASA Headquarters.

Special Thanks

I owe a particular mention of Jay Miller, author of the popular *The X-planes: X-1 to X-45,* (Hinckley, England: Midland Publishing, 2001), among many other works. Anybody interested in reading about the other X-planes should pick up a copy of this excellent book. Jay was responsible for the first photograph I ever had published, and published my first book—a short monograph on the Space Shuttle. Somehow, I feel I have him to blame for the quagmire of aerospace history I find myself embroiled in. I truly appreciate the help and friendship from Jay and his lovely wife Susan over the past 25 years or so.

Thankfully, my mother, Mrs. Mary E. Jenkins, encouraged me to seize opportunities and taught me to write and type—such necessary attributes for this endeavor. As for so many things, I owe her a great deal of gratitude, along with my everlasting love and admiration. After listening to my trials and tribulations about this project for a decade, she passed away before publication. I hope she has found the peace and rest she so richly deserves.

A note regarding terminology: In the days before being politically correct became a prime influence on engineering and history, engineers called piloted vehicles "manned" aircraft, and the process of making them safe enough to fly was termed "man-rating." This work continues to use these terms since they are what were in use at the time.

CHAPTER 1

A New Science

The first 50 years of powered human flight were marked by a desire to always go faster and higher. At first, the daredevils—be they racers or barnstormers—drove this. By the end of the 1930s, however, increases in speed and altitude were largely the province of government—the cost of designing and building the ever-faster aircraft was becoming prohibitive for individuals. As is usually the case, war increased the tempo of development, and two major conflicts within 30 years provided a tremendous impetus for advancements in aviation. By the end of World War II the next great challenge was in sight: the "sound barrier" that stood between the pilots and supersonic flight.

Contrary to general perception, the speed of sound was not a discovery of the 20th century. Over 250 years before Chuck Yeager made his now-famous flight in the X-1, it was known that sound propagated through air at some constant velocity. During the 17th century, artillerymen determined that the speed of sound was approximately 1,140 feet per second (fps) by standing a known distance away from a cannon and using simple timing devices to measure the delay between the muzzle flash and the sound of the discharge. Their conclusion was remarkably accurate. Two centuries later the National Advisory Committee for Aeronautics[1]

1 In an unusually far-sighted move, on 3 March 1915 Congress passed a public law establishing an "Advisory Committee for Aeronautics." As stipulated in the act, the purpose of this committee was "to supervise and direct the scientific study of the problems of flight with a view to their practical solution" and to "direct and conduct research and experiment in aeronautics."

(NACA) defined the speed of sound as 1,117 fps on an ISO standard day, although this number is for engineering convenience and does not represent a real value.[2]

The first person to recognize an aerodynamic anomaly near the speed of sound was probably Benjamin Robins, an 18th-century British scientist who invented a ballistic pendulum that measured the velocity of cannon projectiles. As described by Robins, a large wooden block was suspended in front of a cannon and the projectile was fired into it. The projectile transferred momentum to the block, and the force could be determined by measuring the amplitude of the pendulum. During these experiments, Robins observed that the drag on a projectile appeared to increase dramatically as it neared the speed of sound. It was an interesting piece of data, but there was no practical or theoretical basis for investigating it further.[3]

The concept of shock waves associated with the speed of sound also predated the 20th century. As an object moves through the atmosphere, the air molecules near the object are disturbed and move around the object. If the object passes at low speed (typically less than 200 mph), the density of the air will remain relatively constant, but at higher speeds some of the energy of the object will compress the air, locally changing its density. This compressibility effect alters the resulting force on the object and becomes more important as the speed increases. Near the speed of sound the compression waves merge into a strong shock wave that affects both the lift and drag of an object, resulting in significant challenges for aircraft designers.[4]

Austrian physicist Ernst Mach took the first photographs of supersonic shock waves using a technique called shadowgraphy. In 1877 Mach presented a paper to the Academy of Sciences in Vienna, where he showed a shadowgraph of a bullet moving at supersonic speeds; the bow and trailing-edge shock waves were clearly visible. Mach was also the first to assign a numerical value to the ratio between the speed of a solid object passing through a gas and the speed of sound through the same gas. In his honor, the "Mach number" is used as the engineering unit for supersonic velocities. The concept of compressibility effects on objects moving at high speeds was established, but little actual knowledge of the phenomena existed.[5]

None of these experiments had much impact on the airplanes of the early 20th century since their flight speeds were so low that compressibility effects were

---

2 John D. Anderson, Jr., "Research in Supersonic Flight and the Breaking of the Sound Barrier," in *From Engineering Science to Big Science: The NACA and NASA Collier Trophy Research Project Winners,* edited by Pamela E. Mack, NASA publication SP-4219 (Washington, DC: NASA, 1998), p. 62. The actual speed of sound depends on what model is used. It varied from 1,116.4 fps in the 1959 ARDC Model Atmosphere to 1,116.9 fps in the 1954 ICAO Model Atmosphere. For more, see Pierre Simon Marquis de Laplace, "Sur la vitesse du son dans l'aire et dans l'eau," *Annales de Chimie et de Physique*, 1816, and "Minutes of the Meeting of Committee on Aerodynamics, 12 October 1943," p. 9.

3 John V. Becker, *The High-Speed Frontier: Case Histories of Four NACA Programs, 1920–1950*, NASA publication SP-445 (Washington, DC: NASA, 1980), p. 3. The text is also located on the Web at *http://www.hq.nasa.gov/office/pao/History/SP-445/contents.htm*. For more on Robins' work, see his *New Principles of Gunnery* published in 1742.

4 John D. Anderson, Jr., *Modern Compressible Flow: With Historical Perspective* (Washington, DC: McGraw Hill Education, 1990), pp. 92-95. An excellent example of a shock wave is the Prandtl-Glauert singularity. See *http://www.eng.vt.edu/fluids/msc/gallery/conden/pg_sing.htm* for some excellent photographs illustrating this.

5 Anderson, "Research in Supersonic Flight and the Breaking of the Sound Barrier," pp. 62-63; *http://otokar.troja.mff.cuni.cz/RELATGRP/Mach.htm* (accessed 17 July 2002). This Web site has copies of the original shadowgraphs taken in 1877.

effectively nonexistent. However, within a few years things changed. Although the typical flight speeds during World War I were less than 125 mph, the propeller tips, because of their combined rotational and translational motion through the air, sometimes approached the compressibility phenomenon.[6]

To better understand the nature of the problem, in 1918 G. H. Bryan began a theoretical analysis of subsonic and supersonic airflows for the British Advisory Committee for Aeronautics at the Royal Aeronautical Establishment. His analysis was cumbersome and provided little data of immediate value. At the same time, Frank W. Caldwell and Elisha N. Fales from the Army Air Service Engineering Division at McCook Field in Dayton, Ohio, took a purely experimental approach to the problem.[7] To investigate the problems associated with propellers, in 1918 Caldwell and Fales designed the first high-speed wind tunnel built in the United States. This tunnel had a 14-inch-diameter test section that could generate velocities up to 465 mph, which was considered exceptional at the time. This was the beginning of a dichotomy between American and British research. Over the next two decades the United States—primarily the NACA—made most of the major experimental contributions to understanding compressibility effects, while the major theoretical contributions were made in Great Britain. This combination of American and British investigations of propellers constituted one of the first concerted efforts of the fledgling aeronautical community to investigate the sound barrier. [8]

Within about five years, practical solutions, such as new thin-section propeller blades (made practical by the use of metal instead of wood for their construction) that minimized the effects of compressibility, were in place. However, most of the solution was to avoid the problem. The development of reliable reduction-gearing systems and variable-pitch, constant-speed propellers eliminated the problem entirely for airplane speeds that were conceivable in 1925 because the propeller could be rotated at slower speeds. At the time, the best pursuit planes (the forerunners of what are now called fighters) could only achieve speeds of about 200 mph, and a scan of literature from the mid-1920s shows only rare suggestions of significantly higher speeds in the foreseeable future. Accordingly, most researchers moved on to other areas.[9]

---

6 Becker, *The High-Speed Frontier,* pp. 3-5. For more see John William Strutt (the Third Baron Rayleigh), *The Theory of Sound*, a landmark of acoustics originally published in 1877. An online version is available at *http://www.measure.demon.co.uk/docs/Strutt.html.* The book was republished in 1976 by Dover Publications, Mineola, NY.

7 On 18 October 1917, the U.S. Army established McCook Field outside Dayton as the military aviation research and development site, based largely on its proximity to the American aviation industry (i.e., the Wright brothers). However, within 10 years the facility had become too small and offered no room for expansion. The citizens of Dayton, not wanting to lose the activity, collected donations and purchased 4,000 acres of land they subsequently donated to the government. The Army dedicated the new Wright Field on 12 October 1927. On 1 July 1931, the portion of Wright Field east of Huffman Dam was redesignated Patterson Field in honor of Lieutenant Frank Stuart Patterson. Patterson Field was the home of Air Force logistics; Wright Field was the home of research and development. The adjacent Wright Field and Patterson Field were again joined on 13 January 1948 to become Wright-Patterson AFB. However, most development activities continued on the "Wright Field" part of the base, and most contemporary literature (and official correspondence) generally called it Wright Field until the late 1950s.

8 G. H. Bryan, "The Effect of Compressibility on Streamline Motions," R & M No. 555, Technical Report of the Advisory Committee for Aeronautics, December 1918; G. H. Bryan, "The Effect of Compressibility on Streamline Motions, Part II," R & M No. 640, Technical Report of the Advisory Committee for Aeronautics, April 1919; Becker, *The High-Speed Frontier*, pp. 3-5.

9 Becker, *The High-Speed Frontier*, pp. 6-7. Surprisingly, one 1924 French document envisioned aircraft flying at Mach 0.8 or more by 1930, as well as the development of some wholly new but unspecified type of propulsion and appropriate new high-speed wind tunnels to support these developments. See the English translation of *La Technique Aeronautica*, December 1924, by E. Huguenard, "High-Speed Wind Tunnels," NACA Technical Memorandum 318, 1925.

The public belief in the "sound barrier" apparently had its beginning in 1935 when the British aerodynamicist W. F. Hilton was explaining to a journalist about high-speed experiments he was conducting at the National Physical Laboratory. Pointing to a plot of airfoil drag, Hilton said, "See how the resistance of a wing shoots up like a barrier against higher speed as we approach the speed of sound." The next morning, the leading British newspapers were referring to the "sound barrier," and the notion that airplanes could never fly faster than the speed of sound became widespread among the public. Although most engineers refused to believe this, the considerable uncertainty about how significantly drag would increase in the transonic regime made them wonder whether engines of sufficient power to fly faster than sound would ever be available.[10]

Since the beginning of powered flight, wind tunnels had proven to be useful tools, but it appeared in the 1930s that simulation of the transonic regime was not possible due to the physical characteristics of the test sections. However, the beginning of the Second World War increased the urgency of the research. Therefore, on a spring morning in 1940, John V. Becker and John Stack, two researchers from the NACA Langley Memorial Aeronautical Laboratory in Hampton, Virginia,[11] drove to a remote beach to observe a Navy Brewster XF2A-2 attempting to obtain supercritical aerodynamic data in free flight over Chesapeake Bay. After it reached its terminal velocity in a steep dive—about 575 mph—the pilot made a pull-up that was near the design load factor of the airplane. This flight did not encounter any undue difficulties and provided some data, but the general feeling was that div-

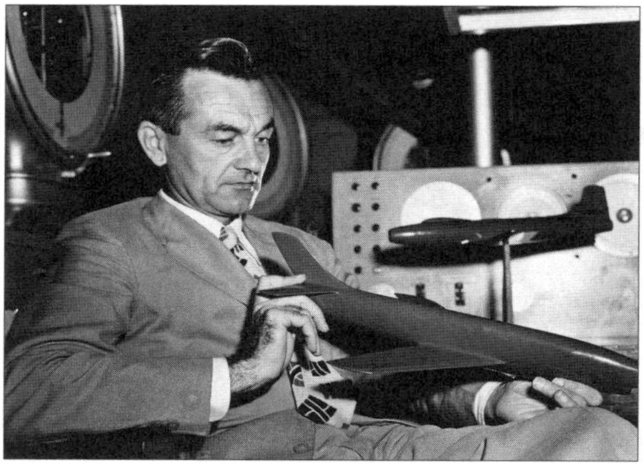

John Stack, head of the Compressibility Research Division at NACA Langley, was one of the driving forces behind the original set of experimental airplanes, such as the Bell X-1 and Douglas D-558 series. Although he lent expertise and advice to the groups developing the X-15, he remained in the background and did not repeat the pivotal roles he had played on earlier projects. (NASA)

10 W.F. Hilton, "British Aeronautical Research Facilities," *Journal of the Royal Aeronautical Society*, volume 70, Centenary Issue, 1966, pp. 103-104.

11 In July 1948 the word "Memorial" was dropped and the facility became the Langley Aeronautical Laboratory. It would subsequently be renamed the Langley Research Center (LaRC) when NASA came into existence on 1 October 1958. John Stack (1906-1972) graduated from MIT in 1928 and joined the Langley Aeronautical Laboratory as an aeronautical engineer. In 1939 he became director of all high-speed wind tunnels and high-velocity airflow research at Langley. Three years later he became chief of the Compressibility Research Division there, was promoted to assistant chief of research in 1947, and subsequently had that title changed to assistant director of the research center. He guided much of the research that paved the way for transonic aircraft, and in 1947 he was awarded the Collier Trophy together with the pilot of the X-1 who broke the sound barrier (by then) Major Charles E. Yeager. He won the award again in 1952 and later won the Wright Brothers Memorial Trophy, among other awards. From 1961 to 1962 he was director of aeronautical research at NASA Headquarters before retiring from NASA to become vice president for engineering at Republic Aircraft Corp. (later part of Fairchild Industries), from which he retired in 1971.

ing an operational-type airplane near its structural limits was probably not the best method of obtaining research information.[12]

X-PLANES

As it happened, John Stack had already considered other alternatives. The idea of a modern research airplane—one designed strictly to probe unknown flight regimes—came in a 1933 proposal by Stack. On his own initiative, Stack went through a preliminary analysis for "a hypothetical airplane which, however, is not beyond the limits of possibility" to fly well into the compressibility regime. Stack calculated that a small airplane using a 2,300-horsepower Rolls-Royce piston engine could obtain 566 mph in level flight—far beyond that of any airplane flying at the time. Ultimately, the NACA did not pursue the suggestion, and it would be another decade before the idea would come of age.[13]

Ezra Kotcher at the Army Air Corps Engineering School at Wright Field made the next proposal for a high-speed research airplane. In 1939 Kotcher pointed out the unknown aspects of the transonic flight regime and the problems associated with the effects of compressibility. He further discussed the limitations of existing wind tunnels and advised that a full-scale flight research program would be an appropriate precaution. By early 1941 John Stack had confirmed that data from wind tunnels operating near Mach 1 were essentially worthless because of a choking problem in the test section. He again concluded that the only way to gather meaningful data near the speed of sound would be to build a vehicle that could fly in that regime. Again, no action resulted from either Kotcher's or Stack's suggestions and determining the effects of compressibility on airplanes remained a largely theoretical pursuit.[14]

The real world intervened in November 1941 when Lockheed test pilot Ralph Virden died trying to pull a P-38 Lightning out of a high-speed dive that penetrated well into the compressibility regime. By 1942 the diving speed of the new generation of fighters exceeded the choking speed of the wind tunnels then in use. Researchers increasingly supported the idea of an instrumented airplane operating at high subsonic speeds. Those involved do not remember that any one individual specifically championed this idea, but John Stack soon became the chief Langley proponent.[15]

Interestingly, there was little interest within the NACA in flying through the sound barrier. It appeared that one of the early turbojet engines could push a small airplane to about Mach 0.9, but the only near-term way to go faster was to use a rocket engine—something that was considered too risky by the NACA.

---

12 Becker, *The High-Speed Frontier*, p. 88.

13 John Stack, "Effects of Compressibility on High Speed Flight," *Journal of the Aeronautical Sciences*, January 1934, pp. 40-43; James R. Hansen, *Engineer in Charge: A History of the Langley Aeronautical Laboratory, 1917–1958*, NASA publication SP-4305 (Washington, DC: NASA, 1987), p. 256.

14 Hansen, *Engineer in Charge*, p. 259. Choking was primarily a transonic issue, since even a small model in the test section could act as an obstruction that prevented the calculated mass of air from flowing through. Some models also produced shock waves that extended almost perpendicular to the flow, reflecting off the tunnel walls and impinging back on the model or instrumentation. Such an effect meant that data from the tests were largely worthless.

15 Jay D. Pinson, ed., *Diamond Jubilee of Powered Flight: The Evolution of Aircraft Design* (New York: American Institute of Aeronautics and Astronautics, 1978), pp. 51-64; Becker, *The High-Speed Frontier*, pp. 89-90; telephone conversation, John V. Becker with Dennis R. Jenkins, 11 April 2002.

A posed group portrait of early X-planes at the NACA High-Speed Flight Station in August 1953. Clockwise from the bottom are the Douglas D55-1, Douglas D-558-2, Northrop X-4, Convair XF-92A, and Bell X-5. This group represents a wide variety of research programs, and only the D558-2 was a true high-speed airplane. (NASA)

The Army, however, wanted a supersonic airplane and appeared willing to accept rocket propulsion. In fact, Ezra Kotcher had listed this as an option in his 1939 proposal, and it became increasingly obvious that a rocket engine represented the only hope for achieving supersonic speeds in level flight in the near future.[16]

Possible Navy interest in the undertaking also appeared during 1942–1944. However, significant differences of opinion came to the forefront during a 15 March 1944 meeting of Army, NACA, and Navy personnel. The NACA thought of the airplane as a facility for collecting high-subsonic speed aerodynamic data that were unobtainable in wind tunnels, while the Army thought it was a step toward achieving a supersonic combat aircraft. The Navy supported both views, wanting to dispel the myth of the impenetrable sound barrier, but was also interested in gathering meaningful high-speed data. Despite the NACA's concerns, the Army soon announced its intention to develop a rocket-powered research airplane.[17]

As John Becker remembers, "The NACA continued to emphasize the assumed safety aspects and relatively long-duration data-gathering flights possible with a turbojet engine compared to the short flights of any reasonably sized rocket plane. Furthermore, the turbojet would have obvious applicability to future mili-

16 Becker, *The High-Speed Frontier,* pp. 90–91; telephone conversation, John V. Becker with Dennis R. Jenkins, 11 April 2002.

17 Becker, *The High-Speed Frontier,* pp. 91–92.

tary aircraft while the rocket propulsion system might not. This apparently irreconcilable difference was easily resolved; the Army was putting up the money and they decided to do it their way."[18]

The beginning of supersonic flight research likely occurred when Robert J. Woods from Bell Aircraft met with Ezra Kotcher at Wright Field on 30 November 1944. After they discussed the basic specifications, Kotcher asked Woods if Bell was interested in designing and building the airplane. Woods said yes, and in late December Bell began contract negotiations with the Army to build the rocket-powered XS-1 research airplane.[19]

Melvin N. Gough, the chief test pilot at Langley, dismissed the rocket-plane concept: "No NACA pilot will ever be permitted to fly an airplane powered by a damned firecracker." When it became clear in early 1944 that the Army was going to insist on rocket propulsion, John Stack began lobbying the Navy to procure the type of airplane the NACA wanted. The Navy was more receptive to the turbojet-powered airplane, and the Navy Bureau of Aeronautics (BuAer) began negotiations with Douglas Aircraft for the D-558 Skystreak in early 1945.[20]

These were the beginnings of the cooperative research airplane program. In reality, until the advent of the X-15 there were two distinct programs: one with the Army and one with the Navy. Just because the NACA did not agree with the path the Army had elected to pursue did not mean the Agency would not cooperate fully in the development of the XS-1. The Navy enjoyed the same level of cooperation for the D-558. John Stack noted in 1951 that "the research airplane program has been a cooperative venture from the start.... The extent of the co-operation is best illustrated by the fact that the X-1, sponsored by the Air Force, is powered with a Navy-sponsored rocket engine, and the D-558-1, sponsored by the Navy, is powered with an Air Force-sponsored turbojet engine." [21]

WHAT WAS ACHIEVED?

Initially the primary justification for a manned research airplane was the choking problems of the wind tunnels, but, as it turned out, this limitation disappeared prior to the beginning of high-speed flight tests. Although this largely eliminated the need for the X-planes, it is unlikely that the progress in developing transonic ground facilities would have occurred without the stimulus begun by the X-1 and D-558. Clearly, there was an important two-way flow of benefits.

---

18 Ibid. The quote was slightly edited by John Becker during the preparation of this manuscript.

19 Richard P. Hallion, *Supersonic Flight* (New York: Macmillan, 1972), p. 34; Becker, *The High-Speed Frontier,* pp. 91-92. Woods worked at Langley during 1928–1929 but he left the NACA and in 1935 teamed with Lawrence D. Bell to form the Bell Aircraft Corporation in Buffalo, New York. The original designation of the X-1 and X-2 was "XS" for "experimental supersonic." This was subsequently simplified to just "X" for "experimental."

20 Becker, *The High-Speed Frontier,* pp. 92-93. Ironically, it was the turbojet-powered D-558-1 that ultimately killed NACA pilot Howard C. Lilly due to engine failure. With further irony, it was the supersonic flights of the rocket-powered X-1 that brought John Stack and the NACA a share of the Collier Trophy.

21 John Stack, "Methods for Investigation of Flows at Transonic Speeds" Aeroballistics Research Facilities Dedication Symposium, 27 June–1 July 1949. See also an updated version presented at the 3rd International Aero Conference, London, 7–11 September 1951. The XS-1 was powered by a Reaction Motors XLR11 rocket engine, which was a redesignated version of the LR8 developed for the Navy. An Air Force-funded Allison J35-A-11 turbojet powered the D-558-1. The United States Air Force superseded the Army Air Forces by virtue of the National Security Act of 1947, which became law on 26 July 1947.

Stimulated by the problems encountered by the research airplanes during flight, researchers created new ground facilities and techniques that in turn provided the data necessary to develop yet faster airplanes. Comparing the results of flight tests at ever-increasing speeds allowed the wind tunnels to be refined, producing yet better data. It was a repetitive loop.[22]

The programs proceeded remarkably rapidly, and the first supersonic flights showed nothing particularly unexpected, much to the relief of the researchers. The most basic result, however, was dispelling the myth of the "sound barrier." The fearsome transonic zone became an ordinary engineering problem, and allowed the designers of operational supersonic aircraft to proceed with much greater confidence.[23]

When people think of X-planes, record-setting vehicles like the X-1 generally come to mind. In reality, most X-planes investigated much more mundane flight regimes, and there were only a handful of high-speed manned experimental aircraft, built mainly during the late 1940s and early 1950s. Specifically, there were five designs (only three of which carried X" designations) intended for the initial manned assault on high-speed flight: the Bell X-1 series, the Bell X-2, the Douglas D-558-1 Skystreaks, the Douglas D-558-2 Skyrockets, and the North American X-15. Of the five, one probed high subsonic speeds, two were supersonic, and one pushed the envelope to Mach 3. The fifth design would go much faster.[24]

The X-planes gave aviation its first experience with controlled supersonic flight. On 14 October 1947, Air Force Captain Charles E. Yeager became the first human to break the sound barrier in level flight when the XS-1 achieved Mach 1.06 at 43,000 feet. It took six additional years before NACA test pilot A. Scott Crossfield exceeded Mach 2 in the D558-2 Skyrocket on 20 November 1953. The Bell X-2 proved to be the fastest and highest-flying of the "round one" X-planes and the most tragic, with the two X-2s logging only 20 glide and powered flights between them. Nevertheless, Captain Iven C. Kincheloe, Jr., managed to take one of the airplanes to 126,200 feet on 7 September 1956. Twenty days later, Captain Milburn G. Apt was killed during his first X-2 flight after he reached Mach 3.196 (1,701 mph), becoming the first person to fly at three times the speed of sound, albeit briefly.[25]

The contributions of the early high-speed X-planes were questionable, and the subject of great debate within the NACA and the aircraft industry. Opinions on how successful they were depend largely on where one worked. The academics and laboratory researchers, and a couple of aerospace-industry designers, are on record indicating the contributions of the X-planes were minimal. On the other side, however, many of the hands-on researchers and pilots are certain the pro-

---

22 Becker, *The High-Speed Frontier*, pp. 93-94. General hypothesis confirmed by John Becker in a telephone conversation with Dennis R. Jenkins on 12 March 2002.

23 Becker, *The High-Speed Frontier,* pp. 93-94.

24 For a look at all of the X-planes, please see Jay Miller, *The X-Planes: X-1 to X-45* (Hinckley, England: Midland Publishing, 2001). Miller is currently working on a companion volume for the same publisher that will deal with experimental aircraft not directly in the "X" designation category (such as the Douglas D-558). For a photo essay on the X-planes, see *X-planes Photo Scrapbook,* compiled by Dennis R. Jenkins (North Branch, MN: Specialty Press, 2004). See also *American X-Vehicles: X-1 through X-50*, NASA monograph SP-2000-4538 (Washington, DC: NASA, September 2003).

25 *The X-Planes: X-1 to X-45*, pp. 9–11; Richard P. Hallion, *On The Frontier*, NASA publication SP-4303 (Washington, DC: NASA, 1984).

grams provided solid, real-world data that greatly accelerated progress in the design and manufacture of the Mach 1 and Mach 2 combat aircraft that followed.[26]

For instance, the X-1 was the first aircraft to purposely break the sound barrier in level flight, but other aircraft were doing so in shallow dives soon afterwards.[27] The first combat type designed from the start as a supersonic fighter—the Republic XF-91 "Thunderceptor"—made its maiden flight only 19 months after Yeager's flight. How much the X-1 experience contributed to Alexander Kartveli's design is unknown.[28] The same thing happened at Mach 2. By the time Scott Crossfield took a D-558-2 to twice the speed of sound, Kelly Johnson at Lockheed had already been developing what would become the F-104 Starfighter for over a year. It is unlikely that the rocket-powered X-planes actually assisted Johnson much—something he would make clear during later deliberations.[29]

The X-1E complemented the heating research undertaken by the X-1B, but the F-104 was already flying and could more easily acquire data at Mach 2. Even at the Flight Research Center (FRC), there was debate over how appropriate this exercise was. FRC research engineer Gene Matranga later recalled, "We could probably fly the X-1E two or three times a month, whereas Kelly [Johnson] was flying his F-104s two or three times a day into the same flight regimes, so it really didn't make sense for us to be applying those kinds of resources to [obtain] that kind of information." However, it is unfair to judge the X-1E program too harshly since its major purpose was simply to keep a cadre of rocket-powered experience at the FRC in anticipation of the upcoming X-15.[30]

Even John Becker recognized the dichotomy represented by the experience: "[T]he cooperative research-airplane program pursued by the Air Force, NACA, and Navy had not been an unqualified success.... Some had lagged so seriously in procurement that their designs had become obsolescent before they were flown. In a few cases tactical designs superior to the research aircraft were in hand before the research aircraft flew." It was not anybody's fault—technology was simply changing too fast. Trying to sort out the detailed story is nearly impossible and well beyond the scope of this book.[31]

Nevertheless, although most believed that the concept of a dedicated research airplane still held promise, researchers decided that the next design would need to offer a significant increment in performance to leapfrog the combat types then in development. Chuck Yeager's October 1947 assault on the sound barrier had

---

26 Telephone conversations with Scott Crossfield and John Becker, various dates, plus writings in a multitude of books, letters, and memos. The debate is probably never ending and largely moot since what happened has already happened.

27 The XP-86 officially broke the sound barrier in a shallow dive on 26 April 1948. Some sources maintain that this event actually took place slightly before Yeager's flight, and Scott Crossfield suggests—as do others—that the first Mach 1 dive by an F-86 occurred "within weeks" of Yeager's first supersonic flight (telephone conversation, Scott Crossfield with Dennis R. Jenkins, 31 October 2002).

28 The XF-91 was hardly a successful attempt, although it did record the "first supersonic rocket-powered flight by a U.S. combat-type airplane" in December 1952. A single General Electric J47-GE-9 jet engine and four Curtiss-Wright XLR27-CW-1 rocket engines powered the aircraft. The Curtiss-Wright rockets were traded for a Reaction Motors XLR11-RM-9 in the modified XF-91A that apparently was never tested.

29 The first flight of an XF-104 powered by a Wright XJ65-W-6 engine was on 7 February 1956, but this prototype aircraft was only capable of Mach 1.79. The General Electric J79-GE-3-powered YF-104A exceeded Mach 2 on 27 April 1956.

30 Interview with Gene Matranga, 3 December 1976, transcript in the files at the DFRC History Office; *http://www.dfrc.nasa.gov/History/Publications/SP-4303/ch4-6.html* (accessed 18 July 2002).

31 John V. Becker, "The X-15 Project: Part 1—Origins and Research Background," *Astronautics & Aeronautics*, February 1964, pp. 53.

The X-1E was the last rocket-powered X-plane at the NACA High-Speed Flight Station until the arrival of the three X-15s. There is considerable debate over the economics of flying the X-1E given that some jet-powered aircraft could attain the same velocities, but the primary purpose of the X-1E was to maintain a cadre of rocket experience at the HSFS pending the arrival of the X-15. (NASA)

ignited a billion-dollar race to build ever-faster aircraft, and directly affected every combat aircraft design for the next two decades. However, a few aeronautical researchers had always been certain that the sound barrier was simply a challenge for the engineers, not a true physical limitation. The X-1 had proven it was possible for humans to fly supersonically. The next goal was so much faster.

HYPERSONICS

Hypersonic. Adj. (1937). Of or relating to velocities in excess of five times the speed of sound.[32]

Between the two world wars, hypersonics was an area of great theoretical interest to a small group of aeronautical researchers, but little progress was made toward defining the possible problems, and even less in solving them. The major constraint was power. Engines, even the rudimentary rockets then available, were incapable of propelling any significant object to hypersonic velocities. Wind tunnels also lacked the power to generate such speeds. Computer power to simulate the environment had not even been imagined. For the time being, hypersonics was something to be contemplated, and little else.

By the mid-1940s it was becoming apparent to aerodynamic researchers in the United States that it might finally be possible to build a flight vehicle capable of achieving hypersonic speeds. It seemed that the large rocket engines developed

32 *Webster's Ninth New Collegiate Dictionary* (Springfield, MA: Merriam-Webster, 1986).

in Germany during World War II might allow engineers to initiate development with some hope of success. Indeed, the Germans had already briefly toyed with a potentially hypersonic aerodynamic vehicle, the winged A-4b version of the V-2 rocket. The only "successful" A-4b flight had managed just over Mach 4 (about 2,700 mph) before apparently disintegrating in flight.[33] Perhaps unsurprisingly, in the immediate post-war period most researchers believed that hypersonic flight was a domain for unmanned missiles.[34]

When the U.S. Navy BuAer provided an English translation of a technical paper by German scientists Eugen Sänger and Irene Bredt in 1946, this preconception began to change. Expanding upon ideas conceived as early as 1928, Sänger and Bredt concluded in 1944 that they could build a rocket-powered hypersonic aircraft with only minor advances in technology. This concept of manned aircraft flying at hypersonic velocities greatly interested researchers at the NACA. Nevertheless, although there were numerous paper studies exploring variations of the Sänger-Bredt proposal during the late 1940s, none bore fruit and no hardware construction was undertaken.[35]

One researcher who was interested in exploring the new science of hypersonics was John V. Becker, the assistant chief of the Compressibility Research Division at the NACA Langley Aeronautical Laboratory in Hampton, Virginia.[36] On 3 August 1945, Becker proposed the construction of a "new type supersonic wind tunnel for Mach number 7." Already a few small supersonic tunnels in the United States could achieve short test runs at Mach 4, but the large supersonic tunnels under construction at Langley and Ames had been designed for Mach numbers no higher than 2. Information captured by the Army from the German missile research facility at Peenemünde had convinced Becker that the next generation of missiles and projectiles would require testing at much higher Mach numbers.[37]

As the basis for his proposed design, Becker extrapolated from what he already knew about supersonic tunnels. He quickly discovered that the compressible-flow theory for nozzles dictated a 100-fold expansion in area between Mach 1 and Mach 7. Using normal shock theory to estimate pressure ratio and compressor requirements, Becker found that at Mach 7 the compressor system would have to grow to impractical proportions.[38]

Hope for alleviating the compressor problem had first appeared in the spring of 1945 when Becker gained a fresh understanding of supersonic diffusers from

33 Supersonic velocities are usually expressed as "Mach numbers," a term honoring Austrian mathematician and physicist Ernst Mach, who was the first to assign a numerical value to the ratio between a solid object passing through a gas and the speed of sound through the same gas. The speed of sound varies with atmospheric conditions (temperature and pressure) and hence is different at every altitude on every day. At sea level on a standard day the speed of sound is 761.6 miles per hour. By convention, at altitudes of above 40,000 feet the speed of sound is a constant 660.4 miles per hour.

34 Despite this apparent success, most engineers on the program believed that heat transfer problems would ultimately doom the A-4b; there were no provisions for cooling the airframe, and little was understood about potential heating effects. For further information, see Michael Neufeld's interview of Karl Werner Dahm, 25 January 1990. In the files at the National Air and Space Museum.

35 Becker, "The X-15 Program in Retrospect," p. 1.

36 The Compressibility Research Division was created in July 1943 as one of the first steps toward breaking the sound barrier. The division included all of the high-speed wind tunnels at Langley and a small section under Arthur Kantrowitz that studied fundamental gas dynamics.

37 Letter, John V. Becker to the Langley Chief of Research, subject: Proposal for new type of supersonic wind tunnel for Mach number 7.0, 3 August 1945. In the Becker Archives, Virginia Polytechnic Institute, Blacksburg, Virginia; letter, John V. Becker to Dennis R. Jenkins, 29 July 2002.

38 Letter, John V. Becker to Dennis R. Jenkins, 29 July 2002.

John V. Becker was the lead of the NACA Langley team that accomplished much of the preliminary work needed to get a hypersonic research airplane approved through the NACA Executive Committee and Department of Defense. Becker continued to play an import role with the X-15 throughout the development and flight programs. (NASA)

a paper by Arthur Kantrowitz and Coleman duPont Donaldson.[39] The paper focused on low-Mach-number supersonic flows and did not consider variable geometry solutions, but it was still possible to infer that changing the wall contours to form a second throat might substantially reduce the shock losses in the diffuser. Unfortunately, it appeared that this could only be accomplished after the flow had been started, introducing considerable mechanical complexity. The potential benefits from a variable-geometry configuration were inconsequential at Mach 2, but Becker determined that they could be quite large at Mach 7. In the tunnel envisioned by Becker, the peak pressure ratios needed to start the flow lasted only a few seconds and were obtained by discharging a 50-atmosphere pressure tank into a vacuum tank. Deploying the second throat reduced the pressure ratio and power requirements, allowing the phasing-in of a continuously running compressor to provide longer test times. It was a novel concept, but a number of uncertainties caused Becker to advise the construction of a small pilot tunnel with an 11 by 11-inch test section to determine experimentally how well the scheme worked in practice.[40]

Not everybody agreed that such a facility was necessary. The NACA chairman, Jerome C. Hunsaker,[41] did not see any urgency for the facility, and Arthur Kantrowitz, who designed the first NACA supersonic wind tunnel, did not believe that extrapolating what little was known about supersonic tunnels would allow the development of a hypersonic facility. The most obvious consequence

39 Arthur Kantrowitz and Coleman duP. Donaldson, "Preliminary Investigation of Supersonic Diffusers," NASA wartime report L713, May 1946 (originally published as L5D20, 1945). Becker was serving as the chairman of the technical editorial committee when he first read the paper.

40 Letter, John V. Becker to Dennis R. Jenkins, 29 July 2002.

41 Hunsaker was chairman of the NACA from 1941 to 1956. Among the notable achievements in a long and accomplished career, his work in aircraft stability was published as NACA Technical Report No. 1 in 1915.

of the rapid expansion of the air necessary for Mach 7 operation was the large drop in air temperature below the nominal liquefaction value. At the time, there was no consensus on the question of air liquefaction, although some preliminary investigations of the condensation of water vapor suggested that the transit time through a hypersonic nozzle and test section might be too brief for liquefaction to take place. Nevertheless, Kantrowitz, the head of Langley's small gas-dynamics research group, feared that "real-gas effects"—possibly culminating in liquefaction—would probably limit wind tunnels to a maximum useful Mach number of about 4.5.[42]

Nevertheless, Becker had his supporters. For instance, Dr. George W. Lewis,[43] the Director of Aeronautical Research for the NACA, advised Becker, "Don't call it a new wind tunnel. That would complicate and delay funding," so for the next two years it was called "Project 506." The estimated $39,500 cost of the pilot tunnel was rather modest, and given Lewis's backing, the facility received quick approval.[44]

In September 1945 a small staff of engineers under Charles H. McLellan began constructing the facility inside the shop area of the old Propeller Research Tunnel. They soon discovered that Kantrowitz's predictions had been accurate—the job required more than extrapolation of existing supersonic tunnel theory. The pilot tunnel proposal had not included an air heater, since Becker believed he could add it later if liquefaction became a problem. As work progressed, it became increasingly clear that the ability to control air temperature would greatly improve the quality and scope of the research, and by the end of 1945 Becker had received approval to include an electric heater. This would maintain air temperatures of about 850°F, allowing Mach 7 temperatures well above the nominal liquefaction point.[45]

The first test of the "11-inch" on 26 November 1947 revealed uniform flow at Mach 6.9, essentially meeting all of the original intents. An especially satisfying result of the test was the performance of the variable-geometry diffuser. McLellan and his group had devised a deployable second throat that favored mechanical simplicity over aerodynamic sophistication, but was still very effective. The benefit appeared as an increased run duration (in this case an increase from 25 seconds to over 90 seconds).[46]

For three years the 11-inch would be the only operational hypersonic tunnel in the United States and, apparently, the world. Several basic flow studies and aerodynamic investigations during this period established the 11-inch as an efficient tool for general hypersonic research, giving Langley a strong base in the new field of hypersonics. Without this development, Langley would not have been

42 John V. Becker, "Results of Recent Hypersonic and Unsteady Flow Research at the Langley Aeronautical Laboratory," *Journal of Applied Physics*, volume 21, number 7, July 1950, pp. 619-628; letter, John V. Becker to Dennis R. Jenkins, 29 July 2002.

43 In 1919 Lewis became the first executive officer of the NACA; in 1924 he received the title of director of aeronautical research, which he kept until 1947. Lewis died at his summer home at Lake Winola, Pennsylvania, on 12 July 1948.

44 Letter, John V. Becker to Dennis R. Jenkins, 29 July 2002. The $39,500 estimate contained in the 3 August 1945 memo seems ridiculous by today's standards. However, it did not include any NACA overhead costs, and construction would take place in NACA shops using NACA personnel. Adding the heater increased the expenditure to over $200,000.

45 Letter, John V. Becker to Dennis R. Jenkins, 29 July 2002.

46 Becker, "Results of Recent Hypersonic and Unsteady Flow Research," pp. 619-628; letter, John V. Becker to Dennis R. Jenkins, 29 July 2002.

The 11-inch at NACA Langley was intended as a pilot tunnel for a larger hypersonic wind tunnel when it opened in 1947. However, it proved so useful that it stayed in service until 1973, and the research documented in it resulted in over 230 publications. Much of the early work on what became the X-15 was accomplished in this wind tunnel. (NASA)

able to define and support a meaningful hypersonic research airplane concept in 1954. Throughout the entire X-15 program, the 11-inch would be the principal source of the necessary hypersonic tunnel support.[47]

Despite the fact that it was a pilot facility, the 11-inch hypersonic tunnel operated until 1973, resulting in over 230 publications from tests and related analysis (about one paper every 5 weeks for its 25 years of operations). Few major wind tunnels have equaled that record. After it was decommissioned, NASA donated the tunnel to the Virginia Polytechnic Institute in Blacksburg, Virginia.[48]

As the 11-inch tunnel at Langley was demonstrating that it was possible to conduct hypersonic research, several other facilities were under construction. Alfred J. Eggers, Jr., at the NACA Ames Aeronautical Laboratory at Moffett Field, California,[49] began to design a 10 by 14-inch continuous-flow hypersonic tunnel in 1946, and the resulting facility became operational in 1950. The first hypersonic tunnel at the Naval Ordnance Facility, constructed largely from German material captured from the uncompleted Mach 10 tunnel at Peenemünde, also became operational in 1950.[50]

47 Letter, John V. Becker to Dennis R. Jenkins, 29 July 2002. For an example of the investigations made during this period, see Charles H. McLellan, "Exploratory Wind Tunnel Investigations of Wings and Bodies at M=6.9," *Journal of the Aeronautical Sciences*, volume 18, number 10, October 1951, pp. 641-648.

48 Hansen, *Engineer in Charge*, p. 347.

49 The Ames Aeronautical Laboratory became the Ames Research Center when NASA came into being on 1 October 1958.

50 Hansen, *Engineer in Charge*, p. 560.

Interestingly, NASA did not authorize a continuously running hypersonic tunnel that incorporated all of the features proposed in the 1945 Becker memo until 1958. Equipped with a 1,450°F heater, the design velocity increased from Becker's proposed Mach 7 to 12. As it ended up, although the tunnel attained Mach 12 during a few tests, severe cooling problems in the first throat resulted in a Mach 10 limit for most work. The enormous high-pressure air supply and vacuum tankage of the Gas Dynamics Laboratory provided blow-down test durations of 10–15 minutes. Together with improved instrumentation, this virtually eliminated the need to operate the tunnel in the "continuously running" mode, and nearly all of Langley's "continuous-running" hypersonic tunnel operations have been conducted in the "blow-down" mode rather than with the compressors running.[51]

THE MISSILE INFLUENCE

Not surprisingly, during the early 1950s the top priority for the hypersonic tunnels was to support the massive development effort associated with the intercontinental missiles then under development. Initially it was not clear whether the resulting weapon would be a high-speed cruise missile or an intercontinental ballistic missile (ICBM), so the Air Force undertook programs to develop both. Much of the theoretical science necessary to create a manned hypersonic research airplane would be born of the perceived need to build these weapons.

Long-range missile development challenged NACA researchers in a number of ways. The advancements necessary to allow a Mach 3 cruise missile were relatively easily imagined, if not readily at hand. The ballistic missile was a different story. A successful ICBM would have to accelerate to 15,000 miles per hour at an altitude of perhaps 500 miles, and then be guided to a precise target thousands of miles away. Sophisticated and reliable propulsion, control, and guidance systems were essential, as was keeping the structural weight at a minimum. Moreover, researchers needed to find some method to handle aerodynamic heating. As the missile warhead reentered the atmosphere, it would experience temperatures of several thousand °F. The heat that was generated by shock-wave compression outside the boundary layer and was not in contact with the structure would dissipate harmlessly into the surrounding air. However, the part that arose within the boundary layer and was in direct contact with the missile structure would be great enough to melt the vehicle. Many early dummy warheads burned up because the engineers did not yet understand this.

During this time, H. Julian Allen was engaged in high-speed research at Ames and found what he believed to be a practical solution to the aerodynamic heating problems of the ICBM. In place of the traditional sleek configuration with a sharply pointed nose (an aerodynamic concept long since embraced by missile designers, mostly because the V-2 had used it), Allen proposed a blunt shape with a rounded bottom. In 1951 Allen predicted that when the missile reentered the atmosphere,

51 Letter, John V. Becker to Dennis R. Jenkins, 29 July 2002.

In 1951, NACA Ames researcher H. Julian Allen postulated the concept of a "blunt body" reentry vehicle for intercontinental missiles. Pushing the shock wave away from the missile body removed most of the aerodynamic heating from being in direct contact with the structure. The reentry profiles developed at NASA Langley used the idea of "sufficient lift," which were a new manifestation of the blunt-body concept. (NASA)

its blunt shape would create a powerful bow-shaped shock wave that would deflect heat safely outward and away from the structure of the missile. The boundary layer on the body created some frictional drag and heating, but this was only a small fraction of the total heat of deceleration, most of which harmlessly heated the atmosphere through the action of the strong shock wave. As Allen and Eggers put it, "not only should pointed bodies be avoided, but the rounded nose should have as large a radius as possible." Thus the "blunt-body" concept was born.[52]

Allen and Eggers verified the blunt-body concept by studying the aerodynamic heating of miniature missiles in an innovative supersonic free-flight tunnel, a sort of wind-tunnel-cum-firing-range that had become operational at Ames in 1949. The researchers published their classified report on these tests in August 1953, but the Air Force and aerospace industry did not immediately embrace the concept since it ran contrary to most established ideas. Engineers accustomed to pointed-body missiles remained skeptical of the blunt-body concept until the mid-to-late-1950s, when it became the basis for the new ICBM warheads and all of the manned space capsules.[53]

In the meantime, Robert J. Woods, designer of the Bell X-1 and X-2 research airplanes, stirred up interest in hypersonic aircraft. In a letter to the NACA

---

52 H. Julian Allen and Alfred J. Eggers, Jr. "A Study of the Motion and Aerodynamic Heating of Ballistic Missiles Entering the Earth's Atmosphere at High Supersonic Speeds," NACA confidential research memorandum A53D28, August 1953. The NACA published updated versions of the same report as TN4047 and TR1381 in 1958; Edwin P. Hartmann, *Adventures in Research: A History of the Ames Research Center*, 1940–1965, NASA publication SP-4302 (Washington, DC: NASA, 1972), pp. 216-218. Allen had worked at Langley in Eastman Jacobs's Variable-Density Tunnel group between 1936 and 1940 before joining the team on the West Coast. As told by John Becker, Allen's given name was "Harry," but he disliked the name and always used "H. Julian" instead. Occasionally he used "Harvey" as a nickname, leading to the use of that name in many publications.

53 Allen and Eggers, "A Study of the Motion and Aerodynamic Heating;" Hartmann, *Adventures in Research*, pp. 218.

Committee on Aerodynamics[54] dated 8 January 1952, Woods proposed that the committee direct some part of its research to address the basic problems of hypersonic and space flight. Accompanying the letter was a document from Dr. Walter R. Dornberger, former commander of the German rocket test facility at Peenemünde and now a Bell employee, outlining the preliminary requirements of a hypersonic aircraft. The "ionosphere research plane" proposed by Dornberger was powered by a liquid-fueled rocket engine and capable of flying at 6,000 feet per second (fps) at an altitude of 50–75 miles.[55] It was apparent that the concept for an "antipodal" bomber proposed near the end of the war by his colleagues Eugen Sänger and Irene Bredt still intrigued Dornberger.[56] According to the Sänger-Bredt study, this aircraft would skip in and out of the atmosphere (called "skip-gliding") and land halfway around the world.[57] Dornberger's enthusiasm for the concept had captured Woods's imagination, and he called for the NACA to develop a manned hypersonic research airplane in support of it. At the time, the committee declined to initiate the research advocated by Woods, but took the matter under advisement.[58]

At the 30 January 1952 meeting of the Committee on Aerodynamics, Woods submitted a paper that noted growing interest in very-high-speed flight at altitudes where the atmospheric density was so low as to eliminate effective aerodynamic control. Since he believed that research into this regime was necessary, Woods suggested that "the NACA is the logical organization to carry out the basic studies in space flight control and stability" and that the NACA should set up a small group "to evaluate and analyze the basic problems of space flight." Woods went on to recommend that the NACA "endeavor to establish a concept of a suitable manned test vehicle" that could be developed within two years. Again, the NACA took the matter under advisement.[59]

Smith J. DeFrance, an early Langley engineer who became the director of NACA Ames when it opened in 1941, opposed the idea for a hypersonic study group because "it appears to verge on the developmental, and there is a question

---

54 The NACA received its direction via a committee system. The committees and their subcommittees were composed of representatives from industry, the military, and NACA scientists and engineers. A subcommittee that had the most direct contact with the "real world" might recognize a new area of research and pass a resolution recommending further efforts. The overarching committee would then take up the resolution and, after discussion at a higher level in the food chain, either table it or pass its own resolution. This in turn would pass to the executive committee, which was composed of distinguished members of industry, high-ranking military officers, and government officials appointed by the president. If the executive committee endorsed the resolution, it would direct the NACA laboratories (Ames, Langley, and Lewis) and stations (the Auxiliary Flight Research Station and later the High-Speed Flight Station) to conduct the research. Usually, funding came from the various military services, although the NACA also had a separately appropriated budget.

55 The accepted standard at the time was to report extreme altitudes in statue miles; this equated to 264,000–396,000 feet, almost exactly foretelling the performance ultimately obtained by the X-15.

56 According to *Webster's*—antipodal: of or relating to the antipodes; *specif*: situated at the opposite side of the Earth. Or, points on opposite sides of a sphere. The original Sänger concept was that the Silverbird would land on the opposite side of the Earth from where it took off, dropping its bombs midway through the mission.

57 Eugen Sänger, *Rocket Flight Engineering*, NASA translation TTF-223 (Washington, DC: NASA, 1965). Sänger's concepts for skip-glide aircraft date back as far as his doctoral thesis of 1928, and formed the basis for several postwar American projects, such as BoMi and RoBo. His "dynamic-soaring" terminology for this flight path also inspired the name "Dyna-Soar" given to the Step III hypersonic research program, and later the X-20 vehicle.

58 Letter, Robert J. Woods to the NACA Committee on Aerodynamics, "Establishment of a Study Group on Space Flight and Associated Problems," 8 January 1952. A few weeks later, Dornberger outlined an even more ambitious version of the aircraft launched from a B-47 and capable of 6,210 fps (4,250 mph) and 564,000 feet. It was, for all intents, a version of the A-4b or A-9 investigated by the Germans at Peenemünde during the war. See a letter from Walter R. Dornberger to Robert J. Woods of 18 January 1952. In the files at the NASA History Office.

59 Minutes of the Meeting, NACA Committee on Aerodynamics, 30 January 1952. In the files at the NASA History Office.

as to its importance. There are many more pressing and more realistic problems to be met and solved in the next ten years." DeFrance concluded in the spring of 1952 that "a study group of any size is not warranted." This reflected the position of many NACA researchers who believed the committee should only undertake theoretical and basic research, and leave development projects to the military and industry.[60]

Further discussion ensued during the 24 June 1952 meeting of the Committee on Aerodynamics. Other factors covered at the meeting included Allen's unanticipated discovery of the blunt-body concept and a special request from a group representing 11 missile manufacturers.

The NACA Subcommittee on Stability and Control had invited the same manufacturers to Washington in June 1951 to present their ideas "on the direction in which NACA research should move for greatest benefit in missile development." In this case the weapons in question were more often than not air-to-air and surface-to-air missiles rather than ICBMs. During this meeting, Maxwell W. Hunter, an engineer who was developing the Sparrow and Nike missiles at the Douglas Aircraft Company, suggested that the NACA should begin to explore the problems missiles would encounter at speeds of Mach 4 to Mach 10. Hunter pointed out that several aircraft designers, notably Alexander Kartveli at Republic, were already designing Mach 3+ interceptors.[61] For an air-to-air missile to be effective when launched from an aircraft at Mach 3, the missile itself would most probably need to be capable of hypersonic speeds.[62]

Hunter and Woods repeated their requests during the June 1952 meeting of the Committee on Aerodynamics. In response, the committee passed a resolution largely penned by Air Force science advisor Albert Lombard. The resolution recommended that "(1) the NACA increase its program dealing with the problems of unmanned and manned flight in the upper stratosphere at altitudes between 12 and 50 miles, and at Mach numbers between 4 and 10, and (2) the NACA devote a modest effort to problems associated with unmanned and manned flight at altitudes from 50 miles to infinity and at speeds from Mach number 10 to the velocity of escape from Earth's gravity." The NACA Executive Committee ratified the resolution on 14 July. NACA Headquarters then asked the Ames, Langley, and

---

60 Memorandum, Smith J. DeFrance, Director, Ames Aeronautical Laboratory, to NACA, subject: Report on Research of Interest to Committee on Aerodynamics, 29 May 1952.

61 In early 1948 Alexander Kartveli at Republic Aviation began designing the Mach 3 AP-44A all-weather high-altitude defense fighter, less than a year after the first XS-1 supersonic flight. Republic sent preliminary data to the Air Force in January 1951, and in September received a phase I development contract for the WS-204A. Although the entire aircraft was extremely futuristic, perhaps its most notable feature was the Wright J67 dual-cycle turbojet engine. The engine installation provided a large bypass duct that fed air directly into the afterburner, allowing it to function as a ramjet at high speed. An 18-month extension of the phase I contract provided further studies of titanium fabrication, high-temperature hydraulics, escape capsules, and periscopic sights. The Air Force continued to fund the program despite a variety of technical problems. By July 1954 the program had advanced to the point where the Air Force awarded Republic a contract to manufacture three prototypes. However, technical problems continued, and a low funding level made it difficult to apply sufficient resources to overcome them. In early 1957 the Air Force reduced the program to a single prototype and two flight engines, but little progress had been made by 21 August 1957 when the Air Force canceled the XF-103 and Wright engine entirely. The program had cost $104 million over nine years.

62 Joseph Adams Shortal, *A New Dimension: Wallops Island Flight Test Range—The First Fifteen Years*, NASA publication SP-1028 (Washington DC: NASA, 1978), p. 238.

Lewis[63] laboratories for comments and recommendations concerning the implementation of this resolution.[64]

This resolution had little immediate effect on existing Langley programs, with the exception that it inspired the Pilotless Aircraft Research Division (PARD)[65] to evaluate the possibility of increasing the speeds of their test rockets up to Mach 10. Nevertheless, the resolution did have one very important consequence for the future: the final paragraph called for the laboratories "to devote a modest effort" to the study of space flight.[66]

The concepts and ideas discussed by Dornberger, Hunter, and Woods inspired two unsolicited proposals for research aircraft. The first, released on 21 May 1952, was from Hubert M. "Jake" Drake and L. Robert Carman of the NACA High-Speed Flight Research Station (HSFRS) and called for a two-stage system in which a large supersonic carrier aircraft would launch a smaller, manned research airplane. The Drake-Carman proposal stated that by "using presently available components and manufacturing techniques, an aircraft having a gross weight of 100,000 pounds could be built with an empty weight of 26,900 pounds. Using liquid oxygen and water-alcohol propellants, this aircraft would be capable of attaining Mach numbers of 6.4 and altitudes up to 660,000 feet. It would have duration of one minute at a Mach number of 5.3. By using this aircraft, an aircraft of the size and weight of the Bell X-2 could be launched at Mach 3 and an altitude of 150,000 feet, attaining Mach numbers up to almost 10 and an altitude of about 1,000,000 feet. Duration of one minute at a Mach number of 8 would be possible." The report went into a fair amount of detail concerning the carrier aircraft, but surprisingly little toward describing the heating and structural problems expected for the smaller research airplane.[67]

David G. Stone, head of the Stability and Control Branch of the PARD, released the second report in late May 1952. This report was somewhat more conservative and proposed that the Bell X-2 itself could be used to reach speeds approaching Mach 4.5 and altitudes near 300,000 feet if it were equipped with two JPL-4 Sergeant solid-propellant rocket motors. Stone also recommended the formation of a project group that would work out the details of actual hardware development, flight programs, and aircraft systems. Langley director Henry J. E.

---

63 The Aircraft Engine Research Laboratory was founded on 23 June 1941 in suburban Cleveland, Ohio. In April 1947 it was renamed the Flight Propulsion Research Laboratory, and a year later it was renamed the Lewis Flight Propulsion Laboratory. When NASA came into being on 1 October 1958, the laboratory was renamed the Lewis Research Center (abbreviated LeRC to differentiate it from the Langley Research Center (LaRC)). On 1 March 1999 it was renamed the John H. Glenn Research Center at Lewis Field.

64 Minutes of the Meeting, Committee on Aerodynamics, 24 June 1952. In the files at the NASA History Office.

65 The PARD was established in June 1946 at the Auxiliary Flight Research Station (AFRS) on Wallops Island, off the eastern shore of Virginia. This group had been set up during World War II to launch "pilotless aircraft" (the military's name for all guided missiles of the time) to obtain research data on them. On 4 July 1945, the AFRS launched its first test vehicle, a small two-stage, solid-fuel rocket, to check out the installation's instrumentation. At the end of the war, a typical model weighed about 40 pounds and could attain a maximum speed of Mach 1.4 before it crashed into the Atlantic Ocean. The instrumented models provided telemetry back to the ground during their flights. Despite the fact that PARD launched 386 models from 1947 to 1949, the "real" researchers in the Langley wind tunnels never believed that the operation obtained much useful data. Nevertheless, the PARD continued and soon began launching large-scale models of aircraft on top of its rockets, obtaining data at speeds the wind-tunnel operators could only dream of at the time. Many types of aircraft were evaluated; for instance, tests of the Convair F-102 Delta Dagger helped verify the effectiveness of Richard T. Whitcomb's area rule principle.

66 Hansen, *Engineer in Charge*, pp. 350-351.

67 Hubert M. Drake and L. Robert Carman, "A Suggestion of Means for Flight Research at Hypersonic Velocities and High Altitudes," unpublished, 21 May 1952. In the files at the Dryden History Office.

Reid and John Stack generally supported this approach, but believed that further study of possible alternatives was required.[68]

Meanwhile, in response to the 1952 recommendation from the NACA Committee on Aerodynamics, Henry Reid set up a three-man study group consisting of Clinton E. Brown (chairman) from the Compressibility Research Division, William J. O'Sullivan, Jr., from the PARD, and Charles H. Zimmerman from the Stability and Control Division. Curiously, none of the three had any significant background in hypersonics. Floyd L. Thompson, who became associate director of Langley in September 1952, had rejected a suggestion to include a hypersonic aerodynamicist or specialist in thermodynamics in the study group. Thompson's plan was to bring together creative engineers with "completely fresh, unbiased ideas." The group was to evaluate the state of available technology and suggest possible programs that researchers could initiate in 1954, given adequate funding.[69]

This group reviewed the ongoing ICBM-related work at Convair and RAND,[70] and then investigated the feasibility of hypersonic and reentry flight in general terms. Not surprisingly, the group identified structural heating as the single most important problem. The group also reviewed the earlier proposals from Drake-Carman and Stone, and agreed to endorse a version of Stone's X-2 modification with several changes. In the Langley concept, the vehicle used a more powerful internal rocket engine instead of strap-on solid boosters, with the goal of reaching Mach 3.7 velocities. Dr. John E. Duberg, the chief of the Structural Research Division, noted, however, that "considerable doubt exists about the ability of the X-2 airplane to survive the planned trajectory because of the high thermal stresses." The study group released its report on 23 June 1953, and in a surprisingly conservative vein, agreed that unmanned missiles should conduct any research in excess of Mach 4.5.[71]

Originally, the plan was to have an interlaboratory board review the findings of the study group, but this apparently never happened. Nevertheless, hypersonic specialists at Langley frequently had the opportunity to talk with the group, and heard Brown formally summarize the findings at a briefing in late June 1953. While listening to this summary, the specialists "felt a strong sense of *déja-vu*,"

---

68 Letter, David G. Stone to Chief of Research, subject: Preliminary study of the proposal for the flight of manned vehicles into space, 21 May 1952. In the files at the Dryden History Office. The High-Speed Flight Research Station (HSFRS) became the High-Speed Flight Station (HSFS) on 1 July 1954, the Flight Research Center (FRC) on 27 September 1959, and the Hugh L. Dryden Flight Research Center (usually abbreviated DFRC) on 26 March 1976. On 1 October 1981, it was administratively absorbed into the Ames Research Center and its name was changed to the Ames-Dryden Flight Research Facility (DFRF). It reverted to Center status on 1 March 1994 and again became DFRC. At some point between 1954 and 1959, the hyphen between "High" and "Speed" seems to have been dropped, but no official evidence of this could be found.

69 Clinton E. Brown, William J. O'Sullivan, and Charles H. Zimmerman, "A Study of the Problems Relating to High-Speed, High-Altitude Flight," 25 June 1953. Copy in the Langley Technical Library under code CN-141,504; Lloyd S. Swenson, Jr., James M. Grimwood, and Charles C. Alexander, *This New Ocean: A History of Project Mercury,* NASA publication SP-4201 (Washington DC: NASA, 1966), p. 57.

70 E. P. Williams, et al., RAND report 174, "A Comparison of Long-Range Surface-to-Surface Rocket and Ram-Jet Missiles," May 1950. From http://rand.org/about/history/: "On 1 October 1945, General Henry H. "Hap" Arnold and Donald Douglas set up Project RAND ('research and development') under special contract to the Douglas Aircraft Company. However, this arrangement was not ideal, and in February 1948 the chief of staff of the newly created United States Air Force wrote to Donald Douglas approving the evolution of RAND into a nonprofit corporation, independent from Douglas. On 14 May 1948, RAND incorporated as a nonprofit corporation under the laws of the State of California. RAND's charter was remarkably brief: 'To further and promote scientific, educational, and charitable purposes, all for the public welfare and security of the United States of America.'"

71 Brown et al., "A Study of the Problems Relating to High-Speed, High-Altitude Flight." The Duberg quote is in Appendix VI.

especially on hearing Brown's pronouncement that "the main problem of hypersonic flight is aerodynamic heating." They disagreed, however, with the group's conclusion that the NACA would have to rely on flight-testing, rather than on ground-based approaches, for research and development beyond Mach 4.[72]

Brown, O'Sullivan, and Zimmerman found it necessary to reject the use of traditional ground facilities for hypersonic research because they were "entirely inadequate" in accounting for the effects of high temperatures.[73] John Becker later wrote that "much of the work of the new small hypersonic tunnels was viewed with extreme skepticism" because they could not simulate the correct temperatures and boundary-layer conditions. The Brown study anticipated there would be significant differences between the "hot" aerodynamics of hypersonic flight and the "cold" aerodynamics simulated in ground facilities. The study concluded that "testing would have to be done in actual flight where the high-temperature hypersonic environment would be generated" and recommended extending the PARD rocket-model testing technique to much higher speeds. This would also mean longer ranges, and the study suggested it might be possible to recover the test models in the Sahara Desert of northern Africa.[74]

This was another case of the free-flight-versus-wind-tunnel debate that had existed at Langley for years. Ground facilities could not simulate the high-temperature environment at very high Mach numbers, admitted the hypersonics specialists, but facilities like the pilot 11-inch hypersonic tunnel at Langley and the 10-by-14-inch continuous-flow facility at Ames had proven quite capable of performing a "partial simulation." Selective flight-testing of the final article was desirable—just as it always had been—but, for the sake of safety, economy, and the systematic parametric investigation of details, the hypersonics specialists argued that ground-based techniques had to be the primary tools for aerodynamic research. Similar debates existed between the wind-tunnel researchers and the model-rocket researchers at PARD.[75]

Although Langley had not viewed their May 1952 proposal favorably, in August 1953 Drake and Carman wrote a letter to NACA Headquarters calling for a five-phase hypersonic research program that would lead to a winged orbital vehicle. Dr. Hugh L. Dryden, the director of the NACA, and John W. "Gus" Crowley, the associate director for research at NACA Headquarters, shelved the proposal as being too futuristic.[76] Nevertheless, in its bold advocacy of a "piggyback" two-stage-to-orbit research vehicle, the Drake-Carman report presented one of the earliest serious predecessors of the Space Shuttle.

72 John V. Becker, "Development of Winged Reentry Vehicles, 1953-1963," unpublished, dated 23 May 1983, p. 30. In the Becker Archives at Virginia Polytechnic Institute, Blacksburg, Virginia.

73 Shortal, *A New Dimension*, p. 208.

74 Becker, "Development of Winged Reentry Vehicles, 1953-1963," p. 30.

75 Hansen, *Engineer in Charge*, p. 353.

76 Dr. Dryden resigned from the Bureau of Standards to become director of aeronautical research at the NACA in 1947, and two years later became the director of the 8,000-person agency.

MILITARY SUPPORT

At the October 1953 meeting of the Air Force Scientific Advisory Board (SAB) Aircraft Panel, Chairman Clark B. Millikan asked panel members for their ideas on future aircraft research and development programs. The panel decided that "the time was ripe" for another cooperative (USAF-NACA) research airplane project to further extend the frontiers of flight. Millikan released a statement declaring that the feasibility of an advanced manned research aircraft "should be looked into." The panel member from NACA Langley, Robert R. Gilruth, would later play an important role in coordinating a consensus between the SAB and the NACA.[77]

Contrary to Sänger's wartime conclusions, by 1954 most experts within the NACA and industry agreed that hypersonic flight would not be possible without major advances in technology. In particular, the unprecedented problems of aerodynamic heating and high-temperature structures appeared to be a potential "barrier" to sustained hypersonic flight. Fortunately, the perceived successes enjoyed by the X-planes led to increased political and philosophical support for a more advanced research aircraft program. The most likely powerplant for the hypersonic research airplane was one of the large rocket engines from the missile programs. Most researchers now believed that manned hypersonic flight was feasible, but it would entail a great deal of research and development. Fortunately, at the time there was less emphasis than now on establishing operational requirements prior to conducting basic research, and, perhaps even more fortunately, there were no large manned space programs that would compete for funding. The time was finally right.[78]

The hypersonic research program most likely originated during a meeting of the NACA Interlaboratory Research Airplane Projects Panel held in Washington, D.C., on 4–5 February 1954. The panel chair, Hartley A. Soulé, had directed the NACA portion of the cooperative USAF-NACA research airplane program since 1946. In addition to Soulé, the panel consisted of Lawrence A. Clousing from Ames, Charles J. Donlan from Langley, William A. Fleming from Lewis, Walter C. Williams from the HSFS, and Clotaire Wood from NACA Headquarters. Two items on the agenda led almost directly to the call for a new research airplane. The first was a discussion concerning Stone's proposal to use a modified X-2, with the panel deciding that the aircraft was too small to provide meaningful hypersonic research. The second was a proposal to develop a new thin wing for the Douglas D-558-2. This precipitated a discussion on the "advisability of seeking a completely new research airplane and possible effects on such a proposal on requests for major changes to existing research airplanes." The panel concluded that the research utility of the D-558-2 and X-2 was largely at an end, and instead recommended that NACA Headquarters request detailed goals and requirements for an

77 The NACA actually had two cooperative efforts under way in the early 1950s, and Soulé was involved with both. The first was testing the Bell X-1, X-2, X-5, etc., in cooperation with the Air Force. The other was testing the Douglas D-558 series in cooperation with the Navy.

78 Becker, "The X-15 Program in Retrospect," p. 2.

entirely new vehicle from each of the research laboratories. This action was, in effect, the initial impetus for what became the X-15.[79]

On 15 March 1954, Bob Gilruth sent Clark Millikan a letter emphasizing that the major part of the research and development effort over the next decade would be "to realize the speeds of the existing research airplanes with useful, reliable, and efficient aircraft under operational conditions" (i.e., developing Mach 2–3 combat aircraft). Gilruth further noted that a "well directed and sizeable effort will be required to solve a number of critical problems, by developing new materials, methods of structural cooling and insulation, new types of structures, and by obtaining a thorough understanding of the aerodynamics involved." Because many of the problems were not then well defined, "design studies should be started now for manned research aircraft which can explore many of these factors during high-speed flight" and which would be capable of "short excursions into the upper atmosphere to permit research on the problems of space flight and reentry." It was a surprising statement.[80]

During the late 1940s and early 1950s, the overwhelming majority of researchers thought very little about manned space flight. Creating a supersonic airplane had proven difficult, and many researchers believed that hypersonic flight, if feasible at all, would probably be restricted to missiles. Manned space flight, with its "multiplicity of enormous technical problems" and "unanswered questions of safe return" would be "a 21st Century enterprise."[81]

Within a few years, however, the thinking had changed. By 1954 a growing number of American researchers believed that hypersonic flight extending into space could be achieved much sooner, although very few of them had the foresight to see it coming by 1960. Around this time, the military became involved in supporting hypersonic research and development with a goal of creating new weapons systems. During 1952, for example, the Air Force began sponsoring Dornberger's manned hypersonic boost-glide concept at Bell as part of Project BoMi.[82]

BoMi (and subsequently RoBo) advanced the Sänger-Bredt boost-glide concept by developing, for the first time, a detailed thermal-protection concept. Non-load-bearing, flexible, metallic radiative heat shields ("shingles") and water-cooled, leading-edge structures protected the wings, while passive and active cooling systems controlled the cockpit temperature. NACA researchers, including the Brown study group, read the periodic progress reports of the Bell study—classified Secret by the Air Force—with great interest. Although most were skeptical,

79 Minutes of the Meeting, Interlaboratory Research Airplane Projects Panel, NACA headquarters, 4-5 February 1954; letter, John W. Crowley to distribution, subject: Request for comments on possible new research airplane, 9 March 1954. The Research Airplane Projects Panel was formed by NACA Associate Director for Research Gus Crowley in September 1948 to coordinate the efforts of Ames, Langley, Lewis, Wallops Island, and the HSFS. Each laboratory reported quarterly to the panel detailing what research was being performed in support of each specific airplane, and the outcome of the research. The panel met in formal session annually. This was different from the Research Airplane Program Committee headed by Langley's John Stack, which included representatives from the Army Air Forces and the Navy Bureau of Aeronautics.

80 Letter, Robert R. Gilruth to Dr. Clark B. Millikan, subject: Air Force Research and Development Effort for the Next Decade in the Field of the Aircraft Panel, 15 March 1954. In the files at the Air Force Historical Research Agency. John Becker remembers that at the time the consensus was that "space" began where the dynamic pressure was less than one pound per square foot. See the interview of John V. Becker by J. D. Hunley, 3 October 2000, written transcript in the files at the DFRC History Office.

81 Becker, "Development of Winged Reentry Vehicles, 1953-1963."

82 BoMi was an acronym for "Bomber-Missile," and RoBo stood for "Rocket-Bomber." Both would be consolidated into the HYWARDS program that later evolved into the Boeing X-20 Dyna-Soar.

a few thought that the project just might work. The Air Force would also fund similar studies by other contractors, particularly Convair and, later, Boeing.[83]

In response to the recommendation of the Research Airplane Projects Panel, NACA Headquarters asked its field installations to explore the requirements for a possible hypersonic research aircraft. Based on the concerns of the 1952 Langley study group, as well as data from Bell regarding BoMi research, it was obvious that a primary goal of any new research airplane would be to provide information about high-temperature aerodynamics and structures. The missile manufacturers concurred.[84]

In response to NACA Headquarters' request, all of the NACA laboratories set up small ad hoc study groups during March 1954. A comparison of the work of these different NACA groups is interesting because of their different approaches and findings. The Ames group concerned itself solely with suborbital long-range flight and ended up favoring a military-type air-breathing (rather than rocket-powered) aircraft in the Mach 4–5 range. The HSFS suggested a larger, higher-powered conventional configuration generally similar to the Bell X-1 or Douglas D-558-1 research airplanes. The staff at Lewis questioned the need for a piloted airplane at all, arguing that ground studies and the PARD rocket-model operation could provide all of the necessary hypersonic information at much less cost and risk. Lewis researchers believed that possible military applications had unduly burdened previous research airplane programs, and there was no reason to think anything different would happen in this case.[85]

On the other hand, Langley chose to investigate the problem based largely on the hypersonic research it had been conducting since the end of World War II. After the 11-inch hypersonic tunnel became operational in 1947, a group headed by Charles McLellan began conducting limited hypersonic research. This group, which reported to John Becker, who was now the chief of the Aero-Physics Division, provided verification of several newly developed hypersonic theories while it investigated phenomena such as the shock–boundary-layer interaction. Langley also organized a parallel exploratory program into materials and structures optimized for hypersonic flight. Perhaps not surprisingly, Langley decided to determine the feasibility of a hypersonic aircraft capable of a 2- to 3-minute excursion out of the atmosphere to create a brief period of weightlessness in order to explore the effects of space flight. Hugh Dryden would later liken this excursion to the leap of a fish out of water, and coined a new term: space leap.[86]

---

83 Becker, "Development of Winged Reentry Vehicles, 1953-1963." The quotes are Becker's recollections of how other engineers felt at the time, not his personal feelings on the subjects.

84 John E. Duberg, "Remarks on the Charts Presenting the Structural Aspect of the Proposed Research Airplane," 9 July 1954. In the files at the NASA History Office.

85 Letter, Floyd L. Thompson/Langley to NACA, 3 May 1954, enclosing a copy of a memo from John V. Becker titled "Research Airplane Study;" letter, HSFS to NACA, 5 May 1954, enclosing an informal report titled "Suggested Requirements for a New Research Airplane"; letter, Ames to NACA, no subject, 7 May 1954; memorandum from Lewis/Associate Director to NACA, 7 May 1954 (actually written 27 April 1954); Hansen, *Engineer in Charge*, p. 357. According to Hard D. Wallace, Jr., *Wallops Station and the Creation of an American Space Program*, NASA publication SP-4311 (Washington, DC: NASA, 1997) p. 19, note 41: "Note that unlike the earlier X-series aircraft, no models of the X-15 appear to have been tested at Wallops."

86 Letter, John V. Becker to Dennis R. Jenkins, 12 June 1999; Becker, "Development of Winged Reentry Vehicles, 1953-1963," p. 30.

Three men that played important parts in the X-15 program. On the right is Walter C. Williams, the head of the High-Speed Flight Station and a member of the Research Airplane Projects panel that guided the X-15 through its formative stages. In the middle, Hugh L. Dryden, the Director of the NACA. At left is Paul F. Bikle, who came late to the X-15, but guided it through most of its flight program as the director of the Flight Research Center. (NASA)

Langley's ad hoc hypersonic aircraft study group consisted of John Becker (chairman); Maxime A. Faget,[87] a specialist in rocket propulsion from the Performance Aerodynamics Branch of PARD; Thomas A. Toll, a control specialist from the Stability Research Division; Norris F. Dow, a hot-structures expert from the Structures Research Division; and test pilot James B. Whitten. Unlike the earlier Brown study group, this group intentionally included researchers with previous experience in hypersonics.[88]

The group reached a consensus on the objectives of a hypersonic research aircraft by the end of its first month of study. Although one of the original goals was to investigate the effects of weightlessness, the members soon realized "that the problems of attitude control in space and the transition from airless flight to atmospheric flight during reentry were at least equally significant." The group also began to consider the dynamics of the reentry maneuvers and the associated problems of stability, control, and heating as the most pressing research need. However, another objective would come to dominate virtually every other aspect of the aircraft's design: research into the related fields of high-temperature aero-

87 Max Faget would be instrumental in the mid-to-late 1960s in defining the configuration of the Space Shuttle orbiter.

88 Letter, John V. Becker to Dennis R. Jenkins, 12 June 1999; Hansen, *Engineer in Charge*, p. 357.

dynamics and high-temperature structures. Thus, it would become the first aircraft in which aero-thermo-structural considerations constituted the primary research problem, as well as the primary research objective.[89]

Eventually, Becker and the group selected a goal of Mach 7, noting that this would permit investigation of "extremely wide ranges of operating and heating conditions." By contrast, a Mach 10 vehicle "would require a much greater expenditure of time and effort" yet "would add little in the fields of stability, control, piloting problems, and structural heating." Considering that no human had yet approached Mach 3, even Mach 7 seemed a stretch.[90]

By the end of April 1954, Becker's group had completed a tentative design for a winged aircraft and an outline of proposed experiments. The group kept the configuration as conventional as possible to minimize the need for special low-speed and transonic developments without compromising its adequacy as a hypersonic, aerodynamic, and structural research vehicle. However, acknowledging what would become a continuing issue; the group did not consider any of the large rocket engines then under development entirely satisfactory for the airplane. In the absence of the rapid development of a new engine, the group hoped a combination of three or four smaller rocket motors could provide hypersonic velocities.[91]

At this point Floyd Thompson, by now the associate director at Langley, influenced the direction of the Becker study. He made a suggestion that echoed John Stack's 1945 recommendation that the Bell XS-1 transonic research airplane use a 12% thick wing that would force it to encounter the compressibility efforts that aerodynamicists were most interested in studying. Since the hypersonic airplane would be the first in which aero-thermal-structural considerations constituted the primary research problem, Thompson argued that the aim of the aircraft "should be to penetrate as deeply as possible into the region of [high aerodynamic] heating and to seek fresh design approaches rather than makeshift modifications to conventional designs." His suggestion became policy.[92]

Wind-tunnel testing began in mid-1954 and continued through the end of 1955 using the basic Becker design. David E. Fetterman, Jr., Jim A. Penland, and Herbert W. Ridyard led the tests, mainly using the 11-inch tunnel at Langley. The researchers noted that previous hypersonic designs had "been restricted mainly to missile types which were not required to be able to land and which, therefore, had relatively small wings or wings of very low aspect ratio." The researchers concentrated on extrapolating existing data to the Becker design while making sure the concept would be acceptable for a manned aircraft, including the ability to land.[93]

---

89 Letter, John V. Becker to Dennis R. Jenkins, 12 June 1999.

90 Letter, Floyd L. Thompson/Langley to NACA, 3 May 1954, enclosing a copy of a memo from John V. Becker titled "Research Airplane Study." The quotes are from the attached memo.

91 Although it had always been assumed that air-drop would be the preferred launch method, the original "Research Airplane Study" did not specifically mention any launch method.

92 Letter, John V. Becker to Dennis R. Jenkins, 12 June 1999; Hansen, *Engineer in Charge*, p. 357.

93 A variety of reports came from these tests. See, for example, Jim A. Penland et al., "Lift, Drag, and Static Longitudinal Stability Data from an Exploratory Investigation at a Mach Number of 6.86 of an Airplane Configuration Having a Wing of Trapezoidal Plan Form," NACA research memorandum L54L03b, 18 January 1955; Herbert W. Ridyard et al., NACA research memorandum L55A21a, "Static Lateral Stability Data from an Exploratory Investigation at a Mach Number of 6.86 of an Airplane Configuration Having a Wing of Trapezoidal Plan Form," 15 February 1955; Jim A. Penland et al., "Static Longitudinal and lateral Stability and Control Characteristics of an Airplane Configuration Having a Wing of Trapezoidal Plan Form with Various Tail Airfoil Sections and Tail Arrangements at a Mach Number of 6.86," NACA research memorandum L55F17, 15 August 1955.

One particular feature, however, differed from later concepts. The initial wind-tunnel tests used a design that incorporated relatively large leading-edge radii for both the wing and vertical stabilizer. The large radii were believed necessary to keep the heat transfer rates within feasible limits. Eventually the researchers discovered the beneficial effects of a leading-edge sweep and found materials capable of withstanding higher temperatures. These allowed smaller radii, resulting in less drag and generally better aerodynamic characteristics. Although the baseline design changed as a result, by this time the researchers were concentrating on evaluating various empennage configurations and elected not to change the wing design on the wind-tunnel models to avoid invalidating previous results.[94]

While performing the original heating analysis of the proposed reentry from the "space leap," Becker and Peter F. Korycinski from the Compressibility Research Division ran head-on into a major technical problem. At Mach 7, reentry at low angles of attack appeared impossible because of disastrous heating loads. In addition, the dynamic pressures quickly exceeded, by large margins, the limit of 1,000 pounds per square foot (psf) set by structural demands. New tests of the force relationships in the 11-inch tunnel provided Becker and Korycinski with a surprising solution to this problem: if the angle of attack and the associated drag were increased, deceleration would begin at a higher altitude. Slowing down in the thinner (lower-density) atmosphere made the heat-transfer problem much less severe. In other words, Becker and Korycinski surmised, by forcing deceleration to occur sooner, the increased drag associated with the high angle of attack would significantly reduce the aircraft's exposure to peak dynamic pressure and high heating rates. Thus, by using "sufficient lift," the Langley researchers found a way to limit the heat loads and heating rates of reentry. Interestingly, this is the same rationale used 15 years later by Max Faget when he designed his MSC-002 (DC-3) space shuttle concept at the Manned Spacecraft Center.[95]

On reflection, it became clear to the Becker group that the sufficient-lift concept was a "new manifestation" of Allen's blunt-body theory and was as applicable to high-lift winged reentry as to the non-lifting missile warheads studied at Ames during 1952. As the group increased the angle of attack to dissipate more of the kinetic energy through heating of the atmosphere (and less in the form of frictional heating of the vehicle itself), the configuration became increasingly "blunt." Some form of speed brakes, again in accord with Allen's concept, could increase drag and further ease the heating problem.[96]

Throughout 1954 the heating problems of high-lift, high-drag reentry came under increasing scrutiny from key Langley researchers. However, another problem soon outweighed the heating consideration: making the configuration stable and controllable at the proposed high-angle-of-attack reentry attitude. Because they were venturing into a new flight regime, the researchers could not determine

94 Penland, "Static Longitudinal and Lateral Stability and Control Characteristics."

95 Unpublished paper, "11-Inch Tunnel Contributions to the X-15," no author (probably Becker), no date. In the Becker Archives at Virginia Polytechnic Institute, Blacksburg, Virginia; Becker, "Development of Winged Reentry Vehicles, 1953-1963," p. 10. For a detailed look at Faget's design, including some of his rationale for slowing down at high altitude, see Dennis R. Jenkins, *Space Shuttle: The History of the National Space Transportation System – The First 100 Missions* (North Branch, MN: Specialty Press, 2001), pp. 102-108.

96 Hansen, *Engineer in Charge*, p. 359.

the exact hypersonic control properties of such a configuration. Nor were they certain they could devise a structure that would survive the anticipated 2,000°F equilibrium temperatures.[97]

The HSFS had forewarned Langley about potential hypersonic stability problems. In December 1953, Air Force Major Chuck Yeager had pushed the Bell X-1A far beyond its expected speed range. As the aircraft approached Mach 2.5, it developed uncontrollable lateral oscillations that nearly proved disastrous.[98] While Yeager frantically tried to regain control, the airplane tumbled for over a minute, losing nearly 10 miles of altitude. At subsonic speed, the aircraft finally entered a conventional spin from which Yeager managed to recover. This incident led to a systematic reinvestigation of the stability characteristics of the X-1A. By mid-1954, findings indicated that the problem that had almost killed Yeager was the loss of effectiveness of the X-1A's thin-section horizontal and vertical stabilizers at high speed. The HSFS was not equipped to conduct basic research into solutions, but it coordinated with Langley in an attempt to overcome this problem. At the same time, Langley and the HSFS began investigating the inertial-coupling phenomenon encountered by the North American F-100A Super Sabre.[99]

The Becker group faced a potential stability problem that was several times more severe than that of the X-1A. Preliminary calculations based on data from X-1A wind-tunnel tests indicated that the hypersonic configuration would require a vertical stabilizer the size of one of the X-1's wings to maintain directional stability—something that was obviously impractical. Stumped by this problem, Becker sought the advice of his 11-inch hypersonic tunnel researchers. The consensus, reached by wind-tunnel testing and evaluating high-speed data from earlier X-planes, was that an extremely large vertical stabilizer was required if the thin-section stabilizers then in vogue for supersonic aircraft were used. This was largely because of a rapid loss in the lift-curve slope of thin airfoil sections as the Mach number increased. In a radical departure, however, Charles McLellan suggested using a thicker wedge-shaped section with a blunt trailing edge. Some time before, McLellan had conducted a study of the influence of airfoil shape on normal-force characteristics, and his findings had been lying dormant in the NACA literature. Calculations based on these findings indicated that at Mach 7 the wedge shape "should prove many times more effective than the conventional thin shapes optimum for the lower speed." By modifying the proposed configuration

---

97 John V. Becker, "The X-15 Project, Part I: Origins and Research Background," *Astronautics and Aeronautics*, February 1964, p. 56; letter, John V. Becker to Dennis R. Jenkins, 29 July 2002. The temperatures in the boundary layer at Mach 7 exceed 3,000°F. The 2,000°F "equilibrium" temperature is the surface temperature of the underside of the wing where heat loss due to radiation away from the surface balances the imposed heating. Although the angle of attack was between 11 and 26 degrees, the reentry flight path was generally around –32 degrees, meaning that the airplane was actually flying between 21 and 6 degrees nose-down.

98 The wind-tunnel tests of the X-1A had extended only to Mach 2.

99 Arthur Henderson, Jr., "Wind Tunnel Investigation of the Static Longitudinal and Lateral Stability of the Bell X-1A at Supersonic Speeds," NACA research memorandum L55I23, October 1955; and Hubert M. Drake and Wendell H. Stillman, "Behaviors of the X-1A Research Airplane During Exploratory Flights at Mach Numbers Near 2.0 and at Extreme Altitudes," NACA research memorandum H55G26, October 1955; Herman O. Ankenbruck and Chester H. Wolowicz, "Lateral Motions Encountered With the Douglas D-558-2 All-Rocket Research Airplane During Exploratory Flights to a Mach Number of 2.0," NACA research memorandum H54I27, December 1954.

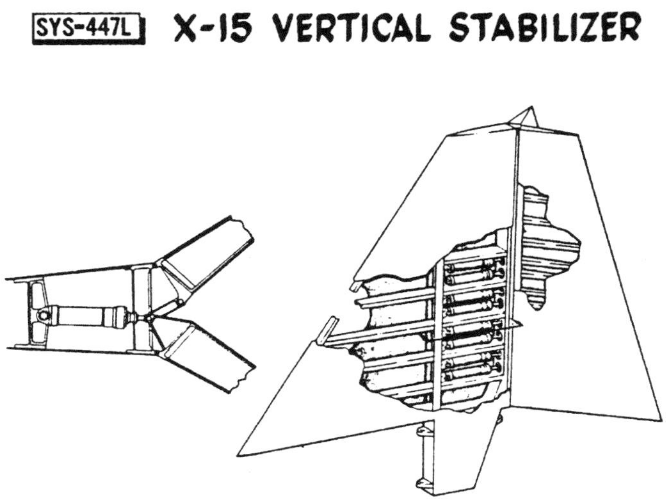

Charles H. McLellan at NACA Langley, one of the researchers that defined much of the X-15 configuration, proposed the use of a split training edge on the vertical stabilizer to form speed brakes. Perhaps even more importantly, these could also be opened to form a variable-wedge vertical stabilizer as a means of restoring the lift-curve slope at high speeds, thus permitting much smaller surfaces that were easier to design and imposed a smaller drag penalty at lower speeds. The ultimate X-15 configuration did not incorporate the split trailing edge, but the much-later space shuttles did. (NASA)

to include the wedge-shaped vertical stabilizer, McLellan believed that a reasonably sized vertical stabilizer could correct most directional instability.[100]

A new series of experiments in the 11-inch tunnel verified that a vertical stabilizer with a 10-degree wedge angle would allow the proposed aircraft to achieve the range of attitudes required by heating considerations for a safe high-drag, high-lift reentry. Further, it might be possible to use a variable-wedge vertical stabilizer as a means of restoring the lift-curve slope at high speeds, thus permitting much smaller surfaces that would be easier to design and would impose a smaller drag penalty at lower speeds. McLellan calculated that this wedge shape should eliminate the disastrous directional stability decay encountered by the X-1A.[101]

Becker's group also included speed brakes as part of the vertical stabilizers to reduce the Mach number and heating during reentry. Interestingly, the speed brakes originally proposed by Langley consisted of a split trailing edge; very similar to the one eventually used on the space shuttles. As the speed brakes opened, they effectively increased the included angle of the wedge-shaped vertical stabi-

100 Becker, "The X-15 Project, Part I," p. 56. Charles H. McLellan had outlined the findings of his original study in an "Investigation of the Aerodynamic Characteristics of Wings and Bodies at a Mach Number of 6.9," a paper presented at an NACA conference on supersonic aerodynamics held at Ames in early 1950. A version of this paper appeared in the October 1950 edition of the *Journal of the Aeronautical Sciences*, volume 18, number 10, pp. 641-648. In 1963 McLellan received a $2,000 award for the development of "wedge tails for hypersonic aircraft" under Section 306 of the National Aeronautics and Space Act of 1958 (see Jane Van Nimmen and Leonard C. Bruno with Robert L. Rosholt, *NASA Historical Data Book Volume I: NASA Resources 1958-1968*, NASA publication SP-4012, Washington, DC, 1988, p. 556).

101 Charles H. McLellan, "A Method for Increasing the Effectiveness of Stabilizing Surfaces at High Supersonic Mach Numbers," NACA research memorandum L544F21, August 1954.

lizer, and variable deflection of the wedge surfaces made it possible to change the braking effect and stability derivatives through a wide range. The flexibility this made possible could be of great value because a primary use of the airplane would be to study stability, control, and handling characteristics through a wide range of speeds and altitudes. Furthermore, the ability to reenter in a high-drag condition with a large wedge angle greatly extended the range of attitudes for reentry that were permissible in view of heating considerations.[102]

Up until this time, the designers of supersonic aircraft had purposely located the horizontal stabilizer well outside potential flow interference from the wings. This usually resulted in the horizontal stabilizer being located partway up the vertical stabilizer, or in some cases (the F-104, for example) on top of the vertical stabilizer. However, researchers at the HSFS suspected that this location was making it difficult, or at times impossible, for aircraft to recover from divergent maneuvers. The same investigations at Langley that verified the effectiveness of the wedge-shape also suggested that an X-shaped empennage would help the aircraft to recover from divergent maneuvers.[103]

The Becker group recognized that the change from a conventional "+" empennage to the "X" configuration would present at least one major new problem: the X-shape empennage projected into the high downwash regions above and below the wing plane, causing a potentially serious loss of longitudinal effectiveness. Researchers at Langley looked for solutions to this new problem. By late 1954 they had an unexpected answer: locate a conventional "+" horizontal stabilizer *in* the plane of the wing, between the regions of highest downwash. This eliminated the need to use an X-shaped empennage, allowing a far more conventional tail section and control surfaces.[104]

Although it would come and go from the various preliminary designs, the use of a ventral stabilizer was beginning to gain support. Charles McLellan observed, "At high angles of attack, the effectiveness of the upper and lower vertical stabilizers were markedly different. Effectiveness of the upper tail decreases to zero at about 20 degrees angle of attack. The lower tail exhibits a marked increase in effectiveness because of its penetration into the region of high dynamic pressure produced by the compression side of the wing. Assuming the wing is a flat plate and the flow is two-dimensional, the dynamic pressure below the wing increases with angle of attack. Since only a part of the lower tail is immersed in this region its gain in effectiveness is, of course, less rapid, but the gain more than offsets the loss in effectiveness of the upper tail."[105]

---

102 John V. Becker, "Review of the Technology Relating to the X-15 Project," a paper presented at the NACA Conference on the Progress of the X-15 Project, Langley Aeronautical Laboratory, 25-26 October 1956, pp. 4-5.

103 McLellan, "A Method for Increasing the Effectiveness of Stabilizing Surfaces at High Supersonic Mach Numbers."

104 Becker, "The X-15 Project, Part I: Origins and Research Background," p. 56-57. Downwash is a small velocity component in the downward direction that is associated with the production of lift, as well as a small component of drag. At hypersonic speed, the flow behind a wing is characterized by a shock pattern. Immediately behind the shock is a region of high dynamic pressure and high downwash, which intersected the lower tail surfaces of the original X-tail concept. The upper tails were in a region of low dynamic pressure and low downwash. This situation had the adverse effect of greatly increasing the yaw (or side-to-side movement) of the lower tails relative to the upper tails, causing directional instability. See McLellan, "A Method for Increasing the Effectiveness of Stabilizing Surfaces at High Supersonic Mach Numbers."

105 McLellan, "A Method for Increasing the Effectiveness of Stabilizing Surfaces at High Supersonic Mach Numbers."

On the structural front, the Becker study evaluated two basic design approaches. In the first, a layer of assumed insulation protected a conventional low-temperature aluminum or stainless steel structure. The alternative was an exposed "hot structure." This design approach and the materials used permitted high structural temperatures without insulation.[106]

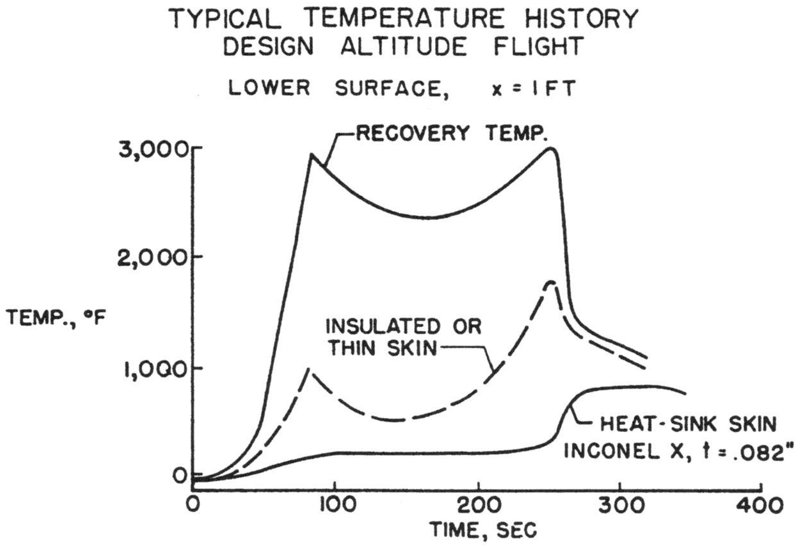

Surprisingly, the temperatures expected on the high-altitude "space leap" were significantly higher than for the basic hypersonic research flights. Establishing a design that could withstand the 2,000°F equilibrium temperature was a challenge, and ultimately resulted in the hot-structure concept shown on the lower line of this chart. (NASA)

Analysis of the heating projections for various trajectories showed that the airplane would need to accommodate equilibrium temperatures of over 2,000°F on its lower surface. Unfortunately, no known insulating technique could meet this requirement. Bell was toying with a "double-wall" concept in which a high-temperature outer shell and a layer of insulator would protect the underlying low-temperature structure. This concept would later undergo extensive development, and several contractors proposed it during the X-15 competition, but in 1954 it was in an embryonic state and not applicable to the critical nose and leading-edge regions. However, the Becker group believed that the possibility of local failure of any insulation scheme constituted a serious hazard, as was later tragically demonstrated on the Space Shuttle *Columbia*. Finally, the problem of accurately measuring heat-transfer rates—one of the primary objectives of the new research

106 Becker, "The X-15 Project, Part I: Origins and Research Background," p. 56-57. These same trade studies would be repeated many times during the concept definition for the Space Shuttle.

aircraft program—would be substantially more difficult to accomplish with an insulated structure.[107]

At the start of the study, it was by no means obvious that the hot-structure approach would prove practical either. The permissible design temperature for the best available material was about 1,200°F, which was far below the estimated equilibrium temperature of 2,000°F. It was clear that some form of heat dissipation—either direct internal cooling or absorption into the structure itself—would be necessary. It was thought that either solution would bring a heavy weight penalty.

The availability of Inconel X and its exceptional strength at extremely high temperatures made it, almost by default, the structural material preferred by Langley for a hot-structure design.[108] In mid-1954, Norris Dow began an analysis of an Inconel X structure while other researchers conducted a thermal analysis. In a happy coincidence, the results showed that the skin thickness needed to withstand the expected aerodynamic stresses was about the same as that needed to absorb the thermal load. This meant that it was possible to solve the structural problem for this transient condition of the Mach 7 research aircraft with no serious weight penalty for heat absorption. This was an unexpected plus for the hot structure. Together with the fact that none of the perceived difficulties of an insulated-type structure (particularly the difficulty of studying structural temperatures) were present, this led the study group to decide in favor of an uninsulated hot-structure design.

Unfortunately, it later proved that the hot structure had problems of its own, especially in the area of non-uniform temperature distribution. Detailed thermal analyses revealed that large temperature differences would develop between the upper and lower wing skins during the pull-up portions of certain trajectories, resulting in intolerable thermal stresses in a conventional structural design. To solve this new problem, researchers devised wing shear members that did not resist unequal expansion of the wing skins. The wing thus was essentially free to deform both span-wise and chord-wise with asymmetrical heating. Although this solved the problem for gross thermal stresses, localized thermal-stress problems still existed near the stringer attachments. The study indicated, however, that proper selection of stringer proportions and spacing would produce an acceptable design that would be free of thermal buckling.[109]

The analyses produced other concerns as well. Differential heating of the wing leading edge resulted in changes to the natural torsional frequency of the wing unless the design used some sort of flexible expansion joint. The hot leading edge expanded faster than the remaining structure, introducing a compression that destabilized the section as a whole and reduced its torsional stiffness. To negate these phenomena, researchers segmented and flexibly mounted the leading edge to reduce thermally induced buckling and bending. Similar techniques found use on the horizontal and vertical stabilizers.

---

107 Ibid. Possible insulators included water, several different liquid metals, air, and various fibrous batt materials. The liquids would require active pumps and large reservoirs, making them exceptionally heavy concepts.

108 Inconel X® is a temperature-resistant alloy whose name is a registered trademark of Huntington Alloy Products Division, International Nickel Company, Huntington, West Virginia. It is, for all intents, an exotic stainless steel. Inconel X is 72.5% nickel, 15% chromium, and 1% columbium, with iron making up most of the balance.

109 Becker, "The X-15 Project, Part I: Origins and Research Background," p. 57-58.

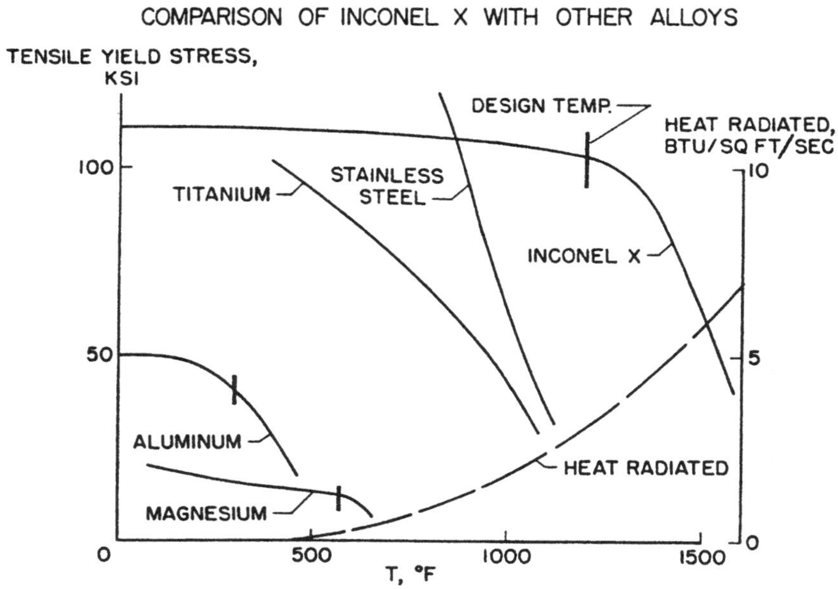

Langley evaluated many materials for the proposed hypersonic research airplane, but the availability of Inconel X and its exceptional strength at extremely high temperatures, made it, almost by default, the preferred material for a hot-structure design. Coincidently, the researchers at NACA Langley discovered that the skin thickness needed to withstand aerodynamic stress was about the same as the amount of structure needed to absorb the thermal load from the high-altitude mission. (NASA)

Perhaps more worrisome was the question of potential propulsion systems. The most promising configuration was found to be four General Electric A1 or A3 rocket engines, due primarily to the "thrust stepping" this configuration provided.[110] At the time, rocket engines could not be throttled (even today, most rocket engines cannot be). Several different techniques can be used to throttle a rocket engine, and each takes its toll in mechanical complexity and reliability. However, a crude method of throttling did not actually involve changing the output of the engine, but rather igniting or extinguishing various numbers of small engines. For instance, in a cluster of three 5,000-lbf engines, the available thrust levels (or "steps") would be 5,000, 10,000, and 15,000 lbf. Since most rocket engines were not restartable (again, the concept adds considerable mechanical complexity to the engine), once an engine was extinguished it could not be restarted. Thrust

110 The General Electric A1 and A3 engines powered the Hermes A-3, also designated XSSM-A-16, which was designed as a tactical surface-to-surface missile capable of carrying a 1,000-pound warhead 150 miles. Project Hermes was the first major U.S. ballistic missile program. It encompassed several different configurations and tested both liquid and solid-fuel rockets, and ramjet propulsion systems. Hermes began in 1944 as an Army effort to study the German V-2 rocket. The project soon led to hardware development, and the first of five Hermes A-1s was launched at the White Sands Proving Grounds on 19 May 1950. The program was canceled on 31 December 1954.

stepping or throttling allowed a much more refined flight profile, and largely defined the propulsion concept for the eventual X-15.[111]

At this stage of the study, the vehicle concept itself was "little more than an object of about the right general proportions and the correct propulsive characteristics" to achieve hypersonic flight. However, in developing the general requirements, the Langley group envisioned a conceptual research aircraft that would serve as a model for the eventual X-15. The vehicle they conceived was "not proposed as a prototype of any of the particular concepts in vogue in 1954...[but] rather as a general tool for manned hypersonic flight research, able to penetrate the new regime briefly, safely, and without the burdens, restrictions, and delays imposed by operational requirements other than research." [112]

Although the Becker group was making excellent progress, their continued investigation of the "space leap" caused considerable controversy. The study called for two distinct research profiles. The first–the basic hypersonic research flights—consisted of a variety of constant angle-of-attack, constant-altitude flights to investigate aero-thermodynamic characteristics. However, the second flight profile explored the problems of future space flight, including investigations into "high-lift and low-L/D [lift over drag] during the reentry pull-up maneuver." Researchers recognized that this was one of the principal problems for manned space flight from both a heating and piloting perspective.[113]

This brought yet more concerns: "As the speed increases, an increasingly large portion of the aircraft's weight is borne by centrifugal force until, at satellite velocity, no aerodynamic lift is needed and the aircraft may be operated completely out of the atmosphere. At these speeds the pilot must be able to function for long periods in a weightless condition, which is of considerable concern from the aeromedical standpoint." By employing a high-altitude ballistic trajectory to roughly 250,000 feet, the Becker group expected that the pilot would operate in an essentially weightless condition for approximately 2 minutes. Attitude control was another problem since traditional aerodynamic control surfaces would be useless at very high altitudes. To solve this problem, the group proposed using small hydrogen-peroxide thrusters for attitude control outside the sensible atmosphere.

While the hypersonic research aspect of the Langley proposal enjoyed virtually unanimous support, it is interesting to note that in 1954 most researchers viewed the space-flight aspect with, at best, cautious tolerance. There were few who believed that any space flight was imminent, and most believed that manned space flight in particular would not be achieved until many decades in the future, probably not until the 21st century. For instance, John Becker remembers that even the usually far-sighted John Stack was "not really interested in the reentry problem or in space flight in general." Several researchers opined that the

111 Thrust stepping was not a new idea. The XLR11 used on the X-1 and other early X-planes had four "chambers" that could be started and extinguished individually. This allowed the thrust to be tailored for any given flight to one of four levels. There was an ongoing effort to develop a throttleable engine for the Bell X-2 research airplane. Originally assigned to Bell, the contract was moved to Curtiss-Wright. The resulting engine was the XLR25-CW-1 which was continuously variable from 2,500 to 15,000 lbf. Unfortunately, the engine fell significantly behind schedule and proved to be unsatisfactory.

112 Becker, "The X-15 Program in Retrospect," p. 2.

113 Ibid.

space-flight research was premature and recommended it be eliminated. Fortunately, it remained.[114]

Langley's work throughout 1954 demonstrated one thing: the need for flexibility. Since their inceptions, the Brown and Becker groups had run into one technical problem after another in the pursuit of a conceptual hypersonic aircraft capable of making a space leap. Conventional wisdom had provided experimental and theoretical guidance for the preliminary design of the configuration, but had fallen far short of giving final answers. Contemporary transonic and supersonic aircraft designs dictated that the horizontal stabilizer should be located far above or well below the wing plane, for example, but that was wrong. Ballistics experts committed to pointy-nosed missiles had continued to doubt the worth of Allen's blunt-body concept, but they too were wrong. Conversely, the instincts of Floyd Thompson, who knew very little about hypersonics but was a 30-year veteran of the vicissitudes of aeronautical research, had been sound. The design and research requirements of a hypersonic vehicle that could possibly fly into space were so radically new and different, Thompson suggested, that only "fresh approaches" could meet them. He was correct.

A CONVINCING CASE

After three months of investigations, the Becker group believed that the development of a Mach 7 research aircraft was feasible. Those at NACA Headquarters who followed the progress of their work, as well as the parallel work on hypersonic aircraft concepts at the other NACA laboratories, agreed. It was time to formally present the results to the NACA upper echelon and the Department of Defense.[115]

The preliminary specifications for the research airplane were surprisingly brief: only four pages of requirements, plus six additional pages of supporting data. As John Becker subsequently observed, "it was obviously impossible that the proposed aircraft be in any sense an optimum hypersonic configuration." Nevertheless, Langley believed the design would work. At the same time, a new sense of urgency was present: "As the need for the exploratory data is acute because of the rapid advance of the performance of service [military] aircraft, the minimum practical and reliable airplane is required in order that the development and construction time be kept to a minimum." In other versions of the requirements, this was even more specific: "It shall be possible to design and construct the airplane within 3 years." The researchers were nothing if not ambitious.[116]

On 4 May 1954, Hugh Dryden sent a letter to Lieutenant General Donald L. Putt at Air Force Headquarters stating that the NACA wanted to initiate a new manned hypersonic research aircraft program. The letter suggested a meeting between the NACA, Air Force Headquarters, and the Air Force Scientific Advi-

114 Hugh L. Dryden, "Toward the New Horizons of Tomorrow," 1st von Kármán Lecture, Astronautics, January 1963; James R. Hansen, *Spaceflight Revolution: NASA Langley Research Center from Sputnik to Apollo*, NASA publication SP-4308 (Washington DC: NASA, 1995), p. 98.

115 Letter, Hartley A. Soulé to NACA, no subject, 3 June 1954.

116 Becker, "The X-15 Program in Retrospect," p. 2; "Preliminary Outline Specification for High-Altitude, High-Speed Research Airplane," NACA Langley, 15 October 1954; "General Requirements for a New Research Airplane," NACA Langley, 11 October 1954.

sory Board to discuss the project. Putt responded favorably and recommended inviting the Navy as well. The general also noted that "the Scientific Advisory Board has done some thinking in this area and has formally recommended that the Air Force initiate action on such a program." On 11 June 1954, Dryden sent letters to the Air Force and Navy inviting them to a meeting on 9 July 1954 at NACA Headquarters.[117]

Attendees included Clark Millikan, Ezra Kotcher from the WADC, and a variety of Air Force and Navy technical representatives. The Air Research and Development Command (ARDC) and Air Force Headquarters also sent policy representatives. During the meeting, Hartley Soulé and Walt Williams reviewed the history of previous research airplanes. Hugh Dryden reported the reasons why the NACA believed a new research aircraft was desirable, and said the time had come to determine whether an agreement existed on the objectives and scope of such a project. Dryden emphasized the need for information on full-scale structural heating and on stability and control issues at high speeds and high altitudes. He also indicated that the NACA thought that actual flight-testing combined with theoretical studies and wind-tunnel experiments produced the best results. The Langley study became the starting point for further discussions since it was the most detailed available, with John Becker and John Duberg, who was substituting for Norris Dow, leading the discussions.[118]

Those in attendance were in general agreement that a new project was feasible. However, Hugh Dryden, reflecting what John Becker described as "his natural conservatism," stated that the fact it was feasible to build such a research airplane did not necessarily make it worth building; he wanted further study before deciding. The Navy representative indicated that some "military objective" should be included in the program, but Clark Millikan stressed the need for a dedicated research airplane rather than any sort of tactical prototype. The group agreed the performance parameters discussed by the Langley study represented an adequate increment over existing research airplanes, and that a cooperative program would be more cost-effective and more likely to provide better research data at an earlier time. The meeting closed with an agreement that the military would continue studying the NACA proposal, and that Hugh Dryden would seek Department of Defense approval for the project.[119]

117 Letter, Hugh L. Dryden to USAF Headquarters, no subject, 4 May 1954; letter, Lieutenant General Donald L. Putt to Dryden, no subject, 26 May 1954; letter, Hugh L. Dryden to USAF Headquarters (invitation), 11 June 1954; letter, Hugh L. Dryden to Navy Bureau of Aeronautics (invitation), 11 June 1954. Donald L. Putt (1905-1988) was a career U.S. Air Force officer who specialized in the management of aerospace research and development activities. Trained as an engineer, he entered the Army Air Corps in 1928 and worked in a series in increasingly responsible posts at the Air Materiel Command and Air Force Headquarters. From 1948 until 1952 he was director of research and development for the Air Force, and between 1952 and 1954 he was first vice commander and then commander of the Air Research and Development Command. Thereafter, until his retirement in 1958 he served as deputy chief of the development staff at Air Force Headquarters.

118 Memorandum for the files (NACA Headquarters), subject: Minutes of joint USAF-USN-NACA new research airplane briefing, 3 September 1954. In the files at the NASA History Office.

119 Memorandum for the files, John V. Becker, subject: Note on the July 9, 1954 Meeting, no date; Hugh L. Dryden, "General Background of the X-15 Research Airplane Project," a paper presented at the NACA Conference on the Progress of the X-15 Project, Langley Aeronautical Laboratory, 25-26 October 1956, pp. xvii-xix; memorandum, J. W. Rogers, Liquid Propellant and Rocket Branch, Rocket Propulsion Division, ARDC, to Lieutenant Colonel L. B. Zambon, Power Plant Laboratory, WADC, no subject, 13 July 1954. In the files at the AFMC History Office. The difference between the Air Force and NACA budgets showed why DoD support was necessary. In fiscal year 1955 the NACA was appropriated $56 million; the Air Force received $16,600 million.

Unexpectedly, the Office of Naval Research (ONR) announced at the meeting that it had already contracted with the Douglas Aircraft Company to investigate a manned vehicle capable of achieving 1,000,000 feet altitude and very high speeds. The configuration evolved by Douglas "did not constitute a detailed design proposal," but was only a "first approach to the problem of a high-altitude high-speed research airplane." Representatives from the NACA agreed to meet with their ONR counterparts on 16 July to further discuss the Douglas study.

THE DOUGLAS MODEL 671

The "High Altitude and High Speed Study" by the El Segundo Division of the Douglas Aircraft Company had been funded by the ONR as a follow-on to the D-558 research aircraft that loosely competed with the Air Force X-1 series. Duane N. Morris led the study under the direction of the chief of the Aerodynamic Section, Kermit E. Van Every. Although the concept is generally mentioned—briefly—in most histories of the X-15, what is almost always overlooked is how insightful it was regarding many of the challenges that would be experienced by the X-15 a few years later.[120]

By the spring of 1954, when the X-15 approval process began, Douglas had not accomplished a detailed design for a new airplane, but recognized many of the same problems as John Becker and the researchers at Langley. The Douglas engineers also examined peripheral subjects—carrier aircraft, landing locations, etc.—that the initial Langley studies did not address in any detail.[121]

One interesting aspect of the Douglas Model 671 was that the contractor and the Navy had agreed that the aircraft was to have two mission profiles: high speed and high altitude (with the emphasis on the latter). This was in distinct contrast to the ongoing Langley studies that eventually led to the X-15. Although the Becker team at Langley was interested in research outside the sensible atmosphere, there was a great deal of skepticism on the part of others in the NACA and the Air Force. Douglas did not have this problem—the ONR strongly supported potential high-altitude research.

Excepting the Langley work, the Douglas study was probably the first serious attempt to define a hypersonic research airplane. Most of the other companies investigating hypersonics were oriented toward producing operational vehicles, such as the ICBMs and BoMi. Because of this, they usually concentrated on a different set of problems, frequently at the expense of a basic understanding

120 Office of Naval Research contract Nonr-1266(00). The "D-558-3" designation was never used in any of the official reports describing the concept, although it was widely used in the more popular press and most historical works.

121 Several reports on the Douglas study were published. See, for instance, Douglas report ES-17657, "High Altitude and High Speed Study," 28 May 1954; and Douglas report ES-17673, "Technical Report on High Altitude and High Speed Study," 28 May 1954; One of the few contemporary articles about the concept was written by Irwin Stambler in the May 1959 *Aircraft & Missile Engineering Journal*, pp. 20-21 and 77-79. Copies supplied by Bob Bradley, San Diego Aerospace Museum. For a slightly more in-depth look at the Douglas Model 671, see Dennis R. Jenkins, "Douglas D-558-3," *Aerospace Projects Review*, volume 3, number 6, November-December 2001, pp. 14-27.

of the challenges of hypersonic flight. The introduction from the Douglas study provides a good background:[122]

> The purpose of the high altitude study…is to establish the feasibility of extending human flight boundaries to extreme altitudes, and to investigate the problems connected with the design of an airplane for such flights.
>
> The project is partially a result of man's eternal desire to go higher, faster, or further than he did last year. Of far more importance, however, is the experience gained in the design of aircraft for high-speed, high-altitude flight, the collection of basic information on the upper atmosphere, and the evaluation of human tolerance and adaptation to the conditions of flight at extreme altitudes and speeds.
>
> The design of an airplane for such a purpose cannot be based on standard procedures, nor necessarily even on extrapolation of present research airplane designs. Most of the major problems are entirely new, such as carrying a pilot into regions of the atmosphere where the physiological dangers are completely unknown, and providing him with a safe return to Earth. The type of flight resembles those of hypersonic, long-range, guided missiles currently under study, with all of their complications plus the additional problems of carrying a man and landing in a proper manner.
>
> The study consists of a first approach to the design of a high-altitude airplane. It attempts to outline most of the major problems and to indicate some tentative solutions. As with any preliminary investigation into an unknown regime, it is doubtful that adequate solutions have been presented to every problem of high-altitude flight, or even that all of the problems have been considered. It would certainly appear, however, that the major difficulties are not insurmountable.

The Model 671 was 41.25 feet long (47.00 feet with the pitot boom), spanned only 18 feet with 81 square feet of area, and had an all-up weight of 22,200 pounds. In many respects, it showed an obvious family lineage to the previous D-558s. The fuselage consisted of a set of integral propellant tanks, and dive brakes were located on each side aft, as in most contemporary fighters.

> A conventional configuration was deliberately chosen for the study, and no benefits have yet been discovered for any unconventional arrangement. Actually, for the prime objective of at-

122 "Technical Report on High Altitude and High Speed Study," p. 6.

> taining very high altitudes, the general shape of the airplane is relatively unimportant. Stability and control must be provided, and it must be possible to create sufficient lift for the pullout and for landing; but, in contrast to the usual airplane design, the reduction of drag is not a critical problem and high drag is to some extent beneficial. The planform of the wing is unimportant from an aerodynamic standpoint at the higher supersonic Mach numbers. Therefore, it was possible to select the planform based on weight and structure and landing conditions. These considerations led to the choice of an essentially unswept wing of moderate taper and aspect ratio.[123]

The empennage of the Model 671 was completely conventional and looked much like that of the Mach 2 D-558-2 that preceded it. However, Douglas realized that the design of the stabilizers was one of the greater unknowns of the design. "The tail surfaces are of proper size for stability at the lower supersonic Mach numbers, but there is some question of their adequacy at very high supersonic speeds. Further experimental data in this speed range are necessary before modifications are attempted. In addition, it may be possible to accept a certain amount of instability with the proper automatic servo controls." Unlike the Becker group, Douglas did not have access to a hypersonic wind tunnel.[124]

Nevertheless, preliminary investigations at Douglas indicated that "extremely large tail surfaces, approaching the wing area in size, are required to provide complete stability at the maximum Mach number of about 7." Engineers investigated several methods to improve stability, with the most obvious being to increase the size of the vertical stabilizer. However, placing additional area above the fuselage might introduce lateral directional dynamic stability problems "due to an unfavorable inclination in the principle axis of inertia and the large aerodynamic rolling moment due to sideslip (the dihedral effect)." The preferred arrangement was to add a ventral stabilizer and keep the ventral and dorsal units as symmetrical as possible. However, Douglas recognized that a large ventral stabilizer would present difficulties in ground handling and during landing. The engineers proposed that the fin should be folded on the ground, unfold after takeoff, and then be jettisoned just before touchdown. Alternately, Douglas believed that some sort of autopilot could be devised that would allow the use of more conventional-sized control surfaces.[125]

Douglas conducted an evaluation of available power plants, and reached much the same conclusions the X-15 program would eventually come to. The desired engine should produce about 50,000 lbf with a propellant consumption of about 200 pounds per second. The only powerplant that met the requirements was the Reac-

123 "High Altitude and High Speed Study," p. 7; "Technical Report on High Altitude and High Speed Study," p. 7.

124 "Technical Report on High Altitude and High Speed Study," p. 7. The wedge principle that would play such an important role in the X-15 design was still languishing in the archives, and the Bell X-2 had not provided its own contribution to understanding "high speed instability."

125 "Technical Report on High Altitude and High Speed Study," p. 40; "High Altitude and High Speed Study," pp. 18-19. The eventual X-15 design took a somewhat similar approach, at least for the ventral stabilizer. By the 1970s, of course, augmentation systems were finally beginning to allow inherently unstable aircraft to fly—the Space Shuttle being a prime example.

tion Motors XLR30-RM-2 rocket engine, which used liquid oxygen and anhydrous ammonia propellants. The high (245 lbf-sec/lbm) specific impulse (thrust per fuel consumption) was desirable since it provided "a maximum amount of energy for a given quantity of propellant." The high density of the propellants allowed a smaller tank size for a given propellant weight, allowing a smaller airframe. However, the researchers worried that since the original application was a missile, it would be difficult to make the engine safe enough for a manned aircraft.[126]

Douglas had some interesting observations about drag and power-to-weight ratios:[127]

> The function of drag in the overall performance must be reconsidered. The effect of drag is practically negligible in the power-on ascending phase of flight (for a high altitude launch), because of the very large thrust to weight ratio. Throughout the vacuum trajectory, the aerodynamic shape of the airplane is completely unimportant. During the descending phase of flight, a large drag is very beneficial in aiding in the pullout, and the highest possible drag is desired within the limits of the pilot and the structure. In fact, during the pullout it has been assumed that drag brakes would be extended in order to decelerate as soon as possible. However, because of excessive decelerative forces acting upon the pilot, it is necessary to gradually retract the brakes as denser air is entered, until they are fully retracted in the later stages of flight.
>
> For a given propulsion unit (i.e., fixed thrust and fuel consumption), the overall performance of the present design [Model 671] is much more dependent upon the ratio of fuel weight to gross weight that it is upon the minimum drag or the optimum lift-drag ratio. Even though the fuel is expended in approximately the first 75 seconds of flight (a relatively small fraction of the total flight time), the ultimate performance as measured by the maximum altitude is affected to a great extent by small changes in the fuel to gross weight ratio. As an example, an increase in fuel weight/gross weight from 0.65 to 0.70 results in an increase in peak altitude of about 35% for a typical vertical flight trajectory, other parameters remaining constant.

To better understand the nature of the various propellants then available for rocket engines, engineers reviewed numerous reports by the Caltech Jet Propulsion Laboratory, the NACA, and RAND. Only two oxidizers—oxygen and either red fuming or white fuming nitric acid—seemed to offer any increase in performance. Douglas was seeking better propellants than the liquid oxygen and alcohol

126 "High Altitude and High Speed Study," pp. 1-14. Reaction Motors, Inc., began operations near Danville, New Jersey, in December 1941, only a few months before the founding of Aerojet on the West Coast in March 1942.

127 "Technical Report on High Altitude and High Speed Study," p. 15.

used in the Reaction Motors LR8, effectively ruling out nitric acid since it was less dense than oxygen. The available fuels were alcohol (CH3OH or C2H5OH), anhydrous ammonia (NH3), hydrazine (N2H4), and gasoline. Alcohol offered no improvement, and hydrazine was too expensive and too difficult to handle safely, narrowing the choice to anhydrous ammonia and gasoline. Interestingly, Douglas ruled out liquid hydrogen because "on the basis of density, hydrogen is seen to be a very poor fuel." It would be 20 years before the Centaur upper stage would prove them wrong.[128]

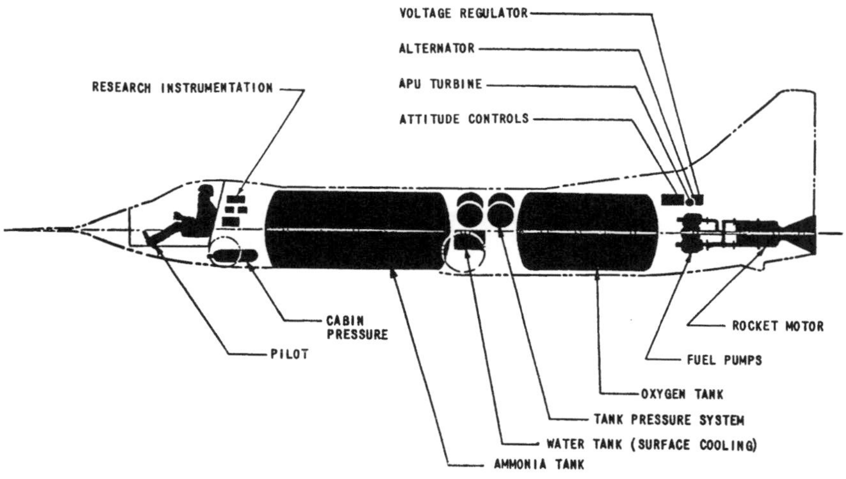

The Douglas Model D-671 was a proposed follow-on to the successful D-558 series of research airplanes developed under Navy auspices and flown at the High-Speed Flight Station. Preliminary investigation showed the concept was capable of roughly the same performance as the eventual X-15, but the Navy declined further development of the Douglas concept when it joined the X-15 program in late 1954. (Douglas Aircraft Company)

An auxiliary power unit (APU) rated at about 8 horsepower was necessary to support the electrical requirements of the instruments, controls, and radio. Investigation showed that the lightest alternative would be a small turbine generator using hydrogen peroxide or ethylene oxide monopropellant. The Walter Kidde Company and American Machine and Foundry Company were develop-

128 "Technical Report on High Altitude and High Speed Study," pp. 64-65. The history of JPL dates to the 1930s when Caltech professor (and head of the Guggenheim Aeronautical Laboratory) Theodore von Kármán began experimenting with rocket propulsion. Von Kármán persuaded the Army Air Corps to fund the development of "jet-assisted take-off" rockets to help underpowered aircraft get off the ground. This was the beginning of the laboratory's rocket-related work for the Army Ordnance department, helping to explain the names of early JPL rockets (Private, Corporal, and Sergeant). By 1945, the JPL had a staff approaching 300 people. JPL was largely responsible for the flight and ground systems of Explorer I successfully launched on 31 January 1958. On 3 December 1958, the laboratory was transferred from Army control to the newly formed NASA.

ing units that could satisfy the requirements. Both companies claimed they could develop a 10-horsepower hydrogen peroxide unit that weighed about 56 pounds, including propellants for 30-horsepower-minutes. Given the trouble of the future X-15 APUs, perhaps North American should have better reviewed this part of the Douglas report.[129]

Douglas recognized that high temperatures would be a major design problem, although they indicated that "it is impractical in the present study to make a complete survey of the temperatures expected on the airplane [since] the calculations are quite complicated and tedious to obtain reasonable estimates." They continued that "it is unfortunate that the largest contributing factor to the high temperatures of reentry, the convective heating from the boundary layer, is the one about which there is the least knowledge." Nevertheless, they took some educated guesses.[130]

The expected average heat level approached 1,400°F, with peak temperatures above 3,300°F on the wing leading edges and nose. Douglas believed "it would be impossible to design a structure for this temperature [1,400°F] which satisfies both the stress and weight requirements…." To overcome this, engineers recommended the use of some as-yet-undeveloped "good insulating material" with a density of 20 pounds per cubic foot and an insulating value of 0.20 British Thermal Units (Btu) per pound. For the purposes of the study, Douglas used a C-110M titanium-alloy structure and skin protected by an unspecified ablative coating. Water sprayed into stainless-steel sections of the wing leading edges and nose area allowed superheated steam to remove unwanted heat, keeping these areas below their melting points. Alternately, Douglas investigated injecting cool gas (bottled oxygen) into the boundary layer to provide cooling. The study noted, however, that "none of these systems have yet been proven by practical application." The designers protected only a few areas, such as the cockpit, with batt insulation since the study assumed no heat transfer to the interior of the aircraft.[131]

Not surprisingly, Douglas chose an air-launch configuration. What is interesting is that the launch parameters were Mach 0.75 at 40,000 feet—well beyond the capabilities of anything except the Boeing B-52, which was still in the early stages of testing. Douglas summarized the need for an air launch by noting that "[t]he performance is increased, but the prime reason for the high altitude launch is the added safety which 40,000 feet of altitude gives the pilot when he takes over under his own rocket power." Trade studies conducted by Douglas indicated that an increase in launch altitude from sea level to 40,000 feet would result in a 200,000-foot increment in maximum altitude on a typical high-altitude mission. Additional benefits of a higher launch altitude diminished rapidly above 40,000 feet since most of the initial improvement was due to decreasing air density.[132]

Engineers spent a great deal of time studying possible flight paths, but "no attempt has been made in the present study to determine an absolute optimum flight

129 "Technical Report on High Altitude and High Speed Study," p. 65.

130 "Technical Report on High Altitude and High Speed Study," pp. 54 and 58. In 1954 calculations of this nature normally were done by hand since general-purpose electronic computers were not widely available, and were quite slow in any case.

131 "High Altitude and High Speed Study," pp. 1-14 and 20-21; "Technical Report on High Altitude and High Speed Study," pp. 55-57.

132 "Technical Report on High Altitude and High Speed Study," pp. 7 and 15-16. Over half the atmosphere lies below 40,000 feet.

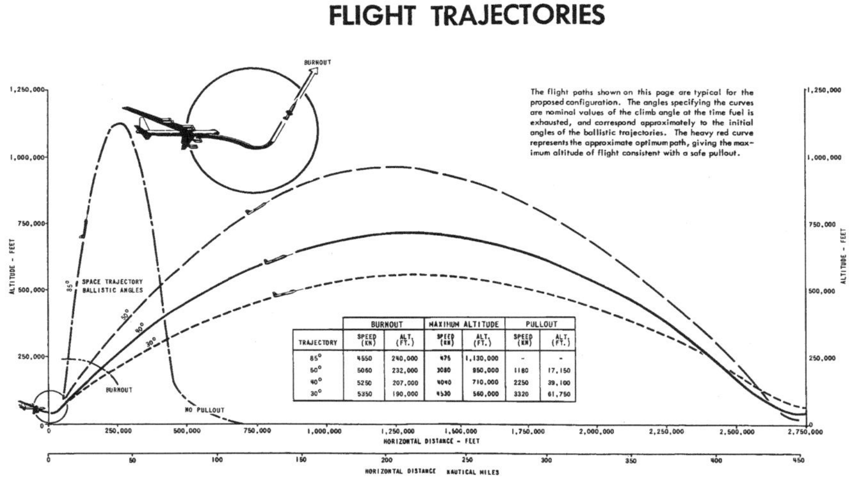

Like the NASA Langley concept, the Douglas D-671 had two separate research flight profiles – one for maximum velocity and one for maximum altitude. Douglas and the Navy were particularly interested in the high-altitude research and at one point estimated the D-671 could reach 1,000,000 feet altitude. Although Douglas only conducted a minimal amount of research into the concept before it was cancelled, they foresaw many of the issues that would ultimately confront the X-15 development effort. (Douglas Aircraft Company)

path, because of the large number of variables involved." The designers noted that the airframe and propulsion systems could theoretically support a maximum altitude in excess of 1,130,000 feet; however, based on a conservative pullout altitude of 30,000 feet, the vehicle was more realistically limited to 770,000 feet. The pullout altitude (and the limiting decelerations, which were really the issue) was "directly traceable to the single limiting factor of the presence of a human pilot." The 770,000-foot, 84-degree profile resulted in a 10-g pullout maneuver, about the then-known limit of human tolerance.[133]

Some thought was given to using a "braking thrust," which would allow a small amount of propellant to be saved and used during reentry. Either a mechanical thrust reverser would be installed on the rocket engine, or the airplane would reenter tail-first. This technique would have allowed slightly higher flights by reducing the stresses imposed by the pullout maneuver, although less propellant would be available for the ascent. The designers did not pursue this concept since entering tail-first involved undesirable risks, and the mechanical complexity of a thrust reverser seemed unnecessary, at least initially.[134]

The theoretical maximum performance was 6,150 mph and 190,000 feet for the speed profile, and 5,200 mph and 1,130,000 feet for the altitude profile (but limited, as discussed above). Landings would be made at Edwards AFB because of its "long runways and considerable latitude in the choice of direction and position of touchdown." The study noted that there would be little opportunity to

133 "Technical Report on High Altitude and High Speed Study," pp. 16-18.

134 "Technical Report on High Altitude and High Speed Study," pp. 18-19.

control either the range or the heading by any appreciable amount after engine burnout. "Since the airplane must land without power at a specified landing site, it is obvious that it must be aimed toward the landing site at launch." Douglas estimated that a misalignment of 5 degrees in azimuth at burnout would result in a lateral miss of over 45 miles.[135]

One of the concerns expressed by Douglas was that "rocket thrust will not be sufficiently reproducible from flight to flight, either in magnitude or in alignment." Engineers estimated a thrust misalignment of less than one-half of a degree could impart 500 pounds of side force on the aircraft, causing it to go significantly off course. Researchers investigated several possible solutions to thrust misalignment, including using a larger rudder, using the auxiliary reaction control system, installing movable vanes in the exhaust,[136] performing gas separation in the nozzle,[137] and mounting the rocket engine on a gimbal. All of these methods contained various problems or unknowns that caused the engineers to reject them. Further consideration showed that thrust misalignment was largely a non-issue since early low-speed flights would uncover any deficiencies, allowing engineers to correct them prior to beginning high-speed flights.[138]

The estimated landing speed was 213 mph, with a stall speed of 177 mph. Engineers accepted this relatively high speed "given the experimental nature of the aircraft and the high skill level of the pilots that will be flying it." The study noted that the slower speeds were possible if high-lift leading-edge devices were used or the area of the wing was increased. However, the increased weight and/or the resulting complications in the leading-edge cooling system appeared to make these changes undesirable.[139]

The high-altitude profile would use "flywheels, gyroscopes, or small auxiliary jets" for directional control outside the atmosphere, with Douglas favoring hydrogen peroxide jets in the wing tips and at the rear of the fuselage. Flywheels were rejected because they were too complex (for a three-axis system), and gyroscopes were too heavy. Each of the hydrogen peroxide thrusters would generate about 100 lbf and use 1 pound of propellant per second of operation. The engineers arbitrarily assumed that a 25-pound supply of propellant was required since no data existed on potential usage during flight. A catalyst turned the liquid hydrogen peroxide to steam at 400-psi pressure.[140]

The projected performance of the airplane caused Douglas engineers to investigate escape capsules for the pilot: "Because of the high altitude and high speed performance of the aircraft, it is believed that all ordinary bailout procedures, such as escape chutes and ejection seats, are of no value to the pilot." At the time, Douglas believed that ejection seats were only "suitable up to a Mach number of

135 "High Altitude and High Speed Study," pp. 15-17 and 23; the quote is from "Technical Report on High Altitude and High Speed Study," p. 37.

136 The same technique used by the V-2 and several other early rockets.

137 This involves injecting a small amount of gas along one wall of the exhaust nozzle, causing a flow separation that results in slightly asymmetrical thrust. The solid rocket motors for the Titan III/IV launch vehicle later used the same technique.

138 "Technical Report on High Altitude and High Speed Study," pp. 37-39.

139 "Technical Report on High Altitude and High Speed Study," p. 21.

140 "Technical Report on High Altitude and High Speed Study," pp. 42-43. In 1954, manned space flight was still seven years in the future, and no airplane had yet flown above the sensible atmosphere. This made it impossible to guess accurately how much control a pilot would want, or need, at extremely high altitudes.

approximately one at sea level, with somewhat higher speeds being safe at higher altitudes." Instead, the engineers decided to jettison the entire forward section of the fuselage, including the pilot's compartment, much like the Bell X-2. The total weight penalty for the capsule was about 150 pounds. The study dismissed pressure suits, stating that "it is very doubtful that sufficient pressurization equipment could be carried by the pilot during...ejection...to sustain suit pressurization from the maximum altitude to a safety zone within the earth's lower atmosphere." Douglas stated flatly that "an ejection seat or other ordinary bailout techniques will be inadequate in view of the problem of high speeds and high altitudes." Scott Crossfield would later disagree.[141]

In order to withstand the reentry temperatures, the cockpit windscreen used two 0.5-inch layers of quartz with a 0.25-inch vented air gap between them. This would keep the inner windscreen below 200°F. A thin sheet of treated glass placed inside the inner quartz layer reduced ultraviolet and other harmful radiation. Although the potential dangers of radiation above the atmosphere were largely unknown, Douglas predicted that little harm would come from the short flights (a few minutes) envisioned for the D-558-3. However, "proper precautions to prevent any one pilot from making too many successive flights in a weeks or months time interval should be taken...."[142]

One of the technical innovations of the eventual X-15 program was the "ball nose" that sensed the angle of attack and angle of sideslip during high-speed and high-altitude flight. The Douglas study foresaw the need for a new pitch and yaw sensor "capable of sensing exceedingly low forces or pressures, but capable of withstanding the maximum dynamic pressures encountered during the complete pullout." However, Douglas thought that "the instrument need not be precise, for it is only to serve as a guide for pointing the nose into the wind at heights where a pilot might otherwise lose all sense of orientation." Four possible solutions emerged:[143]

1. A weathervane, either direct or remote-reading
2. A pitch or yaw indicator that measured the relative Mach number or pressure ratio on opposite sides of a symmetrical sphere, cone, or other convenient shape
3. A vane inside a conventional instrument case that indicated the direction of the resultant momentum from two jets of air brought in by a pair of symmetrical external tubes
4. A device similar to the Reichardt gage

Douglas dismissed the first two (although the second one is what was eventually built for the X-15) since they did "not seem very satisfactory." The external weathervane would need to feature rugged construction to resist the high aero loads and would therefore be too insensitive at high altitudes. Douglas discount-

141 "High Altitude and High Speed Study," p. 28; quotes from "Technical Report on High Altitude and High Speed Study," pp. 79-80. Most subsequent analyses estimated that an escape capsule would impose a much larger weight penalty than 150 pounds.

142 "Technical Report on High Altitude and High Speed Study," p. 77.

143 Ibid, pp. 45-46.

ed the sensing sphere since engineers doubted they could construct one rugged enough to survive reentry. The third alternative was satisfactory, although the issue of how to protect the system from reentry heat appears to have been ignored. Ultimately, Douglas decided the fourth idea was best. Here is the description of their modified Reichardt gage:[144]

> Air is picked up by the yawed total head tubes and carried into the two chambers L [left] and R [right] of the meter. The chambers are separated by a pivoted flat plate [shown on the accompanying drawing as the vane and pointer] which has a small clearance on all four sides so that it is completely free to pivot. The pivot is quite free and without any spring restraint. When the pressure is higher at R than L the needle will move to the left to allow more air to flow through the porous or perforated plate. The complete flow system has been analyzed, and the equations show that the needle position will be a function only of the ratio of the pressure rises, independent of the dynamic pressure. The needle fluctuation is almost proportional to the pressure ration. The vane system used can be very sensitive...since there is neither torque nor load on the vane, it should be satisfactory at very high indicated speeds.

Considering the short time they had to work on the study, the engineers considered a wide variety of details. For instance, they considered the chances of a meteor hitting the aircraft: "For a projected area of 225 square feet, the chances of being hit by a meteor capable of penetrating more than 0.08-inches of aluminum are about one in 450,000 in any one flight." Given that there were no data on the number or size of high-altitude micrometeorites at the time, exactly how the engineers arrived at this probability is uncertain.[145]

Nevertheless, despite the seemingly thorough study, Douglas noted that there were many uncertainties since they were entering previously unknown areas of aeronautical science. Highlighting this, the final report contained statements such as "[t]here is no method available for the calculation of the supersonic, zero-lift, pressure drag of a finite wing with a laminar flow airfoil section" and "no theoretical methods have been devised for the calculation of the theoretical supersonic section drag coefficient of a blunt nose airfoil." It was all very speculative.[146]

Other areas of concern were calculating (or even understanding) the compressibility effects of turbulent flow at high speeds. The compressibility effects in laminar flow were calculated using factors corresponding to the results of Crocco and Van Driest, but engineers noted that the corresponding correction for turbulent flow was "difficult to determine." At the time there were a number of different theories for the turbulent corrections, all of which appeared equally valid but led

144 Ibid, pp. 44-46.

145 "High Altitude and High Speed Study," p. 26. At the time, almost no data actually existed on the number or size of micrometeorites, or the likelihood of their striking an orbiting object.

146 "Technical Report on High Altitude and High Speed Study," pp. 11-12.

to widely divergent results when extended to higher Mach numbers. The proper choice of a compressibility correction was important because between Mach numbers 3 and 10 the uncorrected skin friction accounted for 40–50% of the total zero-lift drag. Douglas chose to use the Van Driest results that predicted a relatively large decrease in turbulent skin friction as Mach numbers increased, although the engineers noted that the results "may be somewhat optimistic." These were many of the same problems investigated by John Becker, Charles McLellan, and others at Langley.[147]

According to the Douglas representative at the 16 July meeting with the NACA and ONR, the next step would be a more detailed study that would cost $1,500,000 and take a year to complete. Given that a new joint project was about to be undertaken, the ONR declined to further fund the Douglas study, and the company began to concentrate its high-speed efforts on the Model 684 that would be proposed to the Air Force for Project 1226.

Overall, Douglas anticipated many of the problems that were ultimately encountered during the development of the eventual hypersonic research airplane. It would not have surprised any of the engineers working on the Douglas study that the solutions they proposed for some of the problems were not the ones that were ultimately implemented. Still, they touched on almost all of the pitfalls that would hamper the development of the eventual X-15. It is difficult to say whether Douglas could have done the job better, faster, or cheaper (to use a much later vernacular). It is likely, however, that they ultimately would have succeeded in building a useful research aircraft if the government had continued down that road.

147 Ibid, p. 13. Luigi Crocco and E. R. Van Driest had conducted a great deal of research into boundary-layer compressibility at North American Aviation. See, for instance: Luigi Crocco, North American report CF-1038, "The Laminar Boundary Layer in Gases," December 1946; Luigi Crocco, NACA technical note 2432, "Transformations of the Hodograph Flow Equation and the Introduction of Two Generalized Potential Functions," August 1951; and E. R. Van Driest, NACA technical note 2597, "Investigation of the Laminar Boundary Layer in Compressible Fluids Using the Crocco Method," January 1952.

CHAPTER 2

A Hypersonic Research Airplane

The 9 July 1954 meeting at NACA Headquarters and the resulting release of the Langley study served to announce the seriousness of the hypersonic research airplane effort. Accordingly, many government agencies and aircraft manufacturers sent representatives to Langley to examine the project in detail. On 16 July three representatives from the Air Research and Development Command (ARDC)—the Air Force organization that would be responsible for the development of the airplane—visited John Becker to acquaint themselves with the NACA presentation and lay the groundwork for a larger meeting of NACA and ARDC personnel.[1]

Independently of any eventual joint program, approval for the first formal NACA research authorization was granted on 21 July 1954. This covered tests of an 8-inch model of the Langley configuration in the 11-inch hypersonic tunnel to obtain six-component, low-angle-of-attack and five-component, variable-angle-of-attack (to about 50 degrees) data up to Mach 6.86.[2] Research authorizations were the formal paperwork that approved the expenditure of funds or resources on a research project. At the time, it was not unusual—or worthy of comment—for the NACA laboratories to conduct research without approval from higher headquarters or specific funding. This type of oversight would come much later.

1 Memorandum for the files (Langley), subject: minutes of the meeting with ARDC representatives, 16 July 1954.

2 Letter, NACA Headquarters to Langley, subject: research authorization, 21 July 1954.

During late July, Richard V. Rhode from NACA Headquarters visited Robert R. Gilruth to discuss the proposed use of Inconel X in the new airplane. Rhode indicated that Inconel was "too critical a material" for structural use, and the program should select other materials more representative of those that would be in general use in the future. Rhode later put this in writing, although Langley appears to have ignored the suggestion. This harkened back to the original decision that the research airplane was not meant to represent any possible production configuration (aerodynamically or structurally), but instead was to be optimized for its research role.[3]

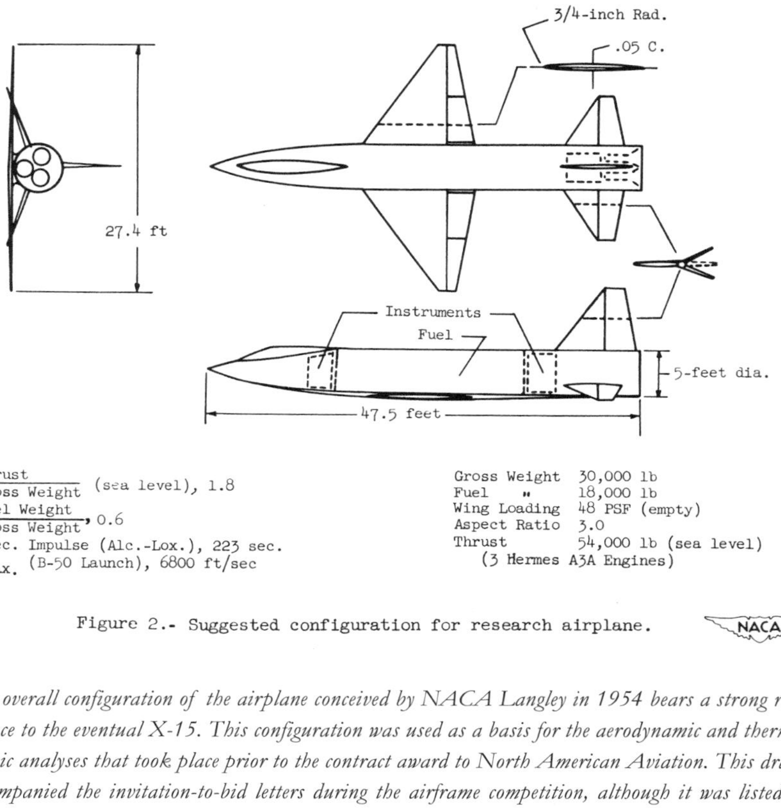

Figure 2.- Suggested configuration for research airplane.

The overall configuration of the airplane conceived by NACA Langley in 1954 bears a strong resemblance to the eventual X-15. This configuration was used as a basis for the aerodynamic and thermodynamic analyses that took place prior to the contract award to North American Aviation. This drawing accompanied the invitation-to-bid letters during the airframe competition, although it was listed as a "suggested means" of complying with the requirements. (NASA)

On 29 July, Robert J. Woods and Krafft A. Ehricke from Bell Aircraft visited Langley as part of the continuing exchange of data with the industry. On 9 August, the Wright Air Development Center (WADC) sent representatives from the Power Plant Laboratory to discuss rocket engines, in particular the Hermes A1 that Langley had tentatively identified for use in the new research airplane. The

3 Letter, Richard V. Rhode, NACA Headquarters, to Robert R. Gilruth, Langley, no subject, 4 August 1954; telephone conversation, John V. Becker with Dennis R. Jenkins, 7 March 2002.

WADC representatives went away unimpressed with the selection. The next day Duane Morris and Kermit Van Every from Douglas visited Langley to exchange details of their Model 671 (D-558-3) study with the Becker team, providing a useful flow of information between the two groups that had conducted the most research into the problem to date.[4]

The Power Plant Laboratory emphasized that the proposed Hermes engine was not a man-rated design, but concluded that no existing engine fully satisfied the NACA requirements. In addition, since the Hermes was a missile engine, it could only operate successfully once or twice, and it appeared difficult to incorporate the ability to throttle or restart during flight. As alternatives to the Hermes, the laboratory investigated several other engines, but suggested postponing the engine selection until the propulsion requirements were better defined.[5]

The Hermes engine idea did not die easily, however. As late as 6 December 1954, K. W. Mattison,[6] a sales engineer from the guided-missile department of the General Electric Company, visited John Becker, Max Faget, and Harley Soulé at Langley to discuss using the A1 engine in the new airplane. Mattison was interested in the status of the project (already approved by that time), the engine requirements, and the likely schedule. He explained that although the Hermes engines were intended for missile use, he was certain that design changes would increase the "confidence level" for using them in a manned aircraft. He was not sure, however, that General Electric would be interested in the idea.[7]

DEVELOPING A CONSENSUS

The WADC evaluation of the NACA proposal arrived at ARDC Headquarters on 13 August. Colonel Victor R. Haugen, director of the WADC laboratories, reported that his organization believed the proposal was technically feasible. The only negative comment referred to the absence of a suitable engine. The WADC estimated that the development effort would cost $12,200,000 and take three or four years. The cost estimate included $300,000 for studies, $1,500,000 for design, $9,500,000 for the development and manufacture of two airplanes, $650,000 for engines and other government-furnished equipment, and $250,000 for modifications to a carrier

4 Memorandum for the files (Langley), subject: new research airplane visits, 18 August 1954.

5 Letter, Colonel Paul F. Nay, Acting Chief, Aeronautics and Propulsion Division, Deputy Commander of Technical Operations, ARDC, to Commander, WADC, subject: New Research Aircraft, 29 July 1954. In the files at the AFMC History Office; memorandum, E. C. Phillips, Chief, Operations Office, Power Plant Laboratory, to Director of Laboratories, WADC, subject: NACA Conference on 9 July 1954 on Research Aircraft-Propulsion System, 5 August 1954; letter, Colonel Victor R. Haugen, Director of Laboratories, WADC, to Commander, ARDC, subject: new research aircraft, 13 August 1954. In the files at the ASD History Office; memorandum, J. W. Rogers, Liquid Propellant and Rocket Branch, Rocket Propulsion Division, Power Plant Laboratory, to Chief, Non-Rotating Engine Branch, Power Plant Laboratory, WADC, subject: conferences on 9 and 10 August 1954 on NACA Research Aircraft-Propulsion System, 11 August 1954. In the files at the AFMC History Office.

6 It was common practice in the 1950s to record only the last name and initials for individuals on official correspondence. First names are provided whenever possible, but in many cases a first name cannot be definitively determined from the available documentation.

7 Memorandum, John V. Becker to the Associate Director/Langley, subject: new rocket engines, 8 December 1954.

aircraft. Somewhat prophetically, one WADC official commented informally: "Remember the X-3, the X-5, [and] the X-2 overran 200%. This project won't get started for twelve million dollars."[8]

A four-and-a-half-page paper titled "NACA Views Concerning a New Research Airplane," released in late August 1954, gave a brief background of the problem and attached the Langley study as a possible solution. The paper listed two major problems: "(1) preventing the destruction of the aircraft structure by the direct or indirect effects of aerodynamic heating; and (2) achievement of stability and control at very high altitudes, at very high speeds, and during atmospheric reentry from ballistic flight paths." The paper concluded by stating that the construction of a new research airplane appeared to be feasible and needed to be undertaken at the earliest possible opportunity.[9]

A meeting between the Air Force, NACA, Navy, and the Office of the Assistant Secretary of Defense for Research and Development took place on 31 August 1954. There was general agreement that research was needed on aerodynamic heating, "zero-g," and stability and control issues at Mach numbers between 2 and 7 and altitudes up to 400,000 feet. There was also agreement that a single joint project was appropriate. The group believed, however, that the selection of a particular design (referring to the Langley proposal) should not take place until mutually satisfactory requirements were approved at a meeting scheduled for October.[10]

Also on 31 August, and continuing on 1 September, a meeting of the NACA Subcommittee on High-Speed Aerodynamics was held at Wallops Island. Dr. Allen E. Puckett from the Hughes Aircraft Company was the chair. John Stack from Langley gave an overview of the proposed research airplane, including a short history of events. He reiterated that the main research objectives of the new airplane were investigations into stability and control at high supersonic speeds, structural heating effects, and aeromedical aspects such as human reactions to weightlessness. He also emphasized that the performance of the new airplane must represent a substantial increment over existing research airplanes and the tactical aircraft then under development. In response to a question about whether an automatically controlled vehicle was appropriate, Stack reiterated that one of the objectives of the proposed program was to study the problems associated with humans at high speeds and altitudes. Additionally, the design of an automatically controlled vehicle would be difficult, delay the procurement, and reduce the value of the airplane as a research tool.[11]

The subcommittee subsequently recommended that the project begin as soon as practical, but recognized that the preliminary Langley concept might not prove to be the best solution. It also recommended the "skill of all the principle design teams in the country be brought to bear in the design of the airplane" and that the

8 A published summary of the 9 July NACA presentations did not appear until 14 August; letter, Colonel Victor R. Haugen to Commander, ARDC, no subject, 13 August 1954; memorandum, R. L. Schulz, Technical Director of Aircraft, to Chief, Fighter Aircraft Division, WADC, no subject, not dated (presumed about 13 August 1954). Both in the files at the AFMC History Office. Budget quote from Houston, Section I.

9 "NACA Views Concerning a New Research Airplane," August 1954. In the files at the NASA History Office.

10 Memorandum, Thomas C. Muse to the Deputy Assistant Secretary of Defense (R&D), no subject, 1 September 1954. In the files at the Air Force Historical Research Agency.

11 Minutes of the Meeting of the NACA Subcommittee on High-Speed Aerodynamics, 31 August-1 September 1954.

establishment of a design competition was the most desirable course of action. The subcommittee forwarded the recommendation to the Committee on Aerodynamics for further consideration.[12]

Major General Floyd B. Wood, the ARDC deputy commander for technical operations, forwarded an endorsement of the NACA proposal to Air Force Headquarters on 13 September 1954, recommending that the Air Force "initiate a project to design, construct, and operate a new research aircraft similar to that suggested by NACA without delay." Wood reiterated that the resulting vehicle should be a pure research airplane, not a prototype of any potential weapon system or operational vehicle. The ARDC concluded that the design and fabrication of the airplane would take about 3.5 years. In a change from how previous projects were structured, Wood suggested that the Air Force should assume "sole executive responsibility," but the research airplanes should be transferred to the NACA after a short Air Force airworthiness demonstration program.[13]

During late September, John R. Clark from Chance-Vought met with Ira H. Abbot at NACA Headquarters and expressed interest in the new project. He indicated that he personally would like to see his company build the aircraft. It was ironic since Chance-Vought would elect not to submit a proposal when the time came. Many other airframe manufacturer representatives would express similar thoughts, usually with the same results. It was hard to see how anybody could make money building only two airplanes.[14]

The deputy director of research and development at Air Force Headquarters, Brigadier General Benjamin S. Kelsey, confirmed on 4 October 1954 that the new research airplane would be a joint USAF-Navy-NACA project with a 1-B priority in the national procurement scheme and $300,000 in FY55 funding to get started.[15]

At the same time, the NACA Committee on Aerodynamics met in regular session on 4 October 1954 at Ames, with Preston R. Bassett from the Sperry Gyroscope Company as chairman. The recommendation forwarded from the 31 August meeting of the Subcommittee on High-Speed Aerodynamics was the major agenda item. The following day the committee met in executive session at the HSFS to come to some final decision about the desirability of a manned hypersonic research airplane. During the meeting, various committee members, including De Elroy Beeler, Walt Williams, and research pilot A. Scott Crossfield, reviewed historic and technical data. Williams's support was crucial. Crossfield would later describe Williams as "the man of the 20th Century who made more U.S. advanced aeronautical and space programs succeed than all the others together.... He was a very strong influence in getting the X-15 program launched in the right direction." Williams would later do the same for Project Mercury.[16]

12 Ibid.

13 Letter, Major General Floyd B. Wood, Deputy Commander of Technical Operations, ARDC, to Director of R&D, USAF, subject: new research aircraft, 20 September 1954. In the files at the ASD History Office.

14 Memorandum for the files (NACA Headquarters), from Ira H. Abbott, no subject, 1 October 1954. Scott Crossfield remembers that none of the contractors were thrilled with the prospects of a two-airplane contract. Unlike today, companies generally made little money on research and development; the profits came from large production quantities.

15 Letter, Brigadier General Benjamin S. Kelsey, Deputy Director of R&D DCS/D, to Commander, ARDC, subject: new research aircraft, 4 October 1954. In the files at the AFMC History Office.

16 Letter, Scott Crossfield to Dennis R. Jenkins, 30 June 1999. Largely because he wanted to become more involved in the X-15 development, Crossfield would leave the NACA in 1955 to work for North American Aviation.

The session at the HSFS stirred more emotion than the earlier meeting in Washington. First, Beeler discussed some of the more general results obtained previously with various research airplanes. Then Milton B. Ames, Jr., the committee secretary, distributed copies of the NACA "Views" document. Langley's associate director, Floyd Thompson, reminded the committee of the major conclusion expressed by the Brown-O'Sullivan-Zimmerman study group in June 1953: that it was impossible to study certain salient aspects of hypersonic flight at altitudes between 12 and 50 miles in wind tunnels due to technical limitations of the facilities. Examples included "the distortion of the aircraft structure by the direct or indirect effects of aerodynamic heating" and "stability and control at very high altitudes at very high speeds, and during atmospheric reentry from ballistic flight paths." The study admitted that the rocket-model program at Wallops Island could investigate aircraft design and operational problems to about Mach 10, but this program of subscale models was not an "adequate substitute" for full-scale flights. Having concluded that the Brown group was right, and that the only immediate way known to solve these problems was to use a manned aircraft, Thompson said that various NACA laboratories had then examined the feasibility of designing a hypersonic research airplane. Trying to prevent an internal fight, Thompson explained that the results from Langley contained in the document Milton Ames had just distributed were "generally similar" to those obtained in the other NACA studies (which they were not), but were more detailed than the other laboratories' results (which they were).[17]

Williams and Crossfield followed with an outline of the performance required for a new research airplane and a discussion of the more important operational aspects of the vehicle. At that point, John Becker and Norris Dow took over with a detailed presentation of their six-month study. Lively debate followed, with most members of the committee, including Clark Millikan and Robert Woods, strongly supporting the idea of the hypersonic research airplane.

Surprisingly, Clarence L. "Kelly" Johnson, the Lockheed representative, opposed any extension of the manned research airplane program. Johnson argued that experience with research aircraft had been "generally unsatisfactory" since the aerodynamic designs were inferior to tactical aircraft by the time research flights began. He felt that a number of research airplanes had developed "startling performances" only by using rocket engines and flying essentially "in a vacuum" (as related to operational requirements). Johnson pointed out that "when there is no drag [at high altitude], the rocket engine can propel even mediocre aerodynamic forms to high Mach numbers." These flights had mainly proved "the bravery of the test pilots," Johnson charged. The test flights generated data on stability and control at high Mach numbers, Johnson admitted, but aircraft manufacturers could not use much of this information because it was "not typical of airplanes actually designed for supersonic flight speeds." He recommended that they use an unmanned vehicle to gather the required data instead of building a new manned airplane. If aeromedical problems became "predominant," Johnson

17 "Minutes of the Meeting, Committee on Aerodynamics," 4-5 October 1954. In the files at the NASA History Office.

Clarence L. "Kelly" Johnson, the legendary founder of the Lockheed Skunk Works, was the only representative on the NACA Committee on Aerodynamics to vote against proceeding with the development of the X-15. Previous X-plane experience had left Johnson jaded since the performance of the research airplanes was not significantly advanced from operational prototypes. As it turned out, the X-15 would be the exception, since no operational vehicle, except the Space Shuttle, has yet approached the velocity and altitude marks reached by the X-15. (Lockheed Martin)

said, a manned research airplane could then be designed and built, and it should have a secondary role as a strategic reconnaissance vehicle.[18]

Various members of the committee took issue with Johnson. Gus Crowley from NACA Headquarters explained that the NACA based its proposal on the X-1 concept "to build the simplest and soundest aircraft that could be designed on currently available knowledge and put into flight research in the shortest time possible." In comparing manned research airplane operations with unmanned, automatically controlled vehicles, Crowley noted that the X-1 and other research air-

18 Ibid, Appendix I, p. 2. Johnson is one of the modern legends in the aerospace community. Founder of the Lockheed "Skunk Works," Johnson was largely responsible for such landmark designs as the P-80, U-2, F-104, and SR-71.

planes had made hundreds of successful flights despite numerous malfunctions.[19] In spite of the difficulties—which, Crowley readily admitted, had occasionally caused the aircraft to go out of control—research pilots had successfully landed the aircraft an overwhelming percentage of the time. In each case the human pilot permitted further flights to explore the conditions experienced, and in Crowley's opinion, automated flight did not allow the same capabilities.[20]

After some further discussion, and despite Johnson's objections, the committee passed a resolution recommending the construction of a hypersonic research aircraft:[21]

RESOLUTION ADOPTED BY NACA
COMMITTEE ON AERODYNAMICS, 5 OCTOBER 1954

WHEREAS, The necessity of maintaining supremacy in the air continues to place great urgency on solving the problems of flight with man-carrying aircraft at greater speeds and extreme altitudes, and

WHEREAS, Propulsion systems are now capable of propelling such aircraft to speeds and altitudes that impose entirely new and unexplored aircraft design problems, and

WHEREAS, It now appears feasible to construct a research airplane capable of initial exploration of these problems,

BE IT HEREBY RESOLVED, That the Committee on Aerodynamics endorses the proposal of the immediate initiation of a project to design and construct a research airplane capable of achieving speeds of the order of Mach Number 7 and altitudes of several hundred thousand feet for the exploration of the problems of stability and control of manned aircraft and aerodynamic heating in the severe form associated with flight at extreme speeds and altitudes.

The "requirements" of the resolution conformed to the conclusions from Langley, but were sufficiently general to encourage fresh approaches. Appended to the specification under the heading of "Suggested Means of Meeting the General Requirements" was a section outlining the key results of the Becker study.[22]

Kelly Johnson was the only member to vote nay. Sixteen days after the meeting, Johnson sent a "Minority Opinion of Extremely High Altitude Research Air-

---

19 If Crowley was talking about high-speed X-planes, he was stretching the point. By the end of 1954, the high-speed research airplanes had barely made 200 flights and, excluding the X-15, would never get to 300 flights.

20 "Minutes of the Meeting, Committee on Aerodynamics," 4-5 October 1954.

21 Resolution, 5 October 1954. In the files at the NASA History Office.

22 Hugh L. Dryden, "General Background of the X-15 Research Airplane Project," a paper presented at the NACA Conference on the Progress of the X-15 Project, Langley Aeronautical Laboratory, 25-26 October 1956, pp. xvii-xix.

plane" to Milton Ames with a request that it be appended to the majority report, which it was.[23]

On 6 October 1954, Air Force Headquarters issued Technical Program Requirement 1-1 to initiate a new manned research airplane program "generally in accordance with the NACA Secret report, subject: 'NACA Views Concerning a New Research Aircraft' dated August 1954." The entire project was classified Confidential. The ARDC followed this on 26 October with Technical Requirement 54 (which, surprisingly, was unclassified).[24]

In the meantime, Hartley Soulé and Clotaire Wood held two meetings in Washington on 13 October. The first was with Abraham Hyatt at the Navy Bureau of Aeronautics (BuAer) to obtain the Navy's recommendations regarding the specifications. The only significant request was that provisions should exist to fly an "observer" in place of the normal research instrumentation package. This was the first (and nearly the only) official request from the Navy regarding the new airplane, excepting the engine. In the second meeting, Soulé discussed the specifications with Colonel R. M. Wray and Colonel Walter P. Maiersperger at the Pentagon, and neither had any significant comments or suggestions.

With an endorsement in hand, on 18 October Hugh Dryden conferred with Air Force (colonels Wray and Maiersperger) and Navy (Admiral Robert S. Hatcher from BuAer and Captain W. C. Fortune from the ONR) representatives on how best to move toward procurement. The parties agreed that detailed technical specifications for the proposed aircraft, with a section outlining the Becker study, should be presented to the Department of Defense Air Technical Advisory Panel by the end of the year. The Navy reiterated its desire that the airplane carry two crew members, since the observer could concentrate on the physiological aspects of the flights and relieve the pilot of that burden. The NACA representatives were not convinced that the weight and cost of an observer could be justified, and proposed that the competing contractors decide what was best. All agreed this was appropriate. Again, the Air Force requested little in the way of changes.[25]

Hartley Soulé met with representatives of the various WADC laboratories on 22 October to discuss the tentative specifications for the airplane. Perhaps the major decision was to have BuAer and the Power Plant Laboratory jointly prepare a separate specification for the engine. The complete specification (airplane and engine) was to be ready by 17 November. In effect, this broke the procurement into two separate but related competitions: one for the airframe and one for the engine.

During this meeting, John B. Trenholm from the WADC Fighter Aircraft Division suggested building at least three airplanes, proposing for the first time more than the two aircraft contained in the WADC cost estimate. There was also a discussion concerning the construction of a dedicated structural test article. It seemed like a good idea, but nobody could figure out how to test it under meaningful temperature conditions, so the group deferred the matter.

---

23 Letter, Clarence L. Johnson to Milton B. Ames, secretary, Committee on Aerodynamics, subject: Minority Opinion of Extremely High Altitude Research Airplane, 21 October 1954.

24 USAF Technical Program Directive 1-1, 6 October 1954; ARDC Technical Requirement 54, 26 October 1954. Both in the files at the Air Force Historical Research Agency.

25 Memorandum for the files (NACA Headquarters), from Clotaire Wood, 26 October 1954; invitations from NACA to Colonel Wray, Colonel Maiersperger, Admiral Hatcher, and Captain Fortune dated 11 October 1954.

Also on 22 October, Brigadier General Benjamin Kelsey and Dr. Albert Lombard from Air Force Headquarters, plus admirals Lloyd Harrison and Robert Hatcher from BuAer, visited Hugh Dryden and Gus Crowley at NACA Headquarters to discuss a proposed Memorandum of Understanding (MoU) for conducting the new research airplane program. Only minor changes to a draft prepared by Dryden were suggested.[26] The military representatives told Dryden that a method of funding the project had not been determined, but the Air Force and Navy would arrive at a mutually acceptable agreement for financing the design and development phases. During the 1940s and 1950s it was normal for the military services to fund the development and construction of aircraft (such as the X-1 and D-558, among others) for the NACA to use in its flight research programs. The aircraft resulting from this MoU would be the fastest, highest-flying, and by far the most expensive of these joint projects.

The MoU provided that technical direction of the research project would be the responsibility of the NACA, acting "with the advice and assistance of a Research Airplane Committee" composed of one representative each from the Air Force, Navy, and the NACA. The New Developments Office of the Fighter Aircraft Division at Wright Field would manage the development phase of the project. The NACA would conduct the flight research, and the Navy was essentially left paying part of the bills with little active roll in the project, although it would later supply biomedical expertise and a single pilot. The NACA and the Research Airplane Committee would disseminate the research results to the military services and aircraft industry as appropriate based on various security considerations. The concluding statement on the MoU was, "Accomplishment of this project is a matter of national urgency."[27]

The final MoU was originated by Trevor Gardner, Air Force Special Assistant for Research and Development, in early November 1954 and forwarded for the signatures of James H. Smith, Jr., Assistant Secretary of the Navy for Air, and Hugh L. Dryden, director of the NACA, respectively. Dryden signed the MoU on 23 December 1954 and returned executed copies to the Air Force and Navy.[28]

John Becker, Norris Dow, and Hartley Soulé made a formal presentation to the Department of Defense Air Technical Advisory Panel on 14 December 1954. The panel approved the program, with the anticipated $12.2 million cost coming from Department of Defense contingency funds as well as Air Force and Navy research and development funds.[29]

---

26 Memorandum of Understanding, signed by Hugh L. Dryden, Director of NACA, James H. Smith, Jr., Assistant Secretary of the Navy (Air), and Trevor Gardner, Special Assistant for R&D, USAF, subject: Principles for the Conduct by the NACA, Navy, and Air Force of a Joint Project for a New High-Speed Research Airplane, 23 December 1954. In the files at the NASA History Office; Walter C. Williams, "X-15 Concept Evolution," a paper in the *Proceedings of the X-15 30th Anniversary Celebration*, Dryden Flight Research Facility, Edwards, California, 8 June 1989, NASA report CP-3105, p. 11.

27 System Development Plan, X-15 Research Aircraft, Supporting Research System Number 447L, 22 March 1956, In the files at the AFFTC History Office; Memorandum of Understanding for the X-15. The Research Airplane Committee was separate from the Research Airplane Projects Panel or the Research Airplane Program Committee.

28 Memorandum of Understanding for the X-15; letter, James H. Smith Jr. Assistant Secretary of the Navy (Air), to Hugh L. Dryden, Director of NACA, 21 December 1954; letter, Hugh L. Dryden to Trevor Gardner returning a signed copy of the MoU, 23 December 1954. In the files at the NASA History Office.

29 Memorandum, A. L. Sea, Assistant Chief, Fighter Aircraft Division, to Director of Weapons Systems Office, WADC, subject: new research aircraft, 29 December 1954. In the files at the ASD History Office.

After the Christmas holidays, on 30 December, the Air Force sent invitation-to-bid letters to Bell, Boeing, Chance-Vought, Convair, Douglas, Grumman, Lockheed, Martin, McDonnell, North American, Northrop, and Republic. Interested companies were asked to attend the bidders' conference on 18 January 1955 after notifying the procurement officer no later than 10 January. An abstract of the NACA Langley study was attached with a notice that it was "representative of possible solutions" but not a requirement to be satisfied.[30]

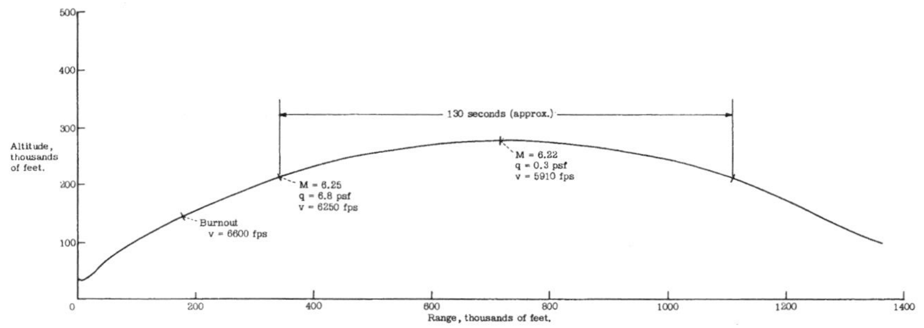

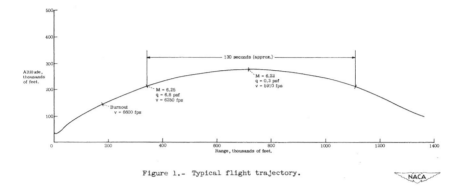

Figure 1.- Typical flight trajectory.

Also accompanying the invitation-to-bid letters was a simple chart that showed the expected flight trajectory for the new research airplane. It was expected that each flight would provide about 130 seconds of good research data after engine burnout. This performance was almost exactly duplicated by the X-15 over the course of the flight program. (NASA)

This was undoubtedly the largest invitation-to-bid list yet for an X-plane, but many contractors were uncertain about its prospects. Since it was not a production contract, the potential profits were limited. Given the significant technical challenges, the possibility of failure was high. Of course, the state-of-the-art experience and public-relations benefits were potentially invaluable. It was a difficult choice even before Wall Street and stock prices became paramount. Ultimately, Grumman, Lockheed, and Martin expressed little interest and did not attend the bidders' conference, leaving nine possible competitors. At the bidders' conference, representatives from the remaining contractors met with Air Force and NACA personnel to discuss the competition and the basic design requirements. The list of participants read like a *Who's Who* of the aviation world. Robert Woods and Walter Dornberger from Bell attended. Boeing sent George Martin, the designer of the B-47. Ed Heinemann from Douglas was there. Northrop sent William Ballhaus.[31]

During the bidders' conference the Air Force announced that each company could submit one prime and one alternate proposal that might offer an un-

30 Letter, Colonel Carl F. Damberg, Chief, Aircraft Division, Air Materiel Command, to Bell Aircraft Corporation et al., subject: competition for new research aircraft, 30 December 1954; memorandum, A. L. Sea, to Director of WSO, WADC, no subject, 29 December 1954; letter, John B. Trenholm, Chief, New Development Office, Fighter Aircraft Division, WADC, to Commander, ARDC, subject: New Research Aircraft, 13 January 1955. In the files at the AFMC History Office.

31 Minutes from the X-15 Bidder's Conference, 18 January 1955. The attendance sheet was attached as an exhibit. In the files at the AFMC History Office.

conventional but potentially superior solution. The Air Force also informed the prospective contractors that an engineering study only would be required for a modified aircraft in which an observer replaced the research instrumentation, per the stated Navy preference. A significant requirement was that the aircraft had to be capable of attaining a velocity of 6,600 fps and altitudes of 250,000 feet. Other clarifications included that the design would need to allocate 800 pounds, 40 cubic feet, and 2.25 kilowatts of power for research instrumentation. A requirement that would come back to haunt the procurement was that flight tests had to begin within 30 months of contract award.

ENGINE OPTIONS

The engine situation was somewhat more complicated. Given that everybody now agreed that the General Electric A1 (Hermes) engine was unacceptable, the Power Plant Laboratory listed the Aerojet XLR73, Bell XLR81, North American NA-5400, and Reaction Motors XLR10 as engines the airframe contractors could use. The four engines were a diverse collection.[32]

The Aerojet XLR73-AJ-1 had a single thrust chamber that used white fuming nitric acid and jet fuel as propellants. As it then existed, the engine developed 10,000 lbf at sea level, but a new nozzle was available that raised that to 11,750 lbf. The engine was restartable in flight by electric ignition and was infinitely variable between 50% and 100% thrust. A cluster of several engines was necessary to provide the thrust needed for the new research airplane. At the time the Power Plant Laboratory recommended the engine, it had passed its preliminary flight rating qualification, with a first flight scheduled for April 1956.[33]

The development of the Bell XLR81-BA-1, usually called the Hustler engine, was part of Project MX-1964—the Convair B-58 Hustler. The B-58 was a supersonic bomber that carried its nuclear weapon in a large external pod, and the XLR81 was supposed to provide the pod with extra range after it was released from the bomber. The engine was a new design based on the engine used in the GAM-63 RASCAL missile. A single thrust chamber used red, fuming nitric acid and jet fuel to produce 11,500 lbf at sea level and 15,000 lbf at 70,000 feet. Sufficient thrust for the hypersonic research airplane would come from a cluster of at least three engines. The existing XLR81 was not throttleable or restartable in flight. Since ignition occurred after the B-58 dropped the weapons pod, the engine included a minimum number of safety components to save weight. At the time the

32 Memorandum, J. W. Rogers to Chief, Power Plant Laboratory, 4 January 1955. In the files at the AFMC History Office; WADC report 54MCP-199342, Confidential, no date. In the files at the AFFTC History Office. Discussions concerning the Reaction Motors LR8 and XLR11 get confusing. They were essentially identical engines, both based on the Reaction Motors 6000C4. Within each family some variants used turbopumps, while others relied on pressurized propellant tanks. All of the engines provided "thrust stepping" by igniting and extinguishing various combinations of the four thrust chambers. The Air Force evaluated the XLR11 since they had that engine under contract; the results were equally applicable to the LR8. At the time, Navy rocket engines used even numbers in the designations, and Air Force engines used odd numbers.

33 WADC confidential report 54MCP-199342, no title, no date, no page numbers. In the files at the AFFTC History Office.

Power Plant Laboratory recommended the engine, it had passed its preliminary flight rating qualification, with a first flight scheduled for January 1957.[34]

Although the Power Plant Laboratory included the engine on its list of candidates, and history papers often mention it, the NA-5400 apparently had little to offer the program. North American was using the effort as the basis for component development, with no plans to assemble a complete engine. If they had, it would only have developed 5,400 lbf at sea level (hence its company designation). The turbopump assembly was theoretically capable of supporting engines up to 15,000 lbf, and the power plant proposed for the new research airplane consisted of three separate engines arranged as a unit. The engine was restartable in flight using a catalyst ignition system. The propellants were hydrogen peroxide and jet fuel, with the turbopump driven by decomposed hydrogen peroxide.[35]

The Reaction Motors XLR10 Viking engine presented some interesting options, although Reaction Motors had already abandoned further development in favor of the more powerful XLR30 "Super Viking" derivative. As it existed, the XLR10 produced 20,000 lbf at sea level using liquid oxygen and alcohol propellants. The XLR30 then under development produced 50,000 lbf using liquid oxygen and anhydrous ammonia. The Power Plant Laboratory preferred to connect two XLR10 thrust chambers to a single XLR30 turbopump, believing this arrangement took better advantage of well-developed components and lowered the risk. The fact that the XLR10/XLR30 discussion used over two pages of the four-and-a-half-page engine report showed the laboratory's enthusiasm. Interestingly, as designed, the engine was not throttleable or restartable in flight, nor was it man-rated.[36]

In response to one contractor's comment that three of the four engines appeared unsuitable because they lacked a throttling capability, the government indicated it would undertake any necessary modifications to the engine selected by the winning airframe contractor.[37]

Between the time of the airframe bidders' conference and the 9 May submission deadline, Boeing, Chance-Vought, Grumman, and McDonnell notified the Air Force that they did not intend to submit formal proposals. This left Bell, Convair, Douglas, North American, Northrop, and Republic. It would seem that Bell and Douglas would have the best chances, given their history of developing X-planes. The Navy D-558-3 study would also appear to provide a large advantage to Douglas. On the other hand, although Convair, North American, and Republic had no particular experience in developing X-planes, they were in the process of either studying or developing high-speed combat aircraft or missiles. Northrop had little applicable experience of any sort, but had a long history of producing innovative designs.

---

34 Bell report 02-945-106, "Project 1226: X-15 Liquid Rocket Engine Proposal," Secret, 25 February 1955. Courtesy of Benjamin F. Guenther; WADC confidential report 54MCP-199342.

35 WADC confidential report 54MCP-199342.

36 WADC confidential report 54MCP-199342; Reaction Motors report TR-9405-C, "Rocket Engine for New Research Airplane," Secret, 26 February 1955. Courtesy of Benjamin F. Guenther. This was the engine used by the Martin Viking sounding rocket, which eventually formed the first stage of the Vanguard launch vehicle. Reaction Motors had begun developing the engine for this vehicle on 1 October 1946, and the first launch was on 3 May 1949. Fourteen Vikings were launched at White Sands Missile Range in New Mexico.

37 Letter, Colonel Carl F. Damberg, Chief, Aircraft Division, AMC, to Bell et al., subject: Project 1226 competition, 2 February 1955. In the files at the AFMC History Office.

During this period, representatives from the airframe contractors met with NACA personnel on numerous occasions and reviewed technical information on various aspects of the forthcoming research airplane. The NACA also provided data from tests in the Ames 10-by-14-inch and Langley 11-inch tunnels. Coordination on the NACA side became easier when Arthur W. Vogeley, an aeronautical research scientist from the Flight Research Division at Langley, became the NACA project engineer on 10 January 1955. Vogeley would act as a single point of contact for the NACA, with offices at both Langley and Wright Field.[38]

On 17 January 1955, NACA representatives met with Wright Field personnel and were informed that the research airplane was identified as Air Force Project 1226, System 447L, and would be officially designated the X-15.[39] The Fighter Aircraft Division of the WADC managed the project since the requirements for the aircraft most closely resembled those for a contemporary jet fighter. In reality, except for some procurement and oversight functions, the division would have little to do because the X-15 Project Office and the Research Airplane Committee actually controlled most aspects of the project. The X-15 enjoyed a national priority of 1-B, with a category of A-1. The Air Force also announced that the WADC project engineer would be First Lieutenant (soon to be Captain) Chester E. McCollough, Jr. BuAer subsequently selected George A. Spangenberg[40] as the Navy project engineer.[41]

Early in March the NACA issued a research authorization (A73L179) that would cover the agency's work on Project 1226 during the design competition and evaluation. The contractors concentrated on preparing their proposals and frequently consulted with both the NACA and WADC. For instance, on 15 April John I. Cangelosi from Republic called John Becker to obtain information on the average recovery factors used for swept-wing heat transfer. Later that day Becker transmitted the answer to NACA Headquarters, which then forwarded it to each of the competing contractors on 26 April.[42]

The Air Force and the NACA also were working on the procedures to evaluate the proposals. During March the NACA Evaluation Group was created with Hartley Soulé (research airplane project leader), Arthur Vogeley (executive secretary), John Becker (Langley), Harry J. Goett (Ames), John L. Sloop (Lewis), and Walt Williams (HSFS) as members.

In early February, ARDC Headquarters sent a letter to all parties emphasizing that the evaluation was a joint undertaking, and the ultimate selection needed to satisfy both the military and the NACA. The evaluation involved the X-15 Project

38 Letter, Clotaire Wood to Ames, Lewis, Langley, HSFS, NACA Liaison Office, no subject, 2 February 1955.

39 Interestingly, the designation was "Confidential" until after the mockup was approved.

40 Spangenberg joined the Naval Air Factory in Philadelphia, Pennsylvania, in 1935. In 1939 he transferred to the then Bureau of Aeronautics (BuAer) in Washington, DC, and became director of the Evaluation Division of the Naval Air Systems Command in 1957, serving in that position until his retirement in 1973.

41 R&D Project card, DD-EDB(A)48, Project 1226, 7 March 1955. In the files at the AMC History Office; A "rewritten" project card dated 22 March 1956 can be found in the AFFTC History Office. The latter card lists the requirements as "to provide exploratory data on the aerodynamic, structural, and physiological problems of manned flight at speeds up to 6,600 fps [Mach 6.0] and at altitudes up to 250,000 feet."

42 Letter, Clotaire Wood to Bell, Convair, Douglas, North American, Northrop, and Republic, no subject, 26 April 1955. It is normal in competitive environments for the contractors to ask questions to clarify various points of the competition. Under the procurement rules, the government must make the answers to all questions available to every contractor in order to keep the playing field level.

Office, the WADC laboratories, and the NACA, while the Air Materiel Command and Navy played subordinate roles. The four evaluation areas were the capability of the contractor, the technical design, the airplane performance, and the cost.[43]

The Research Airplane Committee would begin evaluating the proposals when it met on 17 May at Wright Field. Slightly complicating matters, the Air Force raised the security classification on most X-15-related activities from Confidential to Secret. This restricted access to the evaluation material by some engineers and researchers, but mostly placed additional controls on the physical storage locations for the material.[44]

THE COMPETITION

The airframe proposals from Bell, Douglas, North American, and Republic arrived on 9 May 1955. Convair and Northrop evidently decided they had little to offer the competition. Two days later the various evaluation groups (the WADC, NACA, and Navy) received the technical data, and the results were due to the X-15 Project Office by 22 June.[45]

In mid-May, Soulé, as chair of the NACA evaluation group, sent the evaluation criteria to the NACA laboratories. The criteria included the technical and manufacturing competency of each contractor, the schedule and cost estimates, the design approach, and the research utility of each airplane. Each NACA laboratory had specific technical areas to evaluate. For instance, Ames and Langley were assigned to aerodynamics; Ames, the HSFS, and Langley to flight control; HSFS to crew provisions and carrier aircraft; and the HSFS and Lewis to the engine and propulsion system. Soulé expected all the responses no later than 13 June, giving him time to reconcile the results before submitting a consolidated NACA position to the Air Force on 22 June. Later arrangements ensured that engine evaluations, also coordinated among the WADC, NACA, and Navy, would be available to the

---

43 Letter, Brigadier General Donald R. Ostrander, Director of Development, Deputy Commander of Technical Operations, ARDC, to Commander, WADC, subject: X-15 Special Research Airplane, 2 February 1955. letter, Brigadier General Donald R. Ostrander to Commander, WADC, no subject, 2 February 1955; letter, Brigadier General Howell M. Estes, Jr., Director of WSO, WADC, to Commander, ARDC, subject: X-15 research aircraft, 11 April 1955. Both in the files at the AFMC History Office; letter, Brigadier General Howell M. Estes, Jr., to Commander, ARDC, no subject, 11 April 1955. In the files at the ASD History Office. At first the X-15 was coordinated by the WADC Project Office staff since it was not yet an officially-funded program. Once Project 1226 was created as its own entity, the X-15 Project Office was created within Detachment One of the WADC Project Office to oversee the new research airplane. On 2 April 1951, a collection of independent Air Force laboratories located at Wright Field were consolidated to form the WADC. When the WADC became the Wright Air Development Division (WADD) on 15 December 1959, the WADC Project Office became the Weapon System Project Office (WSPO) and reported to ARDC Headquarters. The X-15 entity was renamed the X-15 WSPO. Some of the WSPOs became system program offices (SPOs) on 9 January 1961, but the X-15 office does not appear to have been one of these. When the Aeronautical Systems Division came into being on 17 March 1961, the X-15 WSPO again became the X-15 Project Office and moved under the Deputy for Systems Management, Defense Systems Program Office (ASZDX). For simplicity, this text uses X-15 Project Office throughout.

44 Letter, Colonel Paul F. Nay, Chief, Aeronautics and Propulsion Division, Deputy Commander of Technical Operations, ARDC, to Commander, WADC, subject: X-15 research aircraft, 26 April 1955. In the files at the ASD History Office.

45 Letter, Hugh L. Dryden, Director of NACA, to Deputy Director of R&D DCS/D, USAF, no subject, 20 May 1955; letter, Rear Admiral Robert S. Hatcher, Assistant Chief of R&D, BuAer, USN, to Commander, WADC, subject: Agreements Reached by 'Research Airplane Committee' on Evaluation Procedure for X-15 Research Airplane Proposals, 31 May 1955. In the files at the Navy History Center.

Research Airplane Committee on 12 July. The final evaluation would take place during a meeting at Wright Field on 25 July.[46]

Given the amount of effort that John Becker and the Langley team had put into their preliminary configuration, one might have thought that all of the contractors would use it as a starting point for their proposals. This was not necessarily the case. The Air Materiel Command had made it clear from the beginning that the Becker concept was "representative of possible solutions." Becker agreed with this; he in no way thought that his was an optimal design, and the bidders were encouraged to look into other configurations they believed could meet the requirements.[47]

As it turned out, each of the four proposals represented a different approach to the problem, although to the casual observer they all appeared outwardly similar. This is exactly what the government had wanted—the industry's best responses on building the new airplane. Two of the bidders selected the Bell XLR81 engine, and the other two chose the Reaction Motors XLR30. Despite this, all of the airplanes were of approximately the same size and general configuration. In the end, the government would have to evaluate these varied designs and determine which would most likely allow the desired flight research.

The Bell Proposal

Bell would have seemed a logical choice to develop the new research airplane since the company had developed the X-1 series and X-2 high-speed research aircraft that had ushered in a new era of flight research. They were also doing studies on much faster vehicles in search of the BoMi boost-glide bomber. The company had direct experience with advanced heat-resistant metals and with the practical issues of powering manned aircraft using liquid-fueled rocket engines. In fact, Bell had an in-house group that built rocket engines, including one under consideration for the X-15. Lawrence Bell, Robert Woods, and Walter Dornberger were already legends. Somehow, all of this was lost in the proposal.[48]

Unsurprisingly, Bell engineers decided the Bell-manufactured XLR81 was the most promising engine, and it became the baseline; however, the XLR30 offered certain advantages and Bell proposed the alternative D-171B variant using this engine. The design had three XLR81s arranged in a triangular pattern with one engine mounted above the others, much like the later Space Shuttle Orbiter. Bell believed that the ability to operate a single XLR81 at its 8,000-lbf "half-thrust" setting was an advantage, based on a reported comment from the NACA

46 Suborder, John B. Trenholm, Chief, New Development Office, Fighter Aircraft Division, to Chief, Rocket Section, Power Plant Laboratory, WADC, subject: X-15 Research Aircraft, 20 June 1955. In the files at the ASD History Office; memorandum, Brigadier General Howell M. Estes, Jr., Director of WSO, to Director of Laboratories, WADC, subject: X-15 Evaluation, 28 June 1955. In the files at the Air Force Historical Research Agency.

47 Dryden, "General Background" pp. xvii-xix; letter John V. Becker to Dennis R. Jenkins, 29 June 2003.

48 Author's note. Reading the Bell proposal and accompanying data, it is easy to see why the company was scored low in the evaluation. Although it was readily apparent that Bell had a great deal of talent, the proposal never offered the reader a sense that the Bell representatives had their hands wrapped around the problem of building a hypersonic research aircraft. Almost every innovation they proposed was hedged in such a manner as to make the reader doubt that it would work. The proposal itself seemed rather poorly organized, and was internally inconsistent (i.e., weights and other figures frequently differed between sections). The design appeared to be an attempt to build an operational aircraft instead of one intended to do research into the high-temperature structural environment.

that "a high percentage of the flight testing would be conducted in the lower speed and altitude ranges." Bell did not record who made the comment, but given that only 36 of the eventual 199 X-15 flights were below Mach 3, it was obviously incorrect. Unfortunately, it seemed to influence the Bell proposal throughout.[49]

A throttle lever controlled engine thrust by actuating a series of switches arranged so that thrust increased as the pilot pushed the lever forward in the conventional manner. The initial switch fired the first engine at its 8,000-lbf half-power setting. The second switch caused this engine to go to 14,500-lbf full power. The next switch fired the second engine at its 14,500-lbf setting, resulting in a 29,000-lbf thrust. The last switch started the third engine, resulting in a full thrust of 43,500 lbf. The engineers did not consider the slightly asymmetrical thrust provided by the triangular engine to be a problem.[50]

The selection of a conventional aerodynamic configuration simplified the arrangement of the fuselage and equipment systems. The fuselage had six major sections. The forward section contained the pilot's compartment, nose gear, and research instrumentation, followed by the forward oxidizer tank. A center section housed the wing carry-through, main landing skids, and pressurization systems, followed by the aft oxidizer tank and fuel tank. The aft section contained the engine and empennage. A pressurized area just behind the cockpit contained the hydraulic and electrical systems, environmental control equipment, and research instrumentation. The hydrogen peroxide supply, the main landing gear, and the structure for suspending the research airplane from the carrier aircraft were located in the center of the fuselage between the two oxidizer tanks. A flush-mounted canopy minimized drag and avoided discontinuities in the airflow that could result in thermal shocks on the glass.[51]

One of the unfortunate consequences of selecting the XLR81 was that the red, fuming nitric acid required a large storage volume, which caused the oxidizer to be stored in two tanks (one on either side of the wing carry-through). This was necessary to maintain the center of gravity within acceptable limits, but complicated the attachment of the wing to the fuselage. Bell investigated bolting the wing directly to the oxidizer tank or passing the structure through the tank. This, however, was not considered ideal "since it would present a hazard in the form of a possible fatigue failure as the result of the combination of localized wing loads and tank pressurization loads." The 61S-T aluminum propellant tanks were generally similar to those used on the Bell MX-776 (GAM-63) RASCAL missile program.[52]

The wing had a leading-edge sweep of 37 degrees to moderate center-of-pressure shifts at subsonic and transonic speeds. Engineers had discovered that higher sweep angles resulted in pitch-up and damping-in-roll difficulties that Bell wanted to avoid. At the same time, researchers found that the aspect ratio was not particularly important, so it was set to provide decent subsonic and landing

49 Bell report D171-945-004, "X-15 Research Airplane Proposal Aircraft Design Report," 6 May 1955, pp. 11-12; Bell report D171-945-003, "X-15 Airplane Proposal Summary Report," 5 May 1955, p. 8.

50 "X-15 Airplane Proposal Summary Report," p. 8.

51 "X-15 Research Airplane Proposal Aircraft Design Report," pp. 15-16.

52 "X-15 Airplane Proposal Summary Report," pp. 9-10.

attitudes. The total wing area was 220 square feet, allowing a reasonable landing speed of 170 mph.[53]

Approximately one-third of the vertical stabilizer area was located under the fuselage to maintain high-speed stability. This ventral stabilizer was added "to provide sufficient directional stability to M=7.0. This lower surface is very effective at high Mach numbers because of the compressive flow field below the wing." Bell attempted to provide as much area as possible while still maintaining sufficient clearance for the D-171 to be loaded into the carrier aircraft without resorting to a folding or retractable design. Before the airplane could land, the pilot would jettison the ventral stabilizer to provide sufficient clearance for the landing gear. A parachute lowered the ventral to a safe landing, although Bell noted that deleting the parachute would save a little weight, with the ventral becoming expendable.[54]

Landing skids were a logical choice to save weight but the exact nature of these skids was the subject of some study. A two-skid arrangement—one forward and one aft—was considered too unstable during landing, although a drag chute could be used to overcome this, as was done on the SM-62 Snark missile. Still, the arrangement was undesirable. A nose wheel with a single aft skid was statically stable, but model tests showed that it was dynamically unstable. A good pilot could land the aircraft with this arrangement, but Bell rejected the configuration because it placed too placed a great burden on the pilot. Two forward skids and a single aft skid offered neutral stability, but experience with the Sud-Est SE5003 Baroudeur showed that it still placed a high burden on the pilot. Bell finally selected a conventional tricycle arrangement with a nose wheel and two main skids located midway aft on the fuselage. Both the nose gear and skids were retractable and covered with doors, unlike the eventual X-15 where the rear skids did not retract inside the fuselage.[55]

The fully loaded airplane weighed 34,140 pounds at launch, including 21,600 pounds of propellants. The estimated landing weight was 12,595 pounds. Based on a launch at Mach 0.6 and 40,000 from a B-36 carrier aircraft, Bell estimated that the D-171 could exceed the basic performance requirements. The projected maximum altitude during the "space leap" was 400,000 feet. At altitudes between 85,000 and 165,000 feet, the velocity was in excess of 6,600 fps, with a maximum of 6,850 fps at 118,000 feet.[56]

A set of reaction controls used eight hydrogen peroxide thrusters: one pointed up and another down at each wing tip for roll control, one up and one down at the tail for pitch control, and one pointing left and one right at the tail for yaw control. A single control stick in the cockpit controlled the thrusters and aerodynamic control systems. Bell noted that "no criteria are available for the design of such

53 Ibid, p. 14.

54 Ibid, p. 15.

55 Ibid, p. 3. The Baroudeur was a small lightweight fighter designed by the French during the early 1950s. The nationalized SNCASE Company (later shortened to Sud-Est, a predecessor of Aerospatiale) set out to produce a conventional, swept-wing, transonic fighter that could operate out of pastures and plowed fields that were too rough for most other aircraft. The resulting aircraft took off using a rocket-propelled sled and recovered using a skid landing gear consisting of two forward units and another built into its ventral stabilizer. The prototype SE 5000 first flew on 1 August 1953. The results were encouraging enough that the French government ordered three pre-production SE 5003 aircraft. The SE 5003s passed their initial operational tests, but a combination of political and budget problems forced the cancellation of the program before production began.

56 "X-15 Airplane Proposal Summary Report," 5 May 1955, p. 16.

controls," so the company arbitrarily assumed that aerodynamic controls would be ineffective at dynamic pressures below 10 psf. Bell expected the X-15 to operate in flight regimes that required reaction controls for about 115 seconds per high-altitude mission, and provided 550 pounds of hydrogen peroxide. Operating all of the thrusters for the entire 115-second flight (something that obviously would not happen) used only 49% of the available propellant.[57]

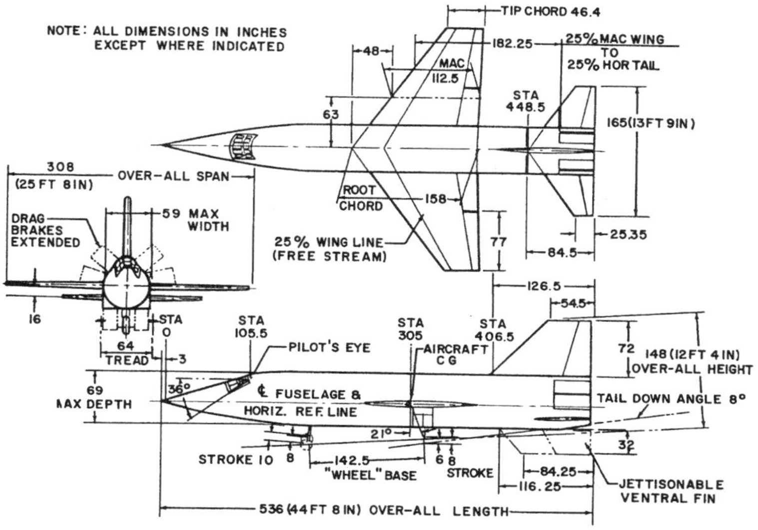

Three View of Airplane, Model D171

The Bell entry in the X-15 competition bore a subtle resemblance to their X-2 research airplane that had such an unhappy career. Bell had considerable theoretical experience with thermal protection systems as part of its ongoing work on the Air Force BoMi and RoBo programs, and much practical experience with high-speed X-planes such as the X-1 and X-2. Ultimately, the Bell proposal finished third in the competition. (Bell Aircraft Company)

The researchers at Bell did not believe the hot-structure data provided by the NACA from the Becker studies. This may have reflected a bias on the part of Bell engineers who had been working on alternate high-speed structures for several years. The Bell proposal contained a detailed discussion on why conventional or semi-conventional structures would not work, and the hot-structure concept fell into the latter category.

A survey of available materials showed that Inconel X was the best available high-temperature alloy for a conventional structure—the same conclusion reached at Langley. Bell estimated that an Inconel X airframe would weigh approximately 180% as much as an equivalent structure made from aluminum 75S-T. Bell noted that the "usual expedient" of adding additional material would not relieve all of the thermal stresses unless sufficient material were added to absorb the entire expected heat load, leading to a structure that would be too

57 Ibid, pp. 17-18.

heavy to accomplish its assigned mission. The Bell engineers also thought that "the stresses and deformations produced by temperature gradients cannot generally be reduced by the simple addition of more material."[58]

The second approach was to use what Bell called semi-conventional structures. In addition to adding sufficient material to absorb the heat load, the designers attempted to develop structures that would be free to warp and bend as they heated. Bell believed that all of the design approaches they tried would fail in operation. For instance, Bell designers decided it would be impossible to use integral propellant tanks in a hot-structure airframe because "no suitable structural arrangement has been found for attaching propellant tank ends and baffles to the outer shell without introducing serious thermal stresses." When they investigated the use of separate tanks, they found the weight penalty to be severe.

Bell also briefly investigated actively cooled structures, such as the "water wall" concept developed early in the BoMi studies. The basic structure weighed little more than a conventional aluminum airframe, but including the weight of coolant and pumping equipment resulted in the concept being 200–300% heavier.[59]

In a fuzzy look at things to come for the Space Shuttle, Bell investigated a structure protected by external insulation and concluded that "[c]eramic materials would seem attractive for insulation, except that the present state of development for this application is not well enough advanced…."[60]

As it turned out, Bell had an alternative, developed during the ongoing BoMi studies. This unique double-wall structure used air as an insulator, permitting heat transfer by radiation in addition to conduction. The outer wall consisted of a 0.005-inch-thick Inconel X skin panel, approximately 4 inches long and 8 inches wide, welded to a corrugated sheet of Inconel X. The corrugations were 0.3125 inch deep with 0.3125-inch spacing. An outside retaining strip of Inconel X (approximately 1.25 inches wide and 0.056 inch thick), running along each edge, held each panel in place. The edges of the corrugations, top and bottom, were joggled 0.056 inch so that the outer surface was flush. In the bottom, joggled portion of each of the corrugations, 0.015-inch-deep protruding dimples provided support for the outer wall panels to the inner structure. The combination of the dimple and joggle raised the outer wall panel to a height slightly over 0.375 inch from the inner structure, providing the necessary air space for insulation. The retaining strip was broken into 4-inch lengths to permit expansion relative to the inner structure, and two screws and two floating inverted-type anchor nuts held each retaining strip to the structure. These provided the required air space between the inner and outer walls to minimize heat conduction into the inner structure. Narrow strips of fibrous insulation located beneath the retaining strips prevented boundary air from leaking between the outer panels and their retaining strips.[61]

This arrangement allowed the outer wall panels to expand in the direction parallel to the corrugations simply by sliding further under the retaining strips. Separating the skin into elements only 4 inches wide accommodated the thermal

---

58 Ibid, pp. 20-23.

59 Ibid, pp. 19-23.

60 Ibid, p. 23.

61 Ibid, pp. 23-24.

expansion of the outer skin of the outer wall. In order to prevent the parallel, free edges of this very thin skin from lifting due to aerodynamic forces, "Pittsburgh" joints interconnected the edges of adjacent panels. This is a standard sheet-metal joint, but in this application "considerable clearance" was used so that the adjacent panels were free to move relative to one another to permit thermal expansions.[62]

Two pins set in the basic structure restrained each of the 4-by-8-inch outer wall panels against lateral movement. One of these pins fit snugly into a hole in a small square plate welded to the bottom of two adjacent corrugations, thus preventing any translations. The other pin fit into a slotted hole, permitting expansion but preventing rotation. Thus the outer wall had complete freedom of expansion relative to the underlying aluminum alloy structure. Its shallow depth (0.3125 inch) and uniformity minimized thermal gradients through the wall. Although they cost considerably more to manufacture, Bell proposed using Haynes 188 or similar alloys in areas where temperatures exceeded the capability of Inconel X. Researchers expected that ceramic panels or various sandwich materials could eventually replace the Inconel outer wall.[63]

The primary advantage of the double-wall system was that it weighed some 2,000 to 3,000 pounds less than an Inconel X hot structure. The double-wall construction also minimized development time, according to Bell, since the primary structure of the airframe was conventional in every way, including its use of aluminum alloys. This limited, in theory, any development problems for the outer wall. Interestingly, Bell believed that the double-wall construction provided an advantage when it came to research instrumentation. Since the outer panels were easily removable, it greatly simplified the installation of thermocouples, strain gages, pressure orifices, and other sensors.[64]

The wing and empennage used the same double-wall construction, but the leading edges were of unique construction. Bell noted that "it cannot be assumed that the optimum design has been selected since the evaluation…requires a greater time than afforded in this proposal period." Bell engineers did not believe they could accurately predict the heat transfer coefficients, but noted that the equilibrium temperature of the leading edges could approach 2,500°F. At this temperature, Bell was not sure that any metallic alloy would be sufficient, or whether a ceramic was necessary instead. Nevertheless, Bell proposed a metal heat sink. A 0.040-inch-thick Inconel X shell formed the desired leading-edge shape with a chord-wise dimension of approximately 6.5 inches (normal to the leading edge). Properly spaced, welded ribs provided attachment fittings, and intermediate ribs provided support to ensure that air pressure would not deform the shell. Lithium, beryllium, magnesium, or sodium (listed in descending order of preference) filled the leading edge shell as a heat sink.[65]

All of the leading edges were easily removable, facilitating the substitution of various types of leading-edge designs for flight research and evaluation. The

62 Ibid, p. 23. Essentially, a "Pittsburgh" joint is made by folding a length of the edge of two pieces of sheet metal back upon itself (bending the sheet 180 degrees), and then with one sheet upside down relative to the other, sliding the folds together.

63 Ibid, pp. 23-25.

64 Ibid, p. 25.

65 Ibid, pp. 27-30.

wing leading edges were single-piece structures on each side of the airplane. The inboard attachment was fixed, but the other attach points were designed to allow span-wise motion to accommodate differences in linear expansion between the wing structure and the leading edge.[66]

At first, Bell selected a Boeing B-50 Superfortress for its carrier aircraft, mainly because it had experience with this type of airplane from the X-1 and X-2 programs. It soon became apparent, however, that the B-50 did not have the capability to carry the D-171 and its support equipment to the altitudes required. Attention then turned to the Convair B-36. A comparison of the two aircraft showed that the B-36 had a much better rate of climb, and could launch the D-171 at Mach 0.6 and 40,000 feet compared to Mach 0.5 and 30,000 feet for the B-50.[67]

The basic installation in the B-36 was straightforward, and Convair already had data on the B-36 carrying large aircraft in its bomb bays from Project Fighter Conveyer (FICON).[68] Loading the D-171 was the same as loading the X-1 or X-2: a pair of hydraulic platforms under the B-36 main landing gear allowed the ground crew to tow the research airplane underneath the raised bomber. Alternately, the bomber straddled an open pit in the ground and crews raised the research airplane into the bomb bays. The D-171 took up the forward three of the four B-36 bomb bays in order to keep the mated center of gravity at an acceptable position. This also minimized B-36 control problems when the D-171 dropped away from the bomber.[69]

As had been the case with previous research airplanes, the mated pair would take off with the research airplane pilot in the carrier aircraft—not in the D-171. As the carrier climbed through 15,000 feet, the pilot would climb into the research airplane and the canopy would close. Equipment checks of the research airplane would begin as the carrier climbed through 35,000 feet. When the checks were completed, the carrier aircraft would drop the research airplane.[70]

Along with the baseline D-171 design, Bell proposed two slight variations. The D-171A two-seat version was a required response to the government request for proposal. Bell noted that that since the equipment compartment had a differential pressure of 2.5 psi to support the instrumentation, a small increase in structural weight would allow the higher pressure differential necessary to carry a second crew member. The observer would be seated on an upward-firing ejection seat and have two small side windows in a separate canopy. The gross weight was unchanged at 34,140 pounds since the weight of the observer and the ejection seat exactly matched the research instrumentation load normally carried. Performance was also unaffected because the propellant load was identical.[71]

---

66 Ibid, pp. 30-31.

67 Ibid, p. 51.

68 Beginning in January 1954 Convair had modified 10 GRB-36Ds to carry a Republic RF-84K Thunderflash reconnaissance fighter in their bomb bays as part of Project FICON. This was a method of extending the range of the B-36 and presenting a smaller target to the Soviets for reconnaissance or strike missions against heavily defended targets. The program progressed with little difficulty, but was operational for only a short time during the late 1950s before being phased out in favor of the Lockheed U-2 spy plane. For further details on the B-36 and FICON, see Dennis R. Jenkins, *Magnesium Overcast: The Story of the Convair B-36*, (North Branch, MN: Specialty Press, 2001).

69 "X-15 Airplane Proposal Summary Report," 51-53.

70 Ibid, pp. 51-53.

71 Ibid, pp. 63-64.

The second variant was the D-171B powered by a Reaction Motors XLR30 "Super Viking" engine. Although Bell preferred to use three XLR81 engines, it realized that the XLR30 offered some advantages. The D-171B had an empty weight about 200 pounds more than the baseline configuration, but a launch weight of some 1,000 pounds less. Bell listed the fact that the XLR30 used liquid oxygen as its oxidizer as its greatest disadvantage since this would require a top-off system in the carrier aircraft, which Bell believed would add "considerable greater weight" to the B-36.[72] Bell also thought that the minimum thrust capability of the XLR30 (13,500 lbf) was unsatisfactory compared to the Hustler engine (8,000 lbf). On the positive side, the internal propellant tank arrangement for the XLR30-powered airplane was superior because only a single oxidizer tank would be needed, greatly simplifying propellant management for center-of-gravity control. Bell agreed that the single XLR30 thrust chamber (versus three for the XLR81 installation) was also an advantage. Although no two-seat XLR30 aircraft was described in the proposal, it is easy to imagine a two-seat variant since the forward fuselage was identical to that of the D-171.[73]

Bell expected to have the basic design established six months after the contract was signed, and to finalize the design after 18 months. The first airplane would be available for ground tests 34 months after the start of the contract. Bell indicated that they attempted to compress the schedule into the required 30 months, but were unable to do so. It would take 40 months to get to the first glide flight, and six additional months before the first powered flight. Bell expected the government to provide a complete test engine in the 27th month, and a final propulsion system had to be delivered to Bell simultaneously with the first aircraft entering ground tests.[74]

The Douglas Proposal

The Model 684 was a conceptual follow-on to the successful D-558-1 and D-558-2 research airplanes that Douglas had built under Navy sponsorship beginning in 1944. It also benefited from the experience Douglas gained from investigating the Model 671, which is generally referred to as the D-558-3, during the "High Altitude and High Speed Study."[75]

Douglas took a unique approach to designing the structure of the Model 684, somewhat following the hot-structure concept developed at NACA Langley, but adding several new twists. The most obvious was that instead of Inconel X, Douglas chose a magnesium alloy "of sufficient gage that the structure [sic] tem-

72 Exactly why Bell thought carrier aircraft weight was an issue is not clear. The B-36 had a maximum bomb capacity of 84,000 pounds, not including several tons of 20-mm cannon and ammunition, plus military electronics (radar, ECM, etc.), all of which would have been removed. The 34,000-pound research airplane, with or without a liquid-oxygen top-off system, was hardly pushing the lifting ability of the bomber.

73 "X-15 Airplane Proposal Summary Report," pp. 65-66.

74 Ibid, pp. 57-58.

75 The information presented here came from the various Douglas proposal documents. See, for example, Douglas report ES-17926, "USAF Project 1226, Douglas Model 684 High Altitude Research Airplane," 20 May 1955; Douglas report ES-17918, "Strength Analysis and Criteria," 29 April 1955; Douglas report 19720, "Estimated Weight and Balance, Substantiation of Weights, and Moment of Inertia," 29 April 1955. All were originally classified Secret and provided courtesy of Benjamin F. Guenther. For a slightly more in-depth look at the Douglas Model 684, see Dennis R. Jenkins, "The X-15 Research Airplane Competition: The Douglas Aircraft Proposal," *Aerospace Projects Review*, volume 4, number 2, March-April 2002, pp. 10-23.

perature will not exceed 600°F." The use of copper for the leading edges permitted temperatures approaching 1,000°F. All of the proposed structure could be manufactured using conventional methods.[76]

The Model 684 weighed only 25,300 pounds fully loaded and had a landing weight of 10,450 pounds, making it the lightest of the competitors. The single Reaction Motors XLR30 allowed the airplane to exceed the performance specifications, with a maximum 6,655 fps velocity at 110,000 feet altitude expected. Douglas noted that it appeared "possible to explore altitudes up to approximately 375,000 feet without exceeding the structural limits of the airplane or the physiological limits of the pilot."[77]

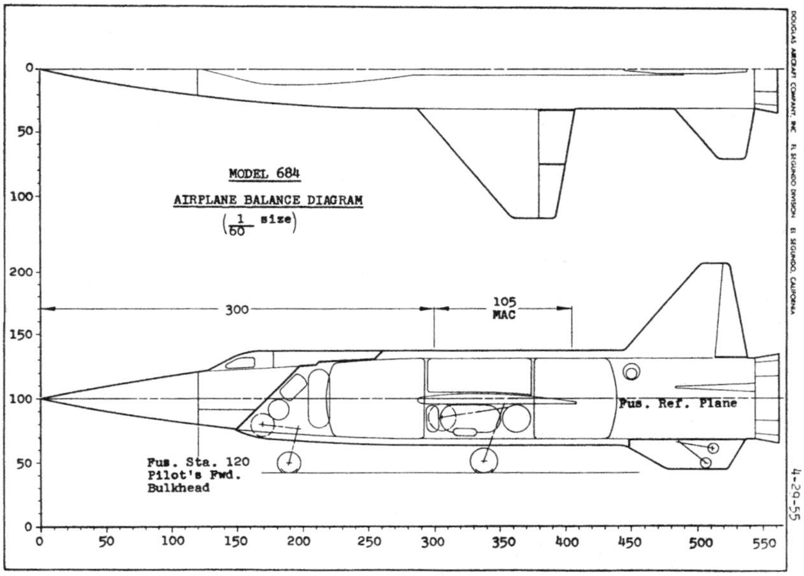

Oddly, Douglas did not just dust off the work it had accomplished for the Navy on the D-671 and submit it for the X-15 competition. The D-684 was a much different design that intrigued many of the evaluators during the competition, and Douglas ultimately lost largely because the Inconel X hot-structure on the North American entry better supported thermal research. The Douglas proposal finished second in the competition. (Douglas Aircraft Company)

The most controversial aspect of the Douglas proposal was the material selected for the hot structure. In advance, Douglas defended this action: "a careful study was made of all the various metals that have satisfactory strength properties at elevated temperatures." During this study Douglas eliminated everything except Inconel X and a thorium-zirconium alloy of magnesium called HK31.[78]

76 "USAF Project 1226, Douglas Model 684 High Altitude Research Airplane," no page numbers.

77 Ibid.

78 Ibid. Interestingly, thorium is slightly radioactive, and in 2006 the U.S. Air Force decided that objects constructed from the various thorium-magnesium alloys could no longer be displayed in public museums.

Douglas noted that the structural properties of Inconel X and HK31 fell off rapidly as the temperature approached 1,200°F and 600°F, respectively, and observed that "[s]ince we are concerned with heating of short duration, not with stabilized temperature, the specific heat[79] of the material becomes a very important factor." The study showed that HK31 had twice the specific heat of Inconel X. Since the strength-to-weight ratios of the two metals were roughly equal, Douglas believed the magnesium alloy was a better choice. "One must realize that less heat will be re-radiated by magnesium because of its lower temperature," allowing less internal insulation around critical components such as the instrumentation and pilot.[80]

Inconel X is difficult to machine, making Douglas engineers skeptical they could provide the exact thickness for a specific heat region. The magnesium alloy, on the other hand, was easy to machine, "so that the minimum required thickness at each point on the structure could be attained." Douglas also found that less internal structure was required to support the magnesium skin. Combined with the ability to machine the metal more precisely, Douglas estimated that a magnesium airframe would weigh approximately 25% less than an equivalent Inconel X airframe. The weight of the Model 684 seemed to confirm this.[81]

The choice of magnesium was not a surprise, since Douglas had manufactured the fuselage for both the D-558-1 and D-558-2 from a similar alloy. Nevertheless, it was a departure from the C-110M titanium-alloy structure investigated for the earlier Model 671. Of course, that airplane would have required an ablative coating—something that was not desirable on the X-15 because of the desire to do research into high temperature structures.[82]

Douglas summarized the advantages of HK31 as follows:[83]

1. There will be far fewer parts due to the greater skin thickness and all of the parts can be manufactured and assembled with existing manufacturing facilities. An Inconel airplane would require special tooling and techniques [further details omitted].
2. The reduction in the required amount of internal structure provides greater access to all control and instrumentation equipment, wiring, hydraulic actuators and piping, and allows better placing of this equipment.
3. The 600°F temperature limit for the magnesium greatly eases the temperature problem for the pilot and equipment in the airplane. This should result in less design time.
4. A psychological advantage in favor of magnesium might

79 The heat required to raise one unit of mass one degree of temperature.

80 "USAF Project 1226, Douglas Model 684 High Altitude Research Airplane," no page numbers.

81 Ibid.

82 Ibid; Douglas report ES-17657, "High Altitude and High Speed Study," Navy contract Nonr-1266(00), 28 May 1954, pp. 1-14 and 20-21; Douglas report ES-17673, "Technical Report on High Altitude and High Speed Study," Navy contract Nonr-1266(00), 28 May 1954, pp. 55-57.

83 "USAF Project 1226, Douglas Model 684 High Altitude Research Airplane," no page numbers.

be that the pilot would prefer to fly in a gray airplane at 600°F rather than in one that is glowing red at 1200°F.

The last point was probably questionable, but the reduction in internal structure was striking. Photographs accompanying the proposal showed a typical wing panel constructed of each material. The HK31 panel used skin almost 0.5 inch thick and needed support only along the four edges of the panel. The Inconel X structure, on the other hand, used skin only 0.1 inch thick and needed support across its entire surface. Both samples could withstand the same aero and thermal loads.[84]

The HK31 skin was thick throughout the vehicle. Skin gages on the upper half of the fuselage varied from 0.38 inch near the nose to 0.12 inch at the end of the ogive. On the lower surface, the gage varied from 0.92 inch near the nose to 0.25 inch at the end of the ogive on the bottom centerline. The skin on the upper surface of the wing was 0.35 inch thick over the entire exposed area, and 0.25 inch thick where the wing crossed inside the fuselage. The lower surface of the wing tapered from 0.64 inch near the leading edge to 0.43 inch 4 feet aft of the leading edge.[85]

The wing used seven truss-type spars that ran continuously through the fuselage. The skin used thick, tapered sheets stiffened by the spars and truss-type chord-wise ribs. Increasing the skin thickness at the wing-fuselage intersection created heat sinks to absorb the heating load. All of the leading edges (wing, empennage, and canopy frame) were made of copper that extended far enough aft to conduct the extremely high temperatures in the stagnation areas away to cooler areas of the airframe.[86]

The forward part of the fuselage consisted of the pressurized instrumentation compartment and the cockpit. If desired, the airplane could carry an observer in lieu of the normal research instrumentation, although the accommodations were cramped, and the observer had no visibility and sat in an awkward position. Another small, pressurized compartment (2.5-psi differential) was located in the aft fuselage to contain the gyros, accelerometers, and other subsystems.[87]

In case of an emergency, the entire forward fuselage separated from the rest of the airplane via explosive bolts and a JATO bottle located near the center of gravity of the nose section. Afterwards, a 5-foot-diamter metal drogue chute would deploy in the reefed position. When the load reached a predetermined level, the reefing device would automatically release and the metal drogue chute would fully open. A 50-foot-diamter fabric main parachute deployed when the load on the open drogue chute dropped below a predetermined value or the altitude reached 15,000 feet.[88]

Douglas hedged its bets slightly: "It is too early to determine whether this escape system will be satisfactory in the event of an emergency at extremely high altitudes, but no other system will be as good.… The jettisonable nose will be the most satisfactory system for escape under the high Mach number, high Q, and high G conditions at which this airplane is most likely to get into trouble." As

84 Ibid.

85 Ibid.

86 Ibid; Douglas report ES-17918, "Strength Analysis and Criteria," 29 April 1955, p. 3.

87 "USAF Project 1226, Douglas Model 684 High Altitude Research Airplane," no page numbers.

88 Ibid.

events with the Bell X-2 would later show, the capsule concept did not significantly alter the chance of survival. Of course, the Douglas system did have one advantage over the X-2: as proposed for the Model 684, the entire nose would descend to the ground, at which time the pilot would unbuckle and walk out of the capsule. In the X-2, the pilot had to unbuckle and jump out of the capsule after it separated but before it hit the ground. This assumed that the pilot had remained conscious during what was sure to be violent tumbling and accelerations during the escape. The pilot of the Model 684 had a small back-type parachute "in case he prefers to bail out in the conventional manner." [89]

A liquid air supply provided a maximum differential pressure of 5 psi for the cockpit and instrumentation compartment. The pressurized areas were insulated from the structural heating by a 0.25-inch layer of high-temperature fiberglass insulation located near the skin, followed by a light-gage stainless-steel radiant barrier that was covered by another 1.5 inches of batt insulation. The liquid air also cooled a heat exchanged that conditioned the recirculated cockpit air to a constant 80°F, and the instrumentation compartment to 150°F. There was sufficient liquid air for 30 minutes of full-load operation, and a warning system told the pilot to turn off the instrumentation if the liquid air supply ran low. The pilot's pressure suit used air diverted from the cockpit supply, and a small electric heater warmed the air to maintain the pilot's comfort.[90]

The windshield consisted of a 0.75-inch panel of high-temperature glass insulated by a 0.25-inch air gap from a 0.25-inch safety glass panel on the inside of the cockpit. Douglas calculated that the outer panel would not exceed 500°F, which was well within the capabilities of the glass. The tinted inner panel resisted radiant heat and ultraviolet light. One of the items Douglas had trouble with was developing a canopy seal. The heat surrounding the cockpit structure made a normal inflated rubber seal impractical. Engineers discovered that the preferred Teflon seal gave off a "small quantity of fluorine" between 400°F and 600°F. This was considered toxic and corrosive, but might be tolerable given that the cabin pressure differential was in the right direction (i.e., fumes would be expelled overboard). If a Teflon seal was used, it would have to be replaced after every flight.[91]

Unlike the other competitors, Douglas proposed a conventional landing gear consisting of two main wheels, a nose wheel, and a tail wheel. The nose gear was located far back on the fuselage (behind the cockpit), while the main gear retracted into compartments under the wing. The ventral stabilizer housed the tail wheel, which was needed because of the relatively high approach attitude of the research airplane. Ground-clearance issues during takeoff dictated that the ventral and tail wheels be retracted on the ground prior to loading in the carrier aircraft. They automatically rotated into the proper position for flight when the pilot started the auxiliary power units prior to launch.[92]

A single liquid-oxygen tank was located forward of the wing, but to maintain the correct center of gravity there were two ammonia tanks: one in the upper fu-

89 Ibid. For additional information of the Bell X-2 see Jay Miller, *The X-Planes: X-1 to X-45*, (Hinckley, England: Midland Publishing, 2001).

90 Ibid.

91 Ibid.

92 Ibid.

selage over the wing carry-through and another behind the wing. All of the main propellant tanks were integral parts of the structure. Three hydrogen peroxide tanks were located under the wing carry-through between the main gear wells. A single 62-gallon tank powered the XLR30 turbopump, and two smaller tanks supplied the reaction control system. The Douglas proposal noted that the compartment that contained these tanks "must be kept clean to prevent combustion in the event of fuel spillage and it is therefore sealed, vinyl coated and vented to an adjacent compartment through a filter that will prevent dirt contamination."[93]

Two completely independent power systems each used a separate Walter Kidde ethylene-oxide auxiliary power unit with sufficient propellant for a 30-minute flight. Each auxiliary power unit drove a hydraulic pump and an AC/DC generator, and operated simultaneously, although either could provide all the required power.[94]

The flight controls were completely conventional, with the all-moving horizontal stabilizer, rudder, and ailerons all being power-boosted. Hydraulically operated two-position speed brakes located in the extreme aft end of the fuselage provided a constant deceleration of 1.5-g when opened. The speed brakes automatically closed at pressures above 1,000 psf.[95]

The Douglas proposal acknowledged that "there are many formidable problems in the design of an airplane to operate over the wide Mach number and altitude ranges encountered by this airplane." Douglas embraced the wedge principle developed by Charles McLellan at Langley, and used the shape for the vertical and horizontal stabilizers. Douglas also flared the aft fuselage to provide additional stability at high Mach numbers.[96]

"Flight out of the atmosphere is another new problem" that caused Douglas to provide a reaction control system with 12 hydrogen peroxide thrusters, two in each direction about each axis. Two completely independent systems were provided (hence the two thrusters at each location), and either system was capable of maneuvering the airplane. The thrusters were powerful enough to rotate (and stop) the airplane through an angle of 90 degrees in 14 seconds when both systems were operational. The pitch and yaw thrusters were rated at 50 lbf each, while the roll thrusters were rated at 12.5 lbf each. Because of the large uncertainties involved, Douglas provided 640% of the amount of propellant estimated necessary for a single flight. In a note of caution, Douglas "recommended that a device be constructed for the purpose of training the pilot in this type of flight."[97]

The Model 684 was light enough that a Boeing B-50 Superfortress was a satisfactory carrier aircraft. This seemingly ignored the maintenance problems and low in-service rate of the B-29 and B-50 carrier aircraft experienced at Edwards, and was a radical step backwards from the apparent use of a B-52 in the earlier D-558-3 study. Surprisingly, the existing X-2 carrier aircraft required very little

---

93 Ibid.

94 Ibid.

95 Ibid.

96 Ibid.

97 Ibid.

modification to accommodate the Model 684—mainly the front and rear bomb bay openings had to be made a little larger.[98]

Douglas conducted preliminary wind-tunnel tests on the Model 684 on 21-22 April 1955 in the company-owned facility in El Segundo. Normally, Douglas would have used the more elaborate tunnel at the Guggenheim Aeronautical Laboratory at the California Institute of Technology (GALCIT), but there was insufficient time to build the more sophisticated model required at GALCIT. The El Segundo tunnel had a test cell that measured 30 by 45 inches and could generate a dynamic pressure of 60 psf. The tests did not generate any truly useful data, but demonstrated that the 6.5% scale model was reasonable stable at low speeds.[99]

The North American Proposal

North American seemed to be at a disadvantage, having never built an X-plane of any description. The company, however, did have a great deal of experience in building early missile prototypes. Their Missile Development Division conducted Project NATIV experiments during the late 1940s using captured German V-2 rockets, and then built major parts of similar vehicles itself. The company had almost completed the design of the Navaho, a large intercontinental cruise missile designed to fly at Mach 3. In addition, the company had developed what were arguably the three highest-performance fighters of their eras: the P-51 Mustang of World War II; the F-86 Sabre, which made its mark in Korea; and the F-100 Super Sabre, the first operational supersonic aircraft. North American was also involved in studies that would eventually lead to the fastest and most advanced bomber ever built: the XB-70A Valkyrie. They were on a roll, and the designers embraced the idea of building a hypersonic aircraft.[100]

Unlike the other competitors, who went in their own directions, Hugh Elkin and the North American Advanced Design Group stayed fairly true to the configuration that John Becker and the team at Langley had proposed; in fact, the resemblance was striking. Their goal was also similar: "the design objective must be to provide a minimum practical and reliable vehicle capable of exploring this regime of flight. Limiting factors are time, safety, state of the art, and cost."[101]

---

98 Ibid.

99 Ibid.

100 The information presented here came from the various North American proposal documents. See, for example: North American report NA-55-221, "X-15 Advanced Research Airplane Design Summary," 9 May 1955; North American report NA-55-223, "Preliminary Structural Data for a X-15 Research Aircraft, Project 1226 (NAA Designation ESO-7487), 13 May 1955; North American report NA-55-224, "Aerodynamic Characteristics Report for a X-15 Research Aircraft, Project 1226 (N.A.A. ESO-7487)," 9 May 1955; North American report NA-55-226, "Ground Handling Equipment and Procedures for a X-15 Research Aircraft, Project 1226 (NAA Designation ESO-7487)," 9 May 1955; North American report NA-55-227, "Carrier Modification Data for a X-15 Research Aircraft, Project 1226 (NAA Designation ESO-7487)," 9 May 1955; North American report NA-55-228, "Alighting Gear Data for a Research Airplane X-15 (NAA Designation ESO-7487)," 9 May 1955; North American report NA-55-229, "Space Control System Data for the X-15 Research Airplane (NAA Designation ESO-7487)," 9 May 1955; North American report NA-55-574, "Propulsion System Operation for a X-15 Research Aircraft, Project 1226 (NAA Designation ESO-7487)," 9 May 1955; North American report NA-55-577, "Structure Thermal Suitability Data for a X-15 Research Aircraft, Project 1226 (NAA Designation ESO-7487)," 9 May 1955. All were originally classified Secret and provided courtesy of Benjamin F. Guenther.

101 "X-15 Advanced Research Airplane Design Summary," pp. 1-2.

North American truly grasped what the government was trying to accomplish with the project. The other competitors—even Douglas, who otherwise came closest—worked at designing an airplane that met the performance requirements. North American, on the other hand, "determined that the specification performance can be obtained with very moderate structural temperatures; however, the airplane has been designed to tolerate much more severe heating in order to provide a practical temperature band within which exploration can be conducted." Put another way, "This performance is attained without recourse to untested or complicated solutions to design problems. This should allow the major effort to be expended on obtaining the desired research information." This was, after all, the point of the whole exercise.[102]

North American engineers spent a great deal of time talking to the researchers and other personnel at Edwards, recognizing that "a secondary, but important, factor considered in preliminary design is the desirability of meshing with the present operational pattern for research aircraft. By following the established pattern of operations, a considerable saving in learning time should be achieved." Given the significant increase in performance promised by the X-15, this was not completely possible, but it showed that North American was attempting to eliminate as many variables as possible. Along the same lines, North American did not attempt to design an operational aircraft, recognizing that a "compromise in favor of extreme simplicity in order to assure a high degree of ruggedness and reliability" would go a long way toward improving the aircraft's research utility.[103]

An interesting passage from the proposal, especially considering the current trend toward trying to eliminate all programmatic risk, is found in the summary: "Detailed definition and solution of all problems which will be encountered in this program are believed impossible for a proposal of this scope; indeed, if this were possible, there would be little need for a research airplane." Nevertheless, North American attempted to mitigate the inherent risk "by allowing for easy modification of critical areas if the need arises," again showing an understanding of the fundamental intent of the program. An example was that the forward nose section, the leading edges, and the wing tips were made easily replaceable "to allow panel structures and aerodynamic shapes to be tested economically." Unfortunately, some of these innovations would never make it off the drawing board.[104]

All of the bidders, as well as the NACA and Air Force, recognized that structural heating would be the major design problem. "At a Mach number of 7, the boundary layer recovery temperature will be on the order of 3,499°F and the skin equilibrium temperature, where heat input is balanced by radiation output, will exceed 1,200°F even at altitudes above 100,000 feet." North American noted that this approached the upper limits of Inconel X, but believed the conditions were

102 Ibid. Authors' note: As an engineer for several large aerospace companies working on NASA contracts, I both wrote and reviewed too many proposals over the years. Reading through the X-15 proposals, two things struck me. The Bell proposal (as mentioned in that section) was terrible—you walked away not entirely sure that Bell had committed themselves to the project. The opposite was true of the North American proposal. From the opening page, you knew that North American understood the goals of the X-15 program and would attempt to design an airplane that would help accomplish the task, not just meet the performance specifications (which did not fully describe the intent of the program).

103 North American report NA-55-221, "X-15 Advanced Research Airplane Design Summary," p. 2.

104 Ibid, pp. 2 and 6.

survivable "if flight duration is low and the skins are thick enough to form a heat sink of sufficient capacity."[105]

North American noted that the wing leading edges might experience temperatures of 1,400°F during extreme conditions, well beyond the ability of Inconel. To allow this without causing permanent damage to the aircraft, the company proposed to use a laminated glass cloth that would "melt or burn locally during these extreme cases." The flight-test group could replace the leading-edge sections after each flight, and alter the shape and material as desired or necessary.[106]

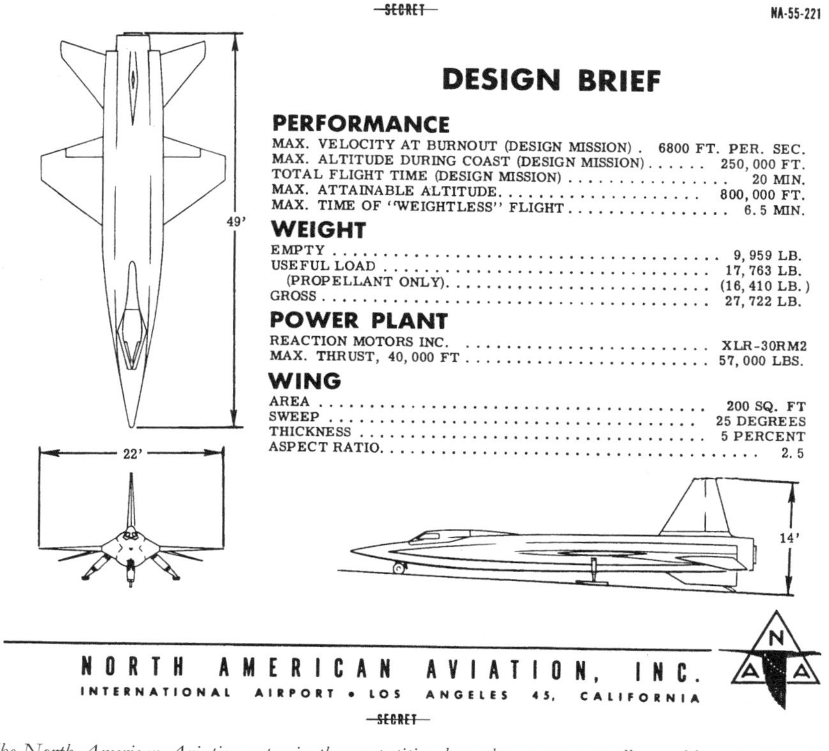
SECRET
NA-55-221
DESIGN BRIEF
PERFORMANCE
MAX. VELOCITY AT BURNOUT (DESIGN MISSION) . . . 6800 FT. PER. SEC.
MAX. ALTITUDE DURING COAST (DESIGN MISSION) . . . 250,000 FT.
TOTAL FLIGHT TIME (DESIGN MISSION) . . . 20 MIN.
MAX. ATTAINABLE ALTITUDE . . . 800,000 FT.
MAX. TIME OF "WEIGHTLESS" FLIGHT . . . 6.5 MIN.
WEIGHT
EMPTY . . . 9,959 LB.
USEFUL LOAD . . . 17,763 LB.
(PROPELLANT ONLY) . . . (16,410 LB.)
GROSS . . . 27,722 LB.
POWER PLANT
REACTION MOTORS INC. . . . XLR-30RM2
MAX. THRUST, 40,000 FT . . . 57,000 LBS.
WING
AREA . . . 200 SQ. FT
SWEEP . . . 25 DEGREES
THICKNESS . . . 5 PERCENT
ASPECT RATIO . . . 2.5
49'
22'
14'
NORTH AMERICAN AVIATION, INC.
INTERNATIONAL AIRPORT • LOS ANGELES 45, CALIFORNIA
SECRET

The North American Aviation entry in the competition bore the greatest overall resemblance to the original NACA Langley study, but the company had refined the concept into a vehicle that would support all of the required research without compromising the safety of the pilot. The North American proposal placed first in the evaluation. (North American Aviation)

The North American design was structurally similar to the one developed at Langley. Fabricating the basic wing as a complete semi-span assembly ensured rigidity, and fuselage ring frames transferred the wing skin loads across the fuselage. The ring frames were made of titanium alloy with numerous web beads to minimize thermal stresses. The wing structural box extended from the 25% chord line to the 75% chord line, and a span-wise series of shear beams made from cor-

105 Ibid, pp. 6-7.

106 Ibid, p. 7.

rugated 24S-T aluminum and titanium-manganese alloy attach points provided the support for the taper-milled Inconel X skins. The spar corrugations resisted the normal crushing loads and served to relieve thermal stresses. The relatively low modulus of elasticity of the titanium-manganese attach angles reduced the thermal stresses induced from the hot Inconel X skins. The skin panels varied from 0.060 inch thick at the tips to 0.125 inch thick at the fuselage fairing intersection.[107]

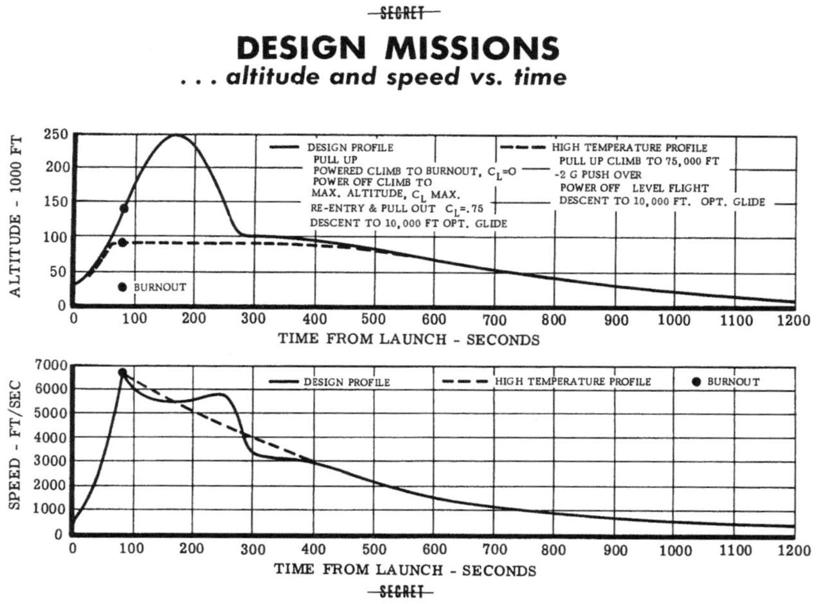

North American met the required performance requirements with an anticipated maximum altitude of 250,000 feet and a velocity of 7,000 fps. In reality, the eventual X-15 would greatly exceed the predicted altitude, while not quite meeting the velocity estimate. Still, the slight performance shortfall did not compromise the research data and the airplane met the expectations of the researchers. (North American Aviation)

One controversial aspect of the North American design was the use of large fuselage side fairings to carry propellant lines, control cables, and wiring around the integral propellant tanks. Oddly, a similar fairing located on top of the Douglas Model 684 received much less comment from the government. Insulation was required around the liquid-oxygen tank to keep the cold temperatures out of the tunnel, and all along the outer skin to protect against the hot temperatures. Segmenting the Inconel X fairings every 20 inches reduced the thermal deflections and stresses.[108] Initially the government was concerned about possible aero- and thermodynamic effects of the tunnels, but early wind-tunnel studies helped North American reshape them slightly and they actually ended up providing beneficial

107 Ibid, p. 9.

108 Ibid, pp. 10 and 12.

lift. It was later determined that the panels were susceptible to hypersonic panel flutter, and additional stiffeners were added during the flight program.

Unlike Bell, which did not believe that a hot structure was compatible with integral propellant tanks, North American proposed such an arrangement from the beginning. The liquid-oxygen and anhydrous-ammonia tanks each consisted of four sections (top, bottom, and beaded sides) welded together with intermediate Inconel X bulkheads and end-dome bulkheads. Beading the sides of the liquid-oxygen tank reduced stress in areas shielded from the temperature of the air stream by the fuselage side tunnels. One bulkhead in each tank had a manhole that allowed access to the tank for maintenance.[109]

In the sections of the fuselage that were not part of the propellant tanks, North American decided to use a series of bulkheads spaced 25 inches apart as the primary support for a semi-monocoque structure. The bulkheads used a series of radial beads to stiffen them and reduce thermal stresses. Engineers worried that using conventional longerons and stiffeners would lead to unwanted temperature gradients that would cause the structure to warp or fail, so they avoided this technique. Instead, thick Inconel skins covered a simple Inconel X structure.[110]

The pressurized areas used an aluminum-alloy inner shell to retain compartment pressurization. The canopy seal was isolated from the hot skins, permitting the use of a conventional "blow-up" seal operated by nitrogen. This was in contrast to the problems Douglas expected with their Teflon canopy seal. The windshield consisted of heavy fused silica or Pyrex outer panes and stretched acrylic inner panes. The inner low-temperature panels provided the normal pressure seal. All of the panes were flat to simplify fabrication and eliminate distortion.[111]

Although it was a landmark preliminary design, the Langley study intentionally ignored many of the details necessary to build an airplane. One such detail was keeping the internal temperatures at an acceptable level for the pilot and instrumentation. North American noted that "the lack of any convenient source of large quantities of either compressed air or ram air, such as is associated with conventional jet aircraft, requires that a new and different approach be taken to the solution of pressurization and cooling." The company's approach—using compressed gas (in this case nitrogen)—was hardly unique, being similar to that taken by the other competitors. The cryogenic nitrogen, plus the available heat absorption inherent in its vaporization, formed the necessary heat sink for refrigeration. The resulting gaseous nitrogen served as the atmosphere and pressurizing agent for the cockpit and equipment compartments.[112]

This led directly to one North American proposal that occupied quite a bit of discussion after contract award. The company also wanted to pressurize the pilot's full-pressure suit with nitrogen, providing breathing oxygen to the pilot through a separate inner breathing mask.[113] Done partly for simplicity, engineers believed that keeping oxygen exposure to the minimum was the simplest method to guard

109 North American report NA-55-577, "Structure Thermal Suitability Data for an X-15 Research Aircraft, Project 1226 (NAA Designation ESO-7487)," 9 May 1955, pp. 30-31.

110 North American report NA-55-221, "X-15 Advanced Research Airplane Design Summary," p. 10.

111 Ibid, p. 11.

112 Ibid, p. 8.

113 Ibid, p. 8.

against fire in the cockpit or suit. Many within the NACA and the Air Force disagreed with this approach, and discussions surrounding the full-pressure suits (and the use of a neck seal or a face seal) would come up many times during the first year of development, with Scott Crossfield leading the charge for North American.

Like the choice of a face-mask oxygen system, North American's decision to provide a simple ejection seat and a full-pressure suit for the pilot would later prove controversial. This combination resulted in "minimum weight and complexity" and exceeded the survival probabilities of "any capsule of acceptable weight which could be developed within the allowable time period." North American went on:[114]

> In the event the pilot is required to bail out, the normal procedure will be to use the ejection seat. The design dynamic pressures encountered are not higher than those assumed for present-day high performance aircraft, so the pilot in his seat should be able to clear the aircraft satisfactorily at any altitude. The protection afforded by the pressure suit will probably conserve body heat and provide sufficient oxygen for a free fall from very high altitudes. However, the two relatively unknown effects of high stagnation temperatures attained on the exterior of the suit upon entering the atmosphere after falling through space, and the possible high rates of angular rotation of the pilot's body during free fall will have to be studied in detail to determine the maximum altitudes at which it is feasible to bail out. Current developments at NAA [North American Aviation] indicate that with the protection against the air stream afforded by a full pressure suit, a suitably stabilized ejection seat may be designed which will assure escape under extreme conditions.

The wedge principle developed at Langley was evident in the vertical stabilizer proposed by North American. The dorsal stabilizer had a 10% wedge section; the ventral used a 15-degree wedge. Like the Douglas entry, the vertical was nominally a double-edge shape with the thickest part at 50% chord. A split trailing edge could open to form a "relatively obtuse blunt wedge" that greatly increased the lift curve slope at high Mach numbers and provided "sufficient directional stability without actual increase of tail area."[115]

Another innovative feature that was the subject of some debate after the contract was awarded was the use of all-moving "rolling" horizontal stabilizers instead of conventional ailerons and elevators.[116] These operated symmetrically for pitch control and differentially for roll control. "Available aerodynamic data indicates that the configuration presented is reasonable when the complete speed range is considered. The all-movable surfaces for pitch, roll, and directional control are

114 Ibid, pp. 11 and 40.

115 Ibid, p. 14.

116 Other competitors bid all-moving horizontal stabilizers, but only North American proposed to operate them differentially ("rolling") for roll control instead of providing conventional ailerons.

known to be satisfactory at the higher Mach numbers. Negative dihedral is incorporated on the horizontal tail to lessen abrupt trim changes due to shock impingement or wake immersion." There was an all-moving dorsal stabilizer that provided directional control, and a smaller fixed smaller ventral stabilizer. Split speed brakes were located on the sides of both the dorsal and ventral stabilizers.[117]

A separate "space control system" for use outside the atmosphere used Reaction Motors XLR32-RM-2 thrusters (four 90-lbf units in a cruciform arrangement at the nose, and one 17-lbf thruster at each wing tip). Unlike several of the other competitors that used the same control stick for the aerodynamic and reaction systems, North American used a separate lever on the right console. The amount of propellant for the reaction controls seemed low by comparison with the other competitors: whereas Bell provided 47 gallons of hydrogen peroxide and Douglas provided nearly the same amount, North American provided only 3.15 gallons (36.2 pounds). The company expected this to be sufficient for "five gross attitude changes about each axis at approximately 6 degrees per second."[118] This shows the amount of uncertainty that existed regarding the amount of use the reaction controls would receive—the first manned space flight was still six years away.

Like Douglas (and the alternate, Bell), North American chose the Reaction Motors XLR30 engine, but stated that "it appears feasible to use any engine or engines in the same performance category." Propellants would be stored in seam-welded Inconel X tanks, with the liquid-oxygen and main ammonia tanks being integral parts of the fuselage. A smaller, nonstructural ammonia tank slightly increased the fuel supply. Helium for propellant system pressurization was stored at 3,000 psi and –300°F in an Inconel X tank located on the centerline inside the liquid-oxygen tank. Surprisingly, there were only sufficient pressurizing gas and igniter propellants for three starts.[119]

Electrical and hydraulic power came from a pair of Reaction Motors X50AP-1 monopropellant gas turbine auxiliary power units in the aft fuselage. The systems were redundant, and either could provide sufficient power to operate the airplane. North American used two bladder-type tanks for both the APU and reaction control propellant, with 68.5% allocated to the APUs.[120]

North American believed it had a handle on the problem of acquiring air data in the hypersonic flight regime, and that "development time for this system will be minimized." The multipurpose air data system used existing components to measure pitot-static pressures, differential dynamic pressures due to angle of attack and angle of sideslip, and air-stream temperatures. North American never stated

117 North American report NA-55-229, "Space Control System Data for the X-15 Research Airplane (NAA Designation ESO-7487)," 9 May 1955, pp. 1-5; North American report NA-55-221, "X-15 Advanced Research Airplane Design Summary," 9 May 1955, pp. 2 and 19; Bell report D171-945-003, "X-15 Airplane Proposal Summary Report," 5 May 1955, pp. 9-10;

118 Ibid.

119 North American report NA-55-574, "Propulsion System Operation for a X-15 Research Aircraft, Project 1226 (NAA Designation ESO-7487)," 9 May 1955, pp. 2-5; North American report NA-55-221, "X-15 Advanced Research Airplane Design Summary," 9 May 1955, p. 2 and 22.

120 North American report NA-55-221, "X-15 Advanced Research Airplane Design Summary," 9 May 1955, p. 16.

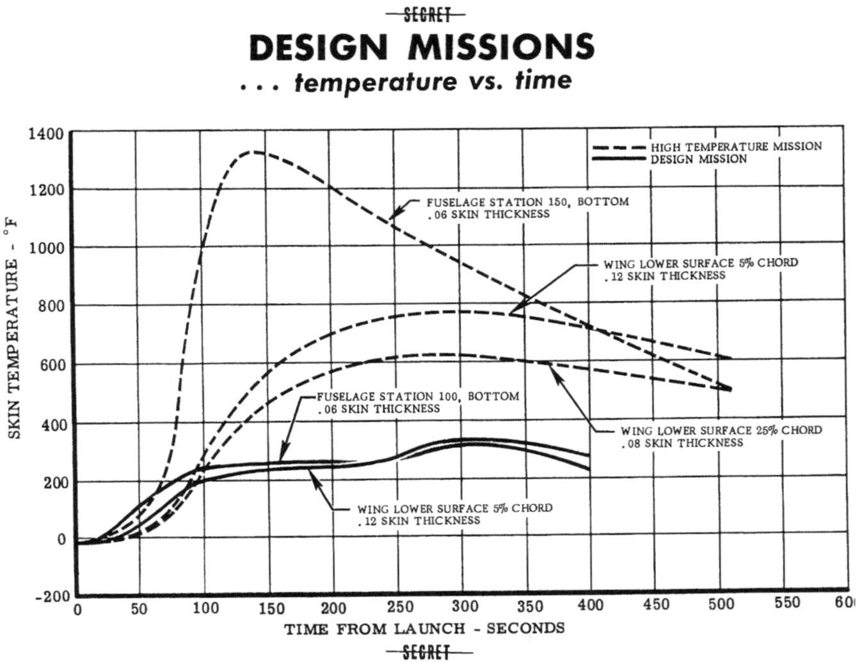

The temperature-versus-time estimates generated by North American essentially agreed with those made earlier at NACA Langley. The North American proposal used the same non-insulated Inconel X hot-structure air-frame conceived at Langley, and this was one of the primary criteria that resulted in North American winning the competition. (North American Aviation)

exactly where the pressure data would be sensed, although two devices originally designed for the Navaho missile program were the basis for the system.[121]

The landing gear consisted of two strut-mounted skids that retracted against the outside of the fuselage beneath the wing leading edge and a two-wheel nose gear located far forward. The pilot deployed the landing gear via a manual cable release of the uplocks, with gravity and a bungee spring taking care of the rest. A small "tail bumper" skid in the aft edge of the ventral stabilizer protected the aft fuselage during landing. North American solved the problem of developing a landing system that was compatible with the large ventral stabilizer "by simply allowing the airplane to touch down and 'rotate in' about the tail bumper and providing adequate energy absorption in the main and nose gears." No retraction mechanisms existed, and the ground crew manually retracted the landing gear after each flight.[122]

North American chose the skids as much because they saved space inside the relatively small airframe as for any other reason: "the stowage of a wheel would

121 Ibid, p. 25. The two Navaho devices would be the North American static error compensator (NASEC) and the North American rate of descent indicator (NARODI). Each of these instruments was meant for fast-moving vehicles, and was believed to be accurate up to 100,000 feet (well beyond the operating altitude of the Navaho). Given the failure of the Navaho flight program, neither device received much actual flight testing.

122 North American report NA-55-228, "Alighting Gear Data for a Research Airplane X-15 (NAA Designation ESO-7487)," 9 May 1955, pp. 1-2; "X-15 Advanced Research Airplane Design Summary," pp. 2 and 23.

not adapt itself to the configuration of the airplane without increasing the cross section area and wetted area." The friction between the skid and the ground accomplished braking, and the estimated landing rollout was 8,000 feet, well within the limits of the dry lakes at Edwards.[123]

In order to accommodate ease of maintenance, North American attempted to "incorporate the absolute minimum of systems and components which require servicing." Access to most wiring, cables, and hydraulic lines was gained through the easily removable side fairing panels. The research instrumentation was concentrated in a single equipment compartment equipped with large doors on each side. The fuselage panels around the engine were removable for service and inspection. All hydraulic components were concentrated in the aft fuselage.[124]

As required by the government, North American performed an engineering study on a two-seat X-15 to meet the Navy's desire to "provide an observer." A second cockpit and ejection seat took the place of the research instrumentation, and an entirely new one-piece clamshell canopy covered both cockpits and faired into the upper fuselage further back than the normal canopy. The observer had large flat-pane side windows, an intercom, and "an abbreviated presentation of flight and research data." The engineers estimated that "inasmuch as the launch and burn-out weights and airplane drag are identical to those of the single-place version, no change in performance will result."[125]

The proposal and its included reports contained an extensive discussion on carrier aircraft. Of course, North American was the only company without some directly related experience with carrier aircraft. Bell and Douglas had both built research airplanes that were air launched, while Republic was manufacturing the RF-84Ks that were carried in the bomb bay of Convair GRB-36Ds as part of the FICON project.

North American chose a B-36 mostly because the only other available aircraft—the Boeing B-50 Superfortress—could not lift the X-15 above 25,000 feet, and North American wanted a higher launch altitude. From a modification perspective, the B-36 appeared to be excellent; only one bulkhead needed to be replaced, and the FICON project had already accomplished the basic engineering. The flight profiles developed by North American assumed a launch at Mach 0.6 and 30,000 feet, but the proposal suggested that the B-36 could actually achieve 38,000 feet with no difficulty. North American expected the separation characteristics to be excellent.[126]

The Republic Proposal

Republic also seemed at a disadvantage in the X-15 competition, for many of the same reasons North American was. However, the company was working on a Mach 3+ interceptor, the XF-103, and had developed the first supersonic combat-

123 "Alighting Gear Data for a Research Airplane X-15 (NAA Designation ESO-7487)," pp. 1-2; "X-15 Advanced Research Airplane Design Summary," pp. 2 and 23.

124 "X-15 Advanced Research Airplane Design Summary," pp. 33-35.

125 Ibid, pp. 44-45.

126 Ibid, p. 39; North American report NA-55-227, "Carrier Modification Data for an X-15 Research Aircraft, Project 1226 (NAA Designation ESO-7487)," 9 May 1955, pp. 1-2.

type aircraft, the experimental XF-91. With the XF-91, the company had gained experience in integrating a liquid-fueled rocket engine into a manned aircraft. The XF-103 was providing a wealth of experience (most of it unhappy), including information concerning the effects of high-speed heating on aircraft structures. In addition, Republic had Alexander Kartveli, one of the most innovative aircraft designers in the world.[127]

The Republic AP-76 was the heavyweight of the competitors, with a launch weight of 39,099 pounds. Nevertheless, Republic expected the design to exceed very slightly the speed specification at 6,619 feet per second, although it fell somewhat short of the altitude requirement at only 220,000 feet.[128]

Like Bell, Republic opted for XLR81-BA-1 engines, although the heavyweight AP-76 used four of them. Each of the engines produced 14,500 lbf, so a total of 58,000 lbf was available at 40,000 feet. Republic justified their choice by noting that "a sacrifice in weight was made in order to use these four units in place of a single thrust chamber engine. The increased safety of numbers as well as the increased reliability of starting one or more units influenced this choice." The engines used a fuel called JP-X that consisted of 40% unsymmetrical dimethylhydrazine (UDMH) and 60% jet fuel. The oxidizer was red, fuming nitric acid. The combination was hypergolic, so no ignition system was required. The thrust line of each engine chamber passed through the center of gravity of the airplane, eliminating any directional component of single- or multiple-chamber operations.[129]

A switch panel at the normal throttle location on the left console controlled the engines, based on experience gained on the XF-91 interceptor. The XF-91 had both switches and a conventional throttle quadrant, but the pilots preferred using the switches. A fixed handgrip next to the switches ensured that the pilot's hand would be near the switches at all times. There were nine two-position switches on the panel: a "master arm" switch, four individual "arm" switches, and four "on" switches. Igniting varying numbers of the engines varied the thrust, just as it had on the X-1 and D-558. Republic did not seem to incorporate the ability to use the "half-thrust" feature of the XLR81.[130]

Much like the XF-103, Republic eliminated the conventional canopy enclosure and submerged the pilot inside the fuselage. Three glass panels on each side of the fuselage provided side vision from launch until the airplane had descended to approximately 25,000 feet. Once the AP-76 had slowed to Mach 0.7, a hatch on the upper surface of the cockpit raised 13 degrees at its leading edge to expose a mirror system that provided forward vision during approach and landing. The

127 The information presented here came from the various Republic proposal documents. See, for example: Republic report ED-AP76-101, "Static and Dynamic Stability and Control for the Republic AP-76 Airplane," 6 May 1955; Republic report ED-AP76-200, "Estimated Weight and Balance and Mean Aerodynamic Chord for AP-76," 6 May 1955; Republic report ED-AP76-900, "Summary of Engineering Data for Republic AP-76 Research Airplane Under Project 1226 Competition," 6 May 1955; Republic report 55WCS-9231-A, "AP-76: Project 1226 Summary Brochure," 6 May 1955; Republic report 55WCS-9231-AA, "Preliminary Model Specification (ES-348): Republic Model AP-76 Research Airplane," 6 May 1955. All were originally classified Secret and provided courtesy of Benjamin F. Guenther. For an slightly more in-depth look at the Republic AP-76, see Dennis R. Jenkins, "The X-15 Research Airplane Competition: The Republic Aviation Proposal," *Aerospace Projects Review*, volume 4, number 3, May-June 2002, pp. 3-19.

128 "AP-76: Project 1226 Summary Brochure," p. 6.

129 Ibid, p. 40.

130 "Preliminary Model Specification (ES-348): Republic Model AP-76 Research Airplane," pp. 74-75; "AP-76: Project 1226 Summary Brochure," p. 41.

system used two mirrors—one in the front of the hatch reflected an image downward to a second mirror on top of the instrument panel. The pilot looked at the second image. This system was similar to the one that had been developed for the XF-103 and had received favorable comments from the pilots during simulations. Surprisingly, the system offered good depth perception and minimal loss of brightness. Republic chose this unique system "because the problem of protecting the pilot from the high temperatures and, if need be, from cosmic radiation in a [conventional] canopy arrangement seem almost impossible." The cockpit and forward instrument compartment used gaseous nitrogen to maintain 40–100°F at a 5-psi differential, while the aft compartment had a 2.5-psi differential.[131]

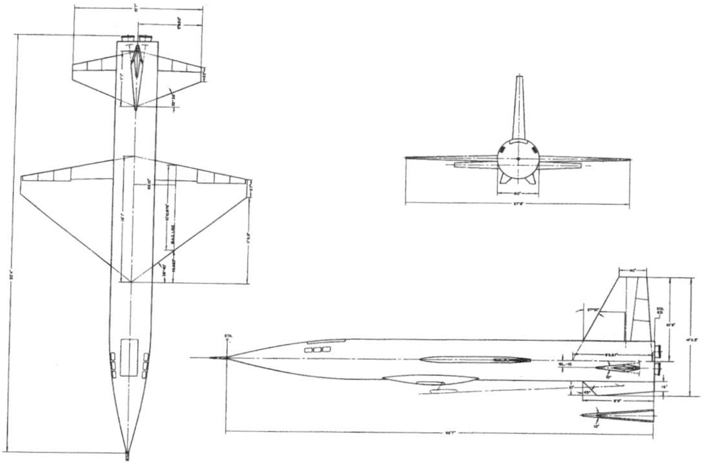

The Republic AP-76 was large, heavy, and although Republic indicated it could slightly exceed the velocity requirements, it fell about 15 percent short of the desired altitude capability. In reality, very few believed it could attain the performance numbers generated by Republic, especially given the weight gains that seem to occur during any development exercise. The Republic entry placed last in the evaluation. (Republic Aviation)

To assist the pilot in flying the predetermined trajectory, Republic proposed installing a "flight program indicator." This display presented the pilot with a second-by-second trace that showed the proper speed, altitude, angle of attack, and path angle during powered flight. The pilot simply guided the airplane to match the cues on the display. It would have been a useful tool.[132]

Normal Air Force fighter standards (+7.33/–3.00 g at burnout weight, but a great deal lower at full gross weight) provided the structural requirements for the AP-76, in contrast to the other competitors that only stressed their designs for +5 g. To accomplish this, and to withstand the expected heating environment, Republic proposed a novel structure for the fuselage. The main structure consisted

131 "Summary of Engineering Data for Republic AP-76 Research Airplane Under Project 1226 Competition," pp. 10-11; "AP-76: Project 1226 Summary Brochure," pp. 6-7 and 20.

132 "Summary of Engineering Data for Republic AP-76 Research Airplane Under Project 1226 Competition," p. 86.

of longitudinal titanium "Z" stringers. The structural titanium skin attached to the inner leg of the stringers, and the outer leg held a series of 0.020-inch-thick corrugated Inconel X shingles that formed a heat shield. The corrugations were very mild, with a 0.08 depth-to-length ratio, and permitted circumferential growth resulting from high transient temperatures. In between the heat shield and inner skin were 0.5-inch-thick blocks of Marinite insulation made by the Johns Manville Company. The 2-foot-wide Inconel outer skin sections stretched over three frames and used elongated attachment holes that allowed the sheets to expand and contract without warping. With the Inconel outer skin at its full 1,200°F, the interior titanium structure would never exceed 300°F.[133]

Aft of the rear instrument compartment were two nitric acid tanks, separated by the wing carry-through structure. In the space above and below the carry-through structure were two hydrogen peroxide tanks to power the APUs and the reaction control system. Liquid nitrogen pressurized all of the propellant tanks, and storage bottles were located below the wing carry-through structure. To the rear of the second nitric acid tank was the JP-X tank. The titanium oxidizer and fuel tanks were an integral part of the fuselage, but because nitric acid reacts with titanium at elevated temperatures, the acid tanks had removable aluminum liners.[134]

The trapezoidal wing used a slightly rounded leading edge with a flat airfoil between the 20% and 80% chord lines and a blunt trailing edge. Unlike the fuselage, Republic did not attempt to insulate the wing structure, and designed it to carry the design loads at elevated temperatures without developing high thermal stresses. The wing used three main sections: 1) the main wing structure, 2) the leading edge, and 3) the trailing edge, which consisted of a conventional single-slotted landing flap and a conventional aileron. The primary load-carrying structure was a tapered multi-cell box that ran from tip to tip and attached to the fuselage at four points (two per side). Intermediate spars were located on 5.5-inch centers with 15 spars at the root and four at the tip. The Inconel X skins were on average 0.10 inch thick. The leading edges were made of kentanium (a titanium carbide alloy) castings segmented into six parts per wing.[135]

The vertical and horizontal stabilizers were "of conventional size made possible by the use of double wedge type sections with rounded leading edges." The included angles were 10 and 12 degrees, respectively. The horizontal surfaces were all moving, but the airplane used conventional ailerons instead of the differentially moving horizontals found on the North American design. The vertical surfaces consisted of a dorsal stabilizer and a jettisonable ventral stabilizer. Wind-tunnel data from the XF-103 provided data for the rudder design, although the overall shape was different. The rudder consisted of the upper 46% of the surface and the entire trailing edge aft of the 70% chord line. Spilt flaps, consisting of the trailing 30% and 35% of the vertical and horizontal stabilizers, respectively, opened through a maximum angle of 50 degrees to increase drag and reduce the speed of the aircraft during reentry. Like the ailerons, these split flaps were each

133 "Summary of Engineering Data for Republic AP-76 Research Airplane Under Project 1226 Competition," pp. 12-13; "AP-76: Project 1226 Summary Brochure," pp. 20-21.

134 "AP-76: Project 1226 Summary Brochure," pp. 7 and 21-23.

135 "Summary of Engineering Data for Republic AP-76 Research Airplane Under Project 1226 Competition," p. 14; "AP-76: Project 1226 Summary Brochure," pp. 6 and 23.

divided into three sections to permit operation while under thermal stresses. The stabilizers were generally of the same construction as the wings, and, like the wing, the leading edges of the empennage were made of cast kentanium.[136]

The landing gear consisted of two main skids and one tail skid. The 48-by-5-inch main skids, installed externally on the side of the fuselage bottom just ahead of the center of gravity, extended 18.5 inches using pneumatic shock absorbers. Just before landing, the tail skid automatically extended when the pilot jettisoned the ventral stabilizer. The landing gear could accommodate descent velocities of only 6 feet per second, considerably less than the 9 fps that tactical aircraft were design to absorb. The rationale was that "highly experienced pilots only are expected to fly this airplane." In fairness to Republic, the NACA had conducted an analysis of earlier research airplane landings and found that the majority were well below the 6-fps figure.[137]

Two hydrogen peroxide auxiliary power units each drove an alternator and hydraulic pump. A 60-gallon supply of the monopropellant could drive the power units for 30 minutes and operate the reaction control system for 3 continuous minutes. The reaction control system used six 90-lbf thrusters (one on each wing tip and four at the rear of the fuselage). Republic linked the thrusters to the same control column that the aerodynamic controls used, and a switch in the cockpit activated them when necessary. At the time of the proposal, the thrusters were throttleable, but Republic noted that "studies of a 'bang-bang' system, that is 'full-on' or 'full-off'...appear very promising."[138]

Given the amount of effort committed to developing an encapsulated escape system during the protracted XF-103 program, it is surprising that Republic opted for a simple ejection seat for the AP-76. "Consideration was given to the use of a pilot's escape capsule in the AP-76. It was found to be extremely difficult to design a capsule which would have the necessary stability characteristics in the low density air of the high altitudes attained by the AP-76." Similarly, Republic found it was almost impossible to provide drag devices that would retard the capsule's descent to the degree necessary to prevent excessive skin temperatures. In its place was an escape seat with leg (but no arm) restraints; the pilot would rely on his partial-pressure suit for protection during ejection.[139]

Not surprisingly, given the weight of the AP-76, Republic chose a Convair B-36 bomber as the carrier aircraft. Republic had some experience in using the B-36 since the company manufactured the RF-84K parasite fighter used in the FICON project. The AP-76 was sufficiently large that it took up the majority of all four B-36 bomb bays. The lifting frame and main attach points were mounted on the B-36 wing box and attached to the AP-76 on top of the fuselage over its wing. It was necessary to modify two main bomb bay frames on the B-36 to clear the

136 "Summary of Engineering Data for Republic AP-76 Research Airplane Under Project 1226 Competition," p. 16; "AP-76: Project 1226 Summary Brochure," p. 6.

137 "Summary of Engineering Data for Republic AP-76 Research Airplane Under Project 1226 Competition," pp. 17 and 68; for the landing data, see Wendell H. Stillwell, NACA Research Memorandum H54K24, "Results of Measurements Made During the Approach and Landing of Seven High-Speed Research Airplanes, 4 February 1955; "Preliminary Model Specification (ES-348): Republic Model AP-76 Research Airplane," p. 23.

138 "Summary of Engineering Data for Republic AP-76 Research Airplane Under Project 1226 Competition," pp. 10-11; "AP-76: Project 1226 Summary Brochure," p. 44.

139 "AP-76: Project 1226 Summary Brochure," pp. 47-48.

research airplane, and to add sway braces to "suitable strong points on the lower longerons of the bomb bay truss." A fairing with a soft gasket sealed the bomb bay when the B-36 was carrying the AP-76.[140]

Unfortunately, Republic appears to have misread the intentions of NACA and the Air Force, and its proposal stated that "the achievement of the speed [6,600 fps] is paramount whereas flight at very high altitudes has a secondary role." Because of this, Republic concentrated on designing an aircraft that would be capable of meeting the velocity requirement, while ignoring the altitude requirement to some degree. Although the proposal listed 220,000 feet as the maximum altitude of the aircraft, other data submitted with the proposal indicated that the company believed the aircraft could achieve almost 300,000 feet if necessary.[141]

The typical high-speed flight profile for the AP-76 began with the airplane being carried aloft by a B-36H[142] carrier from Edwards AFB. The research airplane pilot would be riding in the comparative comfort of the pressurized compartment of the bomber. The B-36 would carry the AP-76 to a predefined release point approximately 540 miles from Edwards and launch the airplane at an altitude of 40,000 feet and a true air speed of 350 knots. After the AP-76 dropped clear of the B-36, the pilot would ignite all four rocket engines and pull into a 20-degree climb before running out of propellants after 105 seconds at approximately 140,000 feet. The AP-76 would then continue a free-flight trajectory to a peak altitude of 220,000 feet about 69 seconds after burnout. During the climb through 100,000 feet, the pilot would activate the switch that armed the reaction control system; thereafter, the movement of the control column and/or rudder pedals would activate the thrusters in addition to the now-useless aerodynamic controls.

The airplane would continue on a ballistic trajectory until it reached an altitude of 150,000 feet, where the aerodynamic controls would regain effectiveness. The airplane would go through a series of pull-ups and glides while the pilot maintained the angle of attack at a constant 6 degrees. The speed brakes on the horizontal and vertical stabilizers would open as needed. When the descent reached 25,000 feet and the speed reduced to Mach 0.7, the pilot would jettison the ventral stabilizer since it was no longer required for directional stability, and raise the hatch to expose the mirror system to provide forward visibility. Finally, the airplane would glide to a landing on its skids on Rogers Dry Lake.[143]

The Republic approach to the required two-seat engineering study was a little different from and decidedly more useful than the other proposals. All of the other competitors had simply deleted all of the research instrumentation and installed accommodations for an observer, although North American, at least, had provided a proper canopy arrangement. Republic, however, stretched the constant-section of the fuselage just ahead of the forward propellant tank by 29 inches. On the single-seat aircraft, two compartments held the research instrumentation (550 pounds ahead of the pilot and 250 pounds behind the pilot). For the two-seat

140 Ibid, pp. 50-53.

141 Ibid, pp. 10 and 14.

142 Republic was the only competitor to specify an explicit model for the carrier aircraft. Given the priorities in the Strategic Air Command at the time of the proposals, it is unlikely that an H-model (which was the latest in the inventory) would have been made available. More likely, it would have been a D-model similar to the FICON GRB-36Ds.

143 "AP-76: Project 1226 Summary Brochure," pp. 10 and 51.

airplane the 250 pounds in the rear compartment were deleted, and, combined with the 29-inch extension, this provided a full-size cockpit for the observer. The airplane could still carry the other 550 pounds of instrumentation—in fact, it was the only proposed two-seat aircraft that could carry any. The empty weight of the airplane increased 380 pounds and the launch weight increased 610 pounds, resulting in a degradation of performance of 170 fps.[144]

144 Ibid, pp. 52-53.

Comparison of Physical Characteristics				
	Bell	**Douglas**	**NAA**	**Republic**
	D-171	Model 684	ESO-7487	AP-76
Fuselage:				
Length (feet):	44.42	46.75	49.33	52.58
Frontal area (square feet):	25.00	21.00	?	?
Maximum diameter (feet):	5.15	5.16	4.50	5.00
Fineness ratio:	8.62	9.06	?	10.5
Wing:				
Airfoil:	biconvex (mod)	Clark Y (mod)	66005 (mod)	hexagonal
Span (feet):	25.67	19.50	22.36	27.66
Root section (percent):	5.0	7.0	5.0	5.0
Tip section (percent):	6.0	4.5	1.0	7.5
Root chord (feet):	13.16	10.40	10.80	16.00
Tip chord (feet):	3.86	2.75	3.00	2.25
Area (square feet):	220.0	150.3	200.0	254.0
Flap area (square feet):	15.25	14.44	?	28.80
Aileron area (square feet):	16.00	9.88	n/a	15.80
Angle of incidence (degrees):	0	0	0	0
Dihedral (degrees):	0	0	0	0
Aspect ratio:	3.00	2.53	2.50	3.00
Taper ratio:	0.30	0.22	?	0.14
Aileron deflection (degrees):	±15	±20	n/a	+17/–12
Flap deflection (degrees):	–45	–45	–40	–38
Leading-edge sweep (degrees):	37.0	40.0	25.0	38.4
MAC (inches):	112.50	105.26	123.23	130.87
Horizontal Stabilizer:				
Airfoil:	biconvex (mod)	5° wedge	66005 (mod)	10° wedge
Span (feet):	13.75	11.83	17.64	15.70
Root chord (feet):	7.05	7.66	7.02	7.08
Tip chord (feet):	2.11	1.66	2.10	1.83
Area (square feet):	63.00	55.20	51.76	69.70
Aspect ratio:	3.00	2.54	2.81	3.48
Taper ratio:	0.30	0.22	0.22	0.26
Leading-edge sweep (degrees):	35.5	40.0	45.0	22.3
Deflection (degrees):	+10/–20	+5/–20	+15/–45	+7/–20

	Bell	**Douglas**	**NAA**	**Republic**
	D-171	Model 684	ESO-7487	AP-76
Dorsal Stabilizer:				
Airfoil:	biconvex (mod)	diamond (mod)	10° wedge	12° wedge
Area (square feet):	45.30	39.25	38.14	47.60
Rudder area (square feet):	13.5	7.85	?	32.0
Aspect ratio:	0.8	1.277	1.25	1.6
Leading-edge sweep (degrees):	45.0	40.0	52.0	27.9
Rudder deflection (degrees):	±20	±30	±45	±20
Ventral Stabilizer:				
Airfoil:	10° diamond	7° edge	15° wedge	10° wedge
Area (square feet):	22.70	12.08	11.42	12.30
Leading-edge sweep (degrees):	45.0	60.0	52.0	45.0
Weights:				
Launch (pounds):	34,140	25,300	27,722	39,099
Burnout (pounds):	12,942	10,600	10,433	15,300
Landing (pounds):	12,595	10,450	10,200	14,800
Empty (pounds):	11,964	9,208	9,959	14,388
Propellants (pounds):	21,600	14,700	16,410	23,660
Propulsion:				
Number of engines:	3	1	1	4
Engine type:	XLR81	XLR30	XLR30	XLR81
Total thrust (lbf):	43,500	57,000	57,000	58,000
Fuel type:	JP-X	NH3	NH3	JP-X
Fuel quantity (gallons):	704	1,142	1,239	710
Oxidizer type:	RFNA	LOX	LOX	RFNA
Oxidizer quantity (gallons):	1,358	816	907	1,430
Performance (estimated):				
Maximum speed (fps):	6,850	6,655	6,950	6,619
Maximum altitude (feet):	400,000	375,000	800,000	220,000
Cost and Schedule:				
R&D plus three aircraft (millions):	$36.3	$36.4	$56.1	$47.0
Estimated First flight:	Jan. 59	Mar. 58	Nov. 57	Feb. 58

THE AIRFRAME EVALUATION

The airframe evaluation process lasted from mid May until late July, with the Air Force, NACA, and Navy conducting independent evaluations based on a number of preestablished criteria. The preliminary NACA evaluation of the proposals consumed the better part of three weeks before each of the laboratories forwarded preliminary results to Hartley Soulé. On 3 June 1955, Ames tentatively ranked the submissions as 1) Douglas, 2) North American, 3) Bell, and 4) Republic. The Douglas ranking resulted from "the completeness and soundness of design study, awareness of factors in speed and altitude regime, and relative simplicity of approach." Ames, however, expressed skepticism over the Douglas magnesium hot-structure wing because it would preclude the study of problems associated with insulated-type structures that would potentially be used in future aircraft intended for greater flight duration. This seemed to be a major disconnect between Ames and Langley. It appears that Ames wanted to test a structure that would be representative of some future production aircraft; Langley just wanted to test a structure that would survive. Another problem that worried the Ames evaluators was the flammability of magnesium. It seemed that "only a small area raised to the ignition temperature would be sufficient to destroy the aircraft." The researchers at Ames held that if Douglas should win the competition, the company should build two aircraft with the proposed HK31 structure, but a third aircraft "should have a wing based upon the alternative higher temperature insulated type of design approach." The Ames report continued to stress the need for a wing of greater leading-edge sweep angle (at least 53 degrees) "for the purpose of minimizing the rate of heat transfer to the leading edge."[145]

At Langley, on 6 June, researchers rated the North American proposal number one, followed by Douglas, Bell, and Republic. According to the Langley assessment, led by John Becker, the research utility of the North American hot-structure approach outweighed the advantages of the simplicity of the magnesium structure proposed by Douglas. Slightly rebuffing Ames, Langley noted that the 21% reduction in heat transfer gained by increasing the leading-edge sweep from the proposed 40 degrees to 53 degrees did not seem to justify the alteration of the planform. This was particularly true because the structure appeared capable of handling the heat load.[146]

In a reminder to the evaluation teams, also on 6 June, Arthur Vogeley and Captain McCollough reiterated that the purpose of the evaluation was "to select a contractor rather than a particular design." Although certain features of the winning design could be unsatisfactory, it was the basic design approach as described in the proposal that might best be relied upon to produce an acceptable research airplane.[147]

---

145 Letter, Harry J. Goett/Ames Evaluation Group to Hartley A. Soulé/Research Airplane Project Leader, no subject, 3 June 1955.

146 Letter, John V. Becker/Langley Evaluation Group, to Hartley A. Soulé/Research Airplane Project Leader, no subject, 6 June 1955.

147 Memorandum, William J. Underwood to the Director/NACA, no subject, 6 June 1955.

On 10 June 1955, the HSFS sent its airframe results to Soulé, detailing the design approach and research utility aspects of the airframe, flight control system, propulsion unit, crew provisions, handling and launching, and miscellaneous systems. Researchers at the HSFS ranked the proposals as 1) Douglas, 2) North American, 3) Bell, and 4) Republic, although the proposals from Douglas and North American were essentially equal.[148]

The final evaluation by Ames, on 10 June, ranked the proposals as 1) North American, 2) Douglas, 3) Bell, and 4) Republic. This represented a change from the earlier Ames evaluation, based largely on researchers considering the North American structure superior in terms of research utility—an opinion voiced earlier by Langley. The Ames evaluators had apparently changed their minds about wanting to test a production-representative structure. The laboratory had also finally given up on advocating an insulated structure since no serious support for their earlier recommendation of equipping the third aircraft with a different wing structure had materialized (sufficient funds to construct an alternate wing were simply not available).[149]

The final evaluation from Langley on 14 June ranked the proposals as 1) North American, 2) Douglas, 3) Republic, and 4) Bell. Although researchers at Langley thought the magnesium wing structure of Douglas was feasible, they feared that local hot spots caused by irregular aerodynamic heating could weaken or destroy the structure. The use of Inconel X by North American presented an advantage with regard to thermal limits—not only from the standpoint of margins for maneuverability within the design temperatures, but also from a safety viewpoint if the airplane ever exceeded its design temperature.

A few days after receiving all of the final evaluations, Soulé sent copies of each to the WADC Project Office, along with a consolidated result. The final NACA ranking was (points based on a scale of 100) as follows:[150]

	Design Approach				**Research Utility**			
	B	**D**	**N**	**R**	**B**	**D**	**N**	**R**
Airframe	70	80	85	75	70	80	90	80
Flight controls	70	80	75	70	70	75	75	75
Propulsion	80	80	90	30	75	40	40	75
Crew provisions	55	85	80	40	55	85	80	35
Handling/launching	95	65	75	65	90	70	70	70
Miscellaneous	70	85	70	70	70	85	70	70
Average	**73**	**79**	**79**	**58**	**72**	**73**	**71**	**68**

148 Letter, Walter C. Williams/HSFS Evaluation Group, to Hartley A. Soulé/Research Airplane Project Leader, 10 June 1955. In the files at the DFRC History Office.

149 Letter, Harry J. Goett/Ames Evaluation Group to Hartley A. Soulé/Research Airplane Project Leader, no subject, 10 June 1955.

150 Letter, Hartley A. Soulé/Research Airplane Project Leader to NACA Liaison Officer at Wright-Patterson AFB, 17 June 1955. The average scores shown were not broken out in the letter, but are shown here to ease understanding of the ultimate ratings.

Oddly, the final order representing the overall NACA evaluation was 1) North American, 2) Douglas, 3) Bell, and 4) Republic, despite the fact that Douglas scored slightly more points in the evaluation (152 versus 150 for North American). Soulé pointed out that although Ames, Langley, and the HSFS did not rank the four proposals in the same order, the final ranking did represent an overall NACA consensus. All of the laboratories involved in this portion of the evaluation considered both the Douglas and North American proposals to be much superior to those submitted by Bell and Republic. While researchers preferred the Inconel X structure of the North American proposal, the design was not without fault. For instance, the NACA thought that the landing-gear arrangement was undesirable, the differentially-operated horizontal stabilator design in lieu of ailerons was an overly complicated arrangement, and (at least at Langley) the replaceable fiberglass leading edges were unacceptable.

John Becker wrote to Hartley Soulé on 16 June attempting to clarify why the North American design was superior to that of Douglas. The letter listed the thermal limits expected for the new aircraft, and showed that the Inconel X structure on the North American design was "impressively superior" to the magnesium alloy used by Douglas. The data were shown for three categories: 1) performance within the design temperature limits in terms of allowable velocity, altitude, and dependence on speed brakes; 2) reserve heat capacity (in case the design temperatures were exceeded by a moderate margin) such that the structure would still have a fair possibility of remaining intact; and 3) the possibility of melting or burning in case the design temperatures were greatly exceeded in local hot spots. There appears to be no further correspondence on this subject, so Becker's explanation seems to have answered whatever unasked questions existed.[151]

During the first two weeks in July, the WADC evaluation teams sent their final reports to the WADC Project Office. As with the NACA evaluations, the Air Force found little difference between the Douglas and North American designs, point-wise, with both proposals considered significantly superior to those of Bell and Republic.

George Spangenberg was in charge of the Navy evaluations, which got off to a late start and ended up being cursory. In the end, the Navy found much the same thing as the NACA and ranked the airframe proposals as 1) Douglas, 2) North American, 3) Republic, and 4) Bell. Given the Navy's long—and successful—association with Douglas airplanes, the order was not surprising. Most Navy concerns centered on the selection of an engine. As Clotaire Wood explained, "the airframe-engine combination was to be evaluated and not the engine alone, since it had been agreed that the engine of the winning design would be the engine supported by the special development program." This was not how the Power Plant Laboratory saw the process, but it seemed to put the Navy at ease.

151 Memorandum, John V. Becker to John W. Crowley, no subject, 16 June 1955. In the Becker Archives, Virginia Polytechnic Institute, Blacksburg, VA. John Becker has no specific memory of why he wrote this letter, but assumes that Harley Soulé wanted technical justification for North American being considered better than Douglas, despite the point system.

In addition, Wood indicated that "it would be of real value to have the Bureau's [BuAer] recommendations regarding an engine development program once the winner of the competition is determined."[152]

In early July the Navy began to raise questions about the various airframe proposals. For instance, the BuAer electronics group did not believe the Bell design had a satisfactory electrical power system, and Navy researchers rated the North American design last from an equipment (e.g., life support) perspective. The Douglas and Republic designs had the best potential flying qualities, and BuAer researchers felt that North American had incorrectly assumed laminar flow over much of their design, and had therefore underestimated the heating values. It was a bit late to be raising concerns, but most of the issues were minor and did not materially affect the outcome of the competition. After conferring with his Air Force and NACA counterparts, on 15 July George Spangenberg finalized the Navy's position as Douglas, North American, Republic, and Bell.[153]

On 26–28 July, the Air Force, NACA, and Navy evaluation teams met at Wright Field to select an airframe contractor. George Spangenberg stated that it was unfortunate that the point system used in the evaluation "appeared to give no conclusive winner," since a contractor could score highly in one area and low in another yet still have a winning score, while another that was satisfactory in all areas would be rated lower. He also indicated that the goals of the project seem to have shifted somewhat, resulting in a "firm requirement" for 1,200°F skin temperature research instead of the previous "desire" for high temperatures.[154]

Presaging events to come, discussions ensued concerning the amount of work recently awarded to North American and Republic, and whether additional awards would spread their engineering groups too thin. Other discussions included the possibility of selecting Douglas but directing it to redesign its aircraft using an Inconel hot structure instead of magnesium. In the end, the Air Force and the NACA concluded that the North American proposal best accommodated their requirements. The Navy did not want to cast the only dissenting vote and, after short deliberation, agreed to go along with the decision.[155]

During the week of 1–5 August 1955, the WADC Project Office prepared the final evaluation summary and oral presentation: "the evaluation of the proposals submitted in competition was made in five areas: performance, technical design, research suitability, development capability, and cost." It is interesting to note that this competition was not about the "lowest bidder," and none of the proposals were anywhere near the original $12.2 million estimate. The results of these evaluations were as follows:[156]

---

152 Letter, Clotaire Wood to George A. Spangenberg, no subject, 19 June 1955. In the files at the Naval History Center.

153 Letter, Clotaire Wood to Langley, no subject, 13 July 1955; memorandum, George A. Spangenberg to the BuAer assistant chief for R&D, no subject, 15 July 1955; Memorandum, George A. Spangenberg to the BuAer assistant chief for R&D, no subject, 15 July 1955. Both in the files at the Naval History Center.

154 Memorandum, George A. Spangenberg to the BuAer assistant chief for R&D, no subject, 1 August 1955. In the files at the Naval History Center.

155 Ibid.

156 Air Force report RDZ-280, "Evaluation Report on X-15 Research Aircraft Design Competition," 5 August 1955, no page numbers. In the files at the Air Force Historical Research Agency.

Performance: The performance evaluation consisted of a check of the probability of the different designs, considering present uncertainties, of meeting the specified speed and altitude requirements. The probabilities were calculated to be best for the North American proposal, equal for the Bell and Douglas proposals, and least for the Republic proposal; but because of the assumptions of the analysis, all designs were judged able to meet the requirements.

Technical Design: This factor was judged on the awareness shown by the contractor of the problems of high-speed, high-altitude flight and of the means, as indicated by the airplane designs, the contractor proposed for exploring and studying these problems. The general design competency of the contractor also was judged from the designs submitted: North American 81.5 points; Douglas 80.1 points; Bell 75.5 points; and Republic 72.2 points. No design, as submitted, was considered safe for the use intended. The Douglas design was considered best in this regard, but did not include adequate margins for ignorance factors and operational errors.

Research Suitability: In this area, the fundamental differences in the proposed structures were examined and rated because of their decisive importance in the research uses of this aircraft. North American was rated acceptable because of the Inconel X "hot-structure" heat-sink, which was most suitable for research and which was potentially the simplest to make safe for the mission. Republic and Bell were considered unsatisfactory because of the hazardous aspects associated with the insulated structures used, and Douglas was considered unsatisfactory because of the low safety margins available and because of the limited future usefulness of the "cool" magnesium heat-sink principle.

Development Capability: Ratings were based on the physical equipment and manpower the contractor had available for pursuing the project, and the resulting time proposed for development. Evaluation of this factor resulted in the following ratings: (1) Douglas was acceptable; (2) North American was acceptable; (3) Bell was less acceptable; (4) Republic was less acceptable. North American, Republic, and Douglas estimated that the first flight date would be within 30 months, but the Republic estimate was not believed to be credible, hence their lower score. Bell promised a first flight date within 40 months.

Costs: Costs for three aircraft plus static test article, engines, and spares as adjusted by AMC to a comparable basis are: Bell,

$36.3 million; Douglas, $36.4 million; Republic, $47.0 million; and North American, $56.1 million.

On 9 August, Captain McCollough presented the results of the evaluation to Brigadier General Howell M. Estes, then chief of the Weapons Systems Division, under whose jurisdiction the WADC Project Office fell, and a select group of senior Air Force officers. McCollough made a second presentation in Baltimore on 11 August for Generals John W. Sessums and Marvin C. Demler, who were the commanders of the WADC and ARDC, respectively, and Hartley Soulé from the NACA.[157]

The final briefing to a combined meeting of Air Force, NACA, and Navy personnel was at NACA Headquarters on 12 August. The attendees included Hugh Dryden, Gus Crowley, Ira Abbott, Richard Rhode, and Hartley Soulé from the NACA; Brigadier General Kelsey, Colonel Donald H. Heaton, Lieutenant Colonels Gablecki and Maiersperger, and Major Heniesse from the Air Force; and Captain R. E. Dixon, Abraham Hyatt, and George Spangenberg from BuAer. Following this, the Research Airplane Committee met, accepted the findings of the evaluation groups, and agreed to present the recommendation to the Department of Defense.[158]

Because the estimated costs submitted by North American were far above the amount tentatively allocated for the project, the Research Airplane Committee included a recommendation for a funding increase before signing the final contract. A further recommendation—one that would later take on greater importance—called for relaxing the proposed schedule by up to 18 months. The committee approved both recommendations and forwarded them to the Assistant Secretary of Defense for Research and Development.

SECOND THOUGHTS

Events took an unexpected twist on the afternoon of 23 August 1955 when the North American representative in Dayton verbally informed the WADC Project Office that his company wished to withdraw its proposal. Captain McCollough notified Hartley Soulé, Air Force Headquarters, and BuAer of this decision, touching off a series of discussions concerning future actions. Within a week the Air Force asked North American to reconsider its decision. The Air Materiel Command recommended that Douglas be declared the winner if North American did not reconsider. The Research Airplane Committee, however, cautioned that the Douglas design would require considerable modification before

157 Memorandum, Hartley A. Soulé/Research Airplane Project Leader to the Members of Project 1226 Evaluation Group, 23 September 1955. In the files at the NASA History Office. The ARDC was activated in April 1951 from the engineering assets of the Air Materiel Command at Wright-Patterson AFB, and in June 1951 it moved its new headquarters to Baltimore, MD. In January 1958 the ARDC moved to Andrews AFB, MD, and was redesignated the Air Force Systems Command in 1961.

158 Dryden, Kelsey, and Dixon were members of the Research Airplane Committee. Captain Dixon had replaced Rear Admiral Robert Hatcher when he retired.

it satisfied Air Force and NACA requirements. On 30 August, North American sent a letter to the Air Force formally withdrawing its proposal because sufficient resources were not available to complete the X-15 program within the 30-month schedule.[159]

On 1 September Hugh Dryden informed Soulé that he and General Kelsey had decided to continue the procurement, pending receipt of official notification from North American. The letter arrived sometime later in the week, and on 7 September, Soulé contacted Dryden and recommended that the Research Airplane Committee consider the second-place bidder. Dryden responded that he wanted to reopen the competition rather than award the contract to Douglas.

Despite North American's request to withdraw, the procurement process continued. A presentation to the Defense Air Technical Advisory Panel on 14 September presented the selection of North American for formal approval. Naturally, the Air Force recommended approval, but the Army representative to the panel flatly opposed the project if it required more Department of Defense funds than previously discussed. This prompted the Air Force to reduce project costs below earlier estimates. The panel was also concerned that the program could not be completed in 30 months, and concurred with the earlier Research Airplane Committee recommendation that the schedule be relaxed.[160]

By 21 September the Department of Defense had approved the selection of North American, with a caveat: a reduction in annual funding. The same week General Estes met with John Leland "Lee" Atwood, the president of North American, who announced that an extended schedule would allow North American to reconsider its position.[161]

Two days later, the vice president and chief engineer for North American, Raymond H. Rice, explained that the company had decided to withdraw from the competition because it had recently won new bomber (WS-110A) and long-range interceptor (WS-202A) studies, and had increased activity relating to its ongoing YF-107 fighter program. Having undertaken these projects, North American said it would be unable to accommodate the fast engineering labor build-up that would be required to support the desired 30-month schedule. Rice went on to say that "due to the apparent interest that has subsequently been expressed in the North American design, the contractor [North American] wishes to extend two alternate courses which have been previously discussed with Air Force personnel. The engineering man-power work load schedule has been reviewed and the contractor wishes to point out that Project 1226 could be handled if it were permissible to extend the schedule…over an additional eight month period. In the event the

159 Letter, North American to Commander, ARDC, no subject, 6 September 1955. In the files at the Boeing Archives.

160 X-15 WSPO Weekly Activity Report, 22 September 1955; Interview, William J. Underwood, NACA Liaison Officer, 1 October 1955, by Robert L. Perry, Chief, History Branch, WADC. In the files at the AFMC History Office.

161 John Leland Atwood began work as an aeronautical engineer for Douglas in 1930, and moved to North American in 1934. He became assistant general manager in 1938, and in 1941 was named North American's first vice president. He became president in 1948 and served continually until he retired in 1970.

above time extension is not acceptable and in the best interest of the project, the contractor is willing to release the proposal data to the Air Force at no cost."[162]

The approval granted by the Research Airplane Committee and the Defense Air Technical Advisory Panel to extend the schedule allowed North American to retract its previous decision to withdraw from the competition once the Air Force notified the company of its selection. Accordingly, on 30 September, Colonel Carl F. Damberg, chief of the Aircraft Division at Wright Field, formally notified North American that the company had won the X-15 competition. The company retracted its letter of withdrawal, and the Air Force thanked the other bidders for their participation. In the competitive environment that exists in the early 21st century, this course of events would undoubtedly lead to protests from the losing contractors, and possibly congressional investigations and court actions. However, as business was conducted in 1955, it was not considered cause for comment and the award went forward uncontested.[163]

Within North American, the program had also been the subject of discussions of which the government was probably unaware. The internal concerns were much the same as those related to the government, but they showed a marked divide between technical personnel and corporate management. Harrison Storms, who would be the chief engineer for the North American Los Angeles Division during the design of the X-15, remembers:[164]

> My position at that time was that of manager of research and development for the Los Angles Division.... I was told that top corporate management wanted to reject the [X-15] program since it was small and they were concerned that too many of the top engineering personnel would be absorbed into the program and not be available for other projects that they considered more important to the future of the corporation. There was considerable objection to this position in the technical area. I was finally called into Mr. Rice's office, the then chief engineer, and told that we could have the program on the condition that none of the problems were ever to be brought into his office. He further elaborated that it would be up to me to seek all the solutions and act as the top NAA representative for the program. This was fine with me.

Funding was another issue, and on 5 October 1955 a meeting was held at Wright Field to discuss how to pay for the program. The Defense Coordinating

162 Letter, Raymond H. Rice, Vice President and Chief Engineer, North American Aviation, to Commander ARDC, no subject, 23 September 1955. In the files at the Boeing Archives. The WS-110A and WS-202A studies would eventually become the B-70 and F-108 programs. In addition, North American was in the midst of a major Navy competition that eventually resulted in the North American A3J (A-5) Vigilante. The YF-107A program had started as an improved F-100 Super Sabre in October 1953, and nine prototypes were ordered in August 1954. Only three were ever completed. The first YF-107A (55-5118) would not make its maiden flight until 10 September 1956, and the program was canceled in February 1957.

163 X-15 WSPO Weekly Activity Report, 22 September 1955; letter, Colonel Carl F. Damberg, Chief, Aircraft Division, AMC, to North American Aviation, subject: X-15 Competition, 30 September 1955. In the files at the Air Force Historical Research Agency; letters, from Colonel Carl F. Damberg to Bell, Douglas, and Republic, no subject, 30 September 1955.

164 Storms, "X-15 Hardware Design Challenges," p. 33.

Committee for Piloted Aircraft had tentatively allocated $30,000,000 to the program from the Department of Defense general contingency fund, with an expected burn rate of approximately $10,000,000 per year. The problem was that the new program estimate was $56,100,000, including a first-year expenditure of almost $26,000,000. The X-15 Project Office began to reduce expenditures by eliminating the static-test article (nobody was sure how to test it in any case), reducing the modifications to the B-36 carrier aircraft, and eliminating some previously required studies and evaluations. The agreed-upon eight-month extension also eased the peak annual expenditures somewhat. After some juggling, the revised cost estimates were $50,063,500–$38,742,500 for the airframes, $9,961,000 for the engine, and $1,360,000 for the new flight test range at Edwards. The peak expenditure ($16,600,000) would occur in the third year of the project.[165]

Contract negotiations followed. The Air Materiel Command took revised budget figures to a meeting on 11 October at the Pentagon. By that time, the reduced estimate was approximately $45,000,000 and the maximum annual expenditure was less than $15,000,000. The Air Force presented these figures to the Defense Coordinating Committee for Piloted Aircraft on 19 October. Support for the project was reconfirmed, although no additional funds were allocated. Nevertheless, the Department of Defense released funds to continue the procurement process.[166]

The AMC Directorate of Procurement and Production drafted a $2,600,000 letter contract for North American on 7 November 1955. Higher headquarters approved the letter contract on 15 November, and North America returned a signed copy on 5 December. The detailed design and development of the hypersonic research airplane had been under way for just under a year at this point. Reaction Motors returned a signed copy of its $2,900,000 letter contract on 14 February 1956.[167]

At this point, the X-15 program budget was (in millions):[168]

	FY56	FY57	FY58	FY59	FY60	Total
Airframe	6.0	10.3	13.9	6.9	0.6	37.7
Engine	2.9	2.8	0.5	0.0	0.0	6.2
Range	0.4	0.9	0.1	0.0	0.0	1.4
Total	9.3	14.0	14.5	6.9	0.6	45.3

165 Memorandum, Arthur W. Vogeley to Hartley A. Soulé/Research Airplane Project Leader, no subject, 13 October 1955; letter, Major General Howell M. Estes, Jr., Assistant Deputy Commander for Weapons Systems at ARDC to Brigadier General J. Stanley Holtoner, Commander AFFTC, no subject, 10 May 1957. In the files at the AFFTC History Office.

166 X-15 WSPO Weekly Activity Report, 13 October; 20 October; 27 October; and 15 December 1955; memorandum, Colonel Bruce C. Downs, Chief, Fighter Branch, to Chief, Aircraft Division, Director of Procurement and Production, AMC, 7 November 1955, subject: Request for permission to negotiate a CPFF [cost-plus-fixed-fee] type contract P. R. No. 636317 and 198558; Letter, N. Shropshire, Director of Contract Administration, North American Aviation, to Commander, AMC, subject: Letter Contract AF33(600)-31693, 8 December 1955. In the files at the ASD History Office.

167 Ibid; memorandum, Colonel B. C. Downs to Chief, Aircraft Division, no subject, 7 November 1955. In the files at the ASD History Office; Memorandum, Captain Chester E. McCollough, Jr., X-15 Project Officer, ARDC, to Chief, Non-Rotating Engine Branch, Power Plant Laboratory, Director of Laboratories, WADC, subject: Engine for X-15, 1 December 1955; letter contract AF33(600)-32248, 14 February 1956.

168 Memorandum, Hartley A. Soulé/Research Airplane Project Leader to Members of the Project 1226 Evaluation Group, no subject, 21 October 1955.

However, the available funds were only (in millions):[169]

	FY56	FY57	FY58	FY59	FY60	Total
Air Force	9.5	8.0	4.0	3.0	0.0	24.5
Navy	0.5	1.8	1.7	1.0	0.0	5.0
Total	10.0	9.8	5.7	4.0	0.0	29.5
Surplus/Deficit	0.7	–4.2	–8.8	–2.9	–0.6	–15.8

There was still less than $30,000,000 available for the project, and an additional $16,000,000 needed to be found. In reality, this amount would become trivial as the project progressed.

The Air Force completed the definitive $5,315,000 contract for North American on 11 June 1956. The contract included three X-15 research airplanes, a full-scale mockup, various wind-tunnel models, propulsion system test articles, preliminary flight tests, and the modification of a B-36 carrier aircraft. The costs did not include government-furnished equipment, such as the engine, research instrumentation, fuel, and oil, or expenses to operate the B-36. The delivery date for the first X-15 was 31 October 1958.[170]

All parties signed the final contract for the major piece of government-furnished equipment, the Reaction Motors engine, on 7 September 1956. The "propulsion subsystem" effort became Project 3116, which was carried on the books separately from the Project 1226 airframe. The final $10,160,030 contract, plus a fee of $614,000, required Reaction Motors to deliver one engine and a full-scale mockup. Amendments to the contract would cover the procurement of additional engines.[171]

169 Ibid.

170 Air Force contract AF33(600)-31693.

171 Air Force contract AF33(600)-32248; System Development Plan, X-15 Research Aircraft, Supporting Research System Number 447L, 22 March 1956. In the files at the AFFTC History Office. As events later demonstrated, even this erred badly on the side of underestimation. The final fee paid to Reaction Motors was greater than the original estimate for the total engine development program. The definitive contract exceeded more than 20 times the original estimate, and more than twice the original total program approval estimate.

CHAPTER 3

Conflict and Innovation

Although it gave the appearance of having a rather simple configuration, the X-15 was perhaps the most technologically complex single-seat aircraft yet built. The airplane would require the development of the largest and most sophisticated man-rated rocket engine yet, and a heated debate took place regarding the escape system for the pilot. Given the extreme environment in which it was to operate, engineers had to either invent or reinvent almost every system in the airplane. North American's Harrison A. "Stormy" Storms, Jr., and Charles H. Feltz had a difficult job ahead of them. Both men were widely admired by their peers, who considered them among the best in the business (a fact confirmed much later when both men played key roles during the development of the Apollo spacecraft).

Harrison Storms had studied aeronautical engineering under Theodore von Kàrmàn at the California Institute of Technology during the 1940s before joining North American Aviation. He was chief engineer for the entire Los Angeles division, and although he was greatly interested in the X-15 he had other responsibilities that precluded daily contact with the X-15 program. Nevertheless, he would be a powerful ally when bureaucratic hurdles had to be overcome or the customer needed to be put at ease.[1]

1 Scott Crossfield, *Always Another Dawn: The Story of a Rocket Test Pilot*, (New York: The World Publishing Company, 1960), pp. 219-221; letter, Scott Crossfield to Dennis R. Jenkins, 30 June 1999. Crossfield's book was later republished, without change (North Stratford, NH: Ayer Company Publishers, 1999).

Charles H. Feltz had joined North American Aviation just before the beginning of World War II and had worked on several high-profile projects prior to being assigned as the lead of the X-15 development effort. Feltz would go on to lead North American's Apollo Command and Service Module and Space Shuttle efforts. (Boeing)

Feltz had joined the company in 1940, working on the P-51 Mustang and B-25 Mitchell during World War II, and later the B-45 Tornado and F-86 Sabre. As the X-15 project engineer, Feltz would lead the day-to-day activities of the design team. In those days at North American, the project engineer was in charge of the entire work force assigned to his airplane. Surprisingly, the 39-year-old Feltz had never heard of the X-15 until Storms pulled him off the F-86 program to be the project engineer, meaning that he had not been involved in the proposal effort and needed to catch up. Fortunately, Storms and Crossfield were there to help.[2]

Directly assisting Storms and Feltz was the already legendary NACA test pilot A. Scott Crossfield, who had joined North American specifically to work on the X-15. Crossfield had been a Navy instructor pilot stationed at Corpus Christi, Texas, during World War II before receiving a bachelor of science degree in aeronautical engineering and a master's in aeronautical science from the University of Washington. Crossfield describes Storms as "a man of wonderful imagination, technical depth, and courage…with a love affair with the X-15. He was a tremendous ally and kept the objectivity of the program intact…." According to Crossfield, Charlie Feltz was "a remarkable 'can do and did' engineer who was very much a source of the X-15 success story." In 2001, Crossfield called Feltz "the flywheel of common sense engineering who educated the world with the X-15, Apollo, and the Space Shuttle."[3]

The day Crossfield reported for work at North American, he defined his future role in the program. As he recounted in his autobiography, "I would be the X-15's chief son-of-a-bitch. Anyone who wanted Charlie Feltz or North American to capriciously change anything or add anything…would first have to fight Crossfield and hence, I hoped, would at least think twice before proposing grand inventions." He played an essential role, for instance, in convincing the Air Force that an encapsulated ejection system was both impractical and unnecessary. His arguments

2 Crossfield, Always Another Dawn, pp. 219-221; telephone conversation, Charles H. Feltz with Dennis R. Jenkins, 14 June 1999.

3 Letter, Scott Crossfield to Dennis R. Jenkins, 30 June 1999; "flywheel" quote from the foreword to, Dennis R. Jenkins and Tony R. Landis, *Hypersonic: The Story of the North American X-15*, (North Branch, MN: Specialty Press, 2001).

in favor of an ejection seat capable of permitting safe emergency egress at speeds between 80 mph and Mach 4, and altitudes from sea level to 120,000 feet saved significant money, weight, and development time. Crossfield also championed the development of a full-pressure suit for the X-15 pilot.[4]

There has been considerable interest in whether Crossfield made the right decision in leaving the NACA, since it effectively locked him out of the high-speed, high-altitude portion of the X-15 flight program. Crossfield had no regrets: "I made the right decision to go to North American. I am an engineer, aerodynamicist, and designer by training...While I would very much have liked to participate in the flight research program, I am pretty well convinced that I was needed to supply a lot of the impetus that allowed the program to succeed in timeliness, in resources, and in technical return.... I was on the program for nine years from conception to closing the circle in flight test. Every step: concept, criteria, requirements, performance specifications, detailed design, manufacturing, quality control, and flight operations had all become an [obsession] to fight for, protect, and share—almost with a passion." Crossfield seldom lacked passion.[5]

A. Scott Crossfield resigned as a NACA test pilot and joined North American Aviation specifically to work on the X-15 project. Although an accomplished test pilot with many rocket-powered flights under his belt, Crossfield was primarily an engineer and wanted to apply what he had learned to the most advanced research airplane of the era. Crossfield led the charge on keeping the escape system simple and the airplane reliable, and later proved his mettle by flying the X-15's first flights. (NASA)

Essential members of the North American team included assistant project engineers Roland L. "Bud" Benner, George Owl, and Raun Robinson. Others included powerplant engineer Robert E. Field, regulators and relief-valve expert John W. Gibb, chief of aerodynamics Lawrence P. Greene, project aerodynamicist Edwin W. "Bill" Johnston, and test pilot Alvin S. White. Storms remembers that "Al White went through all the required training to be the backup pilot to Crossfield and trained for several years—and was not even allowed one flight; that's dedication!" In addition, L. Robert Carman, who (along with Hubert Drake) developed one of the earliest NACA ideas for a hypersonic airplane, had left the NACA and joined North American to work on the X-15.[6]

4 The quote is from Crossfield, *Always Another Dawn*, p. 225.

5 Letter, Scott Crossfield to Dennis R. Jenkins, 30 June 1999.

6 Telephone conversation, Alvin S. White with Dennis R. Jenkins, 8 April 2001; Harrison A. Storms, "X-15 Hardware Design Challenges," a paper in the *Proceedings of the X-15 30th Anniversary Celebration*, Dryden Flight Research Facility, Edwards, CA, 8 June 1989, NASA CP-3105, p. 33.

Years later Storms remembered his first verbal instructions from Hartley Soulé: "You have a little airplane and a big engine with a large thrust margin. We want to go to 250,000 feet altitude and Mach 6. We want to study aerodynamic heating. We do not want to worry about aerodynamic stability and control, or the airplane breaking up. So, if you make any errors, make them on the strong side. You should have enough thrust to do the job." Added Storms, "And so we did."[7]

Soon after the contract was awarded, Storms and Soulé began to know each other much better as North American and NACA began to interact in technical and management meetings. Storms insisted that the contractor team members stay in their own area of responsibility and not attempt to run each other's areas. Soulé agreed with the approach and directed the NACA members similarly. At least initially, Storms and Feltz were somewhat surprised that Soulé insisted on frequent meetings between small groups—seldom more than 10 to 12 people. Nevertheless, Storms remembers, "[S]urprisingly, we managed to get much accomplished, and we all left the meetings with a good concept of what had to be accomplished and when." In later years, Storms was appreciative of the work done by Soulé, and in 1989 commented that "I can't say enough about how well, in my opinion, Hartley did his job. He was a very outstanding program manager and has been greatly neglected in recognition."[8]

When North American signed the final contract, the X-15 was some three years away from its first flight. Although most of the basic research into the materials and structural science was complete, largely thanks to the researchers at Langley, a great deal of work remained. This included the development of fabrication and assembly techniques for Inconel X and the new hot-structure design. North American and its subcontractors met the challenge of each problem with a practical solution that eventually consumed some 2,000,000 engineering man-hours. These included 4,000 hours logged in 15 different wind tunnels that provided more than 2 million data points.[9]

The Air Materiel Command had excluded the Langley study as a requirement in the invitation-to-bid letter circulated to the airframe contractors. Nevertheless, the influence of the Becker study was evident in North American's winning proposal. The North American vertical stabilizers used the thick-wedge airfoil developed by Charles McClellan, and the dihedral in the horizontal stabilizer had been a feature of the Langley configuration. In addition, North American used Inconel X and a multi-spar wing with corrugated webs.

One major difference between the Becker study and that of North American was that the latter used all-movable horizontal stabilizers, resulting in the elimination of separate elevators and ailerons. The "rolling tail" allowed the horizontal stabilizers to deflect differentially to provide roll control, or together for pitch control. During the proposal evaluation the government considered this a "potential risk," and several evaluators believed that it represented an overly complicated approach. However, the rolling tail allowed North American to eliminate the pro-

7 Storms, "X-15 Hardware Design Challenges," p. 27.

8 Ibid, pp. 27 and 33.

9 Harrison Storms, "The X-15 Rollout Symposium," 15 October 1958. Released statements in the files at the AFFTC History Office.

tuberances covering the aileron actuators in the thin wing, and allowed a generally simpler structure for the entire wing. Although the additional drag of the protuberances was of little concern, they would have created another heating problem.[10]

Another significant difference between the two designs was that North American chose to use tunnels on the fuselage sides to house the various propellant lines and wiring ordinarily located inside the fuselage. This was because North American used full-monocoque propellant tanks instead of the separate tanks inside a semi-monocoque fuselage envisioned by Langley. The monocoque tanks were lighter and stronger than separate tanks, but challenged the designers to find ways to route plumbing, wiring, and control cables—hence the tunnels.[11]

In mid-October 1955, both Ames and the HSFS sent comments to Hartley Soulé expressing concerns about the North American design. Ames wanted to change the structure of the wing leading edge, the fuselage nose, and the ventral stabilizer, as well as to add an augmentation system to help control longitudinal damping. Ames also suggested additional study into the overall shape of the fuselage and the location of the horizontal stabilizer. Further, as they had during the proposal evaluation, researchers at Ames continued to believe that North American had overly simplified the heat transfer analysis. The HSFS recommended changing the design dynamic pressure, the load factors, the wing leading edge, the aerodynamic and ballistic control systems, the propellant system, the landing procedure, and various crew provisions. Engineers at the HSFS took this opportunity, again, to recommend using an interim LR8 engine during the early flight tests.[12]

These and other concerns about the North American configuration prompted a meeting at Wright Field on 24–25 October 1955 that was attended by representatives from North American, Reaction Motors, the Air Force, and the NACA. The Navy did not attend. Subsequent meetings at the North American Inglewood plant took place on 27–28 October and 14–15 November; again, the Navy was not in attendance. Major discussion items included the fuselage tunnels and rolling tail. NACA researchers worried that vortices created by the side tunnels might interfere with the vertical stabilizer, and suggested making the tunnels as short as possible. North American agreed to investigate the tunnels' effects during an early wind-tunnel model-testing program. The company also assured the government that the rolling tail had proven effective in wind-tunnel testing and appeared to offer significant benefits with few, if any, drawbacks.[13]

In early November, Bill Johnston and members of the North American aerodynamic staff met with John Becker, Arthur Vogeley, and Hartley Soulé to discuss

---

10 *Research Airplane Committee Report on the Conference on the Progress of the X-15 Project*, a compilation of the papers presented at the Langley Aeronautical Laboratory, 25-26 October 1956, pp. 23-31 (hereafter called the *1956 Research Airplane Committee Report*); letter, Colonel Carl F. Damberg to Bell, no subject, 30 December 1954. In the files at the ASD History Office.

11 *1956 Research Airplane Committee Report*, pp. 23-31; letter, Colonel Carl F. Damberg to Bell, no subject, 30 December 1954.

12 Letter, Harry J. Goett/Ames to Hartley A. Soulé/Research Airplane Project Leader, no subject, 19 October 1955; memorandum, HSFS to Hartley A. Soulé/Research Airplane Project Leader, no subject, 20 October 1955.

13 Memorandum, Hartley A. Soulé/Research Airplane Project Leader to Members of the Project 1226 Evaluation Group, no subject, 10 November 1955; memorandum, Arthur W. Vogeley to Hartley A. Soulé/Research Airplane Project Leader, no subject, 20 October 1955; North American report NA-55-1237, "Supplementary Data X-15 Technical Evaluation Meeting," 22 November 1955. Eventually, an Air Force-NACA study team journeyed to France to study the prototype Sud-Ouest Trident interceptor, which also used a rolling tail. For more information on the airplane, see "Beyond the Frontiers, Sub-Quest Trident: Mixed-Powerplant Fighter," *Wings of Fame*, Aerospace Publishing Ltd. London, volume 10, p. 32.

NACA wind-tunnel support for the X-15. North American proposed acquiring data at Mach numbers between 0.7 and 3.5 with a 1/10-scale model in the Ames Unitary Tunnel. High-speed information, obtained between Mach numbers 3.0 and 6.3, would come from a 1/50-scale model in the Ames 10 by 14-inch hypersonic tunnel. The use of Ames was logical because it was nearer to the North American facilities than Langley, and in the days of travel by car or piston-powered airliners, distance counted. John Becker and his staff believed that more tests were required, and proposed two different programs depending upon which facilities were available:[14]

Plan A:	Mach Number	Laboratory	Facility	Scale
	0.6–1.4	Langley	8-foot transonic tunnel	1/15
	1.4–5.0	Langley	4x4-foot unitary complex	1/15
	3.0–6.3	Ames	10x14-inch hypersonic tunnel	1/50
	6.9	Langley	11-inch hypersonic tunnel	1/50
Plan B:	0.6–1.4	Langley	8-foot transonic tunnel	1/15
	1.6, 1.8, 2.0, 2.2	Langley	4x4-foot supersonic pressure tunnel	1/15
	2.5, 3.0, 3.5, 4.0	Langley	Mach 4 jet facility	1/50
	3.0–6.3	Langley	10x14-inch hypersonic tunnel	1/50
	6.9	Langley	11-inch hypersonic tunnel	1/50

Not surprisingly, these tests were concentrated in Langley facilities. The meeting also covered dynamic stability tests, but researchers agreed that the desirability of such tests would be determined after information from Mach 5 flights at the PARD was evaluated. Two models would be tested—one based on the original Langley configuration, and the other based on the North American configuration. North American wanted to obtain the 1/50-scale results quickly to incorporate them into the 1/15-scale model used to test speed brake and control surface hinge moments.[15]

The new rocket engine also came under scrutiny. Meetings held during early November among the HSFS, Lewis, and Reaction Motors included discussions about converting the XLR30 from anhydrous ammonia to a hydrocarbon fuel (JP-4 or kerosene). An earlier analysis had allowed Lewis to determine that the thrust and specific impulse would be almost identical between the two fuels. Lewis pointed out that pressure gages containing copper consistently failed within six months when used in a test cell with anhydrous ammonia, even though the gages were never in direct contact with the fuel. Researchers suggested converting the XLR30 to JP-4 to eliminate the perceived toxicity, corrosion, and handling problems entailed by the use of ammonia. Lewis also recommended that North American actively participate in the engine development program to ensure airframe

14 Memorandum, Hartley A. Soulé/Research Airplane Project Leader to Members of the Project 1226 Evaluation Group, no subject, 10 November 1955.

15 Ibid; memorandum, Harry J. Goett/Ames to the Ames director, 23 November 1955.

compatibility. The researchers further suggested that a large number of engine parameters in the aircraft and on the ground should be recorded during each flight, and the engine should not be throttled below 50%.[16]

At the same time, John Sloop at Lewis wrote to Hartley Soulé seconding the HSFS's recommendation to use the LR8 as an interim engine for the initial flight tests. It was already evident that the airframe would be ready long before the engine. For its part, Reaction Motors believed that using the LR8 made a great deal of sense since the early flights would need little power, and it might be difficult to throttle the larger engine to such low levels.[17]

On an almost humorous note, it appears that when the issuing agency wrote the contracts for North American and Reaction Motors, it did not understand that North American had proposed to use integral propellant tanks for their X-15 design. The contracts stated that the engine manufacturer would supply the entire propulsion system, including the necessary propellant tanks. This resulted in some initial concerns over what parts of the propulsion system would be provided by which contractor. It obviously made no sense for Reaction Motors to provide major structural pieces of the airframe. A meeting on 7 November resulted in North American agreeing to furnish all of the tanks for the propulsion system, while Reaction Motors would supply all of the necessary valves and regulators. At the same meeting, everybody agreed that Reaction Motors would supply 12 engines for the program, subject to a contract modification from the Air Force to provide funds. Of these, two would be used for testing (one a spare), and one equivalent engine would be used as component spares, leaving nine engines for the flight program. As it turned out, the government later purchased a few more.[18]

CHANGES

The engineers never expected that the design proposed by North American would be the one actually built—it seldom works that way even for operational aircraft, much less research vehicles. True to form, the design evolved substantially over the first year of the program, and on 14-15 November 1955 researchers gathered in Inglewood to resolve several issues. For instance, the North American proposal used 1,599 psf for the minimum design dynamic pressure, while the NACA wanted at least 2,100 psf and preferably 2,500 psf. It would take 100 pounds of additional structure to accommodate the higher pressure. On the other hand, increasing the design load factor from 5.25 g to 7.33 g would cost another 135 pounds, but everybody agreed that raising the design dynamic pressure was a better use of the weight. Nevertheless, as built, the X-15 was rated at 7.33 g, and

16 Memorandum, John L. Sloop/Lewis to Hartley A. Soulé/Research Airplane Project leader, no subject, undated (received at Langley on 7 November 1955).

17 Memorandum, Hartley A. Soulé/Research Airplane Project Leader to Members of the Project 1226 Evaluation Group, no subject, 10 November 1955.

18 Ibid.

the change was incorporated when it became obvious that the additional weight was rather trivial after various other upgrades were incorporated.[19]

Researchers also spent considerable effort on evaluating the structural materials proposed by North American, but a lack of detailed information made it impossible to reach a final decision on the wing leading-edge material. The group discussed various ceramic-metallic (cermet), copper, fiberglass, plastic, and titanium carbide materials without conclusion. North American had proposed a wing leading edge that was easily detachable, and the researchers considered this a desirable capability even though it drove a slightly more complex structure and a little additional weight. A weight increase of 13 pounds allowed the use of Inconel X sandwich construction for the speed brakes and provided additional speed brake hinges to handle the higher dynamic pressure already approved. The use of 0.020-inch titanium alloy for the internal structure of the wings and stabilizers instead of 24S-T aluminum gained support, although it involved a weight increase of approximately 7 pounds.

Other structural discussions included changing the oxygen tank to Inconel X due to the low-impact strength of the original titanium at cryogenic temperatures. At the same time, researchers reviewed the need to include a pressurization system to stabilize the propellant tanks. Initially the engineers had considered this undesirable, and North American had not provided the capability in the original design. However, the additional stresses caused by increasing the design dynamic pressure made it necessary to accept a large increase in structural weight or include a pressurization system, and the attendees endorsed the latter. In fact, during the flight program, pilots routinely repressurized the propellant tanks after they jettisoned any remaining propellants to provide an extra margin of structural strength while landing.[20]

When the researchers considered a random-direction, 1-inch thrust misalignment, it became obvious that the original large dorsal vertical stabilizer was unsatisfactory for the altitude mission profile. Based on experience with the X-1, the researchers knew that an installed engine could be a couple of degrees out of perfect alignment, although aerodynamic trim easily corrected this. However, in the case of the X-15, the thrust of the engine and the extreme velocities and altitudes involved made the issue a matter of some concern, and the government and North American agreed to include provisions correcting potential thrust misalignment. Along with several other issues, this caused engineers to modify the configuration of the vertical stabilizer.[21]

Researchers also concluded that the design would suffer from some level of roll-yaw coupling, and agreed upon acceptable limits. The government also pointed out the need for a rate damping (stability augmentation) system in pitch

19 Memorandum for the engineering files (HSFS), Walter C. Williams, 18 November 1955; memorandum, Hartley A. Soulé/Research Airplane Project Leader to the Members of the Project 1226 Evaluation Group, no subject, 7 December 1955; North American report NA-55-1237, "Supplementary Data X-15 Technical Evaluation Meeting," 22 November 1955.

20 Ibid.

21 Lawrence P. Greene and Rolland L. Benner, "X-15 Experience from the Designer's Viewpoint," a paper in the *1956 Research Airplane Committee Report*, p. 321; memorandum for the engineering files (HSFS), Walter C. Williams, 18 November 1955; memorandum, Hartley A. Soulé/Research Airplane Project Leader to the Members of the Project 1226 Evaluation Group, 7 December 1955; North American report NA-55-1237, "Supplementary Data X-15 Technical Evaluation Meeting," 22 November 1955, no page numbers.

and yaw for a weight increase of 125 pounds. The need to make the dampers redundant would be the subject of great debate throughout the development phase and early flight program, with the initial decision being not to. Attendees also decided the ballistic control system did not require a damping system, something that would change quickly during the flight program.[22]

North American agreed to provide redundant ballistic control systems and to triple the amount of hydrogen peroxide originally proposed. Engineers agreed to provide separate sources of peroxide for the ballistic controls and auxiliary power units (APUs) to ensure that the power units always had propellant. These changes added about 117 pounds.[23]

The configuration of the pilot's controls was finally established. A conventional center stick mechanically linked to a side-controller on the right console operated the aerodynamic control surfaces, while another side-controller on the left console above the throttle operated the ballistic control system. These were among the first applications of a side-stick controller, although these were mechanical devices that bore little resemblance to the electrical side-sticks used in the much later F-16.[24]

In an unusual miscommunication, the attendees at the November meeting believed the WADC had already developed a stable platform and would provide this to North American as government-furnished equipment. Separately, the NACA agreed to supply a "ball nose" to provide angle-of-attack and angle-of-sideslip data. The ball nose, or something functionally similar, was necessary because the normal pitot-static systems would not be reliable at the speeds and altitudes envisioned for the X-15. Although North American proposed a system based on modified Navaho components, the NACA believed that the ball nose represented a better solution.[25]

Per a recent service-wide directive, the Air Force representative had assumed that the X-15 would be equipped with some sort of encapsulated ejection system. On the other hand, North American had proposed a rather simple ejection seat. The company agreed to document their rationale for this selection and to provide a seat capable of meaningful ejection throughout most of the expected flight envelope, although all concerned realized that no method offered escape at all speeds and altitudes.[26]

The November meetings ended with a presentation by Douglas engineer Leo Devlin detailing their second-place proposal. A presentation on the advantages of HK31 magnesium alloy for structural use was interesting but provided no compelling reason to switch from Inconel X. Afterwards, Rocketdyne presented a 50,000-lbf rocket engine concept based on the SC-4 being designed for a high-

22 North American report NA-55-1237.

23 Memorandum for the engineering files (HSFS), Walter C. Williams, 18 November 1955; memorandum, Hartley A. Soulé/Research Airplane Project Leader to the Members of the Project 1226 Evaluation Group, 7 December 1955; "Supplementary Data X-15 Technical Evaluation Meeting."

24 Memorandum for the engineering files (HSFS), Walter C. Williams, 18 November 1955; memorandum, Hartley A. Soulé/Research Airplane Project Leader to the Members of the Project 1226 Evaluation Group, 7 December 1955; North American report NA-55-1237.

25 "Supplementary Data X-15 Technical Evaluation Meeting." A stable platform is a gyroscopically stabilized mechanism that aligns itself to the local vertical to provide a reference plane that can be used for the derivation of altitude, attitude, velocity, and rate-of-climb information. In essence, it was an early form of an inertial measurement unit.

26 "Supplementary Data X-15 Technical Evaluation Meeting."

altitude missile; this was a matter of only passing interest, given that a modified XLR30 was already under contract. Separately, Hartley Soulé and Harrison Storms discussed the proposed wind-tunnel program, attempting again to agree on which facilities would be used and when.[27]

The research instrumentation for the X-15 was the subject of a two-day meeting between personnel from Langley and the HSFS on 16-17 November. The group concluded that strain gauges would be required on the main wing spars for the initial flights, where temperatures would not be extreme, but that wing pressure distributions were not required. The HSFS wanted to record all data in the aircraft, while Langley preferred to telemeter it to the ground. Unfortunately, a lack of funds prevented the development of a high-speed telemetry system. The day following the NACA meeting, representatives from North American drove to the HSFS and participated in a similar meeting. Charlie Feltz, George Owl, and D. K. Warner (North American chief of flight test instrumentation) participated along with Arthur Vogeley, Israel Taback, and Gerald M. Truszynski from the NACA. The participants quickly agreed that the NACA would provide the instruments and North American would install them. The first few flights would use a more or less standard NACA airspeed boom on the nose of the X-15 instead of the yet-to-be-completed ball nose. North American desired to have mockups of the instrumentation within nine months to facilitate the final design of the airplane, and the NACA indicated this should be possible.[28]

The debate regarding engine fuels flared up again briefly at the end of November when John Sloop at Lewis wrote to Captain McCollough recommending the use of a hydrocarbon fuel instead of ammonia. Lewis had concluded that it would be no more difficult to cool a hydrocarbon fuel than ammonia, and the fuel would be cheaper, less toxic, and easier to handle. No information was available on repeated starts of a JP-4-fueled rocket engine, but researchers at Lewis did not expect problems based on recent experience with a horizontally mounted 5,000-lbf engine. The researchers repeated their warning that anhydrous ammonia would attack copper, copper alloys, and silver, all of which were standard materials used in research instrumentation. At the same time, the HSFS wrote that tests exposing a standard NACA test instrument to anhydrous ammonia vapor had proven disastrous. Both NACA facilities repeated their request for a change to a hydrocarbon fuel.[29]

Later the same day, Captain McCollough notified Hartley Soulé that the Power Plant Laboratory had reviewed the data submitted by Reaction Motors on the relative merits of substituting a hydrocarbon fuel for ammonia. The laboratory concluded that Reaction Motors had grossly underestimated the development

---

27 Memorandum, Arthur W. Vogeley to Hartley A. Soulé/Research Airplane Project Leader, subject: Project 1226 meetings to discuss changes in the North American Proposal—Wright-Patterson Air Force Base meeting of 24-25 October, and North American Aviation meetings in Inglewood on 27-28 October and 14-15 November 1955, 30 November 1955. In the files at the NASA History Office. Rocketdyne was a division of North American that was set up to develop rocket engines for the Navaho missile program; the company went on to develop many successful rocket engines, including the Space Shuttle main engines.

28 Memorandum for the files (Langley), Israel Taback, no subject, 9 December 1955; letter, Hartley A. Soulé/Research Airplane Project Leader to the NACA Liaison Officer at WPAFB, no subject, 21 December 1955. Even if Northrop had completed the ball nose in time for the first flights, it is likely the instrumentation boom would have been used since it provided a well-established reference for airspeed and attitude.

29 Letter, John L. Sloop/Lewis, to Captain Chester E. McCollough, Jr., no subject, 28 November 1955; letter, HSFS to Commander WADC, no subject, 28 November 1955.

time for conversion, and recommended the continued use of anhydrous ammonia as the most expeditious method of meeting the schedule. A meeting on 1 December at Wright Field brought all of the government representatives together to finalize the fuel issue. The conclusions were that 1) one fuel had no obvious advantage over the other insofar as performance was concerned, 2) the corrosive character of anhydrous ammonia was annoying but tolerable, 3) it would take 6 to 12 months to switch fuels, and 4) the engine development program should continue with anhydrous ammonia. This finally put the issue to rest, although the NACA facilities still believed the requested change was justified.[30]

November also saw an indication that Inconel might have unforeseen problems. A test of the tensile strength of the alloy was published by Langley, and the results differed significantly (in the wrong direction) from the specifications published by the International Nickel Company, the manufacturer of Inconel. NACA Headquarters asked Langley to explain the discrepancies. The reason was unknown, but researchers though it could be related to variations in the material, milling procedures, heat treatment, or testing procedures. Fortunately, further testing revealed that the results from the first test were largely invalid, although researchers never ascertained the specific reasons for the discrepancy. Still, the episode pointed out the need to precisely control the entire life cycle of the alloy.[31]

In December, North American engineers visited both Ames and Langley to work out details of the wind-tunnel program. The participants agreed that Langley would perform flutter tests on the speed brakes using the 1/15-scale model. The PARD would make a second flutter investigation, this one of the wing planform, since North American required data from a large-scale model at Mach 5 and a dynamic pressure of 1,500 psf—something no existing tunnel could provide. North American was supplied with additional requirements for a rotary-derivative model to be tested at Ames, and NACA personnel suggested that two 1/50-scale models be constructed—one for testing at Ames and one for Langley. The North American representatives agreed to consider the suggestion, but pointed out that no funds existed for two models. Ames also announced that they would take the 10 by 14-inch hypersonic tunnel out of service on 1 May for several months of modifications. The location was important since the tunnels were not identical and researchers could not directly compare the results from the two facilities.[32]

Ultimately, funds were found to build two 1/50-scale models—one for use at Langley in the 11-inch hypersonic and 9-inch blowdown tunnels, and one for the North American 16-inch wind tunnel. It was decided not to use the Ames tunnel prior to its closing. Langley also tested a 1/15-scale high-speed model while Ames tested a rotary-derivative model. The wind-tunnel investigations included evaluating the speed brakes, horizontal stabilizers, vertical stabilizer, fuselage tunnels, and rolling-tail. Interestingly, the tests at Langley confirmed the need for control

---

30 Memorandum, Hartley A. Soulé/Research Airplane Project Leader to the Members of the Project 1226 Evaluation Group, no subject, 7 December 1955.

31 Philip J. Hughes, John E. Inge, Stanley B. Prosser. NACA technical note 3315, "Tensile and compressive stress-strain properties of some high-strength sheet alloys at elevated temperatures," November 1954; various correspondence between NACA Headquarters and Langley between 15 November and 30 November 1955.

32 Memorandum, Harry J. Goett/Ames to the Ames Director, no subject, 1 December 1955; North American report NA-55-1264-1, "Proposed Wind Tunnel Test Program, X-15 Research Airplane, Project 1226," 1 December 1955.

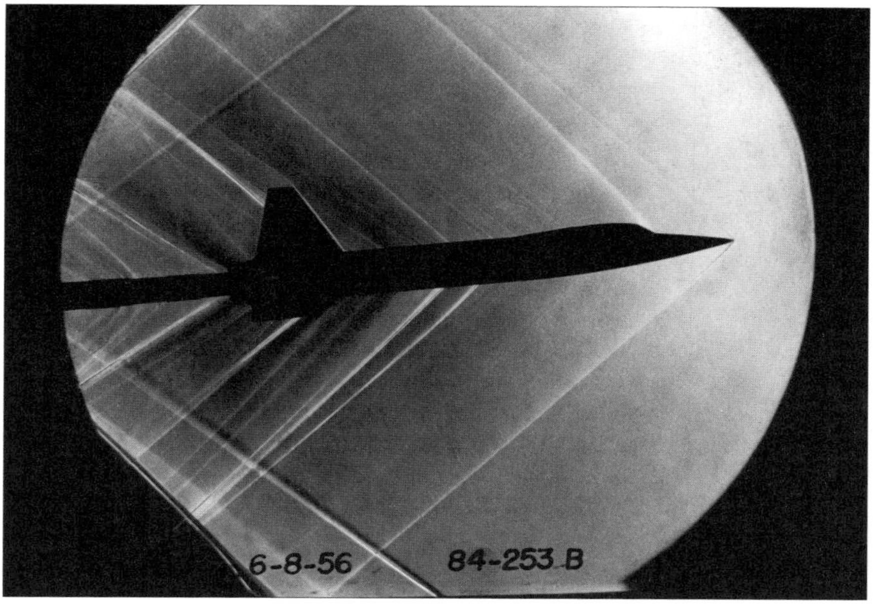

Various wind tunnels around the country participated in the X-15 development effort. This 1956 photo shows an original "high tail" configuration. Note the shock waves coming off the wing leading edge and a separate showck wave just behind it coming off the front of the landing skid. Very soon, this configuration would change substantially as the fuselage tunnels were made shorter, the vertical surfaces reconfigured, and the skids moved further aft. (NASA)

system dampers, while North American concluded they were not necessary. This was not the final answer, and researchers would debate the topic several more times before the airplane flew.[33]

North American had based its design surface temperatures on achieving laminar flow during most of the flight profile. However, most of the heat-transfer theories in general use at the time assumed fully turbulent flow on the fuselage. Researchers had previously raised the same issue with no particular solution. Ultimately, researchers used the Unitary Plan tunnel at Langley and the Air Force Arnold Engineering Development Center at Tullahoma, Tennessee, to resolve the discrepancy. These tests provided heat-transfer coefficients that were even higher than the theoretical values, particularly on the lower surface of the fuselage. Because of these results, the Air Force directed North American to modify the design to withstand the higher temperatures. This proved particularly costly in terms of weight and performance, adding almost 2,000 pounds of additional heat-sink material to the airframe. This is when the program changed its advertising. Instead of using 6,600 fps (Mach 6.5) as a design goal, the program began talking about Mach 6; it was obvious to the engineers that the airplane would likely not attain

33 North American report NA-55-1264-1, "Proposed Wind Tunnel Test Program, X-15 Research Airplane, Project 1226," 1 December 1955.

the original goal. Later, measurements from the flight program indicated that the skin temperatures of the primary structural areas of the fuselage, main wing box, and tail surfaces were actually several hundred degrees lower than the values predicted by the modified theory; in fact, they were below predictions using the original theories. However, resolving these types of uncertainties was part of the rationale for the X-15 program in the first place.[34]

By January 1956, North American required government guidance on several issues. A meeting on 18 January approved the use of a removable equipment rack in the instrument compartment. North American would still permanently mount some instrumentation and other equipment in the fuselage tunnels, but everybody agreed that a removable rack would reduce the exposure of the majority of research instruments and data recorders to ammonia fumes during maintenance.[35]

It soon became evident, contrary to statements at the November meeting, that no suitable stable platform existed, although the WADC had several units under development. It was a major blow, with no readily apparent solution.[36]

Other topics discussed at the 18 January meeting included the speed brake design and operation. Full extension of the speed brakes at pressures of 2,500 psf would create excessive longitudinal accelerations, so North American revised the speed brakes to open progressively while maintaining 1,500-psf pressure until they reached the full-open position. All in attendance thought that this was an appropriate solution.[37]

Pilot escape systems came up again during a 2-3 May 1956 meeting at Wright Field among Air Force, NACA, Navy, and North American personnel. WADC personnel pointed to a recent Air Force policy directive that required an encapsulated escape system in all new aircraft. Researchers from the WADC argued that providing some sort of enclosed system would comply with this policy and allow the gathering of research data on such systems. (This seemed an odd rationale in that it appeared to assume that the pilot would use the capsule at some point—an entirely undesirable possibility.) Those opposed to the Air Force view objected to any change because it would add weight and delay development. The opposing group, including Scott Crossfield, believed that the safety features incorporated in the X-15 made the ejection seat acceptable. After the meeting, the Air Force directed North American to justify its use of an ejection seat, but did not direct the company to incorporate a capsule.[38]

During a 24 May meeting at Langley, representatives from Eclipse-Pioneer briefed researchers from the NACA, North American, and the WADC on a stable

34 Joseph Weil, NASA technical note D-1278, "Review of the X-15 Program," June 1962, p. 7; telephone conversation, Charlie H. Feltz with Dennis R. Jenkins, 12 May 2002; telephone conversation, Scott Crossfield with Dennis R. Jenkins, 8 August 2002.

35 Memorandum, Walter C. Williams/HSFS to Hartley A. Soulé/Research Airplane Project Leader, subject: Visit to North American Aviation, Inc. to discuss Project 1226, 27 January 1956.

36 Ibid.

37 Ibid.

38 In reality, very few U.S. aircraft were ever designed with encapsulated escape systems. The Convair B-58 Hustler and General Dynamics F-111 were the only two that made it to operational service. In addition, the two North American XB-70A prototypes and first three B-1As were so equipped (but the fourth B-1A and production B-1Bs were not). Capsules were also investigated for the Republic XF-103, North American XF-108, and were even toyed with for advanced models of the Lockheed F-104 Starfighter and Republic F-105 Thunderchief, but these did not materialize. The X-2 and D-558s used partial escape capsules (the forward fuselage separated from the remainder of the airplane, but the pilot had to jump clear and parachute to a landing).

platform that weighed 65 pounds and could be ready in 24 months. Later events would show that these estimates were hopelessly optimistic.[39]

On 11 June 1956, the government approved a production go-ahead for the three X-15 airframes, although North American did not cut metal for the first aircraft until September. Four days later, on 15 June 1956, the Air Force assigned three serial numbers (56-6670 through 56-6672) to the X-15 program. The Contract Reporting and Bailment Branch furnished this data by phone on 28 May and confirmed it in writing on 15 June.[40]

THE FIRST INDUSTRY CONFERENCE (1956)

The public law that established the NACA required the agency to disseminate information to the industry and the public. One of the methods used to accomplish this was to hold periodic conferences with representatives of the industry to discuss the results of research into specific areas. By the beginning of July, Hugh Dryden concluded there had been sufficient progress on the development of the X-15 to hold an industry conference at one of the NACA facilities in October.[41]

Langley hosted the first Conference on the Progress of the X-15 Project on 25-26 October 1956, providing an interesting insight into the X-15 development effort. There were 313 attendees representing the Air Force, NACA, Navy, various universities and colleges, and most of the major aerospace contractors. Approximately 10% of the attendees were from various Air Force organizations, with the WADC contributing over half. Oddly, however, Air Force personnel made none of the presentations at the conference. The majority of the 27 authors of the 18 technical papers came from various NACA organizations (16), while the rest were from North American (9) and Reaction Motors (2). The papers confirmed a considerable amount of progress, but made it clear that a few significant problems still lay ahead.[42]

Another paper summarized the results of tests in eight different wind tunnels. These tests were conducted at velocities between low subsonic speeds to Mach 6.9, somewhat in excess of the projected maximum speed of the airplane. One of the surprising findings was that the controversial fuselage tunnels generated nearly half of the total lift at high Mach numbers. However, another result confirmed the NACA prediction that the original fuselage tunnels would cause longitudinal

39 Memorandum, Hartley A. Soulé/Research Airplane Project Leader, subject: Project 1226—Progress report for month of May 1956, 7 June 1956. In the files at the NASA History Office.

40 Memorandum, M. A. Todd, Acting Chief, Contractor Reporting and Bailment Branch, Support Division, to Chief, Fighter Branch, Aircraft Division, Director Procurement and Production, AMC, subject: Confirmation of Serial Numbers Assigned, 15 June 1956. In the files at the AFMC History Office.

41 Letter, Hugh L. Dryden, Director of NACA, to Chief, Fighter WSPO, ARDC, no subject, 6 July 1956. In the files at the NASA History Office.

42 1956 *Research Airplane Committee Report*, passim.

instability. In subsequent testing, researchers shortened the tunnels ahead of the wing, greatly reducing the problem.[43]

One of the more interesting experiments was "flying" small (3- to 4-inch) models in the hypervelocity free-flight facility at Ames. The models, which were made of cast aluminum, cast bronze, or various plastics, were fragile. Despite this, the goal was to shoot the model out of a gun at tremendous speeds in order to observe shock-wave patterns across the shape. As often as not, what researchers saw were pieces of X-15 models flying down the range sideways. Fortunately, enough of the models remained intact for them to acquire meaningful data.[44]

The hypervelocity free-flight facility at NACA Ames fired small (3-4-inch-long) models of the X-15 to observe shock-wave patterns. It was more of an art than a science to get the models to fly forward and not break apart, but enough survived to gain significant insight into shock patterns surrounding the X-15. (NASA)

Other papers dealt with the ability of the pilot to fly the airplane. Pilots had flown the preliminary exit and reentry profiles using fixed-base simulators at Langley and North American. Alarmingly, the pilots found that the airplane was nearly uncontrollable without damping and only marginally stable during some maneuvers with dampers. A free-flying model program at the PARD showed that

43 Herbert W. Riyard, Robert W. Dunning, and Edwin W. Johnston, "Aerodynamic Characteristics From Wind Tunnel Studies of the X-15 Configuration," a paper in the *1956 Research Airplane Committee Report*, pp. 39-56. The list of wind tunnels included the North American 8.75 by 11-foot tunnel, the Langley 8-foot transonic tunnel, the North American 16-inch tunnel, the Massachusetts Institute of Technology supersonic tunnel, the Langley 9 by 9-inch Mach 4 blowdown jet, the Ames 10 by 14-inch tunnel, and the Langley 11-inch hypersonic tunnel.

44 Dale L. Compton, "Welcome," a paper in the *Proceedings of the X-15 30th Anniversary Celebration*, Dryden Flight Research Facility, Edwards, CA, 8 June 1989, NASA CP-3105, p. 3. The free-flight tunnel at Ames was conceived by H. Julian Allen and opened in 1949 at a cost of about $20,000. Its test section was 18 feet long, 1 foot wide, and 2 feet high. By forcing a draft through the tunnel at a speed of about Mach 3 and firing a model projectile upstream, one could simulate velocities of up to Mach 18. Schlieren cameras were set up at seven locations along the test section (three on the side and four on the top) to make shadowgraphs that showed the airflow over the models. The facility proved to be an important tool not only for the X-15 but also for Project Mercury.

low-speed stability and control were adequate. Since some aerodynamicists had questioned the use of the rolling tail instead of ailerons, free-flying models had investigated that feature, proving that the rolling tail would provide the necessary lateral control.[45]

Researchers also reported on the state of the structural design. Preliminary estimates showed that the airplane would encounter critical loads during the initial acceleration and during reentry, but would experience maximum temperatures only during the latter. Because of this, the paper primarily dealt with the load-temperature relationships anticipated for reentry. The selection of Inconel X was justified based on its strength and favorable creep characteristics at 1,200°F. The leading edge would use a bar of Inconel X, since that portion of the wing acted as a heat sink. This represented a radical change from the fiberglass leading edge originally proposed by North American. In another major change, the leading edge of the wing was no longer easily removable, although this fact seemed to escape the attention of most everybody in attendance, particularly Harry Goett from Ames.[46]

The main landing gear brought its own concerns. Originally, it consisted of two narrow skids attached to the fuselage under the front part of the wing and stowed externally along the side tunnels during flight. When unlocked, the skis fell into the down position, with help from airflow and a bungee. Further analysis indicated that the X-15 would land more nose-high than expected, and that the rear fuselage would likely strike the ground before the skids. A small tail-skid had been proposed, but this was found to be inadequate. In its place, engineers moved the skids aft to approximately the leading edge of the vertical stabilizers, solving the ground-strike problem. However, the move introduced a new concern. Now the nose-down rotation after main-skid contact would be particularly jarring, placing a great deal of stress on the pilot and airframe. In fact, it would lead directly to one early landing accident and be a source of problems throughout the flight program. Nobody had a suitable solution.[47]

The expected acceleration of the X-15 presented several unique human-factor concerns early in the program. It was estimated that the pilot would be subjected to an acceleration of up to 5 g. Because of this, North American developed a side-stick controller that used an armrest to support the pilot's arm while still allowing full control of the airplane. Coupled with the fact that there were two separate attitude-control systems on the X-15, this resulted in a unique control-stick arrangement. A conventional center stick, similar to that installed in most fighter-type aircraft of the era, operated the aerodynamic control surfaces through the newly required stability augmentation (damper) system. Mechanical linkages connected a side-stick controller on the right console to the same aerodynamic control surfaces and augmentation system. The pilot could use either stick interchangeably, although the flight manual described the use of the center stick "during normal periods of longitudinal and vertical acceleration." Another side-stick controller

45 Herbert W. Riyard, Robert W. Dunning, and Edwin W. Johnston, "Aerodynamic Characteristics From Wind Tunnel Studies of the X-15 Configuration," a paper in the *1956 Research Airplane Committee Report*, pp. 39-56.

46 Richard L. Schleicher, "Structural Design of the X-15 Research airplane," a paper in the *1956 Research Airplane Committee Report*, pp. 143-146.

47 Wendell H. Stillwell, *X-15 Research Results*, NASA publication SP-60 (Washington, DC: NASA, 1965).

above the left console operated the ballistic control system that provided attitude control at high altitudes. Describing one of the phenomena soon to be discovered in space flight, the flight manual warned that "velocity tends to sustain itself after the stick is returned to the neutral position. A subsequent stick movement opposite to the initial one is required to cancel the original attitude change." Isaac Newton was correct after all.[48]

From the left, North American test pilot Alvin S. White, Air Force X-15 Project Pilot Captain Iven C. Kinchloe, and Scott Crossfield discuss the design of the side stick controller for the new research airplane. The design of these controllers caused quite a bit of controversy early in the program, but the pilots generally liked them once they acclimated. Crossfield's influence on the program showed early in the flight program when some pilots complained the configuration of the cockpit was tailored to Crossfield's size and was not sufficiently adjustable to accommodate other pilots. Later modifications solved these issues. (Alvin S. White Collection)

Engineers had not firmly established the design for the X-15 side-stick controller, but researchers discussed previous experience with similar controllers in the Convair F-102, Grumman F9F, Lockheed TV-2, and North American YF-107A, as well as several ground simulators. The pilots who had used these controllers generally thought that the engineers needed to provide a more "natural" feel for the controllers.[49]

Based largely on urgings from Scott Crossfield, the Air Force agreed to allow North American to use an ejection seat instead of a capsule system. The company

48 Sigurd A. Sjoberg, "Some Experience With Side Controllers," a paper in the *1956 Research Airplane Committee Report*, pp. 167-171; X-15 Interim Flight Manual, FHB-23-1, 18 March 1960, changed 12 May 1961. At the time the terms "ballistic control system" (BCS) and "reaction control system" (RCS) were used interchangeably; however, since "ballistic" seemed to show up in more of the documentation, that is what will be used here.

49 Sjoberg, "Some Experience With Side Controllers," pp. 167-171.

had investigated four escape systems in depth, including cockpit capsules, nose capsules, a canopy-shielded seat, and a stable-seat with a pressure suit. Engineers had tried capsule-like systems before, most notably in the X-2, where the entire forward fuselage could be detached from the rest of the aircraft. Douglas had opted for this approach in all of the D-558s and their X-15 proposal. Model tests showed that these were unstable and prone to tumble at a high rate of rotation, and they added weight and complexity to the aircraft. Their potential success rate was unknown at the time.[50]

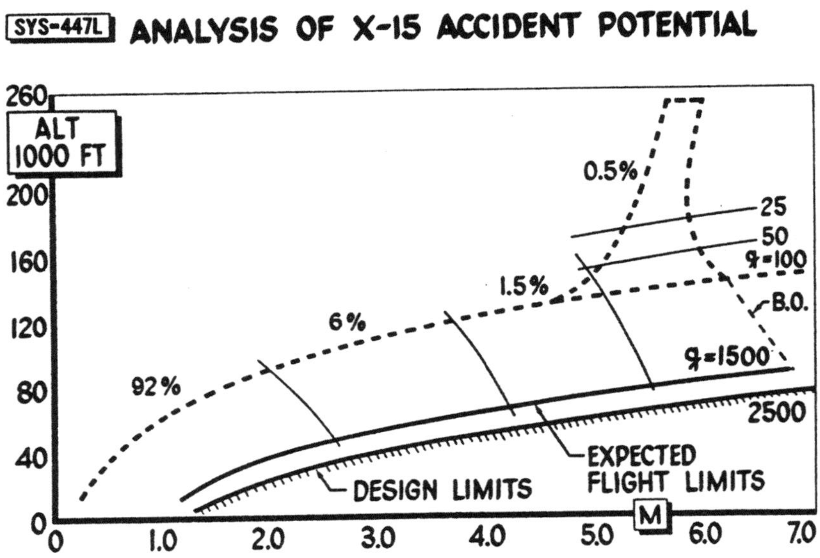

North American performed a seemingly endless series of analyses to support their selection of an ejection seat over an encapsulated system. The company determined there was only a 2-percent likelihood of an accident occurring at high altitude or high speed, eliminating much of the perceived need for the complicated and heavy encapsulated system. The stabilized ejection seat, coupled with the David Clark Company full-pressure suit, provided meaningful ejection up to Mach 4 and 120,000 feet. (North American Aviation)

Surprisingly, an analysis by North American showed that only 2% of the accidents would occur at high altitude or speed. Because engineers expected most potential accidents to occur at speeds less than Mach 4, North American had decided to use a stable-seat with a pressure suit. The perceived benefits of this combination were its relative simplicity, high reliability, and light weight. North American

50 Walter C. Williams, "X-15 Concept Evolution" a paper in the *Proceedings of the X-15 30th Anniversary Celebration*, Dryden Flight Research Facility, Edwards, CA, 8 June 1989, NASA CP-3105, p. 13. On 27 September 1956, Captain Milburn G. Apt lost control of the X-2 on its first Mach 3 flight (Mach 3.196 was achieved at 70,000 feet). The escape capsule successfully separated at approximately 40,000 feet, but apparently Apt was unable to jump clear of the capsule before it impacted the desert. (The capsule was meant to get the pilot away from the aircraft and to a survivable altitude and speed. Then the pilot needed to jump from the capsule and use his backpack parachute for the final descent.) Apt was killed, and the X-2 program was terminated.

acknowledged that the seat did not provide meaningful escape at altitudes above 120,000 feet or speeds in excess of Mach 4. However, the designers (particularly Scott Crossfield) believed that when the seat-suit combination was inadequate, the safest course of action was for the pilot to simply ride the airplane down to an altitude and velocity where the ejection seat could function successfully.[51]

Lawrence P. Greene, the chief of aerodynamics at North American, presented the final paper at the 1956 industry conference. This was an excellent summary of the development effort to date and a review of the major known problems. Researchers considered flutter to be a potential problem, largely because little experimental data regarding flutter at hypersonic Mach numbers were available, and there was a lack of basic knowledge on aero-thermal-elastic relationships. Greene pointed out that engineers had derived the available data on high-speed flutter from experiments conducted at less than Mach 3, and not all of it was applicable to the X-15. As it turned out, the program did encounter panel flutter during the early flights, leading to a change in the design criteria for high-speed aircraft.[52]

Inconel X also presented a potential problem because fabrication techniques for large structures did not exist. By using various alloys of titanium, North American saved considerable weight in parts of the internal structure that were not subject to high temperatures. Titanium, while usable to only about 800°F, weighed much less than Inconel X. Ultimately, the requirements for processing and fabricating these materials influenced some aspects of the structural design. Inconel X soon stopped being a laboratory curiosity as the X-15 program developed techniques to form, machine, and heat-treat it.[53]

Overall, the conference was a success and disseminated a great deal of information to the industry, along with frank discussions about unresolved issues and concerns. It also provided a short break for the development team that had been working hard to meet an extremely ambitious schedule.

MOCKUP INSPECTION

The previous year had resulted in some major configuration changes to the X-15. The wing size and shape were similar to those proposed by North American, but engineers increased the leading-edge radius (along with the radius on the empennage and nose) to satisfy aerodynamic heating concerns. The leading edge was also changed from replaceable fiberglass to a nearly solid piece of Inconel X. NASA had always harbored concerns about the use of ablative materials on the leading edge, but this change also eliminated the removable-leading-edge concept

---

51 Memorandum, Arthur W. Vogeley, to Hartley A. Soulé/Research Airplane Project Leader, subject: Project 1226 meetings to discuss changes in the North American Proposal—Wright-Patterson AFB meeting of 24-25 October, and North American Aviation meetings in Inglewood on 27-28 October and 14-15 November 1955, 30 November 1955; Scott Crossfield, "X-15 Crew Provisions and Escape," a paper in the *1956 Research Airplane Committee Report*, pp. 193-212.

52 Lawrence P. Greene, "Summary of Pertinent Problems and Current Status of the X-15 Airplane," a paper in the *1956 Research Airplane Committee Report*, pp. 193-212.

53 Stillwell, *X-15 Research Results*; Greene, "Summary of Pertinent Problems," pp. 239-258.

that was highly prized by Ames. The final configuration also increased the diameter of the fuselage by about 6% in order to increase the propellant capacity.[54]

A revised landing gear eliminated tail-strikes during landing and improved directional stability during slide-out. The side fairings, always a point of contention between North American and the NACA, were shortened ahead of the wing. The horizontal stabilizer was moved rearward 5.4 inches, the wing was moved forward 3.6 inches, and the center of gravity was brought forward 10 inches to improve longitudinal stability. However, perhaps the most visible change was that the area of the vertical stabilizers was increased from 50 square feet to 75 square feet. Full 10-degree wedge airfoils replaced the original double-wedge configuration for the vertical stabilizers. The area for the verticals was also redistributed (55% for the dorsal stabilizer and 45% for the ventral, instead of the original 73/27 configuration). In addition, both the dorsal and ventral stabilizers now had rudders that were nearly symmetrical and operated together at all times (except after the ventral had been jettisoned during landing). Originally, only the dorsal stabilizer had a rudder.[55]

The development engineering inspection (DEI) took place in Inglewood facility on 12-13 December 1956. In the normal course of development, the Air Force inspected full-scale mockups to ensure the design features were satisfactory before construction of the first airplane began. Of the 49 people who took part in the inspection, 34 were from the Air Force, with the WADC contributing 22. The inspection committee consisted of Major E. C. Freeman from the ARDC, Mr. F. Orazio of the WADC, and Lieutenant Colonel Keith G. Lindell from Air Force Headquarters. The NACA and the Navy each contributed a single voting member. Captain Chester E. McCollough, Jr., from the X-15 Project Office, Captain Iven C. Kincheloe, Jr. (already selected as the first Air Force X-15 pilot), and three NACA researchers served as technical advisors.[56]

The inspection resulted in 84 requests for alterations, of which the board rejected 12 and deferred 22 others for further study. Surprisingly, the board rejected some of the more interesting of the proposed changes. These included suggestions that the aerodynamic center stick should be capable of controlling the ballistic controls at the press of a switch, the motions of the aerodynamic and ballistic side sticks should be similar, or a third controller that combined both functions should be installed on the right console. The committee rejected these suggestions since it seemed inappropriate to make decisions on worthwhile improvements or combinations before evaluating the controllers already selected under actual flight conditions. Given that two of the three controller suggestions came from future X-15 pilots (Iven Kincheloe and Joseph A. Walker), it appeared that improvements were necessary.[57]

---

54 Benjamin F. Guenther, "X-15 Research Airplane," an unpublished manuscript written in 1982, no page numbers. Supplied by Ben Guenther at LaRC.

55 Guenther, "X-15 Research Airplane."

56 Air Force report (no numbers), "Development Engineering Inspection of the X-15 Research Aircraft – 13 December 1956," Director of Systems Management, ARDC. A "request for alteration" is the form used to request changes as the result of a mockup or engineering inspection within the Air Force.

57 Air Force report, "Development Engineering Inspection" Director of Systems Management, ARDC.

An even more surprising rejection occurred concerning changeable leading edges. North American had disclosed at the 1956 industry conference six weeks earlier that the leading edges were no longer removable, with little comment. Nevertheless, Harry Goett from Ames did not agree with the change. Goett wanted to widen the front spar lower flange and locate the ballistic roll thrusters at the back of the same spar. In addition, Goett argued that North American had initially proposed providing interchangeable wing leading edges. In spite of these logical arguments, the inspection committee decided the required changes would add 3 pounds to the design and rejected the request. At least one participant opined that deleting this feature would significantly decrease the value of the hypersonic research airplane.[58]

The X-15 mockup as it was inspected in December 1956. At this point, the airplane looked substantially as it would in final form with short fuselage tunnels and shorter vertical surfaces. This inspection cleared the way for North American to produce the final manufacturing drawings and begin to cut metal. (U.S. Air Force)

Additional wind-tunnel testing resulted in modifications to the vertical stabilizer, but North American essentially built the configuration inspected in mockup form during December 1956. However, while the design and construction of the airframe progressed relatively smoothly, other systems were running into serious difficulties.

58 Ibid.

STRUCTURAL FABRICATION

The X-15 was breaking new ground when it came to structural materials, since it was obvious from the start that most of the wetted surface would be subjected to temperatures up to 1,200°F. Exotic materials made from the rare elements had not advanced sufficiently to permit quantity production of these expensive alloys, so the list of candidate materials was narrowed to corrosion resistant steels, titanium, and nickel-base alloys ("stainless steels"). The following table shows the strength properties of the candidate materials at room temperature; various aluminum alloys are included as a comparison. All properties are for bare sheet stock, except for the AM-355 bar stock. Materials marked with an asterisk were heat-treated.[59]

	Material	**Ultimate Tensile Strength (ksi)**	**Yield Tensile Strength (ksi)**	**Compressive Yield (ksi)**	**Ultimate Shear Strength (ksi)**	**Bearing Yield (ksi)**	**Modulus (x1000 psi)**
Nickel base	Inconel X *	155	100	105	018	186	31.0
	Inconel	80	30	32	56	–	31.0
Corrosion-resistant steel	AM-350 CRES *	185	150	164	125	268	28.7
	AM-355 CRES *	200	165	178	131	295	28.7
	A-286 CRES *	150	95	99	91	136	29.0
	4130 (HT125-Mo)	125	103	113	82	180	29.0
Titanium	8-Mn	120	110	115	79	180	15.5
	5A1-2.5Sn	115	110	110	72	175	15.5
	6A1-4V *	160	145	145	99	230	16.3
Aluminum	2024-T4 *	62	40	40	37	63	10.5
	7075-T6 *	78	69	70	47	110	10.3
	6061-T6 *	42	36	35	27	58	10.2

Although 6A1-4V titanium and AM-350 CRES had good strength efficiencies over a wide temperature range, both of the alloys tended to fall off rapidly above 800°F. Inconel X, on the other hand, had only a gradual drop in strength up to 1,200°F. Because of this stability, North American chose Inconel X for the outer skin for the entire airplane. Regular Inconel (as opposed to Inconel X) was not heat-treatable, but it could be welded and was used in locations where high strength was not of paramount importance or where final closeout welds were necessary following heat treatment of the surrounding structures. To accomplish this, Inconel lands were incorporated into Inconel X structures prior to final heat treatment, and access-hole cover plates made from Inconel were welded to these lands.[60]

59 Richard L. Schleicher, "Structural Design of the X-15," North American Aviation, 1963, pp. 13-14. In the files at the San Diego Aerospace Museum. In the U.S. system in place at the time, material strengths were measured in kips per square inch (ksi). A kip (1914) was a unit of measure equal to 1,000 pounds used to express deadweight load.

60 Schleicher, "Structural Design of the X-15," pp. 13-14.

North American used high-strength aluminum (2024-T4) to form the inner pressure shell of the cockpit and part of the instrumentation bay. As a relief from high thermal stresses, the company used titanium for the structure of the fuselage and wings. Originally, the company used two titanium alloys: 8-Mn, which was the highest strength alloy then available but was not recommended for welding, and 5A1-2.5Sn, which had acceptable strength and was weldable. Later, North American began using a high-strength and weldable alloy, 6A1-4V, in some areas. To combat the high concentrated loads from the engine, most of the aft fuselage structure used titanium framing. The majority of the structure used fusion welding, although the company also used a limited amount of resistance welding. North American radiographically inspected all critical welds to ensure quality.[61]

The material that presented the most problems was probably the 5Al-2.5Sn titanium, which proved to have inconsistent tensile properties that made it difficult to work with. It also exhibited low ductility and notch sensitivity, and had a poor surface condition. These problems existed in both rolled and extruded forms of the metal. The surface condition was the most important factor governing the formability of titanium, so North American had to remove all oxygen contamination, inclusions, and grind marks by machining, polishing, or chemically milling the metal prior to the final finishing. As a result, North American procured titanium extrusions for the X-15 with sufficient extra material in all dimensions to allow technicians to machine all surfaces prior to use.[62]

The limited amount of stretch and shrink that was possible with a titanium extrusion during stretch wrapping presented a different problem when North American went to form the side fairing frames. Each frame was composed of four titanium 5Al-2.5Sn extrusions. One of the problems was that the inside flanges were located in areas that had small bend radii, and it was necessary to prevent compression failure. The small bend radii were "relieved" (some material was removed prior to bending), and a gusset was later welded in to fill the relieved area. The alternative would have been to reduce compression by increasing the pull on the forming machine, thus shifting the bend axis closer to the inboard edge. This, however, would have resulted in a tension failure on the outboard flange.[63]

North American found that one of the more interesting aspects of titanium was that a formed part was prone to crack until the residual stresses resulting from the forming had been removed. This delayed cracking could occur within a few minutes, or it might not become evident until weeks later. In response, North American initiated a process that provided stress relief for all parts except "slightly" formed parts, such as skin panels, since they exhibited few problems.[64]

Forming the seven different pressure vessel configurations in the X-15 presented its own problems. When compatibility with the contained fluid permitted, titanium was the first choice of material. North American used a 26-inch Cincinnati Hydroform for the hemispherical ends of the 14-inch cylindrical nitrogen tanks

61 Richard L. Schleicher, "Structural Design of the X-15," p. 14.

62 I. J. Wilson, North American report NA58-973, "Forming and Fabrication Methods for the X-15 Airplane," 18 July 1958, no page numbers; confirmed by telephone conversation between Charles H. Feltz and Dennis R. Jenkins on 23 May 2002.

63 "Forming and Fabrication Methods for the X-15 Airplane."

64 Ibid.

with little difficulty. The company also attempted to form the 16-inch hemispheres for the helium tanks on this machine, but the optimum blank size was greater than the maximum machine capacity of 26 inches. Using a smaller-than-optimum blank required excessive hold-down pressure that resulted in small surface cracks. The alternative was to "spin form" the hemispherical ends. Engineers heated the blanks to approximately 1,600°F and used an internally heated spinning chuck to shape the disc. Unfortunately, this resulted in a surface with significant oxygen contamination, so North American used thicker parts and machined them to the correct thickness to eliminate the contamination. Machining was also required to match the hemispheres for each end of the tank prior to welding.[65]

Finding the correct material for the main propellant tanks, especially the liquid-oxygen tank, took some investigation. Most steel and common heavy structural alloys gain strength but lose ductility when operated at low temperatures, although Inconel proved to be relatively insensitive to this. The martensitic alloys, such as heat-treated 4130 low-alloy steel and AM-350 CRES precipitation-hardened corrosion-resistant steel, followed predictable curves that showed severe ductility loss as the temperature decreased below –100°F. A titanium alloy containing 5% aluminum and 2.5% tin handled the low temperatures well, but did not have the requisite strength at 1,200°F. North American finally decided to manufacture the primary barrels of the tanks from Inconel X.[66]

Initially, engineers used AM-350 CRES, formed on a 7,000-ton hydraulic press using a deep-draw process, for the 32-inch hemispheres of the main propellant tanks. Excessive thinning occurred until the optimum pressure on the press draw ring was determined. Even then, North American encountered some difficulty due to uneven forces from the pressure pins used to secure the blanks, resulting in non-uniformity around the periphery of the hemisphere. The engineers subsequently decided to discard the CRES hemispheres and to remanufacture them from Inconel X.[67]

Inconel X proved to be remarkably easy to work with considering its hardness, although the engineers had to make severely formed parts in multiple stages, with annealing accomplished between each stage. Nevertheless, problems arose. One of the first concerned fabricating the large Inconel propellant tank hemispheres. The propellant tanks comprised a large portion of the fuselage and were composed of an outer cylindrical shell and an inner cylinder. Inconel X semi-torus hemispheres at each end of the tank joined these two parts. The hemispheres were formed in two segments, with the split located midway between the inner and outer cylinders. Technicians welded the inner torus segment to the inner cylinder, and the outer torus segments to the outer tank, before joining the two assemblies.[68]

After initial attempts to spin the bulkheads from a single, heated Inconel X blank were unsuccessful, the technicians built up the cones by welding smaller pieces together, and performed a complete X-ray inspection of each weld. After

---

65 Ibid.

66 F. R. Kostoch, "X-15 Material and Process Development," a paper in the *Research Airplane Committee Report on the Conference on the Progress of the X-15 Project*, A Compilation of the Papers presented in Los Angeles, CA, 28-30 July 1958, p. 259 (hereafter called the *1958 Research Airplane Committee Report*).

67 "Forming and Fabrication Methods for the X-15 Airplane."

68 Ibid.

the cones were formed to the approximate size, they went through several stages of spinning, with a full annealing process performed after each stage. The first spin blocks used for the hemispheres were made from hardwood, and cast iron was used for the final sizing. A problem developed when transverse cracks began to appear during the spinning of the hemispheres.[69]

Both North American and the International Nickel Company investigated the cracks, but determined that the initial welds were nearly perfect and should not have contributed to the problem. Nevertheless, engineers tried different types of welding

Fabricating the X-15 gave North American engineers some of the first large-scale experience with the newest high-strength alloys of titanium and stainless steel. The main propellant tanks formed an integral part of the fuselage, and after a great deal of investigation, North American manufactured the barrels from Inconel X. The experience gained from building the X-15 provided lessons used during the construction of the Apollo capsules and space shuttle orbiters. (North American Aviation)

69 Ibid.

wire, and varied the speed, feed, and pressure of the spinning lathe, but the welds continued to crack. It was finally determined that the welds were—ironically—too good; they needed to be softer. North American developed a new process that resulted in slightly softer but still acceptable welds, and the cracking stopped.[70]

North American gained experience in manufacturing the propellant tanks and fuselage structure long before it manufactured the first flight airplane. The company constructed three partial fuselages as ground-test articles for the rocket engines. Reaction Motors at Lake Denmark received two of these, while the third went to the Rocket Engine Test Facility at Edwards. Although not intended as "practice," they did allow the workers in Inglewood to gain a certain level of expertise on a less-critical assembly before building the real flight articles.[71]

Forming the ogive section of the forward fuselage also presented some problems for North American. The usual method to construct such a structure was to form four semicircular segments of skin and weld them together. However, due to the size of the structure and the need to maintain a precise outer mold line, the engineers decided that the most expedient production method was to make a cone and bulge-form it into the final shape in one operation. The initial cone was made from four pieces of Inconel X welded together and carefully inspected to ensure the quality of the welds. It was then placed in a bulge-form die and gas pressure was applied that forced the part to conform to the shape of the die. This process worked well, with one exception. For reasons that were never fully understood, one of the four pieces of Inconel X used for one cone had a tensile strength about 28,000 psi greater than the others. During formation this piece resisted stretching, causing the welds to distort and creating wrinkles. North American eventually discarded the piece and made another one using four different sheets on Inconel; that one worked fine.[72]

Both titanium and Inconel were hard metals, and the tools used to form and cut them tended to wear out faster than equivalent tools used in the production of steel or aluminum parts. In addition, it took considerably longer to cut or polish compared to other metals. For instance, it took approximately 15 times longer to machine Inconel X than aluminum. This did not lead to any particular problems during the manufacture of the X-15 (unlike some of the tool contamination issues faced by Lockheed on the Blackbird), but it did slow progress and force North American to rethink issues such as machining versus polishing.[73]

The windshield glass originally installed on the X-15 was soda-lime-tempered plate glass with a single outer pane and double inner panes. Engineers had based this choice on a predicted maximum temperature of 740°F. Data obtained on early flights indicated that the outer face would encounter temperatures near 1,000°F, with a differential temperature between panes of nearly 750°F. It was apparent that soda-lime glass would not withstand these temperatures. The engineers subsequently selected a newly developed alumino-silicate glass that had higher strength and better thermal properties as a replacement. The 0.375-inch-thick alumino-silicate outer

70 Ibid.

71 Crossfield, *Always Another Dawn*, p. 292.

72 "Forming and Fabrication Methods for the X-15 Airplane."

73 "Forming and Fabrication Methods for the X-15 Airplane," I. J. Wilson, "X-15 Forming and Fabrication Methods," a paper in the *1958 Research Airplane Committee Report*, p. 249.

pane withstood temperatures up to 1,500°F during one test. The next test subjected the glass to a surface temperature of 1,050°F with a temperature gradient from the outer to inner surface of 790°F without failure. In actuality, the thermal environment on the X-15 glass was more complicated, although slightly less severe. The outer surface could reach 800°F, while the inner surface could reach 550°F; however, the inner temperature lagged behind the outer temperature. During rapid heat build-up on high-speed missions, the maximum temperature differential reached 480°F at a time when the outer glass was only 570°F. At this point, both the outer and inner panes began to rise in temperature rapidly.[74]

Technicians at the Flight Research Center installed the alumino-silicate glass in the outer pane of all three X-15s, although they continued to use soda-lime plate glass for the inner panes until the end of the program. Corning Glass Company supplied all of the glass. The thermal qualification test was interesting. Corning heated an 8.4 by 28-inch panel of the glass to 550°F in a salt bath for 3 minutes, and then plunged it into room-temperature tap water. If it did not shatter, it passed the test.[75]

Harrison Storms summed up the North American efforts during the X-15 roll-out ceremony: "Inconel X was considered a weldable alloy; however no detailed experience with it, as a weldable structure, was available. The development had to be done by North American Aviation in forming, welding, and otherwise joining this material to make a practical machine." Storms described special techniques for contouring the skins that involved hot machining, cold machining, ovens, freezers, cutters, slicers, and rollers. For instance, one special tool fixture needed to control the contour during a heat-treating cycle of the wing skin weighed 4,300 pounds, while the skin it held weighed only 180 pounds. Despite the publicity normally associated with the use of Inconel X, Charlie Feltz remembered that titanium structures gave North American the most trouble. Fortunately, the use of titanium on the X-15 was relatively small, unlike what Lockheed was experiencing across town on the Blackbird.[76]

HIGH-ALTITUDE GIRDLES

Pressure suits, more often called "space suits" by the public, are essentially taken for granted today. Fifty years ago they were still the stuff of science fiction. These suits serve several necessary purposes, with supplying the correct partial pressure of oxygen being the most obvious (although masks or full-face helmets can also accomplish this). The most important purpose, however, is to protect the pilot against the increasingly low atmospheric pressures encountered as altitude

74 Kordes et al., "Structural Heating Experiences of the X-15," pp. 33-34; Greene and Benner, "X-15 Experience from the Designer's Viewpoint," pp. 318-319.

75 Richard L. Schleicher, "Structural Design of the X-15," North American Aviation, 1963, pp. 37-38. Copy provided courtesy of Gerald H. Balzer Collection.

76 Storms, "The X-15 Rollout Symposium;" telephone conversation, Charles H. Feltz with Dennis R. Jenkins, 19 February 2002.

increases—pressures that reach essentially zero above about 250,000 feet. At high altitudes, the blood and water in the human body want to boil—not from heat, but from the pressure differential between the body and the environment.[77]

A distant precursor of the full-pressure suit was, arguably, the dry suits used by turn-of-the-century commercial salvage divers, complete with their ported brass helmets and valve fittings. In 1920, renowned London physiologist Dr. John Scott Haldane apparently was the first to suggest that a suit similar to the diver's ensemble could protect an aviator at high altitudes. There appeared, however, to be little immediate need for such a suit. The normally aspirated piston-powered airplanes of the era were incapable of achieving altitudes much in excess of 20,000 feet, and the major concern at the time was simply keeping the pilot warm. However, the increasing use of supercharged aircraft engines during the late 1920s led to the first serious studies into pressure suits. Suddenly, aircraft could fly above 30,000 feet and the concern was no longer how to keep the aviator warm, but how to protect him from the reduced pressure.[78]

During the early 1930s Mark E. Ridge determined that a suitably constructed pressurized suit would allow him to make a record-breaking altitude flight in an open balloon. His efforts to interest the United States military in this endeavor failed, and instead he contacted John Haldane in London for help. At the time, Haldane was working with Sir Robert Davis of Siebe, Gorman & Company to develop deep-sea diving suits. Together, Haldane and Davis constructed a hypobaric protection suit for Ridge. For a number of reasons, Ridge was never able to put the suit to actual use, although he tested it in a pressure chamber at simulated altitudes up to 90,000 feet.[79]

In 1934 famed aviator Wiley Post commissioned the B. F. Goodrich Company to manufacture a pressure suit of his own design. Unfortunately, the rubberized fabric suit did not work all that well. The basic design was modified by B. F. Goodrich engineer Russell Colley, and after some trial and error, Post was able to use it successfully on several record-breaking flights to altitudes of 50,000 feet.[80]

While work on derivatives of the Ridge-Haldane-Davis suit continued in England, the U.S. Army Air Corps finally recognized, somewhat belatedly, the need for a pressurized protective garment for military aviators and started the classified MX-117 research program in 1939. This drew several companies into pressure-suit development, including B. F. Goodrich (with Russell Colley), Bell Aircraft, the Goodyear Rubber Company, the U.S. Rubber Company, and the National Carbon Company. From 1940 through 1943, engineers produced a number of designs that all featured transparent dome-like plastic helmets and airtight, rubberized fabric garments that greatly restricted mobility and range of motion when fully pressurized. The development of segmented, bellows-like joints at the knees, hips, and elbows improved mobility, but still resulted in an

77 Crossfield, *Always Another Dawn*, p. 236. Crossfield gives an interesting look at his involvement (which was great) in early pressure-suit development in the chapter titled, "Girdles, Brassieres, Shattered Sinuses."

78 Christopher T. Carey, "Supporting Life at 80,000 feet: Evolution of the American High Altitude Pressure Suit." *http://www.lanset.com/aeolusaero/Articles/SSuits.htm*. Accessed on 9 April 2002.

79 Ibid. A suit based upon the Ridge-Haldane-Davis design was eventually flown to a British altitude record of 50,000 feet in 1936.

80 Ibid.

extremely clumsy and uncomfortable ensemble. The striking visual aspect of these suits resulted in their being called "tomato worm suits," after the distinctive tomato hornworm.[81]

By 1943 the Army Air Corps had largely lost interest in the concept of a full-pressure suit. The newest long-range bomber, the Boeing B-29 Superfortress, was pressurized and seemed less likely to require the suits than earlier aircraft. As Scott Crossfield later opined, "During World War II the armed services, absorbed with more vital matters, advanced the pressure suit not a whit."[82]

After the war, Dr. James P. Henry of the University of Southern California began experimenting with a new concept in aircrew protection. The capstan-type partial-pressure suit operated by imposing mechanical pressure on the body directly, compressing the abdomen and limbs much like the anti-g suits then entering service. The compression was applied by inflatable bladders in the abdominal area and pneumatic tubes (capstans) running along the limbs. A tightly fitting, rubber-lined fabric hood that was fitted with a neck seal and a transparent visor fully enclosed the head.[83]

In Worcester, Massachusetts, a small company named after its founder, David Clark, produced anti-g suits for the Air Force and experimental pressure suits for the Navy. Scott Crossfield described Clark as "one of the most interesting men I have ever met in the aviation world." Although Henry had approached the David Clark Company for assistance in developing his suit concept, contracts for anti-g suits between David Clark and the U.S. government made direct cooperation appear to be a conflict of interest. Instead, Clark sent materials and an experienced seamstress, Julia Greene, to help Henry continue his development in California. Just after the war, the Air Force asked Clark to observe a test of the Henry partial-pressure suit in the altitude chamber at Wright Field. Henry demonstrated the suit to a maximum altitude of 90,000 feet, and remained above 65,000 feet for more than 30 minutes; everybody was suitably impressed. The Air Force asked David Clark to produce the Henry design, and all parties soon reached an agreement that included Julia Greene returning to Worcester. David Clark produced the first suit for Jack Woolams, a Bell test pilot scheduled to fly the XS-1, and made additional suits for Chalmers "Slick" Goodlin and a little-known Air Force captain named Chuck Yeager.[84]

These early partial-pressure suits did, in fact, work. On 25 August 1949, Major Frank K. "Pete" Everest was flying the first X-1 on an altitude flight when the canopy cracked and the cockpit depressurized. The laced partial-pressure suit automatically activated, squeezing Everest along the torso, arms, and legs, supporting his skin and keeping his blood from boiling. He landed, uncomfortable but unhurt. This was the first recorded use of a partial-pressure suit under emergency conditions.[85]

---

81 Ibid.

82 Quote is from Crossfield, *Always Another Dawn*, p. 237.

83 Corrections to the Henry suit description supplied by Jack Bassick at the David Clark Company in a letter to Dennis R. Jenkins, 3 June 2002.

84 David M. Clark, *The Development of the Partial Pressure Suit*, (Worcester, MA: David Clark Company, 1992), pp. 168-169. The Crossfield quote is from *Always Another Dawn*, p. 239.

85 Crossfield, *Always Another Dawn*, pp. 237-238; Jay Miller, *The X-Planes: X-1 to X-45*, (Hinckley, England: Midland Publishing, 2001), pp. 31-32.

Continued improvements resulted in the T-1 suit, the first standardized partial-pressure suit used by the Air Force. The Air Force used the T-1 suit in a variety of aircraft, including the stripped-down "featherweight" versions of the Convair B-36 intercontinental bomber that frequently flew missions lasting in excess of 24 hours at altitudes above 50,000 feet. Unfortunately, the T-1 suit was not a particularly comfortable garment.[86]

The discomfort of the so-called "Henry suit" was an unfortunate aspect of the fundamental design of partial-pressure suits. This was at least partially eliminated in the subsequent MC-1, MC-3, and MC-4 series (the MC-2 suit was an experimental full-pressure suit to be discussed later) by the placement and adjustment of panels during customized fitting. However, the suits did accomplish their main purpose: to protect the wearer from the effects of emergency decompression at altitude.[87]

Taking a different route, after the war the U. S. Navy began investigating the possibility of developing a full-pressure suit in cooperation with B. F. Goodrich and Russell Colley. This led to a progressive series of refinements of the basic design that resulted, in the early 1950s, in the first practical U.S. full-pressure suit. At the same time, the David Clark Company was also experimenting with full-pressure suits under Navy auspices. On 21 August 1953, Marine Corps Lieutenant Colonel Marion E. Carl took one of the D-558-2 aircraft to an unofficial record altitude of 83,235 feet while wearing a David Clark full-pressure suit.[88]

The Navy's adventures in full-pressure suit development took some intriguing turns, and Scott Crossfield covers them well in his autobiography. The Navy ended up concentrating on the Goodrich designs. One of these was the Model H, an early developmental suit that the Navy considered unacceptable for operational use but showed a great deal of promise. Consequently, in a perfect example of interservice rivalry, the Air Force and Navy began separate development efforts—both based on the Model H—to perfect an operational full-pressure suit. By the early 1960s the Navy had progressed through a series of developmental models to the Mark IV, Model 3, Type 1, a production suit that Navy aircrews wore on high-altitude flights for several years.[89]

Air Force experience at high altitudes in the B-36 confirmed the need for a full-pressure suit to replace the partial-pressure suits used by the bomber crews. In response, the Air Force drafted a requirement for a suit to provide a minimum of 12 hours of protection above 55,000 feet. The goal was to construct a "fully mobile suit" that would weigh less than 30 pounds, operate with an internal pressure of 5 psi, and provide the user with sufficient oxygen partial pressure for breathing, adequate counterpressure over the body, and suitable ventilation.[90]

---

86 Carey, "Supporting Life at 80,000 feet."

87 Ibid; amplification of the T-1 suit development supplied by Jack Bassick at the David Clark Company in a letter to Dennis R. Jenkins, 3 June 2002.

88 Crossfield, *Always Another Dawn*, pp. 240-241; *http://www.nasm.edu/nasm/aero/aircraft/douglas_D-558.htm*, accessed on 24 April 2002.

89 Carey, "Supporting Life at 80,000 feet."

90 Edwin G. Vail and Richard G. Willis, "Pilot Protection for the X-15 Airplane," a paper in the *1958 Research Airplane Committee Report*, pp. 117-118.

Whatever the political nuances involved, in 1955 the Air Force issued a request for proposals for a full-pressure suit. Several contracts were awarded and the two leading designs were designated the XMC-2-ILC (International Latex Corporation) and the XMC-2-DC (David Clark Company). The ILC approach resulted in an unwieldy garment that used convoluted metal joints and metal bearing rings, and had limited mobility under pressure; it was known, however, to provide the required pressure protection. Unfortunately, the joint bearings produced painful pressure points on the body and were hazardous during bailout or ejection—hardly an ideal solution.[91]

On the other hand, the David Clark suit featured a major breakthrough in suit design with the use of a new "distorted-angle fabric," called Link-Net, to control inflation and enhance range of motion. This eliminated the need for the tomato-worm bellows at the limb joints. David Clark had been developing this same basic suit with the Navy before that service opted to go with the Goodrich design. The Air Force selected the David Clark suit for further development.[92]

The new Link-Net fabric was the result of an intensive effort by the company to develop a new partial-pressure suit fabric using both Navy and company money. Originally, David Clark had constructed several torso mockups using different unsupported sheet-rubber materials, but quickly discarded these when it became evident that a rupture in the material could cause the entire suit to collapse. The company began looking for a supported-rubber material that would meet the sealing requirements but would not collapse when punctured. Ultimately, David Clark selected a neoprene-coated nylon. A puncture in this material would result in a small leak, but not a sudden expulsion of gas.[93]

The enormous advantages offered by the Link-Net fabric were hard to grasp. Coupled with advances in regulators and other mechanical pieces, David Clark could now produce a workable full-pressure suit that weighed about 35 pounds. Previously, during the early X-15 proposal effort, North American had estimated a suit would weigh 110 pounds.[94]

Further tests showed that two layers of nylon marquisette arranged with opposite bias provided the maximum strength in high-stress areas. This improved Link-Net material consisted of a series of parallel cords that looped each other at frequent intervals. The loops were interlocked but not connected so that the cords could slide over each other and feed from one section of the suit to another to allow the suit to deform easily as the pilot moved. The main characteristic required of the Link-Net was the lowest possible resistance to bending and twisting, but the elasticity had to be minimal since the suit could not increase appreciably in volume while under pressure. The use of a relatively non-elastic cord in the construction of Link-Net made it possible to satisfy these seemingly

91 Ibid. The use of the XMC-2 designation for multiple designs was unusual and confusing.

92 Ibid. Link-Net is a trademark of the David Clark Company.

93 Air Force report ASD-61-116, "Development of a Full Pressure Suit System," May 1961, p. 1. Supplied by Jack Bassick at the David Clark Company.

94 Crossfield, *Always Another Dawn*, pp. 253-254.

The X-15 provided the first impetus to develop a workable full-pressure suit, and Scott Crossfield and Dr. David M. Clark were instrumental in the effort. The first X-15 full-pressure suit, the XMC-2 (S794-3C) was demonstrated by Scott Crossfield in the human centrifuge at the Aero Medical Laboratory on 14 October 1957. Two 15-second runs were made at 7 g, and the following day an additional 23 tests were conducted to demonstrate the anti-g capability of the suit. (U.S. Air Force)

contradictory requirements. Clark chose nylon for the Link-Net because of its high tensile strength, low weight, and low bulk ratio.[95]

The first prototype David Clark Model S794 suit provided a learning experience for the company. For instance, the initial anti-g bladders were fabricated using neoprene-coated nylon, but failed during testing. New bladders incorporated a nylon-oxford restraint cover, and these passed the pressure tests. Materials evaluated for the gloves included leather/nylon, leather/nylon/Link-Net, and all leather. Eventually, the company found the best combination was leather covering the hand, a stainless-steel palm restrainer stitched inside nylon tape supported by nylon tape around the back, Link-Net from the wrist up to the top zipper, and a black cabretta top seam. However, pilots quickly found that gloves constructed in the straight position made it impossible to hold an object, such as a control stick, for more than 15–20 minutes while the glove was pressurized. When the company used a natural semi-closed position to construct the glove, the pilots could hold an object for up to 2 hours without serious discomfort. Perhaps the most surprising

95 "Development of a Full Pressure Suit System," pp. 1-2. The nylon marquisette had a tensile break strength of 64 psi on the fill and 130 psi on the warp.

material used in the prototype suit was the kangaroo leather for the boots, which turned out to be soft and comfortable as well as sufficiently durable.[96]

The construction of two "production" full-pressure suits (S794-1 and S794-2) followed. These suits were an improvement in terms of production and mobility but were, in reality, still prototypes. One of the major changes was extending the use of Link-Net material further from the joints to increase the amount of "draw" and provide additional mobility. Eventually David Clark concluded that the entire suit should use Link-Net. David Clark delivered these two suits to the Aero Medical Laboratory at Wright Field for testing and evaluation, and used the lessons learned to construct the first X-15 suit for Scott Crossfield.[97]

Crossfield's Crusade

By the beginning of the X-15 program, the WADC Aero Medical Laboratory had only partly succeeded in developing a full-pressure suit, almost entirely with the David Clark design. This led to a certain amount of indecision regarding the type of garment needed for the X-15. However, North American proposed the use of a full-pressure suit as a means to protect the pilot during normal operations and emergency escape.

Despite the early state-of-development of full-pressure suits, Scott Crossfield was convinced they were necessary for the X-15. Crossfield also had great confidence in David Clark—both the company and the man. In fact, the detail specification of 2 March 1956 required North American to furnish just such a garment, and the company issued a specification for a full-pressure suit to the David Clark Company on 8 April 1956. Less than a month later, however, the X-15 Project Office, on advice from the Aero Medical Laboratory, advised North American to plan to use a partial-pressure suit. It was the beginning of a heated debate.[98]

North American, and particularly Scott Crossfield, refused to yield, and during a meeting in Inglewood on 20-22 June 1956 the Air Force began to concede. David Clark demonstrated a full-pressure suit, developed for the Navy, during preliminary X-15 cockpit mockup inspection. Although the suit was far from perfected, the Aero Medical Laboratory believed that "the state-of-the-art of full pressure suits should permit the development of such a suit satisfactory for use in the X-15."[99]

During a meeting on 12 July 1956, representatives from the Air Force, Navy, and North American reviewed the status of full-pressure suit development, and the Aero Medical Laboratory committed to make the modifications necessary to support the X-15. The North American representative, Scott Crossfield, agreed that the Aero Medical Laboratory should provide the suit for the X-15. Crossfield insisted

96 "Development of a Full Pressure Suit System," pp. 3-4. At rest, the human hand tends to be in a semi-closed position as the muscles relax. The kangaroo leather boots eventually gave way to standard flying boots that were modified to interface with the pressure suit. The Hyde Athletic Shoe Company provided the model Z100 boots.

97 "Development of a Full Pressure Suit System," pp. 4-5.

98 North American Aviation detail specification NA5-4047, 8 April 1956. In the files at the Boeing Archives; memorandum, Lieutenant Colonel K. F. Troup, Chief, Aircrew Effectiveness Branch, Aero Medical Laboratory, to Chief, New Development WSPO, Fighter Aircraft Division, ARDC, no subject, 4 May 1956. In the files at the Air Force Historical Research Agency; telephone conversation, Scott Crossfield with Dennis R. Jenkins, 5 June 2000.

99 X-15 WSPO Weekly Activity Report, 28 June 1956.

that the laboratory design the garment specifically for the X-15 and make every effort to provide an operational suit by late 1957 to support the first flight. The X-15 Project Office accepted responsibility for funding the development program. Crossfield could not legally change the suit from a contractor-furnished item to government-furnished equipment, but agreed to recommend that North American accept such a change. There was little doubt that Charlie Feltz would concur.[100]

Although the 12 July agreement effectively settled the issue, the paperwork to make it official moved somewhat more slowly. The Air Force did not change the suit from contractor-furnished to government-furnished until 8 February 1957. At the same time, the Aero Medical Laboratory issued a contract to the David Clark Company for the development of a full-pressure suit specifically for the X-15.[101]

The first X-15 suit was the S794-3C, which incorporated all of the changes requested after a brief period of evaluating the first two "production" S794 suits. The complete suit with helmet, boots, and back kit weighed just 37 pounds. David Clark shipped this third suit to Inglewood for evaluation in the X-15 cockpit mockup from 7-13 October 1957. While at North American, the suit underwent pressure checks, X-15 cockpit compatibility evaluations, ventilation checks, and altitude-chamber runs. Unfortunately, the altitude-chamber runs proved pointless since the North American chamber only went to 40,000 feet and the suit controller had been set to pressurize above 40,000 feet.[102]

The suit was then taken to the Aero Medical Laboratory for evaluation, and on 14 October was demonstrated in the Wright Field centrifuge during two 15-second runs at 7 g. The following day, 23 more centrifuge runs demonstrated the anti-g capability of the suit, which proved satisfactory. On 16 October, the suit underwent environmental testing at temperatures up to 165°F. The ventilation of the suit at these temperatures was unsatisfactory, but David Clark engineers understood the issue and the government did not consider it significant. Mobility tests were conducted in the centrifuge on 17 October at flight conditions up to 5 g with satisfactory results, and altitude chamber tests ended at 98,000 feet for 45 minutes. As a result of these evaluations, the Air Force requested numerous minor modifications for subsequent suits, but the Aero Medical Laboratory formally accepted the S794-3C on 12 November 1957.[103]

The list of modifications required for the S794-4 suit took four pages, but they were mostly minor issues and did not represent a significant problem for the David Clark Company, although the resulting suit was almost 3 pounds heavier. Scott Crossfield demonstrated this suit during a cockpit inspection on 2 December 1957 when he put the suit on, inflated it to 3 psi, walked from one end of the

---

100 AMC Form 52 (Record of Verbal Coordination), 12 July 1956, subject: Personal Equipment for X-15 Weapons System; telephone conversation, Scott Crossfield with Dennis R. Jenkins, 5 June 2002.

101 Letter, R. L. Stanley, Deputy Chief, Fighter Aircraft Branch, Aircraft and Missiles Division, Director of Procurement and Production, AMC, to Air Force Plant Representative, North American Aviation, subject: Contract AF33(600)-31693, X-15 Airplane—ECPs NA-X15-1, NA-X15-7, NA-X15-8, NA-X15-12,16 January 1957. In the files at the Air Force Historical Research Agency; letter, S. C. Hellman, Manager, Contracts and Proposals, North American Aviation, to Commander, AMC, subject: Contract AF33(600)-31693 (X-15) NA-240 Contractual Document—Request for Full Pressure Pilot's Suit—Change from CFE to GFAE, ECP NA-X-15-8, 8 February 1957. In the files at the Boeing Archives; Air Force report ASD-61-116, pp. 7-8. The David Clark contract was AF33(616)-3903 as part of Project 6333. The effort was subsequently transferred to Project 6336.

102 "Development of a Full Pressure Suit System," pp. 5-6.

103 Ibid. Between 18 September and 26 November the S794-3C suit spent 66 hours and 40 minutes pressurized without failure at David Clark Company, Firewel Company, North American, and Wright Field.

room to the other (a distance of some 100 feet), and then entered the X-15 cockpit without assistance. Those in attendance were favorably impressed.[104]

On 16 December 1957, David Clark took the S794-4 suit to Wright Field for further evaluation, and then to NADC Johnsville for centrifuge testing on 17-18 December. These centrifuge tests were much more realistic than the limited evaluations conducted at Wright Field on the previous suit, and included complete simulated X-15 flights. After some minor modifications, the Aero Medical Laboratory formally accepted the suit on 20 February 1958.[105]

The S794-5 suit, the first true "production MC-2," incorporated 34 changes. The Air Force sent the completed suit to Wright Field on 17 April 1958, and then to Edwards for flight evaluations. Personnel at Edwards had modified the back cockpits of a T-33 and F-104B to accommodate the suit for the tests. The first flight in the T-33 on 12 May 1958 resulted in several complaints, primarily citing a lack of ventilation because no high-pressure air source was available. Initial concerns about a lack of mobility eased after the third flight as the pilot became more familiar with the suit. The suit seemed to offer adequate anti-g protection up to the 5-g limit of the T-33. Tests in the F-104B proved to be more comfortable, primarily because high-pressure air was available for suit ventilation, but also because the cockpit was somewhat larger, improving mobility even further. The pilots suggested various improvements (many concerning the helmet and gloves) after these flights, but overall the comments were favorable. The suit accumulated 8.25 hours of flight time during the tests.[106]

The Aero Medical Laboratory advised the X-15 Project Office on 10 April 1958 that David Clark would deliver the first suit for Scott Crossfield on 1 June 1958. The laboratory cautioned, however, that the X-15 project would receive only four suits under the current contract. The laboratory would receive other full-pressure suits for service testing in operational aircraft, but these were not compatible with the X-15 cockpit. If additional suits were required, the X-15 Project Office would need to provide the Aero Medical Laboratory with additional funds.[107]

Given the lack of funds for additional suits, the X-15 Project Office investigated the feasibility of using a seat kit instead of the back kit used on the first four suits. This would allow the use of suits designed for service testing, and allow X-15 pilots to use the suits in operational aircraft. The benefits of using a common suit would have been substantial, but by May 1958 it was too late since the X-15 design was too far along to change. Although the X-15 Project Office continued to pursue the idea, the X-15 suit remained different from similar suits intended for

104 Ibid, pp. 8-12.

105 Ibid, p. 13; X-15 WSPO Weekly Activity Report, 30 October 1957; "Full Pressure Suit Assembly," Physiology Branch, Aero Medical Laboratory, WADC, 1 January 1958; memorandum, G. Kitzes, Assistant Chief, Physiology Branch, Aero Medical Laboratory, WADC, to Chief, Fighter Aircraft Division, ARDC, subject: Status of MC-2 Full Pressure Altitude Suits for the X-15 Research Aircraft, 10 April 1958. In the files at the Air Force Historical Research Agency; Air Force report ASD-61-116, p. 13.

106 "Development of a Full Pressure Suit System," pp. 13-17.

107 X-15 WSPO Weekly Activity Report, 30 October 1957; "Full Pressure Suit Assembly," Physiology Branch, Aero Medical Laboratory, WADC, 1 January 1958; memorandum, G. Kitzes, Assistant Chief, Physiology Branch, Aero Medical Laboratory, WADC, to Chief, Fighter Aircraft Division, ARDC, subject: Status of MC-2 Full Pressure Altitude Suits for the X-15 Research Aircraft, 10 April 1958. In the files at the Air Force Historical Research Agency.

operational aircraft. The X-15 Project Office subsequently found funds for two more suits.[108]

On 3 May 1958, the configuration of the suit to be delivered to Crossfield was frozen during a meeting in Worchester among representatives of the Air Force, David Clark, and North American. The decision was somewhat premature since the suit configuration was still in question during a meeting three months later at Wright Field. This indecision had already resulted in a two-month delay, and the need for further tests was apparent.[109]

The X-15 Project Office advised the newly assigned chief of the Aero Medical Laboratory, Colonel John P. Stapp, that the suit delays might postpone the entire X-15 program. To maintain the schedule, the X-15 project needed to receive Crossfield's suit by 1 January 1959, a second suit by 15 February, and the remaining four suits by 15 May. Simultaneously, the X-15 Project Office informed Stapp of the growing controversy concerning the use of a face seal (actually a separate oral-nasal mask inside the pressurized helmet) instead of the neck seal preferred by the Aero Medical Laboratory.[110]

North American believed the pilot should be able to open the faceplate on his helmet, using the face seal as an oxygen mask. The Aero Medical Laboratory disagreed. Since the engineers had long since agreed to pressurize the X-15 cockpit with nitrogen to avoid risks associated with fire, a neck seal meant that the pilot could never open his faceplate under any conditions. North American and the NACA had already ruled out pressurizing the cockpit with oxygen, for safety reasons. Eventually, the program adopted a neck seal for the MC-2 suit, although development of the face seal continued for the highly successful A/P22S-2 suit that came later.[111]

Crossfield finally received his MC-2 pressure suit on 17 December 1958. In a report dated 30 January 1959, the X-15 Project Office attributed much of the credit for the successful development of the full-pressure suit to Crossfield.[112]

David Clark tailored the resulting MC-2 suits for the individual pilots. Each suit consisted of a ventilation suit, upper and lower rubber garments, and upper and lower restraint garments. The ventilation suit also included a porous wool insulation garment. The edges of the upper and lower rubber garments were folded together three times to form a seal at the waist. The lower half of the rubber garment incorporated an anti-g suit that was similar in design

---

108 Interview of Captain Jerry E. Schaub X-15 WSPO, Director of Systems Management, ARDC, 28 May 1959, by Robert S. Houston, History Branch, WADC. Written transcript in the files at the AFMC History Office. X-15 WSPO Weekly Activity Report, 2 May 1958. In a seat kit the pilot sits on the controller unit, parachute, and survival kit, whereas in a back kit these items are located (naturally enough) on his back. This necessitates different seat configurations, which can have a major impact on the design of the ejection seat and supporting equipment.

109 X-15 WSPO Weekly Activity Report, 9 May 1958; Lieutenant Colonel Burt Rowen, "Biomedical Monitoring of the X-15 Program," AFFTC report TN-61-4, May 1961, p. 2. Attendees included representatives of the Aero Medical Laboratory, X-15 Project Office, WADC Crew Station Office, North American, The David Clark Company, Bill Jack Scientific Company, and Firewel Company.

110 Memorandum, Lieutenant Jerry E. Schaub, X-15 WSPO, to Chief, Aero Medical Laboratory, WADC, 19 August 1958, subject: X-15 Full Pressure Suit Program. In the files at the AFMC History Office; X-15 WSPO Weekly Activity Report, 5 September 1958 and 7 November 1958; Lieutenant Colonel Burt Rowen, "Human-Factors Support of the X-15 Program," *Air University Quarterly Review*, Air War College, volume X, number 4, Winter 1958-59, p. 38.

111 Report, "Survey of the X-15 Research Aircraft, 30 September-7 October 1958," ARDC Inspector General, not dated. In the files at the ASC History Office.

112 X-15 WSPO Weekly Activity Report, 21 November and 5 December 1958, and 9 January, 30 January, and 3 April 1959; memorandum, Colonel F. A. Holm to Chief, Programs and Evaluations Office, ARDC Inspector General, 13 February 1958. In the files at the AFMC History Office; Rowen, "Biomedical Monitoring of the X-15 Program," pp. 2-3.

to standard Air Force-issue suits and provided protection up to about 7 g. The X-15 provided gaseous nitrogen to pressurize the portion of the suit below the rubber neck seal. The suit accommodated in-flight medical monitoring of the pilot.[113]

The outer garment was not actually required for altitude protection. An aluminized reflective outer garment contained the seat restraint, shoulder harness, and parachute attachments; protected the pressure suit during routine use; and served as a sacrificial garment during high-speed ejection. It also provided a small measure of additional insulation against extreme temperature. This was the first of the silver "space suits" that found an enthusiastic reception on television and at the movies.[114]

The X-15 supplied the modified MA-3 helmet with 100% oxygen for breathing, and the same source inflated the anti-g bladders within the suit during accelerated flight. The total oxygen supply was 192 cubic inches, supplied by two 1,800-psi bottles located beneath the X-15 ejection seat during free flight. The NB-52 carrier aircraft supplied the oxygen during ground operations, taxiing, and captive flight. A rotary valve located on the ejection seat selected which oxygen source (NB-52 or X-15 seat) to use. The suit-helmet regulator automatically delivered the correct oxygen pressure for the ambient altitude until the absolute pressure fell below 3.5 psi (equivalent to 35,000 feet), and the suit pressure then stabilized at 3.5 psi absolute. Expired air vented into the lower nitrogen-filled garment through two one-way neck seal valves and then into the aircraft cockpit through a suit pressure-control valve. During ejection the nitrogen gas supply to the suit below the helmet

Here Scott Crossfield sits in a thermal-vacuum chamber during tests of a prototype XMC-2 (S794-3C) suit. These tests used temperatures as high as 165°F and the initial suits suffered from inadequate ventilation at high temperatures. Production versions of this suit were used for 36 early X-15 flights, and in a number of other high-altitude Air Force aircraft. (Boeing)

113 "Biomedical Monitoring of the X-15 Program," pp. 2-3; Edwin G. Vail and Richard G. Willis, "Pilot Protection for the X-15 Airplane," a paper in the *1958 Research Airplane Committee Report*, pp. 117-118.

114 Vail and Willis, "Pilot Protection for the X-15 Airplane," p. 119.

was stopped (since the nitrogen source was on the X-15), and the suit and helmet were automatically pressurized for the ambient altitude by the emergency oxygen supply located in the backpack.[115]

Despite the fact that it worked reasonably well, the pilots did not particularly like the MC-2 suit. It was cumbersome to wear, restricted movement, and allowed limited peripheral vision. It was also mechanically complex and required a considerable amount of maintenance. Nevertheless, there was only one serious deficiency noted in the suit: the oxygen line between the helmet and the helmet pressure regulator (mounted in the back kit) caused a delay in oxygen flow such that the pilot could reverse the helmet-suit differential pressure by taking a quick, deep breath. Since the helmet pressure was supposed to be greater than the suit pressure to prevent nitrogen from leaking into the breathing space, this pressure reversal was less than ideal, but no easy solution was available.[116]

Improved Girdles for the Masses

Fortunately, development did not stop there, and the first of the improved A/P22S-2 (David Clark Model S1023) full-pressure suits arrived at Edwards on 27 July 1959. The development by the David Clark Company of a new method to integrate a pressure-sealing zipper made it possible to incorporate all of the layers of the MC-2 suit into a one-piece garment, significantly simplifying handling and maintenance. A separate aluminized-nylon outer garment protected the suit and provided mounting locations for the restraint and parachute harness. A face seal that was more comfortable and more robust replaced the neck seal, which had proven relatively delicate and subject to frequent damage. A modified helmet mounted the oxygen pressure regulator inside the helmet, eliminating the undesirable time delay in oxygen flow. This time David Clark mounted the suit pressure regulator in the suit to eliminate some of the plumbing.[117]

The consensus among X-15 pilots was that the A/P22S-2 represented a huge improvement over the earlier MC-2. However, it would take another year before the Aero Medical Laboratory delivered fully qualified versions of the suit to the X-15 program. By July 1960, the A/P22S-2 pressure suits started arriving at Edwards and familiarization flights in the JTF-102A began later in the year, along with additional X-15 cockpit mockup evaluations and simulator runs. North American also subjected the first suit to wind-tunnel tests in the company facility in El Segundo.[118]

Joe Walker made the initial attempt at using the A/P22S-2 in the X-15 on 21 March 1961; unfortunately, telemetry problems forced Walker to abort the flight (2-A-27). Nine days later Walker made the first flight (2-14-28) in the A/P22S-2.

115 Ibid, pp. 119-120. The MC-2 was pressurized in the X-15 in a slightly different manner compared to MC-2 suits used in other aircraft.

116 Bratt, "Biomedical Aspects of the X-15 Program, 1959-1964," pp. 6-7.

117 Ibid, pp. 7-8. Corrections to the A/P22S-2 description supplied by Jack Bassick at the David Clark Company in a letter to Dennis R. Jenkins, 3 June 2002

118 James E. Love, "History and Development of the X-15 Research Aircraft," not dated, p. 13. In the files at the DFRC History Office. Pressure suit designations continued to be misleading. For instance, the A/P22S-2 was a David Clark Company suit, but the A/P22S-3 was a completely different suit manufactured by the B. F. Goodrich Company.

Walker reported that the new suit represented an improvement in comfort and vision over the MC-2. By the end of 1961, the A/P-22S-2 had a combined total of 730 hours in support of X-15 operations; these included 18 X-15 flights, 171 flight hours in the JTF-102A, and 554 hours of ground time.[119]

The A/P22S-2 was clearly superior to the earlier MC-2, particularly from the pilot's perspective. The improvements included the following:[120]

1. Increased visual area—The double curvature faceplate in the A/P22S-2, together with the use of a face seal in place of the MC-2 neck seal, allowed the face to move forward in the helmet so that the pilot had a lateral vision field of approximately 200 degrees. This was an increase of approximately 40 degrees over the single contoured lens in the MC-2 helmet, with an additional increase of 20 percent in the vertical field of view.
2. Ease of donning—The MC-2 was put on in two sections: the lower rubberized garment and its restraining coverall, and the upper rubberized garment and its restraining coverall. This was a rather tedious process and depended on folding the rubber top and bottom sections of the suit together to retain pressure. The A/P22S-2 was a one-piece garment with a pressure-sealing zipper that ran around the back portion of the suit and was zippered closed in one operation. It took approximately 30 minutes to properly don an MC-2; only 5 minutes for the newer suit.
3. Removable gloves—In the MC-2 the gloves were a fixed portion of the upper rubberized garment. The A/P22S-2 had removable gloves that contributed to general comfort and ease of donning. This also prevented excessive moisture from building up during suit checkout and X-15 preflight inspections, and made it easier for the pilot to remove the pressure suit by himself if that should become necessary. Another advantage was that a punctured glove could be changed without having to change the entire suit.

The A/P22S-2 also featured a new system of biomedical electrical connectors installed through a pressure seal in the suit, avoiding the snap-pad arrangement used in the MC-2 suit. The snap pads had proven to be unsatisfactory for continued use, since after several operations the snaps either separated or failed to make good

119 X-15 Status Reports, Paul F. Bikle/FRC to H. Brown/NASA Headquarters, 15 July 1960, p. 6; 29 July 1960 p. 7; and 3 April 1961, pp. 13-14. In the files at the DFRC History Office; Lieutenant Colonel Burt Rowen, Major Ralph N. Richardson, and Garrison P. Layton, Jr., "Bioastronautics Support of the X-15 Program," a paper in the *Research Airplane Committee Report on the Conference on the Progress of the X-15 Project*, a compilation of the papers presented at the Flight Research Center, 20-21 November 1961, p. 255 (hereafter called the 1961 *Research Airplane Committee Report*). A slightly expanded version of this paper was subsequently republished as AFFTC technical report FTC-TDR-61-61, "Bioastronautics Support of the X-15 Program," December 1961.

120 Rowen et al., "Bioastronautics Support of the X-15 Program," pp. 255-256.

contact because of metal fatigue. This resulted in the loss of biomedical data during the flight. In the new suit, biomedical data were acquired through what was essentially a continuous electrical lead from the pilot's body to the seat interface.[121]

The number of details required to develop a satisfactory operational pressure suit was amazing. Initially the A/P22S-2 suit used an electrically heated stretched acrylic visor procured from the Sierracin Corporation. The visors were heated for much the same reason a car windshield is: to prevent fogging from obscuring vision. Unfortunately, on the early visors the electrical coating was applied to only one side of the acrylic and the coating was not particularly durable, requiring extraordinary care during handling. Polishing would not remove scratches, so the Air Force had to replace the scratched visors. David Clark solved this with the introduction of a laminated heated visor in which the electrical coating was sandwiched between two layers of acrylic. This required a new development effort since nobody had laminated a double-curvature lens, although a Los Angeles company called Protection Incorporated had done some preliminary work on the idea at its own expense. The David Clark Company supplied laminated visors with later models of the A/P22S-2 suit.[122]

Initially, the MC-2 suit used visors heated at 3 W per square inch, but the conductive film overly restricted vision. The Air Force gradually reduced the requirement to 1 W in an attempt to find the best compromise between heating the visor and allowing unimpeded vision. Tests in the cold chamber at the Aerospace Medical Center during late January 1961 established that the 1-W visors were sufficient for their expected use.[123]

Another requirement came from an unusual source. Researchers evaluating the effects of the high-altitude free fall during Captain Joseph Kittinger's record balloon jump realized that the X-15 pilot would need to be able to see after ejecting from the airplane. This involved adding a battery to the seat to provide electrical current for visor heating during ejection.[124]

Like the MC-2 before them, the A/P22S-2 suits were custom made for each X-15 pilot, necessitating several trips to Worcester. It is interesting to note that although the X-15 pilots were still somewhat critical of the lack of mobility afforded by the full-pressure suits (particularly later pilots who had not experienced the MC-2); this was only true on the ground. When the suits occasionally inflated for brief periods during flight, an abundance of adrenaline allowed the pilot to easily overcome the resistance of the suit. At most, it rated a slight mention in the post-flight report.

As good as it was, the A/P22S-2 was not perfect, and David Clark modified the suit based on initial X-15 flight experience. The principle modifications included rotating the glove rings to provide greater mobility of the hands; improved

121 Ibid, pp. 256-257.

122 Minutes of Meeting, X-15 Human Factors Subcommittee, 30 December 1960.

123 Ibid.

124 Minutes of Meeting, X-15 Human Factors Subcommittee, 28 March 1961. Joseph W. Kittinger, Jr., was appointed test director of Project Excelsior to investigate escape from high altitude. During this project, three high-altitude jumps were made from a balloon-supported gondola. The first was from 76,400 feet on 16 November 1958, the second from 74,700 feet 25 days later, and the third from 102,800 feet on 16 August 1960, the highest altitude from which man had jumped. In free-fall for 4.5 minutes at speeds up to 714 mph and temperatures as low as –94°F, Kittinger opened his parachute at 18,000 feet. In addition to the altitude record, he set records for the longest free-fall and fastest speed achieved by a man (without an aircraft!).

The MC-2 suit led to the David Clark Company A/P22S suit that became the standard military and NASA high-altitude suit. The A/P22S and its variants have had a long career, and were used by SR-71 and U-2 pilots, as well as space shuttle astronauts. Here, NASA test pilot Joseph A. Walker stands in front of an X-15 after a flight. (NASA)

manufacturing, inspection, and assembly techniques for the helmet ring to lower the torque required to connect the helmet to the suit, and the installation of a redundant (pressure-sealing) restraint zipper to lower the leak rate of the suit. Other changes included the installation of a double face seal to improve comfort and minimize leakage between the face seal and suit, and modifications to the tailoring of the Link-Net restraint garment around the shoulders to improve comfort and mobility. David Clark also solved a weak point involving the stitching in the leather glove by including a nylon liner that relieved the strain on the stitched leather seams.[125]

Ultimately, only 36 X-15 flights used the MC-2 suit; the remainder used the newer A/P22S-2. Variants of the A/P22S-2 would become the standard operational full-pressure suit across all Air Force programs.

125 Rowen et al., "Bioastronautics Support of the X-15 Program;" "Biomedical Aspects of the X-15 Program: 1959-1964," pp. 8-9.

Post X-15

The X-15 was not the only program that required a pressure suit, although it was certainly the most public at the time. The basic MC-2 suit underwent a number of one-off "dash" modifications for use in various high-performance aircraft testing programs. Many of the movies and still photographs of the early 1960s show test pilots dressed in the ubiquitous aluminized fabric-covered David Clark MC-2 full-pressure suits.

The A/P22S-2 suit evolved into a series of variants designated the A/P22S-4, A/P22S-6, and A/P22S-6A (David Clark models S1024, S1024A, and S1024B, respectively) for use in most high-altitude Air Force aircraft, including the SR-71. Regardless of the success of the A/P22S-2 suit and its modifications for Air Force use, the cooperation between the Navy and Russell Colley at Goodrich continued. The Navy full-pressure suits included the bulky Mark I (1956); a lighter, slightly reconfigured Mark II; an even lighter Mark III (some versions with a gold lamé outer layer) with an improved internal ventilation system; and three models of the final Mark IV, which went into production in 1958 as the standard Navy high-altitude suit.[126]

The original Mercury space suits were reworked Mark IV suits that NASA designated XN-1 through XN-4, but the engineers usually referred to them as the "quick-fix" suits. The A/P22S-2 formed the basis for the Gemini suits, and ILC returned to the fray to produce the EVA suits used for Apollo. In March 1972, the Air Force became the lead service (the Life Support Special Project Office (LSPRO)) for the development, acquisition, and logistics support efforts involving pressure suits for the Department of Defense. This resulted in the Navy agreeing to give up the Mark IV full-pressure suit and adopt versions of the A/P22S-4/6. Today, the standard high-altitude, full-pressure suits used for atmospheric flight operations (including U-2 missions), as well as those used during space shuttle ascent and reentry, are manufactured by the David Clark Company.[127]

ESCAPE SYSTEM DEVELOPMENT

The development of an escape system had been the subject of debate since the beginning of the X-15 program. North American's decision to use a combination of an ejection seat and a full-pressure suit was a compromise based largely on the ejection seat being lighter than the other alternatives. It was also heavily lobbied for by Scott Crossfield.

The Aero Medical Laboratory had recommended an escape capsule, as prescribed by existing Air Force regulations, as early as 8 February 1955. However, the laboratory admitted that an escape capsule would require a long development period and would probably be unacceptably heavy. The laboratory's alternative

126 Carey, "Supporting Life at 80,000 feet."

127 Ibid.

was an ejection seat with limb restraints used together with a full-pressure suit. Meetings held during October and November 1955 resulted in a direction to North American to develop an ejection seat that would incorporate head and limb restraints. The Air Force also told North American to document the rationale for adopting such a system.[128]

Privately, Scott Crossfield had already decided he did not like capsule designs. Part of this came from experience with the Douglas D-558-2 program. According to Crossfield, "We had a capsule nose on the Skyrocket but knew from the wind-tunnel data that if you separated the nose from the fuselage, the g-force would be so great it could kill you. I made up my mind I would never use the Skyrocket capsule. I would ride the ship down and bail out." Later events with a similar system on the X-2 would prove this fear correct.[129]

The North American analysis of potential accidents that could cause the pilot to abandon the X-15 produced some surprising results. Despite the high-altitude and high-speed nature of the mission profiles, North American determined that 98% of potential accidents were likely to occur at dynamic pressures below 1,500 psi, Mach numbers below 4.0, and altitudes less than 120,000 feet. Using these as criteria, North American investigated four potential escape systems: fuselage-type capsules, cockpit capsules, encapsulated seats, and open ejection seats. The comparison included such factors as cockpit mobility, escape potential, mechanical reliability, post-separation performance, and airframe compatibility. This effort took some 7,000 man-hours to complete. The results showed that an open ejection seat imposed the fewest performance penalties on the aircraft and took the least time to develop. The estimates from North American showed that a satisfactory escape capsule would add 9,000 pounds to the 31,000-pound airplane. Just as importantly, North American—and Scott Crossfield, who would be making the first flights in the airplane—believed the ejection seat offered a better alternative in the event of an emergency, mainly due to its relative mechanical simplicity.[130]

Despite the report, the Air Force was not completely convinced. During a meeting at Wright Field on 2-3 May 1956, the laboratory again emphasized the perceived limitations of ejection seats. Primarily due to the efforts of Scott Crossfield, the Air Force finally agreed that "the X-15 was probably its own best capsule." The meeting also resulted in another action for North American, once again, to document its rationale for selecting the stable-seat and full-pressure suit combination.[131]

North American held the first formal cockpit inspection in July 1956 at its facility in Inglewood. This inspection featured a fully equipped cockpit mockup, complete with instruments, control sticks, and an ejection seat. The seat was a custom design that featured a new type of pilot restraint harness and small sta-

128 Memorandum, H. E. Savely, Chief, Biophysics Branch, Aero Medical Laboratory, WADC, to Chief, New Development Office, Fighter Aircraft Division, 8 February 1955, subject: Acceleration Tolerance and Emergency Escape. In the files at the Air Force Historical Research Agency; memorandum, Arthur W. Vogeley, to Hartley A. Soulé/Research Airplane Project Leader, no subject, 30 November 1955. In the files at the NASA History Office.

129 Crossfield, *Always Another Dawn*, p. 231; telephone conversations, Scott Crossfield with Dennis R. Jenkins, 12 July, 14 July, 20 July, and 1 August 2001.

130 J. F. Hegenwald, "Development of X-15 Escape System," a paper in the *1958 Research Airplane Committee Report*, p. 129; Crossfield, *Always Another Dawn*, p. 232.

131 Memorandum, Hartley A. Soulé/Research Airplane Project Leader to Members of the NACA Research Airplane Project Panel, 7 June 1956. In the files at the NASA History Office.

bilizers to "weather-vane" it into the wind blast and prevent fatal tumbling or oscillation. A solid rocket motor provided about 3,000 lbf to ensure that the seat would clear the X-15. Despite Air Force policy to the contrary, nobody raised any objections about the seat during the inspection. By default, it became part of the official design.[132]

By November 1956, North American had tested a 0.10-scale isolated pilot-seat model of its design in the Naval Supersonic Laboratory wind tunnel at the Massachusetts Institute of Technology (MIT). Although the seat seemed to stabilize randomly in different orientations, the results were generally encouraging. In itself, this did not represent a serious problem, although all participants wanted to understand the dynamics involved. North American conducted additional tests in the Southern California Co-Operative Wind Tunnel in Pasadena to develop the final stabilization system configuration and determine the influence of the forward fuselage without the cockpit canopy.[133]

The debate over the X-15 ejection seat intensified on 27 September 1956 when Captain Milburn G. Apt was killed in the X-2. However, the accident also weakened the case for an escape capsule. The X-2 used a semi-encapsulated system whereby the entire nose of the aircraft, including the cockpit, was blown free of the main fuselage in an emergency. Unfortunately, Bell engineers had expected the pilot to be able to unbuckle his seat straps and manually bail out of the capsule after it separated, something Apt was unable to do. It demonstrated that an encapsulated system was not necessarily the best solution, but then neither was an ejection seat. Almost by definition, piloting X-planes was—and would remain—a dangerous occupation.[134]

During early 1958, researchers began testing the X-15 ejection seat on the rocket sleds at Edwards, with the preliminary runs concluding on 22 April. The series got off to a good start, with the first test seat ejected at 230 knots and the parachute successfully opening at 120 feet, lowering the anthropomorphic dummy gently to the ground. The dummy was equipped with telemetry that relayed data from rate gyros, accelerometers, and pressure transducers. The second test, this one at 620 knots and a dynamic pressure of 1,130 psf, also went well. The third test, under similar conditions, was again satisfactory. However, during the fourth run the shock-wave generator catapult exploded at Mach 1.26 and 2,192 psf. The accident damaged the seat, suit, and anthropomorphic dummy beyond repair. Engineers fired another seat during a static test on 24 April, but the post-ejection operation failed because of a mechanical problem in the initiation hardware. During the second static test on 14 May 1958, the parachute and parachute lines became tangled with the seat. In all, the test series provided mixed results. North American made several minor modifications in preparation for a second series of tests scheduled for June.[135]

---

132 Crossfield, *Always Another Dawn*, pp. 232-233.

133 Memorandum, Hartley A. Soulé/Research Airplane Project Leader, to Members of the NACA Research Airplane Project Panel, NACA, subject: Project 1226—Progress Report for months of September and October 1956, 15 November 1956; J. F. Hegenwald, "Development of X-15 Escape System," a paper in the *1958 Research Airplane Committee Report*, pp. 129-130.

134 Miller, *The X-planes*, pp. 62-67.

135 X-15 WSPO Weekly Activity Report, 2 May and 21 May 1958; Hegenwald, "Development of X-15 Escape System," pp. 136-137.

The high cost of the rocket-sled runs, coupled with the damaged seat hardware, was quickly exceeding the budget for the escape-system tests. Because of this, the X-15 Project Office decided to conduct only two tests, at 125 psf and 1,500 psf. Despite the earlier difficulties, Air Force and North American engineers believed these two tests could adequately demonstrate seat reliability.[136]

The Air Force conducted the test at 125 psf on 4 June 1958, and the results appeared to be satisfactory. Three successful tests took place during June, but the fourth test, on 3 July, revealed serious stability problems. North American discontinued further tests until it could determine a cause for the failures. A detailed analysis revealed that the seat would need several major modifications.[137]

The ejection seat for the X-15 was a remarkable engineering achievement, and was the most sophisticated ejection seat yet developed at the time of the first X-15 flight. Still, it was much simpler than an encapsulated ejection system would have been. (U.S. Air Force)

The Air Force conducted the first test of the revised North American seat on 21 November 1958, but several of the sled rockets failed to ignite and reduced the desired 1,500-psf pressure to about 800 psf. Two tests during December also suffered from the failure of sled rockets. The only test conducted during January failed when the right-hand boom and fin failed to deploy. The leg restraints also failed during the test, but North American believed an instability caused by the boom malfunction caused this. The parachute failed to open until just before the test dummy hit the ground, causing significant damage to the dummy.[138]

The schedule was getting tight since the X-15 was nearly ready to begin captive-carry flights. On 12 January, the Aircraft Laboratory verbally approved the seat for the initial captive and glide flights between

136 Ibid.

137 X-15 WSPO Weekly Activity Report, 11 June, 11 July, 3 October 1958. The Convair "B" seat was designed by the Industry Crew Escape Committee and initially manufactured by Stanley. For a variety of reasons, the manufacturing contract was later moved to Aircraft Mechanics, Inc. The seat was used in the Convair F-106 Delta Dart, was capable of zero-zero operation (zero speed at zero altitude), and provided meaningful ejection up to 790 knots and about 60,000 feet.

138 X-15 WSPO Weekly Activity Report, 7 November 1958, 28 November 1958, 9 January 1959, and 6 February 1959.

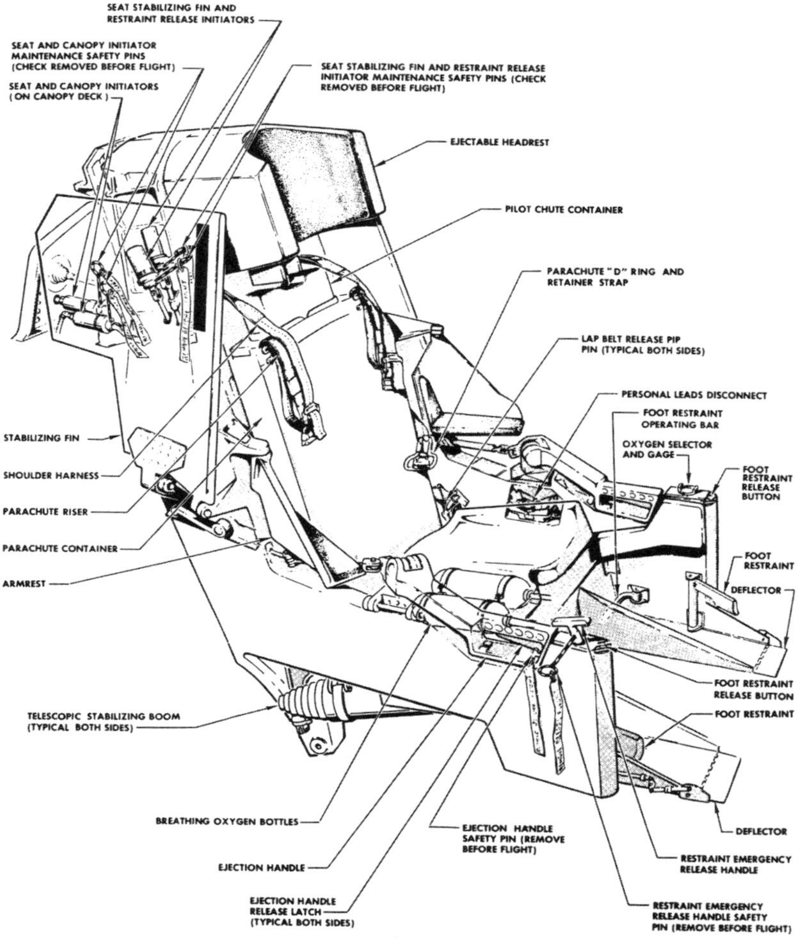

As developed by North American, the ejection seat contained provisions to restrain the pilot's arms and legs to keep them from flailing in the airstream after leaving the aircraft, and also booms and canards to stabilize the seat during separation. After the seat left the aircraft, the pilot unbuckled and jumped from the seat, coming down on his own parachute. (North American Aviation)

Mach 0.377 and Mach 0.720 at dynamic pressures between 195 and 715 psf. The X-15 Project Office considered this satisfactory given the inability of the NB-52 to go much faster.[139]

Because of the unsuccessful January test, North American carefully re-checked and strengthened the booms and pressure-tested the seat's gas system. The Air Force conducted the final sled-test on 3 March 1959 at Mach 1.15 and 1,600 psf—conditions somewhat in excess of requirements. Despite the failure of the leg manacles, the test was the most successful to date. North American pro-

139 X-15 WSPO Weekly Activity Report, 16 January 1959.

posed additional tests and a parachute program in April 1959, but the X-15 Project Office was happy with the results of the tests already run and declined. The X-15 finally had an ejection seat.[140]

The pilot used a backpack-type parachute after he separated from the seat. However, because of the design of the pressure suit, seat, and cockpit, neither the Air Force nor North American considered the standard quarter-deployment bag and 28-foot-diameter C-9 parachute acceptable. Instead, North American produced a special 24-foot-diameter chute and "skirt bag" specifically for the X-15. The company extensively tested this combination on a whirltower to verify the design of the skirt bag, the optimum pilot-parachute bridle length, and the effect of having the seat headrest permanently attached to the pilot chute. The tests in early 1958 included opening speeds up to 300 knots, and subsequent free-fall tests with an anthropomorphic dummy released from a Fairchild C-119 Flying Boxcar over the National Parachute Range in El Centro, California. During the initial tests, the C-119 released the dummy in a head-down attitude at 125 knots and 1,200 feet. These tests were unsuccessful because the pilot chute deployed into a low-pressure zone in the wake of the dummy and was not capable of pulling the main chute from the pack. North American extended the bridle length to 70 inches, allowing the pilot chute to escape the low-pressure area, and subsequent tests were successful.[141]

Initially North American used the 24-foot diameter chute because it was the largest they could easily accommodate in the backpack and the engineers thought it would open more quickly, allowing safe ejection at lower altitudes. However, several flight surgeons had concerns that it would allow too high a descent rate for the pilot, and urged the certification of a larger parachute for use on the X-15. During October 1960, North American tested a repackaged 28-foot-diameter parachute at the National Parachute Range. These tests were successful and indicated no significant difference in opening time between the smaller and larger chutes. It became policy that each pilot could select whichever size parachute he wished to use. Most continued to use the 24-foot chute because the reduced thickness of the backpack made it more comfortable to sit on in the cockpit.[142]

In June 1965, NASA authorized North American to purchase five new 28-foot parachutes to replace the 24-foot units that had reached their 7-year service limit. The new chutes had a disconnect device that allowed the pilots to release one-half of the shroud lines during descent. They were less comfortable because they were thicker than the original parachutes, but as personnel at Edwards discarded the smaller units, they became standard.[143]

Despite the confidence Scott Crossfield and the North American engineers had in the ejection seat, apparently it was not universal. Pete Knight once commented, "They tell me that the seat is good for Mach 4 and 120,000 feet. I take it with a grain of salt, but I think the safest place to be is inside the airplane until we get to a more reasonable environment.... If you had to, as a last resort certainty you would take the chance, but I think most of the pilots have felt that we...would

140 X-15 WSPO Weekly Activity Report, 13 February 1959, 13 March 1959, and 17 April 1959.

141 Hegenwald, "Development of X-15 Escape System," p. 132.

142 Minutes of Meeting, X-15 Human Factors Subcommittee, 30 December 1960.

143 X-15 Status Report, Paul F. Bikle/FRC to J. Martin/NASA Headquarters, 2 June 1965, p. 7.

The X-15 ejection seat, like all other seats of the era, was tested on the rocket sled track at Edwards AFB, California. The sled test results were mixed, with many failures of both the sled and the seat for various reasons, but ultimately the Air Force, NASA, and North American were satisfied that the seat would work as advertised. (U.S. Air Force)

stay with [the airplane] as long as possible." At least everybody agreed that the cockpit was a safe place. Crossfield demonstrated that when the X-15-3 exploded on the ground while he was testing the XLR99 engine.[144]

STABLE PLATFORM DEVELOPMENT

Another major piece of government-furnished equipment was the all-attitude inertial system, called a "stable platform" at the time. Early on, researchers realized the performance of the research airplane required a new method to determine altitude, speed, and attitude information. The original Langley study, as well as each of the contractor proposals, had suggested the use of a stable platform. Unfortunately, such as system was not readily available.

A meeting held at Wright Field on 14–15 November 1955 implied that the WADC would furnish the stable platform. Arthur Vogeley, the NACA representa-

144 Major William J. "Pete" Knight, "Increased Piloting Tasks and Performance of X-15A-2 in Hypersonic Flight," *The Aeronautical Journal of the Royal Aeronautical Society*, volume 72, September 1968, p. 799 (derived from a lecture given to the Test Pilot's Group of the Society on 30 January 1968); general thoughts confirmed with Pete Knight in a telephone conversation with Dennis R. Jenkins, 27 September 2002.

tive, assumed that the Air Force had already developed a suitable device since his report stated that a newly developed Bendix platform weighed only 28 pounds and occupied less than a cubic foot of volume. Others within the NACA and North American were not as certain. During a meeting with North American personnel, Walt Williams specifically asked who was responsible for the stable platform, and no answer was immediately forthcoming.[145]

Researchers apparently did not discuss the requirements for a stable platform until 24 May 1956 during a meeting at Langley. In attendance were representatives from Eclipse-Pioneer (a division of Bendix), the NACA, North American, and the WADC. This group discussed the platform mentioned at the November 1955 meeting, and Eclipse-Pioneer acknowledged that it was only a conceptual design and not a forthcoming product. Nevertheless, the meeting attendees thought that development of a suitable platform would take only 24 months. Since the platform provided research data in addition to flight data, the NACA agreed to charge 40 pounds of the estimated 65-pound weight against research instrumentation. There was no mention as to why the original 28-pound estimate had grown to 65 pounds.[146]

Despite its early participation, Eclipse-Pioneer did not exhibit any further interest, so the Flight Control Laboratory asked the Sperry Gyroscope Company if it was interested. By August 1956, Sperry had prepared a preliminary proposal, and on 4 October the X-15 Project Office held a technical briefing for Sperry at Wright Field.[147]

On 26 December 1956, the Flight Control Laboratory began the process to procure eight inertial flight data systems (six "Type A" units for the X-15 and two "Type B" units for ground research). The laboratory recommended awarding the $1,030,000 contract to the Sperry Gyroscope Company.[148]

For unexplained reasons, the Air Materiel Command did not take immediate action and did not release a formal request for proposal to Sperry until 6 February 1957. Two weeks later Sperry replied, and the Flight Control Laboratory approved the technical aspects of the proposal on 28 March. In the meantime, however, a controversy had developed over contracting details. The negotiations reached a deadlock on 11 April 1957 and the Air Materiel Command informed the X-15 Project Office that it intended to find another contractor. The Flight Control Laboratory and X-15 Project Office argued that Sperry was the only company that stood a chance of meeting the X-15 flight schedule, but procurements were the domain of the Air Materiel Command and the warnings fell on deaf ears.[149]

It was evident that the issue was rapidly exhausting the patience of all concerned. On 22 April 1957, the director of development at the WADC, Brigadier

145 Memorandum, Arthur W. Vogeley to Hartley A. Soulé/Research Airplane Project Leader, no subject, 30 November 1955; memorandum, Walter C. Williams to Hartley A. Soulé/Research Airplane Project Leader, no subject, 27 January 1956. In the files at the NASA History Office.

146 Memorandum, Hartley A. Soulé/Research Airplane Project Leader to Members of the NACA Research Airplane Project Panel, no subject, 7 June 1956. In the files at the NASA History Office.

147 Proposal number A. E. 1752, "Development of Flight Research Stabilized Platform," Sperry Gyroscope Co. August 1956; Memorandum, Hartley A. Soulé/Research Airplane Project Leader to Members of the NACA Research Airplane Project Panel, 15 November 1956. In the files at the NASA History Office.

148 Memorandum, M. L. Lipscomb, Instrumentation Branch, Flight Control Laboratory, WADC, to Chief, Accessories Development Section, Accessories Branch, Aerospace Equipment Division, AMC, no subject, 26 December 1956.

149 Letter, H. L. Kimball, Chief, Accessories Development Section, Accessories Branch, Aerospace Equipment Division, AMC, to Sperry Gyroscope Company, no subject, 6 February 1957; negotiation summary, C. E. Deardorff, Accessories Development Section, Accessories Branch, Aerospace Equipment Division, AMC, 25 April 1956.

General Victor R. Haugen, informed the Air Materiel Command that Sperry was the only company capable of developing the stable platform within the schedule constraints of the X-15 program. Having a general officer intervene was apparently the answer, and a cost-plus-fixed-fee contract signed on 5 June 1957 provided $1,213,518.06 with an $85,000 fee.[150]

Because of the contracting delays, the expected December 1958 delivery of the initial Sperry unit would not support the first flight of the X-15. This was not a significant problem since the initial X-15 flights would be low and slow enough to use a standard NACA flight test boom to provide the data ultimately supplied by the stable platform and ball nose. In fact, the NACA would likely have used the flight test boom even if the other instruments had been available, since it provided a known, calibrated source for acquiring initial air data. Most experimental aircraft use similar booms during early testing.[151]

More disturbing, however, was that it quickly became apparent that the weight of the stable platform had been seriously underestimated. In May 1958, Sperry undertook a weight-reduction program that, unfortunately, was particularly unsuccessful. By August, Sperry was reporting that the weight was approximately twice the original specification.[152]

It was just the beginning of serious trouble. By June 1958, the estimated cost was up to $2,741,375 with a $105,000 fee. Less than a year later the cost reached $3,234,188.87 with an $119,888 fee, mostly due to efforts to reduce the weight of the stable platform.[153]

The Air Materiel Command asked Sperry for additional data on their weight-reduction exercise on 7 August 1958. Sperry replied that with a shock mount capable of meeting the vibration specification, the system weighed 185.25 pounds. An alternate shock mount that did not meet the requirements but was probably acceptable brought the weight down to 165.25 pounds. Interestingly, Sperry admitted it had known about the weight problem for some time, but did not explain why it had not brought the issue to the government's attention at an earlier date.[154]

Sperry defended its actions by listing the changes it had made to eliminate excess weight. These included substituting aluminum for stainless steel in some locations, reducing the thickness of various covers, and reducing component weight wherever practical. The need to include power supplies not anticipated in the original proposal also increased the weight of the system. Finally, Sperry also concluded that the stable platform was lighter and more accurate than any com-

---

150 Memorandum, Brigadier General Victor R. Haugen, WADC, to Chief, Aerospace Equipment Division, Director of Procurement and Production, AMC, subject: Flight Data System for the X-15, 22 April 1957; purchase request DE-7-S-4184. In the files at the AFMC History Office; Contract AF33(600)-35397, 5 June 1957. In the files at the Air Force Historical Research Agency.

151 X-15 WSPO Weekly Activity Report, 2 May 1958.

152 Memorandum, W. W. Bailey, Programming Branch, Flight Control Laboratory, WADC and Captain Chester E. McCollough, Jr., Assistant Chief, X-15 WSPO, to Chief, Flight Data Section, Accessories Branch, Aerospace Equipment Division, AMC, no subject, 5 August 1958.

153 Supplemental Agreements 1 through 10, Contract AF33(600)-35397, 5 June 1957 and subsequent. In the files at the ASC History Office.

154 Memorandum, W. W. Bailey, Programming Branch, Flight Control Laboratory, WADC and Captain Chester E. McCollough, Jr., Assistant Chief, X-15 WSPO, to Chief, Flight Data Section, Accessories Branch, Aerospace Equipment Division, AMC, no subject, 5 August 1958. In the files at the AFMC History Office; letter, J. J. Slamer, Deputy Chief, Flight Data Section, Accessories Branch, Aerospace Equipment Division, AMC, to AFPR, Sperry Rand Corporation, subject: Letter Contract AF33(600)-35397, 7 August 1958. In the files at the Air Force Historical Research Agency.

peting system. Apparently, Sperry's justification was satisfactory since the X-15 Project Office accepted that the system was going to remain overweight and took no further action on the subject.[155]

As finally delivered, the stable platform was an Earth-slaved, Schuler-tuned system aligned in azimuth to a guidance vector coincident with X-15 centerline. The unit provided attitude, velocity, and altitude to the pilot with reference to these coordinate systems. There were three major components to the stable platform: the stabilizer, computer, and displays. Together they weighed approximately 165 pounds, occupied about 3 cubic feet of volume, and required a peak electrical load of 600 W. The stabilizer used three self-balancing accelerometers and three single-degree-of-freedom gyroscopes. A four-gimbal system provided complete attitude freedom in all axes. An analog computer computed velocity and position data, and applied the necessary acceleration corrections. The computer was shock-mounted and shaped to conform to the contours of the X-15 instrumentation compartment. Gaseous nitrogen from the X-15 cooled the stabilizer and computer to counteract the internal heat generated by the units, and the extreme external temperatures. The system was "designed to operate over a limited portion of the Earth's surface." Specifically, it could accept a launch point anywhere within a 275-mile-wide corridor extending 620 miles uprange and 205 miles downrange from Edwards AFB.[156]

Sperry shipped the first stabilizer and computer to Edwards in late January 1959, and the Air Force intended to use the NB-52 carrier aircraft as a test vehicle. This was delayed for unknown reasons, so the Air Force made a KC-97 that was already being used for similar purposes by the Convair B-58 program available to the X-15 project. The first flights in the KC-97 took place in late April, but were of limited value given the low speed of the piston-powered Stratocruiser. In June 1959, North American successfully installed the Sperry system in X-15-3 prior to its delivery to Edwards. By the end of May 1960, there were four complete stable platforms at Edwards: one in X-15-1, one in X-15-3, one spare, and one undergoing repair.[157]

---

155 Letter, G. W. Schleich, Aerospace Equipment Division, Sperry Gyroscope Company, to Commander, AMC, subject: Contract AF33(600)-35397, 4 September 1958. In the files at the Air Force Historical Research Agency.

156 M. L. Lipscomb and John A. Dodgen, "All-Attitude Flight-Date System for the X-15 Research Airplane," a paper in the *1958 Research Airplane Committee Report*, p. 161; Jay V. Christensen and John A. Dodgen, "Flight Experience with X-15 Inertial Data System," a paper in the *1958 Research Airplane Committee Report*, p. 204. Quote from the 1958 paper; Jack Fischel and Lannie D. Webb, NASA technical note D-2407, "Flight-Informational Sensors, Display, and Space Control of the X-15 Airplane for Atmospheric and Near-Space Flight Missions," August 1964, p. 5; Kenneth C. Sanderson, NASA technical memorandum X-56000, "The X-15 Flight Test Instrumentation," 21 April 1964, pp. 10-11. The 1965 flight manual says that the corridor was 240 miles wide and 720 miles long. This probably represents the design for the improved FRC-66 or IFDS system, although the documentation is unclear.

157 NASA technical note D-2407, p. 5; X-15 WSPO Weekly Activity Report, 23 January, 13 March, and 1 May 1959; interview, Lieutenant Ronald L. Panton, X-15 WSPO Director of Systems Management, ARDC, 1 June 1959, by Robert S. Houston, History Branch, WADC. Written transcript in the files at the Air Force Museum archives; James E. Love, "History and Development of the X-15 Research Aircraft," not dated, p. 20. In the files at the DFRC History Office; X-15 Status Report, Paul F. Bikle/FRC to H. Brown/NASA Headquarters, 15 May 1960, p. 7. In the files at the DFRC History Office.

As delivered, the stable platforms could provide the following data:[158]

Measurement	Range	Accuracy (rms)	Display	Record
Pitch angle (degrees)	unlimited	0.5	√	√
Roll angle (degrees)	unlimited	0.5	√	√
Yaw angle (degrees)	unlimited	0.5	√	√
Altitude (feet)	0–500,000	5,000	√	
Total velocity (fps)	±7,000	70		√
Downrange velocity (fps)	±7,000	50	√	
Crossrange velocity (fps)	±3,000	50		√
Vertical velocity (fps)	±5,000	20	√	

However, Sperry had made several compromises during the development of the X-15 stable platform, either to meet schedule or reduce weight. The designers knew that 300 seconds after launch (i.e., as the airplane decelerated to land) the pressure instruments would be adequate for vehicle altitude and velocity data, and that a system capable of operating from carrier aircraft takeoff to X-15 landing would be too heavy and bulky for the X-15. The final design had a very limited operating duration. The pilot aligned the system just before the X-15 separated from the NB-52, and the stable platform provided just 300 seconds of velocity and altitude data, along with 20 minutes of attitude data. This limited operating duration provided some relief for the weight problem.[159]

As it turned out, the lighter shock mount developed by Sperry was not adequate for the X-15. It performed fine during the XLR11 flights, but vibration tests in October 1960 prior to the beginning of XLR99 tests showed that the mount would not withstand more than 1.5 g at 110 cycles. North American redesigned the mount, since by this time saving weight had become a non-issue for the most part; having a reliable airplane was worth more than the few miles per hour the weight cost.

Over the course of the flight program, the stable platform was the subject of several other changes that greatly improved its reliability. Many of these were the result of suggestions from John Hursh at the MIT Instrumentation Laboratory and Dr. Allen Smith from Ames, both of whom spent a great deal of time at the Flight Research Center during late 1960 working on the problems. As an example of these changes, NASA changed all critical germanium transistor amplifiers to silicon during November 1960. NASA also made changes to operating procedures as well as to hardware. Initially, a gyroscope failure required that the entire stable platform be returned to Sperry for repair, taking the unit off flight status for three to six weeks. In response, the FRC developed an in-house repair capability that significantly shortened turnaround times. Even better, during late 1960 NASA

158 Lipscomb and Dodgen, "All-Attitude Flight-Date System for the X-15 Research Airplane," p. 159; Christensen and Dodgen, "Flight Experience with X-15 Inertial Data System," pp. 203 and 209.

159 Christensen and Dodgen, "Flight Experience with X-15 Inertial Data System," pp. 203-204.

The X-15 was one of the first aircraft to require what is today called an inertial measurement unit, or stable-platform. Gyroscopes of the era were large, heavy, and consumed a considerable amount of power. This model shows the three interlocked rings required to determine position in three dimensions. (NASA)

substituted a higher-quality gyroscope manufactured by Minneapolis-Honeywell, which resulted in fewer failures.[160]

In retrospect, the performance specifications established in 1956 were well beyond the state of the art with respect to available gyros, accelerometers, transistors, and circuit techniques. However, the system as originally built was able to perform at levels that, although marginal or subpar compared to the original specification, still allowed the X-15 to realize its full performance capabilities. Compared to modern laser-ring-gyro and GPS-augmented systems, the X-15 stable platform was woefully inaccurate, but it routinely bettered its 70-fps error specification for velocity. Initially its altitude-measuring ability was somewhat substandard, averaging about 2,200 feet (rms) uncertainty. The requirement was 2,000 feet, but the system eventually improved and met its specification. Reliability was initially poor, but by mid-1961 the overall reliability was approaching the high 90th percentile, with the altimeter function proving to be the most unreliable. Unfortunately, this improved reliability proved to be short-lived.[161]

The initial operational experience with the stable platform showed that it had a large error potential that grew as time passed from the initial alignment due to drift and integration noise. The unit integrated velocities to provide distance (X, Y, and Z) and specifically altitude, which had even more error buildup with time.

---

160 Ibid, pp. 204-207; X-15 Status Reports, Paul F. Bikle/FRC to H. Brown/NASA Headquarters, 1 November and 15 November 1960. In the files at the DFRC History Office. Sperry provided spares and support under contract AF33(600)-35397.

161 Christensen and Dodgen, "Flight Experience with X-15 Inertial Data System," pp. 209-213.

Early flight tests showed that the displayed velocities were marginal even after the 90-second engine burn, and that the altitude was undependable for determining peak altitude or reentry setup. Because of this, the flight planners and pilots began to consider two other sources for controlling the energy imparted to the airplane: 1) engine burn time, as measured by a stopwatch in the NASA-1 control room, and 2) radar-measured velocity, as displayed in the control room.[162]

For the first government flight (2-13-26) with the XLR99 engine, the flight planners decided to use radar velocity as the primary indication with a radio call to Bob White at the desired engine shutdown condition. After the successful flight, researchers calculated that the airplane had exceeded the intended speed by about half a Mach number. Further analysis showed that the radar velocity display in the control room incorporated considerable smoothing of the data to provide a readable output. This introduced a lag of 4 seconds between the actual speed and the displayed speed, thus accounting for the overshoot. For the next few flights, NASA-1 started a stopwatch in the control room at the indication of chamber pressure on the telemetry, and radioed the pilot when it was time to shut down the engine.[163]

Using a stopwatch to measure powered flight time proved to be the simplest and yet most accurate method of controlling energy, so a stopwatch was installed in the cockpit of all three airplanes. A signal from the main propellant valves started and stopped the stopwatch so that it displayed the total burn time even after shutdown. The pilot could then assess whether he had more or less energy than planned, and evaluate his energy condition and best emergency lake in the event of a premature shutdown. Although the reliability of the stable platform increased considerably during the course of the program and was eventually operating within its design specifications, the pilots continued to use the stopwatch (with a backup stopwatch in the control room) for most flights. It was cheap and easy, and almost never failed.[164]

By 1963 an increasing number of stable platform failures began to occur—some because of design deficiencies, others simply due to component deterioration. This led to NASA placing a new set of restrictions on X-15 flights, keeping them below 160,000 feet. Progress by Sperry to resolve the issues was slow, so an analysis was undertaken at the FRC to determine what in-house efforts could be made to bolster system performance and improve reliability.[165]

Beginning in late 1963, the FRC began redesigning critical components to improve both accuracy and reliability. Eventually, NASA engineers redesigned some 60% of the subassemblies in the stable platform. Overall, the volume used by the accelerometers, accelerometer electronics, and power supplies was reduced over 50%, and an accompanying reduction in power and cooling requirements was also realized. Although some of the improvements resulted from correcting deficiencies in the original design, most were achieved because the state of the art had improved considerably in the four years since work had begun. NASA

162 Letter, Robert G. Hoey to Dennis R. Jenkins, 20 May 2002.

163 Ibid.

164 Ibid.

165 Melvin E. Burke and Robert J. Basso, "Résumé of X-15 Experience Related to Flight Guidance Research," a paper in the *Progress of the X-15 Research Airplane Program*, a compilation of the papers presented at the Flight Research Center, 7 October 1965, NASA publication SP-90, (Washington, DC: NASA, 1965), pp. 75-76.

completed the initial redesign efforts on the accelerometer loops and power supplies during the summer of 1964, and the first flight of the new components was in X-15-2 on 14 August 1964 (2-33-56). Technicians subsequently installed the revised components in X-15-3 also. This system allowed NASA to cancel the 160,000-foot altitude restriction on the airplanes.

Although the initial performance of the revised components was a little erratic, the increase in accuracy was substantial. For instance, 400 seconds into the flight the original system would have a +8,000-foot error in altitude; the revised system generally had a –1,000-foot error. (In both cases the specification required a less than –5,000-foot error; nothing on the positive side was satisfactory.) Eventually the engineers tuned the erratic performance out of the system. By May 1966, components designed at the FRC had essentially replaced the entire Sperry stable platform, and the system was redesignated the "FRC-66 Analog Inertial System."[166]

At the same time, NASA began making plans to replace the stable platform with surplus Honeywell digital inertial guidance systems from the now-canceled X-20. This inertial flight data system (IFDS) consisted of an inertial measurement unit, a coupler electronics unit, a digital computer, and a set of pilot displays. This system was even smaller and required less power and cooling than the redesigned FRC-66 analog system. In addition, the X-20 IFDS could automatically erect itself and perform an alignment cycle on the ground while the NB-52 was taxiing, and completely eliminated the need for information from the N-1 compass and APN-81 Doppler radar on the NB-52. This made it somewhat easier to pilot the carrier aircraft as the X-15 approached the launch position; the APN-81 took 90 seconds to stabilize after even a gentle turn, requiring the NB-52 pilot to think well ahead of the drop time. To improve accuracy, however, the IFDS altitude loop was synched to the NB-52 pressure altimeter until 1 minute before launch.[167]

The inertial measurement unit was a gyrostabilized, four-gimbaled platform that maintained local vertical orientation throughout the flight. The inner platform contained three pendulous accelerometers that formed an orthogonal triad. The coupler electronics unit contained the power supplies and interface equipment, and a dual-function digital computer performed all computations. NASA first checked out the digital system in X-15-1 on 15 October 1964 (1-50-79), with satisfactory results.[168]

The overall performance of the IFDS during its first 16 flight attempts was excellent, with only two failures. However, problems with the IFDS caused two attempted launches in a row (1-A-105 and 1-A-106) to abort during June 1966. After the first abort, technicians replaced a relay and fixed a loose wire, but the second flight attempt a week later ended the same way. Engineers from Autonetics (a division of North American), Honeywell, the FRC, and Wright Field began

166 James E. Love and Jack Fischel, "Status of X-15 Program," a paper in the *Progress of the X-15 Research Airplane Program*, p. 6; Burke and Basso, "Résumé of X-15 Experience Related to Flight Guidance Research," pp. 76-77 and 83; X-15 Status Reports, Paul F. Bikle/FRC to J. Martin/NASA Headquarters, 4 May and 12 July 1966. The new designation was simply the abbreviation for the Flight Research Center (FRC) and the year the work was completed (66).

167 X-15 Status Reports, Paul F. Bikle/FRC to H. Brown/NASA Headquarters, 3 April 1961, p. 10; Love and Fischel, "Status of X-15 Program," p. 6; and Burke and Basso, "Résumé of X-15 Experience Related to Flight Guidance Research," pp. 77-78 and 84.

168 Burke and Basso, "Résumé of X-15 Experience Related to Flight Guidance Research," pp. 77-78 and 84; X-15 Status Reports, Paul F. Bikle/FRC to J. Martin/NASA Headquarters, 12 January and 4 February 1965.

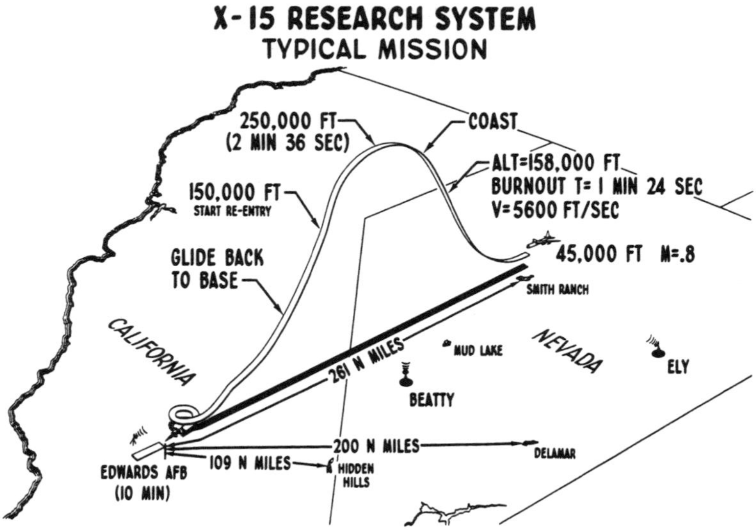

Because of limitations in both the gyroscopes and onboard computers, the X-15 stable platform could only function for a limited amount of time in a 275-mile-wide corridor extending 620 miles uprange and 205 miles downrange from Edwards AFB. Later modifications to the system were more reliable and versatile, and at the end of the program, two of the X-15s were using digital inertial flight data systems developed for the Air Force Dyna-Soar program. (NASA)

investigating the problem. The failures were determined to be the result of yet more wiring problems, all easily corrected.[169]

At the same time, the installation in X-15-3 was not going as well as it had in X-15-1. On 6 January 1965, representatives from Honeywell met with FRC personnel to discuss problems with the installation. There were four primary concerns: cooling and thermal conditions, space availability, cabling, and the interface to the MH-96 adaptive control system. This latter issue was surprising since the X-20 also used a version of the MH-96. Also discussed was the relative accuracy expected from the new system versus data from the ball nose. It was pointed out by the Honeywell representative that at low velocities there would be a significant difference between the IFDS-computed angle of sideslip and that sensed by the ball nose, but at high velocities the difference should be small.[170]

By April 1965 the FRC had made little progress installing the system in X-15-3, and only X-15-1 was flying with the Honeywell inertial system. Fortunately, by this time the modified Sperry systems were proving to be reliable, and no substantial problems had been experienced by X-15-2 or X-15-3 since December 1964. Engineers finally installed the Honeywell IFDS in X-15-3 during a weather-induced down period at the end of 1965.[171]

169 X-15 Status Report, Paul F. Bikle/FRC to J. Martin/NASA Headquarters, 12 July 1966, p. 5.

170 X-15 Status Report, Paul F. Bikle/FRC to J. Martin/NASA Headquarters, 4 February 1965, p. 6.

171 X-15 Status Reports, Paul F. Bikle/FRC to J. Martin/NASA Headquarters, 1 April 1965 and 3 January 1966.

Although the Honeywell IFDS was considered an improvement over the modified Sperry stable platform, the FRC decided that the FRC-66 system was preferred for the Mach 8 flights in the modified X-15A-2, so that airplane never received an IFDS. By the end of 1965, engineers had modified one of the Sperry computers to have Mach 8 scaling coefficients in preparation for the X-15A-2 envelope-expansion program.[172]

The improvements did not stop there. Eventually the FRC modified X-15-3 to include an Ames-developed guidance system that was applicable to future aerospace vehicles. This system coupled the IFDS inertial system, MH-96 adaptive control system, and ball nose to an Alert digital computer to investigate boost guidance command techniques. The navigation functions continued to be performed by the inertial system while the Alert computer handled the research objectives, including providing new displays to the pilot. This program allowed the pilot to fly a velocity-altitude window during boost, a bounded corridor during hypersonic cruise, and a precise corridor during reentry. It was an advanced system, and one that Space Shuttle only duplicated in its waning years.[173]

BALL NOSE DEVELOPMENT

The heating rates and low pressures encountered by the X-15 ruled out the use of traditional vane-type sensors to measure angle of attack (α) and sideslip (β). Based on a preliminary design completed by Langley in June 1956, NASA awarded a contract to the Nortronics Division of Northrop Aircraft Corporation for the detailed design and construction of a prototype and five production ball noses. The sensor and its supporting, sealing, and hydraulic-actuating mechanisms were an integral assembly mounted in the extreme nose of the X-15. The afterbody located behind the sphere contained the electronic amplifiers, power supplies, and control valves, with the electrical, hydraulic, and pneumatic connections between the sphere and the afterbody passing through a single supporting member. Rotary hydraulic actuators provided the required two degrees of freedom.[174]

Officially called the "high-temperature flow-direction sensor," the device was 16.75 inches long with a base diameter of 13.75 inches. The total weight of the ball nose was 78 pounds, half of which was contributed by the thick Inconel X

172 X-15 Status Report, Paul F. Bikle/FRC to J. Martin/NASA Headquarters, 3 January 1966, p. 3.

173 Burke and Basso, "Résumé of X-15 Experience Related to Flight Guidance Research," pp. 79-80.

174 Israel Taback and Gerald M. Truszynski, "Instrumentation for the X-15," a paper in the *1956 Research Airplane Committee Report*, pp. 183-192; memorandum, Hartley A. Soulé/Research Airplane Project Leader, subject: Project 1226—Progress report for month of May 1956, 7 June 1956; William D. Mace and Jon L. Ball, "Flight Characteristics of X-15 Hypersonic Flow-Direction Sensor," a paper in the *1961 Research Airplane Committee Report*, pp. 196-197; Nortronics report NORT-60-46, pp. 3-6. Unfortunately the copy of the report in the DFRC History Office is missing the first two pages, so the title and exact date (the "60" in the report number probably establishes 1960 as the year) could not be ascertained; Kenneth C. Sanderson, NASA technical memorandum X-56000, "The X-15 Flight Test Instrumentation," 21 April 1964, pp. 8-9. The ball nose was also known, somewhat inaccurately, as the "Q-ball"; some documentation also called it the "hot nose," "flow direction sensor," or "NACA nose." A gimbal is a device that allows a body to incline in predefined directions. In this case, the sphere could move both left–right and up–down in relation to the nose. Hydraulic servomotors (servos) provided the power to move the sphere as necessary.

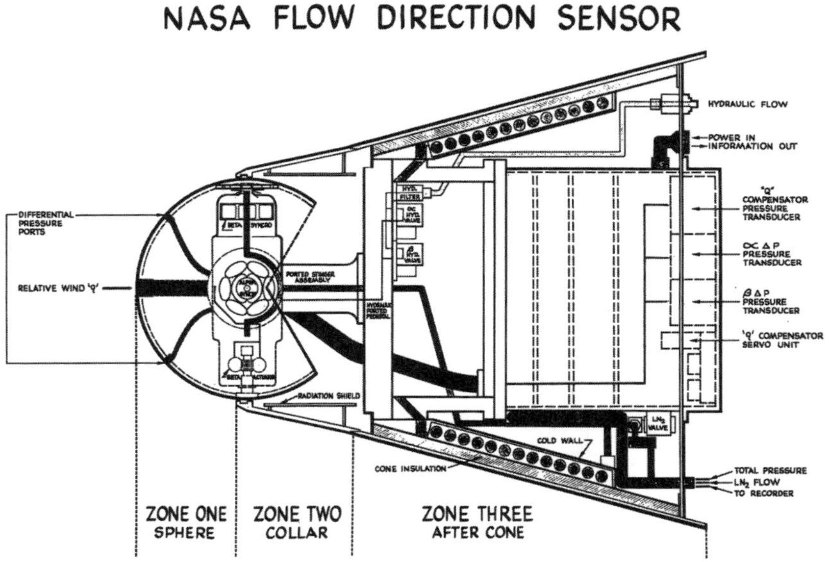

The ball nose, or more officially, the high-temperature flow-direction sensor, was mounted on the nose of the airplane and provided angle of attack and angle of sideslip information to both the pilot and the research instrumentation. This elaborate mechanism was required since the pressure and temperature environment encountered by the X-15 ruled out more conventional vane-type sensors. (NASA)

outer skins of the lip, cone, and sphere. In addition, 13 chromel-alumel thermocouples were located within the sphere to measure skin temperature during flight, and five other thermocouples measured selected internal temperatures. Nitrogen gas from the aircraft supply cooled the sensor. The ball nose was physically interchangeable with the standard NACA flight-test boom nose, and all connections to the sensor were made through couplings that automatically engaged when the ball nose (or boom) was mounted to the aircraft.[175]

The core of the ball nose consisted of a 6.5-inch-diameter Inconel X sphere mounted on the extreme tip of the X-15 nose. The sphere contained two pairs of 0.188-inch diameter orifices (one pair in the vertical plane (α orifices) and one pair in the horizontal plane (β orifices)), each 42 degrees from the stagnation point. Two functionally identical hydraulic servo systems, powered by the normal X-15 systems, rotated the sphere about the α and β axes to a position such that the impact pressures seen by all sensing orifices were equal. When this condition existed, the sphere was oriented directly into the relative wind. Two synchro transducers detected the position of the sphere with respect to the airframe, and this signal fed the various instruments in the cockpit and the recorders and telemetry system. Since the dynamic pressure during flight could vary between 1 psf and 2,500 psf, a major gain adjustment was required in the servo loop to main-

175 Mace and Ball, "Flight Characteristics of X-15 Hypersonic Flow-Direction Sensor," pp. 196-197; Nortronics report NORT-60-46, pp. 3-6.

tain stability and accuracy. Measuring the pressure difference between the total-pressure port and one angle-sensing port provided a signal that adjusted the gain of the sphere-positioning loop. The ball nose could sense angles of attack from –10 to +40 degrees, and angles of sideslip within ±20 degrees. The unit was capable of continuous operation at a skin temperature of 1,200°F. A 0.5-inch-diameter orifice located at the sphere stagnation point provided a total pressure source for the aircraft. Based on ground tests, the angular accuracy of the sensor was within ±0.25 degree for dynamic pressures above 10 psf.[176]

In early 1960 the FRC developed a simple technique for thermal testing the newly delivered ball noses: expose them to the afterburner exhaust from a North American F-100 Super Sabre. This seemed to work well until one of the noses suffered a warped forward lip during testing. Engineers subsequently determined the engine was "operated longer than necessary," resulting in temperatures in excess of 2,400°F instead of the expected 1,900°F. Ultimately, the FRC tested the ball nose "many consecutive times" with "satisfactory results."[177]

The sphere mounted on the extreme nose of the ball nose was machined from Inconel X to very precise tolerances. The X-15 was manufactured before the advent of modern computer-controlled milling machines, so such precise work was accomplished by human operators on traditional lathes and drill presses. The ball noses for the X-15A-2 were manufactured from TAZ-8A cermet since the temperatures in the Mach 8 environment were even more severe. (NASA)

The ball nose performed satisfactorily throughout the flight program, encountering only occasional minor maintenance problems. Late in the program, various parts began to wear out, however, and the need to replace some of them presented difficulties. For instance, the procurer of replacement dynamic-pressure transducers found that the original vendor was not interested in fabricating new parts, and no suitable alternate vendor could immediately be located. Eventually NASA found a new vendor, but this illustrates that the "vanishing vendor" phenomenon frequently encountered during the early 21st century is not new.[178]

As the modified X-15A-2 was being prepared for flight, however, there began a concern over whether the Inconel X sphere in the original ball noses could handle

176 Jack Fischel and Lannie D. Webb, NASA technical note D-2407, "Flight-Informational Sensors, Display, and Space Control of the X-15 Airplane for Atmospheric and Near-Space Flight Missions," August 1964, p. 5; Nortronics report NORT-60-46, pp. 3-10.

177 X-15 Status Report, Paul F. Bikle/FRC to H. Brown/NASA Headquarters, 15 May 1960, p. 8; X-15 Status Report, Paul F. Bikle/FRC to H. Brown/NASA Headquarters, 1 June 1960, p. 10.

178 "X-15 Semi-Annual Status Report No. 6," 1 November 1966, p. 15.

The ball nose had to withstand pressures up to 2,500 psf and temperatures up to 1,200°F. NASA researchers developed a relatively straight-forward heating test using the afterburned exhaust of a jet engine on the ramp at the Flight Research Center. The original ball noses were tested using Pratt & Whitney J57 engines from North American F-100 Super Sabres, while the later X-15A-2 noses used General Electric J79 engines from Lockheed F-104 Starfighters. (NASA)

the additional heat generated at Mach 8. Researchers at NASA Lewis developed a TAZ-8A cermet that Rohr Corporation used to manufacture a new sphere specifically for the X-15A-2. This sphere was delivered in mid-1966, but did not initially pass its qualification test due to a faulty braze around the beta pressure port. Rohr subsequently repaired the sphere and it passed its qualification test. Interestingly, the FRC tested this new sphere (and the forward lip of the cone, which was also manufactured from TAZ-8A) in much the same way as the original ball noses were qualified—this time in the afterburner exhaust of a General Electric J79 engine at 1,850°F. During November 1966, the FRC tested the new sphere, as well as a slightly modified housing necessary to accommodate the ablative coating on the fuselage, in the High-Temperature Loads Calibration Laboratory. NASA installed the new nose on X-15A-2 to support flight 2-52-96 on 21 August 1967.[179]

The ball nose only provided angle of attack, angle of sideslip, and total pressure; like all aircraft, the X-15 needed additional air data during the landing phase.

179 "X-15 Semi-Annual Status Report No. 6," 1 November 1966, p. 15; X-15 Status Report, Paul F. Bikle/FRC to J. Martin/NASA Headquarters, 5 May 1967, p. 10; telephone conversation, Rodney K. Bogue/DFRC with Dennis R. Jenkins, 6 June 2002. The status report says that the new nose was tested in the exhaust of a Lockheed F-104 Starfighter, but photographic evidence shows it was just a J79 engine (probably from an F-104) on the test stand.

North American had installed a total-head tube (also called the alternate probe) ahead of the canopy to provide the total pressure during subsonic flight, and static pressure ports were located on each side of the fuselage 1 inch above the aircraft waterline at station 50.[180]

A different pitot-static system was required for the X-15A-2 since the MA-25S ablator would cover the normal static locations. Engineers chose a vented compartment behind the canopy as the static source, and found it to be suitable during flight tests on the X-15-1. The standard dogleg pitot tube ahead of the canopy was replaced by an extendable pitot because the temperatures expected at Mach 8 would exceed the thermal limits of the standard tube. The retractable tube remained within the fuselage until the aircraft decelerated below Mach 2; the pilot then actuated a release mechanism and the tube extended into the airstream. This was very similar in concept to the system eventually installed on the space shuttle orbiters.[181]

FLIGHT CONTROL SYSTEMS

One of the unique items included in the X-15 design was a side-stick controller. Actually, the airplane included two side sticks: one on the right console for the aerodynamic controls, and one on the left console for the ballistic controls. The right and center controllers were linked mechanically and hydraulically to provide simultaneous movement of both sticks; however, the side stick required only one-third as much movement to obtain a given stabilizer motion.[182]

NASA had installed a similar side stick in one of the North American YF-107A aircraft to gain experience with the new controller. A review of early X-15 landing data (using the side-stick) revealed a "striking similarity" with landings made in the YF-107. Despite large differences in speed and L/D ratios, the variations in angle of attack, normal acceleration, pitching velocity, and horizontal stabilizer position exhibited the same tendencies for the pilot to over-control the airplane using the side stick. During the YF-107 program, several flights were generally required before a pilot became proficient at using the controller and could perform relatively smooth landings; the same was true of the X-15.[183]

Regarding the side-stick controller, Bob White commented that "the side aerodynamic control stick designed for the X-15 has received the usual critical analysis associated with a departure from the conventional." As pilots reported their experiences using the side stick, North American began making minor modi-

---

180 "Advanced Development Plan for X-15 Research Aircraft, Advanced Technology Program 653A," 17 November 1961, pp. 43-44. In the files at the AFFTC History Office.

181 Johnny G. Armstrong, AFFTC technology document FTC-TD-69-4, "Flight Planning and Conduct of the X-15A-2 Envelope Expansion Program," July 1969, p. 26; X-15 Status Report, Paul F. Bikle/FRC to J. Martin/NASA Headquarters, 12 July 1966, p. 9. In the files at the DFRC History Office.

182 Gene J. Matranga, "Analysis of X-15 Landing Approach and Flare Characteristics Determined from the First 30 Flights," NASA technical note D-1057, July 1961, pp. 4-5.

183 X-15 Status Report, Paul F. Bikle/FRC to H. Brown/NASA Headquarters, 15 August 1960, p. 3. In the files at the DFRC History Office

fications to correct undesirable characteristics. In the end, the company found that most of the initial design features were satisfactory. The most frequent complaint was the location of the stick in relation to the pilot's arm, since the stick had been located based on Scott Crossfield's input, and other pilots differed in size and proportions. However, Crossfield was a strong proponent of the side stick and North American soon devised a way to adjust the stick into one of five different fore-aft locations prior to flight based on individual pilot preference. After this, the side stick gained favor rather quickly.[184]

The all-moving horizontal stabilizers deflected symmetrically for longitudinal control (elevators) and differentially for lateral control (ailerons). The rolling tail that had caused so much controversy within the government early in the program proved to be quite satisfactory in operation. According to Bob White, "the pilot is not aware of what specific type of lateral control is allowing the roll motion. His only concern is in being able to get the aircraft response he calls for when deflecting the control stick.... From experience to date [after 45 flights], the rolling tail has provided a good rolling control for the X-15, and there have been no undesirable aircraft motions coupled in any axis because of lateral-control deflection."[185]

Conventional rudder pedals actuated the movable portions of the dorsal and ventral vertical stabilizers. Just prior to the landing flare, the pilot would jettison the lower portion of the dorsal stabilizer to provide sufficient ground clearance; otherwise, the dorsal rudder would contact the ground before the landing skids. Speed brakes were located on each side of the fixed portion of the dorsal and ventral stabilizers. Irreversible hydraulic actuators actuated all of the aerodynamic control surfaces.[186]

The aerodynamic controls were effective up to about 150,000 feet. Nevertheless, many X-15 pilots manually used the ballistic control system in addition to the aerodynamic controls above 100,000 feet, and the MH-96 on X-15-3 automatically began blending in the ballistic control system thrusters above 90,000 feet. As Neil Armstrong, who was a principle engineer on the MH-96, commented, "a rule of thumb is that when dynamic pressure on control surfaces reduces to 50 psf, there should be a switchover from aerodynamic to reaction control." Despite some early concerns about controlling a vehicle above the sensible atmosphere, in practice it quickly became routine.[187]

The Westinghouse-manufactured stability augmentation system (SAS) dampened the aerodynamic controls in all three axes. The system consisted of three rate gyros, two pitch-roll servocylinders, one yaw servocylinder, and various electronics, displays, and controls. Essentially, the system included a channel for each axis that sensed the aircraft rate of change in pitch, roll, and yaw, and automati-

---

184 Major Robert M. White, Glenn H. Robinson, and Gene J. Matranga, "Résumé of X-15 Handling Qualities," a paper in the *1961 Research Airplane Committee Report*, p. 120; telephone conversation, Alvin S. White with Dennis R. Jenkins, 13 June 2002.

185 White et al., "Résumé of X-15 Handling Qualities," p. 132.

186 Gene J. Matranga, "Analysis of X-15 Landing Approach and Flare Characteristics Determined from the First 30 Flights," NASA technical note D-1057, July 1961, pp. 4-5; Lawrence W. Taylor, Jr., and George B. Merrick, "X-15 Augmentation System;" White et al., "Résumé of X-15 Handling Qualities," pp. 118-119.

187 Interview with Neil A. Armstrong and James E. Love by Scholer Bangs, "X-15 pilot evaluates hydraulic system performance," *Hydraulics & Pneumatics*, December 1962, pp. 82-84.

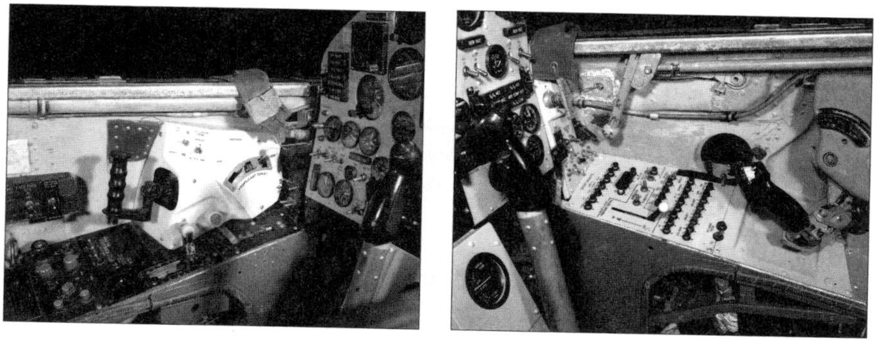

North American incorporated two side-stick controllers in the X-15 cockpit. The controller on the right console operated the aerodynamic flight control systems while the controller on the left operated the ballistic control system thrusters. The aerodynamic controller was mechanically linked to the conventional center stick. In X-15-3, the MH-96 adaptive flight control system automatically blended the ballistic thrusters in when needed, eliminating the need for the pilot to use the left side-controller. (NASA)

cally provided signals to the respective servocylinders to move the horizontal and vertical stabilizers to oppose the airplane angular inputs. An additional interconnect damper, called "yar," provided a crossfeed of the yaw-rate signal to the roll damper. This interconnection was necessary for stability at high angles of attack, primarily because of the high roll input of the lower rudder. The yar interconnect was disabled when the lower rudder was removed during later flights. The authority of the SAS was equal to the pilot's authority in pitch and yaw, and to twice the pilot's authority in roll. The pilot could turn dampening on or off for each individual axis, and select the damping gain for each axis. Originally, the SAS gyro package was located in the instrument compartment behind the pilot. However, a vibration at high gains reported by Scott Crossfield during the first X-15 captive flight resulted in North American moving the gyros to the center of gravity compartment under the wings, thus removing the gyro from a point influenced by fuselage bending.[188]

The SAS caused numerous pilot comments. During early flights below Mach 3.5, the dampers used moderate gains and the pilots quickly expressed a desire for "a stiffer aircraft," particularly in pitch and roll. North American subsequently increased the gain, resulting in generally favorable pilot opinions. It is interesting to note that at angles of attack above 8 degrees with low damper gain or with the roll damper off, pilots had great difficulty in controlling the lateral and directional motions to prevent divergence. This was primarily because of an adverse dihedral effect that was present above Mach 2.3. Although this was of some concern to the pilots, and the subject of a great deal of investigation by the researchers, the airplane exhibited acceptable handling characteristics as long as the dampers were functioning. In general, the airplane exhibited about the same handling qualities expected based on extensive simulations at Ames, and the pilots thought

188 Robert A. Tremant, "Operational Experiences and Characteristics of the X-15 Flight Control System," NASA technical note D-1402, December 1962, pp. 5 and 10; Euclid C. Holleman, "Summary of High-Altitude and Entry Flight Control Experience With the X-15 Airplane," a proposed technical memorandum, 23 December 1965, p. 3. Typescript available in the AFFTC Access to Space Office Project Files.

the damper-off handling was slightly better than the simulator predicted, but still considered the natural stability to be marginal.[189]

The SAS was unique for the time because it provided 10 pilot-selectable gain rates for each axis. However, the system experienced some annoying problems during development and early operations. During the first studies using the fixed-base simulator, the dampers sustained unwanted limit cycles (or continuous oscillations) from linkage lags and rate limiting. Pilots later observed the phenomenon in flight. The frequency of the limit cycle was about 3.2 cycles per second, resulting in changes in bank angle of about 1 degree. This limit cycle was not constant, changed due to control input, and had a tendency to "beat." North American was unable to identify a way to eliminate the limit cycles, but modified the electronic filter to reduce its lag. This greatly lowered the amplitude of the limit cycles, and the pilots found the results acceptable.[190]

Although the modified filter greatly improved the issue with the limit cycles in roll, a new problem soon arose. It became apparent during ground tests that it was possible to excite and sustain a SAS-airplane vibration at 13 cycles per second with the modified filter. A breadboard of the modified filter was flown (flight

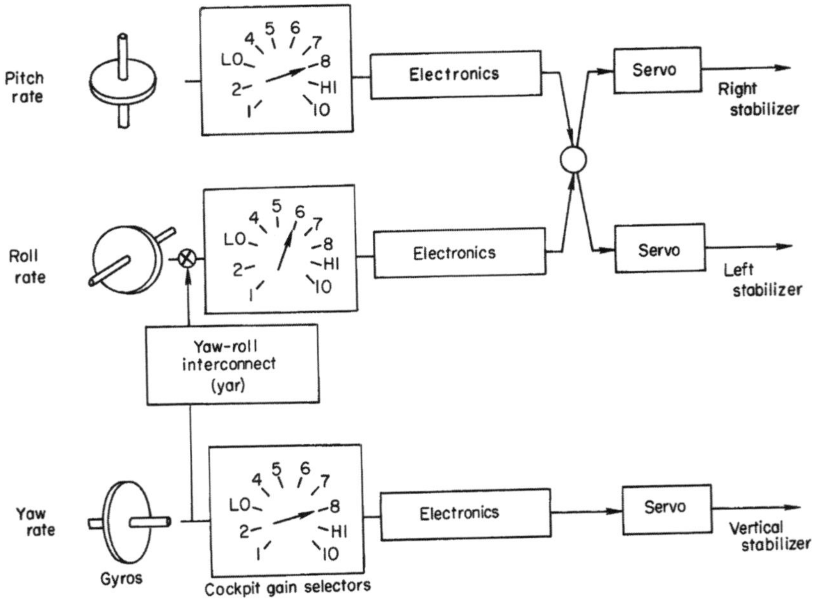

The X-15 made extensive use of a stability augmentation system to dampen the aerodynamic controls in all three axes. The SAS was unique for the time since it provided ten pilot-selectable gain rates for each axis via rotary switches in the cockpit. Flight simulations showed that it would be nearly impossible for a pilot to control the X-15 in some flight regimes without the SAS. (NASA)

189 White et al., "Résumé of X-15 Handling Qualities," pp. 118-119.

190 Taylor and Merrick, "X-15 Augmentation System," pp. 173-174.

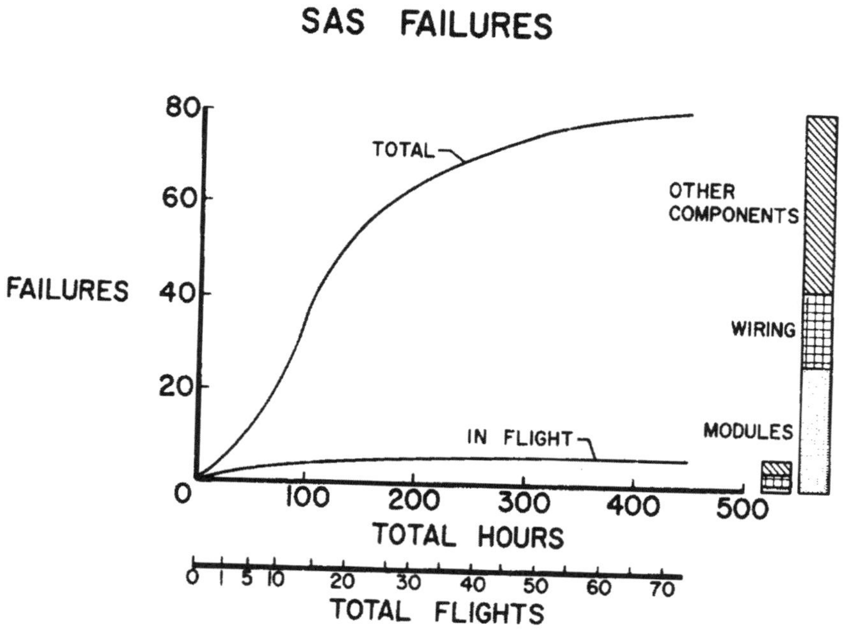

Failures of the stability augmentation system contributed to the maintenance woes suffered by the X-15 early in the flight program, but oddly, most of the failures were on the ground; the system seldom failed in flight. Nevertheless, an auxiliary stability augmentation system was added to the first two airplanes as insurance against an SAS failure. The X-15-3 did not carry an SAS or ASAS since the mH-96 adaptive flight control system performed both functions. (NASA)

2-12-23) at higher damper gains, but Scott Crossfield failed to excite the vibration. During the rollout after landing, however, Crossfield encountered a severe vibration that required disabling the SAS. This experience led to the mistaken belief that the vibration could only occur on the ground. To prevent a recurrence, North American installed a switch that automatically lowered the gain whenever the pilot extended the landing gear. However, five flights later (2-14-28), Joe Walker encountered a 13-cps vibration during reentry from 169,600 feet. After the flight, Walker reported that the vibration was the most severe he had ever encountered (or ever wanted to). The shaking was triggered by pilot inputs at 130 psf dynamic pressure and continued until the damper gain was reduced and the dynamic pressure climbed above 1,000 psf. Fortunately, the amplitude of the shaking was constrained by the rate limits of the control surface actuators. North American and NASA began investigating the problem again.[191]

The problem was that the lightly damped horizontal stabilizers were excited at their natural frequency (13 cps) by pilot inputs to the control system. The gyro

191 Joseph A. Walker, "Pilot Report for Flight 2-14-28," 3 April 1961; Taylor and Merrick, "X-15 Augmentation System," pp. 173-174.

picked up this vibration and the dampers were able to sustain the vibration with input to the control surfaces. Engineers also found a second natural frequency for the stabilizers at 30 cps. North American subsequently installed notch filters in the SAS and pressure feedback valves in the control surface actuators, eliminating the vibrations.[192]

The SAS proved to be unreliable in the beginning, but fortunately most failures occurred during ground testing. The program recorded only seven in-flight failures during the first 78 flights (defined as NB-52 takeoff to X-15 landing). Of these failures, one was an electronic module, three were malfunctioning cockpit gain switches, and three were broken wires in the X-15. Engineers ultimately traced all except the failed electronics module to human error.[193]

LANDING GEAR EVOLUTION

The X-15 landing gear was somewhat unusual, both in its approach and in its simplicity. The system consisted of a dual nose wheel and a pair of aft skids. Initially the cast magnesium nose wheels were fitted with standard aircraft tires pressurized with 240-psi nitrogen. The skids consisted of a 4130-steel skid and an Inconel X strut that was attached to the fuselage by trunnion fittings and through bell crank arms that were attached to shock struts inside the aft fuselage. The skids were free in pitch and roll, but fixed in yaw for parallel alignment. Drag braces attached to the fuselage ahead of the trunnion fittings and to the skids at the strut attachment pin. Bungee springs kept the skid in a nose-up position just before landing. Instead of retracting inside the fuselage, the skids and struts folded forward against the outside of the fuselage when retracted. The pilot lowered the landing gear by pulling a handle in the cockpit that attached via cable to the up-lock hooks and released the gear. North American designed the landing gear for an 11,000-pound airplane with a sink rate of 9 fps, touching down between 190 and 230 mph at an angle of attack of approximately 6 degrees.[194]

Three major test series of the landing-gear system were conducted prior to the first glide flights: 1) a dynamic-model test of stability during the landing run, 2) nose-wheel shimmy tests using the actual nose gear, and 3) full-scale skid tests at the lake-bed landing site.[195]

North American used the model tests to investigate the stability of the tricycle arrangement. Engineers constructed a 1/10-scale model that accurately reflected the size, weight, and mass moments of inertia for yaw and roll, but did

192 Taylor and Merrick, "X-15 Augmentation System," pp. 174-175.

193 Ibid, pp. 172-173.

194 James M. McKay and Eldon E. Kordes, "Landing Loads and Dynamics of the X-15 Airplane," a paper in the *1961 Research Airplane Committee Report*, pp. 61-62; Schleicher, "Structural Design of the X-15," pp. 11 and 33. It should be noted that the main gear touched down at roughly 9 fps; by the time the large moment arm was factored in, the nose gear touched down at 18 fps, providing a somewhat jarring landing (about 3.9-g vertical) for the pilots.

195 L. L. Rhodes, "Landing-Gear Design and Development Testing for the X-15 Airplane," a paper in the *1958 Research Airplane Committee Report*, pp. 314-316.

not simulate the aerodynamic characteristics of the X-15. Scale-size metal skids were manufactured so that they could be installed in either the original mid-fuselage location proposed by North American, or the aft fuselage location eventually built. North American catapulted the model along a concrete runway using a 100-foot length of 0.625-inch-diameter shock cord. High-speed movie cameras on overhead towers recorded each run. The tests revealed some minor nose-wheel instability, which the company subsequently corrected.[196]

Researchers at Langley then tested the revised full-scale nose gear using the landing-loads track facility at speeds up to 125 mph. These tests evaluated the nose gear on smooth concrete, uneven concrete, wet pavement, sandy pavement, uneven tire pressure, one flat tire, and unbalanced wheels. Given that the X-15 was to land only on dry lake beds, some of the tests seemed extreme. Throughout the tests the co-rotating wheel arrangement proved extremely stable, with no tendency to shimmy. Researchers, therefore, concluded the shimmy damper and torque links were unnecessary and North American subsequently removed them, saving 25 pounds.[197]

North American conducted the landing-gear-skid tests on Rogers Dry Lake during April 1958. For these tests, researchers mounted the complete main gear on a two-wheel trailer vehicle and towed it behind a truck at speeds up to 70 mph. After the truck reached full speed, an electric switch actuated a bomb-release solenoid that dropped a 6,000-pound load on the skid landing gear. Instruments on the gear recorded vertical and drag loads, and shock-strut position. High-speed cameras mounted in the truck and trailer recorded the motion of the gear and skids. Test runs included straight-line landing on smooth lake surfaces, "fishtail" runs on rutted and bumpy areas near the edges of the lake, and one landing on the concrete runway just to make sure. The results of all the tests were satisfactory. Skid wear on the lake beds was light, and engineers determined that the skids would last for three or four landings. The tests revealed that the X-15 should leave depressions approximately 0.03 inch deep in the lake bed. As expected, wear on the concrete runway was severe, but the tests showed the X-15 could land on concrete if necessary.[198]

Despite all the tests, the first four actual landings pointed out several deficiencies in the landing gear, mainly because the aircraft was heavier than anticipated and sink rates were slightly higher. North American replaced the shock struts with higher-capacity units, and strengthened some of the structure inside the fuselage. The fourth landing resulted in X-15-1 breaking in half. This was not strictly a design error; Scott Crossfield had been unable to fully jettison the propellants prior to an emergency landing, and the airplane was significantly overweight. However, the landing gear contributed because the gas and oil mixture in the shock strut foamed, keeping the rear skids from absorbing as much of the impact as they should have. This forced a higher than normal load on the nose gear, aggravating the structural problem caused by being overweight.[199]

196 Ibid.

197 Ibid.

198 Ibid.

199 McKay and Kordes, "Landing Loads and Dynamics of the X-15 Airplane," pp. 61-62

The X-15 was unique, even among X-Planes, in using a landing gear consisting of rear skids and a nose wheel. The skids solved several problems for designers since they were relatively small and could be stowed mostly outside the airframe. Interestingly, the X-15 landing gear was lowered by the pilot pulling a mechanical handle that was connected to a cable that released the uplock hooks and allowed a bungee to extend the skids. A similar system would have been used on the X-20 Dyna-Soar if that program had not been cancelled. (NASA)

In addition, during some of the early landings, engineers found that the nose wheel tire marks left on the dry lake bed were not continuous. After initial contact, the tire marks became very faint or disappeared for short distance and then reappeared. This puzzled the engineers since all of the early drop tests of the landing gear had been satisfactory.[200]

The engineers became concerned that the nose-gear extension mechanism was not working properly. Normally, technicians manually retracted the nose gear after attaching the X-15 to the NB-52, and then they pumped dry nitrogen gas into the shock strut to preload it to 1,404 psi. Charlie Feltz had suggested this method as a way to minimize the size and weight of the nose gear compartment. What the engineers discovered was that upon lowering the landing gear, an orifice in the strut trapped the nitrogen gas below it and most of the shock-absorption

200 Schleicher, "Structural Design of the X-15," pp. 35-36.

oil above it. The design of the metering valve was such that it prevented a rapid change in position of the oil and nitrogen in the 10 seconds between gear extension and wheel touchdown. To better understand the problem, engineers conducted additional dynamic tests using the original test apparatus. Initial tests operated the apparatus with the nose gear serviced in the extended position, as had been done in the original tests. The performance appeared normal. The engineers then modified the test rig to allow the gear to be serviced in the retracted position, as was done on the airplane. A delay of 10 seconds was introduced between the gear being lowered and touching down, and the abnormal behavior was reproduced almost exactly.[201]

At first, engineers modified the orifice in the shock, but this failed to resolve the problem. After additional tests, the engineers determined that they could not pressurize the strut in its retracted (compressed) position. Unfortunately, the nose wheel compartment was not large enough to allow the nose gear to be retracted in its extended position. The final solution was to mount redundant nitrogen bottles on the gear strut itself. When the gear reached its fully extended position, a valve actuated and released the nitrogen to pressurize the strut. This worked and the first modified nose gears were available in July 1960. However, the engineers kept evaluating the problem and, later in the program, changed the design again. This time they installed a floating piston inside the strut that kept the oil and gas separated. Technicians could now pressurize the strut in the compressed position before flight, allowing the removal of the nitrogen bottles.[202]

During 1961, engineers instrumented the skids to gather additional data on skid landing gear in support of the Dyna-Soar program and possible future vehicles, such as the space shuttle. Standard NASA instrumentation was used to provide airplane upper-mass response, shock-strut force and displacement, main- and nose-gear drag forces, nose-gear vertical force, horizontal- and vertical-stabilizer setting, horizontal stabilizer load, airplane angle of attack, and airplane pitch velocity during the impact and slideout portion of a landing. Tests were conducted at the end of normal research flights while the pilots landed normally and performed specific control movements during slideout. Phototheodolite cameras on the ground furnished data for landing coordinates, airplane altitude, flight-path velocity, and vertical velocity at touchdown. The instrumentation remained on all three airplanes for the remainder of the flight program to monitor the severity of each landing.[203]

Landing-gear loads continued to be high, despite the minor modifications made early in the flight program. An analytical study of the landing dynamics showed that several important parameters affecting the landing loads were actually aerodynamic factors. One of the primary culprits was a down-load from the horizontal stabilizer caused by both the pilot and SAS. Immediately prior to touchdown, the stabilizer trim position was set to between 4 and 5 degrees with the leading edge down. If the pilot pulled back on the stick and put the leading edge further down, the landing loads increased. If the pilot pushed the stick forward to get the leading edge up, the loads decreased. Another factor affecting the gear loads was lift from

201 Ibid, pp. 36-37.

202 Ibid; X-15 Status Report, Paul F. Bikle/FRC to H. Brown/NASA Headquarters, 1 July 1960, p. 7. In the files at the DFRC History Office.

203 James E. Love (manager), "X-15 Program," NASA FRC, October 1961. pp. 29-30. In the AFFTC Access to Space Office Project Files.

The nose gear was more conventional, consisting of a pair of wheels and tires. Note how short the nose gear strut is, resulting in severe loads during landing. The length of the nose strut was largely dictated by the amount of room available to stow it when retracted. Space shuttle orbiters suffer from a similarly short nose gear strut. (NASA)

the wing. Unfortunately, the severe nose-down angle of the X-15 after nose-gear touchdown effectively pushed the airplane into the ground, further increasing the stress on the landing gear. Unfortunately, this was an unchangeable consequence of the airplane configuration, and a similar problem occurred on the space shuttle orbiters.[204]

The most severe problem, however, was weight. The design landing weight had been 11,000 pounds. The initial landing weight of the airplane was 13,230 pounds, and by 1965 this had crept up to 15,500 pounds on a routine basis. Emergency landings with a partial propellant load could be as high as 17,000 pounds. The only way to execute safely a landing at 17,000 pounds was for the pilot to perform an active push maneuver to obtain low horizontal stabilizer settings. This would still exceed the design load on the airplane, but would most probably be below the yield (destructive) limit.[205]

By 1965 the problem was no longer one of understanding the nature of the loads, but rather one of how best to reduce them. North American introduced a near-constant series of minor modifications to the skids, their struts, and the surrounding structure in an effort to provide additional margin for the landing gear. Of all the factors that affected gear loads, the most difficult to control—without restricting the research role of the airplane—was weight. Engineers determined they could reduce landing gear loads if they prevented the stabilizer angle from moving in the leading-edge-down direction during landings. Training the pilots to perform a push maneuver during landing accomplished this. In addition, North American installed a switch in the cockpit that disengaged the SAS at main gear touchdown to prevent the dampers from forcing the stabilizer leading edge down. Experience showed that under normal circumstances the pilots were efficient at pushing the stick at the right moment, even though the maneuver had to occur within 0.4 second after main gear touchdown to be effective in reducing gear loads. However, this maneuver was unnatural for the pilots, who tended to revert to habits formed

204 James M. McKay and Richard B. Noll, "A Summary of the X-15 Landing Loads," a paper in the *Progress of the X-15 Research Airplane Program*, A Compilation of the Papers presented at the Flight Research Center, 7 October 1965, NASA publication SP-90, (Washington, DC: NASA, 1965), pp. 36-38.

205 Ibid, pp. 37-38.

through long hours of previous experience during emergencies and pull back on the stick. For this reason, the FRC began developing an automatic stick-kicker.[206]

In fact, this very condition occurred during the Jack McKay's accident in X-15-2. The airplane was 1,000 pounds heavy with residual propellants, and as he landed, McKay pulled back on the stick, driving the stabilizer leading edge down to its maximum value. As it happened, the flaps failed on this flight and resulted in a down-load on the main wing, and therefore on the main landing gear. The combined resulted was a severely overstressed gear that, of course, failed.[207]

Following the accident with X-15-2, engineers considered designing a new landing gear for the modified X-15A-2. The original location of the nose gear was approximately 23 feet ahead of the center of gravity, and moving the landing gear back could significantly reduce main-gear loads, with the forward bulkhead of the liquid-oxygen tank representing the rear-most location in the existing airframe. One of the ideas engineers investigated was moving the nose landing gear rearward to the instrumentation compartment behind the pilot. The nose gear would occupy the lower half of the compartment, with most of the instrumentation that normally resided there being moved forward to the old nose-gear compartment ahead of the pilot.[208]

However, fiscal and schedule constraints involved with repairing the aircraft precluded such major modifications, and the existing gear locations were reused on the modified airplane. Nevertheless, engineers made some basic changes, such as increasing the shock strut stroke from 3.66 inches to 5.03 inches, and modifying the relief valve setting from 17,000 pounds to 22,000 pounds. North American manufactured two sets of strengthened struts—one set that was the same length as the original units, and another set that was lengthened from 53.6 inches to 59.0 inches. The longer units provided sufficient ground clearance to land with the functional ramjet sill attached to the ventral, but it appears that all flights of the X-15A-2 used the shorter units. Engineers also lengthened the skid 6.75 inches. In addition, engineers made some changes to the nose gear, primarily increasing the shock strut stroke to accommodate the increased length of the airplane. North American lowered the trunnion 9 inches to allow an attitude at nose-gear touchdown similar to that of the basic X-15. Despite these changes, the landing dynamics of the new gear were not appreciably changed, and X-15A-2 inherited most of the deficiencies of the basic system.[209]

In addition, during the first part of 1965, North American investigated increasing the capability of the X-15A-2 gear. NASA wanted the maximum landing weight with the "short" main landing gear to increase to 16,374 pounds normal and 18,519 pounds emergency. The "long" gear used with the ramjet would increase to 17,855 pounds normal and 20,000 pounds emergency. A preliminary analysis indicated that incorporating the stick-kicker and changing the shock-strut relief valve setting would allow these increases. However, at 20,000 pounds there

206 Richard B. Noll, Calvin R. Jarvis, Chris Pembo, Wilton P. Lock, and Betty J. Scott, NASA technical note D-2090, "Aerodynamic and Control-System Contributions to the X-15 Airplane Landing-Gear Loads," October 1963; McKay and Noll, "A Summary of the X-15 Landing Loads," pp. 37-38.

207 McKay and Noll, "A Summary of the X-15 Landing Loads," p. 38.

208 Ibid, pp. 39-40.

209 Ibid, pp. 39-40; Adkins and Armstrong, "Development and Status of the X-15A-2 Airplane," p. 114.

were concerns about whether the fuselage structure just behind the cockpit would be strong enough.[210]

Researchers installed a prototype stick-kicker in the FRC fixed-base simulator in May 1965 to determine the optimum stick forces. Subsequently, engineers installed the first stick-kicker in X-15-3 during the weather down period at the beginning of 1966, and in X-15-1 by the end of that year. Apparently, NASA never installed the stick-kicker in X-15A-2. An emergency landing at 17,700 pounds, the highest landing weight yet encountered by the program, illustrated the effectiveness of the stick-kicker.[211]

North American also conducted an investigation during early 1965 to determine the modifications needed to increase the landing weight of X-15-1 and X-15-3 to 16,000 pounds normal and 17,000 pounds emergency. The analysis included the use of the stick-kicker to rotate the horizontal stabilizer at landing to reduce main skid loads, although this would not eliminate the need to modify the skids for the higher weights. Preliminary studies showed that relocating the nose gear trunnion (as done on X-15A-2) would appreciably reduce landing loads on the other two airplanes, even without the addition of a stick-kicker.[212]

At the same time, engineers studied the feasibility of incorporating a third main skid attached to the fixed portion of the ventral stabilizer. This third skid could redistribute the landing loads and relieve the critically stressed gear components, particularly if either the stick-kicker of the landing flaps failed to operate. NASA installed the skid on X-15-3 in time for flight 3-52-78 on 18 June 1966, and by the end of 1966 it had used the third skid for four landings. These landings, however, were not at a sufficient weight to require the skid, and during the slideout the third skid contacted the lake surface with little or no load applied to it. Nevertheless, the third skid seemed like a good idea and NASA modified X-15-1 in time for flight 1-71-121 on 22 March 1967. NASA did not install the third skid on X-15A-2 since it would have interfered with the ramjet installation.[213]

The X-15A-2 experienced some of the more bizarre problems with landing gear. On the second flight (2-33-56) of the modified aircraft, after obtaining a maximum Mach number of 5.23, the nose gear unexpectedly extended as the airplane decelerated below Mach 4.2. William P. Albrecht, the X-15 project engineer for the flight, wrote that "[u]pon arrival in the Edwards area, chase aircraft confirmed that the nose gear was extended fully, and that the tires appeared badly burned, although still inflated. Major Rushworth elected to land the X-l5, and skillfully did so. The tires remained intact on touchdown but disintegrated after approximately 300 feet of rollout, the remainder of the 5,630 foot rollout being taken by the magnesium rims of the nose wheels." Considering the circumstance, it was a good landing.[214]

The subsequent investigation revealed that the nose-gear uplock hook was severely bent, the point of the hook having opened by approximately 0.25 inches.

210 "X-15 Semi-Annual Status Report No. 4," 1 April 1965, pp. 10-11.

211 X-15 Status Report, Paul F. Bikle/FRC to J. Martin/NASA Headquarters, 2 June 1965 and 1 March 1966; letter, William J. Knight to Dennis R. Jenkins, 14 August 2002.

212 "X-15 Semi-Annual Status Report No. 4," 1 April 1965, p. 10.

213 "X-15 Semi-Annual Status Report No. 6," 1 November 1966, p. 14; McKay and Noll, "A Summary of the X-15 Landing Loads," pp. 39-40.

214 William P. Albrecht/X-15 Project Engineer, "X-15 Operations Flight Report for Flight 2-33-56," 19 August 1964.

However, engineers determined the hook had not bent far enough to release the gear without the occurrence of some other deflection. The pilot lowered the X-15 landing gear via a simple cable arrangement that connected the landing gear extension handle in the cockpit to the uplock hook. Engineers measured the slack in the landing gear actuating cable (used to compensate for fuselage expansion due to heating effects) at 1.18 inches after the flight, within the specified limits. However, an analysis by North American indicated that the thermal growth of the fuselage was approximately 1.90 inches for this flight. This pointed out that the slack allowance was inadequate. Since the same mechanism operated all three landing gear components, it could not be ascertained in advance which of the three landing gears (left main, right main, or nose) would be first affected by partial actuation of the extension system, since that one with the least cable loading (due to friction, air loads, etc.) would tend to operate first. NASA duplicated the failure in the High-Temperature Loads Calibration Laboratory by simulating the fuselage expansion and applying heat to the nose-gear door. As Albrecht observed afterward, "Needless to say some modification to the landing gear mechanism seems to be in order."[215]

North American modified the cable to provide 2.25 inches of slack to compensate for thermal expansion. Although the engineers did not believe the problem affected the other two airplanes, they also received the modification. The only major drawback to this modification was that the pilot now had to pull the gear handle through almost 14 inches of travel to release the landing gear, which led to several complaints. Subsequently, engineers at the FRC designed a differential pulley that shortened the pull to 11 inches.[216]

These modifications, however, did not totally fix X-15A-2. During the next flight (2-34-57) on 29 September 1964, Bob Rushworth experienced a similar, but less intense, noise and aircraft trim change at Mach 4.5: the small nose-gear scoop door opened. This had already happened several times during the flight program on all three airplanes, fortunately without disastrous results. There were two initial thoughts on how to fix the problem. The first was to eliminate the scoop door altogether; except for inspection and servicing, the door would be bolted shut prior to flight. Alternately, engineers could design a new uplock for the scoop door that featured a positive retention of the door roller on the uplock hook. In the end, NASA selected the second route and installed a new uplock hook, scoop door hook, and associated bell cranks.[217]

NASA conducted two captive-carry flights of X-15A-2 to verify proper deployment of the redesigned nose scoop door and nose landing gear after cold soak. During flight 2-C-58 the nose gear required approximately 5.4 seconds to lock down—an unacceptably long time. Subsequent inspection showed that an incorrect orifice had been installed in the nose-gear snubber (which controlled the

---

215 Johnny G. Armstrong, AFFTC technology document FTC-TD-69-4, "Flight Planning and Conduct of the X-15A-2 Envelope Expansion Program," July 1969, p. 10; William P. Albrecht/X-15 Project Engineer, "X-15 Operations Flight Report for Flight 2-33-56," 19 August 1964.

216 William P. Albrecht/X-15 Project Engineer, "X-15 Operations Flight Report for Flight 2-35-60," 2 December 1964.

217 Vincent N. Capasso/X-15 Project Engineer, "X-15 Operations Flight Report for Flight 3-36-59," 4 November 1964; Major Robert A. Rushworth, "Pilot Report for Flight 2-34-57," 29 September 1964; William P. Albrecht/X-15 Project Engineer, "X-15 Operations Flight Report for Flight 2-34-57," 1 October 1964; William P. Albrecht/X-15 Project Engineer, "X-15 Operations Flight Report for Flight 2-35-60," 2 December 1964.

deployment rate). NASA installed the correct orifice, and the deployment time on flight 2-C-59 was an acceptable 2.7 seconds. Researchers collected data on both these captive flights data regarding the scoop door hook position and scoop door roller loads. Hook movement was negligible (less than 1/16 inch) and NASA subsequently modified the other two airplanes as well. Jack McKay took X-15A-2 on a perfect flight (2-35-60) on 30 November 1964.

Like the rear skids, the nose wheel was lowered by the pilot pulling a handle that was connected to a cable that released the uplocks. On two separate flights, the nose gear extended while Major Robert A. Rushworth was flying the X-15A-2 above Mach 4, resulting in some interesting flying characteristics and two sets of burned tires. Researchers finally deduced that the fuselage of the airplane was expanding due to heat, and that the landing gear release cable did not have enough slack to compensate. North American increased the slack in the cable, but the pilots now had to pull the release handle more than 14 inches to get the landing gear to deploy. (NASA)

However, it did not end there. Rushworth was in the cockpit again for the next fight (2-36-63) of X-15A-2 on 17 February 1965 when the right main skid extended at Mach 4.3 and 85,000 feet. The chase pilot was able to verify that the gear appeared structurally sound, and Rushworth managed to make a normal landing. Investigation of the right-hand main skid uplock revealed that thermally induced bowing of the main strut caused excessive loading of the main uplock hook. Ground heating tests of the main-gear struts during a "hot-flight" profile caused bending of the hook and release of the gear. Consequently, NASA modified the main-gear uplock to include a stronger hook, a Belleville washer mounting system to accommodate approximately 0.14 inch bowing of the strut, and a stronger support structure. In addition, it was necessary to reinforce the sheet-metal fuselage longeron structure around the main-gear drag-brace anchor fittings. While the repair itself was not complicated, access was extremely difficult since it required much of the hydraulic plumbing in the lower engine bay to be removed.[218]

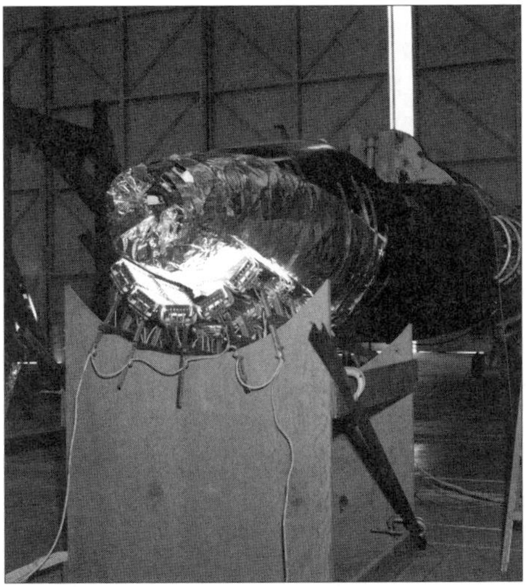

To test the hypothesis that the fuselage expanded more than the release cable, researchers at the Flight Research Center heated one of the X-15 forward fuselages using heat lamps. The test confirmed the theory. (NASA)

This ended the significant problem with the landing gear on the X-15A-2 (and the other airplanes), although the ever-increasing landing weight continued to be a concern and a set of small modifications (such as stronger struts) continued to be implemented until the end of the flight program.

THE SECOND INDUSTRY CONFERENCE (1958)

As North American was completing assembly of the first X-15, the Research Airplane Committee held the second X-15 industry conference at the IAS Building in Los Angeles on 28-29 July 1958. Forty-three authors (15 from North American, 14 from Langley, 6 from the High Speed Flight Station, 3 from the WADC, 2 from Ames, and 1 each from the AFFTC, Reaction Motors, and the Naval Aviation Medical Acceleration Laboratory at NADC Johnsville) presented 28 papers. There were 443 registered participants representing all of the military services and most of the major (and many minor) aerospace contractors. Interestingly,

218 Major Robert A. Rushworth, "Pilot Report for Flight 2-36-63," 17 February 1965; AFFTC technology document FTC-TD-69-4, p. 10; Milton O. Thompson, *At the Edge of Space: The X-15 Flight Program*, (Washington and London: Smithsonian Institution Press, 1992), p. 237; Adkins and Armstrong, "Development and Status of the X-15A-2 Airplane," p. 107; "The Pilot's Panel," a paper in the *Proceedings of the X-15 30th Anniversary Celebration*, Dryden Flight Research Facility, Edwards, CA, 8 June 1989, NASA CP-3105, p. 149; William P. Albrecht/ X-15 Project Engineer, "X-15 Operations Flight Report for Flight 2-37-64," 14 May 1965.

there was no university participation this time. Notable attendees included Dr. David Myron Clark from the David Clark Company, Dr. Charles Stark Draper, and all of the original X-15 pilots. It is interesting to note how at least one of the participants registered; for instance, Harrison Storms listed his affiliation as "NACA Committee on Aircraft, Missile, and Spacecraft Aerodynamics" instead of "North American Aviation."[219]

The 1958 conference began, appropriately, where the 1956 conference had ended. Lawrence P. Greene from North American, who had presented the closing paper at the first conference, gave the technical introduction. One of his first statements summed up the progress: "It can be positively said that through the efforts of all concerned, the development of the X-15 research system has been successfully completed."[220]

The airplane North American was building was the "Configuration 3" that had been inspected by the Air Force in mockup form. Configuration 1 was the initial North American proposal, while Configuration 2 was the one presented during the 1956 industry conference. Greene highlighted the important changes:[221]

1. The side fairings were shortened ahead of the wing to improve longitudinal stability.
2. The horizontal stabilizer was moved 5.4 inches rearward, although the original fuselage location of the hinge line was retained. This modification moved the hinge line from the 37% to the 25% mean aerodynamic chord of the exposed horizontal stabilizer. Although flutter requirements dictated the change, this, combined with a 3.6-inch forward wing movement and the side-fairing changes, provided adequate longitudinal stability near zero lift at the maximum Mach number.
3. The vertical stabilizer area was increased to provide adequate directional stability with the speed brakes retracted and a 10-degree full wedge section was found to be optimum. The planform was then made nearly symmetrical (dorsal and ventral) for dynamic-stability considerations in the exit phase of the mission, since thrust asymmetry considerations in the zero to moderate angle-of-attack range necessitated a reduction in roll due to yaw.
4. Asymmetrical thrust effects also indicated the need for a low value of roll-due-to-yaw control in the low angle-of-attack region. For this purpose, an all-movable directional

219 *1958 Research Airplane Committee Report*, from the Table of Contents and List of Conferees.

220 Lawrence P. Greene, "X-15 Research Airplane Development Status," a paper in the *1958 Research Airplane Committee Report*, pp. 1-2. The final load limits were set at +4.0/-2.0 g at full gross weight and +7.33/-3.0 g at 30% propellants remaining. However, the increase came with restrictions. To avoid a serious increase in weight, pull-outs at 7.33 g at maximum dynamic pressure could only be made once per reentry. During this maneuver the aircraft slowed down appreciably but heated up rapidly. If another pull-up was required, it had to be accomplished at a lower acceleration (g) or lower dynamic pressure (q) to avoid overheating the airframe. See Richard L. Schleicher, "Structural Design of the X-15," a paper presented to the Royal Aeronautical Society on 18 April 1963, and printed in the *Journal of the Royal Aeronautical Society*, volume 67, October 1963, pp. 618-636.

221 Greene, "X-15 Research Airplane Development Status," pp. 2-3.

control was incorporated on the outer span of both the upper and lower vertical stabilizers. Incorporating the control in the lower vertical stabilizer was equally necessary for providing directional control at high angles of attack at high speed because of the ineffectiveness of the upper surface at these conditions. This, in turn, dictated some added complexity in the damper system.

5. In order to avoid compound flutter problems, the speed brakes were reduced in size and relocated on the inboard or fixed parts of the vertical stabilizers.

Although initially it had been decided not to increase the load factor of the airplane from 5 g to 7.33 g, sometime in the intervening two years the change had been made, much to the relief of the pilots and researchers at the HSFS. In mid-1957 the NACA had asked the Air Force to double the amount of research instrumentation carried by the X-15. This became a major design driver. In order to keep the airplane weight (and hence performance) from being too seriously degraded, numerous details were redesigned to save weight. The two areas that received the most rework were the propellant system plumbing and the nose gear. This is when Charlie Feltz came up with the idea of keeping the nose-gear strut compressed when it was stored, allowing a much more compact and lightweight installation.[222]

Changes in configuration also brought changes in weight. To support the additional loads, North American strengthened the structure of the wing, fuselage, and empennage. This resulted in a revised specification that showed an airplane that was 765 pounds heavier than originally expected (184 pounds in empty weight and 581 pounds in useful load; this included the pilot, propellants, and gasses, but not research instrumentation). However, by the time North American began building the airplanes, even this had changed. The empty weight had increased by only 61 pounds (instead of 184), but the useful load had decreased by 196 pounds. The research instrumentation, on the other hand, had increased by 522 pounds. The empty weight increases were the result of the following changes:[223]

1. The wing was changed from 7 to 15 intermediate spars, the skin gage was reduced, and the heat-sink material was changed from titanium carbide with a nickel binder to Inconel X, resulting in a net decrease of 131 pounds.
2. A 17-pound net increase in the empennage resulted from a 58-pound increase to meet thermal requirements and a reduction of 41 pounds for changing the leading-edgheat-sink material from titanium carbide with a nickel binder to Inconel X.

222 Crossfield, *Always Another Dawn*, pp. 263-264; telephone conversation, Charles H. Feltz with Dennis R. Jenkins, 12 May 2002.

223 Gerald H. Johnson, "X-15 Structural Loads," a paper in the *1958 Research Airplane Committee Report*, pp. 197-205.

3. Chem-milling pockets in the skin and reducing the skin gage by adding Z-stiffeners and substituting aluminum for Inconel X in a portion of the intermediate fuel- and oxidizer-tank bulkheads saved 102 pounds in the body ground, but a 15-pound increase was caused by the additional structure to accommodate the engine weight increase. The net fuselage change was a decrease of 87 pounds.
4. The landing gear group was reduced by 73 pounds by eliminating the shimmy damper on the nose wheel and reducing the gage of the main-landing gear skids.
5. A reduction of 12 pounds in surface controls was realized by changing from four direct-acting speed-brake actuators to two actuators with a linkage arrangement.
6. The engine dry weight increased 296 pounds.
7. The addition of an engine purge system increased the propulsion group by 67 pounds. However, this was partially offset by a reduction in the internal liquid oxygen system plumbing of 29 pounds, giving a net propulsion system increase of 38 pounds.
8. The 4-pound increase in the auxiliary powerplant group was due to an increase in the weight of the APUs.
9. Changes in the fixed equipment resulted in a net increase of 9 pounds, consisting of a 76-pound increase in the ejection seat, an 11-pound increase in instruments, a 34-pound decrease in the nitrogen system, and a 44-pound decrease in the air-conditioning system.

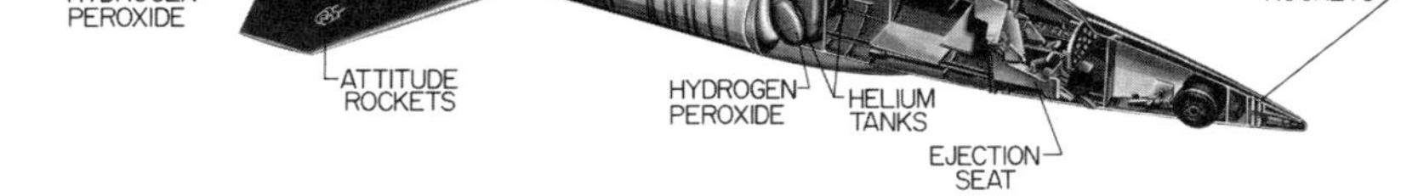

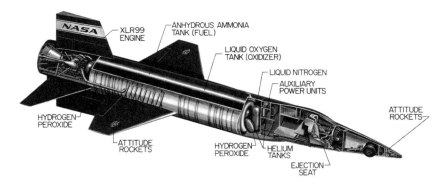

This is the configuration of the X-15 presented at the 1958 Industry Conference, and largely represents the airplane as built. The major components are annotated. The large area immediately behind the cockpit was the primary location for the research instrumentation recorders and other equipment that required a controlled environment. (NASA)

Changes made in the useful load included the following:

1. The turbopump monopropellant was reduced by 196 pounds.
2. Trapped propellants in the engine increased 70 pounds.
3. The helium required to pressurize the propellant tanks increased 13 pounds.
4. The nitrogen required to pressurize the cockpit was reduced by 82 pounds.

All of this resulted in an airplane that had an empty weight of 10,635 pounds, versus an original specification weight of 10,390 pounds and a revised specification of 10,574 pounds. The total gross weight was 31,662 pounds, versus the original target of 30,510 pounds and a revised specification of 31,275 pounds. For high-speed missions, NASA could remove 370 pounds of altitude-related instrumentation, resulting in a gross weight of 31,292 pounds—only 17 pounds over the revised specification.[224]

Perhaps the most notable (though hardly unexpected) item to come out of the second industry conference was that the XLR99 was significantly behind schedule, and initial flight-testing of the airplane would be undertaken using two interim XLR11-RM-5 engines.[225]

224 Johnson, "X-15 Structural Loads," pp. 197-205.

225 De E. Beeler and Thomas A Toll, "Status of X-15 Research Program," a paper in the *1961 Research Airplane Committee Report.*

CHAPTER 4

The Million-Horsepower Engine

Although the hypersonic research airplane concept developed at Langley had met with almost unanimous endorsement by the Air Force, the lack of a suitable powerplant was a major shortcoming in the eyes of the WADC Power Plant Laboratory. The Langley study had determined that an engine (or engines) that could produce roughly 50,000 lbf was needed for the research airplane. The flight profiles developed by John Becker and his researchers showed that the ability to vary the thrust during flight would provide much better data and allow pilots to repeat maneuvers with some precision. The laboratory thought the Hermes A1 engine used in the Becker study was not capable of evolving into a man-rated engine, and suggested several engines it believed were "more suitable" for a manned aircraft. Despite these suggestions, however, the laboratory believed further study was required before any engine could be selected.[1]

By October 1954, researchers from the Air Force, Navy, and the NACA had selected four existing or proposed power plants for possible use in the X-15. These included the Aerojet XLR73, Bell XLR81, North American NA-5400, and Reaction Motors XLR10. Despite the tentative selections, the Power Plant Laboratory thought that any engine would require major modifications to meet the

1 Memorandum, E. C. Phillips to Director of Laboratories, 5 August 1954; memorandum, J. W. Rogers to Chief, Non-Rotating Engine Branch, no subject, 11 August 1954; memorandum, T. J. Keating to Chief, New Development Office, no subject, 15 November 1954; Letter, Colonel Carl F. Damberg, Chief, Aircraft Division, AMC, to Bell et al., Subject: Project 1226 Competition, 2 February 1955.

needs of the X-15. The laboratory also believed the Air Force needed to "accept responsibility for development of the selected engine and...provide this engine to the airplane contractor as government furnished equipment." The primary consideration, for both the laboratory and the NACA, was that the engine be able to operate safely under any condition (acceleration in any axis) the X-15 was likely to experience. Maintenance and reliability (as defined by time between overhauls) did not need to be up to production standards.[2]

The 30 December 1954 invitation-to-bid letter from the Air Materiel Command included summaries of the four engines recommended by the Power Plant Laboratory. However, although the stated preference to use one of these engines did not forbid bidders from using other engines, it did require the bidder and engine manufacturer to justify the selection. The bidder needed to present the justification to the X-15 Project Office for approval.

The powerplant that was ultimately selected for the X-15 was not one of the four recommended ones, but became known during discussions with Reaction Motors concerning the XLR10 from the Viking missile. During a meeting with the Air Force, the company promoted "a larger version of the Viking engine" that was under development for the Navy as the XLR30. After these discussions, the Power Plant Laboratory estimated that Reaction Motors could develop the XLR30 into a suitable engine for less than $5,000,000 in approximately two years. It was not even close.[3]

On 25 January 1955, the Air Force requested additional information from Reaction Motors. The company replied on 3 February 1955 with details on the XLR10 and XLR30, and recommended four possible combinations for the X-15 program. These included an oxygen-ethanol XLR10, an oxygen-ammonia XLR30, an oxygen-hydrocarbon XLR30, and an oxygen-ethanol engine using two XLR10 chambers fed by a single XLR30 turbopump. Each of the engines used hydrogen peroxide to drive the turbopump. After it was briefed on the Becker study, Reaction Motors doubted that a single XLR10 was "adequate to perform the objectives of this type of aircraft."[4]

Although it suggested a combination of XLR10 thrust chambers and an XLR30 turbopump, Reaction Motors believed this engine would be overly complicated and predicted it would weigh 815 pounds (compared to 420 pounds for either of the XLR30 configurations). The company suggested that relatively minor modifications to the XLR30 would allow throttling between 17,000 and 57,000 lbf with a specific impulse of 278 seconds. The XLR30 installation required a

2 Memorandum, T. J. Keating to Chief, New Development Office, no subject, 15 November 1954. The XLR99 was popularly considered to be a million-horsepower engine. According to Webster's, the horsepower of a rocket engine is determined by multiplying the thrust (in pounds) times the speed (in mph), divided by 375. Therefore, the XLR99 would be 57,000 lbf * 4,520 mph / 375 = 687,040 hp (not quite a million, but still impressive for a 900-pound engine).

3 Letter, Colonel Carl F. Damberg to Bell Aircraft, 30 December 1954. In the files at the Air Force Historical Research Agency; memorandum, T. J. Keating to Chief, New Development Office, no subject, 15 November 1954. In the files at the AFMC History Office. In fairness to the laboratory, it must be admitted that such estimates were accompanied by a statement that "less confidence in these estimates exists because the XLR30 engine is at present in a much earlier stage of development." This qualification was justified by later events.

4 Letter, Warren P. Turner to Commander, AMC, no subject, 3 February 1955. In the files at the ASC History Office.

The Reaction Motors XLR30-RM-2 liquid-propellant rocket engine was the leading candidate for the X-15 powerplant. The XLR30 had been developed from the XLR10 that powered the Viking sounding rocket developed for the Naval Research Laboratory. Twelve Vikings were launched between 1949 and 1955. (Reaction Motors Inc.)

space 70 inches long and 30 inches in diameter, considerably less than that required for the larger XLR10-XLR30 combination.[5]

Independently, Reaction Motors determined that the two most important safety requirements were the propellant combination and the means of achieving combustion during ignition and shutdown. The company reviewed seven propellant combinations in depth, and eventually narrowed the choices to liquid oxygen and anhydrous ammonia. Reaction Motors based this choice largely on its significant experience with this combination, which had shown that ammonia had fewer critical starting characteristics than most hydrocarbon fuels. Additionally, the propellants were ideal for the regenerative cooling of the proposed engine's thrust chamber.

The Air Force, however, was still more interested in the XLR10, and on 4 February 1955 it asked Reaction Motors for additional information on that engine. On the same day, however, Reaction Motors and the X-15 Project Office held a meeting during which the company detailed a significant development program to man-rate the XLR-10 for the X-15. Given the development effort required for either engine, the company believed the XLR30 would ultimately be a better engine. After a meeting between the Air Materiel Command and the X-15 Project Office, the government advised Reaction Motors to "make all further estimates on the basis of the XLR30's development." [6]

Concurrently, the Air Materiel Command had also been in discussions with the other three engine manufacturers. The fact that the other manufacturers showed a somewhat lower level of interest than Reaction Motors is understandable–after all, Reaction Motors engines had powered most of the rocket-equipped X-planes since the original XS-1. In fact, by this time North American had already requested that the Air Force withdraw the NA-5400 from consideration. On 18 March 1955, the Air Force supplied the prospective airframe contractors with the specifications on the three remaining engines. The Air Force expected that a flight engine would be available to the winning contractor within 30 months.[7]

The X-15 Project Office released its analysis of the data provided by the engine manufacturers on 22 March 1955. One of the comments was that generating the necessary 50,000 lbf would require multiple Bell and Aerojet engines. The X-15 Project Office made clear that the final engine was not a production item, and that the amount of available propellants was the only limit to the operating time of the engine.[8]

After much discussion, the Air Force decided to release a request for proposal for the X-15 engine that was separate from the airframe competition. On 26 April, Headquarters ARDC requested that "the engine program be subjected to a final critical review apart from, but concurrent with the evaluation of the airframe proposals." The Power Plant Laboratory, NACA, and Navy would complete their engine evaluations by 12 July. The evaluation was to come to one of three conclusions: 1) that one engine was so superior to the others that its use would be

5 Ibid.

6 Letter, Roger W. Walker to Reaction Motors, no subject, 4 February 1955; letter, Lieutenant Colonel W. K. Ashby, Chief, Power Plant Branch, Aeronautical Equipment Division, AMC, to Reaction Motors, Subject: Power Plant for New Research Airplane, 24 February 1955. In the files at the Air Force Historical Research Agency.

7 Letter, John B. Trenholm to Bell et al., no subject, 22 March 1955.

8 Ibid.

mandated, 2) that one engine was so inferior that its use would be forbidden, or 3) that all of the engines were so nearly comparable that the choice would be left to the airframe contractor. The WADC scheduled the final engine evaluation meeting for 28 June, although this later slipped to 6–7 July.[9]

ENGINE PROPOSALS

Three companies–Aerojet, Bell, and Reaction Motors–submitted proposals for the X-15 engine on 9 May 1955, the same day as the airframe competitors. North American had already asked the Air Force and NACA to dismiss the NA-5400 as an alternative. A copy of the Aerojet XLR73 proposal could not be located.

Bell was conservative in its engine proposal and stated that "modifications have been limited to those necessary to permit the engine to be used in a piloted aircraft." The changes to the XLR81 were made primarily in the starting and control systems, mostly to provide additional safety margins. The modified engine would be capable of multiple starts with a safety system based on a similar device provided for use during ground testing. The modifications provided an engine that could operate at an 8,000-lbf thrust level in addition to the normal 14,500-lbf full thrust. The modifications included the addition of a propellant bypass valve just in front of the injector so that, at the reduced thrust level, approximately one-half of the propellants would return to the tanks instead of being injected into the thrust chamber. This eliminated the need to change the pump discharge pressures, and allowed the same amount of propellants to flow through the cooling system. Only one engine in each airplane would have the capability to provide the 8,000-lbf level, although this reflected the removal and capping of the bypass valve and not any major change in engine configuration. Bell also proposed changing the fuel as a safety measure. In an attempt to minimize the risk of mixed propellants accumulating and exploding, Bell wanted to exchange the jet fuel normally used in the XLR81 with a mixture of 40% unsymmetrical dimethylhydrazine (UDMH) and 60% jet fuel (Bell called this combination "JP-X"). This would make the two propellants hypergolic, eliminating the hazard. Bell also pointed out that these propellants would not need to be topped off from the carrier aircraft, since neither had an appreciable vaporization rate. Bell noted that "since tests of the major components of the XLR81-BA-1 engine have been successful, extensive development tests of these components will not be required for the X-15 engine program."[10]

Like the Bell proposal, the proposal from Reaction Motors was brief (Bell used 15 pages, and Reaction Motors used just 14). The XLR30 would be modi-

9 Letter, Colonel Paul F. Nay to Commander, WADC, no subject, 26 April 1955. In the files at the Air Force Historical Research Agency; memorandum, John B. Trenholm to Chief, Rocket Section, no subject, 20 June 1955. In the files at the AFMC History Office; letter, Arthur W. Vogeley to Hartley A. Soulé/Research Airplane Project Leader, no subject, 17 June 1955.

10 Bell report 02-945-106, "Project 1226: X-15 Liquid Rocket Engine Proposal," Secret, 25 February 1955. Courtesy of Benjamin F. Guenther.

fied to "1) emphasize safety and minimum development time, 2) start, operate and shutdown at all altitudes and attitudes, and 3) be capable of at least five successive starts without servicing or manual attention other than cockpit controls." Instead of the thrust-stepping proposed by Bell, Reaction Motors offered an infinitely variable thrust ranging from 13,500 to 50,000 lbf at sea level. Reaction Motors believed that "the highly developed state of the major engine components, i.e., turbopump, thrust chamber and control valves allows RMI to meet the schedule...." Unlike Bell, which extensively discussed the modifications required to make its engine meet the X-15 requirements, Reaction Motors instead gave a technical overview of the XLR30, and it was not possible to determine what the modifications were. Nevertheless, the overall impression was that the state of XLR30 development was far along.[11]

THE ENGINE EVALUATION

On 8 June, John Sloop at Lewis submitted the preliminary NACA engine results to Hartley Soulé. The rankings were 1) XLR81, 2) XLR30, and 3) XLR73. Lewis also commented on various aspects of the airframe proposals, including propellant systems, engine installation, reaction controls, APUs, and fire extinguishing systems, although it drew no conclusions and did not rank the airframe competitors. The airframe manufacturers had concentrated on two of the possible engines: Bell and Republic opted for the Bell XLR81, while Douglas and North American used the Reaction Motors XLR30. Bell had also included an alternate design that used the XLR30 engine. Nobody had proposed using the Aerojet XLR73.[12]

The Power Plant Laboratory believed that minimum thrust was a critical factor. Reaction Motors indicated that its engine was infinitely variable between 30% and 100% thrust. The Bell engine, however, only had thrust settings of 8,000 and 14,500 lbf. However, since the Bell engine had to be used in multiples to provide sufficient thrust for the research airplane, this meant that the equivalent minimum thrust was 18% for the Bell design (which used three engines) and 14% for the Republic airplane (four engines). Initially, the engine evaluation set the desired lower thrust figure at 25%, resulting in a lower score for the Reaction Motors engine. The X-15 Project Office subsequently raised the lower throttle setting to 30%, and the evaluators then ranked the Reaction Motors engine as slightly better.[13]

During the initial evaluation the Power Plant Laboratory found little difference between the Bell and Reaction Motors proposals except for the throttling limits, but the report left the impression that the Air Force favored the Bell design.

---

11 Reaction Motors report TR-9405-C, "Rocket Engine for New Research Airplane," Secret, 26 February 1955. Courtesy of Benjamin F. Guenther.

12 Letter, John L. Sloop/Lewis Evaluation Group to Hartley A. Soulé/Research Airplane Project Leader, no subject, 8 June 1955.

13 Letter, John L. Sloop/Lewis Evaluation Group to Hartley A. Soulé/Research Airplane Project Leader, no subject, 4 June 1955.

Statements such as "the Bell engine would have potential tactical application for piloted aircraft use whereas no applications of the RMI engine are foreseen," and "in the event that the XLR73 development does not meet its objectives, the Bell engine would serve as a 'backup' in the Air Force inventory" made the laboratory's feelings clear.[14] Of course, the idea that rocket engines potentially could be used in operational manned aircraft quickly waned as jet engines became more powerful, and this became a moot point.

The final meeting at Wright Field on 14-15 June finalized the ground rules for the engine evaluation. The engine companies attended the early portion of the meeting to present preliminary results from their proposals. The ground rules established by the Air Force, Navy, and NACA representatives included three major areas of consideration: 1) the development capability of the manufacturer, 2) the technical design (including the design approach and the research utility), and 3) the cost.[15]

On 24 June 1955, NACA Lewis issued a revised ranking of the engine competitors. From a technical perspective (not considering management and other factors), the Lewis rankings were now 1) XLR30, 2) XLR81, and 3) XLR73. The reason given for reversing the rankings of the XLR30 and XLR81 was a shift in the engine-evaluation ground rules. Previously researchers rated the XLR30 lower because of its unsatisfactory throttling limits, but new ground rules relaxed the requirements and elevated the engine's ranking.

There still seemed to be some confusion over the engine-evaluation process, and yet another meeting at NACA Headquarters on 27 June attempted to ensure that everybody was on the same page. The meeting ended with an understanding that the engine evaluation should determine whether any of the engines was unsuitable for use in the airplane, or whether any engine was so clearly superior that it should be selected regardless of the choice of the winning airframe contractor. If neither of these conditions existed, then whichever engine the airframe contractor selected would be chosen. This was the same conclusion reached previously on 14-15 June, and all of the attendees appeared to be satisfied with the result.[16]

On 1 July, the HSFS sent its engine evaluation to Hartley Soulé, ranking the power plants as 1) XLR30, 2) XLR73, and 3) XLR81. The transmittal letter, however, expressed concern about "the lack of development of all three of the proposed engines." Walt Williams again strongly recommended an interim engine for the initial flights of the new research airplane (he suggested the Reaction Motors LR8 based on previous HSFS experience). Since the early flights would be primarily concerned with proving the airworthiness of the airplane, they would not need the full power provided by the final engine. The HSFS believed that the development of the new engine would take longer than most expected, and using an interim engine would allow the flight-test program to begin at an earlier date. To minimize the hazards to personnel and instruments, researchers at the HSFS

---

14 This indicated that the funded Aerojet engine and the Bell engine could substitute for each other in operational aircraft if needed, while the much more powerful Reaction Motors engine was in a class by itself and would have little operational potential. See Air Force report (unnumbered), "Evaluation of Engines–Project 1226," 15 July 1955, Power Plant Laboratory. In the files at the Air Force Historical Research Agency.

15 Letter, Arthur W. Vogeley to Hartley A. Soulé/Research Airplane Project Leader, no subject, 17 June 1955.

16 Letter, John L. Sloop/Lewis Evaluation Group to Hartley A. Soulé/Research Airplane Project Leader, no subject, 24 June 1955; Letter, Clotaire Wood to William J. Underwood, no subject, 29 June 1955.

also recommended that Reaction Motors change the fuel for the XLR30 from anhydrous ammonia to gasoline or jet fuel.[17]

The Air Force evaluation group pointed out that using two fuels interchangeably in the Bell gas generator systems would overly complicate the fuel system. The use of a separate system to meet the restart requirement was also expected to create safety and reliability problems. On the other hand, although the Reaction Motors engine was more orthodox than the Bell design, the company had not yet performed many tests on it, and the evaluators correctly predicted that it would have a difficult development. The evaluators noted that both engines would need substantial development being man-rated.[18]

A meeting at Wright Field on 6-7 July attempted to sort out the engine selection. De Beeler, John Sloop, and Arthur Vogeley represented the NACA, Oscar Bessio represented the Navy, and Joseph Rogers led the Air Force contingent. The representatives from the Power Plant Laboratory indicated a preference for the XLR73, with the XLR81 as their second choice, but the NACA participants argued that finishing the development of the Aerojet engine would consume a great deal of time. The Navy considered the XLR30 the best (not surprisingly, since it was a Navy engine), followed by the XLR81. The XLR73 was not considered worthy of further consideration because of unspecified "extremely difficult development problems."

The final evaluation report stated that none of the engines was clearly superior or deficient, and therefore the airframe contractor would select the most advantageous engine. The XLR73 was effectively eliminated from the competition since none of the airframe proposals used it, although the Power Plant Laboratory supported the continued development of the XLR73 for other uses. The elimination of the XLR73 was ironic because, of the engines under consideration, only the Aerojet XLR73 was a fully funded development engine, and it was the only one that, theoretically at least, would not have entailed additional costs. The evaluators felt that the development timeline of the Bell engine better matched the program schedule by a small margin. The Bell cost estimate was $3,614,088 compared to $2,699,803 for Reaction Motors. Both were hopelessly optimistic.[19]

In the last portion of the report, the Power Plant Laboratory presented its minority opinion justifying its choice of the XLR73 rocket engine, and the NACA included a recommendation to use an interim powerplant, specifically the Reaction Motors LR8-RM-8, for the initial X-15 flight program until the final powerplant was ready.[20]

17 Letter, Walter C. Williams/HSFS Evaluation Group, to Hartley A. Soulé/Research Airplane Project Leader, no subject, 5 July 1955.

18 Ibid.

19 Letter, Clotaire Wood to Langley, no subject, 13 July 1955.

20 Air Force report RDZ-280, "Evaluation Report on X-15 Research Aircraft Design Competition," 5 August 1955, no page numbers. In the files at the Air Force Historical Research Agency.

ENGINE AWARD

During late October 1955, the Air Force notified Reaction Motors that the winning North American entry in the airframe competition was the one that used the XLR30. On 1 December, the New Developments Office of the Fighter Aircraft Division directed the Power Plant Laboratory to prepare a $1,000,000 letter contract with Reaction Motors. However, at the same time the Power Plant Laboratory was further questioning the desirability of the Reaction Motors engine. During preliminary discussions with Reaction Motors, researchers from the NACA expressed concern that anhydrous ammonia would adversely affect the research instrumentation, and again brought up the possibility of converting to a hydrocarbon fuel. The Power Plant Laboratory did not support the change. Even during the initial evaluation the laboratory had not really believed the 2.5-year development estimate, and thought that was at least 6 months short. Changing the propellants would cost at least another year. The laboratory felt that if a 4-year development period was acceptable, the competition should be reopened, since anything over 2.5 years had been penalized during the original evaluation.[21]

To complicate matters further, the end of 1955 saw the Air Force and Navy in disagreement over which agency should control the engine development effort. The BuAer assistant chief for research and development, Rear Admiral William A. Schoech, sent a letter to Air Force Headquarters proposing to develop the X-15 engine as a continuation of the three years already spent on the XLR30. The admiral believed this arrangement would expedite development, especially since the Navy already had a satisfactory working relationship with Reaction Motors. The Navy could also make the Reaction Motors test stands at Lake Denmark available to the X-15 program.[22]

On 9 December, Air Force Headquarters forwarded the letter to General Marvin C. Demler, commander of the ARDC. Demler forwarded the Navy request to the Power Plant Laboratory and X-15 Project Office for comment. On 29 December, ARDC Headquarters and the X-15 Project Office held a teletype conference (the predecessor of today's conference call) to develop arguments against BuAer retaining the engine program. Demler summarized these and forwarded them to Air Force Headquarters on 3 January 1956. The ARDC rejected the Navy position because it felt a single agency should have management responsibility for the entire X-15 program. The Air Force argued that it was already familiar with

21 Letter, Lieutenant Hugh J. Savage, Non-Rotating Engine Branch, Power Plant Laboratory, WADC, to Reaction Motors, Subject: Engine for the X-15 Airplane, 26 October 1955. In the files at the Air Force Historical Research Agency; memorandum for files, Captain Chester E. McCollough to Chief, Non-Rotating Engine Branch, 1 December 1955. In the files at the AFMC History Office; letter, Roger W. Walker, Chief, Power Plant Development Section, Power Plant Branch, Aeronautical Equipment Division, AMC, to Reaction Motors, Subject: Request for Proposal X-15 Aircraft Engine Development, 8 December 1955. In the files at the Air Force Historical Research Agency; Memorandum, T. J. Keating, Chief, Non-Rotating Engine Branch, Power Plant Laboratory, WADC, to Project Officer, New Development Office, Fighter Aircraft Division, Director of Systems Management, ARDC, Subject: The X-15 Airplane Engine, 15 December 1955. In the files at the Air Force Historical Research Agency. Oddly, it was the Power Plant Laboratory that first suggested (in July 1955) that Reaction Motors switch from ammonia to a hydrocarbon fuel. No record of which engines these might have been could be found.

22 Letter, Rear Admiral William A. Schoech, Assistant Chief for Research and Development, BuAer, to the Air Force Chief of Staff, Subject: Cognizance over development of rocket powerplant for NACA X-15 research airplane, 28 November 1955. In the files at the Naval History Center.

the XLR30 and was well experienced in the development of man-rated rocket engines, such as the XLR11 (ignoring the fact that it was a derivative of the Navy XLR8). The Air Force also pointed out that it was already using the Reaction Motors at Lake Denmark. These arguments apparently put the matter to rest, since no additional correspondence on the subject seems to exist.[23]

Reaction Motors submitted this technical proposal on 24 January 1956, followed by the cost proposal on 8 February. The company expected to deliver the first engine "within thirty (30) months after we are authorized to proceed." Reaction Motors assigned the new engine the TR-139 company designation. The Air Force also realized the engine needed a new designation, and on 21 February it formally requested assignment of the XLR99-RM-1 designation. This became official at Wright Field on 6 March and received Navy approval on 29 March. The Reaction Motors cost proposal showed that the entire program would cost $10,480,718 through the delivery of the first flight engine.[24]

During all of this, the NACA was becoming increasingly worried over the seemingly slow progress of the procurement negotiations. On 15 February, the deputy commander for development at the WADC, Brigadier General Victor R. Haugen, wrote to reassure Hugh Dryden that the process was progressing smoothly. Haugen reminded Dryden that one month of delay had been caused by the necessary studies associated with the NACA's suggestion to change from anhydrous ammonia to a hydrocarbon fuel. Haugen assured Dryden that the procurement agency would issue a letter contract no later than 1 March. As it turned out, his letter was sent the day after the Reaction Motors letter contract had been signed.[25]

THE TR-139

The TR-139 engine proposed by Reaction Motors was an extensively modified version of the Navy-developed XLR30-RM-2. Reaction Motors liked to call it a "turborocket" engine because it used turbopumps to supply its propellants, a relatively new concept. The XLR30 dated back to 1946 when Reaction Motors initiated the development of a 5,000-lbf engine to prove the then-new concepts of high-pressure combustion, spaghetti-tube construction, and turbine drive using main combustion propellants. By 1950, engineers believed these principles were sufficiently well established to initiate the development of a 50,000-lbf engine. The turbopump and its associated valves completed approximately 150

23 Letter, Colonel Donald H. Heaton, Chief, Aeronautical Division, Director for R&D DCS/D, USAF, to Commander ARDC, Subject: Cognizance Over Development of Rocket Power Plant for NACA X-15 Research Airplane, 9 December 1955; teletype conference between personnel of Director of Systems Management and Headquarters, ARDC, 29 December 1955, Subject: BuAer Letter on the XLR30; Letter, Colonel E.N. Ljunggren, Assistant for Aircraft Systems, ARDC, to Director for R&D, USAF, Subject: Cognizance Over Development of Rocket Power Plant for NACA X-15 Research Airplane, 3 January 1956. In the files at the Air Force Historical Research Agency.

24 Letter, Warren P. Turner, Manager, Customer Relations and Contracts Division, Reaction Motors, to Commander, AMC, Subject: Rocket Engine System for X-15 Research Aircraft, 7 February 1956. In the files at Thiokol Corporation. The new engine used an "odd" Air Force designation to replace the "even" Navy designation.

25 Letter, Brigadier General Victor R. Haugen to NACA-Washington, 15 February 1956; Letter Contract AF33(600)-32248, 14 February 1956. In the files at the Air Force Historical Research Agency.

tests, and Reaction Motors considered it fully developed, with the exception of additional malfunction-detection and environmental tests that were required before a flight-approval test could be undertaken. The evaluation of a "breadboard" engine had demonstrated safe and smooth thrust-chamber starting, achieved 93–94% of the theoretical specific impulse, and shown satisfactory characteristics using film cooling.[26]

The engine consisted of a single thrust chamber and a turbopump to supply the liquid oxygen and liquid anhydrous ammonia propellants from low-pressure tanks on the aircraft. These propellants had boiling points of –298°F and –28°F, respectively. That meant that after the propellants were loaded into the X-15 tanks, they would immediately begin to boil off at rates that were dependent upon the nature of the tank design and ambient conditions. In an uninsulated tank, liquid oxygen has a boil-off rate of approximately 10% per hour on a standard day. Even the crudest insulation significantly lowers this, and a well-insulated tank can experience less than 0.5% per hour of boil-off. Reaction Motors pointed out that insulating a tank usually required a great deal of volume, and that the airframe manufacturer would need to conduct a trade study to find the best compromise between volume and boil-off. Since the B-36 carrier aircraft had sufficient volume to carry additional liquid oxygen to top off the X-15, this was not a major issue. Anhydrous ammonia, on the other hand, has a relatively high boiling point and very low evaporation losses. Simply sealing the tank by closing the vent valve would minimize losses to the point that the ammonia would not have to be topped off before launch.[27]

Reaction Motors did have some cautions regarding the hydrogen peroxide that powered the TR-139 turbopump and the X-15 ballistic control system. It was necessary to maintain the propellant below 165°F to prevent it from decomposing, and Reaction Motors believed that it would be necessary to insulate all the valves, lines, and tanks. North American thought that only the main storage tank required insulation, because of the relatively short exposure to high temperatures. However, not insulating the entire system allowed small quantities of propellant (such as found in the lines supplying the reaction control system) to potentially reach elevated temperatures. To counter this, Reaction Motors recommended installing a continuous-circulation system whereby the propellant was kept moving through the lines in order to minimize its exposure to high compartment temperatures, particularly in the wings. If the engineers found the circulation system

---

26 Robert W. Seaman, H. A. Barton, V. Cortese, Reaction Motors report TR-9405-E, "Rocket Engine for New Research Airplane," 3 February 1956, pp. 1-2. In the files at the AFFTC History Office. The use of turbopumps on early rocket engines was somewhat unusual because it was much easier to simply pressurize the propellant tanks and let a combination of pressure and gravity feed the propellants into the combustion chambers. Of course, this did not work well if the vehicle was not going more or less straight up, or when it was maneuvering. It was also much less efficient in terms of the thrust that could be provided by the engine and required heavy propellant tanks to provide adequate pressure. Nevertheless, turbopumps tend to be one of the more difficult items to develop on a rocket engine because they operate under extreme pressures and temperatures. As late as the development of the Space Shuttle Main Engines, thought was given to using pressure-fed engines instead of turbopumps. Given the problems experienced by the Space Shuttle Program with the development of its advanced turbopumps, sometimes it seems it might have been a wiser decision. Many of the early engines that did use turbopumps used a separate propellant (usually a monopropellant such as hydrogen peroxide) to drive the turbopumps. Most modern engines decompose one of the normal main propellants into steam to drive the turbopump, eliminating the need to carry a separate propellant.

27 Seaman et al., "Rocket Engine for New Research Airplane," pp. 3-5. Interestingly, North American included provisions for an ammonia top-off system until an agreement was reached that the ammonia vent valve could simply be closed after fueling, and the tank would be allowed to stabilize at the vapor pressure of ammonia.

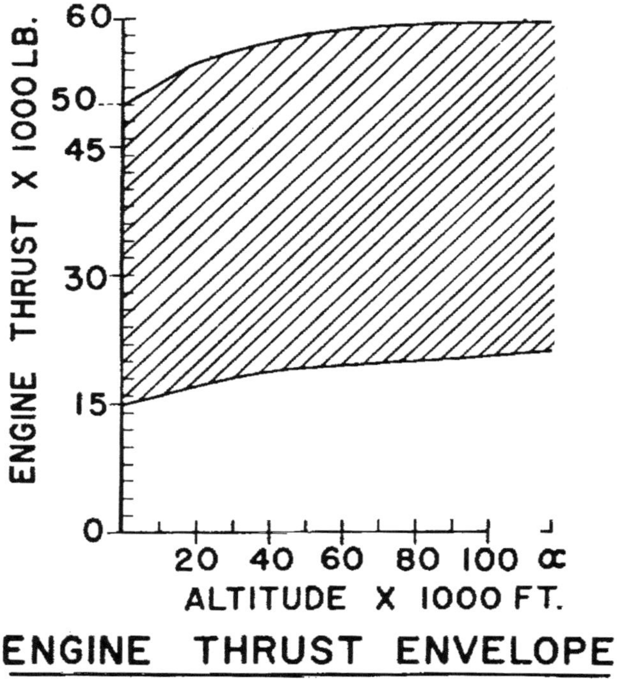

The final Reaction Motors contract called for an engine capable of being throttled between 15,000 lbf and 50,000 lbf, although this was later raised to 57,000 lbf. Some engines actually produced more than 60,000 lbf. The engine needed to operate for 90 seconds at full power or 249 seconds at 15,000 lbf. (NASA)

to be insufficient, it was possible to install a rudimentary cooling system on the main tank.[28]

Engineers considered the TR-139 thrust chamber very lightweight at 180 pounds. Furthermore, it used an assembly of "spaghetti tubes" as segments of the complete chamber, and, as it turned out, the spaghetti tubes would prove to be one of the more elusive items during engine development. The thrust chamber used ammonia as a regenerative coolant, but the exhaust nozzle was uncooled and configured to optimize thrust at high altitude. Reaction Motors expected to use a slightly altered XLR30 thrust chamber. The modifications included the incorporation of a liquid propellant igniter (for restarts) and derating to operate at 600 psia instead of 835 psia. The lower chamber pressure was desired to improve local cooling conditions at low thrust levels.[29]

In order to improve safety, Reaction Motors proposed the simplest igniter the engineers could think of. The igniter was located along the centerline at the top of the chamber and had two sections. The first section contained a catalyst bed that used activated silver screens to decompose hydrogen peroxide into steam and oxygen at 1,360°F. The second section consisted of a ring of orifices where

28 Seaman et al., "Rocket Engine for New Research Airplane," pp. 5-6.

29 Ibid.

fuel was injected; when the fuel and superheated oxygen mixed, they combusted. The resulting flame was used to ignite the propellants in the combustion chamber. Reaction Motors believed this simple igniter would not be subject to the kind of failures that could occur in electrical ignition systems. Despite the apparent desirability of this arrangement, a more traditional electrical ignition system was used in the final engine.[30]

The XLR30 turbopump was a two-stage, impulse-type turbine driving fuel and oxidizer pumps. The turbine operated at a backpressure of 45 psia at full thrust. The designers matched the pump characteristics to allow varying engine thrust over a wide range of thrust simply by varying the power input to the turbine. Varying the flow of hydrogen peroxide to a gas generator controlled the speed of the turbine. The gas generator consisted of a simple catalyst bed that decomposed the hydrogen peroxide into steam. Reaction Motors expected that the engine would need only 2.5 seconds to go from ignition to maximum thrust, and only 1 second to go from minimum to maximum thrust. On the other side, it would take about 1 second to go from maximum to minimum thrust, and not much more to complete a shutdown.[31]

However, using a single turbine to drive both the fuel and oxidizer pumps resulted in the XLR30 liquid-oxygen pump operating at too high a speed for the new XLR99. Haakon Pederson, who became the principal designer of the XLR99 turbopumps, modified the original XLR30 oxidizer pump section to have a single axial inlet impeller operating in conjunction with a directly driven cavitating inducer. This required a new impeller design, new casting patterns, a new inducer, and a new pump case. Essentially, this was a new liquid-oxygen pump, and it became one of the major new developments necessary for the XLR99.[32]

At this point, Reaction Motors expected to take 24 months to develop the new engine, followed by six months of testing and validation. The company would deliver the first two production engines in the 30th month, and manufacture 10 additional engines at a rate of one per month.[33]

All parties finally signed the Reaction Motors contract on 7 September 1956, specifying that the first flight-rated engine was to be ready for installation two years later. The Air Force called the "propulsion subsystem" Project 3116 and carried it on the books separately from the Project 1226 airframe. The final $10,160,030 contract authorized a fee of $614,000 and required that Reaction Motors deliver one engine and a mockup, as well as various reports, drawings, and tools. The 50,000-lbf engine would be throttleable between 30% to 100% of maximum output. The 588-pound engine had to operate for 90 seconds at full power or 249 seconds at 30% thrust.[34]

---

30 Ibid.

31 Preliminary Model Specification for the TR-139 Turborocket Engine, Reaction Motors Specification No. 91, February 1956, p. 15; Seaman et al., pp. 7-8.

32 Seaman et al., pp. 7-8; Paul Gwozdz, Reaction Motors report TR-4085-1, "A Study to Determine Modifications Which Extend the Low and High Thrust Range of the YLR99 Turborocket Engine," undated (but signed on 11 October 1966), p. 3. In the files at the DFRC History Office.

33 Seaman et al., p. 36.

34 Air Force contract AF33(600)-32248, 7 September 1956. In the files at the Air Force Historical Research Agency; System Development Plan, X-15 Research Aircraft, Supporting Research System Number 447L, 22 March 1956. In the files at the AFFTC History Office. As events later demonstrated, even this erred badly on the side of underestimation. The final fee paid to Reaction Motors was greater than the original estimate for the total engine development program. The definitive contract exceeded the original estimate by more than 20 times, and more than doubled the original total program approval estimate.

Less than two months after the Air Force issued the letter contract, the NACA began to question the conduct of Reaction Motors. On 11 April 1956, John Sloop from Lewis visited the Reaction Motors facilities and reported a multitude of potential development problems with the ignition system, structural temperatures, and cooling. Sloop reported that approximately 12 engineers were working on the engine, and that Reaction Motors expected to assemble the first complete engine in May 1957. However, Sloop believed that the Reaction Motors effort was inadequate and questioned whether the appropriate test stands at Lake Denmark would be available in late 1956. Sloop suggested that the company needed to assign more resources to the XLR99 development effort.[35]

Despite the issues raised by Sloop, the Air Force did not seem to be concerned until 1 August 1956, when the Power Plant Laboratory inquired why scheduled tests of the thrust chamber had not taken place. It was not explained why four months had elapsed before the Air Force questioned the schedule slip.[36]

Reaction Motors explained that much of the delay was due to the fact that other projects were taking longer than originally anticipated. The company also admitted delaying hardware manufacturing until a series of design studies were completed, believing that these studies were important for maintaining the schedule. Reaction Motors also attributed part of the delay to modifications of two available test chambers to accommodate the high-powered engine.[37]

THE 1956 INDUSTRY CONFERENCE

The XLR99 presented several unique challenges to Reaction Motors. Perhaps the major one was that the engine was being developed for a manned vehicle, which entailed more safety and reliability requirements than unmanned missiles. However, perhaps even more challenging were the requirements to be able to throttle and restart the engine in flight–something that had not yet been attempted with a large rocket engine. The Reaction Motor representative at the 1956 industry conference concluded his presentation with the observation that developing the XLR99 was going to be challenging. Subsequent events proved this correct.[38]

Robert W. Seaman from Reaction Motors presented preliminary specifications for the XLR99-RM-1 at the conference. The oxygen-ammonia engine could vary its thrust from 19,200 lbf (34%) to 57,200 lbf at 40,000 feet, and had a specific impulse between 256 seconds and 276 seconds depending on the altitude and throttle setting. The engine fit into a space 71.7 inches long and 43.2 inches in di-

35 Memorandum, John L. Sloop, Chief, Rocket Branch, Lewis Laboratory, to Headquarters, NACA, 16 April 1956, Subject: Visit to Reaction Motors, Incorporated, re: Powerplant for the X-15. In the files at the NASA History Office.

36 Letter, H. P. Barfield, Assistant Chief, Non-Rotating Engine Branch, Power Plant Laboratory, WADC, to Reaction Motors, 1 August 1956, Subject: Contract AF33(600)-32248. In the files at the Air Force Historical Research Agency.

37 Letter, A. G. Thatcher, Manager, Division Engineering, Reaction Motors, to Commander, WADC, 17 August 1956, Subject: Contract AF33(600)-32248. In the files at Thiokol Corporation.

38 Some smaller rocket engines could be throttled. The most significant was the man-rated Curtiss-Wright XLR25-CW-1 being developed for the Bell X-2. This engine used two separate thrust chambers (one producing 5,000 lbf and the other producing 10,000 lbf) and was continuously variable from 2,500 to 15,000 lbf. Unfortunately, the engine fell significantly behind schedule and proved to be very unsatisfactory in service.

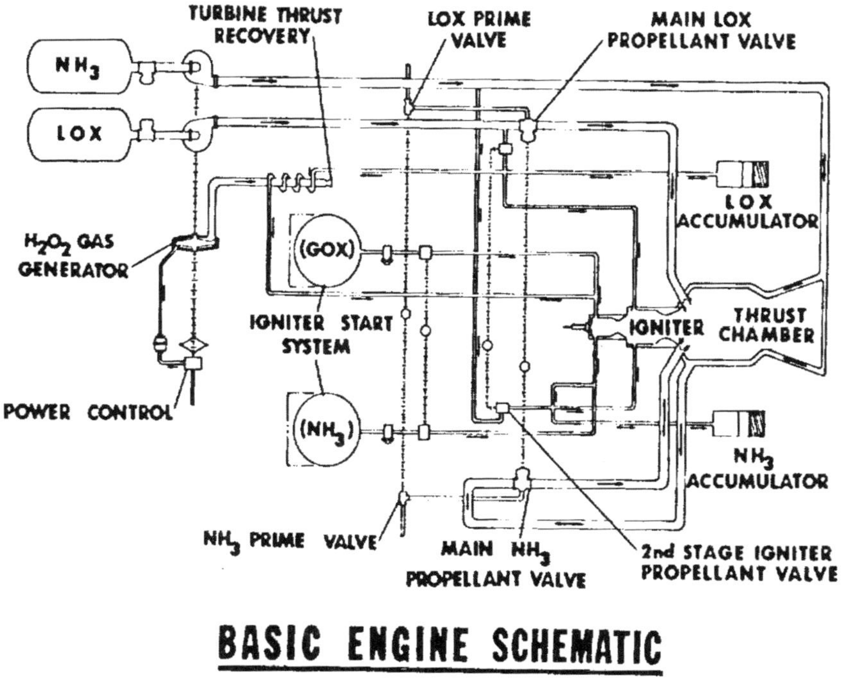

Although not the most powerful rocket engine of its era, the XLR99 was the most advanced and used a sophisticated turbopump to supply liquid oxygen and anhydrous ammonia propellants to the combustion chamber. The engine was capable of being restarted in flight, an unusual feature for the time (or even today) and numerous safety systems automatically shut down the engine in the event of a problem. (NASA)

ameter. At this point, Reaction Motors was predicting a 618-pound dry weight and a 748-pound gross weight. A two-stage impulse turbine drove the single-inlet oxidizer pump and two-inlet fuel pump. The hydrogen-peroxide-driven turbopump exhausted into the thrust chamber. Regulating the amount of hydrogen peroxide that was decomposed to drive the turbopump provided the throttle control.[39]

Engineers decided to control thrust by regulating the speed of the turbopump because the other possibilities resulted in the turbopump speeding up as pressure decreased, resulting in cavitation. Controlling the propellant to the turbopump also required fewer controls and less instrumentation. However, varying the fuel flow led to other issues, such as how to provide adequate coolant (fuel) to the thrust chamber.[40]

The engineers also had to give engine compartment temperatures more consideration than they did for previous engines due to the high heat transfer expected from the X-15 hot-structure. This was one of the first instances in which the surrounding airframe structure would be hotter than the engine. Since North

39 William P. Munger and Robert W. Seaman, "XLR99-RM-1 Rocket Engine for the X-15," a paper in the *1956 Research Airplane Committee Report*, pp. 215-235. The engine was eventually to undergo numerous changes of detail, but its basic design, as described to the 1956 industry conference (excepting its weight), was not greatly altered.

40 Ibid, pp. 215-224.

American was designing the hot structure of the X-15 to withstand temperatures well in excess of those the engine produced, the engineers were not planning to insulate the engine compartment.[41]

Another paper discussed engine controls and instruments, accessory installation, and various propellant system components. The 1,000-gallon liquid-oxygen tank was located just ahead of the aircraft center of gravity, and the 1,400-gallon anhydrous-ammonia tank was just behind it. A 3,600-psi helium supply tube within the liquid-oxygen tank supplied the gas to pressurize both tanks. A 75-gallon hydrogen-peroxide tank behind the ammonia tank provided the monopropellant for the turbopump, using a small, additional supply of helium.[42]

The liquid-oxygen and ammonia tanks had triple compartments arranged to force the propellants toward the center of gravity during normal operations and during jettisoning. The design needed to compensate for the acceleration of the X-15, which tended to force propellants toward one end of the tanks or the other. Further complicating the design of the tanks was the necessity for efficient loading and minimizing the remaining propellant after burnout or jettisoning. Fortunately, the tanks did not present any insurmountable problems during early tests.[43]

Because the engineers did not yet fully understand the vibration characteristics of the XLR99, they designed a rigid engine mount without any special vibration attenuation. The engine-mount truss attached to the fuselage at three fittings, and by adjusting the lower two fittings the engineers could tailor the thrust vector of the engine. Three large removable doors in the aft fuselage provided access to the engine and allowed closed-circuit television cameras to observe the engine during ground testing. Ultimately, this mounting technique would also make it much easier to use the interim XLR11 engines.[44]

MORE PROBLEMS

However, North American was becoming concerned about the engine development effort, echoing many of the same concerns expressed by John Sloop at the NACA. At the 1956 industry conference, North American vice president Raymond H. Rice announced that the XLR99 was four months behind schedule. On 1 February 1957, Rice asked the ARDC assistant deputy commander, Major General Howell M. Estes, Jr., to investigate the apparent delays.[45]

The Air Force and Reaction Motors held meetings on 12 and 18 February, and the Air Force, the NACA, North American, and Reaction Motors met on 19 February. Data presented at these meetings confirmed that the engine was approx-

---

41 Ibid.

42 Bruce O. Wagner, "X-15 Airplane Engine Installation," a paper in the *1956 Research Airplane Committee Report*, pp. 225-235.

43 Ibid.

44 Ibid.

45 Letter, Raymond H. Rice, Vice President and General Manager, North American Aviation, to Assistant Deputy Commander for Weapons Systems, ARDC, no subject, 1 February 1957. In the files at the Boeing Archives.

imately four months behind schedule and overweight. Although the performance estimates were decreasing, the deterioration appeared to be relatively minor. General Estes wrote Hugh Dryden (and copied Rice) that "every effort will be expended to prevent further engine schedule slippage."[46]

The NACA's reaction to the February meeting was different. Hartley Soulé reported that the Air Force accepted the four-month delay, but that Reaction Motors would deliver two engines by 1 September 1958 instead of one. The Air Force also accepted a decrease from 241 to 236 seconds of specific impulse, and a weight increase from 588 to 618 pounds. Soulé pointed out that Reaction Motors had not yet conducted any thrust-chamber tests, and expressed doubt that the revised schedule was achievable. He also noted that the Air Force had scheduled additional engine progress meetings for June and September. On the other hand, the NACA agreed to help Reaction Motors optimize the engine nozzle for high-altitude operations in an attempt to recover some performance. Separately, on 29 March 1957 the X-15 Project Office reported that engine costs had increased to an estimated $14,000,000, plus fee.[47]

Unfortunately, Hartley Soulé's premonitions proved correct. Reaction Motors informed the Air Force on 10 July 1957 that a nine-month schedule slip would be necessary to meet the February specifications. In addition, the development would cost $21,800,000–a 50% increase in only 100 days. Alternately, for $17,000,000 Reaction Motors could develop a compliant engine within the established schedule if the weight could be increased to 836 pounds from the original 618 pounds. Representatives from the Air Force, the NACA, North American, and Reaction Motors met at Wright Field on 29 July to discuss alternatives. The participants generally considered the performance penalty a lesser concern than the increased cost and schedule slip needed to develop the "specification" engine, and the Air Force elected to pursue the heavier engine. Reaction Motors mitigated some concerns when it subsequently reported that the turbopump was exceeding its performance goals, allowing a 197-pound reduction in hydrogen-peroxide propellant. In effect, this resulted in an engine that was only 51 pounds heavier than the original 588-pound specification.

Unfortunately, serious problems arose during development of the thrust chamber and injector assemblies. Primarily, the oxidizer tubes of the spaghetti-type injector tended to burn through at low thrust levels. The Air Force encouraged the company to redouble its efforts, but agreed to raise the minimum thrust requirement if necessary. The Air Force and Reaction Motors also discussed changing to a spud-type injector, but did not reach a final decision.[48]

Despite the increase in weight, the engine program continued to fall behind. On 11 December 1957, during a meeting at the newly formed Propulsion Labo-

46 Letter, Major General Howell M. Estes, Jr., Assistant Deputy Commander for Weapons Systems, ARDC, to NACA, no subject, 7 March 1957. In the files at the NASA History Office.

47 Report, Hartley A. Soulé, Research Airplane Project Leader, to Members, NACA Research Airplane Project Panel, Subject: Project 1226–Progress report for months of January and February 1957, 19 March 1957. In the files at the NASA History Office; ARDC Form 111 (Management Report), Project 3116, Subject: X-15 Propulsion Subsystem, 29 March 1957. In the files at the AFMC History Office. The 618-pound figure had been reported at the industry conference the previous October.

48 Memorandum, Arthur W. Vogeley to Hartley A. Soulé/Research Airplane Project Leader, subject: X-15 Airplane–Discussions at Air Research and Development Command, Detachment #1, Wright-Patterson Air Force Base, Dayton, OH, 29-30 July 1957, 3 August 1957. In the files at the NASA History Office.

ratory, the company reported an additional six-month delay.[49] Reaction Motors attributed this to an explosion that destroyed the first developmental engine, and a series of turbopump failures. The company also confirmed that it had failed to develop a spaghetti-type injector that met the performance and reliability requirements. Overall, the picture was rather bleak.

The spaghetti-type injector consisted of bundled tubing, with each metal tube going to an individual fuel injector. However, Lieutenant K. E. Weiss, the XLR99 project engineer for the Power Plant Laboratory, designed a spud-type injector that used small, perforated disks instead of tubes. Wright Field machine shops built several of the Weiss designs, and researchers ran preliminary tests in early 1958. By March, Reaction Motors was investigating using the spud-type injector on the XLR99.

The mounting engine delays were beginning to threaten the entire X-15 project. In response, WADC commander Major General Stanley T. Wray and Brigadier General Haugen ordered an investigation of the technical and managerial problems. On 7 January 1958, the Air Force asked Reaction Motors to provide a revised schedule and explain how it would correct the various problems. The company submitted the schedule in mid-January, showing a new five-month delay and an increase in costs to $34,400,000–nearly double the July estimate.[50]

Accompanied by personnel from the X-15 Project Office and Propulsion Laboratory, generals Haugen and Wray visited Reaction Motors on 28 January 1958 to discuss the various concerns. Haugen commented on the company's poor record of accomplishment up to that time, which was especially troubling given the importance of the X-15 project. Reaction Motors admitted to its "past deficiencies" and assured the generals that it could meet the current cost and schedule estimates. Haugen and Wray left only partly convinced.[51]

The Propulsion Laboratory and the X-15 Project Office reported their recommendations to the ARDC and WADC commanders in mid-February, and to the director of research and development in Air Force Headquarters, Major General Ralph P. Swofford, Jr., on 21 February 1958. These recommendations included continuing the Reaction Motors development program, using XLR11 engines for initial X-15 flights, approving overtime, assigning the project a top Department of Defense priority (DX rating), establishing a Technical Advisory Group, and initiating an alternate engine development program.

Of these recommendations, the Air Force approved the use of XLR11 engines, an increased Reaction Motors effort, additional funds to cover the increased effort, and the establishment of the advisory group. The XLR11 decision hardly came as a surprise to the engineers at the HSFS and Lewis–they had suggested the same thing nearly three years earlier, as had some at Wright Field. Officials at Air Force headquarters denied the request for a top priority, although they approved a slightly improved priority. The X-15 Project Office postponed the decision concerning the development of an alternate engine, and made it clear that there was a

49 The Power Plant Laboratory and Propeller Laboratory were combined into the Propulsion Laboratory on 17 June 1957.

50 Report, Status of XLR99-RM-1, 9 January 1958 through 27 June 1958, prepared by Propulsion Laboratory, WADC. In the files at the Air Force Historical Research Agency.

51 X-15 WSPO Weekly Activity Report, 29 January 1958.

clear distinction between proposals for an interim engine for the initial flight tests and an alternate engine to replace the XLR99 in the final X-15.[52]

North American had already investigated the idea of installing a pair of XLR11s at the suggestion of L. Robert Carman. Scott Crossfield was not impressed with the idea and said, "I think we'd be making a big mistake." Crossfield was afraid that once the Air Force approved the change, the troublesome larger engine would never be installed, leaving the X-15 a Mach 3+ airplane instead of one twice that fast. Charlie Feltz and Harrison Storms, however, thought the concept had merit. The XLR11 used liquid oxygen, like the XLR99, so the oxidizer tank required no changes. The smaller engine used alcohol instead of ammonia, but the two liquids were roughly comparable and only minor changes were necessary. Feltz, for one, was slightly relieved: "I've been a little concerned about busting into space all at once with a brand-new airplane and a brand-new untried engine.... We're trying to crack space, with a new pressure suit, reentry, new metal, landing—everything at once. I've got a real good buddy [Crossfield] who's going to be flying that airplane for the first time, and I'd just as soon have him around for a while." After a few weeks, even Crossfield came around: "We should learn to crawl before we enter the Olympic hundred-yard dash." Once the government approved the concept of using XLR11s, the technicians at Edwards began assembling a dozen XLR11s from pieces and parts of various XLR11 and LR8 engines left over from previous programs.[53]

The recommendations also resulted in the establishment of a Technical Advisory Group consisting of representatives from the ARDC, BuAer, NACA, and WADC. The first meeting was held at the Reaction Motors facility on 24 February 1958, and the group immediately determined that the thrust chamber was the item that could benefit the most from this advice, since it represented the greatest risk.[54]

In addition to the Technical Advisory Group, the government enlisted the help of other rocket engineers to develop an alternate thrust chamber. North American, which owned Rocketdyne, was reluctant to become involved given its role as the X-15 airframe contractor. Eventually, however, generals Wray and Haugen convinced Lee Atwood to allow Rocketdyne to assist Reaction Motors and begin development of an alternate thrust chamber and injectors. Once North American overcame its corporate reluctance, Rocketdyne immediately began adapting the thrust chamber and injector from the Atlas ICBM XLR105-NA-1 sustainer engine to the XLR99.[55]

---

52 Interview, Captain Chester E. McCollough, Jr., Assistant Chief, X-15 WSPO, Director of Systems Management, ARDC, 14 May 1959, by Robert S. Houston, History Branch, WADC. In the files at the Air Force Historical Research Agency.

53 Crossfield, *Always Another Dawn*, pp. 292-296. The government got its money's worth from these engines, many of which went on to power the various lifting bodies that came after the X-15. Confirmed in phone calls with Charlie Feltz and Scott Crossfield, 9 June 2002.

54 Report, Status of XLR99-RM-1, 9 January to 27 June 1958. In the files at the Air Force Historical Research Agency; Crossfield, *Always Another Dawn*, p. 295.

55 Letter, Major General Stanley T. Wray, Commander, WADC, to Commander, ARDC, no subject, 17 June 1958; report, Status of XLR99-RM-1, 9 January to 27 June 1958. In the files at the Air Force Historical Research Agency. Interestingly, a similar event occurred during the service life of the Space Shuttle main engine. Continuing difficulties with the Rocketdyne-designed turbopumps led NASA to contract with Pratt & Whitney to design and build alternate turbopumps that ultimately proved to be much simpler and vastly superior in terms of reliability.

An additional complication soon developed, although it apparently did not significantly affect the development effort; Reaction Motors and the Thiokol Chemical Corporation began merger negotiations in the early part of 1958. During this period the anticipated reorganization undoubtedly created a distracting uncertainty among Reaction Motors management and employees. Reaction Motors Incorporated (RMI) stockholders approved the merger on 17 April 1958, and the company subsequently became the Reaction Motors Division (RMD) of Thiokol Chemical Corporation.[56]

The Air Force decision to bring Rocketdyne into the fray motivated Reaction Motors to consider alternate designs. However, by the end of April the Air Force acknowledged there were not sufficient funds to develop alternate designs from Rocketdyne and Reaction Motors. Believing that the Rocketdyne XLR105 derivative offered the best chance of success, the Powerplant Laboratory urged Reaction Motors to subcontract with Rocketdyne for its development. Reaction Motors evaluated which design offered the most promise and presented the results at a meeting of Reaction Motors, Rocketdyne, NACA, and WADC representatives on 27 May 1958 at Wright Field. The participants concluded that the Reaction Motors concentric shell thrust chamber would not solve the chamber burnout issue, and Reaction Motors did not believe it could complete the design in time to support the flight program in any case. Since this was obviously not acceptable, all parties agreed that Reaction Motors should discontinue its efforts and subcontract with Rocketdyne for the XLR105 derivative. Two days later the Air Force officially transmitted the 27 May decisions to Reaction Motors.[57]

The next day Reaction Motors and Rocketdyne agreed that $500,000 would fund the development effort through mid-July. Rocketdyne estimated it would cost $1,746,756 to develop the alternate thrust chamber. Producing 14 chambers for initial testing would cost $811,244, and 14 flight chambers would add $657,300.[58]

Despite the appearance of progress, neither the Air Force nor the NACA was completely happy with the progress of the engine development effort. The Propulsion Laboratory prepared two letters intended to provide additional motivation for Reaction Motors. The first was from General Wray to General Anderson, dated 17 June 1958:[59]

> For some time, General Haugen and I have been concerned by the poor progress made by Reaction Motors Division on the development of the XLR99 rocket engine for the X-15 airplane program. This engine was one that had been recommended…on the strength of a supposed advanced state of development of the LR30 rocket engine.… In spite of this state of development,

56 Letter, Lieutenant Colonel L. Schaffer, ARDC New York Regional Office, to Commander, ARDC, Subject: Management Changes at Reaction Motors, Incorporated, Danville, NJ, 7 March 1958. In the files at the Air Force Historical Research Agency; John Sherman Porter, editor, *Moody's Industrial Manual for 1958* (New York: D. F. Shea, 1958).

57 Report, Status of XLR99-RM-1, 9 January to 27 June 1958; Letter, F. W. Tangeman, Deputy Chief, Power Plant Development Section, Power Plant Branch, AMC, to Reactions Motors Division, subject: Contract AF33(600)-32248, XLR99-RM-1 Back-up Chamber Development, 29 May 1958. In the files at the Air Force Historical Research Agency.

58 Report, Status of XLR99-RM-1, 9 January to 27 June 1958.

59 Letter, Major General Stanley T. Wray to Commander, ARDC, no subject, 17 June 1958. In the files at the Air Force Historical Research Agency.

> Reaction Motors Division has experienced continual schedule slippage and financial overruns.... It is by their own admission, as well as the conclusions of our project engineers, that Reaction Motors Division has used poor judgment and management during the early stages of the engine development program. Inability to meet performance and original Preliminary Flight Rating Test initiation date, which was a contractor deficiency, has resulted in submission of supplemental proposals. This by acceptance or rejection has placed the Air Force in the undesirable position of making program decisions which we would have preferred the contractor, through better management, to have made at a much earlier date.

Wray also wrote a second letter addressed to Thiokol president Joseph W. Crosby, but felt it would have more impact if Anderson signed it. Anderson shortened the four-page draft to two pages before he sent it to Crosby on 27 June. Anderson had tempered Wray's adversarial tone somewhat, but still left little doubt that the Air Force was upset. The letter implied, but never explicitly stated, that cancellation of the entire contract for nonperformance was an option. In retrospect, it was high unlikely that the Air Force would ever have taken such drastic action since it likely would have spelled the end of the X-15 program as well.[60]

It is difficult to determine whether the letters, or even the implied threat to cancel the Reaction Motors contract, had any effect on the program. Regardless, things began to improve. Test engines at Lake Denmark accumulated more firing time during the first two weeks of July than during the entire program to date. The tests showed that performance was somewhat low, but by 7 August 1958, engine performance increased to within 2.5% of the specification. Of course, the "specification" had and would change over the course of the contract, as illustrated below:[61]

	Proposal	**Specification 91F**	**Specification 91M**
	February 1956	**June 1958**	**March 1961**
Maximum thrust at 45,000 feet (lbf)	57,000	57,000	57,000
Minimum thrust at 45,000 feet (lbf)	19,500	19,500	31,500
Specific impulse at sea level (sec)	241	238	230
Specific impulse at 45,000 feet (sec)	278	272	265
Engine dry weight (pounds)	540	856	910
Engine wet weight (pounds)	625	990	1,025

60 Letter, Lieutenant General Samuel E. Anderson, Commander, ARDC, to President, Thiokol Chemical Corporation, no subject, 27 June 1958; letter (draft), Commander, ARDC, to Thiokol Chemical Corporation, no subject, approximately 17 June 1958, (used to compose the letter of 27 June 1958, but not actually sent to addressee). In the files at the AFMC History Office.

61 Red Flag Report, X-15 Powerplant XLR99-RM-1, D. McKee, Non-Rotating Engine Branch, Propulsion Laboratory, WADC, 18 July 1958. In the files at the AFMC History Office; Richard G. Leiby, Donald R. Bellman, and Norman E. DeMar, "XLR99 Engine Operating Experience," a paper in the *1961 Research Airplane Committee Report*, pp. 217 and 222.

Although the maximum thrust remained constant, the decrease in specific impulse along with the increased weight had serious performance implications for the X-15. The change in the minimum thrust had less effect, and greatly simplified the development effort, but even so, the flight program seldom used low throttle settings.

By August it was obvious that Rocketdyne had been rather optimistic. At this point the Reaction Motors subcontract with Rocketdyne had already cost $3,125,000–almost double the original estimate. The Propulsion Laboratory believed this was unreasonable given that the original premise was that the XLR105 was a well-established design that needed only minor changes to adapt it to the XLR99. There had been so little progress that the Propulsion Laboratory suggested the Rocketdyne effort be canceled "as soon as possible."[62]

A meeting held at Reaction Motors on 15 August 1958 included Hartley Soulé, Brigadier General Haugen, Brigadier General Waymond A. Davis, and representatives from Air Force Headquarters, the ARDC, and the WADC. Reaction Motors and Rocketdyne provided briefings on the status of their respective efforts, and the participants agreed to freeze the engine design using the Reaction Motors thrust chamber. Reaction Motors was encouraged to continue making minor changes to the injector in an attempt to improve performance, but was cautioned not to delay the schedule or to sacrifice reliability. Surprisingly, given the Propulsion Laboratory's recommendation, the group postponed making any decision on the Rocketdyne effort until October.[63]

Reaction Motors made encouraging progress during September as the company continued to test the engine and injectors. The Rocketdyne program, however, failed to make any significant contributions, primarily because the company could not figure out how to mate its thrust chamber with the Reaction Motors ignition system. The X-15 Project Office conceded that the Rocketdyne effort was an "expensive and apparently fruitless" activity.[64]

On 7 October 1958, the Technical Advisory Group reviewed the engine programs and concluded that although the Rocketdyne effort might offer higher performance at some point in the future, Reaction Motors was well on its way to producing an acceptable engine that would be available sooner. As a result, on 10 October 1958 the Propulsion Laboratory again recommended terminating the Rocketdyne effort, but this time Headquarters WADC and the X-15 Project Office agreed. Reaction Motors subsequently terminated the Rocketdyne subcontract.[65]

Development progress continued at a reasonable pace during the remainder of 1958, despite several failures. For instance, Reaction Motors traced a destructive failure on 24 October to components that had already been recognized as

---

62 Red Flag Report, Engine Testing of the XLR-99, Prepared in Non-Rotating Engine Branch, Propulsion Laboratory, WADC, 7 August 1958; interview, Major Arthur Murray, Chief, X-15 WSPO, Director of Systems Management, ARDC, 18 July 1959, by Robert S. Houston, History Branch, WADC. Written transcript in the files at the AFMC History Office.

63 Memorandum, Colonel J. M. Silk, Chief, Propulsion Laboratory, to Commander, WADC, 20 August 1958, subject: XLR99 Engine for X-15 Aircraft. In the files at the AFMC History Office.

64 X-15 WSPO Weekly Activity Report, 5 September, 13 September, 19 September, and 26 September 1958.

65 X-15 WSPO Weekly Activity Report, 3 October, 10 October, 17 October, and 24 October 1958.

inadequate. Since Reaction Motors was already redesigning the parts, the Air Force did not consider the failure significant.[66]

Despite the best efforts of all concerned during 1958, problems remained at the beginning of 1959. At a 20 January meeting of the Technical Advisory Group, Reaction Motors admitted the engine still suffered from injector failures at low power settings, excessive heat buildup during idle, and minor leakage from various components. A few days later, on 23 January, excessive vibration in a test engine at Lake Denmark resulted in a fuel-manifold failure. Despite the seemingly long list of deficiencies, it was apparent that the development effort would ultimately produce an acceptable engine.[67]

Static testing of prototype XLR99s and associated systems took place at the Reaction Motors facility in Lake Denmark, New Jersey. The test program used four test stands: three at Lake Denmark and stand E1 at the Picatinny Arsenal. The largest stand (R2 at Lake Denmark) was set up to test a complete aircraft system, including a structurally accurate aft fuselage, at all attitudes. Stands R2W and R3 at Lake Denmark were capable of horizontal firing only. The former was used for durability testing and environmental testing, and the latter was used for delivery acceptance tests because it was equipped with an elaborate thrust-vector mount. The test area at Lake Denmark contained support facilities with a storage capacity of 30,000 gallons of liquid oxygen, 18,000 gallons of anhydrous ammonia, and 4,000 gallons of hydrogen peroxide.

Reaction Motors began engine-system testing during the fall of 1958, and by the beginning of 1959 eight flight-representative engines were undergoing some level of testing. Engine run time progressed consistently, and the engines accumulated approximately 340 minutes of operation during the first quarter of 1959. Various components logged even greater run times, with the thrust chamber accumulating nearly 1,800 minutes and the turbopump over 4,200 minutes. The oxidizer pump, loosely based on the oxidizer pump used on the XLR30, operated at approximately 13,000 rpm. The fuel pump operated at 20,790 rpm and was essentially identical to the XLR30 unit. Each pump generated nearly 1,500 horsepower and had an output pressure of approximately 1,200 psi. The combined oxidizer/fuel flow rate at maximum thrust was 13,000 pounds per minute, exhausting the 18,000-pound propellant supply in 85 seconds.

The company finally reached a long-sought goal on 18 April 1959 when the first XLR99 completed its factory acceptance tests. This was the engine scheduled for use in the formal preliminary flight rating test (PFRT), which was based on an MIL-E-6626 modified to include "man-rating" requirements,. The completion of the PFRT series formed the basis of the engine's approval for use in the X-15. The PFRT began the same day the factory acceptance tests were completed, and ran through 5 May 1960. The tests used four engines on test stands R2 and R3 at Lake Denmark, and E1 at Picatinny. Additional component tests took place at the Reaction Motors Component Laboratories and the Associated Testing Laboratories in Cadwell, New Jersey. Reaction Motors personnel conducted all of the

66 X-15 WSPO Weekly Activity Report, 31 October, 14 November, and 28 November 1958.

67 X-15 WSPO Weekly Activity Report, 30 January 1959.

The XLR99 was a great deal more complicated than the XLR11 engines used in most other X-planes. Reaction Motors conducted training classes for the Air Force and NASA personnel who would be responsible for operating and maintaining the engines at Edwards AFB. This was long before computer-aided instruction had even been dreamed of, and the classes were conducted using mimeographed course material and chalkboards. (U.S. Air Force)

tests under the watchful eye of Air Force engineers and inspectors. Captain K. E. Weiss, the XLR99 project engineer, was present for about half of the tests.[68]

In order to obtain a high level of confidence in the service life of the engine, the Air Force required two engines to each accumulate 60 minutes of operational time. Some of the tests were challenging: "[T]he engine shall be run at thrust levels of 50,000, 37,500, and 25,000 pounds for the corresponding durations of 87, 110, and 156 seconds. In addition, one run will be made at 90% of minimum thrust for 170 seconds duration and one run at 110% of maximum thrust for 80 seconds duration." In addition, to demonstrate the "all attitude" capability, an engine performed a series of tests while being fired with the thrust vector 90 degrees up and also 30 degrees down.[69]

Unfortunately, the PFRT got off to a somewhat less than ideal start. The PFRT began with engine 012 performing the attitude test series. After it successfully completed nine 90-degree tests, Reaction Motors repositioned the engine for the

68 X-15 WSPO Weekly Activity Report, 24 April 1959; Captain K. E. Weiss and First Lieutenant R. G. Leiby, Air Force report AFFTC-TR-60-36, "Preliminary Flight Test Rating Test XLR99-RM-1 Rocket Engine," October 1960. In the files at the AFFTC Access to Space Office Project Files. The engines used in the PFRT were serial numbers 011, 012, 014, and 102.

69 Weiss and Leiby, "Preliminary Flight Test Rating Test XLR99-RM-1 Rocket Engine," pp. 9-10.

30-degree nose-down test. After several runs, a faulty weld in the second-stage igniter liquid-oxygen feed line developed a leak that resulted in a fire. The damage to the engine caused Reaction Motors to withdraw it from the test program for extensive repairs. To prevent further occurrence of this type of failure, engineers redesigned the igniter line to eliminate the weld, and the company revised its weld inspection program. The redesigned igniter line subsequently accumulated 1 hour of operation in engines 012 and 102 without incident. Since the original engine had not completed the 30-degree test series, all of those tests were repeated using engine 102.[70]

Another problem was more serious, and continued throughout the flight program. During the PFRT, approximately 80 square inches of the Rokide Z[71] ceramic coating used to insulate the firing chamber peeled off from engine 014. A heat-transfer analysis indicated that the loss of the Rokide coating would not produce a chamber burn-through, but the engineers did not understand why it came off. However, the engine successfully completed its 1 hour of operation, so Reaction Motors revised the acceptable Rokide loss specification based on this performance. Other problems included a transient vibration problem during start that could not be isolated. Fortunately, the built-in vibration cutoff circuit demonstrated that it would shut down the engine before a hazardous condition developed, and restarting the engine after the cutoff was usually successful. The test series experienced a variety of other minor problems, mostly resulting from faulty welds in various components, such as the turbine inlet and exhaust cases. The Air Force did not believe any of these were serious enough to terminate the tests or reject the engine.[72]

Reaction Motors conducted over 200 successful firings during the test program, accumulating 146 minutes of main chamber operation. In the end, one engine ran for 64 minutes and 100 starts; another ran for 65 minutes and 137 starts. The 231 seconds of specific impulse was 7 seconds below specification, but the engine met all other requirements. Engineers explained the low specific impulse by noting that "to expedite the development program, injector design was frozen before the optimum design was achieved." However, nobody expected the slight reduction in specific impulse to have any particular effect on the X-15 program.[73]

Reaction Motors subsequently demonstrated the engine's durability by accumulating more than 60 minutes of operating time on two different engines. One engine fired 108 times without having any more than routine maintenance. In addition, a series of 93 tests demonstrated that the engine would react safely under imposed malfunction conditions, and 234 engine tests demonstrated performance and safety requirements. Of these, 192 were full engine-firing demonstrations, and the remaining 42 were safety-limit tests that did not require thrust-chamber operation. The PFRT cleared the engine to operate between 50% and 100% of full

70 Ibid, pp. 10-11.

71 Rokide is a registered trademark of the Norton Company Corporation and licensed to Plasma-Tec Incorporated.

72 Weiss and Leiby, "Preliminary Flight Test Rating Test XLR99-RM-1 Rocket Engine," p. 11. Cutoffs immediately after launch happened several times during the flight program. The engine would be started after the airplane dropped from the NB-52, only to be automatically shut down because of excessive vibration. The pilot would then immediately initiate a restart, which would be successful and the flight would continue normally, albeit from a slightly lower altitude than planned.

73 Weiss and Leiby, "Preliminary Flight Test Rating Test XLR99-RM-1 Rocket Engine," p. 10; Richard G. Leiby, Donald R. Bellman, and Norman E. DeMar, "XLR99 Engine Operating Experience," a paper in the *1961 Research Airplane Committee Report*, p. 217.

thrust. Testing continued, however, and the Air Force subsequently cleared the engine to operate at 30% of full thrust, meeting the initial contract specification.[74]

It is interesting to note that early in the proposal stage, North American determined that the aerodynamic drag of the X-15 was not as important a design factor as was normally the case with contemporary jet-powered fighters.[75] This was largely due to the amount of excess thrust expected to be available from the engine. Engineers considered weight the largest driver in the overall airplane design. Only about 10% of the total engine thrust was necessary to overcome drag, and another 20% was required to overcome weight. The remaining 70% of engine thrust was available to accelerate the X-15.[76]

At the time it was built, the XLR99 was the largest man-rated rocket engine yet developed. Of course, this would soon change as the manned space program accelerated into high gear. The 915-pound XLR99 could produce 50,000 pounds of thrust (lbf) at sea level, 57,000 lbf at 45,000 feet, and 57,850 lbf at 100,000 feet. The nominal oxidizer-to-fuel ratio was 1.25:1, and the engine had a normal chamber pressure of 600 psi. Playing with the oxidizer-to-fuel ratio could slightly increase the thrust, and the amount of thrust varied somewhat among engines because of manufacturing tolerances. Some engines produced over 61,000 lbf at specific altitudes. The engine had a specific impulse of 230-lbf-sec/lbm at sea level and 276-lbf-sec/lbm at 100,000 feet. The engine was throttleable from 30% to 100%, although the first couple of engines were limited to 50% on the low end until early 1962. Even after Reaction Motors modified the engines and the Air Force approved the use of 30% thrust, a high vibration level meant that they were operationally restricted to no less than 40% thrust. The amount of available propellant was all that limited the duration of any given run. Reaction Motors estimated the service life (mean time between overhaul) of the engine at 1 hour or 100 starts.[77]

ROCKETS IN THE HIGH DESERT

In June 1959, the $450,000 Rocket Engine Test Facility at Edwards AFB came on line to provide local testing of the XLR99, although it would be almost a year before an XLR99 was available to use in it. This test facility provided a capability for engine checkout and pilot and maintenance-crew familiarization, as well as limited development firings. There were two test areas with a large blockhouse between them that contained various monitoring equipment and provided safe shelter for the ground crew during engine runs. During the early portion of

---

74 Weiss and Leiby, "Preliminary Flight Test Rating Test XLR99-RM-1 Rocket Engine," p. 10; Leiby et al., "XLR99 Engine Operating Experience," p. 217; C. Wayne Ottinger and James F. Maher, "YLR99-1 Rocket Engine Operating Experience in the X-15 Research Aircraft," a proposed, but apparently unpublished, NASA technical note prepared during May 1963. Typescript in the files at the DFRC History Office.

75 All of the airframe competitors had noted this, as had Douglas in the D-558-3 study.

76 Charles H. Feltz, "Description of the X-15 Airplane, Performance, and Design Mission," a paper in the *1956 Research Airplane Committee Report*, pp. 28.

77 Weiss and Leiby, "Preliminary Flight Test Rating Test XLR99-RM-1 Rocket Engine;" Leiby et al., "XLR99 Engine Operating Experience," p. 216; Ottinger and Maher, "YLR99-1 Rocket Engine Operating Experience in the X-15 Research Aircraft."

the program, Reaction Motors used one area to test uninstalled engines, while the Air Force fired engines installed in one of the X-15s in the other area. Several "pillboxes" were also located near each area that provided shelter for other ground crews so that they could observe the operation of the engine.[78]

In preparation for the X-15 program, the Air Force constructed the Rocket Engine Test Facility at Edwards AFB to provide local testing of the XLR99. There were two test areas, each capable of supporting an X-15 during engine tests. For most of the flight program, the XLR99 had to be fired prior to every flight attempt, leading several engineers to complain they were testing the engines to death. Later in the program an engine could fly a second flight if no anomalies had occurred on the first. (U.S. Air Force)

In December 1959, the Air Force formally approved the XLR99 for flight in the X-15. Reaction Motors delivered a ground-test engine to Edwards at the end of May 1960, and the first flight engine at the end of July. Initially, the Air Force procured 10 flight engines, along with six spare injector-chamber assemblies. Later, the Air Force procured one additional flight engine. However, in January 1961, shortly after the first XLR99 test flight, only four engines were available to the flight program while Reaction Motors was assembling four others for delivery later in 1961. Reaction Motors continued to use four engines for ground tests, including two flight engines. Three of these engines were involved in tests to isolate and eliminate vibrations at low power levels, while the fourth investigated extending the Rokide loss that was affecting the life of the thrust chamber.[79]

78 System Package Program, System 653A, 18 May 1964, p. 7-1; Leiby et al., "XLR99 Engine Operating Experience," pp. 216-217; e-mail, Bill Arnold (former Reaction Motors engineer) to Dennis R. Jenkins, various dates in September 2002. North American operated the PSTS until it turned over the last XLR99-equipped airplane to the government. At that time the AFFTC Rocket Engine Group, under the Maintenance Division, took over the operation and maintenance of the PSTS and all engine maintenance and overhaul. NASA performed all engine operations, including minor engine maintenance, while the engine was installed in the airplanes.

79 James E. Love, "History and Development of the X-15 Research Aircraft," not dated, p. 18; X-15 Status Report, Paul F. Bikle/FRC to H. Brown/NASA Headquarters, 30 December 1960, pp. 5-6. Serial numbers 006 and 012 were the dedicated ground-test engines; flight engines were serial numbered 101–111, although 101 and 102 were never flown and were always used as ground-test engines. Engine 105 was destroyed in the explosion that damaged X-15-3 on the PSTS, and engine 111 was lost with Mike Adams on flight 3-65-97.

CONTINUING CHALLENGES

Unfortunately, the reliability demonstrated during the PFRT program did not continue at Edwards. Early in the flight program, vibrations, premature chamber failures, pump seal leaks, and corrosion problems plagued operations. Potentially the most serious problem was a 1,600-cycle vibration. Fortunately, the natural frequencies of the engines dampened the vibration below 100 g. However, between 100 and 200 g, the vibration could be dampened or could become divergent, depending on a complex set of circumstances that could not be predicted in advance, and the vibration always diverged above 200 g.[80]

The vibrations caused a great deal of concern at Edwards. On 12 May 1960, as the program was trying to get ready for the first XLR99 flight, the Air Force called a meeting to discuss the problem. Although Reaction Motors had experienced only one vibration shutdown every 50 engine starts at Lake Denmark, personnel at Edwards reported that there had been eight malfunction shutdowns out of 17 attempted starts. The vibration began when the main-propellant valves opened for final chamber start, although the engines had not experienced vibrations during the igniter phase. Since the demonstrated rate of occurrence had jumped from 2% at Lake Denmark to 47% at Edwards, nobody could ignore the problem. Engineers discovered that the 1,600-cycle vibration corresponded to the engine-engine mount resonant frequency, and that Reaction Motors had not seen the vibration using the earlier non-flight-rated engine mounts at Lake Denmark. As a temporary expedient, Reaction Motors installed an accelerometer that shut the engine down when the vibration amplitude reached 120 g, a move the company believed would permit flight-testing to begin.[81]

The engine (serial number 105) used at Edwards differed only slightly in configuration from those used at Lake Denmark; for example, it used an oxidizer-to-fuel ratio of 1.15:1 instead of 1.25:1. The desired operating ratio at altitude was 1.25:1, and this is what Reaction Motors had used during their tests. However, to simulate the 1.25:1 ratio on the ground, the engine had to run at 1.15:1 to compensate for atmospheric and propellant density differences at the lower altitude. Reaction Motors had tested this reduced oxidizer-to-fuel ratio only twice at Lake Denmark, and had not encountered vibrations either time. The company recommended a series of actions, including checking for purge gas leaks at the PSTS, changing the propellant ratio back to 1.25:1, and performing more engine test firings.[82]

By the beginning of June 1960, the problem did not seem to be getting any better. The Air Force conducted two tests with 17 starts on engine 105 at Edwards, with two vibration shutdowns using the ground orifice (1.15:1 ratio). When engineers reinstalled the flight orifice (1.25:1 ratio), three of five starts resulted in vibration shutdowns. Reaction Motors conducted 18 starts on engine 104, and

80 Leiby et al., "XLR99 Engine Operating Experience," pp. 218-219.

81 X-15 Status Report, Paul F. Bikle/FRC to H. Brown/NASA Headquarters, 15 May 1960, pp. 5-6.

82 Ibid; e-mail, Bill Arnold (Reaction Motors) to Dennis R. Jenkins, various dates in September 2002.

three of the four initial starts resulted in vibration shutdowns, but all restarts were successful.[83]

A series of minor changes made to engine 104 by Reaction Motors seemed to ease the problem, and between the middle of July and the middle of August 1960, the engine accumulated 25 starts at Edwards without any vibration-induced shutdowns. In fact, only a single malfunction shutdown of any type was experienced, which was attributed to a severe "throttle chop" that the turbopump governor could not keep up with. Other XLR99s had experienced similar problems, and Reaction Motors warned the pilots to move the throttle slowly to avoid the situation.[84]

The Propulsion System Test Stand was the unlikely name for a non-flight X-15 fuselage that was used to test rocket engines. At least two of the fuselages were manufactured, one for Reaction Motors and one for Edwards AFB. Here technicians install an XLR99 in the PSTS in preparation for a test. (NASA)

Still, as late as the meeting of the Technical Advisory Group on 9-10 November 1960, the vibration problem persisted and the Air Force launched an effort to solve the problem. This program used two engines (006 and 012) at Lake Denmark and completed a series of baseline tests by the end of November that showed a 30% incidence rate of vibration shutdowns with the flight orifices installed. Reaction Motors found that modifying the liquid-oxygen inlet substantially lowered

83 X-15 Status Report, Paul F. Bikle/FRC to H. Brown/NASA Headquarters, 1 June 1960, p. 8-9.

84 X-15 Status Report, Paul F. Bikle/FRC to H. Brown/NASA Headquarters, 15 August 1960, pp. 5-6.

the incident rate of vibration shutdowns. Since this modification did not seem to have any other noticeable effect on the engine, the Air Force adopted it as a temporary fix.[85]

Separately, Reaction Motors determined that o-ring deterioration at the casing joint caused fuel pump seal leaks. Replacing the o-ring was difficult because it took technicians two or three shifts to remove the turbine exhaust duct, stator blades, rotor, and inlet housing; just to remove the exhaust duct necessitated the removal and re-safety-wiring of 60 bolts. Thus, although the o-ring failure itself was not serious, since it simply resulted in a steam leak, the repair required removing the engine from the aircraft, performing a time-consuming engine disassembly, and revalidating the engine installation. This process directly contributed to early flight delays using the XLR99.[86]

Ironically, the corrosion problem appeared to be the result of the unusually long engine life. With a few exceptions, the materials used by Reaction Motors for the turbopump were compatible with the various propellants, but those in contact with the hydrogen peroxide were experiencing more corrosion than desired. There were also some instances of galvanic action between the magnesium pump case and steel parts with decomposed peroxide as an electrolyte. As one researcher noted, "the only thing really compatible with peroxide is more peroxide." There were no obvious fixes, so the program lived with the problem.[87]

The premature failure of the thrust chambers was of more concern. To insulate the stainless-steel cooling tubes from the 5,000°F flame, Reaction Motors used a 0.005-inch-thick, flame-sprayed Nichrome®[88] undercoat with 0.010 inch of oxygen-acetylene flame-sprayed Rokide Z zirconia as an insulating, erosion-resistant top coating. In service, the Rokide coating began to spall or flake due to thermal cycling from the large number of engine starts, and from vibration effects from an unstable flame. For instance, by January 1961 about 50 square inches of Rokide coating had peeled off engine 108 at Edwards, including 14 inches during a single vibration shutdown. The loss of the coating exposed the cooling tubes to the heat and erosive effects of the flame, overheating the ammonia coolant within the tubes and reducing the amount of cooling available. The superheated ammonia vapors also attacked the stainless steel and formed a very brittle nitrided layer. At the same time, the combustion gases began to melt and erode the tube surface. As this condition continued, the effective thickness of the tube wall gradually decreased until it burst. Raw ammonia then leaked into the chamber, causing more hot spots and eventually the complete failure of the chamber.[89]

In January 1961 the X-15 Project Office and the Materials Central Division of the Aeronautical Systems Division at Wright Field initiated a study of methods to improve the chamber life of the XLR99. Two possible approaches were to

85 X-15 Status Reports, Paul F. Bikle/FRC to H. Brown/NASA Headquarters, 15 November, 30 November, and 15 December 1960.

86 Leiby et al., "XLR99 Engine Operating Experience," pp. 218-219.

87 Ibid, p. 219.

88 Nichrome is a registered trademark of D. H. Alloys, Inc.

89 Lawrence N. Hjelm and Bernard R. Bornhorst, "Development of Improved Ceramic Coatings to Increase the Life of the XLR99 Thrust Chamber," a paper in the *1961 Research Airplane Committee Report*, p. 227; X-15 Status Report, Paul F. Bikle/FRC to H. Brown/NASA Headquarters, 1 February 1961, p. 6. In the files at the DFRC History Office. At the time, the acceptable limit was a loss of 12 square inches; this was raised to 68 square inches based on a 350°F cooling limit.

attempt to improve the Rokide coating system, or to develop an improved coating. The Air Force contract with Reaction Motors already included an effort to improve the Rokide coating, but researchers expressed little faith that this would achieve any measurable results. This resulted in the Air Force initiating a program to develop an alternate coating. In the meantime, engineers at the NASA Flight Research Center (FRC) surveyed other rocket engine manufacturers to find out whether they had developed workable processes. Both Rocketdyne and Aerojet were doing extensive laboratory testing of ceramics applied with plasma-arc devices, but neither had put the process into production. Both companies indicated that their experience with flame-sprayed alumina and zirconia had been unsatisfactory. Instead, Rocketdyne was working on metal-ceramic graduated coatings, and Aerojet was investigating the use of refractory metal (molybdenum and tungsten) overcoats on top of ceramics.[90]

At the time, the Air Force already had a contract with the Plasmakote Corporation to study graduated coatings in general, and this contract was reoriented to solving the XLR99 problem specifically. A second contract, this one with the University of Dayton, was reoriented to provide realistic techniques for laboratory evaluations of the coatings.[91]

A graduated coating consisted of sprayed layers of metal and ceramic; the composition changed from 100% metal at the substrate to 100% ceramic at the top surface. This removed the traditionally weak, sensitive interface between the metal and ceramic layers. Researchers produced the coatings by spraying mixed powders with an arc-plasma jet and gradually changing the ratio of metal and ceramic powders, with most of the coatings using combinations of zirconia with Nichrome, molybdenum, or tungsten. The FRC recommended adopting the new technique immediately as a way to repair damaged chambers at Edwards. They noted that engine 101 had been patched using Rokide coating, but the engine would soon need to be repaired again since the coating was not lasting. The Air Force and NASA decided that the next patch on engine 101 would use the new process, and NASA built a special fixture at the FRC to allow the chamber of a fully assembled engine to be coated.[92]

Before the new coating was applied, NASA tested an existing Rokide chamber for 5.5 minutes, and 25 square inches of Rokide coating was lost during the test. Engineers then applied a graduated coating segmented into areas using several different top coats, including tantalum carbide, titanium carbide, titanium nitride, zirconia with 10% molybdenum, and zirconia with 1% nickel. This chamber ran for 5.75 minutes, and only 3 square inches of the new coatings were lost. However encouraging, the tests were of relatively short duration and researchers did not consider them conclusive. One thing that became apparent during the tests

90 Letter, Donald R. Bellman, M. Alan Covington, and C. Wayne Ottinger/FRC to Paul Bikle/FRC, subject: Ceramic Coatings for the XLR99, 16 February 1961; Hjelm and Bornhorst, "Development of Improved Ceramic Coatings to Increase the Life of the XLR99 Thrust Chamber," pp. 229-230.

91 Hjelm and Bornhorst, "Development of Improved Ceramic Coatings to Increase the Life of the XLR99 Thrust Chamber," pp. 227-228. Plasmakote was operating under Air Force contract number AF33(616)7323. The University of Dayton was operating under Air Force contract number AF33(616)7838.

92 Letter, Donald R. Bellman, M. Alan Covington, and C. Wayne Ottinger/FRC to Paul Bikle/FRC, 16 February 1961, subject: Ceramic Coatings for the XLR99; Hjelm and Bornhorst, "Development of Improved Ceramic Coatings to Increase the Life of the XLR99 Thrust Chamber," pp. 229-230.

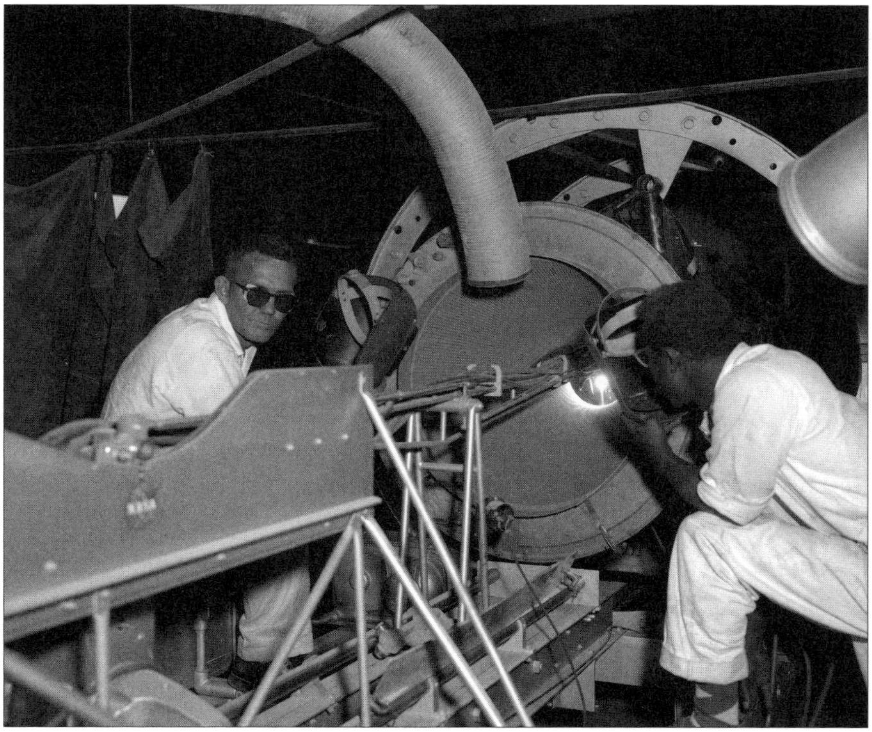

One of the most significant issues experienced by the XLR99 during the flight program was the premature failure of the thrust chambers. Researchers eventually traced this to the spalling or flaking of the Rokide Z zirconia coating that had been applied to the inside of the chamber as an insulator. Although improved coatings were eventually developed, the Flight Research Center also developed an in-house capability to recoat the chambers when necessary, resulting in a significant cost savings compared to sending the chambers back to Reaction Motors or procuring new chambers. (NASA)

was that it would be extremely difficult or impossible to reclaim failed chambers if the coating wore thin or was lost, since the internal damage to the tube might be sufficient to cause it to fail with no visible damage.[93]

The Technical Advisory Group met on 11–12 January 1961 at the Reaction Motors facility at Lake Denmark. All in attendance agreed that chamber durability needed to be increased, and supported the development of a quick-change orifice to simplify ground runs. The group also recommended that the X-15 Project Office initiate the procurement of six spare chambers and sufficient long-lead material to construct six more. It could not be determined whether these chambers were actually procured.[94]

Some documentation indicates that the XLR99 was redesignated YLR99 on 29 December 1961, although nothing appears to have changed on the engines

93 Hjelm and Bornhorst, "Development of Improved Ceramic Coatings to Increase the Life of the XLR99 Thrust Chamber," pp. 230-232.

94 X-15 Status Report, Paul F. Bikle/FRC to H. Brown/NASA Headquarters, 1 February 1961, p. 5.

themselves. The original source documentation from the period is inconsistent in its use of XLR99 or YLR99; this history will use XLR99 throughout simply to avoid confusion.[95]

By March 1962, technicians at the FRC had the necessary equipment and training to recoat the chambers as needed. The cost of the tooling had come to almost $10,000, but the cost to recoat a chamber was only about $2,000–much less than the cost of procuring a new chamber from Reaction Motors. The coating finally approved for use consisted of 30 mils of molybdenum primer in the throat and 10 mils elsewhere, followed by 6 mils of a graduated Nichrome-zirconia coating and then 6 mils of a zirconia topcoat. NASA used this coating process for the duration of the flight program with generally satisfactory results.[96]

As is the case with almost any new technology, some things can never be fully understood. One of the harder things to grasp when dealing with complex mechanical devices is component matching (or mismatching), i.e., why some items will work in a particular assembly and other seemingly identical items will not. For example, during the initial checkout of engines 108 and 111 at Edwards, both engines exhibited excessive vibrations. NASA replaced the igniter in engine 108 with a spare that reduced the vibration to acceptable levels. The igniter that had been removed from 108 was then installed in 111 and its vibration was reduced to acceptable levels. Compatibility was not a particular problem, but scenarios such as this did point out some puzzling inconsistencies.[97]

RETROSPECT

After the first 50 flights with the XLR99 engine, researchers at the FRC took a step back and reflected on the problems they had experienced. Excepting the single incident on the ground that gave Scott Crossfield his wild ride at the Rocket Engine Test Facility, the engine had proved to be remarkably safe during operation. Although there had been a multitude of problems, large and small, the program described itself as "engine safe."[98]

One of the major factors in successful engine operation in the X-15 after launch was the amount of checkout the engine went through on the ground beforehand. This had its drawbacks, however, since "operating cycles on the hardware for ground assurance checks take a relatively large portion of the hardware life," according to C. Wayne Ottinger and James F. Maher. Illustrating this is the fact that 350 ground runs, including 100 with the XLR99 installed in the X-15, had been necessary to achieve the first 50 flights. For the first dozen flights, the FRC conducted a test of the engine installed in the X-15 before each mission. After the

95 System Package Program, System 653A, 18 May 1964, p. 6-14, In the files at the DFRC History Office.

96 X-15 Status Report, Paul F. Bikle/FRC to H. Brown/NASA Headquarters, 2 January 1962, p. 4.

97 Leiby et al., "XLR99 Engine Operating Experience," p. 219.

98 C. Wayne Ottinger and James F. Maher, "YLR99-1 Rocket Engine Operating Experience in the X-15 Research Aircraft," a proposed, but apparently unpublished, NASA technical note prepared during May 1963, no page numbers. Typescript in the files at the DFRC History Office.

12th flight, a flight attempt could follow a successful flight without a test firing–a process that saved 18 ground runs during the next 38 missions.[99]

Between the conclusion of the PFRT and May 1963, 90 modifications were made to the engine configuration. In order to meet the safety criteria imposed by the Air Force, Reaction Motors used the "single-malfunction" concept, i.e., it designed the engine so that no single malfunction would result in a hazardous condition. The company used a dual-malfunction concept with regard to structural failure, meaning that if one member failed, another would carry its load. The PFRT series of tests convincingly demonstrated these capabilities, since 47 different malfunctions resulted in a safe shutdown.[100]

Despite all of the effort that went into developing a restartable engine, this capability was not used during the first 50 flights, except for four flights on which it was used to start an engine that had failed on the first attempt. However, another feature proved to be a welcome addition: the ability to operate the pump and both igniter stages while the research airplane was attached to the carrier aircraft. This allowed verification of over 90% of the moving components in the engine before the research airplane was dropped.[101]

When the engines first arrived at Edwards, several components (particularly leaking pumps and malfunctioning hydrogen-peroxide metering valves) accounted for an abnormally high percentage of the flight delays. Relaxing the operating requirements regarding certain pump leaks and limiting the duration of the pump run time did as much to reduce pump delays as did the ultimate fixes themselves. NASA also noted that "excessive time lag in obtaining approval for correction" and "excessive time required to develop the correction and complete flight hardware incorporation of fixes after approval" were significant contributors to the delays caused by the XLR99.[102]

The control box was the heart of the engine and was responsible for the control and sequencing of the engine. This was not a computer by the modern definition of the term, but rather a mechanical sequencer with some electronic components. The major problem experienced by this device during the first 50 flights was the failure of pressure switches due to ammonia corrosion of the silver contacts–echoes of the original warnings on the effects of ammonia exposure. Reaction Motors finally eliminated this problem by switching to gold contacts. In addition, there were random wiring discrepancies, servo amplifier failures, and timer failures.[103]

During the latter part of 1962, several in-flight oxidizer depletion shutdowns resulted in second-stage igniter damage because reduced liquid-oxygen injector pressure allowed the reverse flow of ammonia into the oxidizer inlet. The subsequent minor explosion either bulged the igniter inlet manifold or blew the face off the second-stage igniter. Reaction Motors installed an auxiliary purge system to correct the problem. In addition, several sensing-line detonations had defied correction throughout the summer of 1963. These occurred in the second-stage

99 Leiby et al., "XLR99 Engine Operating Experience," pp. 216-217; Ottinger and Maher, "YLR99-1 Rocket Engine Operating Experience in the X-15 Research Aircraft."

100 Ottinger and Maher, "YLR99-1 Rocket Engine Operating Experience in the X-15 Research Aircraft."

101 Ibid.

102 Ibid.

103 Ibid.

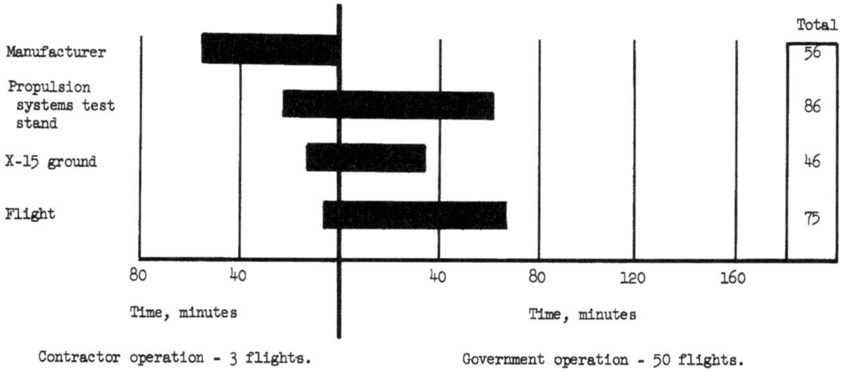

The XLR99s were extensively tested, especially early in the flight program. For the first 53 XLR99 flights, the engines were tested for 188 minutes before being flown for 75 minutes, more than two minutes of testing for each minute of flight. (NASA)

chamber sense line during any thrust decrease when unburned combustible gas from the previous increasing pressure cycle entered the sense line. Interestingly, engineers initially attributed this problem to a lubricant used in the main propellant valve. They believed that the "liquid-oxygen safe" lubricant was impact-sensitive and responsible for the second-stage igniter explosions. Although further investigation later proved this theory incorrect, analysis of the lubricant revealed that some batches were out of specification on impact sensitivity.[104]

The hydrogen-peroxide system that powered the turbopump experienced several problems, including erratic metering valve operation, catalyst-bed deterioration, seal failures, and corrosion. Engineers corrected the metering valve problem by increasing the clearance around the valve. The substitution of electrolytically produced hydrogen peroxide for organically produced product solved the catalyst-bed deterioration, although it technically violated the engine qualification since the PFRT had been run with electrolytically produced hydrogen peroxide. The development of improved gaskets and seals relieved the seal failures and solved most of the corrosion problems. The turbopump itself suffered only minor problems, mainly steam and propellant leaks. The lowering of specifications governing the allowable leakage rate provided the most progress in working with the problem.[105]

The oxidizer system also created some headaches, even though it was largely a copy of the original XLR30 system. The major problems were propellant valve leakage and the need for a quick-change orifice. Improved lip and shaft seals initially helped control the leakage, and eventually Reaction Motors introduced a redesigned valve that eliminated the problem. Prior to the incorporation of the quick-change orifice, it was necessary to remove the engine from the aircraft in order to change the oxidizer-to-fuel ratio. Engineers changed the ratio based on the proposed altitude for the next flight to maximize the performance of the en-

104 Ibid.
105 Ibid.

gine. Once Reaction Motors incorporated the quick-change modification, engineers at Edwards could insert different-sized probes into the orifice while the engine was in the aircraft. This eliminated the need to conduct a ground run after reinstalling the engine. Tailoring the oxidizer-to-fuel ratio actually allowed the engine to produce slightly over 61,000 lbf at some altitudes.[106]

Although nearly everybody considered the XLR99 a good research airplane engine, the engine was far from perfect. Milt Thompson observed that "the LR99 was amazingly reliable if we got it lit, and if we did not move the throttle while it was running." Joe Vensel, the director of FRC flight operations echoed the advice: "[I]f you get the engine lit, leave it alone, don't screw with it." This is perhaps overstating the case, but not by much. During the early part of the flight program, the XLR99 had a remarkably poor record of starting when the pilot wanted. Part of the problem was that the early flight rules said to start the engine at minimum throttle (50% for the very early engines, and 30% for the later ones). The engine simply did not like to start at those throttle settings. After the program decided to start the engine at 100% throttle, things got much better.[107]

Still, even after the engine lit, it did not particularly like to throttle. As a result, Joe Vensel directed the pilots not to throttle the engine until after the X-15 had sufficient energy to make it back to Edwards. Milt Thompson talked him into changing his mind for one flight (3-29-48) in order to accommodate a research request, and Thompson ended up on Cuddeback Lake when the engine quit as he throttled back 42 seconds after launch. After that, the restriction was rigorously enforced: no throttle movement until the airplane could glide back to Edwards. Although the lower throttle limit on later engines was 30%, the program decided not to go below 40% because of the persistent vibration problem. The pilots also learned to move the throttle slowly to minimize the chances of the engine quitting. It mostly worked, and flight planner Bob Hoey does not remember any significant problems occurring later in the program.[108]

During the flight program, eight in-flight propulsion problems resulted in emergency landings. These included one due to no ignition, one because the engine hung at 35% thrust, one shutdown when the throttle was retarded, two due to low fuel-line pressures, one turbopump-case failure, one ruptured fuel tank, and one due to a perceived lack of fuel flow from the external tanks on X-15A-2. Overall, it was not a bad record for a state-of-the-art engine over the course of 199 flights.

Although 11 flight engines were manufactured, only eight were available to the flight program. One (s/n 105) was lost in the ground explosion that seriously damaged the X-15-3 before the XLR99 had even flown, and two other flight engines were dedicated to the ground-test program. Making 199 flights on eight engines was an outstanding achievement.

106 Ibid.

107 Milton O. Thompson, *At the Edge of Space: The X-15 Flight Program*, (Washington and London: Smithsonian Institution Press, 1992), p. 221.

108 E-mail, Robert G. Hoey to Dennis R. Jenkins, 5 July 2001.

XLR99 Flight Engine Run Time Summary (Minutes per Year)									
Year	**s/n 103**	**s/n 104**	**s/n 106**	**s/n 107**	**s/n 108**	**s/n 109**	**s/n 110**	**s/n 111**	**No. of flights**
Pre Del	13.47	31.23	7.90	8.63	6.29	4.64	4.45	4.43	–
1960	11.42	5.88	0	0	0	0	0	0	3
1961	16.66	0	12.05	4.78	13.34	5.98	1.53	5.75	13
1962	8.72	6.13	7.02	18.32	5.77	9.45	11.75	11.87	30
1963	1.43	8.52	0	16.27	5.58	2.55 (9.10)*	11.22	6.32	21
1964	12.03	11.05	6.08	6.52	7.68	6.58	0 (6.33)*	3.24 (20.03)*	27
1965	12.03	7.86	3.26	14.22	15.10	7.73	8.40	5.93	32
1966	2.72	0	15.07	9.98	0.52	2.37	8.85	4.65	20
1967	11.45	3.98	1.23	2.63	5.50	2.72	4.72	2.30	15
1968	3.80	3.60	2.60	0.70	3.63	3.25	1.22	Lost+	8
Total	73.73	78.25	55.21	82.05	63.41	45.77 (54.87)*	52.14 (58.49)*	44.49 (64.52)	169

*Additional time used for ground testing of second-stage igniter purge modification.
+Lost in X-15-3.
Data courtesy of Robert G. Hoey.

As was done for most components on the X-15, all XLR99 maintenance was performed at Edwards using a local, depot-level maintenance approach. With few exceptions, the engines ran for a brief period in the PSTS before NASA installed them in one of the X-15s or stored them for future use. Since the X-15 maintenance philosophy was to provide sufficient spare engines and maintenance personnel to ensure 100% flight engine availability, it was normal to have a backlog of engines in flight-ready storage (essentially spares). The engine activity was divided into three categories: 1) installed in an X-15, 2) active maintenance, and 3) flight-ready storage. Early in the program, NASA conducted one or more ground engine runs (leak checks) after installing the engine in the airplane and before every flight. This requirement for an aircraft engine run between flights was relaxed later in the program, assuming there were no engine problems on the previous flight.[109]

109 Robert G. Hoey, in excerpts from a term paper submitted in January 1976, provided to the author.

Milton O. Thompson had more than his fair share of experience with the XLR99, and enjoyed sharing it during discussions with various groups after the X-15 program ended. One of his favorite stories concerned the emergency landing he had to make on Flight 3-29-48 when the XLR99 quit as he throttled back 42 seconds after launch. (NASA)

The staff of the AFFTC Rocket Engine Maintenance Shop from 1961 to 1968 in support of the XLR99 averaged about 37 people. Interestingly, in 1965 these technicians made about $4 per hour on average. This shop was responsible for all maintenance of all uninstalled XLR99s; the FRC handled minor repairs of installed engines. Every 30 operating minutes, on a test stand or in the airplane, each XLR99 had to undergo a "30-minute" inspection that took just over two weeks to complete. The Air Force overhauled the engines when needed, a process that took just over a month. Recoating the thrust chamber, done by the FRC, took a few days.[110]

Unlike many rocket engines of that era, the XLR99 was equipped with a malfunction-detection and automatic-shutdown system. For most engines, reliability is based on the number of start attempts. However, since one of the primary features of the XLR99 was its ability to restart in flight, its total reliability was

110 Ibid.

defined as the number of successful engine operations per flight attempt, regardless of the number of start attempts. The resulting X-15 data and point estimates of reliability were as follows:[111]

XLR99/X-15 flight attempts[112]	169
Successful engine operations	165
Successful first-start attempts	159
Overall reliability	97.6%
First-start reliability	94.0%

Over the course of the X-15 program, the flight engines accrued a total of 550.53 minutes of run time, plus an undetermined amount on ground-test engines. A total of 1,016 engine starts were recorded for the flyable engines (dedicated ground-test engines incurred many more). Although there were numerous automatic shutdowns, there were no catastrophic engine failures. The safety of the XLR-99 engine (defined as the probability of non-catastrophic engine operation) may be conservatively estimated by dividing the number of successful starts (1,016) by the number of starts plus one (1,017) (assuming the next start to be catastrophic for the worst case). The resulting estimate of the probability of non-catastrophic engine operation is approximately 0.99902.[113]

In retrospect, the engine still casts a favorable impression. The XLR99 pushed the state of the art further than any engine of its era, yet there were no catastrophic engine failures in flight or on the ground. There were, however, many minor design and manufacturing deficiencies, particularly with the Rokide coating on the thrust chamber. Surprisingly, the primary source of problems on most large rocket engines–the turbopump–proved to be remarkably robust and trouble free.

POST X-15

Of the 11 XLR99 flight engines that were produced during 1958–1960 to support the flight program, one (s/n 105) was destroyed in the 1959 ground accident and another (111) was destroyed in the 1967 crash of the X-15-3. During September 1975, researchers at Edwards conducted an inventory of existing engines and engine spares in anticipation that the engine might possibly be used in a future flight program. Seven flight-rated and one ground-test engine remained at Edwards, but the Air Force had already scrapped the others or given them to museums. Although the engineers thought most piece-parts were available from various sources, three high-cost spares (thrust chamber/injector assemblies, turbopump cases, and igniters) were in short supply.[114]

111 Ibid.

112 This is the number of times an XLR99-equipped X-15 was dropped from one of the NB-52s.

113 Robert G. Hoey, in excerpts from a term paper submitted in January 1976, provided to the author. Assuming that the next instance will be a failure is a standard statistical method of determining the probability of failure.

114 Robert G. Hoey, in excerpts from a paper written in January 1976, provided to Dennis R. Jenkins.

For instance, each thrust chamber/injector assembly cost $125,000 in 1965, and 17 were available in 1975. However, the X-15 flight program had gone through 18 similar units, usually because of cracks in the tubing or injector spud. Six pump cases ($12,000 each) had been replaced during the X-15 flight program, mainly due to corrosion, and there were eight cases available for future use. Only 10 igniters ($4,000) were available, but the flight program had used 17, mainly due to detonation at shutdown–a condition that Reaction Motors had largely corrected.[115]

In addition to the possibility of using existing engines in another program, several proposals had been made for augmented or improved versions of the XLR99 to support various projects. The first serious effort was to support the hypersonic research engine (HRE) experiment on the X-15A-2. On 30 October 1963, Douglas E. Wall, the project manager for airborne hypersonic research at the Aeronautical System Branch at the FRC, wrote to James E. Love, the NASA X-15 program manager, advising him that the X-15A-2 would likely fall far short of the performance requirements for the HRE program.[116]

The region of interest for supersonic combustion testing was from 7,000 to 8,000 fps at dynamic pressures between 1,000 and 2,000 psf. Although Wall cautioned that he could not ascertain the extent of the performance shortfall until after preliminary flight tests, at the time it looked like the X-15A-2 would fall approximately 1,000 fps short. At a meeting held at Wright-Patterson on 25 September 1963, researchers recommended that the X-15 Project Office fund an upgrade to the XLR99, and the AFFTC and FRC representatives proposed three different modifications. The first was the use of an extended nozzle to increase performance at the mid-altitudes (≈100,000 feet) for the expected ramjet experiments. The other modifications included a modified injector assembly and the use of a hydrazine fuel additive. Researchers expected that these modifications would take between 12 and 14 months to develop and implement. The X-15 Project Office agreed to look into the matter; however, there appears to be no record indicating that any action was taken.[117]

Nevertheless, Reaction Motors did conduct several studies during 1964–1965 on possible improvements to the XLR99. At least one of these investigated the use of axisymmetric and two-dimensional nozzles, and another studied possible improvements to the thrust chamber. Reaction Motors engineers also kept up with the published reports from other rocket-engine manufacturers to see if any of their developments might be applicable to the XLR99.[118]

---

115 Ibid. The 17 available thrust chambers consisted of four new, one rebuilt, five used assemblies in spares, and seven assemblies installed in the available engines. The eight pump cases consisted of one spare and seven installed in the engines. The 10 igniters included three spares and seven installed units.

116 Memorandum, Douglas E. Wall/FRC to James E. Love/X-15 Program Manager at the FRC, subject: Performance uprating of the YLR99 rocket engine in the X-15A-2 airplane for flight test of the USAF/NASA advanced ramjet engine, 30 October 1963. In the files at the DFRC History Office.

117 Ibid.

118 For the Reaction Motors work, see, for example, Wolfgang Simon, Thiokol (RMD) internal report DS-100-12, "Nozzle Performance Program for Axisymmetrical and Two-Dimensional Contoured Nozzles," 1964; for examples of other reports looked at by Reaction Motors personnel, see, for example, a report by Aerojet General produced under NASA contract NAS7-136, "Study of High Effective Area Ratio Nozzles for Space Craft Engines," June 1964.

The FRC already had some experience with increasing rocket-engine performance by using nozzle extensions on the Douglas D-558-2. These extensions were small, radiation-cooled members that permitted the rocket exhaust gases to attain higher exit velocities by expanding within the nozzle to ambient pressures. Because of their small size, the extensions had no serious aerodynamic effect or structural design implications. It appeared to researchers at the FRC that a lightweight, radiation-cooled nozzle extension could provide a desirable performance increase for the X-15A-2. The researchers admitted, however, that it would be more difficult to design such a nozzle for the XLR99 than for the XLR11 because of the former's larger size and more severe operating environment. The size issue loomed largest because there was a possibility of adverse aerodynamic interference with the afterbody flow.[119]

In order to evaluate this potential, researchers ran a series of wind-tunnel tests that used several different nozzle extension designs. The tests were quite extensive and included various speed brake and horizontal stabilizer positions, ventral stabilizer shapes, and ramjet installations. Tests were conducted over free-stream Mach numbers from 2.3 to 8.0 using the Unitary Plan Tunnel at Langley (Mach numbers up to 4.63) and the von Kármán Gas Dynamics Facility Tunnel B at the Air Force Arnold Engineering Development Center (AEDC) at Mach numbers 6.04 and 8.01. To withstand the high Mach numbers, researchers modified the 1/15-scale model to withstand temperatures of 900°F for up to 30 minutes.[120]

The tests included nozzle extensions of various exit diameters and lengths representing expansion ratios of 22.1:1 to 33.6:1, along with various aerodynamic shrouds to reduce interference effects. In all, researchers investigated nine candidate nozzles, and the tests indicated that none of the nozzle extensions had any appreciable affect on overall drag or static margin, although the 22.2:1 nozzle was most suitable. The use of this nozzle increased the burnout velocity by 400 fps with no other changes to the airplane or engine.[121]

During January 1966, researchers at Langley ran more tests on the 1/15-scale model of the X-15A-2 in the 4 by 4-foot unitary tunnel. These obtained data on various XLR99 nozzle extensions, including ones with area ratios of 11.2:1, 28.8:1, and 33.6:1 at Mach numbers up to 4.63. The X015 models used in the wind tunnels included various other modifications, including a redesigned aft fuselage boat-tail meant to smooth over the larger engine nozzle. All of the nozzle extensions actually improved the base drag coefficients over the basic configuration, and all exhibited less drag than the boat-tail configurations. Despite the seemingly minor cost of the nozzle modifications, neither the Air Force nor NASA took any action to produce any hardware or perform actual engine or flight tests.[122]

In early 1967, Reaction Motors began another investigation of an improved nozzle for the XLR99 designed to increase thrust at high altitudes. The Air Force

119 Earl J. Montoya and Jack Nugent, NASA technical memorandum X-1759, "Wind-Tunnel Force and Pressure Tests of Rocket-Engine Nozzle Extensions on the 0.0667-Scale X-15A-2 Model at Supersonic and Hypersonic Speeds," 15 November 1968.

120 Conversations between Dr. Heibert, AEDC Historian, and Dennis R. Jenkins, 28 October 2004; NASA technical memorandum X-1759.

121 Montoya and Nugent, "Wind-Tunnel Force and Pressure Tests."

122 X-15 Status Report, Paul F. Bikle/FRC to J. Martin/NASA Headquarters, 2 February 1966, p. 3 and attachments.

issued a work order for the study as an extension of the XLR99 engineering support contract, but did not record the exact reason for the study. The new nozzle had an expansion ratio of 22.5:1 instead of the 9.8:1 used on the existing XLR99s, resulting in an increase in vacuum thrust and vacuum-specific impulse of approximately 7% at a chamber pressure of 600 psi. Two percent of that improvement was the result of using a contoured nozzle instead of the 20-degree conical nozzle used on the original 9.8:1 extension.[123]

During the investigations of the new nozzle, all other parts of the engine remained unchanged, so it would have been easily possible to retrofit existing engines. The new engine produced a specific impulse of 298-lbf-sec/lbm and a thrust of 63,378-lbf in a vacuum. The new engine could be operated at sea level without flow separation, although its performance was somewhat below the standard XLR99 at low altitudes. The recommended nozzle design was an overturned bell nozzle composed of tangent circular arcs with a length and end diameter roughly equivalent to the normal 20-degree conical nozzle. The nozzle was designed with an exit angle of approximately 5 degrees rather than zero. This is because the last few degrees of wall-turning only added weight, since friction losses canceled out the theoretical thrust gain. Again, no further action resulted from the study.[124]

Perhaps the most ambitious upgrade was the one proposed to support the delta wing X-15 concept. One of the desired missions for the delta-wing airplane was a sustained 1-g Mach 7 cruise capability, and Reaction Motors sought a way to allow the XLR99 to act as a "sustainer" engine producing 8,000–10,000 lbf for several minutes at a time. The company investigated two different possibilities to provide the sustainer capability. The first used the existing XLR99 chamber to provide the same 57,000-lbf thrust and a separate, remotely located chamber to provide additional thrust during main engine operation and sustainer thrust during cruise. This was conceptually similar to the system used on the Atlas ICBM and the ill-fated Curtiss-Wright XLR25 in the Bell X-2. The second idea was to modify the existing chamber to both provide increased thrust and allow the sustainer function, and to use the previously investigated 22.5:1 expansion ratio nozzle. This second concept was similar to what the 1963 meeting at Wright-Patterson had recommended to fix the X-15A-2 performance shortfall. Reaction Motors estimated that it would take two years to develop and test the modified engine.[125]

Surprisingly, Reaction Motors preferred using a separate sustainer chamber since it presented less risk and required less development time. Throttling the main chamber produced between 26,000 and 62,000 lbf, and the remote chamber produced between 8,000 and 21,000 lbf. This would have provided an engine capable of infinite throttling between 8,000 and 83,000 lbf. The Air Force disagreed

123 W. Simon, Reaction Motors report DS-100-112, "Performance Analysis: YLR99-RM-1 Turbo Rocket Engine with Increased Area Ratio (22.5:1) Nozzle Extension (W.O. 8407-39-3000)," 22 August 1967, p. i.

124 Simon, "Performance Analysis," pp. 1, 10, 14, and 18.

125 Paul Gwozdz, Reaction Motors report TR-4085-1, "A Study to Determine Modifications Which Extend the Low and High Thrust Range of the YLR99 Turborocket Engine," undated (but signed on 11 October 1966), p. 2.

with the risk assessment and considered the problem of integrating a second thrust chamber and nozzle into the X-15 too great, so the delta-wing program selected the single-chamber design despite the longer development time required.[126]

The major constraint imposed in considering the maximum thrust available from modifications to the XLR99 was the number of changes that had to be made to the turbopump. Unlike some other components of the XLR99, the turbopumps had been relatively trouble-free during development and operation. However, because of this lack of problems, nobody was thoroughly familiar with the pumps and their operation. To address this, Reaction Motors brought the original turbopump engineer, Haakon Pedersen, out of retirement. Pedersen proposed relatively modest changes to the turbopump that could provide a 40% increase in pumping capacity. The solution was deceptively simple: speed up the pump. This increased speed was not expected to "generate difficulties with the seals, bearings, or critical speed" or to "affect cavitation adversely." Pedersen did caution that he based these predictions on his own intuition since Reaction Motors had never tested the turbopumps at greater than 100% power. The increased speed, however, required a new turbine because the existing one could not accommodate the 72.5% increase in hydrogen-peroxide flow.[127]

There is no record that Reaction Motors ever accomplished any testing on the modified XLR99 or its components. Given that NASA terminated the delta-wing X-15 project early in its development, it is likely that Reaction Motors never modified any hardware.

AEROJET LR91

Although the XLR99 proved to be a remarkably capable research engine given its relatively short development period and limited operational experience, proposals were made from time to time to replace it. Usually these revolved around the idea of using a derivative of the Aerojet LR91 engine. In October 1966, Aerojet-General submitted an unsolicited proposal to North American that detailed the use of the LR91-AJ-7 engine in the X-15. Aerojet probably intended the proposal to support the concept of using an LR91 in the delta-wing modification.[128]

The LR91 powered the Titan II ICBM, the Titan II Gemini Launch Vehicle, and the Titan III family of space launch vehicles. Aerojet had delivered over 180 engines at the time of the proposal, and had run more than 1,400 engine tests. The engine was man-rated for the Gemini application and the Titan IIIM developed for

126 Letter, Paul Gwozdz/RMD to O. E. Holt/RMD, subject: X-15 Sustainer Engine Studies, 8 September 1966; Reaction Motors report TR-4085-1, p. 2. At these thrust ratings and Mach 7, the XLR99 would have finally lived up to its media hype as a million-horsepower engine.

127 Reaction Motors report TR-4085-1, p. 2 and attachment (letter from Pedersen to Reaction Motors).

128 Aerojet-General proposal, "X-15 Application of Gemini Stage II Engine," 28 October 1966, no page numbers. Copy provided by Aerojet.

the Manned Orbiting Laboratory (MOL). The LR91-AJ-7 developed 100,000 lbf at 250,000 feet using nitrogen tetroxide and Aerozine-50 propellants.[129]

Aerojet believed that the engine offered several advantages for the X-15. The storable propellants provided a higher bulk density, allowing additional specific impulse to be stored in the same volume, although Aerojet suggested limiting the X-15 to 92 seconds of powered flight. The propellants also eliminated the liquid-oxygen top-off system in the NB-52s since they had a very low boil-off rate and would not have to be replenished in flight. An autogenous pressurization system provided tank pressurization gases from the engine in proportion to propellant consumption, eliminating the need for separate pressurization gases and their mechanical systems (regulators, valves, etc.).[130]

Aerojet pointed out that since the engine was in large-scale (for a rocket engine) and continuous production, costs would be lower, and a continuous-improvement program was in place that could benefit the X-15 program. The major changes to the LR91 configuration for the X-15 included modifying it to operate in a horizontal attitude and strengthening the engine to allow it to be reusable. These changes (especially the one to allow horizontal operation) were not as straightforward as they might seem, and a simple description of them took several pages. The modifications to make the engine reusable also took several pages to describe. Nevertheless, Aerojet believed it could provide an engine quickly–beginning by July 1967 allowed the first X-15 flight in March 1969.[131]

The government did not take any action on this proposal or others made along similar lines. Although working with liquid oxygen and anhydrous ammonia presented some issues for the ground crews, it was decidedly simpler than dealing with the hypergolic propellants in the LR91. Moreover, nobody readily believed that the engine would be as reliable and reusable as the XLR99 without a major development effort, something the X-15 program could not afford. Although an additional 40,000 pounds of thrust would have more than restored the performance lost due to the continual weight gains on the X-15, in the final analysis it just was not worth the time and money. Maybe it would have been worth it for the delta wing; but then, perhaps not.

129 These are considered hypergolic propellants because they ignite on contact with each other and do not require an ignition source. Nitrogen tetroxide (N2O4) became the storable liquid propellant of choice after the late 1950s. It consists principally of the tetroxide in equilibrium with a small amount of nitrogen dioxide (NO2). N2O4 has a characteristic reddish-brown color in both liquid and gaseous phases, and an irritating, unpleasant acid-like odor. It is a very reactive, toxic oxidizer that is nonflammable with air; however, it will inflame combustible materials. It is not sensitive to mechanical shock, heat, or detonation. Unsymmetrical dimethylhydrazine (UDMH) became the storable liquid fuel of choice by the mid-1950s. Aerojet used a variation called Aerozine-50 that was a 50-50 mixture of hydrazine and UDMH developed for use in the Titan II. At some point North American had also proposed installing the YLR91 in the X-15A-2 as a means of increasing its performance. It should be noted that at 4,000 mph, the 100,000-lbf LR91 was truly a million-horsepower engine.

130 Aerojet-General proposal, "X-15 Application of Gemini Stage II Engine."

131 Ibid.

REACTION MOTORS XLR11

In order to get flight-testing under way, North American completed the first two aircraft with interim Reaction Motors XLR11-RM-5 engines. Two XLR11s were installed in each aircraft, producing a total of 11,800 lbf at sea level. These engines were quite familiar to personnel working in the experimental rocket aircraft programs at Edwards, since the Bell X-1, Douglas D-558-2, and Republic XF-91 all used the same powerplant (or its XLR8 Navy equivalent).[132]

The basic XLR11 configuration was called G6000C4 by Reaction Motors and consisted of four thrust chambers producing 1,475 lbf each with a turbopump unit, valves, regulators, and controls mounted forward of the chambers. Other variants of the XLR8/XLR11 family used pressure-fed propellants instead of a turbopump. The four chambers were mounted on a support beam assembly that was the main structural member of the engine. A single turbopump provided the pressure to inject the liquid-oxygen and ethyl-alcohol-water propellants, while valves in the oxidizer and fuel lines controlled the flow of the propellants to the chambers. Each thrust chamber contained an igniter, and the pilot could ignite or shut down individual chambers in any sequence, allowing a measure of "thrust stepping." However, once the pilot shut down a chamber, he could not restart that chamber. Fuel circulated through passages in each exhaust nozzle and around each combustion chamber individually for cooling, and then into the firing chambers to be burned. Each engine weighed 345 pounds dry (including pumps) and was approximately 60 inches long, 36 inches high, and 24 inches wide. On paper each engine (including the turbopumps) cost about $80,000, although technicians at Edwards assembled all of the engines used in the X-15 program on site from components left over from earlier programs.[133]

It was surprisingly easy to install the XLR11 in the X-15, considering that the designers had not intended the aircraft to use the engine. Part of this was due to the mounting technique used for the XLR99: the engine was bolted onto a frame structure, which was then bolted into the engine compartment of the aircraft. A new frame was required to mount the two XLR11 engines, but the structural interface to the aircraft remained constant. However, the XLR11 used ethyl alcohol-water for fuel instead of the anhydrous ammonia used in the XLR99. This necessitated some modifications to the system, but none of them were major–fortunately, the two liquids had a similar consistency and temperature. Surprisingly, no documentation describing the changes seems to have survived; however, as Scott Crossfield remembers:[134]

> [S]ince the XLR11 engines were installed as two units including their own fuel pumps, the X-15 needed only to supply the

132 The reported thrust of these engines varied widely. The X-15 Interim Flight Manual (FHB-23-1, 18 March 1960, changed 12 May 1961) listed a thrust of 5,900 lbf per engine, while other sources list 7,000 or 8,000 lbf.

133 "Handbook: Operation, Service, and Overhaul Instructions, with Parts Catalog, for Liquid Rocket Engines Model XLR11," 1 April 1955; Purchase Order L-96-233(G), 6 October 1961. Although called a purchase order, this was actually a disposal form that showed "unlisted excess experimental project support property." Many of these XLR11 engines would go on to power the lifting bodies as they began their test program.

134 E-mail, Scott Crossfield to Dennis R. Jenkins, 7 February 2002.

When it became obvious that the XLR99 would not be available for the initial flight tests, the Reaction Motors XLR11 was selected as an interim engine. The XLR11 had been used, in varying forms, in the Bell X-1 series, Douglas D558-2, and Republic XF-91 programs at Edwards AFB. All of the engines used for the X-15 were made from leftover components from earlier programs. (NASA)

> tank pressures to meet the pumps inlet pressure requirement and the engines didn't know what airplane they were in. There were, of course, structural changes, i.e., engine mounting and I believe some ballast but nothing very complex. That is a relative statement. The difference in mixture would make the ideal fuel/lox load different but I don't remember that was a significant problem.

Charlie Feltz remembers that there were no modifications to the fuel tanks. North American had already built and sealed them by the time NASA decided to use the XLR11s. It was determined that both the metal and the sealant were compatible with alcohol, so there was no need to reopen the tanks. There were some minor changes to the plumbing and electrical systems to accommodate the new engines, along with cockpit modifications to provide the appropriate instrumentation and controls.[135] Nevertheless, considering that North American had designed the airplane with no intention of installing anything but the XLR99, the changes were of little consequence and did not materially delay the program.[136]

In the final installation, the two engines were mounted on a single tubular-steel mounting frame attached to the airplane at three points. The mount canted the upper engine slightly nose-down and the lower engine in a slightly nose-up attitude so that their thrust vectors intersected at the airplane's center of gravity.[137]

After the last XLR11 flight, NASA placed the remaining engines, spare parts, and special tools into long-term storage. Despite being almost 20 years old, the engines later found their way into the heavyweight lifting bodies.[138]

135 These were not so much modifications as an entirely new instrument panel and throttle quadrant. North American supplied two instrument panels for each airplane (one for the XLR11 flights and one for the XLR99 flights), although the X-15-3 never flew with the smaller engines.

136 Telephone conversation, Charles H. Feltz with Dennis R. Jenkins, 19 February 2002.

137 X-15 Interim Flight Manual, FHB-23-1, 18 March 1960, changed 12 May 1961.

138 X-15 Status Reports, Paul F. Bikle/FRC to H. Brown/NASA Headquarters, 15 February 1961, pp. 6.

CHAPTER 5

High Range And Dry Lakes

There was never any doubt that the X-15 flight program would take place at Edwards AFB, California. However, Edwards would play a key role as infrastructure was developed to support the X-15. The program was an involved undertaking, and the operational support required was extensive. Logistically, Edwards would become the linchpin of the entire effort.

MUROC TO EDWARDS

The Mojave Desert–called the "high desert" because of its altitude–is approximately 100 miles northeast of Los Angeles, just on the other side of the San Gabriel Mountains. First formed during the Pleistocene epoch, and featuring an extremely flat, smooth, and hard surface, Rogers Dry Lake is a playa, or pluvial lake, that spreads out over 44 square miles of the Mojave, making it the largest such geological formation in the world. Its parched clay and silt surface undergoes a cycle of renewal each year as desert winds sweep water from winter rains to smooth the lakebed out to an almost glass-like flatness.[1]

Lieutenant Colonel Henry H. "Hap" Arnold decided that Rogers Dry Lake would make a "natural aerodrome," and in September 1933 the Army Air Corps established the Muroc Bombing and Gunnery Range as a training site for squadrons based at March Field near Riverside, California. It continued to serve in that capacity until 23 July 1942, when it became the Muroc Army Air Field. During World War II the primary mission at Muroc was to provide final combat training for aircrews before their deployment overseas.[2]

Until the beginning of World War II, the Army Air Corps conducted the majority of its flight-testing at Wright Field, Ohio. However, the immense volume of testing created by the war was one of the factors that led to a search for a new location to test the first American jet fighter, the Bell XP-59A Airacomet. The urgent need to complete the program immediately dictated a location with year-round flying weather. In addition, the risks inherent in the radical new technology used in the aircraft dictated an area with many contingency landing areas, and one that minimized the danger of crashing into a populated area. After examining a number of locations around the country, the Army Air Forces selected a site along the north shore of Rogers Dry Lake about six miles away from the training base at Muroc.[3]

When Bell test pilot Robert Stanley arrived at the base in August 1942, he found just three structures: an unfinished hangar, a wooden barrack, and a water tower. Things would begin to change quickly as more than 100 people arrived at the base to support the project. On 2 October 1942, Stanley made the first "official flight" of the XP-59A (it had actually lifted off for the first time on the previous day during high-speed taxi tests), introducing flight-testing to the high desert. Only five years later, on 14 October 1947, Captain Charles E. "Chuck" Yeager became the first man to exceed (barely) the speed of sound in level flight when he achieved Mach 1.06 (approximately 700 mph) at 42,000 feet in the Bell XS-1 research airplane. Muroc's place in the history books was firmly established.[4]

However, with the arrival of the X-1, flight-testing at Muroc began to assume two distinct identities. The Air Force typically flew the research airplanes, such as the X-3, X-4, X-5, and XF-92A, in conjunction with the NACA in a methodical fashion to answer largely theoretical questions. The bulk of the testing, however, focused on highly accelerated Air Force and contractor evaluations of prototype operational aircraft, and was often much less methodical as they tried to get new equipment to combat units as quickly as possible at the height of the Cold War.[5]

Not surprisingly, the rather informal approach to safety that prevailed during the late 1940s, and even into the 1950s, was one of the factors that contributed to a horrendous accident rate. There were, of course, a number of other factors.

---

1 Ibid. For additional history of the area see Michael H. Gorn, *Expanding the Envelope: Flight Research at NACA and NASA*, (Lexington, KY: University Press of Kentucky, 2001).

2 Ibid. Despite its usage, legal title for the land did not pass to the Army until 1939.

3 *http://www.edwards.af.mil/history/docs_html/center/pre-military_history.html*, accessed 25 January 2002.The Army Air Forces had superseded the Army Air Corps on 20 June 1941.

4 *http://www.edwards.af.mil/history/docs_html/center/flight_evolution.html*, accessed 25 January 2002; Michael H. Gorn, *Expanding the Envelope: Flight Research at NACA and NASA*, (Lexington, KY: University Press of Kentucky, 2001), p. 181.

5 *http://www.edwards.af.mil/history/docs_html/center/flight_evolution.html*, accessed 25 January 2002.

Edwards AFB, California, hosted the X-15 flight program. The "new" main base complex is located at the center left in this photo, with the NASA Flight Research Center being slightly above the main base on the edge of the lakebed. Rogers Dry Lake was the planned site for all X-15 landings, and 188 times, it worked out that way. Two would land at Cuddeback, one at Delamar, four at Mud, one at Rosamond, one at Silver, and one at Smith Ranch; the X-15-3 broke up in flight and did not land on its last flight. (U.S. Air Force)

The corps of test pilots at Muroc remained small and commonly averaged more than 100 flying hours per month. They flew a wide variety of different types and models of aircraft, each with its own cockpit and instrument panel configuration. Chuck Yeager, for example, reportedly once flew 27 different types of airplanes in a single one-month period. The year 1948 was particularly tragic, with at least 13 fatalities recorded at or near the base. One such fatality was that of Captain Glen W. Edwards, who was killed in the crash of a Northrop YB-49 flying wing on 4 June 1948. In December 1949 the Air Force renamed the base in his honor, while other pilots have streets named after them.[6]

On 25 June 1951, the government established the Air Force Flight Test Center (AFFTC) at Edwards, and a $120 million master plan was unveiled for construction at the base. Part of the appropriation paid to remove the Atcheson, Topeka, and Santa Fe railroad from the northern portion of Rogers Dry Lake and bought out the silt mines that had been located along the route. However, the major undertaking was to relocate the entire base two miles west of the original South Base location and construct a 15,000-foot concrete runway. With the increased number of flight test programs at the base, the natural surfaces of the Rogers and

6 Ibid. Surprisingly, the surviving records are somewhat incomplete, and it is possible that other pilots were also killed during 1948.

Rosamond dry lakebeds took on even greater importance as routine and emergency landing sites. The first AFFTC commander, Brigadier General Albert Boyd, later commented that the dry lakes were nothing less than "God's gift to the U.S. Air Force." That same year, the USAF Test Pilot School moved from Wright Field to the high desert.[7]

THE HIGH-SPEED FLIGHT STATION

On 30 September 1946, Walter C. Williams and four other engineers from NACA Langley arrived at the Muroc Army Air Field to assist in flight-testing the XS-1. It was supposed to be a temporary assignment, and the group did not even have an official name, although they called themselves the NACA Muroc Flight Test Unit. This marked the beginning of the joint USAF-NACA research airplane program that would culminate with the X-15. The NACA Muroc Flight Test Unit received permanent status from Hugh Dryden on 7 September 1947, with Walt Williams named as head of a group that now numbered 27 people.[8]

By the time the NACA redesignated the unit the High-Speed Flight Research Station (HSFRS) on 14 November 1949, roughly 100 people worked for Williams, who was named chief of the station. In February 1953, the Air Force formally leased 175 acres at the north end of the main taxiway to the NACA for a permanent installation.[9]

On 26 June 1954, the now-200-strong NACA contingent moved from its primitive quarters on South Base to a new headquarters, located in Building 4800 on the north side of the new Edwards flight line. This building still serves as the core of the Dryden Flight Research Center (DFRC). The new facility cost $3.8 million. In contrast to the small NACA station at Edwards, the Air Force contingent at the AFFTC numbered over 8,000. The NACA organization was renamed the High-Speed Flight Station (HSFS) on 1 July 1954, with Williams still in charge.[10]

On 1 October 1958, the National Aeronautics and Space Administration (NASA) replaced the NACA, and on 27 September 1959, NASA Headquarters redesignated the HSFS the Flight Research Center (FRC). By the time the sta-

7 *http://www.edwards.af.mil/history/docs_html/center/lakebeds.html*, accessed 25 January 2002; Gorn, *Expanding the Envelope*, p. 204.

8 *http://www.dfrc.nasa.gov/Dryden/mistone.html* accessed 25 January 2002. Many sources say that 13 personnel arrived on 30 September, but DFRC Historian J.D. Hunley says only five (Williams, Cloyce E. Matheny, William S. Aiken, George P. Minalga, and Harold B. Youngblood) arrived on this date and the total of 13 was not reached until early December. The Muroc Flight Test Unit from Langley had been informally established by Walter C. Williams on 30 September 1946 in support of testing the XS-1, and achieved permanent status on 7 September 1947. It was redesignated the High-Speed Flight Research Station (HSFRS) on 14 November 1949, the High-Speed Flight Station (HSFS) on 1 July 1954, the Flight Research Center (FRC) on 27 September 1959, and the Hugh L. Dryden Flight Research Center (usually abbreviated DFRC) on 26 March 1976. On 1 October 1981 it was administratively absorbed into the Ames Research Center and changed its name to the Ames-Dryden Flight Research Facility (DFRF). It reverted to Center status on 1 March 1994 and again became DFRC. At some point between 1954 and 1959, the hyphen between "High" and "Speed" seems to have been dropped, but no official evidence of this could be found.

9 Jane Van Nimmen and Leonard C. Bruno, with Robert L. Rosholt, *NASA Historical Data Book, 1958-1968, Volume I: NASA Resources 1958-1968*, NASA publication SP-4012 (Washington, DC: NASA, 1988), pp. 297-298; *http://www.dfrc.nasa.gov/Dryden/milestone.html*, accessed 25 January 2002.

10 *http://www.dfrc.nasa.gov/Dryden/milestone.html*, accessed 25 January 2002.

On 27 January 1953, a ground-breaking ceremony was held at the site of the future NACA High-Speed Flight Station on the new main base at Edwards AFB. Shown in the photo are (left to right) Gerald Truszynski, Head of Instrumentation Division; Joseph Vensel, Head of the Operations Branch; Walter Williams, Head of the Station, scooping the first shovel full of dirt; Marion Kent, Head of Personnel; and California state official Arthur Samet. (NASA)

tion became a center, Williams was gone. At the behest of Hugh Dryden, on 14 September 1959 he had joined Project Mercury (the first American manned space effort) as its operations director. In his place came Paul F. Bikle, a Pennsylvanian with long experience in flight-testing at the nearby AFFTC. Bikle replaced Williams on 15 September 1959, oversaw its transition to the FRC, and remained for the next 12 years. Bikle believed in doing things quietly and with a minimum of fuss and outside attention. "Under Paul Bikle," one engineer recalled, "we were well aware that headquarters was 3,000 miles away." Like Williams before him, Bikle impressed those who encountered him with his bluntness, drive, and engineering sense.[11]

The first challenge faced by Bikle was shifting from planning for the X-15 program to conducting it. He needed people, and asked Ira Abbott at Headquarters for authority to add 80 new positions to the rapidly growing X-15 team. The personnel and facilities at the FRC expanded throughout the 1960s, with the budget going from $3.28 million in 1959 to $20.85 million in 1963, and to $32.97

11 Richard P. Hallion, *On the Frontier: Flight Research at Dryden, 1946-1981*, NASA publication SP-4303, (Washington, DC: NASA, 1984), p. 101; Robert L. Rosholt, *An Administrative History of NASA, 1958-1963*, NASA publication SP-4101 (Washington, DC: NASA, 1966), p. 79. Within the NACA the pecking order was 1) headquarters, 2) research laboratories, and 3) stations. NASA maintained a similar caste system, calling them centers and facilities instead. Paul F. Bikle (1916-1991) earned a B.S. in aeronautical engineering from the University of Detroit in 1939 and was employed by Taylorcraft Aviation Corp. for a year before working for the Air Corps and Air Force as a civilian from 1940 to 1959, both at Wright Field and at the Flight Test Center at Edwards AFB. At Edwards, he rose to the position of technical director of the center. In 1959 he became director of the NASA Flight Research Center, a position he held until his retirement in 1971.

The employees of the NACA High-Speed Flight Station are gathered for a 1954 photo shoot on the front steps of building 4800, the new NACA facility at Edwards AFB. This new building was considerably larger than the earlier NACA buildings on South Base to support a staff that had increased from 132 in 1950 to 250 in 1954. As the workload increased and more research flights were completed the complement of employees grew to 662 in 1966, largely the result of the X-15 flight program. (NASA)

million in 1968. The staff went from 292 to a peak of 669 in 1965; by the end of the X-15 program, the staff was down to 566.[12]

THE HIGH RANGE

Previous rocket planes, such as the X-1 and X-2, had been able to conduct the majority of their flight research directly over Edwards and the lakebeds immediately surrounding the base. The capabilities of the X-15, however, would need vastly more airspace. The proposed trajectories required an essentially straight flight corridor almost 500 miles long, and the need to acquire real-time data necessitated the installation of radar, telemetry, and communications sites along the entire path. There was also a need for suitable emergency landing areas all along the flight corridor. Fortunately, the high desert was an ideal location for such requirements since many of the ancient lakes had long since vanished, leaving behind dry and hard-packed contingency landing areas.[13]

12 Van Nimmen et al., *NASA Historical Data Book, 1958-1968*, pp. 90-91.

13 Stillwell, *X-15 Research Results*. Collectively, the land, equipment, and personnel that support this type of activity are known as a "range." The High Range discussed in this chapter is just one of many test ranges operated by the United States for a variety of purposes–mainly military. The most visible ranges are the Eastern Range at Cape Canaveral, FL (stretching to Ascension Island in the South Atlantic), and the Western Range at Vandenberg AFB, CA. However, there are also major test ranges at Edwards AFB, NAS Pt. Mugu, Eglin AFB, the Utah Test and Training Range (UTTR), White Sands Missile Range, and a host of others.

As early as 7 April 1955 Brigadier General Benjamin S. Kelsey wrote to Hugh Dryden (both were members of the Research Airplane Committee) suggesting a cooperative agreement on the construction and operation of a new range to support the X-15 program. A range had been included in the initial Air Force cost estimates, with $1,500,000 budgeted for its construction. At a meeting of the Research Airplane Committee on 17 May 1955, the NACA agreed to cooperate with the WADC and AFFTC in planning the range: the Air Force would build and equip it, and the NACA would operate it after its completion. It was much the same agreement that governed the X-15 itself.[14]

However, this decision was not favorably received by AFFTC personnel, who felt they were "being relegated to the position of procurement agent" for the NACA. On 15 June, Walt Williams met with the AFFTC commander, Brigadier General J. Stanley Holtoner, to discuss the concept for the new X-15 range. Williams began by updating Holtoner on the status of the X-15 program since the general had not heard any details since the previous October. During this discussion, Holtoner indicated his willingness to cooperate in developing the range and agreed with Williams that the AFFTC should not become actively involved until the NACA was able to discuss "detailed items of hardware" and support. Nevertheless, he felt the AFFTC "should have a somewhat stronger position in the project."[15]

Despite the apparent lack of enthusiasm for the arrangements within the AFFTC, on 28 July 1955 an amendment to the original X-15 development directive was issued that clearly established the AFFTC's responsibilities for building the range. However, since neither document discussed which organization would operate the range, the AFFTC renewed its efforts to acquire this responsibility.

A conference at ARDC Headquarters in Baltimore on 15 September 1955 set in place the basic architecture of the range. Technical personnel reviewed the availability of various types of radar and decided that all of the range stations should be similar and include telemetry receivers as well as radar equipment. Although no decision was made regarding the specific radar equipment, the choices were narrowed to the AFMTC Model II used on the Atlantic Missile Range, and the Canoga Mod 3 used by North American at White Sands. On 13 October the HSFS proposed expanding the use of telemetry beyond that used on earlier X-planes. In addition to the normal engine-related information that was traditionally monitored, the HSFS wanted to obtain aircraft information (structural, flight path, temperature, etc.), research data (cosmic ray concentrations, etc.), and pilot physiological effects. This was a stretch for the available technology.[16]

---

14 Letter, Brigadier General Benjamin S. Kelsey, Director for Research and Development DCS/D, USAF, to Director of the NACA, no subject, 7 April 1955; letter, Hugh L. Dryden to Deputy Director for Research and Development, no subject, 20 May 1955. In the files at the NASA History Office.

15 Memorandum for record, Major J. E. Downhill, Assistant Chief, Test Project Section, Aeronautics & Propulsion Division, ARDC, subject: Flight Test Range for the X-15, 28 July 1955. In the files at the AFFTC History Office; memorandum, Walter C. Williams/HSFS to Hartley A. Soulé/Research Airplane Project Leader, no subject, 15 June 1955.

16 Memorandum for the Files (HSFS), 13 October 1955; transmitted to Langley on 18 October 1955. In the files at the DRFC History Office; Gerald M. Truszynski and W. D. Mace, "Status of High-Range and Flow-Direction Sensor," a paper in the *1958 Research Airplane Committee Report*, pp. 151-152. This radar was also known as the PAFB (Patrick AFB) Mod 2.

Developing the final specifications for the new range was the subject of a meeting on 16 November 1955. This is when the AFFTC made its move for control, stating that the Air Force would like to operate and maintain the range on the condition that the NACA could also use it for the X-15. The NACA reminded the Air Force that the verbal agreement between Hugh Dryden and General Kelsey had already settled the issue. The NACA representatives also pointed out that the safe operation of the X-15 would depend heavily upon data acquired by the ground stations, and that a division of responsibility would not be desirable. The issue, however, would not go away, and on 2 December 1955 the AFFTC deputy chief of staff for operations at the AFFTC, Lieutenant Colonel Bentley H. Harris, Jr., wrote to the commander of ARDC formally requesting that his center "be assigned the responsibility for operating, as well as developing, the test range." The ARDC reiterated that the NACA would operate the range, but the AFFTC could use it on a non-interference basis.[17]

Despite this contentious beginning, in the end the NACA and AFFTC cooperated in planning and using the range. The HSFS instrumentation staff under Gerald M. Truszynski largely determined the requirements based on experience gained during prior research programs. In November 1955, Truszynski informed the Research Airplane Committee that the range should be at least 400 miles long, with three radar stations able to furnish precise data on aircraft position, reentry prediction, geometric altitude, and ground speed. The X-15 required a launch site located near an emergency landing area, intermediate landing sites, intermediate launch sites (for less than full-power/full-duration flights), airfields near the radar sites that could be used for support, and a "reasonably straight course" for the high-speed flight profile.[18]

Besides the technical issues, many other factors determined where the range and its associated ground facilities would be located. Because of the sonic booms, it was not desirable to have the X-15 fly over major metropolitan areas, at least not routinely. Avoiding commercial airline corridors would make flight planning easier, and avoiding mountains would make the pilots happier. Ground stations needed proper "look angles" so that at least one of them could "see" the X-15 at all times. Emergency landing sites had to be spaced so that the X-15 would always be within gliding distance of one of them. The parameters seemed endless.

Truszynski and his staff concluded that the best course lay on a straight line from Wendover, Utah, to Edwards, with tracking stations near Ely and Beatty, Nevada, and at Edwards. The range would take the X-15 over some of the most beautiful, rugged, and desolate terrain in the Western hemisphere, flying high over

17 Letter, Hartley A. Soulé/Research Airplane Project Leader, to NACA Liaison Officer, WPAFB, subject: Air Force-North American-NACA conference on Project 1226 Range, 20 December 1955. In the files at the NASA History Office; letter, Lieutenant Colonel Bentley H. Harris, Jr., DCS/O, AFFTC, to Commander, ARDC, subject: X-15 Research Aircraft, 2 December 1955. In the files at the AFFTC History Office.

18 Letter, Gerald M. Truszynski to Dennis R. Jenkins, 9 May 2002; memorandum, John L. Sloop/HSFS to Hartley A. Soulé/Research Airplane Project Leader, no subject, 7 November 1955; memorandum for the files (HSFS), unsigned, 10 November 1955. Gerry Truszynski had arrived at Muroc in 1947 and remained there until mid-1960 when he left to join the Office of Space Flight Operations in the Space Sciences Directorate at NASA Headquarters. This organization later became the Office of Tracking and Data Acquisition, with Truszynski as its chief; the group's primary legacy was the development of the Mercury tracking and communications network.

Death Valley before swooping down over the Searles basin to a landing on Rogers Dry Lake.[19]

All of this led to construction of the High Altitude Continuous Tracking Range, which is generally known simply as the High Range. Officially, the effort was known as Project 1876. The Electronic Engineering Company (EECo) of Los Angeles accomplished the design and construction of the range under an Air Force contract awarded on 9 March 1956. The requirements noted that the "range will consist of a ground area approximately 50 miles wide and 400 miles long wherein a vehicle flying at altitudes up to 500,000 feet can be tracked continuously."[20]

Despite the hopelessly optimistic original budget of $1,500,000, the three tracking stations did not come cheap–the more-sophisticated Edwards station cost $4,244,000, and the costs of the other two together were about the same. The Air Force spent another $3.3 million on initial High Range construction, and the NACA would spend a similar amount for improvements over the first few years of operations. An office at Patrick AFB, Florida, managed the procurement of the radar equipment under a modification to an existing contract for the Atlantic Missile Range (later the Eastern Range).[21]

The agreement between the NASA and the AFFTC stated that the Air Force would "retain title to the land, buildings, and equipment, except those physically located within NASA facilities." In addition, "control, operation and support of High Range will revert to USAF upon the conclusion of X-15 Flight Research or earlier if the Research Airplane Committee judges that the National Situation so dictates."[22]

Although Truszynski and his staff at the HSFS had developed the basic configuration of the High Range, it was up to the EECo–with the advice and consent of the government–to select the actual sites for the tracking stations. Since the HSFS staff had already made rough site selections, the next step was developing a radar coverage map. This map showed considerations such as obstructions on the horizon, the curvature of the Earth, and the range in which a target could be "seen" by radar at specified altitudes. This map narrowed down the area that the EECo needed to investigate in detail. Next came a lot of field work.[23]

---

19 Letter, Hartley A. Soulé/Research Airplane Project Leader, to NACA Liaison Officer, WPAFB, subject: Air Force-North American-NACA conference on Project 1226 Range, 20 December 1955. In the files at the NASA History Office.

20 System Development Plan, X-15 Research Aircraft, Supporting Research System Number 447L, 22 March 1956; Engineering Plan, Project High Range, Electronic Engineering Company of California, not dated (but probably late 1956). In the files at the AFFTC History Office; Walter C. Williams, "X-15 Concept Evolution" a paper in the *Proceedings of the X-15 30th Anniversary Celebration*, Dryden Flight Research Facility, Edwards, CA, 8 June 1989, NASA CP-3105, p. 14; R&D Project Card, Project 1876 (part of Project 1226), 27 March 1956. The EECo contract was AF04(611)-1703. The range appears to have had two official names. The NACA called it the High Altitude Continuous Tracking Range, while the Air Force referred to it as the X-15 Radar Range. Fortunately, both agreed on the "short term" of High Range.

21 X-15 WSPO Weekly Activity Report, 21 June 1956; "Advanced development Plan for X-15 Research Aircraft, Advanced Technology Program 653A," 17 November 1961, pp. 19-20. In the files at the AFFTC History Office; Van Nimmen et al., *NASA Historical Data Book, 1958-1968*, p. 300. The Air Force paid for the construction of the physical facilities, radar equipment, roads, and the communication system; the NACA paid for procurement of the telemetry systems, consoles, recorders, strip charts, and other items of "instrumentation." Ely cost $2,688,000, and Beatty cost $2,122,000 according to the Data Book.

22 "Advanced Development Plan for X-15 Research Aircraft, Advanced Technology Program 653A," 17 November 1961, pp. 19-20. In the files at the AFFTC History Office.

23 "Engineering Plan, Project High Range," Electronic Engineering Company of California, not dated (but probably late 1956), pp. 2-1 through 2-7. In the files at the AFFTC History Office; "X-15 Range Facility," prepared by the NASA Flight Research Facility, November 1959. In the files at the DFRC History Office.

Preliminary investigations by AFFTC, NACA, and EECo personnel indicated a possible site called VABM 8002 located 1.5 miles northwest of Ely, Nevada (the number referred to the site's elevation: 8,002 feet above sea level). However, measurements and photographs from this site taken by EECo personnel indicated that it would not provide the required radar sight lines because of an extremely wide and high blockage angle almost directly downrange from the site. In addition, constructing an access road would have required a "considerable amount" of rock blasting. EECo ruled out using the site.[24]

An alternate site in Ely was on Rib Hill. This 8,062-foot-high location was a considerable improvement over VABM 8002 in terms of radar sight lines and the ability to build a road and construct the site itself. The downside was that it was adjacent to the Ruth Copper Pit, and the Kennecott Copper Corporation was already planning to extend the operation into the side of Rib Hill. Even if the hill went untouched, the mining operation would have created too much earth movement for a precision radar installation, so again the EECo ruled out the site.[25]

Fortunately, while investigating the Rib Hill site, EECo personnel ventured to the south ridge of the Rib Hill range. This site was promising because the radar sight lines were excellent. The civil engineering firm of F. W. Millard and Son conducted a detailed land survey, mapping out the best location of the buildings and the access road. The EECo estimated that a 5.65-mile-long, 12-foot-wide road from U.S. Highway 50 to the site would cost approximately $72,400, which included installing culverts and drainage ditches, cutting and filling slopes, clearing and compacting the base, and finishing the gravel road.[26] The road would take advantage of southerly exposures to gain maximum natural snow removal, and arrangements with the White Pine County Road Department and the Nevada Highway Department provided additional mechanical snow removal. It was 10 miles southeast to the town of Ely from the junction of the site access road and Highway 50. The Ely Airport, which was a scheduled stop for several commercial airlines, was five miles east of the town. There were some drawbacks, however. The Kennecott Copper Company offered to supply electricity for a nominal cost, but an evaluation of the mining company's generators showed that the current could fluctuate ±10%, which was unacceptable for the sensitive electronic equipment at the site. EECo estimated that voltage regulators and power lines would cost more than procuring primary and backup generators and generating the required power on-site. In addition, there was no water available at the site, so tank trailers would have to haul water from Ely and store it in a tank at the site.[27]

The site at Beatty was somewhat easier to locate. Preliminary investigations by the AFFTC and NACA resulted in the selection of a location approximately six miles northwest of Springdale, Nevada. Further investigation by EECo personnel substantiated this selection. The site was at an elevation of 4,900 feet, approximately three miles west of U.S. Highway 95. The radar sight lines were excellent,

24 Engineering Plan, Project High Range," p. 2-8. A vertical angle bench mark (VABM) is a USGS accuracy code that provides a standardization of observed gravity precision, elevation control, and latitude and longitude control. VABM was also the nearest name on the map to the desired location.

25 Engineering Plan, Project High Range," pp. 2-8 and 2-9.

26 The other mile and a half used an existing gravel road that exited Highway 50 at an opportune location.

27 Engineering Plan, Project High Range," pp. 2-9 through 2-10, 3-4, and 3-10 to 3-11.

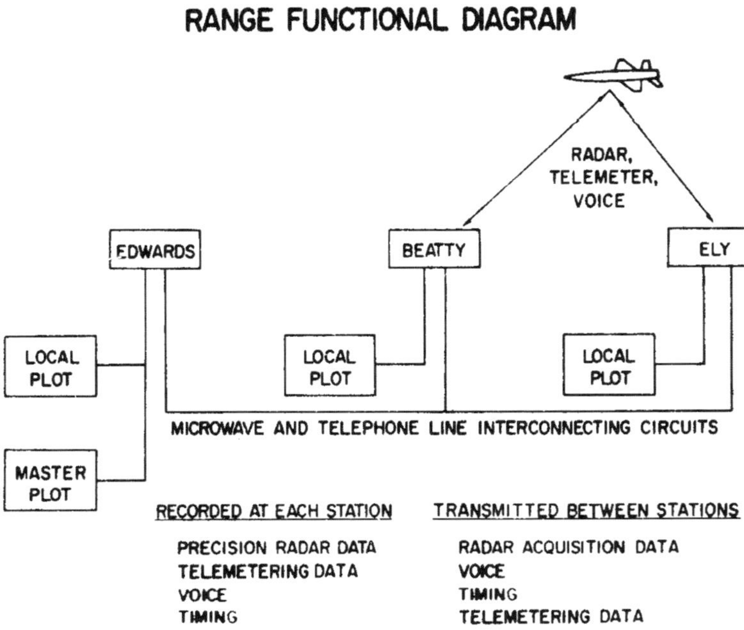

The High Range consisted of three stations: one at Beatty, Nevada, one at Ely, Nevada, and the main station at the High-Speed Flight Station at Edwards. All three sites were interconnected by a sophisticated (for 1955) communications network. Each of the Nevada sites had a "local plot" that could track the course of the X-15 if needed. The general concept of the High Range formed the basis of the later manned spaceflight control networks, not surprising since the same man – Gerald Truszynski – was responsible for the High Range and the initial Mercury network. (U.S. Air Force)

and the civil engineering firm of F. W. Millard and Son prepared a detailed survey of the area. Only 1.75 miles of new gravel road would be required to connect the site to Highway 95 at the cost of $30,500, including the installation of culverts and ditches. The site was 20 miles by road from Beatty, and an additional five miles to the Beatty airfield. No commercial power or water was available at the site, so the EECo again installed diesel generators. Water (at no cost, initially) from the Beatty city water supply was trucked to the site.[28]

The third site, an extension added to the back of the third floor of building 4800 at the HSFS, was the easiest to select. The construction would extend the building toward the airfield ramp from the existing "Flight Control" room using the exterior doorway as the entrance to the new addition. Initial estimates indicated that 1,200 square feet would be adequate for the intended purpose, but further investigation showed that structural constraints required the addition of at least 1,500 square feet. The additional 300 square feet was necessary to take advantage of the existing second-floor columns for greater support of the third-floor addition. After reviewing the plans, the Air Force and NACA requested that EECo further enlarge

28 Ibid, pp. 2-10 through 2-11.

the addition to 2,500 square feet, which was the maximum the building could accommodate. The addition contained four rooms of roughly equal size: a monitor room with plotting boards, a radar room, a telemetry and communications room, and a utility/work area. No plumbing was required in the addition since the main building housed adequate restroom facilities and photographic dark rooms.[29]

EECo subcontracted the administration and supervision of the construction of the two remote sites and the modifications to the NACA building to F. W. Millard and Son. A local contractor selected by competitive bid would perform the actual construction after the Air Force secured the land for the two remote sites. For unexplained reasons, the acquisition was not as straightforward as expected. For instance, the original schedule showed completion of the access road to the Ely site by 15 December 1956, but the Air Force ran into unexpected difficulties in withdrawing the site from the public domain, which delayed construction. In the end, it was October 1957 before the road was completed.[30]

At both remote sites, a 100-by-100-foot area was graded and hard-surfaced with asphalt paving and a sealant coat. This graded area was large enough to accommodate the radar shelter, vehicle parking area, and such items as the diesel generator, fuel tanks, etc. Because of the remote locations, officials decided to station permanently a Dodge Power Wagon four-wheel-drive truck at each site to provide transportation to the airfield. These trucks had sufficient towing capability to haul the water trailers, and the four-wheel drive allowed access to the site during inclement weather.[31]

Interestingly, the way the Air Force had written the High Range contracts, EECo was responsible for constructing 800 square feet of each shelter to house the telemetry equipment and "housekeeping" rooms, but the Reeves Instrument Company was responsible for constructing another 800 square feet at each shelter to house the radar equipment. Smartly, in order to avoid too much duplication of effort and to ensure a uniform appearance, the companies decided that one or the other should build the entire shelter. Since Reeves was not interested in facility construction, the honor fell to EECo. This was probably not the optimum solution, however, since Reeves retained the responsibility to construct the radar pedestal itself (which was an integral part of the building structure) because the exact position of the radar antenna was important to the final operation of the radar, and both contractors believed that the radar contractor should build the pedestal.[32]

EECo developed a generic 1,760-square-foot floor plan for the remote sites, although each would diverge somewhat from the ideal due to site-specific considerations. In essence, each building consisted of four large rooms: a radar room, a telemetry room, a room for data transmitting and receiving equipment, and a utility/work area. The building also included a smaller telephone-equipment room and dark room, and even smaller restrooms and closets. Oddly, the telephone room could only be accessed from outside the building. EECo calculated that each site would use approximately 155 gallons of water per day (5 gallons for personnel

29 Ibid, pp. 2-12 and 3-8 to 3-9.

30 Ibid, pp. 3-3 and 3-4.

31 Ibid, pp. 3-4 and 3-5.

32 Ibid, p. 3-5.

use, 50 for the dark room, and 100 gallons for the flush-type toilet). A 1,000-gallon tank meant that each site would need weekly water deliveries if it was manned continuously. Extreme weather conditions at Ely dictated that the water be stored inside the shelter to keep it from freezing. The shelters consisted of a metal exterior over an insulated framework and drywall interior, with a wooden false floor installed above a concrete slab to provide a location to run wires and cables.[33]

The Ely, Beatty, and Edwards tracking stations had radar and telemetry tracking with oscillograph recording, magnetic-tape data collection, and console-monitoring services. Especially early in the flight program, a backup "communicator" was located at each station in case the communication links went down. Each ground station overlapped the next, and communications lines allowed voice communication, timing signals, and radar data to be available to all. Each station recorded all acquired data on tape and film, and strip charts and plotting boards displayed some of the data locally for the backup communicator.[34]

The radar equipment ultimately selected for the High Range was a minor modification of equipment already used by the Atlantic Missile Range. The radars were World War II vintage SCR-584 units modified to improve their azimuth, elevation, and range accuracy. The Reeves Instrument Corporation modified the three Model II radars (generally called Mod II) and the Air Force supplied them to the EECo as government-furnished equipment. The radars had two selectable range settings: 768,000 yards (436 miles) and 384,000 yards (218 miles). The normal method for acquiring the initial target was to use a remote optical tracker. The antenna pedestal also had provisions for mounting an 80-inch boresight camera. Using a unique (for the period) range-phasing system, two or more Mod 2 radars could simultaneously track the same target without mutual interference.[35]

The radar used a 10-foot parabolic dish that transmitted a 2.5-degree wide beam. Peak power was 350 kilowatts with a pulse width of 0.8 microsecond and a selectable pulse-repetition frequency between 205 and 1,707 pulses per second. The maximum slewing rates were approximately 5 degrees per second in azimuth and 2.5 degrees per second in elevation. These were considered adequate for the X-15, although these limitations were considerations during the selection of launch and contingency landing lakes.[36]

Precision azimuth and elevation information was obtained from two optical encoders, and range data came from one electromechanical encoder attached directly to the radar. The optical encoders were 16-digit analog-to-digital converters produced by the Baldwin Piano Company that used coded glass disks to produce a reflected binary (Gray)[37] code. The output of these units was a 16-digit parallel code produced by an internally synchronized flashlamp actuated 10 times per second by the master timing signal. This was the primary precision tracking information obtained

33 Ibid, pp. 3-6 through 3-8.

34 Hallion, *On the Frontier*, pp. 110-111.

35 "Engineering Plan, Project High Range," p. 2-3; "X-15 Range Facility," apparently unpublished typescript, prepared in November 1959, no page numbers. In the files at the DFRC History Office.

36 "X-15 Range Facility."

37 The reflected binary code, also known as Gray code after Frank Gray who patented the concept in 1947, is a binary numeral system where two successive values differ in only one digit. The code was originally designed to prevent spurious output from electromechanical switches. Today, Gray codes are widely used to facilitate error correction in digital communications such as digital terrestrial television and some cable TV systems.

from the radar system, and an Ampex FR-114 magnetic tape recorder recorded it in digital format. In addition, a data camera photographed the selsyn dial indications of azimuth, elevation, and range for coarse trajectory information.[38]

The AFFTC Project Datum system at Edwards provided automated processing for the radar and telemetry data recorded on the magnetic tapes. This was a general-purpose data-reduction computer system developed by the Air Force to accept a variety of input data tapes and generate output tapes compatible with the IBM 704 computers used for data processing. The IBM computer, in turn, provided data on factors such as the geometric altitude, plan position, trajectory position, and velocity. Project Datum was a post-test analysis tool, not a real-time system. Another IBM 704 computer was located at the FRC for processing the oscillograph data from the X-15. Operators transferred the raw data on the oscillograph and photorecorders to IBM punched cards by using manually operated film recorders, and the punched cards generated magnetic tapes.[39]

Each of the three tracking sites had a "local" Electronic Associates Model 205J plotting board that showed the position of the X-15 as reported by its local radar, and the station at Edwards had a "master" board that correlated all of the results and plotted the vehicle along the entire trajectory. The local boards at each site could alternately display parallax-corrected data from another station. It is interesting to note that the technology of the day did not allow the parallax from the Ely station to be corrected digitally at Edwards because the results would cause the data receiver register to overflow (i.e., the resulting number would be too large for the available space). Since it was necessary to correct the parallax before displaying the data on the master plotting board, engineers devised a method to alter the analog voltage signals at the input to the polar-to-Cartesian coordinate converter. It was an innovative solution to a technological limitation. The coordinate converter itself was an Electronics Associates Model 484A computer.[40]

The X-15 made extensive use (for that time) of telemetry data from the vehicle to the ground. As originally installed, the telemetry was a standard pulse duration modulation (PDM) system capable of receiving up to 90 channels of information in the FM frequency band. A servo-driven helical antenna was located at each range station to receive telemetry data. The antenna was slaved to the radar to track the vehicle, although it could also be positioned manually using a hand crank. Later in the program, NASA installed auto-tracking telemetry antennas at each site. Ampex FR-114 magnetic tape machines recorded 40 analog real-time outputs from an Applied Science Corporation Series M telemetry decommutator. Immediately after each flight, the receiving station processed the recorded information onto strip chart recorders. At the very end of the flight program, X-15-3 received a modern pulse-code modulation (PCM) telemetry system, and NASA modified the Ely and FRC sites to process the data (NASA had decommissioned Beatty by that time).[41]

---

38 Ibid.

39 Ibid; Kenneth C. Sanderson, NASA technical memorandum X-56000, "The X-15 Flight Test Instrumentation," 21 April 1964, pp. 16-17.

40 "Engineering Plan, Project High Range," pp. 4-21 through 4-23; "X-15 Range Facility."

41 "X-15 Range Facility." This is in direct contrast to planning for the X-33 program during the late 1990s, when several thousand parameters at rates up to 10,000 samples per second were required. Still, the X-15 pushed its state of the art; the X-33 was within the capability of commercial off-the-shelf equipment. Forty years of technical progress showed.

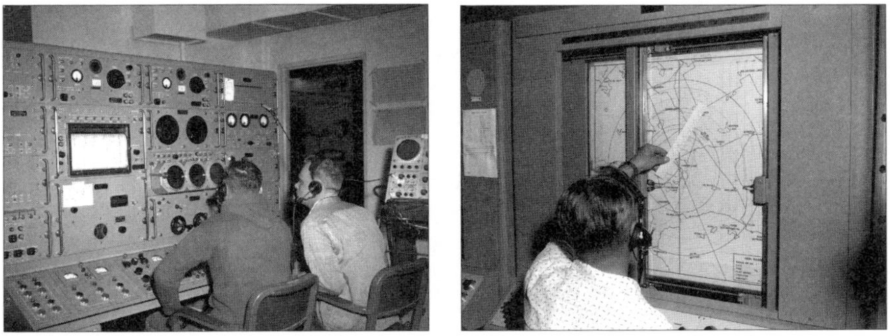

When thinking about radar operators, generally a large "radarscope" comes to mind. However, that was not the case during the 1950s, and the output from a radar was generally a small set of oscilliscopes as shown here on the Mod II unit. (It takes a computer to convert raw radar data into a plan-view for display on a radarscope, and such computers largely did not exist during the late 1950s.) For the most part, on the High Range the radar data was processed and displayed on a set of large paper charts that traced the flight progress on a pre-printed map. The position was plotted using one color of ink for position and another for altitude. (NASA)

Engineers and researchers on the ground needed to look at some of the telemetry data in real time to assist the X-15 pilot if necessary. They could look at this information in various forms on the data monitor consoles located at all three stations, although Edwards generally conducted the critical analyses. All parameters were presented in the form of vertical bar graphs on two center-mounted oscilloscopes, which allowed rapid assessment of a group of parameters to determine whether the operation was within predetermined limits. Of the total parameters transmitted, researchers could look at any 40 at one time, and the strip charts could display an additional 12 channels.[42]

Standard military ground-to-air AN/GRC-27 UHF equipment provided voice communications with the X-15. Originally, the Air Force indicated that it would provide the radios as government-furnished equipment; however, the long lead times caused the AFFTC to ask EECo to bid on supplying them separately. EECo found a Collins unit with 1,750 channels that it could acquire within nine months. The radio was fully compatible with the AN/ARC-34 UHF transmitter-receiver set that North American would install in the X-15.[43]

To ensure positive contact between any of the tracking sites and the X-15 regardless of its location over the High Range, EECo installed a network communications system. Each range station contained two UHF transmitters and receivers (one of each was a spare) and a specially designed communication amplifier and switching unit. When an operator keyed a transmitter at any location, all three stations transmitted the same information simultaneously. The receivers at all three stations fed their outputs onto a telephone line and, regardless of which station

42 Ibid.

43 "Engineering Plan, Project High Range," pp. 6-41 through 6-45; "X-15 Range Facility;" System Development Plan, X-15 Research Aircraft, Supporting Research System Number 447L, 22 March 1956, p. 18. The ARC-34 would be replaced by an AN/ARC-48 before the X-15 was actually built; this in turn was replaced by an AN/ARC-51 during September-October 1966.

received the information, all stations could hear the transmission. The EECo also installed dedicated station-to-station communications links.[44]

The development of the UHF communications system actually presented something of a challenge for the High Range team. The problem was that since all three stations transmitted the same data simultaneously, the airborne receiver experienced an "audible beat or tone" interference. The solution to this heterodyne interference problem was to offset each transmitter frequency by a small amount without drifting outside the frequency bandwidth of the receiver. Experimentation led the team to adopt offsets of 0.005–0.010% of the operating frequency as nearly ideal. It was also determined that each transmitter should be offset by an unequal amount to avoid creating a noticeable "beat" in the audio. In the end, technicians tuned the Edwards transmitter 22 kilocycles below the center frequency, while the Ely site transmitted at 14 kilocycles above the center frequency. Beatty, being in the middle, used the center frequency for its transmitter.[45]

Since a microphone at any one of the stations modulated all three transmitters simultaneously, the signal arrived at the aircraft at slightly different times because of differing distances from the station to the aircraft. In addition, signals originating on the aircraft took slightly different times to reach each of the ground stations. Consequently, some slightly different delays affected each signal. Given that such signals travel at the speed of light (186,000 miles per second), the time difference for an actual transmission was a maximum of approximately 4 milliseconds. A slightly longer delay was encountered in sending the keying signals between stations, resulting in a total delay of about 12 milliseconds between the two outermost sites (Edwards and Ely).[46]

It was found, however, that the time delay was not totally undesirable. The human voice contains a multitude of continuously varying harmonic frequencies. The time delay canceled out a small number of these frequencies since they were 180 degrees out of phase with each other. The only effect this had was to introduce a slight flutter in the reproduced sound that did not seriously degrade speech intelligibility. The second effect the time delay brought was a slight echo effect. Due to the acuity of the human ear, there must be a spacing of approximately 30 milliseconds between signals for the ear to detect that an echo is present. Researchers discovered that a small echo effect actually increases the intelligibility of a voice because of the slight lengthening of word syllables. Analysis indicated that the maximum predicted 12-millisecond time delay would not be sufficient to cause undesirable effects, so the X-15 program elected to ignore the issue.[47]

In the course of determining solutions to the various communications challenges, EECo discovered that it was not the first to confront these issues. Commercial airlines had been using similar systems (operating in VHF instead of UHF) for approximately five years after they had installed communications networks under their frequently traveled routes to allow aircraft to be in constant

44 "Engineering Plan, Project High Range," p. 6-3; "X-15 Range Facility."

45 "Engineering Plan, Project High Range," pp. 6-5 through 6-6. Prior to the early 1960s, scientific convention was to describe frequency in cycles per second (cps). During the mid-1960s this was changed to Hertz (Hz) in honor of German physicist Heinrich Rudolph Hertz, who conducted research on electricity and electromagnetism.

46 Ibid, pp. 6-8 through 6-11.

47 Ibid, pp. 6-8 through 6-11.

touch with their home offices. Each of these networks was composed of several transmitter-receiver sets that contained between two and six stations tied together by a transmission link. Several groups made up a complete network.[48]

United Airlines had designed a similar communications system and contracted its operation to the Aeronautical Radio Company to make it available for other airlines. As Aeronautical Radio expanded and upgraded the original network, it contracted the work to Bell Telephone. Aeronautical Radio leased the system from Bell, and in turn leased the services to the airlines. Collins Radio worked with the service providers and airlines to create a series of radios specifically tailored to operate in the multiple-transmitter environment. Aeronautical Radio, Bell Telephone, Collins Radio, and United Airlines all provided information and assistance to EECo at no charge.[49]

In order to evaluate a working communications system of this type before committing to the use of one on the High Range, EECo arranged for a demonstration using one of the airline VHF networks that ran in a line between Oceanside near San Diego to San Francisco, California. The NACA flew a Boeing B-47 Stratojet from Los Angeles to San Francisco at an altitude of 15,000 feet, returning to Los Angeles at 40,000 feet. The pilot made contact with the ground at 10-minute intervals while Air Force, NACA, and EECo representatives located at the Los Angeles International Airport monitored the two-way communications.[50]

The network spanned a distance of 400 miles, but used six stations (instead of the three planned for the High Range) to provide communications down to an altitude of 1,000 feet. Coverage for the High Range was concentrated above 7,000 feet, and one of the goals of the evaluation was to determine how the concept worked at high altitudes. On the return flight at 40,000 feet, it was likely that the B-47 received signals from all six ground stations, and that all six ground-stations received signals from the aircraft. Thus, potential interference was even greater than it would be with the three-station network planned for the High Range. The only effect noted during the evaluation was a flutter or warble at certain locations in the flight path. Researchers played tapes recorded during the flight for numerous pilots and ground personnel at Edwards, and nobody voiced any serious objections. This validated the concept for the High Range, and the EECo began procurement of the various radios, switching units, and other components.[51]

The three High Range stations could share radar and telemetry data to automatically direct the next radar in line to the target, and to plot radar data from a remote station on a local plotting board if desired. It was necessary to convert the data from each station into the correct relative position using a set of fixed translation equations, which is one reason why the exact position of each radar antenna had to be precisely determined during construction.[52]

48 Ibid, pp. 6-12 through 6-14.
49 Ibid, pp. 6-12 through 6-14.
50 Ibid, pp. 6-12 through 6-14.
51 Ibid, pp. 6-14 through 6-17.
52 X-15 Range Facility."

The High Range stations were positioned on top of mountains to provide the best look angles for the radar and telemetry receivers. The Beatty, Nevada station was closed when the X-15 program ended and nothing remains at the site except for the concrete slabs where the buildings once stood. (NASA)

There were three likely ways to transmit data between the three sites: a leased wire facility, a scatter propagation system, or microwave transmission.[53] The contract with EECo specifically stated that "the contractor shall investigate the possibility of using a microwave service link for radar data transmission originating at the Ely site, passing through the Beatty site, and terminating at Edwards Air Force Base." To satisfy this requirement, EECo personnel discussed possible microwave solutions with the Collins Radio, Pacific Telephone & Telegraph Company (PT&T), Philco Corporation, and Raytheon Manufacturing. EECo also discussed the possibility of a scatter propagation system with the same companies, although only Collins provided any meaningful data.[54]

A typical solution to the microwave system provided three main terminals at Ely, Beatty, and Edwards linked together by 10 repeater stations located approximately 30 miles apart. Each location had complete standby power and radio frequency (RF) equipment to ensure reliability. Engineers estimated the propagation delay from Ely to Edwards at 1.8 milliseconds. There were, however, substantial costs to build the system. For instance, each of the repeater sites needed power generators (at least primary, and probably backup). Then there was the cost to build roads to each repeater site; at an average cost of $3,000 per mile for an estimated three miles per site, this came to $90,000. The roads were to be of the

53 In plain English, a "leased wire facility" is a group of telephone lines. Surprisingly, radar data between tracking sites on most of the major test ranges were transferred using standard 2400- and 9600-baud telephone lines well into the 1990s.

54 "Engineering Plan, Project High Range," pp. 6-27 through 6-29.

same quality as a typical "pole maintenance" road not intended for regular vehicle traffic. The estimated cost of the microwave system was $396,000, and estimated operating expenses were $33,000 per year, not including amortization of the initial installation costs.[55]

The propagation scatter system would have involved placing 28-foot-diameter antennas at each of the three sites and bouncing signals off the troposphere. Collins Radio recommended using a UHF system for distances up to 350 miles, and VHF for distances up to 1,200 miles. At the time, the Federal Communications Commission (FCC) had not made any licensing provisions for tropospheric scatter systems since it appeared only the government would be interested in using them. Collins pointed out that each system was custom-made, and the only way to determine whether such a system would work between any two or more locations was to try a Collins Transhorizon System in a van setup between each of the sites. Collins estimated the original system cost at $287,600, not including installation or spare parts. Collins also pointed out that the system was very susceptible to atmospheric disturbances and weather.[56]

The leased wire facility would provide telephone lines from Edwards through Los Angeles and Sacramento to Reno, Nevada. From Reno the lines would branch off through Tonopah, Nevada, to the Beatty site, and through Wendover, Utah, to the Ely site. The estimated propagation delay from Edwards to Ely was 10 milliseconds. The standard telephone facilities at Ely and Beatty would be "semi public toll service stations," meaning that they would be on a party-line hookup with the towns of Ely and Beatty. All calls from these telephones would be toll calls (10 cents minimum) with a minimum charge of $5.00 per month. The transmission links were semi-permanently connected lines that would not go through an operator's patch panel, avoiding the chance of accidental disconnections. Pacific Telephone would provide all of the maintenance.[57]

Ma Bell, being Ma Bell, had charges for everything. The initial construction charge (running the necessary land lines and terminal equipment) would be $55,000, but there was also an "installation charge" of $95 per site to have a technician actually connect the equipment. The total annual operating costs would be $113,790, not including the cost of two standard telephones at Ely and Beatty, which would run an additional $5 each per month. Pacific Telephone also informed the government that if it selected a microwave system, the telephone company would not find it profitable to provide only standard telephone service to the two remote sites–this would be economically practical only if Pacific Telephone provided the entire data transmission contract.[58]

Armed with this information, the AFFTC, NACA, and EECo compared the telephone and microwave systems to determine which was more practical. The group eliminated the scatter propagation system since it did not seem to offer any great cost advantage and represented a largely unknown operational quantity. The microwave system offered low annual operating costs, assuming the system con-

55 Ibid, pp. 6-27 through 6-29.

56 Ibid, pp. 6-29 and 6-33 through 6-34.

57 Ibid, pp. 6-29 and 6-34 through 6-36.

58 "Engineering Plan, Project High Range," p. 6-41.

tinued to be used for at least six or seven years to amortize the installation costs. Additional channels were readily available with minor expenditures, and engineers considered the link more secure since it was unlikely anybody would attempt to "tap" it. The principal disadvantages of the microwave system were its high initial costs, the possibility that the repeater sites would be inaccessible during bad weather, and that maintenance was the responsibility of the end user (the NACA).[59]

On the other hand, leased telephone facilities offered high reliability and low initial costs, and the telephone company would provide all maintenance. Its principal disadvantages were high annual operating costs and the inability to easily add more channels, particularly high-bandwidth ones.[60]

EECo conducted a cost analysis that included amortization of the initial costs over 5-, 10-, and 20-year periods. The results of this analysis for the "Cost per Channel per Mile per Year" were as follows:[61]

	Initial Cost	20-Year	10-Year	5-Year
Microwave (Philco)	$396,000	$21.90	$30.10	$46.60
Telephone (PT&T)	$55,000	$48.44	$49.57	$51.81

The total annual operating costs, also based on the three possible amortization options were:[62]

	20-Year	10-Year	5-Year
Microwave (Philco)	$52,825	$72,650	$112,299
Telephone (PT&T)	$118,680	$121,434	$126,947

The microwave cost curve dropped sharply in the early years and then leveled off to some degree after 10 years. Additional channels, however, dropped the per-channel cost considerably. This was because the basic investment in a microwave system was in the initial installation; additional channels only required more relatively low-cost multiplex equipment. This reduction, however, only extended until expansion filled the full bandwidth of the microwave system. At this point, the cost would increase greatly because additional microwave equipment would be required. This was not a major concern since the proposed system provided a bandwidth of 100 kilocycles, and the seven required channels only used 21 kilocycles.[63]

Nevertheless, the Air Force was in the position to make the final decision, and it selected the telephone system. There were four reasons for this choice:

59 Ibid, pp. 6-36 through 6-37.

60 This was decades before the advent of high-speed analog modems or DSL technology.

61 Ibid, pp. 6-36 through 6-37.

62 Ibid, pp. 6-36 through 6-37.

63 Ibid, p. 6-42.

1) the high reliability offered by a utility-maintained system, 2) the high initial cost of the microwave system, 3) the distance and inaccessibility of the microwave repeater sites for maintenance, and 4) the fact that the telephone company maintained all telephone facilities. These reasons were unquestionably valid. However, in reality, the more likely rationale was the simple fact that although the Air Force was responsible for funding the installation of the chosen system, the NACA was responsible for maintaining the system once it was operational. The Air Force, therefore, chose the system that would cost it the least amount of up-front money, with little consideration given to future capabilities or operating costs. By March 1961, even before the Ely station came on line (in April 1961), NASA had opted to install a microwave system between the stations on the High Range. The microwave capability from Beatty was operational in June 1961, with Ely following in January 1962.[64]

A master timing system at Edwards provided a constant time reference for all the tracking stations using three separate timing signals: 1,000 parts per second (pps), 100 pps, and 10 pps. An operator at any station could record timing marks on recordings at all three stations to indicate a significant event for later reference.[65]

Early in the program, a pilot staffed each of the High Range sites in addition to the engineers and technicians necessary to run the equipment. The pilot at Beatty used the call sign NASA-2, and the one at Ely used NASA-3. For later flights, pilots often did not staff the remote sites as the communications links between the sites acquired more bandwidth and all involved gained more confidence in the reliability of the systems. Normally, important information from the control room passed to the pilot through the NASA-1 controller, who was usually another X-15 pilot. However, other ground-control personnel had the capability to transmit directly to the pilot in the event of an emergency where there might be insufficient time to relay information through NASA-1, or, as happened on several occasions, the radio at Edwards did not work properly.[66]

Although they were not designed as part of the original control room, researchers added various specialized devices during the flight program. For instance, engineers programmed a small analog computer to take radar-derived altitude, velocity, and vertical velocity measurements and compute the resulting range footprint to assist ground personnel in understanding which contingency landing sites were available at every moment during the flight. A scope-type map display presented the data in the control room. The analog flight simulator generated the data to program this computer. The flight surgeons also gained a dedicated biomedical console.[67]

---

64 Ibid, p. 6-42; Minutes of Meeting, X-15 Operations Subcommittee, 20 March 1961. In the AFFTC Access to Space Office Project Files.

65 "Engineering Plan, Project High Range," p. 4-22; "X-15 Range Facility." During the late 1950s, as each military range came on line, it seemed to reinvent the wheel when it came to things like distributing timing signals. In an early (and very successful) attempt to create standards, the Range Commanders Council (RCC) developed the Inter-Range Instrumentation Group (IRIG) standards. These defined formats and electrical properties for timing signals, telemetry, and radar which were subsequently adopted by all U.S. ranges and many foreign ones.

66 Milton O. Thompson, *At the Edge of Space: The X-15 Flight Program*, (Washington and London: Smithsonian Institution Press, 1992), p. 58; Robert G. Hoey and Richard E. Day, "X-15 Mission Planning and Operational Procedures," a paper in the *1961 Research Airplane Committee Report*, pp. 160-161.

67 Hoey and Day, "X-15 Mission Planning and Operational Procedures," p. 161.

The station at Ely was functionally identical to the one at Beatty, although the physical layout of the two sites differed somewhat due to local environmental conditions. At the end of the X-15 program, the Ely station reverted to the Air Force and continued to play a part in test operations until 1992 when it was finally closed. (NASA)

The High Range underwent a series of modifications over the years. For instance, on 10 March 1967, NASA replaced the Mod II radar at Ely with an improved Reeves Instrument Corporation MPS-19C unit that became operational on 2 May. Wallops Island shipped another MPS-19C during March 1967 for installation at the FRC. At the FRC, the original Mod II had been located on top of building 4800, but engineers deemed this unacceptable because the increased accuracy of the new radar required a firmer base to eliminate vibration and flex. As a result, the new radar was installed a mile or so west, primarily in a new facility with a stiffer base. In addition, in early 1967 NASA upgraded the microwave relay system from Ely to Edwards to handle the higher-bandwidth PCM data from X-15-3. The first successful test (at 144 Kbs) was on 29 March 1967, and the system successfully supported flight 3-58-87 on 26 April.[68]

68 X-15 Status Reports, Paul F. Bikle/FRC to J. Martin/NASA Headquarters, 4 April 1967, p. 6 and 5 May 1967, p. 5; telephone conversation, Jack Kittrell with Dennis R. Jenkins, 1 August 2002; e-mail, Jack Kittrell to Dennis R. Jenkins, 19 August 2002. The MPS-19 at Ely was replaced by an FPQ-5 in the early 1970s when the site was transferred to Air Force control.

DRY LAKES

Although they had one of the most ideal test locations in the world, the Air Force and NACA could not simply go out and begin conducting X-15 operations. Several hurdles had to be overcome before the X-15 could ever do more than just conduct short flights over the Edwards reservation.

It had been recognized early during planning for the X-15 flights that suitable contingency landing locations would need to be found in the event of an abort after separation from the B-52 carrier aircraft, or if problems during the flight forced the pilot to terminate the mission before reaching Edwards. Since North American had designed the X-15 to land on dry lakebeds, the logical course of action was to identify suitable lakebeds along the flight path–in fact, these lakebeds had been one of the factors used to determine the route followed by the High Range.

The Air Force and NACA had to identify lakebeds that would enable the X-15 to always be within gliding range of a landing site. In addition, the flight planners always selected a launch point that allowed the pilot a downwind landing pattern. Normally, the launch point was about 19 miles from the lakebed runway and the track passed the runway 14 miles abeam. To establish the proper launch point, flight planners used the fixed-base simulator to determine the gliding range of the airplane, including both forward glides and making a 180-degree turn and returning along its flight path. Another consideration was that the flight planners needed to selected lakes that would provide an overlap throughout the entire flight.[69]

The first hurdle for the Air Force was to secure permission from the individuals and several government agencies that owned or controlled the lakebeds. Next was seeking permission from the Federal Aviation Agency (FAA–it became an administration later) to conduct flight operations over public land.

Although responsibilities concerning the lakebeds continued throughout the life of the X-15 program, there were several spurts of activity (two major and one minor) concerning them. The first occurred, logically enough, just before the beginning of the flight program when efforts began to secure the rights to the lakebeds needed for the initial flight tests. The second involved securing the lakes needed for the higher-speed and higher-altitude flights made possible by the introduction of the XLR99 engine. One final push later in the program tailored the set of lakes for the improved-performance X-15A-2 and its external tanks.

Eventually, 10 different launch locations would be used, including eight dry lakes: Cuddeback supported a single launch; Delamar was the most used, with 62 launches; Hidden Hills saw 50 launches; Mud hosted 34; Railroad was used for only 2; Rosamond was used for 17, Silver hosted 14, and Smith Ranch was used for 10. In addition, the Palmdale VOR (OMNI) hosted eight launches, and a single flight originated over the outskirts of Lancaster. Hidden Hills was usually the intended site for the abortive 200th flight. The vast majority of these flights (188) would land on Rogers Dry Lake. Two would land at Cuddeback, one at Delamar,

69 Hoey and Day, "X-15 Mission Planning and Operational Procedures," pp. 155-157; letter, Johnny Armstrong to Dennis R. Jenkins, 5 July 2002.

four at Mud, one at Rosamond, one at Silver, and one at Smith Ranch. The X-15-3 broke up in flight and did not land on its last flight.[70]

Rosamond Dry Lake, several miles southwest of Rogers, offered 21 square miles of smooth, flat surface that the Air Force used for routine flight test and research operations and emergency landings. This dry lakebed had served as the launch point for many of the early rocket-plane flights at Edwards. It is also the first lakebed that most visitors to Edwards see, since the road from Rosamond (and Highway 14) to Edwards crosses its northern tip on its way to the main base area. Scott Crossfield would make the X-15 glide flight over Rosamond Dry Lake, and no particular permission was necessary to use Rosamond since the lakebed was completely within the restricted area that made up the Edwards complex. Unfortunately, the lake was only 20 miles away from the base, so it did not allow much opportunity for high-speed work.

The Rogers and Rosamond lakebeds are among the lowest points in Antelope Valley, and they collect seasonal rain and snow runoff from surrounding hills and from the San Gabriel Mountains to the south and the Tehachapi Mountains to the west. At one time, the lakebeds contained water year-round, but changing geological and weather patterns now leave them wet only after infrequent rain or snow. A survey of the Rosamond lakebed surface showed its flatness, with a curvature of less than 18 inches over a distance of 30,000 feet.[71]

Beginning in early 1957, North American, AFFTC, and NACA personnel conducted numerous evaluations of various dry lakes along the High Range route to determine which were suitable for X-15 landings. The initial X-15 flights required 10 dry lakes (five as emergency landing sites near launch locations, and five as contingency landing sites downrange) spaced 30–50 miles apart.[72]

The processes to obtain permission to use the various lakebeds outside the Edwards complex were as diverse as the locations themselves. For instance, permission to use approximately 2,560 acres of land at Cuddeback Lake as an emergency landing location was sought beginning in early 1957, with first use expected in January 1959. The lakebed was within the land area reserved for use by the Air Force at George AFB, California, but the Department of the Interior controlled the lakebed itself. Since the Air Force cannot acquire land directly, officials at the AFFTC contacted the Los Angeles District of the Army Corps of Engineers, only to find out that George AFB had already requested the Corps to withdraw the land from the public domain. The Bureau of Land Management controls all land in the public domain, although control may pass to other government agencies (such as

---

70 For those who care about such things, the longitude and latitude of the lakes are as follows:

Cuddeback Lake, California	117.5 W	35.3 N
Delamar Dry Lake, Nevada	114.9 W	37.4 N
Hidden Hills, California	116.0 W	36.0 N
Lancaster (Fox Field), California	118.2 W	34.8 N
Mud Lake, California	117.1 W	37.9 N
Palmdale OMNI, California	118.1 W	34.6 N
Railroad Valley Lake, Nevada	116.0 W	38.0 N
Rogers Dry Lake, California	117.8 W	34.9 N
Rosamond Dry Lake, California	118.1 W	34.8 N
Silver Lake, California	116.1 W	35.3 N
Smith Ranch Lake, Nevada	117.5 W	39.3 N

71 *http://www.edwards.af.mil/history/docs_html/center/lakebeds.html*, accessed 25 January 2002.

72 Stillwell, *X-15 Research Results*.

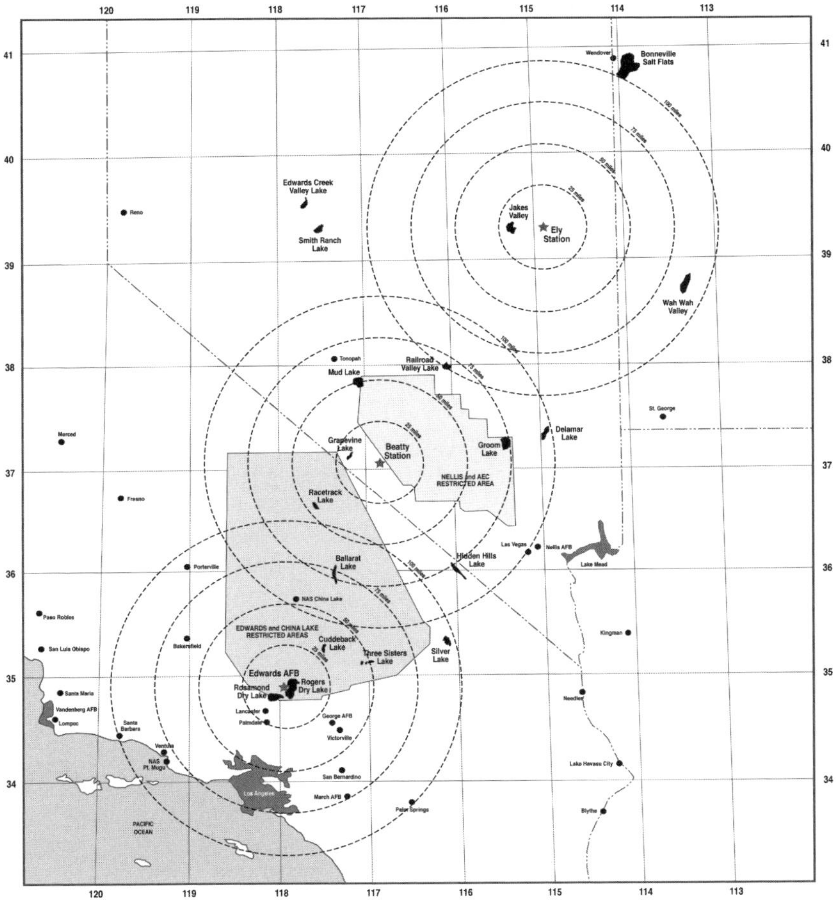

This map shows the general location of the lakebeds as well as the radar coverage afforded by the three High Range stations. The two primary restricted airspace areas are shaded, although the entire flight path of the X-15 was restricted on flight day. (Dennis R. Jenkins)

the military) as stipulated in various laws (U.S. Code Title 43, for example). At the time, the Corps of Engineers acted as the land management agent for the U.S. Air Force, and John J. Shipley was the chief of the real estate division for the Los Angeles District.

Officials at George intended to use the lakebed as an emergency landing site. In turn, on 17 May 1957 the Corps wrote to the Bureau of Land Management on behalf of the Secretary of the Air Force, requesting a special land-use permit for Air Force operations at the lake. When the Los Angeles District received the request from the AFFTC, Shipley contacted Lieutenant Colonel C. E. Black, the installations engineer at George AFB, requesting that a joint-use agreement be set up that would permit sharing the lake with the AFFTC for X-15 operations.[73]

By the end of July 1959, the Bureau of Land Management had approved the permit, and George AFB had agreed in principle to the sharing arrangement. The special-use permit gave George AFB landing rights for several years, and permitted the lakebed to be marked as needed to support flight operations. John Shipley, very intelligently, decided that the joint-use agreement between the AFFTC and George was an internal Air Force affair and bowed out of the process after the issuance of the Bureau of Land Management permit. Although there seemed to be no particular disagreement, the joint-use agreement had a long gestation period. The special-use permit was granted at the beginning of August, but at the end of September Colonel Carl A. Ousley, the chief of the Project Control Office at the AFFTC, questioned why a written joint-use agreement had not been signed. Major Resiner at George replied on 14 October that he had received verbal approval from all parties, but written approval was required from two separate Air Force commands (the ARDC and the Tactical Air Command (TAC)), the Corps of Engineers, and the Bureau of Land Management. He foresaw no difficulties in obtaining the signatures, and apparently the process worked itself out within a suitable period since there appears to have been no further correspondence on the matter. The joint-use agreement with George AFB essentially stated that the AFFTC was responsible for any unique preparations and marking of the lakebed required to support X-15 operations, although George did offer to supply emergency equipment and personnel as needed.[74]

Simultaneously with the request to use Cuddeback, the AFFTC issued a similar request for Jakes Lake and Mud Lake, both in Nevada. Originally, the X-15 program had wanted to use Groom Lake, Nevada, as a launch site instead of Mud Lake. However, the security restrictions in place at Groom Lake (also known as "The Ranch") to protect the CIA-Lockheed reconnaissance programs led the AFFTC and NASA to abandon plans to use this facility. Officials at Nellis suggested Mud Lake as a compromise between the needs of the X-15 program and the highly classified CIA programs.[75]

The AFFTC asked for approximately 2,500 acres of land in the public domain at Jakes Lake; at Mud Lake, the request was for 3,088 acres. The indefinite-term special-use permits sought the right to install fencing to keep cattle from grazing in certain areas. Several ranchers had grazing rights on the public domain land, so this required modifying these agreements and compensating the ranchers with Air Force funds. In this case the Air Force did not want to remove the land from the

73 The expected first-use date is contained in a letter, Colonel Carl A. Ousley, Chief of Project Control Office at AFFTC, to Richard J. Harer, AFFTC, 17 February 1958; various letters from John J. Shipley, Chief of the Real Estate Division, Los Angles District of the Army Corps of Engineers, to the Commander, George AFB, the Bureau of Land Management, and the AFFTC, dated 17 and 20 May 1957. All in the AFFTC Access to Space Office Project Files. The original public domain includes the land ceded to the federal government by the 13 original states, supplemented with acquisitions from native Indians and foreign powers. It encompasses major portions of the land area of 30 western states.

74 Letter from Colonel Carl A. Ousley, Chief of Project Controls at AFFTC to distribution (internal AFFTC codes), 17 February 1958. In the AFFTC Access to Space Office Project Files; Disposition Form (DD96), Colonel Carl A. Ousley, AFFTC to Phyllis R. Actis, also at AFFTC, requesting she make contact with George AFB, 26 September 1957; Reply to Colonel Carl A. Ousley from Major John W. Young, Jr., AFFTC, 16 October 1957. In the AFFTC Access to Space Office Project Files.

75 Memorandum for Record, Richard J. Harer, Chairman X-15 Operations Committee, 4 October 1960.

public domain, but it did want to use approximately 9,262 acres of land at Mud Lake that had already been withdrawn from the public domain for use as part of the Las Vegas Bombing and Gunnery Range.[76]

These two areas were under the purview of the Sacramento District of the Army Corps of Engineers. The district began the process by preparing Real Estate Requirements Estimates for the two lakes detailing the anticipated costs, and forwarding these to ARDC Headquarters on 15 October 1957 for approval and funding. By the end of January 1958, however, Lieutenant Colonel Donald J. Iddins at the AFFTC began to worry that the process was taking too long. The X-15 needed the lakes in July 1959, and there was no evidence of final action. Part of the problem was that land actions involving over 5,000 acres (which the two actions together did) required approval from the House Armed Services Committee. The AFFTC reminded the chief of engineers that they did not want to remove the land from the public domain, which seemingly eliminated the need for congressional approval, and brought the situation to the attention of the X-15 Project Office during a management review at Wright Field on 5 February 1958. The result was a renewed effort to ensure that all three lakes (Cuddeback, Jakes, and Mud) were available for X-15 use on schedule, including the right to build roads to the lakes, marking approach and landing areas, and fencing certain areas if necessary to ensure the safety of the X-15.[77]

On 14 February 1958, the chief of engineers responded that he had initiated the process to grant special-use permits, but had terminated the effort when he noted that the AFFTC wanted to fence off the land. However, the law did not permit fencing to be erected on special-use permitted land. This meant that the land would have to be withdrawn from the public domain after all, or go unfenced. It appears that the answer to the problem was obtained by the AFFTC agreeing to a reduction in the Mud Lake acquisition to just under 2,500 acres (versus the original 3,088), bringing the total to under 5,000 and circumventing congressional approval. This allowed the land to be withdrawn from the public domain, and some of it was fenced as needed to keep stray cattle from wandering onto the marked runway.[78]

Simply getting access to the lakebeds was not always sufficient. For instance, Mud Lake was in the extreme northwest corner of Restricted Area R-271, meaning that Sandia Corporation, which controlled R-271 for the Atomic Energy Commission (AEC), had to approve its use. A "Memorandum of Understanding between the Air Force Flight Test Center and Sandia Corporation" allowed AFFTC support aircraft to operate in the immediate vicinity of Mud Lake during X-15 flights.

---

76 Disposition Form (DD96) from Lieutenant Colonel Donald J. Iddins, Acting Deputy Chief of Staff, ATTFC, to Mrs. Phyllis R. Actis, also at AFFTC, 30 January 1958; letter from Colonel Carl A. Ousley, Chief of Project Controls at AFFTC to distribution (internal AFFTC codes), 17 February 1958; memorandum for the record, Phyllis R. Actis, Planning Specialist, 17 February 1958; memorandum for the Chief of Engineers, Department of the Army, not signed or dated (but received in the files on 19 February 1958). All in the AFFTC Access to Space Office Project Files.

77 Ibid. The Corps of Engineers was responsible for acquiring the land from the landowners, but the Air Force was still expected to pay for it since it was required for AFFTC use.

78 Disposition Form (DD96) from Lieutenant Colonel Donald J. Iddins, Acting Deputy Chief of Staff, ATTFC, to Mrs. Phyllis R. Actis, also at AFFTC, 30 January 1958; letter from Colonel Carl A. Ousley, Chief of Project Controls at AFFTC to distribution (internal AFFTC codes), 17 February 1958; memorandum for the record, Phyllis R. Actis, Planning Specialist, 17 February 1958; memorandum for the Chief of Engineers, Department of the Army, not signed or dated (but received in the files on 19 February 1958). All in the AFFTC Access to Space Office Project Files.

The AFFTC had to furnish flight schedules to Sandia one week before each anticipated mission, and Sandia made the point that it had no radar search capability and could not guarantee that the area was clear of traffic. Sandia also agreed not to schedule any tests within the restricted area that might conflict with X-15 flights. Once approved by Sandia, the AFFTC sought additional approval from Nellis AFB since Mud Lake was also within the Las Vegas Bombing and Gunnery Range. This approval was somewhat easier to negotiate because it was obtained from another Air Force organization.[79]

On 3 November 1958, a team from the AFFTC visited Mud Lake to conduct a preliminary study of lakebed conditions and to determine what action would be required to clear areas of the lakebed for use as a landing strip. When the group from the Flight Test Operations Division and Installations Engineer Division arrived over the lake, the pilot made several low passes to orient the group and obtain a general knowledge of the various obstructions that might conflict with landing on the lakebed. What the group saw was a general pattern of obstructions running east to west in a straight line across the center of the lakebed. The team landed at the Tonopah airport and proceeded by car to the lake, 16 miles away, for a closer inspection.[80]

They found that the obstructions observed down the center of the lake were a series of old gunnery-bombing targets dating from World War II. Practice bodies, wooden stakes, and good-sized rocks used to form bull's-eyes for bombing practice littered the lakebed. The targets were in a narrow straight band down the center of the lake from west to east, but the debris covered a considerably wider area. As would become standard practice on all the lakes, the group dropped an 18-pound steel ball from a height of 6 feet and measured the diameter of the resulting impression. This gave a good indication of the relative hardness of the surface and its ability to support the weight of the X-15 and other aircraft and vehicles. At the edges of the lake, the ball left impressions of 3.25 inches or so, while toward the center of the lake the impressions were only 2.25–3.0 inches in diameter. At the time, the Air Force believed that impressions of 3.125 inches or less were acceptable. The general surface condition of the lakebed varied from relatively smooth and hard to cracked and soft. Although it was not ideal, the group thought the lakebed could be made useable with minor effort.[81]

More lakebed evaluations followed on 13-14 July 1959. X-15 pilot Bob White and the AFFTC chief of flight test operations, Colonel Clarence E. "Bud" Anderson, used a Helio L-28 Super Courier aircraft to visit 12 dry lakes along the High Range route. At each lake, Anderson and White dropped the "imperial ball" from six feet and measured the diameter of the resulting impression. By this time, the Air Force had changed the criteria slightly: a diameter of 3.25 inches was acceptable, and anything above 3.5 inches was unacceptable. The survey included an evaluation of the surface hardness, surface smoothness, approximate elevation,

79 Memorandum of Understanding Between the Air Force Flight Test Center and Sandia Corporation, undated. In the AFFTC Access to Space Office Project Files.

80 Memorandum for the record, Captain Byron E. Hanes, First Lieutenant John T. Craddock, and Glendon Johnson, AFFTC, 10 November 1958. In the AFFTC Access to Space Office Project Files.

81 Ibid. Other documentation says that the ball weighed 17 pounds 9 ounces and was 5 inches in diameter. Many of those involved referred to this as the "imperial ball."

length and direction of possible runways, and obstacles. Anderson remembers that there was "only one lake where we had to make a full power go-around as we watched the tires sink as we landed." Many future surveys would take personnel from AFFTC, NASA, and North American to most of the larger dry lakes along the High Range route.[82]

In addition, on 13 July 1959, four FAA representatives and two members of the AFFTC staff held a meeting at the FAA 4th Region Headquarters in Los Angeles to discuss using Silver Lake as a launch site for the X-15. Since some of the X-15 flight corridor would be outside existing restructured airspace, FAA approval was necessary. The FAA claimed jurisdiction under Civil Aeronautics Regulation 60.24, but was anxious to assist the Air Force within the limits of the law. The Air Force intended to use Silver Lake launches for early X-15 flights with the XLR11 engines. The proposed 100-mile flight path consisted of Silver Lake, Bicycle Lake, Cuddeback and/or Harpers Lake, and then on to landing at Edwards. The FAA had no particular problem with the concept, but since its charter was to protect the safety of all users of public airspace, it believed that certain restrictions needed to be in place before the flights could be approved. The participants spent most of the meeting discussing possible operational problems and concerns, and then developing limitations or restrictions that mitigated the concerns.[83]

For Silver Lake launches, both the launch and the landing were performed in a restricted airspace called a "test area." Silver Lake was inside Flight Test Area Four, while Edwards was at the center of Flight Test Area One. However, none of the test areas surrounding Edwards were restricted 24 hours per day, or seven days per week. In fact, they were open to civilian traffic most of the time, and their closure had to be coordinated with the FAA (the airspace immediately around Edwards was always closed to civilian traffic). In addition, the flight path from Silver Lake to Edwards would take the X-15 out of restricted airspace and into civilian airspace for brief periods. Future flights using the northern portion of the High Range would also be outside normal test areas. The FAA, therefore, needed to approve the plans and procedures for using that airspace.[84]

On 1 September 1959, L. N. Lightbody, the acting chief of the General Operations Branch of the Los Angeles office (4th Region) of the FAA wrote to Colonel Roger B. Phelan, deputy chief of staff for operations at the AFFTC. The letter contained a "certificate of waiver covering the release of the X-15 research vehicle over Silver Lake" subject to some special limitations. The FAA imposed the limitations to ensure "maximum safety not only to your AFFTC personnel and equipment, but also to other users of the immediate airspace. Further, the communications requirements will insure the blocked airspace may be returned to its normal use with minimum delay." The FAA approved the certificate of waiver (form ACA-400) on 1 September 1959 and listed the period of waiver as 1

82 E-mail, Clarence E. "Bud" Anderson to Dennis R. Jenkins, 28 January 2002; Trip Report, Colonel Clarence E. Anderson, Chief of the Flight Test Operations Division, AFFTC, 17 July 1959. In the AFFTC Access to Space Office Project Files. The Helio L-28 Super Courier was redesignated U-10A in 1962.

83 Letter, Colonel Roger B. Phelan/AFFTC to Administrator, 4th Region, FAA, 24 July 1959, subject: Proposed X-15 Operation Involving Controlled Airspace in the Vicinity of Silver Lake, California; letter, R. D. Freeland, Chief General Operations Brach, 4th Region, FAA, to Colonel Roger B. Phelan, AFFTC, 29 July 1959.

84 Ibid.

October 1959 to 31 March 1961, although it was subsequently extended to 1 July 1963, and later still through the end of 1969.[85]

Given the effort that accompanied the acquisition of Cuddeback Lake in late 1957 and early 1958, it is surprising that the first serious survey of the lake does not appear to have taken place until 7 October 1959. Of course, conducting detailed surveys significantly ahead of the anticipated use was not a particularly useful exercise since the periodic rains that kept the lakebeds useable also changed their character each time, as did the effects of other vehicles (such as cars). By this time, the X-15 had already made its first two flights from over Rosamond Dry Lake, landing each time at Rogers. Since the Air Force expected the X-15 to begin rapidly to expand its flight envelope, North American sent George P. Lodge to Cuddeback in an Air Force Piasecki H-21 Shawnee helicopter.[86]

Lodge conducted the standard hardness tests by dropping the same "imperial ball" used in the other surveys. He found that the ball left an impression of about 3 inches (which was considered acceptable) at the southern end of the proposed runway, but quickly degraded to 4–4.5 inches by the northern end. He noted that these measurements compared unfavorably to tests on Rogers (2 inches) and Rosamond (2 inches) conducted after the last rains. A note emphasized that there were a set of deep ruts running the length of the runway made by a vehicle when the lake was wet, and that although it was only a single set of ruts, they "wander around to some extent." The nature of the lakebeds was such that grading or other mechanical methods could not repair major damage–only nature could do that. Lodge recommended that "Cuddeback lake, in its present condition, not be considered as an alternate landing site for the X-15 airplane and should be used only as a last resort in an extreme emergency." He warned that "should a landing be attempted with the X-15 airplane on Cuddeback lake in its present condition, there would be more than a 50-50 chance of wiping out the nose gear." It was clear that the lakes had both good and bad qualities: they were largely self-repairing each time it rained, but they could also be self-destroying by the same process.[87]

Two weeks later, Lodge, who was a flight safety specialist for North American, performed a survey of Silver Lake and nine other lakes to determine their suitability as emergency landing sites. At Silver, Lodge found that the prevailing wind was out of the north, with the best landing heading estimated at 200–310 degrees magnetic. The southern portion of the lake was soft with numerous sinkholes, and not satisfactory for touchdown. Lodge also found an abandoned railroad bed, approximately 2 feet high and 10 feet wide, running north to south across the east side of the lakebed. There was also a dirt road with deep ruts running east to west across the northern part of the lake, a paved road going from Baker to Death Valley along the eastern perimeter, and another dirt road (this time with no ruts) running diagonally northwest to southeast.[88]

---

85 Letter, L. N. Lightbody/FAA to Colonel Roger B. Phelan/AFFTC, 1 September 1959. In the files at the AFFTC History Office.

86 Memorandum, George P. Lodge, North American Aviation, to Roy Ferren, North American Aviation, 8 October 1959, subject: Survey of Cuddeback Lake. Piasecki was later absorbed into Boeing Vertol.

87 Ibid. Emphasis in the original.

88 Memorandum, George P. Lodge, North American Aviation, to Roy Ferren, North American Aviation, 23 October 1959, subject: Survey of Silver and Miscellaneous Dry Lakes.

Despite these obstacles, there was approximately 16,000 feet of satisfactory lakebed between the soft southern portion and the northern road. There were a few sinkholes, most measuring about 7 inches across and 3–4 inches deep, but the Air Force would fill these before use. The usual imperial-ball tests resulted in impressions between 2.9 and 3.7 inches in diameter, although the main area was on the lower end of that range. In addition, Lodge pounded both 3/8-inch and 1/2-inch steel rods into the ground with 200 pounds of force to determine what the condition of the soil was under the upper crust. The 3/8-inch rod generally penetrated between 1 and 3 inches, while the 1/2-inch rod penetrated between 0.25 and 1.5 inches. The results of the tests led Lodge to recommend a location for a marked runway. Of the other nine lakebeds visited, Lodge landed only on the east and west lakes in the Three Sisters group, and determined that both were satisfactory for emergency use despite having "a few rocks and ammo links strewn about."[89]

As 1959 ended, George Lodge was a busy man, and at the end of November he conducted yet another lake survey, this time of approximately 50 lakes in California, Nevada, and Utah. Again, the intent was to find suitable emergency landing sites for the X-15 as it expanded its flight-test program. The test methods Lodge used on the lakes were the same as he had used the previous month at Silver Lake.[90]

The Air Force and NASA continued to survey the established and previously used lakebeds periodically, particularly after it rained to determine that the lakebed was dry enough to support operations and that no sinkholes or gullies existed. Changing the direction of the available runways on a lakebed also required a revised survey. For instance, in early December 1959 Lodge conducted a new survey of Rosamond Dry Lake to determine whether the lake would support a marked runway running northeast to southwest. Marked runways already existed on headings of 10–190 degrees and 70–250 degrees. Starting from a location in the southwest corner of the lakebed, Lodge inspected a heading of approximately 30 degrees, roughly toward the telemetry station located on the edge of the lake. He found that the lakebed was hard and smooth for 2 miles, moderately smooth at 2.5 miles, smooth again at 3 miles, moderately rough at 3.5 miles, and rough from 4 miles to the edge of the lakebed. Imperial-ball drop tests yielded diameters of about 2.5 inches across the route. The conclusion was that the runway was practical, and, as viewed from above, would result in a runway approximately halfway between the two existing runways, with all three converging at the southwest edge of the lakebed.[91]

The second round of lake acquisitions began when the XLR99 engine came on line. First up was securing rights to use Hidden Hills dry lake, slightly west of the Hidden Hills Ranch airstrip. Simulator studies had confirmed that Hidden Hills would be ideal as an emergency landing site during the launches for the initial XLR99 flights that needed to be conducted further uprange than the XLR11 flights. The lakebed would continue to be used as a contingency site as the program

89 Ibid.

90 Memorandum, George P. Lodge, North American Aviation, to Roy Ferren, North American Aviation, 1 December 1959, subject: Survey of Dry Lakes in California, Nevada, and Utah.

91 Memorandum, George P. Lodge, North American Aviation, to E. R. Cokeley, North American Aviation, 7 December 1959, subject: Survey of Rosamond Dry Lake.

continued to launch further uprange into Utah. At the beginning of 1960, it was expected that the program would need access to the lake by 1 October 1960.[92]

However, schedules change, and the XLR99 flight dates kept slipping. A revised plan showed that the XLR99 research buildup flights would use Silver Lake and Hidden Hills Lake in California, Mud Lake in Nevada, and Wah Wah Lake in Utah as launch sites. The program needed various intermediate lakes along the upper portion of the High Range to provide complete coverage for emergency landings along the route. The Air Force would staff the intermediate lakes with crash and emergency personnel during flights. Additional contingency lakes would have runways marked on them, but would not be staffed with support personnel. At first the AFFTC and NASA had wanted to mark "all lakes with a satisfactory 10,000 feet landing surface" to provide an additional factor of safety for the X-15 program. Although no plans existed to use these lakes, the planners believed that marking them would also allow continued X-15 operation when a primary intermediate lake was wet. However, legal personnel indicated that there was "NO possibility" (emphasis in original) of marking any lake unless a right-to-use permit was obtained. Since personnel and funds did not exist to negotiate all the required permits, this plan was abandoned and a list of essential contingency sites was drawn up.[93]

The 30 September 1960 plan included launching immediate flights from Silver Lake, with the west lake at Three Sisters and Cuddeback acting as intermediate emergency sites. By 1 February 1961, operations would move to Hidden Hills, with Cuddeback as the intermediate site. On 1 April, Mud Lake would become the primary launch lake, with Grapevine and Ballarat as the intermediate sites, and contingency sites located at Panamint Springs and Racetrack. Two months later the launches would move to Wah Wah Lake, with Groom Lake, Delamar, and Hidden Hills becoming the intermediate sites, and Dogbone and Indian Springs the contingency sites. The AFFTC sought permission from Nellis to use the last two sites because they were located on the Las Vegas range, as was Mud Lake.[94]

Planners had always considered Smith Ranch Lake as a backup site to Wah Wah Lake, using Mud Lake as the intermediate site and the same contingency sites used during Mud Lake launches. This was still true at the end of February 1961. The program expected to begin launches from Hidden Hills in March 1961, and the launch lake still needed to be surveyed and marked. NASA expected to begin using Mud Lake in April 1961 and two of the support lakes (Grapevine and Panamint) still required use permits, while Ballarat had replaced Racetrack as the second contingency site. The program still needed to survey and mark all three of the support lakes. Launches from Wah Wah would begin in June 1961, and all of the sites along that route (except for Hidden Hills) still had to be "acquired," surveyed, and marked. As the program continued, however, it abandoned plans to use Wah Wah Lake, in part because of difficulties in obtaining permission to use the Nellis contingency sites (particularly Groom Lake) and airspace rights

92 Letter, Richard J. Harer AFFTC to Phyllis R. Actis, AFFTC, 3 May 1960, subject: Hidden Hills Dry Lake Right-To-Use Permit.

93 Memorandum for Record, Richard J. Harer, Chairman X-15 Operations Committee, 4 October 1960.

94 Ibid.

Determining if a lakebed could support the weight of an X-15 and its support airplanes was a relatively non-technical endeavor. A large steel ball, nicknamed the "imperial ball" was dropped from a height of six feet and the resulting impression was measured. For most of the program, a diameter of 3.25 inches or less was considered acceptable to support operations. Neil Armstrong is kneeling beside the ball in this June 1958 photo at Hidden Hills. (NASA)

over Nevada's restricted areas. Instead, the government eventually acquired the alternate launch site at Smith Ranch Lake, although flights from this point did not begin until June 1963.[95]

Supporting the High Range

As the X-15 program moved on to higher and faster flights, support became more difficult because it required more time to travel to the sites and more lakes for each flight. The minutes of the X-15 Operations Subcommittee on 9 March 1961 give some insight into the coordination required. The subcommittee membership included Richard J. Harer, Colonel Bud Anderson, Major Robert M. White, Major K. Lewis, Captain J. E. Varnadoe, Lieutenant R. L. Smith, Captain F. R. O'Clair, Joseph R. Vensel, Stanley P. Butchart, C. E. Sorensen, and Lieutenant Commander Forrest S. Petersen. White and Petersen were X-15 pilots, and several of the other members had long and distinguished flying careers (especially

95 Ibid; letter, Colonel Clay Tice to distribution, subject: Acquiring, Surveying, and Marking Lakebeds in Support of X-15 Flight Test Program, 27 February 1961. Flights from Hidden Hills actually did begin in March 1961.

Anderson and Butchart), so the group was not without a certain amount of applicable expertise.[96]

The previous October Paul Bikle had written a letter to the X-15 Operations Subcommittee and the AFFTC outlining an increase in support that would be required as the X-15 program moved uprange to the more remote lakes. The letter provides insight into how complicated it really was to conduct X-15 flights. For instance, each of the uprange stations (Beatty and Ely) had an operating crew of eight people, and the Air Force had to arrange transportation for the crew "a few days prior to each X-15 flight and for their return to Edwards after the flight." Given that NASA frequently scheduled flights once per week, this required a constant movement of personnel. Beatty supported all launches, while the program only used Ely for the high-speed flights scheduled out of Wah Wah Lake beginning in June 1961.[97]

The subcommittee did not think that supporting Hidden Hills launches would place any additional burden on the AFFTC since the effort required was generally similar to that needed for Silver Lake. However, flights from Mud Lake and farther uprange would require a much greater level of support. In its letter, NASA increased the amount of support requested, largely based on the unknown factors of never having launched from uprange. The AFFTC agreed that the equipment and personnel requirements for the uprange lake sites (as listed in the NASA letter) were valid and, at least initially, appropriate. The Air Force hoped, however, that subsequent experience could reduce some of the requirements.[98]

One of the attachments to Bikle's letter provided the details of the support he was requesting. This example uses a launch from Wah Wah Lake because it was the most comprehensive. The X-15 launch would take place 20 miles north of Wah Wah Lake and would require the X-15, NB-52, and two chase aircraft. An emergency team would be located at Wah Wah Lake in case the X-15 engine did not start or some other emergency required an immediate landing. This team would consist of two Air Force 500-gallon fire trucks, an H-21 helicopter, eight firemen, an Air Force pilot as lake controller, an Air Force crew chief, an Air Force doctor, an Air Force pressure-suit technician, and a NASA X-15 specialist. Delamar Lake, the next contingency landing site, was 120 miles away. One Air Force 500-gallon fire truck, four firemen, four Air Force flight crew, two Air Force paramedics, and a NASA X-15 specialist would staff it. A Jeep would carry a nitrogen purge system to safe the X-15 after landing. One hundred and fifteen miles closer to Edwards was Hidden Hills, the primary emergency site in case the pilot had to shut down the engine early. Orbiting this lake were two F-104 chase aircraft that were intended to pick up the X-15 as it slowed down at the nominal end-of-mission, but could also provide assistance in the event of emergency. An Air Force C-130 waited on the lake to evacuate the X-15 pilot in case of an emergency landing, along with an Air Force 500-gallon fire truck, four

96 Minutes of Meeting, X-15 Operations Subcommittee, 20 March 1961. In the AFFTC Access to Space Office Project Files.

97 Letter, Paul F. Bikle to AFFTC, 12 October 1960, subject: AFFTC Operation Support of Remote Launches for the X-15 Program.

98 Minutes of Meeting, X-15 Operations Subcommittee, 20 March 1961. In the AFFTC Access to Space Office Project Files.

firemen, two pilots, four Air Force flight crew, two Air Force paramedics, and a NASA X-15 specialist.[99]

Back at Edwards, the NASA radio van, an H-21 helicopter, the NASA lake controller, two Air Force fire trucks, eight firemen, two Air Force flight crew, the Air Force flight surgeon, a pressure-suit technician, and a NASA X-15 specialist awaited. In addition, staged between Wah Wah Lake and Delamar were a NASA-provided Jeep and three NASA X-15 specialists in case the X-15 had to set down unexpectedly at a lake other than those manned for the flight. An F-104 also orbited between Delamar and Hidden Hills to provide chase if the X-15 had to slow down during mid-flight. It was a complex ballet.

As it turned out, however, the increase in support that NASA was requesting was not possible. For instance, NASA wanted three C-130 aircraft and four paramedics dedicated to each launch, but the AFFTC did not have these resources. The AFFTC only had four C-130s assigned, and two were normally at El Centro supporting activities at the National Parachute Range. The base flight surgeon indicated that he believed it would be acceptable to provide a capability for a flight surgeon to be on the scene of an accident "within one hour," and the AFFTC adopted this suggestion. In general, however, the level of support provided by the AFFTC was consistent with that requested by Bikle; it differed primarily in some convenience items, not in essential services. On the other hand, NASA had proposed sending crews to the uprange sites the morning of each flight (meaning in the dark, since the X-15 often flew near first light). The AFFTC believed it was easier to send the uprange crews up the day prior to each flight. In most cases the personnel stayed in hotels in the towns near the support sites and reported to the site by 0800 hours in order to be ready by 0830 to support a 0900 takeoff of the NB-52.[100]

By early 1961 the X-15 Operations Subcommittee reported that security restrictions concerning Groom Lake seemed to be easing, and everybody agreed that Groom Lake was a preferable landing site compared to Delamar Lake. The program hoped to gain permission to use Groom Lake in the future, and Captain Varnadoe agreed to contact the appropriate offices to determine the likelihood of that happening. As it ended up, although one black project (the U-2) was ending at Groom, another (the Blackbird) was getting set to begin, and the X-15 program never would obtain permission to use the lakebed.[101]

By this time the Edwards and Beatty sites of the High Range were operational and had supported 34 X-15 flights. The Ely station became operational in April 1961. One of the concerns of the X-15 Operations Subcommittee involved directing rescue forces to a downed X-15 pilot. The H-21 rescue helicopters did not have onboard navigation equipment, and required direction to within five miles of the crash site. From that point they could use radio homing equipment to find the rescue beacon on the pilot. The beacon itself was relatively new and at that time NASA had only installed it on X-15-2; however, it would later install the beacon

99 Letter, Paul F. Bikle to AFFTC, 12 October 1960, subject: AFFTC Operation Support of Remote Launches for the X-15 Program.

100 Minutes of Meeting, X-15 Operations Subcommittee, 20 March 1961. In the AFFTC Access to Space Office Project Files.

101 The CIA-Lockheed A-12 Blackbird would arrive at Groom Lake in early 1962.

JAN '66

LAKE	RUNWAY LENGTH	RUNWAY HEADING	RUNWAY ELEV	TACAN STA	TACAN CHAN	TACAN RAD	TACAN N MI
Bonneville	7-8 mi	3-21	4250	BVL	70		
Delamar	2.5	0-18	4000	MLF	58	215	110
Edwards	7-8	17-35	2300	EDW	68		
	5	18-36	(X-15)				
	6	5-23	(North)				
	5	7-25	(South)				
	4	9-27	(Navaho Trail)				
Grapevine	2	1-19	4000	BTY	94	300	30
Hidden Hls	3	15-33	2000	LAS	116	250	40
Mud	5	6-24	5000	OAL		90	35
Silver	2	12-30	1000	LAS	116	215	65
Smith's	4	4-22	5700	NFL	82	90	55
Three Sis (W)	2.5	3-21	3500	LAS	116	210	110
(E)	2.5	5-23					
Wah Wah	3.5	2-20	4500	MLF	58	290	20

MISC. LAKEBED INFORMATION

Each X-15 pilot was issued a typed summary of lakebed information, along with hand-drawn sketches of the lakes and the marked runways. These were the lakes available in January 1966. (North American Aviation)

on the other two airplanes. North American had promised a 30-mile range for the beacon, but testing at Edwards revealed much less capability. The beacon was returned to North American and discovered to have only half-power in its battery (range is a square function, so this resulted in only one-quarter of the projected distance). The H-21 used an AN/ARA-25 direction (homing) finder to locate the beacon. The subcommittee believed it would be desirable to install an ARA-25 receiver on the NB-52s also to allow the carrier aircraft to locate the pilot and direct the H-21s to the site. In addition, the NASA budget included funds to install auto-trackers on the High Range telemetry antennas. Once installed, the antennas could be set to 2.443 MHz and automatically track the pilot rescue beacon.[102]

Expeditious recovery of the X-15 pilot by an H-21 or C-130 required a detailed knowledge of each lakebed, and this implied that all the rescue pilots would need to fly practice approaches at each possible recovery site. The recovery of the X-15 itself from uprange locations would be handled by NASA, although an AFFTC crane would be provided to lift the airplane onto a flatbed trailer.[103]

More Lakes

Jack McKay conducted a short lake survey in late March 1961 to investigate possible launch lakes for the maximum speed flights. During this trip he visited Tonopah, Nevada, on 22 March to discuss communication requirements, refueling capabilities, and storage requirements. The officer in charge of the Tonopah site stated that F-104 proficiency flights would not be a problem. A 500-gallon fuel truck was available with 91-octane gasoline to refuel H-21 helicopters. The pilot would sign a Form 15, committing the AFFTC to reimburse Tonopah for the fuel. Storage facilities at the airport were limited to a small U.S. Navy installation that consisted of one small, corrugated-metal building leased to the Atomic Energy Commission for the storage of classified materials. However, a fenced area around the building appeared suitable for securing X-15 support equipment if necessary. The manager of the civilian airport informed McKay that 91-octane fuel was available for purchase from a 2,000-gallon fuel truck.[104]

McKay also visited Smith Ranch Lake, located 100 miles north-northwest of Mud Lake. The Air force initially acquired this site as a backup to Wah Wah Lake and removed a total of 25,000 acres from the public domain, although some privately owned land also existed on the southwest portion of the lakebed. A five-mile-long runway was marked on a heading of 025-205 degrees. McKay also investigated the use of Edwards Creek Valley Dry Lake, 26 miles northwest of Smith Ranch during the March 1961 trip, but took no further action.[105]

The increased performance of the "advanced X-15" (the X-15A-2) and its use of recoverable drop tanks necessitated that NASA and the AFFTC acquire rights

102 Minutes of Meeting, X-15 Operations Subcommittee, 20 March 1961. In the AFFTC Access to Space Office Project Files.

103 Ibid.

104 Memorandum, Jack B. McKay to Chief of the Operations Division, 27 March 1961, subject: Periodic Inspection and Markings (March 22, 1961) of X-15 High Range Emergency Sites. In the files at the DFRC History Office.

105 Ibid.

to additional property. All of this land was in Nevada. Most of it was owned by the federal government, and a great deal of it was already out of the public domain.[106]

The X-15A-2 would use drop tanks on the high-speed flights, something that researchers had not anticipated for the original X-15 flight program. The X-15 jettisoned the tanks at approximately Mach 2.1 and 65,000 feet. After some free-fall, the parachutes opened at 15,000 feet and lowered the empty tanks to the ground. With the chutes deployed, the heavier tank had a descent rate of 25 feet per second (17 mph), while the lighter tank fell at 20 fps (14 mph). A helicopter recovered the tanks and placed them on flatbed trucks for the trips back to Edwards. Obviously, the program could not allow the tanks to fall onto civilians or their property. The possible impact areas for the tanks were quite large due to possible dispersions in the X-15 flight conditions at the time of tank jettison, as well as unknown wind effects.[107]

Despite its increased performance potential, the initial of the acceleration of X-15A-2 with full external tanks was considerably less than that of the standard X-15. This caused a reevaluation of the emergency lake coverage for flights with external tanks. Flight planners Robert G. Hoey and Johnny G. Armstrong used the AFFTC X-15A-2 hybrid simulator to conduct a parametric study of the glide capability of the aircraft for different engine burn times along the design profile to 100,000 feet. This study concluded that, of the originally selected launch points, only Mud Lake was suitable for flights using the external tanks. However, since Mud Lake was only 215 miles from Edwards, it was not suitable for the high-speed flights that required more distance. The use of Smith Ranch as a launch point was desirable, but unfortunately the distance between Smith Ranch and Mud Lake was too great for the glide capability of the airplane, and thus for a period of time X-15A-2 would have been without a suitable landing site. NASA wanted to find a usable lake between Smith Ranch and Mud Lake to fill the gap.

NASA conducted a new survey in May 1965 and again focused on Edwards Creek Valley Dry Lake, something that Jack McKay had mentioned as early as March 1961. This lake was 23 miles northwest of Smith Ranch; in a change of rules, there would be no plan to land at Edwards Creek, even in the event the engine failed to ignite immediately after launch. The lake did not provide the desired emergency coverage, but allowed a straight-in approach to Smith Ranch if an engine shutdown occurred at the worse possible time. In addition, if an emergency occurred at the time of tank ejection, the pilot could always land at Smith Ranch.[108]

Johnny Armstrong carried out a further analysis of X-15A-2 flight profiles in early 1965 using the hybrid simulator. For instance, Armstrong studied the glide capability of the X-15A-2 by terminating engine thrust at different times along the Mach 8 profile. For X-15A-2 flights with external tanks, there were two critical

---

106 Memorandum, Colonel Guy M. Townsend, AFFTC Deputy for Systems Test to Phyllis R. Actis, Planning Specialist, 10 May 1965, subject: Land Requirements for Flight Test of the Advanced X-15. In the AFFTC Access to Space Office Project Files.

107 Ibid.

108 Johnny G. Armstrong, AFFTC technology document FTC-TD-69-4, "Flight Planning and Conduct of the X-15A-2 Envelope Expansion Program, July 1969, pp. 13-15; Johnny G. Armstrong, AFFTC Flight Research Division office memorandum AV-64-4, "Geographical Impact Areas for the X-15A-2 Drop Tanks," 22 July 1964. In the AFFTC Access to Space Office Project Files

points along the flight profile with regard to emergency landing sites. The first point was the decision to either to continue straight ahead to a forward landing site or initiate a turn to a landing site behind the airplane. The geographical location of potential emergency landing sites determined the length of this period. Second, the flight planners had to consider emergency lake coverage from the tank drop point. In all cases, it was desirable to arrive at the emergency landing lake at an altitude of 20,000 feet or greater.[109]

In his preliminary study the previous summer, Armstrong had concluded that launches from Mud Lake needed to be conducted from the east side of the lake because of external tank impact considerations, and this condition still held true. If a pilot was considering contingency landing sites, the critical time for a launch from Mud Lake was after 53 seconds of engine thrust; at that point it was possible to either continue forward to Grapevine Lake or turn around and land at Mud Lake. If the pilot elected to continue forward, he would arrive at Grapevine at an altitude of 43,000 feet. Returning to Mud Lake would result in an altitude of 11,000 feet (or 6,000 feet above Mud Lake).[110]

The simulations also showed that adequate emergency lake coverage was not available for a Smith Ranch launch. There was a period of 29–31 seconds (depending upon the exact launch point) during which the X-15 could not go forward or turn around and arrive at the emergency landing site at 20,000 feet altitude. Worse, there was a period of 4–7 seconds in which it was not even possible to arrive at the emergency lakes at 5,000 feet altitude. In other words, given that Mud Lake was at 5,000 feet altitude, the pilot could not even make a straight-in approach if the engine shut down during the critical time. Additionally, if the engine shut down during external tank separation, the X-15A-2 could not go forward to Mud Lake and would have to return to Smith Ranch, arriving with only 5,000 feet altitude.[111]

The use of Edwards Creek Valley as a launch lake allowed the pilot to attempt a straight-in approach at either Smith Ranch or Mud Lake if the engine shut down at a critical time. There was even a small period in which the pilot could elect to abort to either lake. Once the pilot jettisoned the tanks, he could turn the airplane back to Smith Ranch, arriving at 5,000 feet. Given this analysis, the program decided that X-15A-2 high-speed flights would proceed from either Mud Lake or Edwards Creek Valley. The tank recovery area for Mud Lake launches was entirely within Restricted Area R-4907 and posed only minor problems for securing use rights; however, the Air Force needed to acquire use rights for civilian property in the anticipated drop areas for Edwards Creek Valley (and Smith Ranch) launches.[112]

The Air Force would launch the initial X-15A-2 flights from Mud Lake, but would not exploit the full potential of the advanced aircraft because of the limited distance between Mud Lake and Edwards. The program now expected to launch subsequent flights from Edwards Creek Valley based on two considerations: first, the airplane had slightly better gliding performance than anticipated, eliminating

109 AFFTC Flight Research Division memorandum AV-65-6, pp. 3-4.

110 Ibid, p. 4.

111 Ibid.

112 Ibid, p. 5.

most of the gaps in emergency lake coverage from Smith Ranch; second, there had been some difficulties obtaining adequate external tank drop areas from Edwards Creek Valley. As it turned out, there never were any launches from Edwards Creek Valley since the X-15A-2 program stopped at Mach 6.7 instead of proceeding to Mach 8. Of the four flights with external tanks, the program launched the first (with empty tanks) from Cuddeback, and the three flights with full tanks from Mud.[113]

Rogers Dry Lake was the designated landing site for all flights. Initially, the runways on Rogers were marked in typical fashion, showing left and right extremes, and thresholds on each end. A meeting of the original X-15 pilots on 19 October 1960 established a standard operational procedure for releasing the ventral stabilizer before landing. North American decided the pilots should jettison the ventral below 800 feet altitude and less than 300 knots to ensure recovery in a reusable condition. The pilots established that if the touchdown point on runway 18 (the most frequently used) was two miles from the north end, then the ideal jettison queue would be when the pilot passed over the railroad tracks located one mile from the end of the runway. The pilots asked Paul Bikle to request the AFFTC to mark all Rogers runways with chevron patterns one mile from each end (to indicate the ventral jettison point), and also two miles down each runway (to indicate the touchdown point). The program subsequently adopted these markings for most of the lakebed runways.[114]

The markings on the lakebed were not paint, but a tar-like compound on top of the soil. The Air Force standardized the runways at 300 feet wide and at least 2 miles (often 3 miles) long. The tar strips outlining the edges of the runways were 8 feet wide. The width of the strips was critical because they provided a major visual reference for the pilot to judge his height (many of the lakebeds were completely smooth and provided no other reference). The chevron patterns were marked at the appropriate places on each lakebed with the same compound. The Air Force was responsible for keeping each of the active lakebeds marked, and laid new tar at least once per year after the rainy season. If the pilots complained the markings were not visible enough during the approaches practiced in the F-104s, the Air Force would re-mark the runway. As Milt Thompson remembered, "over the years, the thickness of the tar strips increased with each new marking until they exceeded 3 or 4 inches in height…."[115]

The FRC was primarily responsible for checking the lakebeds during the course of the flight program. As often as not, this involved landing the NASA DC-3 on the lakebed for a visual inspection (usually performed by Walter Whiteside riding a motorcycle). If the lakebed appeared damp, the pilot of the DC-3 would make a low pass and roll its wheels on the surface, making sure not to slow down enough to become stuck. He would then fly a slow pass and observe how far the wheels had sunk in the mud. If the DC-3 was not available, the pilots used a T-33 or whatever other airplane they could get, although obviously they could not

113 Memorandum, Colonel Guy M. Townsend, AFFTC Deputy for Systems Test to Phyllis R. Actis, Planning Specialist, 10 May 1965, Land Requirements for Flight Test of the Advanced X-15. In the AFFTC Access to Space Office Project Files.

114 Letter, Paul F. Bikle/FRC to Commander/AFFTC, subject: Rogers Lake Runway Markings for X-15 Flights, 21 October 1960.

115 Thompson, *At the Edge of Space*, pp. 51-52.

carry the motorcycle in those instances. On at least one occasion, the pilots (Neil Armstrong and Chuck Yeager) became stuck in the mud when the lakebed turned out to be softer than they had anticipated.[116]

The National Park Service declared Rogers Dry Lake a national historic landmark because of its role in the development of the nation's space program. Since 1977, NASA has used the lakebed as a landing site for many Space Shuttle test and operational flights.[117]

Despite the time and effort spent on locating, acquiring, and marking many launch and intermediate lakes, none of the X-15 pilots had any real desire to land on any of them, although several did. The pilots considered a landing at the launch lake or an intermediate lake an emergency, while landing on Rogers Dry Lake was normal. Both were deadstick landings, so what was the difference? Milt Thompson summed it up well in his book: "[Rogers] was where God intended man to land rocket airplanes. It was big. It had many different runways. It was hard. It had no obstructions on any of the many approach paths. It had all of the essential emergency equipment. It was territory that we were intimately familiar with and it had a lot of friendly people waiting there." In other words, it was home.[118]

116 Ibid, p. 52. The NASA DC-3 was really a former Navy R4D, which was the Navy equivalent of the Army/Air Force C-47.

117 http://www.edwards.af.mil/history/docs_html/center/lakebeds.html, accessed 25 January 2002.

118 Thompson, *At the Edge of Space*, p. 152.

CHAPTER 6

Preparations

Although most histories consider the development of the three flight vehicles the high mark of the X-15 program, in reality several ancillary areas were perhaps as important as the actual airplanes and left a more lasting legacy. Early in the program, engineers recognized the need for a carrier aircraft, although this was largely an extension of previous X-plane practice. Nevertheless, the two Boeing B-52s used by the X-15 program would go on to long careers carrying a variety of vehicles that researchers had not even dreamed of during the X-15 development. Most important, however, was the development of extensive engineering and mission simulation systems. Although it was crude by today's standards, the X-15 pioneered the use of simulators not just to train pilots, but also to engineer the aircraft, plan the missions, and understand the results. Not surprisingly, given the involvement of Charlie Feltz, Harrison Storms, and Walt Williams in both the X-15 and Apollo programs, the X-15 pointed the way to how America would conduct its space missions. Simulation is one of the enduring legacies of the small black airplanes.

SIMULATIONS

Immediately after World War II, the Air Force developed rudimentary simulators at Edwards AFB for the later phases of the X-1 and X-2 programs. In fact, an X-1 simulation powered by an analog computer led to an understanding of the roll-coupling phenomena, while another simulation accurately predicted the X-2 control problems at Mach 3. The importance of these discoveries led the NACA HSFS to acquire an analog computer capability in 1957, mostly because the engineering staff anticipated that simulation would play an important role in the upcoming X-15 program.[1]

Fixed-Base Simulators

Simulation in the X-15 program meant much more than pilot training. It was perhaps the first program in which simulators played a major role in the development of an aircraft and its flight profiles. The flight planners used the simulators to determine heating loads, assess the effects of proposed technical changes, abort scenarios, and perform a host of related tasks. In this regard, the term "flight planner" at the AFFTC and FRC encompassed a great deal more than someone who sat down and wrote out a plan for a launch lake and a landing site. It is very possible that the flight planners (such as Elmore J. Adkins, Paul L. Chenoweth, Richard E. Day, Jack L. Kolf, John A. Manke, and Warren S. Wilson at the FRC, and Robert G. Hoey and Johnny G. Armstrong at the AFFTC) knew as much as (or more than) the pilots and flight-test engineers about the airplanes.[2]

The initial group of X-15 pilots worked jointly with research engineers and flight planners to develop simulations to study the aspects of flight believed to present the largest number of potential difficulties. During late 1956, North American developed a fixed-base X-15 simulator at their Inglewood facility that consisted of an X-15 cockpit and an "iron bird" that included production components such as cables, push rods, bellcranks, and hydraulics. The iron bird looked more or less like an X-15 and used flight-representative electrical wiring and hydraulic tubing, but otherwise did not much resemble an aircraft. The simulator included a complete stability augmentation system (dampers), and ultimately added an MH-96 adaptive flight control system. Controlling the simulator were three Electronics Associates, Inc. (EAI) PACE 231R analog computers that contained 380 operational amplifiers, 101 function generators, 32 servo amplifiers, and 5 electronic multipliers. None of the existing digital systems were capable of performing the computations in real time, hence the selection of analog computers. The simulator could also compute a real-time solution for temperature at any one of numerous

1 John P. Smith, Lawrence J. Schilling, and Charles A. Wagner, NASA technical memorandum 101695, "Simulation at Dryden Flight Research Facility from 1957 to 1982," February 1989, p. 1.

2 NASA has published several looks into simulation during the X-15 period. See, for example, Gene L. Waltman, *Black Magic and Gremlins: Analog Flight Simulations at NASA's Flight Research Center,* NASA Monographs in Aerospace History No. 20, SP-2000-4520 (Washington, DC: NASA, 2000) and John P. Smith, Lawrence J. Schilling and Charles A. Wagner, NASA technical memorandum 101695, "Simulation at Dryden Flight Research Facility from 1957 to 1982," February 1989; flight planner names remembered by Johnny G. Armstrong and William H. Dana, told to the author via e-mail, April 2002.

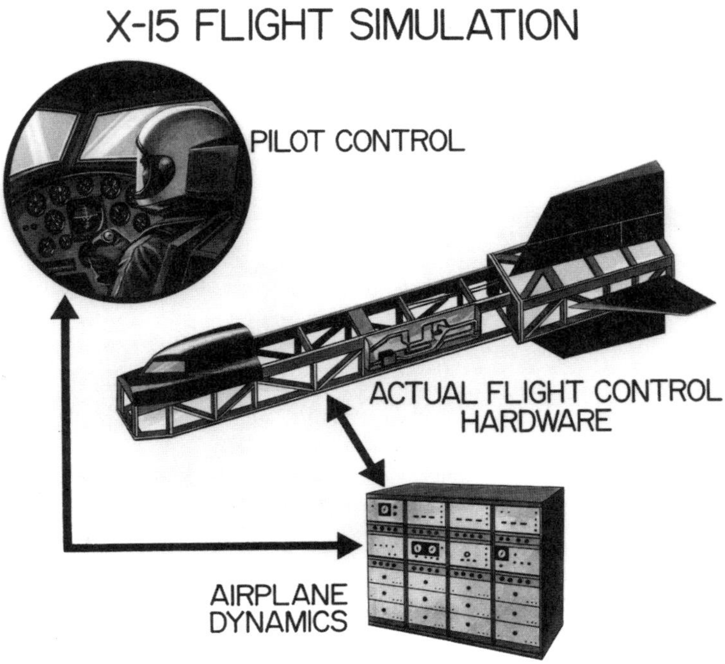

*Simulation in the X-15 program meant much more than pilot training and was the first program where simulators played a major role in the development of the aircraft and its flight profiles. Engineers used the simulators to determine heating loads, the effects of proposed technical changes, and to develop abort scenarios. Controlling the simulator were three Electronics Associates, Inc. (EAI) PACE 231*R *analog computers that contained 380 operational amplifiers, 101 function generators, 32 servo amplifiers, and 5 electronic multipliers. None of the existing digital systems was capable of performing the computations in real time, hence the selection of analog computers.* (NASA)

points on the fuselage and wing. Simulations were initiated in October 1956 using five degrees of freedom, and the simulator was expanded to six degrees of freedom (yaw, pitch, roll, and accelerations vertically, longitudinally, and radially) in May 1957.[3]

The simulator covered Mach numbers from 0.2 to 7.0 at altitudes from sea level to 1,056,000 feet (200 miles), although it was not capable of providing meaningful landing simulations. The initial round of simulations at Inglewood showed that the X-15 could reenter from altitudes as high as 550,000 feet as long

3 Edward N. Videan, Richard D. Banner, and John P. Smith, "The Application of Analog and Digital Computer Techniques in the X-15 Flight Research Program," a paper presented at the International Symposium on Analog and Digital Techniques Applied to Aeronautics, 9-12 September 1963, pp. 2-3; Lieutenant Colonel Burt Rowen, "Human-Factors Support of the X-15 Program," *Air University Quarterly Review*, Air War College, vol. X, no. 4, Winter 1958-59, pp. 36-37; George B. Merrick and C. H. Woodling, "X-15 Flight Simulation Studies," a paper in the *1958 Research Airplane Committee Report*, pp. 94-96. There is considerable disagreement among written papers on the number of components (e.g., function generators) in the simulator. It is likely that the simulator was constantly being modified and the numbers changed frequently. For instance, the numbers quoted in the text come from the paper by Videan, Banner, and Smith; Merrick and Woodling say there were 70 arbitrary 90-diode function generators, 35 computing servos, 330 computing amplifiers, and other associated pieces of computing equipment.

as everything went well. If done exactly right, a reentry from this altitude would almost simultaneously touch the maximum acceleration limit, the maximum dynamic pressure limit, and the maximum temperature limit. The slightest error in piloting technique would exceed one of these, probably resulting in the loss of the airplane and pilot. An angle of attack of 30 degrees would be required with the speed brakes closed, or only 18 degrees with the speed brakes open. The normal load factor reentering from 550,000 feet would reach 7 g, and a longitudinal deceleration of 4 g would last up to 25 seconds. Simulations in the centrifuge confirmed that pilots could maintain adequate control during these maneuvers, and considerations for the physical well-being of the pilot did not limit the flight envelope.[4]

These first simulations indicated the need for a more symmetrical tail to reduce aerodynamic coupling tendencies at low angles of attack, and potential thrust misalignment at high velocities and altitudes. This resulted in the change from the vertical-stabilizer configuration proposed by North American to the one that was actually built. Reentry studies indicated that the original rate-feedback-damper configuration was not adequate for the new symmetrical tail, and an additional feedback of yaw-rate-to-roll-control (called "yar") was required for stability at high angles of attack.[5]

Initially, the North American fixed-base simulator was computation-limited, and researchers could only study one flight condition at a time. The first three areas investigated were the exit phase, ballistic control, and reentry. Later, upgrades allowed complete freedom over a limited portion of a mission, and by mid-1957 unlimited freedom over the complete flight regime. By July 1958, the fixed-base simulator at North American already had over 2,000 simulated flights and more than 3,500 hours of experience under various flight conditions, and the airplane would not fly for another year.

As crude as it may seem today, the simulator nevertheless provided the flight planners with an excellent tool. The flight planner first established a detailed set of maneuvers that resulted in the desired test conditions. He then programmed a series of test maneuvers commensurate with the flight time available to ensure that the maximum amount of research data was obtained. Since the simulator provided a continuous real-time simulation of the X-15, it enabled the pilot to fly the planned mission as he would the actual flight, allowing him to evaluate the planned mission from a piloting perspective and to recommend changes as appropriate. Certain data, such as heating rates and dynamic pressures, required real-time computations to verify that the desired maneuvers were within the capability of the airplane.[6]

---

4 Rowen, "Human-Factors Support of the X-15 Program," pp. 36-37; Merrick and Woodling, "X-15 Flight Simulation Studies," pp. 94-98. The simulator was overly optimistic. In theory, the X-15 could reach a maximum altitude of 700,000 feet; however, 550,000 feet represented the peak altitude without exceeding the 7.33-g load factor or the 2,500-psf dynamic pressure limit during reentry. Thermal studies indicated that something around 550,000 feet would also be the limit from a thermodynamic perspective. See Gerald H. Johnson, "X-15 Structural Loads," a paper in the *1958 Research Airplane Committee Report*, p. 202; letter, Robert G. Hoey/AFFTC Flight Planner to Dennis R. Jenkins, 20 May 2002.

5 Merrick and Woodling, "X-15 Flight Simulation Studies," p. 94.

6 Videan et al., "The Application of Analog and Digital Computer Techniques in the X-15 Flight Research Program," pp. 3-4.

The fixed-base simulator at North American was hardly a fancy affair, just a mocked-up cockpit with a full set of instruments and a television screen. The original cadre of pilots, including Joseph A. Walker, spent a considerable amount of time in the North American simulator before the one at the Flight Research Center was ready. Although crude by today's standards, the X-15 pioneered the use of simulators not just to train pilots, but also to engineer the aircraft, plan the missions, and understand the results. Not surprisingly, given the involvement of Charlie Feltz, Harrison Storms, and Walt Williams in both the X-15 and Apollo programs, the X-15 pointed the way to how America would conduct its space missions. (NASA)

Engineers also used the simulator to develop vehicle systems before committing them in flight. One of the most notable was the MH-96 adaptive flight control system. Exhaustive tests in the simulator, conducted largely by Neil Armstrong, allowed researchers to optimize system parameters and develop operational techniques. Similarly, engineers used the simulators to investigate problems associated with the use of the dampers, and devised modifications to install on the airplane. Researchers then incorporated the results of flight tests into the simulator.[7]

At first, the FRC did not have an iron bird and had to make do with the crude cockpit used in the centrifuge at the Naval Air Development Center (NADC)

7 Ibid.

Johnsville, Pennsylvania. This was a cost-saving measure since the X-15 contract required North American to deliver its simulator (excepting the computers) to the FRC before turning the first airplane over to the government. Unlike the Inglewood installation, at the FRC the cockpit and analog computers were in the same room: not much to look at, but functional. The Air Vehicle Flight Simulation Facility was located in building 4800 at the FRC in an area that later became the center director's office. Like many early computer rooms, it used a linoleum-covered plywood false floor to cover the myriad of cables running beneath it. Large air conditioners installed on the building roof kept the computers cool. The X-15 simulator used a set of EAI analog computers procured for earlier simulations at the FRC, including one model 31R, one 131R, and one 231R that were generally similar to the computers used by North American. John P. Smith had begun mechanizing the original equations in the simulator, but Gene L. Waltman completed the task during the last three months of 1960 after Smith was promoted to a new job. The X-15 simulator became operational at the FRC on 3 January 1961. The X-15 simulator was the largest analog simulation ever mechanized at the FRC. The initial Air Vehicle Flight Simulation Facility at the FRC cost $63,000 and upgrades accounted for a further $1,700,000 by the end of 1968.[8]

Because the FRC simulator was not yet operational, the flight planning for the first 20 flights used the North American simulator. Dick Day and Bob Hoey spent a considerable amount of time during 1959 and 1960 in Inglewood on flight planning and training the first cadre of pilots.[9] Initially, North American was to transfer the simulator from Inglewood to the FRC in January 1961, but the move was delayed for various reasons, including the need to integrate the MH-96 adaptive flight control system into X-15-3. By March 1961, however, Paul Bikle was becoming concerned: "With the performance envelope expansion program now underway, the requirement of traveling to NAA [North American Aviation] to use the X-15 simulator is becoming unduly restrictive in time and in obtaining the close working relationships essential to a sound flight panning effort." Something needed to change.[10]

Bikle knew that North American did not want to transfer the simulator until the MH-96 integration was complete. In an effort to determine the consequences of moving earlier, Bikle called Dave Mellon at Minneapolis-Honeywell, who said he did not think the move would have an adverse affect on his schedule. Bikle also commented that "if a program delay is inevitable, it is preferable to delay the X-15-3 rather than the present program with the X-15-2." Bikle pushed to have the simulator moved to the FRC during April 1961. "We again want to emphasize that once the transfer has been accomplished, the NASA will make the simulator

8 Waltman, *Black Magic and Gremlins*, pp. 46-49; X-15 Status Report, Paul F. Bikle/FRC to H. Brown/NASA Headquarters, 13 January 1961, p. 2; Jane Van Nimmen and Leonard C. Bruno, with Robert L. Rosholt, *NASA Historical Data Book, 1958-1968, Volume I: NASA Resources 1958-1968*, NASA publication SP-4012 (Washington, DC: NASA, 1988), p. 300. Support for the X-15 did not account for the entire cost of the simulation facility; however, an exact cost breakdown could not be ascertained.

9 The Air Vehicle Flight Simulation Facility was renamed the Flight Simulation Laboratory at some point in the mid-1960s. Bob Hoey remembers that Day and Hoey generally traveled to Inglewood two or so days per week, accompanied by one of the initial pilots, when the detailed flight planning was being finalized. The team often flew from the FRC to Inglewood in the NASA DC-3 (R4D).

10 Letter, Paul F. Bikle/FRC to Major Arthur Murray/X-15 Project Office, subject: X-15 Simulator Transfer, 17 March 1961.

At first, the Flight Research Center made do with the crude cockpit that had been used in the centrifuge at NADC Johnsville. This was a cost-saving measure since the X-15 contract required North American to deliver their simulator (excepting the computers) to the FRC before turning the first airplane over to the government. Unlike the Inglewood installation, the cockpit and analog computers were in the same room at the FRC. The Air Vehicle Flight Simulation Facility was located in Building 4800 at the FRC in an area that later became the center director's office. (NASA)

available for whatever additional simulator effort is required by NAA, M-H [Minneapolis-Honeywell], and other contractors...."[11]

When the iron bird finally arrived in April 1961, engineers installed it along the east wall of the calibration hangar next door to the computer facility. A wall around the simulator provided some separation from the operations in the hangar. The cockpit faced away from the hangar door, and pilots discovered that sunlight coming through the windows caused visibility issues, so paint soon covered the windows. One of the unfortunate aspects of this installation was that the iron bird was located a little over 200 feet from the computers. This caused a number of signal-conditioning problems that a better grounding system eventually corrected. The hydraulic stand for the iron bird was originally located next to the mockup inside the hangar, but technicians subsequently relocated the unit to a small shed just outside, eliminating most of the noise from the simulator laboratory.[12]

To provide simulations that were more realistic, engineers at the FRC added a "malfunction generator" that could simulate the failure of 11 different cockpit

11 Ibid; X-15 Status Report, Paul F. Bikle/FRC to H. Brown/NASA Headquarters, 1 May 1961, p. 4.

12 Ibid, pp. 48-49.

The final simulator at the Flight Research Center was functionally identical to the one at North American, and used the same analog computers. The structure behind the cockpit is the "iron bird" that included production components such as cables, push rods, bellcranks, and hydraulics. The iron bird looked more or less like an X-15 and used flight-representative electrical wiring and hydraulic tubing, but otherwise did not much resemble an aircraft. The simulator included a complete stability augmentation system (dampers), and ultimately added an MH-96 adaptive flight control system. (NASA)

instruments and 23 different aircraft systems. The instruments included a pressure altimeter, all three attitude indicators, and pressure airspeed, dynamic pressure, angle-of-attack, angle-of-sideslip, inertial altitude, inertial velocity, and inertial rate-of-climb indicators. The vehicle systems that could be failed included the engine, ballistic control system, both electrical generators, and any axis in the damper system. Later, the simulator could duplicate the failure of almost any function of the MH-96 adaptive control system. Almost all X-15 flights were preceded by practicing various emergency procedures in the simulator using these malfunction generators.[13]

Contrary to many depictions of flight simulators in movies, the fixed-base simulator for the X-15 was not glamorous. The iron bird stretched behind the cockpit, but other than in size, it did not resemble an X-15 at all. The cockpit was open, and the sides of the "fuselage" extended only high enough to cover the side consoles and other controls inside of it. A canopy over the cockpit became

13 Videan et al., "The Application of Analog and Digital Computer Techniques in the X-15 Flight Research Program," pp. 2-3 and 14; Waltman, *Black Magic and Gremlins*, p. 52.

necessary when researchers installed some instruments and controls (particularly for the experiments) there for later flights, but even then, it was made of plywood.[14]

However, unlike most of the previous simulators at the FRC, the X-15 cockpit did have an accurate instrument panel. On one occasion, technicians inadvertently switched the location of the on/off switches for the ballistic control system and the APUs between the simulator and the airplane. It was normal procedure for the pilot to turn off the ballistic controls after reentry, and he practiced this in the simulator before each flight. During the actual flight, the pilot reached for the APU switch instead of the switch he thought was there. Fortunately, he caught himself and avoided an emergency. Everybody redoubled their efforts to ensure that the simulator accurately reflected the configuration of the airplane.[15]

When X-15-3 came on line with a completely different instrument panel arrangement, it presented some challenges for the simulator. Since the pilots needed to train on the correct instrument panel layout, the simulator support personnel had to swap out instrument panels to accommodate each different airplane. The technicians eventually installed a crank and pulley lift in the ceiling, along with cannon plugs for the electrical connections, to assist in making the change. On at least three occasions the program decided to make the instrument panels in the three airplanes as similar as possible, but they quickly diverged again as new experiments were added.[16]

In addition to its simulation tasks, the iron bird found another use as the flight program began. Engineers and technicians at the FRC soon discovered that it was a relatively simple task to remove troublesome components from the flight vehicles and install them on the iron bird in an attempt to duplicate reported problems. Given the initial lack of test equipment available for the stability augmentation system and some MH-96 components, this proved a useful troubleshooting method. The simulator also played an important role in demonstrating the need for advanced display and guidance devices, and found extensive use in the design and development of new systems.[17]

The simulator had a variety of output devices in addition to the cockpit displays, including several eight-channel stripchart recorders and a large X/Y flatbed plotter. The plotter had two independent pens: one showed the X-15 position on a 3-foot-square map of the area, and the other indicated altitude. This plotter was identical to ones used in the control room and at the uprange stations. There were different maps for each launch lake showing the various contingency landing sites and prominent landmarks.[18]

Eventually the FRC simulator grew to encompass six analog computers, and the patch panels needed to operate them contained 500 patch cords. The addition of a Scientific Data Systems SDS-930 digital computer in 1964 allowed the generation of nonlinear coefficients for the X-15A-2. This required an additional

14 John P. Smith, Lawrence J. Schilling and Charles A. Wagner, NASA technical memorandum 101695, "Simulation at Dryden Flight Research Facility from 1957 to 1982," February 1989, p. 3.

15 Ibid.

16 Letter, Johnny G. Armstrong to Dennis R. Jenkins, 3 August 2002.

17 NASA technical memorandum 101695, p. 3.

18 Ibid.

analog computer as an interface between the new digital computer and the rest of the simulator. The SDS-930 was somewhat unusual in that it was a true real-time computer, complete with a real-time operating system and a real-time implementation of Fortran.[19]

Despite its advanced specifications the SDS-930 was not initially satisfactory, which forced the flight planners to use the modified Dyna-Soar hybrid simulator at the AFFTC for the early X-15A-2 flights. The SDS-930 was generally unreliable, normally because of memory-parity errors that the computer manufacturer attempted to fix on numerous occasions during 1965, with little success. The problem was not only affecting flight planning for the X-15A-2, it was also delaying simulations needed for the energy-management system scheduled to fly on X-15-3. During early 1966, the SDS-930 was extensively modified to bring it up to the latest configuration, including the addition of two magnetic-tape units and a line printer to assist in the energy-management simulations. While this was going on, the FRC took advantage of the downtime to upgrade the SAS and ASAS implementation on the iron bird, including replacing all of the computer interface equipment for both systems. Technicians also brought all of the mechanical rigging up to the same standard as the three airplanes. However, Johnny Armstrong and Bill Dana both recall that no actual flight planning or flight simulation was "totally digital."[20]

The hybrid (analog-digital) simulator at the AFFTC initially provided a tool that enabled studies of the performance and handling of the X-20 glider, complete mission planning, and pilot familiarization. It was a logical outgrowth of the analog fixed-base simulators for the X-15. Although they had been ordered long before, the digital computers did not arrive at Edwards until July 1964, six months after the cancellation of the Dyna-Soar program. The equipment sat mostly unused until the flight planners decided to adapt it to the X-15A-2 Mach 8 flight expansion program. This was done as much to provide Air Force personnel with some hands-on experience as for any demonstrated need for another X-15 simulator.[21]

The analog section of the hybrid simulator used PACE 231R-V and 231R computers similar to those used at the FRC and North American installations. Each computer had approximately 75 operational amplifiers, 170 potentiometers, 36 digitally controlled analog switches, and 26 comparators, and the 231R-V had a mode-logic group that supported an interface to a digital computer. The digital subsystem used a Control Data Corporation DDP-24 that had 8,192 words of ferrite core memory, a 5-microsecond access time, and a 1-MHz clock. Although a Fortran II compiler was available on the machine, engineers coded the real-time programs in assembly language to maximize the performance of the relatively

19 Waltman, *Black Magic and Gremlins*, pp. 51-53. The Scientific Data Systems 900-9000 series consisted of the SDS 910, 920, 925, 930, 940, 945, and 9300 computers. The 24-bit machine at the FRC had 8K words of ferrite core memory, one eight-track magnetic-tape reader, a punched-card reader, a paper-tape reader, and one operator-console teletype. It did not include any printer or card punch. The unit delivered to the FRC was among the first 930s to be delivered.

20 X-15 Status Report, Paul F. Bikle/FRC to J. Martin/NASA Headquarters, 1 March 1966, p. 2; various e-mails between Johnny G. Armstrong and Dennis R. Jenkins, March 2002.

21 Captain Austin J. Lyons, Air Force report FTC-TR-66-44, "AFFTC Experiences with Hybrid Computation in a Real-Time Simulation of the X-15A-2," March 1967, pp. iii, and 3-4; conversations among Robert G. Hoey, Johnny G. Armstrong, and Dennis R. Jenkins, various dates in 2001 and 2002.

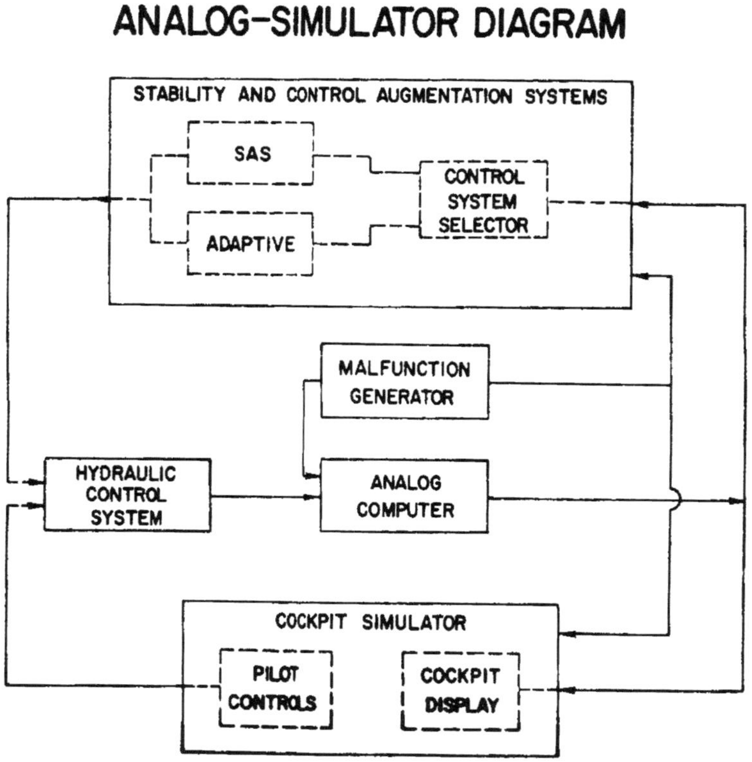

The fixed-base simulators at Inglewood and the FRC consisted of four major parts. The simulator included both controls and displays that were nearly identical to what the pilot found in the X-15 cockpit. The analog computer and malfunction generator were the heart of the system that provided the sequencing and control of the other components. The hydraulic control system was the "iron bird" and actually contained other flight components in addition to the hydraulic system including a complete stability augmentation system (or, later, a complete MH-96 adaptive flight control system). (NASA)

slow machines. Two large patch panels connected the analog subsystem and digital subsystem.[22]

Like the other fixed-base simulators, the AFFTC device had a functional X-15 instrument panel, although it was not as exact as the ones used at the FRC. This was because its intended use was to investigate heating and control problems related to the X-15A-2, not to conduct pilot training. Ultimately, the program did use the AFFTC simulator for some X-15A-2 pilot training, but the final "procedures" training was conducted at the FRC.

Since the X-15 program technically did not need the simulator, the AFFTC engineers were able to develop a "generic" simulation that was usable for other aircraft, not just the X-15. This was an extremely astute idea, and the engineers subsequently used the simulator for the M2-F2, SR-71, X-24A, X-24B, and

22 Ibid, pp. 5-6. The "DDP" stood for digital data processor, and the 24 indicated the number of bits per word.

EF-111. The hybrid simulator was also the only one available to perform heating predictions during reentry simulations of the Space Shuttle Orbiter during the early 1970s, providing valuable input to that program.[23]

At the FRC, the simulation team kept busy maintaining the computers and updating the programming to reflect actual flight results. During most of the flight program the simulation lab was busy for at least two shifts, and often three shifts, per day. The first shift performed pilot training and flight planning, the second shift conducted control-system and other studies, and maintenance and reprogramming occupied the third shift as needed. However, the team generally took weekends off. This was not necessarily a good thing for the simulator since it took the analog computers quite a while on Monday morning to warm up.[24]

Despite the apparent success of the fixed-base simulators, everybody recognized their limitations. The primary concern was that they were fixed-base and not motion-base, and therefore were inappropriate for landing training. For instance, the lack of a high-quality visual presentation meant that critical visual cues were not available to the pilots. The analog computer also had limitations. For example, the precision needed to calculate altitude and rate of climb for the landing phase was not readily achievable with the parameter scaling used for the rest of the flight. The parameter scaling was critical, and analog computers were accurate to about one part in 10,000. For the X-15 simulation, with the altitude scaled such that 400,000 feet equaled 100 volts, one-tenth of a volt was equal to 40 feet. Any altitude less than this was down in the noise of the analog components and barely detectable. It was simply not possible to calculate accurate altitudes for the landing phase and the rest of the flight profile at the same time. All of this necessitated maintaining a fleet of Lockheed F-104 Starfighters as landing trainers, something the X-15 pilots did not seem to mind at all.[25]

Nevertheless, Larry Caw and Eldon Kordes did mechanize a simple four-degrees-of-freedom simulation to study landing loads early in the program. The simulation only covered the last few seconds of a flight, and was not particularly useful as a pilot training tool. However, it allowed Jack McKay and other engineers to look at the variety of forces generated during an X-15 landing, and prompted the first round of landing-gear changes on the airplane.[26]

The lack of a motion-base simulator presented several interesting problems. For instance, some phenomena experienced in the JF-100C variable-stability airplane during the summer of 1961 indicated that using the beta-dot technique in the X-15 might be more difficult than anticipated. Consequently, a cooperative program was initiated with NASA Ames to use its three-axis motion-base simulator. The objective was to investigate further the effect of g-loading on the pilot while he performed beta-dot recovery maneuvers. Four pilots–Forest Petersen, Bob Rushworth, Joe Walker, and Bob White–participated in the tests during September 1961. Paul Bikle reported that, "With fixed-base simulation, the ventral-on condition was uncontrollable, using normal techniques; however, it could be con-

23 Ibid, p. iii; letter, Robert G. Hoey to Dennis R. Jenkins, 20 May 2002.

24 Waltman, *Black Magic and Gremlins*, pp. 51-53.

25 Ibid; Videan et al., "The Application of Analog and Digital Computer Techniques in the X-15 Flight Research Program," p. 5.

26 Waltman, *Black Magic and Gremlin*, pp. 56-57.

trolled by using the special beta-dot control technique. With the moving cockpit simulation, control using either normal or beta-dot techniques was more difficult for the pilot than with the fixed-base cockpit simulation. These results were in general agreement with the ground and flight tests conducted with the variable-stability F-100 airplane."[27]

By the end of the X-15 program, the FRC had established simulation as an integral part of the flight program. Today, the Walter C. Williams Research Aircraft Integration Facility (RAIF) provides a state-of-the-art complex of computers, simulators, and iron-bird mockups. As an example of the extent to which simulations were used, during the X-33 program, pilot Stephen D. Ishmael flew countless missions while engineers evaluated vehicle systems, flight profiles, and abort scenarios. What is ironic is that the X-33 was to be an unmanned vehicle—Ishmael was just another computing device, one with a quick sense of reason and excellent reflexes.

The Wheel

The Navy, an otherwise silent partner, made a notable contribution to flight simulation for the X-15 program. Primarily, the Aviation Medical Acceleration Laboratory (AMAL) at NADC Johnsville provided a unique ground simulation of the dynamic environment.[28]

Even prior to the beginning of World War II, researchers recognized that acceleration effects experienced during high-speed flight would require evaluation, and by 1944 the BuAer became convinced that it would require a long-term commitment to understand such effects completely. The centerpiece of what became the AMAL was a new $2,381,000 human centrifuge. Work on the facility at Johnsville began in June 1947, with the McKiernan-Terry Corporation of Harrison, New Jersey, constructing the centrifuge building under the direction of the Office of Naval Research. The chief of naval operations established the AMAL on 24 May 1949, and during validation of the facility on 2 November 1951, Captain J. R. Poppin, the director of AMAL, became the first human to be tested in the centrifuge.[29]

27 X-15 Status Reports, Paul F. Bikle/FRC to H. Brown/NASA Headquarters, 1 September 1961, p. 3 and 15 September 1961, p.4.

28 The Naval Air Development Center (known as NADEVCEN at the time), Johnsville, PA, was established after World War II to meet a growing need for research and development in naval aviation. In 1944 the Navy acquired the Brewster Aircraft plant located on approximately 370 acres in Bucks County, PA, about midway between Philadelphia and Trenton, NJ. The Navy designated the plant the Naval Air Modification Unit (NAMU), a branch of the Naval Air Materiel Center (NAMC) in Philadelphia. The NAMU converted and modified newly produced aircraft prior to delivery to the fleet for combat use. With the capitulation of the Axis powers, the need for NAMU vanished. However, the growing need for a centralized research and development activity resulted in the redesignation of NAMU, effective 1 August 1947, as the Naval Air Development Station (NADS), an independent activity under the Bureau of Aeronautics. On 1 August 1949 the station was reorganized into the NADEVCEN. The mission of the NADEVCEN was expanded to include three laboratories: the Pilotless Aircraft Development Laboratory (PADL), the Aeronautical Electronic and Electrical Laboratory (AEEL), and the Aircraft Armament Laboratory (AAL). In July 1950, the Aeronautical Computer Laboratory (ACL) was added, first as a small engineering team and later as a laboratory using the Typhoon computer. At the time the Typhoon was the world's largest analog computer and was used for theoretical studies and analyses of missile flight and performance. The addition of an IBM magnetic drum electronic data processing machine (IBM 650) provided digital problem-solving techniques. Eventually the Typhoon was modernized by adding GALE A and B analog computers to provide a large, versatile hybrid facility. The Aviation Medical Acceleration Laboratory (AMAL) became a part of the center on 17 June 1952, when the world's largest human centrifuge was dedicated. This laboratory was created to conduct research into aviation medicine. It soon began supporting space medicine and dynamic flight simulation studies involving the X-15.

29 *http://www.vnh.org/FSManual/AppendixA.html*, accessed 8 February 2002.

When the facility officially opened on 17 June 1952, it was the most sophisticated of its kind in the world, and was capable of producing accelerations up to 40 g to investigate the reaction of pilots to accelerations. A 4,000-horsepower vertical electric motor in the center of the room drove the centrifuge arm. Depending on the exact requirements of the test, researchers could position a gondola suspended by a double gimbal system at one of several locations along the arm. The outer gimbal permitted rotation of the gondola about an axis tangential to the motion of the centrifuge, while the inner gimbal allowed rotation about the axis at right angles to the tangential motion. Separate 75-horsepower motors connected through hydraulic actuators controlled the angular motions of the gondola, and continuous control of the two axes in combination with rotation of the arm produced somewhat realistic high-g accelerations for the pilot.[30]

Initially, electromechanical systems controlled the centrifuge since general-purpose computers did not, for all intents, yet exist. In the centrifuge, large Masonite discs called "cams" controlled the acceleration along the three axes. A series of cam followers drove potentiometers that generated voltages to control the various hydraulic actuators and electric motors. The cams had some distinct advantages over manual control: they automated complex motions and allowed precise duplication of the motions. However, the process of cutting the Masonite discs amounted to little more than trial and error, and technicians had to produce many discs for each test.[31]

Researchers demonstrated the capabilities of the centrifuge in a series of experiments, including a joint Navy-Air Force study during 1956 that revealed that chimpanzees were able to sustain 40 g for 60 seconds. Two years later R. Flanagan Gray of the NADC set a human record of 31.25 g, which he sustained for 5 seconds in the "iron maiden," a water-filled protective apparatus attached 40 feet out on the arm. In 1957 the X-15 program became the first user of the combined human centrifuge and NADC computer facility, marking the initial step in the development of dynamic flight simulation.[32]

The X-15 represented the most extensive, and by far the most elaborate, use of the cams for centrifuge control. Technicians at Johnsville cut the cams based on acceleration parameters defined by researchers at North American. Initially, the tests concentrated on routine flights, measuring the pilot's reactions to the accelerations. Before long, the tests were expanded to emergency conditions, such as an X-15 returning from a high-altitude mission with a failed pitch damper. The concern was whether the pilot could tolerate the accelerations expected under these conditions, which included oscillations between 0 g and 8 g on a cycle of 0.7 seconds. Other conditions included oscillations between 4 g and 8 g with periods as long as 12 seconds. Researchers found that these conditions represented something near the physiological tolerance of the pilots. Even with the best support apparatus the engineers could provide, the pilots found it difficult to operate

30 Carl C. Clark, "Centrifugal Simulation of the X-15," a paper in the *1958 Research Airplane Committee Report*, pp. 107-108.

31 James D. Hardy and Carl C. Clark, "The Development of Dynamic Flight Simulation," *Aero/Space Engineering*, vol. 18, no. 6, June 1959, pp. 48-52.

32 James E. Love, "History and Development of the X-15 Research Aircraft," not dated, p. 10. In the files at the DFRC History Office.

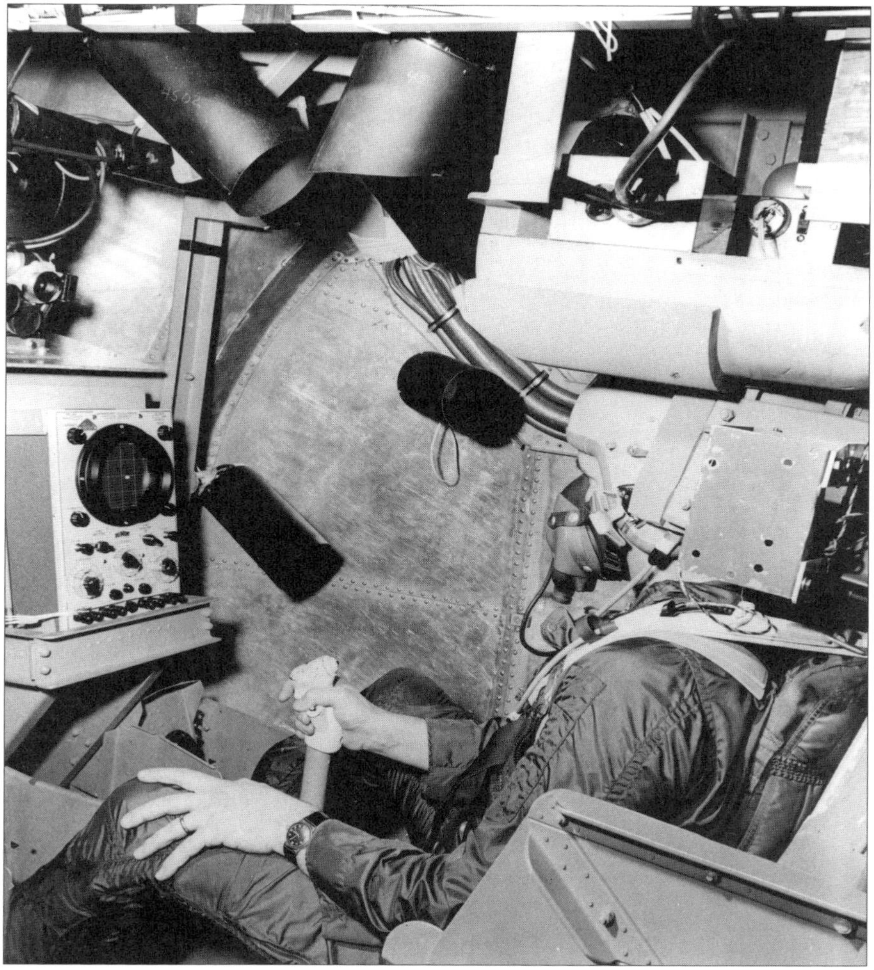

When NADC Johnsville officially opened on 17 June 1952 it was the most sophisticated human centrifuge in the world, capable of producing accelerations up to 40 g to investigate the reaction of pilots to accelerations. The initial runs at Johnsville used a generic cockpit that did not resemble an X-15 at all. During an early series of tests, researchers mounted an oscilloscope in front of the pilot, and asked him to move the gondola to match a trace on the scope. For the first runs, the pilot used a conventional center stick; later tests used a side-stick controller. (U.S. Navy)

the controls, and small, purplish hemorrhages known as petechiae would form on their hands, feet, and back. In one experiment, Scott Crossfield actually blacked out due to a malfunction in his g-suit.[33]

With the use of the Masonite disc cam followers, the gondola was able to maintain a programmed and precisely reproducible acceleration pattern. This was a flaw in some people's minds since the pilot did not influence the motion of the

33 Hardy and Clark, "The Development of Dynamic Flight Simulation," pp. 48-52.

gondola–he was, in effect, a passenger. However, the X-15 pilot had to maintain precise control while being forced backward or forward under the high accelerations, and it was important to find out how well he could perform. This was especially true during marginal conditions, such as a damper failure during reentry. There were no guidelines for defining the degree of control expected from a pilot under those conditions.[34]

To address this issue, researchers subsequently modified the centrifuge to incorporate responses to pilot input into the preprogrammed acceleration curves. During an early series of tests, researchers mounted an oscilloscope in front of the pilot and asked him to move the gondola to match a trace on the scope. For the first runs the pilot used a conventional center stick; later tests used a side-stick controller. Eventually the complexity of the acceleration patterns moved beyond the capabilities of the Masonite discs and researchers began using punched paper tape, something that found widespread use on early computers. The results of these experiments indicated that under extreme conditions the side-stick controller allowed the pilot to brace his arm against the cockpit side console to maintain better control of the aircraft.[35]

Researchers at Johnsville soon installed a complete X-15 instrument panel in the gondola, with the instruments receiving data from analog computers to emulate the flight profile being "flown" by the centrifuge. These simulations led to a recommendation to rearrange some of the X-15 instruments to reduce eye movement. As acceleration increased, the pilot's field of view became narrower, and under grayout conditions the pilots could not adequately scan instruments that were normally in their field of view. Moving a few instruments closer together allowed the pilot to concentrate on one area of the instrument panel without having to move his head, an often difficult and occasionally impossible task under heavy g-loading.[36]

Another important conclusion drawn from this set of experiments was that the centrifuge was sufficiently flexible to use as a dynamic flight simulator. To enable this, in June 1957 researchers linked the centrifuge to the Typhoon analog computer, which was generally similar to the units used in the X-15 fixed-base simulators. This made dynamic control possible, and pilots in the centrifuge gondola could actually "fly" the device, simulating the flight characteristics of any selected type of aircraft. The computer output drove the centrifuge in such a manner that the pilot experienced an approximation of the linear acceleration he would feel while flying the X-15 if he made the same control motions. Unfortunately, the centrifuge only had three degrees of freedom (one in the main arm and two in the gondola gimbal system), whereas the X-15 had six degrees of freedom (three of rotation and three of translation). This meant that the angular accelerations were unlike those experienced in flight; however, researchers believed this limitation was of secondary importance. The perceived benefit of simulating even somewhat unrealistic movements was that they could introduce the pilot to the large accelerations he would experience during flight. The computer also drove the cockpit instruments to reflect the "reality" of flight. Engineers had not previously

34 Stillwell, *X-15 Research Results*; Hardy and C Clark, "The Development of Dynamic Flight Simulation," pp. 48-52.

35 Hardy and Clark, "The Development of Dynamic Flight Simulation," pp. 48-52.

36 Clark, "Centrifugal Simulation of the X-15," p. 108.

attempted this type of closed-loop simulation (pilot to computer to centrifuge), and it was a far more complex problem than developing the fixed-base simulators. Interestingly, in an experiment that was years ahead of its time, researchers using the X-15 simulation computer at NASA Langley controlled the Johnsville centrifuge over a telephone line on several occasions. The response time from this arrangement was less than ideal because of the low data rates possible at the time, but the overall concept worked surprisingly well.[37]

Certain inadequacies in the X-15 simulation were noted during these initial tests, particularly concerning the computation of aircraft responses at high frequencies, the pilot restraints, and the lack of simulated speed brakes. In May 1958 the Navy modified the centrifuge in an attempt to cure these problems, and researchers completed three additional weeks of X-15 tests on 12 July 1958. During this time the pilots (Neil Armstrong, Scott Crossfield, Iven Kincheloe, Jack McKay, Joe Walker, Al White, and Bob White) and various other personnel, such as Dick Day and Bob Hoey, flew 755 static simulations using the cockpit installed in the gondola but with the centrifuge turned off. The pilots also completed 287 dynamic simulations with the centrifuge in motion. The primary objective of the program was to assess the pilot's ability to make emergency reentries under high dynamic conditions following a damper failure. The results were generally encouraging, although the accelerations were more severe than those experienced later during actual flight.[38]

A typical centrifuge run for a high-altitude mission commenced after the pilot attained the exit flight path and a speed of Mach 2, and terminated after the pilot brought the aircraft back to level flight after reentry. During powered flight, the thrust acceleration gradually built up to 4.5 g, forcing the pilot against the seat back. However, the pilot could keep his feet on the rudder pedals with some effort, and still reach the instrument panel to operate switches if required. Researchers also simulated the consequences of thrust misalignment so that during powered flight the pilot would know to apply aerodynamic control corrections with the right-hand side stick and the rudder pedals.[39]

At burnout, the acceleration component dropped to zero and the pilot's head came off the backrest. The pilot attempted to hold the aircraft heading using the ballistic control system. In the design mission, the aircraft would experience less than 0.1 g for about 150 seconds, but the best the centrifuge could do was to remain at rest (and 1 g) during this period since there was no way to simulate less than normal gravity.[40]

37 Hardy and Clark, "The Development of Dynamic Flight Simulation," pp. 48-52; Clark, "Centrifugal Simulation of the X-15," p. 112; *http://www.vnh.org/FSManual/AppendixA.html*, accessed 8 February 2002.

38 Clark, "Centrifugal Simulation of the X-15," p. 108; Love, "History and Development of the X-15 Research Aircraft," p. 10; Robert G. Hoey, "Riding 'The Wheel'," in Fred Stoliker, Bob Hoey, and Johnny Armstrong, *Flight Testing at Edwards: Flight Test Stories–1946-1975*, (Edwards, CA: Flight Test Historical Foundation, 2001), pp. 166-167; letter, Robert G. Hoey to Dennis R. Jenkins, 20 May 2002. There is some disagreement in the numbers. Stillwell in X-15 *Research Results* indicates that over 400 dynamic flights were conducted during this initial series of tests. Harrison Storms ("The X-15 Rollout Symposium," 15 October 1958) supplied the numbers used here, and these are also contained in the Clark paper. Bob Hoey would later talk his way into a ride on "The Wheel" during centrifuge simulations for the X-20 Dyna-Soar program.

39 Clark, "Centrifugal Simulation of the X-15," pp. 109-110.

40 Ibid, pp. 109-110.

A 4,000-horsepower vertical electric motor in the center of the room drove the centrifuge arm that had a gondola suspended by a double gimbal system at one of several locations along the arm. The outer gimbal permitted rotation of the gondola about an axis tangential to the motion of the centrifuge; the inner gimbal allowed rotation about the axis at right angles to the tangential motion. Continuous control of the two axes in combination with rotation of the arm produced somewhat realistic high-g accelerations for the pilot in the gondola. Johnsville would gain fame when the Mercury program used the centrifuge for much the same purposes the X-15 had pioneered several years earlier. (U.S. Navy)

As the aircraft descended, the pilot actuated the pitch trim knob and the aerodynamic control stick at about 200,000 feet to establish the desired angle of attack, but continued to use the ballistic control system until the aerodynamic controls became effective. As the dynamic pressure built, the pullout acceleration commenced and the centrifuge began to turn. If the speed brakes were closed, the drag deceleration reached about 1 g. With the speed brakes open, this would increase to 2.8 g for the design mission and about 4 g for a reentry from 550,000 feet. The pilot gradually reduced the angle of attack to maintain the designed g-value until the aircraft was level, at which time the simulation stopped. During reentry, in addition to the drag acceleration, the pilot also experienced 5–7 g of normal acceleration, so the total g-vector was 6–8 g "eyeballs down and forward"–a very undesirable physiological condition.[41]

Tests on the centrifuge established that, with proper restraints and anti-g equipment, the pilot of the X-15 could tolerate the expected accelerations. These included such oscillating accelerations as 5 g ± 2 g at one cycle per second for 10

41 Letter, Robert G. Hoey to Dennis R. Jenkins, 20 May 2002; Clark, "Centrifugal Simulation of the X-15," pp. 109-110.

seconds, which might occur during reentry from 250,000 feet with failed dampers, and 7 g normal and 4 g "into the straps" for 25 seconds, which might occur during reentry from 550,000 feet. The pilots' ability to tolerate oscillating accelerations was unknown prior to the centrifuge tests, and this information contributed not only to the X-15 but also to Mercury and later space programs.[42]

The tests at Johnsville confirmed that a trained pilot could not only tolerate the acceleration levels, he could also perform all tasks reasonably expected of him under those conditions. This was largely due to the North American design of pilot supports and restraints, and the use of side-stick controllers. The accommodations included a bucket seat without padding adjusted in height for each pilot, and arm and elbow rests also fitted for each pilot. Restraints included an integrated harness with the lower ties lateral to the hips to minimize "submarining" and rolling in the seat, a helmet "socket" to limit motion posteriorly, laterally, and at the top, and a retractable front "head bumper" that could be swung down to limit forward motion of the head. When using the speed brakes or when the dampers were off, the pilots generally found it desirable to use the front head bumper. The pilots used the centrifuge program to evaluate two kinematic designs and three grip designs for the side-stick controller before an acceptable one was found. Despite an early reluctance, the pilots generally preferred the side stick to the center stick under dynamic conditions. Researchers quickly established the importance of careful dynamic balancing and suitable breakout and friction forces for the side stick.[43]

The centrifuge program also pointed out the need for pilot experience under high-acceleration conditions. For example, pilots who had at least 15 hours of practice on the static simulator at Inglewood and previous high-acceleration experience made five successful dynamic reentries out of five attempts, while pilots with 4–10 hours of simulator time had only seven successes in 15 attempts. Another group of pilots who had less than 4 hours of simulator time or no previous high-acceleration experience made only two successful dynamic reentries out of 14 attempts. Most of the failures were due to unintentional pilot control inputs, including using the rudder pedals during drag deceleration, roll inputs while making pitch corrections using the center stick because of the lack of arm support, and inadvertent ballistic control system firings due to leaving the left hand on the side-stick during acceleration. The more experienced pilots would detect these unintended control inputs more rapidly than the other pilots, and could correct the mistakes in time to avoid serious consequences.[44]

Researchers also evaluated physiological responses in the centrifuge. The drag decelerations of the speed brakes, when combined with the normal pullout loads, increased the blood pressure in the limbs. When the resultant acceleration was below 5 g, there was no particular discomfort; however, when the acceleration was above 7 g (including a drag component of more than 3 g), petechiae were noted in the forearms and ankles, and a tingling, numbness, and in some cases definite pain were noted in the limbs. The symptoms became more severe when a pilot made several centrifuge runs in quick succession, something that would

42 Clark, "Centrifugal Simulation of the X-15," pp. 109-110.

43 Ibid, pp. 110-111.

44 Ibid.

obviously never happen during the X-15 program. One pilot stopped the centrifuge when he experienced severe groin pains because of a poorly fitted harness. In two cases of reentry using open speed brakes, the pilots reported pronounced oculogravic illusions, with the visual field seeming to oscillate vertically and to be doubled vertically for a few seconds toward the end of the reentry. Despite this, Scott Crossfield made nine dynamic runs in one day on the centrifuge, but generally the pilots were limited to two runs on the centrifuge per day.[45]

Despite the demonstrated benefits of a pilot being able to experience the unusually high accelerations produced by the X-15 prior to his first flight, only the initial group of pilots actually benefited from the centrifuge simulations. Later pilots received the surprise of their life the first time they started the XLR99 in the X-15. Granted, the Johnsville accelerations were not a realistic replica of the ones experienced in flight, due to the limitations of the centrifuge concept, but they still provided some high-acceleration experience. As Milt Thompson noted in a paper in 1964:[46]

> Prior to my first flight, my practice had been done in a relaxed, head forward position. The longitudinal acceleration at engine light forced my head back into the headrest and prevented even helmet rotation. The instrument-scan procedure, due to this head position and a slight tunnel vision effect, was quite different than anticipated and practiced. The acceleration buildup during engine burn (4-g max) is uncomfortable enough to convince you to shut down the engine as planned. This is the first airplane I've flown that I was happy to shut down. Engine shutdown does not relieve the situation, though, since in most cases the deceleration immediately after shutdown has you hanging from the restraint harness, and in a strange position for controlling [the airplane].

The X-15 closed-loop program was the forerunner of centrifuges that NASA built at the Ames Research Center and the Manned Spacecraft Center (later renamed the Johnson Space Center) to support the manned space programs. Perhaps the most celebrated program of AMAL was the flight simulation training for Project Mercury astronauts, based largely on the experience gained during the X-15 simulations. Beginning in June 1959 the seven Mercury astronauts participated in centrifuge simulations of Atlas booster launches, reentries, and abort conditions ranging up to 18 g (transverse) at NADC Johnsville.[47]

---

45 Ibid, pp. 111-112. The paper actually states that one pilot made nine runs in a single 2-hour period. Conversations with Scott Crossfield and Bob Hoey, as well as simple mathematics, make this hard to believe. If each run took 10 minutes to set up and 5 minutes to run, then nine runs would have taken over 2 hours. Crossfield vaguely recalls that he made nine runs in a single day, which seems much more likely.

46 Waltman, *Black Magic and Gremlins*, p. 57; the quote is from Milton O. Thompson, "General Review of Piloting Problems Encountered During Simulations and Flights of the X-15," a paper presented at the Society of Experimental Test Pilots Symposium, Beverly Hills, CA, 1964. Thompson's paper was also published as NASA technical memorandum X-56884, and the story is related on page 57 of Waltman's monograph.

47 Hardy and Clark, "The Development of Dynamic Flight Simulation," pp. 48-52; *http://www.vnh.org/FSManual/AppendixA.html*, accessed 8 February 2002.

Heating Simulations

At the beginning of the X-15 program, researchers used the methods developed by Edward Van Driest and Ernst Eckert to determine the heat-transfer coefficients for temperature calculations. However, the measured heat-transfer coefficients during the early flight program were considerably lower than the predicted values. Based on these preliminary results, derived primarily from the initial low-angle-of-attack flights, engineers modified Eckert's turbulent-flow method to produce the adiabatic-wall reference-temperature method.[48]

The first, and possibly the most difficult, step in computing surface temperatures was to calculate the local flow conditions. Initially, researchers used the conventional attached-shock Prandtl-Meyer expansion method for the wing and empennage, and a tangent-cone approximation for the fuselage. The boundary-layer transition was completely unpredictable, but since researchers expected turbulent flow during the major portion of most flights, they normally used turbulent-flow calculations for the entire flight. Next came determining the heat-transfer coefficients, and finally calculating the skin temperature. Due to the tedious work involved in this process, which was done mostly by hand since general-purpose computers were not yet in widespread use, the researchers made many assumptions that simplified the procedure. For instance, it was assumed that temperature did not vary through the thickness of the skin, no heat was transferred along the skin, the specific heat of the skin was constant, solar radiation to the skin was negligible, the emissivity of the skin was constant, and no net heat transfer occurred between surfaces by radiation.[49]

Temperatures calculated using the adiabatic-wall reference-temperature method tended to agree closely with measured data from the flight program. In several instances the calculated temperature was somewhat higher because the analytical method assumed turbulent flow all of the time. This was considered reasonable and sufficient for flight-safety purposes since it erred on the side of caution.[50]

In 1957, Lockheed Aircraft Company developed a thermal analyzer program that ran on an IBM 704 digital computer, the largest of its type then available. This program was capable of running the heating prediction equations, including the effects of transient conduction, convection, radiation, and heat storage, that researchers had previously omitted for the sake of expediency. With Lockheed's assistance, researchers modified the program to reflect the X-15 configuration. The program estimated the heat input to the skin elements using the attached-shock Prandtl-Meyer expansion method for flow conditions, and the adiabatic-wall reference-temperature method for heat transfer. Researchers used the laminar-flow

48 Joe D. Watts and Ronald P. Banas, NASA confidential technical memorandum X-883, "X-15 Structural Temperature Measurements and Calculations for Flights to Maximum Mach Numbers of Approximately 4, 5, and 6," 17 May 1963, pp. 5-6. For information on the Van Driest methods, see "The Problem of Aerodynamic Heating," *Aerospace Engineering Review*, vol. 15, no. 10, October 1956, pp. 26-41; for background on Eckert, see his "Survey on Heat Transfer at High Speeds," WADC technical report 54-70, April 1954.

49 NASA confidential technical memorandum X-883, pp. 6-7. For details on the Prandtl-Meyer method, see "Equations, Tables, and Charts for Compressible Flow, NACA Ames report 1135, 1953.

50 Ibid, pp. 7-8.

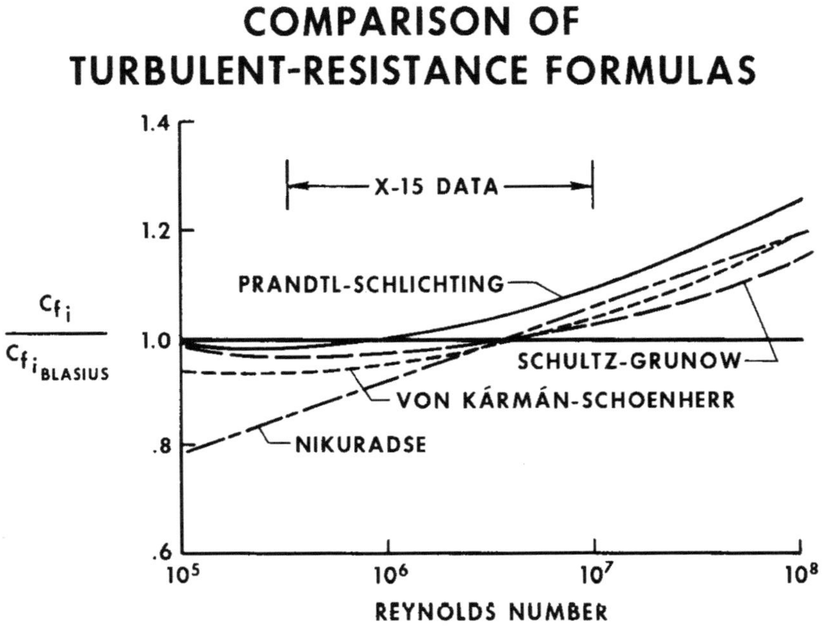

One of the primary goals of the X-15 program was to validate the various heat-transfer methods with actual flight results. Many of the early X-15 flights were dedicated to gathering data that the researchers would spend years comparing against wind tunnel and theoretical results. The results were vastly improved heat-transfer models that were used during the Apollo and space shuttle programs. (NASA)

theory of Fay and Riddell to compute the heat input to the stagnation points, with curves developed by Lester Lees used to weight the periphery.[51]

To accompany the Lockheed-developed software, North American developed two other programs to predict structural heating values and their distribution along the airframe. The first program computed local-flow conditions on the aircraft, and the second program used the local-flow conditions to calculate the aerodynamic heat transfer to the skin. The program developed by Lockheed calculated the transient heating of internal structure based on the results of the other two programs.[52]

To evaluate the acceptability of the thermal analyzer program, researchers compared calculated results with actual flight results on several occasions. The values always compared favorably, and were usually slightly better than

51 J. R. Gardner, "Use of Thermal Analyzer Program," Lockheed report 12870, 5 February 1958. In the files at the Lockheed Martin Corporation; NASA confidential technical memorandum X-883, pp. 7-8. For details on Fay and Riddell, see "Theory of Stagnation Point Heat Transfer in Dissociated Air," *Journal of the Aeronautical Sciences*, vol. 25, no. 2, February 1958, pp. 73-85 and 121; For more on Lees, see "Laminar Heat Transfer Over Blunt-Nose Bodies at Hypersonic Flight Speeds, *Jet Propulsion*, vol. 26, no. 4, April 1956, pp. 259-269.

52 Videan et al., "The Application of Analog and Digital Computer Techniques in the X-15 Flight Research Program," pp. 6-7. In 1956 the IBM 704 became the first mass-produced digital computer capable of performing floating-point arithmetic. A typical 700-series (the 704 was a scientific machine; the closely-related 705 was a business machine) installation would be in a specially built room of perhaps 2,000 square feet with substantial air conditioning and cables running under a raised floor. The computer used core (wire-wound ferrite) memory instead of solid state, did not have disk drives (they did not exist yet), and recorded most of its data on seven-track magnetic tape, punched paper tape, or punched-card devices. Incidentally, the first Fortran compiler was written for use on the 704.

the hand-calculated values for the same conditions. North American and NASA quickly adopted the automated process based largely on the tremendous labor savings it offered.

After the flight planners established a flight profile on the fixed-base simulator, they digitized the results of a clean flight and input them into the IBM 704 to predict the skin and structural temperatures and thermal gradients for the flight. This was a time-consuming process. Researchers then compared the resulting data with the design conditions to ensure that the X-15 did not violate any structural margins. If any exceptions were uncovered during the comparison, researchers modified the flight profile and the entire process was repeated. Emergency and contingency flight profiles went through the same rigorous process. After the flight, researchers compared the heating predictions with actual flight data and then refined the simulations.[53]

Airborne Simulators

In addition to ground simulators and the centrifuge, pilots and researchers used aircraft to simulate various aspects of the X-15. For instance, the Lockheed F-104 Starfighter closely approximately the wing loading of an X-15 during landing, and with the right combination of extended landing gear, flaps, and speed brakes, the F-104 at idle thrust did an excellent job of simulating the X-15. For the first 50 or so flights, the pilots dedicated an entire F-104 mission to practicing landing procedures. As new pilots entered the program, they conducted similar practices. Throughout the program, pilots used the F-104s to establish geographic checkpoints and important altitudes around the landing pattern at all the possible landing lakes.[54]

Scott Crossfield and Al White conducted similar work very early in the program using the North American YF-100A equipped with an eight-foot drag chute. Combined with extended gear and speed brakes, the F-100 at idle thrust did an adequate job of simulating the X-15 during landing, although not quite as well as the F-104. The entire process was a bit trickier since it required the in-flight deployment and release of the drag chute.[55]

As Al White later remembered, "With gear down, speed brake extended, at idle power, and that drag chute deployed, the airplane was comparable to the X-15 on approach. I would start at about 25,000 feet, pick a spot on the lakebed, and see how close I could come to touching down on that spot. With all the room on the lakebed, it was not necessary to hit a spot, but it is always nice to have that much margin for error. I flew this trainer as much as I could, in preparation for that day

---

53 Videan et al., "The Application of Analog and Digital Computer Techniques in the X-15 Flight Research Program," pp. 7-8.

54 White et al., "Résumé of X-15 Handling Qualities," p. 120; Gene J. Matranga, NASA technical note D-1057, "Analysis of X-15 Landing Approach and Flare Characteristics Determined from the First 30 Flights," July 1961, pp. 18-19.

55 Letter, Al White to Dennis R. Jenkins, 8 June 2002; Lieutenant Colonel Burt Rowen, "Human-Factors Support of the X-15 Program," *Air University Quarterly Review*, Air War College, vol. X, no. 4, winter 1958-59, p. 37; NASA technical note D-1057, pp. 18-19.

that never came." Not flying the X-15 was one of the few disappointments during White's significant career.[56]

Much of the X-15 flight planning took place prior to the first manned space flight. Since no one had ever left the atmosphere and returned in a winged vehicle (or anything else), there had been concern that the rapidly changing stability and control characteristics in the X-15 as it reentered the atmosphere might pose an unusually demanding piloting task. To address this question, engineers in the Flight Research Department of the Cornell Aeronautical Laboratory conceived the idea of simulating this brief (about 60 seconds duration) but unfamiliar X-15 piloting task in a NT-33A that was owned by the Air Force but operated by Cornell as a variable-stability trainer.[57]

The NT-33A already had been equipped with a larger internal volume F-94 nose section that contained a three-axis (pitch, roll, and yaw) variable-stability and control system for in-flight simulation purposes. To support the X-15 program, Cornell modified the front cockpit to superficially resemble the X-15, with a side-stick controller on the right-hand console for atmospheric flight control and another side-stick on the left-hand console simulating the ballistic controls. An "instructor" pilot sat in the back cockpit with a normal set of T-33 controls. Jack Beilman at Cornell designed a programmable, non-linear function generator that changed the gains of 32 sensed aerodynamic and rigid-body-motion feedback variables. It also changed the flight-control sensitivities continuously during the simulated reentry so that the NT-33A stability and control characteristics would match the predicted X-15 characteristics.[58]

The flight plan had the NT-33A entering a shallow dive at about 17,000 feet altitude and then pulling up to a ballistic trajectory that produced about 60 seconds of 0 g–about the same as the initial part of the X-15 reentry. At the same time, the variable-stability system on the NT-33A changed the flight-control sensitivities to simulate going from the vacuum of space to the rapidly increasing dynamic pressure of the atmosphere. Since the normal aerodynamic controls of the X-15 would be ineffective outside the atmosphere, the pilot used the ballistic controller to establish the correct reentry pitch attitude.[59]

In the NT-33A simulation the "ballistic controller" produced no physical response whatsoever—it only changed the displayed pitch attitude on the instrument panel. (At this point in the simulation, the NT-33A was at 0 g.) In order to maintain the fidelity of the simulation, the X-15 pilot in the front cockpit wore a hood and had no view of the outside world, since there would be little view of the real world in the X-15 at the simulated altitudes. This deception was necessary for the high-angle-of-attack deceleration at the end of the simulated reentry because although the front cockpit instrumentation indicated the pilot was flying an unbanked steep descent (in the X-15), he was actually flying a steep 5-g turn

56 Letter, Alvin S. White to Dennis R. Jenkins, 1 July 2002.

57 Jack Beilman, 5 September 1999, a short unpublished paper supplied to the author via e-mail, 31 March 2002. Calspan was originally formed in 1946 as the Cornell Aeronautical Laboratory, Inc, part of Cornell University located in Ithaca, NY. In 1972 the laboratory was reorganized as the publicly held Calspan Corporation. In 1978 Calspan was acquired by Arvin Industries, and in 1995 it merged with the Texas-based Space Industries, Inc., to form Space Industries International. The company merged with Veda in 1997 to become Veridian Corporation.

58 Ibid.

59 Ibid.

in the NT-33A. The simulator achieved this deception by gradually biasing the attitude indicator to a bank angle of 75 degrees while the X-15 pilot used the ballistic controller to maintain wings-level flight at the proper airspeed, angle of attack, and descent rate on his cockpit instruments. It was a carefully choreographed ballet between the "student" in the front seat and the safety pilot in the back who was trying to keep the NT-33 from becoming a smoking crater in the high desert.[60]

Accordingly, a Cornell team headed by engineering test pilots Bob Harper and Nello Infanti arrived at Edwards in May 1960 to begin a series of flights in the NT-33A in order to provide reentry training for six X-15 pilots (Neil Armstrong, Jack McKay, Forrest Petersen, Bob Rushworth, Joe Walker, and Bob White). Each pilot was to receive six flights in the NT-33A that included a matrix of simulated Mach numbers, altitudes, and various control malfunctions (principally failed dampers) both separately and simultaneously.[61] Infanti was the "instructor pilot" for each of the X-15 simulation flights in the NT-33A, and the rest of the Cornell team consisted of crew chief Howard Stevens, electronics technician Bud Stahl, and systems engineer Jack Beilman. As Beilman remembers:

> During one of the flights, with Neil Armstrong in the front seat, we were simulating failed dampers at something like Mach 3.2 and 100,000 feet altitude. Neil had great difficulty with this simulated undamped X-15 configuration and lost control of the airplane repeatedly. Nello had to recover from each one of these "lost-control" events using the controls in the back cockpit. [Infanti later recalled that some of these recoveries were "pretty sporty."] The ground crew was monitoring the test radio frequency as usual and followed these simulated flight control problems with great interest.
>
> After landing, the NT-33A taxied to the ramp and Howard Stevens attached the ladder to the cockpits and climbed up to talk to Infanti about the airplane status. I climbed up the ladder front side to talk to Neil Armstrong. He handed me his helmet and knee-pad, got down from the cockpit and we talked about the flight and walked toward the operations building. As we arrived at the door Armstrong extended his right hand to grasp the door handle–but his hand still held the side-stick that he had broken during his last battle with the X-15 dampers-off simulation. I was unaware of any report of this incident during the flight and had not noticed the stick in Armstrong's hand when he exited the cockpit. Addressing the matter for the first time, Armstrong said–without additional comment—"Here's your stick!"

---

60 Ibid.

61 Jack Beilman, 5 September 1999, a short unpublished paper supplied to the author via e-mail, 31 March 2002; X-15 Status Report, Paul F. Bikle/FRC to H. Brown/NASA Headquarters, 29 July 1960, p. 2.

> [It developed that Infanti had been aware of the broken side-stick after it happened because Armstrong had held it up over his head in the front cockpit for Nello to see.]
>
> After the debriefing, we took the broken side-stick to the NASA workshop where Neil found the necessary metal tubing and repaired the stick while I mostly watched him work. The side-stick was reinstalled and ready for the first flight the next morning. Really good test pilots fix what they break!

In general, the pilots considered the NT-33 flights worthwhile, but there were some "obvious discrepancies or malfunctions" during the early flights. There were also a fair number of delays in the flights due to various system malfunctions caused by the high temperatures at Edwards. Eventually the Cornell crew corrected the malfunctions, but the X-15 pilots considered the first 10 flights unsatisfactory since they did not adequately simulate the X-15 flight profile. This was largely because the programmed trajectories required the NT-33 to fly close to its maximum capabilities: something that was not as easy as it sounds, especially in the heat over the high desert.[62]

The X-15 pilots considered the final six flights, flown during the first half of September 1960, reasonably satisfactory. In fact, the pilots discovered a novel control technique for the divergent closed-loop lateral-directional oscillation encountered at Mach 3.5 and 10 degrees angle of attack with the SAS off during these flights. By using the rudder in conjunction with the turn and bank indicator (which was, in effect, a yaw-rate meter) the pilot was able to damp the oscillations. With this technique, the ailerons were only a steady-state controller; in fact, any attempt to use the ailerons for control caused an immediate divergence. Researchers further investigated this technique on the North American fixed-base simulator with good results.[63]

A few hundred miles away, Bill Dana made a check flight in a specially modified JF-100C (53-1709) at Ames on 1 November 1960, and delivered the aircraft to the FRC the following day. Researchers at Ames had modified the aircraft into a variable-stability trainer that could simulate the X-15 flight profile somewhat more convincingly than the NT-33, making it possible to investigate new piloting techniques and control-law modifications without using an X-15. The most limiting factor was that the JF-100C was a single-seat aircraft, meaning that no safety pilot was available to lend assistance if things went wrong. To establish the X-15 flight characteristics on the JF-100C, technicians connected two portable analog computers to the airplane so that the combination became, essentially, a fixed-base simulator. One analog computer simulated the basic F-100C flight characteristics, and researchers manipulated the variable-stability gains until the motion traces matched those obtained from the North American X-15 simulator. Joe Walker and

62 X-15 Status Reports, Paul F. Bikle/FRC to H. Brown/NASA Headquarters, 29 July 1960, p. 3, 31 August 1960, pp. 3-4, and 14 September 1960, p. 3.

63 X-15 Status Report, Paul F. Bikle/FRC to H. Brown/NASA Headquarters, 30 September 1960, p. 3. Obviously, the NT-33 did not actually fly at Mach 3.5 but was simulating the control responses based on known aerodynamic data.

Much of the X-15 flight planning took place prior to the first manned space flight. There was concern that the rapidly changing stability and control characteristics in the X-15 as it reentered the atmosphere might pose an unusually demanding piloting task. To address this, the Cornell Aeronautical Laboratory developed a method of simulating this environment using an NT-33A operated by Cornell as a variable stability trainer. The simulations were hardly ideal, but provided much needed confidence to the original cadre of X-15 pilots. (U.S. Air Force)

Bob White flew these pseudo fixed-base simulations until they were satisfied that the JF-100C adequately represented the X-15.[64]

The first actual flight of the JF-100C with the new mechanization was made on 24 March and was considered generally satisfactory. The major discrepancies were that the Dutch-roll and roll-subsidence modes appeared to be less stable than those of the actual X-15. Nevertheless, the JF-100C was capable of performing some interesting simulations. For instance, six flights in late July 1961 simulated the X-15 at Mach 3.5, 84,000 feet, and 10 degrees angle of attack; later flights extended this to Mach 6 and angles of attack of 20 degrees. The aircraft returned to Ames on 11 March 1964 after making 104 flights for pilot checkout, variable-stability research, and X-15 support.[65]

One of the tasks assigned to the JF-100C was investigating the effects of damper failure on the controllability of the X-15. Researchers had obtained the

64 X-15 Status Reports, Paul F. Bikle/FRC to H. Brown/NASA Headquarters, 3 April 1961, pp. 4-5 and 1 August 1961, pp. 2-3.

65 E-mail, Peter W. Merlin/DFRC History Office to Dennis R. Jenkins, 18 November 1999; X-15 Status Reports, Paul F. Bikle/FRC to H. Brown/NASA Headquarters, 3 April 1961, pp. 4-5 and 1 August 1961, pp. 2-3. The JF-100 was obviously not actually flying at these velocities.

early wind-tunnel data on sideslip effects with the horizontal stabilizer at zero deflection, and used this data in the 1958 centrifuge program at Johnsville. Based on these data, reentries using an angle of attack of less than 15 degrees were possible even with the roll damper off. On the other hand, reentries at angles greater than 15 degrees (which were required for altitudes above 250,000 feet) with the roll damper off showed a distinct tendency to become uncontrollable because of a pilot-induced oscillation (PIO).[66]

As with a typical PIO, if the pilot released the control stick, the oscillations damped themselves. Nevertheless, researchers suspected that a large portion of the X-15 flight envelope was uncontrollable with the roll dampers off or failed. Investigations were initiated to find a way to alleviate the problem. The first method tried (perhaps because it would have been the easiest to implement) was pilot-display quickening. Sideslip and bank-angle presentations in the cockpit were quickened (i.e., presented with less delay) by including the yaw rate and roll rate, respectively. Researchers experimented with various quickening gains during investigation on the fixed-base simulator, but found no combination that significantly improved the pilot's ability to handle the instability.[67]

Shortly after the centrifuge program was completed, researchers conducted a wind-tunnel test to gather sideslip data with the horizontal stabilizer closer to the normal trim position (which was a large leading-edge-down deflection of –15 to –20 degrees). When researchers programmed the results of these tests into the fixed-base simulator at North American, it showed that the PIO boundary for reentry with the roll damper off had dropped from 15 degrees to only 8 degrees, adding new urgency to finding a solution.[68]

To verify the magnitude of the problem in flight, several X-15 pilots explored the fringes of the expected uncontrollable region by setting the airplane up at the appropriate angle of attack and turning the roll and yaw dampers off. In each case, lateral motions began immediately. The pilots experimented with various combinations of angle of attack and control inputs in both the X-15 and the JF-100C to better define the problem.[69]

Lawrence W. Taylor and Richard E. Day from the FRC, and Arthur F. Tweedie from North American independently investigated using the rolling tail to control sideslip angle during certain types of instability. An unconventional control technique, called "beta-dot," evolved from these investigations and showed considerable promise on the fixed-base simulator. This technique consisted of sharp lateral control inputs to the left as the nose swung left through zero sideslip (or vice versa to the right). The pilot kept his hands off the stick except when making the sharp lateral inputs, which eliminated the instability induced by inadvertent inputs associated with merely holding onto the center stick. However, when pilots used this technique in the JF-100C, it did not seem to work as well. Further investigations

66 Letter, Robert G. Hoey to Dennis R. Jenkins, 20 May 2002.

67 Lieutenant Commander Forrest S. Petersen, Herman A. Rediess, and Joseph Weil, "Lateral Directional Control Characteristics," a paper in the *1961 Research Airplane Committee Report*, pp. 135-138. (This paper was later republished as NASA classified technical memorandum X-726, March 1962.)

68 Letter, Robert G. Hoey to Dennis R. Jenkins, 20 May 2002.

69 Petersen et al., "Lateral-Directional Control Characteristics of the X-15 Airplane," pp. 134-135; telephone conversation, Richard E. Day with Dennis R. Jenkins, 3 May 2002.

showed that it worked somewhat better in the X-15 when the pilot used the side-stick controller instead of the center stick.[70]

It appeared that the beta-dot technique might allow reentries from high altitudes with the dampers failed, if anybody could figure out how to perform the maneuver successfully. As Bob Hoey, the flight planner who later discovered the ventral-off stability fix for the same problem, recalled, "the beta-dot technique is one of those things that is really difficult to explain. You could watch someone make 20 simulated reentries and still not understand what they were doing. The method was based on making a very sharp aileron pulse, timed exactly right, and totally foreign to normal, intuitive piloting technique. Properly timed, this pulse would completely stop the rolling motion, although not necessarily at wings level. With a little finesse, you could herd the thing back to wings level flight, but, if at any time you reverted to a normal piloting technique, even for a second, you were in big trouble. Art Tweedie [who discovered this method] and Norm Cooper [a North American flight controls expert] could make successful simulator reentries with the dampers off while drinking a cup of coffee! This obviously became a big challenge for the rest of us." Hoey became pretty good at the technique himself, at least in the simulator.[71]

Dick Day later wrote that "Robert Hoey, lead Air Force engineer on the X-15 project, introduced the control technique to some of the X-15 pilots. Two pilots in particular, Major Robert White and Captain Joe Engle, became so adept at controlling ground and flight simulators that they considered the method would serve as a backup in case of roll damper failure. Fortunately, the beta-dot technique was not required because removing the ventral solved the dampers-off controllability problem. It is worth noting, however, that the complete beta-dot equation was later used in the yaw channel of the Space Shuttle control system to overcome unstable control coupling." It is another enduring legacy of the X-15 program.[72]

All of the X-15 pilots trained using this technique, but the actual usefulness of the beta-dot maneuver was questionable. Furthermore, a lateral input in the wrong direction, which was conceivable considering other potential problems clamoring for the attention of the pilot, could be disastrous. One of the reasons the technique was so foreign to the pilot was that the aileron pulse had to be in the same direction as the roll, which is hardly intuitive for most pilots. Then the pilot had to remove the pulse just as the needle on the sideslip indicator hit the null mark. As Hoey remembers, "about half the pilots were dead-set against [the beta-dot maneuver] and essentially refused to consider it as an option. Others conquered the technique and actually became fairly proficient in its use on the fixed-base and in-flight simulations." Pilots flew the in-flight simulations using the NT-33 and JF-100C variable-stability airplanes, which somehow managed to survive the program.[73]

---

70 Ibid, pp. 138-139.

71 E-mail, Robert G. Hoey to Dennis R. Jenkins, 6 June 2002.

72 Richard E. Day, *Coupling Dynamics in Aircraft: A Historical Perspective*, NASA publication SP-532, (Washington, DC: NASA, 1997), p. 22; telephone conversation, Richard E. Day with Dennis R. Jenkins, 3 May 2002.

73 Letter, Robert G. Hoey to Dennis R. Jenkins, 4 June 2002; telephone conversation, Robert G. Hoey with Dennis R. Jenkins, 8 June 2002.

Researchers at Ames modified a North American JF-100C (53-1709) Super Sabre into a variable-stability trainer that could simulate the X-15 flight profile somewhat more convincingly than the NT-33, making it possible to investigate new piloting techniques and control-law modifications without using an X-15. The most limiting factor was that the JF-100C was a single-seat aircraft, meaning there was not a safety pilot to assist if things went wrong. (NASA)

There were two other answers to the PIO problem at high angles of attack. The first was to make the stability augmentation system truly redundant, at least in the roll axis, by installing the alternate stability augmentation system (ASAS); however, this took almost a year to accomplish. Another answer–discovered by Dick Day and Bob Hoey using the simulator–proved to be remarkably easy, and unexpected: remove the ventral rudder. With the lower rudder on, a considerable portion of the reentry from an altitude mission would be within the uncontrollable region should a damper fail. However, a similar reentry with the lower rudder removed would not enter the predicted uncontrollable region at all. The downside was that the pilots faced significantly reduced flying qualities at low angles of attack without the rudder. Despite a few gripes from the pilots, everybody eventually agreed to remove the lower rudder for almost all of the high-altitude missions. Only a few missions of the X-15A-2 used the ventral rudder, which in this case provided an adequate stand-in for the eventual dummy ramjet. In all, the program would make 73 flights with the ventral rudder on and 126 with it off.[74]

By the time of the 1961 industry conference, researchers had determined that the fixed-base simulator and the F-104 in-flight landing pattern simulator were the two most valuable training tools available to the program. The centrifuge and variable-stability aircraft contributed to the overall pilot experience level, but were not necessary for use on a flight-by-flight basis. This mostly explains why only the first group of pilots got the thrills of "riding the wheel" at Johnsville and flying the NT-33 trainer.[75]

74 Petersen et al., "Lateral Directional Control Characteristics," pp. 139-140.

75 Robert G. Hoey and Richard E. Day, "X-15 Mission Planning and Operational Procedures," a paper in the *1961 Research Airplane Committee Report*, p. 163.

CARRIER AIRCRAFT

The concept of using a large aircraft to carry a smaller one aloft was not necessarily new, but the X-1 program was the first research effort that made extensive use of the idea. The original series of X-planes used two modified Boeing B-29s and three Boeing B-50s as carrier aircraft. However, despite the fact that thousands of B-29s and B-50s had been built, by the end of 1950 maintenance personnel at Edwards were finding that it was difficult to obtain replacement parts, especially for the B-29s. The performance of the aircraft had proven adequate for the original X-1 aircraft, but as the research airplanes got heavier, the performance of even the more-powerful B-50s became marginal. In addition, the ability to take off at high gross weights was limited in the heat that was typical of the high desert during the summer months. Obviously, the research programs needed to find a better solution.[76]

B-36

Three of the four competitors had sized their X-15 concepts around the premise of using a Convair B-36 as the carrier aircraft (Douglas had chosen a B-50). Easily the largest piston-powered bomber to enter operational service, the B-36 could fly over 400 mph and some versions could climb well above 50,000 feet. Convair manufactured 385 of the giant bombers between June 1948 and August 1954. The B-36 would have carried the X-15 partially enclosed in its bomb bays, much like the X-1 and X-2 had been in earlier projects. This arrangement had several advantages, particularly that the pilot could move freely between the X-15 and B-36 during the cruise to the launch location. This was extremely advantageous if problems developed that required jettisoning the X-15 prior to launch. The B-36 was also a large aircraft with more than adequate room for a propellant top-off system (liquid oxygen and ammonia), power sources, communications equipment, breathing oxygen, and monitoring instruments and controls. Launch would have occurred at approximately Mach 0.6 at altitudes between 30,000 and 50,000 feet. At the first industry conference in 1956, engineers at North American anticipated that a B-36 would be modified beginning in the middle of 1957 and ready for flight tests in October 1958.[77]

During their proposal effort, North American evaluated four different schemes for loading the research airplane into the bomber, which were generally similar to those of the other bidders. Engineers quickly rejected the idea of using a pit (like the X-1 and operationally for the GRB-36D/RF-84K FICON project) because of the potential "fire hazard and accumulation of fumes." Similarly, they

---

76 Miller, *The X-planes*, pp. 398-399; *http://www.dfrc.nasa.gov/gallery/photo/D-558-2/HTML/E-2478.html*, accessed 20 April 2002. A few other bombers were used a carrier aircraft for various missile and unmanned X-plane programs, but they are not listed here.

77 System Development Plan, X-15 Research Aircraft, Supporting Research System Number 447L, 22 March 1956, p. 19. In the files at the AFFTC History Office; Lawrence P. Greene, "Summary of Pertinent Problems and Current Status of the X-15 Airplane" a paper presented at the NACA Conference on the Progress of the X-15 Project, Langley Aeronautical Laboratory, 25-26 October 1956, p. 250; Captain Charles C. Bock, Jr., "B-52/X-15 Flight Operations," undated (but probably late 1958), no page numbers. In the files at the AFFTC History Office.

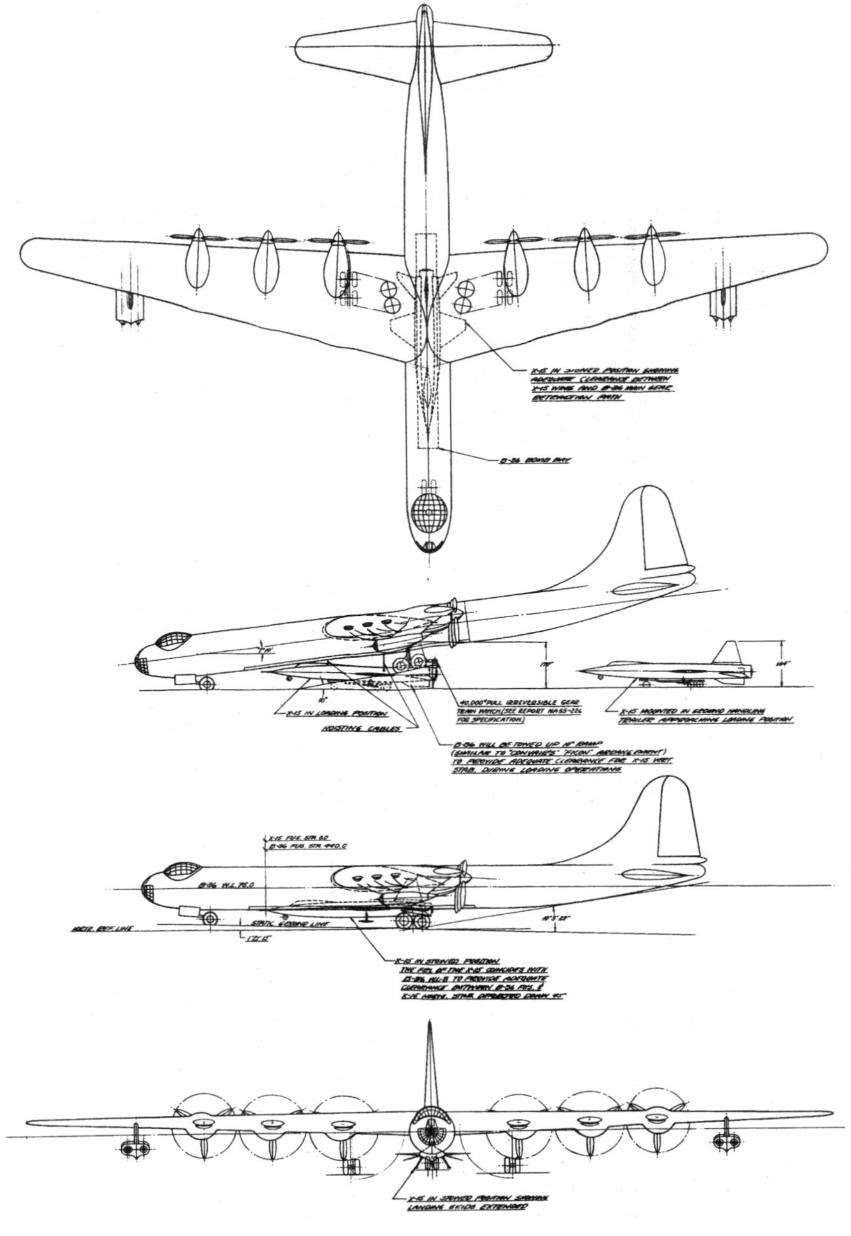

North American had originally selected a Convair B-36 very heavy bomber as the carrier aircraft for the X-15. However, just before modifications were to begin, NASA and the Air Force decided to replace the B-36 with a much newer Boeing B-52 Stratofortress. The B-52 was a good deal faster than the B-36, providing a better launch environment for the research airplane and reducing maintenance requirements for the ground crew. (North American Aviation)

eliminated a plan to jack up the carrier aircraft nose gear, because of "the jockeying necessary to position the research aircraft plus the precarious position of the B-36." The most complicated scheme involved physically removing the vertical stabilizer from the research airplane, sliding the X-15 under the bomber, and then reattaching the vertical once the airplane was in the bomb bay. The potential loss of structural integrity that would result from frequently removing the vertical eventually eliminated this option.[78]

Ramp loading, which was similar to another method used in the FICON project, became the chosen solution.[79] Loading the X-15 into the carrier aircraft began with "running the B-36 main landing gear bogies up on permanent concrete ramps by use of commercially available electric cable hoists attached to the gear struts." The ground crew then towed the research airplane under the bomber and hoisted it into the bomb bays.[80]

The X-15 was suspended from three points: one on either side of the aft fuselage attached to the rear wing spar, and a third on the centerline behind the canopy firmly supported by the structure of the forward liquid-oxygen tank bulkhead. The same types of cartridges used by tactical aircraft to jettison external fuel tanks were used to explosively separate the shackles.[81]

The only major structural modification made to the B-36 would be the removal of bulkhead no. 7, which separated bomb bays 2 and 3, along with some compensating structural stiffening.[82] The X-15 would occupy most of the three forward bomb bays. Since the B-36 used a single set of doors to cover the aft two bomb bays, shorter doors were necessary to cover only bay no. 4.[83] Interestingly, the remaining 16-foot doors covering the last bomb bay would still be functional. A small, fixed fairing replaced the doors that normally covered bomb bay nos. 1 and 2. North American proposed installing a 9-foot-diameter, 6.5-foot-long heated compartment in the front of bomb bay no. 1, equipped with its own entrance hatch on the bottom of the fuselage. The compartment could seat three crewmembers, and included oxygen and intercom connections. A 36-inch hatch opened into the bomb bay, and a catwalk on both sides of the bomb bay allowed access to the X-15 in flight. An aerodynamic fairing with a rubber-sealing strip ran the full length of the bomb-bay opening.[84]

---

78 North American report NA-55-221, "X-15 Advanced Research Airplane Design Summary," 9 May 1955, p. 35; North American report NA-55-227, "Carrier Modification Data for a X-15 Research Aircraft, Project 1226 (NAA Designation ESO-7487)," 9 May 1955, pp. 3-9.

79 At the operational FICON base at Fairchild AFB the RF-84K was parked in a large pit. The GRB-36D was then towed over the pit and the fighter was hoisted into position in the bomb bays. All other sites (mainly Edwards AFB and the Convair plant in Fort Worth) used a large set of ramps. The B-36 was towed up the ramps and the fighter was then towed under the B-36 and raised into position. Interestingly, the Air Force also investigated removing the vertical from the F-84, but this was more in case the mated pair landed at a site not equipped with either normal method and it was imperative to remove the F-84 for some reason. For more information on FICON, see Dennis R. Jenkins, *Magnesium Overcast; The Story of the Convair B-36*, (North Branch, MN: Specialty Press, 2001).

80 "X-15 Advanced Research Airplane Design Summary, p. 35; "Carrier Modification Data for a X-15 Research Aircraft," p. 3.

81 "Carrier Modification Data for a X-15 Research Aircraft," pp. 4-9.

82 The B-36 had four bomb bays, but there was no permanent structure separating nos. 1 and 2, or nos. 3 and 4. In each case a removable bulkhead separated the bays, which allowed large bombs to be carried without structural changes. There was a bulkhead between nos. 2 and 3, but since the wing carry-through structure was immediately above this bulkhead, removing it did not seriously compromise the structural integrity of the airplane.

83 This was not a major issue since various versions of the reconnaissance version of the B-36 used short bomb bay doors.

84 "Carrier Modification Data for a X-15 Research Aircraft," pp. 10-12.

One of the more interesting suggestions concerning the carrier aircraft was that "a bank of powerful lights be turned on several minutes prior to launching so that the pilot [of the research airplane] will not be blinded by the sudden glare of daylight during launching."[85]

The B-36 was equipped with a 1,000-gallon liquid-oxygen tank and a 100-gallon ammonia tank to top off the research airplane's propellants. This was surprising because Bell and Douglas, as well as Reaction Motors, believed the rate of ammonia boil-off was so slow that no topping-off would be required. Suspended in the bomb bay above the X-15, the tanks allowed the propellants to be gravity-fed into the airplane. A nitrogen bottle pressurized and purged the tanks, and lines running outside the fuselage to the former tail turret allowed the carrier aircraft to jettison and vent the rocket propellants.[86]

A Replacement

In early 1957, just as North American was preparing to begin modifications on the B-36, the X-15 Joint Operations Committee began considering replacements for the B-36 for various reasons. There were some concerns that the research airplane would not be as stable as desired during launch because of the relatively slow speed of the B-36. Another reason was that as the weight of the X-15 and its subsystems grew, the Air Force and NACA began to look for ways to recover some of the lost performance; a faster carrier would compensate somewhat for the increased X-15 weight. Perhaps most vocally, personnel at Edwards believed that the 10-engine B-36 would quickly become a maintenance nightmare since the Air Force was already phasing it out of the inventory. A lack of spare parts and depot maintenance capabilities for the B-29 and B-50 carrier aircraft had already delayed the X-1 and X-2 programs on several occasions.[87]

A survey by North American identified the Boeing B-52 Stratofortress, Convair B-58 Hustler, and Boeing KC-135 Stratotanker as possible B-36 replacements. It is interesting to note that Douglas had apparently chosen the B-52 for their model 671 study four years earlier.[88]

The supersonic B-58 was attractive from a performance perspective, but looked less attractive from the maintenance and availability standpoint. Nevertheless, on 22 January 1957, future X-15 pilot Neil Armstrong traveled to the Convair plant in Fort Worth to discuss the possibility of using a B-58 to launch the research airplane. The first problem was that the 22-foot wingspan and 18-foot tail-span of the X-15 both intersected the plane of the rearward-retracting main gear on the B-58. This would have necessitated moving the entire X-15 forward of the desired location. Convair engineers believed that this might be possible,

85 "X-15 Advanced Research Airplane Design Summary," p. 38.

86 "Carrier Modification Data for a X-15 Research Aircraft," pp. 15-19.

87 Harrison A. Storms, "X-15 Hardware Design Challenges" a paper in the *Proceedings of the X-15 30th Anniversary Celebration*, Dryden Flight Research Facility, Edwards, CA, 8 June 1989, NASA CP-3105, p. 27; Bock, "B-52/X-15 Flight Operations."

88 Douglas report ES-17673, "Technical Report on High Altitude and High Speed Study," 28 May 1954, pp. 7 and 15-16. Based on the performance parameters specified in the Douglas study, the B-52 was the most likely platform.

but it would require designing a new nose gear for the B-58 since the X-15 would block the normal nose gear. Another possibility was to beef up the X-15 nose gear and use it while the pair was on the ground. The inboard engine nacelles on the B-58 would likely need to be "toed" outward or simply moved further out on the wing, and either would have necessitated major structural changes. Engineers would need to design a way to fold the X-15 vertical stabilizer because they could not make room for it within the B-58 fuselage without severing a main wing spar. The design of the B-58 included a weapons/fuel pod that weighed 30,000 pounds, only slightly less than the X-15. However, the baseline mission included using the fuel in the pod prior to dropping the pod, and the maximum drop weight was only 16,000 pounds. This would necessitate a new series of tests to validate that a heavier object would separate cleanly, especially at supersonic speeds. However unfortunately, the B-58 was obviously not going to work.[89]

The landing-gear configuration on the KC-135 and B-52 precluded carrying the X-15 under the fuselage, as had been the practice in all earlier research programs. Although the performance and availability of the KC-135 made it attractive, nobody could figure out where to carry the research airplane since the Stratotanker had a low-mounted wing and relatively short landing gear. Engineers quickly dropped the KC-135 from consideration.[90]

The B-52 also offered an excellent performance increment over the B-36, and since the Boeing bomber was still in production, the availability of spare parts and support should not become an issue. There was a large space on the wing between the fuselage and inboard engine nacelle that could be adapted to carry a pylon, and investigations were already under way to install similar pylons on later B-52s to carry air-to-surface missiles. In May 1957, NASA directed North American to perform an initial feasibility study on using the B-52 as an X-15 carrier. The study lasted several weeks and the results were favorable. At a meeting on 18-19 June 1957, the program officially adopted the B-52 as a carrier aircraft. Representatives from the FRC discussed concerns about maintenance and availability issues, and NASA recommended procuring two carrier aircraft to ensure that the flight program would proceed smoothly. The Air Force subsequently authorized North American to modify two B-52s in lieu of the single B-36.[91]

The North American investigations showed that the X-15, as designed, would fit under the wing between the fuselage and inboard engine pylon at an 18% semi-span location. The wing structure in this location was capable of supporting up to 50,000 pounds, so the 31,275-pound research airplane did not represent a problem. Nevertheless, this was not the ideal solution. The X-15 pilot would have to be in the research airplane prior to takeoff, and the large weight

89 Memorandum, Neil A. Armstrong to Walter C. Williams, subject: Visit to Convair, Fort Worth, on 22 January 1957, to discuss possible utilization of a B-58 aircraft as a research vehicle launcher, 31 January 1957. In the files at the DFRC History Office.

90 Bock, "B-52/X-15 Flight Operations."

91 Contract change notice no. 11, "Replacement of a B-52 Airplane in lieu of a B-36 for use as X-15 Carrier Airplane, 30 August 1957; Bock, "B-52/X-15 Flight Operations;" letter, Harrison A. Storms/North American Aviation, to Commander/Air Materiel Command, subject: Contract AF-31693, Modification of B-52A For Use as X-15 Carrier Airplane, 28 June 1957. In the files at the AFFTC History Office.

transition when the B-52 released the X-15 would present some interesting control challenges.[92]

Lawrence P. Greene, the North American chief aerodynamicist wrote, "One item which caused considerable concern in the early evaluation was the fact that in this installation, the pilot could not enter the airplane in flight as had been possible in the B-36. This limitation was of concern from both the fatigue and safety aspects; however, the time from take-off of the B-52 to launching the X-15 is about 1.5 hours, and considerable effort has been expended in plans for making the pilot comfortable during this time. In the event of an emergency, the configuration permits the pilot to eject safely while the X-15 and B-52 are still connected."[93]

Further analysis and wind-tunnel tests indicated that the potential problems were solvable, and that the increase in speed and altitude capabilities was desirable. Researchers conducted additional wind-tunnel tests of a 1/40-scale model in the Langley 7 by 10-foot tunnel and the University of Washington wind tunnel to explore possible flutter problems, but did not discover any critical issues. Researchers installed six-component strain-gage balances in both the B-52 and X-15 models, and the B-52 model had additional strain gages and a pressure gage located in the horizontal stabilizer to obtain measurements of possible tail buffet created by the X-15 installation.[94]

Initially the X-15 was to be carried under the left wing of the B-52. It was moved to the right wing to "permit easier servicing of the X-15 when installed on the B-52," although exactly what was easier to service was not described. Researchers had conducted most of the wind-tunnel tests with models of the X-15 under the left wing. However, since both aircraft were largely symmetrical, researchers decided that the test results were equally as valid for the right-wing configuration. The initial design also had an anti-buffet fairing that partially shielded the pylon from the airflow, but wind-tunnel tests showed that the fairing did not significantly help anything, and the engineers subsequently deleted it.[95]

Originally, the Air Force indicated that it could make the two prototype B-52s (the XB-52 and YB-52) available to the X-15 program. Personnel at Edwards feared that the use of these two non-standard aircraft would result in the same maintenance and parts availability problems they were attempting to avoid. By

---

92 Letter, Harrison A. Storms/North American, to Commander/Air Materiel Command, subject: Contract AF-31693, Modification of B-52A For Use as X-15 Carrier Airplane, 28 June 1957. In the files at the AFFTC History Office; Gene J. Matranga, unpublished NASA technical report, "Launch Characteristics of the X-15 Research Airplane as Determined in Flight," undated but sometime in May 1960, no page numbers. Typescript the AFFTC Access to Space Office Project Files; Greene, "X-15 Research Airplane Development Status," p. 4; William J. Alford, Jr., and Robert T. Taylor, "Aerodynamic Characteristics of the X-15/B-52 Combination," a paper in the *1958 Research Airplane Committee Report*, p. 69.

93 Greene, "X-15 Research Airplane Development Status," p. 4. No other reference could be found that indicated ejection was possible in the mated configuration. The flight manual states that the X-15 would be dropped and then the pilot would eject, although this obviously would not help during an emergency on the takeoff roll or shortly after rotation. The X-15 pilots and the flight planners, however, remember that ejection was possible while the plane was still attached to the NB-52.

94 Alford and Taylor, "Aerodynamic Characteristics of the X-15/B-52 Combination," p. 70; Harry L. Runyan an Harold R. Sweet, "Flutter, Noise, and Buffet Problems Related to the X-15," a paper in the *1958 Research Airplane Committee Report*, p. 235.

95 Quote is from Letter, Harrison A. Storms, North American, to Commander, Air Materiel Command, subject: Contract AF-31693, Modification of B-52A For Use as X-15 Carrier Airplane, 28 June 1957. In the files at the AFFTC History Office; Matranga, "Launch Characteristics of the X-15 Research Airplane as Determined in Flight." The change from the left wing to the right wing happened sometime between June 1957 and June 1958, but exactly when could not be determined. The wind-tunnel models were eventually updated for continued testing, but the initial tests were not repeated.

August 1957 the Strategic Air Command agreed to make an early-production B-52A available, and the Air Force subsequently assigned serial number 52-003 to the program in October 1957. In May 1958 the Air Force also assigned an early RB-52B (52-008) to the X-15 program. Both aircraft had been involved in isolating problems with the B-52 defensive fire control system, and Boeing delivered each aircraft to North American after the completion of their test programs.[96]

On 29 November 1957 the B-52A arrived at Air Force Plant 42 in Palmdale, California, after a flight from the Boeing plant in Seattle. North American placed the aircraft into storage pending modifications. On 4 February 1958, technicians moved the aircraft to the North American hangar and began modifying it to support the X-15 program. The aircraft, now designated NB-52A, flew to Edwards on 14 November 1958 and was subsequently named "The High and Mighty One." The RB-52B arrived in Palmdale for similar modifications on 5 January 1959, and, as an NB-52B, flew to Edwards on 8 June 1959; the airplane briefly wore the name "The Challenger."[97]

The major modifications to the two NB-52s included the following:[98]

1. The no. 3 right main wing fuel cell was removed to allow the installation of pylon tie fittings and supports in the front and rear wing spars.
2. The inboard flap mechanism on both wings was disconnected, and the flaps were bolted to the flap tracks. A cutout through the right inboard flap provided clearance for the X-15 vertical stabilizer.
3. A pylon was installed between the right inboard engine nacelle and the fuselage. The pylon contained a primary hydraulic and a secondary, pneumatic-release mechanism for the research airplane.
4. Changes to the NB-52 avionics included the addition of an AN/APN-81 Doppler radar system to provide ground-speed and drift-angle information to the stable platform in the X-15, an auxiliary UHF communications system to provide additional communications channels, and a change in the AN/AIC-10 interphone system to provide an AUX UHF position.

---

96 Bock, Jr., "B-52/X-15 Flight Operations;" various B-52 history cards and reports in the files at the Boeing Archives.

97 The "N" designation indicated that the aircraft had undergone permanent modifications to a non-standard configuration. Some sources show this as an NRB-52B, which would have been correct. However, the RB-52 configuration did not actually change anything substantial on the aircraft other than adding the capability to carry a self-contained reconnaissance capsule in the bomb bay. The Strategic Air Command quickly decided that it had little use for the RB-52s, and all were subsequently redesignated B-52s. The reconnaissance capability was deleted from future procurements.

98 Procurement specification amendment no. 1 to specification NA57-802, "Procurement Specification, Carrier Airplane Modification Program, X-15 Research Aircraft, 19 September 1957; letter, Harrison A. Storms/North American, to Commander/ARDC, subject: Contract AF33(600)-31693, X-15 Research Airplane, Revision–Procurement and Model Specification, 7 November 1957; North American report NA-58-824D, "Operating and Maintenance Instructions for B-52A Carrier Airplane AF52003 and B-52B Carrier Airplane AF52008," 15 May 1959 (changed 18 August 1961), pp. 1-1 through 1-24C. Copy courtesy of Mick Roth; Bock, "B-52/X-15 Flight Operations;" Captain John E. Allavie, Captain Charles C. Bock, Jr., and First Lieutenant Charles E. Adolph, AFFTC report TR-60-33, "Flight Evaluation of the B-52 Carrier Aircraft for the X-15," September 1960. In the AFFTC Access to Space Office Project Files.; internal letter (North American Rockwell), Charles C. Bock, Jr., to G. Boswell, subject: B-52 and X-15 Launch Programs, 12 November 1973; letter, Charles C. Bock, Jr., to Dennis R. Jenkins, 20 May 2002.

The Air Force initially contributed the third production B-52A (serial number 52-003) to the X-15 program. This airplane had been used in initial B-52 testing at Boeing in Seattle, and came to Edwards when its testing duties were completed. The airplane was modified by North American to support carrying and launching the X-15. The aircraft, now designated NB-52A, flew to Edwards on 14 November 1958 and was subsequently named The High and Mighty One. (NASA)

5. The fuselage static ports were removed from the right side of the NB-52 to allow installation of the forward television camera. The airspeed system was recalibrated to use only the left static ports. This worked surprisingly well, even during sideslip maneuvers, with "no measurable difference" noted.
6. Two television cameras were installed in streamline fairings on the right side of the NB-52. The rear camera pointed generally forward and was equipped with the zoom lens to allow the launch operator to focus on areas of interest on the rear of the X-15. The forward camera used a fixed-length lens pointed outward and slightly rearward to allow a view of the X-15 forward fuselage. Two monitors were located at the launch operator position, and either could show the view from either camera. Four floodlights and three 16-mm motion picture cameras were also installed. Two of these were Millikan DBM-5 high-speed units located in a window on the right side of the fuselage at station 374 and in an astrodome at station 1217. The third was an Urban GSAP gun camera mounted in the pylon pointed downward to show X-15 separation.
7. The NB-52 forward-body fuel cell was removed to provide space for inspecting and maintaining various fluid and gas lines installed in the wing. The mid-body fuel cell was removed and the fuselage area above the bomb bay was reworked to provide space for 15 nitrogen and nine helium

storage cylinders. Early during the flight program, a separate liquid-nitrogen supply was added to the pylon to cool the stable platform on the X-15.

8. Two stainless-steel liquid-oxygen tanks (a 1,000-gallon "climb" tank and a 500-gallon "cruise" tank) were installed in the bomb bay. The tanks were not jettisonable, although the contents could be vented through a streamlined jettison line protruding from the forward left side of the bomb bay. Liquid oxygen would be sucked into the right rear landing gear well if the doors were opened while liquids were being jettisoned; this was procedurally restricted.
9. A launch operator station replaced the normal ECM compartment located on the upper rear flight deck. After the first flew flights with X-15-1, an astrodome-type viewing window was added to the NB-52 above the forward television camera in case the video system failed, and a duplicate set of controls for the liquid-oxygen top-off system were located above the window to allow the launch operator to top off the X-15 while looking out the window. A defrosting system was provided for the window, and two steel straps across the window provided safety for the launch operator in case the window blew out.
10. Changes to the NB-52 flight deck included the addition of a master launch panel on the lower left side of the main instrument panel, launch-indicating lights in the pilot's direct field of vision, a normal launch switch on the left console, and an emergency launch handle below and to the left of the master launch panel. Changes were also made to the B-52 fuel control panel in both aircraft to reflect the removal of the fuel cells and eliminate the external tank position.
11. Breathing oxygen was made available to the NB-52 crewmembers at all times. In addition, oxygen was tapped from the NB-52 oxygen system to supply the X-15 research pilot with breathing oxygen until flight release.
12. A high-speed wheel, tire, and braking system was installed on the NB-52 because the original landing gear was only rated to 174 knots. The new system incorporated an adequate margin for no-flap takeoffs and landings at heavy weights, and was rated to 218 knots.
13. All military systems, including the tail turret and defensive fire-control system, were removed. The modifications to the rear fuselage to delete the tail turret differed between the two aircraft. The ability to carry the reconnaissance pod on the RB-52B was also deleted.
14. Later in the flight program, additional instrumentation was added to the launch operator position to allow monitoring

> of the MH-96 adaptive flight control system and X-20 inertial flight data system. A "stable platform control and monitoring unit" was also added to the NB-52B to allow the launch operator to monitor and control the stable platform during captive-carries of the pod-mounted system used for post-maintenance validation.

These changes differed somewhat from those initially proposed for the NB-52. For instance, the original design had a pressurized compartment in the bomb bay for an observer. When North American deleted this from the design, engineers moved the liquid-oxygen top-off tank there instead. The launch operator position was moved from the left side of the aircraft to the right side to permit "continuous observation of the research vehicle" after the X-15 itself was moved to the right side. This also allowed the launch operator to remain in his ejection seat for the entire launch process (previously he had to stand up occasionally to visually check the X-15).[99]

The change from a B-36 to a B-52 did not come cheaply. Although the basic aircraft was provided at no charge to the program, North American submitted a bill for an additional $2,130,929.06 for the modification of the first B-52. The second airplane cost somewhat less since it did not require wind-tunnel testing and the basic engineering was already complete.

The Air Force named Captain Edward C. Gahl as the project pilot for the NB-52 carrier aircraft in 1957. Gahl was well up to the task. He was a graduate of the Experimental Test Pilot School and had been involved in flight-testing the B-52 and KC-135 prior to joining the carrier program. Unfortunately, Gahl perished in a mid-air collision on 16 June 1958, long before the NB-52A had completed its modifications. Captain Charles C. Bock, Jr., replaced him as the chief carrier pilot.[100]

After the modifications to the NB-52A were completed, engineers from the Air Force, Boeing, NASA, and North American conducted a ground vibration test on the pylon using the X-15-1. The tests built on data already accumulated by Boeing-Wichita while the B-52F was being integrated with the North American GAM-77 Hound Dog missile.[101] Technicians constructed a structural steel frame to make the NB-52 wing as rigid as possible, effectively preventing any movement by the NB-52 wing, pylon, horizontal stabilizer, or fuselage. The X-15 was excited by electromagnetic shakers and sensors mounted on the X-15 fuselage, wing, horizontal stabilizer, and vertical stabilizers measured the amplitude of motion for

---

99 Procurement specification amendment no. 1 to specification NA57-802, "Procurement Specification, Carrier Airplane Modification Program, X-15 Research Aircraft, 19 September 1957; letter, Harrison A. Storms/North American, to Commander/ARDC, subject: Contract AF33(600)-31693, X-15 Research Airplane, Revision–Procurement and Model Specification, 7 November 1957; letter, Walter C. Williams, to Commander/ARDC, subject: Modification of B-52A airplane for use as X-15 carrier airplane, 6 August 1957.

100 Biography, "Captain Edwards C. Gahl." In the files at the AFFTC History Office; "Two Center Pilots Lost in Mid-Air Crash Here," an article in the *Desert Wings* paper published at Edwards AFB. Gahl was the copilot on a Martin B-57 piloted by Lieutenant Colonel Boyd L. Grubaugh when the aircraft collided with an North American F-100 piloted by Captain Cecil D. Crabb about 30 miles northwest of Edwards. Crabb managed to limp his damaged Super Sabre home to George AFB, but the B-57 crashed, killing both Edwards pilots.

101 The GAM-77 was a large jet-powered cruise missile that was originally designated B-77 and later redesignated AGM-28. Specially modified B-52s could carry a single Hound Dog on a pylon under each wing in a location very similar to where the X-15 pylon was mounted.

various frequencies. Researchers used these data to determine the natural vibration frequencies of the pylon to verify data obtained from a series of flutter model tests of the NB-52/X-15 combination conducted by Boeing in a low-speed wind tunnel. The results from these two tests demonstrated that the flutter speed of the NB-52 when carrying the X-15 was well above the required launch conditions.[102]

However, there was some concern about the jet exhaust from engine nos. 5 and 6 of the NB-52 impinging on the X-15 empennage. Specifically, the engineers worried that the engine acoustics would detrimentally affect the X-15's structural fatigue life. To mitigate this concern, at least initially, the engineers decided the NB-52 pilots would restrict engine nos. 5 and 6 to 50% thrust while carrying the X-15. The engineers and pilots believed this was an acceptable compromise between protecting the X-15 and the need to provide adequate power and control of the NB-52 during takeoff. At 50% power on these two engines, the tip of the X-15 horizontal stabilizer was exposed to 158 decibels and the sides of the vertical stabilizers were exposed to 144 decibels; at 100% power each value was about 10 decibels greater.[103]

Although it appeared feasible to operate the carrier aircraft engines at reduced power, it was not desirable, so North American began redesigning some parts of the X-15 to increase their fatigue life. The modifications to the vertical stabilizers consisted of increasing the rivet diameter, using dimpled-skin construction instead of countersunk rivets, and increasing the gage of the corrugated ribs along the edge where they flanged over to attach to the cap strip. The horizontal stabilizer used larger rivets and dimpled construction.[104]

To verify the effectiveness of the modifications, researchers conducted several acoustic tests to establish the structural fatigue life of both the original and modified aft X-15 structures. A static ground test was run on a simulated X-15 empennage to determine the sound levels beneath the pylon (the hastily-constructed structure could not be attached to the pylon) with the B-52 engines operating at 85% rpm (equivalent to 50% thrust). Both the original and modified test panels withstood 20 hours of operation with no failure. Subsequent analysis indicated that the original panels would be adequate for operation at 50% power, and the new panels would allow operation at 100% power. North American decided to retrofit all three X-15s with the new structure, which would take several months.[105]

Following completion of these tests, Captain Bock and Captain John E. "Jack" Allavie tested the NB-52A along with launch panel operator, William "Bill" Berkowitz from North American. To eliminate possible interference with the X-15, the engineers decided to bolt the inboard flaps in the closed position, meaning that the NB-52 pilots would have to fly the airplane without flaps. Therefore, the pilots dedicated the initial flights to developing techniques for no-flap

102 Bock, "B-52/X-15 Flight Operations;" "B-52/X-15 Ground Vibration Test," Boeing Report D3-2121, 29 January 1959.

103 Gareth H. Jordan, Normal J. McLeod, and Lawrence D. Guy, "Structural Dynamic Experiences of the X-15," a paper in the *1961 Research Airplane Committee Report*, pp. 48-49 (this was later republished as NASA technical note D-1158, March 1962); Bock, "B-52/X-15 Flight Operations."

104 Harry L. Runyan an Harold R. Sweet, "Flutter, Noise, and Buffet Problems Related to the X-15," a paper in the *1958 Research Airplane Committee Report*, pp. 235-236; Jordan et al., "Structural Dynamic Experiences of the X-15," pp. 48-49.

105 Bock, "B-52/X-15 Flight Operations;" Jordan et al., "Structural Dynamic Experiences of the X-15," pp. 48-49.

operations and measuring various performance parameters of the modified NB-52. The takeoffs were conducted using 50% power on engine nos. 5 and 6 since it appeared that initial flights would be restricted to this power setting until all three X-15s were modified. The NB-52 also accomplished qualitative stability tests over the speed and altitude ranges anticipated for the X-15 program.[106]

There was very little no-flap, takeoff-and-landing experience with the B-52 available to draw on, so Bock and Allavie conducted the initial tests using predicted information and recommendations from Boeing personnel. Engineers based the anticipated takeoff speeds and distances on a lift coefficient of 0.75, meaning that the NB-52 had to be rotated about the aft main gear to an attitude that would produce the correct amount of lift. This was contrary to normal B-52 takeoffs where all four main gear lift at the same time. The pilots also realized that the 10% chord elevator used on the B-52 would have limited authority and that the horizontal-stabilizer trim setting would be important if reasonable takeoff distances were to be attained.[107]

The flight tests involved a fair amount of trial and error. For instance, on the first test at a gross weight of 315,000 pounds (the maximum predicted weight for an actual X-15 flight), Bock set the stabilizer trim 0.5 degrees more than the normal recommended trim of 0 degrees. The pilots ran engine nos. 5 and 6 at 50% power, and fuel loading simulated the weight (but not the drag) of the X-15 on the right wing. The predicted takeoff distance was 10,500 feet at a speed of 176 knots. However, the NB-52 would not rotate, even with the control columns pulled all the way back. After the airplane passed the 10,000-foot marker on the runway, the pilots went to full power on engine nos. 5 and 6, and the aircraft broke ground at 12,650 feet at 195 knots. Engineers later calculated the actual lift coefficient for this takeoff at 0.639. During a normal B-52 takeoff with the flaps down, all four main gear leave the ground simultaneously and the lift coefficient is approximately 0.55.[108]

Subsequent takeoff tests established that a trim setting of 2 degrees nose up was the optimum setting (this represented one-half of the available trim). This setting produced reasonable takeoff distances and a rapid but controllable rotation just prior to liftoff, with the pilot holding the column all the way back. The maximum lift coefficients were later determined to be approximately 0.71.[109]

Landings also proved challenging. Again, the airplane needed higher than normal lift coefficients during landing in order to produce reasonable touchdown speeds and landing distances. Unlike the traditional B-52 landing on all four main gear at once, the NB-52s landed on their two aft main gear. The problem was that the designers had not intended the B-52 to do this. Very little control could be achieved as the aircraft rotated to a level attitude, and the forward main gear usually hit with a noticeable impact. Accelerometers installed in the pylon after the initial landing tests measured impact loads of 1.5–1.8 g. The engineers considered these annoying but acceptable.[110]

---

106 Bock, Jr. "B-52/X-15 Flight Operations."

107 Ibid.

108 Ibid; telephone conversation, Charles Bock with Dennis R. Jenkins, 12 June 2002.

109 Ibid.

110 Ibid.

After the front main gear touched down, the pilots fully extended the NB-52 air brakes and the drag chute deployed at 140 knots. When landing at heavier weights, such as when returning with the X-15 still attached, the pilots used moderate braking. When these techniques were used with a 300,000-pound airplane, the touchdown speed was 172 knots and the landing roll took 10,800 feet. At 250,000 pounds, touchdown occurred at 154 knots and light braking used only 9,300 feet of runway. The importance of the drag chute was telling: one landing at 267,000 pounds with a failed drag chute required over 12,000 feet to stop even with heavy braking, and resulted in one brake being severely warped, necessitating its replacement.[111]

The NB-52 pilots now felt confident that they could control their airplane with the X-15 attached, so the first captive flight was attempted. The right wing sat on its outrigger wheel during the initial takeoff roll in order to keep spoiler extension and the associated drag at a minimum. The engineers did not expect the additional drag of the X-15 to result in any serious degradation of low-speed performance; however, there existed some concerns about the possible impingement of the X-15 wake on the right horizontal stabilizer of the NB-52.[112]

Despite the concerns about exhaust impingement from engine nos. 5 and 6, the X-15 program had not taken a firm stand on what power levels to use. Bock and Allavie therefore decided to use full power on all eight engines for the flight on 10 March 1959. The takeoff gross weight was 258,000 pounds and the center of gravity was located at 26.5% mean aerodynamic chord (MAC). The actual takeoff distance was 6,085 feet and liftoff occurred at 172 knots. The lift coefficient developed on this takeoff was 0.66 since the pilots did not attempt to achieve maximum performance. Bock just wanted to demonstrate that the mated pair would actually fly as predicted, which it did for 1 hour and 8 minutes. The second flight (which was supposed to result in an X-15 glide flight, but did not due to a radio failure) produced largely similar results. On the third flight (another unsuccessful attempt at a glide flight) engine nos. 5 and 6 were set to 50% thrust until an indicated airspeed of 130 knots was reached, and then they were advanced to full power. This procedure extended the takeoff distance to 7,100 feet at the same gross weight and similar atmospheric conditions.[113]

Following takeoff, engine nos. 5 and 6 were set to 50% thrust at 5,000 feet altitude and the mated pair continued to climb using a circular pattern around Rogers Dry Lake. This kept Scott Crossfield in the X-15 within gliding distance of a suitable lake in the event of a possible emergency jettison. The NB-52 pilots flew all of these early tests to an altitude of 45,000 feet and Mach 0.85, which was pretty much the maximum performance of the mated pair. Bock and Allavie flew simulated launch patterns and practiced emergency and aborted launch procedures, and Crossfield accomplished X-15 propellant jettison tests using a water-alcohol mixture that included red dye. Before each flight, technicians covered the

111 Ibid.

112 Ibid; telephone conversation, Charles Bock with Dennis R. Jenkins, 12 June 2002.

113 Ibid; telephone conversation, Charles Bock with Dennis R. Jenkins, 12 June 2002.

underside of the right horizontal stabilizer of the NB-52 with a powdery substance so that the impingement would be easy to identify.[114]

Since the X-15 horizontal and vertical stabilizers used for these initial carry flights were the original design, the engineers decided to inspect them after the third flight. The inspection revealed several structural failures in the upper vertical stabilizer. For the most part, the corrugated ribs had failed where they flanged over to attach to the cap strip, but the most extensive failure was an 18-inch separation of the rib from the flange on the side away from the NB-52 engines. Subsequent investigation showed that the failures were largely a result of a previously unsuspected source: the turbulent airflow created by the X-15 pylon and the B-52 wing cutout. Researchers made pressure measurements to determine the exact environment around the wing cutout. Fortunately, the subsequent analysis indicated an acceptable fatigue life for the modified X-15 structures, even though the engineers had not factored this particular environment into the design. After this round of tests and analysis was completed, the pilots made most subsequent takeoffs with all eight B-52 engines operating at 100% power.[115]

Nevertheless, it was recognized that heavyweight takeoffs (≈315,000 pounds) with no flaps were going to require a considerable amount of runway during the summer heat. Most flight operations at Edwards during the summer were conducted in the early morning in any case, and if the takeoff roll was computed to be too long, one of the lakebeds could always be used (although this only happened once during actual flight operations). The NB-52B eliminated this particular deficiency. Unlike the A-model, the NB-52B was quipped with water injection for its engines. Bock and Allavie tested the NB-52B using water injection on just the outer four engines, and on all engines except nos. 5 and 6, with promising results. Bock noted that the use of water injection "appreciably increases take-off performance and is considered mandatory for take-off from the paved runway at a weight of 300,000 pounds when the ambient temperature exceeds 90 degrees Fahrenheit."[116]

Takeoffs were initially made using runway 04 at Edwards because that runway had several miles of lakebed overrun available. This allowed the pilots to fly a better pattern during climb-out, but more importantly, it avoided the use of heavy braking in case of an aborted takeoff. Engineers considered the use of maximum braking "undesirable" because of potential damage to the X-15 if one of the NB-52 tires failed. The other direction, runway 22, has a road at the end of it instead of lakebed.[117]

Pilots found the lateral and directional control systems of the carrier aircraft capable of trimming out the unbalance of the NB-52/X-15 combination. Most of the pilots noted that lateral control became sensitive above Mach 0.8, but believed that launches were possible up to Mach 0.85 with no particular problems. The evaluations did not reveal any buffeting in level flight. It was possible to induce a minor airframe buffet in maneuvering flight at 1.6 g (80% of the pylon load limit), but only at speeds well below the normal operating range. It was discovered that

114 Ibid.

115 Jordan et al., "Structural Dynamic Experiences of the X-15," pp. 48-49.

116 Bock, "B-52/X-15 Flight Operations;" AFFTC report TR-60-33, p. 6.

117 AFFTC report TR-60-33, p. 6. Runway 22, the other direction of the same piece of concrete, ends in one of the main base access roads.

The Air Force also provided the second production RB-52B (the fifth B-model) to the X-15 program. The RB-52B (52-008) arrived in Palmdale for similar modifications on 5 January 1959, and as an NB-52B, flew to Edwards on 8 June 1959; the airplane briefly wore the name The Challenger. The NB-52B went on to a long career at the Flight Research Center before being retired in 2005. (U.S. Air Force)

the specific range deterioration of the NB-52 was about 7% with an empty pylon; with the X-15 attached, the specific range decreased by approximately 16%. Given that researchers never planned to launch the X-15 from a distance of more than 500 miles, and the B-52 was an intercontinental bomber, nobody considered this decrease in range significant. Nevertheless, a nonstop flight in May 1962 demonstrated that the pair could fly 1,625 miles from Edwards to Eglin AFB, Florida.[118]

The engineers and pilots predicted that launching the X-15 would result in an instantaneous rearward shift of the NB-52 center of gravity, coupled with a tendency for the carrier aircraft to roll to the left. The X-15 glide flight (i.e., with no fuel) was expected to result in a 4.5% shift in the center of gravity, while full-fuel flights would result in a 9% shift (which rose to about 12% on the later X-15A-2 flights). Engineers calculated that the rolling tendency and pitch-up were well within the capabilities of the NB-52 to counter, and in fact actual operations revealed no particular problems. Under "normal" conditions, the center of gravity actually shifted approximately 7% and required a 40-pound push force on the control column to compensate, but the resulting pulse usually dampened in one cycle.[119]

Some other minor problems were discovered during the NB-52 flight tests. For instance, the aft alternator cooling air duct on the right-wing leading edge and the air ducts on the right side of the NB-52 fuselage ingested hydrogen peroxide residue during pre-launch operation of the X-15 nose ballistic control system. Engineers did not consider the residue hazardous since it was composed primarily of water. Interestingly, while the X-15 was attached to the NB-52, operation of the X-15 ballistic control system had no noticeable effect on the bomber. Operation of the X-15 aerodynamic flight control also had no appreciable effect on the NB-52; however, a slight airframe buffet was noted when the X-15 speed brakes were extended. A flap extension on the X-15 caused a small nose-down trim change, and extension of the X-15 main landing skids was not even apparent in the bomber. Initially, extension of the X-15 nose gear resulted in a "thump" that was felt and

118 Bock, "B-52/X-15 Flight Operations;" AFFTC report TR-60-33, p. 7; telephone conversations, John E. Allavie and Robert M. White with Dennis R. Jenkins, various dates in May and June 2002.

119 Bock, "B-52/X-15 Flight Operations;" AFFTC report TR-60-33, p. 9.

heard in the NB-52, but later changes to the X-15 extension mechanism eliminated the event.[120]

On the other side of the equation, the NB-52 had some effects on the X-15. For instance, the NB-52 fuselage and wing created noticeable upwash and sidewash on the X-15. Because of the NB-52 wing sweep, the right wing of the X-15 was nearer to the B-52 wing leading edge and, consequently, flow over the X-15 right wing was deflected downward more than over its left wing. This difference in effective angle of attack of the right and left wings resulted in a right rolling moment. There were also some concerns that the X-15 might strike the carrier aircraft during separation. Because there was only two feet of clearance between the X-15 dorsal stabilizer and the cutout in the NB-52 wing, the X-15 could potentially strike the cutout if the X-15 bank angle exceeded 20 degrees before the airplane dropped below the NB-52 fuselage level (about 2.5 feet vertically). It was decided that all X-15 controls should be in the neutral position when the airplane was dropped, allowing the automatic dampers to take care of correcting the attitude. The first few X-15 launches experimented with the settings needed for the dampers to do this, but Scott Crossfield soon developed a consistent set of settings.[121]

Scott Crossfield unexpectedly demonstrated the effects of not using the dampers on the third flight (2-3-6) when the roll damper failed at launch. The X-15 rolling velocity increased rapidly to a peak value of 47 degrees per second and a peak bank angle of 40 degrees. The X-15 dorsal stabilizer dropped below the NB-52 wing cutout within 0.5 second, with the tail barely clearing the cutout. Crossfield finally managed to get the X-15's wings level about 7 seconds after launch.[122]

The most obvious modification was a large pylon under the right wing to carry the X-15. This was in contrast to all earlier X-planes, which had been carried partially submerged in the bomb bay of the carrier aircraft, something that was not possible given the B-52 configuration. The pylon worked satisfactorily and allowed the NB-52s to carry other research airplanes, such as the lifting bodies, later in their careers. (NASA)

The damper generally applied a left-aileron input of 6–8 degrees, reducing the peak right-roll velocity to about 25 degrees per second. The pilot could do the same if the damper failed. Aileron inputs of only 2 degrees, however, resulted in peak roll velocities in excess of 50 degrees per second, with corresponding bank angles of over 40 degrees. This risked a tail strike during launch. As the

120 AFFTC report TR-60-33, p. 8.

121 Gene J. Matranga, unpublished NASA technical report, "Launch Characteristics of the X-15 Research Airplane as Determined in Flight," undated but sometime in May 1960. In the AFFTC Access to Space Office Project Files; North American report NA-67-344, "Technical Proposal for a Conceptual Design Study for the Modification of an X-15 Air Vehicle to a Hypersonic Delta-Wing Configuration," 17 May 1967, vol. I, pp. 39-40. In the files at the JSC History Office.

122 Matranga, "Launch Characteristics of the X-15 Research Airplane as Determined in Flight."

Another modification to the two NB-52s was a notch in the right wing to accommodate the X-15 vertical stabilizer. Because there was only 2 feet of clearance between the X-15 dorsal stabilizer and the cutout in the NB-52 wing, the X-15 could potentially strike the cutout if the X-15 bank angle exceeded 20 degrees before the airplane dropped below the NB-52 fuselage level (about 2.5 feet vertically). Fortunately, this was never an issue during the flight program. (U.S. Air Force)

X-15 cleared the NB-52 flow field, it tended to roll left, so the damper and/or pilot had to be prepared to correct this sudden opposite movement. It took approximately 0.8 second for the X-15 to drop 10 feet below the NB-52.[123]

The first few seconds were quite a ride, at least during the first time for each pilot. However, it quickly became routine. Bob White described it as "what might be expected and, after the very first experience, is of no concern to the pilot as normal 1.0-g flight is regained within 2 seconds. The rolloff at launch stops as the X-15 emerges from the B-52 flow field. Since the bank-angle change is small, it is easily and quickly corrected. Launch has been made by using either the center or side aerodynamic control stick with equal satisfaction in both cases."[124]

During initial planning, the engineers set the X-15 launch parameters at Mach 0.78 and 38,000 feet. However, before the first flight, North American decided to raise the launch altitude to 40,000 feet to provide additional performance and increased safety margins. During early launches from 40,000 feet, the X-15 generally needed about 3,000 feet to recover before beginning its climb. After the first

123 Matranga, "Launch Characteristics of the X-15 Research Airplane as Determined in Flight." The engineers talked in terms of aileron input even though the X-15 used a rolling tail instead of conventional ailerons; it was largely indistinguishable to the airplane.

124 White et al., "Résumé of X-15 Handling Qualities," pp. 113-116.

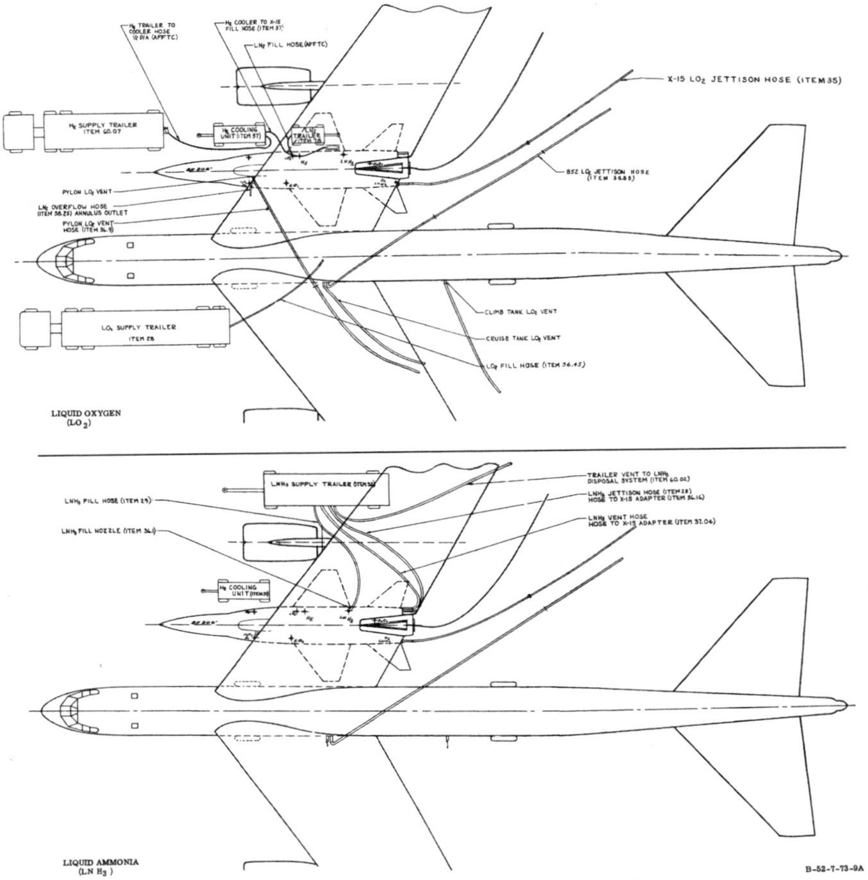

Although simplistic by modern standards, preparation of the X-15 for flight was still a complicated procedure involving many people and pieces of ground- support equipment. These drawings show the relative placement of tank trucks and other equipment during the loading of liquid oxygen and anhydrous ammonia prior to flight. (NASA)

few flights, researchers decided to increase the launch parameters yet again, this time to Mach 0.80 and 45,000 feet, just below the previously determined buffet boundary for the NB-52/X-15 combination. Interestingly, when researchers raised the launch altitude to 45,000 feet, the research airplane needed between 4,000 and 9,000 feet to recover, negating much of the value of the higher launch altitude.[125]

In June 1960 the Air Force installed an AN/APN-41 radar transponder in the NB-52A that allowed the High Range to track the carrier aircraft more accurately. This beacon was similar to the one installed in the X-15. The problem had been that the B-52 fuselage was often located between the X-15 beacon and the radar site before launch and acted as an effective shield. Installing a beacon on the B-52 avoided the problem. A series of test flights that made simulated launches from Silver Lake (the NB-52 did not carry the X-15 for the tests) showed that using the beacon to position the B-52 resulted in a more accurate launch location than had previously been attained. This provided an extra margin of safety should the X-15 pilot have to make an emergency landing, and also allowed flight profiles to be repeated more accurately, helping post-flight analysis. The NB-52B received a similar beacon during July 1960. Flight 1-9-17 on 4 August 1960 was the first flight to use the new beacon.[126]

In June 1965 the FRC estimated that the full-up weight of the X-15A-2 with a real ramjet and fuel had grown to 56,000 pounds. This was more than 1,000 pounds greater than the most recent analysis showed the NB-52 wing/pylon could safely tolerate. In January and February 1966 the Air Force modified the NB-52A to increase the allowable pylon weight to 65,000 pounds, allowing for the heaviest expected X-15A-2 flight with some reserve for gusts or other contingencies. The modifications consisted primarily of installing doublers and additional fasteners on various parts of the wing and pylon structure. Although the modifications allowed the NB-52 to carry the X-15A-2 safely, performance suffered. For instance, the maximum launch altitude was 1,500 feet lower and the maximum launch speed was restricted to about Mach 0.8 when the research airplane carried the external tanks and ramjet. The Air force installed the same modifications on the NB-52B during its next major maintenance period.[127]

XB-70

During the course of the X-15 program, various drawings and artist concepts were released that showed the research airplane–particularly the proposed delta-wing version–carried by a North American XB-70 bomber. The use of this Mach 3+ capable aircraft would have greatly extended the performance envelope of the X-15. However, given the theoretical uncertainties of launching an object from the back of a larger aircraft traveling at Mach 3, it is unlikely that the Air Force or NASA ever seriously considered this concept. After the fatal crash on 30 July 1966 of a Lockheed M-21 Blackbird while launching a D-21 drone from

125 Matranga, "Launch Characteristics of the X-15 Research Airplane as Determined in Flight;" Jordan et al., "Structural Dynamic Experiences of the X-15," p. 49.

126 X-15 Status Report, Paul F. Bikle/FRC to H. Brown/NASA Headquarters, 29 July 1960, pp. 1 and 5.

127 X-15 Status Report, Paul F. Bikle/FRC to J. Martin/NASA Headquarters, 2 June 1965, p. 2; Knight, "Increased Piloting Tasks and Performance of X-15A-2 in Hypersonic Flight," pp. 793-802.

The use of the Mach 3+ capable XB-70A as a carrier aircraft would have greatly extended the performance envelope of the X-15. However, given the theoretical uncertainties of launching an object from the back of a larger aircraft traveling at Mach 3, coupled with the fact that only two Valkyries were manufactured, it is unlikely that the Air Force or NASA ever seriously considered this concept. (North American Aviation)

a similar configuration, it became even more unlikely. Nevertheless, sometime during 1966 North American conducted a study (logically called "XB-70/X-15"); unfortunately, however, no copy could be found in any archive, so its contents and conclusions are unknown.[128]

CHASE AND SUPPORT AIRCRAFT

In addition to the NB-52s there were numerous chase and support aircraft, mostly provided by the Air Force. The number of chase aircraft differed depending on what the flight profile looked like. The program generally used three chase aircraft on the early low-speed X-15 flights, four on most research flights, and five for the very long-range flights. Of course, all things were variable and additional chase aircraft were not uncommon, particularly during the middle years of the program.

Chase-1 was the prelaunch chase, and was usually a North American F-100F Super Sabre during the early years and a Northrop T-38A Talon later, although NASA used a Douglas F5D Skyray on a couple of occasions. Al White frequently flew this chase during the North American flights, but an Air Force pilot generally flew the airplane once the government took over. Chase-1 took off with the NB-52 and flew formation during the climb-out and cruise to the launch lake. The chase pilot visually verified various parts of the X-15 checklist, such as control

128 For more information on the crash of the M-21, see Tony R. Landis and Dennis R. Jenkins, *Lockheed Blackbirds*, WarbirdTech Series Vol. 10, (North Branch, MN: Specialty Press, 2004), p. 50-52; various e-mails, Michael J. Lombardi, Boeing historian, to Dennis R. Jenkins, May and June 2002 confirming that the report could not be located in the Boeing archives. It also could not be located in the DFRC archives, National Archives II, the Air Force Historical Research Agency, or any of the major aerospace museums.

surface movements, propellant jettison, ballistic system checks, APU start, and engine priming. The use of the F-100 presented some problems at the beginning of the program because the aircraft could not maintain a low enough speed to fly formation with the NB-52 during a right-hand turn; however, the T-38 proved to be more satisfactory.

Chase-2 was the launch chase and provided assistance for the X-15 pilot in the event of an emergency landing at the launch lake. Chase-2 was usually a Lockheed F-104 Starfighter flown by either another X-15 pilot or a NASA test pilot. The F-100 and T-38 could not produce enough drag to fly the steep final approach used by the X-15, which largely dictated the use of the Starfighter for this role. Conversely, the F-104 could not cruise at 45,000 feet due to its high wing loading, which made it unsuitable as Chase-1. Chase-2 normally stayed below 35,000 feet until 3 minutes before launch, and then went into afterburner and climbed to 45,000 feet just before the X-15 dropped. The pilot trailed the NB-52 during launch and then tried to keep up with the X-15 as it left the launch lake area. It was a futile gesture, but it proved useful on the few occasions in which the X-15 engine failed soon after ignition.

Chase-3 covered landings at the intermediate lakebeds and was usually an F-104 flown by either another X-15 pilot or an Air Force test pilot. Unlike Chases 1 and 2, which took off with the NB-52, Chase-3 waited until 30 minutes before X-15 launch to take off so that it would have enough fuel to loiter for a while. On flight profiles that had multiple intermediate lakes, Chase-3 would orbit between them. In the event the X-15 had to make an emergency landing, the F-104 would attempt to join up to provide support for the X-15 pilot during final approach and touchdown. For flights out of Smith Ranch there were two intermediate chases, usually called 3 and 4 (the Edwards chase became Chase-5 in these cases).

Chase-4 covered the Edwards landing area, usually with an Air Force pilot. Again, only an F-104 could keep up with the X-15 in the landing pattern. This chase took off at the same time as Chase-3 and orbited 30-40 miles uprange along

The Lockheed F-104 Starfighter was used as a chase airplane and to practice landing maneuvers. In addition to the F-104Ns owned by NASA, various F-104s from the Air Force Flight Test Center were used as needed. (NASA)

Ferrying men and supplies to the contingency landing sites and High Range stations kept the NASA Douglas R4D (C-47/DC-3) Skytrain busy. In addition, the Air Force used Lockheed C-130 Hercules to move fire trucks and other heavy equipment. The C-130s also carried rescue teams during flight operations to ensure help would arrive swiftly in the event of a major accident. (NASA)

the flight path. The pilot began accelerating on cue from NASA-1 in an attempt to intercept the X-15 at the maximum possible speed and altitude as the X-15 descended into the Edwards area. Usually the chase pilot took his cues from the vapor trail left as the X-15 pilot jettisoned his residual propellants, since the research airplane was too small and too dark to acquire visually until the chase pilot was right on top of it. Chase-4 would make a visual inspection of the X-15 as it descended and provide airspeed and altitude callouts to the X-15 pilot during the final approach, in addition to verifying that the ventral had successfully jettisoned and the landing gear extended.[129]

At times there were other chase aircraft, with a photo-chase or a "rover" being the most frequent. The photo-chase filmed the X-15, although Chase-1 was frequently a two-seater and carried a photographer in the back seat as well. Rover was usually another X-15 pilot who just felt like tagging along. All of the X-15 pilots flew chase aircraft, as did many AFFTC test pilots, and students and instructors from the test-pilot schools at Edwards. The chase pilots (particularly other X-15 pilots) tended to use first names for themselves and the X-15 pilot during radio chatter; alternately, they simply used "chase" (without a number) since there was seldom more than one chase aircraft in the vicinity.

A number of other aircraft provided various support functions. In particular, the program used the NASA Gooney Bird (R4D/DC-3) to ferry men and supplies to the uprange stations and to inspect the lakebeds as necessary. The Air Force used several Lockheed C-130 Hercules turboprops to transport fire engines and other material to the lakebeds and High Range stations for each flight. These aircraft often made several trips per day carrying men and equipment. During the actual flight one of them orbited midway down the flight corridor, usually with a flight surgeon and response team in case the X-15 had to make an emergency landing. The program took safety very seriously.

Piasecki H-21 Shawnee helicopters were also shuttled to the primary emergency landing lake in case of an emergency, and additional H-21s were located at Edwards. These provided a quick means of moving emergency personnel to an

129 Letter, Johnny G. Armstrong to Dennis R. Jenkins, 5 July 2002.

accident scene, surveying the runways, and evacuating the X-15 pilot if necessary. The H-21 pilots also knew how to disperse fumes from a damaged X-15 by hovering near the crashed airplane, and they used this technique on at least one occasion, probably saving the life of the X-15 pilot.

IMPLICATIONS OF SPUTNIK

In mid-1955 the Soviet Union and the United States separately announced intentions to orbit satellites as part of the 1957 International Geophysical Year. Nevertheless, when the Soviet Union launched the first Earth artificial satellite–*Sputnik* (later called *Sputnik 1*)–on 4 October 1957, the event created a stir among the popular press. The seeming lack of response by President Dwight D. Eisenhower further antagonized the fourth estate and soon the American people as well. However, it was the 1,100-pound *Sputnik 2* that ultimately caused the administration to take action, since it graphically portrayed the capability of Soviet launch vehicles and, directly, their ICBM program.

The Soviet achievements damaged American scientific and technological prestige, and the satellite was widely regarded as a threat to national security. Robert Gilruth later wrote, "I can recall watching the sunlight reflecting off the *Sputnik 1* carrier rocket as it passed over my home on the Chesapeake Bay, Virginia. It put a new sense of value and urgency on the things we had been doing."[130]

Over a year before, the Air Force had begun Project HYWARDS (Hypersonic Weapon and Research & Development Supporting System) to design a successor to the X-15. Researchers considered this round III of the research airplane program. Round I had been the X-1 and D-558 series, while round II consisted of the X-15. The goal of round III was to design a vehicle capable of achieving at least Mach 12 and perhaps as much as Mach 18. HYWARDS is outside the scope of this history, but it created an enormous debate between researchers at Ames and Langley, and between the NACA and the Air Force. The Air Force soon combined HYWARDS with the remaining work on BoMi/RoBo and other projects into the Boeing X-20 Dyna-Soar program. Ultimately, the experimental research conducted for HYWARDS and Dyna-Soar, combined with the flight results from X-15, formed the technical foundation for the development of a space shuttle.

Although HYWARDS was the next logical step in the progressive effort to fly a man into space, other programs, such as Project 7969, were under way concurrently. The organizations that proposed these programs intended then to put a man into space as soon as possible, mainly as a publicity ploy, and offered little in the way of a long-term solution to space flight. The X-15 figured into some of these programs, and at least two proposals for orbital X-15s were made during 1957 and 1958 (see the "X-15B" section for more details).

---

130 Robert R. Gilruth, "From Wallops Island to Project Mercury, 1945-1958: A Memoir," in *History of Rocketry and Astronautics*, American Astronautical Society History Series, vol. 7, part 2, R. Cargill Hall, editor (San Diego, CA: American Astronautical Society, 1986), p. 462.

In the meantime, the NACA Executive Committee met in its regular annual session on 10 October 1957, less than a week after the launch of *Sputnik*. Interestingly, the committee did not discuss the Soviet satellite at any length. But the NACA Committee on Aerodynamics met on 18-20 November 1957 aboard the aircraft carrier USS *Forrestal* (CVA-59) and paid a great deal of attention to crafting a response to *Sputnik*. The committee noted that "[t]he big question to be answered now is how can these views [on accelerating space research] be put across to the NACA and to the Government in order that the NACA be recognized as the national research agency in this field, and be provided with the necessary funds ... the NACA should act now to avoid being ruled out of the field of space flight research." The committee suggested highlighting the hypersonics program in general and the X-15 program specifically in order to make that case.[131]

This threw a great deal more attention onto the X-15 program than it was ready for. North American was making good progress with its development effort, but the first airframe was still almost a year away from being completed. The XLR99 engine was much further away. Nevertheless, the media–and indeed, some within the NACA and military–saw the X-15 as the most promising American response to *Sputnik*. The North American plant in Inglewood, which was clearly visible from the Los Angeles International Airport, soon sported a huge "Home of X-15" neon sign and articles began to appear in periodicals ranging from popular newsstand magazines to serious industry journals. It was a spotlight the X-15 program was ill prepared to handle.[132]

Nevertheless, the publicity probably made some aspects of the X-15 program somewhat easier, particularly securing funding at a time when the program was seriously over budget. In his essay on the 1961 Collier trophy, W. D. Kay wrote:[133]

> After the launch of *Sputnik 1* in 1957, interest in the [X-15] project on the part of the military, political leaders, and the public at large grew rapidly... media coverage of the first flights was the most intense ever seen at Edwards, and even led to some public relations mix-ups between NASA and the Air Force. Once the first Mercury flights were underway, public attention shifted to the events at Cape Canaveral. This might, however, have ultimately worked to the [X-15] program's benefit. A major contributor to the X-15's success over the long run was its emphasis on incremental development and its use in highly specialized scientific and technical research. As experience with many later space projects ... has shown, the general public tends to lose interest in such "routine" undertakings rather quickly. In short, it appears the X-15 got a needed boost of public fanfare at precisely the right point in its history–the later development and early flight test stage–and then became regarded as a low-key

131 Minutes of the meeting, NACA Committee on Aerodynamics, 18-20 November 1957. Quote is on p. 17.

132 Crossfield, *Always Another Dawn*, p. 287.

133 W. D. Kay, "The X-15 Hypersonic Flight Research Program: Politics and Permutations at NASA," in *From Engineering Science to Big Science: The NACA and NASA Collier Trophy Research Project Winners*, edited by Pamela E. Mack, NASA publication SP-4219 (Washington, DC: NASA, 1998), p. 163.

effort worthy of only occasional interest just as it was entering its less "flashy" research phase. These shifts in external perception probably could not have been planned any better.

Scott Crossfield might not completely agree that the program wanted the publicity, especially as he spent too many hours in an uncomfortable MC-2 full-pressure suit in the hot desert sun providing encouragement for the technicians working to get the X-15 ready for its first glide flight. Overall, however, events probably turned out as well as anybody could have expected.

There were a variety of proposals (some legitimate, most not) to use the X-15 to put a man into orbit before the Soviets. However, there was a flaw with all of these ideas: the lack of a suitable booster. The ICBMs then under development had two significant problems. First, none had the "throw weight" to launch a complicated lifting reentry vehicle, be it an X-15 derivative or one of the round III concepts under study at Ames, Langley, or Wright Field. Second, the early ICBMs did not work very well; they tended to blow up.

Project 7969

The Air Force initiated Project 7969, the manned ballistic rocket research system, in February 1956 with a stated goal of orbiting and recovering a manned space capsule. By the end of 1957, a joint Air Force-NACA team had evaluated at least 10 serious proposals during a conference held at Wright Field on 29–31 January 1958. Avco, Convair, Goodyear, Lockheed, Martin, and McDonnell proposed spherical reentry vehicles or blunt capsules, while Bell, North American, Republic, and Northrop all proposed winged vehicles.[134]

The North American proposal included a "stripped" X-15 with an empty weight of 9,900 pounds. Cape Canaveral would launch the vehicle on a two-stage booster that allowed a single orbit with an apogee of 400,000 feet and a perigee of 250,000 feet. The launch vehicle consisted of four Navaho boosters. Three were clustered together in the first stage and one acted as the second stage. The XLR99 in the X-15 was the third stage. The X-15 would be equipped with beryllium oxide leading edges and a René 41 alloy shingle heat shield, plus a thicker Inconel X hot structure. Due to the low perigee and aerodynamics of the X-15, no retro-rocket was required for reentry. The pilot would eject and descend by parachute just before ditching the X-15 in the Gulf of Mexico, with the aircraft being lost. North American expected that it could conduct the first manned orbital flight 30 months after a go-ahead, at a cost of $120 million.[135]

---

134 House Report 1228, Project Mercury, First Interim Report, 86th Congress, 2nd Session, p. 2; comments by Clotaire Wood, NACA, 26 January 1960, on Draft, NIS Meeting at ARDC Headquarters, 19 June 1958; memorandum, Maxime A. Faget, NACA Langley, to Hugh L. Dryden, Director, NACA, no subject, 5 June 1958; comments by Maxime A. Faget on "Outline of History of USAF Man-in-Space R&D Program," *Missiles and Rockets*, vol. 10, no. 13, 26 March 1962, pp. 148-149; Mark Wade, *http://www.astronautix.com/craftfam/mercury.htm*, accessed 7 April 2002; Lloyd S. Swenson, Jr., James M. Greenwood, and Charles C. Alexander, *This New Ocean: A History of Project Mercury*, (Washington, DC: NASA, 1966), pp. 77-78.

135 E-mail, Scott Crossfield to Dennis R. Jenkins, 28 June 2002; Mark Wade, *http://www.astronautix.com/craft/x15b.htm*, accessed 7 April 2002; "Outline of History of USAF Man-in-Space R&D Program," pp. 148-149; memorandum, Clarence A. Syvertson to Director, Langley Aeronautical Laboratory, subject: Visit to WADC, Wright-Patterson AFB, Ohio, to Attend Conference on January 29-31, 1958, concerning research problems associated with placing a man in a satellite vehicle, Moffett Field, 18 February 1958.

Given the early state of development of the X-15, there was almost no real engineering associated with this proposal. Nevertheless, it was further along than many of the others since researchers already knew that the basic X-15 shape was stable in most flight regimes, and both the airframe and XLR99 were at least under active development.

After the launch of *Sputnik 1*, Project 7969 was reoriented into the Man In Space Soonest (MISS) project to ensure that a U.S. Air Force pilot would be the first human in outer space. On 27 February 1958, General Curtiss E. LeMay, the Air Force vice chief of staff, was briefed on three alternatives that included the X-15 derivative, speeding up the Dyna-Soar program, and building a simple non-lifting ballistic capsule that could be boosted into low orbit by an existing ICBM-derived booster. LeMay apparently expressed no preference, and although it was a long and complicated process, the result was that a ballistic capsule appeared to offer the best hope of immediate success. This idea formed the basis for Project Mercury after NASA was formed on 1 October 1958 and the first American manned space effort was transferred to the civilian agency.[136]

X-15B

Nevertheless, engineers at North American continued to refine their Project 7969 concept. A few days after the Soviet Union orbited *Sputnik 1* on 4 October 1957, North American packaged everything into a neat report and Harrison Storms took the idea to Washington. This version used two Navaho boosters clustered together as the 830,000-lbf first stage, a single Navaho booster as the 415,000-lbf second stage, and an X-15B powered by a 75,000-lbf Rocketdyne XLR105 Atlas sustainer engine as the third stage. Unlike the 7969 proposal, this one had a great deal more engineering in it, although it was still very preliminary since North American had not conducted wind-tunnel tests or detailed calculations on heating or aero loads.[137]

The X-15B was larger than the basic X-15 and was capable of carrying two pilots. The Inconel X skin was made thicker to withstand the increased reentry heating, and the vehicle had larger propellant tanks to feed the Atlas sustainer engine that replaced the XLR99. However, the shape and many of the internal systems were identical to those of the basic X-15 then under construction. Engineers had already demonstrated the supersonic and subsonic stability of the X-15 during numerous wind-tunnel tests, and keeping the same shape eliminated the need to repeat many of them.

The flight plan was simple. Eighty seconds after launch from Cape Canaveral, the first stage would drop away and the second stage would fire. At an altitude of about 400,000 feet, the second stage would burn out and the X-15B would continue using its own power. The vehicle would eventually get up to 18,000 mph, enough for three orbits. The pilot would fire the XLR105 at a point that would allow the X-15B to land at Edwards using the reentry profiles already developed

136 Swenson et al., *This New Ocean*, pp. 78-81.

137 Crossfield, *Always Another Dawn*, pp. 280-281. Unfortunately, a copy of the report could not be located, and neither Scott Crossfield nor Charlie Feltz had any particular memories of the concept. The X-15B designation was rather arbitrarily used by Storms and was not an official Air Force designation.

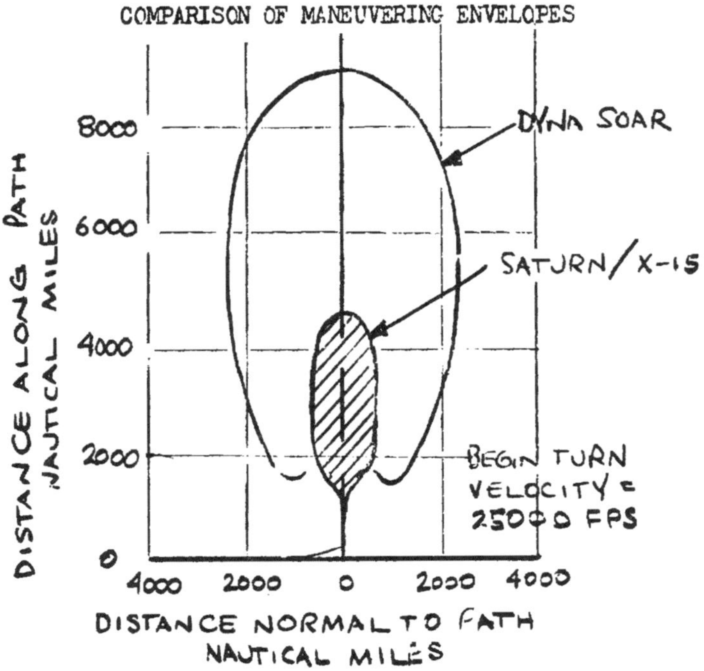

In the excitement caused by the Soviet launch of Sputnik, North American proposed a heavily modified X-15B as an early orbital vehicle. Although the aerodynamics of the X-15 were well-understood by this time, the X-15B did not have nearly the maneuverability of the Air Force Dyna-Soar while returning from orbit, and in fact, many X-15B proposals had the pilot ejecting over water instead of attempting to land. (North American Aviation)

for the basic X-15. It was a grand plan, and years ahead of its time. Unfortunately, when Storms got back from Washington he reported that "there were exactly 421" other people who had competing proposals. Eventually the X-15B just quietly faded from sight.[138]

Becker's Lament

Despite the variety of artists' concepts and popular press articles on an orbital X-15, in the end the new National Aeronautics and Space Administration (NASA) would decide to endorse a concept that had been initiated by the Air Force and use a small ballistic capsule for the first U.S. manned space program, renamed Mercury. Nevertheless, a small minority within NASA, mainly at Langley, continued to argue that lifting-reentry vehicles would be far superior to the non-lifting capsules. In fact, at the last NACA Conference on High-Speed Aerodynamics in March 1958, John Becker presented a concept for a manned 3,060-pound

138 Crossfield, *Always Another Dawn*, pp. 281-282, and 287. The "421" was undoubtedly an exaggeration by Storms or Crossfield, but the general sentiment was correct.

winged orbital satellite. According to Becker, this paper, which dissented from the consensus within the NACA favoring a ballistic capsule, created more industry reaction–"almost all of it favorable"–than any other he had ever written, including the initial X-15 study.[139]

What ruled out acceptance of his proposal, even more than the sheer momentum behind the capsules, was the fact that the 1,000 pounds of extra weight (compared to the capsule design presented by Max Faget) was beyond the capability of the Atlas ICBM. If the Titan had been further along, Becker's concept would have worked, but the simple fact was that Atlas was the only game in town. If it had all happened a year or two later, when the Titan became available, Becker believes that "the first U.S. manned satellite might well have been a [one-man] landable winged vehicle." The decision to adopt the capsule concept made the X-15 a dead end, at least temporarily. It would be a decade later when the aerospace community again decided that a winged lifting-reentry vehicle was feasible; the result would be the space shuttle.

There was one other orbital X-15 proposal. At the end of 1959, Harrison Storms presented a version of the X-15B launched using a Saturn I first stage and an "ICBM-type" second stage. According to Storms, "We figure the X-15, carrying two pilots...could be put into orbit hundreds of miles above the earth. Or with a scientific or military payload of thousands of pounds...into a lower orbit." Storms estimated that it would take three to four years of development and presented the idea to both the Air Force and NASA, but neither organization was interested. NASA was too busy with Mercury, and the Air Force was occupied with Dyna-Soar and fighting off Robert McNamara.[140]

MORE X-15S?

During the development of the X-15, many wanted to expand the program beyond the three airplanes covered under the original agreements. This opinion obviously did not prevail, but the proposals are nonetheless of passing interest. Early on, North American suggested using X-15 as part of an extensive training program for astronauts and test pilots, believing that such a program could familiarize pilots with rocket-powered aircraft, the use of reaction controls, and the physiological sensations of space flight. The Air Force did not express any particular interest.[141]

Early in 1958, researchers at the HSFS wanted to procure one additional X-15 for flight-control research, but NACA Headquarters did not concur. It was the first of several such proposals.[142]

---

139 James R. Hansen, *Engineer in Charge: A History of the Langley Aeronautical Laboratory–1917-1958*, NASA publication SP-4305 (Washington, DC: NASA, 1987), pp. 377-381. Becker quote from p. 381. The subject was confirmed in a telephone conversation, John V. Becker with Dennis R. Jenkins, 17 June 2001.

140 Ibid, pp. 374-375.

141 Letter, John W. Crowley, Associate Director for Research, NACA/Washington, to HSFS, 28 February 1958, subject: Flight control research for hypersonic airplanes. In the files at the DFRC History Office.

142 Ibid.

In mid-1958 the first serious proposal to expand the X-15 program came when Air Force Headquarters asked the ARDC if there was any merit to expanding the X-15 program. On 8 April 1958, headquarters requested recommendations for "configuration changes, estimated costs, aircraft availability, the increased performance expected, the test results to be obtained, and a brief substantiation of their value." Headquarters wanted the results of the study at an early date because it needed to make a decision before North American disbanded the engineering team.[143]

The X-15 Project Office asked the AFFTC, North American, and WADC for recommendations. By 29 April, these organizations concluded that the best approach would be to improve performance using new structural materials and an improved rocket engine instead of the XLR99. The development difficulties with the XLR99 apparently influenced the call for a new engine, although the WADC suggested that any new engine should "be obtained as a result of across the board BMD [Ballistic Missile Division] and other efforts, and not as a sole X-15 effort."[144]

The Navy verbally concurred with expanding the program on 19 May, and the NACA agreed a day later. On 13 June the X-15 Project Office recommended to the ARDC that three additional airplanes be constructed using higher-temperature structural materials than those used in the original design. The ARDC forwarded this recommendation to Air Force Headquarters on 16 June.[145]

Apparently, the seeming urgency in the 8 April letter from headquarters had evaporated. On 18 November 1958, Major General Marvin C. Demler, director of research and development at Air Force Headquarters, finally informed the ARDC that the X-15 program would not be expanded. In the interim, the Research Airplane Committee had met on 31 October and Hugh Dryden concluded the three original airplanes were adequate for NASA's purposes. Ultimately, the Research Airplane Committee recommended against procuring additional airplanes.[146]

There was, however, another fleeting prospect. After an explosion seriously damaged the X-15-3 during an XLR99 ground test, the X-15 Project Office had to solicit additional funds from the Pentagon to rebuild the aircraft. This prompted a renewed interest in the X-15 and the data it might deliver for future use in the Air Force space program. On 12 August 1960, Air Force Headquarters ordered a complete review of the X-15 program. The X-15 Project Office presented its results at the 17-18 October 1960 X-15 program review. The briefing identified original program objectives that were no longer valid, new objectives to consider, continuing objectives, and funding requirements. Surprisingly, the general officers who were briefed agreed that the X-15 promised to be considerably more important to the Air Force space effort than had been foreseen when the program was initially conceived in 1954, or when the program expansion was rejected in late 1958. The Pentagon advised the ARDC that it would "entertain" proposals for additional X-15s to be operated exclusively by the Air Force.

As part of the ongoing discussion, the AFFTC put together its own recommendation for the program. On 26 October 1960 the AFFTC released a report

143 X-15 WSPO Weekly Activity Report, 23 April 1958.

144 X-15 WSPO Weekly Activity Report, 2 May 1958.

145 X-15 WSPO Weekly Activity Report, 18 June 1958.

146 Letter, Major General Marvin C. Demler, Director of Research and Development, USAF, to Commander, ARDC, 18 November 1958, subject: Further Development of X-15 Aircraft. In the files at the Air Force Historical Research Agency.

that called for three additional X-15s and one more NB-52 "to carry out R&D objectives not presently covered by the present NASA-AF-Navy X-15 program." The AFFTC expected to "own and operate" these aircraft. Based on a 1 January 1961 start, the AFFTC expected the first aircraft to be delivered (along with a third NB-52) in September 1961, with the others following in March and June 1962. The flight program was to average 60 flights per year through December 1965. Some of the research objectives for the new aircraft included flight control and guidance, aero-thermo-elasticity, supersonic boundary-layer turbulence, sonic fatigue, landing-impact data, and electromagnetic propagation. The AFFTC expected that it would need an additional 330 people to support the X-15, plus 37 more to operate the High Range during AFFTC flights.[147]

Another proposal, originating from Brigadier General Donald R. Flickinger at ARDC Headquarters, was for a two-place biomedical research version of the airplane.[148]

The Air Force called a meeting at Wright Field on 14 November that brought together representatives from the ARDC, the WADC,[149] the command and control division of the Air Force Cambridge Research Laboratories, and the Army Corps of Engineers.[150] It was immediately apparent to the X-15 Project Office that if all of the stated requirements for X-15-type aircraft were to be satisfied, "several additional X-15s will be required." Two weeks earlier the government had notified North American of the meeting, and Charlie Feltz prepared a briefing outlining several advanced X-15 configurations. Feltz presented his briefing on the afternoon of 14 November and provoked further interest in a comprehensive extension program.[151]

Although a two-seat X-15 engineering study had been required in the original proposals, the government had not taken any action on the idea. Nevertheless, it loomed in the background during much of the early X-15 program. The variant shown during the November 1960 meeting differed somewhat from the one originally proposed. North American optimized this version for "space training and biomedical research." Instead of simply deleting the research instrumentation and extending the canopy over the second cockpit, the new configuration extended the fuselage by approximately 14 inches and added a second cockpit with a separate canopy. The company deleted the aero-thermo research equipment, but the extension provided space for a variety biomedical equipment.[152]

North American environmentally separated the second cockpit from the primary cockpit so that it could study alternate atmospheres (i.e., not nitrogen-

147 Memorandum, Lieutenant Colonel Harold G. Russell (interestingly, Russell was the director of the AFFTC Dyna-Soar Test Force), subject: Additional X-15 Aircraft Assigned to AFFTC, 26 October 1960. In the files at the AFFTC History Office.

148 Letter, USAF Headquarters to ARDC Headquarters, subject: X-15 Development Plan, 3 November 1960; "Advanced Development Plan for X-15 Research Aircraft, Advanced Technology Program 653A," 17 November 1961, p. 2. In the files at the AFFTC History Office; Geiger et al., "History of the Wright Air Development Division: July 1960-March 1961," pp. I-40 to I-42.

149 By this time, this was technically the Wright Air Development Division (WADD), not the WADC.

150 Exactly what the Army Corps of Engineers was doing there could not be ascertained. The Cambridge Research Laboratories are now the Electronic Systems Center at Hanscom AFB, MA.

151 Geiger et al., "History of the Wright Air Development Division: July 1960-March 1961," pp. I-40 to I-42; Charles H. Feltz, North American report NA-60-1, "X-15 Research Capability," 11 November 1960, no page numbers. In the files at the USAF Test Pilot School, Edwards AFB.

152 North American report NA-60-1.

purged). A separate set of dummy controls could be installed that would allow the second pilot to react independently from the pilot flying the aircraft. His responses would be recorded and reconstructed on the ground to evaluate performance under acceleration and weightless conditions. It was expected that flight profiles could be developed that would allow five minutes under essentially weightless conditions during flights to altitudes in excess of 500,000 feet. The change added 354 pounds to the aircraft, but the use of an uprated XLR99 would have increased performance by 120 fps.[153]

The meetings resulted in NASA rearranging the existing X-15 program slightly to accommodate the Air Force research priorities, and relegating excess work to the new research extension program. The product was a revised System 605A plan released on 1 February 1961. Essentially, the X-15 Project Office requested approval for the construction of two additional aircraft, both of them slightly stretched two-seat versions similar to one proposed by Charlie Feltz in November. For the moment, the question of additional single-seat aircraft or advanced models was not considered pressing and was deferred. The two-seat aircraft would satisfy the need for biomedical research and training of future aerospace research pilots and Dyna-Soar astronauts.[154]

The idea was short-lived. On 20 March 1961, Major General Marcus F. Cooper, chief of research and engineering at ARDC Headquarters, disapproved the development plan. Cooper instructed the X-15 Project Office to revise the existing (October 1960) development plan to reflect funding changes proposed by the Pentagon. Nevertheless, in one paragraph Cooper instructed Wright Field to "give consideration to the election of the best type of vehicle to use in training future Aerospace Research Pilots.... The possibility of using the existing X-15s for this purpose after completion of the test program should be explored. In addition the need for additional X-15 aircraft or other vehicles, such as Dyna-Soar, for this purpose should be considered." The concept could potentially require additional X-15s.[155]

Although this kept hopes alive for an expanded X-15 program, it essentially buried the two-seat X-15. As Cooper explained, funding shortages for FY61 and FY62 would prevent "the additional heavy funding required in those years to support the proposed additional X-15 aircraft." It had also become apparent that the existing X-15s, with some additional equipment and telemetry installations, could acquire the majority of the desired biomedical data at far less cost. The X-15 Project Office had also begun to worry that stretching the X-15 fuselage might involve more engineering and development work than anticipated, although the subsequent development of X-15A-2 proved this concern to be unfounded.[156]

The ARDC Commanders Program Management Review in March 1961 tasked the X-15 Project Office to review "identified problem areas which might

153 North American report NA-60-1.

154 Geiger et al., "History of the Wright Air Development Division: July 1960-March 1961," pp. I-42 to I-43.

155 Letter, Major General Marcus F. Cooper, DCS/R&E, ARDC, to Director, Systems Management, WADD, subject: Advanced Development Plan for X-15 Research Aircraft, System 605A, 20 February, 1961. The letter was dated 20 February, but the RDRA Endorsement was dated 20 March, marking the actual disapproval.

156 Letter, Major General Marcus F. Cooper, DCS/R&E, ARDC, to Director, Systems Management, WADD, subject: Advanced Development Plan for X-15 Research Aircraft, System 605A, 20 February, 1961; Geiger, "History of the Wright Air Development Division: July 1960-March 1961," pp. I-42 to I-43.

require investigation by X-15 type aircraft with particular attention given to the relationship between the problem areas and presently authorized advanced aerospace programs and studies." The response indicated that two additional single-place X-15s would be useful for investigating a variety of Air Force-specific areas of interest. The ARDC rejected this recommendation on 2 August 1961, and all thoughts of additional X-15s seemed to fade.[157]

COST OVERRUNS

Not surprisingly by today's standards, the original cost estimates for the X-15 and the XLR99 had been hopelessly optimistic. The first Air Force estimate for development and two airplanes totaled only $12,200,000. By the time the Air Force issued the letter contracts, the estimates stood at $38,742,500 for the airframe, $9,961,000 for the engine, and $1,360,000 for the High Range.

By the time the government and North American signed the final contract, the total cost had already risen to $40,263,709 plus $2,617,075 in fee. This had increased to $64,021,146 by the beginning of 1959. During the next six months, the estimates increased first to $67,540,178, then to $68,657,644, and by 1 June to $74,500,000–almost double the letter contract amount. The three airframes ended up costing $23.5 million; the rest represented research and development expenses.[158]

The engine was worse. In 1955 the Air Force estimated the engine costs would ultimately be about $6,000,000. The letter contract was for $9,961,000, and by the time the Air Force and Reaction Motors signed the final engine contract this had risen to $10,160,030, plus an additional $614,000 fee. At the end of FY58, the amount was over $38,000,000, and FY59 brought the total to $59,323,000. The cost for FY60 alone was $9,050,000. As of June 1959, the engine costs were $68,373,000–over five times the 1955 estimate for the entire program and almost a sevenfold increase over the initial Reaction Motors contract value. Each of the 10 "production" engines cost just over $1 million.[159]

While it was not nearly as bad as the engine, the stable platform ran significantly over budget as well. The original contract price was $1,213,518 plus an $85,000 fee. By May 1958, the cost had increased to $2,498,518 and a year later was at $3,234,188 plus $119,888 in fee. The auxiliary power units cost $2.7

157 Letter, X-15 Project office to ARDC Headquarters, subject: Procurement of two additional X-15 aircraft, 26 May 1961; letter, AFSC Headquarters to X-15 Project Office, subject: Procurement of two additional X-15 aircraft, 2 August 1961.

158 Cost projections, Contract AF33(600)-31693, prepared quarterly by North American Aviation Department of Pricing, 1955-59. In the files at the Boeing Archives; interview, Captain Chester E. McCollough, Jr., Assistant Chief, X-15 WSPO, Director of Systems Management, ARDC, 12 June 1959, by Robert S. Houston, History Branch, WADC. Written transcript in the files at the AFMC History Office; James E. Love and William R. Young, NASA technical note D-3732, 10 August 1966, p. 6.

159 Interview, Captain Chester E. McCollough, Jr., Assistant Chief, X-15 WSPO, Director of Systems Management, ARDC, 12 June 1959, by Robert S. Houston, History Branch, WADC. Written transcript in the files at the AFMC History Office; NASA technical note D-3732, p. 6.

million, the ball nose another $600,000, the MH-96 adaptive control system $2.3 million, and the David Clark full-pressure suits more than $150,000.[160]

During the first five years of development, the government spent $121.5 million on the X-15 program, not including laboratory and wind-tunnel testing at Wright Field, the Arnold Engineering Development Center, NADC Johnsville, and the various NACA/NASA laboratories. The funding was broken down as follows: [161]

	FY56	FY57	FY58	FY59	FY60	Total
Air Force	8.8	18.3	39.1	36.3	13.6	116.1
Navy	0.5	1.8	2.1	1.0	0.0	5.4
Total	**9.3**	**20.1**	**41.2**	**37.3**	**13.6**	**121.5**

Together with approximately $11,500,000 for the High Range, it was obvious that the cost of the X-15 project was going to exceed $150,000,000 before the flight program got underway. When the original development and manufacturing contracts were closed out in FY63 (replaced by sustaining engineering and support contracts), the total came to $162.8 million. By the time it was all over in 1968, the total would almost double when all operational costs and modifications were included. Most published comparisons use the final program cost of approximately $300 million, but this is an unfair comparison to the original $12.2 million because the scope was extremely different.[162]

160 James E. Love and William R. Young, "Operational Experience of the X-15 Airplane as a Reusable Vehicle System," a paper presented at the SAE Second Annual Space Technology Conference, Palo Alto, CA, 9-11 May 1967, p. 3; NASA technical note D-3732, p. 6. The cost of the MH-96 was just that portion charged to the X-15 program; other parts were paid for by the Dyna-Soar program.

161 [signed W.T.G.] "X-15: The World's Fastest and Highest-Flying Aeroplane," *Flight*, 8 May 1959.

162 Love and Young, "Operational Experience of the X-15 Airplane as a Reusable Vehicle System," p. 3; NASA technical note D-3732, p. 6. The cost of the MH-96 was just that portion charged to the X-15 program; other parts were paid for by the Dyna-Soar program. The original $12.2 million included a flight program to achieve "a few" flights at the design speed and altitude, not the extensive experimental research program that was actually flown. To compare apples to apples, it would probably be fair to compare this with the $162.8 million expended up through FY63–still a huge overrun by any standard.

CHAPTER 7

THE FLIGHT PROGRAM

By January 1958, everything had moved into high gear and North American was assembling the three model NA-240 airplanes at its facility in Inglewood, adjacent to the Los Angeles International Airport. The company had released over 6,000 engineering drawings–including one that was 50 feet long–by the end of 1957, although it continued to make minor changes to the configuration. North American subcontracted about 200 items to various vendors, but manufactured the majority of the airplane on the premises.[1]

ROLLOUT

On 15 October 1958, North American rolled out the first X-15 (56-6670) in Inglewood to great pomp and circumstance. It was ironic, in a way. The NACA had given birth to a concept and had nurtured the X-15 for over four years, but two weeks earlier the committee itself had ceased to exist. In its place, the National Aeronautics and Space Administration (NASA) was created effective 1 October

1 Scott Crossfield, *Always Another Dawn: The Story of a Rocket Test Pilot* (New York: The World Publishing Company, 1960), p. 289.

X-15-1 was presented during the roll-out ceremony. The air-data boom on the nose would be used until the ball nose was ready. The bug-eye camera ports located behind the canopy and under the fuselage in the center-of-gravity compartment would provide some breathtaking views of the early flights courtesy of National Geographic. (North American Aviation).

1958. The X-15 had been the largest development program at the NACA; it would soon be one of the smallest at a moon-destined NASA.

The master of ceremonies at the rollout was Raymond H. Rice, vice president and general manager of the Los Angeles division of North American Aviation. The keynote speakers included Major General Victor R. Haugen, deputy commander of the ARDC; Brigadier General Marcus F. Cooper, commander of the AFFTC; Walt Williams, chief of the HSFS; and Harrison Storms, chief engineer for the Los Angeles division. Also in attendance were six future X-15 pilots: Neil A. Armstrong, A. Scott Crossfield, John B. McKay, Captain Robert A. Rushworth, Joseph A. Walker, and Captain Robert M. White.[2]

Congressmen and senators sat in the grandstands and Vice President Richard M. Nixon was on hand to proclaim that the X-15 had "recaptured the U.S. lead in space." There were special exhibits featuring a David Clark full-pressure suit and a mockup of the Reaction Motors XLR99 engine. Guests could sit in the X-15 fixed-base simulator, and attend a gala luncheon where everybody praised the efforts of all involved. For the X-15 team it was a moving occasion and a much-needed respite from the years of hard work.[3]

Bob White, the man who felled every Mach number and altitude milestone in the X-15, later remembered eloquently, "The X-15 … was in the public eye from its inception and grew almost asymptotically from the day of its manufacture. Witness the presence of the vice president of the United States at the X-15 rollout ceremony. The X-15 was not controversial; it was audacious. It literally vibrated the imagination that this aircraft would double the fastest speed by more than three whole Mach numbers and … fly out of the atmosphere, into space, and back again to an on-Earth landing. The X-15 did these things and many more …."[4]

2 Raymond H. Rice, "The X-15 Rollout Symposium," 15 October 1958. Released statements in the files of the AFFTC History Office.

3 Crossfield, *Always Another Dawn*, pp. 303-304. The Nixon quote is as Crossfield remembered it on page 303.

4 "The Pilot's Panel," a paper in the *Proceedings of the X-15 30th Anniversary Celebration*, Dryden Flight Research Facility, Edwards, CA, 8 June 1989, NASA CP-3105, p. 145.

The space race had already begun, and the United States was eager to show any progress toward besting the Soviet accomplishments. Newspapers, magazines, and newsreels all heralded the X-15 as the American entry in the space race. Considering that only four years earlier researchers had wanted to remove the "space leap" from the X-15 concept, it was ironic that many now portrayed this small black airplane as America's response to the Soviet threat. It may have been small, but it had not come cheaply. Despite the original $12,200,000 estimate prepared by the WADC in 1954, at the time of the rollout Major General Haugen estimated that the government had spent nearly $120 million–and the airplane had not yet flown.[5]

Haugen also pointed out that the X-15 rollout was taking place two weeks ahead of the schedule established in June 1956, calling this "a tribute to all of the government and industry team." The general then summed up the spirit of the program: "It has been said that there are two extremes to research or exploratory flying–the approach that, for example, would strap a man on an ICBM and see what happens, and the super safe approach that would have us take tiny steps into the unknown and be absolutely sure of each step. We believe the solution is neither of these but rather a bold step into the future within the known technical capabilities of our engineers. We believe that the X-15 represents such a bold step … that will help us build better air and space vehicles in the future."[6]

Perhaps because his base would host the flight testing, Brigadier General Cooper was a little more cautious in his remarks: "I wish to point out here that this research program will be one of long duration, and the type of flights which

Given the recent successes of the Soviets with Sputnik, the rollout of the X-15 was considered sufficiently important for the vice president of the United States to show up. Richard M. Nixon presided over the ceremonies along with distinguished speakers from the Air Force and the state of California. (North American Aviation)

5 Cost estimate from Victor R. Haugen, "The X-15 Rollout Symposium," 15 October 1958. Released statements in the files of the AFFTC History Office. Ironically, as a colonel, Haugen was the director of the WADC laboratories when the NACA proposal that eventually became the X-15 was evaluated, and he concurred with the original $12,200,000 estimate for the project.

6 Major General Victor R. Haugen, "The X-15 Rollout Symposium," 15 October 1958. Released statements in the files of the AFFTC History Office.

excite the imagination and make newspaper headlines are many, many months away." However, the general could not resist riding the space bandwagon, at least a little, by calling the program "the first major breakthrough in sustained piloted space flight."[7]

Not to be outdone, Stormy Storms was even more direct: "The rollout of the X-15 marks the beginning of man's most advanced assault on space. This will be one of the most dramatic, as in the X-15 we have all the elements and most of the problems of a true space vehicle." Describing the potential performance of the airplane, Storms said, "The performance of the X-15 is hard to comprehend. It can out fly the fastest fighters by a factor of three, a high-speed rifle bullet by a factor of two, and easily exceed the world altitude record by many times."[8]

Following the conclusion of the official ceremonies, North American moved the first X-15 back inside and prepared it for delivery. On the night of 16 October, covered completely in heavy-duty wrapping paper, X-15-1 traveled overland by truck through the Los Angeles foothills to Edwards for initial ground-test work.

FLIGHT PROGRAM OVERVIEW

The primary objective of the flight program was to explore the hypersonic flight regime and compare the results against various analytical models and wind-tunnel results. The physical X-15 configuration was of only passing interest and was not an attempt to define what any future operational aircraft might look like; it was simply a means to obtain the necessary thermal environment and dynamic pressures. The researchers wanted to understand heating rates, stagnation points, laminar and turbulent flow characteristics, and stability and control issues. Later, the X-15 would become a carrier for various experiments, and the airplane configuration would be of even less interest.

During the 10 years of operations, five major aircraft were involved in the X-15 flight program. The three X-15s were designated X-15-1 (Air Force serial number 56-6670), X-15-2 (56-6671), and X-15-3 (56-6672). The second airplane became X-15A-2 after North American extensively modified it following an accident midway through the flight program. The two carrier aircraft were an NB-52A (52-003) and an NB-52B (52-008); although not identical, they were essentially interchangeable.[9]

The program used a three-part designation for each flight. The first number represented the specific X-15 ("1" was for X-15-1, etc.). There was no differentia-

7 Brigadier General Marcus F. Cooper, "The X-15 Rollout Symposium," 15 October 1958. Released statements in the files of the AFFTC History Office.

8 Harrison Storms, "The X-15 Rollout Symposium," 15 October 1958. Released statements in the files of the AFFTC History Office.

9 Contrary to many sources, the basic X-15s never carried an "A" suffix (i.e, they were "X-15" not "X-15A"). During the 1950s it was not unusual for the first development model of an aircraft to not carry a suffix (e.g., YF-102, YF-105, etc.). The "A" was applied to the first major modification of the design (in this case the rebuilt X-15A-2). It should also be noted that according to the DoD designation system, the number after the designation was normally reserved for a "production block" number that was used to track minor changes on the production line. In the case of the X-15, that was not strictly true, and each airplane was simply numbered sequentially.

tion between the original X-15-2 and the modified X-15A-2. The second position was the flight number for that specific X-15 (this included free flights only, not captive carries or aborts); the first flight was 1, the second was 2, etc. If the flight was a scheduled captive carry, the second position in the designation was a C; if it was an aborted free-flight attempt, it was an A. The third position was the total number of times that either NB-52 had carried aloft that particular X-15, including captive carries, aborts, and actual releases. A letter from Paul Bikle established this system on 24 May 1960 and retroactively redesignated the 30 flights that had already been accomplished.[10]

FLIGHT DESCRIPTION

X-15 flights did not begin with a pilot waking up and deciding he wanted to fly that day. Weeks or months before, a researcher would develop requirements for data gathered under specific conditions. One of the flight planners (Johnny Armstrong, Dick Day, Bob Hoey, Jack Kolf, or John Manke, among others) would take these requirements and lay out a flight plan that defined the entire mission. The term "flight planner" does not begin to describe the expertise of the engineers who performed this function. These engineers lived in the simulator and were experts on the airplane. They determined the thrust settings, climb angles, pushover times, and data-gathering maneuvers; they also evaluated stability and control issues and heating concerns. In addition to laying out specific flights, the flight planners performed parametric studies that were not related to a particular flight or pilot training. Some of these included glide performance, peak altitude versus pitch angle, speed-optimization techniques, and reentry trades involving dynamic pressure, load factors, angle of attack, and temperatures.[11]

The flight planners would then present their plan to the pilot selected for the flight. The flight planners and the pilot would spend the next week or month, depending on the complexity of the mission, in the simulator choreographing every second of the flight. After extensive practice with the nominal mission, the pilot flew off-design missions to acquaint himself with the overall effect of changes in critical parameters, including variations in engine thrust or engine shutdown times.[12]

At this point, the primary ground controller (called "NASA-1") joined the flight planners and pilot for additional simulations so that they could all become familiar with the general timing of the flight. After practicing the off-design missions, the team evaluated various anomalous situations, including failures of the

10 Memorandum, Paul F. Bikle to NASA Headquarters (RSS/Mr. H. Brown), subject: X-15 flight designation, 24 May 1960. In the files at the DFRC History Office. The 30 flights included 13 carries of X-15-1 that had resulted in eight free flights, and 17 carries of X-15-2 that also had resulted in eight free flights.

11 Letter, Johnny G. Armstrong to Dennis R. Jenkins, 5 July 2002; letter, Robert G. Hoey to Dennis R. Jenkins, 12 August 2002.

12 Letter, Johnny G. Armstrong to Dennis R. Jenkins, 5 July 2002; Robert G. Hoey and Richard E. Day, "X-15 Mission Planning and Operational Procedures," a paper in the *1961 Research Airplane Committee Report*, pp. 158-159. (This paper was later published as NASA technical note D-1159, March 1962.)

engine, stable platform, ball nose, radio and dampers, and variations in the stability derivatives. For instance, the flight planners would insert simulated premature engine shutdowns at critical points to acquaint the pilot with the optimum techniques for returning to the lake behind him or flying to an alternate lake ahead of him. Normally the failure of the velocity or altitude instrument would not affect a flight; however, in the event of an attitude presentation failure during the exit phase of an altitude mission, the pilot had to initiate an immediate pushover from about 30 degrees pitch attitude to 18 degrees so that he could visually acquire the horizon. Failures of the ball nose were usually not terminal since the pilot could still fly the mission using normal acceleration, attitudes, and stabilizer-position indications, but the results were not as precise. Radio failure meant the pilot had to be self-sufficient–an undesirable situation, but not a tremendous problem for most test pilots.[13]

A simple flight would encompass 15–20 hours of simulator time, and a complex mission could easily double that. Given that each flight was only 8–10 minutes long, this represented a lot of training. By far, these were the most extensive mission simulations attempted during the X-plane program, and would point the way to how the manned space program would proceed. Although the drill at times seemed tedious and time-consuming to all involved, it undoubtedly played a major role in the overall safety and success of what was unquestionably a potentially dangerous undertaking. All of the pilots praised the flight planners and the simulators, and nobody believes the program would have succeeded nearly as well without it. Milt Thompson later observed, "[W]e were able to avoid many pitfalls because of the simulation. It really paid off. I personally do not believe that we could have successfully flown the aircraft without a simulation, particularly in regard to energy management." Simulation and mission planning are some of the enduring legacies of the X-15 program.[14]

FLIGHT DAY

X-15 flights generally began early in the morning; indeed, most flight-testing at Edwards began early in the morning when the temperatures and winds in the high desert were lower. The ground crew had mated the X-15 to the NB-52 the day before and stayed all night or arrived early to prepare the airplane for the flight. Floodlights lit the scene as propellants and gases were loaded onto both the carrier aircraft and research airplane, and liquid-oxygen vapor drifted around the area, lending a surreal fog. When the X-15 pilot arrived, he generally went straight to the physiological support van to get into the David Clark full-pressure suit. Getting the suit on and hooking up the biomedical instrumentation took

13 Hoey and Day, "X-15 Mission Planning and Operational Procedures," pp. 159-160; letter, Robert G. Hoey to Dennis R. Jenkins, 12 August 2002.

14 Thompson, *At the Edge of Space*, p. 70.

about 15 minutes once the program switched to the A/P22S-2 suits; the MC-2 suits had taken considerably longer.[15]

When the ground crew was ready for the pilot to enter the cockpit, two technicians carried a portable cooling system and other equipment while they escorted the pilot from the van to the airplane–a scene vaguely similar to Cape Canaveral before a space flight. Oddly, the driver of the physiological support van in which the pilot donned the pressure suit made no particular effort to park near the X-15, forcing the pilot to walk across the ramp. A large ladder and platform were located alongside the X-15 to allow the pilot and his handlers easy access to the cockpit. The cockpit itself was large for a single-seat airplane, but the bulk of the pressure suit made it seem somewhat smaller. Nevertheless, most pilots found it had more than adequate room and some of the smaller pilots even had difficulty reaching all of the controls mounted far forward, since the seat was not adjustable. Once the pilot was in the cockpit, the ground crew hooked up a myriad of lines, hoses, and straps that provided life support and monitored the pilot's biomedical data. While this was happening, the pilot began going through the preflight checklist to verify the status of all the aircraft systems. Once this was completed (usually a 30-minute process), the ground crew closed the X-15 canopy. The cockpit suddenly seemed smaller since the canopy fit snugly around the pressure-suit helmet.

While this was happening, the ground crew was disconnecting the servicing carts used to prepare the NB-52 and X-15 for flight. At this point, the NB-52 started its engines and the carrier aircraft pilots went through their preflight checklist, taking about 10 minutes to complete the activity. The ground crew then closed up the NB-52 hatches and the mated pair taxied toward the runway accompanied by a convoy of a dozen or so vehicles. Edwards is a large base, and the aircraft had to taxi for 2 or 5 miles depending on which runway was active. One of the H-21 helicopters took off and performed a visual check of the runway to make sure no debris was present, then took up a position beside and slightly behind the bomber, preparing to follow it down the runway for as long as possible.

At the end of the runway, the ground crew removed the safety pins from the X-15 release hooks. When everybody signaled they were ready, the NB-52 took off and climbed to 25,000 feet while circling over Edwards to make sure the X-15 could make an emergency landing on Rogers Dry Lake. Once above 25,000 feet, the NB-52 turned toward the launch lake and began climbing to 45,000 feet, since at this altitude the X-15 could glide to an alternate lakebed if necessary. The NB-52 supply topped off the X-15 liquid-oxygen tank, and the inertial platform was receiving alignment data, but otherwise things were quiet. Chase-1 flew in formation with the B-52, observing the X-15 for leaks or other anomalies that might signal a potential problem.

The mission rules dictated that if a serious problem occurred on the NB-52 while the mated pair was on the way to the launch lake, the carrier aircraft would jettison the research airplane since the extra 30,000 pounds of dead weight under the right wing would undoubtedly be detrimental to saving the NB-52. Similarly, if something happened on the X-15 that looked like it would endanger the NB-52, the research airplane would be jettisoned. As Scott Crossfield later observed, "It

15 Letter, Johnny G. Armstrong to Dennis R. Jenkins, 5 July 2002.

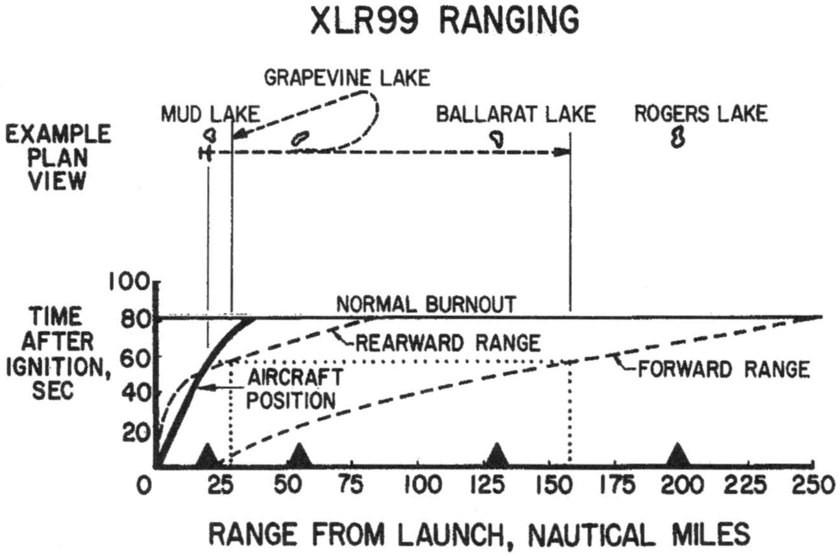

The need for the various lakebeds was largely driven by a program requirement to always have a landing site available to the X-15 pilot if he needed it for any reason. Therefore, each flight was planned such that the X-15 could glide to an emergency landing site from any point on the flight path, although frequently the nearest site was behind the airplane and required the pilot to turn around, as illustrated in this drawing. The program used the emergency landing sites 10 times. (NASA)

was not heroics; it was simple mathematics. Better to lose one man than four." In reality, the X-15 stood a chance of surviving if it was jettisoned, especially if the X-15 pilot had some advanced notice. The major problem was that neither of the APUs aboard the X-15 was running during captive carry since there was not enough propellant to last more than about 30 minutes. During the climb-out, the NB-52 supplied all of the X-15's electrical needs, as well as breathing oxygen and pressurization gas. If the carrier aircraft jettisoned the X-15, the pilot would have his hands full trying to get the APUs started using a small emergency battery since without the APUs the pilot had no flight controls, no radio, no anything. If the APUs started, the pilot could try to fly (with or without the engine) to a lakebed. Of course, the ejection seat was always an option. Fortunately, the program never had to find out what would happen in that scenario.[16]

At 12 minutes before the scheduled launch time, things began to happen. The X-15 pilot started both APUs and began to run through the prelaunch checklists. The pilot checked all of the X-15 systems, exercised the flight controls, tested the ballistic control system, and set all switch positions. Chase-1 observed the results of these tests and reported them back to the X-15 pilot. During this time, radar and radio communication with NASA-1 guided the carrier aircraft into position near

16 Thompson, *At the Edge of Space*, pp. 186-187; Scott Crossfield, during an interview in the NBC documentary film *The Rocket Pilots*, 1989.

the launch lake. Eight minutes before launch the NB-52 began a long sweeping turn back toward Edwards, coming onto the final heading about 4 minutes later. At the same time, the X-15 pilot began activating the propulsion system. At 2 minutes prior to launch the X-15 pilot started the data recorders, checked the ball nose one last time, and turned on the cameras. One minute prior to launch the XLR99 was set to precool and the igniter was set to idle. More checks were performed to make sure the engine looked ready to fire. The X-15 pilot took a deep breath.[17]

Three, two, one: launch. The X-15 separated from the NB-52 and began to fall. The launch was harder than most pilots initially expected because the X-15 went from normal 1-g flight while attached to the carrier aircraft to 0-g flight instantaneously. The X-15 also wanted to roll to the right because of downwash from the NB-52 wing and interference from the fuselage. The X-15 pilots usually had left roll input applied at the moment of launch, but the airplane still rolled—more so on some occasions than others.

The XLR99 start sequence was remarkably simple, a necessary attribute in the days before computerized control systems. The first step was to pressurize the propellant tanks with gaseous helium to ensure a smooth flow of propellants to the turbopump. Then the oxidizer system was precooled to ensure that the liquid oxygen did not vaporize between the propellant tank and the turbopump (vaporized liquid oxygen caused the turbopump to cavitate and go into an overspeed condition that resulted in an automatic shutdown). It required about 10 minutes to chill the oxidizer system. Next was the engine prime sequence that fed a small amount of liquid oxygen and ammonia to the turbopump. The igniter-ready light came on when the prime cycle began and the pilot turned on the igniter switch. This all happened before the X-15 dropped away from the NB-52. As the X-15 was falling, the pilot continued the engine start procedure. There were about 10 seconds available to light the engine before the pilot had to abort to the launch lake; that was time for two ignition attempts.[18]

Pressing the pump-idle button to start the turbopump initiated the ignition cycle. The turbopump spooled up quickly and forced propellants into the first-stage igniter, where a spark plug ignited them. The propellants were then fed into the second-stage igniter chamber, where the flame generated by the first-stage igniter caused them to combust. The second-stage igniter produced 1,500 lbf–as much as one chamber on the XLR11.

The throttle quadrant was a "backwards L" slot located on the left console. The outer corner was the "idle" position, the bottom inside corner of the L corresponded to minimum throttle, and the most forward position was 100% power. Moving the throttle inboard opened the main propellant valves and forced 30 gallons per second of propellants into the main chamber, where they were ignited by the flame from the second-stage igniter. The pilots found early in the flight program that the engine did not ignite reliably at low-power settings, so they usually immediately advanced the throttle to the 100% position. Although the XLR99 proved to be a remarkably reliable engine, it really did not like to throttle. Still, the capability provided a certain amount of research utility that would not otherwise have been

17 Letter, Robert G. Hoey to Dennis R. Jenkins, 12 August 2002.

18 Ibid.

available, although it also contributed to several in-flight emergencies when the engine decided it no longer wanted to work as its designers had intended.[19]

In an attempt to ensure that the entire propulsion system was in working order, NASA conducted a ground run before almost every flight. Although it was comforting to the X-15 pilot to know the engine indeed seemed to work, these tests also added a great deal of wear and tear to the engines and other systems. During ground runs, the pilot would allow the engine to stabilize at 100% thrust for 8 seconds, and then retard it to idle for 5 seconds before shutting the engine down. The pilot would then perform an emergency restart sequence that relit the main chamber at 75% thrust. The pilot would stabilize the engine for 5 seconds, reduce it to idle for a couple of seconds, and then shut it down. It all became routine.

Energy management started the instant the NB-52 released the X-15. If the XLR99 did not light in two attempts, the pilot would make an emergency landing at the launch lake. If the engine died within the first 30–40 seconds of flight, the pilot would turn around and make an emergency landing at the launch lake. After about 40 seconds of burn, the airplane would be too far away to make it back to the launch lake, but if the engine burned less than 70 seconds, it was unlikely the pilot could make it to Rogers Dry Lake. The 30-second period in between was why the program had a large assortment of intermediate lakebeds available.

Unfortunately, the technology did not exist to provide the pilot with an energy-management display, although NASA installed a rudimentary unit in X-15-3 toward the end of the flight program. It was up to the ground controller (NASA-1) to advise the pilot where to land if a problem developed during the flight. As flight attendants are fond of saying on every commercial airline flight, the nearest exit may be behind you. In many cases, the best landing site was an intermediate lake that the airplane had already passed at hypersonic velocities.

The intermediate lakes were more important for the high-speed flights than for the altitude flights. Given enough altitude, the X-15 could glide for over 400 miles–more than enough distance to make it back to Edwards from almost any point on the High Range. Every flight was supposed to have excess energy as the airplane arrived over Edwards, allowing some flexibility during the final approach. Nevertheless, part of why the program had an excellent safety record was that the pilots and flight planners always had contingency plans—even for the contingency plans.

Most X-15 flights were essentially in the vertical plane, and it was important to establish the proper heading back toward Edwards during the first 20 seconds after launch. Once the engine shut down, the ballistics was pretty well established for the next few minutes of flight. If there was a wind at the launch altitude (and usually there was), the NB-52 would crab as necessary to maintain the proper ground track during the final 10-minute turn. At 1 minute to launch, the NB-52 pilot would turn to the desired launch heading and allow the carrier aircraft to drift. Since winds at launch did not seriously affect the X-15 trajectory, this minimized the workload on the X-15 pilot to obtain, and hold, the desired heading. After launch, any necessary heading corrections were made by the X-15 pilot using small bank angles while performing a 2-g rotation and accelerating from Mach

19 Ibid.

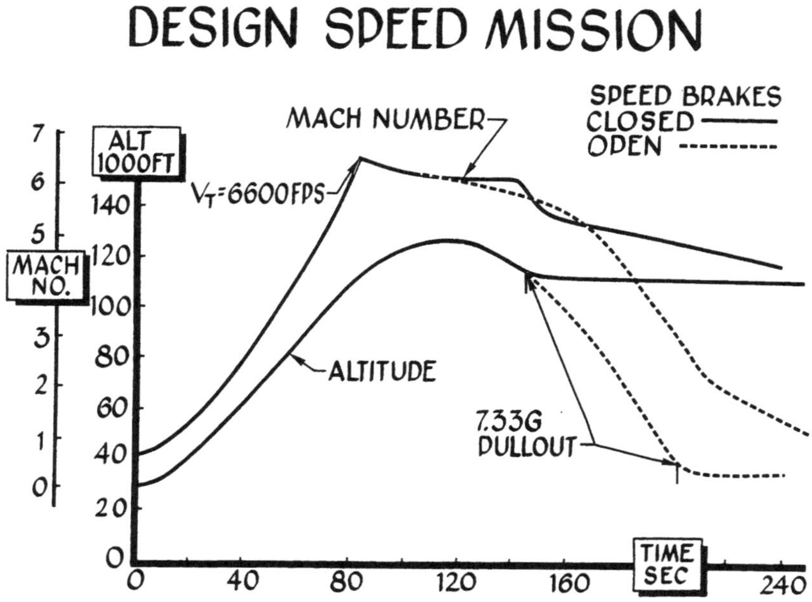

The design speed mission was flown at relatively low altitudes – from 100,000 to 110,000 feet. These were the essential heating flights that were used to validate the various theoretical and experimental (wind tunnel) results. The time at maximum speed was not spent flying straight and level since the pilot was conducting a series of rudder pulses and other maneuvers to optimize the heating on the side of the aircraft that was instrumented. The ability to exactly repeat these maneuvers from one flight to the next was critical for the ultimate success of the flight program and a tribute to the flying skills of the pilots. (NASA)

1 to 2 in about 20 seconds. Once the X-15 reached the desired pitch angle, the g-level was less than one, and no further turning corrections could be made until after completion of the reentry.[20]

The thrust from the XLR99 could be terminated by one of two routine ways at the nominal end of burn. The most frequently used method was called "shut-down." When a specific set of flight conditions had been reached, the pilot would manually shut down the engine. Normally the pilot did this after a precalculated amount of time based on a stopwatch in the cockpit that started when the main propellant valves opened. After NASA installed the X-20 inertial systems later in the program, the pilot could also use inertial velocity to shut down the engine, and several of the high-altitude flights used the altitude predictor installed in X-15-3. The other type of thrust termination was called "burnout." In this method the pilot just let the engine burn until the propellants were exhausted and the engine quit.[21]

20 E-mail, Robert G. Hoey to Dennis R. Jenkins, 19 August 2002; telephone conversation, William J. "Pete" Knight with Dennis R. Jenkins, 4 September 2002.

21 Letter, Johnny G. Armstrong to Dennis R. Jenkins, 5 July 2002; letter, Robert G. Hoey to Dennis R. Jenkins, 12 August 2002.

The high-speed flights were conducted at fairly low altitudes (a relative term since the altitudes would have been considered extraordinary before the X-15 program began). For these flights, the X-15 was essentially an airplane; its wings generated lift, maneuvering was accomplished via a set of aerodynamic control surfaces, and the atmosphere created a great deal of drag and friction on the airframe. The pilot would begin a 2-g rotation to the desired pitch angle immediately after the engine lit. During this rotation the primary piloting task was to adjust the bank angle to attain and hold the desired heading back to Edwards. As he approached 70,000 feet, the pilot initiated a gentle pushover to come level at something between 100,000 and 110,000 feet. As the airplane came level, the pilot either stabilized his speed at some preset value to conduct various research maneuvers, or continued to accelerate to attain more speed. The X-15 liked to accelerate; even at the top end, it took only 6 seconds to accelerate from Mach 5 to Mach 6. The research maneuvers continued after engine burnout until the airplane decelerated to the point that no more useful data were forthcoming. These were the essential heating flights.[22]

Altitude flights began much the same way, except that the pilot continued a steep climb out of the atmosphere. The engine shut down on the way up and the airplane coasted over the top on a ballistic trajectory. The pitch angle, in conjunction with the shutdown velocity, established both the range and maximum altitude of the arc that would follow. As the airplane continued on the ballistic trajectory, it was committed to a steep descent back into the atmosphere. The pilot set up the angle of attack for reentry, performed a pullout to level flight after reentry, and then began a shallow descent during the glide back to Rogers Dry Lake. A combination of dynamic pressure (q), load factor (g), and structural temperature limited the reentry since the relaxation of one parameter resulted in an excess of one of the others. These flights spent between 2 and 5 minutes outside the atmosphere, much of that time in a weightless (i.e., no accelerations) environment. The ballistic control system allowed the pilot to maintain attitude control, but he could not change the flight path of the airplane. Contrary to popular lore, as fast as it was, the X-15 never flew anywhere near fast enough to attain orbital velocities or altitudes.[23]

For the next few minutes, the calls from NASA-1 were primarily comparisons between the planned profile (on the plot boards) and the actual radar track of the airplane. These let the X-15 pilot know how well he had flown the exit phase and, more importantly, what maneuvers might be required during reentry. If he was "high and long," he would expect to make an immediate turn and apply the speed brakes during the latter part of the reentry. If he was "low and short," he would expect a straight-ahead glide with brakes closed. A "left of course" call would alert him to expect a right turn to a new heading after reentry. The ability to comprehend some of these energy-management subtleties while simultaneously controlling the aircraft's attitude and subsystems, and accomplishing test maneuvers was one of the goals of the X-15 simulator training.[24]

---

22 E-mail, Robert G. Hoey to Dennis R. Jenkins, 25 August 2002.

23 Letter, Johnny G. Armstrong to Dennis R. Jenkins, 5 July 2002; letter, Robert G. Hoey to Dennis R. Jenkins, 12 August 2002. Escape (orbital) velocity is generally considered to be 17,500 mph at altitudes over 93 miles to maintain even a marginally stable orbit.

24 E-mail, Robert G. Hoey to Dennis R. Jenkins, 25 August 2002.

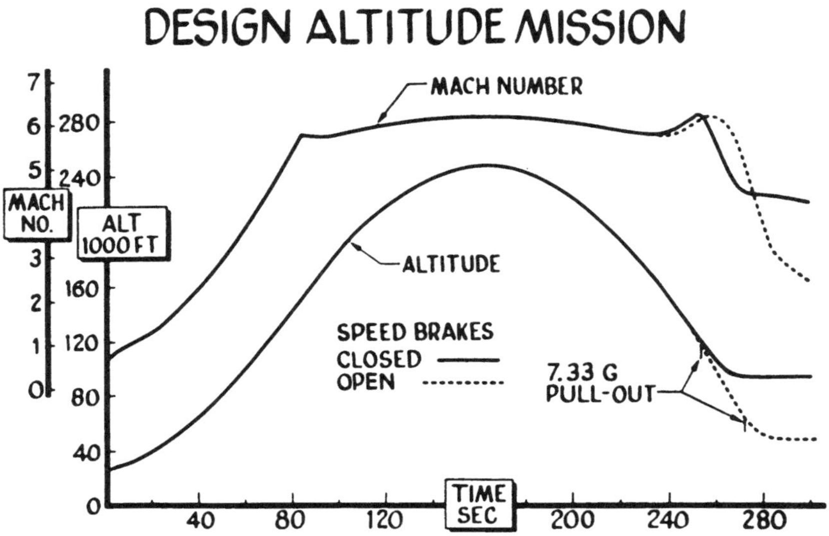

Surprisingly, the X-15 spent more time at higher Mach numbers during the altitude missions than it did during the speed missions. This is because there is less aerodynamic drag at high altitudes and the airplane coasted at high velocities for longer while it was outside the atmosphere. The altitude missions were particularly demanding on the pilot since even small deviations from the planned profile could result in overshooting the target altitude. The ballistic control system was required to control the attitude of the airplane during these missions, most of which were flown by X-15-3 since the MH-96 adaptive control system provided more redundancy. (NASA)

Perhaps surprisingly, the altitude flights required a longer ground track than the high-speed flights. This was primarily because the airplane covered many miles while it was outside the atmosphere. Let us use the two maximum performance flights as comparative examples. Joe Walker's 354,200-foot altitude flight required a ground track of 305 miles to climb out of the atmosphere, coast to peak altitude, reenter, make the pullout, and then slow to land. On the other hand, Pete Knight's 4,520-mph speed flight only took 225 miles, mainly because the airplane slowed quickly after engine burnout since the speed flights occurred in a relatively dense atmosphere.[25]

During the envelope expansion and heating flights, the pilots performed a specific set of maneuvers (rudder pulses, angle-of-attack changes, and rolls) to evaluate the stability and control of the airplane in various flight regimes. Many times these maneuvers were near the limits of controllability for the airplane, and well-practiced contingency plans were always at the ready. Other tests provided information on control effectiveness, aerodynamic performance, lift-to-drag ratio, and aero-thermo loads. All of these maneuvers required that the pilot fly at a

25 Joseph A. Walker, "Pilot Report for Flight 3-22-46," 22 August 1963; Major William J. Knight, "Pilot Report for Flight 2-53-97," 3 October 1967; Thompson, *At the Edge of Space*, p. 53; letter, Johnny G. Armstrong to Dennis R. Jenkins, 5 July 2002. Despite the thicker atmosphere, the speed brakes were frequently used to decelerate into the Edwards area on speed flights.

specific speed, attitude, and altitude while gathering the data. Often, the program needed to exactly duplicate the profile on subsequent flights to eliminate variables from the data, a decided challenge before the advent of computerized flight-control systems.[26]

As Milt Thompson later observed, "This is the kind of thing a research pilot is required to do to earn his money–accomplishing good maneuvers for data purposes. Flying the airplane is just something the pilot does to get the desired test maneuver. He can be the greatest stick and rudder pilot in the world, but if he cannot do the required data maneuvers, he is worthless as a research pilot." Most of the X-15 pilots were very good research pilots.[27]

Assuming all went as planned, the X-15 arrived back at Edwards and set up a high key (the highest point of the final approach to a runway) at approximately 35,000 feet and 290 to 350 mph. As he approached Edwards, the X-15 pilot began dumping any residual propellants to lower the landing weight and to get rid of potentially explosive substances. It also made a convenient way for the chase planes to find the small X-15 in the vast skies over the high desert. The X-15 then entered a 35-degree banking turn while maintaining 250 to 300 knots. The pilots normally turned to the left, although each pilot seemed to develop a preference, and it really did not matter much. At the completion of the turn, the X-15 was approximately 4 miles abeam of the intended touchdown point at 18,000 feet altitude headed in the opposite direction of the landing runway (this was low key). The pilot then continued around 180 degrees, turned onto final at about 8,000 feet and 300 knots, and flared at around 1,000 feet. The pilot jettisoned the ventral rudder, lowered the landing flaps as the airplane came level at about 100 feet, and deployed the landing gear at 215–225 knots. Touchdown was generally made at around 190–200 knots. The pilot judged the possible crosswinds by the simple expedient of looking at the smoke from flares beside the runway.[28]

Unsurprisingly, not all flights arrived at high key exactly as planned. At least one flight arrived at high key at 80,000 feet and over Mach 3.5, another made high key at only 25,000 feet, and one made a straight-in approach because it was too low on energy when it arrived at Edwards. Despite these variances, the majority of X-15 touchdowns were made within 2,000 feet of the intended spot, although a couple of flights missed by over 4,000 feet. Neil Armstrong managed to miss by 12 miles–fortunately, Rogers is a large dry lake. The X-15 generally slid for 8,000–10,000 feet before coming to a stop, chased by a convoy of rescue and support vehicles.[29]

The general concept was similar to that ultimately adopted as the terminal area energy-management maneuver used by the Space Shuttle. The proven ability of the X-15 (and later the heavyweight lifting bodies) to make unpowered approaches was one reason the Space Shuttle program decided it could eliminate the

---

26 Letter, Johnny G. Armstrong to Dennis R. Jenkins, 5 July 2002. A notable exception to this was flight 3-7-14, which was always intended as a record flight (that still stands today) although research data were also collected during the flight.

27 Thompson, *At the Edge of Space*, p. 53.

28 Letter, Johnny G. Armstrong to Dennis R. Jenkins, 5 July 2002. Even if the engine had been run to burnout, there were usually propellants left in the tanks since the sump system was not 100% effective, especially at some flight attitudes.

29 Letter, Johnny G. Armstrong to Dennis R. Jenkins, 5 July 2002; Radio transcript for flight 3-7-14, 17 July 1962. In the files at the DFRC History Office

complexity of landing engines and make the Orbiter a glider. It is another enduring legacy of the X-15 program.[30]

THE ORIGINAL CONTRACTOR PLAN

To make sure everything went as smoothly as possible, North American selected Q. C. Harvey to run its X-15 operations at Edwards. Harvey had come to the high desert a decade earlier to work on the odd McDonnell XF-85 Goblin, and then migrated to Bell to work on the X-1 program. He had joined North American in 1953 to work on the F-86 and later the F-100 and YF-107 programs. Considered a good manager with excellent technical skills, he also worked well with Scott Crossfield. In everybody's opinion, he was a good choice.[31]

According to the production contract, North American had to demonstrate each airplane's general airworthiness above Mach 2 before delivering it to the Air Force, which would then turn it over to NASA. Mach 3 and beyond were part of the government flight program. Initially, North American planned to demonstrate the basic capabilities of the first two airplanes using the XLR11 engines while the third airplane waited in Inglewood for the arrival of the XLR99. At this point, all three airplanes were essentially identical in configuration except for the engines–the MH-96 adaptive flight control system was not part of the plan yet. After the company checked out the first two airplanes, the government would use them for the envelope expansion tests and the research program. North American would then demonstrate X-15-3 with the XLR99 engine for a couple of flights before turning it over to the government. Once the government accepted the third airplane with the XLR99, North American would install the ultimate engine in the first two airplanes. North American would then fly one or two flights in each airplane with the XLR99 and turn them back over to the government.[32] It all seemed so simple.

This carefully orchestrated plan suffered a fatal blow in June 1960 when X-15-3 blew up on the Propulsion System Test Stand (PSTS) during a ground test of the XLR99. In the end, Scott Crossfield would fly one glide flight and one XLR11-powered flight in X-15-1 before turning the airplane over to the government. Crossfield made nine contractor flights in X-15-2 with the XLR11s, and three more with the XLR99 before North American turned that airplane over to the government. The company never flew X-15-3, and Neil Armstrong took the airplane for its first flight after North American finished rebuilding it after the XLR99 ground explosion.

---

30 Letter, Johnny G. Armstrong to Dennis R. Jenkins, 5 July 2002. Similar unpowered approaches were later demonstrated in the lifting-body program, usually landing on the concrete runway instead of a lakebed. The lifting-body contributions have received a great deal more attention in the popular press than the X-15 landings, which were arguably closer in profile.

31 Crossfield, *Always Another Dawn*, pp. 298-299.

32 At this point the XLR99 was often referred to as the "ultimate" engine or the "X-15 engine" to differentiate it from the "interim" XLR11s.

THE ORIGINAL GOVERNMENT PLAN

As North American continued to manufacture the three X-15s, personnel at the High Speed Flight Station (HSFS) began to plan how they would test the new airplane. During the admittedly brief history of the research airplane program, flight research had been conducted as a cooperative venture of varying degrees with the Air Force and/or Navy. Usually the contractor would first demonstrate the basic flight worthiness of the aircraft and then turn it over to the military service that had funded its development (the Air Force for the X-planes, or the Navy for the Douglas D-558 series). The military would then conduct a flight-envelope-expansion program with some NACA participation. For instance, the civilian agency normally supplied the instrumentation and research expertise. At some point after the military had obtained the data it desired, it would turn the airplanes over to the NACA, which then conducted a series of purely research-oriented flights to validate wind-tunnel and other predictive techniques. The flight tests at the HSFS had followed a predictable pattern. All flight operations, maintenance, instrumentation, data reduction, research engineering, reporting, and project control were accomplished by NACA personnel. The Air Force supplied support services such as engine overhaul, chase aircraft, carrier aircraft operations, and the usual air base functions (crash trucks, medical services, etc.).[33]

In the case of the X-15, the original memorandum of understanding signed by the members of the Research Airplane Committee stated simply that "upon acceptance of the airplane and its related equipment from the contractor, it will be turned over to the NACA, who shall conduct the flight tests and report the results of same." There was no provision in the MoU for Air Force flights. From experience, however, Walt Williams believed that the Air Force would want to conduct a program of its own. The Air Force substantiated this when it briefly proposed building a fourth airplane for the exclusive use of the AFFTC. The Research Airplane Committee, and others, did not agree and instead believed that the best arrangement would be to operate the three X-15s on a cooperative basis.[34]

The NACA was not sure it really wanted the Air Force to be involved in the flight program. The NACA in general, and Walt Williams in particular, had a severe lack of confidence in the Air Force based largely on the poor management of the X-2 envelope-expansion program, which had resulted in the loss of both airplanes and the death of Mel Apt. It was a long and uphill battle for the AFFTC to establish a relationship wherein the HSFS management would appreciate the necessity for AFFTC support, and thus the need to allow some level of AFFTC participation.[35] It eventually succeeded.

As the flight program neared, the Air Force wanted to formalize the responsibilities delegated to each organization. The AFFTC, in particular, wanted to expand its role, and expressed on several occasions a desire to change the original

33 Memorandum, Walter C. Williams to Hugh L. Dryden, subject: NACA-Air Force cooperation program, X-15 airplanes, 5 June 1957. In the files at the NASA History Office.

34 Ibid.

35 Letter, Robert G. Hoey to Dennis R. Jenkins, 12 August 2002.

MoU. Failing to do that, the AFFTC rather arbitrarily assigned itself the duties of operating the Rocket Engine Test Facility and the carrier aircraft. Williams did not consider this "of any serious consequence" since similar arrangements had worked satisfactorily in the past.[36]

On 24 May 1957, Walt Williams met with Captain Iven C. Kincheloe, Jr., who was designated to be the first Air Force X-15 pilot, and Richard J. Harer, the AFFTC X-15 project engineer, to discuss the division of responsibilities for the X-15 program. Paul F. Bikle, the AFFTC technical director, was unable to attend. Williams, true to form, bluntly asked the Air Force representatives exactly what the Air Force's desires were. Kincheloe stated that the AFFTC would like to take over the entire job—it wanted everything it could get. On the other hand, Kincheloe stated that he did not believe the AFFTC personnel were technically qualified to conduct such a program, and as a result they wanted to work with the NACA. The underlying tone was that the AFFTC personnel felt uninformed on the progress of the program, something Williams indicated that he would try to correct. All in attendance agreed, however, that Edwards should present a unified view to the outside world, and that the AFFTC and HSFS should internally coordinate their answers before publicly announcing them.[37]

Actually, the two groups had already taken this tack during the mockup inspection. Engineers from the AFFTC and HSFS had met prior to and again during the inspection to discuss what items needed to be changed. Several other items, particularly the switch from a B-36 to a B-52 carrier aircraft, had also resulted from pre-coordinated joint action. In spite of this, the AFFTC representatives still felt that they were not receiving sufficient consideration on the program and wanted a more formal agreement finalized.[38]

This led to a discussion of missions and objectives. The AFTTC pointed out that it wanted its engineering staff to benefit from active participation in the entire program. This would allow the Air Force engineers to become familiar with advanced technology for evaluating future weapons systems, which was, after all, their primary job. Of particular concern was that the NACA was specifying the research instrumentation without AFFTC input. Williams pointed out that the main reason NASA had not consulted AFFTC personnel concerning instrumentation was that they lacked the experience to make any significant contributions. Indeed, the researchers at the HSFS were largely dependent on the scientists at Langley and Lewis for advice since nobody had ever designed instrumentation to measure the aero-thermo environment expected for the X-15.[39]

At the end of the meeting, Williams pointed out that the NACA was primarily responsible for research into structures, handling qualities, and flight techniques, and therefore needed to have the primary responsibility for the X-15 program. This had been the rationale behind the original MoU. Nevertheless, Williams was

36 Memorandum, Walter C. Williams to Hugh L. Dryden, subject: NACA-Air Force cooperation program, X-15 airplanes, 5 June 1957. In the files at the NASA History Office.

37 Ibid. Paul Bikle would eventually replace Walt Williams as the director of the newly renamed NASA Flight Research Center.

38 Ibid.

39 Ibid.

smart enough to know that he needed the support of the AFFTC personnel, and besides, many of their observations were valid–they needed to be involved in the program in order to sharpen their skills for evaluating future weapons systems. Much more so than NASA, the NACA existed primarily to provide data that were useful to the industry and the military services that paid most of the bills.[40]

In an attempt to satisfy everybody concerned, Williams agreed to set up the X-15 Flight Test Steering Committee as a logical successor to similar committees used on previous programs. However, Williams emphasized that the NACA "had no intention whatsoever" of relinquishing the technical direction of the program per the original MoU. To ensure that this was the case, Williams appointed himself chairman of the committee and reserved the controlling vote. Other members of the committee were the AFFTC X-15 project engineer, the HSFS X-15 project engineer, and a test pilot from each organization. Initially the NACA personnel were Kenneth S. Kleinknecht, Joseph A. Walker, and Hubert M. Drake, respectively; Richard Harer, Iven Kincheloe, and an undetermined engineer represented the Air Force. The Air Force's Paul Bikle would act as an advisor to the committee, somewhat countering Williams and his unilateral veto authority. It was the beginning of a long association between Bikle and the X-15.[41]

Walt Williams wrote a letter to Hugh Dryden on 5 June 1957 explaining his reasons for setting up the committee. It took four months for Dryden to respond formally, but when he did, Dryden cautioned Williams not to exceed the scope of his authority: "Any major changes in the scope or intent of the [X-15] program have to be cleared with NACA Headquarters. It is presumed there are similar restrictions on the [Air Force] Flight Test Center. It should be understood at the outset, therefore, that the steering committee would have jurisdiction only in regard to matters that would normally come under the jurisdiction of the Flight Test Center or the High-Speed Flight Station." At the same time, Dryden wrote to Lieutenant General Donald L. Putt on 2 October 1957 indicating he had authorized Williams to participate in such a committee, and urged Putt to authorize the AFFTC to participate. Eventually this group morphed into the X-15 Joint Operations Committee and was responsible for coordinating most of the X-15 flight program. Some references indicate that the Navy had membership on the X-15 Joint Operations Committee.[42]

Soon after Dryden wrote this, the Soviet Union launched *Sputnik*, diverting the attention of Headquarters elsewhere. At the end of 1957, NASA disbanded the Interlaboratory Research Airplane Projects Panel; for the next decade, over-

---

40 Ibid.

41 Ibid; "Advanced Development Plan for X-15 Research Aircraft, Advanced Technology Program 653A," 17 November 1961, pp. 19-20. In the files at the AFFTC History Office. See the letter from Dryden to Putt, 2 October 1957 in the files at the DFRC History Office. A copy of the letter was sent to Brigadier General Marcus F. Cooper at the AFFTC over the signature of Colonel W. Gordon Duncan some time later. A copy is in the files at the AFFTC History Office. Kenneth S. Kleinknecht started his career in 1942 at the Lewis Research Center after graduating from Purdue University with a B.S. in mechanical engineering. In 1951, Kleinknecht transferred to the Flight Research Center. After NASA was formed, he transferred to the Manned Spacecraft Center in 1959. Before being named the manager of Project Mercury, Kleinknecht was active in the National Air Races, served as supervisor for a number of avionics tests at Lewis, and was the Head of the Project Engineering Station for the X-1E. Additionally, Kleinknecht served on the X-15 project and as the technical assistant to the director of the Manned Spacecraft Center. Some documentation calls the original committee the HSFS-FTC Steering Committee. In addition, some sources also call this the X-15 Joint Operating Committee (instead of "operations").

42 Letter, Hugh L. Dryden to Walter C. Williams, no subject, 2 October 1957; letter Hugh L. Dryden to Lieutenant General Donald L. Putt, subject: new flight test steering committee, 2 October 1957.

sight for the X-15 would come from the Research Airplane Committee run by Hugh Dryden.

Although the development of the X-15 had carried the System 644L designation, the initial flight program was designated System 605A. An R&D project card was prepared that outlined the extent of the test series, as well as the anticipated funding requirements. At the time, the AFFTC optimistically expected that 300 flights would be made over a five-year period beginning in July 1959 from air-launch sites located above Cuddeback Lake, Silver Lake, Mud Lake, Jakes Lake, and the Bonneville Salt Flats. The anticipated funding was $2,400,000 in FY60, $2,386,000 in FY61, and $2,325,000 for each of the next three years.[43]

The X-15 Joint Operations Committee coordinated the flight program and could call on support from other organizations as needed. The FRC was responsible for the maintenance and logistics of the three X-15s, while the AFFTC maintained the two NB-52s. An exception to this was that the FRC maintained the unique launch equipment on the NB-52s. Technically, flying the NB-52s was a joint project, but in reality a NASA pilot never flew the airplanes; the FRC did, however, supply the launch panel operators. NASA was responsible for data collection and analysis, with support from the Air Force as needed (or desired by the Air Force). All aircraft instrumentation, as well as High Range operation and maintenance, was the responsibility of NASA. The AFFTC was responsible for the biomedical instrumentation package, and maintained the David Clark full-pressure suits and rescue apparatus (parachutes, etc.). The Air Force provided most support aircraft (C-130s, H-21s, and chase aircraft), although NASA began to provide more chase aircraft as the program continued, and the Navy briefly contributed a Douglas F5D Skyray. It was not unusual for NASA pilots to fly AFFTC chase planes.[44]

The AFFTC supplied all of the propellants and gases necessary for X-15 and NB-52 operation, and was responsible for all maintenance of uninstalled engines (XLR11 and XLR99) and engine overhauls. The Air Force maintained and operated the Rocket Engine Test Facility used for ground-engine runs. NASA was responsible for installing engines in the X-15s, performing maintenance and inspections of installed engines, and conducting the ground runs using the AFFTC test stands. As the program continued, NASA began to perform more maintenance on the XLR99 engines, including recoating the nozzles. The AFFTC maintained the X-15 APUs and was responsible for all engine, APU, and stable-platform logistics.[45]

The Air Force marked and maintained the lakebeds; provided inter-agency coordination (e.g., with the FAA); supplied medical, fire, and security personnel

---

43 R&D Project Card, System 605A, 10 September 1959. In the files at the AFFTC History Office. The project card was not finally approved until 17 December 1959. Among the more interesting tidbits of information on the card were the detailed costs for each year. For instance, in FY60 a total of 48,000 gallons of anhydrous ammonia were to be purchased at $0.55 per gallon. Hydrogen peroxide (208,000 gallons needed) cost $0.67 per gallon. Liquid oxygen cost $13.25 for each of the 3,568 tons expected to be used. The grand total was $357,007 for propellants and gases. Another $1,362,871 would be spent on other supplies, and 182,321 hours of military time and 156,831 hours of civilian time would be used during the year. The cost of the civilian time was $506,708, or an average of $3.23 per hour (no cost was given for the military time). $56,054 would be spent on travel, mainly to visit Wright Field and the various contractor facilities. The other years were similar.

44 R&D Project Card, System 605A, 10 September 1959. In the files at the AFFTC History Office. Interestingly, although a NASA pilot never flew the NB-52s during the X-15 program, squadron leader David Cretney from Royal Air Force did. Also, North American supplied one launch panel operator for some of the contractor flights.

45 Ibid.

as needed; and operated the long-range camera facilities. The Air Force also operated and maintained several radar facilities that were not part of the High Range but nonetheless generated data to support the flight program. NASA provided maintenance for the stable platform (and later the inertial systems) and the ball nose, since both of these were considered research instrumentation. It was a complicated agreement but it worked remarkably well.[46]

The AFFTC expected the ARDC (and later the Systems Command) to "establish, fund, and monitor an open call type contract with North American Aviation, Inc. to furnish such articles and supplies and perform for the Government such services as may be required." Similar contracts existed with Reaction Motors for the engines, and with Sperry for the stable platform.[47]

REVISIONS

As it turned out, the initial flight plan was modified somewhat as the program progressed. The envelope-expansion program was eventually broken into two parts: the basic research program and the basic program extension. The first category consisted mostly of the original plan that covered the aerodynamic, stability and control, and structural aspects of the basic X-15. The government expected that it would take only 17 flights to reach the design conditions of Mach 6 and 250,000 feet; the rest of the early flights would be for pilot familiarization.

Nevertheless, intermediate progress deviated considerably from the plan, since during the course of the program observations sometimes indicated the need for extreme caution and at other times permitted larger increments than planned. In the end, partially because of the delay resulting from X-15-3 blowing up at the Rocket Engine Test Facility, it took 45 flights to reach Mach 6, and 52 flights to reach 246,700 feet (close enough to 250,000).

The basic program extension was essentially similar but was concerned with answering a few lingering questions and conducting the same evaluations of the "advanced" X-15A-2. In the meantime, a separate program began that used the X-15 as a flying test bed and as a carrier for a variety of follow-on experiments.[48]

It is interesting to note that the X-15 program lacked much of the drama of the earlier X-planes. Although it was pushing performance levels and the state of art further than any previous airplane, the X-15 did not experience the catastrophic technical problems that had plagued earlier programs. The XLR99 worked, if not perfectly, well enough for its intended purpose, unlike the Curtiss-Wright XLR25 in the X-2. The Inconel X hot structure seemed to suffer little ill effect from its prolonged exposure to high temperatures and dynamic pressures. The inertial coupling phenomena that had caused the loss of the X-2, and almost the

46 Ibid.

47 Ibid.

48 "X-15 Semi-Annual Status Report No. 3," 1 December 1964, p. 1. In the files at the DFRC History Office; Thomas A. Toll and Jack Fischel, "The X-15 Project: Results and New Research," *Astronautics & Aeronautics*, March 1964, pp. 21-22.

X-1A, had been addressed by a combination of aerodynamic design, an efficient damper system, and some restrictions on flight maneuvers. The explosive effects of Ulmer leather and liquid oxygen were well understood and avoided.[49]

However, these conclusions were not obvious as the envelope-expansion program began. The researchers–and pilots–worried about many things. Would the hot structure survive the tremendous heating rates? Would the wings remain attached to the fuselage during a 6-g pullout from high altitude after the structure was heated to 1,200°F? Would the ballistic control system provide sufficient control while outside the atmosphere?

The flight program expanded speed and altitude concurrently. Normally, the speed flights came first to ensure that the airplane was controllable at the velocity necessary for the next altitude flight. During the high-speed flights, the pilot pulled up to an angle of attack that simulated the expected pullout from the next high-altitude flight, allowing a relatively safe evaluation of the effects of the pullout. It took only 12 flights for the X-15 to expand its envelope from the Mach 3.5 and 136,500 feet attained with the XLR11 (and basically representative of the best the earlier X-planes had managed) to Mach 6.06 and 246,700 feet. It was an amazing feat.

Perhaps not so amazingly to the designers, John Becker and the researchers at Langley had done a lot of basic research, and Charlie Feltz and his team at North American had taken that, added to it, and developed a very robust airframe. North American took Hartley Soulé's comments to Harrison Storms about making errors on the strong side seriously. The airplane ended up a bit overweight, resulting in slightly diminished performance, but it could take a great deal of punishment and survive. The simulation program run by North American and later by the FRC and AFFTC flight planners correctly predicted almost every nuance of the flight program. As the pilots learned to trust the simulator, most of the initial worries disappeared. Still, it was incredible that the program accomplished the envelope expansion so apparently effortlessly.

This is not to say the program did not experience problems. As Bob Hoey remembers, "[T]he X-15 had a significant inertial coupling problem for roll rates that were easily within the capability of the control system. The boundaries were reasonably well established on the simulator, and everyone recognized that there was no need to perform rapid rolls on an X-15 mission, so the pilots were advised 'don't do that!' and they didn't." The auxiliary power unit provided more than its share of challenges early on, and was never completely satisfactory. The stable platform got off to a marginal start, got better, and then got a lot worse. In the end, a more modern unit originally designed for the canceled X-20 Dyna-Soar replaced it. The ballistic control system was particularly troublesome during the initial flights, so much so that researchers purposely turned it off on some of the early altitude buildup flights. Fortunately, the bugs had been worked out and it performed satisfactorily by the time it was really needed.[50]

The XLR99 had its share of minor problems (mainly sensitivity to throttling) and a worrisome habit of shedding some of the insulating coating inside its

49 Letter, Robert G. Hoey to Dennis R. Jenkins, 12 August 2002.

50 Ibid.

exhaust nozzle. Then there was the landing gear, which underwent a constant set of modifications right up until the final year of the flight program. In this case, it was not the components' fault, at least not completely. The airplane was overweight when North American delivered it, and it continued to get heavier over the years. Upgraded struts, skids, nose wheels, tires, and stronger supporting structures never caught up with the weight increases. Still, few of the problems were show-stoppers, and the X-15 program continued at a blistering pace.

Each of the initial X-15 pilots had spent many hours in the fixed-base simulator at North American and had undergone centrifuge training at NADC Johnsville. Prior to his first flight in the X-15, each pilot went through a ground dry run with the X-15 mated to the NB-52 to familiarize himself with the complete prelaunch checklist and cockpit procedures. Each pilot also performed engine runs at the Rocket Engine Test Facility prior to his first X-15 flight. In addition, the pilots flew missions in the NT-33 and JF-100C variable-stability trainers to become familiar with the low-speed handling characteristics of the X-15. The pilots practiced landings in F-104s, including approaches to each of the uprange lakebeds in service at the time. There should be no surprises.[51]

CAN IT FLY?

As conceived at the time of the rollout in 1958, the contractor flight program consisted of four phases. The first was called "B-52 and X-15 Lightweight Captive Flight Evaluation" and was intended to verify the mated flight characteristics with an unfueled X-15, operational procedures, jettison characteristics (using dye), systems (APU, hydraulic, heat and vent, and electrical) operations, B-52 communications and observation, and carrier aircraft performance at launch speed and altitude. The second phase was the "X-15 Lightweight Glide Flight Evaluation" and involved launching an unfueled X-15 on an unpowered glide flight to verify the launch procedure, low-speed handling characteristics, and landing procedures.[52]

The third phase was the "B-52 and X-15 Heavyweight Captive Flight Evaluation," which was intended to replicate the first series of tests with a fully loaded X-15, demonstrate topping off the liquid-oxygen system, and verify that a full propellant load could be jettisoned using actual propellants. The last phase involved the initial "X-15 Powered Flight Evaluation" using the interim XLR11 engines. The schedule showed the first captive flight on 31 January 1959, with the first glide flight on 9 February 1959 and the first powered flight on 2 April 1959. Somehow, it would not work that way.[53]

X-15-1 arrived at Edwards on 17 October 1958, trucked over the foothills from the North American Inglewood plant. The second airplane joined it in April 1959,

51 Hoey and Day, "X-15 Mission Planning and Operational Procedures," pp. 160-161.

52 North American report NA58-190, "X-15 Research Airplane NAA Model NA-240 Flight Test Program," 1 August 1958, p. I-3. In the AFFTC Access to Space Office Project Files.

53 North American report NA58-190, p. I-3.

and the third would arrive later. As Air Force historian Dr. Richard P. Hallion later observed, "In contrast to the relative secrecy that had attended flight tests with the XS-1 a decade before, the X-15 program offered the spectacle of pure theater." It was not that the X-15 program necessarily relished the limelight–it simply could not avoid it after *Sputnik*.[54]

Beginning in December 1958, North American conducted numerous ground runs with the APUs installed in X-15-1 at Edwards. The company intended this to build confidence in the units before the first flights, but it did not turn out that way. Bearings overheated, turbines seized, and valves and regulators failed, leaked, or did not regulate. The mechanics would remove the failed part, rebuild it, and try again. More failures followed. Scott Crossfield later described this period as "sleepless weeks of sheer agony." Harrison Storms eventually got together with the senior management at General Electric, who sent Russell E. "Robby" Robinson to Edwards to fix the problem. For instance, Robinson noted that invariably after one APU failed, the other would follow within a few minutes. The engineers finally deduced that a sympathetic vibration transferred through the shared mounting bulkhead caused the second one to fail. North American devised a new mounting system that separated the APUs onto two bulkheads.[55]

The North American pilot was Scott Crossfield, the person who arguably knew more about the airplane than any other individual did. After they performed various ground checks, technicians mated X-15-1 to the NB-52A and then conducted additional ground tests. All of this delayed the original schedule by about 60 days. When the day for the first flight arrived, Crossfield described it as a "carnival at dawn." Things were different during the 1950s. Crossfield and Charlie Feltz shared a room in the bachelor officer quarters (BOQ) at Edwards; there was no fancy hotel in town. They each dressed in a shirt and tie before driving to the flight line–nothing casual, even though Crossfield soon changed into a David Clark MC-2 full-pressure suit. When they got to the parking lot next to the NB-52 mating area, more than 50 cars were already waiting. The flight had been scheduled for 0700 hours. Based on his previous rocket-plane experience, Crossfield predicted they would take off no earlier than noon, and maybe as late as 1400.[56]

Crossfield was pleasantly surprised. At 1000 hours on 10 March 1959, the mated pair took off on its scheduled captive-carry flight (retroactively called program flight number 1-C-1). It had a gross take-off weight of 258,000 pounds, and lifted off at 172 knots after a ground roll of 6,085 feet. During the 1 hour and 8 minute flight, Captains Charlie Bock and Jack Allavie found that the NB-52 was an excellent carrier for the X-15, as was expected from numerous wind-tunnel and simulator tests.[57]

During the captive flight, Crossfield exercised the X-15 flight controls, and the recorders gathered airspeed data from the flight test boom to calibrate the

---

54 Richard P. Hallion, editor, *The Hypersonic Revolution: Case Studies in the History of Hypersonic Technology* (Wright-Patterson AFB, OH: Aeronautical Systems Division, 1987), vol. I, "Transiting from Air to Space: The North American X-15," p. 129.

55 Crossfield, *Always Another Dawn*, pp. 311-313.

56 James E. Love, "History and Development of the X-15 Research Aircraft," not dated, p. 12. In the files at the DFRC History Office; Crossfield, *Always Another Dawn*, pp. 322-323.

57 Love, "History and Development of the X-15 Research Aircraft," p. 12; Crossfield, *Always Another Dawn*, pp. 322-323.

Scott Crossfield spent many hours in his David Clark full-pressure suit while the X-15-1 was prepared for its initial flights. Despite the daytime temperatures in the desert, Crossfield believed that his presence, ready to go, kept ground crew morale high. (NASA)

instrumentation. Bock and Allavie found that the penalties imposed by the X-15 on the NB-52 flight characteristics were minimal, and flew the mated pair up to Mach 0.85 at 45,000 feet. Part of the test sequence was to make sure the David Clark full-pressure suit worked as advertised, although Crossfield had no doubts. This was a decidedly straightforward test. The suit should inflate as soon as the altitude in the cockpit went above 35,000 feet. As the mated pair passed 30,000 feet, Crossfield turned off the cabin pressurization system and opened the ram air door to equalize the internal pressure with the outside air. Once the airplanes climbed above 35,000 feet, Crossfield felt the suit begin to inflate, and "from that point on [his] movements were slightly constrained and slightly awkward." Still, Crossfield could reach all of the controls, including the hardest control in the cockpit to reach: the ram air door lever. Crossfield closed the door, and as the cockpit repressurized, the suit relaxed its grip. Pilots repeated this test on every X-15 flight until the end of the program. Near the end of the flight, Crossfield lowered the X-15 landing gear just to make sure it worked, even if it looked a little odd while still mated to the NB-52.[58]

The next step was to release the X-15 from the NB-52 to ascertain its gliding and landing characteristics. North American rescheduled the first glide flight for 1 April 1959, but aborted it when the X-15 radio failed. The NB-52A and X-15 spent 1 hour and 45 minutes airborne conducting further tests in the mated configuration. A combination of radio failure and APU problems caused a second abort on 10 April. Yet a third attempt aborted on 21 May 1959 when the X-15 stability augmentation system failed and a bearing in the no. 1 APU overheated after approximately 29 minutes of operation.[59]

The problems with the APU were the most disturbing. All of these flights encountered various valve malfunctions, leaks, and speed-control problems with the APUs, all of which would have been unacceptable during research flights. Tests conducted on the APU revealed that extremely high surge pressures were occurring at the pressure relief valve (actually a blowout plug) during the initial peroxide tank pressurization. The installation of an orifice in the helium pressurization line immediately downstream of the shut-off valve reduced the surges to acceptable levels. Engineers decided that other problems were unique to the captive-carry flights and deemed them of little consequence to the flight program since the operating scenario would be different. Still, reliability was marginal at best. The APUs underwent a constant set of minor improvements during the flight program, but continued to be a source of irritation until the end.[60]

On 22 May, North American conducted the first ground run of the interim XLR11 engine using X-15-2 at the Rocket Engine Test Facility. Scott Crossfield was in the cockpit for the successful test, clearing the way for the eventual first powered flight–if X-15-1 could ever make its unpowered flight. Another attempt at the glide flight on 5 June 1959 aborted even before the NB-52 left the ground, when Crossfield reported smoke in the cockpit. Investigation showed that a cockpit ventilation fan motor had overheated. The continuing problems with the first glide flight were beginning to take their toll, both physically and mentally, on all involved.[61]

Because of the lessons learned on the aborted glide flights and during the XLR11 ground runs, engineers modified numerous pieces of equipment on the X-15. These included the APUs, their support brackets, the mounting bulkheads, and the bearings inside them. North American also improved the flight control system's mechanical responsiveness. In addition, technicians accomplished a great deal of work on the various regulators and valves, particularly in the hydrogen-peroxide systems. Storms remembered, "[I]n the final analysis, the regulators and valves were the most troublesome hardware in the program insofar as reliability was concerned."[62]

---

58 Ibid.

59 Love, "History and Development of the X-15 Research Aircraft," p. 13; Crossfield, *Always Another Dawn*, pp. 323-324.

60 Ibid.

61 Because the NB-52 never left the ground, this attempt was not assigned a program flight number.

62 Harrison A. Storms, "X-15 Hardware Design Challenges" a paper in the *Proceedings of the X-15 30th Anniversary Celebration*, Dryden Flight Research Facility, Edwards, CA, 8 June 1989, NASA CP-3105, p. 31.

1959 FLIGHT PERIOD

Finally, at 0838 hours on 8 June 1959, Scott Crossfield and X-15-1 dropped from the NB-52A at Mach 0.79 and 37,550 feet. Just prior to launch, the SAS pitch damper failed, but Crossfield elected to proceed with the flight and switched the pitch channel to standby. At launch, the X-15 separated cleanly and Crossfield rolled to the right with a bank angle of about 30 degrees. Usually the obedient test pilot, on this flight Crossfield allowed himself to deviate slightly from the flight plan and perform one unauthorized aileron roll. However, not all was well. On the final approach to landing, the X-15 began a series of increasingly wild pitching motions. Crossfield: "[T]he nose of the X-15 pitched up sharply. It was a maneuver that had not been predicted by the simulator ... I was frankly caught off guard. Quickly I applied corrective elevator control. The nose came down sharply. But instead of leveling out, it tucked down. I applied reverse control. The nose came up but much too far. Now the nose was rising and falling like the bow of a skiff in a heavy sea ... I could not subdue the motions." The X-15 was porpoising wildly, sinking toward the desert at 175 knots.[63]

The airplane touched down safely at 150 knots and slid 3,900 feet while turning slightly to the right. After he landed, Crossfield said he believed that the airplane exhibited a classic case of static instability. Harrison Storms, on the other hand, was sure that the cure was a simple adjustment. In the end, Storms was right. As he would on all of his flights, Crossfield had used the side-stick controller during the flare instead of the center stick, and this subsequently proved to be the contributing cause of the oscillations. The side-stick controller used small hydraulic boost actuators to assist the pilot since it would have been impossible (or at least impractical) to move the side stick through the same range of motion required for the center stick. However, the engineers had decided to restrict the authority of these hydraulic cylinders somewhat, based on a best guess of the range of movement required. The guess had been wrong, and because of this a cable in the control system was stretching and retracting unexpectedly. What appeared to be pilot-induced oscillations during landing actually reflected the mechanics of the control system. The fix was to provide more authority to the hydraulic cylinder by changing an orifice—a simple adjustment.[64]

Although the impact at landing was not particularly hard, later inspection revealed that bell cranks in both main landing skids had bent. Unfortunately, North American had not instrumented the main skids on this flight, so no specific impact data were gathered. However, the engineers generally believed that the shock struts had bottomed and remained bottomed because of higher-than-predicted landing loads. Excessive rebound loads caused by a foaming of the oil in the nose gear strut compounded the issue, although it took several more landings to realize

63 The aileron roll was confirmed in an e-mail, Scott Crossfield to Dennis R. Jenkins, 14 May 2002; Scott Crossfield and Harrison Storms, during an interview in the NBC documentary film *The Rocket Pilots*, 1989; Crossfield, *Always Another Dawn*, pp. 342-343.

64 Crossfield and Storms, *The Rocket Pilots*; Crossfield *Always Another Dawn*, pp. 343-346; telephone conversation, Scott Crossfield to Dennis R. Jenkins, 8 August 2002. The side and center sticks were mechanically interconnected to the control system cables through bell cranks; this was years before an electric side stick would be flown. Crossfield had long believed the center stick should be "cut off and thrown away."

Scott Crossfield climbs out of X-15-1 after the first captive-carry flight. The X-15 landing gear had been deployed during the flight to demonstrate it would work after being cold-soaked at altitude. A member of the ground crew installs protective covers on the nose-mounted air data boom. (AFFTC History Office)

this. As a precaution against the main skid problem occurring again, the metering characteristics of the shock struts were changed, and engineers conducted additional lakebed drop tests at even higher loads with the landing-gear test trailer used to qualify the landing-gear design. The landing gear would continue to be a concern throughout the flight program. All other airplane systems operated satisfactorily on this flight, clearing the way for the first powered flight using X-15-2. The following day North American moved X-15-1 into the hangar to hook up its

XLR11s and propellant system and make other changes in preparation for its first powered flight.[65]

While the NB-52 was carrying X-15-1 as expensive wing cargo, engineers were testing the XLR11s at the Rocket Engine Test Facility using X-15-2. Despite the successful 22 May test, things were not going particularly well. Perhaps the engines had been out of service for too long between programs, or maybe too much knowledge had been lost during the coming and goings of the various engineers and technicians over the years, but the initial runs were hardly trouble-free. Various valves and regulators in the propellant system also proved to be surprisingly troublesome. Moreover, sometimes things just went to hell. After one engine run, the ground crew began purging the hydrogen-peroxide lines of all residual liquid by connecting a hose from a ground nitrogen supply to a fitting on X-15-2. On this day, it was a new hose. Despite the careful procedures and great caution used, the hose had a slight residue of oil. When the technician applied gas pressure to the hose, the film of oil ran into the hydrogen-peroxide lines. The only thing truly compatible with peroxide is more peroxide, not oil. The result was an immediate explosion and fire that raced through the X-15 engine compartment. As always, the Edwards fire crew was standing by and quickly extinguished the fire, but not before gutting the engine bay. One X-15 crewman was badly burned; if he had been standing two feet closer, he likely would have been killed. It took weeks to repair the airplane.[66]

Forty-six days after the first glide flight, and after the damage from the explosion was repaired, the NB-52A took X-15-2 for a captive-carry flight with full propellant tanks on 24 July 1959. One of the purposes of this flight was to evaluate the liquid-oxygen top-off system between the NB-52 and X-15. It proved to be erratic. Another test was to measure the time it took to jettison the propellants at altitude. While still safely attached to the wing of the NB-52, Crossfield jettisoned the hydrogen peroxide, which took 140 seconds. He then jettisoned the liquid oxygen and alcohol simultaneously, which took 110 seconds. The times matched predictions. The APUs and pressure suit performed flawlessly. Despite the failure of the top-off system, researchers considered the flight a success. The original contract had specified that North American would turn the first airplane over to the government in August 1959. For a while it looked like the company might deliver the first X-15 on schedule, but it was not to be.[67]

During August and early September, engineers canceled several attempts to make the first powered flight before the aircraft left the ground, due to leaks in the APU propellant system and hydraulic problems. There were also several failures of propellant tank pressure regulators, and on at least one occasion, liquid oxygen streamed out of the safety vent while the NB-52 carried the X-15. No flight occurred on that day. Charlie Feltz, Bud Benner, and John Gibb, along with a variety

65 Love, "History and Development of the X-15 Research Aircraft," pp. 12-13; letter, Robert G. Hoey to Dennis R. Jenkins, 12 August 2002. Although the XLR11s had been "installed" for the glide flight, in reality they were little more than ballast. They were not hooked up to the propellant system or capable of being ignited.

66 Crossfield, *Always Another Dawn*, pp. 348-350.

67 Ibid, pp. 352-353.

of other North American engineers and technicians, worked to eliminate these problems, all of which were irritating but not critical—other than to the morale.[68]

At the 30th anniversary celebration, Storms described the mood at the time:[69]

> A typical launch attempt would start the night before, and the crews would work all night preparing the X-15 and fueling it. About 8 a.m., Scott Crossfield would be in his flight gear and, after walking around the operation, get into the cockpit and start his checkout. Scott would stay in the ready condition as the countdown continued. This, unfortunately, might be as late as 3 or 4 in the afternoon before the B-52 would be allowed to take off. By the time it had reached launch altitude and attempted to hold for the required length of time with all systems in operation, sometime during this period a regulator would fail, a valve would fail, or the bearings on one or both APUs would go out. Then back to Edwards. When Scott returned, we would be scheduled to go to a press conference and meet many tired, and by that time somewhat edgy, reporters that always wanted answers that were just not available. These were not happy meetings for any of the participants.
>
> Shortly after about the fourth such encounter, I was gathered up by General John McCoy of Wright Field and taken over to Mr. [James Howard 'Dutch'] Kindelberger's office, the then chairman of the board. The general explained that the country was in a bad spot with the Sputnik success and that our false starts were not very much of a positive boost to the national position. In short, "when were we going to launch that X-15?" This one time in my life all eyes were on me. Not the most desirable position. The answer I gave was to go over the conditions that we and the NASA had set up for a launch. Also, I gave my support to this approach and pointed out that we were attempting to put a new type of flying machine in the air without the loss of either millions of dollars worth of equipment or the pilot. However, if they wanted to, I would take them to the task force that set up the launch ground rules and they could either convince them of a different approach or overrule them, if possible. The whole meeting ended up with the Air Force's plea for increased effort on out part and hope for early success. Fortunately for all concerned, the next attempt turned out to be a winner.

---

68 Ibid, pp. 350-357.

69 Storms, "X-15 Hardware Design Challenges" pp. 30-31. In June 1955, General John Louis McCoy became the commander of the ARDC Directorate of Systems Management at Wright-Patterson AFB, serving until January 1960. James Howard "Dutch" Kindelberger retired as chief executive officer of North American in 1960. Although he remained as chairman of the board until his death in 1962, he never got to see the ultimate success of the X-15 program. He was succeeded by John Leland "Lee" Atwood in both jobs.

At last, Scott Crossfield made the first powered flight using X-15-2 on 17 September 1959. The NB-52A released the research airplane at 0808 in the morning while flying at Mach 0.80 and 37,600 feet. X-15-2 reached Mach 2.11 and 52,341 feet during 224.3 seconds of powered flight using the two XLR11 engines. Crossfield surprised everybody, including most probably himself, by performing another aileron roll, this time all the way around. As Crossfield remembers, "Storms was tickled." On a more serious note, he observed, "With the rolling tail one would expect very clean 'aileron' rolls without the classical adverse yaw from ailerons, and that is the way it rolled. No big deal at all." The government's concerns about the rolling tail were for naught.[70]

Crossfield landed on Rogers Dry Lake 9 minutes and 11 seconds after launch, despite some concerns about a crosswind on the lake. Following the landing, ground crews noticed a fire in the area around the ventral stabilizer, but quickly extinguished it. A subsequent investigation revealed that the upper XLR11 fuel pump diffuser case had cracked after engine shutdown and sprayed fuel throughout the engine compartment. Alcohol collected in the ventral stabilizer and some unknown cause ignited it during landing. Crossfield noted that "the fire had burned through a large area, melting aluminum tubing, fuel lines, valves, and other machinery." For the second time in less than six months, X-15-2 went back to Inglewood. It took about three weeks to repair the damage.[71]

Edwards was not the only place where the X-15 created interest, although it was certainly the most visible. Back at Langley Research Center, just a month after the first powered flight, approximately 20,000 visitors attended the first anniversary inspection, held on Saturday, 24 October 1959. The crowds had come at NASA's invitation, and local newspapers had spread the word that for the first time in its 42-year history Langley would be open to the public. NASA scientists, engineers, and technicians showed the public just what the new agency was doing to launch their country into space. The attractions included full-scale mockups of the X-15, XLR99, and a dummy in an MC-2 full-pressure suit. A small group of Langley secretaries acted as the hostesses for the exhibit, while both John Becker and Paul Bikle were nearby to answer questions. The event was a success with both the public and the media.[72]

Back in the high desert, the third flight (2-3-9) of X-15-2 took place on 5 November 1959 when the NB-52A dropped the X-15 at Mach 0.82 and 44,000 feet. The flight got off to a bad start; during the engine start sequence, one chamber in the lower engine exploded. Chase planes reported external damage around the engine and base plate, and the resulting fire convinced Crossfield to land on Rosamond Dry Lake. Crossfield shut down both engines, but the 13.9 seconds

---

70 E-mails, Scott Crossfield to Dennis R. Jenkins, 13 and 14 May 2002; The roll was captured by the camera chase, and video can be seen in the NBC documentary film *The Rocket Pilots*, 1989. "Aileron" is in quotes because the X-15 did not have ailerons and used the rolling tail for control instead. Still, aerodynamicists continue to use the term "aileron" to describe motion.

71 Love, "History and Development of the X-15 Research Aircraft," p. 13; Crossfield, *Always Another Dawn*, pp. 365-366.

72 James R. Hansen, *Spaceflight Revolution: NASA Langley Research Center from Sputnik to Apollo*, NASA publication SP-4308 (Washington, DC: NASA, 1995), pp. 28-30. Langley had held "inspections" since 1926, but previously they had been closed conferences for invited members of the aeronautic community. In most cases, the laboratories were open on the day after the conference to family and friends of employees, plus a few invited guests. Normally these inspections attracted about 400 people.

A minor explosion during Flight 2-3-9 on 5 November 1959 resulted in an emergency landing on Rosamond Dry Lake that broke the back of X-15-2. As built, the X-15 was heavier than originally intended, and it did not help that Scott Crossfield was unable to jettison all of the unused propellants before the emergency landing. The airplane was repaired in time for its fourth flight on 11 February 1960. (AFFTC History Office)

of powered flight had been sufficient to accelerate the X-15 to Mach 1. Unfortunately, the flight attitude necessary to descend to the lakebed made it impossible to dump most of the remaining propellants. Crossfield initiated the landing flare at about 950 feet altitude and 253 knots. The aircraft touched down near the center of the lake at approximately 161 knots and a 10.8-degree angle of attack with a descent rate of 9.5 feet per second. Crossfield noted: "The skids dug in gently. The nose slammed down hard and the airplane plowed across the desert floor, slowing much faster than usual. Then she came to a complete stop within 1,500 feet instead of the usual 5,000 feet." When the nose gear had bottomed out, the fuselage literally broke in half at station 226.8, shearing out about 70% of the bolts at the manufacturing splice. The broken fuselage dug into the lakebed, creating a very effective brake.[73]

A contributing factor to the hard landing was the 15,138-pound touchdown weight. During development, engineers had established a limiting rate of sink of 9 fps based on design weight of 11,500 pounds. However, the as-built airplane had increased to 13,230 pounds. In addition, Crossfield had been unable to jettison some of the propellants because of the steep descending attitude necessary to reach the landing site, which further increased the landing weight. Crossfield later

73 Crossfield, *The Rocket Pilot*; Gene J. Matranga, NASA technical note D-1057, "Analysis of X-15 Landing Approach and Flare Characteristics Determined from the First 30 Flights," July 1961, pp. 13-14; Crossfield, *Always Another Dawn*, pp. 381-382. Fuselage stations are measured in inches from a fixed point somewhat ahead of the nose of the aircraft.

stated that the damage was the result of a structural defect that probably should have broken on the first flight.[74]

Yet again, X-15-2 went to the Inglewood plant for repairs, and returned to Edwards in time for its fourth flight on 11 February 1960. North American repaired the damaged fuselage and strengthened the manufacturing splice by doubling the number of fasteners and adding a doubler plate, top and bottom, at the fuselage joint. The company also modified the other two airplanes to prevent similar problems.[75]

1960 FLIGHT PERIOD

While X-15-2 was undergoing repairs, X-15-1 became the primary flight vehicle and made its first powered flight on 23 January 1960. The performance of the airplane was beginning to show: Crossfield reached 1,669 mph (Mach 2.53) and 66,844 feet during 267.2 seconds of powered flight. Engineers installed the stable platform for the first time, and its performance was encouraging. This was also the first X-15 flight that used the NB-52B as a carrier aircraft. Tensions were beginning to ease, and Crossfield could not resist kidding around a bit with Q.C. Harvey, who was the ground controller for the flight. After the airplane landed, and before the convoy arrived on the scene, this was the radio chatter: Crossfield: "Does steer real good. Look at that. You can steer it all over. Want me to park it at NASA?" QC: "Yes, Scott." Crossfield: "Oh, I'm in the mud. Bogged down." QC: "Bogged down?" Crossfield: "Full in the mud." QC: "Don't do that to our lake Scott. Scott, you still with me? This is QC." Crossfield: "Bet your life." QC: "How badly dug in are you?" Crossfield: "I was just kidding you, buddy."[76]

Under the terms of the contract, the X-15 "belonged" to North American until it demonstrated its basic airworthiness and operation. Everybody agreed this flight adequately satisfied the criteria, and although X-15-1 had made only two flights the government was anxious to get started. Engineers performed a pre-delivery inspection a few days after the flight, and on 3 February 1960 the Air Force formally accepted X-15-1 and subsequently turned the airplane over to NASA on long-term loan.[77]

With the earlier X-planes, the Air Force had conducted an envelope-expansion program before turning the research airplanes over to the NACA. For the X-15 program, however, nobody could figure out how to expeditiously conduct the envelope-expansion and research programs in a serial manner, so the government decided to conduct them in parallel. After some initial organizational squabbles,

74 Crossfield, *The Rocket Pilots*, 1989; NASA technical note D-1057, pp. 13-14; letter, Robert G. Hoey to Dennis R. Jenkins, 12 August 2002.

75 Love, "History and Development of the X-15 Research Aircraft," p. 14.

76 Radio transcript for X-15 no. 1, first powered flight (later redesignated flight 1-2-7). In the files at the DFRC History Office; "Advanced Development Plan for X-15 Research Aircraft, Advanced Technology Program 653A," 17 November 1961, p. 1. In the files at the AFFTC History Office.

77 "Advanced Development Plan for X-15 Research Aircraft, Advanced Technology Program 653A," 17 November 1961, p. 1.

the Air Force and the NACA agreed to cooperate. The organizations selected two pilots to conduct the envelope expansion: Joseph A. Walker from NASA would concentrate on altitude expansion, and Major Robert M. White would conduct the high-speed flights. Four other pilots would be "checked out and utilized in a routine manner on research flights not directly involved with the expeditious expansion of the X-15 flight envelope." Paul Bikle believed that "the use of more than two pilots in the part of the program devoted to expanding the envelope cannot be justified from a technical standpoint and would seriously interfere with the timely completion of the research objectives associated with this part of the program."[78]

Despite the generally good cooperation between NASA and the Air Force, occasionally minor disputes did pop up. One of these centered around which organization would make the first government flight in the X-15. Paul Bikle tells it best in the minutes of a 1 October 1959 meeting between himself and Brigadier General John W. Carpenter III, the commander of the AFFTC:[79]

> The point of which pilot would make the first flight in the first X-15 to be turned over to NASA was then raised. On the proposed schedule, Walker was listed as the pilot. General Carpenter felt that there was no technical reason why Walker should be selected instead of White and I agreed that this was the case. He felt that the Air Force had spent about one hundred million dollars for the X-15 airplanes and that the Air Force was spending roughly four million dollars per year in support of the X-15 program and that, for this reason, the Air Force pilot should make the first flight so that the Air Force could extract the maximum benefits from the publicity which will be associated with the flight. I could appreciate his point of view but told him that NASA had conceived the program back in 1952, had devoted a large percentage of their efforts to the program over the past seven years, had the responsibility for conducting the research program, and I felt for these reasons it would be more appropriate for an NASA pilot to make the first flight. General Carpenter could appreciate my point of view on this and said that he would feel the same way if he was in my position. However, he could not accept this decision for the Air Force and he felt that we would have to agree to disagree on this point. He plans to contact Headquarters, ARDC and have them contact Headquarters, USAF to determine if the Air Force position is such that they will bring the matter before the Research Airplane Committee. I would anticipate that the Air Force will

78 Letter, Paul F. Bikle/FRC to NASA Headquarters (copy to Hartley A. Soulé/Research Airplane Committee). subject: Participation of USAF pilots in X-15 flights, 2 October 1959; Letter, Robert G. Hoey to Dennis R. Jenkins, 12 August 2002. The other four pilots were Neil Armstrong, Jack McKay, Forrest Petersen, and Bob Rushworth.

79 Letter, Paul F. Bikle/FRC to NASA Headquarters (copy to Hartley A. Soulé/Research Airplane Committee), subject: Participation of USAF pilots in X-15 flights, 2 October 1959. In the files at the DFRC History Office. Carpenter had replaced General Cooper as commander of the AFFTC in March 1959. Cooper had come to the desert on 1 July 1957, and left to become assistant administrator of the FAA on 20 February 1959. Carpenter arrived in March 1959 and left in June 1961 for a tour at Air Force Headquarters.

> approach NASA Headquarters on this matter, probably at the Administrator's level.[80]

There is no record that Carpenter officially brought the matter to the attention of Hartley Soulé and the Research Airplane Committee, or to T. Keith Glennan, the NASA administrator at the time. Interestingly, Carpenter also did not agree with assigning specific flight profiles to each of the two pilots during the envelope-expansion program, believing that the pilots should each fly a portion of both types of flights. NASA had discussed this idea at some length on previous occasions, and always concluded it was better to assign a single pilot to each flight profile in order to gain experience more quickly. As it turned out, Walker and White would each fly both profiles. The X-15s, however, would be somewhat specialized: X-15-1 would be used to expand the flight envelope to the design objectives, while X-15-2 would be used for pilot familiarization and the early research flights.

At the FRC itself, the X-15 program was having major impacts on the culture and staffing. To stay abreast of the workload, an increasing number of people at the FRC found themselves working on the X-15 program; within a year or two, it would seem that *everybody* at the FRC was working on the X-15. However, the increasing number of personnel and the visibility created by the program were driving away the informality that had traditionally characterized the desert facility. Walt Williams had thought nothing of issuing verbal instructions to a team of engineers, who in turn would ask technicians, flight crews, and mechanics for help as needed. This no longer worked. Paul Bikle needed to be able to trace the money. This meant paperwork such as had never been imagined at the FRC–paper to monitor the intense contractor involvement, paper to monitor agreements with the Air Force, and paper to account for the progress of the flight program itself. In addition, more paper meant the need for more people to manage it, which itself meant more paper. It was a vicious circle, and the FRC would never be quite the same.[81]

When X-15-2 returned to Edwards, North American and the government struggled to get the ballistic control system operational. So far, neither airplane had required the system since the altitudes were low enough for the aerodynamic flight controls to remain effective. For a variety of reasons, the system proved unreliable, primarily because of leaks and poor centering characteristics in the metering valves. In fact, based on the difficulties in activating the system in the second airplane, NASA decided the initial XLR99 flights in X-15-3 would take place without the ballistic controls. To make matters worse, on 26 April 1960 the bladder inside the peroxide tank of X-15-2 failed, further delaying efforts.[82]

---

80 The quote has some errors of fact in it. Brigadier General Marcus E. Cooper had stated at the rollout ceremony that the Air Force had spent $120 million on the program, not the $100 million used here. Records show that AFFTC was spending about $2.5 million per year at this point, not $4 million. In addition, the NACA had conceived what became the X-15 program during 1954, not 1952, although the basic idea had been floated two years earlier. Still, the general sentiment of the meeting is insightful.

81 Michael H. Gorn, *Expanding the Envelope: Flight Research at NACA and NASA* (Lexington, KY: University Press of Kentucky, 2001), p. 243.

82 X-15 Status Report, Paul F. Bikle/FRC to H. Brown/NASA Headquarters, 1 May 1960. In the files at the DFRC History Office.

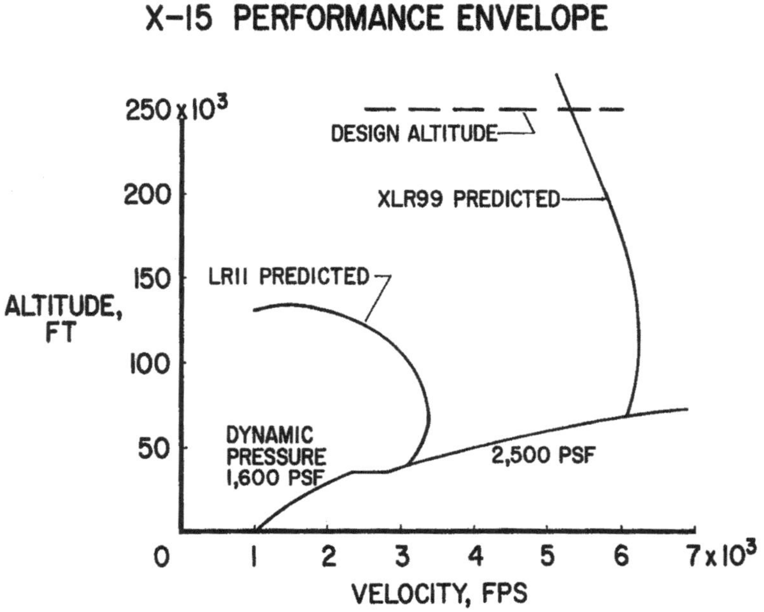

The predicted performance of the XLR11 was, as could be expected, significantly lower than that of the XLR99. However, the XLR11 flight provided valuable experience in operating the airplane and uncovered many problems with various systems such as the stability augmentation system and auxiliary power units. The availability of the interim engines allowed the program to be in a better position to exploit the performance of the XLR99 once it arrived. (NASA)

In any event, Joe Walker made the first government X-15 flight (1-3-8) on 25 March 1960. The NB-52 dropped X-15-1 at Mach 0.82 and 45,500 feet, although the stable platform had malfunctioned just prior to release. Two restarts were required on the top XLR11 before all eight chambers were firing, and the flight lasted just over 9 minutes, reaching Mach 2.0 and 48,630 feet. Overall, Walker was impressed with the flight. The Air Force finally flew the airplane on 13 April 1960, when Bob White took X-15-1 to Mach 1.90 and 48,000 feet on flight 1-4-9.[83]

The next six months saw Walker and White taking turns flying X-15-1. Most of the early flights flown with the XLR11 engines did not include an operable ballistic control system, mostly because there was no need for one and the program engineers had enough "new" things on their hands without worrying about systems they did not need. The ballistic control system used eight 113-lbf thrusters located in the nose (two pointed in each of the major directions) and two 40-lbf thrusters in each wing tip. Each of the nozzles used a 1.40-inch-diameter hole in the skin. The ballistic control system was always used whenever the dynamic pressure was below 25 psf (approximately 180,000 feet and above), although

83 Love, "History and Development of the X-15 Research Aircraft," p. 14; Joseph A. Walker, "Pilot Report for Flight No. 3 (later redesignated 1-3-8)," 25 March 1960; Robert M. White, "Pilot Report for Flight No. 12 (later redesignated 1-4-9)," 13 April 1960.

many pilots began using it as low as 100,000 feet (approximately 50 psf). At this pressure, the effectiveness of the ballistic controls approximated the effectiveness of the aerodynamic controls. The maximum propellant flow was 0.06 gallon per second for the pitch thrusters and 0.02 gallon per second for the roll thrusters. A typical high-altitude mission consumed about 2 gallons of hydrogen peroxide.[84]

On 5 May 1960, Scott Crossfield tested the ballistic control system for the first time, with X-15-2 securely mounted to the wing of the NB-52B. The flight suffered an APU failure before launch and aborted back to Edwards (flight 2-A-17). Nevertheless, North American considered the ballistic control-system test successful, but noted that the initial use of the upper nose thrusters coated the cockpit windscreen with peroxide, which promptly turned to opaque frost. Because the catalyst beds had not come up to temperature, the first use of the thrusters expelled a small amount of undecomposed hydrogen peroxide. The solution was simple: install heaters on the catalyst beds. This was accomplished on all three airplanes before the first free flight that used the ballistic controls.[85]

Surprisingly, there was still some debate over exactly how the ballistic control system should operate. North American conducted a series of studies in the fixed-base simulator to compare different techniques. These included having the thrusters operate proportionally to stick input, on-off at full thrust, or on-off at half thrust, and a proportional system with an on-off damping loop. The simulations used the baseline altitude mission to 250,000 feet with angles of attack varying between 5 and 25 degrees. Eventually North American and the government decided the proportional system was best.[86]

Joe Walker made the first flight (1-7-12) from a remote location (instead of Rosamond) on 12 May 1960. The use of Silver Lake by this flight represented not only the first X-15 launch from a remote lake, but also the first launch of any rocket plane from a remote lake, since all previous X-plane flights took place over the Edwards reservation. The stable platform failed just before launch, and NASA had decided to omit the ballistic control system because of continuing problems, but all other systems performed satisfactorily. X-15-1 dropped away from the NB-52 at Mach 0.83 and 44,800 feet. Walker ignited all eight chambers on the two XLR11s, and set an 8-degree angle of attack to a maximum altitude of 77,882 feet. After a pushover at peak altitude and entry into a slight dive, the aircraft accelerated more than expected. Walker turned off three chambers of the XLR11, but this resulted in an abrupt deceleration that caused the propellant pumps to cavitate and the other five chambers to shut down seconds later. Walker reached a maximum speed of Mach 3.19, marking the first Mach 3+ flight for the X-15 program. During this flight, Walker recalled, his "intention to utilize the side stick for some evaluation during the glide back to base was abandoned after being initiated as

84 George B. Merrick, North American, "X-15 Controlled in Space by Reaction-Control Rocket System," *SAE Journal*, August 1960, pp. 38-41; Robert D. Reed and Joe D. Watts, "Skin and Structural Temperatures Measured on the X-15 Airplane During a Flight to Mach Number of 3.3," NASA confidential technical memorandum X-468, January 1961, pp. 2-3; Bruce O. Wagner, "X-15 Auxiliary Power Units and Reaction Controls," a paper in the *1958 Research Airplane Committee Report*, p. 303. The Bell Aircraft-developed "ring-slot pintle" nozzles had a relatively high heat capacity and caused local heat-sink effects in the skin around them. But they were the only nozzles that were thin enough to fit in the wing without some sort of fairing and the attendant aero-thermal problems.

85 X-15 Status Report, Paul F. Bikle/FRC to H. Brown/NASA Headquarters, 15 May 1960, p. 7.

86 X-15 Status Report, Paul F. Bikle/FRC to H. Brown/NASA Headquarters, 1 June 1960, p. 5.

a result of very strained arm position required in order to grasp the hand grip of the control stick and it was thought that any evaluation of its capabilities would be clouded by this aspect." Walker concluded with, "Having established that the powerplant can be started dependably and that the systems function adequately in the aircraft, it is felt that the remote lake launching yields the desired benefits of performance and resulting expansion of the envelope at rather small cost of operational complications."[87]

The XLR11 flight profiles–both speed and altitude–differed from those achieved later with the XLR99 because of the lower available thrust and slower speed buildup. Eventually, 30 flights used the interim XLR11 engines. X-15-1 would make 21 of these flights, while the other nine would be flown by X-15-2. The third X-15 was equipped with the XLR99 engine from the start. In general the XLR11 flights stayed below 100,000 feet, although several were barely above that altitude and Bob White took X-15-1 to 136,500 feet on 12 August 1960 (flight 1-10-19), establishing a new altitude record for piloted aircraft. The maximum speed recorded with the XLR11 engines was Mach 3.50 (2,275 mph) on flight 1-21-36, again with Bob White at the controls.[88]

For the XLR11 altitude missions, the NB-52 generally launched the X-15 approximately 100 miles from Edwards on a near straight-in heading at an altitude of approximately 45,000 feet and a launch speed of Mach 0.85. This was the scenario for Bob White's record flight: After separating from the NB-52, White started all eight chambers and initiated a climb at the maximum lift-drag ratio by flying at a nearly constant 8 degrees angle of attack. As the airplane neared 60,000 feet, White brought it to level flight and increased to Mach 1.9. He then initiated a 1.5-g pull-up to an angle of attack of 15–19 degrees. This condition simplified the longitudinal piloting task, although the stick force was still high, but complicated the roll control task because of the limited available differential control. Propellant exhaustion occurred 256.2 seconds after engine ignition at an altitude of 116,500 feet and a Mach number of 1.93. The aircraft continued ballistic over the top, with White decreasing the angle of attack to about 10 degrees. The deflection of the stabilizer initiated a ±4 degree pitching oscillation with a period of about 8 seconds, but the combined efforts of White and the pitch damper managed to reduce this to ±1 degree after four cycles. The flight reached a maximum pressure altitude of 133,900 feet at a static pressure of 5.6 psf. Based on the U.S. extension to the ICAO atmosphere charts, this corresponded to 136,500 feet geometric altitude. The Mach number at the peak altitude was 1.63 at a dynamic pressure of 10.6 psf. The nominal acceleration remained below 0.1 g for 57 seconds at an angle of attack of 11 degrees. During reentry the airplane experienced a maximum dynamic pressure of 785 psf until White came level at 46,000 feet and began preparing for his landing.[89]

---

87 X-15 Status Report, Paul F. Bikle/FRC to H. Brown/NASA Headquarters, 1 June 1960, p. 2; Joseph A. Walker, "Pilot Report for Flight No. 15 (later redesignated 1-7-12)," 12 May 1960.

88 One of the 21 X-15-1 flights was unpowered, although the XLR11s were physically installed in the airplane.

89 Euclid C. Holleman and Donald Reisert, NASA confidential technical memorandum X-514, "Controllability of the X-15 Research Airplane with Interim Engines During High Altitude Flights," March 1961, pp. 6-7.

The XLR99 Arrives

The first ground-test XLR99 (s/n 101) arrived at Edwards on 7 June 1959, and the first hot test was accomplished without an actual X-15 at the Rocket Engine Test Facility on 26 August 1959. X-15-3 arrived at Edwards on 29 June 1959. It was essentially identical to the other two airplanes in that it was equipped with a standard Westinghouse stability augmentation system, a stable platform, and a normal cockpit instrument panel. What made it different, at this point, was that it had the XLR99 engine. X-15-3 was never equipped with the XLR11 engines. At the same time, North American removed the second X-15 from flight status after its ninth flight (2-9-18) on 26 April 1960 in anticipation of replacing the XLR11 engines with the XLR99. This left only X-15-1 on active flight status, although the XLR99-powered X-15-3 would soon be joining it.[90]

North American made the first ground run with the XLR99 in X-15-3 on 2 June 1960 at the PSTS. Subsequent inspection revealed damage to the liquid-oxygen inlet line brackets, the result of an unexpected, but easily corrected, water-hammer effect. After repairs were completed, the company conducted another ground run with satisfactory results. For all of the ground runs during the program, a pilot had to be in the cockpit since the nearby blockhouse could not operate the engine by remote control. For the early tests, the pilot was Scott Crossfield, although all of the pilots would participate in ground runs prior to their first flights. The MC-2 full-pressure suit was an order of magnitude more comfortable than earlier pressure suits, but Crossfield still had little desire to wear it more than necessary. Since there was no need for altitude protection during the engine runs on the ground, Crossfield generally wore street clothes in the cockpit. All other personnel required for the tests were in the blockhouse, with the exception of Air Force fire crews a relatively safe distance away.[91]

The third ground run began on 8 June at approximately 1930 hours. The objectives were to demonstrate the restart capability and throttling characteristics of the XLR99. All pre-test operations, servicing, and APU starts were successful and all systems were operating normally. The engine was primed, set to idle, and then ignited at 50% thrust. After the chamber pressure stabilized for 7 seconds, Crossfield advanced the throttle to 100% for 5 seconds and then moved the throttle to idle for 5 seconds before shutting down the engine. Nobody noted anything abnormal during these events. After 15 seconds, Crossfield moved the throttle to the 50% position. The turbopump started normally, first-and second-stage ignition occurred, and the main chamber start appeared normal. After the main chamber pressure stabilized, it rapidly fell off and the engine shut down automatically. At this time, a valve malfunction light came on in the cockpit, so Crossfield moved the throttle to the off position and the light went out. In order to restart the XLR99

90 E-mail, Bill Arnold (Reaction Motors) to Dennis R. Jenkins, various dates in September 2002. North American operated the PSTS until it turned over the last XLR99-equipped airplane to the government. At that time, the AFFTC Rocket Engine Group under the maintenance division took over the operation and maintenance of the PSTS and all engine maintenance and overhaul. NASA performed all engine operations, including minor engine maintenance, while the engine was installed in the airplanes. The lack of the MH-96 in X-15-3 at this point can be derived from various documents, but it was confirmed by Scott Crossfield in an e-mail to the author on 28 May 2002.

91 Crossfield, *Always Another Dawn*, p. 400; telephone conversation, Scott Crossfield with Dennis R. Jenkins, 8 August 2002.

after a malfunction shutdown, the pilot had to push a switch that reset the automatic safety devices. As Crossfield wrote in his accident statement, "the reset button was depressed at which time the airplane blew up." It was approximately 1945 hours.[92]

Crossfield later observed, "During this entire sequence except for the malfunction shut down, there was no evidence in the cockpit of difficulty." The explosion appeared to be centered forward of the engine compartment, and caused the aircraft to separate around fuselage station 483.5, just forward of the liquid-oxygen tank. Don Richter, who was in the main blockhouse, indicated that he observed the explosion originating 5 feet forward from the aft end of the airplane, with the fireball quickly expanding to about 30 feet in diameter.[93]

The explosion threw the entire forward fuselage about 30 feet forward. Crossfield said, "In the explosion, which is not describable, the cockpit translated abruptly forward and to the right with an acceleration beyond the experience of this pilot." The basic X-15 airframe had been designed–largely at Crossfield's urging–to protect the pilot in case of an emergency; it appeared to work well. Ever the competent test pilot, Crossfield turned on his Scott airpack, turned off the engine switches, and pulled all the circuit breakers. He attempted to contact personnel inside the blockhouse, but the explosion had severed communications with the ground.[94]

The fire truck that had been standing by was on the scene within 30 seconds, water pouring from its overhead nozzle, and a second fire truck arrived a minute or two later to help extinguish the fires. Art Simone and a suited fireman rushed to the cockpit and Crossfield was rescued uninjured. Simone had inhaled ammonia fumes and received minor burns to his hands, but suffered no lasting effects. The fires were largely out within a few minutes of the explosion, and Crossfield was safe. It was time to figure out what had happened.[95]

Representatives from the Edwards provost marshal's office, the North American industrial security office, and the Edwards air police arrived on the scene and roped off the area pending an investigation. Around 2110 hours, North American photographer Stan Brusto arrived to photograph the wreckage; after this was complete, the Air Force removed the data recorders from the aircraft for analysis. The air police withdrew after putting into place procedures to limit access to the area, leaving one fire truck on standby just in case. Personnel spent the next 24 hours finding all the bits and pieces blown from the aircraft, tagging them, and preparing to move the remains of the aircraft back to Inglewood. Major Arthur Murray from the X-15 project office authorized the move on 10 June.[96]

Engineers removed the XLR99 from the wreckage on 13 June and took it to hangar 1870 at Edwards for inspection. North American transported the remains of X-15-3 by truck from Edwards on 15 June, parking overnight at the intersection

92 Accident investigation report 60-RWRL-568, not dated, no page numbers. In the files at the AFFTC Access to Space Office Project Files. The general scenario was confirmed during a telephone conversation, Scott Crossfield with Dennis R. Jenkins, 8 August 2002.

93 Ibid.

94 Ibid.

95 Ibid.

96 Ibid.

of Sepulveda and San Bernardo Road before continuing on to Inglewood on 16 June.[97] By 4 August the company had assessed the damage and determined that the airframe would have to be replaced from fuselage station 331.9 aft. The dorsal and ventral stabilizers, all four speed brakes, both horizontal stabilizers, both main landing skids, and both propellant tanks would be replaced. The company considered the wings repairable, as were the APUs and stable platform. All of the miscellaneous equipment in the rear and center fuselage, along with most of the research instrumentation in the aft fuselage, also required replacement. Reaction Motors did not consider the XLR99 repairable, although the company salvaged some parts for future use. The Rocket Engine Test Facility required major repairs, but was back on line by the end of June.[98]

Subsequent investigation revealed that the initiating cause of the explosion was an overpressurization of the ammonia tank. Because of the toxic nature of ammonia fumes, the Air Force had incorporated a vapor-disposal system into the PSTS to allow the ammonia fumes to be vented from the airplane during engine testing without endangering people. Essentially the disposal system consisted of a 90-foot pipe that connected the airplane ammonia vent to a water pond where the ammonia was diluted. At the time of the explosion, the ammonia tank pressurizing gas regulator froze or stuck in the open position while the vent valve was operating erratically or modulating only partially open. North American had considered this condition a potential failure on the airplane itself, and had addressed the problem during development. However, when combined with the back pressure created by the vapor-disposal system attached to the ammonia vent, the tank pressure surged high enough to rupture the tank. In the process, debris damaged the hydrogen-peroxide tank, and the mixing of the peroxide and ammonia caused an explosion.[99]

Post-accident analysis indicated that there were no serious design flaws in either the XLR99 or the X-15. The Air Force determined that the cause of the accident was a failure of the pressure regulator, exacerbated by the unique configuration required for the ground test. Nevertheless, North American devised several modifications to preclude similar failures in the future. These included redesigning the pressurizing gas regulator to reduce maximum flow through an inoperable regulator, providing the regulator with additional closing forces in the event of freezing, relocating the regulator to minimize the chances of moisture accumulation and subsequent freezing, and redesigning the relief valve and its surrounding plumbing.[100]

Rebuilding the aircraft was not as straightforward as it sounded. Besides the estimated $4.75 million cost, there would be a considerable delay in obtaining suitable replacement parts. The X-15s were not mass-produced items, and structural spares were nonexistent. The time required to repair the airplane meant it would miss most of the envelope expansion program and was, therefore, somewhat redundant.

97 This was to ease traffic problems in the area.

98 Accident investigation report 60-RWRL-568; X-15 Status Report, Paul F. Bikle/FRC to H. Brown/NASA Headquarters, 1 July 1960, p. 5.

99 Lawrence P. Greene and Rolland L. Benner, "X-15 Experience from the Designer's Viewpoint," a paper in the *1961 Research Airplane Committee Report,* pp. 315-316.

100 Ibid, pp. 315-316.

Scott Crossfield was at the controls of X-15-3 when it suffered a catastrophic explosion during a ground run of the XLR99. Fortunately, Crossfield was not injured. Subsequent investigation showed there was nothing wrong with either the engine or airframe design and that the explosion had been caused by the failure of a minor component and the unique configuration required for ground testing. The X-15-3 was subsequently rebuilt to include the advanced MH-96 adaptive flight control system. (AFFTC History Office)

There had been considerable interest in testing a new Minneapolis-Honeywell MH-96 adaptive flight control system in a high-speed vehicle prior to its use on the X-20 Dyna-Soar. Given the unfortunate event, the Air Force took this opportunity to modify X-15-3 to include the system. Complicating this was the fact the X-15 program was operating under a "reduced budget"–$8.6 million for FY61 instead of the $10.5 million that had been requested. However, the X-15 program still enjoyed considerable support within the Pentagon, and in early August, Air Force Headquarters authorized the ARDC to release $1 million from existing funds (i.e., the $8.6 million) to cover the procurement of long lead items needed for the repairs. The remaining $3.75 million, along with the restoration of the $1.9 million removed from the program earlier, was to follow "at a later date." In the interim, the Pentagon directed the X-15 program to "operate on a fiscal 1961 schedule compatible with … funds of $10.5 million plus an additional $4.75 million to cover the repair of the damaged aircraft." Although money never came easily for the X-15 program, it always came.[101]

101 Clarence J. Geiger, Albert E. Misenko, and William D. Putnam, "History of the Wright Air Development Division: July 1960-March 1961," AFSC historical publication 61-50-2, August 1961, pp. I-38 to I-40. In the files at the Air Force Historical Research Agency (K234.011).

On 10 August, the Air Materiel Command requested that North American submit an estimate for the repair of X-15-3. Twelve days later the Air Materiel Command ordered the repair using the $1 million authorized by the Pentagon, and North American proceeded with the work. The company estimated that the aircraft could be completed in August 1961 and available for flight in October. The Pentagon came through at the end of March 1961, funding the X-15 program at $15.25 million–the original $10.5 million request plus the cost of rebuilding the damaged airplane.[102]

The new money allowed the AFFTC to increase the propellants it had ordered because of 1) the high consumption of propellants required for component testing at the PSTS, 2) the high level of development testing of the APU and ballistic control system, and 3) the increased development testing of the XLR99 at the Rocket Engine Test Facility. A quick review shows the quantities and costs involved in this usually overlooked matter:[103]

Item	Original FY61	Revised FY61
Alcohol (gal)	48,000 @ $0.51 = $24,480	60,000 @ $0.51 = $30,600
Ammonia (gal)	140,000 @ $0.28 = $39,200	256,000 @ $0.28 = $71,680
Peroxide (lbs)	261,000 @ $0.60 = $156,600	420,000 @ $0.60 = $252,000
Helium (sfc)	2,400,000 @ $0.02 = $48,000	5,400,000 @ $0.02 = $108,000
Nitrogen (tons)	1,500 @ $15.00 = $22,500	3,500 @ $15.00 = $52,500

At Inglewood, North American was installing the XLR99 in X-15-2 and incorporating several other changes at the same time. These included a revised vent system in the fuel tanks as an additional precaution against another explosion, revised ballistic control system components, and provisions to install the ball nose instead of the flight-test boom used so far in the program. The company had been looking to conduct the first flight in early September, but discovered corrosion in the engine hydrogen-peroxide tank. While North American was taking care of the corrosion, Reaction Motors tore down one of the ground-test engines to determine the condition of the individual components after 2 hours of engine operation. The inspection revealed no outstanding deficiencies or indications of excessive wear, clearing the way for the first X-15 flight with the million-horsepower engine.[104]

The installation of the ball nose presented its own challenges since it had no capability to determine airspeed. The possibility of a failure in the ball-nose steering mechanism also made it unsuitable as a total-pressure port to derive airspeed. The X-15 was designed with an alternate airspeed probe just forward of the cockpit, although two other locations–one well forward on the bottom centerline of the aircraft, and one somewhat aft near the centerline–had also been

102 Ibid, pp. I-38 to I-40.

103 ARDC Form 111, Management Report, "X-15 Research Aircraft," 5 August 1960, signed by Colonel Carl A. Ousley, Deputy Chief of Staff/Operations, AFFTC. In the files at the AFFTC History office.

104 William Beller, "Turbopump Key to New X-15 Engine," *Missiles and Space*, 15 August 1960, p. 33; James E. Love, "History and Development of the X-15 Research Aircraft," not dated, p. 17. In the files at the DFRC History Office.

considered. Several early flights compared the data available from each location, while relying on the data provided by the airspeed sensors on the flight-test boom protruding from the extreme nose. The primary location exhibited some velocity-indication sensitivity at speeds over 345 mph and angles of attack over 4 degrees. At 8 degrees alpha the indicated airspeeds were generally about 25 mph low. The tests indicated that the data from all three locations were about the same, so the engineers decided to retain the original location. An interesting discovery was that the error was substantially less after the ball nose was installed, which led to a theory that the extended nose boom was contributing to the errors. Fortunately, the airspeed indications were consistent at the speeds and angles of attack encountered in the landing pattern, so researchers simply adjusted the instruments to compensate. After NASA installed the ball nose, engineers compared angle-of-attack data (based on the horizontal stabilizer position) with those from previous flights using the flight-test boom. The data were generally in good agreement, clearing the way for operational use of the ball nose.[105]

Back to Flying

In its own way, the X-15 program was "politically correct," even if the term did not yet exist. Paul Bikle had decided that a NASA pilot should make the first government X-15 flight, but he would later give the honor of performing the first government XLR99 flight to an Air Force pilot. The initial piloting duties were split evenly between one NASA pilot and one Air Force pilot. It seemed only fitting, therefore, that the third government pilot to qualify in the X-15 should be from the Navy.

Forrest Petersen checked out in the airplane while Joe Walker and Bob White conducted the envelope-expansion phase with the XLR11 engine. Like all of the early pilot familiarization flights, Petersen's first flight would be low and slow, if that describes Mach 2 and 50,000 feet. The flight plan showed Petersen launching over Palmdale, heading toward Boron, turning left to fly back toward Mojave, and making another left turn toward Edwards. The launch went well, but as the airplane approached Boron the upper engine began to fail; soon it stopped altogether. Petersen reported that he "believed erroneously that the lower engine was still running, but the inability to hold altitude, and airspeed variations from values expected for single engine operation forced the pilot to the inevitable conclusion that both engines were shut down." Milt Thompson, who was NASA-1 for the flight, advised Petersen to head directly for Rogers Dry Lake. Petersen arrived at high key with only 25,000 feet altitude, much lower than desired, and Joe Walker tucked a chase plane into formation and coached Petersen through a tight turn onto final. The landing was almost perfect, and Petersen handled the entire incident with his usual aplomb. Petersen's final report was understated: "Nothing during the flight surprised the pilot with the exception of early engine shutdown." The only Navy pilot was an excellent addition to the team.[106]

---

105 X-15 Status Reports, Paul F. Bikle/FRC to H. Brown/NASA Headquarters, 13 January 1961, pp. 3-4 and 28 February 1961, p. 3.

106 Lieutenant Commander Forrest S. Petersen, "Pilot Report for Flight 1-13-25," 23 September 1960. In the files at the DFRC History Office; Thompson, *At the Edge of Space*, pp. 93-94.

It was time for Crossfield to go back to work with the ultimate engine. The first flight attempt of X-15-2 with the XLR99 was on 13 October 1960, but a peroxide leak in the no. 2 APU ended the day prior to launch. Just to show how many things can go wrong on a single flight, there was also liquid-oxygen impingement on the aft fuselage during the prime cycle, manifold pressure fluctuations during engine turbopump operation, and fuel-tank pressure fluctuations during the jettison cycle. Two weeks later, Crossfield again entered the cockpit with the goal of making the first XLR99 flight. More problems with the no. 2 APU forced an abort.

On 15 November 1960, everything went right and Crossfield made the first flight (2-10-21) of X-15-2 powered by the XLR99. The primary flight objective was to demonstrate engine operation at 50% thrust. The launch was at Mach 0.83 and 46,000 feet, and the X-15 managed to climb to 81,200 feet and Mach 2.97 using somewhat less than half the available power. The second XLR99 flight (2-11-22) tested the engine's restart and throttling capability. Crossfield made the flight on 22 November, again using the second X-15. During the post-flight inspection of the aircraft and its engine, engineers found that, like most of the ground-test engines, the XLR99 was beginning to shed some of the Rokide coating on the exhaust nozzle.[107]

Despite being fast-paced, the X-15 program was never reckless. As North American prepared X-15-2 for its next flight during December 1960, AFFTC commander Brigadier General John Carpenter heard rumors about the Rokide coating and called a meeting to discuss the matter. Representatives from the Air Force, NASA, North American, and Reaction Motors were present. Each gave his opinion, which was that it appeared safe to continue. Carpenter dismissed the meeting but asked Scott Crossfield and Harrison Storms to stay. During this session he questioned Crossfield on his feelings about making the flight given the condition of the engine. Scott did not show any concern and indicated he was willing to go ahead with the flight. Carpenter excused Crossfield but asked Storms to stay.[108]

Storms recalled, "When we were alone, General Carpenter asked my opinion. I told him that earlier this day on my arrival at Edwards that I had inspected the thrust chamber in question and did not have any great concerns. Yes, some of the insulation was gone, but not to any great extent and the individual areas were small. It had not all been lost in one area, but the loss was fairly evenly well distributed over the entire area. Further, it certainly had not caused any negative comments from the manufacturer or their test engineers. The General's comment was, 'Very well, we will make it a joint decision to proceed with the flight.' … Seriously, there is a point to be made here. That is, there is a very fine line between stopping progress and being reckless. That the necessary ingredient in this situation of solving a sticky problem is attitude and approach. The answer, in my opinion, is what I refer to as 'thoughtful courage.' If you don't have that, you will very easily fall into the habit of 'fearful safety' and end up with a very long and tedious-type solution at the hands of some committee. This can very well end up

107 Love, "History and Development of the X-15 Research Aircraft," pp. 15-16.

108 Storms, "X-15 Hardware Design Challenges," pp. 32-33.

giving a test program a disease commonly referred to as 'cancelitis,' which results in little or no progress." It was an excellent observation, and is as applicable today as it was in 1960.[109]

With the blessing of Carpenter and Storms, North American conducted the third and final XLR99 demonstration flight (2-12-23) using X-15-2 on 6 December 1960. Crossfield successfully accomplished the engine-throttling, shutdown, and restart objectives. This marked the last X-15 flight for North American Aviation and Scott Crossfield. The job of flying the X-15 was now totally in the hands of the government test pilots. Crossfield, the engineer, transferred to testing the Hound Dog cruise missile and then to the Apollo program.[110]

After this flight, the program established a work schedule that would allow an early XLR99 flight with a government pilot using North American maintenance personnel. Bob White would make the flight as early as 21 December 1960, assuming North American could accomplish the necessary maintenance work in time. This included replacing the engine, which had suffered excessive chamber coating loss; installing redesigned canopy hooks and a reinforced vertical stabilizer; rearranging the alternate airspeed system; and relocating the ammonia tank helium pressure regulator into the fixed portion of the upper vertical. The company made good progress until engineers found a pinhole leak in the chamber throat of the replacement engine during a ground run. Although Reaction Motors considered the leak acceptable, it became increasingly worse during a subsequent test. Since a spare XLR99 was not available, the program canceled the flight and established a schedule to deliver the aircraft to the government prior to another flight. As a result, North American formally delivered X-15-2 to the Air Force and turned the airplane over to NASA on 7 February 1961. On the same day, X-15-1 was returned to the North American plant for conversion to the XLR99, having completed the last XLR11 flight (1-21-36) of the program the day before with Bob White at the controls.[111]

The first two years of the flight program showed five major reasons for flight cancellations: problems with the APUs and their fuel system, XLR11 problems, propellant system (less engine) difficulties, weather, and heating and ventilation troubles. When the ultimate engine came on line, the top five reasons changed slightly to XLR99 problems, propulsion system (less engine) difficulties, miscellaneous, problems with the APU and its fuel system, and stable platform failures. It was not surprising that the engine became a major source of delays, since the XLR99 was a major leap forward in rocket engine technology and growing pains were to be expected. Many of the propulsion-system problems were a direct result of the XLR99, such as some plastic seal materials being incompatible with anhydrous ammonia. Although the XLR99 was performing satisfactorily in flight, by

109 Ibid.

110 Love, "History and Development of the X-15 Research Aircraft," pp. 15-16.

111 X-15 Status Report, Paul F. Bikle/FRC to H. Brown/NASA Headquarters, 30 December 1960, pp. 1; North American report NA-65-1, "X-15 Research Airplane Flight Record," revised 15 May 1968; "Advanced Development Plan for X-15 Research Aircraft, Advanced Technology Program 653A," 17 November 1961, p. 1. The North American report says that X-15-2 was delivered on 8 February 1961; the Air Force report says 7 February. Engine 103 was removed and replaced with engine 104. These were the only two flight engines available at the time (105 had been destroyed in the X-15-3 ground accident, 106 and 108 were in acceptance testing, and 107, 109, and 111 were in assembly).

Major Robert M. White flew the last XLR11 flight of the program (1-21-36) on 7 February 1961. This was the fastest XLR11 flight, reaching 2,275 mph and Mach 3.50. Six months earlier White had gone to 136,500 feet using the XLR11s. Bob White holds the distinction of being the first man to fly Mach 3, Mach 4, Mach 5, and Mach 6, and the first pilot to fly to 200,000 feet and 300,000 feet, all in the X-15. (NASA)

the end of December 1960, maintenance personnel had discovered ammonia leaks in the thrust chambers of three engines. Reaction Motors dispatched technicians to Edwards to correct the problems while the Air Force, NASA, North American, and Reaction Motors all looked for a cause.[112]

From the beginning of the X-15 flight program in 1959 until the end of 1960, seven pilots had made 31 flights with the first two airplanes. The NB-52s had carried the two X-15s 55 times, including two scheduled captive flights and 22 aborted launch attempts. However, X-15-1 was experiencing an odd problem. When the pilot started the APU, the hydraulic pressure was either slow in coming up or dropped off out of limits when he moved the control surfaces. The solution to the problem was found after researchers placed additional instrumentation on the hydraulic system. The bootstrap line that pressurized the hydraulic reservoir was freezing, causing a flow restriction or stoppage. Under these conditions the hydraulic pump would cavitate, resulting in little or no pressure rise. The apparent cause of this problem was the addition of a liquid-nitrogen line to cool the stable platform. Since North American had installed the nitrogen line adjacent to the hydraulic lines, it caused the Orinite hydraulic oil to freeze. The solution was to add

112 Geiger et al., "History of the Wright Air Development Division: July 1960-March 1961," pp. I-48 to I-51; James E. Love and John A. Palmer, "Operational Reliability Experience with the X-15 aircraft," a paper in the *1961 Research Airplane Committee Report*, pp. 279-280.

electric heaters to the affected hydraulic lines, since there was not enough room in the side tunnel to separate the lines sufficiently to prevent the problem.

Some problems defied all efforts to fix them. For example, North American tested the APU and its fuel system for many hours on an exact replica of the airplane installation. Yet, over the course of the program, the APUs caused more schedule delays and cancellations than any other system. One of the major problems was a critical pressure switch. Although the switch had been thoroughly (and correctly) qualified by the vendor, the program had to replace it by the dozen. Even with improvements, the switch continued to be a problem.[113]

Paul Bikle closed the year by saying that he was generally pleased with the progress made: "The data coverage within this envelope has been fairly complete in the areas of performance, flight dynamics, control, and structural loads, but somewhat limited in structural heating due to the low heating rates encountered." Bikle cautioned, however, that the short duration and transient nature of each flight had generally precluded the acquisition of extensive or systematic measurements under selected flight conditions, as was possible with conventionally powered aircraft.[114]

1961 FLIGHT PERIOD

The first government flight (2-13-26) with the XLR99 finally took place on 7 March 1961 with Bob White at the controls. This was the first time a manned aircraft had flown faster than Mach 4, reaching Mach 4.43 and 77,450 feet. The objectives of the flight were to obtain additional aerodynamic and structural heating data, as well as information on stability and control of the aircraft at high speeds. The flight was generally satisfactory. Post-flight examination showed a limited amount of buckling to the side-fuselage tunnels, attributed to thermal expansion (the temperature difference between the tunnel panels and the primary fuselage structure was close to 500°F). The damage was not significant because the panels only carried air loads and were not primary structure. However, the buckling continued to become more severe as Mach numbers increased in later flights, and eventually NASA elected to install additional expansion joints to minimize the buckling.[115]

It was a complicated ballet, and many things could go wrong. On 21 March, Joe Walker took off in X-15-2 mated to the NB-52B (2-A-27). The telemetry system failed soon after takeoff, and the NB-52B landed with the hope of affecting a repair for another attempt later in the day. Unfortunately, during the landing the NB-52 drogue chute failed to operate properly, resulting in damage to the chute compartment. Heavy braking was required, causing the brakes on the forward

113 Love and Palmer, "Operational Reliability Experience with the X-15 aircraft," pp. 280-281.

114 X-15 Status Report, Paul F. Bikle/FRC to H. Brown/NASA Headquarters, 30 December 1960, pp. 2.

115 James E. Love, "History and Development of the X-15 Research Aircraft," not dated, p. 20. In the files at the DFRC History Office; letter, Major General Robert M. White (USAF, Retired) to Dennis R. Jenkins, 13 June 2002.

truck to overheat and the safety fuses of the tires to blow to relieve the air pressure. The repairs took a week. During the next attempt, on 29 March, a failure in the NB-52 landing-gear steering mechanism–possibly a residual effect of the earlier landing incident–delayed the flight for a day.[116]

Joe Walker's flight (2-14-28) on 30 March 1961 marked the first Hidden Hills launch and the first use of the new David Clark A/P22S-2 full-pressure suit instead of the earlier MC-2. Walker reported that the suit was much more comfortable and afforded better vision. The flight began rather inauspiciously with an engine failure immediately after the NB-52 released the X-15, but Walker successfully restarted the XLR99. During the "coast" portion of the flight between 100,000 feet and 169,000 feet, Walker experienced about 2 minutes of weightlessness, a new record for piloted aircraft. However, the flight revealed a potential problem with the stability augmentation system: as Walker descended through 100,000 feet, a heavy vibration occurred and continued for about 45 seconds until Walker recovered at 55,000 feet. The vibration included incremental acceleration of approximately 1 g in the vertical and transverse axes at a frequency of 13 cps, corresponding to the first bending mode of the horizontal stabilizer. This was one of the first cases of "structural resonance" for the X-15.[117]

Structural resonance can occur when high-gain feedback control systems are linked to lightly damped (welded) structural components, and happens when a control system sensor (in this case a pitch-rate gyro) detects motion at some structural mode frequency and then commands a surface actuator to move at that frequency, thus sustaining the oscillation. The motion transmits directly through the vehicle structure and does not require any aerodynamic response. Program personnel had observed this particular oscillation following one landing and during ground tests on the landing gear.[118]

Engineers originally thought it was associated with landing-gear modes and did not expect it to occur in flight. Subsequent analysis showed the SAS pitch gyro sustained the vibration at the natural frequency of the horizontal stabilizer. Essentially, the oscillations began because of the increased activity of the controls on reentry, which excited the oscillation and stopped after the pilot reduced the pitch-damper gain.[119]

The Air Force, NASA, North American, and Westinghouse (the manufacturer of the SAS) discussed two possible solutions for the vibration problem: a notch filter for the SAS, and a pressure-derivative feedback valve for the horizontal stabilizer hydraulic actuator. The notch filter eliminated SAS control surface input at 13 cps, and the feedback valve damped the stabilizer-bending mode. In essence, the valve corrected the source of the problem, while the notch filter avoided the problem. Although it was believed that either solution would likely affect a cure, the final decision was to use both. The Cornell Aeronautical Laboratory conducted

116 X-15 Status Reports, Paul F. Bikle/FRC to H. Brown/NASA Headquarters, 3 April 1961, pp. 1-2.

117 Love, "History and Development of the X-15 Research Aircraft," p. 21; Geiger et al., "History of the Wright Air Development Division: July 1960-March 1961," pp. I-51 to I-52.; letter, Robert G. Hoey to Dennis R. Jenkins, 12 August 2002.

118 Letter, Robert G. Hoey to Dennis R. Jenkins, 12 August 2002.

119 Joseph A. Walker, "Pilot Report for Flight 2-14-28," 3 April 1961; letter, Robert G. Hoey to Dennis R. Jenkins, 12 August 2002.

an independent assessment of the SAS, specifically looking at the two solutions to the vibration problem. The preliminary results from Cornell agreed with the assessments of Westinghouse and the FRC; however, no final record of the Cornell results could be ascertained.[120]

Joe Walker's flight took place five weeks before Alan Shepard's suborbital Mercury flight in *Freedom 7*, and was of great interest to the media and the public. Congressman Roman Pucinski (D-IL) asked Walker to write a short report on his impressions of the flight. Paul Bikle forwarded the report to Dr. Charles H. Roadman, the acting director of the Office of Life Science Programs at NASA Headquarters:[121]

> I had plenty of time at the peak of the trajectory to make outside observations. The most impressive observation initially was the aspect of the sky overhead. The color I would describe as being a very deep violet blue, not indicative of a black shading, but an extremely dark bluish cast....
>
> The next thing is that you have no doubt from external visual cues that you're really high up ... No difficulty is experienced in observing and identifying geographical features on the surface of the Earth particularly in areas with which one is familiar. An outstanding aspect of this is the appreciation of relative heights or elevations; different levels of the surface. Mountains still stand out as mountains and looking down into the Los Angeles Basin, I could tell the smog as distinct from some low stratocumulus clouds along the seacoast. Areas which are heavily forested or under agricultural development could be separated from those areas where nothing was growing, and once again, if one were familiar with the territory, this is even easier to pick out. The curvature of the Earth was very apparent.

There was a quiet rivalry between some of the X-15 pilots and their counterparts on Project Mercury. Milt Thompson remembered when he and Joe Walker traveled to Cape Canaveral to watch Virgil I. "Gus" Grissom fly the second suborbital Mercury flight in July 1961. Walker told Grissom that the X-15 had almost as much thrust as the Redstone booster that was going to lift *Liberty Bell* 7 (57,000 lbf versus 76,000 lbf for the Redstone), and that the X-15 engine had a throttle. Walker also pointed out that the X-15 pilots were flying the exit profile, while the Mercury astronauts were just along for the ride. In terms of actual performance, the suborbital Mercury flights and the X-15 were roughly comparable. Al Shepard reached a maximum speed of 5,180 mph and an altitude of 116 miles; the X-15 would eventually demonstrate 4,520 mph and 67 miles. Of

120 Love, "History and Development of the X-15 Research Aircraft," p. 21; Geiger et al., "History of the Wright Air Development Division: July 1960-March 1961," pp. I-51 to I-52; X-15 Status Reports, Paul F. Bikle/FRC to H. Brown/NASA Headquarters, 15 May 1961, p. 4 and 1 June 1961, p. 4.

121 Letter, Paul F. Bikle to Dr. Charles H. Roadman, 3 April 1961, attaching a copy of a memorandum from Joseph A. Walker, subject, visual observations during flight 2-14-28, 30 March 1961.

course, Walker was not really arguing; it was obvious that the astronauts would ultimately go much faster and higher than the X-15. Somehow, Tom Wolfe picked up this story and portrayed it in *The Right Stuff* as more of a real argument than it ever was.[122]

By June 1961, government test pilots had been flying the X-15 for just over a year. There were four primary objectives during this period: comparing the predicted hypersonic aerodynamic heating rates against actual flight results, determining the structural characteristics of the X-15 during high heating, investigating hypersonic stability during boost and reentry, and evaluating pilot performance during hypersonic flight and zero g. These objectives were largely satisfied by late 1961, although some specific research continued until 1967 using the X-15A-2.[123]

Physiologists discovered that the heart rates of the X-15 pilots varied between 145 and 185 beats per minute compared to only 70–80 beats per minute on test missions in other aircraft. The researchers ultimately determined that pre-launch anticipatory stress, not post-launch physical stress, was the primary cause of the high heart rate. The researchers determined that the high rates were probably representative of the physiological condition of future astronauts, which was later confirmed on the Mercury flights. Interestingly, the pilots thought little about the weightlessness aspects of some of their mission profiles. Bob White commented that "zero-g, while apparently an interesting area to consider has had no noticeable effect on the pilot control task for the approximate 2-minute period during which the weightless state was experienced."[124]

Although the X-15 researchers at Langley and elsewhere performed years of theoretical analysis and wind-tunnel testing on the airplane configuration and missions, sometimes the best results came from the folks in the trenches. The flight planners and pilots learned early on that the best way to reenter from the high-altitude missions was to establish a constant angle of attack at the top and then allow the acceleration forces to build as the dynamic pressure increased. As the airplane approached the desired g-loading, the pilot gradually decreased the angle of attack and the airplane usually experienced the maximum dynamic pressure just prior to level flight. As the maximum altitude increased, so did the initial angle of attack needed to avoid exceeding the airplane structural limits. The pilots and flight planners practiced this many times in the fixed-base simulators.[125]

The early simulations had showed that reentries with the SAS turned off were possible at initial angles of attack up to 15 degrees, which was adequate to achieve the altitude goals of the X-15 program. Above 15 degrees, a serious instability would develop and the airplane would be uncontrollable without the dampers, and even then would tend to oscillate in sideslip. Researchers programmed the

122 Thompson, *At the Edge of Space*, p. 6; telephone conversation, Scott Crossfield with Dennis R. Jenkins, 1 June 2000.

123 Crossfield, *Always Another Dawn*, pp. 307-366.

124 Stillwell, *X-15 Research Results*, pp. 65; quote from Robert M. White, Glenn H. Robinson, and Gene J. Matranga, NASA confidential technical memorandum X-715, "Résumé of X-15 Handling Qualities," March 1962, p. 5; telephone conversation, Major General Robert M. White with Dennis R. Jenkins, 18 August 2002.

125 Robert G. Hoey, "X-15: Ventral-Off," in Fred Stoliker, Bob Hoey, and Johnny Armstrong, *Flight Testing at Edwards: Flight Test Stories–1946-1975* (Edwards, CA: Flight Test Historical Foundation, 2001), pp. 155-158. Anyone who is interested in getting a better "feel" for how testing progressed at Edwards during this period should find a copy of this collection of short stories written by some of the flight test engineers and flight planners.

simulator with the results of all of the wind-tunnel data accumulated so far in the program. The problem was that the early wind-tunnel tests had the horizontal stabilizer at zero deflection, but the airplane usually flew with a substantial deflection, approximately 15–20 degrees leading-edge down. As the wind-tunnel researchers expanded their tests to include runs at non-zero deflections, serious concerns began to develop. When researchers mechanized the new data into the simulator, they discovered that the maximum angle of attack possible with the dampers failed (or turned off) was only about 8 degrees, not 15 degrees as had been thought. This limited the maximum altitude to about 200,000 feet since the non-redundant roll damper was required for control at higher angles of attack. This limitation was obviously unsatisfactory and the researchers needed to find a solution.[126]

Engineers considered the original SAS fail-safe because it consisted of dual channels; however, these were not redundant channels–each axis had a working channel and a monitor channel. When the system detected a difference between the working and monitor channels in any axis, it inhibited the dampers for that axis, eliminating any possibility it could do something untoward. The system, therefore, was fail-safe but not fail-operational. Discussions (usually initiated by the pilots) on whether the SAS should be truly redundant (fail-operational) had taken place since the beginning of development contract, with the conclusion being that the weight penalty was too severe. By 1961, however, the program had stopped worrying about saving a few pounds, and was concentrating instead on producing the most useful vehicle possible. If the simulations were right, a single failure in the roll channel would result in the loss of the airplane reentering from high altitude. Two flight planners, Richard E. Day from the FRC and Robert G. Hoey from the AFFTC, decided this required further investigation since it potentially could keep the X-15 from achieving its design objectives.[127]

The first step was "to verify the problem was real and not some quirk in the simulation." During flight 1-11-21 on 19 August 1960, Joe Walker intentionally turned off the roll dampers and began to increase the angle of attack. The divergent lateral oscillations experienced by Walker were identical to what the simulator had predicted–the problem was real. Ironically, the cause was an adverse rolling moment created by having too much vertical stabilizer. Although the airplane had adequate directional stability, the dihedral effect was strongly negative at high angles of attack (i.e., left sideslip produced left roll).[128]

Part of the problem lay in the technique used for the original analysis of the flight profiles, which assumed that the airplane spent most of the flight at zero, or very low, angles of attack. Only the reentry pull-up at high-q and high-g was at 15 degrees angle of attack for a short time. North American engineers were well aware that this did not reflect how NASA would use the airplane, and it was obvious to everybody that the most practical method was to establish a constant, high

126 Hoey, "X-15: Ventral-Off," pp. 155-158; letter, Johnny G. Armstrong to Dennis R. Jenkins, 3 August 2002.

127 Robert G. Hoey, AFFTC technology document FTC-TDR-62-7, "Envelope Expansion with Interim XLR11 Rocket Engines," 1962; Hoey, "X-15: Ventral-Off," pp. 155-158; Joseph A. Walker, "A Pilot's Impression of the X-15 Program," a paper in the *1961 Research Airplane Committee Report,* p. 305; Robert A. Tremant, NASA technical note D-1402, "Operational Experiences and Characteristics of the X-15 Flight Control System," December 1962, pp. 10-11.

128 Joseph A. Walker, "Pilot Notes for Flight 1-11-21," 19 August 1960; Hoey, "X-15: Ventral-Off," pp. 155-158; letter, Robert G. Hoey to Dennis R. Jenkins, 20 May 2002.

angle of attack before any buildup in dynamic pressure or acceleration occurred. The North American design missions represented a worst-case structural load, but the engineers were late in assessing the handling qualities and stability problems of setting up and flying through reentry at fairly high angle of attack.[129]

To provide operational redundancy, North American developed a backup roll damper. This alternate stability augmentation system (ASAS) operated at a fixed gain level that was set before each flight based on the pilot's preferences. It contained its own sensors, had minimal electronics, and fed directly to the existing servocylinders. This backup system was for emergency use only and the pilot could engage it at any time. NASA installed the ASAS in X-15-1 and X-15-2 during April 1962. Subsequently, in early 1967 NASA modified the ASAS in X-15A-2 to include the yaw axis in anticipation of flights with the dummy ramjet. This provided an extra margin of safety for the X-15A-2 at Mach numbers above 6, but was subsequently installed in X-15-1 as a matter of commonality. The MH-96 provided its own redundancy, so X-15-3 did not include an ASAS.[130]

However, Hoey and Day were not convinced that the ASAS was the entire answer, although nobody questioned its potential usefulness. Hours in the simulator had convinced the flight planners that the airplane did not fly the high angle-of-attack reentry profile all that well even when all the dampers were functioning properly, and they began exploring possible aerodynamic fixes.[131]

The primary reason for the large, symmetrical vertical stabilizer was to compensate for potential thrust misalignment at the end of the exit phase when dynamic pressure was low. This had been a major concern early on, and the program had even evaluated using the ballistic control system to handle thrust misalignments. As it turned out, Hoey remembers, "the engine guys figured out a clever way of aligning the engines in the airplanes, which essentially eliminated thrust misalignment as a problem. We never experienced any significant thrust misalignment during the flight program." The trouble became that the wedge-shaped dorsal and ventral stabilizers actually prevented the airplane from flying safely at high angles of attack because of a negative dihedral effect.[132]

Since it appeared that the problem was that the ventral stabilizer was too large, Hoey and Day decided to see what would happen if they made it smaller. This was easy to do because the pilot jettisoned the lower rudder at the end of each flight anyway. There was a substantial base of wind-tunnel and flight-test data at low speeds with the ventral off, since this was the standard landing configuration. However, the high-speed investigation of this configuration consisted of a single set of wind-tunnel runs at Mach 3–hardly conclusive data. Nevertheless, Hoey and Day created a temporary modification to the simulator using these data and "some freehand guesses" to fill in the holes at other Mach numbers.[133]

---

129 Letter, Robert G. Hoey to Dennis R. Jenkins, 20 May 2002.

130 X-15 Status Report, Paul F. Bikle/FRC to H. Brown/NASA Headquarters, 16 April 1962, pp. 3; "X-15 Semi-Annual Status Report No. 2," April 1964, p. 6; "X-15 Semi-Annual Status Report No. 6," 1 November 1966, p. 13; "X-15 Semi-Annual Status Report," 10 May 1967, p. 34.

131 X-15 Status Report, Paul F. Bikle/FRC to H. Brown/NASA Headquarters, 16 April 1962, pp. 3; Hoey, "X-15: Ventral-Off," pp. 155-158; letter, Robert G. Hoey to Dennis R. Jenkins, 20 May 2002.

132 Letter, Robert G. Hoey to Dennis R. Jenkins, 20 May 2002.

133 Stillwell, *X-15 Research Results*, pp. 51-52; Gene J. Matranga, NASA technical note D-1057, "Analysis of X-15 Landing Approach and Flare Characteristics Determined from the First 30 Flights," July 1961, pp. 8-9; Hoey, "X-15: Ventral-Off," pp. 155-158.

As could easily be imagined, the directional stability was somewhat less throughout the envelope, but the dihedral effect was normal at all angles of attack and the Dutch roll stability was satisfactory. More importantly, the simulator was easily controllable with the dampers off from altitudes as high as 250,000 feet. Hoey and Day were sufficiently confident in the ventral-off scheme that they proposed to test it on an upcoming Mach 4 flight at 80,000 feet. When the two flight planners first presented their idea to the rest of the technical community, they met with some skepticism. The aerodynamicists wanted to run a complete set of wind-tunnel tests to verify the concept, something that would take a considerable amount of time. However, Paul Bikle and Bob Rushworth believed the risks involved in testing the idea were minimal and worthwhile, and approved the concept.[134]

The technicians at the FRC began building a heat shield to bolt onto the bottom of the fixed portion of the ventral to protect the area from aerodynamic heating, and to clean up the drag in the area to ensure there were no local hot spots. As the proposed flight got closer, however, Hoey and Day became increasingly nervous since they had based their idea on "pretty thin evidence." What bothered the flight planners the most was that the trend in high-speed flight had been to *increase* the vertical surface area, which explains why the X-15 had such large surfaces to begin with. In fact, the vertical surfaces on most of the early supersonic combat aircraft had been increased 15–20% based on initial supersonic flight tests. Hoey and Day were proposing to *decrease* the surface area of the X-15 by 27%. However, the planners had no idea what stability degradation might occur due to rocket plume effects, and no data on the effects of operating the speed brakes. Bob Hoey observed, "On the morning of the flight, I suspect that Bikle and Rushworth had more confidence in Hoey and Day than did Hoey and Day."[135]

There was another concern, one that researchers could not adequately investigate except in the wind tunnel or in flight. With the ventral rudder removed, the X-15 would have no directional control for the first second or two immediately after launch from the carrier aircraft, since the NB-52 wing would blank the dorsal vertical stabilizer and rudder until the airplane had dropped a few feet. It did not seem like a real problem, but it was an unknown.[136]

With complete faith in the flight planners, Bob Rushworth flew the first ventral-off flight (1-23-39) on 4 October 1961, reaching Mach 4.3 and 78,000 feet. The flight went without a hitch. The X-15 had sufficient directional stability during launch, and the handling qualities were similar to those of the ventral-on configuration at low angles of attack, but better at 8 degrees. Rushworth performed several stability pulses that matched the trends seen in the simulator. This apparent success prompted the researchers at Langley to begin wind-tunnel tests of the entire speed and altitude range, but it would be another year before the program began to fly routinely without the ventral.[137]

On 30 April 1962, Joe Walker flew the first flight (1-27-48) to nearly the design altitude, reaching 246,700 feet with the ventral on and the ASAS installed.

134 Hoey, "X-15: Ventral-Off," pp. 155-158; letter, Robert G. Hoey to Dennis R. Jenkins, 20 May 2002.

135 Ibid, pp. 155-158.

136 Major Robert A. Rushworth, "Pilot Report for Flight 1-23-39," 4 October 1961; X-15 Status Report, Paul F. Bikle/FRC to H. Brown/NASA Headquarters, 16 October 1961, p. 5.

137 Ibid. Facts confirmed via e-mail from Bob Hoey to Dennis R. Jenkins, 12 August 2002.

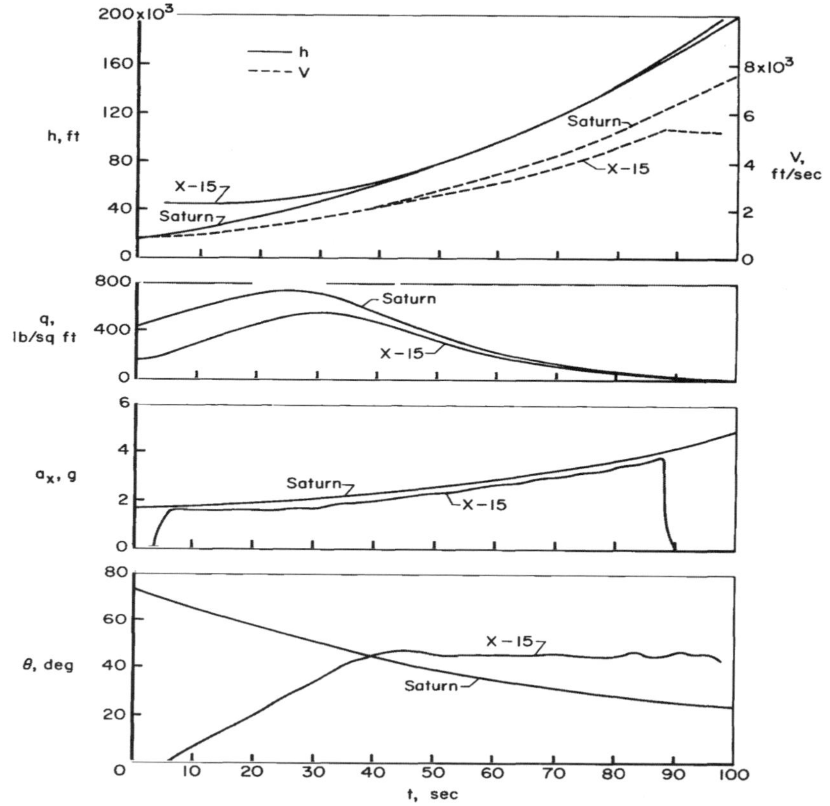

The X-15 pilots and the astronauts at Cape Canaveral were always joking with each other about who had the best ride. The X-15 was incapable of reaching orbital velocities, but within its domain, it gave even the Saturn I used on the early Apollo missions a run for its money. (NASA)

Five months later the researchers had completed the ventral-off wind-tunnel tests and mechanized the results on the simulator. These tests showed that the configuration allowed reentries with the dampers off at angles of attack as high as 26 degrees, equal to 400,000 feet. Wind-tunnel data showed that there were some directional stability problems in the transonic region with the speed brakes deployed, but the flight planners briefed the pilots on how to avoid this area. Jack McKay flew the second ventral-off flight (2-29-50) on 28 September 1962, and the flight was completely nominal.[138]

Eliminating the lower portion of the ventral had another benefit that researchers had recognized as early as 1961: the lift-drag ratio increased from 4.25 to 4.5, offering slightly improved range. Eventually the airplanes flew Mach 6 reentries with trajectories of up to 26 degrees and flight path angles approaching –38 degrees. It would be over three years before the program would use the ventral rud-

138 Joseph A. Walker, "Pilot Report for Flight 1-27-48," 30 April 1962; Jack B. McKay, "Pilot Report for Flight 2-29-50," 28 September 1962; Hoey, "X-15: Ventral-Off," pp. 155-158.

der again in flight, and then only five times–all of them with X-15A-2. In all, the program would make 73 flights with the ventral on and 126 with it off.[139]

Heading back to the flight program, it is interesting to note that things that sound potentially catastrophic, or at least important, in retrospect were not necessarily so at the time. For instance, on 11 October 1961, the left outer windscreen glass on flight 2-20-36 developed a series of longitudinal cracks. In an unusual lapse of procedure, technicians had inadvertently installed one of the original soda-lime windshields in the left panel of X-15-2 and it fractured during reentry from 217,000 feet. The item did not figure at all in the post-flight pilot report, and rated exactly three lines of radio chatter at the time. Bob White to Forrest Petersen, who was NASA-1 that day: "OK, my … outside windshield went …." Petersen responded, "Understand, outside pane?" White confirmed, "That's correct," and both men returned to their duties.[140]

White was not quite as calm on the next flight (2-21-37) when a similar thing happened. The right side of the windshield shattered as he decelerated through Mach 2.7 after White became the first person to pilot an aircraft above Mach 6. In this case, the windshield was the correct alumino-silicate glass. The event even made it into the report this time:[141]

> I would guess at about 2.7 Mach number at 70,000 feet, somewhere in that neighborhood, when I said, "Good Lord, not again," that's where the right windshield panel went. … I could see out the left windshield panel fairly well, and the lake was just off to the left so it looked like it would be real handy for a left-hand circle landing pattern. As I got down lower, I realized I couldn't see out the right side. For all intents and purposes, the visibility out of the right windshield was nonexistent. I asked the chase plane to stay in close, thinking right after it happened that it might also happen on the left side. In that event, I considered going to high face plate heat when I got subsonic, jettison the canopy and see what happened from there. The pattern was as per usual, but on the final approach I was quite surprised at what a compromise it offered being able to see out of only one windshield.

Investigations revealed that the retainer frame buckled near the center of the upper edge of the glass and created a local hot spot, causing the glass to fail. Engineers subsequently changed the retainer from its original 0.050-inch-thick Inconel X design to one that used a 0.100-inch-thick 6A1-4V titanium alloy. The reduced coefficient of expansion of titanium better compensated for the differential expansion associated with the cooler Inconel X substructure. Nevertheless, as the flight envelope expanded and the environment became more severe, the glass deteriorated along the rear edge just forward of the aft windshield frame. Engineers cured

---

139 Stillwell, *X-15 Research Results*, pp. 51-52; NASA technical note D-1057, pp. 8-9; letter, Robert G. Hoey to Dennis R. Jenkins, 12 August 2002.

140 Radio transcript, Flight 2-20-36. In the files at the DFRC History Office.

141 Robert M. White, "Pilot Report from Flight 2-21-37," 9 November 1961. In the files at the DFRC History Office.

this by cutting away the aft retainer, eliminating the lip that was causing the hot spot on the glass.[142]

In 1968, John Becker wrote, "The really important lesson here is that what are minor and unimportant features of a subsonic or supersonic aircraft must be dealt with as prime design problems in a hypersonic airplane. This lesson was applied effectively in the precise design of a host of important details on the manned space vehicles."[143]

During the first year of XLR99 flight operations, nearly all of the flights experienced malfunction shutdowns of the engine immediately after launch, and sometimes after normal engine burnout. The engine always relit on the second attempt, making the former cases more of an annoyance than anything else. The post-burnout malfunction was more perplexing since the only engine system that was active after shutdown was the lube-oil system. Analyses of this condition revealed wide acceleration excursions during the engine-start phase. Engineers created a reasonable simulation of this acceleration by placing an engine on a work stand with the ability to rotate about the Y-axis. Under certain conditions, the lube-oil pump cavitated for about 2 seconds, tripping an automatic malfunction shutdown. To eliminate this problem, Reaction Motors installed a delay timer in the lube-oil malfunction circuit that allowed the pump to cavitate up to 6 seconds without actuating the malfunction shutdown system. After this delay timer was installed in early 1962, the program did not experience any further malfunction shutdowns of this type, although the engine still required two ignition attempts on occasion.[144]

On 11 October 1961, flight 2-20-36 became the first to use the ballistic control system to maintain the attitude of the airplane. Bob White flew the mission to Mach 5.21 and 217,000 feet and reported that the system worked as expected. Post-flight inspections, however, revealed an unexplained high propellant consumption by the no. 2 system. Actually, both systems used more propellant than expected, and this provided an impetus to install a transfer system that transferred residual propellants from the XLR99 turbopump supply to the ballistic control system. North American subsequently installed the transfer system in all three airplanes.[145]

---

142 Eldon E. Kordes, Robert D. Reed, and Alpha L. Dawdy, "Structural Heating Experiences of the X-15," a paper in the *1961 Research Airplane Committee Report*, pp. 33-34; Greene and Benner, "X-15 Experience from the Designer's Viewpoint," pp. 318-319; Love and Fischel, "Status of X-15 Program," p. 6. North American conducted a series of laboratory tests on the new configuration in late 1961. During the last test of the series the glass failed at 1.50 times the temperature and 1.50 times the deflections that had been experienced on flight 2-21-37. However, it was not believed that this represented an accurate test since the longeron on the test sample was made of aluminum (instead of Inconel X) and was very close to its melting point of 1,200°F. It was thought that this produced an excessive concentration of force on the glass. Except for the last test, however, there was no indication that the titanium glass retainer was buckling or lifting away from the glass to create any potential hot spots, so the new configuration was cleared for flight. See X-15 Status Report, Paul F. Bikle/FRC to H. Brown/NASA Headquarters, 2 January 1962, p. 6. In the files at the DFRC History Office.

143 John V. Becker, "The X-15 Program in Retrospect," 3rd Eugen Sänger Memorial Lecture at the Deutsch Geaellschaft Fur Luftfahrforschung, Bonn, Germany, 5 December 1968; and James E. Love, "X-15: Past and Future," paper presented to the Fort Wayne Section, Society of Automotive Engineers, 9 December 1964.

144 Love, "History and Development of the X-15 Research Aircraft," p. 17.

145 X-15 Status Report, Paul F. Bikle/FRC to H. Brown/NASA Headquarters, 16 October 1961, p. 9. Since the ballistic control system shared propellant tanks with the APUs, this change also provided more propellants for the APUs if needed.

Pilot in the Loop

During the late 1950s and early 1960s, the value of a human pilot and redundant systems in space vehicles was a matter of some controversy. There was, and continues to be, a great debate on the relative merits of piloted vehicles versus automated ones. Because it had many similarities to early spacecraft, the X-15 became the subject of several evaluations and studies to determine whether the general design approach taken concerning redundancy and control were appropriate.[146]

The AFFTC conducted one of these evaluations during late 1961. The basic approach of the study was to perform a detailed flight-by-flight engineering analysis of each problem or failure that occurred for the 44 free flights, plus an additional 2 captive flights and 30 aborts, made through 1 November 1961. For each problem, researchers assessed the action taken by the pilot or redundant system with regard to its impact on mission success and vehicle recovery. The researchers then compared the results with those that would be obtained on a hypothetical unmanned and/or non-redundant X-15.[147]

The researchers strictly adhered to several important ground rules during the evaluation and documented every problem, whether it seemed significant or not. The researchers conservatively assessed the benefits of the pilot-in-the-loop and redundancy to avoid any glorification of either of these elements.[148] The researchers also attempted to minimize conjecture, especially in the case of the hypothetical unmanned X-15. For instance, the researchers did not credit a pilot with detection or corrective action that some other element would definitely have provided in his absence. Likewise, he was not marked down for detrimental effects that would have been the same without a pilot. The study used a similar assessment scheme for redundancy. Finally, for the hypothetical unmanned X-15, the study assumed no changes to systems or components other than removing all redundant systems and substituting relatively simple and reliable present-day systems in their place.[149]

The results were not surprising. Of the 44 free flights conducted up to that time, researchers considered 43 successful as flown.[150] Computed as an airplane that carried a pilot but no redundant systems, only 27 would have been successful. The number fell to 24 with redundancy but without a pilot, and to only 23 with no redundancy or pilot. The study noted that 19 flights were completely trouble- free, so they would have been successful in any of the three configurations. Significantly, the evaluation showed that the majority of times the mission was not successful, the aircraft would have been lost. In fact, in the case of a pi-

146 Robert G. Nagel, "X-15 Pilot-in-the-Loop and Redundancy Evaluation," a paper in the *1961 Research Airplane Committee Report*, p. 289. An expanded version of this paper (covering the first 47 flights) was published as AFFTC technical documentary report 62-20, "X-15 Pilot-in-the-Loop and Redundant/Emergency Systems Evaluation," October 1962.

147 Ibid, pp. 289-290.

148 This also required some manipulation of the data. For instance, problems concerning the life support system, and the benefits of its redundancy were only factored into the piloted X-15. It was believed that if it were not for the presence of the pilot, there would have been no need for such systems or redundancy. This approach was taken to keep the results conservative with regard to prohibiting any distortion of the virtues of redundant systems in general.

149 Nagel, "X-15 Pilot-in-the-Loop and Redundancy Evaluation," pp. 289-290.

150 Flight 2-3-9 was not, since it terminated after only 13.9 seconds of powered flight and Crossfield made an emergency landing on Rosamond Dry Lake.

loted but non-redundant X-15, the study showed that 14 aircraft would have been lost in 44 missions.[151]

Around the same time, The Boeing Company conducted a similar study that analyzed the first 60 flights of the Bomarc surface-to-air missile. This large unmanned missile was designed to be relatively non-redundant in order to keep its manufacturing costs low.[152] The Boeing study compared the actual flight results with a theoretical piloted Bomarc that incorporated a level of redundancy mostly equivalent to the X-15. Thus, the Boeing study was roughly the inverse extrapolation of the AFFTC X-15 evaluation, and the results bore an amazing similarity. For the X-15, the total mission success rate had been approximately 98%, which compared well to the computed 97% rate for a piloted and redundant Bomarc. Conversely, for both the actual Bomarc and the theoretical unmanned, non-redundant X-15, the total mission success rate was an identical 43%. This lent credibility to the idea that, with the current state of the art, it was still important to include a pilot in the loop.[153]

The Third Industry Conference

November 1961 saw the first industry conference held in three years (NASA had held previous conferences in 1956 and 1958). The classified conference at the FRC featured 24 papers from 56 authors, including 4 X-15 pilots, and was attended by 442 people. Of the authors, 5 came from North American, 37 from various NASA centers, 13 from the Air Force, and 1 from the Navy. The attendees represented virtually every major aerospace contractor in the country, all of the NASA centers, several universities, the various military services, and the British Embassy.[154]

At the time the papers for the conference were prepared, the program had made 45 flights during the 29 months since the initial X-15 flight. The first of these was a glide flight, and of the subsequent powered flights, 29 had used the XLR11 engines and 15 used the XLR99. A maximum altitude of 217,000 feet (flight 2-20-36) and a velocity of 6,005 feet per second (flight 2-21-37) had been achieved.[155]

Researchers had already accomplished quite a bit of analysis on aerodynamic heating, one of the primary research objectives of the X-15. Several theoretical models had been developed to predict heating rates, but little experimental data were available to validate them since it was uncertain whether wind tunnels were capable of realistically simulating the conditions. The X-15 provided the first real-world experience at high Mach numbers in a well-instrumented, recoverable vehicle. Data from the X-15 showed that none of the models were completely ac-

151 Nagel, "X-15 Pilot-in-the-Loop and Redundancy Evaluation," pp. 291-292.

152 The supersonic Bomarc missiles (IM-99A and IM-99B) were the world's first long-range anti-aircraft missiles. The Bomarc used analog computers, some of which were built by Boeing and had been developed for GAPA experiments during World War II. Authorized by the Air Force in 1949, Bomarc was the result of coordinated research between Boeing (Bo) and the University of Michigan Aeronautical Research Center (marc). Boeing built 700 Bomarc missiles between 1957 and 1964, as well as 420 launch systems. Bomarc was retired from active service during the early 1970s.

153 Nagel, "X-15 Pilot-in-the-Loop and Redundancy Evaluation," pp. 293 and 301.

154 Table of contents and registered guest list in the front of the *1961 Research Airplane Committee Report*.

155 De E. Beeler and Thomas A Toll, "Status of X-15 Research Program," a paper in the *1961 Research Airplane Committee Report*.

curate, although all showed some correlation at different Mach numbers. The data showed that the wind tunnels were reasonably accurate.[156]

A particular area of interest to researchers was how the boundary layer transitioned at different Mach numbers and angles of attack. Researchers used two methods to detect laminar and turbulent areas on the airplane in flight. The first was to use thermocouple data reduced to heat-transfer coefficients, which showed a much higher level of heat transfer in a turbulent boundary layer than in a laminar one. The second method was to use temperature-sensitive "DetectoTemp" paint applied over large areas of the airplane. In general, NASA applied the paint to the left side of the airplane, and the thermocouples were on the right side.[157]

The first use of the paint was on 4 August 1960 for flight 1-9-17, which was the XLR11 maximum speed attempt. The results were promising inasmuch as the paint established a semipermanent pattern of contrasting colors at different temperature levels. The pattern retained on the wing and vertical stabilizer after the flight clearly indicated all of the heat-sink locations and areas of high heating. For instance, the internal spars and ribs stood out as heat sinks, while areas such as the expansion joints on the wing leading edge stood out in the color pattern as concentrated heating areas. Researchers decided that they could use the paint to collect qualitative temperature data, particularly in small areas that were not equipped with thermocouples.[158]

One of the notable discoveries made using the paint was that patterns indicated high-temperature, wedge-shaped areas originating at the wing leading-edge expansion joints and extending for a considerable distance rearward. The 0.080-inch-wide expansion joints appeared to result in a turbulent flow during the entire flight, producing 1,000°F temperatures in an 8-inch wedged-shaped area behind them. The measured heat-transfer data on the other wing supported this view, offering "a classic example of the interaction among aerodynamic flow, thermodynamic properties of air, and elastic characteristics of structure." Although the rates were well within the limits of the airframe, engineers installed small 0.008-inch-thick Inconel X shields over the expansion joints in an attempt to minimize the interference. Flights with these covers showed that the turbulent wedges still existed, although they were smaller, and researchers theorized that they would be present for shorter periods on each flight.[159]

The conclusion drawn from this was that the "boundary layer transition, which may be produced by such discontinuities in the surface of a high-speed vehicle, would be extremely difficult to predict. As yet, for the X-15, there has not been established parametric correlation which would allow the prediction of the

156 Richard D. Banner, Albert E. Kuhl, and Robert D. Quinn, "Preliminary Results of Aerodynamic Heating Studies on the X-15," a paper in the *1961 Research Airplane Committee Report*, pp. 14-15. The theoretical models included ones from Ernst Eckert at Wright Field, Eva Winkler at the Naval Ordnance Laboratory, and E. R. Van Driest.

157 Banner et al., "Preliminary Results of Aerodynamic Heating Studies on the X-15," pp. 16-17. This paint was procured from Curtiss-Wright and turned various colors depending upon the temperatures encountered. The paint was a light green when it was applied. It changed to a light blue at approximately 149°F, light blue to yellow at 293°F, yellow to black at 428°F, and then black to brown at 644°F. Several similar paints, such as Tempilaq (Tempil, Inc.), were also used. For a good description of Tempilaq see *http://www.tempil.com/TempilaqG.htm*, accessed 30 July 2002.

158 X-15 Status Report, Paul F. Bikle/FRC to H. Brown/NASA Headquarters, 15 August 1960, p. 3.

159 Stillwell, *X-15 Research Results*, pp. 65; Banner et al., "Preliminary Results of Aerodynamic Heating Studies on the X-15," pp. 17-18.

transition location on the wing *a priori*. Under these circumstances, it would seem that conservative estimates of transition should still be required."[160]

To show how the preflight estimates and flight data correlated, the authors presented data for one thermocouple on the lower surface of the right wing about 1.4 feet from the leading edge at mid-semispan. For the high-speed flight profile, the measured data indicated an all-turbulent flow with a high skin-heating rate and high maximum temperature. The calculated skin temperature agreed quite well during the high heating period, but slightly overestimated the measured value near its peak and during a period of cooling just afterwards. A close look at the trajectory during this period of disagreement showed a high angle of attack, and researchers believed the differences were due to their inability to properly predict the local flow conditions. For a high-altitude mission, however, this point of the wing appeared to experience laminar flow, at least at times. An all-turbulent flow prediction resulted in a higher temperature than was actually measured during the exit phase of the trajectory, greater cooling during the ballistic portion, and an overestimate of the maximum temperature during reentry. The assumption of laminar flow during the latter part of the exit phase resulted in better agreement between the measured and calculated data. Researchers noted, however, that one of the turbulent wedges originating on a wing leading-edge expansion joint might affect the thermocouple in question. Researchers did not understand exactly what might cause the location to go laminar, but theorized that either the turbulent wedge vanished or its lateral spread was delayed.[161]

The wing leading-edge expansion slots produced problems in addition to the wedge-shaped boundary layer issue. On one flight the area directly behind the expansion slots buckled. One reason for this was that the fastener spacing directly behind the slot was wider than on other sections of the leading edge, providing less support for the area. It was also determined that the original segmentation of the leading-edge heat sink did not adequately relieve the thermal compression loads. The skins at the expansion slots acted as a splice plate for the solid heat-sink bar, and as a result buckled in compression. Engineers made several changes to solve this problem. The shield installed over each expansion slot to help the boundary layer problem minimized the local hot spot, but engineers also added a fastener near each slot and three additional expansion slots (with shields) in the outboard segments of the leading edge. This presented some concern since North American had designed the original expansion slots with shear ties to prevent relative displacement of the leading edge, and it was not cost-effective to provide shear ties for the new slots because the entire wing structure would have required modification. A structural analysis showed that sufficient shear stiffness was present in the leading edge to meet the design requirements without shear ties, but engineers expected some relative displacement at the three new slots. Actual flight tests showed that this displacement averaged about 0.125 inch. Overall,

160 Banner et al., "Preliminary Results of Aerodynamic Heating Studies on the X-15," p. 18.

161 Ibid, pp. 18-19.

The X-15 program was one of the first to employ temperature-sensitive paint that established a semi-permanent pattern of contrasting colors at different temperature levels. The paint clearly showed the different heating loads absorbed by the hot-structure airframe. In general, NASA applied the paint to the left side of the airplane; the thermocouples were on the right side. (NASA)

the modifications prevented any serious leading-edge buckling, although minor distortions continued throughout the flight program.[162]

The conclusion drawn from the available data was that "when the boundary layer is known to be either laminar or turbulent, the skin temperatures can be predicted with reasonable accuracy." The problem was to figure out what the boundary layer would do under different flight conditions.[163]

The effect of temperature is not linear, and at Mach 6 the heating load on the X-15 was eight times that experienced at Mach 3. Unsurprisingly, the front and lower surfaces of the aircraft experienced the highest heating rates. During the conference, researchers discussed several intriguing aspects of the temperature problems. One was surprising, given that the program had always worried about high temperatures: "The first temperature problem occurred on the side-fairing panels along the LOX tank before the X-15 was first flown. Pronounced elastic buckles appeared in the panels as a result of contraction when the tank was filled for the first time." Adding a 0.125-inch expansion joint to the tunnel fairing near the wing leading edge relieved the buckling.[164]

162 Eldon E. Kordes, Robert D. Reed, and Alpha L. Dawdy, "Structural Heating Experiences of the X-15," a paper in the *1961 Research Airplane Committee Report*, pp. 34-35.

163 Banner et al., "Preliminary Results of Aerodynamic Heating Studies on the X-15," pp. 18-19.

164 Kordes et al., "Structural Heating Experiences of the X-15," pp. 31-32; Stillwell, *X-15 Research Results*, pp. 65.

However, after a Mach 4.43 flight (2-13-26) on 7 March 1961, several permanent 0.25-inch buckles formed in the outer sheet of the fairing between the corrugations near the edge of a panel. Since the panel only carried air loads (not structural loads), the buckles did not seriously affect structural integrity. During the flight, the panels that buckled had experienced temperatures between 490°F (near the wing leading edge) to 590°F (near the front of the fairing). On this particular flight, the pilot shut down the engine prior to propellant depletion, leaving about 20% of the liquid oxygen in its tank. The maximum temperatures occurred after shutdown, and it was theorized that the cold tank (–260°F), together with the high outer-skin temperatures, resulted in large thermal gradients that caused the buckles. These gradients were higher than had been calculated for the original design, since the estimates had assumed propellant depletion on all flights. Based on this experience, engineers added four expansion joints in the fairing ahead of the wing that allowed a total expansion of slightly over 1 inch. This modification appeared to prevent any further buckling.[165]

Researchers expected the surface irregularities produced by the buckles to cause local hot spots during high-speed flights. To investigate this, NASA covered the buckled areas with temperature-sensitive paint for flight 2-15-29. The results from the Mach 4.62 flight showed that the maximum temperature in the buckle area was essentially the same as in the surrounding areas with no evidence of local hot spots. The researchers went back to their slide rules to come up with revised theories.[166]

Other heating problems experienced during the early flight program included hot airflow into the interior of the airplane, which caused unexpected high temperatures around the speed brake actuators, and loss of instrumentation wires in the wing roots and tail surfaces. In a separate incident, cabin pressure forced the front edge of the canopy upward, allowing hot air to flow against and damage the seal. NASA resolved the canopy problem by attaching a shingle-type strip to the fuselage just ahead of the canopy joint to prevent airflow under the edge of the canopy. A similar problem developed in the nose landing-gear compartment: a small gap at the aft end of the nose-gear door was large enough to allow the airstream to enter the compartment and strike the bulkhead between the nose-gear compartment and the cockpit. This stream caused a local hot spot that melted some aluminum tubing used by the pressure-measuring system on flight 2-17-33. During the Mach 5.27 flight, the bulkhead heated to 550°F, high enough to scorch the paint and generate some smoke inside the cabin. It was a potentially catastrophic problem, but fortunately no significant damage resulted. In response, engineers added an Inconel compression seal to the aft end of the nose-gear door and installed a baffle plate across the bulkhead.[167]

165 Kordes et al., "Structural Heating Experiences of the X-15," p. 32.

166 Ibid, pp. 32-33.

167 Ibid, p. 33.

Manpower

By late 1961, most of the people involved in the flight program expected it to end in December 1964. This would allow an orderly investigation of the remaining aero-thermo environment, an evaluation of the MH-96 adaptive control system, and a few follow-on experiments. This was in general agreement with the original 1959 Air Force plan, although it consisted of only 100 flights instead of the anticipated 300 flights.[168]

A quick look at the labor required to support the X-15 shows that it was not a small program. The following table counts only government employees, not contractors, in "equivalent" man years, meaning that there may have been more people actually supporting the program than shown, but they were doing so on a less than full-time basis. In general, the Air Force figures consisted of about 55% civil servants and 45% military personnel. The Air Force paid the civilians an average of $8,370 per annum at the ASD and $7,850 at the AFFTC. The FY65 numbers reflect the period between June 1964 and December 1964 (the government fiscal years at the time ran from 1 July to 30 June).[169]

Organization	FY62	FY63	FY64	FY65	Total
ASD	22	16	11	6	55
AFFTC	170	170	170	85	595
NASA-FRC	420	420	420	300	1,560
Total	612	606	601	391	

The next table shows the projected propellant and gas requirements at the same point in the program:[170]

Propellant	FY62	FY63	FY64	FY65	Total
Ammonia (gal)	240,000	240,000	240,000	120,000	840,000
Peroxide (lbs)	420,000	420,000	420,000	210,000	1,470,000
Helium (scf)	5,400,000	5,400,000	5,400,000	2,700,000	18,900,000
Liquid nitrogen (tons)	3,500	3,500	3,500	1,750	12,250
Liquid oxygen (tons)	3,560	3,560	3,560	1,780	12,460

The AFFTC also had a separate budget for support of the X-15 program, including supplies required for the operation of the NB-52s, other support and chase aircraft, propellant analysis and servicing, instrumentation, data processing and acquisition, photo lab, biomedical support, engineering, and test operations.

168 "Advanced Development Plan for X-15 Research Aircraft, Advanced Technology Program 653A," 17 November 1961, pp. 2 and 60; R&D Project Card, System 605A, 10 September 1959. Both in the files at the AFFTC History Office.

169 "Ibid. Naturally, the NASA personnel were civil servants; no equivalent pay scales could be found.

170 "Advanced Development Plan for X-15 Research Aircraft, Advanced Technology Program 653A," p. 60.

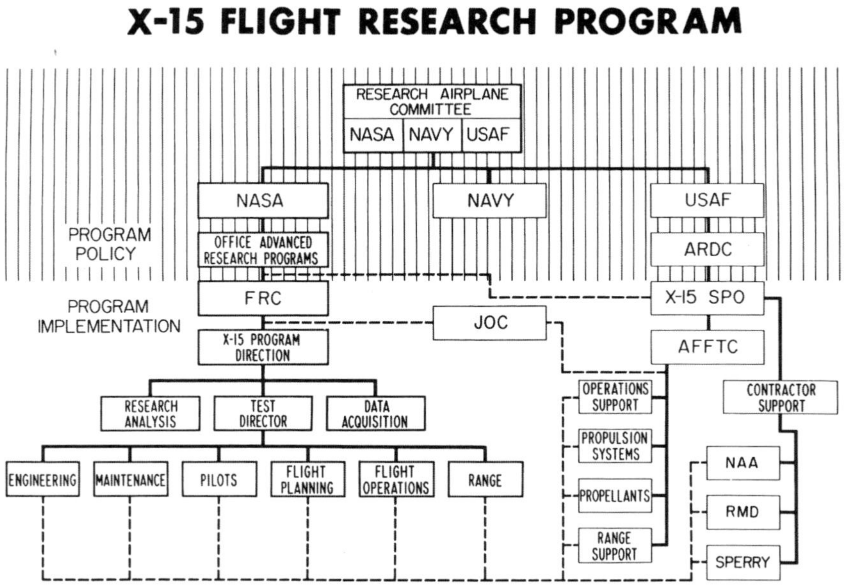

The X-15 program was a joint venture between the Air Force, Navy, and NASA, although the Navy generally played the role of a silent partner. The Air Force developed and paid for the airplanes and operated much of the support infrastructure at Edwards AFB, while NASA flew the airplanes (often with military pilots) and performed the maintenance. This 1961 organizational chart delineates the various interrelationships. In all, it worked well. (NASA)

Additional funds were budgeted for travel. Again, these are only Air Force funds; the equivalent NASA funding could not be ascertained.

	FY62	FY63	FY64	FY65	Total
O&M funds	$1,277,403	$1,277,403	$1,277,403	$638,702	$4,470,911
Travel	$65,000	$59,000	$55,000	$27,000	$206,000

The Adaptive Control System Arrives

By the time North American was manufacturing the X-15 airframes, the Air Force had already selected the Minneapolis-Honeywell MH-96 adaptive control system for use on the upcoming X-20 Dyna-Soar. At the time, Honeywell had tested the system on a McDonnell F-101 Voodoo, but many researchers wanted to get some high-performance experience with the system prior to committing it to space flight on the X-20. When an XLR99 ground test almost destroyed X-15-3, the Air Force seized the opportunity to include a prototype MH-96 when North American rebuilt the airplane.[171]

171 E-mail, Scott Crossfield to Dennis R. Jenkins, 28 May 2002.

The MH-96 was the first command augmentation system with an adaptive gain feature that provided invariant aircraft response throughout the flight envelope. The MH-96 used a rate command control mode whereby a given control-stick deflection would produce a specific rate response for the airplane. For example, a 1-inch pitch stick deflection would result in a 5-degrees-per-second pitch rate, regardless of how far the control surfaces had to deflect to produce that rate. This meant that the response would be the same regardless of airplane speed or flight condition.[172]

In a conventional aircraft of the period, the pitch rate response would vary with airspeed. In an airplane with a large speed envelope, such as the X-15, a 1-inch stick deflection with a conventional system could result in such disparate responses as almost none at low speed to an extremely violent one at high speed. The MH-96 was an attempt to cure this. However, nothing comes free. With an invariant response, the pilot lost the "feel" for the airplane; for example, the controls did not become sloppy as it approached a stall. The system automatically compensated for everything right up to the point that the airplane stopped flying. The same problem would confront the first fly-by-wire systems.[173]

The rate-command system eliminated the need to modify the trim settings because of configuration changes, such as deploying the landing gear or flaps. The system also masked any shifts in the center of gravity. In many respects, these were good things because they eliminated mundane tasks that otherwise needed to be accomplished by a pilot who already had his hands full of rocket plane. On the other hand, they eliminated many of the normal cues the pilots used to confirm that certain things had happened, such as the trim change after the landing gear deployed. It took an open mind–and some experience–to get comfortable flying the MH-96.[174]

The MH-96 was potentially superior to the basic flight-control system installed in the other two airplanes, for a couple of reasons. The first was that it was more redundant than the SAS (even after the ASAS was installed), which eliminated many of the concerns of flying to high altitudes. Also, the MH-96 blended the ballistic controls and the aerodynamic controls together beginning at 90,000 feet. The pilot moved the same stick regardless of altitude and the MH-96 decided which controls were appropriate to command the airplane. The MH-96 also offered a few autopilot modes (such as roll hold, pitch-attitude hold, and angle-of-attack hold) that significantly reduced the pilot's workload during the exit phase.[175]

The system minimized any extraneous aircraft motions by providing much higher damper gains. The pilots appreciated this feature particularly during altitude flights, and X-15-3 was designated the primary airplane for altitude flights.

172 Minneapolis-Honeywell report MH-2373-TM1, "Operation and Maintenance Manual, MH-96 Flight Control System for the X-15 Aircraft," various volumes, 31 May 1961, provided under Air Force contract number AF33(616)-6610, passim; Robert P. Johannes, Neil A. Armstrong, and Thomas C. Hays, "Development of X-15 Self-Adaptive Flight Control System," a paper in the *1961 Research Airplane Committee Report*.

173 Minneapolis-Honeywell report MH-2373-TM1; Johannes et al., "Development of X-15 Self-Adaptive Flight Control System;" letter, Robert G. Hoey to Dennis R. Jenkins, 12 June 2003.

174 Ibid.

175 Minneapolis-Honeywell report MH-2373-TM1; Johannes et al., "Development of X-15 Self-Adaptive Flight Control System."

Neil Armstrong had been heavily involved in the development and evaluation of the MH-96 and made the first four evaluation flights with the system.

North American moved the rebuilt X-15-3 from Inglewood to Edwards on 15 June 1961, and finally delivered the airplane, along with the XLR99 and MH-96, to the government on 30 September. After various ground tests were completed, Neil Armstrong attempted to take the airplane for its first flight on 19 December 1961, but a problem with the XLR99 resulted in an abort. The flight (3-1-2) successfully launched the next day, with additional flights on 17 January and 5 April 1962. As it turned out, the MH-96 worked remarkably well, but Armstrong and others realized the system would require a considerable period of evaluation before researchers could thoroughly understand it. The MH-96 provided good service to the X-15 program until a fateful day in 1967.[176]

1962 FLIGHT PERIOD

The year did not get off to a great start. Forrest Petersen's X-15 experience had begun with an engine failure on his first flight in 1960, and ended the same way on 10 January 1962 during flight 1-25-44 when the XLR99 refused to start–twice. Petersen had no choice but to land at Mud Lake, marking the program's first uprange landing. This was exactly why NASA launched each flight within gliding distance of a suitable emergency landing lake. Other than Crossfield's initial glide flight, this would be the only X-15 flight below Mach 1.[177]

One of Petersen's post-flight comments was that Mud Lake had been marked the same as Rogers, and he stressed the importance of having these markings for depth perception and as a familiar guide. This was the primary reason that the AFFTC attempted to keep all of the lakebed markings as similar as possible. When the X-15 landed at a remote lake, the only way home was to load the craft on a flatbed truck and haul it over the public roads. Fortunately, the 22-foot wingspan made this job considerably easier than it sounds. Milt Thompson, however, related a story about one incident in which the truck driver noted a large camper coming toward him at high speed. Although the trucker pulled as far to the right as possible, the camper managed to hit the wing of the X-15, resulting in a huge gash in the camper but very little damage to the steel wing. Thompson did not record the consequences of this incident, but most likely NASA bought a new camper.[178]

Petersen's departure from the program had nothing to do with his flight experience; the record is complimentary about his contributions to the program. Nevertheless, Petersen was an up-and-coming naval officer, and he needed to return

176 X-15 Status Report, Paul F. Bikle/FRC to H. Brown/NASA Headquarters, 15 June 1961, p. 1; Neil A. Armstrong, "Pilot Report for Flight 3-1-2," 20 December 1961. Both in the files at the DFRC History Office

177 Informal interview (no interviewer noted) with Lieutenant Commander Forrest S. Petersen, 11 January 1962. Written transcript in the files at the DFRC History Office.

178 Informal interview (no interviewer noted) with Lieutenant Commander Forrest S. Petersen, 11 January 1962. Written transcript in the files at the DFRC History Office; camper story in Thompson, *At the Edge of Space*, p. 99. It could not be ascertained on which flight the camper incident happened, but Johnny Armstrong remembers it was later in the program than Petersen's landing.

to active service in order to continue advancing his career. His destination after leaving the program was to command VF-154 at NAS Miramar; subsequently he returned to the "black shoe" Navy, served as executive officer on the USS *Enterprise*, and ultimately retired as a vice admiral.

The program personnel reacted to emergency landings very professionally, and such events seldom slowed things down much. NASA trucked X-15-1 back to Edwards on 13 January 1962 and removed the engine so that engineers could inspect the engine mounts and main landing skids. The inspection revealed no significant damage, so the airplane was prepared for a 23 January flight and performed a satisfactory ground run on 19 January. However, rain on 20 January closed Rogers (not-so) Dry Lake, and all flight activities ceased. The airplane headed to the maintenance shops for minor modifications.[179]

The weather continued to get worse. It rained the following day and snowed the day after that, resulting in over half an inch of water on Rogers and over 12 inches of snow on Mud Lake. By this time only Silver, Hidden Hills, and Three Sisters were still dry and useable. A week of relative sunshine brightened the outlook, but things took a turn for the worse when heavy rains pelted the area from 7 through 12 February. This essentially precluded any flights before 15 April at the earliest. NASA decided to take the opportunity to perform maintenance and modifications to all three airplanes.[180]

When flights resumed on 20 April 1962, Neil Armstrong's fourth MH-96 evaluation flight (3-4-8) in X-15-3 would become the program's longest-duration flight at 12 minutes and 28.7 seconds. The flight plan called for a peak altitude of 205,000 feet, with Armstrong performing various maneuvers during exit and re-entry to evaluate the MH-96. At the conclusion of the flight, Armstrong reported, "In general, aircraft control and damping during ballistic flight and entry were outstanding, and considerably more smooth than had been expected. Unfortunately, this may be at the expense of excessive reaction control fuel consumption." This was confirmed when the APU/BCS low-peroxide warning light came on as the airplane descended through 160,000 feet. Armstrong initiated the transfer of unused turbopump propellant to the APU tank, and the light went out as he descended through 115,000 feet.[181]

Things began to get a bit strange at this point. As Armstrong began his pullout, the airplane began a slight climb, unnoticed by Armstrong. As soon as Joe Walker (NASA-1) saw a slight positive rate of climb on the radar data, he knew Armstrong was in trouble. When Walker told him to make a hard left turn, Armstrong rolled into a 60-degree left bank and pulled up to start the turn. When Walker called for the next hard left turn, Armstrong realized that he was above the atmosphere and was not turning. He sailed right by Edwards at Mach 3 and 100,000 feet headed for Palmdale in a 90-degree bank with full nose-up stabilizer, but the airplane did not want to turn.[182]

179 X-15 Status Report, Paul F. Bikle/FRC to H. Brown/NASA Headquarters, 1 February 1962, p. 1.

180 Ibid; X-15 Status Reports, Paul F. Bikle/FRC to H. Brown/NASA Headquarters, 15 February 1962, p. 1.

181 Neil A. Armstrong, "Pilot Report for Flight 3-4-8," 20 April 1962; e-mail, Neil A. Armstrong to Dennis R. Jenkins, 13 August 2002.

182 Ibid; letter, Robert G. Hoey to Dennis R. Jenkins, 12 August 2002; e-mail, Neil A. Armstrong to Dennis R. Jenkins, 13 August 2002.

The initial cadre of X-15 pilots pose in front of Building 4800 at the Flight Research Center. From left, Forrest S. Peterson (USN), A. Scott Crossfield (NAA), Robert M. White (USAF), and Joseph A. Walker (NASA). (NASA)

Once a "skip" out of the atmosphere starts, there is no choice but to wait until the vehicle peaks in altitude and settles back into the atmosphere. By that time, Armstrong was 45 miles south of Edwards. Ironically, although he had excessive energy when he was over Edwards, he now did not have enough to make it back to Edwards.[183]

Armstrong was not getting much help at this point from Joe Walker in the NASA-1 control room since the planners had never envisioned a landing from the south and there were no checkpoints marked on the maps. Nobody could offer much assistance except for the reassuring voices of the chase pilots. Palmdale was not really a viable option because the Air Force installation there had a concrete runway, which was not an ideal surface for the X-15 skids. Eventually, Armstrong began setting up for a landing on runway 35 at the extreme south end of Rogers Dry Lake. This was about as far away as you could get from the normal runway 18 at the north end of the lake, and the recovery and emergency vehicles were racing at full speed to cover the 12 miles before Armstrong touched down. The landing itself was not dramatic as Armstrong set the record for the longest miss distance during a non-emergency landing (12 miles). Milt Thompson later called this "Neil's cross-country flight."[184]

---

183 Neil A. Armstrong, "Pilot Report for Flight 3-4-8," 20 April 1962; letter, Robert G. Hoey to Dennis R. Jenkins, 12 August 2002.

184 Thompson, *At the Edge of Space*, p. 106; letter, Johnny G. Armstrong to Dennis R. Jenkins, 3 August 2002.

Astronaut Wings

As near as can be determined, the three X-15s spent their entire career in and around Edwards, except for the occasional trip back to Inglewood to be repaired or modified. There was one exception, part of Project Eglin 1-62. On 2 May 1962, Jack Allavie and Bob White, along with a pressure-suit technician and a B-52 crew chief, took the NB-52A and X-15-3 to Eglin AFB in Florida for the 4-hour-long "Air Proving Ground Center Manned Weapons Fire Power Demonstration" attended by President John F. Kennedy. According to Allavie, "[W]e took off with an inert X-15 and flew all the way to Eglin AFB in Florida ... that's 1,625 miles and it was a simple flight. We landed there, put the X-15 on exhibit, and then flew it back to Edwards" on 5 May with a stop at Altus AFB, Oklahoma, for fuel. Photographic evidence shows a mission marking on the NB-52A depicting an X-15 oriented in the opposite direction of the regular launches (indicating, one guesses, a flight eastward) and the inscription "PRES. VISIT EGLIN FLA." Although it was by far the longest captive carry of the program, NASA did not assign the flight a program flight number.[185]

Back at Edwards, during the summer of 1962 Bob White made three flights in X-15-3 that demonstrated the potential problems of matching the preflight profile. On the first flight (3-5-9), White became disoriented during the exit and decided that he needed to push the nose down slightly so that he could visually acquire the horizon: "When we got up to 32 degrees, and at about 60 seconds in time, I guess it was just a small case of disorientation. I say a small case because I didn't lose complete orientation but when I was up at this climb angle, and this is the first time that I've had this feeling, I looked at the ball, I had 32 degrees in pitch, but I had the darndest feeling that I was continuing to rotate. I couldn't resist the urge just to push on back down until the light blue of the sky showed up. I never did get to the horizon, but I was satisfied that it wasn't happening." By the time he was satisfied and began his climb again, his energy was such that he undershot his planned 206,000-foot peak altitude by 21,400 feet.[186]

White's next flight (3-6-10) was only nine days later. This one was much better. White undershot by only 3,300 feet, about average for the program. White reported that the weather obscured most of his view of the ground: "I did look around quite a bit, and I was a little disappointed because of all the low clouds that obscured the coast line. I took a couple of definite looks because I wanted to try and scan up further north, and down along the Mexican coast, and pick out some places, but the cloud cover was so extensive that I couldn't really do that. Then too, when you're up there it feels like everything's right under the nose. It was reassuring again to hear ground saying you're right on profile and track. That eliminates any concern on the pilot's part."[187]

---

185 Telephone conversation, John E. Allavie with Dennis R. Jenkins, 22 May 2002; telephone conversation, Major General Robert M. White with Dennis R. Jenkins, 24 May 2002; e-mail, Tony Landis/DFRC to Dennis R. Jenkins, 5 June 2002; e-mail, Peter W. Merlin/DFRC Archivist to Dennis R. Jenkins, 10 June 2002. The Kennedy Library checked the appointment books and determined that the president had been at Eglin on 4 May 1962. James B. Hill, the audiovisual archivist at the library, reports that the library does not have any photographs showing Kennedy inspecting the X-15, although there are 16 photos of him at the Eglin event.

186 Major Robert M. White, "Pilot Report for Flight 3-7-14," 17 July 1962.

187 Ibid.

If it seemed that White was getting better at hitting his planned altitude, the next flight would dispel any such thoughts. On 17 July 1962, White took X-15-3 on a flight that was supposed to go to 282,000 feet, which was sufficient to qualify him for an Air Force astronaut rating. The MH-96 failed just before launch, which probably should have meant scrubbing for the day. Instead, White reached over and reset the circuit breakers. The MH-96 appeared to function correctly, so White called for a launch. White seemed to be trying to make up for the altitude he had not achieved on his last two flights. The climb angle was a bit steeper than called for, and the engine produced a bit more thrust than usual and burned a bit longer than expected. The result was a flight that was 32,750 feet higher than planned, setting a new Fédération Aéronautique Internationale (FAI) record for piloted aircraft of 314,750 feet and becoming the first winged vehicle to exceed 300,000 feet, the first flight above 50 miles, and the first X-15 flight that qualified its pilot for an astronaut rating. This time, as the first astronaut from Edwards, White was suitably impressed with the view:[188]

> You could just see as far as you looked. I turned my head in both directions and you see nothing but the Earth. It's just tremendous. You look off and the sky is real dark. I didn't think the impression would be much different than it was up around 250,000 feet, but I was impressed remarkably more than I was at 250,000 feet. It amazed me. I looked up and was able to pick out San Francisco bay and it looked like it was down over there off the right wing and I could look out, way out. It was just tremendous, absolutely tremendous. You have seen pictures from high up in rockets, or these orbital pictures of what the guy sees out there. That's exactly what it looked like. The same thing.

White reentered and arrived over the high key at Mach 3.5 and 80,000 feet. The potential for a repeat of Armstrong's excursion to Pasadena was present, but White had learned from Armstrong's mistake: "I was mainly concerned at this time with the possibility of overshooting the landing point. I think that was my overriding consideration at this point. I went by the lake and turned it around, and when I went around in the turn I just pushed in on the bottom rudder so I could get the nose down and stay in where I had some q. I didn't want any bounce in altitude. If I had gotten bounce, I would never have gotten back."[189]

A wide sweeping turn over Rosamond brought White back to a more normal high key at 28,000 feet and subsonic speeds. He continued around for a near-perfect landing at 191 knots. Milt Thompson in the chase plane commented, "Nice, you really hit that … Bob," and Joe Walker in the NASA-1 control room finished by saying, "This is your happy controller going off the air." Despite having over-

188 Ibid. During the course of the X-15 program, the Department of Defense recognized 50 miles (264,000 feet) as the beginning of space, and Air Force pilots flying above this altitude qualified for an astronaut rating. Despite reports that NASA recognizes the international standard of 100 kilometers (62.14 miles, 328,099 feet), this is not the case–NASA does not specifically recognize any standard (telephone conversation, William F. Readdy, associate administrator for manned space flight, with Dennis R. Jenkins, 27 October 2004). Because of this, the civilian X-15 pilots were not awarded "astronaut wings" until late 2005.

189 Major Robert M. White, "Pilot Report for Flight 3-7-14," 17 July 1962.

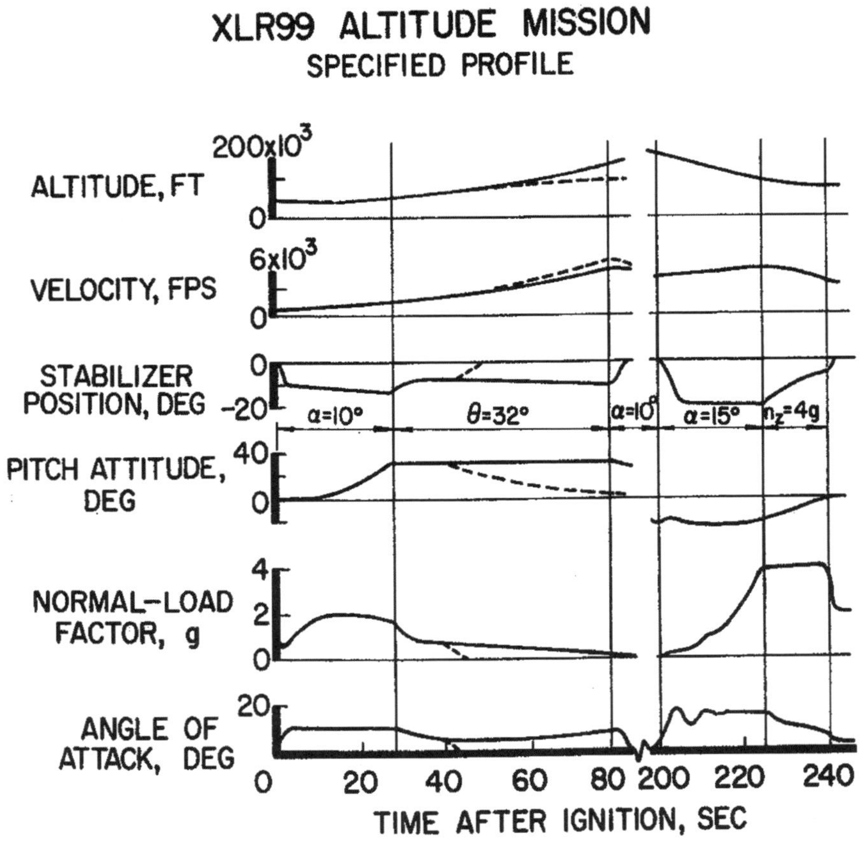

The altitude missions demanded precise piloting, and even then, several variables beyond the control of the pilot could result in significant altitude errors. On 17 July 1962, Bob White took X-15-3 on a flight that was supposed to go to 282,000 feet. The climb angle was a bit steeper than called for, the XLR99 produced a bit more thrust than usual, and it burned a bit longer than expected. The result was a flight that was 32,750 feet higher than planned, setting a new FAI record for piloted aircraft of 314,750 and becoming the first winged vehicle to exceed 300,000 feet, the first flight above 50 miles, and the first X-15 flight that qualified its pilot for an astronaut rating. (NASA)

shot the altitude by more than 10%, White flew the flight nearly perfectly, and data from this flight would be used for several years to check out and calibrate the fixed-base simulator.[190]

Interestingly, this flight will probably remain an altitude record for airplanes as long as the FAI has a category for rocket-powered aircraft. In theory, it is possible to break the record one time. According to the rules, new records must ex-

190 Radio transcript for flight 3-7-14, 17 July 1962. In the files at the DFRC History Office. Use of the data in the fixed-base simulator comes from a telephone conversation, Johnny Armstrong with Dennis R. Jenkins, 30 May 2002; e-mail, Robert G. Hoey to Dennis R. Jenkins, 2 June 2002.

ceed the old mark by 3%, meaning that somebody will have to fly at least 324,193 feet altitude to beat White's record. However, according the FAI, the atmosphere ends at 328,099 feet (100 kilometers). Therefore, it will be impossible to better the subsequent record without going into space, which would disqualify the attempt (as happened with Joe Walker's 354,200-foot flight). The chances of somebody managing to get above 324,194 feet without exceeding 328,098 feet are extremely remote. It has been 40 years and nobody has tried yet.[191]

The next day, on 18 July 1962, President John F. Kennedy presented the Robert J. Collier Trophy to four X-15 pilots–Scott Crossfield, Forrest Peterson, Joe Walker, and Bob White—"for invaluable technological contributions to the advancement of flight and for great skill and courage as test pilots of the X-15." By this point Crossfield had been gone for two years, and Petersen had already left to become the commanding officer at VF-154. Nevertheless, all four pilots journeyed to Washington to accept the trophy on the South Lawn of the White House. The National Aeronautic Association annually awards the Collier Trophy, which is generally considered the most prestigious recognition for aerospace achievement in the United States. In the case of the X-15, the selection of the recipients was not arbitrary; it represented the first pilot from each organization (North American, Navy, NASA, and Air Force) to fly the airplane. The trophy itself was 7 feet tall and weighed 500 pounds, and when Kennedy presented it to Bob White (the spokesman for the group), he commented, "I don't know what you are going to do with it."[192]

Later the same day the Air Force presented White with his astronaut wings during a small ceremony at the Pentagon, and that evening NASA feted all four pilots at a dinner where they received the NASA Distinguished Service Medal from Vice President Lyndon B. Johnson. NASA administrator James E. Webb commented at the dinner that the X-15 program was "a classic example of a most effective way to conduct research."

Since the beginning, the X-15 program had used four North American F-100 Super Sabres as Chase-1. However, the F-100 was getting old, and the AFFTC was happy to begin receiving new Northrop T-38 Talons during October 1961. Pilots reported that the T-38 "appears as good or better than the F-100F for X-15 support." The Air Force conducted several test flights, sans the X-15, to evaluate whether the T-38 could fly close chase at 45,000 feet when the NB-52 was in a right-hand turn–something the F-100 could not do. Such a capability would allow a

---

191 Thompson, *At the Edge of Space*, p. 112. As of 2 September 2006 the Fédération Aéronautique Internationale still regards this flight as a record for the class "Class C-1 (landplanes), group IV (rocket engine), launched from an aircraft." The current status was obtained from an e-mail, Anne-Laure Perret/FAI Executive Officer to Dennis R. Jenkins, 2 July 2002 and 2 September 2006.

192 William MacDougall, "White, 3 Other X-15 Pilots Get Collier Trophy," *Los Angeles Times*, 19 July 1962; Pamela E. Mack, "Introduction," *From Engineering Science to Big Science: The NACA and NASA Collier Trophy Research Project Winners*, edited by Pamela E. Mack, NASA publication SP-4219, 1998, p. xi. The caption for the photo on page 150 of the book incorrectly identifies the event as happening on 18 July 1961 (it was 1962). Mack had some interesting observations concerning the trophy, although none were particularly applicable to the X-15 award. One paragraph is particularly telling: "The United States has had and still has a number of aviation and aerospace organizations, ranging from booster groups to professional societies. The National Aeronautic Association fits somewhere in the middle of that range. In turn, its prize is shaped by the composition of the committee that awards it and by a series of rules, in particular that the prize be given for an achievement in the preceding year. While the Nobel Prize is usually given for an accomplishment whose significance has been proven by years of experience, the Collier Trophy represents an almost concurrent evaluation of an achievement (and like the Pulitzer Prize, it sometimes lacks the wisdom of hindsight)."

right-hand NB-52 pattern prior to a launch, and would greatly improve ground telemetry reception during that period since the NB-52 fuselage would not block the X-15-to-ground line of sight. The previously used left-hand pattern resulted in a loss of telemetry during the turn until approximately 2 minutes prior to launch, but allowed the F-100F to remain in a suitable chase position during activation of the X-15 systems. The problem was that during a right turn the F-100 was on the inside of the turn and had to fly at a slow indicated airspeed. In a left turn on the X-15 side, the F-100 was on the outside of the turn, flying at a higher and more acceptable indicated airspeed. The first flight (1-32-53) to use a T-38 was in July 1962 and the T-38 would be Chase-1 for almost every flight until the end of the program.[193]

On 18 July 1962, president John F. Kennedy presented the Robert J. Collier Trophy to the X-15 program. The award was accepted by Scott Crossfield, Forrest Peterson, Joe Walker, and Bob White in a ceremony on the South Lawn of the White House.. The trophy is seven feet tall and weighs 500 pounds. (NASA)

A Bad Day

On 9 November 1962, Jack McKay launched X-15-2 from the NB-52B on his way to what was supposed to be a routine heating flight (2-31-52) to Mach 5.55 and 125,000 feet. Just after the X-15 separated, Bob Rushworth (NASA-1) asked McKay to check his throttle position, and McKay verified it was full open. Unfortunately, the engine was only putting out about 35% power. In theory, the X-15 could have made a slow trip back to Rogers Dry Lake, but there was no way of knowing why the engine had decided to act up, or whether it would continue to function for the entire trip. The low power setting seriously compounded the problems associated with energy management since the flight planners had calculated the normal decision times for an emergency landing at each of the intermediate lakebeds based on 100% thrust. The computer power at the time was such that there was no way to recompute those decision points in real time, so the mission

193 E-mail, Clarence E. Anderson to Dennis R. Jenkins, 28 January 2002; e-mail, Scott Crossfield to Dennis R. Jenkins, 28 January 2002; Minutes of Meeting, X-15 Operations Subcommittee, 20 March 1961. One flight (2-14-28) on 30 March 1961 had used a T-38 from the Test Pilot School flown by Pete Knight as Chase-2, but 1-32-53 was the first use as Chase-1. A few flights used a Douglas F5D Skyray as Chase-1.

rules dictated that the pilot shut down the engine and make an emergency landing. McKay would have to land at Mud Lake.[194]

As emergency landing sites went, Mud Lake was not a bad one, being about 5 miles in diameter and very smooth and hard. When Rushworth and McKay decided to land at Mud, the pilot immediately began preparing for the landing. The engine was shut down after 70.5 seconds, the airplane turned around, and as much propellant as possible was jettisoned. It was looking like a "routine" emergency until the X-15 wing flaps failed to operate. The resulting "hot" landing (257 knots) caused the left main landing skid to fail, and the left horizontal stabilizer and wing dug into the lakebed, resulting in the aircraft turning sideways and flipping upside down. Luckily, McKay realized he was going over and jettisoned the canopy just prior to rolling inverted. The unfortunate result was that the first thing to hit the lakebed was McKay's helmet.[195]

As was the case for all X-15 flights, the Air Force had deployed a rescue crew and fire truck to the launch lake. Normally it was a dull and boring assignment, but on this day they earned their pay. The ground crew sped toward the X-15, but when they arrived less than a minute later, they found that their breathing masks were not protecting them from the fumes escaping from the broken airplane. Fortunately, the pilot of the H-21 recovery helicopter noted the vapors from unjettisoned anhydrous ammonia escaping from the wreck and maneuvered his helicopter so that his rotor downwash could disperse the fumes. The ground crew was able to dig a hole in the lakebed and extract McKay. By this time, the C-130 had arrived with the paramedics and additional rescue personnel. McKay was loaded on the C-130 and rushed to Edwards, and the ground crew tended to the damaged X-15. At this point the airplane had accumulated a total free flight time of 40 minutes and 32.2 seconds.[196]

It had taken three years and 74 flights, but all of the emergency preparations had finally paid off. In this case, as for all flights, the Air Force had flown the rescue crew and fire truck to the launch lake before dawn in preparation for the flight. The helicopter had flown up at daybreak. The C-130 had returned to Edwards and carried another fire truck to an intermediate lake (they were possibly the most traveled fire trucks in the Air Force inventory). The C-130, loaded with a paramedic and sometimes a flight surgeon, then began a slow orbit midway between Mud Lake and Edwards, waiting. Outside the program, some had questioned the time and expense involved in keeping the lakebeds active and deploying the emergency crews for each mission. The flight program was beginning to seem so routine. Inside the program, nobody doubted the potential usefulness of the precautions. Because of the time and expense, Jack McKay was resting in the

---

194 Armstrong, "Expanding the X-15 Envelope to Mach 6.7," pp. 200-201. In his book, Johnny Armstrong says that Pete Knight was NASA-1 for this flight; however, all other documents, including the radio transcripts, indicate that Bob Rushworth was the communicator. Additionally, although most contemporary documentation (including the flight report) indicates that the engine was at 30% power; subsequent analysis showed it was really at 35%.

195 William P. Albrecht/X-15 Project Engineer, "X-15 Operations Flight Report for Flight 2-31-52," 16 November 1962; William P. Albrecht/X-15 Project Engineer, "X-15 Operations Flight Report Supplement for Flight 2-31-52," 22 May 1964; Armstrong, "Expanding the X-15 Envelope to Mach 6.7," pp. 200-201; Thompson, *At the Edge of Space*, p. 229. The 257-knot landing speed was almost 60 knots higher than normal.

196 Ibid.

Jack McKay made an emergency landing at Mud Lake on 9 November 1962 after the XLR99 stuck at 35-percent power on Flight 2-31-52. Unfortunately, the wing flaps failed and the airplane was heavy with unjettisoned propellant, resulting in a very high 257-knot landing speed. As McKay touched down, the left rear skid failed and the airplane flipped over. Since Mud was a designated emergency landing site for this flight, fire trucks were standing by and paramedics were orbiting in a C-130 transport. McKay was airlifted to the hospital at Edwards with serious injuries. McKay recovered and flew 22 more X-15 flights and the X-15-2 was rebuilt into the advanced X-15A-2. (NASA)

base hospital, seemingly alive and well. Had the ground crew not been there, the result might have been much different.[197]

Although the post-flight report stated that the "pilot injuries were not serious," in reality Jack McKay had suffered several crushed vertebra that made him an inch shorter than when the flight had begun. Nevertheless, five weeks after his accident, McKay was in the control room as the NASA-1 for Bob White's last X-15 flight (3-12-22). McKay would go on to fly 22 more X-15 flights, but would ultimately retire from NASA because of lasting effects from this accident.[198]

X-15-2 had not fared any better–the damage was major, but not total. On 15 November 1962, the Air Force and NASA appointed an accident board with Donald R. Bellman as chair. The board released its findings, which contained no surprises, in a detailed report distributed during December 1962. Six months after the Mud Lake accident, the Air Force awarded North American a contract to modify X-15-2 into an advanced configuration that eventually allowed the program to meet its original speed goal of 6,600 fps (Mach 6.5). Because of the basic airplane's ever-increasing weight, it had been unable to do this, by a small margin.[199]

197 Ibid.

198 Ibid.

199 William P. Albrecht/X-15 Project Engineer, "X-15 Operations Flight Report Supplement for Flight 2-31-52," 22 May 1964; Armstrong, "Expanding the X-15 Envelope to Mach 6.7," p. 201.

1963 FLIGHT PERIOD

On 4 October 1962, the first in-flight failure of an APU had occurred when the no. 1 APU failed 5 minutes after launch on flight 3-10-19. On 17 January 1963, a second failure took place, this time 4 minutes after launch on flight 3-14-24. Almost 3 months passed while a team of specialists from the Air Force, NASA, and General Electric investigated the problem, representing the only significant cessation of flight activities caused by mechanical failure during the X-15 program.[200]

What the engineers found was excessive wear on the high-speed (51,200-rpm) turbine shaft pinion. The solution became obvious when simulated altitude tests revealed that when engineers eliminated seal leakage from the drive-turbine case into the gear-reduction box, the gearbox was no longer pressurized. The lower ambient temperature at altitude reduced the efficiency of the lubricant as a coolant and as a film between the gear teeth. This deficiency caused pinion failure at altitudes in as little as 90 seconds. Engineers devised a way to pressurize the gearbox and effectively solved the problem.[201]

As it became obvious that the program was going to continue past its initial mandate to gather aero-thermo data, the FRC began correcting some of the shortcomings of the original design. For instance, pilots had long complained that the configuration of the instrument panel was less than ideal. During the summer of 1963, NASA made modifications to relieve the panel's visual clutter and improve its scan pattern. At the same time, the agency added a dynamic pressure indicator, heading vernier, altitude predictor, and cross-track position indicator to provide more trajectory-control data. The resulting instrument panel bore little resemblance to the original; in fact, even the original black color had given way to a medium gray that the pilots found contrasted better with the instruments. By the fall of 1963, the dynamic pressure and heading indicators had been used on several flights and found to be "effective piloting aids." Engineers planned more changes for X-15-3 in the form of an energy-guidance display to allow the pilot more precise control of the boost trajectory.[202]

Although the use of dampers was increasing on the aerodynamic controls, there continued to be debate about including some sort of stability augmentation system for the ballistic controls. As early as June 1960, North American had conducted tests on the fixed-base simulator to investigate a proposed reaction augmentation system (RAS). Three pilots–Neil Armstrong, Joe Walker, and Bob White–were involved in the tests. All agreed that the RAS made the airplane a great deal easier to fly, and that the "combination of RAS and SAS affords a considerable improvement in reentry-control characteristics." This seemed to be in direct contradiction to the 1956 findings that dampers were not required for

200 Love and Fischel, "Status of X-15 Program," p. 7.

201 Ibid.

202 "Semi-Annual Summary Status Report of X-15 Program," October 1963, p. 19.

the ballistic control system, but in intervening years the program engineers had learned a great deal more about the actual vehicle flight characteristics.[203]

By 1963 the FRC had decided it was time to modify X-15-1 and X-15-2 to incorporate the RAS. X-15-3 was not so equipped since the MH-96 essentially took care of this function. The RAS was the proportional system with an on-off damping loop. The system apparently worked fairly well, although most of late 1963 and early 1964 were spent developing filter modifications so that the system would not excite any of the natural frequencies on the X-15. The first modified unit was available in the summer of 1964.[204]

Maximum Altitude

Joe Walker would fly the maximum altitude flight (3-22-36) of the program on 22 August 1963, his second excursion above 300,000 feet in just over a month. The simulator predicted that the X-15 could achieve altitudes well in excess of 400,000 feet, but there was considerable doubt as to whether the airplane could successfully reenter from such heights. A good pilot on a good day could do it, but if anything went wrong, the results were usually less than desirable. In order to provide a margin of safety, NASA decided to limit the maximum altitude attempt to 360,000 feet, providing a 40,000-foot pad for cumulative errors. This might sound like a lot, but the flight planners and pilots remembered that Bob White had overshot his altitude by 32,750 feet. The X-15 was climbing at over 4,000 fps, so every second the pilot delayed shutting down the engine would result in a 4,000-foot increment in altitude. The XLR99 also was not terribly precise–sometimes the engine developed 57,000 lbf, while other times it developed 60,000 lbf. An extra 1,500 lbf for the entire burn translated into an additional 7,500 feet of altitude. A 1-degree error in climb angle could also result in 7,500 feet more altitude. Add these all up and it is easy to understand why the program decided a 40,000-foot cushion was appropriate.[205]

Walker had made one build-up flight (3-21-32) prior to the maximum altitude attempt in which he overshot his 315,000-foot target by 31,200 feet through a combination of all three variables (higher-than-expected engine thrust, longer-than-expected engine burn, and a 0.5-degree error in climb angle). Walker commented after the flight, "First thing I'm going to say is I was disappointed on two items on this flight, one was that I was honestly trying for 315,000, the other one was I thought I had it made on the smoke bomb on the lakebed. I missed both of them." Although he missed the smoke bomb on landing, it was well within tolerance. As for missing the altitude, the 40,000-foot cushion suddenly did not seem very large.[206]

The flight was surprisingly hard to launch, racking up three aborts over a two-week period mainly because of weather and APU problems. On the actual flight day, things began badly when both the Edwards and Beatty radars lost track on the

203 X-15 Status Report, Paul F. Bikle/FRC to H. Brown/NASA Headquarters, 1 July 1960, p. 3.

204 "X-15 Semi-Annual Status Report No. 2," April 1964, p. 6.

205 Thompson, *At the Edge of Space*, p. 123; letter, Johnny G. Armstrong to Dennis R. Jenkins, 3 August 2002; letter, Robert G. Hoey to Dennis R. Jenkins, 12 August 2002.

206 Joseph A. Walker, "Pilot Report for Flight 3-21-32," 19 July 1963. In the files at the DFRC History Office.

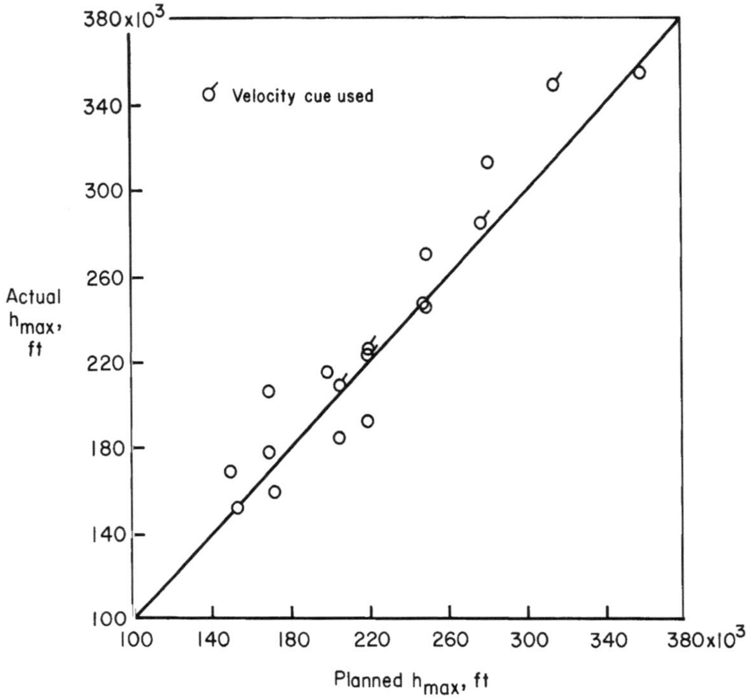

It was not uncommon for X-15 altitude flights to miss their expected altitude. The X-15 climbed at over 4,000 fps, so every second that the pilot delayed shutting down the engine resulted in a 4,000-foot increment in altitude. The XLR99 also was not terribly precise – sometimes the engine developed 57,000-lbf; other times it developed 60,000-lbf. An extra 1,500-lbf for the entire burn translated into an additional 7,500 feet of altitude. A 1-degree error in climb angle could also result in 7,500 feet more altitude.

NB-52 during the flight to the launch lake, but both reacquired it 4 minutes prior to the scheduled launch time. The launch itself was good and Walker began the long climb to altitude. Although this was the first flight for the altitude predictor, Walker flew the mission based on its results, changing his climb angle several times to stay within a predicted 360,000 feet. When the XLR99 depleted its propellants, X-15-3 was traveling through 176,000 feet at 5,600 fps. It would take almost 2 minutes to get to the top of the climb, ultimately reaching 354,200 feet.[207]

To give the reader a sense of what reentry was like on this flight: The airplane was heading down at a 45-degree angle, and as it descended through 170,000 feet it was traveling 5,500 fps–over a mile per second. The acceleration buildup was non-linear and happened rather abruptly, taking less than 15 seconds to go from essentially no dynamic pressure to 1,500 psf, then tapering off for the remainder of reentry, and reaching a peak acceleration of 5 g at 95,000 feet. Walker maintained 5 g during the pullout until he came level at 70,000 feet. All the time the anti-g part of the David Clark full-pressure suit was squeezing his legs and stomach, forcing blood back to his heart and brain. Walker said that "the comment of

207 Ibid.

previous flights that this is one big squeeze in the pullout is still good." The glide back to Edwards was uneventful and Walker made a perfect landing. The flight had lasted 11 minutes and 8 seconds, and had covered 305 ground miles from Smith Ranch to Rogers Dry Lake. Although Walker had traveled more than 67 miles high, well in excess of the 62-mile (100-kilometer) international standard supposedly recognized by NASA, no astronaut rating awaited him. This was apparently reserved for people who rode ballistic missiles at Cape Canaveral, and it would take 42 years to correct the oversight.[208]

By the end of 1963, the program had gathered almost all of the data researchers had originally desired and the basic research program was effectively completed. The program would now push into the basic program extensions phase using X-15A-2 to gather similar data at increasingly high speeds while the other two airplanes continued the follow-on experiments. The basic program extensions were a set of experiments that had not been anticipated when the Air Force and NASA conceived the basic program. Some were truly follow-ons to issues that were uncovered during the basic program; others were the result of new factors, such as the increased capabilities of the modified X-15A-2. In general, researchers continued all of the original research into aerodynamics, structures, and flight controls for the rebuilt airplane. The FRC paid for many of the experiments from general research funds, not from a separate appropriation from Headquarters or Congress.[209]

Despite the progress and future plans, there was no uniform agreement that the X-15 program should continue. At least privately, several officials (including Paul Bikle) argued that the value of the projected research returns was not worth the risk and expense, and that the program should be terminated at the conclusion of the basic research program, or as soon as the X-15A-2 had completed its basic program. This body of opinion was the same that had initially led NASA to argue against modifying X-15-2 into the advanced configuration. However, by this time the X-15A-2 was well under construction and researchers had proposed an entire series of follow-on experiments, making it unlikely that the program would be terminated any time soon.[210]

Although the point would be moot after the Department of Defense canceled the Dyna-Soar on 10 December 1963, at the end of 1963 the X-15 program was making plans for four unnamed future X-20 pilots to make high-altitude familiarization flights in X-15-3 during the first half of 1964. Several of the Dyna-Soar pilots had already flown the X-15 simulator in preparation.[211]

---

208 Ibid; Thompson, *At the Edge of Space*, p. 53; letter, Robert G. Hoey to Dennis R. Jenkins, 12 August 2002.

209 "X-15 Semi-Annual Status Report No. 1," October 1963, p. 22.

210 Letter, Paul F. Bikle to USAF/ASD, no subject, 2 November 1961. In the files at the DFRC History Office.

211 "X-15 Semi-Annual Status Report No. 1," October 1963, p. 43. Surprisingly, nobody seems to remember which X-20 pilots were selected to make the four flights. The six X-20 pilots were Major James W. Wood, Major Henry C. Gordon, Major William J. Knight, Major Albert H. Crews, Major Russell L. Rogers, and Milton O. Thompson. Wood was the lead pilot. Bob Hoey remembers that "I was all in favor of that since there were a lot of similarities between the X-15 and the X-20. The side arm controller was quite similar, although the X-20 stick was all fly-by-wire so the movement was a lot smoother. Landings would have been very similar–same L/D and about the same wing loading." After the Dyna-Soar was canceled, Pete Knight and Milt Thompson joined the X-15 program.

1964 FLIGHT PERIOD

After the 100th X-15 flight (1-44-70), the NASA administrator, James E. Webb, presented a Group Achievement Award to "The X-15 Research Airplane Flight Test Organization" even if such an entity, in reality, did not exist. The award was "for outstanding accomplishments during the X-15 flight research program, from the first flight on June 8, 1959 to the one-hundredth flight on January 28, 1964." Given that these events included flights by Scott Crossfield and the Air Force pilots, Webb meant the award for the entire X-15 team, hence the fictional organizational reference.[212]

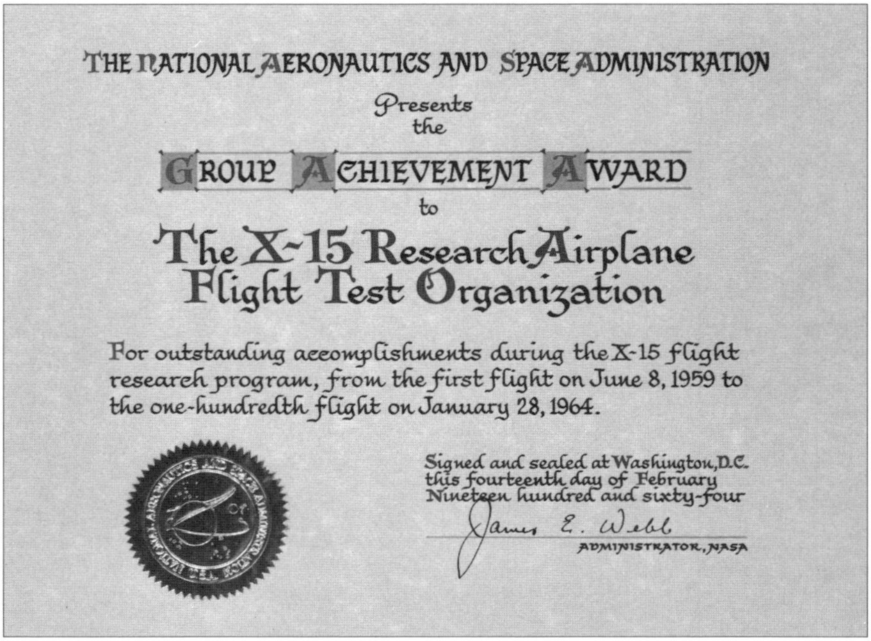

NASA Administrator James E. Webb presented a Group Achievement Award to the "The X-15 Research Airplane Flight Test organization" on 28 January 1964. Oddly, such an organization did not actually exist, but it was a way to honor the entire X-15 community, including the Air Force, Navy, and North American Aviation. (NASA)

The first part of 1964 brought good news and bad news. Captain Joe H. Engle and NASA test pilot Milton O. Thompson joined the program as pilots, which was good, but trouble with the stable platform caused the program to restrict flights to below 200,000 feet. To solve the problem with the stable platform, the Air Force and NASA were modifying a batch of inertial guidance systems originally procured for the Dyna-Soar program. The first unit became available in September 1964, but it was a "low" year, literally. In addition to the Dyna-Soar inertial systems, engi-

212 Copy of the award, in the author's collection.

neers and technicians at the FRC extensively modified the original Sperry stable platform and installed it in X-15A-2 and X-15-3 as an interim measure.[213]

By mid-1964, the FRC was getting serious about obtaining boundary-layer noise data, and finally found microphones that could tolerate the temperatures involved. The precision flying required for these measurements was more demanding than it sounded: the pilot had to maintain a steady-state altitude and speed for about 10 seconds to obtain useful data, something that was not necessarily easy to accomplish with the X-15. These particular data also had to be collected on flights below 100,000 feet since the aerodynamic pressure was a key component of the noise.[214]

One of the nagging problems experienced by the X-15 program was that the research instrumentation–particularly the data recorders–was not keeping up with the performance potential of the aircraft. In addition, the increased complexity of the experiments required a greater quantity of more precise data. The standard data-recording devices, such as oscillographs and manometers, performed well during the flight program, with a reliability of around 94%. However, the limited space within the X-15 often forced researchers to use smaller Parsons tape recorders. Some parameters, such as very low-pressure data, were not suited for the tape recorders, which introduced too much noise and made the data hard to extract. All of the recorders, and the sensors themselves, were analog devices (frequently optical), not modern digital units. Eventually, the FRC decided to reinstall the larger oscillograph recorders that provided better accuracy but resulted in fewer parameters being recorded per flight.[215]

The XLR99 did not particularly like to throttle, and Joe Vensel, the director of FRC flight operations, mandated that the pilots should not throttle the engine until the X-15 had sufficient energy to make it back to Edwards. Thompson talked him into changing his mind for a flight (3-29-48) on 21 May 1964. As Thompson throttled back from 100% to 45%, the XLR99 shut down–only 41 seconds into a planned 120-second burn. The problem was a pressure spike in the second-stage chamber pressure-sensing line, something that had been present for several years. This particular engine had not shown a tendency to generate spikes during the three flights and four ground runs that had been accomplished since the engine was installed in X-15-3. The intensity of the spike was sufficient in this case to deform the switch mechanically, holding the contacts closed and thus preventing an engine restart. Although X-15-3 accelerated to Mach 2.90 at 64,200 feet, Thompson could not make Rogers Dry Lake and opted for an emergency landing on Cuddeback.[216]

If it was not bad enough that Thompson had to make an emergency landing, he touched down with so much speed he nearly ran out of lakebed. Thompson: "I finally get it on the ground and I'm landing way long and there's a road that goes across the lakebed about three miles up the lakebed. I hit that road doing 100 miles per hour, just plowed through the banks that they had up on either side,

213 "X-15 Semi-Annual Status Report No. 2," April 1964, p. 1; "X-15 Semi-Annual Status Report No. 3," 1 December 1964, p. 1.

214 "X-15 Semi-Annual Status Report No. 3," 1 December 1964, p. 8.

215 Ibid, pp. 9-10

216 Vincent N. Capasso/X-15 Project Engineer, "X-15 Operations Flight Report for Flight 3-29-48," 28 May 1964; "X-15 Semi-Annual Status Report No. 3," 1 December 1964, p. 1. Both in the files at the DFRC History Office.

The X-15-3 carried a dorsal rudder with a "sharp leading edge" for many of its later flights. The leading edge of this rudder protruded forward a bit further than the normal rudder and had a small radius. In this photo, the temperature-sensitive paint and two leading-edge expansion slots show up well. (NASA)

and bounced over the road and finally came to a stop about 500 feet beyond the road. There was a fire truck that had pulled up behind me when I landed, and they came roaring across there and hit that road about the same speed. Somebody told me later that fire truck was 10 feet in the air." Milt continued, "Anyway, after that landing I borrowed a line from Jack McKay who had made a similar landing up at Delamar; he landed a bit long and it turned out he ran off the edge of the lakebed and up in the boondocks. Somebody asked Jack after that landing 'How long was the runway on Delamar?' and he said 'Oh, it's about 3 miles long with a 500-foot overrun.' Well, it turns out that Cuddeback is the same thing–three miles long to the road and a 500-foot overrun." This marked the program's first emergency landing at Cuddeback. The landing did not seriously damage the X-15, and Thompson was uninjured.[217]

By the end of 1964, after 120 flights and accumulated flying time of 2 hours at speeds above 3,000 mph, the X-15 airplanes were beginning to show their age. Wrinkles and buckles marred the once-sleek fuselages and engineers had cut gaps elsewhere. Scars were visible where technicians had hammered the skin of the wings back in place. The X-15s appeared old and tired. One of the airplanes had a vertical stabilizer with a sharp leading edge (a radical departure from the others), and none of them had the vertical stabilizer with which it first flew. Other changes were less obvious, such as the added structure that stiffened the fuselage and vertical stabilizer, and the electronics that helped operate the flight controls.[218]

217 "The Pilot's Panel," a paper in the *Proceedings of the X-15 30th Anniversary Celebration,* Dryden Flight Research Facility, Edwards, CA, 8 June 1989, NASA CP-3105, p. 152.

218 Stillwell, *X-15 Research Results*.

At this point, the three X-15s were more different than similar. Originally, the first two aircraft were substantially alike, while the MH-96 in X-15-3 significantly altered its character. However, the modification of the second airplane into the advanced X-15A-2 meant that all three aircraft shared little more than the general configuration. In addition to the originally installed SAS, X-15-1 and X-15-2 also had the independent ASAS, while X-15-3 used the MH-96 adaptive control system and a different damper scheme. A reaction-augmentation system added to the ballistic control system on X-15-1 and X-15-2 provided better vehicle damping at high altitudes, while the MH-96 on X-15-3 performed much the same function.[219]

By now, NASA expected the flight program to continue through the end of calendar year 1968. The FRC would take X-15-1 and X-15-3 out of service at the end of CY67 and mid-CY67, respectively, while the Mach 8-capable X-15A-2 would continue through the end of 1968. Data reduction and analysis would continue for several months after the end of the flight program. However, the X-15 program still had high-level supporters. Senator Clinton P. Anderson (D-NM) said, "During the past four-and-one-half years the program has achieved a very commendable record, providing a wealth of research data for the aeronautical and space programs of the United States. The past accomplishments of the X-15 program reflect a superb job of managing flight-test operations, and cooperation between the NASA, the Air Force, and the Navy." Given that no significant portion of the X-15 program was conducted in New Mexico, this was high praise.[220]

James E. Love, the NASA X-15 program manager, revealed that it cost an average of $270,000 to refurbish the airplane after each flight, approximately 3% of the cost of a new X-15. He based this figure on the annual operating budget of $16.3 million for the program, excluding military salaries. NASA also provided some "cost per pound" information, although its exact relevance is difficult to determine. For example, the X-20 inertial flight data system cost $6,670 per pound, and the X-15 stable platform cost $4,700 per pound. Other X-15 system costs per pound were as follows: airframe, $1,930; engine, $5,900; stability augmentation system, $5,400; auxiliary power unit, $3,750; ball nose, $1,300; and NB-52 carrier aircraft, $170.[221]

High-Temperature Loads Calibration Laboratory

The requirement to measure flight loads on aircraft flying at supersonic and hypersonic speeds led the FRC to construct the High-Temperature Loads Calibration Laboratory in building 4820 during 1964. The facility allowed researchers to calibrate strain-gage installations and test structural components and complete vehicles under the combined effects of loads and temperatures. The laboratory was a hangar-type structure with a small shop and office area attached to one end. A

219 James E. Love and Jack Fischel, "Status of X-15 Program," a paper in the *Progress of the X-15 Research Airplane Program*, A Compilation of the Papers presented at the Flight Research Center, 7 October 1965, NASA publication SP-90 (Washington, DC: NASA, 1965), pp. 3-4.

220 Letter, Albert J. Evans to Hugh L. Dryden, subject: Notification of approval of additions to the X-15 test-bed program, 30 March 1964. In the files at the NASA History Office. Anderson quote in the Evans letter.

221 B. K. Thomas, Jr. "X-15 Flights Providing Baseline Data on Reusable Space Vehicles," *Aviation Week & Space Technology*, 9 January 1967, pp. 67-69.

The High Temperature Loads Calibration Laboratory was established at the Flight Research Center to allow researchers to calibrate strain-gage installations and test structural components and complete vehicles under the combined effects of loads and temperatures. The facility was equipped with a programmable heating system that used infrared quartz lamps available in various lengths from 5 inches to 32 inches. Reflector arrangements were available for heating rates from 0 to 100 Btu per second per second and temperatures up to 3,000 degrees Fahrenheit. This photo shows an X-15 horizontal stabilizer being tested under the lamps. (NASA)

door measuring 40 feet high and 136 feet wide allowed access to an unobstructed test area that was 150 feet long by 120 feet wide and 40 feet high.[222]

A state-of-the-art control room was provided to operate the heating and loads equipment remotely, and a data acquisition system occupied the second floor over the office spaces. Large windows overlooked the hangar floor, and the room included a closed-circuit television system. A high-capacity hydraulic system could operate up to 34 actuators to apply loads to test specimen or entire aircraft. Perhaps more importantly for the X-15 program, the facility had a programmable heating system that used infrared quartz lamps available in various lengths from 5 inches to 32 inches. Reflector arrangements were available for heating rates from 0 to 100 Btu per second per second and temperatures up to 3,000°F.[223]

NASA used this facility for a variety of purposes during the remainder of the flight program. This included testing a set of X-15 horizontal stabilizers as part of the loads program undertaken late in the flight program, and the laboratory proved

222 Walter J. Sefic and Karl F. Anderson, NASA technical memorandum X-1868, "NASA High Temperature Loads Calibration Laboratory," September 1969.

223 Ibid.

to be critical for solving the inadvertent landing-gear extension problem suffered by X-15A-2 when it began its envelope expansion program. NASA later used the laboratory to test portions of the XB-70A and Lockheed Blackbirds.

1965 FLIGHT PERIOD

From 1 December 1964 to 31 March 1965, 12 flight attempts resulted in only eight flights. There were also two scheduled captive flights of the X-15A-2 to verify aerodynamic loads on the landing gear. The Honeywell inertial system in X-15-1 and the landing-gear problems on X-15A-2 were the primary causes of the delays and aborts. Weather also caused 10 delays, ranging from 1 to 10 days each, but this was normal for the winter in the high desert. All launches used the NB-52B since the other carrier aircraft was in Wichita undergoing major maintenance and did not return until 28 April.[224]

Most X-15 flights looked pretty much the same, varying mainly in what experiments were being carried, and what surfaces had temperature-sensitive paint or experimental ablators on them. The large white rectangle on the bottom of the fuselage is condensation from the liquid oxygen tank. (NASA)

Also during this period, the FRC evaluated how to equip each X-15 with the experiments for the follow-on program, and concluded that "[a]ll three X-15s will increase in weight because of the number and variety of experiments and research tests being planned." Engineers at the FRC began investigating modifications to the NB-52 wing/pylon structure and X-15 landing gear to support the heavier

224 "X-15 Semi-Annual Status Report No. 4," 1 April 1965, pp. 1-2; X-15 Status Report No. 65-5, Paul F. Bikle/FRC to J. Martin/NASA Headquarters, 13 May 1965, p. 2.

aircraft. These increases in weight pretty much guaranteed that the program had already reached its maximum altitude; the maximum speed, on the other hand, still lay ahead with the modified X-15A-2.[225]

On 26 February 1965, Jack McKay took X-15-1 on a Mach 5.40 heating flight (1-52-85). Afterwards, McKay commented that there was "quite a bit of pounding over the airplane during the acceleration part of it and this is just that regular banging during the heating run you know. Every time you get used to that and you don't fly that bird for some time that first one will wake you up. It is hard to tell just where it is coming from. It is just like somebody is hitting the airplane with a sledge hammer."[226]

The Fourth Industry Conference

NASA held the fourth and last conference on the progress of the X-15 program at the FRC on 7 October 1965. This conference was considerably smaller than the previous ones, with only 13 papers written by 25 authors. The FRC employed 18 of the authors, while four came from other NASA centers, one from the AFFTC, and the remaining two from other Air Force organizations. Approximately 500 persons attended the event. At this point, the program had conducted approximately 150 flights over 6 years.[227]

By the time of the conference, the X-15 had essentially met or exceeded all of its revised performance specifications. The future would bring no additional altitude marks, and additional speed of less than a Mach number. For the most part, the government was using the X-15 as an experiment carrier, although X-15A-2 continued some additional aero-thermo-dynamic research. Jim Love noted that 10 pilots had used the three X-15s to accumulate almost 1 hour of flight above 200,000 feet and almost 4 hours at speeds in excess of Mach 4.[228]

The follow-on experiments were taking on unanticipated importance. Love observed, "The use of the airplane as an experimental test bed is one of the most significant extensions in the research capability of the X-15 airplanes. They have been utilized to carry various experimental packages to required environments, obtaining measurements with these packages, and then returning the experiment and results to the experimenters ... several experiments were installed on each aircraft for better flight utilization. For this reason, on the X-15-1 airplane, specially constructed [wing] tip pods and tail-cone box have been installed ... to accommodate the experiments .... Three experiments have been completed, five are in progress, and three more are planned for next year."[229]

---

225 "X-15 Semi-Annual Status Report No. 4," 1 April 1965, p. 1.

226 Pilot questionnaire, John B. McKay, flight 1-52-85 (undated, but probably 26 February 1965).

227 *Progress of the X-15 Research Airplane Program*, a compilation of the papers presented at the flight research center, 7 October 1965, NASA publication SP-90 (Washington, DC: NASA, 1965), p. iii; X-15 Status report no. 65-10, Paul F. Bikle/FRC to J. Martin/NASA Headquarters, 14 October 1965, p. 2. The conference had been planned for two days (7-8 October), but was reduced to a single day a few months previously. Unfortunately, this proceedings report did not include a list of attendees. The other industry conferences were held in 1956, 1958, and 1961.

228 Love and Fischel, "Status of X-15 Program," p. 2.

229 Ibid, p. 5. The omitted text is primarily references to figures that do not appear in this history.

Love noted that "the X-15 program has never settled down to a routine operation because of the continued increase in complexity and the nature of experiments and research performed by each aircraft. This attribute is probably characteristic of research programs." The lack of routine, however, undoubtedly increased the cost of the program and placed a heavy burden on personnel to maintain safety.[230]

The X-15A-2

After Jack McKay's emergency landing in X-15-2 on 9 November 1962, North American proposed modifying X-15-2 to an advanced configuration capable of reaching Mach 8 velocities. NASA in general and Paul Bikle in particular were not particularly enthusiastic and felt the Air Force should simply repair the aircraft to its original configuration or retire it altogether. Many researchers believed that the Mach 8-capable X-15A would be of limited value for aero-thermo research. However, NASA did not press its views, and on 13 May 1963 the Air Force directed North American to repair and modify the aircraft at a cost of $4.75 million. The advanced aircraft was intended to evaluate an air-breathing hypersonic research engine (HRE) being developed at Langley. It was designed to reach 8,000 fps at an altitude of 100,000 feet, and a dynamic pressure of 1,000 psf. Heating rates up to 210 Btu per square foot per second were expected, with peak structural temperatures approaching 2,400°F.[231]

The modifications did not significantly alter the physical appearance of X-15A-2. The wingspan was still 22.36 feet, but the airplane was 29 inches longer due to a plug in the center of gravity compartment between the propellant tanks. Perhaps the most obvious change was the addition of external propellant tanks on each side of the fuselage below the wings. These allowed the airplane to carry approximately 70% more propellant, a necessary ingredient in raising performance to 8,000 fps. The tanks provided an additional 60 seconds of engine burn time, for a total of 150 seconds at 100% power. Other modifications included adding hydrogen-peroxide tanks within extended aft-side fairings to supply the turbopump for the longer engine burn times, and additional pressurization gas in a spherical helium tank just behind the vertical stabilizer.[232]

The fuselage extension provided additional internal volume for experiments, and the center-of-gravity compartment access doors could accommodate optical windows looking up or down. The compartment could also accommodate a liquid-hydrogen tank, with a total capacity of 48 pounds, to fuel the ramjet mounted under the fixed portion of the ventral stabilizer, but it appears NASA never actually installed the tank. Perhaps the most difficult part of incorporating this extension

230 Ibid, p. 5.

231 Elmor J. Adkins and Johnny G. Armstrong, "Development and Status of the X-15A-2 Airplane," a paper in the *Progress of the X-15 Research Airplane Program*, a compilation of the papers presented at the FRC, 7 October 1965, NASA publication SP-90 (Washington, DC: NASA, 1965), pp. 103-104; Edwin W. Johnston, "Current and Advanced X-15," a paper presented at the Military Aircraft Systems and Technology meeting, Washington, DC, 21-23 September 1964; Johnny G. Armstrong, AFFTC technology document FTC-TD-69-4, "Flight Planning and Conduct of the X-15A-2 Envelope Expansion Program," July 1969, p. 2. The repair and modifications were accomplished under Air Force contract AF33(657)-11614.

232 Adkins and Armstrong, "Development and Status of the X-15A-2 Airplane," pp. 104-105.

was moving the B-52 pylon attach points to maintain the vertical stabilizer in the appropriate position under (through) the NB-52 wing.[233]

North American strengthened the landing gear using a strut that was 6.75 inches longer than the original. This provided 33 inches of ground clearance to the bottom of the fixed ventral stabilizer; the expected ramjet was 30 inches in diameter. The new strut provided a 1,000-pound increase in allowable landing weights, but there was some concern over the effects of the longer strut on nose-wheel and forward fuselage loads. In an attempt to provide an additional margin of safety, the nose-gear trunnion was mounted 9 inches lower (effectively lowering the nose gear by the same amount), allowing an attitude at nose-gear touchdown that was similar to that of the basic airplanes.[234]

Instead of the trapezoidal windows on the original airplanes, North American installed elliptical windows that used three panes of glass to withstand the increased temperatures at Mach 8. The outer pane was 0.65-inch-thick fused silica, the middle pane was 0.375-inch alumino-silicate, and the inner pane was 0.29-inch laminated soda lime glass. This time the company mounted the outside windshield-retaining frame flush with the glass to prevent the reoccurrence of the flow heating experienced early in the program.[235]

The X-15A-2 modification also included a "skylight" hatch. Two upward-opening doors, 20 inches long by 8.5 inches wide, were installed above the instrument compartment behind the cockpit to expose cameras and other experiments. North American revised the normal research instrumentation elevator so that the upper shelf could extend upward through the open hatch if needed. The modifications also included additional data recorders: five 36-channel oscillographs, eight three-channel oscillographs, two 14-track tape recorders, one 24-cell manometer, and one cockpit camera. In addition, a new 86-channel PDM telemetry system was used to transmit data to the ground in real time.[236]

The accident had seriously damaged the outer portion of the right wing. North American found that it could adequately repair the main wing box, but the outer 41 inches were a total loss. With the government's concurrence, the company modified the wing box to support a replaceable outer panel that allowed the testing of various materials and structures during hypersonic flight. The panel provided with the airplane (and the only one that apparently ever flew) was similar in construction and materials to the standard X-15 wing except that it was equipped with a 26.7 by 23-inch access panel that allowed access to an extensive amount of research instrumentation.[237]

---

233 Ibid, p. 105; Johnston, "Current and Advanced X-15;" letter, Johnny G. Armstrong to Dennis R. Jenkins, 3 August 2002.

234 Adkins and Armstrong, "Development and Status of the X-15A-2 Airplane," p. 105; Johnston, "Current and Advanced X-15;" Major William J. Knight, "Increased Piloting Tasks and Performance of X-15A-2 in Hypersonic Flight," *The Aeronautical Journal of the Royal Aeronautical Society*, vol. 72, September 1968, pp. 793-802 (derived from a lecture given to the test pilots group of the society on 30 January 1968); letter, Johnny G. Armstrong to Dennis R. Jenkins, 3 August 2002.

235 Armstrong, "Flight Planning and Conduct of the X-15A-2 Envelope Expansion Program, " p. 6; Adkins and Armstrong, "Development and Status of the X-15A-2 Airplane," p. 105.

236 Adkins and Armstrong, "Development and Status of the X-15A-2 Airplane," p. 105; AFFTC technology document FTC-TD-69-4, p. 7.

237 Adkins and Armstrong, "Development and Status of the X-15A-2 Airplane," p. 105.

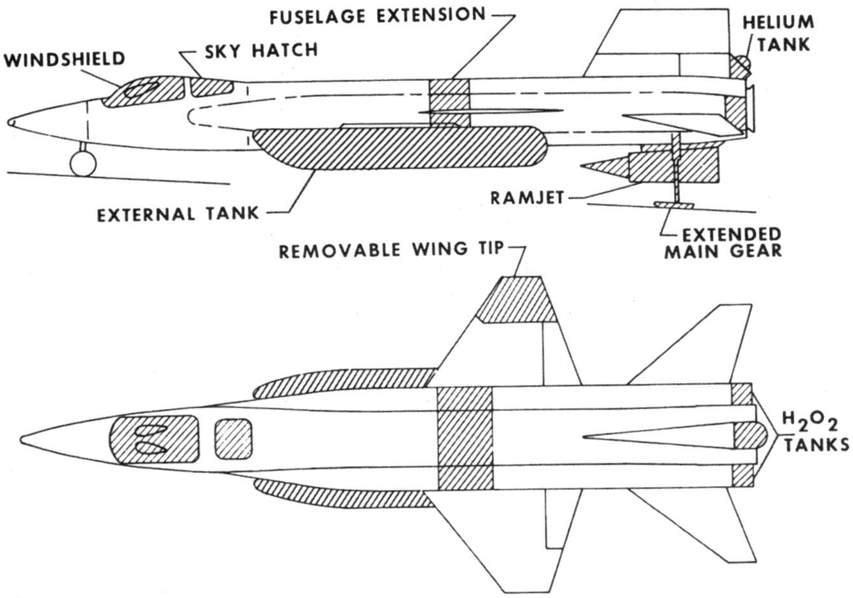

After Jack McKay's emergency landing at Mud Lake, the Air Force had North American rebuild the X-15-2 with several modifications intended to allow flights to Mach 8 to support ramjet propulsion research. The X-15A-2 was designed to reach 8,000 fps at an altitude of 100,000 feet, and a dynamic pressure of 1,000 psf. Heating rates up to 210 Btu per square foot per second were expected, with peak structural temperatures approaching 2,400 degrees Fahrenheit. A 29-inch fuselage extension provided a larger center-of-gravity compartment to hold a liquid hydrogen fuel tank for the proposed ramjet, and external tanks carried additional propellants for the XLR99. (NASA)

NASA conducted wind-tunnel tests of the X-15A-2 during the summer and fall of 1963. The tests indicated that there was little aerodynamic difference between the modified X-15A-2 without external tanks and the basic X-15. Despite the anticipated similarities, engineers decided it was prudent to conduct an abbreviated flight series to verify that the airplane still handled satisfactorily. Stability and control maneuvers conducted during the initial flights of the X-15A-2 largely verified the wind-tunnel predictions. However, the verification took significantly longer than expected when the program encountered trouble with the modified landing-gear system.[238]

North American completed final assembly of X-15A-2 in Inglewood on 15 February 1964, and the Air Force accepted the airplane on 17 February, three weeks ahead of schedule and slightly below budget. The airplane was, however, 773 pounds overweight, a condition that was expected to reduce the maximum velocity somewhat. The design launch weight was 49,640 pounds, and propellants accounted for 32,250 of these pounds (18,750 pounds internally and 13,500

238 Knight, "Increased Piloting Tasks and Performance of X-15A-2 in Hypersonic Flight," pp. 793-802; "Flight Planning and Conduct of the X-15A-2 Envelope Expansion Program," p. 7.

pounds in the external tanks). Subsequent modifications would add another few hundred pounds in empty weight. North American delivered the airplane to the FRC on 18 February and an "official" government acceptance ceremony took place on 24 February.[239]

After NASA conducted the final systems checks, the modified aircraft made its first captive flight (2-C-53) on 15 June 1964 and its first free flight (2-32-55) on 25 June. The main purpose of the flight was to check out the various systems, evaluate the handling qualities of the modified airplane, and gain preliminary experience with the ultraviolet stellar photography experiment (#1).[240]

It was not bad for a "checkout" flight. Using 77% thrust, Bob Rushworth reached Mach 4.59 and 83,300 feet. In an ironic twist, Jack McKay, who had been injured on the flight that damaged the airplane, was the NASA-1 controller. As expected, Bob Rushworth reported that the modified X-15A-2 handled much like a basic X-15. Static longitudinal stability remained about the same, despite a 10% forward shift in the center of gravity. The already low directional stability of the unmodified airplane was somewhat lower in X-15A-2, but Rushworth did not think it posed a significant threat to safety. The longitudinal trim characteristics of the modified airplane were essentially unchanged up through Mach 3 at angles of attack up to 15 degrees. The modified airplane had a trim capability reduced by approximately 3–5 degrees at higher angles of attack and Mach numbers.[241]

Things got more exciting on the second flight (2-33-56). Shortly after a maximum Mach number of 5.23 was obtained, the nose gear unexpectedly extended as the airplane decelerated through Mach 4.2. After the flight Rushworth wrote, "Everything was going along fine and just about the time I was ready to drop it over [lower the nose] I got a loud bang and … the resulting conditions that I had gave me quite a little bit of concern because the airplane began to oscillate wildly and I couldn't seem to catch up with it. I put the dampers back on and stuffed the nose down to about 5 degrees angle of attack and it seemed to be normal then except I had a sideslip and I was then required to use left roll to hold the airplane level. A couple of seconds later I realized that this sound that I had heard was very much similar to the nose gear coming out in the landing pattern so that was the only thing I could think of. I announced that and then a few seconds later I began to get smoke in the cockpit, quite a little bit more than I had ever seen before. This partially confirmed that the nose gear, at least the door was open. I wasn't sure that the gear was out but it was; there was enough of an explosion there to make me think that the gear was out."[242]

For the time being, the chase planes were of no help in confirming the problem since they were some 10 miles below the X-15. Jack McKay as NASA-1 could not help much either, since no emergency procedures existed for this particular failure. McKay did advise Rushworth that it would probably be best if the X-15

---

239 Johnston, "Current and Advanced X-15;" Knight, "Increased Piloting Tasks and Performance of X-15A-2 in Hypersonic Flight," pp. 793-802.

240 "X-15 Semi-Annual Status Report No. 3," 1 December 1964, p. 1; Major Robert A. Rushworth, "Pilot Report for Flight 2-32-55," 25 June 1964.

241 Major Robert A. Rushworth, "Pilot Report for Flight 2-32-55," 25 June 1964; Armstrong, "Expanding the X-15 Envelope to Mach 6.7," pp. 5-6.

242 Armstrong, "Flight Planning and Conduct of the X-15A-2 Envelope Expansion Program," p. 10; Radio transcript, flight 2-33-56, 14 August 1964. In the files at the DFRC History Office.

remained at high altitude until it had slowed considerably, thereby easing the aero-thermo loads on the extended nose gear. At one point NASA-1 advised Rushworth to use the brakes to slow down a bit, but Rushworth had other ideas: "No, I don't want to get brakes out, I want to get the damn thing home." Fifty miles away from Edwards, the X-15 was still traveling at Mach 2.5 and McKay advised Rushworth, "Let's go max L/D, Bob. You're looking OK now. Your heading is good. You're on profile. Looks like you've got plenty of energy."[243]

The chase planes finally spotted the X-15 as it was descending 20 miles north-east of Edwards. Despite the degraded control and increased drag resulting from the extended nose gear, Bob Rushworth was doing fine. Joe Engle in Chase-3 verified that the nose gear appeared to be structurally sound and in the locked-down position. As for the tires, Engle reported, "OK, Bob, your tires look pretty scorched; I imagine they will probably go on landing." There was a worry, however, that the oleo strut had also been damaged by the heat and dynamic pressure; if it failed on landing, the X-15 could break in half or worse. There seemed to be little choice. Engle was right–the tires disintegrated shortly after the nose gear came down, but Rushworth managed to stop the airplane without serious difficulty.[244]

An investigation revealed that aerodynamic heating was the cause of the failure. The expansion of the fuselage was greater than the amount of slack built into the landing gear release cable. This caused an effective pull on the release cable that released the uplock hook. An outward bowing of the nose gear door imposed an additional load on the uplock hook. The load from both of these sources caused the uplock hook to bend, allowing the gear to extend. Engineers duplicated this failure in the High-Temperature Loads Calibration Laboratory by simulating the fuselage expansion and applying heat to the nose-gear door.[245]

The same stability and control data flight plan was duplicated for the next X-15A-2 light (2-34-57) on 29 September 1964. Again, shortly after reaching a maximum Mach number of 5.20, Bob Rushworth experienced a similar but less intense noise and aircraft trim change at Mach 4.5–the small nose-gear scoop door had opened. In his post-flight report Rushworth noted, "Yes, I sensed it was the little door, because the magnitude of the bang when it came open wasn't as large as the other experience." During the normal gear-extension sequence, air loads on the small door pulled the nose gear door open to assist in the extension of the nose gear. Although not as serious a failure as that on the previous flight, it again precluded obtaining dampers-off stability data. NASA redesigned the nose-gear door to provide positive retention of the scoop door regardless of the thermal stresses. Engineers also modified the other two airplanes since the basic failure mode was common.[246]

To check out the modifications to the nose gear, the program decided on a low-speed flight (2-35-60) to a maximum Mach number of 4.66. The flight planners decided to give Bob Rushworth a break after the two previous adventures, so

243 Radio transcript, flight 2-33-56, 14 August 1964. In the files at the DFRC History Office.

244 Major Robert A. Rushworth, "Pilot Report for Flight 2-33-56," 14 August 1964; Radio transcript, flight 2-33-56, 14 August 1964. In the files at the DFRC History Office.

245 Armstrong, "Flight Planning and Conduct of the X-15A-2 Envelope Expansion Program," p. 10.

246 Major Robert A. Rushworth, "Pilot Report for Flight 2-34-57," 29 September 1964. In the files at the DFRC History Office.

Jack McKay made this flight, which went off without a problem. The nose gear performed normally.[247]

Rushworth was in the cockpit again for the next fight (2-36-63) of X-15A-2 on 17 February 1965. In a run of bad luck that is hard to fathom, this time the right main skid extended at Mach 4.3 and 85,000 feet. In his post-flight report Rushworth wrote, "Jack [McKay, NASA-1] was talking away and things were going along real nice and I couldn't seem to get a word in there to tell him that I had a little problem. It took several seconds to get the airplane righted and dampers back on, very much similar to the nose gear coming out. Once I got it righted, I realized that I had a tremendous sideslip, I guess 4 degrees, and it took a lot of rudder deflection to get sideslip to zero. This persisted all the way down until I got subsonic. Once I had gone subsonic the airplane handled reasonably well." Again, the chase pilot was able to verify that the gear appeared structurally sound, and Rushworth managed to make a normal landing. When Rushworth finally got out of the airplane, he turned around and kicked it–enough was enough. Post-flight inspection revealed that the uplock hook had bent, allowing the gear to deploy. Again, aerodynamic heating was determined to be the source of the high load on the uplock hook.[248]

NASA flew five more X-15A-2 flights (2-38-66 through 2-42-74) before the envelope expansion program was begun. These flights were primarily conducted to study stability and control, but they also included landing-gear performance tests. Each flight carried the ultraviolet stellar photography experiment but obtained little useable data because of problems in maintaining the precise attitudes required for the experiment. Fortunately, the landing gear seemed to behave throughout these flights, but it had caused this portion of the flight program to take longer than expected.[249]

The engineers had always had some concerns about operating the X-15A-2 with the 23.5-foot-long, 37.75-inch-diameter external tanks. These attached to the airplane structure within the side fairings at fuselage stations 200 and 411. Propellant and gas interconnects ran through a tank pylon that was located between stations 317 and 397 and was covered by a set of retractable doors after the tanks were jettisoned. The left tank contained about 793 gallons of liquid oxygen in one compartment and three helium bottles with a total capacity of 8.4 cubic feet. The right tank contained about 1,080 gallons of anhydrous ammonia in a single compartment. The empty left tank weighed 1,150 pounds and the empty right tank weighed only 648 pounds; when they were full of propellants, they weighed 8,920 pounds and 6,850 pounds, respectively. Note that the left tank was over 2,000 pounds heavier than the right tank when they were full. To minimize weight and cost, the government had opted not to insulate the liquid-oxygen tank. As a result, the evaporation rate was high enough that the engineers considered the NB-52 top-off supply to be marginal. If a flight encountered a long hold time prior to

247 Armstrong, "Flight Planning and Conduct of the X-15A-2 Envelope Expansion Program," p. 10.

248 Major Robert A. Rushworth, "Pilot Report for Flight 2-36-63," 17 February 1965. In the files at the DFRC History Office; AFFTC technology document FTC-TD-69-4, p. 10; Thompson, *At the Edge of Space*, p. 237; Adkins and Armstrong, "Development and Status of the X-15A-2 Airplane," p. 107; "The Pilot's Panel," a paper in the *Proceedings of the X-15 30th Anniversary Celebration*, Dryden Flight Research Facility, Edwards, CA, 8 June 1989, NASA CP-3105, p. 149.

249 Armstrong, "Flight Planning and Conduct of the X-15A-2 Envelope Expansion Program," p. 12.

launch, it might prove necessary to abort the mission and return to Edwards due to excessive liquid-oxygen boil-off.[250]

The use of external tanks on the X-15A-2 was unique in that the pilot *had* to jettison the tanks from the aircraft. The structural limitations of the aluminum tanks and the degraded handling qualities dictated that the maximum allowable Mach number with the external tanks was 2.6, so the pilot had to jettison the tanks before reaching that speed. In addition, a landing was not possible with the tanks installed because of the increased drag and a lack of ground clearance. Hence, the program expended considerable effort to ensure the tanks would jettison when commanded.[251]

Each tank was forcibly ejected from the airplane during flight through the use of fore and aft gas-cartridge ejectors and a forward solid-propellant sustainer rocket that imparted pitching and rolling moments to the tank after it had been ejected. For a normal empty tank jettison, both sets of gas cartridges fired and the nose rocket ignited. In the case of an emergency jettison when the tanks were full, only the nose gas cartridge fired.

The tanks were relatively expensive, so they were equipped with a recovery system that included a drogue and a main parachute. The drogue chute deployed from its nose compartment immediately after separation, and the main descent parachute deployed when a barometric sensor detected the tanks passing through 8,000 feet. Although the engineers expected some impact damage, they believed it was possible to refurbish the tanks at a reasonable cost.[252]

Wind-tunnel tests indicated that satisfactory separation characteristics existed when the dynamic pressure was less than 400 psf and the angle of attack was less than 10 degrees; acceptable separation probably existed for dynamic pressures up to 600 psf. At higher angles of attack and dynamic pressures, researchers expected the tanks to roll excessively and to pitch up within close proximity to the airplane. Tank separation characteristics with partly expended propellants were unknown and were a potential problem since there were no slosh baffles or compartments for center-of-gravity control. The researchers expected the full-tank ejection characteristics to be satisfactory for any reasonable flight conditions that might occur within 15 seconds of launch.[253]

Prior to the first flight using external tanks, the Air Force conducted two dummy tank jettison tests with X-15A-2 located over a 10-foot-deep pit in the ground beside the ramp. Technicians constructed a pair of beams with similar mass and inertia properties to simulate empty tanks. Preloaded cables attached to the beams applied simulated aerodynamic drag and side loads. The first test used a single set of ejector cartridges at simulated air loads of 400 psf, 5 degrees angle of attack, and 3 degrees of sideslip. The second test used two sets of ejector cartridges at a simulated dynamic pressure of 600 psf. Both tests were successful, and high-speed motion pictures showed good separation characteristics. During the tests,

250 Ibid, p. 5; Adkins and Armstrong, "Development and Status of the X-15A-2 Airplane," p. 107; North American report NA-67-344, "Technical Proposal for a Conceptual Design Study for the Modification of an X-15 Air Vehicle to a Hypersonic Delta-Wing Configuration," 17 May 1967, vol. I, pp. 182-184.

251 Armstrong, "Flight Planning and Conduct of the X-15A-2 Envelope Expansion Program," p. 16.

252 Ibid, pp. 4-5; Adkins and Armstrong, "Development and Status of the X-15A-2 Airplane," p. 107.

253 Adkins and Armstrong, "Development and Status of the X-15A-2 Airplane," p. 108.

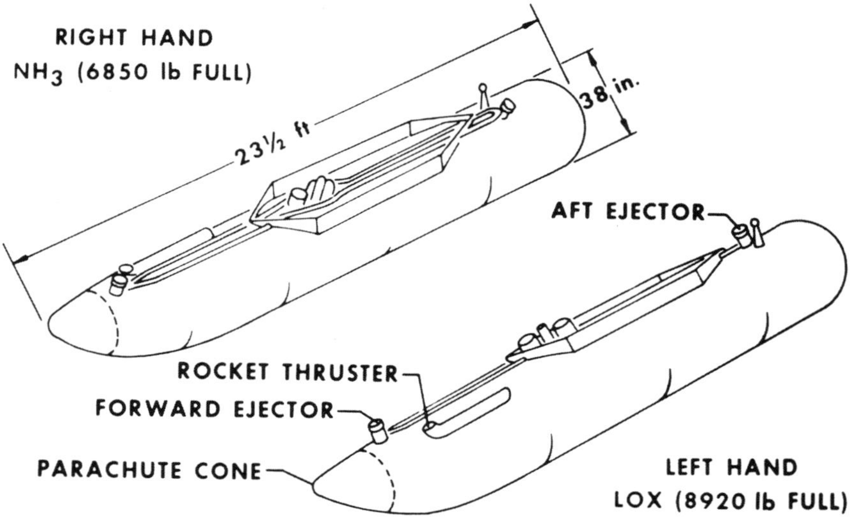

The external tanks allowed carriage of approximately 70 percent more propellant, a necessary ingredient in raising performance to 8,000 fps. The tanks provided an additional 60 seconds of engine burn time, for a total of 150 seconds at 100-percent power. The tanks were 23.5 feet long and 37.75 inches in diameter. The left tank contained about 793 gallons of liquid oxygen in one compartment and three helium bottles with a total capacity of 8.4 cubic feet. The right tank contained about 1,080 gallons of anhydrous ammonia in a single compartment. The empty left tank weighed 1,150 pounds and the empty right tank weighed only 648 pounds; when full, they weighed 8,920 pounds and 6,850 pounds, respectively. (NASA)

the X-15 APU supplied hydraulic and electrical power, and engineers engaged the SAS to observe its reaction to the separation, which was satisfactory.[254]

Despite this, during a review leading up to the first flight, engineers expressed concern over the possible separation of partially filled tanks during an emergency. The wind-tunnel tests and the tank separation system only covered full and empty scenarios. What would happen if the pilot had to abort the flight during the first 60 seconds of powered flight while the engine was siphoning propellants from the external tanks? The initial response was that the tanks, as designed, would not withstand the loads imposed during a separation with a partial load. Engineers at the FRC and AFFTC considered installing a rapid propellant-dump system, installing a set of baffles in the tanks, or even providing a system that would allow the pilot to refill the tanks using internal propellants. All seemed too complicated given the time and money available to the program.[255]

After a great deal of consultation among the engineers, flight planners, and pilots, management decided to continue, at least for the time being. The risk was considered reasonable because the XLR99 had never encountered a premature

254 Ibid.

255 Armstrong, "Flight Planning and Conduct of the X-15A-2 Envelope Expansion Program," p. 18.

shutdown from 100% thrust–all failures had occurred either during ignition or while throttling. If a failure happened during ignition, the tanks would be full and would not present a problem, and the plan called for no throttling during the high-speed runs. Nevertheless, engineers decided to add a third jettison button in the cockpit. This one, intended for use with partial tanks, would fire the forward gas cartridge and ignite the separation rocket–sort of a middle ground between the other scenarios.[256]

Although there were physical differences between the basic X-15 and the X-15A-2 without external tanks, their aerodynamic qualities were similar. With external tanks on the airplane, however, some rather dramatic differences existed, with the general trend toward unfavorable characteristics. The offset center of gravity caused by the external tanks further complicated the overall control task. At launch with full tanks, the vertical center of gravity was approximately 9 inches below the aircraft waterline, moving upward as the engine consumed propellants. The pilot had to use additional nose-up stabilizer trim to counteract the nose-down pitch at engine ignition caused by this offset below the thrust vector. The heavier liquid-oxygen tank on the left side displaced the center of gravity 2 inches to that side, causing a left rolling moment that the pilot also had to counteract.[257]

The nominal flight profile for the speed missions was to maintain the airplane at a 12-degree angle of attack until it reached a pitch attitude of 34 degrees. The pilot held this climb attitude until the external propellant was depleted. Tank ejection occurred at approximately Mach 2.1 and 67,000 feet, and the pilot maintained an angle of attack of 2 degrees until the airplane reached 100,000 feet. The airplane then accelerated to maximum velocity.[258]

As was the case with the basic airplane, the simulator predicted poor handling qualities at high angles of attack, due primarily to the large negative dihedral effect caused by the presence of the ventral rudder. For a yaw damper failure with the speed brakes out, a divergent sideslip oscillation persisted above 6 degrees angle of attack. Although the pilot could damp this divergence, it required almost continuous attention and left little time for other tasks. The simulator showed that turning off the roll damper would eliminate the divergent yaw oscillation, but then the pilot would have to fly the airplane with less lateral directional stability. From the simulator studies it was determined that, because of the relatively low-altitude profiles required, the airplane could be safely flown after a roll and/or yaw damper failure if an angle of attack of less than 8 degrees was maintained. The program accepted this restriction for the initial envelope expansion flights. However, for the projected ramjet tests, which required flights at high dynamic pressures, a divergence of this type could occur too rapidly for the pilot to take corrective action. Hence, NASA decided to provide a redundant yaw damper, similar to the ASAS used for the roll axis. The FRC began initial design work, but the flight program ended before the system was completed.[259]

256 Ibid.

257 Adkins and Armstrong, "Development and Status of the X-15A-2 Airplane," p. 108; Knight, "Increased Piloting Tasks and Performance of X-15A-2 in Hypersonic Flight," pp. 793-802; "Flight Planning and Conduct of the X-15A-2 Envelope Expansion Program," pp. 19-20.

258 Adkins and Armstrong, "Development and Status of the X-15A-2 Airplane," p. 108.

259 Armstrong, "Flight Planning and Conduct of the X-15A-2 Envelope Expansion Program," p. 24.

The final ground-based external tank test took place on the Rocket Engine Test Facility where X-15A-2 had completed a full-duration engine run with the external tanks installed on the aircraft. Engineers had already corrected deficiencies uncovered during several earlier tests.[260]

The expected performance of X-15A-2 represented a significant improvement over the demonstrated 6,019 fps of the basic aircraft. With external tanks and the ventral rudder, the estimated velocity was between 7,600 and 7,700 fps at 120,000 feet. Replacing the ventral with an assumed ramjet configuration would decrease that to about 7,200 fps at 118,000 feet, a result of increased weight and drag for the ramjet configuration. This performance was, however, appreciably less than the design goal of 8,000 fps at 100,000 feet. As a result, Reaction Motors was investigating the development of a new injector and nozzle to provide additional thrust in an attempt to bring the performance back up to 8,000 fps. Again, the end would come before the company completed the work.[261]

The length of time the airplane could remain at high velocity and dynamic pressure determined the amount of useful data about the ramjet that could be obtained. Researchers expected that X-15A-2 could stay above 7,000 fps for 50 seconds and above 6,000 fps for 110 seconds per flight. For ramjet tests that required steady conditions (that is, at a relatively constant velocity and dynamic pressure), the pilot would throttle the XLR99 to minimum and extend the speed brakes so that low acceleration existed. The expected stabilized test time for this configuration was approximately 14 seconds at 7,000 fps and 40 seconds at 6,000 fps.[262]

The first flight (2-43-75) with empty external tanks was on 3 November 1965, the only flight launched from Cuddeback, about 60 miles north of Edwards. Bob Rushworth jettisoned the tanks at Mach 2.25 as the airplane passed through 70,300 feet, and took the airplane to Mach 2.31 and 70,600 feet before landing at Rogers Dry Lake after a flight of only 5 minutes and 1 second (the shortest non-emergency powered flight of the program). Post-flight analysis indicated that the handling qualities were essentially as predicted by the simulator. Rushworth, who for a change was flying without deploying part of the landing gear, commented that he thought the "roll stability was significantly less than I had expected," but the "longitudinal control wasn't quite as bad" as he had anticipated.[263]

Two ground-based mobile trackers, each with 150-inch lenses on 35-mm Mitchell cameras running at 72 and 48 frames per second, provided photographic coverage of the tank separation. In addition, six Askania tracking cameras recorded the tank recovery system. Because the events took place at quite a distance, the resulting image size was small and researchers could only make a qualitative analysis of the event. The tanks separated cleanly from the aircraft; however, it appeared that the tanks did not rotate nose down as much as expected. They

260 Ibid.

261 Adkins and Armstrong, "Development and Status of the X-15A-2 Airplane," p. 110.

262 Ibid.

263 Lieutenant Colonel Robert A. Rushworth, "Pilot Report for Flight 2-43-75," 3 November 1965; AFFTC technology document FTC-TD-69-4, p. 29; Armstrong, "Expanding the X-15 Envelope to Mach 6.7," p. 202; letter, Johnny G. Armstrong to Dennis R. Jenkins, 3 August 2002. Local folklore has it that after Rushworth's February 1965 flight the ground crew installed a cockpit placard that read "Do Not Deploy Landing Gear Above Mach 4," and that this was the solution to the landing-gear problems.

exhibited a tumbling action during flight with the drogue chutes attached, and tended to trim at an angle of attack of about –110 degrees. The drogue chutes occasionally collapsed during flight, so the engineers lengthened the drogue chute riser for future flights. Impact with the desert destroyed the liquid-oxygen tank after the nose cone containing the main descent chute did not separate properly. The Air Force recovered the ammonia tank in repairable condition. The tumbling action of the tanks increased the total drag and the tanks fell short of their predicted impact points–the ammonia tank landed 2.3 miles short and 0.6 mile to the left, while the liquid-oxygen tank landed 2.7 miles short and 1.6 miles to the left. This was still well inside the bounds of the Edwards impact range and did not represent a problem.[264]

Joe Engle ended up being the only X-15 pilot who would get to fly the next lifting-reentry vehicle, the Space Shuttle. He also has the distinction of being the only person to fly back from orbit, on the second Space Shuttle flight (STS-2). Milt Thompson said that "Joe Engle seemed to have a charmed relationship with the X-15" because for the most part all of Engle's flights went according to plan. However, not everybody would agree with that assessment of his 15th flight. On 10 August 1965, Engle took X-15-3 to 271,000 feet–his second flight above 50 miles. Mission rules stated that the X-15 pilot should fly an alternate low-altitude mission if the yaw damper channel on the MH-96 failed during the first 32 seconds of flight. This was because it was unlikely the airplane could make a successful reentry with a failed yaw damper. On this flight (3-46-70), the yaw channel failed 0.6 seconds after the X-15 dropped off the pylon. Engle reset the damper and did not feel obligated to fly the alternate profile since the damper successfully reset. It was a temporary reprieve, however. The damper failed again 19 seconds later; the reset was successful for at least 10 seconds until it failed again. The damper failed three times in the first 32 seconds of flight. Remarkably, Engle successfully flew the mission, although he missed some of the profile for various reasons, including a preoccupation with resetting the failing yaw damper.[265]

At the end of 1965, NASA could see that the end of the X-15 program was in sight. Researchers had long since completed the originally envisioned basic flight research, and the aircraft were now primarily experiment carriers, although X-15A-2 was still extending the flight envelope somewhat. However, plans to use X-15A-2 as a hypersonic ramjet test bed began to unravel when, on 6 August 1965, Secretary of Defense Robert S. McNamara disapproved the funding necessary for the effort.[266]

Under the best-case scenario, the FRC anticipated that the flight program using the basic X-15s would begin winding down at the end of 1967 when X-15-3 began receiving its delta-wing modifications. By the end of 1969, X-15-1 would be retired, leaving only X-15A-2 and the newly redelivered delta-wing X-15-3 in

264 Lieutenant Colonel Robert A. Rushworth, "Pilot Report for Flight 2-43-75," 3 November 1965; Armstrong, "Flight Planning and Conduct of the X-15A-2 Envelope Expansion Program," p. 29; X-15 Status Report 65-12, Paul F. Bikle/FRC to J. Martin/NASA Headquarters, 1 December 1965, p. 3.

265 Joe H. Engle, "Pilot Report for Flight 3-46-70," 23 August 1965; Memorandum, Joseph A. LaPierre/FRC to Chief, Research Division, X-15 Project Office, subject: Flight Research Report on Flight 3-46-70, 23 August 1965.

266 John V. Becker, "A Hindsight Study of the NASA Hypersonic Research Engine Project," 1 July 1976, p. 22. Prepared under contract NAS1-14250 but never published. Copy in the author's collection.

service. X-15A-2 would finish its ramjet tests in mid-1970, transferring all flight activity to the delta wing.[267]

Paul Bikle had long believed that any extended operation of the X-15 program beyond its original objectives was unwise and hard to justify in view of the high cost and risk involved. As early as 1961, he had suggested the end of 1964 as a desirable termination date. As time went on, Bikle felt that continued extensions of the program were becoming increasingly hard to justify, and he personally had strong doubts that either the delta wing or the HRE would ever reach flight status on an X-15. In spite of these personal misgivings, Bikle continued to support the program in his public statements.[268]

1966 FLIGHT PERIOD

January 1966 was much like December 1965 in the high desert–wet. Between 12 November and 1 December 1965 more than 3 inches of rain had fallen, and 2 more inches fell during December. NASA described Rogers, Three Sisters, Silver, and Hidden Hills as "wet," while Mud Lake was only "damp." Over 95% of Cuddeback was under water and there was visible snow at Delamar. A lack of landing sites effectively grounded the X-15 program.[269]

This gave the program time to do maintenance on the airplanes and incorporate various modifications. For instance, engineers installed the Honeywell IFDS, finally, on X-15-3 along with a new Lear Siegler-developed vertical-scale instrument panel. All of the instrumentation wiring on this airplane was removed and replaced with new four-conductor shielded Teflon wire. It received the modifications necessary to carry the wing-tip experiment pods, and the third skid and stick-kicker needed for higher landing weights were installed.[270]

The pilots were not greeting the new X-15-3 instrument panel with overwhelming enthusiasm. Paul Bikle opined that "there has been some evidence of reluctance to accept the vertical-scale, fixed-index [tape] instruments." Bikle noted that previously "no objective evaluation of the suitability of the panel for the X-15 mission had been made." To correct this, engineers installed a duplicate of the panel in the fixed-base simulator and conducted runs using "measurable flight control and pilot performance parameters in a comparison of the Lear panel with the traditional panel."[271]

Of all the performance measures taken, only two showed consistent and significant differences. These were the absolute error in velocity at power reduction and the burnout altitude; in both cases, the statistical results favored the Lear panel.

267 Project Development Plan, "Delta Wing X-15," second draft, December 1965, pp. 36-37. In the files at the DFRC History Office.

268 Letter, Paul F. Bikle to USAF/ASD, no subject, 2 November 1961; John V. Becker, "A Hindsight Study of the NASA Hypersonic Research Engine Project," 1 July 1976, p. 26. Prepared under contract NAS1-14250 but never published. Copy in the author's collection.

269 X-15 Status Reports, Paul F. Bikle/FRC to J. Martin/NASA Headquarters, 1 December 1965, and 3 January 1966.

270 X-15 Status Reports, Paul F. Bikle/FRC to J. Martin/NASA Headquarters, 3 January, 2 February, and 1 March 1966.

271 X-15 Status Report, Paul F. Bikle/FRC to J. Martin/NASA Headquarters, 1 March 1966, p. 3.

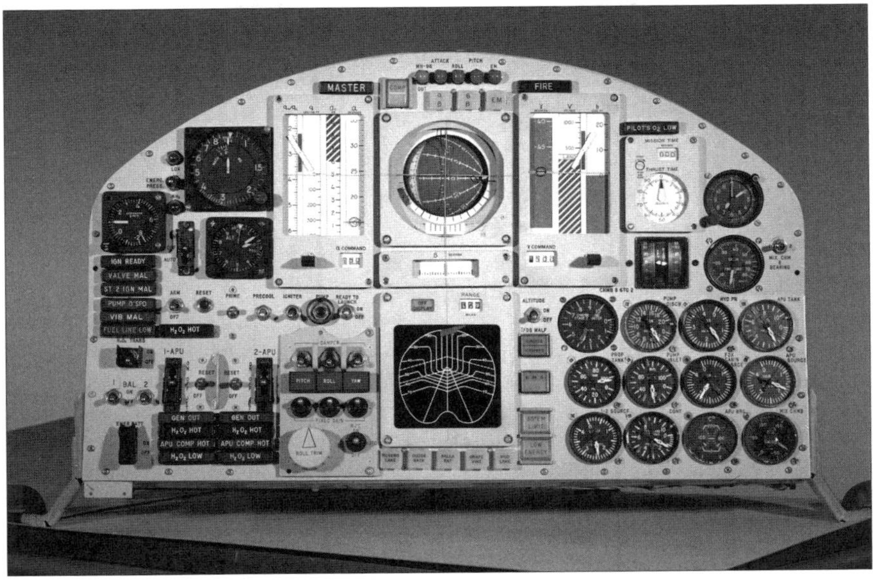

For most of the flight program, the X-15 used an instrument panel that contained conventional instrumentation. In 1965, Lear Siegler developed a new panel for X-15-3 that used vertical-scale instruments that were supposed to provide enhanced situational awareness for the pilot. Similar instruments were being incorporated into the latest generation of Air Force fighters about the same time. At first, the new instrument panel was not met with overwhelming enthusiasm from the X-15 pilots, but eventually they came to accept the new instruments, although having two very different cockpit configurations complicated the simulators and training regiments. (NASA)

An examination of the altitude and velocity indicators on both panels showed that the differences were the result of high-scale resolution on the Lear instruments, which was almost twice that of the traditional panel instruments. The pilots were still not altogether happy with the new panel, but they no longer mistrusted it.[272]

During this down period, X-15A-2 received a new Maurer camera to replace the Hycon unit in the center-of-gravity compartment. This was not as simple as it sounded and took almost eight weeks of work. X-15-1 received a modification that allowed ground personnel to easily remove or replace the wing-tip pods as needed to support various experiments. NASA could now swap the pods between X-15-1 and X-15-3, and was manufacturing a second set of pods.[273]

As January passed with no relief from the wet lakebeds (another half inch of rain fell at Edwards, with more snow on the upper areas of the High Range), NASA performed more modifications on the airplanes. Because the increase in stiffness of the main skids and the addition of the third skid transmitted higher

272 Ibid. The introduction of tape-style instruments into operational aircraft was initially viewed with similar mistrust. The scientific ("human factors") community was sure that the new displays were easier to read and provided better information; the pilots pointed to 50 years of using the older, round instruments without a problem. In the end, the tape-style instruments had a relatively short life in most combat aircraft and were eventually replaced by the old-style round dials–at least until the advent of the "glass cockpit" in the 1980s.

273 X-15 Status Report, Paul F. Bikle/FRC to J. Martin/NASA Headquarters, 3 January 1966. In the end, one set of pods was lost with X-15-3 on flight 3-65-97; the other set is installed on X-15-1 as it is displayed in the NASM.

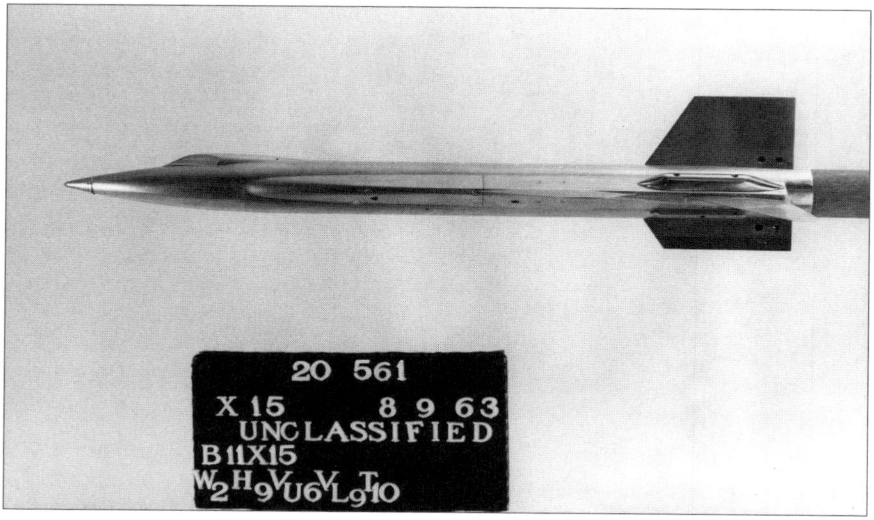

The X-15A-2 configuration was tested in a variety of wind tunnels, including one at the NASA Jet Propulsion Laboratory in Pasadena, California. The JPL tests centered around determining the effects of shock-wave impingement on the proposed ramjet and finding an alternate vertical-stabilizer configuration to provide enhanced stability at Mach 8 while carrying a ramjet under the ventral stabilizer. (NASA)

loads through the structure to the nose gear, engineers decided to reinforce the skin on X-15-1 between fuselage stations 91 and 106. The Air Force sent the NB-52B to Tinker AFB for major maintenance, leaving her older sister to support the flight program, assuming the lakebeds ever dried out. The carrier aircraft returned on 8 April and the AFFTC spent the next five weeks modifying it to carry the heavier X-15A-2.[274]

NASA also used the time to complete various analyses, including a complete simulation of reentry profiles at the increased weights currently flown by the airplanes. The ground rules were that reentries would be limited to 1,600 psf using an angle of attack of 20 degrees. To avoid exceeding the structural limitations of the airplanes, NASA decided to restrict X-15-1 to altitudes under 265,000 feet and X-15A-2 to less than 250,000 feet. Mostly because it was equipped with the MH-96, NASA allowed X-15-3 to operate up to 360,000 feet. These restrictions were not really a problem since the program had already reached the maximum altitude it was planning on, although the first two airplanes would bump into these limits on several future flights.[275]

The simulations showed that, as currently configured, X-15A-2 should be able to reach a maximum velocity of 7,500 fps without the ramjet and 7,100 fps with the ramjet, both at 120,000 feet. These velocities assumed a launch weight

274 X-15 Status Report, Paul F. Bikle/FRC to J. Martin/NASA Headquarters, 2 February 1966, p. 1; X-15 Status Report 66-5, Paul F. Bikle/FRC to J. Martin/NASA Headquarters, 4 May 1966, p. 1.

275 X-15 Status Report, Paul F. Bikle/FRC to J. Martin/NASA Headquarters, 1 March 1966, p. 2. The X-15-1 was restricted to lower altitudes than X-15-3 since it was not equipped with the MH-96 adaptive flight control system; the X-15A-2 was not intended to fly much above 100,000 feet during its maximum speed program. Bob Hoey remembers that the ballistic control system was eventually removed from the X-15A-2 to save weight.

of 51,650 pounds with the use of external tanks and an XLR99 burn time of 152 seconds. Based on these simulations, flight planners decided to conduct the X-15A-2 envelope-expansion program with the ventral on, primarily because it most closely resembled the planned ramjet configuration. However, the program was short of ventral rudders, and it was uncertain whether economic constraints would allow each flight to use one.[276]

More importantly, Langley and the Jet Propulsion Laboratory conducted wind-tunnel tests to investigate shock-wave systems affecting the proposed ramjet installation on X-15A-2. Researchers worried that shock waves impinging on the ramjet could affect inlet and engine performance, structures, and structural heating. The tests provided data for angles of attack between –5 and +20 degrees at Mach numbers between 2.3 and 4.63. A review of the data showed that a shock wave emanating from the forward tip of the landing-gear skid would impinge on the ramjet inlet at all Mach numbers, and did not significantly vary with the angle of attack. These tests also showed that there was a complex shock impingement around the ventral stabilizer in general. Apparently, these data went unnoticed.[277]

By the beginning of April, the weather had improved considerably. The Air Force was in the process of repairing and re-marking Rogers, Grapevine, and Mud Lake. Cuddeback was dry but still too soft to re-mark. All of the other lakes were drying rapidly and were ready to use by the end of the month.[278]

Flying Again

Bob Rushworth's last flight (2-45-81), on 1 July 1966, was also the first flight with full external tanks. As Johnny Armstrong later observed, "with 20-20 hindsight, flight 45 was destined for failure." On X-15A-2, the propellants in the external tanks were pressure-fed to the internal tanks, and the engine received propellants from the internal tanks in the normal fashion. The fixed-base simulator had shown that the X-15 would quickly become uncontrollable if the propellant from one external tank transferred while that from the other tank did not, because the moment about the roll axis would be too large for the rolling tail to counter. If this situation developed, the pilot would jettison the tanks, shut down the engine, and make an emergency landing.[279]

The problem was that, for this first flight with full tanks, there was no direct method to determine whether the tanks were feeding correctly. Instrumentation was being developed to provide propellant transfer sensors (paddle switches), but it was not available for this flight. Instead, a pressure transducer across an orifice in the helium pressurization line provided the only information. Researchers had verified that the pressure transducer worked as expected during a planned captive-carry flight (2-C-80) with propellants in the external tanks.[280]

---

276 X-15 Status Report, Paul F. Bikle/FRC to J. Martin/NASA Headquarters, 1 March 1966, p. 2 and attachments; X-15 Status Report, Paul F. Bikle/FRC to J. Martin/NASA Headquarters, 1 March 1966, p. 2.

277 X-15 Status Report, Paul F. Bikle/FRC to J. Martin/NASA Headquarters, 1 April 1966, p. 2.

278 Ibid, pp. 7-8.

279 Armstrong, "Expanding the X-15 Envelope to Mach 6.7," pp. 202-203; various e-mails and telephone conversations, Johnny G. Armstrong to Dennis R. Jenkins, June/July 2002.

280 Ibid.

During the flight to the launch lake, while still safely connected to the NB-52, Rushworth verified that the pressure transducer was working. Rushworth jettisoned a small amount of propellant from the internal tanks, and NASA-1 watched the helium pressure come up as the external propellants flowed into the airplane (NASA-1 had to do it since nobody had thought to provide the pilot with any indicators). However, 18 seconds after the X-15 dropped away from the NB-52, Jack McKay (NASA-1) called to Rushworth: "We see no flow on ammonia, Bob." Rushworth responded, "Roger, understand. What else to do?" McKay: "Shutdown. Tanks off, Bob." Rushworth got busy: "OK, tanks are away ... I'm going into Mud." Any emergency landing is stressful, but this one ended well. Bruce Peterson in Chase-2 reported, "Airplane has landed, everything OK, real good shape."[281]

Jettisoning the tanks with the "full" button was supposed to initiate only the nose cartridges and not fire the separation rockets. However, in this case, apparently because of faulty circuitry, the separation rockets did fire. Fortunately, the separation occurred without the tanks recontacting the airplane. Engineers obtained a great deal of data on the tank separation because an FM telemetry system in the liquid-oxygen tank transmitted data on accelerations and rotational rates during separation. Post-flight inspection of the ejector bearing points on the aircraft indicated that the ammonia tank briefly hung on the aircraft, marring the ejector rack slightly. The drogue chutes deployed immediately after separation and the dump valve in the tank allowed the propellants to flow out. The main chute deployment was satisfactory; however, the mechanism designed to cut the main chute risers failed and high surface winds dragged the tanks across the desert. Nevertheless, the Air Force recovered both tanks in repairable condition.[282]

Bob Rushworth left the program after this flight, going on to a distinguished career that included a tour as the AFFTC commander some years later. Rushworth had flown 34 flights, more than any other pilot and more than double the statistical average. He had flown the X-15 for almost 6 years and had made most of the heating flights. These flights were perhaps the hardest to get right, and Rushworth did so most of the time.[283]

Major Michael J. Adams, making his first flight (1-69-116) on 6 October 1966, replaced Rushworth in the flight lineup. He started his career with a bang, literally. X-15-1 launched over Hidden Hills on a scheduled low-altitude (70,000 feet) and low-speed (Mach 4) pilot-familiarization flight. The bang came when the XLR99 shut itself down 90 seconds into the planned 129-second burn after the forward bulkhead of the ammonia tank failed. Fortunately, the airplane did not explode and Adams successfully landed at Cuddeback without major incident. Perhaps Adams was just having a bad day. After he returned to Edwards, he jumped in a T-38 for a scheduled proficiency flight. Shortly after takeoff, one of the J85 engines in the T-38 quit; fortunately, the Talon has two engines. Adams

281 Radio transcript for flight 2-45-81; Armstrong, "Expanding the X-15 Envelope to Mach 6.7," pp. 202-203.

282 William P. Albrecht/X-15 Project Engineer, "X-15 Operations Flight Report for Flight 2-45-81," 5 July 1966; memorandum, Lieutenant Colonel Robert A. Rushworth to Chief, Research Projects Office, subject: Preliminary report of X-15 flight 2-45-81, 21 July 1966.

283 Thompson, *At the Edge of Space*, p. 239; letter, Johnny G. Armstrong to Dennis R. Jenkins, 3 August 2002.

The external tanks on X-15A-2 were more than half the size of the airplane itself. The fixed-base simulator had shown that the X-15 would quickly become uncontrollable if propellant from one external tank transferred but the other one did not – the moment about the roll axis was too large for the rolling tail to counter. If this situation developed, the pilot would jettison the tanks, shut down the engine, and make an emergency landing. Unfortunately, this exact scenario played out on 1 July 1966 on the first flight with full tanks. Thankfully, Bob Rushworth managed to jettison the tanks and make an uneventful emergency landing at Mud Lake. (NASA)

made his second emergency landing of the day, this time on the concrete runway at Edwards.[284]

Jack McKay seemed to have more than his share of problems, and holds the record for the most landings at uprange lakes (three). His last emergency landing was made during his last flight (1-68-113), on 8 September 1966. The flight plan showed this Smith Ranch launch going to 243,000 feet and Mach 5.42 before landing on Rogers Dry Lake. However, as McKay began his climb he noticed the fuel-line pressure was low. Mike Adams as NASA-1 recommended throttling back to 50% to see if the fuel pressure would catch up; it did not. McKay shut down the engine and began jettisoning propellants to land at Smith Lake. The landing was uneventful and NASA trucked the airplane back to Edwards.[285]

The program had experienced a few flights where the pilot overshot the planned altitude for various reasons, but Bill Dana added one for the record books on 1 November 1966. On flight 3-56-83, Dana got the XLR99 lit on the first try and pulled into a 39-degree climb, or so he thought, heading for 267,000

284 Major Michael J. Adams, "Pilot report for flight 1-69-116," 6 October 1966. In the files at the DFRC History Office; Thompson, *At the Edge of Space*, pp. 248-249. Note that the "low and slow" familiarization flights performed by the original group of X-15 pilots had gone from Mach 2 and 50,000 feet to Adams' Mach 4 and 70,000 feet.

285 Jack B. McKay, "Pilot Report for Flight 1-68-113," 8 September 1966; Radio transcript for flight 1-68-113. Both in the files at the DFRC History Office.

feet. In reality, the climb angle was 42 degrees. Interestingly, Pete Knight in the NASA-1 control room did not notice the error either, and as the engine burned out he reported, "We got a burnout, Bill, 82 seconds, it looks good. Track and profile are looking very good." As Dana climbed through 230,000 feet, NASA-1 finally noticed and said, "[W]e got you going a little high on profile. Outside of that, it looks good." The flight eventually reached 306,900 feet–39,900 feet higher than planned.[286]

As Dana went ballistic over the top, he asked Knight if "Jack McKay [was] sending in congratulations." The reference was to flight 3-49-73 on 28 September 1965, when McKay had overshot his altitude by 35,600 feet. Dana had been NASA-1 on that flight and had needled McKay ever since. Dana's fun, however, did not stop with the overshoot. As he reached to shut down the engine, Dana apparently bumped the checklists clipped to his kneepad with his arm. Dana later recalled, "At shutdown my checklist exploded. I don't know how it came out of that alligator clamp, but anyway I had 27 pages of checklist floating around the cockpit with me, and it was a great deal like trying to read Shakespeare sitting under a maple tree in October during a high wind. I only saw one instrument at a time for the remainder of the ballistic portion … these will be in the camera film which I think we can probably sell to Walt Disney for a great deal." After an otherwise uneventful landing, Dana could not find the post-landing checklist, "Thank you, Pete," he joked. "Since my page 16 is somewhere down on the bottom of the floor, maybe you could go over the checklist with me?"[287]

1967 FLIGHT PERIOD

As was usual for the high desert during the winter, the rains had begun in late November 1966, and during early 1967 most of the lakebeds were wet, precluding flight operations. This gave North American and the FRC time to perform maintenance and modifications on the airplanes. For instance, X-15-1 was having its ammonia tank repaired and the third skid added, X-15A-2 was having instrumentation modified, and X-15-3 was having an advanced PCM telemetry system installed. By February the lakebeds at Three Sisters, Silver, Hidden Hills, and Grapevine were dry, and Rogers and Cuddeback were expected to be within two weeks. Unfortunately, snow and ice still covered Mud, Delamar, Smith Ranch, and Edwards Creek Valley. It would be late March before all the necessary lakes were dry enough to support flight operations.[288]

The program was also making plans to add new pilots, allowing some of the existing pilots to rotate to other assignments. For instance, John A. Manke, a

286 Conversation, William H. Dana by Dennis R. Jenkins, 12 August 1999; conversation, William H. Dana with Dennis R. Jenkins, 12 September 2002; William H. Dana, "Pilot Report for Flight 3-56-83," 1 November 1966; Radio transcript for flight 3-56-83. Both in the files at the DFRC History Office.

287 Conversation, William H. Dana and Dennis R. Jenkins, 12 August 1999; William H. Dana, "Pilot Report for Flight 3-56-83," 1 November 1966; Radio transcript for flight 3-56-83. Both in the files at the DFRC History Office.

288 X-15 Status Report, Paul F. Bikle/FRC to J. Martin/NASA Headquarters, 10 January 1967, p. 1 and 3 February 1967, p. 9. Both in the files at the DFRC History Office.

NASA test pilot, went through ground training and conducted a single engine run. Unfortunately, Mike Adams's accident would eliminate any chance that Manke would ever fly the X-15.[289]

Pete Knight would eventually set the fastest flight of the program, but before that event he had at least one narrow escape while flying X-15-1. As he related in the pilot's report after flight 1-73-126:[290]

> The launch and the flight was beautiful, up to a certain point. We had gotten on theta and I heard the 80,000-foot call. I checked that at about 3,100 fps. Things were looking real good and I was really enjoying the flight. All of a sudden, the engine went "blurp" and quit. There could not have been two seconds between the engine quit and everything else happening because it all went in order. The engine shut down. All three SAS lights came on. Both generator lights came on and then there was another light came on, and I think it was the fuel low line light. I am not sure. Then after all the lights got on, they all went out. Everything quit. By this time, I was still heading up and the airplane was getting pretty sloppy. As far as I am concerned both APUs quit.

Once the X-15 began its reentry after an essentially uncontrolled exit, Knight managed to get one of the APUs started. Unfortunately, the generator would not engage, which meant Knight had hydraulics but no electrical power. He elected to land at Mud Lake.

> Once I thought I was level enough I started a left turn back to Mud. Made a 6-g turn all the way around … Once I was sure I could make the east shore of Mud Lake with sufficient altitude I used some speed brakes to get it down to about 25,000 [feet altitude] and then varied the pattern to make the left turn into the runway landing to the west. On the final, all this time the trim was still at 5 degrees for the theta that we had. I was getting pretty tired of that side stick so I began to use both hands. One on the center stick and one on the side stick taking the pressure off the stick with the left hand and flying it with the right. Made the pattern and the airplane is a little squirrelly without the dampers but really not that bad. … I settled in and got it right down to the runway and it was a nice landing as far as the main skids were concerned, but the nose gear came down really hard.

289 Letter, John Manke to Tony Landis, 27 October 2004. Manke would go on to make the first supersonic flight of a heavy-weight lifting body and the first runway landing of a lifting body. He served as chief of flight operations at the FRC, and became "site manager" of the short-lived Ames-Dryden Flight Research Facility (when the FRC was administratively attached to the Ames Research Center).

290 Major William J. Knight, "Pilot Report for Flight 1-73-126," 29 June 1967. In the files at the DFRC History Office.

> After I got it on the ground I slid out to a stop. I started to open the canopy. I could not open the canopy. I tried twice and could not move that handle, so I sat there and rested for a while, I reached up and grabbed it again. Finally, it eased off and the canopy came open. Then I started to get out of the airplane and I could not get this connection off over here. I got the hat [helmet] off, to cool off a little bit, and tried it again. Then I was beginning to take the glove off to get a hand down in there also. I never did get that done. I tried it again and it would not come so I said the hell with it, and I'll pull the emergency release. I pulled the emergency release and that headrest blew off and it went into the canopy and slammed back down and hit me in the head. I got out of the airplane and by that time, the C-130 was there. Got into the 130 and came home.

It was one of the few times an X-15 pilot extracted himself from the airplane without the assistance of ground crews. Normally a crew was present at each of the primary emergency lakes, but Mud was not primary for this flight and no equipment or personnel were stationed there. Based on energy management, Knight probably should have landed at Grapevine. At the time, there was no energy-management display in the X-15, so NASA-1 made those decisions based on information in the control room. However, since the airplane had no power, and hence no radio, decisions made by NASA-1 were not much help.[291]

It is likely that the personnel on the ground were more worried than Knight was, because when the APUs failed they took all electrical power, including that to the radar transponder and radio. At the time, the radars were not skin tracking the X-15, so the ground lost track of the airplane. It was almost 8 minutes later when Bill Dana, flying Chase-2, caught sight of the X-15 just as it crossed the east edge of Mud Lake.[292]

The problem was most likely the result of electrical arcing in the Western Test Range launch monitoring experiment. Unlike most experiments, this one connected directly to the primary electrical bus. The arcing overloaded the associated APU, which subsequently stalled and performed an automatic safety shutdown. This transferred the entire load to the other APU, which also stalled because the load was still present. The APUs had been problematic since the beginning of the program, but toward the end they were generally reliable enough for the 30 minutes or so that they had to function. Each one was usually completely torn down and tested after each flight. In this case, something went wrong. After this flight, NASA moved the WTR and MIT experiments to the secondary electrical bus, which dropped out if a single generator shut down; this would preclude a complete power loss to the airplane.[293]

---

291 Ibid.

292 Ibid.

293 Memorandum, Perry V. Row to Paul F. Bikle, subject: Flight suitability of the number one X-15, 30 January 1968; letter, Robert G. Hoey to Dennis R. Jenkins, 12 August 2002.

Paul Bikle commented that Knight's recovery of the airplane was one of the most impressive events of the program. The flight planners had spent many hours devising recovery methods after various malfunctions; all were highly dependent upon the accuracy of the simulator for reproducing the worst-case, bare-airframe aerodynamics. NASA constantly updated the simulator with the results from flights and wind-tunnel tests to keep it as accurate as possible. The flight by Knight was the only complete reentry flown without any dampers. As AFFTC flight planner Bob Hoey remembers, "[W]e would have given a month's pay to be able to compare Pete's entry with those predicted on the sim, but all instrumentation ceased when he lost both APUs, and so there was no data! Jack Kolf told Pete that we were planning to install a hand crank in the cockpit hooked to the oscillograph so he could get us some data next time this happened." Fortunately, it never happened again.[294]

Ablative Coatings

During the early 1960s, major aerospace contractors during the early preconcept phases of space shuttle development were becoming increasingly interested in silicone-based elastomeric ablative coatings as possible heat shields. Engineers believed this type of ablator offered several advantages over the resin ablators used on previous capsules, including ease of application to complex shapes; flexibility over a wide range of temperatures; potential for refurbishment with spray, bonded sheets, or prefabricated panels; and superior shielding effectiveness at low-to-moderate heating rates. This coating would have to be a good insulator, lightweight, and easy to apply, remove, and reapply before another flight. The first real-world opportunity to test the materials on a full-scale reusable vehicle would come on X-15A-2 during its envelope expansion to Mach 8.[295]

It was obvious that the Mach 6.5 structural design of the X-15 was not adequate to handle the aerodynamic heating loads expected at Mach 8. For example, the total heat load for a location on the underside of the nose was approximately 2,300 Btu per square foot at Mach 6, but over 13,000 Btu at Mach 8. Similarly, the wing leading edge absorbed 9,500 Btu per square foot at Mach 6, but 27,500 Btu at Mach 8. It might have been possible to beef up the hot structure to accommodate these heat loads, but this would have amounted to an extensive redesign the program could not afford.[296]

Researchers believed the ability of the ablator to protect the airplane might well be the governing factor during the envelope expansion. To provide an engineering tool to evaluate this problem during the planning of these flights, the AFFTC developed a real-time temperature simulation using the former Dyna-

294 Letter, Robert G. Hoey to Dennis R. Jenkins, 12 August 2002.

295 Joe D. Watts, John P. Cary, and Marvin B. Dow, "Advanced X-15A-2 Thermal-Protection System," a paper in the *Progress of the X-15 Research Airplane Program*, a compilation of the papers presented at the FRC, 7 October 1965, NASA publication SP-90 (Washington, DC: NASA, 1965), p. 117. The early shuttle development programs included contracts from both the Air Force and various NASA centers as part of the Integral Launch and Reentry Vehicle (ILRV) programs. For a further discussion of the early studies into the Space Shuttle and its thermal protection system, see Dennis R. Jenkins, *Space Shuttle: The History of the National Space Transportation System–The First 100 Flights* (North Branch, MN: Specialty Press, 2001) and T. A. Heppenheimer, *The Space Shuttle Decision: 1965-1972* (Washington, DC/London: Smithsonian Institution Press, 2002).

296 Watts et al., "Advanced X-15A-2 Thermal-Protection System," pp. 117 and 123.

Soar hybrid simulator. In conjunction with a complete fixed-base simulation of X-15A-2, the hybrid had ability to predict the temperature at selected points for both protected and unprotected surfaces. Researchers obtained a temperature-time history from these simulations for a point aft of the nose-gear door for a flight to Mach 7.6 at 100,000 feet. They then compared this with the temperature at the same location for an actual Mach 6 flight. Both the effective heating rate and the maximum temperature were significantly more severe at the higher speed.[297]

There had been some minor interest in the use of ablators for the X-15 as early as 1961. For instance, on flight 1-23-39 researchers tested a sample of Avcoat no. 2 on the leading edge of the right wing, directly over the semispan thermocouple. The leading-edge temperature at 144 seconds after launch was only 25°F underneath the test sample, and the thermocouple on either side of it showed 350°F and 315°F. Nevertheless, since the entire point of the X-15 was to gather accurate aero-thermo data, it made no sense to protect the structure, until now.[298]

It appears that the ablator initially chosen by North American for X-15A-2 was Emerson Electric Thermolag 500, and this is the product shown in most reference documentation as late as the end of 1964. North American extensively tested this material in its 2.5-inch, 1-megawatt plasma tunnel for up to 317 seconds at a time, even though only 180 seconds were required for the actual X-15A-2 flight conditions. The material thickness on the leading edge was 0.70 inch, the forward fuselage ranged between 0.20 inch and 0.04 inch, and the wing mid-span quarter-chord thickness was 0.10 inch. A commercial paint spray gun applied the material, which weighed only 303 pounds.[299]

After further evaluation, however, researchers decided the material was unacceptable, primarily because of its cure cycle. The coating had to be subjected to 300°F for a prolonged period to cure properly, and although this had not been a serious problem for small test areas, accomplishing it on the entire airplane would have been a challenge. In addition, researchers found that T-500 was somewhat water-soluble after it cured–not an ideal trait for something that was to be used outdoors, even in the high desert.[300]

In late 1963 the Air Force and NASA formed a joint committee to select a more suitable ablative material, although T-500 continued as the baseline for another year. To determine which ablative materials qualified as candidates for use on the X-15, the committee set up an evaluation program and requested all major ablator manufacturers to provide test samples. The primary factors used in evaluating the materials were the shielding effectiveness, room-temperature cure cycle, bond integrity, operational compatibility with the X-15, and refurbishment. The researchers used three facilities for this evaluation, including the 2-inch arc jet tunnel at the University of Dayton Research Institute, the 2.5-megawatt arc tunnel at Langley, and the X-15 airplanes. They ranked the materials in order of their

297 Adkins and Armstrong, "Development and Status of the X-15A-2 Airplane," p. 106.

298 X-15 Status Report, Paul F. Bikle/FRC to H. Brown/NASA Headquarters, 16 October 1961, p. 7 plus attached photos.

299 Edwin W. Johnston, "Current and Advanced X-15," a paper presented at the Military Aircraft Systems and Technology Meeting, Washington, DC, 21-23 September 1964. The ablator was actually made by the Electronics and Space Division of Emerson Electric, St. Louis, MO.

300 Armstrong, "Flight Planning and Conduct of the X-15A-2 Envelope Expansion Program," pp. 24-25.

shielding effectiveness as measured under a low heat-flux environment, and sent the results to the Air Force Materials Laboratory at Wright-Patterson AFB.[301]

While North American was rebuilding the second airplane, NASA began initial flight tests of various ablative coatings on X-15-1 and X-15-3. Engineers applied the coatings to removable panels behind the ball nose, and directly to locations under the liquid-oxygen tank, on the lower surface of the horizontal stabilizers, and on the canopy, ventral stabilizer, speed brakes, and rudder. The ventral stabilizer and speed brakes provided moderate heating rates in easily accessible locations that could tolerate material failures if they occurred. The liquid-oxygen tank provided a test area for checking the bond integrity at temperatures approaching –300°F during actual flight. The removable nose panels provided measured back-surface temperatures and allowed direct comparison of two materials under the same heating conditions. Researchers expected the canopy application to show whether a windshield-contamination problem existed, but the tests proved inconclusive.[302]

Flight-testing began in late 1963 and concluded in October 1964. NASA wanted to find a material that could provide protection at heating rates of 5–150 Btu per square foot per second and shearing stresses as high as 15 psf at a total weight of less than 400 pounds. The bonding had to be reliable at skin temperatures from –300 to +500°F, and ideally the material should not require special curing or handling.[303]

Eventually, 15 different materials were flight-tested and the more promising included General Electric ESM 1004B, Martin MA-32H and MA-45R, McDonnell B-44, and NASA E-2A-1 Purple Blend. Researchers at Langley were developing the NASA material primarily as a backup in case the commercial products did not prove acceptable. The evaluation group also performed limited tests of alternate forms of the Martin and McDonnell materials, and ultimately selected one of these, MA-25S, for full-scale use.[304]

Flight-testing proved to be an extremely valuable part of the overall evaluation. Researchers discovered numerous deficiencies in materials, bond systems, and spray techniques during the flights that they probably would not have found any other way–another example of the fact that there is no substitute for real-world experience. The flight conditions experienced at Mach 5 showed material problems that had not appeared in ground-facility tests, mainly poor bonding and excessive erosion and blistering on some segments.[305]

Most of these problems, if they had occurred during a Mach 8 flight, would have likely resulted in the loss of the airplane. One of the most serious problems was bond failures of sheet materials, usually because the material was too stiff to conform to skin irregularities, resulting in voids in the bond (glue). This proved to

301 Watts et al., "Advanced X-15A-2 Thermal-Protection System," p. 118. Air Force contract number AF33(615)-1312. For further information on this evaluation, see Dennis Gerdeman and Michael Jolly, "Preliminary Evaluation of Ablative Coatings for X-15 Application," University of Dayton report UDRI-TM-64-108, 15 June 1964.

302 "X-15 Semi-Annual Status Report No. 2," April 1964, pp. 6-7; Watts, Cary, and Dow, "Advanced X-15A-2 Thermal-Protection System," p. 119.

303 "X-15 Semi-Annual Status Report No. 2," April 1964, pp. 6-7; Watts et al., "Advanced X-15A-2 Thermal-Protection System," p. 119.

304 "X-15 Semi-Annual Status Report No. 3," 1 December 1964, p. 2; "X-15 Semi-Annual Status Report No. 4," 1 April 1965, p. 3.

305 Watts et al., "Advanced X-15A-2 Thermal-Protection System," pp. 118-119.

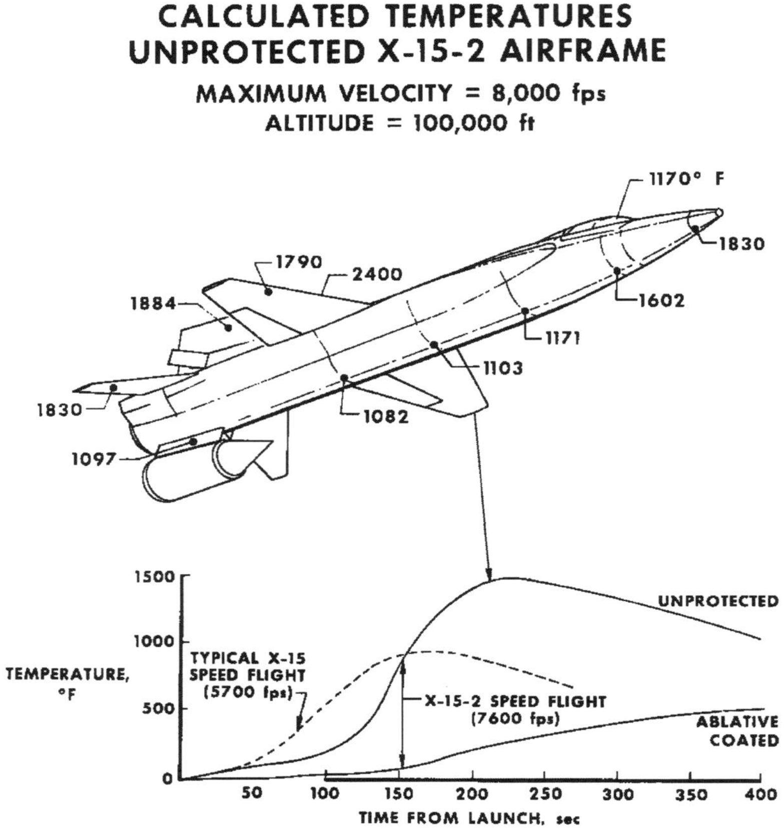

The Mach 6.5 structural design of the original X-15 was not adequate to handle the aerodynamic heating loads expected at Mach 8 for the advanced X-15A-2. For example, the total heat load for a location on the underside of the nose was approximately 2,300 Btu per square foot at Mach 6, but over 13,000 Btu at Mach 8. Similarly, the wing leading edge absorbed 9,500 Btu per square foot at Mach 6, but 27,500 Btu at Mach 8. To protect the airframe, researchers turned to ablative coatings similar to ones being proposed for the space shuttle. (NASA)

be a major blow to the concept of using ablators, since researchers had expected to be able to easily service the sheet materials before and after flight. The alternative was to apply the ablator with a spray gun, but many of the materials responded by delaminating and peeling off during flight. In every case examined in detail, this was the result of improper application, not a material failure. Nevertheless, it pointed out the difficulties of actually using these materials, and the test areas were generally only a couple of square feet–imagine the problems involved with coating an entire airplane.[306]

A few materials eroded very badly on the ventral stabilizer leading edge. This was a sign of inadequate thermal protection since Mach 5 provided a low heating

306 Ibid, p. 119.

environment compared to the expected Mach 8 design requirements. For instance, the test panel under the nose reached a peak surface temperature of 1,000°F on a Mach 5 mission; at Mach 8, this panel would soar to 1,750°F.[307]

Something all the materials had in common was that they were difficult to remove after flight. Char and remaining virgin material required soaking in solvents and manual scraping. One alternative that was tested was applying pressure-sensitive tape to the airframe, and then applying the ablative over the tape. Technicians would simply strip the tape off after a flight and all residual material would come off with it, leaving a clean surface. However, if the tape got too hot–even in small areas–it could start to peel, taking the ablator with it, and leaving the airframe exposed to catastrophic heating levels.[308]

As the flight-testing was nearing completion, researchers began thermal-performance testing using the 2.5-megawatt arc tunnel at Langley to determine the relative shielding effectiveness of the candidate materials. These tests closely simulated the peak heating rates and enthalpy levels expected on the design Mach 8 mission. The material manufacturers provided test samples of their materials installed on identical leading-edge and afterbody models.[309]

The leading-edge tests showed that most of the silicone-based ablators were unable to withstand the severe heating conditions. The three silicone-based materials had densities between 32 and 60 pounds per cubic foot, resulting in a surface between 0.545 inch and 0.294 inch thick. The back surface temperature of all three products was relatively similar, but the materials experienced a variety of erosion, blistering, and cracking problems during the tests. The fourth material tested in the Langley facility was a phenolic-silica ablator with a density of 110 pounds per cubic foot, resulting in a surface thickness of only 0.165 inch. The shape retention of this material was excellent, but its shielding effectiveness was low. All four of the materials passed the afterbody tests, with no significant differences in performance noted.[310]

During the arc-tunnel tests, researchers observed that loosened material from the ablator tended to reattach to surfaces downstream. Flight tests on X-15-1 with a panel of windshield glass mounted on the vertical stabilizer aft of a sample patch of the ablator showed that the glass panel quickly became opaque, which would seriously restrict the pilot's vision. Since the pilot obviously needed to see during landing, researchers considered three different approaches to restore the necessary vision. These included explosive fragmentation of the outer windshield glass after the high-speed run was completed, boundary-layer blowing over the windshield during the entire flight, and a hinged metal "eyelid" that could be opened after the high-speed portion of the flight.[311]

The explosive concept worried everybody and was not pursued very far because there seemed to be too many possible failure modes. The boundary-layer idea was the only one that potentially provided a continuously clear windshield; however, the pilot actually had little reason to need completely clear vision at

307 Ibid, pp. 119 and 125.
308 Ibid, p. 119.
309 Ibid, p. 120.
310 Ibid, pp. 120-121.
311 Armstrong, "Flight Planning and Conduct of the X-15A-2 Envelope Expansion Program," pp. 25-26.

100,000 feet since there was really nothing to run into at that altitude, and the implementation was complex and expensive. Therefore, the program selected the eyelid because it was the easiest to implement. The right windshield was unprotected and provided normal pilot vision during launch and initial climb-out. During the high-speed run, the right windshield would become opaque, allowing the pilot to see little more than light and dark patches of sky. The eyelid was installed over the left windshield; it would remain closed during the climb-out and high-speed flight, and open once the airplane slowed below Mach 3. The pilot would look out of the left side of the windshield for landing. This carried some risks, though. After one of his windshields shattered during a 1961 flight, Bob White reported that his vision had been "compromised" during landing. When flight tests began, the pilots discovered another phenomenon: the open eyelid created a small canard effect, causing the airplane to pitch up, roll right, and yaw right. The effects were small but noticeable.[312]

In the end, the Air Force and NASA determined that the General Electric, Martin, McDonnell, and NASA Purple Blend products were all potentially acceptable and sent requests for proposals to the manufacturers. The source evaluation board received the proposals during late 1965, and in January 1966, NASA awarded a contract to Martin Marietta to design and apply a sprayable ablator to X-15A-2.[313]

The basic MA-25S ablative material had a virgin material density of 28 pounds per cubic foot. Martin had developed MA-25S "specifically for application over complex vehicle configurations," although it had existed well before the X-15 application was proposed. Most significantly, application and curing took place at room temperature (70°F to 100°F). A special premolded fiber-reinforced elastomeric silicone material (ESA-3560-IIA) similar to that used on the Air Force X-23A PRIME reentry vehicles would cover all the leading edges. Martin developed a premolded flexible material (MA-25S-1) to cover the seams around access panels, and used smaller pieces of this material to cover fasteners and other items that required last-minute access.[314]

Interestingly, although Martin considered MA-25S a "mature" product, "all previous applications had been accomplished with laboratory equipment," and in March 1966 the company had to start from scratch to come up with methods to coat an entire airplane. Once the engineers finished writing the procedure, Martin procured several large sheets of Inconel and used them as test subjects. The company also ran compatibility tests with the various liquids and gases found on the X-15. Hydraulic fluid, helium, nitrogen, and ammonia did not seem to present any problems. An outside laboratory had to test the hydrogen peroxide, delaying the results, but no problems were expected. However, the MA-25S material, like all of

312 Knight, "Increased Piloting Tasks and Performance of X-15A-2 in Hypersonic Flight," pp. 793-802; Armstrong, "Flight Planning and Conduct of the X-15A-2 Envelope Expansion Program," p. 26; Lieutenant Colonel Robert M. White, "Pilot Report for Flight 2-21-37," 9 November 1961. In the files at the DFRC History Office.

313 Armstrong, "Flight Planning and Conduct of the X-15A-2 Envelope Expansion Program," p. 25; X-15 Status Report, Paul F. Bikle/FRC to J. Martin/NASA Headquarters, 2 February 1966, p. 6.

314 Martin Marietta design report ER-14535, "Thermal Protection System: X-15A-2," undated (but probably April 1967), pp. 59-60; Armstrong, "Flight Planning and Conduct of the X-15A-2 Envelope Expansion Program," p. 25. Originally, Martin Marietta apparently used a small "s" in the trade name of the ablator (MA-25s). However, it is generally known as MA-25S and seems more readable that way, so that is what will be used here. MA-25S and ESA-3560 have both had long lives and are currently being used to insulate some portions of the Space Shuttle external tank.

the ablators originally tested for the X-15, was impact-sensitive after exposure to liquid oxygen. Tests showed that a local detonation would occur on the material if it was submerged in liquid oxygen and struck with a force as low as 8 foot-pounds. Martin concluded that "the significance of the material being impact sensitive with liquid oxygen is not well understood at this time and this particular material characteristic should be reviewed with X-15A-2 operations personnel."[315]

The sensitivity to liquid oxygen brought several unexpected problems since the casual spilling of liquid oxygen (not an uncommon occurrence) suddenly became a major problem. In response, Martin proposed spraying a white protective wear layer over the ablator to isolate it from any minor liquid-oxygen spillage. Nevertheless, the potential for contaminating the inside of the liquid-oxygen lines, pumps, vents, etc. during the application (spraying and sanding) of the ablator was the most worrisome.[316]

On 18 May 1966, X-15A-2 flight 2-44-79 provided the first relatively large-scale tests of MA-25S and the ESA-3560-IIA leading-edge material. The materials had been applied (as appropriate) to three nose panels (F-3, F-4, and E-4), the UHF antenna, both main landing skids and struts, both sides of the ventral stabilizer, both lower speed brakes, and the left horizontal stabilizer. Researchers instrumented all of these panels to determine the effects of the ablator. Ground handling resulted in ablator damage that technicians repaired using a documented repair procedure; the test would inadvertently provide validation of its reparability. As part of the evaluation, technicians used various application techniques in different locations, providing some validation of the proposed concepts. In general, these tests were successful, although instrumentation failures precluded the gathering of any precise data from the nose panels.[317]

The ablator also forced the program to develop a new pitot-static system. NASA relocated the static pickups since ablative material now covered the normal locations on the sides of the forward fuselage. Engineers moved the static source into a vented compartment behind the canopy that tests on X-15-1 had shown to be acceptable. An extendable pitot tube replaced the standard dogleg pitot ahead of the canopy because the temperatures expected at Mach 8 would exceed the standard tube's limits. The retractable tube would remain within the fuselage until the aircraft decelerated below Mach 2, at which point the pilot would actuate a release mechanism and the tube would extend into the airstream. This was similar in concept to the system eventually installed on the space shuttle orbiters. The ill-fated flight 2-45-81 marked the first use of the retractable pitot tube, in parallel with the normal system. Despite other problems on the flight, Bob Rushworth considered the new system acceptable for flight, and subsequent data analysis confirmed this.[318]

---

315 Martin Marietta monthly letter report no. 3, subject: X-15 thermal protection system, 7 April 1966. In the files at the DFRC History Office; Armstrong, "Flight Planning and Conduct of the X-15A-2 Envelope Expansion Program," p. 25.

316 Letter, Robert G. Hoey to Dennis R. Jenkins, 13 August 2002.

317 Martin Marietta monthly letter report no. 5, subject: X-15 thermal protection system, 10 June 1966. In the files at the DFRC History Office.

318 Armstrong, "Flight Planning and Conduct of the X-15A-2 Envelope Expansion Program," p. 26; X-15 Status Report, Paul F. Bikle/FRC to J. Martin/NASA Headquarters, 12 July 1966, p. 9.

Getting Ready for Maximum Speed

The general cautiousness that was beginning to permeate NASA was also affecting the X-15 program, and the buildup to the maximum speed flight was unusually conservative. Although the program had never been "wild and crazy," it had previously taken reasonable risks when it understood the problems and their consequences. This was not the case during preparations for the maximum speed flight, which really did not represent that large an increment over the Mach 6+ speeds already attained. Nevertheless, in preparation, the program dealt with each individual piece separately.

Pete Knight flew the next X-15A-2 flight (2-49-86) with the ventral on, primarily to familiarize himself with the handling qualities, since all of his previous flights had been with the ventral off. All future X-15A-2 flights would use either the ventral or the ramjet. Flight 2-50-89 was the first flight where the external tanks operated (knowingly) successfully, including the improved instrumentation that let the ground crew and pilot know the propellants were transferring correctly.[319]

The NB-52s required a modification to strengthen the wing in order to carry the X-15A-2 and its external tanks. On 27 June 1066, Bob Rushworth was in the cockpit of a scheduled captive-carry flight (2-C-80) to test the X-15A-2 with full external tanks. (NASA)

After this flight, X-15A-2 went down for the final modifications needed to get ready for the maximum speed flight. Perhaps the most noticeable was the installation of the "eyelid" over the left-hand canopy window. NASA sent the canopy to Inglewood in January 1967 and it returned to Edwards in early April, in time for flight 2-51-92. In addition, NASA relocated the thermocouple recording system from the center-of-gravity compartment to the main instrument bay since it had failed to operate on the previous two flights because of the cold environment. By May 1967, three dummy ramjet shapes had arrived at Edwards, and wind-tunnel

319 Major William J. Knight, "Pilot Report for Flight 2-49-86," 30 August 1966.

tests in the JPL 21-inch hypersonic tunnel had verified the mated ramjet configuration. One of the three dummy ramjets was sent to Inglewood to have a thermal protection system installed, and engineers at the FRC instrumented the other two in preparation for flight. Researchers had already calibrated the flow-field cone probes at Mach numbers of 3.5 and 4.4 in the Ames 1 by 3-foot wind tunnel, with additional tests scheduled at Mach numbers of 5.0 and 7.4.[320]

Pete Knight evaluated the handling qualities of the X-15A-2 with the dummy ramjet installed under the fixed portion of the ventral stabilizer on flight 2-51-92. This flight did not include the external tanks and reached Mach 4.8. Knight jettisoned the ramjet just before landing, much like the ventral rudder, to provide the necessary clearance for the landing gear. Next up for X-15A-2 was a flight with the ablative coating and dummy ramjet, but without the external tanks.[321]

Ablator Application

There had always been questions about exactly how to apply an ablative coating over the surface of an entire airplane, even one as small as the X-15. Even more questions existed on how to maintain the airplane after applying the coating, and how difficult it would be to refurbish the coating between flights. There appears to have been little actual concern about the effectiveness of the ablator; if it was applied correctly, everyone was relatively sure the concept would work.

As part of its initial contract, Martin Marietta developed a comprehensive procedure for applying the coating, maintaining it, and removing it if necessary. Martin accomplished the first complete application of the ablator in general agreement with the schedule and procedures published earlier. Simply because it represents one of the few attempts to use an ablative coating on an entire airplane, it is appropriate to review the application in detail.[322]

The process began with cleaning the airplane, and Martin admitted the preparatory cleaning was "somewhat overdone" for the first application. Technicians masked all joints, gaps, and openings before the cleaning began to prevent solvent from getting into the airplane. The surface condition of the airplane, with its accumulation of contamination and overabundance of lacquer, necessitated the use of a great deal of solvent during the initial cleaning. Technicians accomplished the final cleaning with powdered cleanser and water using a "water-break-free" test to ascertain when the surface was properly clean. Some areas of the aircraft, especially around fastener heads and skin joints, never did achieve a completely water-break-free condition, and Martin noted that "these areas continually bleed hydraulic fluid or other contamination."[323]

---

320 X-15 Status Report, Paul F. Bikle/FRC to J. Martin/NASA Headquarters, 10 January 1967, p. 1 and 4 April 1967, pp. 2 and 5.

321 Major William J. Knight, "Pilot report for flight 2-51-92," 8 May 1967. In the files at the DFRC History Office.

322 For the detailed instructions of how to apply, maintain, and remove the ablative coating, see Martin Marietta report ER-14535, "Thermal Protection System: X-15A-2," undated (but probably April 1967). In the files at the AFFTC and DFRC History Offices.

323 Martin Marietta monthly progress report no. 3, subject: X-15 full scale ablator application, 14 July 1967. In the files at the DFRC History Office; A. B. Price, Martin Marietta report MCR-68-15, "Full Scale Flight Test Report: X-15A-2 Ablative Thermal Protection System," December 1967, pp. 5-6. A clean surface is a "water-break-free" area on which the water sheets out over the surface, while the presence of oil or contaminants will cause water to bead up. This is a standard test used in many industries (particularly the paint industry).

Next, technicians used polyethylene tape to mask all of the seams between panels to keep the ablative material out of the aircraft compartments. The only problem encountered in the initial ablator application was that nobody had anticipated masking the gap between the fixed portion of each vertical stabilizer and the rudders. The installation crew then improvised a solution that was mostly successful. As a means of checking the adequacy of the masking during all phases of ablator operation, technicians placed airborne contamination collectors in nine aircraft compartments before beginning the application process. At the end of the process, quality inspectors from Martin Marietta and NASA checked these collectors and found very little contamination, indicating that the masking worked as expected.[324]

Before turning the airplane over to Martin Marietta, NASA had made a few minor changes to accommodate the ablator installation. The retractable pitot tube (or "alternate pitot" as it was called) was installed, as was a new retaining ring around the ball nose that had a step at its aft end. When the ablator was built up during the application, it would fill up to the top of the step, resulting in a smooth surface.[325]

Next up was installing the molded ablator "details" on the aircraft. This included premolded leading-edge covers made from ESA-3560-IIA for the wing and horizontal stabilizers, and covers for various antennas, the canopy leading edge, and the vertical stabilizer leading edge. Although it was not provided as part of the kit, the installation team fabricated a detail for the leading edge of the dummy ramjet instrumentation rake from a spare piece of the vertical stabilizer leading-edge detail.[326]

After technicians glued the details onto the surface of the leading edges, they covered the majority of the airplane with polyethylene sheeting to protect cleaned areas from overspray during the sequential ablator applications. The airplane was broken down into nine distinct areas that technicians would spray in sequence. Technicians installed marker strips (a vinyl foam tape) over the contamination masking and applied a layer of DC93-027 RTV over fastener heads and peripheral gaps of the seldom-removed panels. The installation team then sprayed the MA-25S ablator using a commercial paint spray gun. Controlling the thickness of the ablator was the most significant difficulty encountered during the application process, but the team got much better toward the end as they became more familiar with the deposition characteristics of the material. Some areas, particularly the middle of the wing root and the crown centerline of the fuselage, proved to be too much of a stretch for the technicians standing on the ground. This condition resulted in a "somewhat cheezy" ablator application in those areas, but the layer was deemed adequate to protect the airframe.[327]

---

324 A. B. Price, Martin Marietta report MCR-68-15, "Full Scale Flight Test Report: X-15A-2 Ablative Thermal Protection System," December 1967, pp. 6-7. The collectors were essentially petri dishes with millipore filters in them that collected any dust that settled in the bottom of the compartments.

325 Martin Marietta design report ER-14535, "Thermal Protection System: X-15A-2," undated (but probably April 1967), passim.

326 Martin Marietta report MCR-68-15, pp. 8-9.

327 Ibid, pp. 9-10.

Applying the MA-25S ablator was more involved than most expected. The airplane had to be scrubbed clean, and then each individual panel had to be taped to ensure ablator did not get into the airplane. The ablator was then sprayed, sanded to a consistent finish, and its depth measured. The amount of time required to coat the relatively small X-15 did not bode well for a large Space Shuttle. (NASA)

Once the entire surface was covered, the next task was to go back and remove the trim marker strips. This proved more difficult than had been expected because the tape was "too thick and possessed too high an adhesive tack." Nevertheless, the team eventually accomplished the task, but decided to use a different tape next time. It was important to avoid disturbing the sealing tape under the marker strips, since it would have to protect the compartments from the effects of the sanding operation still to come.[328]

The ablator was left to cure at room temperature for a few hours, and then technicians sanded the entire surface to remove overspray and irregularities, and to bring the ablator layer down to within ±0.020 inch of its design thickness. This proved to be a very tedious operation. First, the team had to draw grid lines on the airplane to establish precise monitor locations, and a penetrating needle dial gage determined the thickness at each point on the grid. Technicians then sanded the surface. Since this removed the grid lines, they would have to be redrawn and the thickness rechecked. The process continued until the desired thickness was reached. It was evident that there was a need for a better way to establish the grid on the airplane.[329]

328 Ibid, p. 10.
329 Ibid, p. 11.

When the sanding was finished, the team glued 10 test plugs to the ablator surface and cut through the ablator layer around their periphery. A pull test was performed on the plugs to determine whether the ablator had properly bonded to the skin. The first application successfully passed all of its pull tests. Various "hard point inserts" were then installed around the external tank inboard sway brace attach points and the aircraft jacking points. Inserts of MA-25S-1 material also covered the ram air door in the fuselage nose and the engine compartment fire doors on the aft fuselage.[330]

MA-25S had a natural pinkish color and somehow this seemed inappropriate for the world's fastest airplane. Fortunately, the specification called for a layer of Dow Corning DC90-090 RTV over the entire airplane to provide a wear coating and to seal the ablator. The DC90-090 was translucent white and did not completely hide the pink, so NASA asked Martin Marietta to apply an extra coat (or two, in some areas) so that the airplane would have a uniform white finish. This exhausted the available supply of the coating; however, Dow Corning had replaced DC90-090 with a similar product called DC92-007. Martin requested samples of the new product to determine its suitability as a substitute.[331]

At this point, the team applied a limited number of hazard and warning markings to the exterior using standard high-temperature aircraft lacquer paint. The last step was to remove the polyethylene tape that sealed the service panels and install strips of MA-25S-1 around their periphery to provide extra durability during panel removal and replacement. Martin then returned the airplane to the X-15 maintenance crews, who installed instrumentation and prepared it for flight.[332]

Ablator Flights

Because so many unknowns still existed, the Air Force and NASA decided to conduct a thorough post-flight inspection of the entire airplane surface for each mission, and to monitor the ablator char depth and back-surface temperatures throughout the performance buildup. The ablator weighed 125 pounds more than planned and, taken with the expected increase in drag, the maximum speed of airplane was expected to barely exceed Mach 7.[333]

Pete Knight made the first flight (2-52-96) in the ablator-coated, ramjet-equipped X-15A-2 without the external tanks on 21 August 1967. The flight reached Mach 4.94 and the post-flight inspection showed that, in general, the ablator had held up well. The leading-edge details on the wings and horizontal stabilizers had uniform and minor charring along their lengths. A careful examination revealed only minor surface fissuring with all char intact, and good shape retention. The char layers were approximately 0.050 inch deep on the wing leading edge and 0.055 inch deep on the horizontal stabilizer–well within limits.[334]

330 Ibid, pp. 12-13.

331 Martin Marietta monthly progress report no. 3, subject: X-15 full scale ablator application, 14 July 1967. In the files at the DFRC History Office; Martin Marietta report MCR-68-15, p. 13.

332 Martin Marietta report MCR-68-15, pp. 13-15.

333 Watts et al., "Advanced X-15A-2 Thermal-Protection System," p. 121; Knight, "Increased Piloting Tasks and Performance of X-15A-2 in Hypersonic Flight."

334 Martin Marietta report MCR-68-15, pp. 64-65.

The ablator details for the canopy and dorsal vertical stabilizer showed almost no thermal degradation, and local erosion and blistering of the wear layer were the only evidence of thermal exposure. The leading edge of the forward vane antenna suffered local erosion to a depth of 0.100 inch because of shock-wave impingement set up by an excessively thick ablator insert over the ram air door just forward of the antenna. The remainder of the leading-edge detail on the aft vane antenna showed "minor, if not insignificant degradation."[335]

The most severe damage during the flight was to the molded ablator detail on the leading edge of the modified ventral, which showed heavy charring along its entire length. "The increased amount of thermal degradation was directly attributable to the shock wave interactions from the pressure probes and the dummy ramjet assembly." Additional shock waves originated from the leading edges of the skids. The shock impingement had apparently completely eroded the lower portion of the detail, and very little char remained intact. However, it was difficult to ascertain how much of the erosion had taken place during the flight since sand impact at landing had caused similar, although much less significant, erosion during an earlier ablator test flight. Still, this should have been a warning to the program that something was wrong, but somehow everybody missed it.[336]

The primary ablative layer over the airplane experienced very little thermal degradation as the result of this Mach 5 flight. On the wings and horizontal stabilizers, only the areas immediately adjacent to the molded leading edges were degraded. These areas exhibited the normal random reticulation of the surface, there was no evidence of delaminating, and all material was intact. Some superficial blistering of the ablative layer was evident on the outboard lower left wing surface. Martin Marietta believed the blistering was most probably the result of an excessively thick wear-layer application. Not surprisingly, the speed brakes exhibited some wear, but there was no significant erosion or sign of delamination. The only questionable area of ablator performance was the left side of the dorsal rudder. A number of circular pieces of ablator were lost during the flight. A close examination of the area revealed that all separation had occurred at the spray layer interface, and significant additional delamination had occurred. The heavy wear layer, however, had held most of the material in place. The program had seen similar delamination during some of the earlier test flights and traced it to improper application of the material. It then changed the installation procedures to prevent reoccurrence.[337]

After the inspection, Martin Marietta set about repairing the ablator for the next flight. With the exception of the leading-edge details for the ventral stabilizer and the forward vane antenna, refurbishment was minimal. Only the wings and horizontal stabilizers had experienced any degree of charring, and technicians refurbished them by sanding away the friable layer. They did not attempt to remove all of the thermally affected material, and sanding continued only until they exposed resilient material. The canopy leading-edge detail required no

335 Ibid, p. 65.

336 Ibid.

337 Ibid, pp. 65-67.

As it finally rolled out of the paint shop at the Flight Research Center, the MA-25S-covered X-15A-2 was the polar opposite of what an X-15 normally looked like. Instead of the black Inconel X finish, the airplane had a protective layer of white Dow DC90-090. Actually, this was a relief to the pilots since the MA-35S has a natural pink color. (NASA)

refurbishment, but Martin lightly sanded its surface to remove the wear layer to minimize deposition on the windshield during the next flight.[338]

Martin repaired local gouges in the main MA-25S ablator using a troweled repair mix and kitchen spatulas, eliminating most of the sanding usually required for the patches. Technicians sanded the speed brakes to apparent virgin material and resprayed the areas to the original thickness. They also completely stripped the left side of the dorsal rudder and reapplied the ablator from scratch using the revised procedure.[339]

Although the ablator around the nose of the airplane had experienced no significant thermal degradation, a malfunction of the ball nose necessitated its re-

338 Martin Marietta report MCR-68-15, p. 15.

339 Ibid.

placement, and the ablator was damaged in the process. Unfortunately, Martin had depleted the supply of ablator during the refurbishment process, forcing the use of a batch of MA-25S left over from a previous evaluation. For the final preparation the entire surface of the airplane was lightly sanded and a new coating of the replacement DC92-007 wear layer was applied.[340]

Maximum Speed

All was ready on the morning of 3 October 1967 as Colonel Joseph P. Cotton and Lieutenant Colonel William G. Reschke, Jr., started the engines on the NB-52B. Pete Knight had already been in the cockpit of X-15A-2 for over an hour performing the preflight checklist with the ground crew led by Charlie Baker and Larry Barnett and a host of support personnel in the NASA control room. At 1331 hours the mated pair took off from Edwards and headed to Mud Lake. An hour later, Knight "reached up and hit the launch switch and immediately took my hand off to [go] back to the throttle and found that I had not gone anywhere. It did not launch." This was not a good start, but a second attempt 2 minutes later resulted in the smooth launch of flight 2-53-97.[341]

The flight plan showed that X-15A-2 would weigh 52,117 pounds at separation, more than 50% heavier than originally conceived in 1954. As the X-15 fell away, Knight lit the engine and set up a 12-degree angle of attack resulting in about 1.5 g in longitudinal acceleration. As normal acceleration built to 2 g, Knight had to hold considerable right deflection on the side stick to keep X-15A-2 from rolling left due to the heavier liquid-oxygen tank. When the aircraft reached the 35-degree planned pitch angle, Knight began to fly a precise climb angle. The simulator had predicted a maximum dynamic pressure of 540 psf, remarkably close to the 560 psf measured during the rotation. Knight maintained the planned pitch angle within ±1 degree.[342]

Knight jettisoned the external tanks 67.4 seconds after launch at Mach 2.4 and 72,300 feet. Tank separation was satisfactory, but Knight described it as "harder" than it had been on flight 2-50-89. The parachute system performed satisfactorily and the Air Force recovered the tanks in repairable condition. Free of the extra weight and drag of the external tanks, the airplane began to accelerate quickly, and Knight came level at 102,100 feet. As Knight later recalled, "We shut down at 6,500 [fps] and I took careful note to see what the final got to. It went to 6,600 maximum on the indicator."[343]

Seventy-one seconds after engine shutdown, Knight performed the first of a series of planned rudder pulses with the yaw damper off. The sideslip indica-

340 Martin Marietta monthly progress report no. 6, subject: X-15 full scale ablator application, 6 October 1967. In the files at the DFRC History Office; Martin Marietta report MCR-68-15, p. 19.

341 Major William J. Knight, "Pilot Report for Flight 2-53-97," 3 October 1967; memorandum, Major William J. Knight to Chief, Research Projects Office, subject: Preliminary Report of X-15 Flight 2-53-97, 26 October 1967.

342 Flight plan for flight 2-53-97, 19 September 1967; Major William J. Knight, "Pilot Report for Flight 2-53-97," 3 October 1967; memorandum, Major William J. Knight to Chief, Research Projects Office, subject: Preliminary Report of X-15 Flight 2-53-97, 26 October 1967; Armstrong, "Expanding the X-15 Envelope to Mach 6.7," pp. 204-205; X-15 Status Report, Paul F. Bikle/FRC to J. Martin/NASA Headquarters, 8 November 1967, p. 4.

343 Memorandum, Major William J. Knight to Chief, Research Projects Office, subject: Preliminary report of X-15 flight 2-53-97, 26 October 1967; Armstrong, "Expanding the X-15 Envelope to Mach 6.7," pp. 204-205; X-15 Status Report, Paul F. Bikle/FRC to J. Martin/NASA Headquarters, 8 November 1967, p. 4.

This is how the ventral stabilizer and ramjet installation looked on the morning of 3 October 1967 prior to Flight 2-53-97. The skid landing gear is extended in this photograph. (NASA)

tor did not rotate as expected, but post-flight analysis revealed that the aircraft achieved a satisfactory yaw rate and lateral acceleration. Since the maneuver occurred at approximately the same time the unprotected ball nose reached its maximum temperature, researchers theorized that differential expansion in the nose may have resulted in a false instrument reading. Almost amusingly, despite the significant heating experienced by the rest of the airplane, the aft viewing Millikan 16-mm camera installed in the center-of-gravity compartment froze because of a malfunction of the thermal switch that activated the camera heater.[344]

As Knight decelerated through Mach 5.5, the HOT PEROXIDE light came on; unknown to anybody, the intense heat from shock waves impinging on the dummy ramjet were severely damaging the airplane. Unfortunately, the peroxide light distracted Knight from his planned maneuvers and his energy management. As worries mounted, NASA-1 directed Knight to jettison his peroxide and began vectoring him toward high key. The X-15A-2 came across the north edge of Rogers at 55,000 feet and Mach 2.2. When Knight went to jettison the remain-

344 Major William J. Knight, "Pilot Report for Flight 2-53-97," 3 October 1967; memorandum, James R. Welsh (for Elmor J. Adkins/X-15 Research Planning Office) to Assistant Chief, Research Projects, subject: Preliminary report on X-15 flight 2-53-97, 26 October 1967.

ing propellants so that the chase plane could find him, nothing came out. There would be no help from the chase. Knight was high on energy, unable to jettison his propellants, and unsure about the condition of his airplane. He turned through high key at 40,000 feet but was still supersonic. While on final approach, Knight tried to jettison the ramjet, but later indicated that "I did not feel it go at all." The ground crew reported that they did not see anything drop. Something was obviously wrong, but things were happening too quickly to worry about it.[345]

Fortunately, things mellowed out after that and Knight made an uneventful landing. Once on the ground, Knight realized that something was not right when a majority of the ground crew rushed to the back of the airplane. After he finally egressed and walked toward the rear of the X-15, he understood: there were large holes in the side of the ventral with evidence of melting and skin rollback.[346]

Post-flight analysis showed that the airplane had managed to attain Mach 6.70, equivalent to 4,520 mph (6,629 fps), at 102,700 feet, an unofficial speed mark for winged-vehicles that would stand until the return of the Space Shuttle *Columbia* from its first orbital mission in April 1981. This was the only X-15 flight to exceed the original 6,600-fps design goal.[347]

Later analysis showed that the shock wave from the spike nose on the ramjet had intersected the ventral and caused severe heating. Flight planner Johnny Armstrong observed, "So now maybe we knew why the ramjet was not there." The telemetry indicated that the ramjet instrumentation ceased to function 25 seconds after the XLR99 shut down. Later that afternoon several people, including Armstrong, were reviewing the telemetry when they noted an abnormal decrease in the longitudinal acceleration trace that indicated a sudden decrease in drag. The conclusion was that this was when the ramjet had separated. When the flight profile was computed, it was determined that this happened at about the 180-degree point during the turn over the south area of Rogers Dry Lake at about Mach 1 and 32,000 feet. Armstrong began correlating the telemetry with recorded radar data: "I could say that I did a detailed calculation of the drag coefficient for a tumbling ramjet, then a 5th order curve fit of the potential trajectory, corrected for winds–but actually, I just made an engineering estimate." In other words, he guessed.[348]

Not everybody believed Armstrong, but Bill Albrecht, the NASA operations engineer for X-15A-2, and Joe Rief, the AFFTC airfield manager, thought the theory had merit. Albrecht and Armstrong checked out a radio-equipped carryall van, cleared it with the tower, and headed out onto the Edwards impact range. Armstrong had previously marked up a map with some landmarks near where the telemetry and radar indicated the ramjet had separated. As they drove, Armstrong

345 Major William J. Knight, "Pilot Report for Flight 2-53-97," 3 October 1967; Radio transcript for flight 2-53-97. Both in the files at the DFRC History Office; Thompson, *At the Edge of Space*, pp. 243-245.

346 Armstrong, "Expanding the X-15 Envelope to Mach 6.7," pp. 204-205; memorandum, William J. Knight to Chief, Research Projects Office, subject: Preliminary report of X-15 flight 2-53-97, 26 October 1967.

347 Memorandum, James R. Welsh (for Elmor J. Adkins/X-15 Research Planning Office) to Assistant Chief, Research Projects, subject: Preliminary report on X-15 flight 2-53-97, 26 October 1967; Major William J. Knight, "Pilot report for flight 2-53-97," 3 October 1967. Both in the files at the DFRC History Office. This is sometimes shown as 4,534 mph and Mach 4.72. The difference is what atmospheric corrections were applied to convert Mach and dynamic pressure to miles per hour. The official NASA records show 4,520 mph and Mach 6.70; the Air Force tends to use the higher figures. This was the only X-15 flight that actually exceeded the original design goal of 6,600 fps; the next closest was flight 2-50-89 at 6,233 fps. The fastest "basic" X-15 flight was 1-30-51 at 6,019 fps.

348 Armstrong, "Expanding the X-15 Envelope to Mach 6.7," pp. 205-206; telephone conversation, Johnny Armstrong with Dennis R. Jenkins, 12 May 2001.

indicated a place to stop. They got out and walked about 200 yards directly to the ramjet, which was lying in two major pieces. The pair gathered up the nose cone and pressure probes and then headed back to the van (the main body of the ramjet was too heavy for only two men to lift). The next day Albrecht and Armstrong directed a helicopter to retrieve the ramjet. Subsequent inspection showed that three of the four explosive bolts that held the ramjet on had fired, probably due to the excessive temperatures that had melted large portions of the ramjet and ventral.[349]

Did it Work?

From the Martin Marietta post-flight report: "The actual flight environment in the area of the modified ventral fin proved to be much more severe than anticipated. The condition was directly attributable to interaction effects of the shock waves generated by the dummy ramjet, the ventral, and the pressure probes. The ablator applications in this area were inadequate to protect the structure under these flow conditions, and the vehicle suffered localized damage in the area."[350]

The flight had completely eroded the ablator application, including both the molded leading-edge detail and the sprayed MA-25S layer, from the forward portion of the ventral. The vehicle skin sustained major damage due to the excessively high heating in the shock impingement, which burned through at the leading edge and on the sides of the ventral at the torque box assembly. This also damaged the torque box and destroyed the wiring and pressure lines in the forward compartment.[351]

A study of the thermocouple responses in the area of the ventral indicated that the ablator had provided at least some protection for the first 140 seconds of flight. Continual erosion of the ablator surfaces was occurring during this period, and by approximately 160 seconds the degradation was such that all protection broke down. The ablator materials should have had zero surface recession, but instead eroded away. The particles from the forward sections of ablator, in turn, caused severe impact erosion of the downstream ablator layer. The lower speed brakes were bare of ablator, and the material on the inboard edges of the main landing skids and the undersides of the side fairings experienced considerable abrasion.[352]

Otherwise, the ablator had performed well enough. The flight had uniformly charred the details over the leading edges of the wings, horizontal stabilizers, canopy, and dorsal stabilizer along their lengths. All of the parts had retained their shape, and the char layer attachment was firm. There were some signs of localized surface melt in areas of shock impingement during peak heating, but because of a continually varying velocity during the flight, shock presence in any one area was limited and the degradation was "insignificant." The nose-up trim attitude degraded the lower surface of the wing details more heavily than the upper surfaces; the reverse was true for the horizontal stabilizers.[353]

---

349 Ibid, pp. 205-206. Armstrong kept the probes in his desk drawer for years, but presented them to Pete Knight in a ceremony at the AFFTC Museum just before Knight passed away in 2004.

350 Martin Marietta report MCR-68-15, pp. 70-71.

351 Ibid, pp. 78-79.

352 Ibid, pp. 78-79.

353 Ibid, p. 71.

The lower, fixed portion of the dorsal stabilizer leading edge charred more heavily than the upper, movable rudder, and some evidence of unsymmetrical heating of the rudder was present, with the left side sustaining a higher heat load. The ablator details for both vane antennas were heavily charred and experienced local erosion or spallation of the char from their surface. They looked worse than they were; measurements showed that more than half an inch of ablator remained on the antennas, which were undamaged in any case.[354]

The sprayed MA-25S layer over the fuselage and side fairings showed varying degrees of effects. Thermal degradation, with the resultant reticulation of the ablator surface, occurred only on the forward areas of the nose. Ablator fissuring extended along the fuselage belly to approximately the forward vane antenna. The ablator on the crown of the fuselage and the belly aft of the vane antenna showed no evidence of thermal exposure.[355]

Engineers could easily correlate the varying amounts of charring experienced over the fuselage with their location or proximity to the various design features of the airplane. For instance, heavily charred areas were directly behind the pressure orifices in the ball nose. These openings were apparently sufficient to "trip" the flow, causing a rapid transition to turbulent boundary-layer conditions. The holes for the ballistic control-system thrusters greatly increased heating effects in their vicinity. Localized stagnation within the recesses apparently permitted burning of the ablator, evidenced by a surface discoloration. The thickness of the material behind the nose-gear door was seriously degraded.[356]

The various stacks and vents protruding from the airplane caused localized heating problems. Stagnation shock and trailing-wake damage were evident downstream from an external tank disconnect door that failed to close after the tanks were jettisoned. The ablator surface on the lower wing experienced varying degrees of charring over the whole area. This was heaviest adjacent to the molded leading edges, and some blistering was evident near the wing tips. However, the upper wing surfaces thermally degraded only near the leading edge details; the remainder of the surface was unaffected. Again, the ablator on the upper surface of the horizontal stabilizers degraded more heavily than the lower surfaces. Along the inboard edge of the stabilizers, next to the side fairings, sections of ablator were missing from both the top and bottom surfaces, forward of the torque tube. The open cavity of the stabilizer's inboard closing rib and the adjacent fairing formed a channel to trap the airflow during flight. This resulted in severe heating within the cavity and caused degradation of the ablator from the back face.[357]

In addition to the thermal degradation, the stabilizer upper surfaces sustained a significant amount of impact damage. Some of the abrasions obviously occurred during landing since the exposed ablator was virgin material, while others had occurred early in flight and the exposed ablator had become charred. Engineers thought the likely cause was spallation of small pieces of upstream ablator of fluid

354 Ibid, p. 72.

355 Ibid, pp. 72-73.

356 Ibid, pp. 72-73.

357 Ibid, pp. 74-75.

droplets from the various vents and drains. As expected, ablation residue partially covered the unprotected right-hand windshield.[358]

Pull tests were conducted at random locations on the surface of the ablator to determine whether it was still well bonded to the airplane. The results were generally acceptable. In the end, Martin Marietta believed that the ablator "performed satisfactorily except in the area of the modified ventral fin." Nevertheless, Martin went on to suggest a series of minor modifications that would solve some of the problems experienced on these two flights.[359]

The ablator obviously was not completely successful. Unexpectedly, the ablator actually prevented cooling of the airframe by preventing heat from absorbing into the underlying hot structure. The post-flight condition of the airplane was a surprise to Jack Kolf, an X0-15 project engineer at the FRC, who noted, "If there had been any question that the airplane was going to come back in that shape, we never would have flown it."[360]

Engineers had not fully considered possible shock interaction with the ramjet shape at hypersonic speeds. As it turned out, the flow patterns were such that a tremendous shock wave impinged on the ramjet and its supporting structure. Researchers later estimated that the heat in the ventral stabilizer was 10 times higher than normal. The warning signs had been there in various wind-tunnel tests and previous flights, but researchers had not recognized them.[361]

It is interesting to note that post-flight photographs of the X-15A-2 damage normally highlight two areas. The first is the ventral stabilizer and ramjet. Heating effects unquestionably damaged this area, although there had been indications on the previous flight that something was not right. The second area shown is the large fissures around the nose. When NASA replaced the ball nose before this flight, it used an outdated batch of MA-25S because it was all that was available. Although its application characteristics, cure rate, and appearance were the same as those of the "fresh" ablator used elsewhere, thermal exposure resulted in a greater shrink rate than the newer material. This produced much more pronounced fissuring, but it appeared that the ablator provided sufficient protection.[362]

The original contract with Martin Marietta indicated the company was responsible for "touching up" the ablator twice to allow three flights with the initial application. The damage sustained by the ventral stabilizer precluded the aircraft from flying again in the near future. Consequently, the Air Force directed Martin to remove the ablator so that it could return the aircraft to North American for inspection and repair. NASA technicians under the direction of a Martin engineer, however, performed the actual removal. The technicians removed the MA-25S-1 strips from the service panel peripheries, cleaned the panel edges, and then applied polyethylene tape to protect the aircraft interior from contamination. They stripped the ablator layer using plexiglass scrapers and scrubbed the surface to

358 Ibid, pp. 74-75.

359 Ibid, p. 77.

360 John V. Becker, "The X-15 Program in Retrospect," 3rd Eugen Sänger Memorial Lecture at the Deutsch Geaellschaft Fur Luftfahrforschung, Bonn, Germany, 5 December 1968); interview with Jack Koll, 28 February 1977 (interviewer not noted). Transcript in the files at the DFRC History Office.

361 Martin Marietta report MCR-68-15, pp. 77.

362 Ibid, pp. 74-75.

This is the ventral stabilizer after Flight 2-53-97; the ramjet had fallen off during landing. The X-15A-2 skin sustained major damage due to the excessively high heating in the shock impingement, which burned through at the leading edge and on the sides of the ventral at the torque box assembly. This also damaged the torque box and destroyed the wiring and pressure lines in the forward compartment. (NASA)

remove all residual ablator material. The final cleaning was performed with aluminum wool and nylon pads with powdered cleanser, and wooden toothpicks proved useful for dislodging the ablator material from skin gaps and the heads of permanent fasteners.[363]

NASA sent X-15A-2 to North American for repair and general maintenance. The airplane returned to Edwards on 27 June 1968, and a series of nondestructive load and thermal tests on the instrumented right wing began on 15 July in the FRC High Temperature Loads Calibration Laboratory. As it turned out, the airplane would never fly again.[364]

Some of the problems encountered with the ablator were non-representative of possible future uses. North American had designed the X-15 with an uninsulated hot structure, but researchers expected to design any future vehicle with a more conventional airframe that would eliminate some of the problems encountered on this flight. However, other problems were very real. The amount of time it took to apply the ablator was unacceptable. Even considering that after they gained some experience the technicians could cut the application time in half or even more, the six weeks it took to coat the relatively small X-15 bode ill for larger vehicles.[365]

363 Ibid, pp. 20-21.

364 X-15 Status Report, Paul F. Bikle/FRC to J. Martin/NASA Headquarters, 17 July 1968, p. 1. In the files at the DFRC History Office.

365 Dennis R. Jenkins, *Space Shuttle: The History of the National Space Transportation System–The First 100 Flights* (North Branch, MN: Specialty Press, 2001), pp. 160-162.

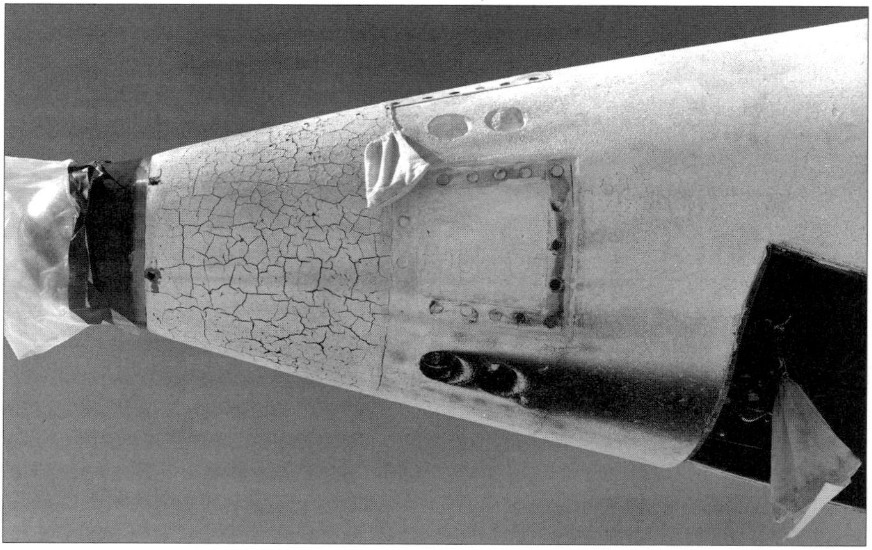

This is the nose of X-15A-2 after Flight 2-53-97. NASA had replaced the ball nose before this flight because of a maintenance issue, and had used an outdated batch of MA-25S to patch the area because it was all that was available. Although its application characteristics, cure rate, and appearance were the same as the "fresh" ablator used elsewhere, thermal exposure resulted in a greater shrink rate than the newer material. This produced much more pronounced fissuring, but analysis indicated that the ablator provided sufficient protection, despite appearances. (NASA)

The use of an ablative coating on X-15A-2 came at an interesting time. The development of what became the space shuttle was just beginning, with various study efforts being initiated under the auspices of NASA and the Air Force. It was obvious that some sort of reusable thermal protection system was going to be required on a space shuttle, and a great deal of attention initially turned to ablatives because they were the most mature technology available at the time. The experience with the X-15 provided very meaningful insights into the problems that the space shuttle undoubtedly would have encountered using this technology. Nevertheless, various contractors continued to propose the use of ablators on their space shuttle concepts, in decreasing quantity, until 1970 when several forms of ceramic tiles and metal "shingles" became the preferred concepts. Based at least partially on the results of the X-15 tests, the space shuttle program decided to go down a different road; whether that road was truly superior is open to debate. At least it represented a different set of problems.

Tragedy

At 10:30:07.4 on 15 November 1967, X-15-3 dropped away from the NB-52B 45,000 feet over Delamar Dry Lake. Major Michael J. Adams was at the controls, making his seventh X-15 flight. Adams had spent slightly over 23 hours in the fixed-base simulator practicing this particular mission (3-67-95), which was intended to evaluate the Ames boost guidance display and conduct several experiments, including measuring the ultraviolet plume of rocket exhausts at high altitude. About 1 minute after launch, as X-15-3 passed through 85,000 feet, an electrical disturbance caused the MH-96 dampers to trip out. It was later determined the disturbance most probably had emanated from electrical arcing in the experiment in the nose of the right wing-tip pod that was being flown for the first time. Adams reset the dampers and continued.[366]

As planned, Adams switched the cockpit sideslip attitude indicator to an alternate display mode. One of the more controversial aspects of the attitude indicator was a second use for the cross-pointers, which were developed late in the program to allow precise pointing of several experiments. In this mode the cross-pointers displayed vernier attitude errors (pitch error on the alpha needle, and bank error on the beta needle). A switch allowed the pilot to control the display mode. During the climb, the pilot switched the display to the vernier-attitude-error mode, and would normally have switched back to the sideslip mode prior to reentry.[367]

Unlike the other two airplanes, X-15-3 automatically blended the ballistic control-system thrusters with the aerodynamic controls as needed using the right side stick, allowing the pilot to largely ignore the dedicated ballistic controller on the left. The electrical disturbances fooled the flight-control system into believing that the dynamic pressure was higher than it actually was, resulting in the system failing to engage the ballistic control system as would normally occur at high altitude. Adams felt the lack of response as the airplane approached maximum altitude and began using the left side stick to operate the thrusters. Unfortunately, Adams reverted to flying the vertical needle on the attitude indicator as if it were still showing sideslip instead of its actual vernier-attitude-error display.[368]

Pete Knight was NASA-1 on the ground. As the X-15 climbed after engine shutdown, Adams initiated a wing-rocking maneuver to sweep the ultraviolet plume experiment up and down across the horizon. Because Adams was apparently interpreting the attitude indicator incorrectly, he began rocking the wings excessively. After Adams stopped the wing rocking, the X-15 began to drift toward its peak altitude, flying with a 15-degree sideslip to the right. As Adams descended, the drift began again and X-15-3 yawed at a right angle to the flight path. The airplane entered a hypersonic spin as it encountered rapidly increasing dynamic pressure at 130,000 feet.[369]

The designers of the NASA control room had not thought to provide a heading indication, so the controllers were unaware of the attitude of the airplane. Everybody knew the ball nose did not accurately align with the relative wind at altitudes above 250,000 feet, so there was little concern when the angle of attack and angle of sideslip began drifting off nominal values near peak altitude. In reality, the airplane was yawing wildly, eventually turning completely around. Fifteen

366 Donald R. Bellman et al., NASA report (no number), "Investigation of the Crash of the X-15-3 Aircraft on November 15, 1967," January 1968, pp. 8-15, and 25; e-mail, Johnny G. Armstrong to Dennis R. Jenkins, 26 July 2002; radio transcript for flight 3-65-97;

367 E-mails, Robert G. Hoey to Dennis R. Jenkins, 24 August and 20 November 2002.

368 Bellman, "Investigation of the Crash," p. 4; e-mails, Johnny G. Armstrong to Dennis R. Jenkins, 26 July and 23 November 2002; e-mail, Robert G. Hoey to Dennis R. Jenkins, 20 November 2002.

369 Bellman, "Investigation of the Crash," pp. 8-15; letter, Robert G. Hoey to Dennis R. Jenkins, 12 August 2002. To date, this is the only hypersonic spin that has been encountered during manned flight research.

At 10:30:07.4 on 15 November 1967, X-15-3 dropped away from the NB-52B 45,000 feet over Delamar Dry Lake with Major Michael J. Adams at the controls. Technical problems combined with possible piloting issues caused the X-15-3 to break-up at approximately 62,000 feet with a velocity of about 3,800 fps and a dynamic pressure of 1,300 psf. The wreckage fell near Johannesburg, California. (NASA)

seconds later Adams reported that the airplane "seems squirrelly" and at 1034 hours he advised, "I'm in a spin, Pete." Adams radioed again, "I'm in a spin," followed by groans as the pilot was subjected to heavy accelerations. Engineers knew very little about the hypersonic spin characteristics of the X-15, and there was no recommended spin recovery technique.[370]

Realizing that X-15-3 would never make it back to Rogers Dry Lake, the chase pilots–Hugh M. Jackson and Bill Dana–shoved their F-104s into afterburner and raced for Ballarat and Cuddeback, the most likely emergency landing lakes. In the X-15, Adams used the combined power of the aerodynamic and ballistic controls against the spin. Eventually, largely through a weathervane effect, the airplane recovered at 120,000 feet and 140 psf. It then entered an inverted Mach 4.7 dive at an angle of nearly 45 degrees. At this point, it looked like Adams might pull out of the dive. However, a technical problem emerged as the MH-96 entered a limit-cycle oscillation when the airplane emerged from the spin. This prevented the system from reducing the pitch gain in response to the increasing dynamic pressure. While descending at over 2,700 fps, the X-15 began to exhibit an increasingly severe rapid pitching motion. The severe oscillations in the flight-control system effectively blocked pilot inputs. As it passed through 65,000 feet, X-15-3 was descending in an inverted dive at Mach 3.93 and approaching both the side-load and normal-load limits. At 1034:57.5, the airplane broke up at approxi-

370 Radio transcript for flight 3-65-97; Bellman, "Investigation of the Crash," pp. 4 and 8-15.

mately 62,000 feet with a velocity of about 3,800 fps and a dynamic pressure of 1,300 psf. An Air Force pilot spotted the wreckage near the town of Johannesburg. Mike Adams was dead, and X-15-3 was destroyed.[371]

The Air Force and NASA convened an accident board. It took two months for the board, chaired by Donald R. Bellman, to prepare its report. During the investigation, personnel searched for additional pieces of wreckage, especially the film from the cockpit camera. The weekend after the accident, an unofficial search party from the FRC found the cockpit camera but not the film cartridge. Since the film cassette was lighter than the camera, engineers theorized that the cassette must have been blown north by winds at altitude. A search party organized by Victor Horton converged on the area on 29 November, and Willard E. Dives found the cassette. The film was flown to the EG&G laboratory in Boston for processing.

Mike Adams flew the X-15 for 13 months from 6 October 1966 until 15 November 1967, making seven flights. All of these were with the XLR99 engine and he reached Mach 5.59, a maximum speed of 3,822 mph, and an altitude of 266,000 feet. Adams died on Flight 3-65-97. The Air Force posthumously awarded Mike Adams an astronaut rating for his last flight in X-15-3, which had attained an altitude of 266,000 feet (50.38 miles). This was the only fatality during the program's 199 flights. (NASA)

371 Bellman, "Investigation of the Crash," pp. 31-32.

Johnny Armstrong and Jack Kolf began analyzing the cockpit film when it returned. Armstrong later recalled, "We had the time history from the flight recorded in the control room. We could see the vertical needle on the attitude indicator in the film and correlated the time of the film and the recorded time history. It became clear to us that the pilot was making manual ballistic inputs as if the vertical needle was sideslip rather than roll angle. His inputs were in the correct direction to make sideslip zero if it had been sideslip. However since it was roll angle his inputs drove the nose further from away from the flight path and eventually into … a spin."[372]

The accident board concluded that Adams misinterpreted his instruments, and combined with distraction and possible vertigo, this led him to allow the heading of the X-15-3 to deviate unexpectedly. The overall effectiveness of the MH-96 had been degraded by the electrical disturbance early in the flight, further adding to the pilot's workload. The MH-96 then caused the airplane to break up. The board made two major recommendations: install a telemetered heading indicator in the control room, visible to the flight controller, and medically screen X-15 pilot candidates for labyrinth (vertigo) sensitivity. Because of the crash, NASA added an attitude indicator in the control room to display real-time heading, pitch, roll, sideslip, and angle-of-attack information. Although it was not specifically called out in the accident report, many engineers came away with a more important lesson: do not use the same instrument to display multiple different indications in a high-workload or high-stress environment.[373]

The Air Force posthumously awarded Mike Adams an astronaut rating for his last flight in X-15-3, which had attained an altitude of 266,000 feet (50.38 miles). This was the only fatality that occurred during the program's 199 flights.[374]

Almost the End

On 13 October 1960, the government established the Aeronautics and Astronautics Coordinating Board (AACB) to coordinate various activities between the Department of Defense and NASA. The deputy administrator of NASA and the assistant secretary of the DDR&E served as cochairmen of the AACB; initially this meant Hugh Dryden and Herbert F. York, respectively. In an indirect way, the Research Airplane Committee that was created in 1954 to manage the X-15 program fell under the auspices of the AACB. However, given that the X-15 program existed prior to the creation of the AACB, the board had little direct impact on the program. The Research Airplane Committee continued to function much as it always had until sometime in 1965.[375]

372 E-mail, Johnny G. Armstrong to Dennis R. Jenkins, 26 July 2002.

373 Bellman, *Investigation of the Crash*, pp. 8-15.

374 Aeronautical order 130, awarding the rating of command pilot astronaut to Major Michael J. Adams, 15 November 1967. In the author's collection.

375 Interview, Dr. Robert C. Seamans, Jr., by Martin Collins, 15 December 1988, electronic transcript available at *http://www.nasm.si.edu/nasm/dsh/trasncpt/seaman10.htm*, accessed 25 April 2002. The AACB also oversaw the Manned Spacecraft Panel, Unmanned Spaceflight Panel, Launch Vehicle Panel, Spaceflight Ground Environment Panel, and Supporting Space Research and Technology Panel.

The AACB Aeronautics Panel began discussing the issue of continued funding for the X-15 in early 1966. Charles W. Harper from NASA made a good case for continuing Air Force funding for the X-15 since both the HRE and delta-wing projects were of potential value to the Air Force as well as to NASA. Both projects were part of a joint national hypersonics program organized in May 1965 by John Becker from NASA Langley and R. E. Supp from the Air Force Systems Command. Becker and Supp made a presentation to the Aeronautics Panel on 13 June 1966 showing that the HRE and delta-wing projects would be the principal users of the X-15 after the end of 1967, although a number of other experiments also continued. After a brief discussion, the Aeronautics Panel endorsed these projects and recommended that the AACB develop a cost-sharing plan that would allow the X-15 program to continue.[376]

The next meeting of the AACB on 5 July 1966, in fact, would influence the X-15 program greatly, but not the way the Aeronautics Panel had expected. Instead, the meeting essentially defined the date the X-15 program would end. In rejecting the recommendation of the Aeronautics Panel, the AACB indicated that the two most important approved Air Force experiments (20 and 24) would conclude at the end of 1967, and the AACB saw little need for continued Air Force support of the program past that date. Beginning on 1 January 1968, the program would become the responsibility of NASA exclusively.[377]

Rather quickly, however, it became apparent that the planned completion of the two Air Force experiments would run well into 1968. Consequently, at the 24 August 1967 meeting of the AACB, the participants attempted to work out some compromise that would allow the X-15 program to continue. The agreement changed little on the surface. From a monetary perspective, NASA agreed to begin funding the sustaining engineering contracts the Air Force maintained with North American, Reaction Motors, and the other original contractors. Both agencies concluded it was easier to allow the Air Force contracts to continue than to terminate them and restart them as NASA contracts. Instead, NASA would reimburse the Air Force for the cost of the contracts. The FRC agreed to continue its maintenance responsibilities for the airplanes and most of their systems, while the AFFTC agreed to continue maintenance of the carrier aircraft, rocket engines, and other systems it had been responsible for.[378]

The largest change was the dissolution of the Research Airplane Committee that had guided the X-15 program since the signing of the original 1954 memorandum of understanding. The X-15 Joint Operations Committee and the X-15 Joint Program Coordinating Committee that had reported to the Research Airplane Committee would now report to the Aeronautics Panel of the AACB.[379]

All in attendance agreed the X-15 program would continue at least through the middle of 1968. How long the program would continue after that depended upon the status of the Air Force experiments and the NASA funding situation. On 26 October 1967, the Air Force and NASA signed a new memorandum of under-

376 Minutes of the Meeting, AACB Aeronautics Panel, 13 June 1966.

377 Memorandum for Dr. John S. Foster and Dr. Robert C. Seamans, Jr., prepared by Thomas C. Muse (Assistant Director OSD, DDR&E) and Charles W. Harper (Deputy Administrator, OART), 26 October 1967.

378 Ibid.

379 Ibid.

standing, replacing the original 1954 MoU that had governed the X-15 program for 13 years. Charles W. Harper (NASA deputy associate administrator for the Office of Advanced Research and Technology) worked with Thomas C. Muse (assistant director OSD, DDR&E) to get the new agreement signed by Dr. John S. Foster (director, DDR&E) and Dr. Robert C. Seamans, Jr. (NASA deputy administrator). The new MoU reestablished Air Force responsibility for X-15 costs, and spelled out the specific responsibilities of the two organizations. However, instead of ending with a statement of national priority, the new MoU contained the ominous proviso, "funds permitting." To most NASA managers, this meant that NASA would still have to face up to the total funding of the X-15 program as soon as the last two Air Force experiments ended.[380]

Charles Harper and his boss at the Office of Advanced Research and Technology, Mac Adams, made one last effort to find funds for the program during the fall of 1967. They solicited help from the NASA Office of Manned Spaceflight (OMSF) because both the HRE and the delta-wing projects would produce new technology for the Space Shuttle. The attempt failed, however, because the OMSF was already having trouble promoting the space shuttle concept and did not want to add to its problems by supporting a potentially attractive-sounding alternative.[381]

The accident involving Mike Adams underscored the concerns long expressed privately by Paul Bikle and others regarding the high costs and risks associated with extending the X-15 program. In the discussions that followed the accident, Bikle convincingly speculated on the enormous costs of the HRE flight program involving years of delay in getting started, malfunctions, and repairs. In December 1967, the Air Force and NASA both agreed to abandon the HRE flight program and to terminate the X-15 program at the end of 1968. On 13 March 1968 the Air Force announced that it would allow its X-15 funding to expire at the end of the year, but that it would continue to support flight tests to the "completion of Air Force IR [24] and WTR [20] experiments."[382]

NASA allocated $1,500,000 for X-15 operations in FY68, with the Air Force contributing another $777,000. It appeared the program could save $150,000 by not returning X-15A-2 to flight status, and by flying a minimum number of other flights using X-15-1. The first six months of 1969 would require approximately $400,000 to catalog and dispose of spare parts, ground equipment, and prepare the two remaining vehicles for shipment to museums. The X-15 program would transfer some parts and ground equipment to other programs, and scrap the remainder.[383]

---

380 Ibid.

381 John V. Becker, "A Hindsight Study of the NASA Hypersonic Research Engine Project," 1 July 1976, p. 27. Prepared under contract NAS1-14250, but never published. Copy in the author's collection.

382 Ibid; "X-15 Program," a briefing prepared by the AFFTC in late October 1968. In the files at the AFFTC History Office. Although this statement indicated that the WTR experiment was #28, in reality it appears to have been #20.

383 "X-15 Program."

1968 FLIGHT PERIOD

The X-15 program would only fly another eight missions. During 1968, Bill Dana and Pete Knight took turns flying X-15-1. However, even within NASA, not everyone was certain the flights were worth the risk and $600,000 cost.[384]

X-15A-2 returned to Edwards on 27 June 1968. On 15 July, a series of non-destructive load and thermal tests began on the instrumented right wing in the FRC High Temperature Loads Calibration Laboratory. The airplane would remain grounded forever.[385]

Nevertheless, during the first part of 1968 the AFFTC and FRC worked together to see if there was sufficient interest to extend the program. By October 1968, they had surveyed the current users of the airplane and potential future researchers, and found some programs that could likely benefit from the X-15 being available. Two of the Air Force experiments (20 and 24) might need more time, especially the WTR launch monitoring, which would require extraordinary luck to get the X-15-1 and an ICBM in the air at the same moment. The groups investigating the impingement heating on the last flight of X-15A-2 also would have been happy to keep that airplane flying, since they had little other means of conducting experiments to understand the problem.[386]

Technically, NASA had already canceled the HRE flight program, but most everybody acknowledged that the ramjet experiments could also benefit from flight testing. However, NASA was a bit gun-shy after the bad experience on X-15A-2, and the flight ramjet development was running well behind schedule. Several other programs within the defense community were studying advanced propulsion concepts (ramjets, turbo-ramjets, or similar engines), and most of them potentially could have used the X-15 as a platform if it was still flying. There was even some talk about reviving the delta-wing concept that had been canceled after the loss of X-15-3.[387]

Despite this minor interest, in the end the AFFTC report concluded that "no known overpowering technological benefits will be lost if [the X-15] program ends on 31 December 1968." It noted that there was a firm requirement for the completion of the two Air Force experiments, and that "many USAF/USN technological activities [were] underway or planned for the Mach 4-6 regime," but the report failed to identify any specific requirements for the use of the small black airplanes. It noted that "the future value of the X-15 as a hypersonic test capability should be more evident by mid-late 1969" and that the "option to use X-15 resources after 1969 should be protected."[388]

384 USAF headquarters development directive no. 32, 5 March 1964, reprinted in System Package Program, System 653A, 18 May 1964, p. 13-7; memorandum, John V. Becker and R. E. Supp, subject: Report of meeting of USAF/NASA working groups on hypersonic aircraft technology, 21-22 September 1966; James E. Love and William R. Young, NASA technical note D-3732, "Survey of Operation and Cost Experience of the X-15 Airplane as a Reusable Space Vehicle," November 1966, pp. 7.

385 X-15 Status Report, Paul F. Bikle/FRC to J. Martin/NASA Headquarters, 17 July 1968, p. 1.

386 "X-15 Program."

387 Ibid.

388 Ibid.

Bill Dana completed the 199th—and as it turned out the last–X-15 flight, reaching Mach 5.38 and 255,000 feet on 24 October 1968. The program made 10 attempts to launch the 200th flight, but maintenance and weather problems forced cancellation every time. The attempt on 12 December actually got airborne (1-A-142), but the X-15 inertial system failed before launch. On 20 December 1968, things looked dismal, but everybody geared up for an attempt. Bill Dana began taxiing an F-104 for a weather flight, but John Manke noted that snow was falling–at Edwards! Manke recalled Dana before he took off and canceled the mission. Later that afternoon, technicians at the FRC demated X-15-1 from the NB-52A for the last time. After nearly 10 years of flight operations, the X-15 program ended.[389]

By the end of the program, the two remaining airplanes were tired. In absolute terms, they were still young airframes–just 10 years old and with only about 10 flight hours each. The total free-flight time for all three airplanes was only 30 hours, 14 minutes, and 57 seconds. Even counting all the time spent under the wing of the two NB-52s, the total barely reached 400 hours. Despite early Air Force estimates of 300–500 flights, that had not been the original idea. Bob Hoey remembers asking North American project aerodynamicist Edwin W. "Bill" Johnston how long North American expected the airplanes to last. Johnston responded that the company had "expected that each airplane would only see 5 or 6 exposures to the design missions [i.e., Mach 6 or 250,000 feet]." They did much better.[390]

The X-15s accumulated much more flight time than most of the high-performance X-planes, and the environment they flew in was certainly extreme. They frequently experienced dynamic pressures as high as 2,000 psf, and as low as (essentially) 0 psf. The airframes endured accelerations ranging from –2.5 g to over +8.0 g. Temperatures varied from –245°F to over 1,200°F. It had been a rough life.

In addition, NASA tested the airplanes–a lot. After each flight, NASA removed, disassembled, and thoroughly checked almost every system. Then each was reinstalled and tested some more. If the technicians noted any anomalies they made the appropriate repairs and retested. Milt Thompson wrote, "[M]y personal opinion is that we wore the airplanes out testing them in preparation for flight." The space shuttle would suffer much the same fate.[391]

It is interesting to note that although the X-15 is generally considered a Mach 6 aircraft, only two of the three airplanes ever exceeded Mach 6, and then only four times. On the other hand, 108 flights exceeded Mach 5 (not including the four Mach 6 flights), accumulating 1 hour and 25 minutes of hypersonic flight. At the other end of the spectrum, only two flights were not supersonic (one of these was the first glide flight), and 14 others did not exceed Mach 2. It was a fast airplane.

389 USAF Headquarters development directive no. 32, 5 March 1964, reprinted in System Package Program, System 653A, 18 May 1964, p. 13-7; memorandum, John V. Becker and R. E. Supp, subject: Report of meeting of USAF/NASA working groups on hypersonic aircraft technology, 21-22 September 1966; James E. Love and William R. Young, NASA technical note D-3732, "Survey of Operation and Cost Experience of the X-15 Airplane as a Reusable Space Vehicle," November 1966, pp. 7.

390 Letter, Robert G. Hoey to Dennis R. Jenkins, 13 August 2002.

391 Thompson, *At the Edge of Space*, p. 223.

Similarly, there were only four flights above 300,000 feet (all by X-15-3), but only the initial glide flight was below 40,000 feet.[392]

Final Dispositions

In November 1968, William P. Albrecht and Vincent N. Capasso inspected X-15A-2, which had been in storage at the FRC since the completion of the thermal tests. The engineers determined what work would be needed to prepare the aircraft for display in a museum, or to return it to flight status if necessary. As the airplane stood, it was missing control surfaces, most of its cockpit displays, and the removable right outer wing panel. All of the pieces were stored nearby.[393]

A cursory inspection of the airplane showed signs of minor corrosion in unprotected areas, and the engineers believed the aircraft needed "a thorough inspection for corrosion with cleaning and repainting as required. A lubrication would be accomplished at the same time to protect moving surfaces .... This would take two men approximately 2 to 4 weeks to accomplish."[394]

To restore the vehicle to flight status, the engineers believed three to four months of work would be required, including installing the engine plumbing, control surfaces, actuators, and SAS pump. All of the wiring would have to be checked and the hydraulic system would need servicing. In addition, the instrument panel would have to be installed and the landing gear made flight-ready. If the airplane went to a museum, the engineers thought that some items (mainly bars to replace the control surface actuators) would have to be fabricated. A rough estimate included three people for a month to prepare the airplane for display, plus time to paint and stencil the exterior.[395]

Officially, the X-15 program simply "expired" at the end of its authorized funding on 31 December 1968. After the New Year holiday, things began to happen quickly. Between the Apollo program and the increasing tempo of the air war in Southeast Asia, neither NASA nor the Air Force seemed particularly interested in the small black airplanes that were stored in the High-Temperature Loads Calibration Laboratory at the FRC.

On 4 January 1969, officials at Edwards formally requested reassignment instructions for the two remaining X-15 airplanes. A response came on 20 February directing that the "number one X-15 be made available for display in the Smithsonian Museum. The Smithsonian is prepared to receive the X-15 and it may be transported to Andrews as soon as it is ready for shipment. In order to protect the option of any future flight test program, extreme care should be taken in handling the X-15 so that it will not be altered or damaged. The Air Force Museum should retain accountability for the aircraft and reassign it to the Smithsonian for

392 At the 3rd Eugen Sänger Memorial Lecture in 1968, John Becker stated that 109 flights exceeded Mach 5. A reevaluation of the flight data shows that only 108 actually did. See John V. Becker, "The X-15 Program in Retrospect," 3rd Eugen Sänger Memorial Lecture at the Deutsch Geaellschaft Fur Luftfahrforschung, Bonn, Germany, 5 December 1968, p. 3 for Becker's original numbers.

393 Memorandum, William P. Albrecht and Vincent N. Spasso to James E. Love/X-15 Program Manager, subject: Status of X-15A-2, 14 November 1968. In the files at the DFRC History Office.

394 Ibid.

395 Ibid.

display." A later message directed NASA to transfer X-15A-2 to the Air Force Museum at Wright-Patterson AFB.[396]

A meeting on 7 January 1969 at North American discussed how best to dispose of the remaining program assets for which North American still had responsibility. Unlike many programs that require the contractor to account for every pencil purchased with government funds, the X-15 ended much more casually. For instance, the "contractor was advised ... that no physical inventory of X-15 assets will be required," and that the North American working inventory would be "accepted by the Air Force as the formal X-15 inventory record." The Air Force justified this casual attitude by noting that "(a) it is a research type program, (b) the last physical inventory was taken less than a year ago, (c) [it is] in the interest of program economy." Nevertheless, North American had to assign class codes (indicating how to dispose of the item) to some 9,000 line items having a monetary value in excess of $6,000,000.[397]

On 18 March 1969, the public affairs officer at the FRC wrote to his counterpart at NASA Headquarters. The opening paragraph was telling: "Sometime this spring, probably May, the number one X-15 will go into the Smithsonian. Because of the haste of the announcements and Apollo 8, the world didn't seem to care much when the program was concluded last December. I'd like to see if we can't remind the world about the X-15 and use the Smithsonian as an excuse."[398]

The Smithsonian Institution's National Air and Space Museum (NASM) had begun its efforts to acquire an X-15 as early as 1962, but nothing was likely to happen as long as the flight program continued. After the funding expired, the Air Force agreed to lend X-15-1 to NASM for two years. NASA partially disassembled X-15-1, loaded it onto a flatbed trailer, and flew it to Andrews AFB inside an Air Force transport. On 13 May 1969, a truck moved X-15-1 from Andrews to the Silver Hill Facility (later the Paul E. Garber Facility) in Maryland. After some minor refurbishment, the Smithsonian installed the X-15 near the original 1903 Wright Flyer on the floor in the north hall of the Arts and Industries building, which housed the NASM at the time. On 7 July 1971, the Air Force officially transferred ownership of X-15-1 to the NASM, which subsequently loaned the airplane to the FAA for display at Transpo 72 in the spring of 1972. The airplane then traveled to the FRC to help commemorate its 25th anniversary. The NASA loan was effective for one year beginning in August 1972, but ultimately was extended until the summer of 1975. The X-15 returned to the Smithsonian for installation in the new NASM building on the mall before it opened to the public

396 TWX 632136Z Jan 69, subject: Termination XB-70, X-15 program, 4 January 1969. This TWX also requested instruction for the reassignment of the remaining XB-70A (62-0001); TWX 202041Z Feb 69, subject: Transfer of X-15 SN56-6670 to the Smithsonian Museum. Both in the files at the DFRC History Office.

397 Meeting minutes, "Disposition of Those X-15 Program Assets for which NR has Accountability," 7 January 1969. At this point North American Aviation had become North American Rockwell (usually abbreviated NAR, but only NR here).

398 Letter, Ralph B. Jackson/FRC to Joseph A. Stein/NASA Headquarters, 18 March 1969. In the files at the NASA History Office.

on 1 July 1976. X-15-1 currently hangs in the Milestones of Flight Gallery at the NASM in Washington, D.C.[399]

X-15A-2, completely refurbished after its unhappy experience with the ablative coatings, became the property of the National Museum of the United States Air Force at Wright-Patterson AFB, Ohio. However, prior to the airplane arriving in Ohio, the museum loaned it to the Alabama Space and Rocket Center in Huntsville (now the U.S. Space & Rocket Center). The airplane arrived on a one-year loan on 27 March 1970, although for some reason the Air Force did not installed the right wing while the airplane was in Huntsville. The airplane now sits—in black Inconel finish—in the Presidential and Research & Development Galleries of the National Museum of the United States Air Force. A set of external tanks and a dummy ramjet are part of the display.

The Air Force buried the remains of X-15-3 at an undisclosed location on the Edwards reservation. In 1991 the Astronaut Memorial at the Kennedy Space Center, Florida, added Mike Adam's name, a tacit reminder of an oft-forgotten manned space program.[400]

The two NB-52s remained at Edwards to support the heavyweight-lifting-body program. Not long after the end of the lifting-body program, NASA retired the NB-52A to the Pima Air & Space Museum outside Tucson, Arizona. The NB-52B continued to serve as a carrier aircraft, launching the X-38 and X-43 vehicles, through the beginning of 2005. NASA finally received a B-52H in mid-2005 to serve as a carrier aircraft, but a lack of requirements resulted in the airplane returning to the Air Force in 2006. At the time of its retirement, the NB-52B was the oldest operational (and lowest flight time) B-52 in the Air Force.[401]

CORRECTING AN OVERSIGHT

On 23 August 2005, 40 years of aerospace controversy ended. For years, many aviation historians and enthusiasts had questioned why the Air Force pilots who flew the X-15 to altitudes above 50 miles received astronaut ratings, while the NASA pilots who accomplished the same feat in the same airplanes did not. The answer came on a small stage at the DFRC when Navy Captain Kent V. Romminger, chief of the NASA Astronaut Office at the Johnson Space Center, presented certificates proclaiming three NASA test pilots as astronauts. NASA administrator Shawn O'Keefe authorized the recognition, and Romminger, associate administrator for the Space Operations Mission Directorate William F. Readdy, and DFRC director Kevin L. Peterson signed the certificates. The purposefully

399 E-mail, F. Robert van der Linden/X-15 curator for the NASM to Dennis R. Jenkins, 6 May 2002. It is not unusual for the NASM to begin the process of obtaining a significant vehicle much earlier than would seem appropriate. For instance, they began attempts to acquire the Space Shuttle *Columbia* as early as 1982, barely a year after it had made its first flight.

400 The author played a key role in getting Mike Adams placed on the memorial.

401 NASA DFRC press release 02-21, " NASA's Historic B-52B and 'New' B-52H Participating in 50th Anniversary Activities, 11 April 2002.

In August 2005, NASA finally recognized three NASA pilots who had flown over 50 miles altitude but had not received astronaut wings like their military counterparts. Three former X-15 pilots joined in the ceremony. From left, Robert M White, William H. Dana (proudly wearing the new wings on his flight jacket), Neil A. Armstrong, and Joe H. Engle. The families of Jack McKay and Joe Walker were present to accept their astronaut wings from Kent Romminger, the Chief of the Astronaut Office. (NASA)

small ceremony was a private moment for a very special group of men and their families.[402]

In the late 1960s, these three men–William H. Dana, John B. McKay, and Joseph A. Walker–had piloted the X-15 to altitudes in excess of 50 miles. Although five of their colleagues had received Air Force astronaut ratings for similar accomplishments, NASA had never recognized the three civilian pilots. Now, 40 years after the fact, the agency did. Only Bill Dana was still alive to receive his certificate, and to have his wife, Judy, place the blue and gold name tag with the astronaut wings emblem on his flight jacket. However, almost the entire McKay and Walker families were on hand to receive the tribute. Joe Walker, who always had a smile on his face, was the first human being to fly into space twice; now his son has a set of astronaut wings to proudly display. On hand to honor their colleagues were three former X-15 pilots: Joe H. Engle, who after his X-15 flights became the only person to fly the space shuttle back from orbit under manual control; Robert M. White, perhaps the least known of the test pilots (odd considering he was the first person to fly to Mach 4, Mach 5, and Mach 6, as well

402 Personal experience of the author, who had the privilege of being present at the ceremony.

as the first person to fly to 200,000 feet and then to 300,000 feet; Bob still holds the world absolute-altitude record at 314,750 feet); and Neil A. Armstrong, who needed little introduction. Unfortunately, Scott Crossfield could not attend due to previous commitments. There was not a dry eye in the house.[403]

403 Oddly, although the recognition of the three X-15 pilots was authorized by one NASA administrator (Sean O'Keefe) and recognized publicly by his successor (Mike Griffin), and the certificates were signed by the head of the Astronaut Office, the associate administrator for Space Flight, and the Dryden Center director, the JSC Public Affairs Department refused to concede that astronauts can come from anywhere but Houston (an example of the small minds of bureaucrats in action).

CHAPTER 8

The Research Program

Because the research program was the rationale for the X-15's existence, flights to obtain basic aero-thermo data began as soon as North American and the government were sure the airplane was relatively safe for its intended purpose. Nevertheless, almost from the beginning, the airplanes carried a few minor experiments that had little to do with its basic aero-thermo research objectives; the B-70 emission coating and a radiation detector were early examples. Still, the first couple of years of the flight program were primarily dedicated to expanding the flight envelope and obtaining the basic data needed by aerodynamicists to validate the wind-tunnel predictions and theoretical models used to build the X-15.

As this goal was increasingly satisfied, more X-15 flights carried unrelated experiments, such as tests of ablative materials and star trackers for the Apollo program. Usually these experiments required little support from the X-15 itself, other than some power and recording capacity. Later in the program, flights began to be conducted for the sole purpose of supporting the "follow-on" experiments, although even these usually gathered aero-thermo or stability and control data to support continued evaluation. In reality, the X-15 as an experiment ended sometime in 1963 (except for the advanced X-15A-2); after that, the airplane was mostly a carrier for other experiments.

RESEARCH INSTRUMENTATION

Previous X-planes had recorded all of the research data onboard, mainly because telemetry systems were in a very early state of development and bandwidth was very limited. Nevertheless, several earlier programs did telemeter a small amount of data to the ground in real time. It was decided early on that all X-15 data would continue to be recorded onboard the aircraft, although much more extensive use of telemetry would also be made. The reason for recording everything onboard was "to eliminate the risk of data loss and degradation inherent in radio-frequency telemetry links." This took on more significance for the X-15 program since the airplane would frequently be out of range of the antennas at Edwards, and would have to rely on the new and untried High Range installations at Beatty and Ely.[1]

Initially, the instrumentation centered on the aero-thermo environment that the researchers intended the X-15 to investigate. When the follow-on experiments began to arrive, more of the instrumentation and recording capacity shifted to support non-aero-thermo investigations. A group of researchers from the HSFS, Langley, and Lewis–with limited input from the WADC and AFFTC–came up with the initial requirement for between 1,000 and 1,100 data points. Per the original specification, instrumentation was limited to 800 pounds and 40 cubic feet, and could use up to 2.25 kilowatts of power. The approved design included 1,050 instrumented points (588 thermocouples, 64 strain gages, 28 control surface position indicators, 136 aerodynamic surface pressures, 22 basic flight parameters (angle of attack, etc.) and 212 airplane condition monitors). By contrast, the X-2 had used only 15 thermocouples and a few electrical pressure transducers, and carried only 550 pounds of research instrumentation.[2]

In mid-1957, the NACA asked the Air Force to modify the X-15 specification to double the amount of research instrumentation carried by the airplanes. Given that North American had already frozen the design by that time, this came as something of a shock. In order to keep the airplane's weight (and hence performance) from being too seriously degraded, numerous structural and subsystem details were redesigned to save weight.[3]

When the X-15 emerged from North American, it could carry 1,300 pounds of research instrumentation, the majority of which were installed in a removable elevator in the instrumentation compartment just aft of the cockpit. Engineers designed the cabling so that they could remove the entire elevator from the airplane, which allowed them to perform all pre- and postflight calibrations more easily. Originally, the engineers intended this feature to remove the instrumentation from

1 Kenneth C. Sanderson, NASA technical memorandum X-56000, "The X-15 Flight Test Instrumentation," 21 April 1964, pp. 2-3. A similar paper was presented by Sanderson at the Third International Flight Test Instrumentation Symposium in Buckinghamshire, England, 13-16 April 1964; letter, Robert G. Hoey to Dennis R. Jenkins, 13 August 2002.

2 Letter, Gerald M. Truszynski to Dennis R. Jenkins, 9 May 2002; NASA technical memorandum X-56000, pp. 2-3. A similar paper was presented by Sanderson at the Third International Flight Test Instrumentation Symposium in Buckinghamshire, England, 13-16 April 1964; Lieutenant Colonel Burt Rowen, "Human-Factors Support of the X-15 Program," *Air University Quarterly Review*, Air War College, vol. X, no. 4, winter 1958-59, pp. 31-39.

3 Scott Crossfield, *Always Another Dawn: The Story of a Rocket Test Pilot* (New York: The World Publishing Company, 1960), pp. 263-264; telephone conversation, Charles H. Feltz to Dennis R. Jenkins, 12 May 2002.

possible ammonia contamination, but NASA seldom used it for that purpose. Within the airframe itself, all of the wiring and tubing were routed through the fuselage side tunnels.[4]

In addition to the instrumentation compartment, North American installed small amounts of equipment in the nose of the airplane, in a center-of-gravity compartment located between the oxidizer and fuel tanks, and in the rear fuselage. The main instrumentation compartment and the nose compartment were pressurized and temperature-controlled. The center-of-gravity compartment was temperature-controlled but unpressurized, and the rear fuselage area was insulated against high temperatures but was otherwise uncontrolled. Individual instruments and equipment were shock-mounted or hard-mounted as necessary; hard mounting was preferred because it saved weight and space.[5]

In many respects, X-15 development occurred at an awkward time. Modern data-processing systems were in their infancy, but they promised to offer a substantial improvement over the largely mechanical systems that had preceded them. However, the simple fact was that they were not ready. This forced the instrumentation engineers to rely on oscillographs and precision photographic recorders for the aircraft instead of modern magnetic tape recorders. Most of the rationale was simple: these devices were available from commercial sources or from NACA stock, lessening the cost of an already over-budget program. The program could also procure and test them within the time available before the first flight.

However, they came with some handicaps. The time associated with processing data from an oscillograph system, especially when large quantities of data were involved, was long and tedious compared to that required for data from magnetic tape systems. The instrumentation community debated this problem at length, but finally decided that the 15,000 data points expected to be collected on each flight would not result in processing times that would be detrimental to the planned flight schedule. It was also a fact that during 1956–1957, a costly, time-consuming development program would have been required to obtain a fully automatic magnetic tape system that could withstand the X-15 environment.[6]

Despite the "design" instrumentation list, as manufactured the first two airplanes each had 656 thermocouples, 112 strain gages, 140 pressure sensors, and 90 telemeter pickups. The thermocouples were 30-gage chromel-alumel leads that were spot-welded to the inside surface of the skin. The leads connected to 20-gage extensions that were routed to the signal-conditioning equipment and recorders. The use of 20-gage extensions was necessary to reduce circuit resistance in the thermocouple loops and to minimize measurement errors due to resistance changes caused by the large temperature variations along the wire. Since the thermocouples were inaccessible after the airplanes were constructed, North American designed the installation to function for the life of the airplane and require no maintenance. A silicone-impregnated fiberglass braid covered the leads and extensions, and those in close proximity to the skin used an outer sleeve of

4 Rowen, "Human-Factors Support of the X-15 Program," pp. 31-39; North American report NA58-190, "X-15 Research Airplane NAA Model NA-240 Flight Test Program," 1 August 1958, pp. II-2 through II-3.

5 NASA technical memorandum X-56000, " p. 4.

6 Ibid, pp. 5-6.

unimpregnated fiberglass. The silicone impregnation slowly sublimated during repeated exposure to elevated temperatures, but retained its electrical insulating properties. Its use, however, created a potential problem since tests showed that out-gassing could result in an explosion if the temperature quickly rose to 1,200°F for the first time. NASA eliminated this hazard on the X-15 by gradually building up to the maximum Mach number during the course of the envelope-expansion program.[7]

The first two airplanes used Bakelite strain gages, but these lost their effectiveness as structural temperatures increased. Consequently, North American completed X-15-3 with Micro-Dot weldable-type strain gages designed for use at higher temperatures. The static pressure taps consisted of 0.3125-inch-outside-diameter tubing installed flush with the outside surface of the skin. A study was made of the lag effects of a tube-connected system, and it was determined that 0.25-inch tubing with lengths as great as 40 feet was acceptable for gradual maneuvers and steady-state data at altitudes up to 100,000 feet.[8]

Most of the instrumentation was located on the right side of the airplane; however, there were minimal corresponding sensors on the left side of the forward fuselage and vertical stabilizer. Since the aircraft was largely symmetrical, researchers assumed the data was equally applicable to either side. Because of installation difficulties, no instrumentation was located near the integral propellant tanks. Similarly, North American did not initially install any pressure instrumentation in the horizontal stabilizers due to the difficulty of running tubing to this location. However, the company did install some strain gages in the horizontal, with the wiring running through the pivot point. As part of a loads study late in the program, North American manufactured a new set of horizontal stabilizers with electrical pressure transducers, loads sensors, and thermocouples. Toward the end of the flight program, researchers also installed instrumentation in the wing-tip pods and ventral stabilizer on some flights.[9]

Precision NACA recorders that employed servo-repeater systems to position a light source on moving film recorded angle-of-attack and angle-of-sideslip data provided by the ball nose. Similar devices recorded the attitude-angle outputs from the stable platform. Electrical transducers sensed all other data. A central patch panel in the main instrumentation compartment collected the data, routed

7 James E. Love (manager), "X-15 Program," NASA FRC, October 1961. pp. 14-15; Richard D. Banner, Albert E. Kuhl, and Robert D. Quinn, "Preliminary Results of Aerodynamic Heating Studies on the X-15," a paper in the *1961 Research Airplane Committee Report*, p. 13; Kenneth C. Sanderson, NASA technical memorandum X-56000, "The X-15 Flight Test Instrumentation," 21 April 1964, pp. 11-12. The instrumentation number varied widely over the course of the program and among the three airplanes. For instance, in early 1961, 750 thermocouples were installed in X-15-1 (293 surface units, 191 located in the substructure, and 266 located in various compartments). The telemetered data included such things as control surface positions (right stabilizer, left stabilizer, vertical stabilizer, upper dive brake, lower dive brake, and right wing flap [since the flaps were mechanically interconnected there was no sensor on the left one]), stability augmentation system servo shaft positions (left/right pitch and roll, and yaw), airplane attitude (pitch, roll, and yaw–all from the stable platform), altitude (three precisions: 0-30 in. Hg, 0-3 in. Hg, and 0-1 in. Hg), airspeed (again, in three precisions: 0-2500 psf, 0-1000 psf, and 0-100 psf), horizontal velocity (0-7000 fps), vertical velocity (0-6000 psf), pilot control positions (longitudinal trim, all three control sticks plus the rudder pedals), accelerations (+8/-1 g normal, ±1 g transverse, and ±5 g longitudinal), and various cameras.

8 Love, "X-15 Program," pp. 14-15; Banner et al., "Preliminary Results of Aerodynamic Heating Studies on the X-15," p. 13; letter, Gerald M. Truszynski to Dennis R. Jenkins, 9 May 2002.

9 Banner et al., "Preliminary Results of Aerodynamic Heating Studies on the X-15," p. 13; North American report NA58-190, "X-15 Research Airplane NAA Model NA-240 Flight Test Program," 1 August 1958, pp. II-2 through II-3; "Advanced Development Plan for X-15 Research Aircraft, Advanced Technology Program 653A," 17 November 1961, pp. 40-41; Love, "X-15 Program," pp. 14-15, and 22.

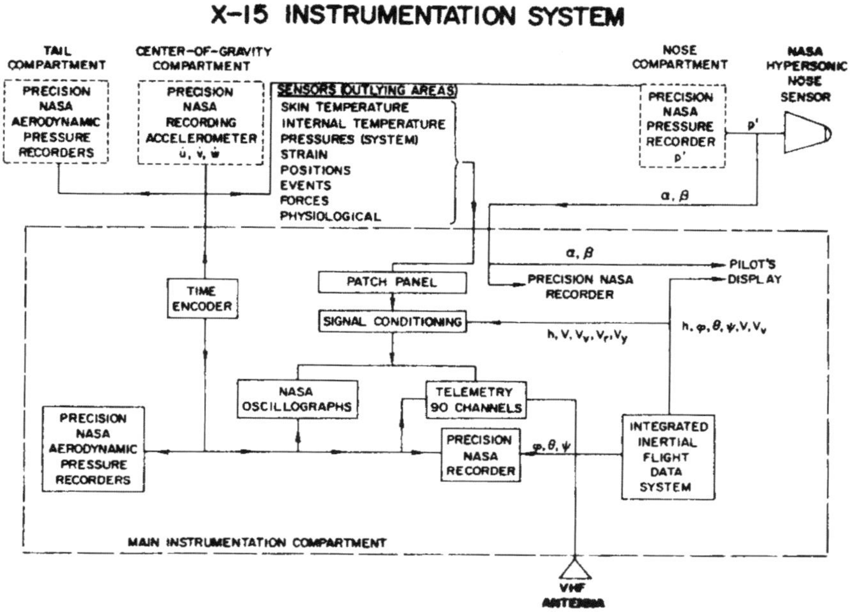

This block diagram shows the basic interrelationship of the various pieces of research instrumentation carried on the X-15. The exact instrumentation varied considerably between airplanes, and flight to flight. Late in the program the X-15-3 received a much more modern PCM telemetry system. (NASA)

it to appropriate signal conditioners, and then sent it to recording oscillographs and the telemetry set. The NACA-developed photo-oscillographs were capable of recording 36 channels each. Recording speeds could be varied from 0.25 inch per second to 4.0 inches per second, resulting in recording times ranging from 56 minutes to only 3.5 minutes using 70-foot film magazines. The photo-oscillographs used a blue-sensitive polyester-based thin film with the trade name Cronar®. A variety of 16-mm motion picture cameras photographed portions of the pilot's instrument panel, and the wings and empennage during flight.[10]

Recorder limitations restricted the number of installed sensors that could be recorded simultaneously. A 12-channel oscillograph recorded 40 thermocouples per channel at 1-second intervals, and four manometer-oscillographs recorded up to 96 pressure transducers. A NACA-designed aneroid-type 24-cell film-recording manometer similar to those used in previous flight programs recorded the surface pressures. Again, recorder limitations restricted the number of pressure measurements that could be recorded simultaneously. The exact data recorded often differed on each flight as researchers and engineers connected different sensors to the recorders and telemetry system. A single switch in the cockpit turned

10 Kenneth C. Sanderson, NASA technical memorandum X-56000, "The X-15 Flight Test Instrumentation," 21 April 1964, pp. 6-7. Cronar® film was first released in 1955 and is still used in various imaging and medical applications. The film is produced (and trademarked) by duPont Teijin Films.

on all of the recorders, and an event switch allowed the pilot to mark the recording when something significant occurred.[11]

Two separate cockpit instrument panels were supplied with each of the first two airplanes: one for the initial low-speed flights using the XLR11 engines and the nose-mounted flight-test boom, the other for hypersonic flights using the XLR99 engine and the ball nose. NASA significantly revised the instrument panel in the first two airplanes early in the flight program based on pilots' comments that the original panel was difficult to scan under all flight conditions, especially when they were wearing the MC-2 full-pressure suit. As initially completed, X-15-3 had an instrument panel identical to the XLR99 panels manufactured for the first two airplanes. However, when North American rebuilt the airplane following its XLR99 ground explosion, the Air Force decided to incorporate the Minneapolis-Honeywell MH-96 adaptive flight-control system, and this necessitated a unique instrument panel. NASA subsequently replaced this panel late in the flight program with a set of vertical-tape displays developed by Lear-Siegler. All of the instrument panels were in a constant state of flux as various switches and indicators were added to almost any available location in the cockpit to support the various experiments and data requirements for any given flight. Every attempt was made to keep the critical displays and switches in constant locations between the three airplanes (at least as much as possible given the radical difference in X-15-3), and twice the program created a "standard X-15" cockpit arrangement and brought the airplanes into compliance. This greatly eased the problems associated with keeping the simulator accurate, and made life much easier for the pilots and flight planners.[12]

Initially, the X-15s used a pulse-duration modulation (PDM) telemetry system that researchers considered state of the art when they selected it. However, the system was insufficient for many types of data that researchers wanted to view on the ground (particularly the biomedical parameters), and the AFFTC Human Factors Subcommittee requested the installation of a more sophisticated FM-FM telemetry system. Initially, the FRC objected to the proposed change because of the size and volume requirements of such a system. However, on 2 December 1960 Paul Bikle stated that he favored the installation of a FM-FM system if it fit into the space then used by the existing North American telemetry system. By then, the state of the art allowed the Air Force to purchase a 12-channel FM-FM system for use in the biomedical package. NASA subsequently installed this system in the X-15s as needed to support biomedical work, and the first flights took place in late 1961.[13]

In May 1967, NASA installed a modern pulse-code modulation (PCM) system in X-15-3. The first flight (3-58-87) for the new system was on 26 April 1967 with Bill Dana at the controls. By all accounts, the new system worked well and

11 North American report NA58-190, pp. II-2 through II-3. See also many of the weekly status reports from Paul Bikle that described the flight-by-flight changes in instrumentation.

12 Air Force flight handbook FHB-23-1, "Interim Flight Manual, USAF Series X-15 Aircraft," 18 March 1960; Air Force technical order 1X-15-1, "Utility Flight Manual, USAF Series X-15 Aircraft," 31 March 1965; North American report NA58-190, pp. II-2 through II-3; e-mail, Scott Crossfield to Dennis R. Jenkins, 28 May 2002.

13 Minutes of Meeting, X-15 Human Factors Subcommittee, 30 December 1960. In the files at the DFRC History Office. At the end of 1960 this subcommittee changed its name to the Bioastronautics Subcommittee because of "the obsolescence of the term human factors."

provided a great deal more bandwidth than the old PDM and FM-FM telemetry systems. It appears that NASA never updated the other two aircraft to PCM.[14]

BIOMEDICAL RESEARCH

One of the few areas of research that were handled almost exclusively by the Air Force was studying the physiological responses of the pilots to the demanding flight profiles required for high-performance aircraft. Although NASA monitored the results of the biomedical program, the Air Force was entirely responsible for the conduct of the research.

Before the beginning of the X-15 flight program, a Convair TF-102A (54-1354, subsequently redesignated JTF-102A) was modified to evaluate the new David Clark MC-2 full-pressure suit (and later the A/P22S-2). The David Clark Company had designed the MC-2 pressure suits with 24 electrical contact points to facilitate connections between the sensors and the telemetry system. The system monitored helmet pressure versus suit-pressure differential, cockpit pressure versus suit pressure differential, body surface temperatures, and electrocardiogram data. Beginning in December 1958, the Air Force used the JTF-102A to familiarize the X-15 pilots with the MC-2 pressure suit and to develop baseline physiological data for each of the pilots. Researchers also used the aircraft to evaluate additional physiological instrumentation and test the operational suitability of the MC-2 for future weapons systems (unrelated to the X-15). This initial JTF-102 test program lasted several months and eventually accumulated approximately 15 hours of flight time by pilots wearing the MC-2 ensemble, although the Air Force continued to use the JTF-102 through the end of the flight program.[15]

Instrumentation

When the Air Force approved the X-15 program in December 1954, the aviation medical community in the United States had already embarked on research into the physiological effects of weightlessness in anticipation of technological developments that would permit manned space flight. This research consisted largely of obtaining physiological measurements from human subjects while they flew Keplerian trajectories in a modified Lockheed F-94C Starfire and attempted to perform certain psychomotor tasks. The maximum duration of weightlessness in these early experiments was 30–40 seconds, and it was difficult to separate the subject's responses to the weightless state from his responses to the pre- and post-trajectory accelerations. Nausea and vomiting, for example, occurred in the majority of test subjects in these experiments, probably due to the relatively rapid

14 X-15 Status Report, Paul F. Bikle/FRC to J. Martin/NASA Headquarters, 5 May 1967, pp. 5-6; Vincent N. Capasso/X-15 project engineer, "X-15 Operations Flight Report for Flight 3-58-87," 3 May 1967; "X-15 Semi-Annual Status Report No. 7," 10 May 1967, p. 29.

15 Lieutenant Colonel Burt Rowen, "Human-Factors Support of the X-15 Program," *Air University Quarterly Review*, Air War College, vol. X, no. 4, winter 1958-59, pp. 31-39.

transitions between hypergravic and hypogravic states. Despite the amount of uncertainty surrounding the experiments, some medical researchers nevertheless concluded that weightlessness would induce nausea and vomiting in most people. The Air Force widely reported this conclusion, which greatly influenced several early manned space studies.[16]

Because the X-15 flight profiles would provide longer periods of weightlessness than were possible with lower-performance aircraft, acquiring physiological data became an early objective of the program. As North American finalized the X-15 configuration, there were additional reasons for monitoring biomedical data from a safety standpoint. Since the cockpit of the X-15 was engineered for a 3.5-psi differential between the inside of the cockpit and the outside atmosphere (or lack thereof), it was not considered feasible to use a breathable atmosphere. At sea level, oxygen accounts for approximately 20% of the normal atmospheric pressure of 14.7 psi. A breathable atmosphere therefore requires 20% of the normal 14.7 psi–about 3 psi of oxygen in the 3.5-psi cockpit.[17] Engineers considered the problems of combustion and fire associated with this 86% oxygen atmosphere to be insurmountable. As a result, North American pressurized the X-15 cockpit and ventilated the full-pressure suit with nitrogen, supplying breathing oxygen to the helmet area only. A neck seal (MC-2 suit) or a face seal (A/P22S-2 suit) separated the breathing space from the remainder of the suit. In order to prevent the leakage of nitrogen into the breathing space, technicians adjusted the breathing-oxygen regulator to deliver oxygen at a pressure 1 inch of water higher than the suit pressure.[18]

The maintenance of this helmet-suit pressure differential was vital, since otherwise the pilot could develop an insidious hypoxia that would lead to serious impairment or unconsciousness. The suit pressure regulator maintained 3.5 psi in the suit, the same pressure maintained in the cockpit. In the event of loss of cockpit pressure, the suit would automatically inflate, thus preventing a catastrophic decompression of the pilot. It was not particularly unusual for the suit to inflate partially as the X-15 cabin differential changed during exit or reentry. The suit/cabin-pressure differential provided an indication of the proper functioning of the suit and suit-pressure regulator, and the cabin-pressure regulator. In the event of failure of the suit regulator or breathing-oxygen regulator, the pilot could select the emergency oxygen system that pressurized both the suit and helmet with oxygen; this was the same emergency system used during ejection.[19]

North American designed and fabricated the original biomedical instrumentation system as part of the basic X-15 contract. The system monitored eight parameters, including the ECG, oxygen flow rate, helmet/suit-pressure differential, cabin/suit-pressure differential, and pilot skin temperature, from four locations. The helmet/suit-pressure differential also served as an excellent respirometer;

16 Lieutenant Colonel Harry R. Bratt, AFFTC technical report FTC-TR-65-24, "Biomedical Aspects of the X-15 Program, 1959-1964," August 1965, p. 1.

17 This is essentially the environment that later contributed to the deaths of three astronauts in the Apollo 1 fire–a pure oxygen atmosphere. Interestingly, the North American engineering team for the Apollo spacecraft included Harrison Storms and Charlie Feltz, the men who had been in charge of the X-15 program.

18 Rowen, "Human-Factors Support of the X-15 Program," pp. 31-39; Bratt, "Biomedical Aspects of the X-15 Program, 1959-1964," p. 2.

19 Ibid.

since the breathing space in the helmet was relatively small, the pilot's respiration produced pressure fluctuations that the 0–0.5-psi transducer could follow, providing a real-time indication of respiratory rate. The ECG, oxygen flow rate, and skin temperatures were recorded using an onboard oscillograph recorder. The two pressure differentials were sent to the ground via PDM telemetry and displayed in the control room, along with cabin pressure (obtained via vehicle, not biomedical, instrumentation) on a heated stylus stripchart recorder. The first physiological and environmental data recorded on the X-15 program were obtained during flight 1-6-11 on 6 May 1960 with Bob White at the controls.[20]

One of the first things that researchers assessed on the X-15 was whether the cockpit environment adequately protected the pilot. The requirement was to keep the pilot's skin temperature below 100°F even though the aircraft's outer skin could heat to nearly 1,000°F. In fact, researchers found that the cockpit outer wall was reaching 750°F, but the cockpit itself remained in a temperature range between 36°F and 81°F. The Air Force removed the skin-temperature sensors after the first round of flights when it became obvious that the mission was not exposing the pilot to any significant thermal stress.[21]

The original biomedical signal-conditioning package, mounted in the instrumentation compartment behind the cockpit, was 5 by 6.5 by 11.5 inches in exterior dimensions and weighed 11 pounds. In general, this instrumentation functioned well, but as researchers gained experience they corrected minor deficiencies and simplified the system. For example, the original ECG used five electrodes that simulated the clinical I, II, III, and V4 leads. However, since the ST segment and T(minus) wave changes are essentially uninterpretable under dynamic conditions, a one-channel ECG gave just as much information as a multi-channel system. Therefore, the ECG was simplified to a three-electrode configuration (two 0.75-inch-diameter stainless-steel screen mid-axillary leads and a reference electrode on the lower abdomen). A silicone potting compound ring surrounded the metal mesh electrode, a conductive paste assured good contact with the skin, and pressure-sensitive adhesive secured a plastic cap over each electrode to keep it in place. Beginning with flight 2-18-34 on 12 September 1961, the Air Force installed a Tabor Instruments amplifier on the ejection seat. Amplifying the signals closer to the pilot resulted in much better data.[22]

Researchers found the pilot's heart rate during flight usually increased from the normal 70–80 beats per minute to 140–150 per minute, but with no apparent physiological effect. One interesting finding, later confirmed on Mercury flights, was that the pilot's heart rate decreased during the period of zero g. The reduction, however, was not great (to about 130 beats per minute). The respiration rate followed similar trends, increasing to three or four times the resting rate, but

---

20 Harry R. Bratt and M. J. Kuramoto, "Biomedical Flight Data Collection," ISA Journal, October 1963, pp. 57-58; Bratt, "Biomedical Aspects of the X-15 Program, 1959-1964," p. 3.

21 Burt Rowen, Ralph N. Richardson, and Garrison P. Layton, Jr., "Bioastronautics Support of the X-15 Program," a paper in the *1961 Research Airplane Committee Report*, pp. 256-257. According to Harry R. Bratt at the AFFTC, this represented "the first in-flight physiological data [acquired] under operational flight conditions in the United States."

22 X-15 Status Report, Paul F. Bikle/FRC to H. Brown/NASA Headquarters, 2 October 1961, p. 4; Rowen et al., "Bioastronautics Support of the X-15 Program," p. 257; Bratt, "Biomedical Aspects of the X-15 Program, 1959-1964," p. 3. Axilla: of or relating to the armpit. The skin temperature sensors would make a return on later versions of the biomedical instrumentation.

researchers considered this less meaningful because talking influences the respiratory system and has a poor dynamic response rate in any case. On almost all flights, there was a large peak in respiration rate during the powered portion of the flight when the pilots tended to breathe rapidly and shallowly.[23]

During the initial phases of the flight program, researchers only installed the biomedical package in the X-15 on a non-interference basis. As a result, it frequently did not work correctly since technicians had not allocated sufficient time to its installation and checkout. Most of the difficulties were traced to shorts and broken wires. Although the biomedical team coordinated with the Air Force and NASA, the next flight frequently suffered the same problems. As a result, in early 1961 the Air Force and NASA assembled a dedicated team to work on biomedical issues, and the system became much more reliable.[24]

The researchers requested that the biomedical instrumentation package fly on all XLR99 flights that expanded the envelope. In a meeting held at the FRC on 2 December 1960, the Air Force and NASA agreed that the acquisition of physiological data was important from both a flight-safety and research perspective. However, NASA did not make the acquisition of biomedical data mandatory, mainly because it did not want to have to cancel a flight because the biomedical package failed.[25]

After Paul Bikle approved the concept of installing an FM-FM telemetry system dedicated to the biomedical package, the Air Force awarded a $79,000 contract to the Hughes Aircraft Company to develop and manufacture the system.[26] The system included an FM radio transmitter rather than a hardwire link to the aircraft telemetry transmitter. This was done to demonstrate the feasibility of the radio link in order to permit the mobility expected on future spacecraft. The final Bendix TATP-350 unit measured 9.30 by 3.95 by 0.70 inches and weighed 0.84 pound. The first unit was delivered in March 1962, and the third and final unit was delivered in July 1962. Researchers demonstrated the system during flights of the JTF-102A using MC-2 suits, and in an unusual test the system received a telemetered ECG from a free-falling parachutist.[27]

NASA installed the new FM-FM system in all three X-15s during the summer of 1962. This installation permitted the ECG to be telemetered and displayed in the control room along with the helmet/suit- and cabin/suit-pressure differentials, cabin pressure, and two axes of aircraft acceleration (vertical and longitudinal). The system multiplexed these signals onto a single FM channel and then displayed them on a six-channel Sanborn stripchart recorder in the control room.[28]

In 1962, the AFFTC began providing biomedical system expertise to the Dyna-Soar program. Because of severe space and weight limitations on the X-20,

---

23 Rowen et al., "Bioastronautics Support of the X-15 Program," pp. 258 and 264.

24 Minutes of Meeting, X-15 Human Factors Subcommittee, 30 December 1960. In the files at the DFRC History Office.

25 Ibid.

26 Air Force contract number AF04(611)6344.

27 Bratt and Kuramoto, "Biomedical Flight Data Collection," pp. 58-59; Bratt, "Biomedical Aspects of the X-15 Program, 1959-1964," p. 4.

28 Bratt, "Biomedical Aspects of the X-15 Program, 1959-1964," p. 3.

miniaturization was an absolute necessity. Based on its success in providing the X-15 FM-FM system, the Air Force awarded Hughes Aircraft a contract to fabricate two prototype signal-conditioning units designed around X-20 requirements. Researchers first used the system to monitor environmental and physiological data during dynamic simulations on the centrifuge at NADC Johnsville. When North American rebuilt X-15-2 into its advanced configuration, the company installed a Hughes signal-conditioning system to test the new system prior to its use on the X-20. After the cancellation of the Dyna-Soar program in December 1963, Hughes modified the design to incorporate interchangeable modules that could meet a variety of requirements. Hughes repackaged the system so that all of the modules were a common size and used identical connectors.[29]

The final package measured 4.0 by 3.5 by 0.7 inches and weighed only 0.6 pound. Like the earlier Hughes system, this package used an FM transmitter link to the aircraft telemetry system, although a hardwire link could also be used if needed. For X-15 use, the package provided the ECG, helmet/suit- and cabin/suit-pressure differentials, Korotkoff sounds, and partial pressure of oxygen in the breathing space. When required, researchers could substitute modules that provided the partial pressure of CO2 and an impedance pneumogram.[30]

During the summer of 1963, the Air Force again modified the biomedical instrumentation, this time by adding a blood-pressure monitoring system developed by the Air Force School of Aerospace Medicine at Brooks AFB, Texas. The system used an occlusive cuff crystal microphone to determine arterial pressure in the upper arm. An electro-pneumatic programmer that cycled once per minute automatically inflated the cuff. During deflation of the cuff, a microphone detected the Korotkoff sounds, and a display showed these sounds simultaneously with the cuff pressure trace and the ECG. The system could be turned on or off by the pilot and had a fail-safe feature that could dump the pressure in the cuff in the event of a power failure, preventing a tourniquet effect from the cuff. Surprisingly, the first few flights of the package did not yield meaningful blood-pressure information, since the pilot's pressures exceeded the maximum reading available on the instrumentation. The school modified the cuff inflation pressure to allow up to 240 millimeters of mercury to obtain useful systolic pressure end-points.[31]

The school had used the blood-pressure monitoring system for in-flight studies using conventional jet aircraft for some time, and it had been very reliable in service. However, the initial use in the X-15 was not completely satisfactory because of a generally inadequate signal-to-noise ratio. The X-15 environment proved to be particularly severe; the combination of frictional noise from the suit, vibration, acoustic noise, and pilot movement artifacts produced a high background noise

29 Bratt and Kuramoto, "Biomedical Flight Data Collection," pp. 60-61; Bratt, "Biomedical Aspects of the X-15 Program, 1959-1964," p. 3.

30 Bratt, "Biomedical Aspects of the X-15 Program, 1959-1964," p. 3.

31 Ibid, pp. 4-5, and 12. The Korotkoff sounds are audible vibrations generated by the turbulent flow of blood beyond an abrupt constriction in an artery, such as produced by an occlusive cuff on the upper arm. As the occlusive cuff pressure is lowered, the pressure at the first audible sound is taken as the systolic pressure (peak pressure at the passage of the pulse wave). The pressure at the last audible sound, or the point at which the amplitude and frequency of the sounds changes abruptly, is taken as the diastolic pressure (relaxation pressure between pulse waves).

and a low signal-to-noise ratio. Researchers experimented with several filters and amplifiers, and eventually found a satisfactory combination.[32]

In addition to the ECG and various cockpit and suit pressures and temperatures, the researchers added blood pressure, skin temperature (on the calf, abdomen, forearm, and axilla), respiratory rate, radiation, and partial pressures of oxygen and carbon dioxide in the helmet. A $47,000 Bendix Aviation mass spectrometer determined the partial pressure of oxygen, carbon dioxide, carbon monoxide, nitrogen, and water vapor.[33] A linear pneumotachometer provided by Spacelabs, Inc., under a $23,000 Air Force contract[34] furnished a rapid method for determining the total oxygen consumed by measuring changes in the pilot's breathing rate.[35]

As researchers evaluated the biomedical data during the flight program, it became apparent that the initial objective of obtaining data on the physiological response to weightlessness was not feasible using the X-15. The duration of weightlessness (3–4 minutes) was too short and the pilot's responses were conditioned by too many uncontrollable variables that occurred simultaneously for any conclusions to be made concerning the physiological response to weightlessness. In addition, the manned space programs initiated shortly after the X-15 began its flight program provided a much longer weightlessness duration without the attendant stresses of having to fly the airplane; this portion of the X-15 data was instantly obsolete. Nevertheless, the X-15 data provided researchers a unique opportunity to observe the basic physiological responses of pilots in manned vehicles flying exit and reentry profiles–something that Mercury did not, since the astronaut was simply along for the ride during those periods.[36]

Some Results

In mid-1965 the X-15 program was roughly three-quarters of the way through its eventual flight program, and flight surgeons at the AFFTC published a report on their findings to date. At the time, nine different pilots had flown the X-15 (Adams, Dana, and Knight had not yet flown); however, researchers only collected data from the six who had flown a sufficient number of flights to be statistically relevant to the analysis (omitting Armstrong, Petersen, and Thompson). The researchers noted that a "potentially very useful comparison of pilot performance and concurrent physiologic response is not possible because the X-15 flight test program is not structured as a psycho-physiological experiment. The aforementioned variability in flight profiles and unpredictable aircraft malfunctions makes possible only a general, qualitative comparison, rather than a specific, quantitative one."[37]

32 Ibid, p. 4. The Air Force and NASA both wanted a means to perform constant blood-pressure monitoring, but nobody could figure out an easy way to do it. The AFFTC did issue a contract to Spacelabs, Inc., in Van Nuys, CA, to study "a system for monitoring cardiovascular dynamics either through blood pressure or by use of physiological parameters having high predictive value." The results of the study indicated that pulse-wave velocity (PWV) had potential to provide the data, but researchers were not sure the results were interpretable in the clinical sense. Although studies continued, the technique was never used on the X-15.

33 Air Force contract number AF04(611)6347.

34 Air Force contract number AF04(611)6341.

35 Robert E. Hedblom and Burt Rowen, "Medical Monitoring of X-15 Pilots in Flight," a paper presented to the X-15 Human Factors Subcommittee on 30 December 1960. In the files at the DFRC History Office; Rowen, "Biomedical Monitoring of the X-15 Program," pp. 3-4.

36 Bratt, "Biomedical Aspects of the X-15 Program, 1959-1964," p. 2.

37 Ibid, p. 9.

It is important when considering the physiological data obtained during the X-15 program to keep in mind the conditions under which researchers collected the data. In addition to the normal variability of physiologic responses, no two X-15 flights were the same. Different flight profiles and random aircraft malfunctions varied the physiological and psychic stresses to which the pilots were exposed.[38]

During an altitude mission, immediately after launch, the X-15 rotated to a preplanned climb angle and accelerated at 3–3.5 g. The pilot experienced a front-to-back ("eyes-in") inertial force that increased the apparent weight of the body, particularly the chest area, and resulted in a prompt increase in respiratory rate that continued until the acceleration subsided. After approximately 40 seconds of acceleration, the pilot pushed over to a "zero-normal" acceleration. The pulse rate, which had been increasing up to and throughout the launch operation, tended to decline during this period. At engine burnout, approximately 80 seconds after launch, the longitudinal acceleration dropped abruptly to zero, followed by a variable period in which all accelerations were essentially zero. The pilot was in an essentially weightless state during this period and the respiration rate showed a prompt decline.[39]

Immediately after engine burnout, the pilot invariably immediately experienced an increased heart rate that tended to decrease during the zero-g period. The increased heart rate at this point was probably a psychic response to the abrupt transition from a hypergravic state (in the normal plane) to a hypogravic ("weightless") state. From this point to the landing phase, the pilot was busily engaged in usually complex flight maneuvers, including "accomplishing deliberate aircraft perturbations in roll, pitch, and yaw for the purpose of collecting stability and control information." Heart rates and respiratory rates tended to reflect the difficulties the pilot encountered in managing the flight.[40]

After the aircraft passed over the top of its trajectory and was descending at a steep angle, the pilot had to pull out of the dive into level flight. This pull-up generated a positive normal acceleration that the pilot experienced as increased body weight. At this point, the anti-g portion of the David Clark full-pressure suit activated to counteract these forces. Nevertheless, during this maneuver, the blood tended to pool in the lower parts of the body, the carotid arteries experienced decreased pressure, and the cardio-accelerator reflex produced a prompt increase in heart rate. The heart rate lowered as the accelerations decreased. The landing maneuver produced only mild accelerations, and the small increase in both heart rate and respiratory rate during this phase was entirely a psychic response to the task of accomplishing the landing. Since steady-state conditions existed for only a few seconds at a time during the brief 8–10-minute flights, physical and psychic stimuli were usually occurring concurrently and independently. This meant that "only the grossest correlation with heart rate and respiratory rate responses [could] be made."[41]

38 Ibid, p. 9.
39 Ibid, pp. 9-10.
40 Ibid, p. 10.
41 Ibid, pp. 10-11.

In most professions, including piloting, there is a general trend for heart rates and respiratory rates to decrease as an individual gains experience in performing a task. However, an analysis showed "no statistically significant difference" between early flights and later flights for each of the six pilots analyzed. Researchers believed a number of factors could explain this failure to adhere to the expected trend. The first, and probably most important, was that there were no "easy" X-15 flights. Trying to obtain the maximum amount of data on each flight kept the pilot very busy performing the required maneuvers at the proper time while maintaining the desired flight profile. This required intense concentration, and the pilot also had to monitor aircraft systems during this period.[42]

In psychological terms, the pilot had a fast-moving, intensive task to perform continuously during his 8–10-minute flight, plus a few minutes on each end. Added to this was the psychic stress of actual or potential system failures, which were not uncommon during the flight program. Another factor was the variation in flight profiles, which meant that the pilots had little or no opportunity to develop a routine for a familiar flight. Furthermore, there was often a considerable interval between flights flown by individual pilots. In the end, the researchers found that it was "not surprising that a rapid reduction in responsiveness" was not seen. The researchers found that, overall, "the spectrum of physiological response of the pilots to X-15 flights, in terms of heart rate, respiratory rate, blood pressure, and pulse pressure, has remained quite stable throughout the X-15 Program regardless of pilot experience level. This pattern of physiological response may be tentatively considered the norm for this type of operation."[43]

In the end, the X-15 program was both a contributor to and a recipient of biomedical instrumentation. It was the first program to generate meaningful requirements in airborne biotelemetry and was the impetus for the development of several pieces of instrumentation that later found their way into standard clinical practice. Although Mercury and Gemini gathered better data, the X-15 nevertheless contributed to the physiological database that helped establish baselines for future programs. However, perhaps the most significant contribution of the X-15 program from a biomedical perspective was "the unequivocal, and at times dramatic, demonstration of the capabilities of the human pilot in managing a vehicle and a flight profile from launch to landing, which is a true space flight in miniature."[44]

MH-96 ADAPTIVE CONTROL SYSTEM

Although it was an integral part of X-15-3, the Minneapolis-Honeywell MH-96 adaptive flight-control system was also an experiment and hence part of the research program. In 1956, researchers performing in-house studies at the Flight Control Laboratory of the Aeronautical Systems Division (ASD) at Wright-

42 Ibid, p. 11.

43 Ibid, p. 11 and 17.

44 Ibid, p. 16.

Patterson AFB determined that it was feasible to design a self-adaptive flight-control system. As the name implies, such a system automatically adapts itself to provide essentially constant damping in flight conditions of varying control-system effectiveness. In other words, a given movement of the control stick would always result in the same airplane response, regardless of how far the control surfaces had to move to accomplish the maneuver. At the time, most aircraft still had simple mechanical linkages to the flight controls, with manually set trim tabs. The new supersonic fighters had more sophisticated system that adjusted their gains as a function of measured and computed air data. However, these functions required extensive flight-testing to perfect, and generally resulted in complex and unreliable systems. Researchers expected that future vehicles would be operating in flight regimes where air data might not be available, and decided to develop a new approach. The Air Force awarded a number of study contracts in 1957 that led to flight-testing of a variety of adaptive concepts on several Lockheed F-94 Starfires by the Massachusetts Institute of Technology (MIT) and the Minneapolis-Honeywell Regulator Company. When government funding ended, Minneapolis-Honeywell continued its effort with a company-funded flight program using a McDonnell F-101A Voodoo. The Air Force subsequently provided limited funding for the F-101 trials, and future astronaut Virgil Grissom flew some of the evaluation flights.[45]

By 1958 the Flight Control Laboratory was convinced of the potential of self-adaptive techniques; however, the performance of the available aircraft was insufficient to test the concepts, particularly the first expected application in the Boeing X-20 Dyna-Soar orbital glider. The logical choice of test platforms was the X-15 because its flight profile was the closest approximation to the Dyna-Soar that was available. Unfortunately, the X-15 program was already in high gear and the Air Force was reluctant to delay the critical hypersonic testing planned for the three airplanes.[46]

Despite the lack of an available test platform, the Flight Control Laboratory continued with its development effort. The Air Force released invitations to bid in late 1958, evaluated proposals during early 1959, and awarded to contract to Minneapolis-Honeywell in June 1959. Although the primary purpose of the program was to test the self-adapting technique in a true aerospace environment, researchers also decided to evaluate several features that were recognized as desirable for any production system. These included dual redundancies for reliability, the integration of aerodynamic and ballistic control systems, rate-command control, and simple outer-loop hold modes for attitude and angle of attack. Within a few months, Honeywell flew the prototype MH-96 in the F-101A at Minneapolis and in the X-15 fixed-base simulator in Inglewood.[47]

The basic system consisted of an adaptive controller that contained the various electronic modules and redundant rate gyro packages (each containing three

45 Robert P. Johannes, Neil A. Armstrong, and Thomas C. Hays, "Development of X-15 Self-Adaptive Flight Control System," a paper in the *1961 Research Airplane Committee Report*, p. 183; David S. Ball, "In Search of X-15 No. 3," Quest, vol. 3, no. 1, spring 1994, p. 27.

46 Johannes et al., "Development of X-15 Self-Adaptive Flight Control System," p. 183. As originally delivered, X-15-3 had the same control system as the other two X-15s; the MH-96 was installed while it was being rebuilt following the ground explosion that destroyed the aft part of the airplane. It should be noted that all X-15-3 flights used the MH-96.

47 Ibid, pp. 183-184.

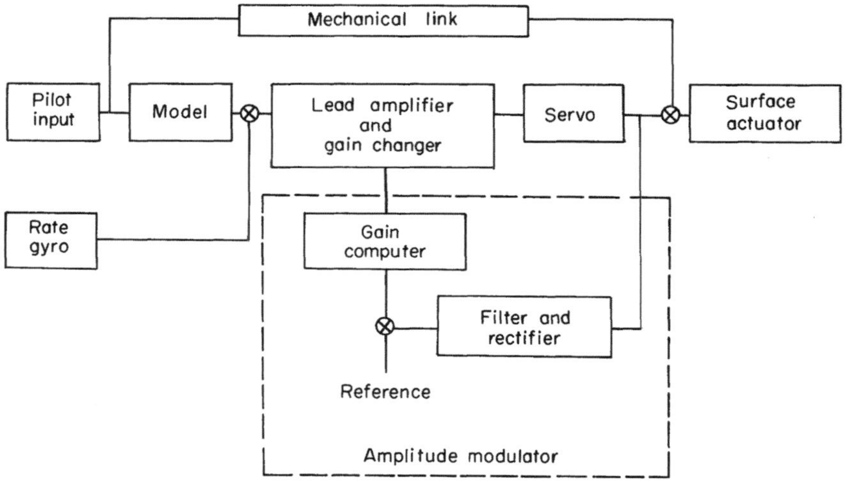

The MH-96 adaptive flight control system installed in X-15-3 was an early attempt at a fly-by-wire concept, although the linkages were still largely mechanical. Pilot inputs were compared to an ideal model running on a small computer, and the MH-96 commanded the control surfaces to move an appropriate amount based on speed, dynamic pressure, and other variables. The system generally worked well, and the MH-96 was used for all of the program's high-altitude flights since it provided better redundancy than the standard stability-augmentation system installed in the other two airplanes. (NASA)

rate gyros–one for each axis). The system also required an attitude reference (i.e., an inertial platform) and angle-of-attack and angle-of-sideslip information. The electronics modules were programmed with an ideal response rate (the "model") for the aircraft, and the MH-96 adjusted the damper gains automatically until the aircraft responded at the ideal rate. Essentially, the gain changer operated by monitoring the limit-cycle amplitude and adjusting the gain to maintain a constant amplitude. A tendency for the amplitude limit cycle to increase resulted in a gain reduction, whereas loss of the limit cycle initiated a gain increase. Lead compensation largely determined the limit-cycle frequency, which had to be higher than the aircraft's natural frequency but lower than its structural frequency. On the X-15, that worked out to about four cycles per second.[48]

Early on, this model presented a problem that was first seen in the X-15 simulator: a quick decrease in gain was necessitated by the rapid buildup of control surface effectiveness during reentry. Delays in the gain reduction, partly caused

48 Ibid, p. 184. On the X-15 the attitude reference was provided by the stable platform (and later the Honeywell IFDS); the alpha and beta information was provided by the ball nose. Bob Hoey provided this observation: "Limit cycle is a natural phenomena associated with high feedback gains. The frequency is primarily a function of the amount of friction and slop in the control linkage. Frequency CAN be tailored to some degree by lead compensation, as mentioned. The key point is that limit cycle occurs VERY, VERY close to the stability boundary of the system. Controlling the gain to a specified limit cycle amplitude is like walking on the edge of a cliff. The slightest miscue that might cause the gain to get a little too high can result in loss of stability and loss of control. We saw that on the simulator often when we were a little ham-fisted with the controls. Milt [Thompson] had a wild few seconds on one of his heating flights, and of course, Mike [Adams] really saw the dark side of the MH-96 system." Letter, Robert G. Hoey to Dennis R. Jenkins, 13 August 2002, with comments on a draft version of this manuscript.

by the lag in the mechanical control linkages, resulted in temporary oscillations as high as 3 degrees, peak to peak, at the servo. Modifications to the gain computer improved the situation but never eliminated it. However, since the X-20 was going to be a fly-by-wire vehicle, it would not have suffered from this problem. A different issue proved easier to resolve. A control problem existed whenever motions about one axis were coupled to another. To address this, the MH-96 contained cross-control circuitry that commanded a roll input proportional to the yaw rate in order to combat the unfavorably high negative dihedral effect demonstrated by the X-15 during wind-tunnel testing. This was, essentially, the MH-96 flying the beta-dot technique.[49]

When a ground test of the XLR99 severely damaged X-15-3, the Air Force agreed to modify the airplane to accommodate the prototype MH-96. The installation of the system into the airplane began in December 1960 and presented something of a challenge. Although it allowed the removal of the original Westinghouse stability augmentation system, the MH-96 required an even greater volume. NASA installed most of the system electronics on the lower instrument-elevator shelf, but this required a "rather extensive revision of the original instrument-recording configuration" since the data recorders normally occupied this area.[50]

One of the significant features of the MH-96 was its redundant design, which would become a feature of many future flight-control systems. This system was one of the first to experience the conflicting objectives of reliability and the ability to "fail safe". Extremely high reliability was a requirement due to the low probability of a successful reentry from high altitude without damping. The ability to fail safe was equally important since a large transient introduced in a high-dynamic-pressure region would result in the destruction of the vehicle. The MH-96 provided completely redundant damper channels, such that either channel could control the vehicle. The adaptive feature of the circuitry permitted one channel to be lost with little or no loss in system performance, since the remaining gain changer would attempt to provide the additional gain required to match the limit cycle. The gain computers were interlocked, when operative, to prevent overcritical gain following a limit-cycle circuit failure, and to provide the desired limiting effect for hard-over failures.[51]

In the case of a model or variable-gain amplifier failure, conventional monitor circuits would disengage either or both channels when required. Combined with the desire of NASA for increased system flexibility, this led to the addition of parallel fixed-gain channels with fail-safe passive circuitry. Since these channels operated simultaneously with the adaptive channels to avoid the time-lag penalties of switching, they effectively limited the minimum gain for adaptive operation. The fixed-gain circuits had to be sufficiently powerful for satisfactory emergency performance throughout the flight envelope, but below the critical level in the high-dynamic-pressure regions. A successful compromise was elusive, and X-15-3 spent most of its career with some restrictions on its flight envelope.[52]

49 Ibid, pp. 186-187; letter, Robert G. Hoey to Dennis R. Jenkins, 13 August 2002.

50 X-15 Status Report, Paul F. Bikle/FRC to H. Brown/NASA Headquarters, 15 December 1960, p. 5.

51 Johannes et al., "Development of X-15 Self-Adaptive Flight Control System," p. 188.

52 Ibid, p. 188.

As installed in X-15-3, the MH-96 provided stability augmentation in the pitch, roll, and yaw axes. The MH-96 controlled both the aero surfaces and the ballistic control system, blending the two as needed to achieve the desired control responses. In addition, autopilot modes provided control-stick steering, pitch and roll attitude hold, heading hold, and angle-of-attack hold. Pilot commands to the system were electrical signals proportional to the displacement of the right side controller or the center stick, and the rudder pedals. Nevertheless, the left-hand controller remained in the cockpit and the pilot could use it if desired to manually control the ballistic control thrusters. Provisions were also incorporated to electrically trim the pitch and roll axes. Trimming presented some problems of its own, mainly because the MH-96 was adapted to use existing X-15 hardware instead of its own newly developed hardware. In order to keep the pitch servos centered, the "trim follow-up" system used a low-rate trim motor to adjust the center point of the pilot's stick. This not only centered the servos, it also physically moved the stick. If the pilot was performing a precise task while the trim motor was moving the stick, it was easy to get out of phase with the trim motor and it would become saturated, oscillating at low amplitude all by itself at about 0.5 Hz, with no pilot input for several seconds. The pilots found this disconcerting.[53]

The reliability of the adaptive system on the X-15 was excellent, despite the fact that it was not a production system. The mean time between failures of the dampers was 360 hours, and the entire system averaged 200 hours, mainly because some servos were not redundant. The adaptive electronics had a failure time of 100,000 hours. All of these figures compared favorably with the 100 hours demonstrated by the Westinghouse SAS in the other two airplanes.[54]

The MH-96 experienced only two persistent failures during its 65 flights, and each involved only a single axis. It also experienced several other momentary failures on one or more axes; however, in each instance the adaptive mode reengaged following the transient disturbance. Milt Thompson observed that "it appears obvious that black-box technology is capable of providing a high degree of reliability through redundancy and improved electronic hardware." Thompson admitted, however, that the quality of maintenance and the caliber of technical support might have had something to do with the reliability.[55]

Although it was not known at the time, 50 years later almost all high-performance aircraft would use some sort of adaptive flight controls. Many of the problems would be eliminated, or at least minimized, by the incorporation of digital fly-by-wire technology, quick-acting hydraulic and electric actuators, and fast digital computers. Nevertheless, given the technology available at the time, the MH-96 was an important first step.

---

53 Minneapolis-Honeywell report MH-2373-TM1, "Operation and Maintenance Manual, MH-96 Flight Control System for the X-15 Aircraft, Volume V, System Description and Bench Test Procedure (Preliminary)," 31 May 1961, provided under Air Force contract number AF33(616)-6610, pp. 3-6; e-mail, Robert G. Hoey to Dennis R. Jenkins, 25 August 2002.

54 Johannes et al., "Development of X-15 Self-Adaptive Flight Control System," p. 188.

55 Milton O. Thompson and James R. Welsh, "Flight Test Experience with Adaptive Control Systems," a paper presented at the AGARD Guidance and Control and Flight Mechanics Panels, 3-5 September 1968, Oslo, Norway).

THE FOLLOW-ON PROGRAM

During the early 1960s, the X-15 was the only platform that could realistically carry a useful payload above the Earth's atmosphere and return. Researchers had been making use of various sounding rockets that provided relatively inexpensive access to the upper atmosphere from a variety of locations around the world. However, in general these rockets had very small payload capabilities, could not provide much in the way of power or controlled flight, and were usually not recoverable. On the other hand, although the X-15 was very limited in where it could fly (over southern California and Nevada), it could provide a fair amount of power, it was at least somewhat controllable for aiming purposes, and, most importantly, it was recoverable.

EXPERIMENT ACCOMMODATIONS

Although the X-15 provided some internal space for experiments, many researchers wanted specific views of the world outside or to have their experiments located away from the "noise" of the airplane. This gave rise to several modifications that ultimately affected all three X-15s.

Wing-Tip Pods

Several experiments (particularly a proposed micrometeorite collection system) had to be located outside the flow field of the X-15 and, it was hoped, outside the zone of contamination from the ballistic control-system thrusters. The most obvious location was the wing tips.

There were several preliminary designs for the wing-tip pods. Initially North American wanted to give the pods a rectangular cross-section, since it would be easier to package the various experiments in them. However, after considering both normal and potential emergency operations in terms of the effects of stability and control, heating, drag, and turbulence, the engineers decided to use circular-cross-section pods constructed of Inconel X. The pods were 8 inches in diameter and 58 inches long, and could weigh a maximum of 96.2 pounds, although the program exceeded this limit on numerous occasions.[56]

There was some initial discussion about equipping the pods with an emergency jettison system in case the micrometeorite collection system stuck open, but the final design had the collection equipment simply burning off during reentry if that occurred. Researchers tested the wing-tip pods in the supersonic and

56 Statement of Work for the Micrometeorite Collection experiment (#13). In the AFFTC Access to Space Office Project Files; "X-15 Semi-Annual Status Report No. 3," 1 December 1964, p. 5; X-15 Status Report, Paul F. Bikle/FRC to J. Martin/NASA Headquarters, 10 January 1967, p. 6. Interestingly, the weight of the pods often differed from side to side. For instance, on flight 3-57-86 the right pod weighed 72.4 pounds with the longitudinal center of gravity at 34% of the wing-tip chord, while the left pod weighed 97.2 pounds at 33% chord.

Wing tip pods were developed for X-15-1 to house experiments that needed to be located outside the flow field of the X-15. The pods were 8 inches in diameter, 58 inches long, and could weigh a maximum of 96.2 pounds. The first flight (1-50-79) with the pods was on 15 October 1964 with Jack McKay at the controls. Similar pods were later manufactured for X-15-3. (NASA)

hypersonic wind tunnels at the Jet Propulsion Laboratory (JPL) on 24–25 October 1962 to verify that they had no adverse effect on the airplane. On 5 November 1962, North American tested the configuration in its low-speed wind tunnel to verify that the landing characteristics were not affected. The test results proved to be satisfactory.[57]

Initially, North American manufactured a single set of the pods for X-15-1. NASA installed the modifications necessary to use the wing-tip pods, including the attachment points and wiring routed through the wing, on X-15-1 during March 1964. The first flight (1-50-79) with the pods was conducted on 15 October 1964 with Jack McKay at the controls. The flight reached Mach 4.56 and 84,900 feet, and the pods did not seem to have any major adverse effect on the handling of the airplane. Subsequently, however, some pilots complained that the pods seemed to introduce a buffet at load factors significantly below the previous buffet boundary. Researchers installed accelerometers in the pods to verify this, but failed to uncover any evidence of buffeting. However, the redistribution of mass due to the

57 Edwin W. Johnston, "Current and Advanced X-15," a paper presented at the Military Aircraft Systems and Technology Meeting, Washington, DC, 21-23 September 1964.

pod installation appeared to result in a 17-cps vibration tied to the wing-bending mode that was excited by some maneuvers and gusts, which likely explained what the pilots felt.[58]

Researchers subsequently determined that having only one set of pods put an unreasonable constraint on scheduling experiments, and decided to manufacture a second, easily removable set of pods. NASA modified the third airplane to carry wing-tip pods, and could switch the pods between X-15-1 and X-15-3 as needed to support the experiments and flight schedule. Frequently the rear compartment on one or both pods contained cameras aimed at various parts of the airplane (usually the ablative panels on the stabilizers) or one of the experiments in the tail-cone box. At some point, the pods on X-15-1 also received a small set of drag braces for unspecified reasons (probably an attempt to cure the vibration problem). Despite the original intent, and the best efforts of all involved, the wing-tip pods did not put the experiments outside the contamination zone of the ballistic control thrusters. Residue from the hydrogen peroxide would render several experiments useless. The pods were also inside the nose shock-wave interference zone at certain angles of attack, further hampering some experiments.[59]

Tail-Cone Box

Several experiments needed to view the sky behind the X-15, so NASA decided to build a "tail-cone box" behind the upper vertical stabilizer. In September 1961, NASA asked North American to investigate whether the installation would have an adverse effect on the aerodynamic stability of the airplane, and after a brief analysis the company concluded that none was expected. North American began detailed engineering for the box on 10 August 1962, with fabrication expected to take about two months. The program often referred to these as "boat-tail" boxes.[60]

The box, which was located immediately behind the upper speed brakes, was the same width as the vertical stabilizer, as high as the speed brakes, and protruded aft to the extreme rear of the fuselage. It was closed on the sides and top, but open on the back to allow the instruments to view behind the airplane. The Inconel X structure provided no environmental control (temperature or pressurization) for the experiments it housed. NASA procured two different types of boxes and installed them on the airplanes as needed to support the specific experiment manifested for a particular flight. The first style of box was equipped with a stabilized platform that allowed precise aiming of the experiment. This box could also be equipped with a removable panel that covered the rear opening during the exit phase to prevent exhaust efflux from contaminating the experiment. The

58 Trip report, Captain Hugh D. Clark/X-15 Project Office, describing a trip on 20-24 August 1962 to the FRC to discuss the Follow-On Experiments Program, report dated 17 September 1962. In the files of the Air Force Historical Research Agency; "X-15 Semi-Annual Status Report No. 3," 1 December 1964, p. 5; X-15 Status Report, Paul F. Bikle/FRC to J. Martin/NASA Headquarters, 1 December 1965, p. 4; Ronald S. Waite/X-15 Project Engineer, "X-15 Operations Flight Report for Flight 1-45-72," 15 April 1964.

59 "X-15 Semi-Annual Status Report No. 3," 1 December 1964, p. 5; X-15 Status Report, Paul F. Bikle/FRC to J. Martin/NASA Headquarters, 1 December 1965, p. 4.

60 Trip report, Captain Hugh D. Clark/X-15 Project Office, describing a trip on 20-24 August 1962 to the FRC to discuss the Follow-On Experiments Program, report dated 17 September 1962. In the files of the Air Force Historical Research Agency.

Several experiments needed to view the sky behind the X-15 so NASA decided to build a "tail-cone box" behind the upper vertical stabilizer. This is the Phase II MIT Apollo Horizon Experiment (#17) on X-15-1. NASA procured two different types of boxes and installed them on the airplanes as needed to support the specific experiment manifested for a particular flight. The first style of box was equipped with a stabilized platform that allowed precise aiming of the experiment. The second style was a "lightweight" box used for experiments that did not require the stabilized platform. Both X-15-1 and X-15-3 ultimately included the capability to carry the tail-cone box. The rebuilt X-15A-2 sported a very similar protuberance, but in this case, the box housed a spherical helium tank that provided additional pressurization gas for the propellant system. (NASA)

second style was a "lightweight" box used for experiments that did not require the stabilized platform. Both X-15-1 and X-15-3 ultimately included the capability to carry the tail-cone box. The rebuilt X-15A-2 sported a very similar protuberance, but in this case the box housed a spherical helium tank that provided additional pressurization gas for the propellant system.[61]

Skylight Compartment

Several of the proposed experiments needed to expose telescopes or other devices to the atmosphere at high altitudes. To accommodate this, North American devised the "skylight" modification, which consisted of a hatch that opened at high altitude to give a portion of the instrument compartment free access to the outside environment. This required the installation of pressure bulkheads around a portion of the instrument elevator to allow the lower portion of the instrument

---

61 Ibid.

compartment that held the data recorders to remain pressurized. The proposed hatch was 18 by 12 inches, with the 18-inch dimension lengthwise of the aircraft, and a pair of 6-inch-wide doors split along the centerline to open. Several of the experiments also required a stabilized platform inside the compartment. Since the University of Wisconsin had the first experiment that needed such a platform, NASA awarded the university a contract to develop a star-tracking, gyro-stabilized platform that would replace the upper portion of the instrumentation elevator. The university estimated that this platform could be available about six months after it received the go-ahead.[62]

Several of the proposed experiments needed to expose telescopes or other devices to the atmosphere at high altitudes. To accommodate this, North American devised the "Skylight" modification that consisted of a hatch that opened at high altitude to give a portion of the instrument compartment free access to the outside environment. A skylight compartment was installed during the rebuilding of X-15A-2 and, somewhat later, on X-15-1. This is the Ultraviolet Stellar Photography Experiment (#1) on X-15A-2. (NASA)

North American anticipated that it would take about two months to perform the modification to X-15-2, with most of that time required for rerouting wiring in the instrument compartment and building the pressure bulkheads. A change order was prepared for the modification and was awaiting approval when Jack McKay's landing accident damaged X-15-2 and put the entire effort on hold. The Air Force decided to press ahead with the skylight modification as part of rebuilding X-15-2 into the advanced configuration, but for some reason the actual implementation changed somewhat. The hatch became slightly larger, with two upward-opening

62 Ibid.

doors that were 20 inches long by 8.5 inches wide. Otherwise, the changes were mostly the same as originally conceived.[63]

North American also installed a similar but slightly smaller compartment on X-15-1 in early 1966 to carry the "Western Test Range (WTR) launch-monitoring" experiment (#20). Only the WTR and MIT experiments used this X-15-1 capability.[64]

Bug-Eye Camera Bays

As completed, each X-15 had four "bug-eye" structural camera bays, named for their odd shape.[65] Two were located on top of the fuselage just behind the cockpit, and two were under the center-of-gravity compartment. Originally, each bay held a 16-mm motion picture camera that ground personnel could aim through a limited field of view to observe the fuselage, wings, or stabilizers. Over the course of the program, researchers used these bays to house a variety of other equipment. Sometimes the bug-eye fairings above the fuselage provided a viewing port for the experiments or simply provided extra volume, and at other times flush plates covered the area. The lower bays were usually faired over later in the flight program with the internal space used by experiments or data recorders.

Although it was not truly an experiment, the National Geographic Society occasionally provided cameras for the upper bug-eye camera bays. Photos looking back at the vertical stabilizer of the X-15 with the curve of the Earth in the background are more often than not ones taken by the Society's cameras.[66]

Early Experiments

During the early portion of the flight program, various small experiments were piggybacked onto the airplanes as time and space permitted. These usually required little, if any, support from the airplane or pilot during the mission since the flight program was concentrating on acquiring aero-thermo and stability and control data.[67]

B-70 Signature Reduction

In what was perhaps the first true "follow-on" experiment, in 1961 researchers used X-15-2 to test a coating material designed to reduce the infrared emissions of the North American B-70 Valkyrie bomber. One of the complaints frequently voiced against the B-70 was that it was a large target. Although the concept of

---

63 Ibid; Elmor J. Adkins and Johnny G. Armstrong, "Development and Status of the X-15A-2 Airplane," a paper in the *Progress of the X-15 Research Airplane Program*, a compilation of the papers presented at the FRC, 7 October 1965, NASA publication SP-90 (Washington, DC: NASA, 1965), p. 105; Johnny G. Armstrong, AFFTC technology document FTC-TD-69-4, "Flight Planning and Conduct of the X-15A-2 Envelope Expansion Program, July 1969, p. 7.

64 X-15 Status Report, Paul F. Bikle/FRC to J. Martin/NASA Headquarters, 5 May 1967; Ronald S. Waite/X-15 Project Engineer, "X-15 Flight Operations report for Flight 1-63-104," 20 May 1966.

65 For some reason, the publicity mockups used by North American and the mockups used in several movies did not get the bug-eye shape correct. They used a rectangular protrusion, whereas the actual aircraft used a rounded shape.

66 See a variety of status reports (e.g., X-15 Status Report, Paul F. Bikle/FRC to H. Brown/NASA Headquarters, 15 January 1962, p. 3. In the files at the DFRC History Office).

67 Captain Ronald G. Boston, "The X-15's Role in Aerospace Progress," a paper prepared at the Department of History of the Air Force Academy, August 1978, p. 36.

"stealth" (a term not yet applied to the idea) was not far advanced in 1960, engineers at Lockheed and North American both understood that reducing the radar and infrared signatures of strategic aircraft would at least delay their detection by the enemy. For instance, Lockheed specifically intended the shape and materials of the A-12/SR-71 Blackbird to lower its radar signature. North American conducted several detailed studies into the infrared and radar signatures of the B-70 to provide a basis for reduction attempts.[68]

During the very short YB-70 development period, the Air Force directed North American to investigate ways to reduce the probability that the B-70 would be detected. The company made preliminary investigations into applying various radar absorbing materials to the airframe, particularly the insides of the air intakes. However, most of the North American effort appears to have concentrated on reducing the infrared signature of the aircraft. Exhausting cool air around the J93 engines was one means of reducing the infrared signature of the B-70.

As part of its research, North American developed a "finish system" (i.e., paint) that provided a low emittance at wavelengths used by Soviet infrared detecting devices, and allowed most of the excess heat to be radiated from the surface in wavelengths that were not normally under surveillance. The finish used a low-emittance basecoat with an organic topcoat that was transparent to energy in the 1–6-micron range. The topcoat was strangely opaque and highly emissive at wavelengths between 6 and 15 microns. This finish was relatively invisible to infrared detecting equipment and still allowed the skin to radiate excess heat overboard to maintain its structural integrity.[69]

North American developed two different coatings: one for areas that reached a maximum of 485°F, and the other for areas up to 630°F. The first (logically called Type I) consisted of Engelhard Industries' Hanovia ceramic metallic coating no. 2, applied 0.004 mils thick. Over this was applied a 1-mil-thick mixture of 85% Ferro Enamaling no. AL-8 Frit and 15% Hommel no. 5933 Frit. The Type II basecoat was a mixture of 40% Hanovia silver resinate and 60% Hanovia L.B. coating no. 6593 applied 0.004 mil thick. The topcoat was a mixture of 74% 3M Kel-F no. 2140, 24% 3M Kel-F no. 601, and 2% Al2O3 applied 1 mil thick. Most probably, the topcoats would have been opaque silver instead of the white finish used on the two XB-70A prototypes.[70]

The finish system was somewhat difficult to apply to an aircraft as large as the B-70, but the engineers expected that further development would yield improvements in the process. The most difficult problem was that the underlying surface had to be highly polished prior to applying the basecoat. In addition, the basecoat of both finishes had to cure at 750°F, while the topcoat of the Type II finish had to cure at 1,000°F (creating almost a ceramic finish). Accelerated environmental tests indicated that the surface would prove durable on the stainless-steel sections of the B-70, but its long-term adhesion to titanium appeared to be weak. Both fin-

68 See, for example, North American report NA-59-53-1, "Thermal Radiation Characteristics of the B-70 Weapon System," 31 July 1959 and North American report NA-59-1887, "B-70 Radar Cross Section, Infrared Radiation, and Infrared Countermeasures," 31 December 1959. Both originally classified Secret.

69 North American report NA61-295 "Development of Coating Materials for Reduction of the Infrared Emission of the YB-70 Air Vehicle," 16 March 1961.

70 Ibid.

ishes were relatively immune to exposure to hydraulic fluid, fuels, oils, and other substances encountered during operational service.[71]

To obtain real-world flight experience, the Type I coating was applied to one panel on the vertical stabilizer of X-15-2 in March 1961 and flown on flight 2-13-26 by Bob White. Since Inconel X is a type of stainless steel, the test was relatively representative of the proposed B-70 installation. No observable physical changes occurred during the Mach 4.43 flight, during which the aircraft's exterior reached 525°F, and the engineers made no attempt to measure the infrared qualities of the coating during this single flight. It was made simply to determine whether the coating would survive the aero-thermo environment, and appears to have been successful.[72]

Radiation Detection

The next experiment came from an unlikely source. On 3 August 1961, the Air Force Special Weapons Center at Kirtland AFB, New Mexico, delivered an ionizing radiation-detection device for use on the X-15. NASA installed the 10-pound package in the left side console of the cockpit outboard of the ejection seat. Actually, the first attempt to install the experiment failed because the space allocated in the cockpit was insufficient, but Kirtland soon repackaged it to fit.[73]

The experiment activated automatically when the pilot turned on the main instrumentation switch during flight. The package contained an ion chamber, two scintillators, a Geiger tube, and a self-contained multi-channel tape recorder. Different thicknesses of human-tissue-equivalent plastic encased the ion chamber and scintillators. With the Geiger tube acting as a count rate monitor, the detectors recorded radiation dose rates on the surface and at depths of 0.25 inch and 1.0 inch in the plastic between 1 millirad per hour and 100 millirads per hour.[74]

The first flight attempt was made on 29 September 1961, but this flight (1-A-38) aborted prior to launch due to a flight-control anomaly in the X-15. The package successfully flew on 4 October 1961 with Bob Rushworth at the controls of flight 1-23-39. The experiment subsequently flew several more times during late 1961. After each flight the taped data went to Kirtland for analysis, and the results ultimately showed that the pilots received essentially a normal background dosage of radiation (0.5 millirads per hour) during the flights. Since there seemed to be no cause for concern, the Air Force deleted the radiation detector from flights beginning in 1962.[75]

The program flew a different radiation experiment on X-15-2 from early 1961 until September 1963. The "Earth cosmic-ray albedo" experiment investigated the cosmic-ray environment at altitudes from 50,000 feet upward to determine the cosmic-ray environment in which future manned space vehicles would operate. The experiment consisted of placing small photographic emulsion stacks in up-

71 Ibid.

72 Ibid.

73 X-15 Status Reports, Paul F. Bikle/FRC to H. Brown/NASA Headquarters, 15 February 1961, p. 6.

74 Burt Rowen, Ralph N. Richardson, and Garrison P. Layton, Jr., "Bioastronautics Support of the X-15 Program," a paper in the *1961 Research Airplane Committee Report*, p. 259; Minutes of Meeting, X-15 Human Factors Subcommittee, 30 December 1960; "Advanced Development Plan for X-15 Research Aircraft, Advanced Technology Program 653A," 17 November 1961, p. 46. In the files at the AFFTC History Office.

75 Bratt, "Biomedical Aspects of the X-15 Program, 1959-1964," p. 16.

per and lower structural (i.e., bug-eye) camera bays to obtain information on the cosmic-ray albedo flux and spectrum, as well as the flux and spectra of electrons and protons leaking out of the Van Allen belts. The X-15-2 carried the stacks to high altitudes on as many flights as practical and placed no restrictions on the flight path or trajectory. The NB-52 carried similar stacks during the same flights to provide lower-altitude references. Researchers at the University of Miami and the University of California at Los Angeles and Berkeley analyzed the film from the stacks.[76]

In a very similar experiment, X-15-1 and X-15-2 carried two nuclear-emulsion cosmic-radiation measurement packages from the Goddard Space Flight Center on the aft ends of their side fairings to investigate the cosmic-radiation environment at extreme altitudes. These emulsion stacks were considerably larger than the Earth cosmic-ray albedo stacks and were located external to the airplane. Several flights carried the packages to altitudes above 150,000 feet. The packages required no special maneuvers and no servicing other than installation just prior to flight, and removal after landing.[77]

And a Couple More

Researchers considered X-ray photographs important for understanding the problems of the solar atmosphere, which led to the "X-ray mapping of the sun" experiment. Instruments on sounding rockets had obtained similar photographs of the sun, but the excessive motion of the vehicle had greatly complicated measurements. NASA installed a small pinhole camera in one of the upper bug-eye camera bays on the X-15 in January 1962. This experiment flew above 150,000 feet several times between March 1962 and September 1963.[78]

The "electron-distribution determination" experiment measured electron distribution in the upper atmosphere using radiofrequency techniques. These measurements of the ionosphere D-layer (often as low as 50 miles) were important for investigators seeking to gain a basic understanding of the ionosphere. Since the temporal variation of the electron distribution was important, a series of flights was desirable; however, there appears to be no record indicating that the experiment actually flew or acquired any useful data.[79]

76 "Advanced Development Plan for X-15 Research Aircraft, Advanced Technology Program 653A," pp. 45-46; X-15 Status Reports, Paul F. Bikle/FRC to H. Brown/NASA Headquarters, 1 August 1961, p. 4 and 1 September 1961, p. 4.

77 "Advanced Development Plan for X-15 Research Aircraft, Advanced Technology Program 653A," p. 46; X-15 Status Report, Paul F. Bikle/FRC to H. Brown/NASA Headquarters, 1 September 1961, p. 4. In the files at the DFRC History Office.

78 "Advanced Development Plan for X-15 Research Aircraft, Advanced Technology Program 653A," p. 46.

79 Ibid.

EARLY PLANNING

During the summer of 1961, the Air Force ASD and NASA Headquarters proposed a new initiative to use the X-15 to carry scientific experiments that were unforeseen when John Becker conceived the aircraft in 1954. For instance, researchers at the FRC wanted to use the X-15 to carry high-altitude experiments for the proposed Orbiting Astronomical Observatory, while others wanted to carry a hypersonic ramjet for air-breathing propulsion studies. Of particular interest was the ability of the X-15 to carry experiments above the attenuating effects of the atmosphere.[80]

On 15 August 1961, the Research Airplane Committee signed a memorandum of understanding (MoU) to form the X-15 Joint Program Coordinating Committee with Air Force and NASA representatives as cochairmen. The MoU included the following statements:[81]

> 1. The X-15 is a program of national importance undertaken in accordance with the terms of a Memorandum of Understanding dated 23 December 1954 among the Department of the Air Force, Department of the Navy, and the NACA (now the NASA). It is recognized that the X-15 flight research program will soon complete the initial phase of flight research.
> 2. It is necessary that an optimum follow-on research program be formulated to insure maximum benefit to the national objectives accrue from the research program.
> 3. An X-15 Joint Program Coordinating Committee with the NASA and USAF representatives in the role of co-chairman is hereby assigned the responsibility to formulate the optimum follow-on research program for the X-15. The program will be transmitted to the participating departments through normal channels and will be jointly reviewed by HQ [Headquarters] USAF and the NASA RAPL [Research Airplane Project Leader (Hartley Soulé)] prior to submittal to the Research Airplane Committee.
> 4. The X-15 Joint Program Coordinating Committee is recognized by the Research Airplane Committee as the focal point of the subject project for continuous evaluation and formulation of program objectives for approval of the Research Airplane Committee. The establishment of a Joint Program Coordinating Committee is not intended to change

80 James E. Love, "History and Development of the X-15 Research Aircraft," not dated, p. 23. In the files at the DFRC History Office.

81 MoU, "X-15 Flight Research Program, signed on 15 August 1961 by the Research Airplane Committee; letter, Hugh L. Dryden to Major General Marvin C. Demler, no subject (but referencing the MoU), 12 July 1961; "Advanced Development Plan for X-15 Research Aircraft, Advanced Technology Program 653A," pp. 2-3. At this point the Research Airplane Committee included Hugh L. Dryden from NASA, Major General Marvin C. Demler from the Air Force, and Rear Admiral John T. Hayward from the Navy.

> the functions or responsibility of the NASA FRC-AFFTC Flight Test Steering Committee [later called the X-15 Joint Operations Committee].

The initial cochairs of the X-15 Joint Program Coordinating Committee were Lieutenant Colonel E. F. Pezda, chief of the X-15 project office at the ASD, and Paul Bikle from the FRC. The committee held its first meeting on 23–25 August 1961, during which the scientific community suggested over 40 experiments as suitable candidates. Hartley Soulé and John Stack proposed separating the experiments into four groups.[82]

- Group I consisted of desirable experiments that did not require special aircraft modifications or special flight profiles. It was also initially limited to experiments that could be prepared within three to four months of approval.
- Group II consisted of experiments that required "appreciable aircraft modifications" or a relatively long lead time for preparation.
- Group III was a holding area for experiments that were not well defined.
- Group IV included experiments that supported other programs (such as the Dyna-Soar or Apollo).

By November 1961, a long list of possible experiments had been divided among the first three groups; the fourth group was not populated pending coordination with other programs. The X-15 Joint Program Coordinating Committee met four more times (9 May 1962, 7-8 January 1963, 18 September 1963, and 16 October 1963), and initially forwarded proposals for 28 experiments to the Research Airplane Committee for approval. The committee subsequently approved at least three other proposals for implementation, and it appears that several others were assigned experiment numbers; however, the nature or purpose of some of them is unknown.[83]

APPROVED TEST-BED EXPERIMENTS

The final name used by the FRC for the follow-on research program was "test-bed experiments," although the Research Airplane Committee and other sources continued to call it the "follow-on program." The effort was formally announced in a news release on 13 April 1962: "The hypersonic X-15 will become a 'service' airplane to carry out new experiments in aeronautical and space sciences, in a program planned to make use of its capabilities for extremely high

82 Memorandum, Homer Newell to Hugh L. Dryden, 18 December 1961, subject: X-15 follow-on program; memorandum, Paul F. Bikle to Hartley A. Soulé, undated (probably November 1961); "Advanced Development Plan for X-15 Research Aircraft, Advanced Technology Program 653A," pp. 2-3 and 45; Love, "History and Development of the X-15 Research Aircraft," p. 23; NASA news release 61-261; Linda Neuman Ezell, *NASA Historical Data Book Volume II: Programs and Projects 1958-1968*, NASA publication SP-4012 (Washington, DC, NASA, 1988), p. 507; System Package Program, System 653A, 18 May 1964, p. 1-3.

83 System Package Program, System 653A, pp. 6-37 through 6-48; NASA news release 62-98; X-15 news release 62-91; letter, Hugh L. Dryden to Lieutenant General James Ferguson, 15 July 1963; NASA news release 64-42.

speeds and altitudes beyond Earth's atmosphere. The new program adds at least 35 flights ... and may take two years to complete." John Stack and Hubert M. Drake announced that an ultraviolet stellar photography experiment from the Washburn Observatory at the University of Wisconsin would be the first.[84]

Experiment #1: Ultraviolet Stellar Photography

The NASA Office of Space Sciences sponsored experiment #1 to investigate the ultraviolet emissions of large, hot stars, and the properties of interstellar media. Researchers had already obtained limited data using sounding rockets, but desired additional data prior to the launch of the Orbiting Astronomical Observatory (OAO). The purpose of the experiment was to obtain measurements of the stellar brightness between 1,800 and 3,200 200 ångstroms (Å). The ozone layer blocks this spectrum from observation by ground-based instruments. Dr. Arthur D. Code and Dr. Theodore E. Houck from the Washburn Observatory at the University of Wisconsin designed the experiment.[85]

During December 1960, North American conducted a few runs in the fixed-base simulator to determine whether a pilot could fly the X-15 precisely enough to allow the experiment to collect useful data; the answer appeared to be yes. The simulations, however, pointed out the need for the reaction augmentation system, and were yet another driver to develop and install the system in the first two airplanes.[86]

Before the experiment began, researchers at the University of Wisconsin wanted to gather information on the ultraviolet intensity of the sky background. To accomplish this, they installed a photomultiplier in one of the upper bug-eye camera bays of X-15-1 in April 1962. The photomultiplier required power and the use of one recording channel, but little else in the way of support. The first flight of the instrument was made on 19 April 1962 (flight 1-26-46). Originally, the university planned to install the complete experiment in the skylight compartment of X-15-2 in August 1962, but scheduling priorities delayed this until December 1962. Unfortunately, Jack McKay's accident on flight 2-31-52 would postpone all future uses of X-15-2.[87]

Ultimately, the experiment consisted of an ultraviolet "star tracker" and horizon scanner installed on a stabilized platform in the skylight compartment on X-15A-2 after it was modified. The star tracker first flew on flight 2-33-56 and functioned properly in the caged mode. The next X-15A-2 flight repeated the same tests. Flight 2-35-60 was intended to check out an uncaged (i.e., free to

---

84 News release 62-91, "X-15 Assigned New Follow-On Research Role," 13 April 1962; System Package Program, System 653A, pp. 6-37 through 6-48; NASA news release 62-98; X-15 news release 62-91; letter, Hugh L. Dryden to Lieutenant General James Ferguson, 15 July 1963; NASA news release 64-42. At this point, the Research Airplane Committee consisted of Hugh L. Dryden, Major General Marvin C. Demler, and Vice Admiral William F. Raborn.

85 System Package Program, System 653A, p. 6-37; "X-15 Semi-Annual Status Report No. 1," October 1963, p. 34; "X-15 Semi-Annual Status Report No. 3," 1 December 1964, p. 16. The OAO was a series of four orbiting observatories launched between 1966 and 1972 by NASA to provide astronomical data in the ultraviolet and X-ray wavelengths normally filtered out by the Earth's atmosphere. Only two of the four launches were successful.

86 System Package Program, System 653A, p. 6-37; "X-15 Semi-Annual Status Report No. 1," October 1963, p. 34; "X-15 Semi-Annual Status Report No. 3," 1 December 1964, p. 16.

87 "Advanced Development Plan for X-15 Research Aircraft, Advanced Technology Program 653A," 17 November 1961, p. 47; X-15 Status Report, Paul F. Bikle/FRC to H. Brown/NASA Headquarters, 16 April 1962, p. 3.

move) stabilized platform without opening the skylight doors, but a blown fuse prevented this. The experiment was successfully checked out on the next two X-15A-2 flights.[88]

The experiment was carried on five additional flights (2-38-66 through 2-41-73); however, little usable star-tracking data were obtained because of problems in maintaining the precise attitudes required for the experiment. Nevertheless, data from flight 2-39-70 confirmed speculation that the sky background was somewhat brighter than originally expected. The brightness gave less contrast between the star or constellation and the sky, making acquisition and observation more difficult. After the last flight in this series, researchers temporarily discontinued the experiment because of the position of the desired stars during the winter in southern California. The position of the stars supported three additional flights (2-46-83 through 2-48-85) the following summer. All of these flights were successful and obtained good data.[89]

Researchers determined that the atmosphere above 45 miles did not absorb the light from stars of moderate or larger magnitude. During flight 2-47-84, the experiment successfully photographed the stars Eta Aurigae, Alpha Aurigae, and Rho Aurigae from altitudes above 246,000 feet, which were some of the first stellar ultraviolet images. In late 1966, NASA removed the experiment from X-15A-2 in preparation for its Mach 8 envelope-expansion program.[90]

Experiment #2: Ultraviolet Earth Background

The Air Force Geophysics Research Directorate sponsored experiment #2 to measure the total Earth background radiation (albedo) and horizon in support of designing missile-warning surveillance satellites. Researchers expected that the Earth's atmosphere would absorb most of the ultraviolet rays and thus appear very black to an ultraviolet sensor. Any missile rising from the surface of the Earth would show as a bright point of light in the ultraviolet, and thus could be easily detected. As originally envisioned, the experiment would use an array of spectrometers installed in the lower bug-eye camera bays. Researchers wanted to obtain data during each of the four seasons and at altitudes above 132,000 feet to be above the ozone ultraviolet absorption level, but otherwise did not require special flight considerations. The experiments would obtain spectral background data in the middle ultraviolet spectrum, high-angular-resolution data relative to the solar-blind ultraviolet horizon gradient, high-angular-resolution data in the solar-blind gradient near 3,100 Å, and vacuum ultraviolet background data. The

---

88 "X-15 Semi-Annual Status Report No. 1," October 1963, p. 34; "X-15 Semi-Annual Status Report No. 3," 1 December 1964, p. 16.

89 Johnny G. Armstrong, AFFTC technology document FTC-TD-69-4, "Flight Planning and Conduct of the X-15A-2 Envelope Expansion Program, July 1969, pp. 12 and 34.

90 X-15 Status Reports, Paul F. Bikle/FRC to J. Martin/NASA Headquarters, 9 July 1965, 1 April, and 8 August 1966; "X-15 Semi-Annual Status Report No. 6," 1 November 1966, p. 15; Captain Ronald G. Boston, "The X-15's Role in Aerospace Progress," a paper prepared at the Department of History of the Air Force Academy, August 1978, pp. 36-37; e-mail, Marilyn Meade/University of Wisconsin to Dennis R. Jenkins, 5 June 2002. Ms Meade indicated that the original X-15 film was reflown onboard Spacelab 1 during STS-9 on 28 November 1983 to commemorate the event.

experiment was scheduled to begin in late 1962, but was postponed almost a year because key Air Force personnel were busy with other projects.[91]

Researchers planned to fly the experiment on X-15-2, but a meeting on 17 September 1962 between Captain Hugh D. Clark and Captain James H. Smith from the ASD, and James E. Love and Lannie D. Webb from the FRC resulted in a decision to use X-15-3 instead. This decision also affected the ultraviolet exhaust-plume characteristics (#3) and infrared-exhaust-signature (#10) experiments.[92]

During the postponement, the Air Force briefly canceled the experiment due to a lack of funding, but ultimately reinstated it. The experiment required at least one flight in excess of 150,000 feet to calibrate the test package, and then six further flights to acquire data. The equipment consisted of a high-resolution Barnes ultraviolet scanning spectrometer and a solar-blind radiometer mounted on a stabilized platform in the tail-cone box on X-15-3. Mechanical problems with the experiment precluded any data collection through the end of 1963, and equipment and scheduling problems continued to conspire against the experiment until the Air Force finally canceled it in early 1965 without acquiring any useful data. Instead, researchers decided to concentrate their efforts on experiment #3, which used the same basic equipment aimed at a specific point behind the X-15 to measure its exhaust.[93]

Experiment #3: Ultraviolet Exhaust-Plume Characteristics

The ASD sponsored experiment #3 to measure the exhaust characteristics from a liquid-oxygen-ammonia rocket engine (the XLR99). It used the same basic equipment as experiment #2, without the stabilized platform. The first flight (3-41-64) was made on 23 April 1965 with Joe Engle at the controls. By the end of 1965, the high-resolution Barnes ultraviolet scanning spectrometer and solar-blind radiometer that had proved so troublesome on experiment #2 had successfully obtained good data. As a follow-up, researchers installed a Millikan dual-channel radiometer in X-15-3 during the weather down period at the beginning of 1966, and installed a vacuum ultraviolet spectrometer later in the year. The Millikan radiometer flew on flight 3-55-82 but froze due to a failed heater, and there is no record of it flying again. Similarly, no record exists of the spectrometer ever being flown.[94]

---

91 "Advanced Development Plan for X-15 Research Aircraft, Advanced Technology Program 653A," p. 48; Statement of work for the ultraviolet earth background experiment (#2).

92 Trip report, Captain Hugh D. Clark/X-15 Project Office, describing a trip on 20-24 August 1962 to the FRC to discuss the follow-on experiments program, report dated 17 September 1962. In the files of the Air Force Historical Research Agency; "X-15 Semi-Annual Status Report No. 1," October 1963, p. 35; "X-15 Semi-Annual Status Report No. 3," 1 December 1964, p. 16.

93 "X-15 Semi-Annual Status Report No. 1," October 1963, p. 35; "X-15 Semi-Annual Status Report No. 3," 1 December 1964, p. 16; X-15 Status Report, Paul F. Bikle/FRC to J. Martin/NASA Headquarters, 1 April 1966, p. 8.

94 Ibid; X-15 Status Reports, Paul F. Bikle/FRC to J. Martin/NASA Headquarters, 4 February 1965 and 1 April 1966; "X-15 Semi-Annual Status Report No. 6," 1 November 1966, p. 15. In the files at the DFRC History Office.

Experiment #4: Langley Horizon Definition

NASA Langley sponsored experiment #4 to examine the visible and far-infrared spectrum to determine whether certain horizon phenomena were sufficiently stable to serve as Apollo space-navigation references. Researchers made the first observations in November 1962 from the top of a 12,000-foot mountain using a simple photometer and several interference filters. The data indicated that the "stable phenomena" hypothesis appeared to be correct, but emphasized the need for observations made from outside the Earth's atmosphere using equipment that was more sophisticated. Researchers flew variations of the experiment on sounding rockets and the X-15.[95]

Researchers installed a radiometer in the tail-cone box of X-15-3 along with a 16-mm motion-picture camera pointing out the rear. The camera provided wide-angle coverage to check for clouds or haze during the data-gathering period. The radiometer included a motor-driven scan mirror that provided a 30-degree field of view, and reflected energy into a parabolic mirror that focused the energy on the detector. The radiation passed through an optical bandpass filter to select the appropriate spectral band. The angle of the scan mirror and the output of the detector were recorded on an FM-FM magnetic tape recorder.[96]

The experiment first flew on 2 May 1963 (flight 3-16-26) and made five additional flights during 1963. Three of these six flights provided meaningful data for the MIT-Apollo horizon photometer experiment (#17). Another successful flight (3-30-50) on 8 July 1964 investigated the near infrared in the 0.8–2.8-micron region. After the flight, the experiment returned to Langley for modifications, and was intended to fly at least three more times. In the end, only two additional flights were flown during 1965 (3-42-65 and 3-44-67), since the more sophisticated MIT experiment had already begun flying aboard X-15-1.

Langley was generally happy with the X-15 as an experiment platform: "Not only is the design of the experiment simplified because there are few restrictions due to size and weight limitations, but also the availability of standard X-15 attitude and position data are an important advantage ... the radiometer is reusable ... and good weather data is available." This was in contrast to sounding rockets that provided comparatively short flights, had minimal onboard instrumentation, and, of course, were not generally recoverable.[97]

This experiment provided the first infrared data gathered on the Earth's limb from above 30 miles. From these data, researchers modeled the horizon profile to an

---

95 Anthony Jalink, Jr., "Radiation Measurements of the Earth's Horizon," a paper in the *Progress of the X-15 Research Airplane Program*, a compilation of the papers presented at the FRC, 7 October 1965, NASA publication SP-90 (Washington, DC: NASA, 1965), p. 95; Carlton R. Gray, "An Horizon Definition Experiment," AIAA paper no. 69-869, presented at the AIAA Guidance, Control, and Flight Mechanics Conference, Princeton, NJ, 18-20 November 1969, p. 1. It is often difficult to differentiate this experiment from experiment #17 (MIT-Apollo Horizon Photometer) in the literature since both were commonly called "horizon definition" and used similar equipment.

96 "X-15 Semi-Annual Status Report No. 1," October 1963, p. 35; "X-15 Semi-Annual Status Report No. 3," 1 December 1964, p. 16. In the files at the DFRC History Office; Jalink, "Radiation Measurements of the Earth's Horizon," pp. 96-98.

97 "X-15 Semi-Annual Status Report No. 1," October 1963, p. 35; "X-15 Semi-Annual Status Report No. 3," 1 December 1964, p. 16; X-15 Status Report No. 66-4, Paul F. Bikle/FRC to J. Martin/NASA Headquarters, 1 April 1966, pp. 8-9; Jalink, "Radiation Measurements of the Earth's Horizon," pp. 98-99.

accuracy of 4 kilometers for use in attitude-referencing systems carried aboard early orbiting spacecraft.[98]

Experiment #5: Photo Optical Degradation

With the appearance of high-performance aircraft and missiles during the mid-1950s, designers began to be concerned with the effects of a turbulent boundary layer on the performance of optical equipment. As early as 1956, wind-tunnel researchers determined that the effects of a narrow beam of light through a turbulent boundary layer were a function of the free-stream Mach number and the density of the stream. The effects of this "light spreading" on the accuracy of star trackers were studied by Autonetics in 1957 and again by North American in connection with the B-70 program. Researchers observed the first actual effects of aerodynamics on aerial photography in 1957 when pictures taken from a McDonnell RF-101 Voodoo at Mach 1.4, viewed stereoscopically, provided a false evaluation of the terrain. This led the Army Corps of Engineers to award a contract to Vidya (a division of Itek Corporation) during 1959–1960 to develop a theory that explained the phenomena. The Navy sponsored similar work at MIT during 1959 to determine the degrading effects of turbulent flow on the resolving power of cameras.[99]

The ASD sponsored this experiment to determine the degradation of optical imagery caused by supersonic and hypersonic shock waves, boundary layers, and rapid frictional heating of the photographic window. Several different experimental packages were employed using well-instrumented aerial cameras and multiple boundary-layer rakes.[100]

Officially called the "induced turbulence experiment," this project sought "to determine the effects of aerodynamics associated with supersonic and hypersonic aircraft, typified by the X-15 research airplane, on the performance of (1) a high-acuity modern camera set, exemplified by the Fairchild KS-25, and (2) a cartographic camera, exemplified by the Fairchild KC-1." The cartographic aspects of the experiment were of interest to the U.S. Army Corps of Engineers, while the Air Force was interested in the possible effects on tactical and strategic aerial reconnaissance. This experiment also used data collected by the small two-camera package installed in X-15-2 as part of experiment #27.[101]

This program was very involved, and significantly funded under an Air Force contract to North American as part of Project 6220, Photographic Reconnaissance Technology. The Reconnaissance Division of the Air Force Avionics Laboratory under the direction of Donald I. Groening coordinated the experiments. Two principle subcontractors were also involved: Aeroflex Laboratories fabricated parts for the ART-15A stabilized mount, and Vidya provided theoretical and image

98 Boston, "The X-15's Role in Aerospace Progress," p. 38.

99 Air Force report AL-TR-64-328, "Influence of High-Speed Flight on Photography," 8 January 1965, pp. x111-xiv. In the AFFTC Access to Space Office Project Files.

100 Donald I. Groening, "Investigation of High-Speed High-Altitude Photography," a paper in the *Progress of the X-15 Research Airplane Program*, a compilation of the papers presented at the FRC, 7 October 1965, NASA publication SP-90 (Washington, DC: NASA, 1965), p. 85.

101 "Influence of High-Speed Flight on Photography," p. xiii; Boston, "The X-15's Role in Aerospace Progress," p. 42.

analysis. Fairchild Camera and Instrument Corporation provided the KS-25 camera under a separate Air Force contract. The Hycon Manufacturing Company provided the camera lens and conducted resolution testing, and the Cornell Aeronautical Laboratory assisted in determining the final target design.[102]

Phase I

The Army Corps of Engineers and the ASD jointly sponsored Phase I. The initial requirement was for three separate flight profiles: high-speed, high-altitude, and one that mimicked the Mach 3 B-70 bomber. The exact profiles were important because the launch lakes had to be established well in advance of the flights so that the Air Force could erect 6 to 10 photo targets along the flight path. This involved removing yet more land from the public domain. The B-70 profile placed another constraint on the program because it required flying the XLR99 at 40% thrust, and the early engines were incapable of doing this reliably. There was also a desire to photograph the same targets during Phase II.[103]

The launch lakes were Delamar and Smith Ranch. The targets would be located along the flight path from Delamar to Edwards with single three-bar targets located near Pahrump and Indian Springs in Nevada, and two sets of three targets straddling the flight path at Pilot Knob and Cuddeback in California. The single target at Pahrump determined the performance of the camera primarily at the maximum altitude point on the high-altitude missions, while the single target at Indian Springs determined performance at the maximum speed point on the high-speed profile. Triple targets at Pilot Knob and Cuddeback allowed for accumulated navigation errors and measured performance at high-supersonic speeds. The Pilot Knob targets also measured the camera performance at the point of reentry from the high-altitude profile. Each target was a collection of white stripes of different widths on a black background (a standard Mil-Std-150A photo-calibration target pattern) with an additional large contract patch and two sharp edges normal to each other to determine the atmospheric attenuation and edge response. The Air Force called this the Delamar camera range.[104]

A photometric van from the Scripps Institute of Oceanography at the University of California was usually set up at the Pahrump site. This van had three photometers that measured the total sky radiance, solar radiance, and radiance of the surface of the target. Researchers located meteorological instrumentation near each target to provide compensation data for the analysis, and the Air Force launched standard radiosondes to support the experiment.[105]

The X-15 package for the cartographic program contained a KC-1 camera, an ART-15A stabilized mount, and photometric and environmental instrumentation to measure the conditions that prevailed during the time of the experiment. The KC-1 had been modified with a GEOCON I lens designed by Dr. J. Baker

---

102 Air Force contract number AF33(600)-40765; "Influence of High-Speed Flight on Photography," p. i; Ronald S. Waite/X-15 project engineer, "X-15 Operations Flight Report for Flight 1-39-63," 5 November 1963.

103 Trip Report, Captain Hugh D. Clark/X-15 Project Office, describing a trip on 20-24 August 1962 to the FRC to discuss the follow-on experiments program, report dated 17 September 1962. In the files of the Air Force Historical Research Agency.

104 "Influence of High-Speed Flight on Photography," pp. 7-9.

105 Ibid, p. 23.

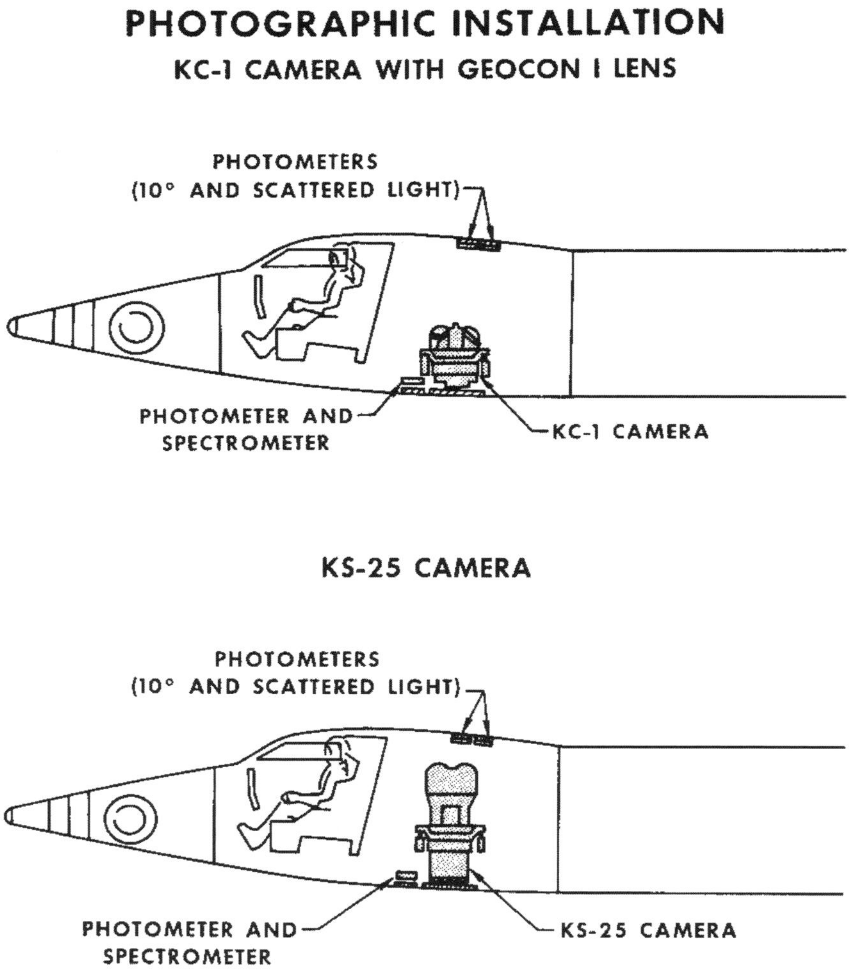

The Photo Optical Degradation Experiment (#5) was used to determine the degradation of optical imagery caused by supersonic and hypersonic shock waves, boundary layers, and rapid frictional heating of the photographic window. Several different experimental packages were employed using well-instrumented aerial cameras and multiple boundary-layer rakes. Two different camera systems were installed in the X-15 for the experiment. (NASA)

of Spica, Incorporated, to combine low distortion with relatively high acuity, and was adapted for operation at high altitude. The experiment package, minus the camera, weighed approximately 156 pounds. The KC-1 camera and lens added another 85–90 pounds depending on the film load, and occupied a space about 16 inches long by 18 inches wide by 21 inches high at the bottom of the instrument compartment. The GEOCON I low-distortion mapping lens had a focal length of 6 inches and a relative aperture of f/5.6, and could provide a resolution of 37 lines per millimeter on Super-XX film. North American modified X-15-1 to accept a KC-1 camera, including modification of the ART-15 mount and the addition of an 18-inch-diameter window that was 1.5 inches thick in the bottom of the instrument compartment. The film was nominally 9 by 9 inches, and 390 feet of it were stored in the magazine.[106]

Bob Rushworth flew the first flight (1-33-54) with the KC-1 on 11 April 1963 and NASA shipped the exposed film to Westover AFB in Massachusetts for processing. The last of six flights (1-38-81) was made on 18 July 1963, again with Rushworth as the pilot. The majority of the detailed results are still classified, but a general overview is given in the Phase II discussion.[107]

Phase II

The Phase II experiment involved six data-gathering flights using X-15-1 beginning with flight 1-42-67 on 5 December 1963, again with Rushworth as the pilot. As it happened, this proved to the fastest flight by a basic X-15, reaching Mach 6.06. Jack McKay flew the last flight (1-49-77) of the experiment on 30 June 1964. Three checkout flights (1-39-62 through 1-41-65) had preceded the data-gathering flights.[108]

The purpose of the experiment was to obtain quantitative data to determine the effects of aero-thermo distortions associated with vehicles flying at hypersonic speeds and extreme altitudes. Researchers believed the results were directly applicable to the Lockheed A-12/SR-71 and North American B-70/RS-70 programs, and to "future hypersonic reconnaissance systems." The Air Force conducted similar experiments (albeit at much lower speeds) using Martin RB-57D aircraft and high-altitude balloons.[109]

The high-acuity experiment package was somewhat more sophisticated than the one flown during Phase I, replacing the original KC-1 camera with a more sensitive KS-25. In addition to the new camera on the same ART-15A stabilized mount, researchers installed a small analog computer that collected signals from the X-15 stable platform to use for image-motion compensation and instrumentation to monitor the mechanical and optical performance of equipment. Seven downward-looking photometers measured the spectral changes in light with respect to altitude and provided a signal to the automatic exposure control system on the KS-25. Two additional upward-looking photometers monitored the amount of visible light remaining in the upper atmosphere. Instrumentation provided a continuous record of the temperature on the inner and outer surfaces of the photographic window. A multiple-pickup boundary-layer rake determined whether the boundary layer was laminar or turbulent and monitored its thickness for subsequent comparison with

106 Ibid, pp. 8, 11-17, and 27; Statement of work for the induced turbulence experiments (#5 and #6). In the AFFTC Access to Space Office Project Files. The X-15 modifications were performed under ECP X-15-155.

107 "Influence of High-Speed Flight on Photography," pp. 8, 11-17, and 27.

108 "X-15 Semi-Annual Status Report No. 1," October 1963, p. 33; "X-15 Semi-Annual Status Report No. 3," 1 December 1964, p. 16.

109 "Influence of High-Speed Flight on Photography," p. iii; "X-15 Semi-Annual Status Report No. 1," October 1963, p. 41; "X-15 Semi-Annual Status Report No. 3," 1 December 1964, p. 20.

photographic quality. A display of delta cross-range using inertial system outputs in the cockpit center pedestal assisted the pilot in maintaining the correct course.[110]

The KS-25 and its additional electronics weighed 325 pounds in addition to the 156-pound experiment support package from the earlier tests. The KC-25 was much larger than the earlier KC-1, occupying a volume approximately 13 inches long, 10 inches wide, and 43 inches high; this camera took up the entire height of the instrument compartment. Again, Dr. J. Baker of Spica built a special lens that had a focal length of 24 inches and a relative aperture of f/4, and could provide a resolution of 70–90 lines per millimeter on Super-XX film. The film was nominally 4.5 by 4.5 inches and 250 feet of it were stored in the magazine. The camera had to undergo several modifications to adapt it to the X-15 environment. The automatic focus control was disabled since its time range was not compatible with the speed of the X-15, and the automatic exposure control was modified to fix the lens at f/4 (instead of varying it between f/4 and f/16). After it was modified, the Air Force tested the camera in a centrifuge at the Rocket Propulsion Laboratory at Edwards to determine the effects of large acceleration on its electromechanical properties.[111]

The X-15 flew both high-speed and high-altitude flights with the experiment, and the Air Force analyzed the photographs to determine the influence of the hypersonic flight environment on the degradation of image quality. Researchers deemed the image quality from four particular flights (1-42-67, 1-45-72, 1-46-73, and 1-47-74) to be the best, and used these data for the analysis. These flights varied in altitude from 101,000 feet (three flights) to 175,000 feet (1-46-73) and in speed from Mach 5.01 (1-46-73) to Mach 6.06 (1-42-67). NASA returned the experiment to the vendor for repair after it malfunctioned prior to launch on abort 1-A-68, and reinstalled it in time for flight 1-45-72. In addition to the support used in Phase I of this experiment, Phase II also used a Boeing RB-47 Stratojet equipped to photograph the same targets just before and after the X-15 flights, providing researchers with a known reference.[112]

Researchers performed a laboratory analysis on the film to determine the extent of the deleterious effects of the flight conditions on the optical performance of the camera system. They determined the resolution for those frames that contained images of the three-bar resolving power targets. They then used these readings to check the values of resolution obtained by making microdensitometer traces of edges appearing in the photographs, converting these edge traces to transfer functions, and finding the intersection of these with the film threshold to estimate system resolution and determine the degradation in optical performance. The resolution ranged from less than 11 to greater than 60 lines per millimeter for a lens-emulsion combination whose low-contrast performance was between 80 and 90 lines under laboratory conditions.[113]

---

110 Groening, "Investigation of High-Speed High-Altitude Photography," pp. 85-86.

111 "Influence of High-Speed Flight on Photography," pp. xiv and 11-21.

112 Ronald S. Waite/X-15 project engineer, "X-15 Operations Flight Report for Flight 1-43-69," 22 January 1964; Ronald S. Waite/X-15 project engineer, "X-15 Operations Flight Report for Flight 1-44-70," 4 April 1964; "Influence of High-Speed Flight on Photography," pp. xv and 27.

113 "Influence of High-Speed Flight on Photography," p. xv.

Regardless of the technical considerations, the photography proved to be rather spectacular. On each flight the camera exposed a frame with the X-15 still attached to the NB-52 to use as a reference. This frame almost always had a resolution of over 80 lines per millimeter. On one flight the X-15 photographed the Indian Springs target while at Mach 5.47 and 101,400 feet, when the temperatures on the camera window were –4 degrees on the inner surface and +287°F on the outer surface. The resolution of the photograph was 60 lines per millimeter.[114]

Other examples included a photograph of Indian Springs AFB taken at Mach 5.43 and 120,000 feet, with inner and outer window temperatures of –1°F and +321°F, respectively. Three aircraft parked on the ramp of the base were readily identifiable. Another photo taken at Mach 4.37 and 169,600 feet also had a 60-line resolution. Researchers determined from these tests that the photographic quality obtained at high speeds and altitudes was acceptable. Researchers also performed a subjective analysis of the image quality for the bulk of the photographs in an effort to find some correlation between image quality and certain data from the flight environment. However, they could not establish any direct relationship.[115]

In the latter part of Phase II, researchers also tested several experimental near-infrared color films for the first time in flight. Various reports indicate that the X-15 flights led directly to the use of near-infrared color film during the conflict in Southeast Asia (the heat-sensitive colored emulsions showed enemy activity under the dense jungle canopy). Researchers soon adopted similar techniques for Earth-resource photography.[116]

Conclusions

The experiment had its share of problems. In addition to the accumulated navigation errors experienced on most flights that often precluded directly overflying the targets, numerous equipment malfunctions plagued the experiment. For instance, both the KC-l and KS-25 incorporated a vacuum system that used a sense line routed from the experiment to ambient pressure in the aircraft's liquid-nitrogen bay. Sporadic malfunctions occurred that resulted in loss of vacuum and, hence, loss of data. A survey of six flights showed that three of them experienced problems with the vacuum system.[117]

The researchers did not believe the experiment was particularly conclusive, since there were many unanswered questions. For instance, researchers found isolated instances of high-quality images being obtained at speeds between Mach 2.5 and 6 at altitudes of 55,000–100,000 feet. However, they also noted nonperiodic image smears that evidently arose from image motion that was not accounted for in the flight data by vibration, aircraft motion, or stabilizer-mount movements. This behavior limited the analysis of the experimental results. Still, researchers concluded that the distortion of the quartz window due to thermal effects had a negligible effect on resolution, and that scattering from the turbulent boundary layer was not severe and its optical effects were slight in any case.[118]

---

114 Groening, "Investigation of High-Speed High-Altitude Photography," pp. 86-87.

115 Ibid, pp. 87-88.

116 Boston, "The X-15's Role in Aerospace Progress," pp. 42-43.

117 Ronald S. Waite/X-15 project engineer, "X-15 Operations Flight Report for Flight 1-38-61," 30 July 1963.

118 "Influence of High-Speed Flight on Photography," pp. xv-xvi.

It was also determined that the mathematical model used to predict the optical performance gave good agreement with the measured performance, and that further improvements in the method could not be made using the results of these X-15 flights. Like Phase I, the detailed results of Phase II remain classified.[119]

However, it is likely that the results of this experiment are no longer terribly applicable. Although the 3-arc-second cameras tested on the X-15 apparently showed a negligible impact from the hypersonic aero-thermo environment, the increased sensitivity of the more-modern 0.5-arc-second (or better) cameras may well be subject to significant degradation from shock waves and boundary-layer flow.

Experiment #6: Earth Atmospheric Degradation Effects

The Air Force combined experiment #6, originally known as the "environmental effects on optical measurements" experiment, with experiment #5.[120]

Experiment #7: Electric Side-Stick Controller

The ASD and FRC jointly sponsored this experiment to address pilots' complaints about the feel of the side-stick controllers in the X-15. Side-stick controllers were of interest because of the relatively small cockpit space they required and the better support they provided for the pilot's arm under accelerated flight conditions. Pilots criticized the side stick in the X-15 because of the adverse feel characteristics caused by connecting it mechanically to the center stick and the power actuators that moved the control surfaces. As in the much-later F-16, there was no mechanical linkage between the electric side stick and the flight-control system, and the electric side-stick would have transmitted instructions to the MH-96 adaptive control system to fly the airplane. In addition to providing a better control system for the X-15, the electric side-stick program would have provided experience applicable to the Dyna-Soar. By the end of 1962, North American had begun flight-testing a modified F-100C equipped with an electric side stick, but these tests were not completely successful. The Air Force put plans to install the electric side stick in the X-15 fixed-base simulator on hold, and then canceled the experiment at the end of 1963 when the Dyna-Soar program abruptly ended. NASA never installed the electric side stick in X-15-3.[121]

Experiment #8: Detachable High-Temperature Leading Edge

The ASD and FRC sponsored experiment #8 to look at various leading-edge concepts suitable for use on future high-speed vehicles. Researchers wanted to evaluate four concepts: 1) a segmented leading edge that allowed thermal ex-

119 "Influence of High-Speed Flight on Photography," pp. xv-xvi; X-15 Status Report, Paul F. Bikle/FRC to J. Martin/NASA Headquarters, 1 April 1966, p. 9.

120 "X-15 Semi-Annual Status Report No. 3," 1 December 1964, p. 16.

121 "Advanced Development Plan for X-15 Research Aircraft, Advanced Technology Program 653A," 17 November 1961, p. 51; Trip report, Captain Hugh D. Clark/X-15 project office, describing a trip on 20-24 August 1962 to the FRC to discuss the follow-on experiments program, report dated 17 September 1962. In the files of the Air Force Historical Research Agency; "X-15 Semi-Annual Status Report No. 3," 1 December 1964, p. 16.

pansion in a number of segments to occur away from the primary restraint; 2) a thin-skin, refractory-metal concept that relied on a low coefficient of expansion to minimize thermal stresses; 3) a prestressed leading edge that used a mechanically or thermally applied prestress system; and 4) a nonmetallic leading edge that contained an ablative material (much like North American's X-15 proposal).[122]

The original X-15 wing and empennage leading edges used a round profile to minimize the effects of heating. NASA (particularly Ames) had wanted removable wing leading edges to allow different designs to be tested during the flight program, but these disappeared early in the development period. After the basic envelope expansion was completed, various researchers in the Air Force and NASA became interested in reviving the idea. Since replacing the wing leading edge would have required an extensive wing redesign, researchers decided to find an alternate way. The selected method was to modify a ventral rudder to accommodate leading edges manufactured from René 41 and tantalum, and the modified rudders were ready for flight in mid-1966. However, it is unlikely that they ever flew, given that X-15A-2 was the only aircraft to fly with the ventral rudder during the time the modified units were available.[123]

Sharp-leading-edge studies that were intended to evaluate various heating theories were also part of this experiment. The standard X-15 rudder had a leading-edge radius of 0.5 inch over the very forward 0.6 inch of chord. The sharp-leading-edge modification extended the leading edge of the dorsal rudder 5.16 inches forward, resulting in an overall chord of 9.00 feet. This sharp 347-stainless-steel leading edge had a radius of only 0.015 inch at the tip, and essentially had a knife-edge shape. To ensure turbulent flow along one side of the rudder, researchers placed boundary-layer trips consisting of spot welds 0.125 inch in diameter and 0.020 inch high on the right side approximately 5 inches from the leading edge.[124]

To gather data on flights with the sharp rudder, researchers mounted an Inconel X shear-layer rake impact probe on the left side of the sharp-leading-edge rudder 27 inches aft of the leading edge and 12 inches from the top. Eleven 30-gage chromel-alumel thermocouples were spot-welded to the inside surface of the skin, equally spaced chord-wise on the right side of the rudder 22 inches from the top. NASA installed six 0.25-inch-diameter pressure orifices near the thermocouples and connected the surface orifices and impact probes to standard NACA manometers in the side fairing of the fuselage. Similar instrumentation on a blunt-leading-edge rudder on X-15-2 collected baseline data; however, in this case the impact probe was on the right side 95 inches from the front of leading edge and 22 inches from the top of the rudder. The location of the probes was changed because the researchers wanted to gather slightly different data.[125]

122 "X-15 Semi-Annual Status Report No. 1," October 1963, p. 36; "X-15 Semi-Annual Status Report No. 3," 1 December 1964, p. 16.

123 System Package Program, System 653A, 18 May 1964, p. 6-39; X-15 Status Report, Paul F. Bikle/FRC to J. Martin/NASA Headquarters, 1 April 1966, p. 9.

124 Ronald P. Banas, NASA technical memorandum X-1136, "Comparison of Measured and Calculated Turbulent Heat Transfer in a Uniform and Nonuniform Flow Field on the X-15 Upper Vertical Fin at Mach Numbers of 4.2 and 5.3," 28 May 1965, pp. 25-26. Often the leading-edge profile is quoted as a diameter instead of a radius; the original leading edge had a diameter of 1.0 inch, and the new one was 0.030 inch in diameter.

125 Ibid, pp. 4, and 25-27.

The sharp rudder first flew on X-15-3 on 7 November 1963 (3-23-39) with Bob Rushworth at the controls. Several flights using X-15-2 had already gathered baseline data with the standard configuration. The X-15-3 would carry the sharp rudder through flight 3-33-54, when NASA removed it to install additional instrumentation. A normal rudder borrowed from X-15-1 replaced it for flight 3-34-55. NASA reinstalled the sharp rudder in time for flight 3-35-57, and X-15-3 continued to fly with it until the airplane was lost. The tests allowed researchers to validate various heating theories for both the blunt- and sharp-leading-edge shapes. In general, the theories fell into two groups: those that closely predicted the flight results (Moeckel and Love), and those that overestimated the heat transfer by 30–50% (Eckert).[126]

Experiment #9: Landing Computer

The ASD sponsored experiment #9 to test a landing computer developed by Sperry in conjunction with the MH-96 installation on X-15-3. The Air Force canceled the experiment prior to completion, but combined elements of it with experiment #14.[127]

Experiment #10: Infrared Exhaust Signature

The Air Force Geophysics Research Directorate sponsored experiment #10, with Leonard P. Marcotte as the principal investigator, to determine the infrared characteristics of a liquid-oxygen-ammonia rocket engine. This was conceptually similar to experiment #3 except that it involved the infrared spectrum instead of the ultraviolet. Measurements had been made of the signatures from Atlas and Titan ICBM engines; however, no measurements from oxygen-ammonia engines were available. Researchers wanted the data to use as part of a missile-detection system. The primary instrument was a Block Associates E-8 infrared radiometer that measured radiation in four spectral regions by focusing radiation through a calcium fluoride lens and four selective filters onto a lead sulfide detector. The range of the detectors was 2.5–7.0 microns. Personnel from the Cambridge Research Laboratory accomplished pre- and postflight checkouts of the package.[128]

The experiment was carried in the tail-cone box of X-15-3 on seven flights during 1963 and early 1964, but because of mechanical problems, data were obtained on only a single mission. Researchers asked for four additional flights

126 Ibid, pp. 9-10.

127 "Advanced Development Plan for X-15 Research Aircraft, Advanced Technology Program 653A," 17 November 1961, p. 51; "X-15 Semi-Annual Status Report No. 3," 1 December 1964, p. 16.

128 "Advanced Development Plan for X-15 Research Aircraft, Advanced Technology Program 653A," 17 November 1961, p. 51; "X-15 Semi-Annual Status Report No. 1," October 1963, p. 34; "X-15 Semi-Annual Status Report No. 3," 1 December 1964, p. 16; Statement of work for the infrared exhaust signature experiment (#10). In the AFFTC Access to Space Office Project files. The Cambridge Research Laboratory and Geophysics Research Directorate at Hanscom Field, MA, are now part of the Space Vehicles Directorate (VS), with headquarters in Kirtland AFB, NM, at the site of the former Philips Laboratory. The Atlas used liquid oxygen and RP-1 (kerosene); the Titan used hypergolic nitrogen tetroxide (N2O4) and Aerozine 50 (a 50/50 mixture of hydrazine and unsymmetrical dimethylhydrazine (UDMH)).

during late 1964, but apparently no flights were made. The detailed results are still classified.[129]

Experiment #11: High-Temperature Windows

The ASD sponsored experiment #11 to investigate various transparent materials in the high-temperature environment. The rapid buildup of temperature and dynamic force as cold structures reentered the atmosphere at hypersonic velocities created severe problems for the window designers. The window design and installation technique were critically important since both affected the heat transfer between the airframe and the transparency, as well as between the outer and inner window surfaces. NASA instrumented the X-15-2 canopy windows, as well as the center-of-gravity compartment windows, to provide precise temperature data. Among other things, the experiment tested the fused silica windows used on the photo optical degradation experiment (#5). The experiment acquired useful data on several flights during 1963.[130]

Proposals were later made to modify the experiment to test an X-20 window and retainer during high-speed flights on the X-15. Researchers wanted to install the window on one of the X-15-2 lower speed brakes and expose it to variable dynamic pressures on several Mach 6 flights during 1964. These plans never came to fruition after Secretary of Defense Robert McNamara canceled the Dyna-Soar program in December 1963. Nevertheless, X-15A-2 carried an instrumented window in the fixed portion of its ventral stabilizer for five flights during early 1966. Among other things, researchers used these flights to investigate whether ablator smoke and residue would adhere to the glass enough to hinder vision through the windshield; they concluded that it would.[131]

Experiment #12: Atmospheric-Density Measurements

Given the increased operations of both high-altitude manned vehicles and military missiles, the Air Force considered it important to determine the atmospheric density at altitudes above 100,000 feet as well as the day-to-day variation. As originally envisioned, the experiment would have used an alphatron ionization gage in a modified wing tip (this experiment predated the wing-tip pod concept) on X-15-2 that was outside the contamination caused by the APU and ballistic control exhausts. The measurements placed no constraints on the flight path or trajectory.[132]

The engineers could not find a reasonable way to mount the ionization gage, so the researchers rescoped the experiment to perform analytical research using

129 "X-15 Semi-Annual Status Report No. 1," October 1963, p. 34; "X-15 Semi-Annual Status Report No. 3," 1 December 1964, p. 16; Statement of work for the infrared exhaust signature experiment (#10). In the AFFTC Access to Space Office Project files.

130 System Package Program, System 653A, 18 May 1964, p. 6-39; "X-15 Semi-Annual Status Report No. 1," October 1963, pp. 36-37; "X-15 Semi-Annual Status Report No. 3," 1 December 1964, p. 17.

131 "X-15 Semi-Annual Status Report No. 1," October 1963, pp. 36-37; "X-15 Semi-Annual Status Report No. 3," 1 December 1964, p. 17; "X-15 Semi-Annual Status Report No. 4," 1 April 1965, p. 12; X-15 Status Report, Paul F. Bikle/FRC to J. Martin/NASA Headquarters, 1 April 1966, pp. 9-10; "X-15 Semi-Annual Status Report No. 7," 10 May 1967, pp. 22-23.

132 "Advanced Development Plan for X-15 Research Aircraft, Advanced Technology Program 653A," 17 November 1961, p. 49.

air data gathered by the normal X-15 ball nose and stable platform. Density-height profiles in the stratosphere and mesosphere were obtained from measurements of impact pressure, velocity, and altitude on two flights (2-14-28 and 2-20-36) in 1961 and four more (3-16-26, 3-20-31, 3-21-32, and 3-22-36) in 1963. The researchers noted that the modern recorders in X-15-3 provided more precise data, but the X-15 pressure-measuring system had a substantial lag in it, which made it difficult to perform an exact analysis. The density computations used a form of the Rayleigh pitot formula, and the data agreed well with measurements made by Arcas rocketsondes launched at Point Mugu around the time of the X-15 flights. The X-15 data generally indicated 5–7% greater densities than the standard predicted values at altitudes between 110,000 and 150,000 feet.[133]

The Air Force Geophysics Research Directorate sponsored a follow-on experiment to determine the atmospheric density at high altitudes to provide data for the designers of future aerospace vehicles. The wing-tip pods finally allowed researchers to measure atmospheric impact pressure with a densatron ionization gage installed in the nose of the right wing-tip pod on X-15-1. The College of Engineering at the University of Michigan built the experiment under Air Force contract. Researchers used two flights (1-50-79 and 1-51-81) to check out the installation and measure temperatures in the instrument. NASA then installed a small amount of radioactive tritium in the gage to measure the atmospheric density above 90,000 feet.[134]

The intended goal of obtaining atmospheric density profiles on a regular basis was never realized; in fact, the experiment only flew on three more flights (five flights in four years). As the researchers later commented, "The research activity undertaken here was valuable if for no other reasons than to point out the numerous restrictions associated with a manned rocket vehicle."[135]

An analysis of the data showed that despite predictions that the wing-tip pods would be outside the interference area, the experiment was limited below 100,000 feet by the bow shock-wave interference, and above 240,000 feet by the residue from the ballistic control-system thrusters. In between those altitudes, the thrusters intermittently biased the gage output; however, researchers could still obtain sufficient data for useful analysis.[136]

Experiment #13: Micrometeorite Collection

The Air Force Geophysics Research Directorate sponsored experiment #13 to collect samples of micrometeorites and extraterrestrial dust at altitudes above 150,000 feet. This was the initial impetus to manufacture the wing-tip pods, and researchers installed a collector in the nose of the left wing-tip pod on X-15-1. At

---

133 Earl J. Montoya and Terry J. Larson, NASA technical memorandum X-56009, "Stratosphere and Mesosphere Density-Height Profiles Obtained with the X-15 Airplane."

134 "X-15 Semi-Annual Status Report No. 1," October 1963, p. 34; "X-15 Semi-Annual Status Report No. 3," 1 December 1964, p. 17; Statement of work for the atmospheric density measurements experiment (#12). In the AFFTC Access to Space Office Project files. Air Force contract number AF19(628)-3313 (Project 6020, Task 606002).

135 Jack J. Horvath and Gary F. Rupert, University of Michigan report 06093-1-F, "Pitot Measurements on an X-15 Rocket Plane," August 1968, pp. 2 and 38.

136 Ibid, pp. 38-39.

high altitude and low dynamic pressure, the lid opened from the rear to a vertical position on top of the wing. As it lifted, rotating upward toward the front, it also swiveled so that the underside of the lid faced the aircraft fuselage and exposed the collector to the air stream. The collector then "broke seal" to expose a rotating collection surface behind an orifice in the side of the collector unit. The unit rotated to six different positions during the collection, and the location served to indicate the time of the event.[137]

During flight 1-50-79 the collector door inadvertently opened during the exit phase and remained so for the remainder of the flight, but fortunately did not cause serious damage. The collector was flown on flight 1-51-81, without exposing the collection device, to determine the amount of contamination resulting from ground handling. The plan was to operate the collector on as many high-altitude flights of the X-15 as possible.[138]

The experiment flew on flight 1-63-104, but the altitude attained on the flight was not sufficient to provide meaningful data, and an engine problem forced an emergency landing on Delamar Lake. After Jack McKay landed the X-15, the ground crew noticed that the collector box had extended, although they could not determine when this occurred. A postflight inspection revealed that the retraction mechanism was not functioning properly, and NASA returned the experiment to North American for repair.[139]

The experiment malfunctioned during preflight testing prior to flight 3-55-82 and NASA removed it from the aircraft. After it was modified to increase its reliability, the experiment flew on flight 1-65-108 to an altitude of 241,800 feet, but the collection rotor jammed in its second position. Subsequently, the experiment flew on both X-15-1 and X-15-3 and collected some particles during six flights. Unfortunately, residue from the ballistic control-system thrusters had contaminated the particles, and the Air Force canceled the experiment.[140]

Experiment #14: Advanced Integrated Flight-Data and Energy-Management Systems

The ASD and FRC jointly sponsored experiment #14. "A [principal] objective of this program is to obtain information to be applied to problems of design and use of advanced flight control equipment for vehicles which reenter the atmosphere from Earth orbits. Accordingly, a primary goal in the EMS design work has been to include the features of advanced orbital re-entry energy management systems to the maximum extent compatible with the X-15 vehicle and the flight control hardware

137 "X-15 Semi-Annual Status Report No. 1," October 1963, p. 33; "X-15 Semi-Annual Status Report No. 3," 1 December 1964, p. 17; Statement of work for the micrometeorite collection experiment (#13); X-15 Status Report 66-8, Paul F. Bikle/FRC to J. Martin/NASA Headquarters, 8 August 1966, p. 6. Initially, NASA and North American studied the installation of some sort of bulge on or near the wing tip; however, subsequent analysis indicated that this led to unexpected aero-thermo problems, and the idea was abandoned. Next came a study of an external store that could be suspended beneath the X-15 wing; this too had aero-thermo problems. The wing-tip solution had the fewest problems and was the easiest to implement, although the wings did have to be largely disassembled so that wires could be run to connect to the pods.

138 "X-15 Semi-Annual Status Report No. 1," October 1963, p. 33; "X-15 Semi-Annual Status Report No. 3," 1 December 1964, p. 17.

139 X-15 Status Report 66-5, Paul F. Bikle/FRC to J. Martin/NASA Headquarters, 4 May 1966, p. 7.

140 "X-15 Semi-Annual Status Report No. 6," 1 November 1966, p. 21; Boston, "The X-15's Role in Aerospace Progress," p. 37.

to be tested." To this end, the Air Force contracted with Bell Aerosystems to develop a suitable unit targeted at the Dyna-Soar program. Robert W. Austin and John M. Ryken at Bell led the work on Advanced Technology Program (ATP) 667A.[141]

James E. Love and Melvin E. Burke from the FRC, and Lieutenant Colonel Elmer F. Smith, director of the X-15 Project Office at Wright-Patterson AFB, worked out an MoU for including the Advanced Integrated Flight Control System (AIFCS) in the X-15 flight program. Smith signed the MoU on 9 September 1963 and Paul Bikle signed it on 12 September.[142]

Essentially the MoU indicated that the Air Force would be responsible for funding the development program, testing the system prior to its installation in an X-15, and maintaining the system after it was delivered. The FRC would handle the actual flight research program and provide a digital computer to upgrade the fixed-base simulator. The MoU stated that the X-15 Joint Program Coordinating Committee would determine the installation and flight schedule after "a reasonable reliability shall be demonstrated ... as evidence in laboratory tests, rocket sled tests and finally flight tests in a Douglas F5D Skyray prior to the initiation of installation modifications of the X-15 airplane."[143]

The Bell system was extensively simulated using an analog system to experiment with different control-loop arrangements, and an IBM 7090 digital computer to work out the problems associated with the digital programming. The results showed that the system performed well in a range of missions covering the X-15 flight envelope. Although Bell would design the system, Litton Industries would program it into one of their digital flight computers. The energy-management system (EMS) used slightly more than 3,000 words of memory and "about 15-percent of real-time on the Litton Flight Data System computer." The X-15-3 carried the system because it required the MH-96 adaptive flight-control system.[144]

Probably the most significant change from the system designed for Dyna-Soar was the use of an artificial dynamic pressure limit to ensure that the X-15 stayed within dynamic (q) and thermal limits. The decision to use a q-limit instead of directly using temperature as a control variable (as in the case of the Dyna-Soar) was the result of discussions among Air Force, Bell, and NASA personnel. The use of q-limits eliminated the need to instrument the exterior of the X-15 to obtain additional temperature data. The only inputs the system needed were dynamic pressure and altitude-rate information. The EMS performed four basic functions:[145]

---

141 Bell report 7176-935002, "An Energy Management System Design for Flight Testing in the X-15," 20 April 1963. The Dyna-Soar system was being developed under Air Force contract AF33(616)-7463 "Study and Preliminary Design of an Energy Management Computer for Winged Vehicles." The X-15 system was developed under Air Force contract AF33(657)-8330 "Advanced Energy Management System for Re-entry Vehicles."

142 Memorandum of Understanding between the NASA Flight Research Center and USAF X-14 Systems Project Office relating to the X-15 airplane and the advanced integrated flight control system, (USAF Advanced Technology Program 667A), 9 September 1963; memorandum, James E. Love/X-15 program manager to Paul F. Bikle, subject: Seventh bi-monthly meeting of participants in RTD advanced integrated flight data system program (ATP 667A), 7 October 1963. Both in the files at the DFRC History Office.

143 Ibid.

144 Bell report 7176-935002, " pp. ii-iii. The IBM 7090 was a transistorized version of the IBM 700-series and was equipped with 32 Kbytes of 36-bit core memory and a hardware floating-point unit. Fortran was its most popular language. IBM 7090s controlled the Mercury and Gemini space flights, the Ballistic Missile Early Warning System (until well into the 1980s), and the CTSS time-sharing system at MIT.

145 Bell report 7176-935002, pp. 4-5. In itself, this was not an issue with the X-15 since it was already well instrumented; however, the idea was to demonstrate a method that could be used on an operational vehicle that might not be equipped with temperature transducers. This concept would prove to be very useful in the development of the Space Shuttle.

1. Computation of vehicle total maneuver potential, formation of a nondimensional ground area attainable, and generation of angle of attack and bank commands for vehicle destination maneuvering.
2. Computation of the minimum value of dynamic pressure attainable at the next pullout (perigee) point and generation of override commands required to insure that pullout conditions do not reach critical values.
3. Computations to nondimensionalize measured dynamic pressure and generation of override commands for α [angle of attack] and $\varnothing$ [bank angle] to ensure that present dynamic pressure and aerodynamic heating do not reach critical values. (A similar loop for control of "g" loading was not contained within the EMS since this was already provided in the Honeywell [MH-96] adaptive flight control system for the X-15.)
4. Computations to nondimensionalize measured rate of change of altitude and generation of commands to damp phugoid motions (long-period oscillations along the longitudinal axis).

The pilot could select either an automatic or manual energy-management mode. In the manual mode, the system displayed the results of the energy-management computations to the pilot but did not take any independent action. This allowed the pilot to fly the correct energy-management profile or to deviate from it as needed. In the automatic mode, the system displayed the same information to the pilot but also sent commands directly to the MH-96 to fly the desired reentry profile. The system was programmed to arrive at high key with "sufficient energy for the pilot to accomplish the final descent and landing with considerable energy reserve." Interestingly, the system did not direct the X-15 toward any particular heading over high key, so the pilot had to use some of the excess energy to establish a heading that would allow him to land.[146]

As development progressed, there were concerns that the system was requiring too much power and cooling. Jim Love and Lannie D. Webb from the FRC first voiced these concerns during a meeting on 17 September 1962 with Captain Hugh D. Clark and Captain James H. Smith from the ASD. Love indicated that the electrical demands were so high that the X-15-3 electrical system would have to be "beefed up" to accommodate the new system. Whereas the original Sperry stable platform required 1.4 pounds per minute of cooling, the new system required over 6.3 pounds per minute. The original Litton computer was finally tested in the NASA F5D (BuNo 142350/NASA 213) in late 1964, despite an initial intent to begin testing in January 1964. The F5D portion of the program ended on 31 March 1965 after 17 flights.[147]

146 Ibid, pp. 7-8.

147 Trip report, Captain Hugh D. Clark/X-15 Project Office, describing a trip on 20-24 August 1962 to the Flight Research Center to discuss the Follow-On Experiments Program, report dated 17 September 1962. In the files of the Air Force Historical Research Agency; "X-15 Semi-Annual Status Report No. 4," 1 April 1965, p. 13.

This experiment was reoriented in October 1964 to use Honeywell equipment instead of the originally procured Litton components. The centerpiece was an H-387 digital computer hooked to a new Lear Siegler instrument panel. In addition to conducting the experiments that were initiated under ATP 667A, researchers later included studies of pilot displays, energy management, and piloting problems during the exit phase of high-performance vehicles. The program expected to make 16 flights in X-15-3 to cover most of the flight envelope.[148]

As finally defined for the X-15 program, this experiment was an evaluation of vertical-tape displays, energy-management concepts and techniques, and command guidance for boost and trajectory control. The equipment consisted of a Honeywell inertial system, coupler, and computer; a Honeywell AN/AYK-5 Alert digital computer; a Lear Siegler cockpit instrument panel with vertical-tape displays; the Honeywell MH-96 adaptive control system; and the ball nose. NASA installed the system in X-15-3 during the weather down period in early 1966.[149]

Another part of the experiment was to test a boost-guidance technique and display that had been developed by the Ames Research Center and was called, logically enough, the Ames boost-guidance evaluation. For the most part, the experiment consisted of additional programming for the Alert computer. Data was displayed on the horizontal pointer of the three-axis attitude indicator, making it a "fly-to-null" display of altitude error plus altitude rate error. This change ultimately confused Mike Adams, and on flight 3-65-97 contributed to the loss of X-15-3. Researchers flew it for the first time on flight 3-58-87 to evaluate needle movement on the display. A postflight review of the cockpit film showed that the cross-pointer was moving as expected since the guidance parameters stored in the computer were not representative of the planned flight. Subsequent flights programmed the boost-guidance software to match the desired flight profile. On future flights, the pilot was to fly the boost portion using the boost-guidance program as long as the display of pitch attitude was within +2 degrees of the planned flight path. The experiment seemed to function as expected.[150]

Overall, the entire integrated flight-data system appeared to work well enough during the next 14 flights. Its performance on its last flight is more open to debate.

Experiment #15: Heat-Exchanger System or Vapor-Cycle Cooling

The ASD sponsored experiment #15 to verify performance estimates for evaporators and condensers at zero gravity. Researchers wanted to mount the experiment in the instrument compartment of X-15-1 during four high-altitude flights with a large zero-g parabola at the top. The first of the Garrett AiResearch heat exchangers (excess units from the canceled Dyna-Soar) arrived in early November 1964. North American conducted the initial performance tests in Inglewood during

148 "X-15 Semi-Annual Status Report No. 1," October 1963, p. 35; "X-15 Semi-Annual Status Report No. 3," 1 December 1964, p. 17; X-15 Status Report, Paul F. Bikle/FRC to J. Martin/NASA Headquarters, 1 April 1965, p. 7; "X-15 Semi-Annual Status Report No. 4," 1 April 1965, p. 13.

149 X-15 Status Report, Paul F. Bikle/FRC to J. Martin/NASA Headquarters, 1 April 1966, p. 10.

150 X-15 Status Reports, Paul F. Bikle/FRC to J. Martin/NASA Headquarters, 3 March 1967, p. 4 and 10 May 1967, p. 4; memorandum, Elmor J. Adkins/X-15 Project Office to Assistant Division Chief, Research Projects, subject: Preliminary report on X-15 flight 3-58-87, 10 May 1967; memorandum, Elmor J. Adkins/X-15 Project Office to Assistant Division Chief, Research Projects, subject: Preliminary report on X-15 flight 3-64-95, 3 November 1967.

late November, and the unit underwent centrifuge tests at the Rocket Propulsion Laboratory at Edwards in mid-December 1964. Engineers tested the units aboard a KC-135 in early 1965 and scheduled the installation in X-15-1 for mid-1965.[151]

However, the experiment faced several challenges. The most pressing was that starting the large compressor needed to cool the equipment required more power than was available on either the X-15 or the NB-52. Engineers thought that installing larger alternators in the NB-52 might be possible, but the wiring on the carrier and the X-15 would have to be upgraded to a heavier gage to handle the load. Another possible method would be to start the compressor using ground power before takeoff since the X-15 APUs could supply the operating load, without starting the compressor. The compressor was equipped with an automatic shutoff feature that could detect a failure of one of the X-15 APUs; a single unit could not supply both the experiment and the airplane, and the airplane came first.[152]

Difficulties in bringing the experiment up to the safety standards demanded by the X-15 program delayed the experiment for over a year. As it ended up, NASA never installed the hardware on an X-15 and the experiment was moved to the Apollo Applications Program, which itself never got off the ground.[153]

Experiment #16: Rarefied Wake-Flow Experiment

The FRC sponsored a rather fanciful concept known as the "rarefied wake-flow" experiment. Initially the plan was to tow an inflatable plastic sphere behind the X-15. By measuring the tension on the tow rope and analyzing photographs, the researchers hoped to determine the atmospheric density above 200,000 feet and the drag characteristics of a towed sphere in free-molecular-flow regions, assess the effect of vehicle flow fields, and study supersonic wakes. Additional investigations included the motion of a towed drag body and the viability of inflatable reentry vehicle deceleration devices.[154]

The experiment was modified so that a small Mylar balloon could be released (instead of towed) from the tail-cone box on X-15-3 at altitudes above 250,000 feet to investigate the properties of supersonic wakes at low densities. The experiment would require two flights above 300,000 feet using balloons originally procured for Project Mercury, and researchers wanted four additional flights above 250,000 feet using somewhat sturdier balloons. Two unsuccessful attempts (flights 3-21-32 and 3-22-36) to release a Mercury balloon occurred in mid-1963, marking the end of this idea.[155]

The experiment ended up using a Pace flow transducer mounted in the forward section of the X-15 left wing-tip pod. This installation negated many of the

151 "X-15 Semi-Annual Status Report No. 1," October 1963, p. 34; "X-15 Semi-Annual Status Report No. 3," 1 December 1964, pp. 17-18.

152 Trip report, Captain Hugh D. Clark/X-15 Project Office, describing a trip on 20-24 August 1962 to the FRC to discuss the follow-on experiments program, report dated 17 September 1962.

153 X-15 Status Report, Paul F. Bikle/FRC to J. Martin/NASA Headquarters, 1 April 1966, pp. 10-11.

154 System Package Program, System 653A, 18 May 1964, pp. 6-40 and 6-41.

155 "X-15 Semi-Annual Status Report No. 1," October 1963, p. 36. These balloons were 30 inches in diameter and could be folded, packaged, and housed with their own gas expansion bottle in a very small space. The balloons had been used on Mercury for various experiments in space. See Lloyd S. Swenson, Jr., James M. Greenwood, and Charles C. Alexander, *This New Ocean: A History of Project Mercury* (Washington, DC: NASA, 1966), pp. 444 and others.

original secondary objectives of the experiment. The revised experiment called for flights above 300,000 feet, which resulted in very few flight opportunities, and by December 1964 it was determined that flights above 250,000 feet would be sufficient. (Only four program flights were above 300,000 feet, while 15 others got above 250,000 feet.) The experiment was an evaluation of a mechanical transducer for rarefied-flow measurement and measured upper-atmosphere ambient density. NASA carried the experiment on a "standby" status to replace experiment #13 if opportunity allowed, but by the end of 1965 the experiment apparently still had not flown. In April 1966 the ballast nose cone for the wing-tip pods was modified to accept the Pace transducer, allowing the experiment to be installed in either wing-tip pod on either X-15-1 or X-15-3. The experiment flew several times on each airplane during 1966 and 1967.[156]

Experiment #17: MIT-Apollo Horizon Photometer

The Office of Manned Space Flight sponsored experiment #17 to measure the Earth's horizon-intensity profile as a function of altitude to different wavelengths in the visible spectrum. This was officially called the "simultaneous photographic horizon scanner experiment," and was in many respects a follow-on to the Langley horizon definition experiment (#4) using much more sophisticated equipment. The MIT project was large and wide-ranging, using various aircraft, sounding rockets, as well as Mercury and Gemini spacecraft, to carry radiometers to measure the Earth's infrared horizon. Of these, the X-15 carried the largest and most sophisticated package to define the Earth's limb for use as an artificial horizon for the space sextant carried aboard the Apollo spacecraft. Researchers designed the sextant as a backup device in the event of a radar or communications failure. NASA installed a single Phase I and two Phase II experiments on X-15-1.[157]

The interim Phase I system was a fixed platform in the tail-cone box supporting three MIT Instrument Laboratory-designed photosensitive instruments (a photomultiplier photometer, a solid-state photometer, and a camera) pointing aft and approximately aligned with the aircraft thrust axis. Researchers evaluated the fixed platform during flight 1-51-81, and flew four additional flights to obtain photometer output levels.[158]

The Phase II experiment contained a spectral photometer, a camera, and a star tracker mounted on a three-axis stabilized platform in the tail-cone box that isolated it from X-15 attitudes. Researchers designed the star tracker to acquire Polaris, and the gimbaled system could control horizon-scan rates to obtain the most useful data independent of aircraft maneuvering. A door that opened above 100,000 feet covered all of the instruments during the X-15 exit phase. NASA installed the Phase II experiment in X-15-1 during the weather down period in early 1966. The initial plan was to fly a single flight to 220,000 feet as a checkout of the system, and then

156 X-15 Status Reports, Paul F. Bikle/FRC to J. Martin/NASA Headquarters, 1 April and 4 May 1966; "X-15 Semi-Annual Status Report No. 3," 1 December 1964, p. 18; "X-15 Semi-Annual Status Report No. 6," 1 November 1966, p. 21.

157 Boston, "The X-15's Role in Aerospace Progress," pp. 38-39.

158 Carlton R. Gray, "An Horizon Definition Experiment," AIAA paper no. 69-869, presented at the AIAA Guidance, Control, and Flight Mechanics Conference, Princeton, NJ, 18-20 November 1969, p. 1; "X-15 Semi-Annual Status Report No. 3," 1 December 1964, p. 18.

fly four data-gathering flights to 250,000 feet under various seasonal sun-angle and atmospheric conditions with the system pointed approximately true north.[159]

Flight 1-63-104 was the checkout for part 1 of Phase II, and postflight inspection showed that the experiment was in good condition despite the emergency landing. The experiment flew on flights 1-65-108, 1-66-111, 1-67-112, and 1-68-113, but did not obtain data on flights 1-65-108 and 1-67-112 because of electrical power problems, or on flight 1-68-113 due to a loss of the scan signal. An evaluation of the data from flight 1-66-111 indicated that the photometer functioned properly but the star tracker did not acquire Polaris as programmed. The experiment subsequently flew on four additional flights and gathered good data on all of them.[160]

Five flights (part 2 of Phase II) added a Barnes infrared edge tracker to measure the 14–40-micron infrared profile. The Manned Spacecraft Center sponsored this part of the experiment using an instrument designed for spacecraft attitude stabilization in the Apollo Applications Program. The Barnes instrument was essentially a telescope employing a 2.4-inch-diameter silicon lens mounted on the elevator under the skylight hatch of X-15-1. North American installed this hardware, collocated with the WTR launch-monitoring experiment, in early 1967. Researchers checked out the experiment on flight 1-76-134, and made four data-gathering flights between June and September 1968. Flight 1-80-140 was the last flight of the experiment, and Paul Bikle reported that "star recognition was not achieved."[161]

One of the more interesting aspects of the experiment was that the High Range could not provide sufficiently accurate radar data to meet the needs of MIT. Instead, NASA arranged for the Sandia Corporation to track the X-15 using the MPS-25 radar at Cactus Flats, Nevada. This radar could track the airplane with 0.10-milliradian-attitude accuracy and a range accuracy of several yards.[162]

The experiment concluded that the concept was feasible for use as a space-navigation technique, but because the most stable portions of the radiance were in the near-ultraviolet range, it was usable only during daylight portions of an orbit. To verify that the idea worked from greater distances, NASA asked the astronauts on Apollo 8, 10, and 11 to make visual sightings of the Earth's horizon using the onboard spacecraft sextant. This exercise was conducted several times en route to and returning from the Moon, and revealed that the sextant had relatively good accuracy compared to radar positioning.[163]

Experiment #18: Supersonic Deceleration Devices

Initially, NASA Langley sponsored experiment #18 to test the concept of inflatable devices. During the late 1950s, engineers thought they could use in-

159 Gray, "An Horizon Definition Experiment," pp. 1-3; X-15 Status Report, Paul F. Bikle/FRC to J. Martin/NASA Headquarters, 1 April 1966, p. 11.

160 X-15 Status Report 66-5, Paul F. Bikle/FRC to J. Martin/NASA Headquarters, 4 May 1966, pp. 7-8; "X-15 Semi-Annual Status Report No. 6," 1 November 1966, p. 22.

161 X-15 Status Reports, Paul F. Bikle/FRC to J. Martin/NASA Headquarters, 1 April 1966, pp. 8-9, 3 March 1967, p. 1, p. 1, 6 September 1968, p. 4, and 7 October 1968, p. 2; Gray, "An Horizon Definition Experiment," p. 2; "X-15 Semi-Annual Status Report No. 1," October 1963, p. 35. The Manned Spacecraft Center was subsequently renamed the Johnson Space Center.

162 Gray, "An Horizon Definition Experiment," p. 2.

163 Ibid, pp. 8-12; Boston, "The X-15's Role in Aerospace Progress," pp. 38-39.

ternal pressure to erect and stabilize structures in space because of the lack of atmosphere and gravity. The inflation of these structures, however, was difficult to investigate on the ground. A test would consist of carrying the structure either internally or externally on the X-15, ejecting it at high altitude under conditions of zero-g and zero dynamic pressure, and then photographing the inflation of the structure. It was expected that the experiment could be packaged in place of the ventral rudder if the equipment was not too large; otherwise, an external store might be required.[164]

After more thought, this concept seemed a bit far-fetched. The experiment was reoriented away from inflatable structures and toward inflatable decelerator devices. In this incarnation, the experiment was sponsored by the FRC to evaluate the drag, stability, and deployment characteristics of various decelerator configurations at Mach numbers as high as 5 and altitudes as high as 200,000 feet. Dr. Heinrich at the University of Minnesota had developed a variety of such devices, and researchers at Langley studied a number of configurations in wind tunnels to determine which ones held the most promise for actual flight tests. The possibilities included inflatable spheres and cones, and various self-inflating parachutes. In December 1964 the plan was to fly the first X-15 decelerator tests during the early summer of 1965 and deploy the decelerator at Mach 4 following burnout. The tests would require the installation of a decelerator tow kit in the tail-cone box. NASA fabricated the modification kits for two X-15 airplanes and gathered preliminary data in April 1965 using an F-104 to drop a decelerator at Mach 1.8 from 57,000 feet. Engineers made some modifications to X-15-3 to support the experiment during the weather down period in early 1966, but apparently never installed the experiment.[165]

Experiment #19: High-Altitude Sky Brightness

The ASD sponsored experiment #19 to determine the intensity, polarization, and spectral distribution of the daytime sky at high altitudes. Researchers would use the information to develop electro-optical tracking systems that were capable of discriminating a star's optical signal from the surrounding sky's brightness. Northrop Nortronics was developing a spectrophotometer for use on a Lockheed U-2 reconnaissance aircraft as part of the High Altitude Daytime Sky Background Radiation Measurement Program to survey the sky at altitudes between 20,000 and 70,000 feet in 10,000-foot increments. The Air Force, however, desired data obtained at up to 200,000 feet, and in 1962 the service modified the Nortronics contract to develop instrumentation for the X-15. The goal was to survey the sky in the range of 3,500–7,500 Å, with a spectral resolution of approximately 2 Å, to support the design of future star trackers. Researchers extrapolated the data gathered by the U-2 to higher altitudes and used it to predict and verify data acquired by

164 "Advanced Development Plan for X-15 Research Aircraft, Advanced Technology Program 653A," p. 56.

165 System Package Program, System 653A, 18 May 1964, p. 6-41; "X-15 Semi-Annual Status Report No. 1," October 1963, p. 36 "X-15 Semi-Annual Status Report No. 3," 1 December 1964, p. 19; "X-15 Semi-Annual Status Report No. 4," 1 April 1965, p. 13; X-15 Status Report, Paul F. Bikle/FRC to J. Martin/NASA Headquarters, 1 April 1966, p. 11.

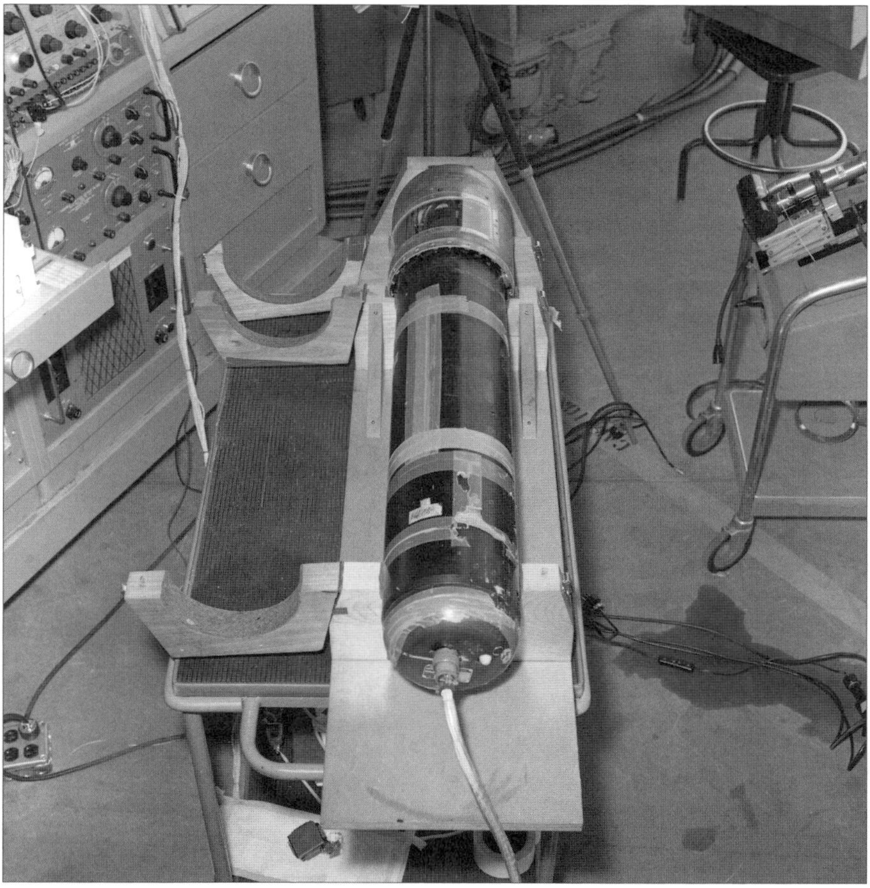

The High-Altitude Sky Brightness Experiment (#19) surveyed the sky in the range between 3,500 to 7,500 angstroms, with a spectral resolution of approximately 2 angstroms to support the designs of future star trackers. Researchers extrapolated the data gathered by the U-2 to higher altitudes and used it to predict and verify data acquired by the X-15. The spectrophotometer sensor was located in the rear portion of the left wing-tip pod, and flew on both X-15-1 and X-15-3. (NASA)

the X-15 since the effects of high-speed aerodynamics were largely unknown. The researchers wanted the X-15 to acquire data from 40,000 feet to 200,000 feet.[166]

Researchers first flew the spectrophotometer in the rear portion of the left wing-tip pod of X-15-1 on flights 1-50-79 and 1-52-85 to check out its operation. The experiment flew on flight 1-63-104, but the emergency landing precluded the

166 System Package Program, System 653A, p. 6-41; letter, Ralph H. Becker/Navigation & Guidance Laboratory, to Ted Little/AMC, subject: High Altitude Daytime Sky Background Radiation Measurement Program, 29 October 1962; "X-15 Semi-Annual Status Report No. 1," October 1963, p. 33; "X-15 Semi-Annual Status Report No. 3," 1 December 1964, p. 19; Boston, "The X-15's Role in Aerospace Progress," p. 39; letter, Ralph H. Becker/Navigation & Guidance Laboratory, to Ted Little/AMC, subject: High Altitude Daytime Sky Background Radiation Measurement Program, 29 October 1962; "X-15 Semi-Annual Status Report No. 1," October 1963, p. 33; "X-15 Semi-Annual Status Report No. 3," 1 December 1964, p. 19. In the files at the DFRC History Office. The Original Nortronics contract was AF33(694)-291 for the Sky Radiation Measurement Program (for use on the Lockheed U-2).

acquisition of any meaningful data. Researchers obtained data on flight 1-65-108, and the experiment flew on flight 1-66-111; however, no useful results were obtained because a slow-blow fuse failed. Engineers conducted several tests in an environmental chamber to investigate the fuse, which consistently failed at 140,000 feet and –158°F. They eventually traced the problem to a power connector on the experiment. After repairs were made, the instrument flew several flights aboard X-15-3 beginning with 3-56-83, and acquired useful data on at least two flights.[167]

Experiment #20: Western Test Range Launch Monitoring

The ASD funded experiment #20 under the name "Pacific Missile Range (PMR) launch monitoring." The goal was to measure from high altitude the signature of an ascending ballistic missile to determine the feasibility of using the ultraviolet spectrum for space-based detection and tracking systems. There was initial concern regarding this experiment because the timing requirements seemed very critical given the short duration of X-15 flights and the acceleration profile of an ICBM. Nevertheless, the Air Force deemed the experiment important for national security and requested six flights in excess of 250,000 feet. In mid-1964 the Air Force awarded a contract to the Northrop Space Laboratories to design and fabricate equipment. A review of the preliminary design revealed that the experiment package and its recording equipment were too large to fit on X-15-1, so the Air Force, NASA, and Northrop were reevaluating the problem as 1965 ended.[168]

Eventually Northrop worked through the problems and NASA installed the experiment during the weather down period in early 1966. The experiment consisted of an optical system, a vidicon camera, a four-spectral-band radiometer, and a servo-driven scanning mirror installed on the extensible elevator under the skylight hatch of X-15-1. The experiment first flew on 15 June 1967 (flight 1-72-125), but an electrical malfunction within the experiment precluded a complete operational checkout. The X-15-1 subsequently carried the experiment on eight additional flights.[169]

The primary target for the experiment would be a Minuteman II ICBM launched from Vandenberg AFB, although some thought was given to trying the experiment against a Titan II target. The Air Force also wanted the X-15 to track multiple Minuteman ICBMs launched from Vandenberg in rapid sequence (simulating an actual wartime response). In each case, the X-15 portion of the experiment would be secondary to other reasons for launching the missiles. Whatever

---

167 X-15 Status Report 66-5, Paul F. Bikle/FRC to J. Martin/NASA Headquarters, 4 May 1966, p. 8; "X-15 Semi-Annual Status Report No. 6," 1 November 1966, p. 23.

168 "X-15 Semi-Annual Status Report No. 1," October 1963, p. 41; X-15 Semi-Annual Status Report No. 3," 1 December 1964, p. 19. There seems to a great deal of confusion in the official documentation concerning the experiment number assigned to the Western test range launch monitoring experiment. Most documents call it experiment #20; however, many Air Force documents refer to it as experiment #28. Since most documents use #20, that is what will be used here.

169 X-15 Status Reports, Paul F. Bikle/FRC to J. Martin/NASA Headquarters, 1 March, 1 April 1966, and 5 May 1967; memorandum, James R. Welsh for E. James Adkins, Subject: Preliminary report on X-15 flight 1-71-121, 16 May 1967.

The most ambitious of the follow-on experiments was the Western Range Launch Monitoring Experiment (#20) installed under the Skylight hatch on X-15-1. The X-15 was supposed to track a Minuteman ICBM launched from Vandenberg AFB, but the timing of getting the X-15 in position at the exact moment the ICBM was launched never worked. (NASA)

experiment the Air Force was conducting involved the use of a B-52 in addition to the target ICBMs.[170]

On 22-23 May 1968, representatives from the Air Force, NASA, and Northrop met to discuss various aspects of the upcoming flights. The first order of business was to discuss the security classification surrounding the project, and the Air Force agreed that the only classified data the FRC would receive would be the actual launch time of the targets. The representative from the Strategic Air Command (SAC), Lieutenant Colonel John McElveen, indicated that SAC "will do everything possible to insure a successful coordination with the exception of compromising their primary objective." This would include allowing Vandenberg to adjust its launch times to coincide with X-15 launches as long as the delays were a reasonable length of time.[171]

The attendees spent most of the meeting discussing how to make sure the ICBM and X-15 would be in position at the right time. They decided that, whenever possible, the experiment should be scheduled for between 1000 and 1400

170 Memorandum, Jack L. Kolf/FRC to James E. Love/X-15 Program Manager, subject: WTR Experiment Coordination, 23 May 1968. Most likely, the "other reasons" for launching the missiles were operational training; real missiles were routinely removed from operational silos, transported to Vandenberg, and launched by operational crews. On several occasions Vandenberg launched multiple Minuteman ICBMs during operational testing; however, no multiple Titan launches were ever conducted. It could not be ascertained exactly what the Air Force B-52 was needed for.

171 Ibid.

hours Pacific daylight time. The X-15 flight planners would purposefully schedule the X-15 so that it would arrive at its launch point either on time or slightly late, since the Air Force could hold off on launching the target but could not recall it once it was launched. For the multiple-target missions, Vandenberg would launch the Minuteman ICBMs 30 seconds apart. Procedures allowed the Air Force B-52 to hold while the NB-52/X-15 got into position for launch, and to time the launch of the target ICBMs. Nevertheless, this experiment would have required extraordinary luck to have everything in place at exactly the right time.[172]

The Air Force apparently put a high priority on this experiment since it was one of the two reasons listed for extending Air Force funding of the X-15 program into 1968. Unfortunately, the first nine attempts to coordinate this aerial ballet failed. On at least two occasions, equipment on the X-15 failed to operate as expected, and on another Vandenberg could not launch the target because of a technical problem. The experiment also required very precise flight-path control. For instance, during flight 1-79-139 the experiment extended 129 seconds after launch. It immediately began searching for the target, but quickly failed after the elevator and azimuth torquers drove against their stops. It was later determined that Bill Dana deployed the experiment slightly before the airplane achieved the 0±2-degree pitch and roll attitude requirement. Engineers warned Dana and Pete Knight not to extend the experiment until the airplane was stable as it approached apogee.[173]

As the flight went on, more difficulties arose. About 208 seconds after launch, NASA-1 requested Bill Dana to retract the experiment. Things appeared normal at first, and the experiment retracted without the delays noted on some previous flights. However, the timing was unfortunate since the call was made a bit later than planned, and the automatic timer interrupted the normal action and initiated an emergency-retract sequence. Nevertheless, the experiment successfully retracted. Since a demonstration of the normal retraction sequence was required before the experiment could become "operational," NASA scheduled a flight to check out the mechanism. On flight 1-80-142, Pete Knight extended the experiment 162 seconds after launch and the sensor went into track mode 5 seconds later. At 240,000 feet, Knight commanded the experiment to retract, but indications at 220,000 feet showed that it had not. Knight activated the emergency mode, with satisfactory results.[174]

Finally, the Air Force and NASA managed the first coordinated launch of the X-15 and a WTR target. Flight 1-81-141 launched from Smith Ranch on a magnetic heading of 169 degrees, within 3 seconds of the optimum time. Bill Dana reached the planned 36-degree pitch angle 30 seconds after launch and held it until burnout at 5,400 fps. The flight experienced a nose-left thrust misalignment that caused 4.5-degree of sideslip, but Dana did not use any rudder input during the exit phase, resulting in a 3-degree error in ground track. The experiment was extended at approximately 235,000 feet as planned (roughly 137 seconds after

172 Ibid.

173 X-15 Status Report, Paul F. Bikle/FRC to J. Martin/NASA Headquarters, 6 September 1968, p. 2. In the files at the DFRC History Office.

174 X-15 Status Report, Paul F. Bikle/FRC to J. Martin/NASA Headquarters, 6 September 1968, p. 2. In the files at the DFRC History Office.

X-15 launch), but 2.8 seconds later all power was lost to the system and the experiment retracted. The flight did not acquire any useful data.[175]

The last attempt was on the 200th X-15 flight. The launch attempt on 21 November 1968 was coordinated with Vandenberg, and the Air Force launched a Minuteman II at 1028 hours; unfortunately, the X-15 never left the ground because of a problem with the NB-52A. By this time the Air Force had spent $700,000 on the experiment, not counting the normal flight costs of the X-15 (which carried other experiments as well) or the cost of the Minuteman ICBMs (which were being launched anyway).[176]

Experiment #21: Structural Research

The FRC sponsored experiment #21 to investigate lightweight structures in the high-temperature environment by using the detachable outer wing panel on X-15A-2. The experiment consisted of two configurations: one for sustained Mach 3 cruise, and one for hypersonic cruise. The hypersonic outer wing panel was required to withstand temperatures beyond Mach 8 without the use of ablative coatings. Both panels needed extensive instrumentation for loads, stresses, and temperatures. The FRC received proposals in late 1964, but never built or tested the panels. By the end of 1965, NASA placed this experiment on "inactive" status.[177]

Experiment #22: Air-Breathing Propulsion

Very early on, a small group of researchers believed that the X-15 was a potentially useful test bed for various air-breathing propulsion system components, including complete ramjet engines. The airplane was capable of speeds in the Mach 3–5 region, in which inlet and exit problems were greatest, and a ramjet engine was considered a desirable method of propulsion. The X-15 would provide testing under true atmospheric conditions (ground-test facilities were seldom able to achieve the proper stagnation temperatures and Reynolds number). The X-15 would also permit closer control of test conditions than was possible with ground-controlled rockets, such as those launched at the Pilotless Aircraft Research Division (PARD).[178]

The most desirable position for the propulsion test package appeared to be in place of the ventral rudder, although it had to be jettisoned before landing to provide adequate clearance for the landing gear. At this point Dick Day and Bob Hoey had not proposed to fly the X-15 with the ventral removed, so this was one of the larger unknowns of the initial engine proposal. Two wing-root tanks, each holding about 100 gallons of liquid hydrogen, carried fuel for the ramjet. Other

---

175 X-15 Status Report, Paul F. Bikle/FRC to J. Martin/NASA Headquarters, 4 November 1968, pp. 1-2. In the files at the DFRC History Office.

176 Memorandum, James R. Welsh to Assistant Chief, Research Projects, Subject: Preliminary report on X-15 flight 1-79-139, 5 September 1968; memorandum, Jack L. Kolf to Assistant Chief, Research Projects, Subject: Preliminary report on X-15 flight 1-81-141, 5 November 1968; e-mail between Jeffery Geiger, 30th Space Wing Historian, and Dennis R. Jenkins, 8 April 2002; "X-15 Program," a briefing prepared by the AFFTC in late October 1968.

177 System Package Program, System 653A, p. 6-42; "X-15 Semi-Annual Status Report No. 1," October 1963, p. 37-40; "X-15 Semi-Annual Status Report No. 3," 1 December 1964, p. 19.

178 "Advanced Development Plan for X-15 Research Aircraft, Advanced Technology Program 653A," p. 54.

positions for the engine would be possible if permanently attached engines were required. For example, a small engine could replace one of the wing root tanks or a pair of engines mounted under the wing tips.[179]

The FRC proposed the first truly serious version of this experiment as "an extensive air-breathing engine development program … in which one or more sub-scale modular experimental engines would be flown in a true flight environment aboard the X-15." Somehow, the experiment took on a life of its own and morphed into the hypersonic research engine (HRE) project (discussed separately below).

Experiment #23: Infrared Scanning Radiometer

The ASD and later the Air Force Research Technology Division sponsored experiment #23 as a follow-on to the infrared exhaust signature experiment (#10) to determine the feasibility of an infrared imaging instrument operating at Mach 3–5 at altitudes between 90,000 and 120,000 feet. NASA installed a Singer scanning radiometer in the lower portion of the instrument compartment of X-15-1 during mid-March 1965. The experiment looked through an Iratran IV window in the lower fuselage and recorded the reflected solar radiation as well as radiation emitted by Earth.[180]

The Infrared Scanning Radiometer Experiment (#10) was used to determine the feasibility of an infrared imaging instrument operating at Mach 3-5 at altitudes between 90,000 and 120,000 feet. A Singer scanning radiometer was installed in the lower portion of the instrument compartment of X-15-1 during mid-March 1965. The experiment looked through an Iratran IV window in the lower fuselage and recorded the reflected solar radiation as well as radiation emitted by Earth. (NASA)

The first of six flights was made on 26 March 1965 (1-53-86); the last was flight 1-60-99 on 30 September 1965. Actually, flight 1-59-98 was supposed to be the last flight, but a broken wire had precluded the acquisition of any useful data. The Air Force decided to leave the experiment on the airplane for Pete Knight's familiarization flight (1-60-99), although Knight did not attempt to fly the profile normally required for the experiment. Despite this, the experiment obtained good data. Although the experiment only generated a

179 Ibid.

180 Ronald S. Waite/X-15 Project Engineer, "X-15 Operations Flight Report for Flight 1-53-86," 13 April 1965; "X-15 Semi-Annual Status Report No. 1," October 1963, p. 41; "X-15 Semi-Annual Status Report No. 3," 1 December 1964, p. 20.

crude, two-dimensional image, it proved that it was possible to perform infrared reconnaissance at hypersonic speeds. The development of a Germanium metal window that was transparent to infrared photography offset the masking effect of an aerodynamically heated window. This work reportedly advanced the development of infrared line scanners, such as the Texas Instruments AN/AAS-18, that went on to operational service on various Air Force reconnaissance aircraft. The Earth Resources Development Agency (ERDA) also capitalized on this technology by contracting with the Mead Corporation to develop several portable suitcase-size scanners for use on general aviation aircraft to detect various forms of pollution.[181]

Experiment #24: High-Altitude Infrared Background Measurements

Experiment #24 was sponsored by the Air Force Research Technology Division to obtain high-altitude infrared measurements of the Earth, horizon, and sky in the 3–5- and 8–14-micron regions for use in various surveillance applications (i.e., target tracking). The measuring device was a simple dual-channel, solid-state radiometer with a flat rotating mirror that provided a circular scan. A self-contained liquid-helium system cooled the experiment. The Autonetics Division of North American built the experiment, and NASA installed it in the right wing-tip pod on X-15-1 during the weather down period in early 1966. Researchers requested three flights to altitudes above 150,000 feet, but the only verifiable attempt was on the aborted 200th flight.[182]

Experiment #25: Optical Background Measurements

The Air Force Research Technology Division sponsored experiment #25 as an extension of the ultraviolet exhaust plume experiment (#3). The objective was to obtain narrow-band optical-background measurements covering the spectral region between 0.3 and 1.3 microns. Northrop modified the existing Barnes high-resolution spectrometer and associated equipment from experiment #3 to operate at visible wavelengths.[183]

Researchers installed the experiment in the X-15-3 tail-cone box to determine the background characteristics of the atmosphere and Earth when viewed with a narrow-band receiver. The data was applicable to future laser systems for space vehicles. The experiment had flown twice by the end of 1965, but had gathered little usable data because of system noise. Researchers modified their equipment and the experiment flew on two additional checkout flights in mid-1966.[184]

Flights 3-53-79 and 3-54-80 carried the experiment. The first flight failed to acquire useful data due to improper instrumentation, and Bill Dana inadvertently

181 Memorandum, Paul L. Chenoweth/X-15 Project Engineer to Chief, Research Division, subject: Preliminary evaluation of X-15 flight 1-60-99, 26 October 1965; X-15 Status Reports, Paul F. Bikle/FRC to J. Martin/NASA Headquarters, 11 March, and 14 October 1965; Boston, "The X-15's Role in Aerospace Progress," p. 41.

182 System Package Program, System 653A, p. 6-43; "X-15 Semi-Annual Status Report No. 3," 1 December 1964, p. 20; X-15 Status Report, Paul F. Bikle/FRC to J. Martin/NASA Headquarters, 1 April 1966, p. 12.

183 Letter, Albert J. Evans to Hugh L. Dryden, subject: Notification of approval of additions to the X-15 test-bed program, 30 March 1964. In the files at the NASA History Office.

184 X-15 Status Report, Paul F. Bikle/FRC to J. Martin/NASA Headquarters, 1 April 1966, p. 13.

turned off the experiment after only 131 seconds on the second. The experimenter reported, however, that the limited data collected was satisfactory. The experiment was last flown on flight 3-56-83, and good data were collected.[185]

Experiment #26: Supersonic Transport (SST) Structural Demonstration Techniques

The Air Force Research Technology Division sponsored experiment #26 to evaluate a new technique for determining the mechanical loads and thermal stress experienced by aerospace vehicles exposed to a thermal environment. Republic Aviation developed an experimental analytical procedure that enabled the determination of loads, deformation, and stresses from given strain and temperature measurements. Laboratory tests on a box beam and frame structure yielded data with a calculated accuracy of ±10%. This procedure could be proof-tested on the X-15 and then used to validate the analytical design methods and structural load criteria used for the SST and other advanced aerospace vehicles.[186]

Researchers proposed to install thermocouples and strain gages in the fuselage-wing attachment structures and fabricate one horizontal stabilizer with strain gages and thermocouples installed on the spars. Approximately 360 sensors would have been required to perform the tests.[187]

The researchers forwarded a suggested program for using this technology to the Federal Aviation Administration (FAA) for possible funding. The FAA endorsed the requirement but thought it would be more appropriate for NASA to fund the experiment. NASA reviewed the experiment and agreed that a well-verified means of interpreting flight loads and thermal stress data was essential for the future SST, and that NASA should be responsible for developing the technique. However, NASA did not believe that a specific experiment of this magnitude was required to assess the Republic method.[188]

Eventually, however, the FRC approved and sponsored at least part of the experiment, which was broken into two parts called, logically enough, Phase I and Phase II. The Phase I program used a slightly instrumented set of horizontal stabilizers during several flights to gather baseline airplane data. The tests began on flight 3-52-78 on 18 July 1966 and concluded on flight 3-61-91 on 20 July 1967. Not every flight collected data, due to a variety of malfunctions, but sufficient data were gathered. On several Phase I flights the pilots noted a slight buffet and beta excursion under some flight conditions, a phenomenon the researchers could not explain.[189]

Phase II included a new set of horizontal stabilizers that were manufactured by North American during May 1966. NASA instrumented the left-hand unit with 128 strain gages and 125 thermocouples, and tested it in the High Temperature

185 "X-15 Semi-Annual Status Report No. 6," 1 November 1966, p. 25.

186 System Package Program, System 653A, p. 6-44.

187 Ibid.

188 Ibid.

189 X-15 Status Report, Paul F. Bikle/FRC to J. Martin/NASA Headquarters, 1 April 1966, p. 12. In the files at the DFRC History Office; memorandum, James R. Welsh (for Elmor J. Adkins, Chief/X-15 Project Office) to Assistant Chief, Research Projects, subject: Preliminary report on X-15 flight 3-61-91, 2 August 1967.

Loads Calibration Laboratory before installing it on X-15-3 in time for flight 3-62-92. To investigate buffet and beta excursions experienced during the Phase I portion of the experiment, pilots performed maneuvers at Mach 2.5, 3.7, and 4.0 with a pull-up to approximately 12 degrees angle of attack made at each Mach number. The pilots did not notice a buffet or beta excursion at the two higher Mach numbers, but at Mach 2.5 they experienced results similar to those encountered on the two previous flights. The beta excursion registered about 3 degrees, but the pilot was not positive that buffet occurred during this maneuver. Buffet had been experienced at 10.5 degrees on the previous flight. The only configuration change that occurred between the flights was the replacement of the Phase I horizontal stabilizer with the Phase II units. To evaluate this, NASA reinstalled the original horizontal stabilizers for flight 3-63-94. The pilot did not notice any buffet, leading researchers to suspect some minor manufacturing flaw in the new horizontal stabilizers. Unfortunately, X-15-3 was lost before researchers could complete any further work. Since the experiment depended on the PCM telemetry system in X-15-3, researchers could not move it to X-15-1.[190]

Another test in this series was to study of the effect of various discontinuities on local surface heating between Mach 4 and Mach 6. To avoid having to make detailed local measurements, the experiment was designed to determine the ratio of the heating rates on two symmetrically located panels under the center fuselage and on the wing tips. One panel in each location would have the discontinuity while the other would not. Discontinuities included forward and aft facing steps, wavy surfaces (sinusoidal distortions), streamwise corners, and antenna posts. At least two X-15-3 flights included the step panels, and the wavy panels made at least three flights.[191]

Experiment #27: Hycon Camera

The Air Force Research Technology Division sponsored experiment #27. It was conceptually an extension of experiment #5, which had used KC-1 and KS-25 cameras to acquire optical data at speeds between Mach 6 and Mach 8. This experiment used X-15-2 and was approximately 80% complete at the time of Jack McKay's accident in the second airplane. The experiment, however, continued after X-15A-2 returned to service.[192]

The first part of this experiment actually preceded experiment #5. NASA installed two instruments–a vertical camera with a 12-inch focal length, and an oblique camera with a 6-inch focal length–in the center-of-gravity compartment (between the propellant tanks) in X-15-2. The resulting data permitted the investigation of contrast attenuation at high altitudes and showed the feasibility of performing aerial photography from supersonic vehicles. These tests began as early as 9 October 1962 (flight 2-30-51) when the 6-inch oblique camera photo-

190 Memorandum, Elmor J. Adkins, Chief/X-15 Project Office to Assistant Chief, Research Projects, subject: Preliminary report on X-15 flight 3-62-92, 14 September 1967; memorandum, Elmor J. Adkins, Chief/X-15 Project Office to Assistant Chief, Research Projects, subject: Preliminary report on X-15 flight 3-63-94, 2 November 1967.

191 "X-15 Semi-Annual Status Report No. 1," October 1963, p. 37; "X-15 Semi-Annual Status Report No. 3," 1 December 1964, p. 19.

192 "X-15 Semi-Annual Status Report No. 1," October 1963, p. 41; "X-15 Semi-Annual Status Report No. 3," 1 December 1964, p. 20.

graphed the Las Vegas area from very high altitude using black and white film. During flight 2-39-70 on 22 June 1965, the 6-inch camera used color film to take a similar photo, and the 12-inch camera photographed Indian Springs AFB using color-infrared Ektachrome film. These tests included the evaluation of a special film, Kodak SO-190, which had a resolution of almost 200 lines per millimeter, a speed index of 6, and very low granularity.[193]

In late December 1965, a new Maurer model 500 camera replaced the Hycon in the center-of-gravity compartment on X-15A-2. NASA installed the camera during the weather down period during early 1966, with the intent to carry it throughout the envelope-expansion flights beginning with flight 2-49-86. Pre-flight tests of the system indicated that the experiment was functioning satisfactorily, but checks of the system before launch showed that the platform would not erect properly. Despite this, the camera data were satisfactory and the quality of the resulting photographs was excellent. The X-15A-2 carried the camera on two more flights, also with satisfactory results.[194]

A Hycon KA-51A "Chicago Aerial" camera then replaced the Maurer, which only flew one time on flight 2-52-96. For the next flight of X-15A-2, NASA removed the Hycon experiment and installed an aft-viewing Millikan 16-mm camera to photograph the dummy ramjet.[195]

Experiment #28: X-Ray Air Density

There is no record of what organization sponsored experiment #28. The experiment consisted of an X-ray tube and detector located in the forward portion of the right wing-tip pod. The wing-tip pod skin scattered the X-rays, and solid-state cells measured the backscatter to determine air density. The design and fabrication of this experiment began in late 1965 and several flights during 1967 and 1968 apparently carried it, although no results could be ascertained.[196]

Experiment #29: JPL Solar-Spectrum Measurements

The JPL sponsored experiment #29, which consisted of a spectrometer containing 12 sensors and a servo-positioning system installed in the rear section of the left wing-tip pod of X-15-1. Researchers wanted to use the data to improve the methods of correcting for atmospheric absorption, determine the absolute energy of the sun, and calibrate solar cells to validate solar simulation. JPL built

193 Groening, "Investigation of High-Speed High-Altitude Photography," pp. 85, 88, and 93; "Influence of High-Speed Flight on Photography," p. 18. IR Ektachrome differs from normal film in that the spectral sensitivity of each emulsion layer is shifted toward the infrared. The blue light is removed by filtering, and in the final reversed image that is printed, naturally green objects are blue, yellow objects are green, and red objects are yellow. Objects that radiate or reflect strongly in the near-infrared, such as healthy vegetation, are red.

194 X-15 Status Reports, Paul F. Bikle/FRC to J. Martin/NASA Headquarters, 3 January and 1 April 1966; "X-15 Semi-Annual Status Report No. 6," 1 November 1966, p. 25.

195 William P. Albrecht/X-15 Project Engineer, "X-15 Operations Flight Report for Flight 2-52-96," 25 August 1967; William P. Albrecht/X-15 Project Engineer, "X-15 Operations Flight Report for Flight 2-53-97," 9 October 1967.

196 X-15 Status Report, Paul F. Bikle/FRC to J. Martin/NASA Headquarters, 1 April 1966, p. 13; "X-15 Semi-Annual Status Report No. 6," 1 November 1966, p. 25. There seems to be a great deal of confusion in the official documentation concerning the experiment number assigned to the WTR launch-monitoring experiment. Most documents call it experiment #20; however, many Air Force documents refer to it as experiment #28. Since most documents use #20, that is what will be used here. Very late in the program the X-ray air density experiment was called #28, as reflected here.

the experiment in early 1966, but a pop-up hatch used to expose the spectrometer failed the qualification test in April 1966. Researchers subsequently redesigned the experiment to use a quartz window in the pod instead of a hatch to eliminate the problem. At the same time, researchers modified the experiment to use the new PCM telemetry system in X-15-3.[197]

The experiment first flew on flight 3-58-87, and later on two additional flights. A preliminary review of the data showed excessive electrical noise on the data channel, but researchers considered the data acceptable.[198]

Experiment #30: Spectrophotometry

In experiment #30, an objective spectrograph and two photometers were used to obtain spectra of the planets and observe day airflow at high altitude. As of April 1966, this experiment did not have a sponsor of formal approval, although it did apparently receive an experiment number. By the end of 1966, NASA had canceled the experiment before any actual hardware development was undertaken.[199]

Experiment #31: Fixed Alpha Nose

The FRC sponsored the fixed-ball-nose experiment to investigate the feasibility of using a fixed-sphere-cone sensor to measure air data parameters in extreme flight environments. Rodney K. Bogue and John P. Cary built the experiment hardware.[200]

The standard X-15 ball nose proved to be remarkably reliable given its operating environment, performing less than satisfactorily on only one of its first 70 flights. Nevertheless, in retrospect, the ball nose was an overly complicated solution to the problem. All that was really needed was a way to compute the difference in pressure between opposing ports, not to drive the entire sensor to seek the null pressure.

Late in the program, NASA flew an experiment that used a non-moving sensor to detect the angle of attack. Researchers attached a fixed ball nose on the left wing-tip pod, permitting the use of the normal ball nose for comparison purposes. The sensor consisted of a ported sphere, 4.36 inches in diameter, mounted on the nose of the pod. The total length of the sensor was 18.75 inches, but it looked like a simple extension of the pod. Five pressure ports were located on the pod. One port was 5 degrees below the zero angle-of-attack stagnation point, and the remaining four ports were located symmetrically around this point in the vertical and horizontal planes. The vertical ports were used to measure the angle of attack. Researchers planned to use the horizontal ports for the angle of sideslip, but this

197 "X-15 Semi-Annual Status Report No. 7," 10 May 1967, p.27; James E. Love and Jack Fischel, "Summary of X-15 Program," a paper in the *Progress of the X-15 Research Airplane Program*, a compilation of the papers presented at the FRC, 7 October 1965, NASA publication SP-90 (Washington, DC: NASA, 1965), p. 14; X-15 Status Reports, Paul F. Bikle/FRC to J. Martin/NASA Headquarters, 1 April and 4 May 1966.

198 X-15 Status Report 66-10, Paul F. Bikle/FRC to J. Martin/NASA Headquarters, 6 October 1966, p. 6.

199 X-15 Status Report, Paul F. Bikle/FRC to J. Martin/NASA Headquarters, 1 April 1966, p. 13.

200 Rodney K. Bogue, FRC working paper 30, "X-15 Fixed Ball Nose Flight Test Results," July 1972. Typescript in the files at the DFRC History Office. Several clarifications to the original narrative were provided in an e-mail from Rodney K. Bogue to Dennis R. Jenkins, 6 June 2002.

was never implemented. The sensor flew on a single flight (1-53-86) to Mach 5.17 with Bob Rushworth at the controls.[201]

The standard ball nose had a demonstrated measurement error of less than 0.25 degree over its entire operating range. On its single flight, the fixed nose did not return the same absolute data as the ball nose. This was not surprising since the wing-mounted device and the nose-mounted unit operated in different flow fields. Several factors affected the performance of the wing-mounted device, including 1) flow disturbances and shock-wave impingement from the forebody of the X-15, 2) rotational flow about the lifting-wing surface (the latter effect was particularly noticeable during approach and landing), and 3) suspected small deflections (bending and twisting) of the wing that created a variable offset between the normal- and fixed-ball-nose devices. Nevertheless, the fixed-ball-nose data showed the same trends as the ball-nose data. Researchers concluded that the fixed ball nose was a feasible alternative to the ball nose.[202]

Confidence was high enough that NASA manufactured a "fixed alpha nose" and installed it on a wing-tip pod for six of the last seven X-15-1 flights. Again, the data did not precisely match those obtained with the ball nose, but were repeatable enough that researchers could make consistent correlations. A conceptually similar system was used on the Apollo launch escape system to provide limited air data to the astronauts in case of an abort forced them to separate the capsule from the Saturn booster. NASA designed and installed a similar system, using ports in the nose cone, on the Space Shuttle *Columbia* as the Shuttle Entry Air Data System (SEADS) experiment between 1986 and 1991.[203]

OTHER FLOWN EXPERIMENTS

In addition to the "numbered" experiments formally approved by the Research Airplane Committee, the X-15s carried several other experiments that were often funded by the FRC as part of its own normal research activities.

Saturn Insulation

The "Saturn insulation" experiment exposed various types of insulation material from the Saturn launch vehicles to the hypersonic environment. Some documentation shows this as experiment #41. The X-15-3 made at least five flights with pieces of Saturn insulation material. By flying the material on the X-15, researchers could examine it after a flight, which was not possible with the expendable Saturn boosters. Generally, researchers installed variable-thickness panels on

201 Ibid.

202 Ibid.

203 For more on the SEADS experiment, see Dennis R. Jenkins, *Space Shuttle: The History of the National Space Transportation System–The First 100 Flights* (North Branch, MN: Specialty Press, 2001), pp. 436-437.

The test of insulation for the Saturn launch vehicles is usually heralded as one of the X-15's contributions, but in reality the tests were minimal and concentrated more on the adhesives behind the insulation. Here the Saturn insulation is installed on the upper speed brakes of X-15-3 on 31 October 1967, just before its last flight. Note the tail cone box behind the speed brakes. (NASA)

the upper speed brakes with two thermocouples on the left side, and seven thermocouples, two static-pressure transducers, and one pitot probe on the right side. They also installed additional constant-thickness insulation panels on the lower speed brakes with two thermocouples on the right side and seven thermocouples on the left side. NASA installed a camera in the right wing-tip pod to look at the upper speed brakes, and a second camera in the left pod pointed at the lower speed brakes. Some of the tests were decidedly unsuccessful. For instance, NASA applied Saturn insulation to the upper left speed brake on the aborted flight attempt on 31 October 1967 (3-A-96); the bond failed and the insulation came off during the captive flight. Researchers replaced the insulation before Mike Adams's fatal flight (3-65-97).[204]

After X-15-3 was lost, NASA transferred the experiment to X-15-1. Researchers installed 16-mm movie cameras in each wing pod to photograph the insulation on the upper speed brakes, and installed 18 thermocouples in the speed brakes

204 X-15 Status Report, Paul F. Bikle/FRC to J. Martin/NASA Headquarters, 8 November 1967, p. 2; Vincent N. Capasso, "X-15 Operations Flight Report for Flight 1-75-133," 9 April 1968; memorandum, James R. Welsh/X-15 Research Project Office to Assistant Chief, Research Projects, subject: Preliminary report on X-15 flight 1-75-133, 17 April 1968; Vincent N. Capasso, "X-15 Operations Flight Report for Flight 1-76-134," 30 April 1968. All in the files at the DFRC History Office. If this was experiment #41, then nothing could be ascertained about experiments #32 through #40.

themselves. Several flights carried the insulation until the end of the program, although sometimes it was on the lower speed brakes (and other times on both).[205]

Since these tests were conducted fairly late in the Saturn development program (1966–1967), it is unlikely that any unexpected information was gained. More probably, the researchers just achieved final confirmation of the material's ability to withstand high dynamic pressures without losing its thermal properties.

Skid Materials

The ASD sponsored an experiment that was essentially a product evaluation program of materials selected for use on the Dyna-Soar. Researchers bonded cermet (ceramic-metallic composite) runners to the rear landing-gear skids on the X-15 for five flights using X-15-3 in early 1964. Two additional flights were conducted using X-15A-2 to evaluate Inconel X skids. Engineers compared these data with those obtained on five earlier flights that used standard 4130-steel skids but carried additional instrumentation to measure landing loads:[206]

Test	Flight	Skid Material	Lakebed Surface	Landing Weight	Distance Main Nose	Nose Gear Impact	Slideout Distance	Touchdown Speed
				(pounds)	(feet)	(seconds)	(feet)	(knots)
1	1-9-17	4130 Steel	Dry-hard	14,700	312	0.70	7,920	207
2	1-10-19	4130 Steel	Dry-hard	14,500	304	0.80	—	196
3	1-11-21	4130 Steel	Dry-hard	14,600	218	0.54	—	196
4	1-12-23	4130 Steel	Dry-hard	14,950	294	0.74	8,170	204
5	1-13-25	4130 Steel	Dry-hard	15,150	205	0.60	4,488	164
6	3-25-42	Cermet	Dry-hard	14,920	252	0.72	5,702	175
7	3-26-43	Cermet	Dry-hard	15,100	253	0.61	4,807	208
8	3-27-44	Cermet	Dry-hard	15,100	310	0.83	5,204	193
9	3-28-47	Cermet	Dry-hard	14,750	320	0.89	5,808	187
10	3-29-48	Cermet	Dry-soft	14,920	172	0.76	3,520	181
11	2-33-56	Inconel X	Dry-hard	17,798	288	0.71	6,056	205
12	2-34-57	Inconel X	Damp-hard	15,855	365	0.72	8,968	221

205 X-15 Status Reports, Paul F. Bikle/FRC to J. Martin/NASA Headquarters, 5 April 1968, p. 2 and 2 May 1968, p. 2. In the files at the DFRC History Office.

206 "X-15 Semi-Annual Status Report No. 1," October 1963, p. 35; "X-15 Semi-Annual Status Report No. 3," 1 December 1964, pp. 8-9; Ronald J. Wilson, NASA technical note D-3331, "Drag and Wear Characteristics of Various Skid Materials on Dissimilar Lakebed Surfaces During the Slideout of the X-15 Airplane," March 1966. Data in the table comes mainly from Wilson. The cermet process is interesting. To coat a standard 4130 steel skid, a 0.1865-inch screen of tungsten-carbide chips is copper-brazed to the skid surface after the surface is precoated with a flux. A 0.020–0.040-inch-thick matrix of tungsten (35%), chrome, nickel, and boron (65%) is flame-sprayed on top of the copper-brazed carbide chips, fused and grit-blasted, and then flame-sprayed with a copper-nickel matrix. The surface is then ground to a nominal thickness of 0.20 inch.

One of the outcomes of the study was an evaluation of skid wear. The amount of skid wear depended on the speed of the sliding, the hardness of the skid material, the strength of the surface material, and the sliding distance. For this evaluation, engineers measured the thickness of the X-15 skids after each flight, generally near the point of attachment to the main strut. The difficulties involved in removing and reinstalling the skids in a timely manner precluded weighing them. The cermet skids experienced a considerable amount of wear during the first landing because of the soft outer layer of copper-nickel, but showed less wear on later landings because the tungsten-carbide chips were uncovered.[207]

The data for the 4130-steel skids showed an increasing amount of skid wear as the sliding distance increased beyond 6,400 feet. The wear characteristics of the Inconel X skids were not determined because of the difficulty of measuring the chemically milled areas inside the skid. However, preliminary data indicated a wear resistance superior to that of the 4130 steel, with or without a cermet coating.[208]

Cold Wall

The X-15 offered investigators a unique opportunity to measure heat transfer and skin friction under quasi-steady flight conditions at high Mach numbers and low wall-to-recovery temperature ratios. This allowed them to make a direct comparison between measured flight data and calculated values. A considerable amount of heat-transfer data and some skin-friction data were obtained during the flight program, and these data indicated that the level and rate of change of turbulent skin friction and heat transfer were lower than predicted by the most widely used theories, such as those of Van Driest and Eckert. However, comparisons of the X-15 data and the theory were inconclusive due to uncertainties about the boundary layer conditions because of non-uniform flow and conduction losses. To evaluate the problem, researchers wanted to use a highly instrumented panel in a location with known flow characteristics. They also wanted the panel to be shielded from aerodynamic heating until the airplane was in a steady-state cruise condition.[209]

Researchers selected the X-15-3 with the sharp-leading-edge modification on the dorsal rudder to carry the experiment. The test panel was located just behind the right-side leading-edge boundary-layer trips 15.1 inches below the top of the rudder, and was constructed of 0.0605-inch-thick Inconel X. Researchers installed a removable panel on the left side of the rudder to provide access to the instrumentation used for the test panel. To obtain the desired wall-to-recovery temperature ratios and ensure an isothermal test surface when the airplane reached the desired speed and altitude, it was necessary to insulate the test panel during the initial phase of the flight. Explosive charges jettisoned the insulating cover from the test panel in approximately 50 milliseconds, resulting in an instantaneous heating of

207 Wilson, "Drag and Wear Characteristics of Various Skid Materials," pp. 21-24.

208 Ibid, pp. 24.

209 Robert D. Quinn and Frank V. Olinger, NASA confidential technical memorandum X-1921, "Flight-Measured Heat Transfer and Skin Friction at a Mach Number of 5.25 and at Low Wall Temperatures," 19 August 1969, pp. 1-20. For data on earlier heat-transfer and skin-friction studies, see, for example, Richard D. Banner and Albert E. Kuhl, "A Summary of X-15 Heat-Transfer and Skin-Friction Measurements," NASA technical memorandum X-1210, 1966.

the test panel (the so-called "cold wall" effect). Researchers instrumented the test panel with thermocouples, static-pressure orifices, and a skin-friction gage with the data recorded on tape by a PCM data acquisition system at a rate of 50 samples per second. A Millikan camera operating at 400 frames per second was in the upper bug-eye camera bay to record the events. The measurements obtained were in general agreement with previous X-15 data.[210]

Researchers used the same general location for another test panel, but without the cold wall. This panel, which was flush with the normal surface of the rudder, had a microphone and static-pressure orifice mounted flush, and an "L"-shaped total pressure probe sticking out and forward. The microphone was located 28.8 inches from the original rudder leading edge (not the sharp extension) and 20.3 inches from the top of the rudder. The data was recorded onboard the airplane and evaluated after the flight. The intent of the experiment was to determine when the boundary layer transitioned to turbulent flow. The highest noise levels occurred during reentry as the Reynolds numbers reached their peak value. The data gathered provided a qualitative indication of the end of the transition that agreed reasonably well with wind-tunnel data. Interestingly, researchers also recorded some data while the NB-52 carried the X-15, and described the noise level as "very high" due to aerodynamic interference with the carrier aircraft. This confirmed predictions made before the first glide flight.[211]

Sonic Booms

Just as the X-15 program was winding down, researchers noted that airplanes flying faster than Mach 3 (the YF-12C/SR-71A and XB-70A) did not generate a sonic-boom noise. NASA had made some measurements at Mach numbers up to 16 during the liftoff and reentry of Apollo spacecraft, but did not consider this representative of future aerospace vehicles, such as the Space Shuttle. Therefore, researchers made measurements during several X-15 flights at Mach numbers up to 5.5 and compared these with results obtained by theoretical methods of determining overpressures.[212]

For flight 1-70-119, instruments were set up at Mud Lake to record the boom generated at Mach 5.3 and 92,000 feet. Researchers obtained satisfactory data even though the airplane was about 6 miles east of the monitoring site. The sonic boom was a typical far-field signature with some slight atmospheric distortion, although this was less than predicted. The boom peak overpressure was about 0.34 psf.[213]

For another flight, researchers installed microphone arrays around Goldstone and Cuddeback dry lakes. Since there were no meteorological facilities at either lake, researchers estimated the environmental conditions based on data obtained

---

210 X-15 Status Report, Paul F. Bikle/FRC to J. Martin/NASA Headquarters, 4 April 1967, p. 2; Robert D. Quinn and Frank V. Olinger, NASA confidential technical memorandum X-1921, "Flight-Measured Heat Transfer and Skin Friction at a Mach Number of 5.25 and at Low Wall Temperatures," 19 August 1969, pp. 5-8.

211 Thomas L. Lewis and Richard D. Banner, NASA technical memorandum X-2466, "Boundary-Layer Transition Detection on the X-15 Vertical Fin Using Surface Pressure-Fluctuation Measurements," 20 August 1971, passim.

212 X-15 Status Report, Paul F. Bikle/FRC to J. Martin/NASA Headquarters, 4 April 1967, p. 4; Karen S. Green and Terrill W. Putnam, NASA technical memorandum X-3126, "Measurements of Sonic Booms Generated by an Airplane Flying at Mach 3.5 and 4.8," 5 September 1974. Note that the X-15 flight program had been terminated nearly six years before this report was issued.

213 X-15 Status Report, Paul F. Bikle/FRC to J. Martin/NASA Headquarters, 4 April 1967, p. 4.

at Edwards. When the airplane arrived over Goldstone at Mach 4.8, the engine was operating at 50% thrust and the speed brakes were extended; at Cuddeback the engine had already shut down, the speed brakes had retracted, and the airplane was at Mach 3.5. Although the flight plan called for the airplane to fly directly over the microphone arrays, in reality it passed 1.7 miles south of the array at Goldstone and 7.9 miles south of the Cuddeback array–not an unusual amount of error for an X-15 flight.[214]

Researchers scaled and corrected the data collected from Goldstone so they could compare it with similar data obtained from an SR-71 flight. The two sets of data were in general agreement. Researchers did not evaluate the data from Cuddeback because of the X-15 miss distance. The results of the experiment also compared favorably to theoretical results, and no unusual phenomena related to the overpressure were encountered.[215]

RECOVERABLE BOOSTER SYSTEM

As early as 1960, some researchers considered the X-15 an ideal recoverable first stage for small launch vehicles, such as the NASA/USAF Blue Scout series. The researchers believed that this could result in significant cost savings and increased reliability compared to four-stage, all-ballistic firings.[216]

Researchers had already gained some limited experience by launching small rockets from high-performance aircraft. Milt Thompson and Forrest Petersen had participated in five launches of Viper I-C sounding rockets from a Lockheed F-104A Starfighter (56-0749). The F-104 carried a hydraulically actuated MB-1 launcher rack equipped with a modified Sidewinder launch rail on the centerline. The researchers expected that the single-stage Viper could reach 800,000 feet, an altitude comparable to that achieved by the ground-launched Nike-Asp sounding rocket. The F-104 was also equipped with a modified MA-2 low-altitude bombing system (LABS) computer from a North American F-100C Super Sabre that automatically launched the sounding rocket when the F-104 reached the proper altitude and pitch angle.[217]

Engineers believed the Viper was sufficiently safe to launch from a manned aircraft, but conducted two flights to verify that the rocket could withstand the stresses of the climb to altitude and the launch maneuver. The Air Force conducted the launches over the Pacific Missile Range at Point Mugu, California, at altitudes between 28,600 feet and 51,100 feet, and the rockets attained altitudes

214 Karen S. Green and Terrill W. Putnam, NASA technical memorandum X-3126, "Measurements of Sonic Booms Generated by an Airplane Flying at Mach 3.5 and 4.8," 5 September 1974, no page numbers.

215 Ibid.

216 "Advanced Development Plan for X-15 Research Aircraft, Advanced Technology Program 653A," p. 55.

217 Victor W. Horton and Wesley E. Messing, NASA technical note D-1279, "Some Operational Aspects of Using a High-Performance Airplane as a First-Stage Booster for Air-Launching Solid-Fuel Sounding Rockets," January 1963, no page numbers.

between 204,000 feet and 383,000 feet. These tests seemed to confirm that the concept was possible.[218]

Along the same lines, North American Aviation and the Aeronutronic Division of the Ford Motor Company conducted a joint study during 1961 to determine the feasibility and desirability of using the X-15 to launch modified RM-89 Blue Scout rockets. The intent was to provide a "recoverable booster system capable of accomplishing a wide variety of space probe and orbital experiment missions."[219]

The NACA conceived the basic Scout in 1958 as part of a study into the development of an inexpensive, lightweight vehicle to launch small satellites or perform high-altitude research. NASA assigned the management of the Scout program to Langley, and the vehicle emerged as a four-stage vehicle. Engineers at Langley decided that all four stages would use solid propellants, citing the relative simplicity and reliability of solid-fuel technology. In April 1959, Langley issued the Scout production contract to the Astronautics Division of Ling-Temco-Vought, a subsidiary of the Chance Vought Corporation. The Air Force modified the original NASA Scout under the names Blue Scout I, Blue Scout II, and Blue Scout Junior.

Essentially, the North American-Ford study defined a three-stage booster. The NB-52 was the first stage, the X-15 was the second stage, and the upper two stages (stages 3 and 4) of the Blue Scout were called the third stage (despite being two physical stages). The study investigated both guided and unguided versions of the Scout, but concentrated on the unguided vehicle as a means of keeping costs at a minimum.[220]

As usual, the NB-52 would launch the X-15 at 45,000 feet, with the research airplane climbing to altitudes between 130,000 and 200,000 feet to launch the Blue Scout. The shutdown of the X-15 engine and ignition of the Blue Scout would occur simultaneously.

Ford and North American engineers believed they could reasonably predict the effects of adding an external store to the X-15, and the entire modification would add approximately 500 pounds to the empty weight of the airplane. With the missile pylon mounted on the bottom centerline of the fuselage, a slight reduction in directional stability was expected. However, engineers anticipated that partial deflection of the speed brakes could maintain a level of directional stability comparable to that of the basic aircraft. Lateral stability would suffer from a slightly greater negative dihedral effect, but North American did not expect this to be a cause for concern since it was within the capability of the SAS to counter. The pylon was about the same height as the normal fixed portion of the ventral stabilizer and extended forward to the leading edge of the wing.[221]

North American did not expect reentry with the launcher pylon installed to present "any particular problems." The study estimated that the temperatures on and around the pylon would be less than 1,000°F, and any local hot spots could be tolerated through the use of ablative materials.[222]

---

218 Ibid.

219 Aeronutronic (a division of Ford Motor Company) report number 12121U, "X-15 Recoverable Booster System," 11 December 1961, p. 1. In the files at the DFRC History Office.

220 Ibid, p. 3.

221 Ibid, pp. 5, 10, 21, and drawings attached to the back of the report.

222 Ibid, p. 6.

Before the X-15 pilot could extend the launcher and fire the missile, he had to arm the missile ignition circuit and the missile destruct system via switches in the cockpit. The launcher was extended and the missile fired by pressing a button on the center stick. Upon activation, the hydraulic actuator unlocked the uplock and extended the launch rail. Shortly before the bottom of the extension stroke the actuator became a snubber, and when it bottomed out it became a drag link. When the extension arms reached 60 degrees arc, the fire circuit for the missile energized and the missile left the launch rails. If the missile did not fire, it automatically jettisoned at the bottom of the extension stroke along with the launch rails. During normal operation, the missile de-energized the jettison circuit as it left the launch rails, and the rails automatically retracted into the pylon.[223]

The Pacific Missile Range tracked the Blue Scout after launch from an X-15 flying from a lake near Wendover AFB heading west. The expended stages would fall into the Pacific off the coast of California. If the missile had to be destroyed during the first-stage boost, the remains would likely fall on government land along the High Range. Engineers expected that the X-15/Blue Scout configuration could launch 150 pounds into a 115-mile orbit, or 60 pounds into a 1,150-mile orbit.[224]

Ford estimated that using the NB-52 and X-15 to launch the Blue Scout could save between $150,000 and $250,000 per mission compared to ground-launching a similar payload. Some figures showed even greater savings. Ford stated, "It is estimated that an orbital mission using the X-15 Recoverable Booster System can be accomplished at a cost of approximately $250,000 as opposed to the $1,000,000 required for an orbital flight of the Scout vehicle. Based on 50 and 100 vehicle launches over a 2-1/2 year period, it is estimated that savings in the order of 12 and 24 million dollars could be achieved. Amortization of vehicle and aircraft modifications and the required development program are reflected in these figures." This did not completely agree with the assessment made a year or two later by the FRC that each X-15 launch alone cost approximately $600,000.[225]

Remembering that 1961 was the height of the Cold War, Ford also pointed out that "[e]xperimental missile launches from the X-15 aircraft in the environment of outer space should provide considerable data toward solving the problem of weapons delivery from a space plane or other orbital vehicle." Interestingly, NASA also conducted wind-tunnel tests of the X-15/Blue Scout carrying an ASSET research vehicle in support of the Dyna-Soar program.[226]

The study also proposed taking the X-15 "on the road" and conducting equatorial launches. The favored scenario apparently had the NB-52 taking off from Cape Canaveral, Florida, and the X-15 landing on Grand Bahama Island. The study continued, "Although it is realized that certain Ground Support Equipment

---

223 Ibid, pp. 10-11.

224 Ibid, pp. 12-16 and 25.

225 Ibid, pp. 18-19; James E. Love and William R. Young, NASA technical note D-3732, "Survey of Operation and Cost Experience of the X-15 Airplane as a Reusable Space Vehicle," November 1966, pp. 7. Interestingly, these are the same cost arguments made by Orbital Sciences Corporation for their current Pegasus launch vehicle. Ironically, the Pegasus first flew from the same NB-52 aircraft that supported the X-15 program.

226 Aeronutronic report number 12121U, p. 16.

and facilities must be made available for landing and recovery of the X-15 in remote places … the cost of achieving a mission … would be considerably less than required for establishing a missile ground launch site." This seemed to ignore the fact that there are very few dry-lake landing sites around the equator, especially in the Bahamas.[227]

Ford and North American expected that the engineering would take only three months after they were given the authority to proceed, and the manufacture of the launch system and modifications to the X-15 and NB-52 would take an additional three months. Two development tests (one at Hidden Hills and one at Silver Lake) were conducted seven months after the go-ahead was received. These tests used an unpowered missile to evaluate the captive-carry and jettison characteristics of the configuration. The first test was performed at a relatively low altitude, peaking at 112,000 feet; the second would go to the full 180,000-foot expected launch altitude.[228]

When Paul Bikle heard about the proposal, he raised several questions, primarily centering on range-safety aspects in the event of a Blue Scout failure, and the possible impact on the X-15 research program that could result from dedicating an airplane to this concept. It appears that the obstacles were too great for the expected return, and the concept just quietly faded from the scene.[229]

RAMJETS

Although the X-15 would eventually play a major role in the Hypersonic Research Engine (HRE) project, researchers had not considered air-breathing propulsion at all during its conceptual development in 1954. At the time, most researchers believed that hypersonic air-breathing engines were improbable or, more likely, impossible. Several military programs undertook subsonic-burning ramjet development, but there appeared to be fundamental obstacles to their use at hypersonic speeds. In 1955, William H. Avery at the Applied Physics Laboratory (APL) of The Johns Hopkins University conducted a survey of ongoing ramjet development efforts and concluded that Mach 4 was about the highest speed achievable by ramjets. Two problems arose at higher speeds: the lack of structural materials for the combustor, and a serious energy loss due to dissociation of the propulsive airflow and the failure of this plasma to recombine in the nozzle.[230]

A remarkable change from pessimism to optimism occurred during the late 1950s and early 1960s. By 1964, researchers believed they could solve the problems encountered previously. In particular, a hydrogen-powered supersonic combustion ramjet appeared to have the dramatic potential of useful performance up

227 Ibid, p. 17; Keith J. Scala, "A History of Air-Launched Space Vehicles," *Quest*, vol. 3, no. 1, spring 1994, p. 38.

228 Aeronutronic report number 12121U, pp. 20-28.

229 X-15 Status Report, Paul F. Bikle/FRC to H. Brown/NASA Headquarters, 15 March 1962, p. 3.

230 John V. Becker, "A Hindsight Study of the NASA Hypersonic Research Engine Project," 1 July 1976, p. 2. Prepared under contract NAS1-14250 but never published. Copy in the author's collection.

to near-orbital velocities. No single breakthrough created this newfound optimism–it sprang from a confluence of results from a number of unrelated research efforts. The first important contribution was a series of external burning studies conducted at the NACA Lewis Flight Propulsion Laboratory and the Marquardt Corporation in Van Nuys, California. These studies appeared to confirm that combustion in a supersonic flow was possible. Similar results had been produced by the APL and Antonio Ferri at the Brooklyn Polytechnic Institute in the late 1950s. The next innovation was the development of hydrogen as a fuel, which was also mainly accomplished at Lewis. Beginning in 1954, Richard J. Weber at Lewis began to think about the possibility of using supersonic combustion, internally, in a ramjet engine. Although he doubted that shock-free combustion would be possible in a supersonic combustor, Weber decided to analyze the ideal performance that would be attainable in a ramjet. The work had a low priority and proceeded slowly, but resulted in the first definitive analytical assessment of a supersonic ramjet.[231]

In a September 1958 report, Weber and John S. Mackay identified several beneficial features of a supersonic combustion ramjet (scramjet), noting that it could relax inlet/diffuser requirements, reduce combustor heating, minimize the nozzle-dissociation problem, alleviate variable-geometry inlet requirements, and provide the potential for performance levels much higher than any other air-breathing engine at speeds above Mach 7. The effects of the combustor area ratio, thermal compression, and other design parameters were determined for the first time. Several other researchers generally confirmed the results of this research by 1960. Ironically, by the time NASA finally published the Weber-Mackay paper in 1958, the authors had moved on to other research, believing there would be little interest in the scramjets and few (if any) applications for them.[232]

This was an interesting time for the NACA laboratories. On 1 October 1958, the NACA ceased to exist and the new NASA came into being. Lewis was beginning to abandon all work on air-breathing engines in favor of rocket engines. Thus, it surprised Weber when in early 1959 he was invited to speak at the 2nd Symposium on Advanced Propulsion Concepts as a specialist in supersonic combustion. Weldon Worth, then technical director of the Aero-Propulsion Laboratory at Wright Field, organized an entire session on the subject. Worth had many interests, including Aerospaceplane, a large single-stage-to-orbit vehicle powered by scramjets. Shortly after the beginning of the Mercury program in 1959, most of the major aerospace companies participated in studies of the Aerospaceplane, although in retrospect it is easy to see that the concept could never have worked given the technology of the era. Nevertheless, the concept was exciting, and Alexander Kartveli at Republic Aviation, for example, enlisted the services of Antonio Ferri to collaborate on orbital concepts. In addition to scramjets, the companies began working on imaginative new schemes, such as the air collection engine system (ACES) and the liquid air collection and enrichment system

231 Ibid. Weber used, logically enough, the acronym SCRJ to describe the device, but this was difficult to pronounce and soon gave way to "scramjet" SCRAM had first been a Navy program to develop a supersonic combustion ramjet missile.

232 Ibid; Richard J. Weber and John S. Mackay, NACA technical note 4386, "An Analysis of Ramjet Engines Using Supersonic Combustion, September 1958. Available online at *http://naca.larc.nasa.gov/reports/1958/naca-tn-4386/*.

(LACES), that would extract air from the atmosphere on the way up to be used as oxidizer by rocket engines when the vehicle left the sensible atmosphere.[233]

The first public discussion of hypersonic propulsion and its possible applications was held at the 4th AGARD Colloquium in Milan during April 1960. Ferri fired the imagination of his audience with the prospects of air-breathing engines that worked all the way to orbit. Many of the older researchers were politely skeptical. The Aerospaceplane concepts would survive for several years within the Air Force before everybody came to realize they were simply too advanced for the state of the art. For a brief time, however, they influenced the road taken by some of the early space shuttle studies.[234]

The scramjet concept, however, survived relatively intact. Between 1959 and 1963, the military spent $10 million on scramjet research, and researchers failed to uncover any "concept killer" obstacles. Perhaps equally important was the appearance of a rapidly growing cult of ardent scramjet enthusiasts of which Ferri was the chief spokesman and Worth the chief benefactor. By all appearances, it seemed that practical scramjet applications were just around the corner. One 1964 summary stated that "scramjets are passing into the development stage" and listed no less than 19 institutions that were working on the concept, including five that were "testing complete engine models."[235]

In 1964 the Air Force released Project Forecast, one of the periodic studies the military conducted into possible advanced concepts for future applications. Largely through the lobbying efforts of Ferri and Worth, the scramjet became an area that merited special emphasis. Consequently, General Bernard A. Schriever, the commander of the Air Force Systems Command, established a special task force to examine scramjet technology and its potential. However, the cards were stacked in favor of the technology because the majority of the members of the task force were members of Worth's staff or representatives of the various contractors working under $22 million worth of scramjet contracts. The final report published in April 1965 envisioned "no unforeseen problems" and recommended initiating a high-priority national development program. There were, of course, skeptics who did not believe the technology was nearly as advanced as its proponents claimed. However, few of them were willing to buck the Air Force hierarchy, which apparently had decided to embark on a crusade.[236]

The origination of large government research and development projects is seldom a logical process, and the HRE was no exception. North American Aviation was always interested in new business, and during the early 1960s it was particularly keen on finding new ways to exploit the X-15 research airplane. Given the newfound interest in scramjet propulsion, project aerodynamicist Bill Johnston decided to marry the two. During May 1962, Johnston visited various Air Force and NASA centers with a proposal to modify an X-15 for use as a flying test bed

233 Becker, "A Hindsight Study of the NASA Hypersonic Research Engine Project," pp. 4-5. For more information on Aerospaceplane, see Dennis R. Jenkins, *Space Shuttle: The History of the National Space Transportation System–The First 100 Missions* (North Branch, MN: Specialty Press, 2001), pp. 52-57. ACES (air-collection engine system) and LACE (liquid air cycle engine) were actually brought to the small demonstrator stage, but no full-scale development was ever undertaken.

234 Becker, "A Hindsight Study of the NASA Hypersonic Research Engine Project," pp. 4-5.

235 Ibid, pp. 5-6.

236 Ibid, pp. 6-7.

for hypersonic air-breathing engines. To many researchers, including some at the FRC, the X-15 seemed like an ideal test bed for such a propulsion system. As envisioned by the FRC in 1961, this idea was "an extensive air-breathing engine development program ... in which one or more sub-scale modular experimental engines would be flown in a true flight environment aboard the X-15." Surprisingly, there were no takers, and the proposal floundered until November 1962 when Jack McKay made an emergency landing in X-15-2, injuring himself and seriously damaging the airplane.[237]

North American took this opportunity to dust off Johnston's concept and reiterated its proposal to modify the airplane for propulsion testing. The Air Force supported the plan and was willing to pay the estimated $4.75 million to rebuild and modify the aircraft. Many within NASA, however, were not in favor of the idea since they considered the proposed Mach 8 speed to be of limited value for propulsion research. Nevertheless, NASA did not press its objections and the Air Force authorized North American to modify the airplane. It thus appeared that a Mach 8 carrier vehicle would be available within a couple of years; however, the propulsion test engines themselves were completely undefined.[238]

To correct this illogical situation, the FRC quickly launched a study aimed at determining what type of engine would be appropriate for testing on the X-15. Recognizing that the expertise for monitoring such a study would be found chiefly at other NASA facilities, the FRC solicited comments on its draft procurement documents; no support was forthcoming. In fact, Kennedy F. Rubert at Langley expressed his opposition to any flight program as "an unwise expenditure of government funds" since engine research "is better done on the ground." Undaunted, the FRC continued with its procurement and stated firmly that it planned "to take an active role in advanced air-breathing propulsion and the X-15 should prove very useful in this regard." This course of action seemed to both prolong the X-15 program and increase the participation of the FRC in basic research projects, despite philosophical misgivings on the part of many at the FRC, including Paul Bikle.[239]

After a brief proposal period, the FRC awarded a four-month study contract to the Marquardt Corporation to generate requirements applicable to 1) subsonic combustion ramjets, 2) LACES, 3) scramjets, 4) ducted rockets, and 5) turboramjets.[240]

When the final report appeared in December 1963, the results bore little resemblance to the dummy ramjet that would ultimately fly on X-15A-2. Marquardt determined that the X-15 was a viable platform for testing ramjets in the speed range of Mach 4 to Mach 8, providing a useful complement to ground testing. The company proposed to test three different types of ramjets that required 33 months to develop and build. Surprisingly, the study investigated using one of the basic X-15s for preliminary testing while North American rebuilt X-15A-2.[241]

237 "X-15 Semi-Annual Status Report No. 1," October 1963, p. 40; Becker, "A Hindsight Study of the NASA Hypersonic Research Engine Project," pp. 8-9.

238 Becker, "A Hindsight Study of the NASA Hypersonic Research Engine Project," p. 9.

239 Ibid.

240 "X-15 Semi-Annual Status Report No. 1," October 1963, p. 40.

241 Marquardt report MP1209, "Hypersonic Airbreathing Propulsion Systems for Testing on the X-15: Feasibility and Preliminary Design Study," prepared under contract NAS4-382, 3 December 1963.

The three proposed engines included a subsonic combustion ramjet, a scramjet, and a "convertible ramjet," all sharing a common external design referred to as MA-131. The convertible engine operated as a subsonic combustion engine between Mach 3 and 5, and with supersonic combustion between Mach 7 and 8; it transitioned from one mode to the other between Mach 5 and 7. Researchers investigated three other engine types—the turboramjet, ducted rocket, and LACE/ACES–and ruled them out, although the ducted rocket returned as part of the later air-augmented rocket propulsion system (AARPS) concept.[242]

Marquardt considered regenerative, radiation, and ablative cooling schemes, and settled on the latter as being the most cost-effective and lowest risk. Unfortunately, this probably doomed the Marquardt proposal since most hypersonic-engine researchers were firmly convinced that testing was not worthwhile unless the engine used regenerative cooling. Another controversial aspect of the Marquardt proposal was the plan to forego a true variable-geometry inlet design in favor of an inlet that could be set to various positions on the ground before flight. In retrospect, this seems like a good compromise. Undoubtedly, any production engine would use a variable-geometry inlet, but it would be expensive and time-consuming to develop one. In addition, given how short a period the X-15 could maintain steady flight conditions, there would be little opportunity to adjust the inlet in flight in any case. Ground personnel could adjust it to allow data to be gathered on successive flights at different geometries. Still, the researchers at Langley and Lewis believed the solution was inelegant and rejected it out of hand.[243]

The engineers at the FRC begged to differ, noting that "the elimination of complex and unproven inlet and exhaust nozzle control systems from the test engine also provides operational simplicity with reasonable assurance for success without a long and costly X-15 flight test program." Nevertheless, the engineers worried that the drag created by the ramjet installation might result in much slower-than-desired acceleration while on the way to the intended flight conditions. Marquardt modified the design so that the inlet would close during the acceleration phase and open only when the correct test conditions were available.[244]

Instead of the round cross-section dummy ramjet that ultimately hung from the ventral stabilizer on X-15A-2, Marquardt proposed a rectangular shape that fit flush against the lower fuselage. The unit would be 188 inches long, 24 inches wide, and 21 inches high. A boundary-layer fence between the inlet and the lower fuselage ensured clean airflow into the inlet. Researchers expected the hydrogen-fueled ramjet could produce up to 1,000 lbf gross thrust. Several mockups were produced and fitted to X-15A-2 at various times, including one airshow at Edwards.[245]

---

242 Irving Stone, "X-15 Use Planned in Ramjet Evaluations," *Aviation Week & Space Technology*, 31 August 1964, pp. 57-58; Marquardt report MP1209, "Hypersonic Airbreathing Propulsion Systems for Testing on the X-15: Feasibility and Preliminary Design Study," prepared under contract NAS4-382, 3 December 1963, no page numbers.

243 Ibid.

244 Memorandum, Douglas E. Wall/FRC (Airborne Hypersonic Research Program manager) to James E. Love/FRC (X-15 Program Manager), subject: Performance uprating of the YLR99 rocket engine in the X-15A-2 airplane for flight test of the USAF/NASA advanced ramjet engine, 20 October 1963.

245 Marquardt report MP1209.

Concurrently, North American conducted a study to determine the structural modifications needed to support the Marquardt concepts. In addition to the three engines proposed by Marquardt, engineers also studied an in-house-developed ramjet called the Typhon. North American estimated that the Typhon installation would weigh 803 pounds, while the three Marquardt engines would average about 900 pounds. The engineers believed all of these were within the capability of the X-15 to handle, although they shifted the center of gravity dangerously rearward.[246]

In addition to the engine package itself, North American needed to install an engine control system, engine jettison system, liquid-fuel storage and transfer system, and fuel pressurization system, as well as a new fire detection system. The engine package would replace the ventral stabilizer on the basic X-15, but would hang from a stub ventral on X-15A-2.[247]

On the basic airplane the entire ventral stabilizer and lower rudder actuator would be removed, a "roller support system" would be installed that actually supported the ramjet, a new frame would be added in the fuselage at station 483.5, and a pair of conformal liquid-hydrogen slipper tanks would be added over the aft portions of the side tunnels. Since North American was including a liquid-hydrogen tank in the center-of-gravity compartment of the rebuilt X-15A-2, the slipper tanks would be unnecessary. The longer rear skids on the advanced airplane would also allow the ramjet to be mounted on the stub ventral stabilizer. This had a couple of desirable effects: the inlet would be farther away from the flow disturbance caused by the X-15 fuselage, and at least a small ventral stabilizer would remain if the ramjet had to be jettisoned at high speeds. North American also suggested using JP-Pentaborane as an alternate fuel, and proposed installing a system that could handle either fuel as necessary.[248]

North American did express a couple of concerns. The modifications would increase landing-gear loads significantly, reducing the factor of safety below the 150% normally maintained. The company suggested beefing up the landing gear on the basic X-15 at a minimum, and perhaps even strengthening the already beefier gear on the advanced airplane. A more disturbing concern was the aft center of gravity that would be created by the ramjet installation, particularly in the basic airplane where the liquid hydrogen (and, more importantly, its tankage) would be mounted far aft. North American advised performing a new series of stability and control wind-tunnel tests to determine how bad the situation might really be. Ultimately, researchers at the JPL conducted these tests during 1966 on both the basic airplane and the advanced X-15A-2.[249]

Assuming a go-ahead in February 1965, North American estimated it would take three months to design the modifications to X-15-1, four months to fabricate the modification kit, and four months to install it, meaning that X-15-1 would be

246 North American report NA-63-1414, "X-15 Propulsion System Test Package Study," December 1963, no page numbers.

247 Ibid.

248 Ibid. Although the report says that the slipper tanks would not be used on the X-15A-2, wind-tunnel studies at the JPL 20-inch hypersonic facility showed that slipper tanks were used on the X-15A-2 as well as several variations of the basic airplane.

249 North American report NA-63-1414.

available to support hypersonic engine testing in January 1966. The advanced X-15A-2 would become available in July 1966. Researchers expected that the flight program would encompass approximately 25 flights spread over a two-year period.[250]

Hypersonic Research Engine

None of the NASA reviewers, excepting the FRC, believed a research program based on the Marquardt engine concept was justifiable. They pointed out that the emphasis on low cost would result in overly simplified designs that provided little valid test data. In addition, the use of ablative materials would produce contaminants that might strongly affect the combustion process. While discussing the problem with Kennedy Rubert, John Becker suggested that Rubert offer an alternative that might be worthwhile. Rubert then described, in general terms, a concept very close to what would eventually become the HRE–a sophisticated dual-mode engine that was thoroughly researched on the ground and used a clean internal metallic structure without ablative coatings. Becker argued that this was a superior alternative.[251]

After the final Marquardt briefing at the FRC, Douglas E. Wall, who was in charge of X-15 research engine activities, called an informal meeting of the NASA participants to discuss the next move. The outside center reviewers were unanimously against the Marquardt engines, and generally against any flight program. Wall argued convincingly that financial support for an extensive scramjet program was unlikely to be forthcoming unless it was tied to an X-15 flight experiment. Although almost everybody still viewed a flight program as unnecessary, all agreed that Wall was probably correct. Everybody recognized, however, that Lewis would present a formidable obstacle; not only was Lewis traditionally unsympathetic to research airplanes, but the center had also recently abandoned almost all air-breathing engine research. To bypass the expected objections, the researchers decided to propose the Hypersonic Research Engine (HRE) program as a joint FRC-Langley effort, with Langley managing the ground phase and the FRC being responsible for the flight phase.[252]

Although he was personally unconvinced, Paul Bikle endorsed this concept and verbally presented it to NASA Headquarters, with Rubert recommended as the program manager. The initial Langley reaction, however, was unfavorable, mainly because Lawrence K. Loftin, Jr., one of the assistant center directors, had recently recommended against such a program. In Becker's Aero Physics Division there was a very different reaction. For years, propulsion-related fluid mechanics and hypersonic inlet/diffuser work in the division had suffered from a dearth of real-life applications. The prospect of involvement with a real engine for X-15 testing offered an exciting infusion of much needed vitality. Becker also pointed

250 Irving Stone, "X-15 Use Planned in Ramjet Evaluations," *Aviation Week & Space Technology*, 31 August 1964, pp. 57-60; North American report NA-63-1414.

251 Becker, "A Hindsight Study of the NASA Hypersonic Research Engine Project," p. 9. This section is largely an abridged version of: John V. Becker, "A Hindsight Study of the NASA Hypersonic Research Engine Project," 1 July 1976. Prepared under contract NAS1-14250 but never published, for a variety of reasons best explained by Becker.

252 Ibid, pp. 9-10.

out that the HRE project would reveal whether any of the performance claims for the scramjet were valid, something that appealed to many Langley managers. Another important consideration was the complete lack in 1964 of ground-test facilities for true-temperature simulation with clean air above Mach 5. Therefore, researchers viewed the X-15 as a unique test facility, and eventually Langley management came around and began supporting the project.[253]

NASA asked Rubert to develop a detailed plan for the HRE program, and on 17 March 1964 he released a preliminary proposal that outlined a three-phase program. Phase I was to define a practical, high-performance, Mach 3–8 hypersonic engine, and to design, develop, and build such an engine; Phase II was to measure the performance of the engine in the laboratory; and Phase III was to measure the performance of the engine in maneuvering flight and to validate the ground-test results. Significantly, the proposal did not discuss the need for scramjet research, assuming (incorrectly) that this was already well known. Rubert stated flatly that the "gaps" in component technology "had been filled," leaving only uncertainties "which can be discovered and resolved only by design and construction of a truly practical research engine." Nobody at Langley challenged these claims, which mainly demonstrated the inflated technical confidence in the concept that existed at the time. Rubert's plan required four years at a cost of $30.4 million, plus the operations costs of the X-15. The proposal "sailed through" its approval process at NASA Headquarters "with no opposition and few questions asked." Significantly, Lewis director Abe Silverstein did not oppose the project, although he stopped short of actually supporting it. Phase I funds were released on 13 June 1964.[254]

As Wall had indicated, tying the HRE proposal to the X-15 lent credibility. The X-15 was still a successful program that enjoyed almost universal approval within NASA; anything related to it, by default, usually enjoyed similar approval. Of course, there should have been questions. Both the schedule and budget were hopelessly optimistic for developing an entirely new type of engine. The lack of coordination with the Air Force and Navy should have been disturbing. Moreover, nobody asked how Langley was going to compensate for its lack of experience in engine development and testing (traditionally a Lewis task). It would not be as easy as it appeared.[255]

The proposed HRE engine was described as a "truly practical complete engine" that would provide "factual" performance data under real-world conditions. If researchers could have fulfilled all of the hopeful claims of the original proposal, this single engine project would have advanced the technology from the early exploratory research stage to an operational system. An elaborate subscale prototype engine was obviously required to fulfill such claims. Unfortunately, this was not what would be specified for the Phase I competition. Instead, the statement of work called for the "best possible research engine." While the Phase I

253 Ibid, pp. 10-11.

254 Ibid, pp. 11-13.

255 Ibid, pp. 13-14. As a matter of fact, the Air Force was also beginning a scramjet flight program, only using rockets as boosters instead of the X-15. NASA received its first inkling of this program on 18 September 1964 in the form of a copy of Technical Development Plan 561E, "Supersonic Combustion Ramjet Propulsion." The Air Force intended to boost a series of incremental scramjet engines to progressively higher speeds starting at about Mach 5 and eventually reaching Mach 9. What is ironic is that the Air Force was using low-cost versions of the simple ramjets originally proposed by Marquardt.

engine would be required to deal with realistic internal flow conditions, it would not be required to consider the critically difficult high-temperature regeneratively cooled structure or to worry about external drag. In fact, the structure and external features were to be "refined only to the extent necessary for compatibility" with the internal flow performance requirements.[256]

Rubert never openly acknowledged the downgrading of the engine concept from the advanced prototype referred to in the original proposal to an aerothermodynamic boilerplate. The rationale for the change was that project personnel soon realized that the limited funding they had requested could not possibly pay for a prototype engine; unfortunately, they continued to portray the engine as a prototype throughout the project. Ironically, the engine specified in the Phase I statement of work closely followed the 18-inch-diameter pod-type engine that had been suggested by Marquardt during the initial FRC study and was uniformly rejected by Langley and the other NASA centers.[257]

The decision to seek the highest possible internal performance and to impose no thrust-minus-drag requirement had several unfortunate consequences. In order to comply, the contractor that eventually won the Phase I competition used a higher-than-optimal degree of external compression, which caused extremely high external cowl drag. In the final design, designers thickened the cowl to house research instrumentation, aggravating the drag problem even further. In the end, the engine was capable of producing essentially zero net thrust (thrust minus drag). When outside researchers realized this, most of the already lukewarm support for the project vanished.[258]

A Phase I request for proposals was issued to 35 potential bidders, calling for a nine-month, 27,500 man-hour (roughly 20 people) study to develop a concept and a preliminary design; determine performance, life, weight, and safety data; and provide a development plan, manufacturing plan, and costs for the Phase II effort. When the proposals arrived on 28 May 1964, only four companies had responded. A team of 50 engineers and researchers from Ames, Langley, Lewis, and the FRC convened to pick a winner. Significantly, there was only a single Air Force representative on the technical review panels. NASA awarded parallel study contracts to Garrett, General Electric, and Marquardt in October. The evaluators never thoroughly understood why Pratt & Whitney had chosen to submit a proposal, since nobody thought it was a "serious effort to compete."[259]

Nine months later, the same small army of evaluators reconvened to look over the results of the three studies. The concepts were essentially unchanged by the nine months of effort, and the results seemed to favor Garrett. John Becker later said that there were "some flaws in the deliberations which led to Garrett's selection," although he maintained they were honest mistakes and not deliberate attempts to mislead.[260]

The Garrett engine was the smallest, simplest, and easiest to cool, and had the best structural approach of the three designs. The evaluators also believed that

256 John V. Becker, "A Hindsight Study of the NASA Hypersonic Research Engine Project," 1 July 1976, p. 16.

257 Ibid, p. 16.

258 Ibid, p. 17.

259 Ibid, p. 18.

260 Ibid, pp. 18-19.

the engine had a very high research potential because of the quasi-two-dimensional nature of the flow in its shallow annular combustor. Researchers thought that this would simplify the analysis of the combustor data for use in any future two-dimensional combustor design. There was another powerful consideration in favor of Garrett: under the leadership of Anthony duPont, Garrett had exhibited an energy and zeal unmatched by the other companies. Drawing on $250,000 in company funds, it had built a full-scale HRE combustor model and later operated it successfully at the Navy Ordnance Aerophysics Laboratory in Daingerfield, Texas, under simulated Mach 6 conditions. This made it seem like the design was well along, and that developing an engine based on it would be a quick and inexpensive process.[261]

The General Electric design, on the other hand, did not appear to offer a two-dimensional approach because its combustor annulus was too deep. The engine was also large, heavy, and hard to cool. The evaluation team also penalized General Electric because of its long development schedule and high cost, although in retrospect they were much more realistic than Garrett's.[262]

The evaluators ranked the Marquardt engine developed by Ferri last because of its complex three-dimensional flows and a general lack of substantiation of the claims made for it. The most serious question revolved around the thermal compression effect used to avoid having a variable-geometry inlet.[263]

As it turned out, there were three serious flaws in the evaluation. The supposedly simple two-dimensional flow expounded by Garrett was illusory. The complex boundary layers, focused shock waves, and resulting separations and complex interactions made the actual flow virtually impossible to analyze, unique to this particular engine and undesirable from all standpoints. The generally better performance actually obtained with the General Electric combustor suggests that it should have received at least an equal rating. It is interesting to note that during his oral briefings to the evaluation board, Antonio Ferri had called attention to the problems of axisymmetrical design, including "focused shocks," "high losses," and "high cowl drag"–the same problems that were actually encountered by the Garrett engine. The evaluators unfortunately dismissed these comments as prejudiced.[264]

The second flaw in the evaluation was the belief that the study would reveal true time and cost estimates in a situation where the government told the contractors what the times and costs should be. The two contractors that fed back what the government wanted to hear were credited with "responsiveness," while the one (Marquardt) that provided more realistic (but unpopular) estimates was penalized. The last flaw was perhaps the most unfortunate. Garrett gave the impression that the already-developed model combustor could be easily made to work. However, its apparent success during early tests was the result of researchers not understanding the test conditions, and in reality the development of the combustor would prove to be the primary problem of the HRE. Garrett later blamed its mis-

261 Ibid, pp. 18-19.
262 Ibid, pp. 18-19.
263 Ibid, p. 20.
264 Ibid, p. 20.

leading experience with this model for its gross underestimates of the true time and cost of the actual engine.[265]

There were also questions, even prior to Phase I, regarding whether Garrett had sufficient expertise to undertake the development of the HRE. The company had little experience with scramjet aerothermodynamics, and both management and technical personnel were inexperienced in this type of development effort. The fact that the company was proceeding with the development of the combustor model at its own expense was the primary consideration that overruled its inexperience.[266]

On 11 July 1966, NASA awarded Garrett the Phase II contract, but things quickly began to unravel during the negotiations for a final contract. Modifications and ground support equipment for X-15A-2 would cost a staggering $8.7 million, vastly more than had been expected. Within six weeks, Garrett was proposing a $10 million increase in overall costs. Given the overall reductions in funding caused by the conflict in Southeast Asia, NASA managers began to question the necessity for the program.[267]

At a meeting of the Aeronautics and Astronautics Coordinating Board on 5 July 1966, the Air Force announced it would stop funding the X-15 program in 1968 and that NASA would take sole responsibility for the majority of operational support (the military would continue to provide minor base support services). The withdrawal of Air Force support for the X-15 program was a serious setback because it meant that the NASA budget would need to find an additional $8 million per year, an enormous increase that was unlikely to occur. At the same time, there was another adverse development on the Air Force side: a gradual decrease in support for hypersonic technology in general, and scramjets in particular. Just before retiring from a long and notable career, General Bernard A. Schriever was unsuccessful in his attempt to obtain $50 million for an ambitious scramjet program.[268]

Finding additional NASA funding would not be easy. This raised significant questions about how to proceed to Phase II. Interestingly, the question of *whether* to proceed seems not to have been raised at all. In September 1966, Langley established a formal project office to oversee Phase II, with Rubert designated as the project manager, and by year's end approximately a dozen people staffed the office.[269]

On the contractor side, the president of Garrett, Harry Wetzel, was getting "politely impatient" with the delay in getting started. In a letter to NASA administrator James E. Webb on 16 December 1966, Wetzel indicated that he might invoke "pre-project costs" under a provision of the contract if delays should continue. This appeared to have the desired effect because a plan was soon devised that split the former Phase II effort into Phases IIA and IIB. The first part would cover development and the manufacture of one pre-prototype, flight-weight engine. Phase IIB would subsequently produce six prototype engines for ground tests, qualification testing, and later flight tests as part of Phase III. NASA for-

265 Ibid, p. 20.
266 Ibid, pp. 20-21.
267 Ibid, pp. 20-21.
268 Ibid, p. 23.
269 Ibid, p. 24.

mally approved Phase IIA with a target cost of $15.6 million (including fee), and researchers estimated that Phase IIB would cost $13 million. However, nobody attempted to define a cost estimate for Phase III because it contained too many unknowns. In addition, project management did not address how to extend the X-15 program long enough to allow the engine to be developed, or how to pay for X-15 operations.[270]

In the high desert, plans to fly a "dummy" ramjet shape on the modified X-15A-2 were taking shape. In order to gain basic aerodynamic data and investigate the effects of carrying a generic ramjet shape on X-15A-2, the FRC had several dummy ramjets constructed. None of these resembled the engine mock-ups that engineers had hung under the X-15 in the past. The FRC fabricated the dummy shapes, about 7 feet long and 2 feet in diameter, from a series of truncated cones. The program flew two different nose configurations: a 20-degree cone on flights 2-51-92 and 2-52-96, and a 40-degree cone on flight 2-53-97.[271]

To accommodate the dummy ramjet, NASA significantly modified the ventral stabilizer on X-15A-2 by removing 2.8 feet from the front and adding a blunt, unswept leading edge. In addition, engineers removed approximately 3 inches of the lower surface for the first 3.3 feet of the ventral to allow the ramjet to be mounted in a semi-submerged location. Ten impact pressure probes were installed on the leading edge. Most of these protruded approximately 5 inches in front of the ventral, although the three closest to the ramjet were progressively shorter. The probes extended through the pylon standoff shock wave except near the ramjet, where they were made shorter to measure pylon-ramjet interference effects.[272]

A removable camera fairing installed over the center-of-gravity compartment interrupted the smooth cylindrical surface of the lower fuselage of X-15A-2. This was the same camera window used for the Hycon/Mauer experiments (#27) and it protruded a maximum of 1.75 inches below the fuselage. This protrusion was located approximately 13 feet ahead of the leading edge of the pylon, or about 10.25 feet ahead of the tip of the 40-degree nose cone. For these tests, researchers installed a Millikan 16-mm movie camera to photograph the ramjet.[273]

Surface static-pressure orifices were located on the right side of the dummy ramjet and pylon. All orifices were normal to the surface and flush with the metal skin. When the ablative coating was used, an insert of higher-density ablative material at each orifice location maintained a sharp edge at the outer surface. The first flight with the 20-degree nose cone did not use any nose probes. The second flight with the 20-degree cone, and the only flight with the 40-degree cone used a rake with two 40-degree cone probes protruding from the extreme nose in an "L" shape. The top cone probe was on the ramjet centerline, and the lower cone was 8 inches below.[274]

---

270 Ibid, p. 24.

271 Frank W. Burcham, Jr., and Jack Nugent, NASA technical note D-5638, "Local Flow Field Around a Pylon-Mounted Dummy Ramjet Engine on the X-15A-2 Airplane for Mach Numbers From 2.0 to 6.7," February 1970, pp. 3-4 and 22-28.

272 Ibid, pp. 3-4 and 22-28.

273 Ibid, pp. 3 and 22-28.

274 Ibid, pp. 4-5 and 22-28.

A wind-tunnel study conducted after the last X-15A-2 flight showed that shock waves generated by the wing leading edge, lower-fuselage camera window, and fuselage side fairing all impinged on the dummy ramjet and pylon. Researchers found that these were very sensitive to the angle of attack, with a 1% increase in free-stream angle of attack resulting in a 10% increase in impact pressure at Mach 6.5.[275]

At the beginning of 1967, the program planners, who had originally expected the program to be completed by the end of 1969, did not expect to begin flight tests of an operable ramjet before 1971 at the earliest. The schedule had begun to slip even before the start of Phase I, when NASA extended the original four-year project 15 months just to accommodate the procurement cycle. However, there was little actual concern among those involved at the time since they believed the Air Force and NASA would extend the X-15 program as required. By 1967, that prospect was beginning to look less likely.[276]

Faced with the long schedule extension, greatly increased costs, the loss of Air Force X-15 funding, waning interest in hypersonic technology in general, and the prospect for austere R&D funding in the years ahead, managers began to doubt they could complete the HRE program at all. In particular, they considered it unlikely that the necessary continuation of the X-15 program could be obtained using only NASA funding. In retrospect, it was obvious to most of those involved that the HRE should have died a natural death at this point. As is often the case, however, the project had developed a life of its own. Some believed that Phase IIA would develop useful scramjet technology regardless of what transpired in the future. Since there was still a minor chance that the X-15 program would continue with the development of the delta-wing cruise vehicle, Langley launched HRE Phase IIA on 3 February 1967 with the signing of the final contract with Garrett.[277]

Any chance of flight-testing a real HRE vanished on 15 November 1967 when X-15-3 crashed, ending the proposed delta-wing program at the same time. Surprisingly, perhaps because researchers had long anticipated it, the actual demise of the X-15 portion of the program seems to have caused only minor distress in the HRE project office. Researchers suggested that the X-15 had served a very useful purpose by imposing "real" design requirements for the engine, but surmised they could realize some 90% of the program objectives even without actual flight tests. By this time roughly half of the Phase IIA costs had been committed, and these would be lost if the HRE program was terminated. There would be other costs associated with terminating the project, possibly totaling the entire cost of Phase IIA; the decision was to let Phase IIA continue unchanged.[278]

Given the lack of a flight vehicle, NASA decided to reorient the HRE into a ground-based program. Ground testing moved from the Navy Daingerfield Facility to a newly completed test stand at the Lewis Plumbrook installation. In early 1968, Rubert told Garrett to stop work on the X-15 modification package and other items related to flight-testing, and the dummy ramjet eventually tested on

275 Ibid, pp. 16-17.

276 Becker, "A Hindsight Study of the NASA Hypersonic Research Engine Project," pp. 24-25.

277 Ibid, p. 25.

278 Ibid, p. 27.

X-15A-2 had little relation to the HRE developed by Garrett. As it turned out, stopping this work saved little money since the development of most flight subsystems continued in an effort to achieve a "realistic" engine. As John Becker later observed, "And thus was HRE adroitly decoupled from the X-15 which gave it birth and left to make its own way, apparently unchanged but actually now stripped of its glamour and its principle reason to exist."[279]

The HRE had survived the loss of the X-15 flight phase by only a few months when mounting cost and schedule overruns forced the abandonment of the original plan to develop and test a complete hydrogen-burning engine. Nevertheless, the program continued–with dubious results–until 22 April 1974, when NASA finally terminated it.[280]

Although the original promoters of the HRE had oriented Phase I only toward an internal aerothermodynamic performance test model of a scramjet, the combination of the ambitious general claims made for the project and the X-15 flight requirements forced it in the direction of a much more costly subscale prototype with realistic structural and other subsystems. Much later John Becker estimated that the total cost of the entire HRE program, including 25 X-15 flights, would have exceeded $125 million, or about four times the original estimate. The total actually expended was $50.8 million, including $7.5 million charged to the rebuilding of X-15A-2 and the construction of the dummy ramjets at the FRC.[281]

Another Ramjet

Despite the HRE debacle, Marquardt did not give up easily. Although NASA had ruled out a ducted rocket in 1963, Marquardt managed to generate enough interest in the concept to get a study contract from the FRC in early 1964, and the AARPS came back as a separate study. The designers of the AARPS contemplated the use of advanced air-breathing propulsion cycles, such as ducted rockets and ejector ramjets. NASA awarded Marquardt a small contract to define a research and development plan for AARPS and to determine the feasibility and usefulness of flight-testing the system on X-15A-2.[282]

On 3 January 1967, the company proposed a different ramjet installation for X-15A-2, actually providing power to allow a "cruise capability of approximately Mach 5." The company proposed installing an "ejector ramjet on X-15A-2 in the area now occupied by the rocket engine." The ramjet would use jet fuel and liquid oxygen as propellants, although hydrogen peroxide was listed as an alternate oxidizer.[283]

The gross weight of the airplane would increase 2,571 pounds (from 35,735 to 38,306 pounds). The amount of liquid oxygen would remain constant at 10,533

279 Ibid, pp. 27-28.

280 Ibid, pp. 28 and 54-58.

281 Ibid, p. 58. Becker's hindsight study traces the HRE project in considerable detail up through its termination, and offers some interesting insight into how and why the program progressed as it did. However, the story past this point is beyond the scope of this history and will be left to some future historian to tell.

282 Irving Stone, "X-15 Use Planned in Ramjet Evaluations," *Aviation Week & Space Technology*, 31 August 1964, pp. 57-60.

283 Marquardt report (no number), "A Study of the Ejector Ramjet Engine for X-15 Propulsion," 3 January 1967, originally classified Confidential.

pounds, but 9,400 pounds of jet fuel would replace the normal 8,199 pounds of anhydrous ammonia. The propulsion system weight would increase from 910 pounds (XLR99) to 2,280 pounds (1,380 pounds for the engine and 900 pounds for the inlet). On the airplane itself, the liquid-oxygen tank would remain unchanged, but the proposal modified the existing ammonia tank to allow room for the inlet ducting. Unfortunately, Marquardt did not specify how it would accomplish this, given that the ammonia tank was a full-monocoque structural member of the fuselage.[284]

Another aspect that the company did not fully explain was exactly how the airplane would get to Mach 5. The ejector ramjet produced only 29,370 lbf, well below the 57,000 lbf provided by the XLR99 (but well above the 16,000 lbf provided by the interim XLR11s). Marquardt estimated that the acceleration to Mach 5 would take 4.21 minutes at 1.04 g (much slower than the 90 seconds or so it normally took to get to Mach 6), covering approximately 150 miles in the process. Once at Mach 5 the ramjet would provide 14.8 minutes of steady-state cruise, covering 840 miles. This 1,000-mile flight would have necessitated a major extension to the High Range, and might well have exceeded the heat-sink capability of the Inconel structure, even with an ablative coating.[285]

Marquardt also suggested that the engine could be adapted to the delta-wing airplane, and that in the future a modified engine could provide additional cruise performance. In either case, the engine featured a large rectangular inlet located under the fuselage that started slightly ahead of the wing. The inlet duct swept upward into the fuselage just ahead of the ventral stabilizer, explaining the required modifications to the fuel tank. The inlet faired into the ventral, and the ramjet engine was located where the normal XLR99 had been.[286]

It appears that NASA did not take any action based on the study results.

THIN DELTA WINGS

During the mid-1960s, a proposed delta-wing modification to X-15-3 might have kept the program flying until 1972 or 1973. Unlike many proposals, such as the "orbital X-15," the delta wing was a real project and was the subject of a great deal of research and engineering.

The delta-wing X-15 grew out of hypersonic cruise research vehicle studies conducted during the early 1960s. A "hypersonic cruise" vehicle would spend minutes or tens of minutes at hypersonic velocities, in contrast to the original X-15 that spent only a few tens of seconds at that velocity. The delta-wing X-15 configuration used the third airplane with the MH-96 and the basic modifications made to X-15A-2. Proponents of the concept, particularly John Becker at Langley, found the idea very attractive. Becker opined that "the highly swept delta

284 Ibid.

285 Ibid.

286 Ibid.

wing has emerged from studies of the past decade as the form most likely to be utilized on future hypersonic flight vehicles in which high lift/drag ratio is a prime requirement i.e., hypersonic transports and military hypersonic cruise vehicles, and certain recoverable boost vehicles as well."[287]

Researchers held a meeting at the FRC on 9-10 December 1964 to determine exactly what research could be undertaken with a delta-wing hypersonic-cruise X-15. Attendees included researchers from Ames and Langley, and of course groups from the AFFTC and FRC. Not surprisingly, Ames and Langley did not necessarily agree on the exact nature of the research, and NASA Headquarters asked each center to submit a position paper outlining its preferences.

The Langley paper included an evaluation of possible aerodynamic and heat-transfer experiments, in-flight engine-inlet tests, and various structural recommendations that might be applicable to the delta-wing X-15. The entire paper was remarkably short–only 11 pages, or about the same size as the original 1954 paper that had been the genesis of the X-15 program.[288]

John Becker and David E. Fetterman, Jr. led the Langley group that defined the aerodynamic and heat-transfer experiments primarily concerned with evaluating the differences between data gathered during full-scale flight tests and the results of wind-tunnel and analytical data. They noted that "[s]ince air-breathing hypersonic cruise vehicles will fly at such large Reynolds numbers that turbulent conditions will occur over the entire wing, it is obviously of great importance to establish the turbulent heat-transfer characteristics of delta wings. The lack of any rigorous theory to turbulent heat transfer places great emphasis on experimental determinations. It has proved impossible, however, to achieve natural turbulent boundary layers on delta wing models in hypersonic ground facilities except over the rearward regions." Becker and Fetterman used similar logic to justify investigations into areas such as turbulent skin friction and Reynolds analogy, turbulent boundary-layer profile surveys, interference heating, and pressure distributions.[289]

The discussion of engine-inlet testing led to a rather surprising conclusion: "an inlet flight test program on the X-15 is not recommended." J. R. Henry believed that ground facilities such as the 20-inch hypersonic tunnel at Langley and the 3.5-foot hypersonic tunnel at Ames were more than adequate for research into inlet configurations up to Mach 8. Henry's case was convincing, and despite the ongoing interest in the HRE experiment, Langley dropped engine-inlet testing from further consideration for the delta wing.[290]

Structural considerations were not so much possible experiments, but rather recommendations prepared by J. C. Robinson representing the views of the Structures Research Division at Langley. The primary recommendation was to manufacture the main wing structure from one of the nickel- or cobalt-base "su-

---

287 Memorandum, John V. Becker to Floyd L. Thompson, 29 October 1964; letter, Paul F. Bikle to C. W. Harper, 13 November 1964.

288 Letter, Floyd L. Thomson/Langley to Albert J. Evans/NASA headquarters, subject "Proposed experiments and structural recommendations for X-15 with delta wing," 25 January 1965, with three attachments. In the files at the DFRC History Office.

289 Ibid. Quote is from attachment (addendum) A, "Proposed Aerodynamic and Heat-Transfer Experiments for X-15 with Delta Wing."

290 Ibid.

peralloys" using simple construction methods such as "corrugated webs welded to machined cap members with a machined waffle plate skin between the cap members and welded or riveted to them." It was also recommended that the leading-edge material "should be refurbishable, fabricated of thoria-dispersed nickel or a refractory metal, radiation cooled, and should have expansion joints to accommodate differences in thermal expansion between it and the main structure."[291]

The Ames position paper submitted by J. Lloyd Jones was more extensive, consisting of 18 pages using much smaller typeface. The paper also levied some criticism of the existing X-15 program.[292]

Ames agreed with Langley that the primary area of research should be turbulent boundary layers "because of the difficulty of providing turbulent boundary layer flow on models in wind tunnel tests at hypersonic speeds." Ames noted that the existing X-15 had already validated wind-tunnel results up to Mach 5, and the Mach 8 data would be a natural extension. Ames also pointed out that the delta-wing X-15 "is more representative of hypersonic cruise aircraft configurations" and would therefore yield more useful data. Ames also believed that "knowledge that will accrue of the handling qualities of a delta winged vehicle representative of current concepts of airbreathing cruise configuration will certainly be of value."[293]

The researchers at Ames seemed to want to take the lead on the delta-wing configuration, much as Langley had done on the original X-15, and their list of potential research areas was a good deal longer. Besides turbulent-boundary-layer research, Ames wanted to look at skin-friction surveys, pressure distributions and local flow fields, boundary-layer-transition definitions, ablative studies, panel-flutter studies, and low-speed and hypersonic-handling qualities. To accompany these experiments, Ames believed that "an increased program of ground based research relating to hypersonic cruise aircraft technology should be initiated."[294]

Although Ames acknowledged that "the X-15 program to date unquestionably has been very successful" and had turned into "a research facility with which to conduct studies never envisioned at its inception," it believed the program was open to some criticism. "For example, measurement of heat transfer was one of the major research experiments conducted on the airplane, but design inflexibility resulted in the acquisition of heat transfer data in an environment which compromised their value to the extent that they cannot be fully explained nor understood."[295]

To overcome this fault on the new airplane, Ames indicated, "the key to the potential benefits … for a delta wing X-15 program lies in the design of the air-

291 Ibid. The thoria-dispersed nickel alloy was usually called a "dispersion-strengthened" alloy. Such allows suitable for use in temperature ranges up to 1,600-2,400°F. At these temperatures, most nickel and cobalt superalloys lost most of their useful strength properties because of the dissolution of the precipitated phases responsible for strength. Consequently, other methods of strengthening nickel and cobalt alloys were required to extend the high-temperature capabilities of these metals. Dispersion strengthening was the most promising because the strengthening component did not lower the melting point of the matrix metal. Unfortunately, in the late 1960s, only two variations were commercially available: 1) a nickel alloy with 2–3% dispersed thoria, which had good strength but poor oxidation resistance, and 2) a nickel alloy with 20% chromium, which was not quite as strong but provided highly superior oxidation resistance.

292 Memorandum, J. Lloyd Jones/Ames to Director/Ames, 3 March 1965 (transmitted to Albert J. Evans at NASA Headquarters on 8 March 1965). In the files at the DFRC History Office.

293 Ibid. Quotes are from page 1 of the original memorandum.

294 Ibid.

295 Ibid.

plane to accomplish well defined experimental tasks as primary objectives." To this end, Ames made several recommendations for the vehicle configuration:[296]

1. Provision for removable test panels in the areas selected for measurements ... to provide for heat transfer, boundary layer and structural tests on both experimental and prototype panels. Design of the test panels and supporting structure should be guided by the requirement to avoid localized heat sinks that withdraw heat away from the boundary layer in a non-uniform manner.
2. Provide a smooth primary test area along the bottom centerline of the airplane free of all protuberances. This consideration may well lead to the requirement for a low-wing configuration to insure a test region with a definable uniform flow field.
3. A removable fuselage nose section ahead of the wheel well with an instrument compartment and a removable tip. This feature would provide for replacement nose sections having different geometry.
4. An instrumentation bullet located at the wing-fin juncture may be advantageous.

Ames went on to describe an elaborate research program that began with wind-tunnel studies, followed by flights using X-15A-2, and finally tests with the delta-wing aircraft. The program would concentrate most of the theoretical and wind-tunnel work at Ames. Based on the scope of the work described, it probably would have been expensive, although the report did not include a cost estimate.

After reviewing the papers submitted by Ames and Langley, with additional input from the Air Force and FRC, NASA defined two primary objectives for the delta-wing X-15 program:[297]

1. Aerodynamic research–The flight tests would provide realistic aerodynamic data under fully developed turbulent flow conditions to supplement ground-based research where such conditions cannot be achieved. Answers would be obtained to key questions relating to hypersonic aerodynamics of delta wings, large-scale behaviors of flap-type controls, tip-fin interference effects, and handling qualities of a configuration typical of present thinking for a future hypersonic air-breathing vehicle. Aerodynamic research on this vehicle would be unclouded by propulsion effects, inasmuch as most of the data would be taken under gliding conditions.

296 Ibid.

297 Paul F. Bikle and John S. McCollom, "X-15 Research Accomplishments and Future Plans," a paper in the *Progress of the X-15 Research Airplane Program*, a compilation of the papers presented at the FRC, 7 October 1965, NASA publication SP-90 (Washington, DC: NASA, 1965), pp. 138-139.

2. Structural research–The delta-wing proposal would permit the evaluation in a practical flight application of a hot radiation-cooled structure designed for repeated flights at temperatures between 1,500 degrees and 2,200 degrees Fahrenheit. It would also focus technical effort on a refurbishable, hot-wing leading edge design.

Paul Bikle concluded that "[i]n general, a delta-wing X-15 program could establish a baseline of confidence and technology from which decisions regarding the feasibility and design of advanced air-breathing vehicles could be realistically made. The proposed time for the delta X-15 fits well with that for an overall hypersonic research vehicle program and the cost does not appear to be unreasonable."[298]

Things seemed to be progressing rapidly. In January 1965 the FRC drafted a statement of work for North American to conduct a detailed study of the delta-wing concept. This document indicated that "NASA is considering a hypersonic cruise vehicle research program which involves a modification of the basic X-15 configuration for study of various aerodynamic, structural, and flight control problems. The program will also include limited investigations of flight to altitudes extending to about 180,000 feet." Extreme high-altitude research was not a requirement.[299]

NASA suggested that an existing "X-15 airplane would be modified to incorporate a representative slender hypersonic wing substituted for the present wing and horizontal tail. The wing structure would be designed for sustained hypersonic flight at a Mach number of 7, but would also be capable of flight to Mach number 8 for limited time periods. The basic X-15 fuselage structure, rocket engine, flight control and other systems would be retained with minimum modification, and the present B-52 launch system and high range facility would be utilized."[300]

The work statement went on to indicate that the airplane should have a load limit of 5 g and a 2,000-psf design dynamic pressure. Potential "improvements" included relocating the wing to be flush with the bottom of the fuselage, increasing the dynamic pressure to 2,500 psi and the load factor to 7.33 g, including external propellant tank(s), and relocating the nose landing gear. Other possibilities included the addition of a permanent thermal-protection system (in lieu of ablative coatings) over the fuselage to prevent contamination of the wing with ablative products.[301]

The delta wing seemed to languish at the FRC for the remainder of the year while engineers put together a project development plan. By the end of the year, the FRC had released the second draft of the plan for internal review, providing more detail on how things might progress. The opening paragraph provided the justification for the program:[302]

298 Ibid, p. 139.

299 Draft statement of work, "Feasibility Study and Cost Analysis of Modifying an X-15 Aircraft to a Slender Hypersonic Configuration," January 1965, n. p. In the files at the DFRC History Office.

300 Ibid.

301 Ibid.

302 Project Development Plan, "Delta Wing X-15," second draft, December 1965, p. 1. In the files at the DFRC History Office.

> Three of the most probable uses for hypersonic airbreathing aircraft are transport over long ranges, military reconnaissance, and as maneuverable reusable first-stage boosters. There are currently no military or civilian requirements of over-riding importance for any one of these. Their potential, however, constitutes a clear justification to proceed with comprehensive programs to develop the required hypersonic technology.

Unfortunately, the justification also included a rationale for not supporting the program, given the budget crunch NASA was experiencing as it continued the Apollo program to the detriment of the aeronautics budget. Nevertheless, the FRC pressed on with detailed plans. The FRC considered the delta-wing project an extension of the X-15 program, and assumed that all existing agreements between the Air Force and NASA would continue. Researchers believed that the manpower requirements for the program could be satisfied "with the present complements of the Langley, Ames, and Flight Research Center."[303]

Researchers at the FRC estimated the program would cost $29,750,000 spread between FY67 and FY73. Of this, the airframe contractor would receive $24,600,000 to build the flight vehicle, while the other $5,150,000 would be "in-house" expenses. The second year represented the largest annual expenditure: $14,500,000 to the contractor and a little over $1,000,000 in-house. The planners warned, however, that "if the military withdraws their operational support from the general X-15 program, this project would be responsible for additional expenses over the 4-1/2 year operational period. These expenses could amount to as much as 17 million dollars." The preliminary schedule showed a request for proposals in August 1966, a contract award in March 1967, modifications to X-15-3 between December 1967 and October 1968, and a first flight in January 1969. The 37-flight research program continued until December 1972.[304]

In the project plan, the FRC had expected the X-15 Project Office at Wright-Patterson AFB to handle the procurement of the modifications, although NASA would pay the bills. Although it would seem logical for North American to perform the modifications, several other contractors (Lockheed, Northrop, and Republic) had expressed interest in the program, so the FRC proposed to make it a competitive process.[305]

The Air Force was not totally in favor of this since they saw their involvement with the X-15 winding down, and had little apparent interest in the delta-wing program. Despite negotiations between the Air Force and NASA at various levels, the X-15 Project Office declined to participate in the expected procurement of the delta-wing airplane; however, it did agree to transfer the X-15-3 airframe to NASA for the modification at the end of its flight program.

After nearly two years of delay, on 13 May 1967 the delta-wing program had progressed far enough for the FRC to issue a request for proposals (PR-7-174) for a formal conceptual design study. The primary objectives of the study were

303 Ibid, pp. 1-2.

304 Ibid, pp. 2-3. In addition to 37 powered flights, the planners envisioned two captive flights and one glide flight.

305 Ibid.

to 1) develop a preliminary design for evaluating the modification of X-15-3 to a delta-wing configuration, and 2) formulate an accurate estimate of performance, weight, cost, and schedule for such modification. A secondary objective was to analyze alternate approaches, such as unsegmented leading edges; eliminate the use of ablatives; and incorporate a fly-by-wire control system, multiplane airfoils, symmetrical tip fins, and different propulsion systems.[306]

There appears have been only a single respondent to the request for proposals. North American submitted a two-volume, 500-page proposal containing detailed engineering concepts and cost data–and that was just the proposal to do the study! By this time, North American had already been testing the delta-wing X-15 in wind tunnels for over a year. The North American low-speed and hypersonic tunnels and the Langley 20-inch hypersonic tunnel had tested 1/15-scale and 1/50-scale models at Mach numbers between 0.2 and 6.9 and Reynolds numbers up to 10,000,000 (equivalent, based on model length).[307]

The proposed North American delta-wing X-15-3 was not a simple conversion. The 603-square-foot delta-wing planform had a 76-degree leading-edge sweep, but the span was the same as that of the original X-15 to ensure that there would be no clearance issues with the NB-52 carrier aircraft. Elevons (30.8 square feet each) at the trailing edge provided longitudinal and roll control by deflecting up to 4.5 degrees up or 5.0 degrees down. The existing dorsal and ventral stabilizers provided directional stability with the addition of wing-tip fins, and the existing dorsal rudder provided directional control. Engineers could adjust the removable tip fins on the ground for cant and tow-in, which allowed them to change the relative levels of directional and lateral stability to investigate the handling qualities of the vehicle. The tip fins compensated for the blanking of the normal centerline vertical stabilizers by the fuselage at hypersonic speeds and large angles of attack.[308]

The position of the wing was the subject of a great deal of study since the HRE was expected to be carried on the ventral stabilizer (as the dummy was on X-15A-2), and the aircraft also had to be stable in flight without the 1,000-pound engine. It proved to be a difficult problem. The final answer before NASA terminated the program was to position the wing in the best location to compensate for the HRE. On flights without the engine, as much research equipment or ballast as possible would be located in a new aft experiment compartment. Likewise, the shape of the wing leading edge was of some concern, but North American noted that "the effect of leading edge radius on the low-speed aerodynamic characteristics of highly swept delta wings is not well understood." Engineers did not think the effect on the leading-edge shape at supersonic speeds would be significant, because positive pressure on the wing lower surface would produce most of the lift. Nevertheless, since the leading-edge shape significantly influenced the landing

306 North American report NA-67-344, "Technical Proposal for a Conceptual Design Study for the Modification of an X-15 Air Vehicle to a Hypersonic Delta-Wing Configuration," 17 May 1967, vol. I, p. 4. In the files at the JSC History Office.

307 North American report NA-67-344, "Proposal for a Conceptual Design Study for the Modification of an X-15 Air Vehicle to a Hypersonic Delta-Wing Configuration," two volumes (Technical and Business Management), 17 May 1967; North American report NA-67-344, "Technical Proposal for a Conceptual Design Study for the Modification of an X-15 Air Vehicle to a Hypersonic Delta-Wing Configuration," 17 May 1967, vol. I, p. 42.

308 North American report NA-67-344, "Technical Proposal for a Conceptual Design Study for the Modification of an X-15 Air Vehicle to a Hypersonic Delta-Wing Configuration," 17 May 1967, vol. I, pp. 2-3 and 28.

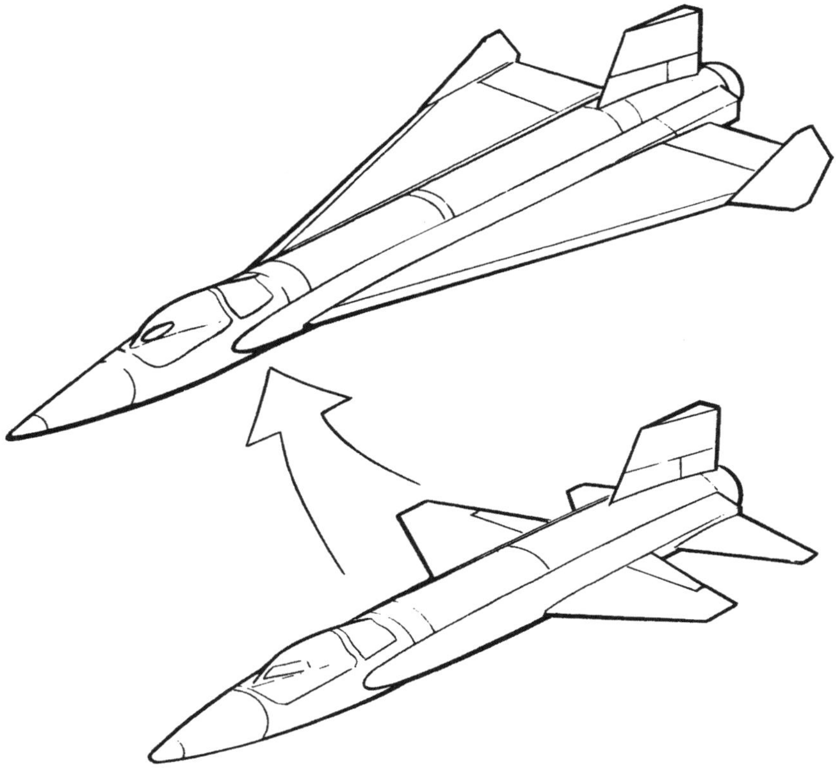

During the mid-1960s, a proposed delta-wing modification to X-15-3 might have kept the program flying until 1972 or 1973. Unlike many proposals, such as the "orbital X-15," the delta wing was a real project and was the subject of a great deal of research and engineering. Despite endorsements from the Flight Research Center and John Becker at Langley, support remained lukewarm within the Air Force and NASA. The FRC was still evaluating the proposals for the delta-wing study on 15 November 1967 when the crash of the X-15-3 effectively ended all thought of such a modification. (NASA)

characteristics, North American investigated various configurations in its low-speed wind tunnel. The company had not found a satisfactory answer, and was awaiting further data from NASA wind-tunnel tests, when the program ended.[309]

North American was also somewhat uncertain about the leading-edge material, mainly because of the expected 2,200°F temperatures encountered on the design mission. North American built a segmented leading edge made from columbium alloy that successfully passed tests at 2,400°F. This appeared satisfactory, at least for initial use. The company expected that no available material would prove satisfactory for the lower surface of the wing, and that some form of thermal protection system would have to be developed. Unsurprisingly, many of the North American ideas looked similar to concepts the company was investigating for the space shuttle. One of the most promising ideas was to use metallic heat

309 Ibid, volume I, p. 34.

shields supported by standoff clips with a layer of low-density insulation sandwiched between the shield and the wing skin. Only an area about 2 feet wide just behind the leading edge needed this type of protection since the airflow further aft smoothed out sufficiently to keep temperatures within the ability of alloys such as TD nickel to survive unprotected.[310]

Originally, North American had envisioned using upswept wing tips to replace the directional stability lost by the removal of the ventral rudder from the delta-wing configuration. Although the X-15 program seldom used the ventral rudder, this was because most missions flew at high angles of attack, where the lower rudder was detrimental to stability. The delta-wing program, on the other hand, wanted to fly sustained high-speed cruise missions that would require little high-angle-of-attack work. The initial round of tests in the North American hypersonic tunnel revealed that the upswept wing tips were inadequate above Mach 6. Researchers tested various configurations in both the North American hypersonic tunnel and the 20-inch Langley hypersonic tunnel until they found a set of tip fins that extended both above and below the wing centerline to be adequate. Nevertheless, engineers decided to make it easy to replace the fins just in case the wind-tunnel tests proved to be inaccurate.[311]

The large-angle-of-attack capability of the basic X-15s was no longer required since researchers did not intend the mission to go to high altitudes. Given that the maximum angle of attack envisioned for the new airplane was less than 15 degrees, engineers decided to use a fixed-flow direction sensor to sense the angle of attack and sideslip. A hemispherical nose with five pressure taps could provide an air-data computer with sufficient information to derive the necessary angles without the complexity and weight of the ball nose. Conceptually, this was identical to the fixed alpha nose flown during six of the last X-15-1 flights.[312]

North American proposed to stretch the fuselage 10 feet to 62.43 feet overall, and to manufacture what was essentially a new fuselage from the cockpit rearward. The company would stretch the propellant tank section 91 inches and provide new mounting provisions for the delta wing. North American manufactured test specimens from René 41 and Inconel 718 to determine which would be the best material for this area; these tests were in progress when NASA canceled the program. The space between the liquid-oxygen and ammonia tanks accommodated the standard center-of-gravity instrumentation compartment, and North American added a new 29-inch-long compartment behind the fuel tank but ahead of the engine to hold fuel and gases for the HRE. Designers also wanted to replace the existing ogive forward fuselage (in front of the canopy) with a 20-degree, included-angle-cone section. This semi-monocoque structure would use René 41 outer skin and Inconel X (or Inconel 718) frames, and titanium would be used for the inner skin of the equipment compartment.[313]

North American investigated several different powerplants for the airplane, with the leading challenger being an Aerojet YLR91-AJ-15 from the second stage

310 Ibid, volume I, pp. 104-108. Office.

311 Ibid, volume I, p. 38.

312 Ibid, volume I, p. 38.

313 Ibid, volume I, p. 128.

of a Titan II ICBM. This engine used unsymmetrical dimethylhydrazine and nitrogen tetroxide as propellants, and had already been man-rated for the NASA Gemini program. When equipped with a 25:1 nozzle, this engine completed the reference mission without the use of external propellant tanks. In fact, at a launch weight of 52,485 pounds and a burnout weight of 18,985 pounds, the YLR91 would have allowed a maximum velocity of 8,745 fps, well in excess of the 7,600 fps required by NASA. The effect of carrying the 1,000-pound HRE would have reduced this by about 400 fps.[314]

North American briefly investigated the idea of using a separate "sustainer" engine to provide thrust to overcome drag during hypersonic cruise. Although the integration issues involved with incorporating a second engine and its propellants into the airframe eventually convinced all concerned that it would be too difficult, the particular engines investigated show how a program could come full circle. One of the engines investigated was the Bell YLR81-BA-11, a variation of the one of the engines proposed to power the X-15 in 1954. North American also investigated several variants of the Reaction Motors LR11 family that had been used for the initial X-15 flights, along with the Aerojet LR52 (AJ-10).[315]

The engine that was ultimately selected was a modified XLR99 that provided 83,000 lbf at 100,000 feet and was throttleable down to 8,000 lbf for sustained cruise. This was the version of the XLR99 that used a single thrust chamber and nozzle, not the Reaction Motors concept that used a second, remotely located alternate chamber. The increased internal fuel would permit sustained flights at Mach 6.5 using the low-thrust "sustainer" capability of the modified XLR99 to overcome drag but not produce any acceleration. The addition of a single centerline external tank would allow Mach 8 flights.[316]

The main landing gear would be a version of the gear developed for the X-15A-2, appropriately strengthened for the almost 19,000-pound normal landing weight of the delta-wing design. As on the X-15-A-2, North American proposed to use both short and long versions of the rear shock struts; the long ones would provide clearance for the HRE under the ventral, while flights that did not carry the HRE would use the short ones. The nose gear would be moved to the instrument compartment behind the pilot, and the recorders and other research instrumentation normally carried there would be moved to a new compartment in front of the pilot where the original nose gear well was.[317]

Although it was not part of the delta-wing baseline, North American was investigating the use of a fly-by-wire control system on the delta-wing X-15. Engineers believed that this would reduce the overall system size, weight, and volume, and provide better overall performance. This system would have used an analog flight-control system, not a digital one. The MH-96 adaptive control

---

314 Ibid, vol. I, pp. 15 and 142. At some point North American had also proposed installing the YLR91 in the X-15A-2 as a means of increasing its performance.

315 Ibid, vol. I, pp. 197-199. In the files at the JSC History Office.

316 Bikle and McCollom, "X-15 Research Accomplishments and Future Plans," pp. 138-139; Paul Gwozdz, Reaction Motors report number TR-4085-1, "A Study to Determine Modifications Which Extend the Low and High Thrust Range of the YLR99 Turborocket Engine," undated (but signed on 11 October 1966), p. 2. In the files at the DFRC History Office. The modified XLR99 (called a YLR99 in the report) would theoretically be capable of producing 87,000 lbf at 100,000 feet, but Reaction Motors recommended slightly derating it to increase reliability.

317 North American report NA-67-344, vol. I, pp. 131-132.

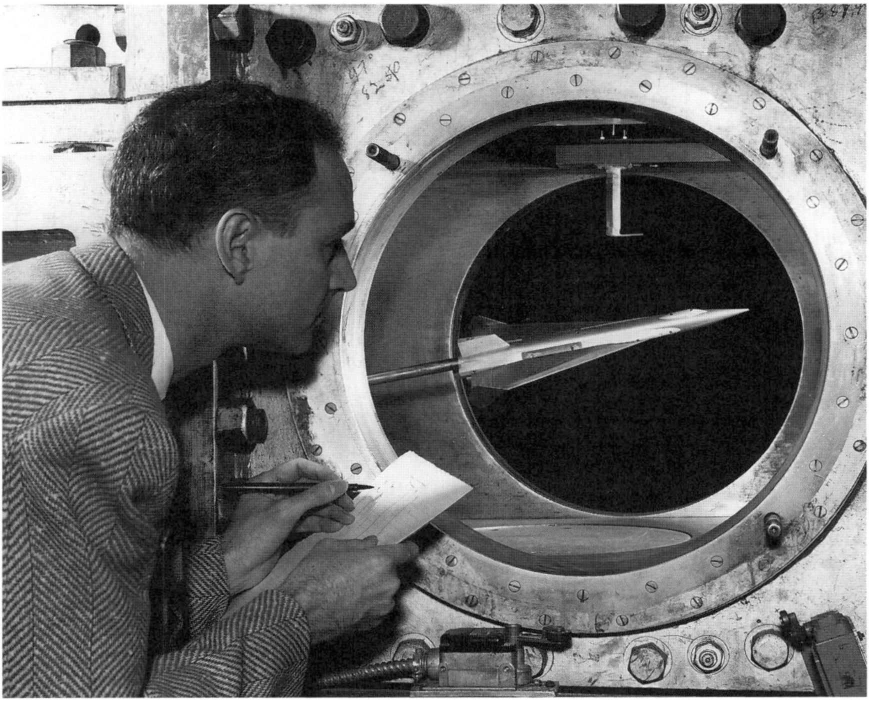

The final delta-wing design spent a considerable amount of time in this NASA Langley wind tunnel before the program was cancelled. (NASA)

system was capable of accepting electrical inputs that were equivalent to flying in a fly-by-wire mode, and Honeywell designed the MH-96 to interface to the fly-by-wire flight-control system in the Dyna-Soar. In X-15-3 these were paralleled with mechanical linkages, and the delta wing could eliminate these mechanical linkages altogether. Given the facts that a fly-by-wire system had never flown, and the delta-wing airplane was flying in a new performance envelope anyway, NASA was not supportive of this effort.[318]

Although the delta-wing airplane was generally described as a modification of X-15-3, about the only structure from the original airplane that would remain would be the cockpit and the aft thrust structure. Most of the electronics (i.e., the inertial system and MH-96) would also remain. However, at least by weight, the majority of the aircraft would be new. Since the North American study had not been completed when X-15-3 was lost, the company had not estimated the final cost, but the amount would probably have been substantial.

Although no formal contracting arrangement existed, North American pressed on with a great deal of research into the delta-wing configuration. By March 1967, wind-tunnel models had accumulated over 300 hours of testing, with a 1/50-scale model used for high-speed tests and a 1/15-scale model used for low-speed tests. According to a North American news release, "the four year research program has

318 Ibid, vol. I, pp. 176-180.

also enabled North American to check out the integrity of components using new super alloys that will be required at hypersonic speeds. Tanks, wing sections, and other components have been fabricated of such materials and put through exhaustive thermal and structural tests."[319]

Despite endorsements from the FRC and John Becker at Langley, support remained lukewarm within the Air Force and NASA. The FRC was still evaluating the proposals for the delta-wing study on 15 November 1967 when the crash of the X-15-3 effectively ended all thought of such a modification. Since the general concept depended upon the use of the electronic systems that were unique to X-15-3, most researchers did not consider it readily possible to convert one of the other airframes; besides, the accident effectively sealed the fate of the entire X-15 program.[320]

HIRES

Perhaps the most unusual concept involving the use of X-15s was also the one that should have made the program most thankful it was never implemented. During the late 1950s and early 1960s, the Air Force investigated a single-stage-to-orbit concept called Aerospaceplane (not to be confused with the later National Aero-Space Plane (NASP)). The vehicles explored during this program included some very exotic propulsion concepts, such as LACES and ACES, that extracted oxygen from the atmosphere during ascent and used it once the vehicle left the sensible atmosphere.[321]

Most of the contractors involved in the program performed parametric evaluations of conventional concepts that carried all of the propellants from the ground–termed "propellants onboard at takeoff" (POBATO)–in addition to the air-collection schemes. However, an even more bizarre concept was called the "hypersonic in-flight refueling system" (HIRES), and designers at Convair, Douglas, and North American each considered trying to refuel the Aerospaceplane in flight at Mach 6. This concept actually advanced far enough that the Air Force and NASA had preliminary discussions about using two X-15s flying in formation to validate the idea. The logistics of getting two X-15s in formation would have been formidable, and the piloting task daunting. On two separate occasions the X-15 program attempted to fly two flights in a single day (but not at the same

319 North American news release GHH031067, 17 March 1967. Provided courtesy of Mike Lombardi, Boeing Historical Archives.

320 It is somewhat difficult to determine which factor had the most effect on the decision not to proceed with the delta-wing program. The MH-96 and other advanced flight-control equipment on X-15-3 could have been replaced. Spare parts and complete systems that had been procured for the Dyna-Soar were available if somebody had wanted to use them, although there would have been integration costs to bring them up to the X-15 configuration. Political support for the program had been declining for some time. Apollo had siphoned off too much of the budget, but was obviously going to succeed despite the disastrous Apollo 1 fire in January 1967. It was probably more a case of too many things going against the program, and the easiest answer was simply to not request continued funding.

321 For a better description of the Aerospaceplane program, see Dennis R. Jenkins, *Space Shuttle: The History of the National Space Transportation System–The First 100 Missions* (North Branch, MN: Specialty Press, 2001), pp. 52-55.

time, since the High Range could not support the concept), and each time one of the X-15s had a system problem that led to the flight being scrubbed. Fortunately for the X-15 program, the refueling demonstration was never attempted.[322]

322 See, for example, Convair report GD/C-DCJ-65-004, "Reusable Space Launch Vehicle Study, 18 May 1965.

APPENDIX A

SELECTED BIOGRAPHIES

Although 15 pilots were assigned to the X-15 program, only 12 of them actually flew the airplane. Al White was the backup pilot for Scott Crossfield and never needed to take over. Iven Kincheloe was the initial Air Force project pilot, but he died in an accident before the first airplane was delivered. NASA reassigned John Manke to the lifting-body program after the loss of X-15-3, before he was able to fly the X-15. In each of the four groups of government pilots, an equal number came from the Air Force and NASA. The following table shows the pilots in the order of their selection by the program:

Name	Pilot at Edwards	Assigned to X-15	Left the X-15
Scott Crossfield	1950–1960	September 1955	December 1960
Al White	1954–1966	September 1955	December 1960
Iven Kincheloe	1955–1958	April 1958	July 1958
Bob White	1955–1963	April 1958	December 1962
Bob Rushworth	1957–1967	April 1958	July 1966
Joe Walker	1951–1966	April 1958	August 1963
Jack McKay	1951–1971	April 1958	September 1966
Neil Armstrong	1955–1962	April 1958	August 1962
Forrest Petersen	1958–1962	August 1958	February 1962
Joe Engle	1962–1966	June 1963	April 1966
Milt Thompson	1956–1967	June 1963	August 1965
Pete Knight	1958-1969/1979–1982	May 1965	December 1968
Bill Dana	1959–1991	May 1965	December 1968
Mike Adams	1963–1967	July 1966	November 1967
John Manke	1963-1975	July 1966	November 1967

There were also plans to allow four Dyna-Soar pilots to fly the X-15 before Robert McNamara canceled that program, and some sources have indicated that Jacqueline Cochran attempted to get permission to fly the X-15 to set the women's speed and altitude records.[1]

MICHAEL J. ADAMS, USAF

Mike Adams flew the X-15 for 13 months from 6 October 1966 until 15 November 1967, making seven flights. All of these were with the XLR99 engine

1 Jacqueline Cochran received her pilot license in 1932, set three major flying records in 1937, and won the prestigious Bendix Race in 1938. In 1941, Cochran selected a group of highly qualified women pilots to ferry aircraft for the British Air Transport Auxiliary. In 1942, Cochran, at the request of Army General Henry "Hap" Arnold, organized the Women's Flying Training Detachment (WFTD), which subsequently merged with Nancy Love's Women's Auxiliary Ferry Squadron (WAFS) to form the Women Airforce Service Pilots (WASP) with Cochran as director. Following the war, Cochran continued to establish speed records into the 1960s. She was the first woman to break the sound barrier, doing so in 1953 in an F-86 Sabre. She was a 14-time winner of the Harmon Trophy, awarded to the best female pilot of the year. Cochran also became the first woman to break Mach 2 in the Lockheed F-104 Starfighter. Cochran authored two autobiographies--*The Stars at Noon and Jackie Cochran*--with Mary Ann Bucknam Brinley.

and he reached Mach 5.59, a maximum speed of 3,822 mph, and an altitude of 266,000 feet. Adams died on flight 3-65-97.

Michael James Adams was born on 5 May 1930 in Sacramento, California, and enlisted in the Air Force on 22 November 1950 after graduating from Sacramento Junior College. Adams earned his pilot's wings and commission on 25 October 1952 at Webb AFB, Texas. He served as a fighter-bomber pilot in Korea, flying 49 missions during four months of combat service. For 30 months Adams served with the 613th Fighter-Bomber Squadron at England AFB, Louisiana, and for six months he served rotational duty at Chaumont Air Base in France.[2]

In 1958 Adams received a bachelor of science degree in aeronautical engineering from Oklahoma University. In 1962, after 18 months of astronautics studies at the Massachusetts Institute of Technology (MIT), Adams attended the Experimental Test Pilot School at Edwards, where he won the Honts Trophy for being the best in his class. He subsequently attended the Aerospace Research Pilot School (ARPS), graduating with honors on 20 December 1963, and was assigned to the Manned Spacecraft Operations Division at Edwards AFB in the Manned Orbiting Laboratory program. During this time he was one of four Edwards aerospace research pilots to participate in a five-month series of NASA Moon-landing practice tests conducted by the Martin Company in Baltimore, Maryland.

In July 1966 Adams came to the X-15 program with 3,940 hours of total flight time, including 2,505 hours in single-engine jets (primarily the F-80, F-84F, F-86, F-104, F-106, and T-33) and an additional 477 hours in multiengine jets (primarily the F-5, T-38, and F-101). Unfortunately, Mike died during flight 3-65-97 on 15 November 1967, and The Air Force posthumously awarded Adams an astronaut rating for his last flight in X-15-3, which had attained an altitude of 266,000 feet (50.38 miles). In 1991, the Astronaut Memorial at the Kennedy Space Center in Florida added Adams to its list of astronauts who had been killed in the line of duty.

NEIL A. ARMSTRONG, NASA

Neil Armstrong flew the X-15 for 20 months from 30 November 1960 until 26 July 1962, making seven flights. These included two flights with the XLR11 and five with the XLR99. Armstrong reached Mach 5.74, a maximum speed of 3,989 mph, and an altitude of 207,500 feet. His accomplishments include making the first flight with the ball nose and the first flight with the MH-96 adaptive control system.

Neil Alden Armstrong was born on 5 August 1930 in Wapakoneta, Ohio. He attended Purdue University, earning his bachelor of science degree in aeronautical engineering in 1955. During Korea, which interrupted his engineering studies, Armstrong flew 78 combat missions in F9F-2 fighters, for which he earned the

2 Biography of Major Michael J. Adams, Air Force Systems Command, Edwards AFB, 12 November 1965; letter, Colonel Clyde S. Cherry/AFFTC to Paul Bikle/FRC, subject: Selection of crew member for X-15 program, 14 July 1966; letter, William H. Dana to Dennis R. Jenkins, 14 June 2002, containing comments to a draft of this manuscript.

Air Medal and two Gold Stars. He later earned a master of science degree in aerospace engineering from the University of Southern California.

Armstrong joined the NACA Flight Propulsion Research Laboratory (now the Lewis Research Center) in 1955. Later that year he transferred to the High-Speed Flight Station (HSFS) as an aeronautical research scientist and then as a pilot. Armstrong served as the project pilot on the F-100A, F-100C, F-101, and F-104A, and flew the X-1B, X-5, F-105, F-106, B-47, KC-135, and Paresev. He left with over 2,450 flying hours.

Armstrong was a member of the USAF-NASA Dyna-Soar Pilot Consultant Group before Robert McNamara canceled that program, and studied X-20 Dyna-Soar approaches and aborts using F-102A and F5D aircraft. In 1962, when he was flying the X-15, Armstrong was one of nine pilots selected for the second NASA astronaut class. In March 1966 he was the commander of Gemini 8, with David Scott as pilot (this mission accomplished the first successful docking of two vehicles in orbit). On 20 July 1969, during the Apollo 11 mission, Armstrong became the first human to land on the Moon. Armstrong has a total of 8 days and 14 hours in space, including 2 hours and 48 minutes walking on the Moon.

After his lunar flight, Armstrong became the deputy associate administrator for aeronautics at NASA Headquarters. He resigned from NASA in August 1971 to become professor of engineering at the University of Cincinnati, a post he held until 1979. Armstrong became chairman of the board of Cardwell International, Ltd., in 1980 and served in that capacity until 1982. During 1982–1992, he was chairman of Computing Technologies for Aviation, and from 1981 to 1999 he served on the board of directors for the Eaton Corporation. He was also vice chair of the Rogers Commission, which investigated the Space Shuttle *Challenger* accident in 1986.

Armstrong has been the recipient of numerous awards, including the Presidential Medal of Freedom and the Robert J. Collier Trophy in 1969, the Robert H. Goddard Memorial Trophy in 1970, and the Congressional Space Medal of Honor in 1978.[3]

JOHN V. BECKER, NASA

John Becker is widely regarded as the father of the X-15, having served as the leader of the Langley researchers who defined the general concept of a hypersonic research airplane.

John Vernon Becker was born in 1913 in Albany, New York. He earned a bachelor of science degree in mechanical engineering (aero option) in 1935 and a master of science degree in aero engineering in 1936, both from New York State University. He joined the NACA Langley Memorial Aeronautical Laboratory as a junior aeronautical engineer in 1936.[4]

---

3 *http://www.dfrc.nasa.gov/PAO/PAIS/HTML/bd-dfrc-p001.html* (accessed 29 April 2002); *http://www.jsc.nasa.gov/Bios/htmlbios/armstrong-na.html* (accessed 29 April 2002).

4 Biography, John V. Becker, 8 April 1959; Resume, John V. Becker, 1976. In the files at the NASA History Office.

Becker served as head of the 16-foot high-speed wind-tunnel branch from 1943 until 1947 and chief of the Compressibility Research Division from 1947 through 1957. During this time Becker contributed to the design and understanding of the Bell X-1, Bell X-2, Douglas X-3, the Century Series fighters, and the XB-70, in addition to his work on the X-15. In 1958 Becker became the division chief of the Aero-Physics Research Division, a position he held until his retirement in 1974. During that time he contributed to the X-20 Dyna-Soar and various lifting-reentry vehicles that led to the Space Shuttle, Mercury, Gemini, and Apollo, as well as Project FIRE, Sprint, the hypersonic cruise vehicle, the hypersonic research engine, and others. After he retired from NASA, Becker was a consultant for the General Applied Sciences Laboratory, Burns and Roe, and the NASA Office of Aeronautics and Space Technology.

Becker authored over 50 research papers in addition to numerous technical journal articles. In 1955, New York University cited Becker as one of its 100 outstanding graduates from the College of Engineering. He received the Sylvanus Reed Award from the American Institute of Aeronautics and Astronautics (AIAA) for 1960, and received other AIAA awards in 1961, 1968, and 1973. Becker delivered the 3rd Eugen Sänger Memorial Lecture at the Deutsch Geaellschaft Fur Luftfahrforschung, Bonn, Germany, in December 1968.[5]

PAUL F. BIKLE, NASA

Paul F. Bikle was born on 5 June 1916 in Wilkensburg, Pennsylvania, and graduated from the University of Detroit with a bachelor of science degree in aeronautical engineering in 1939. His career with the Army Air Forces began in 1940 when he became an aeronautical engineer at Wright Field, and in 1944 he became chief of the aerodynamics branch of the Flight Test Division. While working closely with other government agencies in establishing the first flying qualities specifications for aircraft, he wrote AAF Technical Report 50693 ("Flight Test Methods"), which was used as a standard manual for conducting flight tests for more than five years. During World War II he was involved in more than 30 test projects and flew over 1,200 hours as an engineering observer.

In 1947, Bikle became chief of the performance engineering branch and directed tests of the XB-43, XC-99, and F-86A. When the flight-test mission was transferred to the newly formed Air Force Flight Test Center (AFFTC) at Edwards, Bikle came to the desert and advanced to assistant chief of the flight-test engineering laboratory in 1951. From there, he advanced to the position of AFFTC technical director. He replaced Walt Williams as director of the NASA Flight Research Center (FRC) in September 1959. Like Williams, Bikle had little use for unnecessary paperwork, and often remarked that he would stay with NASA as long as the paperwork level remained below what he had experienced in the Air Force. He was also an avid soaring enthusiast and established two world soaring records during a flight near Lancaster on 25 February 1961 that still stands as of 2006. In July 1962, Bikle received the NASA Medal for Outstanding Leadership

5 Ibid.

for directing the "successful X-15 flight operations and research activities," and he received the 1963 FAI Lilienthal Medal. Bikle retired from NASA in May 1971 and died on 20 January 1991.[6]

A. SCOTT CROSSFIELD, NAA

Scott Crossfield flew the X-15 for 18 months, from 8 June 1959 until 6 December 1960, making 14 flights. These included one glide flight, 10 flights with the XLR11, and three flights with the XLR99. Crossfield reached Mach 2.97, a speed of 1,960 mph, and an altitude of 88,116 feet. His accomplishments include the first X-15 glide flight, the first powered flight, the first flight with the XLR99, and the first emergency landing.

Albert Scott Crossfield was born on 2 October 1921 in Berkeley, California. He began his engineering training at the University of Washington in 1940, but interrupted his education to join the U.S. Navy in 1942. Following flight training, he served as a fighter and gunnery instructor, and maintenance officer before spending six months in the South Pacific without seeing combat duty. After the war, Crossfield was the leader of a Navy acrobatic team that flew FG-1D Corsairs at various exhibitions and airshows in the Pacific Northwest.[7]

He resumed his engineering studies in 1946 and graduated with a bachelor of science degree in aeronautical engineering from the University of Washington in 1949. He earned a master of science degree in aeronautical science the following year from the same university, and received an honorary doctor of science degree from the Florida Institute of Technology in 1982.

Crossfield joined the HSFS as a research pilot in June 1950. During the next five years he flew the X-1, X-4, X-5, XF-92A, D-558-1, and D-558-2 aircraft, accumulating 87 rocket-powered flights in the X-1 and D-558-2, and 12 in the D-558-2 with jet power only. On 20 November 1953, Crossfield became the first pilot to exceed Mach 2, in the D-558-2 Skyrocket. Crossfield left the NACA in 1955 to work for North American Aviation on the X-15 as both pilot and design consultant.[8]

In 1960, Crossfield published his autobiography (written with Clay Blair, Jr.), *Always Another Dawn: The Story of a Rocket Test Pilot* (Cleveland and New York: World Publishing Company, 1960; reprinted New York: Arno Press, 1971; reprinted North Stratford, NH: Ayer Company Publishers, 1999). The book covers his life through the completion of the early X-15 flights and is a fascinating story for anybody who is interested in that period of flight test.

Crossfield also served for five years at North American as the director responsible for systems test, reliability engineering, and quality assurance for the WS-131 Hound Dog missile, the Paraglider, the Apollo command and service

6 Richard P. Hallion, *On the Frontier: Flight Research at Dryden, 1946-1981*, NASA publication SP-4303 (Washington, DC, 1984), p. 104; letter, Richard J. Harer to Dennis R. Jenkins, 15 October 2002; *http://records.fai.org/pilot.asp?from=gliding&id=342* (accessed 23 October 2006).

7 Telephone conversation, Scott Crossfield with Dennis R. Jenkins, 8 August 2002.

8 Thompson quote from Milton O. Thompson, *At the Edge of Space: The X-15 Flight Program*, (Washington, DC: Smithsonian Institution Press, 1992), p. 4.

module, and the Saturn booster. From 1966 to 1967 he served as technical director of research engineering and test at North American Aviation.

Crossfield served as an executive for Eastern Airlines from 1967 to 1973, and as senior vice president of Hawker Siddeley Aviation during 1974–1975. From 1977 until his retirement in 1993, Crossfield served as technical consultant to the House Committee on Science and Technology, advising committee members on matters related to civil aviation. In 1993 he received the NASA Distinguished Public Service Medal for his contributions to aeronautics and aviation over a period spanning half a century.

Crossfield was a joint recipient of the 1961 Robert J. Collier Trophy presented by President John F. Kennedy at the White House in July 1962. Other awards included the International Clifford B. Harmon Trophy for 1960, the Lawrence Sperry Award, the Octave Chanute Award, the Iven C. Kincheloe Award, and the Harmon International Trophy. He has been inducted into the National Aviation Hall of Fame (1983), the International Space Hall of Fame (1988), and the Aerospace Walk of Honor (1990). In 2006 the American Astronautical Society awarded Crossfield and David Clark the Victor A. Prather Award for the development of the full-pressure suit. Crossfield died on 19 April 2006 when his Cessna 210 crashed during a severe thunderstorm over Georgia.[9]

WILLIAM H. DANA, NASA

Bill Dana flew the X-15 for 35 months from 4 November 1965 until 24 October 1968, making 16 flights. All of these were with the XLR99 engine. Dana reached Mach 5.53, a maximum speed of 3,897 mph, an altitude of 306,900 feet, and flew the last flight of the program.

William Harvey Dana was born on 3 November 1930 in Pasadena, California. He received his bachelor of science degree from the U.S. Military Academy in 1952 and served four years as a pilot in the Air Force. He joined NASA after receiving a master of science degree in aeronautical engineering from the University of Southern California in 1958.

During the late 1960s and the 1970s, Dana was a project pilot on the manned lifting-body program, for which he received the NASA Exceptional Service Medal. In 1976 he received the Haley Space Flight Award from the AIAA for his research work on the M2-F3 lifting-body control systems. In 1986 Dana became the chief pilot at the FRC, and later was an assistant chief of the Flight Operations Directorate. He was also a project pilot on the F-15 HIDEC (highly integrated digital electronic control) research program, and a co-project pilot on the F-18 high-angle-of-attack research program. In August 1993, Dana became chief engineer, a position he held until his retirement in 1998.[10]

He was inducted into the Aerospace Walk of Honor in 1993 and received the NASA Distinguished Service Medal in 1997. In 1998 the Smithsonian Insti-

9 *http://www.edwards.af.mil/history/docs_html/people/pilot_crossfield.html* (accessed 29 April 2002); *http://www.dfrc.nasa.gov/PAO/PAIS/HTML/bd-dfrc-p021.html* (accessed 29 April 2002); *http://www.aviationnow.com/avnow/news/channel_awst_story.jsp?id=news/CROSS_spec.xml* (accessed 23 October 2006).

10 Letter, William H. Dana to Dennis R. Jenkins, 14 June 2002.

tution's National Air and Space Museum honored Dana when he delivered the Charles A. Lindbergh Memorial Lecture. On 23 August 2005, Dana finally received astronaut wings for his two X-15 flights above 50 miles altitude.[11]

HUGH L. DRYDEN, NASA

Hugh Latimer Dryden was born 2 July 1898 in Pocomoke City, Maryland. He earned his way through Johns Hopkins University, completing the four-year bachelor of arts course in three years and graduating with honors. Influenced by Dr. Joseph S. Ames, who for many years was chairman of the NACA, Dryden undertook a study of fluid dynamics at the Bureau of Standards while taking graduate courses at Johns Hopkins. In recognition of his laboratory work, the university granted him a doctor of philosophy degree in 1919.[12]

Dryden became head of the bureau's aerodynamics section in 1920. With A. M. Kuethe, in 1929 he published the first of a series of papers on the measurement of turbulence in wind tunnels and the mechanics of boundary-layer flow. He advanced to chief of the Mechanics and Sound Division of the Bureau of Standards in 1934, and in January 1946 became assistant director. Six months later he became associate director.

In 1945 Dryden became deputy scientific director of the Army Air Forces Scientific Advisory Group. In 1946 he received the nation's second highest civilian decoration, the Medal of Freedom, for "an outstanding contribution to the fund of knowledge of the Army Air Forces with his research and analysis of the development and use of guided missiles by the enemy."

In 1947 Dryden resigned from the Bureau of Standards to become director of aeronautical research at the NACA. Two years later the agency gave him additional responsibilities and the new title of director. Dryden held this post until he became deputy administrator of the new National Aeronautics and Space Administration (NASA) in 1958. The National Civil Service League honored Dryden with the Career Service Award for 1958. He served as the deputy administrator of NASA until his death on 2 December 1965.

JOE H. ENGLE, USAF

Joe Engle has the unique honor of having flown the X-15 and the Space Shuttle, bringing lifting-reentry vehicles full circle. Engle flew the X-15 for 24 months from 7 October 1963 until 14 October 1965, making 16 flights with the XLR99 engine. Engle reached Mach 5.71, a maximum speed of 3,888 mph, and an altitude of 280,600 feet.

Joe Henry Engle was born on 26 August 1932 in Abilene, Kansas, and graduated from the University of Kansas at Lawrence with a bachelor of science degree

11 *http://www.edwards.af.mil/history/docs_html/people/pilot_dana.html* (accessed 29 April 2002); *http://www.dfrc.nasa.gov/PAO/PAIS/HTML/bd-dfrc-p002.html* (accessed 29 April 2002).

12 *http://www.hq.nasa.gov/office/pao/History/Biographies/dryden.html* (accessed 2 May 2002).

in aeronautical engineering in 1955. After graduation he worked at Cessna Aircraft as a flight-test engineer before being commissioned through the Air Force ROTC program in 1956. Engle earned his pilot wings in 1958 and flew F-100s for the 474th Fighter Squadron (Day) and later the 309th Tactical Fighter Squadron at George AFB, California.

Engle graduated from the Test Pilot School in 1962 and attended the ARPS at Edwards for training as a military astronaut. He graduated from the ARPS in 1963 and became a project pilot for the X-15 program in June 1963. Engle received an Air Force astronaut rating for making a flight above 50 miles in the X-15.[13]

In 1966, at the age of 32 years, Engle became the youngest person selected to become an astronaut. First assigned to the Apollo program, he served on the support crew for Apollo X and then as backup lunar module pilot for Apollo XIV. In 1977 he was commander of one of two crews that conducted the approach and landing tests with the Space Shuttle *Enterprise*. In November 1981 he commanded the second flight (STS-2) of the *Columbia* and manually flew the reentry, performing 29 flight-test maneuvers from Mach 25 through landing rollout. This was the first (and so far only) time a pilot has flown a winged aerospace vehicle from orbit through landing. He accumulated the last of his 224.5 hours in space when he commanded *Discovery* during mission 51-I (STS-27) in August 1985.

Engle has flown more than 180 different types of aircraft and logged nearly 14,000 flight hours. Among his many honors, Engle has been awarded the Distinguished Flying Cross (1964), the AIAA Lawrence Sperry Award for Flight Research (1966), the NASA Distinguished Service Medal and Space Flight Medal, and the Harmon International, Robert J. Collier, Lawrence Sperry, Iven C. Kincheloe, Robert H. Goddard, and Thomas D. White aviation and space trophies. In 1992 he was inducted into the Aerospace Walk of Honor.[14]

CHARLES H. FELTZ, NAA

Charles Henderson Feltz was born on 15 September 1916 on a small ranch near Channing, Texas. He graduated from Texas Technological College in 1940 with a bachelor of science degree in mechanical engineering. He joined the Los Angeles Division of North American Aviation the same year, serving in a variety of engineering positions for the design and production of the B-25. Following the war, Feltz became the design group engineer in charge of the design of the wing structure for the F-82 and F-86 series of aircraft. Between 1948 and 1956 Feltz was the assistant project engineer for the development of the FJ2 Fury and the F-86D Sabre, and in 1956 he became the project engineer and program manager for the X-15.[15]

In 1962 Feltz became the chief engineer for the Apollo command and service module, and advanced to vice president and deputy program manager by

13 Thompson quote from *At the Edge of Space*, p. 16.

14 *http://www.edwards.af.mil/history/docs_html/people/pilot_engle.html* (accessed 29 April 2002); *http://www.jsc.nasa.gov/Bios/htmlbios/engle-jh.html* (accessed 29 April 2002).

15 Resume provided to Dennis R. Jenkins by Charles H. Feltz, 15 May 2002; biography, Charles H. Feltz, 13 February 1980, In the files of the Boeing Archives; *http://www.charlesfeltz.com/* (accessed 23 October 2006).

1970. When the Apollo program ended, he became the vice president and deputy program manager for the Space Shuttle orbiter. Between 1974 and 1976, Feltz was the vice president and technical assistant to the president of the North American Rockwell Space Division. In 1976 he became vice president of the North American Aerospace Operations Division of Rockwell International, and in 1980 he became president of the Space Transportation System Development and Production Division of Rockwell International. Feltz retired from Rockwell International in 1981.

Texas Tech named Feltz a distinguished engineer in 1967, and a distinguished alumnus in 1972. During his career Feltz received a variety of medals and honors from NASA and industry groups, including a NASA Distinguished Public Service Medal in 1981. Charlie Feltz, the common-sense engineer, passed away on 3 January 2003.

IVEN C. KINCHELOE, JR., USAF

Iven Carl Kincheloe, Jr., was born on 2 July 1928 in Detroit, Michigan. In 1945 he entered Purdue University, where he studied aeronautical engineering as a member of the Air Force ROTC unit. He graduated in 1949 with bachelor of science degree in aeronautical and mechanical engineering.[16]

Kincheloe received his wings at Williams AFB, Arizona, in 1951. In early 1952 he was promoted to captain and entered the Korean War with the 5th Interceptor Wing. He flew 131 missions and shot down five MiG-15s, becoming the 10th jet ace. For his outstanding service he received the Silver Star and the Distinguished Flying Cross with two oak leaf clusters. After he returned to the United States, Kincheloe was a gunnery instructor at Nellis AFB, Nevada, and in 1953 he was accepted into the Empire Test School in Farnborough, England. While in England, he received a master of science degree in aeronautical engineering from Oxford in December 1954.[17]

Kincheloe flew the X-2 to an altitude of 126,200 feet, and became famous as "America's first spaceman." On 27 March Kincheloe was named chief of the manned spacecraft section, fighter operations branch, of the flight-test operations division that was responsible for training the Air Force pilots who were to participate in the X-15 flight program. Kincheloe became the first Air Force project pilot for the X-15; unfortunately, however, he died before he had a chance to fly the airplane. On 26 July 1958, Kincheloe took off on a routine chase mission in an F-104. At 2,000 feet altitude the engine failed. Although Kincheloe was able to roll the airplane inverted to enable the downward-firing ejection seat, he was too low for his parachute to open.

A biography of Kincheloe, *First of the Spacemen: Iven C. Kincheloe, Jr.*, by James J. Haggerty, Jr. (New York: Duell, Sloan and Pearce, 1960), was published in 1960, and a CD-ROM biography of "Kinch" was aboard the Space Shuttle *Discovery* on STS-70 in July 1995.

16 *http://icdweb.cc.purdue.edu/~ivenc/who.html* (accessed 25 April 2002).

17 *http://www.kinsella.org/director/iven.htm* (accessed 25 April 2002).

During the course of his career, Kincheloe accumulated 3,573 flying hours in 70 American and foreign aircraft. Numerous honors followed his death. One of the most meaningful came from his peers, when the Society of Experimental Test Pilots (SETP) renamed its prestigious Outstanding Pilot Award in his honor. His most public tribute, however, took place far away in his home state when Kinross AFB in Michigan's Upper Peninsula was renamed Kincheloe AFB in his memory.[18]

WILLIAM J. KNIGHT, USAF

Pete Knight flew the X-15 for 35 months from 30 September 1965 until 13 September 1968, making 16 flights with the XLR99 engine. Knight reached Mach 6.70, a maximum speed of 4,520 mph, and an altitude of 280,500 feet. His accomplishments include the first flight with the dummy ramjet, the first flight with a full ablative coating, and the maximum speed flight.

William J. "Pete" Knight was born on 18 November 1929 in Noblesville, Indiana. He enlisted in the Air Force in 1951 and completed pilot training in 1953. Flying an F-89D for the 438th Fighter-Interceptor Squadron, Knight won the prestigious Allison Jet Trophy Race in September of 1954. He graduated with a bachelor of science degree in aeronautical engineering from the Air Force Institute of Technology in 1958, and from the Experimental Test Pilot School later that same year. In 1960 he was one of six test pilots selected to fly the Dyna-Soar. After Robert McNamara canceled the X-20 in 1963, he completed the astronaut-training curriculum at the new ARPS in 1964 and went on to fly the X-15.

In 1969, after nearly 10 years of flying at Edwards, Knight went to Southeast Asia, where he completed 253 combat missions in the F-100. Following this, he served as test director for the F-15 System Program Office at Wright-Patterson AFB and became the 10th pilot to fly the F-15 Eagle. Knight returned to Edwards AFB as vice commander of the AFFTC in 1979 and remained an active test pilot in the F-16 Combined Test Force. After 32 years of service and more than 7,000 hours in more than 100 different aircraft, Colonel Knight retired from the Air Force in 1982. In 1984 the people of Palmdale elected Knight to the city council, and he became the city's first elected mayor in 1988. Subsequently, Knight served in the California state assembly in 1992 and the California state senate in 1996.[19]

Among his many honors, Knight received the Legion of Merit with an oak leaf cluster, the Distinguished Flying Cross with two oak leaf clusters, the Air Medal with 10 oak leaf clusters, the Harmon International Trophy, the Octave Chanute Award, and the Air Force Association Citation of Honor. He was inducted into the National Aviation Hall of Fame (1988), the Aerospace Walk of Honor (1990), and the International Space Hall of Fame (1998). Pete Knight died from cancer on 8 May 2004.[20]

---

18 *http://www.edwards.af.mil/history/docs_html/people/bio_kincheloe.html* (accessed 29 April 2002).

19 Total flight time from telephone conversation with William J. Knight to Dennis R. Jenkins, 24 June 2002.

20 *http://www.edwards.af.mil/history/docs_html/people/pilot_knight.html* (accessed 29 April 2002).

JOHN A. MANKE, NASA

John Manke was the last NASA pilot assigned to the X-15 program, but he never flew the airplane. Manke was born on 13 November 1931 in Selby, South Dakota. He attended the University of South Dakota before being selected for the NROTC program in 1951, and graduated from the Marquette University in Milwaukee in 1966 with a bachelor of science degree in electrical engineering. Following graduation, Manke entered flight training and served as a fighter pilot with the Marine Corps. He left the service in 1960 and worked for Honeywell for two years.

NASA hired Manke on 25 May 1962 as a flight research engineer, and he served as an X-15 flight planner. Along with Mike Adams, Manke completed X-15 "ground school" and conducted a test run of the XLR99 in the Rocket Engine Test Facility. Manke left the X-15 program after the X-15-3 accident that claimed Mike Adams's life. On 28 May 1968 he flew the HL-10, the first of his 42 flights in a heavyweight lifting body.

After the X-15 program ended, Manke became chief of flight operations at the FRC in October 1981 and continued in that capacity until he retired on 27 April 1984.

JOHN B. MCKAY, NASA

Jack McKay flew the X-15 for 70 months from 28 October 1960 until 8 September 1966, making 29 flights. These included two flights with the XLR11 and 27 with the XLR99. McKay reached Mach 5.65, a maximum speed of 3,938 mph, and an altitude of 295,600 feet. He made three emergency landings in the X-15, and although was seriously injured on one of them, he returned to fly 22 more X-15 missions.

John Barron "Jack" McKay was born on 8 December 1922 in Portsmouth, Virginia, and graduated from Virginia Polytechnic Institute in 1950 with a bachelor of science degree in aeronautical engineering. During World War II he served as a Navy pilot in the Pacific, earning the Air Medal with two oak leaf clusters and a Presidential Unit Citation while flying F6F Hellcats.

He joined the NACA on 8 February 1951 and worked at Langley as an engineer for a brief period before transferring to the HSFS, where he flew the F-100, YF-102, F-102A, F-104, YF-107A, D-558-1, D-558-2, X-1B, and X-1E. With the exception of Scott Crossfield, McKay accumulated more rocket flights than any other U.S. pilot (46 flights before he joined the X-15 program). As Milt Thompson remembers, "Jack was an excellent stick and rudder pilot, possibly the best of the X-15 pilots." McKay retired from the NASA on 5 October 1971 and died on 27 April 1975, mostly from late complications resulting from his X-15 crash. On 23 August 2005, NASA presented McKay's family with a set of astronaut wings, honoring MacKay's high-altitude flight in the X-15.[21]

---

21 Thompson, *At the Edge of Space*, p. 11.

FORREST S. PETERSON, USN

Forrest "Pete" Petersen flew the X-15 for 15 months from 23 September 1960 until 10 January 1962, making five flights. These included two flights with the XLR11 and three flights with the XLR99. He reached Mach 5.30, a maximum speed of 3,600 mph, and an altitude of 101,800 feet.

Forrest Silas Petersen was born on 16 May 1922 in Holdrege, Nebraska. After he graduated from the Naval Academy in June 1944, he reported to the destroyer USS *Caperton* (DD 650) and participated in campaigns in the Philippines, Formosa, and Okinawa. Petersen switched from the "black shoe" Navy to "brown shoes" when he graduated from flight training in 1947 and was assigned to VF-20A.

Petersen completed two years of study at the Naval Post Graduate School and received a bachelor of science degree in aerospace engineering. He continued his studies at Princeton University and received a master's degree in engineering in 1953. In 1956 he attended the Naval Test Pilot School and remained as an instructor following graduation. The Navy assigned him to the X-15 program in August 1958, and he served with NASA until January 1962. He was a joint recipient of the 1961 Robert J. Collier Trophy presented by President John F. Kennedy at the White House in July 1962, and the NASA Distinguished Service Medal presented by Vice President Lyndon B. Johnson.

Petersen served as commanding officer of VF-154 prior to being assigned to the office of director, Division of Naval Reactors, Atomic Energy Commission, for nuclear power training. He reported to USS *Enterprise* in January 1964 and served as executive officer until April 1966. Petersen received the Bronze Star during *Enterprise's* first combat tour in Vietnam. Afterward, he became an assistant to the director of naval program planning in the office of the chief of naval operations. In November 1967 he assumed command of USS *Bexar* (APA-237) and received the Navy Commendation Medal with Combat V. He later served as deputy chief of naval operations for air warfare, and commander of the Naval Air Systems Command. Vice Admiral Petersen retired from active duty in May 1980 and died of cancer in Omaha, Nebraska, on 8 December 1990.

ROBERT A. RUSHWORTH, USAF

Bob Rushworth flew the X-15 for 68 months from 4 November 1960 until 1 July 1966, making 34 flights. These included two flights with the XLR11 and 32 flights with the XLR99. Rushworth reached Mach 6.06, a maximum speed of 4,018 mph, and an altitude of 285,000 feet. His accomplishments include the first ventral-off flight, the maximum dynamic-pressure flight, the maximum temperature flight, the maximum Mach number (6.06) in the basic X-15, the first flight of X-15A-2, and the first flight with external tanks.

Robert Aitken Rushworth was born on 9 October 1924 in Madison, Maine. He joined the Army Air Forces, flying C-46 and C-47 transports in World War II and later combat missions in Korea. In 1943 he graduated from Hebron Academy, Maine. He received bachelor of science degrees in mechanical engineering from the University of Maine in 1951 and in aeronautical engineering from the Air Force Institute of Technology in 1954. He graduated from the National War College at Fort Lesley J. McNair, Washington, D.C., in 1967.[22]

Rushworth began his flight-test career at Wright Field and transferred to Edwards in 1956. Following graduation from the Experimental Test Pilot School, Rushworth reported to the fighter operations branch at Edwards and later became operations officer in the manned spacecraft section while flying the X-15. Prior to flying the X-15, Rushworth flew the F-101, TF-102, F-104, F-105, and F-106. He received the Distinguished Flying Cross for an emergency recovery of the X-15 after premature extension of the nose gear at near Mach 5 speeds, and the Legion of Merit for overall accomplishments in the national interest of initial space flights.[23]

He graduated from the National War College in August 1967 and attended F-4 Phantom II combat crew training at George AFB. In March 1968, Rushworth went to Cam Ranh Bay Air Base in Vietnam as the assistant deputy commander for operations with the 12th TFW and flew 189 combat missions. From April 1969 to January 1971, he was program director for the AGM-65 Maverick, and in February 1971 he became commander of the 4950th Test Wing at Wright-Patterson AFB. General Rushworth served as the inspector general for the Air Force systems command from May 1973 to February 1974 and returned to the AFFTC as commander until November 1975, when he became commander of the Air Force Test and Evaluation Center at Kirtland AFB, New Mexico. Rushworth retired from the Air Force in 1981 as vice commander of the Aeronautical Systems Division at Wright-Patterson AFB. Bob Rushworth died of a heart attack on 18 March 1993 in Camarillo, California.[24]

HARTLEY A. SOULÉ, NASA

Hartley A. Soulé was born on 19 August 1904 in New York City. He received a bachelor of science degree in mechanical engineering from New York University in 1927 and joined the staff at Langley in October 1927 after working briefly for the Fairchild Airplane Company in Long Island. Soulé concentrated his research on stability and control, and became chief of the Stability Research Division in 1943. He became assistant chief of research in 1947 and assistant director of Langley in August 1952.

Soulé was a coinventor of the stability wind tunnel and directed the construction of three other wind tunnels at Langley. He pioneered the use of computing machinery for analytical and data reduction. He was also instrumental in establishing the Pilotless Aircraft Research Division at Wallops Island. Soulé became chairman of the Interlaboratory Research Airplane Projects Panel, and in that role he directed research on the Bell X-1 program and was instrumental in managing the early years of the X-15 program. Later he became project director for the Mer-

22 *http://www.af.mil/news/biographies/rushworth_ra.html* (accessed 24 June 2002); telephone conversation between William J. Knight and Dennis R. Jenkins, 24 June 2002.

23 *http://www.af.mil/news/biographies/rushworth_ra.html* (accessed 24 June 2002); Thompson, *At the Edge of Space*, p. 13.

24 *http://www.af.mil/news/biographies/rushworth_ra.html* (accessed 24 June 2002).

cury worldwide tracking and ground instrumentation system. Soulé retired from NASA on 16 February 1962 and passed away in 1988.

HARRISON A. STORMS, JR., NAA

Harrison A. "Stormy" Storms, Jr., was born in 1915 in Chicago, Illinois. He attended Northwestern University and graduated with a master of science degree in mechanical engineering in 1938. Storms then attended the California Institute of Technology (Caltech), earning a master of science degree in aeronautical engineering. At Caltech he studied under Theodore von Kármán and worked in the wind tunnels at the Guggenheim Aeronautical Laboratory (GALCIT).

In 1940, Storms went to work on the P-51 Mustang at North American Aviation, where he developed a reputation as an expert on wind flow and high-speed aircraft. He subsequently worked on the F-86 and F-100 jet fighters. In 1957, Storms became vice president and chief engineer of the Los Angeles Division, where he led the development of the XB-70 bomber. In 1959, he became vice president for program development, in charge of the development of the Apollo spacecraft. Between 1961 and 1967, he served as president of the Space and Information Systems Division, an organization that peaked at more than 35,000 employees in 1965. Storms took the brunt of the blame for the Apollo 1 fire and stepped out of the public eye, although he continued as a company vice president. The AIAA honored him with the 1970 Aircraft Design Award. Storms died in Los Angles in July 1992.[25]

MILTON O. THOMPSON, NASA

Milt Thompson flew the X-15 for 22 months from 29 October 1963 until 25 August 1965, making 14 flights with the XLR99 engine. Thompson reached Mach 5.48, a maximum speed of 3,723 mph, and an altitude of 214,100 feet.

Milton Orville Thompson was born on 4 May 1926 in Crookston, Minnesota. Thompson began flying with the Navy and served in China and Japan during World War II. Following six years of active duty, Thompson entered the University of Washington and graduated with a bachelor of science degree in engineering in 1953. After graduation Thompson became a flight-test engineer for the Boeing Aircraft Company, testing, among other things, the B-52.

Thompson joined the HSFS on 19 March 1956 and became a research pilot in January 1958. At the time, there were only five pilots at the station: Joe Walker, Stan Butchart, Jack McKay, Neil Armstrong, and Thompson. In 1962, Thompson became the only civilian pilot on the X-20 Dyna-Soar, but Robert McNamara canceled that program just over a year later. On 16 August 1963, Thompson became the first person to fly a lifting body, the lightweight M2-F1. He flew it 47 times and made the first five flights of the all-metal M2-F2. Thompson concluded his

25 Eve Dumovich, "Harrison Storms: The Quarterback for the Race to the Moon," *Manager* (Boeing internal magazine), issue 5/6, 2000. Copy provided by Charles H. Feltz.

active flying career in 1967 and became chief of research projects two years later. In 1975, he became chief engineer and retained the position until his death on 6 August 1993. Thompson also served on NASA's Space Transportation System Technology Steering Committee during the 1970s. In this role he was successful in leading the effort to design the Space Shuttle orbiters for power-off landings rather than increase weight with air-breathing engines. His committee work earned him the NASA Distinguished Service Medal.

Thompson was a member of the Society of Experimental Test Pilots, and he received the organization's Iven C. Kincheloe Trophy as the outstanding experimental test pilot of 1966 for his research flights in the M2 lifting bodies. He also received the 1967 Octave Chanute award from the AIAA for his lifting-body research. In 1990, the National Aeronautics Association selected Thompson as a recipient of its Elder Statesman of Aviation award (this award has been presented each year since 1955 to individuals who made contributions "of significant value over a period of years" in the field of aeronautics). Milt Thompson died on 6 August 1993.[26]

Thompson wrote about his experiences with the X-15 in *At the Edge of Space: The X-15 Flight Program* (Washington, D.C.: Smithsonian Institution Press, 1992). Anybody who is interested in an inside look at the program should pick up a copy; it is a fascinating read.

JOSEPH A. WALKER, NASA

Joe Walker flew the X-15 for 41 months, from 25 March 1960 until 22 August 1963, making 25 flights. These included five flights with the XLR11 and 20 with the XLR99. Walker reached Mach 5.92, a maximum speed of 4,104 mph, and an altitude of 354,200 feet. His accomplishments include the first government flight, the maximum speed (4,104 mph) flight of a basic X-15, and the maximum altitude (354,200 feet) flight.

Joseph Albert Walker was born on 20 February 1921 in Washington, Pennsylvania, and graduated from Washington & Jefferson College in 1942 with a bachelor of arts degree in physics. During World War II he flew P-38 fighters for the Army Air Forces in North Africa, earning the Distinguished Flying Cross and the Air Medal with seven oak leaf clusters.

He joined the NACA in March 1945 at the Aircraft Engine Research Laboratory (now the Lewis Research Center), where he was involved in icing research and spent many hours flying into the worse weather the Great Lakes region could dish out. He transferred to the HSFS in 1951 and became chief pilot in 1955. He served as project pilot on the D-558-1, D-558-2, X-1, X-3, X-4, X-5, and X-15, and flew the F-100, F-101, F-102, F-104, and B-47. He was the first man to pilot the Lunar Landing Research Vehicle (LLRV) used to develop piloting and operational techniques for lunar landings.

Prior to joining the X-15 program, Walker did some pioneering work on the concept of reaction controls, flying an JF-104A to peak altitudes of 90,000 feet.

---

26 *http://www.dfrc.nasa.gov/PAO/PAIS/HTML/bd-dfrc-p018.html* (accessed 29 April 2002).

The indicated airspeed going over the top of this maneuver was less than 30 knots, providing an ideal environment for evaluating the reaction control system.[27]

Walker was a joint recipient of the 1961 Robert J. Collier Trophy presented by President John F. Kennedy at the White House in July 1962. Walker also received the 1961 Harmon International Trophy for Aviators, the 1961 Iven C. Kincheloe Award, and the 1961 Octave Chanute Award. He received an honorary doctor of aeronautical sciences degree from his alma mater in June 1962, and in 1963 the National Pilots Association named him Pilot of the Year for 1963. He was a charter member of the Society of Experimental Test Pilots, and one of the first to be designated a fellow. Tragically, Walker died on 8 June 1966 in a mid-air collision between his F-104 and the second XB-70A.[28] On 23 August 2005, the Walker family received a set of astronaut wings honoring Joe Walker's flights above 50 miles altitude in the X-15.

ALVIN S. WHITE, NAA

Al White was the second contractor pilot assigned to the X-15 project. He participated in the centrifuge program, attended the training sessions, flew the fixed-base simulator, practiced the landing-approach flights, and flew the photo chase airplane for many of the early X-15 flights. White never flew the X-15.

Alvin S. White was born in December 1918 in Berkeley, California. In 1936, he enrolled in the University of California at Davis to study electrical engineering, transferring to the Berkeley campus two years later. In 1941, he enlisted as an aviation cadet in the Army Air Corps, graduating from flight school at Williams Field, Arizona, in May 1942.[29]

After nearly two years as an advanced flight instructor at Williams Field, White joined the 355th Fighter Group in England on 4 June 1944. He flew two tours as a combat fighter pilot from D-Day until the end of the war in Europe. White returned to the University of California at the end of 1945, earning his degree in mechanical engineering with elective courses in aeronautical engineering in 1947.

In 1948, White reenlisted in the Air Force and spent nearly three years conducting parachute research at Wright-Patterson AFB and the National Parachute Range at El Centro. In 1952, White graduated from the Air Force Test Pilot School at Edwards and joined the fighter test section. In May 1954, he left the Air Force to join North American Aviation.

After four years of testing the F-86 series, the F-100 series, and the F-107, he became backup pilot to Scott Crossfield on the X-15. In 1957, White became project pilot for the XB-70, and concentrated his work on that program after the completion of the North American X-15 flights. After he retired from North American, White became a well-respected aviation consultant until his death on 29 April 2006.[30]

---

27 Thompson, *At the Edge of Space*, p. 5.

28 *http://www.dfrc.nasa.gov/PAO/PAIS/HTML/bd-dfrc-p019.html* (accessed 29 April 2002).

29 Letter, Alvin S. White to Dennis R. Jenkins, 18 June 2002.

30 Letter, Alvin S. White to Dennis R. Jenkins, 8 June 2002.

ROBERT M. WHITE, USAF

Bob White flew the X-15 for 32 months from 13 April 1960 until 14 December 1962, making 16 flights. These included six flights with the XLR11 and 10 with the XLR99. White reached Mach 6.04, a maximum speed of 4,093 mph, and an altitude of 314,750 feet. His accomplishments include the maximum Mach number (3.50) and maximum altitude (136,000 feet) with the XLR11, the first Mach 4 flight (of any manned aircraft), the first Mach 5 flight, the first Mach 6 flight, the first flight over 200,000 feet (of any manned aircraft), the first flight over 300,000 feet, and an FAI record flight of 314,750 feet (which still stands as of 2006).

Robert Michael White was born on 6 July 1924 in New York, New York. He entered the Army Air Forces in November 1942 and received his wings in February 1944. White subsequently joined the 354th Fighter Squadron in July 1944 flying the P-51 Mustang. In February 1945, the Germans shot White down during his 52nd combat mission. He was captured by the Germans and remained a prisoner of war for two months.

White returned to the United States and enrolled in New York University, where he received a bachelor's degree in electrical engineering in 1951. The Air Force recalled him to active duty in May 1951 as a pilot and engineering officer with the 514th Troop Carrier Wing at Mitchel AFB, New York. In February 1952, the Air Force sent him to Japan and assigned him to the 40th Fighter Squadron as an F-80 pilot and flight commander until the summer of 1953.

White became a systems engineer at the Rome Air Development Center in New York. In January 1955, he graduated from the Experimental Test Pilot School and stayed at Edwards to test the F-86K, F-89H, F-102A, and F-105B. He became the deputy chief of the Flight Test Operations Division, and somewhat later became assistant chief of the manned spacecraft branch. Following the death of Iven Kincheloe, backup pilot White was designated the primary Air Force pilot for the X-15 program in 1958.

In October 1963, White became the operations officer for the 36th Tactical Fighter Wing at Bitburg, and then served as the commanding officer of the 53rd Tactical Fighter Squadron. He returned to the United States in August 1965 to attend the Industrial College of the Armed Forces in Washington, where he graduated in 1966. That same year, he received a master of science degree in business administration from The George Washington University. White went to Southeast Asia in May 1967 as deputy commander for operations of the 355th Tactical Fighter Wing, and flew 70 combat missions.

In June 1968, he went back to Wright-Patterson as director of the F-15 Systems Program Office. Brigadier General-selectee White assumed command of the AFFTC on 31 July 1970. White commanded the AFFTC until 17 October 1972 when he assumed the duties of commandant of the Air Force ROTC. In February 1975 he received his second star, and in March he became chief of staff of the Fourth Allied Tactical Air Force. White retired from active duty as a major general in February 1981.[31]

31 *http://www.edwards.af.mil/history/docs_html/people/white_biography.html* (accessed 29 April 2002).

White was a joint recipient of the 1961 Robert J. Collier Trophy presented by President John F. Kennedy at the White House in July 1962. He also received the NASA Distinguished Service Medal, the Harmon International Trophy from the Ligue Internationale des Aviateurs for the most outstanding contribution to aviation for the year, and the Iven C. Kincheloe Award. Among his many military decorations are the Air Force Cross, the Distinguished Service Medal, the Silver Star with three oak leaf clusters, the Legion of Merit, the Distinguished Flying Cross with five oak leaf clusters, and the Knight Commander's Cross of the Order of Merit of the Federal Republic of Germany.[32]

WALTER C. WILLIAMS, NASA

Walter Charles Williams was born on 30 July 1919 in New Orleans, Louisiana. He earned a bachelor of science degree in aerospace engineering from Louisiana State University in 1939 and went to work for the NACA in August 1940, serving as a project engineer to improve the handling, maneuverability, and flight characteristics of World War II fighters. Williams became the project engineer for the X-1 in 1946 and went to the site that eventually became Edwards AFB to set up flight tests for the X-1.[33]

He was the founding director of the organization that became the Dryden Flight Research Center{AQ8}. In September 1959, he became the associate director of the new NASA Space Task Group at Langley, which was created to carry out Project Mercury. He later became director of operations for the project, and then associate director of the NASA Manned Spacecraft Center in Houston (subsequently renamed the Johnson Space Center).

In January 1963, Williams moved to NASA Headquarters as deputy associate administrator of the Office of Manned Space Flight, and received an honorary doctorate of engineering degree from Louisiana State University. From April 1964 to 1975, he was vice president and general manager of The Aerospace Corporation. Williams returned to NASA Headquarters as chief engineer in 1975 and retired from that position in July 1982. Twice Williams received the NASA Distinguished Service Medal. He died at his home in Tarzana, California, on 7 October 1995.

32 Letter, Major General Robert M. White (USAF, Retired) to Dennis R. Jenkins, 13 June 2002, with comments on a draft copy of this manuscript.

33 Biography, Walter C. Williams, 11 October 1995. In the files at the NASA History Office.

APPENDIX B

X-15 Flight Log

Revised 1 July 2006

Compiled by Betty J. Love, Roy G. Bryant,
Tony R. Landis and Dennis R. Jenkins

*This flight log has been compiled with input from many individuals;
We extend our thanks and appreciation to all of you.*

The two NB-52s prepare to launch two X-15s on the same day. The 4 November 1960 attempt resulted in the launch of 56-6670 with Bob Rushworth as pilot, but 56-6671, piloted by Scott Crossfield, aborted due to the failure of the #2 APU. On 18 November 1966 the program would again try to launch two flights in a single day, but again one X-15 would abort due to technical problems.

X-15 Serial Numbers

		First Flight	X-15 Flights	Highest Mach	Highest Speed	Highest Altitude	Notes
X-15-1	56-6670	08 Jun 59	81	Mach 6.06	4,104 mph	266,500	
X-15-2	56-6671	17 Sep 59	31	Mach 6.04	4,093 mph	217,000	Airframe was rebuilt into X-15A-2
X-15A-2	56-6671	25 Jun 64	22	Mach 6.70	4,520 mph	249,000	
X-15-3	56-6672	20 Dec 61	65	Mach 5.73	3,897 mph	354,200	Aircraft lost on flight 191

X-15 Pilots

	Name	X-15 Flights	Highest Mach	Highest Speed	Highest Altitude	Notes
Adams	Major Michael J. Adams, USAF	7	Mach 5.59	3,822 mph	266,000	Killed on flight 3-65-97
Armstrong	Neil A. Armstrong, NASA	7	Mach 5.74	3,989 mph	207,500	Made first flight with ball nose and MH-96
Crossfield	A. Scott Crossfield, NAA	14	Mach 2.97	1,960 mph	88,116	Made first X-15 glide, first XLR11, and first XLR99 flights
Dana	William H. Dana, NASA	16	Mach 5.53	3,897 mph	306,900	Made last X-15 flight
Engle	Captain Joe H. Engle, USAF	16	Mach 5.71	3,888 mph	280,600	
Kincheloe	Captain Iven C. Kincheloe, Jr., USAF	0	—	—	—	Killed in an F-104 accident prior to his first X-15 flight
Knight	Major William J. "Pete" Knight, USAF	16	Mach 6.70	4,520 mph	280,500	Made maximum speed flight
McKay	John B. "Jack" McKay, NASA	29	Mach 5.65	3,863 mph	295,600	
Petersen	Lt. Cdr. Forrest S. Petersen, USN	5	Mach 5.30	3,600 mph	101,800	
Rushworth	Lt. Colonel Robert A. Rushworth, USAF	34	Mach 6.06	4,018 mph	285,000	Made first flight of X-15A-2
Thompson	Milton O. Thompson, NASA	14	Mach 5.48	3,724 mph	214,100	
Walker	Joseph A. Walker, NASA	25	Mach 5.92	4,104 mph	354,200	Made maximum altitude flight
White, Al	Alvin S. White, NAA	0	—	—	—	Scott Crossfield's backup; never flew the X-15
White	Major Robert M. White, USAF	16	Mach 6.04	4,093 mph	314,750	Made FAI record flight to 314,750 feet

Chase aircraft used on the X-15 program

Type	Serial No. (BuNo)	Notes
F-100A	52-5760	Original North American landing trainer.
F-100A	52-5778	NASA support aircraft. Departed 10 Jun 60.
JF-100C	53-1717	NASA support aircraft. Used between 06 Nov 59 and 23 Feb 61.
F-100F	56-3726	AFFTC support aircraft.
F-100F	56-3963	NAA suport aircraft.
F-100F	56-3875	AFFTC support aircraft.
JF-104A	55-2961	NASA support aircraft.
JF-104A	56-0749	NASA support aircraft. Delivered 13 Apr 59; written-off 20 Dec 62.
F-104A	56-0740	AFFTC support aircraft.
F-104A	56-0743	AFFTC support aircraft.
F-104A	56-0744	AFFTC support aircraft.
F-104A	56-0746	AFFTC support aircraft.
F-104A	56-0748	AFFTC support aircraft.
F-104A	56-0749	AFFTC support aircraft.
F-104A	56-0755	AFFTC support aircraft.
F-104A	56-0757	AFFTC support aircraft.
F-104A	56-0760	AFFTC support aircraft.
F-104A	56-0763	AFFTC support aircraft.
F-104A	56-0764	AFFTC support aircraft.
F-104A	56-0766	AFFTC support aircraft.
F-104A	56-0768	AFFTC support aircraft.
F-104A	56-0790/N820NA	AFFTC support aircraft. To FRC on 27 Dec 66 as N820NA.
F-104A	56-0802	AFFTC support aircraft.
F-104A	56-0817	AFFTC support aircraft.
F-104B	56-3722	AFFTC support aircraft.
F-104B	57-1303	NASA support aircraft.
F-104D	57-1314	AFFTC support aircraft.
F-104D	57-1315	AFFTC support aircraft.
F-104D	57-1316	AFFTC support aircraft.
F-104D	57-1331	AFFTC support aircraft.
F-104D	57-1332	AFFTC support aircraft.
F-104N	NASA 011/N811NA *	NASA support aircraft. Delivered on 19 Aug 63.
F-104N	NASA 012/N812NA *	NASA support aircraft. Delivered on 6 Sep 63.
F-104N	NASA 013/N813NA *	NASA support aircraft. Delivered on 22 Oct 63; written-off 8 Jun 66.
F4H-1	145313	Navy support aircraft. Flown during Mar 61. (See next entry)
F-4A	145313	NASA support aircraft. Delivered on 3 Dec 65; departed on 14 Jun 66.
F-4C	63-7651	AFFTC support aircraft.
F5D-1	139208/ NASA 212	NASA support aircraft. Delivered on 16 Jan 61; departed on 4 Mar 63.
F5D-1	142350/NASA 213	NASA support aircraft. Delivered on 15 Jun 61. Later NASA 802.
YT-38A	58-1197	AFFTC support aircraft.
T-38A	59-1596	AFFTC support aircraft.
T-38A	59-1598	AFFTC support aircraft.
T-38A	59-1599	AFFTC support aircraft.
T-38A	59-1600	AFFTC support aircraft.
T-38A	59-1601	AFFTC support aircraft.
T-38A	59-1604	AFFTC support aircraft.
T-38A	59-1606	AFFTC support aircraft.
T-38A	60-0563	AFFTC support aircraft.

Notes:
* The F-104Ns changed from 0xx to 8xx in March 1965
Data supplied by Betty J. Love and Peter W. Merlin, DFRC History Office.

Chase pilots supporting the X-15 program

Adams	Major Michael J. Adams, USAF
Armstrong	Neil A. Armstrong, NASA
Baker	Robert "Bob" Baker, NAA
Collins	Captain Michael Collins, USAF
Crews	Captain Albert H. Crews, Jr., USAF
Crossfield	A. Scott Crossfield, NAA
Curtis	Captain Lawrence C. Curtis, Jr., USAF
Cuthill	Major Fred J. Cuthill, USAF
Dana	William H. Dana, NASA
Daniel	Major Walter F. Daniel, USAF
Davey	Captain Thomas J. Davey, USAF
DeLong	John DeLong, NAA (cameraman)
Enevoldson	Einar Enevoldson, NASA
Engle	Captain Joe H. Engle, USAF
Evenson	Captain Mervin L. Evenson, USAF
Fulton	Lt. Colonel Fitzhugh L. Fulton, Jr., NASA
Gentry	Captain Jerauld A. Gentry, NASA
Gordon	Major Henry C. Gordon, USAF
Haise	Frederick W. Haise, Jr., NASA
Hoag	Captain Peter C. Hoag, USAF
Hover	Captain Robert C. Hover, USAF
Jackson	Hugh M. Jackson, NASA
Knight	Captain William J. "Pete" Knight, USAF
Krier	Gary E. Krier, NASA
Livingston	Captain David W. Livingston, USAF
Looney	Captain William R. Looney, USAF
Mallick	Donald L. Mallick, NASA
Manke	John A. Manke, NASA
Marrett	Captain George J. Marrett, USAF
McDivitt	Major James A. McDivitt, USAF
McKay	John B. McKay, NASA
Parsons	Major Robert K. Parsons, USAF
Petersen	Lt. Commander Forrest S. Petersen, USN
Peterson	Bruce A. Peterson, NASA
Powell	Captain Cecil Powell, USAF
Roberts	J. O. Roberts, NAA
J. Rogers	Major Joseph W. Rogers, USAF
R. Rogers	Major Russell L. Rogers, USAF
Rushworth	Major Robert A. Rushworth, USAF
Shawler	Captain Wendell H. "Wendy" Shawler, USAF
R.W. Smith	Captain Robert W. Smith, USAF
R.J. Smith	Captain Roger J. Smith, USAF
Sorlie	Major Donald M. Sorlie, USAF
Stroface	Captain Joseph F. Stroface, USAF
Thompson	Milton O. Thompson, NASA
Twinting	Major William T. "Ted" Twinting, USAF
Walker	Joseph A. Walker, NASA
Ward	Lt. Colonel Fred Ward, USAF
Whelan	Captain Robert E. Whelan, USAF
A. White	Alvin S. White, NAA
R. White	Major Robert M. White, USAF
Wood	Major James W. Wood, USAF

NB-52 aircraft used on the X-15 program

NB-52A	52-003	"The High and the Mighty One"
NB-52B	52-008	"The Challenger"

NB-52 Significant Dates

29 Nov 57	B-52A (52-0003) arrives at Air Force Plant 42 in Palmdale, California. The aircraft came from Boeing and was placed in storage pending modifications.
04 Feb 58	B-52A was moved into the NAA hangar for start of modification.
14 Nov 58	The modified NB-52A arrives at Edwards AFB.
14 Jan 61	NB-52A was flown to Wichita, Kansas, for major overhaul.
23 Mar 61	NB-52 returns to Edwards from Boeing-Witchita.
17 Apr 61	NB-52A returns to operational status.
06 Jan 59	RB-52B (52-008) is flown to NAA facility in Palmdale for modification.
08 Jun 59	The modified NB-52B arrives at Edwards AFB. (some source indicate this was originally designated NRB-52B)

Launch Panel Operators for the X-15 program

Berkowitz	William "Bill" Berkowitz, NAA
Butchart	Stanley P. Butchart, NASA
Dustin	Allen F. Dustin, NASA
Moise	John W. Moise, NASA
Peterson	Bruce A. Peterson, NASA
Russell	John "Jack" W. Russell, NASA

B-52 Pilots Supporting the X-15 program

Allavie	Captain John E. "Jack" Allavie, USAF
Anderson	Donald C. Anderson, USAF (one flight, 2-A-39)
Andonian	Colonel Harry Andonian, USAF
Archer	Squadron Leader Harry M. Archer, RAF
Bement	Captain Russell P. Bement, USAF
Bock	Captain Charles C. Bock Jr., USAF (later Major)
Bowline	Captain Jerry D. Bowline, USAF (later Major)
Branch	Brigadier General Irving "Twig" Branch, USAF (one flight, 1-44-70)
Campbell	Captain John K. Campbell, USAF
Cole	Major Frank E. Cole, USAF
Cotton	Lt. Colonel Joseph P. Cotton, USAF (later Colonel)
Cretney	Squadron leader David Cretney, RAF
Crews	Major Albert H. Crews Jr., USAF
Cross	Major Carl S. Cross, USAF
Doryland	Major Charles J. Doryland, USAF
Fulton	Major Fitzhugh "Fitz" Fulton, USAF (later Lt. Colonel)
Jones	Colonel Gay E. Jones, USAF
Kuyk	Captain Charles F. G. Kuyk Jr., USAF
Lewis	Colonel Kenneth K. Lewis, USAF
McDowell	Major Edward D. McDowell Jr., USAF
Miller	Squadron Leader John Miller, RAF
Mosley	Captain Robert L. Mosley, USAF
Reschke	Major William G. Reschke Jr., USAF (later Lt. Colonel)
Stroup	Captain Floyd B. Stroup, USAF
Sturmthal	Lt. Colonel Emil "Ted" Sturmthal, USAF
Townsend	Colonel Guy M. Townsend, USAF
Yeager	Colonel Charles E. "Chuck" Yeager, USAF (one flight, 2-A-38)

Notes:
Names taken from flight logs. Only last names and ranks of Air Force personnel were given.
First names supplied by Betty Love and Peter W. Merlin, DFRC/HO based on Test Pilot School and AFFTC History Office files, and personal interviews with Fitz Fulton, Wendell Shawler, and Johnny Armstrong.
On X-15 flight 1-12-23, the B-52 pilot is listed as "Kirk," but this appears to be a misspelling of Kuyk in the original record.

Radio Locations

NASA 1	Bldg. 4800 Control Room, FRC
NASA 2	Beatty Radar Site, High Range
NASA 3	Ely Radar Site, High Range

Personnel Who Served as NASA 1

Adams	Major Michael J. Adams, USAF
Armstrong	Neil A. Armstrong, NASA
Butchart	Stanley P. Butchart, NASA
Dana	William H. Dana, NASA
Engle	Captain Joe H. Engle, USAF
Harvey	Q.C. Harvey, NAA
Knight	Captain William J. "Pete" Knight, USAF
Manke	John A. Manke, NASA
McKay	John B. McKay, NASA
Petersen	Lt. Commander Forrest S. Petersen, USN
Rushworth	Major Robert A. Rushworth, USAF
Thompson	Milton O. Thompson, NASA
Walker	Joseph A. Walker, NASA
White	Major Robert M. White, USAF

Miscellaneous Aircraft Supporting the X-15 program

C-47H (R4D)	N817NA	NASA support aircraft used for lakebed surveys and recovery from remote sites. Originally R4D-5 (BuNo 17136)
C-130A	54-1624	AFFTC support aircraft. Used to ferry X-15 rescue and paramedic personnel to uprange lakebeds.
C-130A	54-1626	AFFTC support aircraft. Used to ferry X-15 rescue and paramedic personnel to uprange lakebeds.
C-130A	53-3132	Assigned to X-15 support.
C-130A	53-3134	Assigned to X-15 program after 20 March 1959.
C-130A	53-3135	Assigned to X-15 support. Used during Mud Lake emergency landing recovery operations on 10 January 1962.
C-130B	57-0525	Assigned to X-15 support. Used during Mud Lake emergency landing recovery operations on 1 July 1966.
C-130E	61-2358	Assigned to X-15 support. Used during the last flight of X-15-3.
UH-1F	63-13143	U.S. Army
YUH-1H	60-6029	U.S. Army
H-21B	51-15855	Originally bailed to Sperry Gyroscope. Became available to AFFTC around February 1959.
H-21B	53-4389	Originally bailed to Prewitt Aircraft Company. Became available to AFFTC around January 1959.
H-21B	??	Became available to AFFTC around September 1959.
JTF-102A	54-1354	Used from 1958 to early 1959 to test X-15 pressure suit and biomedical package.
JF-100C	53-1709	NASA variable-stability aircraft.

Ten Highest Mach X-15 Flights

Program Flight #	Flight ID	X-15 (s/n)	Flight Date	Pilot	Max. Mach	Max. Altitude	Max. Speed
188	2-53-97	56-6671	03 Oct 67	Knight	6.70	102,100	4,520
175	2-50-89	56-6671	18 Nov 66	Knight	6.33	98,900	4,250
97	1-42-67	56-6670	05 Dec 63	Rushworth	6.06	101,000	4,018
45	2-21-37	56-6671	09 Nov 61	White	6.04	101,600	4,093
59	1-30-51	56-6670	27 Jun 62	Walker	5.92	123,700	4,104
44	1-24-40	56-6670	17 Oct 61	Walker	5.74	108,600	3,900
64	1-32-53	56-6670	26 Jul 62	Armstrong	5.74	98,900	3,989
76	3-13-23	56-6672	20 Dec 62	Walker	5.73	160,400	3,793
105	1-47-74	56-6670	29 Apr 64	Rushworth	5.72	101,600	3,906

Ten Highest Speed X-15 Flights

Program Flight #	Flight ID	X-15 (s/n)	Flight Date	Pilot	Max. Mach	Max. Altitude	Max. Speed	Max. Velocity (fps)
188	2-53-97	56-6671	03 Oct 67	Knight	6.70	102,100	4,520	6,629
175	2-50-89	56-6671	18 Nov 66	Knight	6.33	98,900	4,250	6,233
59	1-30-51	56-6670	27 Jun 62	Walker	5.92	123,700	4,104	6,019
45	2-21-37	56-6671	09 Nov 61	White	6.04	101,600	4,093	6,003
97	1-42-67	56-6670	05 Dec 63	Rushworth	6.06	101,000	4,018	5,893
64	1-32-53	56-6670	26 Jul 62	Armstrong	5.74	98,900	3,989	5,851
137	2-39-70	56-6671	22 Jun 65	McKay	5.64	155,900	3,938	5,776
89	1-38-61	56-6670	18 Jul 63	Rushworth	5.63	104,800	3,925	5,757
86	1-36-57	56-6670	25 Jun 63	Walker	5.51	111,800	3,911	5,736
105	1-47-74	56-6670	29 Apr 64	Rushworth	5.72	101,600	3,906	5,729

Ten Highest Altitude X-15 Flights

Program Flight #	Flight ID	X-15 (s/n)	Flight Date	Pilot	Max. Mach	Max. Altitude	Max. Speed
91	3-22-36	56-6672	22 Aug 63	Walker	5.58	354,200	3,794
90	3-21-32	56-6672	19 Jul 63	Walker	5.50	347,800	3,710
62	3-7-14	56-6672	17 Jul 62	White	5.45	314,750	3,832
174	3-56-83	56-6672	01 Nov 66	Dana	5.46	306,900	3,750
150	3-49-73	56-6672	28 Sep 65	McKay	5.33	295,600	3,732
87	3-20-31	56-6672	27 Jun 63	Rushworth	4.89	285,000	3,425
138	3-44-67	56-6672	29 Jun 65	Engle	4.94	280,600	3,432
190	3-64-95	56-6672	17 Oct 67	Knight	5.53	280,500	3,869
77	3-14-24	56-6672	17 Jan 63	Walker	5.47	271,700	3,677
143	3-46-70	56-6672	10 Aug 65	Engle	5.20	271,000	3,550

Speed Summary

The following represents to total time the three X-15s spent above the indicated Mach number. The total time includes time spent below Mach 1. Includes glide flights. Does not include NB-52 carry time. Given as hours:minutes:seconds.

Aircraft	Mach 1	Mach 2	Mach 3	Mach 4	Mach 5	Mach 6	Total
X-15-1	07:35:24	04:40:59	03:17:31	02:12:34	00:27:55	00:00:08	12:40:43
X-15-2	04:31:41	02:48:16	01:56:07	01:11:02	00:12:57	00:01:10	07:51:37
X-15-3	06:09:23	04:41:29	03:37:55	02:35:16	00:44:41	00:00:00	09:42:37
Total	18:16:28	12:10:44	08:51:33	05:58:52	01:25:33	00:01:18	30:14:57

Ten Slowest Mach X-15 Flights

Program Flight #	Flight ID	X-15 (s/n)	Flight Date	Pilot	Max. Mach	Max. Altitude	Max. Speed
1	1-1-5	56-6670	08 Jun 59	Crossfield	0.79	37,550	522
47	1-25-44	56-6670	10 Jan 62	Petersen	0.97	44,750	645
4	2-3-9	56-6671	05 Nov 59	Crossfield	1.00	45,462	660
74	2-31-52	56-6671	09 Nov 62	McKay	1.49	53,950	1,019
7	2-5-12	56-6671	17 Feb 60	Crossfield	1.57	52,640	1,036
22	1-13-25	56-6670	23 Sep 60	Petersen	1.68	53,043	1,108
159	2-45-81	56-6671	01 Jul 66	Rushworth	1.70	44,800	1,061
29	1-18-31	56-6670	30 Nov 60	Armstrong	1.75	48,840	1,155
178	3-58-87	56-6672	26 Apr 67	Dana	1.80	53,400	1,163
31	1-19-32	56-6670	09 Dec 60	Armstrong	1.80	50,095	1,188

Ten Slowest Speed X-15 Flights

Program Flight #	Flight ID	X-15 (s/n)	Flight Date	Pilot	Max. Mach	Max. Altitude	Max. Speed	Max. Velocity (fps)
1	1-1-5	56-6670	08 Jun 59	Crossfield	0.79	37,550	522	766
47	1-25-44	56-6670	10 Jan 62	Petersen	0.97	44,750	645	946
4	2-3-9	56-6671	05 Nov 59	Crossfield	1.00	45,462	660	968
74	2-31-52	56-6671	09 Nov 62	McKay	1.49	53,950	1,019	1,495
7	2-5-12	56-6671	17 Feb 60	Crossfield	1.57	52,640	1,036	1,519
159	2-45-81	56-6671	01 Jul 66	Rushworth	1.70	44,800	1,061	1,556
22	1-13-25	56-6670	23 Sep 60	Petersen	1.68	53,043	1,108	1,625
29	1-18-31	56-6670	30 Nov 60	Armstrong	1.75	48,840	1,155	1,694
178	3-58-87	56-6672	26 Apr 67	Dana	1.80	53,400	1,163	1,706
31	1-19-32	56-6670	09 Dec 60	Armstrong	1.80	50,095	1,188	1,742

Ten Lowest Altitude X-15 Flights

Program Flight #	Flight ID	X-15 (s/n)	Flight Date	Pilot	Max. Mach	Max. Altitude	Max. Speed
1	1-1-5	56-6670	08 Jun 59	Crossfield	0.79	37,550	522
47	1-25-44	56-6670	10 Jan 62	Petersen	0.97	44,750	645
159	2-45-81	56-6671	01 Jul 66	Rushworth	1.70	44,800	1,061
4	2-3-9	56-6671	05 Nov 59	Crossfield	1.00	45,462	660
12	1-4-9	56-6670	13 Apr 60	White	1.90	48,000	1,254
9	1-3-8	56-6670	25 Mar 60	Walker	2.00	48,630	1,320
29	1-18-31	56-6670	30 Nov 60	Armstrong	1.75	48,840	1,155
25	1-16-29	56-6670	04 Nov 60	Rushworth	1.95	48,900	1,287
32	1-20-35	56-6670	01 Feb 61	McKay	1.88	49,780	1,211
10	2-7-15	56-6671	29 Mar 60	Crossfield	1.96	49,982	1,293

XLR11 Maximum Altitude

Program Flight #	Flight ID	X-15 (s/n)	Flight Date	Pilot	Max. Mach	Max. Altitude	Max. Speed
X-15-1							
19	1-10-19	56-6670	12 Aug 60	White	2.52	136,500	1,772
X-15-2							
6	2-4-11	56-6671	11 Feb 60	Crossfield	2.22	88,116	1,466

XLR11 Maximum Speed

Program Flight #	Flight ID	X-15 (s/n)	Flight Date	Pilot	Max. Mach	Max. Altitude	Max. Speed
X-15-1							
33	1-21-36	56-6670	07 Feb 61	White	3.50	78,150	2,275
X-15-2							
6	2-4-11	56-6671	11 Feb 60	Crossfield	2.22	88,116	1,466

X-15 Flight Log Legend and Explanations

Program Flight #: Cumulative X-15 flight number. Includes all glide and powered free-flights.

Flight ID: X-15 flight identification.
First number is which X-15 (1, 2, or 3).
Second number is total number of free flights by that aircraft.
Third number is total number of times that X-15 has been carried aloft by the B-52.

The second number is replaced by an "A" for unplanned aborts, and a "C" for planned captive flights.

X-15 (s/n) The Air Force serial number (tail number) of the X-15.

Flight Date: The date the flight was actually flown.

Pilot (flight #): The pilot, and the number of flights he had made in an X-15.

Launch Lake: The dry lake the launch took place over (all launches took place near a dry lake to serve as an emergency abort landing site).

Launch Time: The time the launch took place. All X-15 times are given as hour:minute:second.tenths on a 24-hour clock.
All times are local to Edwards AFB, California.

Landing Lake: The dry lake the flight landed on.

Landing Time: The time the X-15 touched-down on the landing lake. Computed as the X-15 launch time plus the X-15 Flight Duration.

The following entries have two components.
The "Plan" column contains the preflight planning values.
The "Actual" column contains the values actually achieved on the flight.

Max Mach: The maximum Mach number attained by the X-15 on that flight.

Max Altitude: The maximum altitude (feet; mean sea level) attained by the X-15 on that flight.

Speed (mph): The maximum speed attained by the X-15 on that flight. Listed in miles per hour, figured for a standard day.

X-15 Flight Duration: The total flight time for the X-15 in hours:minutes:seconds.tenths. This information was obtained from flight records (recorded onboard for X-15-1 and X-15-2; telemtered to the ground for X-15-3).

XLR11 (s/n): The serial numbers of the XLR11 engines used on that flight. The first number is the upper engine; then the lower.

XLR99 (s/n): The serial number of the XLR99 engine used on that flight.

Powered Time (sec): The total powered flight time. This disregards any momentary lapses in power due to restarts, etc.
For XLR11 flights, it includes any time at least one chamber on either engine was firing.

These entries may contain one of the following annotations
"B.O." indicates the engine burned-out (I.e. ran out of propellants).
"S.D." indicates the engine was shut down by the pilot.

Thrust (chambers): For XLR11 flights only. The total number of chambers that fired on that flight (of eight possible)

Thrust (pct): For XLR99 flights only. The throttle setting for the flight. May have multiple entries if the flight required changing thrust levels.

Configuration: Major configuration of the X-15 vehicle. Lists items such as the ball nose, MH-96, wing tip pods, etc.

Purpose: The major purpose of this X-15 flight. In later flights this was frequently to exercise non-X-15 related experiments.

Aborts: Any aborts leading up to this flight.
Includes the flight number (with an "A" as the middle component, signifying abort), date, and reason if the NB-52 took-off.
Includes date and reason if the NB-52 did not take off (no program flight number assigned).

NASA 1: The person who acted as the aircraft communicator in the NASA control room. Usually another X-15 pilot.

B-52 - Pilots - LP: The B-52 serial number, followed by the flight crew (pilot first, then copilot), followed by the X-15 launch panel operator in the B-52.

Take-Off Time: The B-52 take off time. The majority of available data only lists this to hour:minute, so that is how it is presented here.
All times are local to Edwards AFB, California.

Landing Time: The B-52 landing time.

B-52 Flight Time: The total flight time for the B-52 in hours:minutes. This is computed as landing time minus take-off time.

Chase 1: The aircraft type, serial number, and pilot of the first chase aircraft.

Chase 2: The aircraft type, serial number, and pilot of the second chase aircraft.

Chase 3: The aircraft type, serial number, and pilot of the third chase aircraft.

Chase 4: The aircraft type, serial number, and pilot of the fourth chase aircraft, if any.

Chase 5: The aircraft type, serial number, and pilot of the fifth chase aircraft, if any.

Rover: The aircraft type, serial number, and pilot of the "rover" chase aircraft, if any.

Notes: Includes any anomalies encountered on the flight, additional chase aircraft, or other notes.

Program Flight #:	1			**Plan**	**Actual**	**NASA 1:**	Harvey			
			Max Mach:	0.80	0.79	**B-52 - Pilots - LP:**	52-003	Bock / Allavie	Berkowitcz	
Flight ID:	1-1-5		**Max Altitude:**	40,000	37,550	**Take-Off Time:**	08:01			
X-15 (s/n)	56-6670	(1)	**Speed (mph):**	—	522	**Landing Time:**	08:58			
Flight Date:	08 Jun 59		**X-15 Flight Time:**	—	00:04:56.6	**B-52 Flight Time:**	00:57			
Pilot (flight #):	Crossfield	(1)								
			XLR11 (s/n):	—	??	**Chase 1:**	F-100F	56-3726	Al White / DeLong	
Launch Lake:	Rosamond		**Powered Time (sec):**	0	0	**Chase 2:**	F-100F	56-3963	Wood	
Launch Time:	08:38:40.0		**Thrust (chambers):**	0	0	**Chase 3:**	F-100F		White	
						Chase 4:				
Landing Lake:	Rogers		**Configuration:**	Ventral on; Nose boom		**Chase 5:**				
Landing Time:	08:43:36.6									

Purpose: Pilot familiarization – Crossfield's first X-15 flight

Aborts:

1-C-1	10 Mar 59	Scheduled captive flight
1-A-2	01 Apr 59	Radio failure
1-A-3	10 Apr 59	Radio and APU failure
1-A-4	21 May 59	APU and SAS failure
—	05 Jun 59	Smoke in cockpit during taxi

Notes: Pitch damper failed pre-launch;
Unauthorized aileron roll
Significant instability duirng landing
First X-15 glide flight

All aborts used NB-52A 52-003; Crossfield was the X-15 pilot for all aborts

Program Flight #:	2			**Plan**	**Actual**	**NASA 1:**	Harvey			
			Max Mach:	2.00	2.11	**B-52 - Pilots - LP:**	52-003	Bock / Allavie	Berkowitcz	
Flight ID:	2-1-3		**Max Altitude:**	50,000	52,341	**Take-Off Time:**	07:31			
X-15 (s/n)	56-6671	(1)	**Speed (mph):**	—	1,393	**Landing Time:**	08:46			
Flight Date:	17 Sep 59		**X-15 Flight Time:**	—	00:09:11.0	**B-52 Flight Time:**	01:15			
Pilot (flight #):	Crossfield	(2)								
			XLR11 (s/n):	—	??	**Chase 1:**	F-100F	56-3963	Al White / DeLong	
Launch Lake:	Rosamond		**Powered Time (sec):**	??	224.3	**Chase 2:**	F-100F		Walker	
Launch Time:	08:08:48.0		**Thrust (chambers):**	8	8	**Chase 3:**	F-104D	57-1316	White	
						Chase 4:				
Landing Lake:	Rogers		**Configuration:**	Ventral on; Nose boom		**Chase 5:**				
Landing Time:	08:17:59.0									

Purpose: First X-15 powered flight;
Aircraft checkout

Aborts:

2-C-1	24 Jul 59	Scheduled full-propellant captive flight
2-A-2	04 Sep 59	Vent malfunction

Notes: Flaps extended only 60 percent;
Roll damper failed during flight;
Unauthorized aileron roll

All aborts used NB-52A 52-003; Crossfield was the X-15 pilot for all aborts

Program Flight #:	3			**Plan**	**Actual**	**NASA 1:**				
			Max Mach:	2.00	2.15	**B-52 - Pilots - LP:**	52-003	Bock / Allavie	Moise	
Flight ID:	2-2-6		**Max Altitude:**	60,000	61,781	**Take-Off Time:**	09:25			
X-15 (s/n)	56-6671	(2)	**Speed (mph):**	—	1,419	**Landing Time:**	10:55			
Flight Date:	17 Oct 59		**X-15 Flight Time:**	—	00:09:37.7	**B-52 Flight Time:**	01:30			
Pilot (flight #):	Crossfield	(3)								
			XLR11 (s/n):	—	??	**Chase 1:**	F-100F	56-3963	Al White / DeLong	
Launch Lake:	Rosamond		**Powered Time (sec):**	??	254.5	**Chase 2:**	F-104D		Walker	
Launch Time:	10:13:07.0		**Thrust (chambers):**	8	8	**Chase 3:**	F-104		White	
						Chase 4:				
Landing Lake:	Rogers		**Configuration:**	Ventral on; Nose boom		**Chase 5:**				
Landing Time:	10:22:44.7									

Purpose: Aircraft checkout

Aborts:

2-A-4	10 Oct 59	LOX topoff failure; Helium leak
2-A-5	14 Oct 59	LOX topoff failure; Cabin Pressure

Notes: Roll damper off at launch - reengaged;
Alcohol fire in engine bay after landing

All aborts used NB-52A 52-003; Crossfield was the X-15 pilot for all aborts

Program Flight #:	4			**Plan**	**Actual**	**NASA 1:**	Harvey			
			Max Mach:	2.00	1.00	**B-52 - Pilots - LP:**	52-003	Allavie / Fulton	Moise	
Flight ID:	2-3-9		**Max Altitude:**	80,000	45,462	**Take-Off Time:**	09:00			
X-15 (s/n)	56-6671	(3)	**Speed (mph):**	—	660	**Landing Time:**	10:02			
Flight Date:	05 Nov 59		**X-15 Flight Time:**	—	00:05:28.0	**B-52 Flight Time:**	01:02			
Pilot (flight #):	Crossfield	(4)								
			XLR11 (s/n):	—	??	**Chase 1:**	F-100F		Baker / DeLong	
Launch Lake:	Rosamond		**Powered Time (sec):**	255	13.9	**Chase 2:**	F-104		White	
Launch Time:	09:39:28.0		**Thrust (chambers):**	8	7	**Chase 3:**	F-104		Walker	
						Chase 4:				
Landing Lake:	Rosamond		**Configuration:**	Ventral on; Nose boom		**Chase 5:**				
Landing Time:	09:44:56.0									

Purpose: Aircraft checkout

Aborts:

2-A-7	22 Oct 59	Pilot's oxygen failure; torn gloves
2-A-8	31 Oct 59	Weather

Notes: Explosion and fire in lower engine;
Roll damper dropped out at launch;
Fuselage failed just forward of LOX tank
(station 226.8) at landing

All aborts used NB-52A 52-003; Crossfield was the X-15 pilot for all aborts

			Plan	Actual				
Program Flight #:	5				**NASA 1:**	Harvey		
		Max Mach:	2.00	2.53	**B-52 - Pilots - LP:**	52-008	Fulton / Kuyk	Berkowitcz
Flight ID:	1-2-7	**Max Altitude:**	65,000	66,844	**Take-Off Time:**	15:42		
X-15 (s/n)	56-6670 (2)	**Speed (mph):**	—	1,669	**Landing Time:**	17:00		
Flight Date:	23 Jan 60	**X-15 Flight Time:**	—	00:09:53.8	**B-52 Flight Time:**	01:18		
Pilot (flight #):	Crossfield (5)							
		XLR11 (s/n):	—	3 and 10	**Chase 1:**	F-100F		Baker / DeLong
Launch Lake:	Rosamond	**Powered Time (sec):**	??	267.2 (B.O.)	**Chase 2:**	F-104		Walker
Launch Time:	16:17:05.0	**Thrust (chambers):**	8	8	**Chase 3:**	F-104		White
					Chase 4:			
Landing Lake:	Rogers	**Configuration:**	Ventral on; Nose boom		**Chase 5:**			
Landing Time:	16:26:58.8							

Purpose: Aircraft checkout;
SAS evaluation;
First powered flight by X-15-1

Notes: First flight of the stable-platform;
First launch from NB-52B 52-008

Aborts: 1-A-6 16 Dec 59 Radio failure; LOX regulator

Abort used NB-52B 52-008; Crossfield was the X-15 pilot on the abort

			Plan	Actual				
Program Flight #:	6				**NASA 1:**	Harvey		
		Max Mach:	2.00	2.22	**B-52 - Pilots - LP:**	52-008	Allavie / Fulton	Moise
Flight ID:	2-4-11	**Max Altitude:**	80,000	88,116	**Take-Off Time:**	09:07		
X-15 (s/n)	56-6671 (4)	**Speed (mph):**	—	1,466	**Landing Time:**	10:34		
Flight Date:	11 Feb 60	**X-15 Flight Time:**	—	00:10:15.5	**B-52 Flight Time:**	01:27		
Pilot (flight #):	Crossfield (6)							
		XLR11 (s/n):	—	??	**Chase 1:**	F-100F	56-3963	Al White / DeLong
Launch Lake:	Rosamond	**Powered Time (sec):**	260	251.2	**Chase 2:**	F-104		Walker
Launch Time:	10:15:04.0	**Thrust (chambers):**	8	8	**Chase 3:**	F-104		White
					Chase 4:			
Landing Lake:	Rogers	**Configuration:**	Ventral on; Nose boom		**Chase 5:**			
Landing Time:	10:25:19.5							

Purpose: Aircraft checkout

Notes: Good flight

Aborts: 2-A-10 04 Feb 60 Loss of source pressure

Abort used NB-52B 52-008; Crossfield was the X-15 pilot on the abort

			Plan	Actual				
Program Flight #:	7				**NASA 1:**	Harvey		
		Max Mach:	2.00	1.57	**B-52 - Pilots - LP:**	52-008	Fulton / Allavie	Moise
Flight ID:	2-5-12	**Max Altitude:**	50,000	52,640	**Take-Off Time:**	08:54		
X-15 (s/n)	56-6671 (5)	**Speed (mph):**	—	1,036	**Landing Time:**	10:02		
Flight Date:	17 Feb 60	**X-15 Flight Time:**	—	00:10:35.9	**B-52 Flight Time:**	01:08		
Pilot (flight #):	Crossfield (7)							
		XLR11 (s/n):	—	??	**Chase 1:**	F-100		White
Launch Lake:	Rosamond	**Powered Time (sec):**	260	309.4	**Chase 2:**	F-104		Walker
Launch Time:	09:41:32.0	**Thrust (chambers):**	8	7	**Chase 3:**	F-104		
					Chase 4:			
Landing Lake:	Rogers	**Configuration:**	Ventral on; Nose boom		**Chase 5:**			
Landing Time:	09:52:07.9							

Purpose: Aircraft checkout;
SAS stability and control evaluation

Notes: Upper engine problems - Restart on 7 chambers was successful

Aborts: None

			Plan	Actual				
Program Flight #:	8				**NASA 1:**	Harvey		
		Max Mach:	2.00	2.15	**B-52 - Pilots - LP:**	52-008	Allavie / Kuyk	Moise
Flight ID:	2-6-13	**Max Altitude:**	50,000	52,640	**Take-Off Time:**	07:55		
X-15 (s/n)	56-6671 (6)	**Speed (mph):**	—	1,419	**Landing Time:**	08:46		
Flight Date:	17 Mar 60	**X-15 Flight Time:**	—	00:08:39.5	**B-52 Flight Time:**	00:51		
Pilot (flight #):	Crossfield (8-6)							
		XLR11 (s/n):	—	??	**Chase 1:**	F-100F	56-3726	Al White / DeLong
Launch Lake:	Rosamond	**Powered Time (sec):**	??	233.5	**Chase 2:**	F-104		White
Launch Time:	08:31:25.0	**Thrust (chambers):**	8	8	**Chase 3:**	F-104		Walker
					Chase 4:			
Landing Lake:	Rogers	**Configuration:**	Ventral on; Nose boom		**Chase 5:**			
Landing Time:	08:40:04.5							

Purpose: Roll stability and control evaluation;
Dampers on and off evaluation

Notes: Good flight

Aborts: None

Program Flight #:	9	
Flight ID:	1-3-8	
X-15 (s/n)	56-6670	(3)
Flight Date:	25 Mar 60	
Pilot (flight #):	Walker	(1)
Launch Lake:	Rosamond	
Launch Time:	15:43:23.0	
Landing Lake:	Rogers	
Landing Time:	15:52:31.0	

	Plan	Actual
Max Mach:	2.00	2.00
Max Altitude:	50,000	48,630
Speed (mph):	—	1,320
X-15 Flight Time:	—	00:09:08.0
XLR11 (s/n):	—	??
Powered Time (sec):	??	272.0 (B.O.)
Thrust (chambers):	8	8, 6
Configuration:	Ventral on; Nose boom	

NASA 1:			
B-52 - Pilots - LP:	52-008	Fulton / Allavie	Russell
Take-Off Time:	14:44		
Landing Time:	16:12		
B-52 Flight Time:	01:28		
Chase 1:	F-100		Crossfield
Chase 2:	F-104		White
Chase 3:	F-100		McKay
Chase 4:			
Chase 5:			

Purpose: Pilot familiarization – Walker's first X-15 flight

Aborts: None

Notes: First government flight;
Stable platform malfunctioned prelaunch;
Two restarts required on top engine;
No roll damper

Program Flight #:	10	
Flight ID:	2-7-15	
X-15 (s/n)	56-6671	(7)
Flight Date:	29 Mar 60	
Pilot (flight #):	Crossfield	(9)
Launch Lake:	Rosamond	
Launch Time:	09:59:28.0	
Landing Lake:	Rogers	
Landing Time:	10:08:38.5	

	Plan	Actual
Max Mach:	2.00	1.96
Max Altitude:	50,000	49,982
Speed (mph):	—	1,293
X-15 Flight Time:	—	00:09:10.5
XLR11 (s/n):	—	??
Powered Time (sec):	267	244.2
Thrust (chambers):	8	8
Configuration:	Ventral on; Nose boom	

NASA 1:	Harvey		
B-52 - Pilots - LP:	52-008	Fulton / Allavie	Moise
Take-Off Time:	08:16		
Landing Time:	10:14		
B-52 Flight Time:	01:58		
Chase 1:	F-100F		White
Chase 2:	F-104D		Knight
Chase 3:	F-104C		Rushworth
Chase 4:			
Chase 5:			

Purpose: Launch characteristics evaluation;
Minus 2-g pushover;
Full throw rudder step evaluation

Aborts: 2-A-14 18 Mar 60 WALC leak

Notes: Good flight

Abort used NB-52B 52-008; Crossfield was the X-15 pilot on the abort

Program Flight #:	11	
Flight ID:	2-8-16	
X-15 (s/n)	56-6671	(8)
Flight Date:	31 Mar 60	
Pilot (flight #):	Crossfield	(10)
Launch Lake:	Rosamond	
Launch Time:	08:42:05.0	
Landing Lake:	Rogers	
Landing Time:	08:51:01.5	

	Plan	Actual
Max Mach:	2.00	2.03
Max Altitude:	50,000	51,356
Speed (mph):	—	1,340
X-15 Flight Time:	—	00:08:56.5
XLR11 (s/n):	—	??
Powered Time (sec):	??	254.5
Thrust (chambers):	8	8
Configuration:	Ventral on; Nose boom	

NASA 1:	Harvey		
B-52 - Pilots - LP:	52-008	Allavie / Fulton	Moise
Take-Off Time:	08:03		
Landing Time:	08:58		
B-52 Flight Time:	00:55		
Chase 1:	F-100		White
Chase 2:	F-104		Rushworth
Chase 3:	F-104		Knight
Chase 4:			
Chase 5:			

Purpose: High-g maneuvers;
SAS gains checkout

Aborts: None

Notes: Good flight;
Landing was intentionally made with all dampers off

Program Flight #:	12	
Flight ID:	1-4-9	
X-15 (s/n)	56-6670	(4)
Flight Date:	13 Apr 60	
Pilot (flight #):	White	(1)
Launch Lake:	Rosamond	
Launch Time:	09:15:11.0	
Landing Lake:	Rogers	
Landing Time:	09:24:03.7	

	Plan	Actual
Max Mach:	2.00	1.90
Max Altitude:	50,000	48,000
Speed (mph):	—	1,254
X-15 Flight Time:	—	00:08:52.7
XLR11 (s/n):	—	??
Powered Time (sec):	??	253.7 (B.O.)
Thrust (chambers):	8	8
Configuration:	Ventral on; Nose boom	

NASA 1:	Walker		
B-52 - Pilots - LP:	52-003	Allavie / Kuyk	Russell
Take-Off Time:	08:28		
Landing Time:	09:33		
B-52 Flight Time:	01:05		
Chase 1:	F-100		Al White / DeLong
Chase 2:	F-104		Walker
Chase 3:	F-104		Rushworth
Chase 4:			
Chase 5:			

Purpose: Pilot familiarization – White's first X-15 flight

Aborts: None

Notes: First Air Force flight;
First flight with stiffened side-tunnel panels;
Flown on center stick;
No research data until High Key (pilot forgot to activate);
No landing data due to film drum failure

Program Flight #:	13		Plan	Actual	**NASA 1:**			
		Max Mach:	2.35	2.56	**B-52 - Pilots - LP:**	52-003	Fulton / Allavie	Russell
Flight ID:	1-5-10	**Max Altitude:**	60,000	59,496	**Take-Off Time:**	08:00		
X-15 (s/n)	56-6670 (5)	**Speed (mph):**	—	1,689	**Landing Time:**	09:10		
Flight Date:	19 Apr 60	**X-15 Flight Time:**	—	00:09:58.6	**B-52 Flight Time:**	01:10		
Pilot (flight #):	Walker (2)							
		XLR11 (s/n):	—	??	**Chase 1:**	F-100		Rushworth
Launch Lake:	Rosamond	**Powered Time (sec):**	??	260.6 (B.O.)	**Chase 2:**	F-104D	(USAF)	McKay
Launch Time:	08:51:44.0	**Thrust (chambers):**	8	8	**Chase 3:**	F-104		Knight
					Chase 4:			
Landing Lake:	Rogers	**Configuration:**	Ventral on; Nose boom		**Chase 5:**			
Landing Time:	09:01:42.6							

Purpose: Performance buildup;
Stability and control buildup;
Fuselage side fairing vibration and flutter data

Aborts: None

Notes: Good flight
No gear data taken

Program Flight #:	14		Plan	Actual	**NASA 1:**	See Notes		
		Max Mach:	2.50	2.20	**B-52 - Pilots - LP:**	52-003	Fulton / Allavie	Russell
Flight ID:	1-6-11	**Max Altitude:**	60,000	60,938	**Take-Off Time:**	09:06		
X-15 (s/n)	56-6670 (6)	**Speed (mph):**	—	1,452	**Landing Time:**	10:11		
Flight Date:	06 May 60	**X-15 Flight Time:**	—	00:09:23.2	**B-52 Flight Time:**	01:05		
Pilot (flight #):	White (2)							
		XLR11 (s/n):	—	??	**Chase 1:**	F-100F		Knight
Launch Lake:	Rosamond	**Powered Time (sec):**	??	246.5 (B.O.)	**Chase 2:**	F-104D		McKay
Launch Time:	09:53:19.0	**Thrust (chambers):**	8	8	**Chase 3:**	F-104A		Rushworth
					Chase 4:			
Landing Lake:	Rogers	**Configuration:**	Ventral on; Nose boom		**Chase 5:**			
Landing Time:	10:02:42.2							

Purpose: Performance buildup;
Stability and control buildup

Aborts: None

Notes: Roll damper failed at launch (reset)
Normal ventral jettison failed; ventral came off when skids deployed
There was not a functional NASA 1 on this flight due to radio problems;
Pete Knight served as a radio relay from a chase aircraft

Program Flight #:	15		Plan	Actual	**NASA 1:**	Armstrong		
		Max Mach:	3.00	3.19	**B-52 - Pilots - LP:**	52-003	Bock / Allavie	Russell
Flight ID:	1-7-12	**Max Altitude:**	73,000	77,882	**Take-Off Time:**	08:08		
X-15 (s/n)	56-6670 (7)	**Speed (mph):**	—	2,111	**Landing Time:**	09:40		
Flight Date:	12 May 60	**X-15 Flight Time:**	—	00:10:10.3	**B-52 Flight Time:**	01:32		
Pilot (flight #):	Walker (3)							
		XLR11 (s/n):	—	??	**Chase 1:**	F-100F		White
Launch Lake:	Silver	**Powered Time (sec):**	??	256.3 (B.O.)	**Chase 2:**	F-104A		Rushworth
Launch Time:	08:47:37.0	**Thrust (chambers):**	8, 5	8, 0	**Chase 3:**	F-104A		Knight
					Chase 4:	F-104D	57-1316	McKay
Landing Lake:	Rogers	**Configuration:**	Ventral on; Nose boom		**Chase 5:**			
Landing Time:	08:57:47.3							

Purpose: Performance buildup;
Stability and control buildup

Aborts: None

Notes: Stable platform inoperative from launch;
First launch (of any X-plane) from a remote lake;
First X-15 Mach 3 flight;
Three chambers intentionally shut down -
remaining 5 shut down seconds later;
Ventral chute failed, ventral extensively damaged

Program Flight #:	16		Plan	Actual	**NASA 1:**	Armstrong		
		Max Mach:	2.20	2.31	**B-52 - Pilots - LP:**	52-003	Bock / Allavie	Russell
Flight ID:	1-8-13	**Max Altitude:**	110,000	108,997	**Take-Off Time:**	08:05		
X-15 (s/n)	56-6670 (8)	**Speed (mph):**	—	1,590	**Landing Time:**	09:20		
Flight Date:	19 May 60	**X-15 Flight Time:**	—	00:11:24.6	**B-52 Flight Time:**	01:15		
Pilot (flight #):	White (3)							
		XLR11 (s/n):	—	??	**Chase 1:**	F-100F		Knight
Launch Lake:	Silver	**Powered Time (sec):**	??	274.7	**Chase 2:**	F-104A		Rushworth
Launch Time:	08:46:47.0	**Thrust (chambers):**	6, 8	6, 8	**Chase 3:**	F-104D		McKay
					Chase 4:			
Landing Lake:	Rogers	**Configuration:**	Ventral on; Nose boom		**Chase 5:**			
Landing Time:	08:58:11.6							

Purpose: Altitude buildup

Aborts: None

Notes: First X-15 flight above 100,000 feet

Program Flight #:	17	
Flight ID:	2-9-18	
X-15 (s/n)	56-6671	(9)
Flight Date:	26 May 60	
Pilot (flight #):	Crossfield	(11)
Launch Lake:	Rosamond	
Launch Time:	09:08:36.0	
Landing Lake:	Rogers	
Landing Time:	09:17:50.4	

	Plan	Actual
Max Mach:	2.30	2.20
Max Altitude:	78,000	51,282
Speed (mph):	—	1,452
X-15 Flight Time:	—	00:09:14.4
XLR11 (s/n):	—	??
Powered Time (sec):	255	243.4
Thrust (chambers):	8	8
Configuration:	Ventral on; Nose boom	

NASA 1:	Harvey		
B-52 - Pilots - LP:	52-008	Bock / Allavie	Moise
Take-Off Time:	08:13		
Landing Time:	09:30		
B-52 Flight Time:	01:17		
Chase 1:	F-100F	56-3963	Al White / DeLong
Chase 2:	F-104		White
Chase 3:	F-104D		Petersen
Chase 4:			
Chase 5:			

Purpose: High-g maneuvers; SAS gains checkout; High alpha stability and control; BCS checkout

Notes: Good flight; Last XLR11 flight of X-15-2

Aborts: 2-A-17 05 May 60 #1 APU failure

Abort used NB-52A 52-003; Crossfield was the X-15 pilot on the abort

Program Flight #:	18	
Flight ID:	1-9-17	
X-15 (s/n)	56-6670	(9)
Flight Date:	04 Aug 60	
Pilot (flight #):	Walker	(4)
Launch Lake:	Silver	
Launch Time:	08:59:13.0	
Landing Lake:	Rogers	
Landing Time:	09:09:35.6	

	Plan	Actual
Max Mach:	3.30	3.31
Max Altitude:	75,000	78,112
Speed (mph):	—	2,196
X-15 Flight Time:	—	00:10:22.6
XLR11 (s/n):	—	??
Powered Time (sec):	260	264.2 (B.O.)
Thrust (chambers):	8	8
Configuration:	Ventral on; Nose boom	

NASA 1:	Butchart		
B-52 - Pilots - LP:	52-003	Fulton / Allavie	Russell
Take-Off Time:	08:15		
Landing Time:	09:40		
B-52 Flight Time:	01:25		
Chase 1:	F-100F		White
Chase 2:	F-104A		Rushworth
Chase 3:	F-104A		Petersen
Chase 4:	F-104D		Knight
Chase 5:			

Purpose: Maximum speed with XLR11; Stability and control data; Aerodynamic heating data

Notes: Good flight

Aborts:

1-A-14	27 May 60	Loss of telemetry
1-A-15	03 Jun 60	#2 APU failure; Hydraulic pressure
1-A-16	08 Jun 60	Source pressure

1-A-14 and 1-A-16 used NB-52A 52-003; 1-A-15 used NB-52B 52-008
Walker was the X-15 pilot for all the aborts

Program Flight #:	19	
Flight ID:	1-10-19	
X-15 (s/n)	56-6670	(10)
Flight Date:	12 Aug 60	
Pilot (flight #):	White	(4)
Launch Lake:	Silver	
Launch Time:	08:48:43.0	
Landing Lake:	Rogers	
Landing Time:	09:00:22.1	

	Plan	Actual
Max Mach:	2.50	2.52
Max Altitude:	133,000	136,500
Speed (mph):	—	1,772
X-15 Flight Time:	—	00:11:39.1
XLR11 (s/n):	—	??
Powered Time (sec):	??	256.2 (B.O.)
Thrust (chambers):	8	8
Configuration:	Ventral on; Nose boom	

NASA 1:			
B-52 - Pilots - LP:	52-003	Fulton / Andoian	Russell
Take-Off Time:	08:06		
Landing Time:	09:15		
B-52 Flight Time:	01:09		
Chase 1:	F-100F		Rushworth
Chase 2:	F-104A		Petersen
Chase 3:	F-104D		Looney
Chase 4:			
Chase 5:			

Purpose: Maximum altitude with XLR11; Stability and control data

Notes: Good flight; Record altitude flight; Highest flight with XLR11 engines

Aborts: 1-A-18 11 Aug 60 Loss of nitrogen source pressure

Abort used NB-52A 52-003; White was the X-15 pilot on the abort

Program Flight #:	20	
Flight ID:	1-11-21	
X-15 (s/n)	56-6670	(11)
Flight Date:	19 Aug 60	
Pilot (flight #):	Walker	(5)
Launch Lake:	Silver	
Launch Time:	08:34:22.0	
Landing Lake:	Rogers	
Landing Time:	08:44:04.4	

	Plan	Actual
Max Mach:	3.00	3.13
Max Altitude:	70,000	75,982
Speed (mph):	—	1,986
X-15 Flight Time:	—	00:09:42.4
XLR11 (s/n):	—	??
Powered Time (sec):	??	251.6 (B.O.)
Thrust (chambers):	8	8
Configuration:	Ventral on; Nose boom	

NASA 1:			
B-52 - Pilots - LP:	52-003	Allavie / Cole	Butchart
Take-Off Time:	07:51		
Landing Time:	09:20		
B-52 Flight Time:	01:29		
Chase 1:	F-100		White
Chase 2:	F-104		Rushworth
Chase 3:	F-104A	56-0764	Petersen
Chase 4:	F-104		Looney
Chase 5:			

Purpose: Aerodynamic heating data; Stability and control data; Performance data

Notes: Alpha cross-pointer hooked up backwards

Aborts: 1-A-20 18 Aug 60 APU #1 Failure

Abort used NB-52A 52-003; Walker was the X-15 pilot on the abort

Program Flight #:	21
Flight ID:	1-12-23
X-15 (s/n)	56-6670 (12)
Flight Date:	10 Sep 60
Pilot (flight #):	White (5)
Launch Lake:	Silver
Launch Time:	11:45:10.0
Landing Lake:	Rogers
Landing Time:	11:55:10.0

	Plan	Actual
Max Mach:	3.20	3.23
Max Altitude:	80,000	79,864
Speed (mph):	—	2,182
X-15 Flight Time:	—	00:10:00.0
XLR11 (s/n):	—	??
Powered Time (sec):	??	264.3
Thrust (chambers):	8	8
Configuration:	Ventral on; Nose boom	

NASA 1:	Walker		
B-52 - Pilots - LP:	52-008	Allavie / Kuyk	Butchart
Take-Off Time:	11:01		
Landing Time:	12:25		
B-52 Flight Time:	01:24		
Chase 1:	F-100F		Looney
Chase 2:	F-104A	56-0760	Armstrong
Chase 3:	F-104A		Rushworth
Chase 4:	F-104D		Knight
Chase 5:			

Purpose: Stability and control data;
Performance data

Aborts:

—	01 Sep 60	Did not take off due to cloud cover
1-A-22	02 Sep 60	Telemetry failure

Notes: APU problem

Taxi used NB-52B 52-008; White was the X-15 pilot
Abort used NB-52B 52-008; White was the X-15 pilot on the abort

---

Program Flight #:	22
Flight ID:	1-13-25
X-15 (s/n)	56-6670 (13)
Flight Date:	23 Sep 60
Pilot (flight #):	Petersen (1)
Launch Lake:	Palmdale VOR
Launch Time:	09:52:06.0
Landing Lake:	Rogers
Landing Time:	09:59:15.6

	Plan	Actual
Max Mach:	2.00	1.68
Max Altitude:	50,000	53,043
Speed (mph):	—	1,108
X-15 Flight Time:	—	00:07:09.6
XLR11 (s/n):	—	??
Powered Time (sec):	??	146.6
Thrust (chambers):	8	8, 4, 0
Configuration:	Ventral on; Nose boom	

NASA 1:	Thompson		
B-52 - Pilots - LP:	52-008	Allavie / Fulton	Russell
Take-Off Time:	09:11		
Landing Time:	10:20		
B-52 Flight Time:	01:09		
Chase 1:	F-100F		Looney
Chase 2:	F-104A		Walker
Chase 3:	F-104D		Rushworth
Chase 4:			
Chase 5:			

Purpose: Pilot familiarization – Petersen's first X-15 flight

Aborts:

1-A-24	20 Sep 60	#2 APU would not stay on

Notes: First launch from Palmdale;
Engines shut down early;
Two unsuccessful restarts on upper engine

Abort used NB-52B 52-008; Petersen was the X-15 pilot on the abort

---

Program Flight #:	23
Flight ID:	1-14-27
X-15 (s/n)	56-6670 (14)
Flight Date:	20 Oct 60
Pilot (flight #):	Petersen (2)
Launch Lake:	Palmdale VOR
Launch Time:	09:30:27.0
Landing Lake:	Rogers
Landing Time:	09:39:53.1

	Plan	Actual
Max Mach:	2.00	1.94
Max Altitude:	50,000	53,800
Speed (mph):	—	1,280
X-15 Flight Time:	—	00:09:26.1
XLR11 (s/n):	—	??
Powered Time (sec):	??	285.4
Thrust (chambers):	8, 5	8, 5
Configuration:	Ventral on; Nose boom	

NASA 1:	Thompson		
B-52 - Pilots - LP:	52-008	Fulton / Kuyk	Russell
Take-Off Time:	08:59		
Landing Time:	09:47		
B-52 Flight Time:	00:48		
Chase 1:	F-100F		White
Chase 2:	F-104A		Rushworth
Chase 3:	F-104D	57-1314	Armstrong
Chase 4:			
Chase 5:			

Purpose: Stability and control data;
Performance data;
Alternate airspeed calibration;
Additional pilot familiarization

Aborts:

—	05 Oct 60	X-15 failed preflight checks
1-A-26	11 Oct 60	Failed engine H2O2 tank regulator

Notes: Good flight

Abort used NB-52B 52-008; Petersen was the X-15 pilot on the abort

---

Program Flight #:	24
Flight ID:	1-15-28
X-15 (s/n)	56-6670 (15)
Flight Date:	28 Oct 60
Pilot (flight #):	McKay (1)
Launch Lake:	Palmdale VOR
Launch Time:	09:43:56.0
Landing Lake:	Rogers
Landing Time:	09:53:01.3

	Plan	Actual
Max Mach:	2.00	2.02
Max Altitude:	50,000	50,700
Speed (mph):	—	1,333
X-15 Flight Time:	—	00:09:05.3
XLR11 (s/n):	—	??
Powered Time (sec):	??	267.5
Thrust (chambers):	8	8
Configuration:	Ventral on; Nose boom	

NASA 1:	Thompson		
B-52 - Pilots - LP:	52-008	Fulton / Cole	Butchart
Take-Off Time:	09:12		
Landing Time:	10:06		
B-52 Flight Time:	00:54		
Chase 1:	F-100		Looney
Chase 2:	F-104		White
Chase 3:	F-104		Petersen
Chase 4:			
Chase 5:			

Purpose: Pilot familiarization – McKay's first X-15 flight
Stability and control data;
Performance data;
Alternate airspeed calibration

Aborts: None

Notes: Ventral chute did not open

			Plan	Actual				
Program Flight #:	25				**NASA 1:**	McKay		
		Max Mach:	2.00	1.95	**B-52 - Pilots - LP:**	52-008	Fulton / Cole	Butchart
Flight ID:	1-16-29	**Max Altitude:**	50,000	48,900	**Take-Off Time:**	12:10		
X-15 (s/n)	56-6670 (16)	**Speed (mph):**	—	1,287	**Landing Time:**	13:15		
Flight Date:	04 Nov 60	**X-15 Flight Time:**	—	00:08:46.3	**B-52 Flight Time:**	01:05		
Pilot (flight #):	Rushworth (1)							
		XLR11 (s/n):	—	??	**Chase 1:**	F-100		Looney
Launch Lake:	Palmdale VOR	**Powered Time (sec):**	??	271.0	**Chase 2:**	F-104		White
Launch Time:	12:43:33.0	**Thrust (chambers):**	8	8	**Chase 3:**	F-104	57-1316	Armstrong
					Chase 4:	F-100F	56-3963	Al White / DeLong
Landing Lake:	Rogers	**Configuration:**	Ventral on; Nose boom		**Chase 5:**			
Landing Time:	12:52:19.3							

Purpose: Pilot familiarization – Rushworth's first X-15 flight
Stability and control data;
Performance data;
Alternate airspeed calibration

Aborts: None

Notes: Good flight

			Plan	Actual				
Program Flight #:	26				**NASA 1:**	Harvey		
		Max Mach:	2.70	2.97	**B-52 - Pilots - LP:**	52-003	Allavie / Kuyk	Moise
Flight ID:	2-10-21	**Max Altitude:**	60,000	81,200	**Take-Off Time:**	08:59		
X-15 (s/n)	56-6671 (10)	**Speed (mph):**	—	1,960	**Landing Time:**	10:16		
Flight Date:	15 Nov 60	**X-15 Flight Time:**	—	00:08:28.4	**B-52 Flight Time:**	01:17		
Pilot (flight #):	Crossfield (12)							
		XLR99 (s/n):	—	103	**Chase 1:**	F-100F	56-3963	Al White / DeLong
Launch Lake:	Rosamond	**Powered Time (sec):**	155	137.3 (B.O.)	**Chase 2:**	F-104		Walker
Launch Time:	09:59:00.0	**Thrust (pct):**	50	50	**Chase 3:**	F-104		White
					Chase 4:			
Landing Lake:	Rogers	**Configuration:**	Ventral on; Nose boom		**Chase 5:**			
Landing Time:	10:07:28.4							

Purpose: XLR99 checkout;
Stability and control evaluation

Aborts:

2-A-19	13 Oct 60	H2O2 leak in #2 APU
2-A-20	04 Nov 60	Failed #2 APU shutoff valve

Notes: First XLR99 flight

All aborts used NB-52A 52-003; Crossfield was the X-15 pilot for all aborts

			Plan	Actual				
Program Flight #:	27				**NASA 1:**	McKay		
		Max Mach:	2.20	1.90	**B-52 - Pilots - LP:**	52-003	Fulton / Allavie	Russell
Flight ID:	1-17-30	**Max Altitude:**	55,000	54,750	**Take-Off Time:**	12:10		
X-15 (s/n)	56-6670 (17)	**Speed (mph):**	—	1,254	**Landing Time:**	13:00		
Flight Date:	17 Nov 60	**X-15 Flight Time:**	—	00:08:58.2	**B-52 Flight Time:**	00:50		
Pilot (flight #):	Rushworth (2)							
		XLR11 (s/n):	—	??	**Chase 1:**	F-100		Looney
Launch Lake:	Palmdale VOR	**Powered Time (sec):**	??	261.9	**Chase 2:**	F-104		Walker
Launch Time:	12:43:07.0	**Thrust (chambers):**	8	8	**Chase 3:**	F-104		Knight
					Chase 4:			
Landing Lake:	Rogers	**Configuration:**	Ventral on; Nose boom		**Chase 5:**			
Landing Time:	12:52:05.2							

Purpose: Aerodynamic data

Aborts: None

Notes: Lower XLR11 engine shutdown and restarted;
Upper XLR11 removed on 24 November 1960

			Plan	Actual				
Program Flight #:	28				**NASA 1:**	Harvey		
		Max Mach:	2.30	2.51	**B-52 - Pilots - LP:**	52-003	Allavie / Fulton	Moise
Flight ID:	2-11-22	**Max Altitude:**	54,000	61,900	**Take-Off Time:**	12:46		
X-15 (s/n)	56-6671 (11)	**Speed (mph):**	—	1,656	**Landing Time:**	13:40		
Flight Date:	22 Nov 60	**X-15 Flight Time:**	—	00:07:31.7	**B-52 Flight Time:**	00:54		
Pilot (flight #):	Crossfield (13)							
		XLR99 (s/n):	—	103	**Chase 1:**	F-100F	56-3963	Al White / DeLong
Launch Lake:	Rosamond	**Powered Time (sec):**	134	125.1 (**)	**Chase 2:**	F-104		Walker
Launch Time:	13:25:55.0	**Thrust (pct):**	50, 75, 100	50, 75, 100	**Chase 3:**	F-104		White
					Chase 4:			
Landing Lake:	Rogers	**Configuration:**	Ventral on; Nose boom		**Chase 5:**			
Landing Time:	13:33:26.7							

Purpose: XLR99 checkout - restart and throttle;
BCS evaluation

Aborts: None

Notes: First demonstration of XLR99 throttle capabilities;
First XLR99 inflight restart

** First engine run was shutdown (S.D.);
Second was a burnout (B.O.)

Program Flight #:	29
Flight ID:	1-18-31
X-15 (s/n)	56-6670 (18)
Flight Date:	30 Nov 60
Pilot (flight #):	Armstrong (1)
Launch Lake:	Palmdale VOR
Launch Time:	10:42:42.0
Landing Lake:	Rogers
Landing Time:	10:52:35.8

	Plan	Actual
Max Mach:	2.00	1.75
Max Altitude:	50,000	48,840
Speed (mph):	—	1,155
X-15 Flight Time:	—	00:09:53.8
XLR11 (s/n):	—	??
Powered Time (sec):	??	309.1
Thrust (chambers):	8	7
Configuration:	Ventral on; Nose boom	

NASA 1:	McKay		
B-52 - Pilots - LP:	52-008	Fulton / Cole	Butchart
Take-Off Time:	10:10		
Landing Time:	11:04		
B-52 Flight Time:	00:54		
Chase 1:	F-100F		Looney
Chase 2:	F-104D	(USAF)	Petersen
Chase 3:	F-104A	(USAF)	Walker
Chase 4:			
Chase 5:			

Purpose: Pilot familiarization – Armstrong's first X-15 flight

Aborts: None

Notes: Upper #3 chamber did not start;
Inertial attitudes incorrect

Program Flight #:	30
Flight ID:	2-12-23
X-15 (s/n)	56-6671 (12)
Flight Date:	06 Dec 60
Pilot (flight #):	Crossfield (14)
Launch Lake:	Lancaster (west of)
Launch Time:	15:29:30.0
Landing Lake:	Rogers
Landing Time:	15:37:37.2

	Plan	Actual
Max Mach:	2.30	2.85
Max Altitude:	54,000	53,374
Speed (mph):	—	1,881
X-15 Flight Time:	—	00:08:07.2
XLR99 (s/n):	—	103
Powered Time (sec):	121	128.9
Thrust (pct):	50, 70	50, 70 (**)
Configuration:	Ventral on; Nose boom	

NASA 1:	Harvey		
B-52 - Pilots - LP:	52-003	Allavie / Cole	Moise
Take-Off Time:	14:50		
Landing Time:	16:00		
B-52 Flight Time:	01:10		
Chase 1:	F-100F	56-3963	Al White / DeLong
Chase 2:	F-104		Petersen
Chase 3:	F-104		White
Chase 4:			
Chase 5:			

Purpose: XLR99 restart demonstration; BCS checks;
High-g maneuvers

Aborts: None

Notes: Last North American Aviation flight of X-15
Two engine inflight restarts;
Last nose-boom flight;
Only Lancaster launch

** First engine run was shutdown (S.D.);
Second was shutdown (S.D.); Third was a burn-out (B.O.)

Program Flight #:	31
Flight ID:	1-19-32
X-15 (s/n)	56-6670 (19)
Flight Date:	09 Dec 60
Pilot (flight #):	Armstrong (2)
Launch Lake:	Palmdale VOR
Launch Time:	11:52:40.0
Landing Lake:	Rogers
Landing Time:	12:03:29.0

	Plan	Actual
Max Mach:	1.90	1.80
Max Altitude:	50,000	50,095
Speed (mph):	—	1,188
X-15 Flight Time:	—	00:10:49.0
XLR11 (s/n):	—	??
Powered Time (sec):	??	270.1
Thrust (chambers):	8	8
Configuration:	Ventral on; Ball-nose	

NASA 1:	McKay		
B-52 - Pilots - LP:	52-008	Allavie / Cole	Russell
Take-Off Time:	11:21		
Landing Time:	12:17		
B-52 Flight Time:	00:56		
Chase 1:	F-100F		Daniel
Chase 2:	F-104D		Petersen
Chase 3:	F-104A		White
Chase 4:			
Chase 5:			

Purpose: Ball nose evaluation;
Stability and control data;
Alternate airspeed sources evaluation

Aborts: None

Notes: First ball-nose flight

Program Flight #:	32
Flight ID:	1-20-35
X-15 (s/n)	56-6670 (20)
Flight Date:	01 Feb 61
Pilot (flight #):	McKay (2)
Launch Lake:	Palmdale VOR
Launch Time:	10:47:32.0
Landing Lake:	Rogers
Landing Time:	10:57:19.7

	Plan	Actual
Max Mach:	2.00	1.88
Max Altitude:	50,000	49,780
Speed (mph):	—	1,211
X-15 Flight Time:	—	00:09:47.7
XLR11 (s/n):	—	??
Powered Time (sec):	??	263.7
Thrust (chambers):	8	8
Configuration:	Ventral on; Ball-nose	

NASA 1:	Thompson		
B-52 - Pilots - LP:	52-008	Fulton / Lewis	Russell
Take-Off Time:	10:13		
Landing Time:	11:08		
B-52 Flight Time:	00:55		
Chase 1:	F-100		White
Chase 2:	F-104		Petersen
Chase 3:	F-104		Wood
Chase 4:			
Chase 5:			

Purpose: Ball nose evaluation;
Side-stick controller evaluation;
Inertial velocity indicator checkout
Alternate airspeed sources evaluation

Aborts:

1-A-33	15 Dec 60	#2 hydraulic system failure	1-A-33 used NB-52A 52-003; White was the X-15 pilot
1-A-34	11 Jan 61	#2 hydraulic system failure	1-A-34 used NB-52A 52-003; McKay was the X-15 pilot

Notes: Good flight

Program Flight #:	33
Flight ID:	1-21-36
X-15 (s/n)	56-6670 (21)
Flight Date:	07 Feb 61
Pilot (flight #):	White (6)
Launch Lake:	Silver
Launch Time:	12:56:10.0
Landing Lake:	Rogers
Landing Time:	13:06:37.8

	Plan	Actual
Max Mach:	3.10	3.50
Max Altitude:	75,000	78,150
Speed (mph):	—	2,275
X-15 Flight Time:	—	00:10:27.8
XLR11 (s/n):	—	??
Powered Time (sec):	??	276.1
Thrust (chambers):	8	8
Configuration:	Ventral on; Ball-nose	

NASA 1:	Armstrong		
B-52 - Pilots - LP:	52-008	Fulton / Mosely	Butchart
Take-Off Time:	12:17		
Landing Time:	13:21		
B-52 Flight Time:	01:04		
Chase 1:	F-100		Daniel
Chase 2:	F-104		Knight
Chase 3:	F-104		Petersen
Chase 4:	F-104		Rushworth
Chase 5:			

Purpose: Stability and control data; Performance data; Flight systems evaluation

Aborts: None

Notes: Last X-15 XLR11 flight; Fastest flight with XLR11 engines

---

Program Flight #:	34
Flight ID:	2-13-26
X-15 (s/n)	56-6671 (13)
Flight Date:	07 Mar 61
Pilot (flight #):	White (7)
Launch Lake:	Silver
Launch Time:	10:28:33.0
Landing Lake:	Rogers
Landing Time:	10:37:07.1

	Plan	Actual
Max Mach:	4.00	4.43
Max Altitude:	84,000	77,450
Speed (mph):	—	2,905
X-15 Flight Time:	—	00:08:34.1
XLR99 (s/n):	—	108
Powered Time (sec):	116	127.0 (S.D.)
Thrust (pct):	50	50
Configuration:	Ventral on; Ball-nose	

NASA 1:	Butchart		
B-52 - Pilots - LP:	52-008	Cole / Kuyk	Russell
Take-Off Time:	09:53		
Landing Time:	10:50		
B-52 Flight Time:	00:57		
Chase 1:	F-100		Rushworth
Chase 2:	F5D-1	212 (139208)	Walker
Chase 3:	F4H-1	145313	Petersen
Chase 4:	F-104		Looney
Chase 5:			

Purpose: Envelope expansion; Stability and control data; Temperature data; B-70 IR emission coating test

Aborts:

2-A-24	21 Feb 61	Inertial platform failure
2-A-25	24 Feb 61	Attitude gyro failure

Notes: First X-15-2 ball-nose flight; First Mach 4 flight (for any aircraft); First government XLR99 flight

All aborts used NB-52B 52-008; White was the X-15 pilot for all aborts

---

Program Flight #:	35
Flight ID:	2-14-28
X-15 (s/n)	56-6671 (14)
Flight Date:	30 Mar 61
Pilot (flight #):	Walker (6)
Launch Lake:	Hidden Hills
Launch Time:	10:05:00.0
Landing Lake:	Rogers
Landing Time:	10:15:16.5

	Plan	Actual
Max Mach:	3.70	3.95
Max Altitude:	150,000	169,600
Speed (mph):	—	2,760
X-15 Flight Time:	—	00:10:16.5
XLR99 (s/n):	—	108
Powered Time (sec):	79	81.9 (S.D.)
Thrust (pct):	75	75
Configuration:	Ventral on; Ball-nose	

NASA 1:			
B-52 - Pilots - LP:	52-008	Fulton / Kuyk	Russell
Take-Off Time:	09:20		
Landing Time:	10:35		
B-52 Flight Time:	01:15		
Chase 1:	F-100		White
Chase 2:	T-38A		Knight
Chase 3:	F-104	(USAF)	Petersen
Chase 4:	F-104		Rushworth
Chase 5:			

Purpose: Altitude buildup; Ballistic control system evaluation; Thermostructures data; Aerodynamic data

Aborts:

2-A-27	21 Mar 61	Telemetry failure; NB-52 brake chute failed on landing

Notes: XLR99 lost fire signal, Restart required; SAS cycle limit; First use of new A/P22S-2 full-pressure suit; First Hidden Hills launch

Abort used NB-52B 52-008; Walker was the X-15 pilot for the abort in an A/P-22S

Program Flight #:	36
Flight ID:	2-15-29
X-15 (s/n)	56-6671 (15)
Flight Date:	21 Apr 61
Pilot (flight #):	White (8)
Launch Lake:	Hidden Hills
Launch Time:	10:05:17.0
Landing Lake:	Rogers
Landing Time:	10:15:20.4

	Plan	Actual
Max Mach:	4.60	4.62
Max Altitude:	105,000	105,000
Speed (mph):	—	3,074
X-15 Flight Time:	—	00:10:03.4
XLR99 (s/n):	—	108
Powered Time (sec):	67	71.6 (S.D.)
Thrust (pct):	100	100
Configuration:	Ventral on; Ball-nose	

NASA 1:	Armstrong		
B-52 - Pilots - LP:	52-003	Allavie / Mosley	Russell
Take-Off Time:	09:19		
Landing Time:	10:32		
B-52 Flight Time:	01:13		
Chase 1:	F-100F		Looney
Chase 2:	F-104A		Walker
Chase 3:	F-104A		Rogers
Chase 4:	F-104D		Wood
Chase 5:			

Purpose: Velocity buildup; Aerodynamic heating data; Stability and control data; Performance data

Aborts: None

Notes: Restart required; Pitch damper dropout; Cabin pressure rose to 46,000 feet

Program Flight #: 37

Flight ID:	2-16-31
X-15 (s/n)	56-6671 (16)
Flight Date:	25 May 61
Pilot (flight #):	Walker (7)
Launch Lake:	Mud
Launch Time:	12:16:35.0
Landing Lake:	Rogers
Landing Time:	12:28:43.1

	Plan	Actual
Max Mach:	5.00	4.95
Max Altitude:	117,000	107,500
Speed (mph):	—	3,307
X-15 Flight Time:	—	00:12:08.1
XLR99 (s/n):	—	103
Powered Time (sec):	73	74.3 (S.D.)
Thrust (pct):	100	100
Configuration:	Ventral on; Ball-nose	

NASA 1:			
B-52 - Pilots - LP:	52-003	Allavie / Fulton	Butchart
Take-Off Time:	11:30		
Landing Time:	12:52		
B-52 Flight Time:	01:22		
Chase 1:	F-100		Looney
Chase 2:	F-104		Daniel
Chase 3:	F-104		Petersen
Chase 4:	F-104		Rushworth
Chase 5:			

Purpose: Velocity buildup;
Stability and control data
Performance data;
Aerodynamic heating data;
SAS resildual oscillation evaluation

Notes: First launch from Mud Lake;
SAS dropped out at launch;
Cabin altitude went to 50,000 feet

Aborts: 2-A-30 19 May 61 Lost Beatty radar

Abort used NB-52A 52-003; Walker was the X-15 pilot for the abort

Program Flight #: 38

Flight ID:	2-17-33
X-15 (s/n)	56-6671 (17)
Flight Date:	23 Jun 61
Pilot (flight #):	White (9)
Launch Lake:	Mud
Launch Time:	14:00:05.0
Landing Lake:	Rogers
Landing Time:	14:10:10.7

	Plan	Actual
Max Mach:	5.30	5.27
Max Altitude:	115,000	107,700
Speed (mph):	—	3,603
X-15 Flight Time:	—	00:10:05.7
XLR99 (s/n):	—	103
Powered Time (sec):	75	78.7 (S.D.)
Thrust (pct):	100	100
Configuration:	Ventral on; Ball-nose	

NASA 1:			
B-52 - Pilots - LP:	52-003	Allavie / Fulton	Butchart
Take-Off Time:	13:08		
Landing Time:	14:33		
B-52 Flight Time:	01:25		
Chase 1:	F-100		Looney
Chase 2:	F-104		Daniel
Chase 3:	F-104		Crews
Chase 4:	F-104		Walker
Chase 5:			

Purpose: Velocity buildup;
Stability and control data
Performance data;
Aerodynamic heating data

Notes: First Mach 5 flight (for any aircraft);
Cabin altitude rose to 56K feet; suit inflated

Aborts: 2-A-32 20 Jun 61 #1 APU failure

Abort used NB-52A 52-003; White was X-15 pilot

Program Flight #: 39

Flight ID:	1-22-37
X-15 (s/n)	56-6670 (22)
Flight Date:	10 Aug 61
Pilot (flight #):	Petersen (3)
Launch Lake:	Silver
Launch Time:	10:27:05.0
Landing Lake:	Rogers
Landing Time:	10:36:29.4

	Plan	Actual
Max Mach:	3.70	4.11
Max Altitude:	75,000	78,200
Speed (mph):	—	2,735
X-15 Flight Time:	—	00:09:24.4
XLR99 (s/n):	—	107
Powered Time (sec):	115	117.7 (S.D.)
Thrust (pct):	50	50
Configuration:	Ventral on; Ball-nose	

NASA 1:	Armstrong		
B-52 - Pilots - LP:	52-003	Allavie / Archer	Russell
Take-Off Time:	09:43		
Landing Time:	10:44		
B-52 Flight Time:	01:01		
Chase 1:	F-100		White
Chase 2:	F-104		Rushworth
Chase 3:	F-104		Walker
Chase 4:			
Chase 5:			

Purpose: XLR99 systems checkout;
Beta-dot control technique evaluation

Notes: First XLR99 flight for X-15-1;
Delayed release from NB-52 due to drop switch problem

Aborts: None

Program Flight #: 40

Flight ID:	2-18-34
X-15 (s/n)	56-6671 (18)
Flight Date:	12 Sep 61
Pilot (flight #):	Walker (8)
Launch Lake:	Mud
Launch Time:	14:40:17.0
Landing Lake:	Rogers
Landing Time:	14:49:00.9

	Plan	Actual
Max Mach:	5.60	5.21
Max Altitude:	120,000	114,300
Speed (mph):	—	3,618
X-15 Flight Time:	—	00:08:43.9
XLR99 (s/n):	—	106
Powered Time (sec):	79	115.0 (B.O.)
Thrust (pct):	100, 50 75	100, 50, 75
Configuration:	Ventral on; Ball-nose	

NASA 1:	Butchart		
B-52 - Pilots - LP:	52-008	Archer / Allavie	Russell
Take-Off Time:	13:44		
Landing Time:	15:10		
B-52 Flight Time:	01:26		
Chase 1:	F-100		White
Chase 2:	F-104		Petersen
Chase 3:	F-104		Daniel
Chase 4:	F-104		Rushworth
Chase 5:			

Purpose: Velocity buildup;
Aerodynamic heating data;
Stability and control data;
Performance data;
Base data for sharp-leading edge experiment on X-15-3

Notes: XLR99 fuel suction pressure switch failure;
Fuel line low light at launch;
Airplane very loose approaching 15 degrees angle of attack

Aborts: None

Program Flight #:	41		**Plan**	**Actual**	**NASA 1:**	Thompson		
		Max Mach:	5.00	5.30	**B-52 - Pilots - LP:**	52-008	Allavie / Archer	Russell
Flight ID:	2-19-35	**Max Altitude:**	80,000	101,800	**Take-Off Time:**	09:04		
X-15 (s/n)	56-6671 (19)	**Speed (mph):**	—	3,600	**Landing Time:**	10:15		
Flight Date:	28 Sep 61	**X-15 Flight Time:**	—	00:08:41.6	**B-52 Flight Time:**	01:11		
Pilot (flight #):	Petersen (4)							
		XLR99 (s/n):	—	106	**Chase 1:**	F-100		Daniel
Launch Lake:	Hidden Hills	**Powered Time (sec):**	90	87.1 (B.O.)	**Chase 2:**	F-104		McKay
Launch Time:	09:50:25.0	**Thrust (pct):**	100, 50	100, 50	**Chase 3:**	F-104		Rogers
					Chase 4:			
Landing Lake:	Rogers	**Configuration:**	Ventral on; Ball-nose		**Chase 5:**			
Landing Time:	09:59:06.6							

Purpose: Heat transfer data; Thermostructural data; Stability and control data; Controllability at low dynamic pressure; Performance and stability data with speed brakes extended

Notes: Good flight

Aborts: None

Program Flight #:	42		**Plan**	**Actual**	**NASA 1:**	Knight		
		Max Mach:	3.70	4.30	**B-52 - Pilots - LP:**	52-003	Allavie / Archer	Russell
Flight ID:	1-23-39	**Max Altitude:**	80,000	78,000	**Take-Off Time:**	09:59		
X-15 (s/n)	56-6670 (23)	**Speed (mph):**	—	2,830	**Landing Time:**	11:10		
Flight Date:	04 Oct 61	**X-15 Flight Time:**	—	00:08:31.3	**B-52 Flight Time:**	01:11		
Pilot (flight #):	Rushworth (3)							
		XLR99 (s/n):	—	103	**Chase 1:**	F-100		Daniel
Launch Lake:	Silver	**Powered Time (sec):**	120	122.0 (S.D.)	**Chase 2:**	F-104		McKay
Launch Time:	10:40:50.0	**Thrust (pct):**	75, 50	75, 50	**Chase 3:**	F-104		White
					Chase 4:			
Landing Lake:	Rogers	**Configuration:**	Ventral off; Ball-nose		**Chase 5:**			
Landing Time:	10:49:21.3							

Purpose: Ventral-off handling quality evaluation; Ventral-off stability study

Notes: First ventral off flight; Leading-edge heating slot shields

Aborts: 1-A-38 29 Sep 61 Stabilizer pulsing / feedback

Abort used NB-52A 52-003; Rushworth was the X-15 pilot for the abort

Program Flight #:	43		**Plan**	**Actual**	**NASA 1:**	Petersen		
		Max Mach:	5.00	5.21	**B-52 - Pilots - LP:**	52-003	Allavie / Fulton	Russell
Flight ID:	2-20-36	**Max Altitude:**	200,000	217,000	**Take-Off Time:**	11:22		
X-15 (s/n)	56-6671 (20)	**Speed (mph):**	—	3,647	**Landing Time:**	12:52		
Flight Date:	11 Oct 61	**X-15 Flight Time:**	—	00:10:14.7	**B-52 Flight Time:**	01:30		
Pilot (flight #):	White (10)							
		XLR99 (s/n):	—	106	**Chase 1:**	F-100		Daniel
Launch Lake:	Mud	**Powered Time (sec):**	79	82.5 (S.D.)	**Chase 2:**	F5D	142350 / NASA 213	McKay
Launch Time:	12:20:00.0	**Thrust (pct):**	100	100	**Chase 3:**	F-104		Wood
					Chase 4:	F-104		Rushworth
Landing Lake:	Rogers	**Configuration:**	Ventral on; Ball-nose		**Chase 5:**			
Landing Time:	12:30:14.7							

Purpose: Altitude buildup; Aerodynamic heating during reentry data; Controllability at low dynamic pressure; Performance and stability data with speed brakes extended

Notes: First aircraft flight above 200,000 feet; First X-15 flight that used BCS for attitude control; Left outer windshield shattered on reentry; The highest Mach number was achieved during descent from max altitude

Pete Knight was NASA 2

Aborts: None

Program Flight #:	44		**Plan**	**Actual**	**NASA 1:**	Petersen		
		Max Mach:	5.70	5.74	**B-52 - Pilots - LP:**	52-003	Allavie / Archer	Butchart
Flight ID:	1-24-40	**Max Altitude:**	113,000	108,600	**Take-Off Time:**	10:01		
X-15 (s/n)	56-6670 (24)	**Speed (mph):**	—	3,900	**Landing Time:**	12:30		
Flight Date:	17 Oct 61	**X-15 Flight Time:**	—	00:10:11.7	**B-52 Flight Time:**	02:29		
Pilot (flight #):	Walker (9)							
		XLR99 (s/n):	—	103	**Chase 1:**	F-100F		White
Launch Lake:	Mud	**Powered Time (sec):**	80	84.6 (S.D.)	**Chase 2:**	F-104D	(USAF)	McKay
Launch Time:	10:57:33.0	**Thrust (pct):**	75, 100	75, 100	**Chase 3:**	F-104		Daniel
					Chase 4:	F-104		Knight
Landing Lake:	Rogers	**Configuration:**	Ventral on; Ball-nose		**Chase 5:**			
Landing Time:	11:07:44.7							

Purpose: Velocity buildup; Aerodynamic heating data; Stability and control data; Performance data

Notes: Laterally out of trim to the right

Aborts: None

Program Flight #:	45
Flight ID:	2-21-37
X-15 (s/n)	56-6671 (21)
Flight Date:	09 Nov 61
Pilot (flight #):	White (11)
Launch Lake:	Mud
Launch Time:	09:57:17.0
Landing Lake:	Rogers
Landing Time:	10:06:48.2

	Plan	Actual
Max Mach:	6.00	6.04
Max Altitude:	110,000	101,600
Speed (mph):	—	4,093
X-15 Flight Time:	—	00:09:31.2
XLR99 (s/n):	—	109
Powered Time (sec):	83	86.9 (B.O.)
Thrust (pct):	100	100
Configuration:	Ventral on; Ball-nose	

NASA 1:			
B-52 - Pilots - LP:	52-008	Allavie / Archer	Russell
Take-Off Time:	09:00		
Landing Time:	10:26		
B-52 Flight Time:	01:26		
Chase 1:	F-100		Rushworth
Chase 2:	F-104		Walker
Chase 3:	F-104		Gordon
Chase 4:	F-104		Daniel
Chase 5:			

Purpose: Maximum velocity flight; Aerodynamic heating data; Stability and control data; Performance data

Notes: First Mach 6 flight (for any aircraft); Right outer window shattered decelerating thru Mach 2.7

Jack McKay was NASA 2

Aborts: None

Program Flight #:	46
Flight ID:	3-1-2
X-15 (s/n)	56-6672 (1)
Flight Date:	20 Dec 61
Pilot (flight #):	Armstrong (3)
Launch Lake:	Silver
Launch Time:	14:45:50.0
Landing Lake:	Rogers
Landing Time:	14:56:15.4

	Plan	Actual
Max Mach:	3.50	3.76
Max Altitude:	75,000	81,000
Speed (mph):	—	2,502
X-15 Flight Time:	—	00:10:25.4
XLR99 (s/n):	—	106
Powered Time (sec):	104	106.3 (S.D.)
Thrust (pct):	75, 50	75, 50
Configuration:	Ventral on; Ball-nose	

NASA 1:	McKay		
B-52 - Pilots - LP:	52-003	Allavie / Bement	Butchart
Take-Off Time:	14:07		
Landing Time:	15:06		
B-52 Flight Time:	00:59		
Chase 1:	F-100		Daniel
Chase 2:	F-104A	56-0749	Petersen
Chase 3:	F-104		Rushworth
Chase 4:			
Chase 5:			

Purpose: MH-96 evaluation; Checkout of X-15-3

Notes: First X-15-3 flight; All three axes disengaged at launch - reset; Yaw limit cycle cuased downmode to fixed gain

Aborts: 3-A-1 19 Dec 61 XLR99 indication failure

Abort used NB-52A 52-003; Armstrong was the X-15 pilot for the abort

---

Program Flight #:	47
Flight ID:	1-25-44
X-15 (s/n)	56-6670 (25)
Flight Date:	10 Jan 62
Pilot (flight #):	Petersen (5)
Launch Lake:	Mud
Launch Time:	12:28:16.0
Landing Lake:	Mud
Landing Time:	12:32:01.7

	Plan	Actual
Max Mach:	5.70	0.97
Max Altitude:	117,000	44,750
Speed (mph):	—	645
X-15 Flight Time:	—	00:03:45.7
XLR99 (s/n):	—	111
Powered Time (sec):	95	3.3 (S.D.)
Thrust (pct):	100	**
Configuration:	Ventral on; Ball-nose	

NASA 1:	Thompson		
B-52 - Pilots - LP:	52-003	Allavie / Bement	Russell
Take-Off Time:	11:29		
Landing Time:	13:20		
B-52 Flight Time:	01:51		
Chase 1:	F-100		Daniel
Chase 2:	F-104		Walker
Chase 3:	F-104		McDivitt
Chase 4:	F-104		Rushworth
Chase 5:			

Purpose: High angle of attack stability and control data; Aerodynamic heating data

Notes: Two engine malfunction shutdowns; Emergency landing at Mud Lake; First uprange landing; Petersen's last flight

** ≈ 238 psia chamber pressure maximum

Aborts:

1-A-41	27 Oct 61	Weather in launch area
1-A-42	02 Nov 61	Cabin pressure
1-A-43	03 Nov 61	XLR99 purge pressure switch failure

All aborts used NB-52A 52-003; White was the X-15 pilot for all aborts

---

Program Flight #:	48
Flight ID:	3-2-3
X-15 (s/n)	56-6672 (2)
Flight Date:	17 Jan 62
Pilot (flight #):	Armstrong (4)
Launch Lake:	Mud
Launch Time:	12:00:34.0
Landing Lake:	Rogers
Landing Time:	12:11:01.7

	Plan	Actual
Max Mach:	5.00	5.51
Max Altitude:	100,000	133,500
Speed (mph):	—	3,765
X-15 Flight Time:	—	00:10:27.7
XLR99 (s/n):	—	107
Powered Time (sec):	100	97.4 (S.D.)
Thrust (pct):	75	75
Configuration:	Ventral on; Ball-nose	

NASA 1:	Thompson		
B-52 - Pilots - LP:	52-003	Allavie / Bement	Butchart
Take-Off Time:	11:05		
Landing Time:	12:34		
B-52 Flight Time:	01:29		
Chase 1:	F-100		Gordon
Chase 2:	F-104		Petersen
Chase 3:	F-104		McDivitt
Chase 4:	F-104		Rushworth
Chase 5:			

Purpose: MH-96 evaluation

Notes: Good flight

Aborts: None

Program Flight #:	49			Plan	Actual	**NASA 1:**	Walker		
			Max Mach:	4.00	4.12	**B-52 - Pilots - LP:**	52-003	Fulton / Allavie	Butchart
Flight ID:	3-3-7		**Max Altitude:**	170,000	180,000	**Take-Off Time:**	09:23		
X-15 (s/n):	56-6672	(3)	**Speed (mph):**	—	2,850	**Landing Time:**	10:30		
Flight Date:	05 Apr 62		**X-15 Flight Time:**	—	00:11:17.0	**B-52 Flight Time:**	01:07		
Pilot (flight #):	Armstrong	(5)							
			XLR99 (s/n):	—	107	**Chase 1:**	F-100		Daniel
Launch Lake:	Hidden Hills		**Powered Time (sec):**	70	79.2 (S.D.)	**Chase 2:**	F-104		McKay
Launch Time:	10:04:25.0		**Thrust (pct):**	75, 100	75, 100	**Chase 3:**	F-104		Rushworth
						Chase 4:			
Landing Lake:	Rogers		**Configuration:**	Ventral on; Ball-nose		**Chase 5:**			
Landing Time:	10:15:42.0								

Purpose: MH-96 evaluation at high and low dynamic pressure

Notes: Engine failed to light on initial attempt; Restart required

Aborts:

3-A-4	29 Mar 62	Inertial platform failure
3-A-5	30 Mar 62	Igniter idle malfunction
3-A-6	31 Mar 62	analyzer test #24 failed

All aborts used NB-52A 52-003; Armstrong was the X-15 pilot for all aborts

Program Flight #:	50			Plan	Actual	**NASA 1:**	White		
			Max Mach:	5.90	5.69	**B-52 - Pilots - LP:**	52-003	Allavie / Archer	Russell
Flight ID:	1-26-46		**Max Altitude:**	153,000	154,000	**Take-Off Time:**	08:58		
X-15 (s/n):	56-6670	(26)	**Speed (mph):**	—	3,866	**Landing Time:**	10:37		
Flight Date:	19 Apr 62		**X-15 Flight Time:**	—	00:08:58.9	**B-52 Flight Time:**	01:39		
Pilot (flight #):	Walker	(10)							
			XLR99 (s/n):	—	109	**Chase 1:**	F-100		McKay (aborted)
Launch Lake:	Mud		**Powered Time (sec):**	83	84.3 (B.O.)	**Chase 2:**	JF-104A	55-2961	Dana (new Chase 1)
Launch Time:	10:02:20.0		**Thrust (pct):**	100	100	**Chase 3:**	F-104		Rushworth
						Chase 4:	F-104		Daniel
Landing Lake:	Rogers		**Configuration:**	Ventral on; Ball-nose		**Chase 5:**	F-104		Knight
Landing Time:	10:11:18.9								

Purpose: ASAS evaluation;
20-degree angle of attack evaluation;
(#1) UV stellar photography experiment preliminary data gathering

Notes: Beta cross-pointer wired backwards;
First flight with ASAS installed (checkout only)

Aborts:

1-A-45	18 Apr 62	Weather in launch area

Abort used NB-52A 52-003; Walker was the X-15 pilot for the abort

Program Flight #:	51			Plan	Actual	**NASA 1:**	Walker		
			Max Mach:	5.35	5.31	**B-52 - Pilots - LP:**	52-008	Allavie / Bement	Butchart
Flight ID:	3-4-8		**Max Altitude:**	205,000	207,500	**Take-Off Time:**	10:35		
X-15 (s/n):	56-6672	(4)	**Speed (mph):**	—	3,789	**Landing Time:**	11:57		
Flight Date:	20 Apr 62		**X-15 Flight Time:**	—	00:12:28.7	**B-52 Flight Time:**	01:22		
Pilot (flight #):	Armstrong	(6)							
			XLR99 (s/n):	—	110	**Chase 1:**	F-100		White
Launch Lake:	Mud		**Powered Time (sec):**	81	82.4 (S.D.)	**Chase 2:**	F-104	(USAF)	McKay
Launch Time:	11:26:58.0		**Thrust (pct):**	100	100	**Chase 3:**	F-104		Gordon
						Chase 4:	F-104		Rushworth
Landing Lake:	Rogers		**Configuration:**	Ventral on; Ball-nose		**Chase 5:**			
Landing Time:	11:39:26.7			Delta-h indicator on I-panel					

Purpose: MH-96 evaluation

Notes: Overshot (bounced) during reentry - ended up 45 miles south of Edwards; Used max L/D glide to get back to Edwards
Longest flight in X-15 program

Aborts: None

Program Flight #:	52			Plan	Actual	**NASA 1:**	Butchart		
			Max Mach:	5.35	4.94	**B-52 - Pilots - LP:**	52-008	Allavie / Bement	Russell
Flight ID:	1-27-48		**Max Altitude:**	255,000	246,700	**Take-Off Time:**	09:34		
X-15 (s/n):	56-6670	(27)	**Speed (mph):**	—	3,489	**Landing Time:**	10:52		
Flight Date:	30 Apr 62		**X-15 Flight Time:**	—	00:09:46.2	**B-52 Flight Time:**	01:18		
Pilot (flight #):	Walker	(11)							
			XLR99 (s/n):	—	109	**Chase 1:**	F-100		Daniel
Launch Lake:	Mud		**Powered Time (sec):**	81	81.6 (S.D.)	**Chase 2:**	F-104		White
Launch Time:	10:23:20.0		**Thrust (pct):**	100	100	**Chase 3:**	F-104B	57-1303	Dana / Thompson
						Chase 4:	F-104		Rushworth
Landing Lake:	Rogers		**Configuration:**	Ventral on; Ball-nose		**Chase 5:**			
Landing Time:	10:33:06.2								

Purpose: Altitude buildup;
Controllability at low dynamic pressure data;
Aerodynamic heating during reentry data;
Performance and stability with speed brakes extended

Notes: Certified altitude record;
First flight of X-15-1 with operational ASAS

Aborts:

1-A-47	27 Apr 62	Weather

Abort used NB-52B 52-008; Walker was the X-15 pilot for the abort

Program Flight #:	53		Plan	Actual	**NASA 1:**	Armstrong		
		Max Mach:	5.00	5.34	**B-52 - Pilots - LP:**	52-008	Allavie / Bement	Russell
Flight ID:	2-22-40	**Max Altitude:**	73,000	70,400	**Take-Off Time:**	09:07		
X-15 (s/n)	56-6671 (22)	**Speed (mph):**	—	3,524	**Landing Time:**	10:26		
Flight Date:	08 May 62	**X-15 Flight Time:**	—	00:08:50.4	**B-52 Flight Time:**	01:19		
Pilot (flight #):	Rushworth (4)							
		XLR99 (s/n):	—	111	**Chase 1:**	F-100		Daniel
Launch Lake:	Hidden Hills	**Powered Time (sec):**	103	97.9 (B.O)	**Chase 2:**	F-104		McKay
Launch Time:	10:01:28.0	**Thrust (pct):**	100, 30	100, 30	**Chase 3:**	F-104		Rogers
					Chase 4:			
Landing Lake:	Rogers	**Configuration:**	Ventral on; Ball-nose		**Chase 5:**			
Landing Time:	10:10:18.4							

Purpose: Heat transfer investigation;
Stability at high-alpha with partial speed brakes;
ASAS checkout

Notes: First XLR99 operation at 30 percent; Vibrations noted;
First X-15 flight above q=2,000 psf
Qbar overshoot due to lack of pilot presentation;
First flight of X-15-2 with operational ASAS

Aborts: 2-A-38 25 Apr 62 Weather
2-A-39 26 Apr 62 XLR99 pump idle too high

All aborts used NB-52A 52-003; White was the X-15 pilot for all aborts

Program Flight #:	54		Plan	Actual	**NASA 1:**	Walker		
		Max Mach:	5.20	5.03	**B-52 - Pilots - LP:**	52-003	Allavie / Campbell	Russell
Flight ID:	1-28-49	**Max Altitude:**	90,000	100,400	**Take-Off Time:**	09:24		
X-15 (s/n)	56-6670 (28)	**Speed (mph):**	—	3,450	**Landing Time:**	10:27		
Flight Date:	22 May 62	**X-15 Flight Time:**	—	00:09:16.2	**B-52 Flight Time:**	01:03		
Pilot (flight #):	Rushworth (5)							
		XLR99 (s/n):	—	109	**Chase 1:**	F-100		Daniel
Launch Lake:	Hidden Hills	**Powered Time (sec):**	77	75.3 (S.D.)	**Chase 2:**	F-104	(USAF)	Dana
Launch Time:	10:04:46.0	**Thrust (pct):**	100	100	**Chase 3:**	F-104		Rogers
					Chase 4:			
Landing Lake:	Rogers	**Configuration:**	Ventral on; Ball-nose		**Chase 5:**			
Landing Time:	10:14:02.2							

Purpose: Local flow investigation

Notes: Premature engine shutdown; Left roll out of trim

Aborts: None

Program Flight #:	55		Plan	Actual	**NASA 1:**	Walker		
		Max Mach:	5.80	5.42	**B-52 - Pilots - LP:**	52-008	Fulton / Bement	Russell
Flight ID:	2-23-43	**Max Altitude:**	162,000	132,600	**Take-Off Time:**	10:00		
X-15 (s/n)	56-6671 (23)	**Speed (mph):**	—	3,675	**Landing Time:**	11:28		
Flight Date:	01 Jun 62	**X-15 Flight Time:**	—	00:10:01.9	**B-52 Flight Time:**	01:28		
Pilot (flight #):	White (12)							
		XLR99 (s/n):	—	104	**Chase 1:**	F-100		Daniel
Launch Lake:	Delamar	**Powered Time (sec):**	93	86.0	**Chase 2:**	F-104		Dana
Launch Time:	10:51:15.0	**Thrust (pct):**	100, 30, 75	100, 30	**Chase 3:**	F-104		Rogers
					Chase 4:	F-104		Collins
Landing Lake:	Rogers	**Configuration:**	Ventral on; Ball-nose		**Chase 5:**			
Landing Time:	11:01:16.9							

Purpose: ASAS checkout;
Stability data at 23 degrees angle of attack

Notes: First launch from Delamar;
Vibrations noted at 30% thrust

Aborts: 2-A-41 25 May 62 Inertial platform and telemetry failure
2-A-42 29 May 62 Inertial platform cooling

All aborts used NB-52B 52-008; White was the X-15 pilot for all aborts

Program Flight #:	56		Plan	Actual	**NASA 1:**	Rushworth		
		Max Mach:	5.60	5.39	**B-52 - Pilots - LP:**	52-003	Allavie / Bement	Peterson
Flight ID:	1-29-50	**Max Altitude:**	100,000	103,600	**Take-Off Time:**	09:45		
X-15 (s/n)	56-6670 (29)	**Speed (mph):**	—	3,672	**Landing Time:**	10:53		
Flight Date:	07 Jun 62	**X-15 Flight Time:**	—	00:08:24.2	**B-52 Flight Time:**	01:08		
Pilot (flight #):	Walker (12)							
		XLR99 (s/n):	—	109	**Chase 1:**	F-100		Daniel
Launch Lake:	Hidden Hills	**Powered Time (sec):**	80	81.5 (S.D)	**Chase 2:**	F-104	(USAF)	McKay
Launch Time:	10:29:20.0	**Thrust (pct):**	100	100	**Chase 3:**	F-104		White
					Chase 4:			
Landing Lake:	Rogers	**Configuration:**	Ventral on; Ball-nose		**Chase 5:**			
Landing Time:	10:37:44.2							

Purpose: Local flow at high angles of attack

Notes: Ammonia check valve in fuel tank stuck;
Rough engine operation

Aborts: None

Program Flight #:	57			**Plan**	**Actual**	**NASA 1:**	Rushworth		
			Max Mach:	5.15	5.02	**B-52 - Pilots - LP:**	52-008	Fulton / Allavie	Russell
Flight ID:	3-5-9		**Max Altitude:**	206,000	184,600	**Take-Off Time:**	10:56		
X-15 (s/n)	56-6672	(5)	**Speed (mph):**	—	3,517	**Landing Time:**	12:41		
Flight Date:	12 Jun 62		**X-15 Flight Time:**	—	00:09:33.9	**B-52 Flight Time:**	01:45		
Pilot (flight #):	White	(13)							
			XLR99 (s/n):	—	106	**Chase 1:**	F-100		McDivitt
Launch Lake:	Delamar		**Powered Time (sec):**	77	81.9 (S.D.)	**Chase 2:**	F-104		McKay
Launch Time:	12:04:00.0		**Thrust (pct):**	100	100	**Chase 3:**	F-104		Collins
						Chase 4:	F-104		Gordon
Landing Lake:	Rogers		**Configuration:**	Ventral on; Ball-nose		**Chase 5:**			
Landing Time:	12:13:33.9								

Purpose: Pilot checkout; Ballistic control system evaluation

Notes: Overshot altitude by 21,400 feet

Aborts: None

Program Flight #:	58			**Plan**	**Actual**	**NASA 1:**	Rushworth		
			Max Mach:	5.40	5.08	**B-52 - Pilots - LP:**	52-008	Allavie / Lewis	Butchart
Flight ID:	3-6-10		**Max Altitude:**	250,000	246,700	**Take-Off Time:**	09:01		
X-15 (s/n)	56-6672	(6)	**Speed (mph):**	—	3,641	**Landing Time:**	10:23		
Flight Date:	21 Jun 62		**X-15 Flight Time:**	—	00:09:33.6	**B-52 Flight Time:**	01:22		
Pilot (flight #):	White	(14)							
			XLR99 (s/n):	—	106	**Chase 1:**	F-100		Daniel
Launch Lake:	Delamar		**Powered Time (sec):**	80	82.3 (S.D.)	**Chase 2:**	F-104	(USAF)	McKay
Launch Time:	09:47:05.0		**Thrust (pct):**	100	100	**Chase 3:**	F-104D	57-1315	Armstrong
						Chase 4:	F-104		Collins
Landing Lake:	Rogers		**Configuration:**	Ventral on; Ball-nose		**Chase 5:**			
Landing Time:	09:56:38.6								

Purpose: Contractual demonstration of MH-96

Notes: Good flight

Aborts: None

Program Flight #:	59			**Plan**	**Actual**	**NASA 1:**			
			Max Mach:	6.00	5.92	**B-52 - Pilots - LP:**	52-003	Allavie / Townsend	Russell
Flight ID:	1-30-51		**Max Altitude:**	107,000	123,700	**Take-Off Time:**	12:13		
X-15 (s/n)	56-6670	(30)	**Speed (mph):**	—	4,104	**Landing Time:**	13:38		
Flight Date:	27 Jun 62		**X-15 Flight Time:**	—	00:09:32.4	**B-52 Flight Time:**	01:25		
Pilot (flight #):	Walker	(13)							
			XLR99 (s/n):	—	107	**Chase 1:**	F-100		Rushworth
Launch Lake:	Mud		**Powered Time (sec):**	84	88.6 (B.O.)	**Chase 2:**	F-104		McKay
Launch Time:	13:08:10.0		**Thrust (pct):**	100	100	**Chase 3:**	F-104		Knight
						Chase 4:	F-104		Daniel
Landing Lake:	Rogers		**Configuration:**	Ventral on; Ball-nose		**Chase 5:**			
Landing Time:	13:17:42.4			Trim on side-stick					

Purpose: High angle of attack stability

Notes: Unofficial world absolute speed record; Ventral chute lost during flight; Pitch damper tripped out during pull-up maneuver

Aborts: None

Program Flight #:	60			**Plan**	**Actual**	**NASA 1:**	Walker		
			Max Mach:	4.20	4.95	**B-52 - Pilots - LP:**	52-008	Allavie / Archer	Peterson
Flight ID:	2-24-44		**Max Altitude:**	84,000	83,200	**Take-Off Time:**	09:57		
X-15 (s/n)	56-6671	(24)	**Speed (mph):**	—	3,280	**Landing Time:**	11:05		
Flight Date:	29 Jun 62		**X-15 Flight Time:**	—	00:08:53.6	**B-52 Flight Time:**	01:08		
Pilot (flight #):	McKay	(3)							
			XLR99 (s/n):	—	110	**Chase 1:**	F-100		Rushworth
Launch Lake:	Hidden Hills		**Powered Time (sec):**	122	112.4 (B.O.)	**Chase 2:**	F-104A	57-1316	Armstrong
Launch Time:	10:41:47.0		**Thrust (pct):**	85, 80, 50	85, 80, 50	**Chase 3:**	F-104		Daniel
						Chase 4:			
Landing Lake:	Rogers		**Configuration:**	Ventral on; Ball-nose		**Chase 5:**			
Landing Time:	10:50:40.6			Q-meter on I-panel					

Purpose: Heating rates at low angle of attack and Mach; Notch filter evaluation

Notes: Speed brake handle seized temporarily; Two SAS tripouts (one pilot induced); Ballistic control system inoperative due to leaking valve

Aborts: None

Program Flight #:	61		Plan	Actual	**NASA 1:**			
		Max Mach:	5.40	5.37	**B-52 - Pilots - LP:**	52-008	Allavie / Archer	B. Peterson
Flight ID:	1-31-52	**Max Altitude:**	105,000	107,200	**Take-Off Time:**	13:23		
X-15 (s/n)	56-6670 (31)	**Speed (mph):**	—	3,674	**Landing Time:**	14:40		
Flight Date:	16 Jul 62	**X-15 Flight Time:**	—	00:09:37.8	**B-52 Flight Time:**	01:17		
Pilot (flight #):	Walker (14)							
		XLR99 (s/n):	—	107	**Chase 1:**	F-100		Daniel
Launch Lake:	Mud	**Powered Time (sec):**	80	83.9 (S.D.)	**Chase 2:**	F-104		Dana
Launch Time:	14:09:25.0	**Thrust (pct):**	100	100	**Chase 3:**	F-104		Engle
					Chase 4:	F-104		Rushworth
Landing Lake:	Rogers	**Configuration:**	Ventral on; Ball-nose		**Chase 5:**			
Landing Time:	14:19:02.8							

Purpose: Notch filter evaluation at high dynamic pressure;
Aerodynamic drag data;
ASAS stability investigation

Aborts: None

Notes: Numerous pitch and roll tripouts;
Ventral chute malfunctioned;
#2 generator tripped out during flight (no reset)

Program Flight #:	62		Plan	Actual	**NASA 1:**	Walker		
		Max Mach:	5.15	5.45	**B-52 - Pilots - LP:**	52-003	Allavie / Archer	Butchart
Flight ID:	3-7-14	**Max Altitude:**	282,000	314,750	**Take-Off Time:**	08:46		
X-15 (s/n)	56-6672 (7)	**Speed (mph):**	—	3,832	**Landing Time:**	10:03		
Flight Date:	17 Jul 62	**X-15 Flight Time:**	—	00:10:20.7	**B-52 Flight Time:**	01:17		
Pilot (flight #):	White (15)							
		XLR99 (s/n):	—	103	**Chase 1:**	F-100		McDivitt
Launch Lake:	Delamar	**Powered Time (sec):**	80	82.0 (B.O.)	**Chase 2:**	F-104	(USAF)	McKay
Launch Time:	09:31:10.0	**Thrust (pct):**	100	100	**Chase 3:**	F-104	(USAF)	Dana
					Chase 4:	F-104B	57-1303	Thompson / Petersen
Landing Lake:	Rogers	**Configuration:**	Ventral on; Ball-nose		**Chase 5:**			
Landing Time:	09:41:30.7							

Purpose: Contractual demonstration of MH-96

Aborts:

3-A-11	10 Jul 62	B-52 landing gear
3-A-12	11 Jul 62	#1 APU pressure regulator
3-A-13	16 Jul 62	Unplugged NB-52 umbilical

Notes: Originally scheduled for Smith Ranch launch (rain)
FAI world altitude record for class;
First aircraft flight above 300,000 feet; First flight above 50 miles;
First Astronaut qualification flight;
Overshot altitude by 32,250 feet

All aborts used NB-52A 52-003; White was the X-15 pilot for all aborts

Program Flight #:	63		Plan	Actual	**NASA 1:**	Armstrong		
		Max Mach:	4.60	5.18	**B-52 - Pilots - LP:**	52-008	Fulton / Bement	B. Peterson
Flight ID:	2-25-45	**Max Altitude:**	73,000	85,250	**Take-Off Time:**	09:11		
X-15 (s/n)	56-6671 (25)	**Speed (mph):**	—	3,474	**Landing Time:**	10:20		
Flight Date:	19 Jul 62	**X-15 Flight Time:**	—	00:08:23.8	**B-52 Flight Time:**	01:09		
Pilot (flight #):	McKay (4)							
		XLR99 (s/n):	—	110	**Chase 1:**	F-100		Rogers
Launch Lake:	Hidden Hills	**Powered Time (sec):**	120	106.2 (B.O.)	**Chase 2:**	F-104D	57-1315	Dana
Launch Time:	09:53:45.0	**Thrust (pct):**	80, 40	80, 40	**Chase 3:**	F-104A		Rushworth
					Chase 4:			
Landing Lake:	Rogers	**Configuration:**	Ventral on; Ball-nose		**Chase 5:**			
Landing Time:	10:02:08.8							

Purpose: Aerodynamic heating rates at low angle of attack and low Mach;
Aerodynamic drag data;
Handling qualities data;
Wing pressure distribution investigation

Aborts: None

Notes: Alpha indicator had oscillations;
Idle stop changed from 45 to 40 percent;
Ventral chute failed

Program Flight #:	64		Plan	Actual	**NASA 1:**	Walker		
		Max Mach:	5.70	5.74	**B-52 - Pilots - LP:**	52-003	Fulton / Bement	Russell
Flight ID:	1-32-53	**Max Altitude:**	111,000	98,900	**Take-Off Time:**	10:34		
X-15 (s/n)	56-6670 (32)	**Speed (mph):**	—	3,989	**Landing Time:**	11:57		
Flight Date:	26 Jul 62	**X-15 Flight Time:**	—	00:10:21.6	**B-52 Flight Time:**	01:23		
Pilot (flight #):	Armstrong (7)							
		XLR99 (s/n):	—	106	**Chase 1:**	T-38A		Rushworth
Launch Lake:	Mud	**Powered Time (sec):**	83	82.8 (B.O.)	**Chase 2:**	F-104		Collins
Launch Time:	11:22:30.0	**Thrust (pct):**	100	100	**Chase 3:**	F-104		Daniel
					Chase 4:	F-104		White
Landing Lake:	Rogers	**Configuration:**	Ventral on; Ball-nose		**Chase 5:**			
Landing Time:	11:32:51.6		Side-stick with beep trim					

Purpose: Aerodynamic stability and drag;
Handling qualities

Aborts: None

Notes: Full back trim only gave 16 degrees of stabilizer;
Smoke in cockpit;
Armstrong's last flight

Program Flight #:	65		Plan	Actual	NASA 1:	White		
		Max Mach:	5.10	5.07	B-52 - Pilots - LP:	52-003	Fulton / Bement	Russell
Flight ID:	3-8-16	Max Altitude:	160,000	144,500	Take-Off Time:	09:05		
X-15 (s/n)	56-6672 (8)	Speed (mph):	—	3,438	Landing Time:	10:31		
Flight Date:	02 Aug 62	X-15 Flight Time:	—	00:09:14.0	B-52 Flight Time:	01:26		
Pilot (flight #):	Walker (15)							
		XLR99 (s/n):	—	107	Chase 1:	T-38A		Daniel
Launch Lake:	Mud	Powered Time (sec):	78	80.0 (S.D.)	Chase 2:	F-104	(USAF)	McKay
Launch Time:	09:56:15.0	Thrust (pct):	100	100	Chase 3:	F-104		Collins
					Chase 4:	F-104		Rushworth
Landing Lake:	Rogers	Configuration:	Ventral on; Ball-nose		Chase 5:			
Landing Time:	10:05:29.0		Q-meter on I-panel					

Purpose: MH-96 fixed gain evaluation

Notes: Theta vernier wired backwards

Aborts: 3-A-15 01 Aug 62 NH3 tank pressure unreadable — Abort used NB-52A 52-003; Walker was the X-15 pilot for the abort

Program Flight #:	66		Plan	Actual	NASA 1:	Walker		
		Max Mach:	4.00	4.40	B-52 - Pilots - LP:	52-008	Fulton / Sturmthal	Russell
Flight ID:	2-26-46	Max Altitude:	84,000	90,877	Take-Off Time:	09:15		
X-15 (s/n)	56-6671 (26)	Speed (mph):	—	2,943	Landing Time:	10:33		
Flight Date:	08 Aug 62	X-15 Flight Time:	—	00:07:42.8	B-52 Flight Time:	01:18		
Pilot (flight #):	Rushworth (6)							
		XLR99 (s/n):	—	111	Chase 1:	T-38A		McDivitt
Launch Lake:	Hidden Hills	Powered Time (sec):	98	95.8 (B.O.)	Chase 2:	F-104		McKay
Launch Time:	10:08:35.0	Thrust (pct):	100, 75, 65, 40	See note	Chase 3:	F-104		Engle
					Chase 4:	F-104		Collins
Landing Lake:	Rogers	Configuration:	Ventral on; Ball-nose		Chase 5:			
Landing Time:	10:16:17.8							

Purpose: Aerodynamic heating rates at high angle of attack and low Mach
RAS checkout;
Aerodynamic drag data

Notes: ASAS engaged with pilot induced yaw damper

Actual engine thrust levels were 100, 75, 65, 52, and 39 percent

Aborts: None

Program Flight #:	67		Plan	Actual	NASA 1:	White		
		Max Mach:	5.80	5.25	B-52 - Pilots - LP:	52-003	Fulton / Crews	Russell
Flight ID:	3-9-18	Max Altitude:	220,000	193,600	Take-Off Time:	09:46		
X-15 (s/n)	56-6672 (9)	Speed (mph):	—	3,747	Landing Time:	11:16		
Flight Date:	14 Aug 62	X-15 Flight Time:	—	00:09:04.9	B-52 Flight Time:	01:30		
Pilot (flight #):	Walker (16)							
		XLR99 (s/n):	—	107	Chase 1:	T-38A		Rushworth
Launch Lake:	Delamar	Powered Time (sec):	83	84.2 (B.O.)	Chase 2:	F-104D	(USAF)	Dana
Launch Time:	10:41:35.0	Thrust (pct):	100	100	Chase 3:	F-104		Engle
					Chase 4:	F-104		White
Landing Lake:	Rogers	Configuration:	Ventral on; Ball-nose		Chase 5:			
Landing Time:	10:50:39.9							

Purpose: Constant theta reentry and stability at minimum yaw gain

Notes: Roll damper dropped off during reentry
Last flight of X-15-3 with ventral on

Aborts: 3-A-17 10 Aug 62 #1 BCS valve failed to open — Abort used NB-52A 52-003; Walker was the X-15 pilot for the abort

Program Flight #:	68		Plan	Actual	NASA 1:			
		Max Mach:	4.90	5.24	B-52 - Pilots - LP:	52-008	Fulton / Andonian	Russell
Flight ID:	2-27-47	Max Altitude:	85,000	88,900	Take-Off Time:	09:20		
X-15 (s/n)	56-6671 (27)	Speed (mph):	—	3,534	Landing Time:	10:34		
Flight Date:	20 Aug 62	X-15 Flight Time:	—	00:08:38.2	B-52 Flight Time:	01:14		
Pilot (flight #):	Rushworth (7)							
		XLR99 (s/n):	—	111	Chase 1:	T-38A		Gordon
Launch Lake:	Hidden Hills	Powered Time (sec):	92	86.5 (B.O.)	Chase 2:	F-104	(USAF)	McKay
Launch Time:	10:08:40.0	Thrust (pct):	100, 75, 65, 40	100, 75, 60, 40	Chase 3:	F-104		Engle
					Chase 4:	F-104		Daniel
Landing Lake:	Rogers	Configuration:	Ventral on; Ball-nose		Chase 5:			
Landing Time:	10:17:18.2							

Purpose: Heating rates at moderate angle of attack and high Mach;
ASAS evaluation
Aerodynamic drag data;
Stability and control data

Notes: Roll SAS failed at launch - would not reengage;
XLR99 second stage igniter injector face damage

Aborts: — 17 Aug 62 Weather prior to taxi

			Plan	Actual				
Program Flight #:	69				**NASA 1:**	Armstrong		
		Max Mach:	4.80	5.12	**B-52 - Pilots - LP:**	52-008	Fulton / Bement	Butchart
Flight ID:	2-28-48	**Max Altitude:**	87,000	97,200	**Take-Off Time:**	09:50		
X-15 (s/n)	56-6671 (28)	**Speed (mph):**	—	3,447	**Landing Time:**	11:00		
Flight Date:	29 Aug 62	**X-15 Flight Time:**	—	00:08:47.1	**B-52 Flight Time:**	01:10		
Pilot (flight #):	Rushworth (8)							
		XLR99 (s/n):	—	110	**Chase 1:**	T-38A		White
Launch Lake:	Hidden Hills	**Powered Time (sec):**	91	92.0 (B.O.)	**Chase 2:**	F-104	(USAF)	Walker
Launch Time:	10:36:03.0	**Thrust (pct):**	100, 80	100, 80	**Chase 3:**	F-104		McDivitt
					Chase 4:	F-104		Knight
Landing Lake:	Rogers	**Configuration:**	Ventral on; Ball-nose		**Chase 5:**			
Landing Time:	10:44:50.1		Cut-away windshield retainer					

Purpose: Heating rates at high angle of attack and high Mach

Notes: Intermittent roll SAS trip-outs;
Speed brake vibrations

Aborts: None

			Plan	Actual				
Program Flight #:	70				**NASA 1:**	Armstrong		
		Max Mach:	4.20	4.22	**B-52 - Pilots - LP:**	52-008	Bement / Sturmthal	Butchart
Flight ID:	2-29-50	**Max Altitude:**	87,000	68,200	**Take-Off Time:**	09:17		
X-15 (s/n)	56-6671 (29)	**Speed (mph):**	—	2,765	**Landing Time:**	10:34		
Flight Date:	28 Sep 62	**X-15 Flight Time:**	—	00:09:27.5	**B-52 Flight Time:**	01:17		
Pilot (flight #):	McKay (5)							
		XLR99 (s/n):	—	108	**Chase 1:**	T-38A		White
Launch Lake:	Hidden Hills	**Powered Time (sec):**	124	128.2 (B.O.)	**Chase 2:**	F-104	(USAF)	Walker
Launch Time:	10:04:55.0	**Thrust (pct):**	87, 44, 35	87, 44, 35	**Chase 3:**	F-104		Engle
					Chase 4:	F-104		Rushworth
Landing Lake:	Rogers	**Configuration:**	Ventral off; Ball-nose		**Chase 5:**			
Landing Time:	10:14:22.5							

Purpose: Heating rates at low angle of attack and low Mach;
Ventral-off stability data;
Base data for sharp-leading edge experiment on X-15-3;
(#1) UV stellar photography experiment preliminary data gathering

Notes: XLR99 igniter malfunction before launch;
First X-15-2 flight without ventral

Aborts: 2-A-49 27 Sep 62 Left-hand ejection lever problems

Abort used NB-52B 52-008; McKay was the X-15 pilot for the abort

			Plan	Actual				
Program Flight #:	71				**NASA 1:**	White		
		Max Mach:	5.00	5.17	**B-52 - Pilots - LP:**	52-008	Fulton / Lewis	Butchart
Flight ID:	3-10-19	**Max Altitude:**	103,000	112,200	**Take-Off Time:**	09:26		
X-15 (s/n)	56-6672 (10)	**Speed (mph):**	—	3,493	**Landing Time:**	10:53		
Flight Date:	04 Oct 62	**X-15 Flight Time:**	—	00:09:50.5	**B-52 Flight Time:**	01:27		
Pilot (flight #):	Rushworth (9)							
		XLR99 (s/n):	—	107	**Chase 1:**	T-38A		Rogers / Daniel
Launch Lake:	Delamar	**Powered Time (sec):**	108	103.2 (B.O.)	**Chase 2:**	F-104		Walker
Launch Time:	10:10:11.0	**Thrust (pct):**	100, 50	100, 50	**Chase 3:**	F-104		Collins
					Chase 4:	F-104		Gordon
Landing Lake:	Rogers	**Configuration:**	Ventral off; Ball-nose		**Chase 5:**			
Landing Time:	10:20:01.5							

Purpose: Pilot checkout;
Ventral-off stability data

Notes: #1 APU failed 5 minutes after launch (first in-flight APU failure)
(Ball-nose and yaw damper lost as a result)

Aborts: None

			Plan	Actual				
Program Flight #:	72				**NASA 1:**	Walker		
		Max Mach:	5.30	5.46	**B-52 - Pilots - LP:**	52-003	Fulton / Lewis	Russell
Flight ID:	2-30-51	**Max Altitude:**	125,000	130,200	**Take-Off Time:**	10:09		
X-15 (s/n)	56-6671 (30)	**Speed (mph):**	—	3,716	**Landing Time:**	11:38		
Flight Date:	09 Oct 62	**X-15 Flight Time:**	—	00:09:40.3	**B-52 Flight Time:**	01:29		
Pilot (flight #):	McKay (6)							
		XLR99 (s/n):	—	108	**Chase 1:**	T-38A		White
Launch Lake:	Delamar	**Powered Time (sec):**	81	79.5 (S.D.)	**Chase 2:**	F-104B	56-3722	Dana
Launch Time:	10:58:32.0	**Thrust (pct):**	100	100	**Chase 3:**	F-104		Rushworth
					Chase 4:	F-104		Rogers
Landing Lake:	Rogers	**Configuration:**	Ventral off; Ball-nose		**Chase 5:**			
Landing Time:	11:08:12.3		LH & RH windshield retainer					

Purpose: Ventral-off stability data;
(#27) Hycon camera experiment

Notes: Roll failed to ASAS at launch - reengaged;
XLR99 second stage igniter injector face damage

Aborts: None

Program Flight #:	73			**Plan**	**Actual**	**NASA 1:**	McKay		
			Max Mach:	5.50	5.47	**B-52 - Pilots - LP:**	52-008	Bement / Cross	Butchart
Flight ID:	3-11-20		**Max Altitude:**	125,000	134,500	**Take-Off Time:**	10:31		
X-15 (s/n)	56-6672	(11)	**Speed (mph):**	—	3,716	**Landing Time:**	12:28		
Flight Date:	23 Oct 62		**X-15 Flight Time:**	—	00:09:46.5	**B-52 Flight Time:**	01:57		
Pilot (flight #):	Rushworth	(10)							
			XLR99 (s/n):	—	107	**Chase 1:**	T-38A		Rogers
Launch Lake:	Mud		**Powered Time (sec):**	79	78.0 (S.D.)	**Chase 2:**	F-104D	57-1315	Dana
Launch Time:	11:30:40.0		**Thrust (pct):**	100	100	**Chase 3:**	F-104B	57-1303	Thompson
						Chase 4:	F-104		Knight
Landing Lake:	Rogers		**Configuration:**	Ventral off; Ball-nose		**Chase 5:**			
Landing Time:	11:40:26.5								

Purpose: Ventral-off stability data;

Notes: B-52 launched X-15 (popped circuit breaker);
Lateral out-of-trim with damper off throughout flight;
Aft windshield retainers removed

Aborts: None

Program Flight #:	74			**Plan**	**Actual**	**NASA 1:**	Rushworth		
			Max Mach:	5.55	1.49	**B-52 - Pilots - LP:**	52-008	Bement / Lewis	Russell
Flight ID:	2-31-52		**Max Altitude:**	125,000	53,950	**Take-Off Time:**	09:28		
X-15 (s/n)	56-6671	(31)	**Speed (mph):**	—	1,019	**Landing Time:**	11:55		
Flight Date:	09 Nov 62		**X-15 Flight Time:**	—	00:06:31.1	**B-52 Flight Time:**	02:27		
Pilot (flight #):	McKay	(7)							
			XLR99 (s/n):	—	103	**Chase 1:**	F-104		White
Launch Lake:	Mud		**Powered Time (sec):**	79	70.5 (S.D.)	**Chase 2:**	F-104		Walker
Launch Time:	10:23:07.0		**Thrust (pct):**	100	35	**Chase 3:**	F-104		Evenson
						Chase 4:	F-104		Daniel
Landing Lake:	Mud		**Configuration:**	Ventral off; Ball-nose		**Chase 5:**			
Landing Time:	10:29:38.1								

Purpose: Ventral-off stability data;
Aerodynamic boundary layer investigations

Notes: Engine stuck at 35% requiring abort;
Flaps did not extend resulting in fast landing;
Left skid failed; aircraft rolled over on ground damaging left wing and horizontal stabilizer
Pilot jettisoned canopy prior to roll-over - sustained crushed vertebrae but later returned to flight status

Aborts: — 7 Nov 62 Ammonia leak prior to taxi

Program Flight #:	75			**Plan**	**Actual**	**NASA 1:**	McKay		
			Max Mach:	5.40	5.65	**B-52 - Pilots - LP:**	52-008	Bement / Cross	Butchart
Flight ID:	3-12-22		**Max Altitude:**	153,000	141,400	**Take-Off Time:**	09:47		
X-15 (s/n)	56-6672	(12)	**Speed (mph):**	—	3,742	**Landing Time:**	11:18		
Flight Date:	14 Dec 62		**X-15 Flight Time:**	—	00:09:36.7	**B-52 Flight Time:**	01:31		
Pilot (flight #):	White	(16)							
			XLR99 (s/n):	—	111	**Chase 1:**	T-38A		Rogers
Launch Lake:	Mud		**Powered Time (sec):**	79	77.7 (S.D.)	**Chase 2:**	F-104	(USAF)	Dana
Launch Time:	10:44:07.0		**Thrust (pct):**	100	100	**Chase 3:**	F-104		Evenson
						Chase 4:	F-104		Knight
Landing Lake:	Rogers		**Configuration:**	Ventral off; Ball-nose Delta-Psi indicator		**Chase 5:**			
Landing Time:	10:53:43.7								

Purpose: Ventral-off stability data;
Heading vernier checkout;
(#2) UV Earth background experiment

Notes: White's last flight

Aborts: 3-A-21 13 Dec 62 Helium leak in cabin source

Abort used NB-52B 52-008; White was the X-15 pilot for the abort

Program Flight #:	76			**Plan**	**Actual**	**NASA 1:**	McKay		
			Max Mach:	5.56	5.73	**B-52 - Pilots - LP:**	52-008	Bement / Fulton	Butchart
Flight ID:	3-13-23		**Max Altitude:**	173,000	160,400	**Take-Off Time:**	10:30		
X-15 (s/n)	56-6672	(13)	**Speed (mph):**	—	3,793	**Landing Time:**	11:55		
Flight Date:	20 Dec 62		**X-15 Flight Time:**	—	00:08:54.4	**B-52 Flight Time:**	01:25		
Pilot (flight #):	Walker	(17)							
			XLR99 (s/n):	—	111	**Chase 1:**	T-38A		Rushworth
Launch Lake:	Mud		**Powered Time (sec):**	90	81.0 (S.D.)	**Chase 2:**	F-104		White
Launch Time:	11:25:04.0		**Thrust (pct):**	100	100	**Chase 3:**	F-104		Daniel
						Chase 4:	F-104		Gordon
Landing Lake:	Rogers		**Configuration:**	Ventral off; Ball-nose		**Chase 5:**			
Landing Time:	11:33:58.4								

Purpose: Ventral-off stability data;
MH-96 limit cycle investigation

Notes: Good flight

Aborts: None

Program Flight #:	77
Flight ID:	3-14-24
X-15 (s/n)	56-6672 (14)
Flight Date:	17 Jan 63
Pilot (flight #):	Walker (18)
Launch Lake:	Delamar
Launch Time:	10:59:16.0
Landing Lake:	Rogers
Landing Time:	11:08:59.9

	Plan	Actual
Max Mach:	5.22	5.47
Max Altitude:	250,000	271,700
Speed (mph):	—	3,677
X-15 Flight Time:	—	00:09:43.9
XLR99 (s/n):	—	109
Powered Time (sec):	77	81.2 (S.D.)
Thrust (pct):	100	100
Configuration:	Ventral off; Ball-nose	

NASA 1:	Rushworth		
B-52 - Pilots - LP:	52-008	Bement / Archer	Butchart
Take-Off Time:	10:07		
Landing Time:	12:08		
B-52 Flight Time:	02:01		
Chase 1:	T-38A		White
Chase 2:	F-104		Dana
Chase 3:	F-104		Gordon
Chase 4:	F-104		Daniel
Chase 5:			

Purpose: Ventral-off altitude buildup;
(#1) UV stellar photography experiment preliminary data gathering;
(#10) IR exhaust signature experiment

Aborts: None

Notes: #1 APU failed four minutes after launch;
Ball-nose and rudder servo failed eight minutes after launch

Since Walker was a NASA pilot, he did not get astronaut wings for a flight above 50 miles (the NASA standard was 62 miles)

Program Flight #:	78
Flight ID:	1-33-54
X-15 (s/n)	56-6670 (33)
Flight Date:	11 Apr 63
Pilot (flight #):	Rushworth (11)
Launch Lake:	Hidden Hills
Launch Time:	10:03:20.0
Landing Lake:	Rogers
Landing Time:	10:12:16.7

	Plan	Actual
Max Mach:	4.00	4.25
Max Altitude:	74,000	74,400
Speed (mph):	—	2,864
X-15 Flight Time:	—	00:08:56.7
XLR99 (s/n):	—	107
Powered Time (sec):	121	120.2 (B.O.)
Thrust (pct):	50	50
Configuration:	Ventral off; Ball-nose Squat switch (1st flight)	

NASA 1:			
B-52 - Pilots - LP:	52-008	Bement / Archer	Russell
Take-Off Time:	09:21		
Landing Time:	10:40		
B-52 Flight Time:	01:19		
Chase 1:	T-38A		Rogers
Chase 2:	F-104		McKay
Chase 3:	F-104		Crews
Chase 4:			
Chase 5:			

Purpose: (#5) Optical degradation phase I (KC-1) experiment;
Auxiliary power unit checkout

Aborts: None

Notes: Roll SAS disengaged at launch - reengaged

Program Flight #:	79
Flight ID:	3-15-25
X-15 (s/n)	56-6672 (15)
Flight Date:	18 Apr 63
Pilot (flight #):	Walker (19)
Launch Lake:	Hidden Hills
Launch Time:	12:16:26.0
Landing Lake:	Rogers
Landing Time:	12:23:39.2

	Plan	Actual
Max Mach:	5.05	5.51
Max Altitude:	75,000	92,500
Speed (mph):	—	3,770
X-15 Flight Time:	—	00:07:13.2
XLR99 (s/n):	—	110
Powered Time (sec):	86	79.0 (B.O)
Thrust (pct):	100	100
Configuration:	Ventral off; Ball-nose	

NASA 1:	McKay		
B-52 - Pilots - LP:	52-008	Fulton / Archer	Butchart
Take-Off Time:	11:36		
Landing Time:	13:38		
B-52 Flight Time:	02:02		
Chase 1:	T-38A		White
Chase 2:	F-104		Dana
Chase 3:	F-104		Sorlie
Chase 4:	F-104		Rogers
Chase 5:			

Purpose: Heat transfer at high Mach and low angle of attack;
Local flow at high Mach and low angle of attack;
(#10) IR exhaust signature experiment

Aborts: None

Notes: Nose gear scoop opened at 55,000 feet and Mach 3.4

Program Flight #:	80
Flight ID:	1-34-55
X-15 (s/n)	56-6670 (34)
Flight Date:	25 Apr 63
Pilot (flight #):	McKay (8)
Launch Lake:	Delamar
Launch Time:	14:04:19.0
Landing Lake:	Rogers
Landing Time:	14:14:51.3

	Plan	Actual
Max Mach:	5.05	5.32
Max Altitude:	98,000	105,500
Speed (mph):	—	3,654
X-15 Flight Time:	—	00:10:32.3
XLR99 (s/n):	—	107
Powered Time (sec):	80	86.1 (B.O.)
Thrust (pct):	100	100
Configuration:	Ventral off; Ball-nose	

NASA 1:	Rushworth		
B-52 - Pilots - LP:	52-008	Bement / Fulton	Russell
Take-Off Time:	13:14		
Landing Time:	14:45		
B-52 Flight Time:	01:31		
Chase 1:	T-38A		White
Chase 2:	F-104		Thompson
Chase 3:	F-104		Wood
Chase 4:	F-104		Knight
Chase 5:			

Purpose: (#5) Optical degradation phase I (KC-1) experiment

Aborts: None

Notes: Roll SAS trip-out at launch - reset

Program Flight #:	81		Plan	Actual	NASA 1:	Rushworth		
		Max Mach:	4.97	4.73	B-52 - Pilots - LP:	52-008	Bement / Archer	Russell
Flight ID:	3-16-26	Max Altitude:	206,000	209,400	Take-Off Time:	09:08		
X-15 (s/n)	56-6672 (16)	Speed (mph):	—	3,488	Landing Time:	10:40		
Flight Date:	02 May 63	X-15 Flight Time:	—	00:09:17.2	B-52 Flight Time:	01:32		
Pilot (flight #):	Walker (20)							
		XLR99 (s/n):	—	110	Chase 1:	T-38A		White
Launch Lake:	Mud	Powered Time (sec):	78	79.2 (S.D.)	Chase 2:	F-104		Dana
Launch Time:	09:59:12.0	Thrust (pct):	100	100	Chase 3:	F-104		Rogers
					Chase 4:	F-104		Knight
Landing Lake:	Rogers	Configuration:	Ventral off; Ball-nose		Chase 5:			
Landing Time:	10:08:29.2							

Purpose: APU altitude checkout;
High angle of attack aerodynamic flow data;
(#2) UV Earth background experiment;
(#10) IR exhaust signature experiment

Notes: Good flight

Aborts: None

Program Flight #:	82		Plan	Actual	NASA 1:	Walker		
		Max Mach:	4.80	5.20	B-52 - Pilots - LP:	52-008	Bement / Archer	Russell
Flight ID:	3-17-28	Max Altitude:	90,000	95,600	Take-Off Time:	11:30		
X-15 (s/n)	56-6672 (17)	Speed (mph):	—	3,600	Landing Time:	12:39		
Flight Date:	14 May 63	X-15 Flight Time:	—	00:07:33.0	B-52 Flight Time:	01:09		
Pilot (flight #):	Rushworth (12)							
		XLR99 (s/n):	—	110	Chase 1:	T-38A		Sorlie
Launch Lake:	Hidden Hills	Powered Time (sec):	84	86.9 (S.D.)	Chase 2:	F-104		Dana
Launch Time:	12:11:56.0	Thrust (pct):	100, 80	100, 80	Chase 3:	F-104		Daniel
					Chase 4:	F-104B	57-1303	McKay
Landing Lake:	Rogers	Configuration:	Ventral off; Ball-nose		Chase 5:			
Landing Time:	12:19:29.0							

Purpose: Aerodynamic heating rates at high Mach and high angle of attack;
(#2) UV Earth background experiment;
(#10) IR exhaust signature experiment

Notes: Engine restart required due to vibration shutdown

Aborts: 3-A-27 10 May 63 Ruptured hydraulic line

Abort used NB-52B 52-008; Rushworth was the X-15 pilot for the abort

Program Flight #:	83		Plan	Actual	NASA 1:	Walker		
		Max Mach:	5.53	5.57	B-52 - Pilots - LP:	52-003	Bement / Archer	Butchart
Flight ID:	1-35-56	Max Altitude:	98,000	124,200	Take-Off Time:	09:57		
X-15 (s/n)	56-6670 (35)	Speed (mph):	—	3,856	Landing Time:	11:28		
Flight Date:	15 May 63	X-15 Flight Time:	—	00:10:20.5	B-52 Flight Time:	01:31		
Pilot (flight #):	McKay (9)							
		XLR99 (s/n):	—	107	Chase 1:	T-38A		Rushworth
Launch Lake:	Delamar	Powered Time (sec):	81	84.1 (B.O.)	Chase 2:	F-104		Dana
Launch Time:	10:50:46.0	Thrust (pct):	100	100	Chase 3:	F-104		Evenson
					Chase 4:	F-104		Daniel
Landing Lake:	Rogers	Configuration:	Ventral off; Ball-nose		Chase 5:			
Landing Time:	11:01:06.5							

Purpose: (#5) Optical degradation phase I (KC-1) experiment;
Traversing probe development

Notes: Nose gear scoop opened at Mach ≈5.2;
Nose tires blew at touchdown

Aborts: None

Program Flight #:	84		Plan	Actual	NASA 1:	Rushworth		
		Max Mach:	5.60	5.52	B-52 - Pilots - LP:	52-008	Bement / Fulton	Butchart
Flight ID:	3-18-29	Max Altitude:	90,000	92,000	Take-Off Time:	09:53		
X-15 (s/n)	56-6672 (18)	Speed (mph):	—	3,858	Landing Time:	11:22		
Flight Date:	29 May 63	X-15 Flight Time:	—	00:11:48.0	B-52 Flight Time:	01:29		
Pilot (flight #):	Walker (21)							
		XLR99 (s/n):	—	110	Chase 1:	T-38A		White
Launch Lake:	Delamar	Powered Time (sec):	86	84.3 (B.O.)	Chase 2:	F-104D	(USAF)	Dana
Launch Time:	10:43:07.0	Thrust (pct):	100, 40	100, 41	Chase 3:	F-104		Knight
					Chase 4:	F-104		Rogers
Landing Lake:	Rogers	Configuration:	Ventral off; Ball-nose		Chase 5:			
Landing Time:	10:54:55.0							

Purpose: Ventral-off stability data;
Aerodynamic heating rates at high Mach and low angle of attack

Notes: Left inner window cracked

Aborts: — 28 May 63 Weather prior to taxi

Program Flight #:	85		Plan	Actual	NASA 1:	Walker		
		Max Mach:	5.20	4.97	B-52 - Pilots - LP:	52-008	Archer / Bement	Russell
Flight ID:	3-19-30	Max Altitude:	220,000	223,700	Take-Off Time:	09:43		
X-15 (s/n)	56-6672 (19)	Speed (mph):	—	3,539	Landing Time:	11:40		
Flight Date:	18 Jun 63	X-15 Flight Time:	—	00:09:49.8	B-52 Flight Time:	01:57		
Pilot (flight #):	Rushworth (13)							
		XLR99 (s/n):	—	110	Chase 1:	T-38A		Gordon
Launch Lake:	Delamar	Powered Time (sec):	78	79.3 (S.D.)	Chase 2:	F-104	(USAF)	Dana
Launch Time:	10:34:21.0	Thrust (pct):	100	100	Chase 3:	F-104		Ward
					Chase 4:	F-104		Rogers
Landing Lake:	Rogers	Configuration:	Ventral off; Ball-nose		Chase 5:			
Landing Time:	10:44:10.8							

Purpose: Altitude buildup;
Vertical stabilizer pressure distribution investigation;
(#2) UV Earth background experiment

Notes: Inertial altitude and altitude rate failed

Aborts: None

Program Flight #:	86		Plan	Actual	NASA 1:	Rushworth		
		Max Mach:	5.50	5.51	B-52 - Pilots - LP:	52-003	Bement / Archer	B. Peterson
Flight ID:	1-36-57	Max Altitude:	102,000	111,800	Take-Off Time:	09:03		
X-15 (s/n)	56-6670 (36)	Speed (mph):	—	3,911	Landing Time:	10:30		
Flight Date:	25 Jun 63	X-15 Flight Time:	—	00:09:59.3	B-52 Flight Time:	01:27		
Pilot (flight #):	Walker (22)							
		XLR99 (s/n):	—	107	Chase 1:	T-38A	59-1601	Daniel
Launch Lake:	Delamar	Powered Time (sec):	83	92.8 (B.O.)	Chase 2:	F-104D	57-1314	McKay
Launch Time:	09:53:50.0	Thrust (pct):	100, 55	100, 55	Chase 3:	F-104		Wood
					Chase 4:	F-104		Rogers
Landing Lake:	Rogers	Configuration:	Ventral off; Ball-nose		Chase 5:			
Landing Time:	10:03:49.3							

Purpose: (#5) Optical degradation phase I (KC-1) experiment;
Traversing probe development

Notes: Good flight

Aborts: None

Program Flight #:	87		Plan	Actual	NASA 1:	Walker		
		Max Mach:	5.10	4.89	B-52 - Pilots - LP:	52-008	Bement / Archer	B. Peterson
Flight ID:	3-20-31	Max Altitude:	278,000	285,000	Take-Off Time:	09:07		
X-15 (s/n)	56-6672 (20)	Speed (mph):	—	3,425	Landing Time:	10:33		
Flight Date:	27 Jun 63	X-15 Flight Time:	—	00:10:28.1	B-52 Flight Time:	01:26		
Pilot (flight #):	Rushworth (14)							
		XLR99 (s/n):	—	110	Chase 1:	T-38A		Daniel
Launch Lake:	Delamar	Powered Time (sec):	79	80.1 (S.D.)	Chase 2:	F-104		McKay
Launch Time:	09:56:03.0	Thrust (pct):	100	100	Chase 3:	F-104		Wood
					Chase 4:	F-104		R. Rogers
Landing Lake:	Rogers	Configuration:	Ventral off; Ball-nose		Chase 5:			
Landing Time:	10:06:31.1							

Purpose: Ventral-off stability data;
Altitude buildup;
(#2) UV Earth background experiment;
(#10) IR exhaust signature experiment

Notes: Rushworth's Astronaut qualification
The highest Mach number was achieved during descent from max altitude

Aborts: None

Program Flight #:	88		Plan	Actual	NASA 1:	Rushworth		
		Max Mach:	5.20	5.07	B-52 - Pilots - LP:	52-008	Archer / Lewis	Russell
Flight ID:	1-37-59	Max Altitude:	220,000	226,400	Take-Off Time:	11:17		
X-15 (s/n)	56-6670 (37)	Speed (mph):	—	3,631	Landing Time:	12:49		
Flight Date:	09 Jul 63	X-15 Flight Time:	—	00:08:58.0	B-52 Flight Time:	01:32		
Pilot (flight #):	Walker (23)							
		XLR99 (s/n):	—	107	Chase 1:	YT-38A	58-1197	Daniel
Launch Lake:	Delamar	Powered Time (sec):	81	83.6 (S.D.)	Chase 2:	F-104D	57-1316	McKay
Launch Time:	12:12:12.0	Thrust (pct):	100	100	Chase 3:	F-104D	57-1314	Rogers
					Chase 4:	F-104A	56-0817	Wood
Landing Lake:	Rogers	Configuration:	Ventral off; Ball-nose		Chase 5:			
Landing Time:	12:21:10.0							

Purpose: (#5) Optical degradation phase I (KC-1) experiment;
Traversing probe development;
RAS checkout;
Cork ablative evaluation on lower right speed brake

Notes: Good flight

Aborts: 1-A-58 03 Jul 63 X-15 radio problem

Abort used NB-52B 52-008; Walker was the X-15 pilot for the abort

Program Flight #:	89	
Flight ID:	1-38-61	
X-15 (s/n)	56-6670	(38)
Flight Date:	18 Jul 63	
Pilot (flight #):	Rushworth	(15)
Launch Lake:	Mud	
Launch Time:	10:07:20.0	
Landing Lake:	Rogers	
Landing Time:	10:16:44.1	

	Plan	Actual
Max Mach:	5.60	5.63
Max Altitude:	112,000	104,800
Speed (mph):	—	3,925
X-15 Flight Time:	—	00:09:24.1
XLR99 (s/n):	—	107
Powered Time (sec):	84	84.1 (S.D.)
Thrust (pct):	100	100
Configuration:	Ventral off; Ball-nose	

NASA 1:	McKay		
B-52 - Pilots - LP:	52-003	Fulton / Bock	B. Peterson
Take-Off Time:	09:17		
Landing Time:	10:42		
B-52 Flight Time:	01:25		
Chase 1:	T-38A		Rogers
Chase 2:	F-104D		Dana
Chase 3:	F-104D		Evenson
Chase 4:	F-104D		Gordon / Wood
Chase 5:			

Purpose: Ventral-off stability data;
(#5) Optical degradation phase I (KC-1) experiment;
Ablator evaluation on upper left speed brake;
Ablator evaluation on fixed ventral leading edge

Notes: Good flight

Aborts: 1-A-60 17 Jul 63 Pilot O2 from B-52 disconnected

Abort used NB-52A 52-003; Rushworth was the X-15 pilot for the abort

Program Flight #:	90	
Flight ID:	3-21-32	
X-15 (s/n)	56-6672	(21)
Flight Date:	19 Jul 63	
Pilot (flight #):	Walker	(24)
Launch Lake:	Smith Ranch	
Launch Time:	10:19:53.0	
Landing Lake:	Rogers	
Landing Time:	10:31:17.9	

	Plan	Actual
Max Mach:	5.40	5.50
Max Altitude:	315,000	347,800
Speed (mph):	—	3,710
X-15 Flight Time:	—	00:11:24.9
XLR99 (s/n):	—	111
Powered Time (sec):	83	84.6 (S.D.)
Thrust (pct):	100	100
Configuration:	Ventral off; Ball-nose	

NASA 1:	McKay		
B-52 - Pilots - LP:	52-008	Fulton / Bement	Butchart
Take-Off Time:	09:20		
Landing Time:	11:04		
B-52 Flight Time:	01:44		
Chase 1:	T-38A		Crews
Chase 2:	F-104A	56-0817	Rogers
Chase 3:	F-104		Daniel
Chase 4:	F-104D	57-1316	Wood / Gordon
Chase 5:	F-104	(USAF)	Dana

Purpose: Expansion of ventral-off reentry;
(#2) UV Earth background experiment;
(#10) IR exhaust signature experiment;
(#16) Rarefied gas experiment (balloon)

Notes: Instrumentation on balloon experiment failed;
First Smith Ranch launch;
Used left-hand side-stick (BCS) part of the flight;
Overshot altitude by 31,200 feet;

Technically, Walker qualified as an Astronaut under NASA's 62-mile rule

Aborts: None

Program Flight #:	91	
Flight ID:	3-22-36	
X-15 (s/n)	56-6672	(22)
Flight Date:	22 Aug 63	
Pilot (flight #):	Walker	(25)
Launch Lake:	Smith Ranch	
Launch Time:	10:05:42.0	
Landing Lake:	Rogers	
Landing Time:	10:16:50.6	

	Plan	Actual
Max Mach:	5.38	5.58
Max Altitude:	360,000	354,200
Speed (mph):	—	3,794
X-15 Flight Time:	—	00:11:08.6
XLR99 (s/n):	—	111
Powered Time (sec):	84.5	85.8 (B.O.)
Thrust (pct):	100	100
Configuration:	Ventral off; Ball-nose Altitude predictor	

NASA 1:	McKay		
B-52 - Pilots - LP:	52-003	Bement / Lewis	Russell
Take-Off Time:	09:09		
Landing Time:	10:53		
B-52 Flight Time:	01:44		
Chase 1:	YT-38A	58-1197	Wood
Chase 2:	F-104D	57-1316	Dana
Chase 3:	F-104		Gordon
Chase 4:	F-104A	56-0817	Rogers
Chase 5:			

Purpose: Expansion of vertical-off reentry;
Altitude predictor checkout;
(#3) UV exhaust plume experiment

Notes: #1 left roll RCS thruster froze;
Unofficial world altitude record; Highest X-15 flight;
Little Joe II nose art;
Walker's last flight;
Technically, Walker qualified as an Astronaut under NASA's 62-mile rule

Aborts:
3-A-33 06 Aug 63 Weather during climbout
3-A-34 13 Aug 63 #1 APU would not keep running
3-A-35 15 Aug 63 Weather, #1 APU, Radio

All aborts used NB-52B 52-008; Walker was the X-15 pilot for all aborts

Program Flight #:	92	
Flight ID:	1-39-63	
X-15 (s/n)	56-6670	(39)
Flight Date:	07 Oct 63	
Pilot (flight #):	Engle	(1)
Launch Lake:	Hidden Hills	
Launch Time:	12:22:56.0	
Landing Lake:	Rogers	
Landing Time:	12:30:33.0	

	Plan	Actual
Max Mach:	4.00	4.21
Max Altitude:	74,000	77,800
Speed (mph):	—	2,834
X-15 Flight Time:	—	00:07:37.0
XLR99 (s/n):	—	107
Powered Time (sec):	122	118.6 (S.D.)
Thrust (pct):	50	50
Configuration:	Ventral off; Ball-nose Delta track indicator	

NASA 1:	Rushworth		
B-52 - Pilots - LP:	52-008	Bement / Jones	Russell
Take-Off Time:	11:22		
Landing Time:	13:00		
B-52 Flight Time:	01:38		
Chase 1:	T-38A		Sorlie
Chase 2:	F-104D		Thompson
Chase 3:	F-104		Rogers
Chase 4:			
Chase 5:			

Purpose: Pilot familiarization – Engle's first X-15 flight;
(#5) Optical degradation phase II (KS-25) experiment checkout;
Delta cross-range indicator checkout;
Emersom T-500 ablator on fixed ventral and lower speed brakes

Notes: Unauthorized 360-degree roll performed by pilot;
Abort called for alpha indicator failure – launched
anyway after it began working again.
Angle of attack indicator failed again at launch

Aborts: 1-A-62 04 Oct 63 Communications failure

Abort used NB-52B 52-008; Engle was the X-15 pilot for the abort

			Plan	Actual				
Program Flight #:	93				**NASA 1:**	McKay		
		Max Mach:	4.00	4.10	**B-52 - Pilots - LP:**	52-008	Fulton / Jones	Butchart
Flight ID:	1-40-64	**Max Altitude:**	74,000	74,400	**Take-Off Time:**	11:59		
X-15 (s/n)	56-6670 (40)	**Speed (mph):**	—	2,712	**Landing Time:**	13:09		
Flight Date:	29 Oct 63	**X-15 Flight Time:**	—	00:08:43.0	**B-52 Flight Time:**	01:10		
Pilot (flight #):	Thompson (1)							
		XLR99 (s/n):	—	107	**Chase 1:**	T-38A		Sorlie
Launch Lake:	Hidden Hills	**Powered Time (sec):**	122	126.1 (S.D.)	**Chase 2:**	F-104		Walker
Launch Time:	12:42:34.0	**Thrust (pct):**	50	50	**Chase 3:**	F-104		Rushworth
					Chase 4:			
Landing Lake:	Rogers	**Configuration:**	Ventral off; Ball-nose		**Chase 5:**			
Landing Time:	12:51:17.0							

Purpose: Pilot familiarization – Thompson's first X-15 flight;
(#5) Optical degradation phase II (KS-25) experiment;
Delta cross-range indicator checkout;
Emersom T-500 ablator on fixed ventral and lower speed brakes

Aborts: None

Notes: Thompson's first flight

			Plan	Actual				
Program Flight #:	94				**NASA 1:**	McKay		
		Max Mach:	4.05	4.40	**B-52 - Pilots - LP:**	52-008	Bement / Jones	Butchart
Flight ID:	3-23-39	**Max Altitude:**	79,000	82,300	**Take-Off Time:**	09:27		
X-15 (s/n)	56-6672 (23)	**Speed (mph):**	—	2,925	**Landing Time:**	10:41		
Flight Date:	07 Nov 63	**X-15 Flight Time:**	—	00:08:51.7	**B-52 Flight Time:**	01:14		
Pilot (flight #):	Rushworth (16)							
		XLR99 (s/n):	—	108	**Chase 1:**	T-38A		Gordon
Launch Lake:	Hidden Hills	**Powered Time (sec):**	115	108.2 (B.O.)	**Chase 2:**	F-104A		Thompson
Launch Time:	10:11:45.0	**Thrust (pct):**	100, 48	100, 48	**Chase 3:**	F-104		Sorlie
					Chase 4:			
Landing Lake:	Rogers	**Configuration:**	Ventral off; Ball-nose Sharp rudder		**Chase 5:**			
Landing Time:	10:20:36.7							

Purpose: Heat transfer with sharp upper rudder;
Damper off controllability;
Sharp leading edge data

Aborts:

—	29 Aug 63	Damaged flap during preflight
3-A-37	14 Oct 63	Stable platform
3-A-38	25 Oct 63	Stable platform

Notes: First flight with sharp leading edge on upper rudder

All aborts used NB-52B 52-008; Rushworth was the X-15 pilot for all aborts

			Plan	Actual				
Program Flight #:	95				**NASA 1:**	McKay		
		Max Mach:	4.50	4.75	**B-52 - Pilots - LP:**	52-008	Bement / Jones	Russell
Flight ID:	1-41-65	**Max Altitude:**	92,000	90,800	**Take-Off Time:**	10:36		
X-15 (s/n)	56-6670 (41)	**Speed (mph):**	—	3,286	**Landing Time:**	11:55		
Flight Date:	14 Nov 63	**X-15 Flight Time:**	—	00:07:46.8	**B-52 Flight Time:**	01:19		
Pilot (flight #):	Engle (2)							
		XLR99 (s/n):	—	104	**Chase 1:**	T-38A		Rushworth
Launch Lake:	Hidden Hills	**Powered Time (sec):**	82	83.1 (S.D.)	**Chase 2:**	F-104		Dana
Launch Time:	11:19:21.0	**Thrust (pct):**	100, 79	100, 79	**Chase 3:**	F-104		Rogers
					Chase 4:			
Landing Lake:	Rogers	**Configuration:**	Ventral off; Ball-nose		**Chase 5:**			
Landing Time:	11:27:07.8							

Purpose: (#5) Optical degradation phase II (KS-25) experiment;
Delta cross-range indicator checkout

Aborts: None

Notes: Good flight

			Plan	Actual				
Program Flight #:	96				**NASA 1:**	McKay		
		Max Mach:	4.50	4.94	**B-52 - Pilots - LP:**	52-008	Fulton / Lewis	Butchart
Flight ID:	3-24-41	**Max Altitude:**	92,000	89,800	**Take-Off Time:**	11:35		
X-15 (s/n)	56-6672 (24)	**Speed (mph):**	—	3,310	**Landing Time:**	12:59		
Flight Date:	27 Nov 63	**X-15 Flight Time:**	—	00:07:04.3	**B-52 Flight Time:**	01:24		
Pilot (flight #):	Thompson (2)							
		XLR99 (s/n):	—	108	**Chase 1:**	T-38A		Rushworth
Launch Lake:	Hidden Hills	**Powered Time (sec):**	86	87.5 (S.D.)	**Chase 2:**	F-104D	57-1314	Dana
Launch Time:	12:18:22.0	**Thrust (pct):**	94, 78	94, 78	**Chase 3:**	F-104A		Sorlie
					Chase 4:			
Landing Lake:	Rogers	**Configuration:**	Ventral off; Ball-nose Sharp rudder		**Chase 5:**			
Landing Time:	12:25:26.3							

Purpose: Pilot checkout

Aborts: 3-A-40 19 Nov 63 Weather

Notes: Inertials failed at launch;
Aircraft rolled left at launch (pilot induced)

Abort used NB-52B 52-008; Thompson was the X-15 pilot for the abort

			Plan	Actual				
Program Flight #:	97				**NASA 1:**	McKay		
		Max Mach:	5.70	6.06	**B-52 - Pilots - LP:**	52-008	Bement / Jones	Russell
Flight ID:	1-42-67	**Max Altitude:**	104,000	101,000	**Take-Off Time:**	10:11		
X-15 (s/n)	56-6670 (42)	**Speed (mph):**	—	4,018	**Landing Time:**	11:39		
Flight Date:	05 Dec 63	**X-15 Flight Time:**	—	00:09:34.0	**B-52 Flight Time:**	01:28		
Pilot (flight #):	Rushworth (17)							
		XLR99 (s/n):	—	104	**Chase 1:**	T-38A		Wood
Launch Lake:	Delamar	**Powered Time (sec):**	78	81.2 (B.O.)	**Chase 2:**	F-104D		Sorlie
Launch Time:	11:04:36.0	**Thrust (pct):**	100	100	**Chase 3:**	F-104N	NASA 012	Dana
					Chase 4:	F-104		Engle
Landing Lake:	Rogers	**Configuration:**	Ventral off; Ball-nose		**Rover:**	F-104N	NASA 011	Petersen
Landing Time:	11:14:10.0							

Purpose: (#5) Optical degradation phase II (KS-25) experiment;
Delta cross-range indicator checkout
Emersom T-500 ablator on LN2 and LO2 tanks and side fairing

Aborts:
— 4 Dec 63 X-15 radio failure
1-A-66 3 Dec 63 X-15 radio failure

Notes: Highest Mach number for unmodified X-15;
Right inner windshield cracked in the pattern

Abort used NB-52B 52-008; Rushworth was the X-15 pilot for the abort

			Plan	Actual				
Program Flight #:	98				**NASA 1:**	McKay		
		Max Mach:	5.20	5.32	**B-52 - Pilots - LP:**	52-008	Fulton / Lewis	Russell
Flight ID:	1-43-69	**Max Altitude:**	130,000	139,900	**Take-Off Time:**	11:15		
X-15 (s/n)	56-6670 (43)	**Speed (mph):**	—	3,616	**Landing Time:**	12:44		
Flight Date:	08 Jan 64	**X-15 Flight Time:**	—	00:08:50.7	**B-52 Flight Time:**	01:29		
Pilot (flight #):	Engle (3)							
		XLR99 (s/n):	—	104	**Chase 1:**	T-38A	59-1599	Rushworth
Launch Lake:	Mud	**Powered Time (sec):**	74	74.4 (S.D.)	**Chase 2:**	F-104D	57-1316	Dana
Launch Time:	12:10:31.0	**Thrust (pct):**	100	100	**Chase 3:**	F-104D	57-1314	Wood
					Chase 4:	F-104D		Sorlie
Landing Lake:	Rogers	**Configuration:**	Ventral off; Ball-nose		**Rover:**	F-104N	NASA 013	Petersen
Landing Time:	12:19:21.7							

Purpose: Pilot evaluation of damper-off stability

Aborts: 1-A-68 18 Dec 63 Optical degradation experiment (#5)
malfunction prior to launch

Notes: Inertial malfunction at peak altitude
KS-25 camera removed due to malfunction during abort

Abort used NB-52B 52-008; Rushworth was the X-15 pilot for the abort

			Plan	Actual				
Program Flight #:	99				**NASA 1:**	Rushworth		
		Max Mach:	4.65	4.92	**B-52 - Pilots - LP:**	52-008	Fulton / Lewis	Russell
Flight ID:	3-25-42	**Max Altitude:**	72,000	71,000	**Take-Off Time:**	09:20		
X-15 (s/n)	56-6672 (25)	**Speed (mph):**	—	3,242	**Landing Time:**	10:30		
Flight Date:	16 Jan 64	**X-15 Flight Time:**	—	00:08:17.0	**B-52 Flight Time:**	01:10		
Pilot (flight #):	Thompson (3)							
		XLR99 (s/n):	—	109	**Chase 1:**	T-38A		Gordon
Launch Lake:	Hidden Hills	**Powered Time (sec):**	104	90.5 (S.D.)	**Chase 2:**	F-104D	57-1315	Peterson
Launch Time:	10:03:29.0	**Thrust (pct):**	100	100	**Chase 3:**	F-104		Crews
					Rover:	F-104N	NASA 013	Walker
Landing Lake:	Rogers	**Configuration:**	Ventral off; Ball-nose		**Rover:**	F-104N	NASA 011	Dana
Landing Time:	10:11:46.0		Sharp rudder					

Purpose: Heat transfer with sharp upper rudder;
Damper off stability;
Cermet skid evaluation;
(#10) IR exhaust signature experiment

Aborts: None

Notes: Premature engine burn-out;
Speed brakes extremely hard to open during high heat phase of flight

			Plan	Actual				
Program Flight #:	100				**NASA 1:**	McKay		
		Max Mach:	5.50	5.34	**B-52 - Pilots - LP:**	52-008	Bement / Branch	Russell
Flight ID:	1-44-70	**Max Altitude:**	102,000	107,400	**Take-Off Time:**	11:15		
X-15 (s/n)	56-6670 (44)	**Speed (mph):**	—	3,618	**Landing Time:**	12:55		
Flight Date:	28 Jan 64	**X-15 Flight Time:**	—	00:10:25.5	**B-52 Flight Time:**	01:40		
Pilot (flight #):	Rushworth (18)							
		XLR99 (s/n):	—	104	**Chase 1:**	T-38A		Engle
Launch Lake:	Delamar	**Powered Time (sec):**	76	76.2 (S.D.)	**Chase 2:**	F-104D	57-1315	Dana
Launch Time:	12:11:36.0	**Thrust (pct):**	100	100	**Chase 3:**	F-104		Crews
					Chase 4:	F-104A	56-0817	Wood
Landing Lake:	Rogers	**Configuration:**	Ventral off; Ball-nose		**Rover:**	F-104N	NASA 012	Petersen
Landing Time:	12:22:01.5		Speed brake link removed					

Purpose: Stability evaluation using upper speed brake only

Aborts: None

Notes: SAS roll mode failed repeatedly

Program Flight #:	101			Plan	Actual	**NASA 1:**	McKay		
			Max Mach:	5.05	5.29	**B-52 - Pilots - LP:**	52-003	Fulton / Jones	Russell
Flight ID:	3-26-43		**Max Altitude:**	75,000	78,600	**Take-Off Time:**	09:16		
X-15 (s/n)	56-6672	(26)	**Speed (mph):**	—	3,519	**Landing Time:**	10:55		
Flight Date:	19 Feb 64		**X-15 Flight Time:**	—	00:07:03.1	**B-52 Flight Time:**	01:39		
Pilot (flight #):	Thompson	(4)							
			XLR99 (s/n):	—	103	**Chase 1:**	T-38A		Rushworth
Launch Lake:	Hidden Hills		**Powered Time (sec):**	93	83.3 (B.O.)	**Chase 2:**	F-104N	NASA 012	Peterson
Launch Time:	09:57:13.0		**Thrust (pct):**	100, 40	100, 40	**Chase 3:**	F-104N	NASA 013	Dana
						Chase 4:			
Landing Lake:	Rogers		**Configuration:**	Ventral off; Ball-nose		**Chase 5:**			
Landing Time:	10:04:16.1			Sharp rudder					

Purpose: Heat transfer with sharp upper rudder;
Boundary layer noise data;
Cermet skid evaluation;
Langley Purple Blend ablator evaluation

Aborts: None

Notes: Premature burn out - LOX line unported

Program Flight #:	102			Plan	Actual	**NASA 1:**	Rushworth		
			Max Mach:	4.20	5.11	**B-52 - Pilots - LP:**	52-003	Bement / Lewis	Butchart
Flight ID:	3-27-44		**Max Altitude:**	71,000	76,000	**Take-Off Time:**	09:01		
X-15 (s/n)	56-6672	(27)	**Speed (mph):**	—	3,392	**Landing Time:**	10:13		
Flight Date:	13 Mar 64		**X-15 Flight Time:**	—	00:07:29.0	**B-52 Flight Time:**	01:12		
Pilot (flight #):	McKay	(10)							
			XLR99 (s/n):	—	103	**Chase 1:**	T-38A		Rogers
Launch Lake:	Hidden Hills		**Powered Time (sec):**	107	105.0 (B.O.)	**Chase 2:**	F-104D	57-1315	Peterson
Launch Time:	09:46:02.0		**Thrust (pct):**	100, 87, 43	100, 87, 43	**Chase 3:**	F-104		Engle
						Chase 4:			
Landing Lake:	Rogers		**Configuration:**	Ventral off; Ball-nose		**Chase 5:**			
Landing Time:	09:53:31.0			Sharp rudder					

Purpose: Heat transfer and skin friction with sharp upper rudder;
Boundary layer noise data;
Cermet skid evaluation

Aborts: None

Notes: Good flight

Program Flight #:	103			Plan	Actual	**NASA 1:**	Thompson		
			Max Mach:	5.70	5.63	**B-52 - Pilots - LP:**	52-003	Bement / Lewis	Butchart
Flight ID:	1-45-72		**Max Altitude:**	103,000	101,500	**Take-Off Time:**	09:16		
X-15 (s/n)	56-6670	(45)	**Speed (mph):**	—	3,827	**Landing Time:**	11:30		
Flight Date:	27 Mar 64		**X-15 Flight Time:**	—	00:09:52.4	**B-52 Flight Time:**	02:14		
Pilot (flight #):	Rushworth	(19)							
			XLR99 (s/n):	—	111	**Chase 1:**	T-38A		Gordon
Launch Lake:	Delamar		**Powered Time (sec):**	81	82.7 (S.D.)	**Chase 2:**	F-104D	57-1315	Peterson
Launch Time:	10:10:18.0		**Thrust (pct):**	100	100	**Chase 3:**	F-104N	NASA 012	Adams
						Chase 4:	F-104A	56-0817	Engle
Landing Lake:	Rogers		**Configuration:**	Ventral off; Ball-nose		**Chase 5:**			
Landing Time:	10:20:10.4								

Purpose: (#5) Optical degradation phase II (KS-25) experiment;

Aborts: 1-A-71 17 Mar 64 Optical degradation experiment (#5) malfunction prior to launch

Notes: Inertial altitude about 10,000 feet off after shutdown

Abort used NB-52A 52-003; Rushworth was the X-15 pilot for the abort

Program Flight #:	104			Plan	Actual	**NASA 1:**	Rushworth		
			Max Mach:	5.20	5.01	**B-52 - Pilots - LP:**	52-003	Fulton / Bement	Russell
Flight ID:	1-46-73		**Max Altitude:**	180,000	175,000	**Take-Off Time:**	09:10		
X-15 (s/n)	56-6670	(46)	**Speed (mph):**	—	3,468	**Landing Time:**	10:38		
Flight Date:	08 Apr 64		**X-15 Flight Time:**	—	00:09:45.7	**B-52 Flight Time:**	01:28		
Pilot (flight #):	Engle	(4)							
			XLR99 (s/n):	—	111	**Chase 1:**	T-38A		Gordon
Launch Lake:	Delamar		**Powered Time (sec):**	78	81.8 (S.D.)	**Chase 2:**	F-104D	57-1314	Thmopson
Launch Time:	10:02:27.0		**Thrust (pct):**	100	100	**Chase 3:**	F-104		Crews
						Chase 4:	F-104		Rogers
Landing Lake:	Rogers		**Configuration:**	Ventral off; Ball-nose		**Rover:**	F-104N	NASA 011	Peterson
Landing Time:	10:12:12.7								

Purpose: (#5) Optical degradation phase II (KS-25) experiment;
Altitude buildup

Aborts: None

Notes: Reference lines were added to the inside windshield to define a 30-degree airplane climb angle relative to the horizon
Flight "missed" Pahrump and Pilot Knob targets, marginal acquaition of Nellis target

Program Flight #:	105			Plan	Actual	**NASA 1:**	Engle		
			Max Mach:	5.70	5.72	**B-52 - Pilots - LP:**	52-003	Fulton / Bock	Russell
Flight ID:	1-47-74		**Max Altitude:**	102,000	101,600	**Take-Off Time:**	09:09		
X-15 (s/n):	56-6670	(47)	**Speed (mph):**	—	3,906	**Landing Time:**	10:40		
Flight Date:	29 Apr 64		**X-15 Flight Time:**	—	00:09:34.6	**B-52 Flight Time:**	01:31		
Pilot (flight #):	Rushworth	(20)							
			XLR99 (s/n):	—	109	**Chase 1:**	T-38A		Sorlie
Launch Lake:	Delamar		**Powered Time (sec):**	84	81.3 (S.D.)	**Chase 2:**	F-104N	NASA 012	Dana
Launch Time:	10:00:27.0		**Thrust (pct):**	100	100	**Chase 3:**	F-104		Crews
						Chase 4:	F-104		Rogers
Landing Lake:	Rogers		**Configuration:**	Ventral off; Ball-nose		**Chase 5:**			
Landing Time:	10:10:01.6			Lines on window					

Purpose: (#5) Optical degradation phase II (KS-25) experiment; Optical attitude indicator checkout

Notes: Right inner windshield cracked; Pilot reported smoke in cockpit; Split-vision mirror installed in cockpit to use Earth horizon as an attitude reference, This optical attitude indicator was deemed unsatisfactory; Flight directly over Nellis, 0.5 mile right of Pahrump, and 1 mile left of Pilot Knob and Cuddeback (all within limits)

Aborts: None

Program Flight #:	106			Plan	Actual	**NASA 1:**	Thompson		
			Max Mach:	4.07	4.66	**B-52 - Pilots - LP:**	52-003	Bement / Jones	Butchart
Flight ID:	3-28-47		**Max Altitude:**	69,000	72,800	**Take-Off Time:**	09:06		
X-15 (s/n):	56-6672	(28)	**Speed (mph):**	—	3,084	**Landing Time:**	10:40		
Flight Date:	12 May 64		**X-15 Flight Time:**	—	00:08:11.3	**B-52 Flight Time:**	01:34		
Pilot (flight #):	McKay	(11)							
			XLR99 (s/n):	—	103	**Chase 1:**	T-38A		Sorlie
Launch Lake:	Hidden Hills		**Powered Time (sec):**	110	108.6 (B.O.)	**Chase 2:**	F-104D	57-1315	Peterson
Launch Time:	09:51:46.0		**Thrust (pct):**	100, 43	100, 43	**Chase 3:**	F-104		Engle
						Chase 4:			
Landing Lake:	Rogers		**Configuration:**	Ventral off; Ball-nose		**Chase 5:**			
Landing Time:	09:59:57.3			Sharp rudder; Seat cutter					

Purpose: Heat transfer and skin friction with sharp upper rudder; Boundary layer noise data; Cermet skid evaluation

Notes: Inertial velocities failed at launch; MH-96 pitch and roll disengaged twice during boost

Aborts:

3-A-45	31 Mar 64	Inertial system, cabin pressure
3-A-46	11 May 64	LOX tank regulator

All aborts used NB-52A 52-003; McKay was the X-15 pilot for all aborts

Program Flight #:	107			Plan	Actual	**NASA 1:**	Rushworth		
			Max Mach:	5.20	5.02	**B-52 - Pilots - LP:**	52-003	Fulton / Jones	Butchart
Flight ID:	1-48-75		**Max Altitude:**	200,000	195,800	**Take-Off Time:**	09:35		
X-15 (s/n):	56-6670	(48)	**Speed (mph):**	—	3,494	**Landing Time:**	11:05		
Flight Date:	19 May 64		**X-15 Flight Time:**	—	00:09:01.2	**B-52 Flight Time:**	01:30		
Pilot (flight #):	Engle	(5)							
			XLR99 (s/n):	—	109	**Chase 1:**	T-38A		Sorlie
Launch Lake:	Delamar		**Powered Time (sec):**	81	78.3 (S.D.)	**Chase 2:**	F-104		Gordon
Launch Time:	10:26:28.0		**Thrust (pct):**	100	100	**Chase 3:**	F-104N	NASA 012	Dana
						Chase 4:	F-104		Daniel
Landing Lake:	Rogers		**Configuration:**	Ventral off; Ball-nose		**Chase 5:**			
Landing Time:	10:35:29.2								

Purpose: (#5) Optical degradation phase II (KS-25) experiment; Altitude buildup

Notes: Good flight; Optical horizon indicator installed in cockpit

Aborts: None

Program Flight #:	108			Plan	Actual	**NASA 1:**	McKay		
			Max Mach:	3.35	2.90	**B-52 - Pilots - LP:**	52-003	Fulton / Jones	Butchart
Flight ID:	3-29-48		**Max Altitude:**	66,000	64,200	**Take-Off Time:**	09:00		
X-15 (s/n):	56-6672	(29)	**Speed (mph):**	—	1,865	**Landing Time:**	10:40		
Flight Date:	21 May 64		**X-15 Flight Time:**	—	00:07:56.5	**B-52 Flight Time:**	01:40		
Pilot (flight #):	Thompson	(5)							
			XLR99 (s/n):	—	103	**Chase 1:**	T-38A		Rushworth
Launch Lake:	Silver		**Powered Time (sec):**	120	41.0 (S.D)	**Chase 2:**	F-104		Dana
Launch Time:	09:39:55.0		**Thrust (pct):**	100, 45	100, 0	**Chase 3:**	F-104A		Sorlie
						Chase 4:			
Landing Lake:	Cuddeback		**Configuration:**	Ventral off; Ball-nose		**Rover:**	F-104N	NASA 011	Petersen
Landing Time:	09:47:51.5			Sharp rudder					

Purpose: Heat transfer with sharp upper rudder; Boundary layer noise data; Cermet skid evaluation

Notes: Premature engine shut down at throttle back; Emergency landing; First Cuddeback landing

Aborts: None

Program Flight #:	109			**Plan**	**Actual**	**NASA 1:**	McKay		
			Max Mach:	4.50	4.59	**B-52 - Pilots - LP:**	52-003	Fulton / Bement	Russell
Flight ID:	2-32-55		**Max Altitude:**	80,000	83,300	**Take-Off Time:**	08:50		
X-15 (s/n)	56-6671	(32 / 1)	**Speed (mph):**	—	3,104	**Landing Time:**	09:58		
Flight Date:	25 Jun 64		**X-15 Flight Time:**	—	00:08:54.7	**B-52 Flight Time:**	01:08		
Pilot (flight #):	Rushworth	(21)							
			XLR99 (s/n):	—	106	**Chase 1:**	T-38A		Engle
Launch Lake:	Hidden Hills		**Powered Time (sec):**	78	77.0 (S.D.)	**Chase 2:**	JF-104A	55-2961	Peterson
Launch Time:	09:34:47.0		**Thrust (pct):**	100	100	**Chase 3:**	F-104		Rogers
						Chase 4:	F-104N		Sorlie
Landing Lake:	Rogers		**Configuration:**	Ventral off; Ball-nose		**Chase 5:**			
Landing Time:	09:43:41.7								

Purpose: Aircraft checkout and stability at low angle of attack

Notes: First flight of modified X-15A-2;
Right roll out-of-trim

Aborts: 2-C-53 15 Jun 64 Scheduled captive flight — Captive used NB-52A 52-003; Rushworth was the X-15 pilot for the captive flight
2-A-54 23 Jun 64 #2 APU overspeed shutdown — Abort used NB-52A 52-003; Rushworth was the X-15 pilot for the abort

Program Flight #:	110			**Plan**	**Actual**	**NASA 1:**	Rushworth		
			Max Mach:	5.20	4.96	**B-52 - Pilots - LP:**	52-003	Fulton / Lewis	Russell
Flight ID:	1-49-77		**Max Altitude:**	182,000	99,600	**Take-Off Time:**	08:59		
X-15 (s/n)	56-6670	(49)	**Speed (mph):**	—	3,334	**Landing Time:**	10:27		
Flight Date:	30 Jun 64		**X-15 Flight Time:**	—	00:11:27.0	**B-52 Flight Time:**	01:28		
Pilot (flight #):	McKay	(12)							
			XLR99 (s/n):	—	107	**Chase 1:**	T-38A		Engle
Launch Lake:	Delamar		**Powered Time (sec):**	80	83.4 (S.D.)	**Chase 2:**	F-104D	57-1314	Peterson / Kennedy
Launch Time:	09:49:40.0		**Thrust (pct):**	100	100	**Chase 3:**	F-104D		Sorlie
						Chase 4:	F-104A	56-0763	Rogers
Landing Lake:	Rogers		**Configuration:**	Ventral off; Ball-nose		**Rover:**	F-104N	NASA 011	Walker
Landing Time:	10:01:07.0								

Purpose: Pilot altitude buildup;
(#5) Optical degradation phase II (KS-25) experiment

Notes: McKay replaced Milt Thompson for this flight;
Inertial malfunction at launch;
Alternate profile flown;
250-foot film magazine for KS-25 (instead of 100-foot)

Aborts: 1-A-76 11 Jun 64 Radio and SAS failure — Abort used NB-52A 52-003; Thomson was the X-15 pilot for the abort

Program Flight #:	111			**Plan**	**Actual**	**NASA 1:**	Rushworth		
			Max Mach:	5.20	5.05	**B-52 - Pilots - LP:**	52-003	Bement / Lewis	Russell
Flight ID:	3-30-50		**Max Altitude:**	180,000	170,400	**Take-Off Time:**	11:59		
X-15 (s/n)	56-6672	(30)	**Speed (mph):**	—	3,520	**Landing Time:**	13:45		
Flight Date:	08 Jul 64		**X-15 Flight Time:**	—	00:09:55.9	**B-52 Flight Time:**	01:46		
Pilot (flight #):	Engle	(6)							
			XLR99 (s/n):	—	104	**Chase 1:**	T-38A		Sorlie
Launch Lake:	Delamar		**Powered Time (sec):**	77.5	78.3 (S.D.)	**Chase 2:**	F-104D	57-1315	Dana
Launch Time:	13:02:57.0		**Thrust (pct):**	100	100	**Chase 3:**	F-104		Smith
						Chase 4:	F-104		Rogers
Landing Lake:	Rogers		**Configuration:**	Ventral off; Ball-nose		**Rover:**	F-104N	NASA 013	Mallick
Landing Time:	13:12:52.9			Sharp rudder					

Purpose: MH-96 pilot checkout;
(#4) LaRC horizon definition experiment;
GE ablator on lower ventral and speed brakes

Notes: Dampers disengaged ~10 seconds after launch;
Had to shut off to reengage;
Flew left hand BCS

Aborts: 3-A-49 02 Jul 64 XLR99 malfunction — Abort used NB-52A 52-003; Engle was the X-15 pilot for the abort

Program Flight #:	112			**Plan**	**Actual**	**NASA 1:**	Rushworth		
			Max Mach:	5.05	5.38	**B-52 - Pilots - LP:**	52-003	Fulton / Bement	Russell
Flight ID:	3-31-52		**Max Altitude:**	78,000	78,000	**Take-Off Time:**	11:12		
X-15 (s/n)	56-6672	(31)	**Speed (mph):**	—	3,623	**Landing Time:**	12:20		
Flight Date:	29 Jul 64		**X-15 Flight Time:**	—	00:07:49.1	**B-52 Flight Time:**	01:08		
Pilot (flight #):	Engle	(7)							
			XLR99 (s/n):	—	104	**Chase 1:**	T-38A		Sorlie
Launch Lake:	Hidden Hills		**Powered Time (sec):**	90	93.6 (B.O.)	**Chase 2:**	F-104	(USAF)	McKay
Launch Time:	11:54:57.0		**Thrust (pct):**	100, Tmin	100, 45	**Chase 3:**	F-104		Rogers
						Chase 4:			
Landing Lake:	Rogers		**Configuration:**	Ventral off; Ball-nose		**Rover:**	F-104N	NASA 011	Petersen
Landing Time:	12:02:46.1			Sharp rudder					

Purpose: Heat transfer data with surface distortion panels;
Local flow experiments;
GE ablator on lower ventral and speed brakes and LO2 tank

Notes: Good flight;
Thermopaint on F-3 and F-4 panels

X-15-3 had been used to film "rescue movies" on 13-14 July

Aborts: 3-A-51 28 Jul 64 GN2 cooling gas depleted — Abort used NB-52A 52-003; Engle was the X-15 pilot for the abort

Program Flight #:	113			Plan	Actual	**NASA 1:**	Engle		
			Max Mach:	5.02	5.24	**B-52 - Pilots - LP:**	52-003	Fulton / Bement	Russell
Flight ID:	3-32-53		**Max Altitude:**	75,000	81,200	**Take-Off Time:**	09:30		
X-15 (s/n)	56-6672	(32)	**Speed (mph):**	—	3,535	**Landing Time:**	10:35		
Flight Date:	12 Aug 64		**X-15 Flight Time:**	—	00:06:42.8	**B-52 Flight Time:**	01:05		
Pilot (flight #):	Thompson	(6)							
			XLR99 (s/n):	—	104	**Chase 1:**	T-38A		Rushworth
Launch Lake:	Hidden Hills		**Powered Time (sec):**	90	82.1 (B.O.)	**Chase 2:**	F-104N	NASA 013	McKay
Launch Time:	10:12:27.0		**Thrust (pct):**	100, Tmin	100, 47	**Chase 3:**	F-104		Sorlie
						Chase 4:			
Landing Lake:	Rogers		**Configuration:**	Ventral off; Ball-nose		**Chase 5:**			
Landing Time:	10:19:09.8			Sharp rudder					

Purpose: Heat transfer data with surface distortion panels;
Boundary layer noise data;
Local flow experiments

Notes: Premature engine burn out;
Thermopaint on F-3 and F-4 panels

Aborts: None

Program Flight #:	114			Plan	Actual	**NASA 1:**	McKay		
			Max Mach:	5.20	5.23	**B-52 - Pilots - LP:**	52-003	Fulton / Bement	Russell
Flight ID:	2-33-56		**Max Altitude:**	96,000	103,300	**Take-Off Time:**	09:04		
X-15 (s/n)	56-6671	(33 / 2)	**Speed (mph):**	—	3,590	**Landing Time:**	10:32		
Flight Date:	14 Aug 64		**X-15 Flight Time:**	—	00:12:06.3	**B-52 Flight Time:**	01:28		
Pilot (flight #):	Rushworth	(22)							
			XLR99 (s/n):	—	106	**Chase 1:**	T-38A		Knight
Launch Lake:	Delamar		**Powered Time (sec):**	82	80.3 (S.D.)	**Chase 2:**	F-104		Dana
Launch Time:	09:54:32.0		**Thrust (pct):**	100	100	**Chase 3:**	F-104		Engle
						Chase 4:	F-104N		Sorlie
Landing Lake:	Rogers		**Configuration:**	Ventral off; Ball-nose		**Rover:**	F-104N	NASA 013	Thompson
Landing Time:	10:06:38.3					**"Guest"**	T-38A	63-8193	Armstrong

Purpose: Stability and control evaluation;
(#1) UV stellar photography experiment checkout

Notes: Nose gear extended above Mach 4.2;
Tires failed at landing;
First flight of redesigned stable platform

Aborts: None

Program Flight #:	115			Plan	Actual	**NASA 1:**	Thompson		
			Max Mach:	5.02	5.65	**B-52 - Pilots - LP:**	52-003	Fulton / Bement	Butchart
Flight ID:	3-33-54		**Max Altitude:**	75,000	91,000	**Take-Off Time:**	10:00		
X-15 (s/n)	56-6672	(33)	**Speed (mph):**	—	3,863	**Landing Time:**	11:23		
Flight Date:	26 Aug 64		**X-15 Flight Time:**	—	00:07:19.6	**B-52 Flight Time:**	01:23		
Pilot (flight #):	McKay	(13)							
			XLR99 (s/n):	—	104	**Chase 1:**	T-38A		Sorlie
Launch Lake:	Hidden Hills		**Powered Time (sec):**	90	94.4 (B.O.)	**Chase 2:**	F-104B	57-1303	Peterson
Launch Time:	10:42:07.0		**Thrust (pct):**	100, Tmin	100, 47	**Chase 3:**	F-104		Knight
						Chase 4:			
Landing Lake:	Rogers		**Configuration:**	Ventral off; Ball-nose		**Chase 5:**			
Landing Time:	10:49:26.6			Sharp rudder					

Purpose: Heat transfer data with surface distortion panels;
Boundary layer noise data;
Local flow experiments

Notes: Alpha indicator incorrect;
Three stripes of green thermopaint across nose wheel door

Aborts: None

Program Flight #:	116			Plan	Actual	**NASA 1:**	McKay		
			Max Mach:	5.05	5.35	**B-52 - Pilots - LP:**	52-003	Bement / Jones	Peterson
Flight ID:	3-34-55		**Max Altitude:**	75,000	78,600	**Take-Off Time:**	09:10		
X-15 (s/n)	56-6672	(34)	**Speed (mph):**	—	3,615	**Landing Time:**	10:16		
Flight Date:	03 Sep 64		**X-15 Flight Time:**	—	00:06:18.1	**B-52 Flight Time:**	01:06		
Pilot (flight #):	Thompson	(4)							
			XLR99 (s/n):	—	104	**Chase 1:**	T-38A		Knight
Launch Lake:	Hidden Hills		**Powered Time (sec):**	92	91.0 (B.O.)	**Chase 2:**	F-104N	NASA 012	Walker
Launch Time:	09:54:59.0		**Thrust (pct):**	100, Tmin	100, 47	**Chase 3:**	F-104		Rogers
						Chase 4:			
Landing Lake:	Rogers		**Configuration:**	Ventral off; Ball-nose		**Chase 5:**			
Landing Time:	10:01:17.1								

Purpose: Heat transfer data with surface distortion panels;
Boundary layer noise data;
Shear layer rakes data;
Center stick evaluation

Notes: U-2 took-off across the path of the X-15 during final approach

Blunt leading-edge rudder from X-15-1 installed for this flight

Aborts: None

Program Flight #:	117			Plan	Actual	**NASA 1:**	Thompson		
			Max Mach:	5.65	5.59	**B-52 - Pilots - LP:**	52-003	Fulton / Lewis	Butchart
Flight ID:	3-35-57		**Max Altitude:**	98,000	97,000	**Take-Off Time:**	12:24		
X-15 (s/n)	56-6672	(35)	**Speed (mph):**	—	3,888	**Landing Time:**	13:54		
Flight Date:	28 Sep 64		**X-15 Flight Time:**	—	00:09:34.3	**B-52 Flight Time:**	01:30		
Pilot (flight #):	Engle	(8)							
			XLR99 (s/n):	—	103	**Chase 1:**	T-38A		Rogers
Launch Lake:	Delamar		**Powered Time (sec):**	82	80.3 (B.O.)	**Chase 2:**	F-104N	NASA 012	McKay
Launch Time:	13:16:18.0		**Thrust (pct):**	100	100	**Chase 3:**	F-104		Parsons
						Chase 4:	F-104	56-0768	Knight
Landing Lake:	Rogers		**Configuration:**	Ventral off; Ball-nose		**Chase 5:**			
Landing Time:	13:25:52.3			Sharp rudder					

Purpose: Martin MA-45R ablator on ventral and lower speed brakes;
Langle Purple Blend ablator on F-3 panel;
GE ESM-1004B ablator on F-4 panel;
Boundary layer noise data;
Skin-friction measurements

Notes: Inertial velocity malfunctioned;
Smoke in the cockpit after burnout

Aborts: 3-A-56 23 Sep 64 Canopy Seal Problems

Abort used NB-52A 52-003; Engle was the X-15 pilot for the abort

Program Flight #:	118			Plan	Actual	**NASA 1:**	McKay		
			Max Mach:	5.20	5.20	**B-52 - Pilots - LP:**	52-008	Fulton / Townsend	Butchart
Flight ID:	2-34-57		**Max Altitude:**	96,000	97,800	**Take-Off Time:**	12:10		
X-15 (s/n)	56-6671	(34 / 3)	**Speed (mph):**	—	3,542	**Landing Time:**	13:30		
Flight Date:	29 Sep 64		**X-15 Flight Time:**	—	00:09:51.0	**B-52 Flight Time:**	01:20		
Pilot (flight #):	Rushworth	(23)							
			XLR99 (s/n):	—	108	**Chase 1:**	T-38A	59-1599	Sorlie
Launch Lake:	Mud		**Powered Time (sec):**	81	79.7 (S.D.)	**Chase 2:**	F-104		Thompson
Launch Time:	13:00:05.0		**Thrust (pct):**	100	100	**Chase 3:**	F-104		Parsons
						Chase 4:	F-104		Engle
Landing Lake:	Rogers		**Configuration:**	Ventral off; Ball-nose		**Rover:**	F-104N	NASA 011	Peterson
Landing Time:	13:09:56.0								

Purpose: Stability and control evaluation;
Landing dynamics;
(#1) UV stellar photography experiment checkout;
(#27) Hycon camera experiment

Notes: Nose gear scoop door came open above Mach 4.5;
Theta vernier and 8-ball did not agree

Aborts: None

Program Flight #:	119			Plan	Actual	**NASA 1:**	Engle		
			Max Mach:	4.30	4.56	**B-52 - Pilots - LP:**	52-008	Fulton / Cotton	Butchart
Flight ID:	1-50-79		**Max Altitude:**	80,000	84,900	**Take-Off Time:**	12:32		
X-15 (s/n)	56-6670	(50)	**Speed (mph):**	—	3,048	**Landing Time:**	13:50		
Flight Date:	15 Oct 64		**X-15 Flight Time:**	—	00:08:40.9	**B-52 Flight Time:**	01:18		
Pilot (flight #):	McKay	(14)							
			XLR99 (s/n):	—	107	**Chase 1:**	T-38A		Rogers
Launch Lake:	Hidden Hills		**Powered Time (sec):**	73	72.9 (S.D.)	**Chase 2:**	F-104N	NASA 011	Peterson
Launch Time:	13:15:40.0		**Thrust (pct):**	100	100	**Chase 3:**	F-104		Knight
						Chase 4:			
Landing Lake:	Rogers		**Configuration:**	Ventral off; Ball-nose; X-20 IFDS		**Chase 5:**			
Landing Time:	13:24:20.9			Tip pods					

Purpose: Honeywell X-20 inertial system checkout;
Tip-pod dynamic stability evaluation;
(#12) Atmospheric density experiment checkout
(#13) Micrometeorite collection experiment;
(#19) High-altitude sky brightness epxeriment checkout

Notes: First flight with wing-tip pods installed;
Micrometeorite collector opened while going
transonic at high-key

Aborts: 1-A-78 02 Oct 64 SAS malfunction

Abort used NB-52A 52-003; McKay was the X-15 pilot for the abort

Program Flight #:	120			Plan	Actual	**NASA 1:**	McKay		
			Max Mach:	4.50	4.66	**B-52 - Pilots - LP:**	52-008	Bement / Lewis	Butchart
Flight ID:	3-36-59		**Max Altitude:**	81,000	84,600	**Take-Off Time:**	09:12		
X-15 (s/n)	56-6672	(36)	**Speed (mph):**	—	3,113	**Landing Time:**	10:27		
Flight Date:	30 Oct 64		**X-15 Flight Time:**	—	00:07:10.1	**B-52 Flight Time:**	01:15		
Pilot (flight #):	Thompson	(5)							
			XLR99 (s/n):	—	103	**Chase 1:**	T-38A		Rushworth
Launch Lake:	Hidden Hills		**Powered Time (sec):**	74	74.4 (S.D.)	**Chase 2:**	F-104D	57-1316	Peterson
Launch Time:	09:51:52.0		**Thrust (pct):**	100	100	**Chase 3:**	F-104		Engle
						Chase 4:			
Landing Lake:	Rogers		**Configuration:**	Ventral off; Ball-nose		**Chase 5:**			
Landing Time:	09:59:02.1			Sharp rudder					

Purpose: Landing gear door mod checkout;
Boundary layer noise data;
Skin-friction measurements;
Center stick evaluation;
McDonnell B-44 ablator on ventral and lower speed brakes

Notes: Fire warning light 54 seconds after shutdown

Aborts: 3-C-58 29 Oct 64 Scheduled captive flight

Captive used NB-52B 52-008; Thompson was the X-15 pilot for the captive flight

				Plan	Actual				
Program Flight #:	121					**NASA 1:**	Thompson		
			Max Mach:	4.50	4.66	**B-52 - Pilots - LP:**	52-008	Bement / Bock	Russell
Flight ID:	2-35-60		**Max Altitude:**	80,000	87,200	**Take-Off Time:**	11:29		
X-15 (s/n)	56-6671	(35 / 4)	**Speed (mph):**	—	3,089	**Landing Time:**	12:42		
Flight Date:	30 Nov 64		**X-15 Flight Time:**	—	00:08:34.8	**B-52 Flight Time:**	01:13		
Pilot (flight #):	McKay	(15)							
			XLR99 (s/n):	—	108	**Chase 1:**	T-38A		Sorlie
Launch Lake:	Hidden Hills		**Powered Time (sec):**	80	75.3 (S.D.)	**Chase 2:**	F-104N	NASA 012	Mallick
Launch Time:	12:09:32.0		**Thrust (pct):**	100	100	**Chase 3:**	F-104		Rogers
						Chase 4:	F-104		Knight
Landing Lake:	Rogers		**Configuration:**	Ventral off; Ball-nose		**Rover:**	F-104		Twinting
Landing Time:	12:18:06.8								

Purpose: Landing gear door modification checkout;
Stability and control data;
(#1) UV stellar photography experiment checkout

Notes: Blown fuse prevented UV experiment (#1) from acquiring data;
Boost performance did not match simulator

Aborts:

2-C-58	06 Nov 64	Scheduled captive flight	
2-C-59	16 Nov 64	Scheduled captive flight	All captive flights used NB-52B 52-008; McKay was the X-15 pilot

				Plan	Actual				
Program Flight #:	122					**NASA 1:**	McKay		
			Max Mach:	5.20	5.42	**B-52 - Pilots - LP:**	52-008	Fulton / Lewis	Russell
Flight ID:	3-37-60		**Max Altitude:**	85,000	92,400	**Take-Off Time:**	09:53		
X-15 (s/n)	56-6672	(37)	**Speed (mph):**	—	3,723	**Landing Time:**	11:05		
Flight Date:	09 Dec 64		**X-15 Flight Time:**	—	00:06:25.7	**B-52 Flight Time:**	01:12		
Pilot (flight #):	Thompson	(6)							
			XLR99 (s/n):	—	106	**Chase 1:**	T-38A		Rushworth
Launch Lake:	Hidden Hills		**Powered Time (sec):**	104	101.4 (S.D.)	**Chase 2:**	F-104N	NASA 012	Peterson
Launch Time:	10:36:17.0		**Thrust (pct):**	100	100, 43	**Chase 3:**	F-104A		Sorlie
						Chase 4:	F-104		Twinting
Landing Lake:	Rogers		**Configuration:**	Ventral off; Ball-nose		**Chase 5:**			
Landing Time:	10:42:42.7			Sharp rudder					

Purpose: Non-uniform 3-dimensional flow field measurements;
Boundary layer noise data;
Skin-friction measurements;
McDonnell Y-7 and B-44 ablators on right lower speed brake

Notes: Purposely shutdown with negative g

Aborts: None

				Plan	Actual				
Program Flight #:	123					**NASA 1:**	Rushworth		
			Max Mach:	5.20	5.35	**B-52 - Pilots - LP:**	52-003	Bock / Fulton	Russell
Flight ID:	1-51-81		**Max Altitude:**	112,000	113,200	**Take-Off Time:**	10:15		
X-15 (s/n)	56-6670	(51)	**Speed (mph):**	—	3,675	**Landing Time:**	11:48		
Flight Date:	10 Dec 64		**X-15 Flight Time:**	—	00:09:44.7	**B-52 Flight Time:**	01:33		
Pilot (flight #):	Engle	(9)							
			XLR99 (s/n):	—	107	**Chase 1:**	T-38A		Sorlie
Launch Lake:	Delamar		**Powered Time (sec):**	78	80.5 (S.D.)	**Chase 2:**	F-104N	NASA 012	McKay
Launch Time:	11:10:26.0		**Thrust (pct):**	100	100	**Chase 3:**	F-104		Parsons
						Chase 4:	F-104		Rogers
Landing Lake:	Rogers		**Configuration:**	Ventral off; Ball-nose; X-20 IFDS		**Chase 5:**			
Landing Time:	11:20:10.7			Tip pods					

Purpose: Honeywell X-20 inertial system checkout;
Tip-pod dynamic stability evaluation;
Center stick controller;
(#12) Atmospheric density experiment;
(#17) MIT horizon definition phase I checkout (fixed platform)

Notes: Originally scheduled for Mud Lake;
Pitch SAS tripout after launch;
Dark green theropaint on left wing-tip pod;
Light green theropaint on right wing-tip pod;
Martin MA-25S ablator on nose BCS panels

Aborts:

1-A-80	04 Dec 64	Fuel vent valve malfunction	Abort used NB-52A 52-003; Engle was the X-15 pilot for the abort

				Plan	Actual				
Program Flight #:	124					**NASA 1:**	McKay		
			Max Mach:	5.18	5.55	**B-52 - Pilots - LP:**	52-003	Fulton / Bock	Russell
Flight ID:	3-38-61		**Max Altitude:**	81,000	81,200	**Take-Off Time:**	09:55		
X-15 (s/n)	56-6672	(38)	**Speed (mph):**	—	3,593	**Landing Time:**	11:08		
Flight Date:	22 Dec 64		**X-15 Flight Time:**	—	00:07:50.0	**B-52 Flight Time:**	01:13		
Pilot (flight #):	Rushworth	(24)							
			XLR99 (s/n):	—	103	**Chase 1:**	T-38A	59-1599	Twinting
Launch Lake:	Hidden Hills		**Powered Time (sec):**	101	88.0 (S.D.)	**Chase 2:**	F-104N	NASA 012	Mallick
Launch Time:	10:44:52.0		**Thrust (pct):**	100, 46	100, 46	**Chase 3:**	F-104A	56-0817	Knight
						Chase 4:			
Landing Lake:	Rogers		**Configuration:**	Ventral off; Ball-nose		**Chase 5:**			
Landing Time:	10:52:42.0			Sharp rudder					

Purpose: Non-uniform 3-dimensional flow field measurements;
Boundary layer noise data;
Skin-friction measurements;
Langley Purple Blend ablator on F-3 panel;
GE ESM-1004B ablator on F-4 panel

Notes: High gear loads due to crosswind landing

Aborts: — 17 Dec 64 Lack of support aircraft

			Plan	Actual				
Program Flight #:	125				**NASA 1:**	Engle		
		Max Mach:	5.10	5.48	**B-52 - Pilots - LP:**	52-003	Fultun / Bement	Butchart
Flight ID:	3-39-62	**Max Altitude:**	92,000	99,400	**Take-Off Time:**	10:03		
X-15 (s/n)	56-6672 (39)	**Speed (mph):**	—	3,712	**Landing Time:**	11:15		
Flight Date:	13 Jan 65	**X-15 Flight Time:**	—	00:06:47.5	**B-52 Flight Time:**	01:12		
Pilot (flight #):	Thompson (10)							
		XLR99 (s/n):	—	103	**Chase 1:**	T-38A	59-1599	Smith
Launch Lake:	Hidden Hills	**Powered Time (sec):**	90	98.5 (B.O.)	**Chase 2:**	F-104A	56-0763	Dana
Launch Time:	10:50:50.0	**Thrust (pct):**	100, 46	100, 46	**Chase 3:**	F-104A	56-0817	Rushworth
					Chase 4:			
Landing Lake:	Rogers	**Configuration:**	Ventral off; Ball-nose		**Chase 5:**			
Landing Time:	10:57:37.5		Sharp rudder					

Purpose: Non-uniform 3-dimensional flow field measurements;
Boundary layer noise data;
Skin-friction measurements

Notes: Rate limiting and loss of pitch and roll damping experienced during pull-up/roll maneuver after burnout

Aborts: — 12 Jan 65 Cancelled, lack of C-130 support

			Plan	Actual				
Program Flight #:	126				**NASA 1:**	Thompson		
		Max Mach:	5.64	5.71	**B-52 - Pilots - LP:**	52-008	Fulton / Bement	Russell
Flight ID:	3-40-63	**Max Altitude:**	94,000	98,200	**Take-Off Time:**	12:00		
X-15 (s/n)	56-6672 (40)	**Speed (mph):**	—	3,885	**Landing Time:**	13:15		
Flight Date:	02 Feb 65	**X-15 Flight Time:**	—	00:09:58.3	**B-52 Flight Time:**	01:15		
Pilot (flight #):	Engle (10)							
		XLR99 (s/n):	—	103	**Chase 1:**	T-38A		Sorlie
Launch Lake:	Delamar	**Powered Time (sec):**	82.5	81.4 (B.O.)	**Chase 2:**	F-104N	NASA 012	Peterson
Launch Time:	12:50:02.0	**Thrust (pct):**	100	100	**Chase 3:**	F-104		Stroface
					Chase 4:	F-104		Rushworth
Landing Lake:	Rogers	**Configuration:**	Ventral off; Ball-nose		**Chase 5:**			
Landing Time:	13:00:00.3		Sharp rudder					

Purpose: MH-96 fixed gain evaluation;
Boundary layer noise data;
Skin-friction measurements;
Martin MA-25S ablator on ventral, lower speed barkes, and F-4 panel;
Langley Purple Blend ablator on F-3 panel;

Notes: Good flight

Aborts: None

			Plan	Actual				
Program Flight #:	127				**NASA 1:**	McKay		
		Max Mach:	5.20	5.27	**B-52 - Pilots - LP:**	52-008	Bement / Fulton	Butchart
Flight ID:	2-36-63	**Max Altitude:**	96,000	95,100	**Take-Off Time:**	09:54		
X-15 (s/n)	56-6671 (36 / 5)	**Speed (mph):**	—	3,539	**Landing Time:**	11:16		
Flight Date:	17 Feb 65	**X-15 Flight Time:**	—	00:09:20.3	**B-52 Flight Time:**	01:22		
Pilot (flight #):	Rushworth (25)							
		XLR99 (s/n):	—	108	**Chase 1:**	T-38A		Sorlie
Launch Lake:	Mud	**Powered Time (sec):**	81.5	79.8 (S.D.)	**Chase 2:**	JF-104A	55-2961	Dana
Launch Time:	10:44:27.0	**Thrust (pct):**	100	100	**Chase 3:**	F-104N	NASA 013	Thompson
					Chase 4:	F-104		Engle
Landing Lake:	Rogers	**Configuration:**	Ventral off; Ball-nose		**Chase 5:**			
Landing Time:	10:53:47.3		Precision Attitude Indicator					

Purpose: Stability and control evaluation;
Landing dynamics data;
(#1) UV stellar photography experiment checkout

Notes: Right main skid extended at Mach 4.3 and 85,000 feet;
Inertial altitude failed; Engine momentarily lost power

Aborts:
2-C-61 15 Feb 65 Scheduled captive flight
2-C-62 15 Feb 65 Scheduled captive flight

All captive flights used NB-52B 52-008; Rushworth was the X-15 pilot
The captive flights were to evaluate X-15 landing gear loads

			Plan	Actual				
Program Flight #:	128				**NASA 1:**	Rushworth		
		Max Mach:	5.20	5.40	**B-52 - Pilots - LP:**	52-008	Fulton / Bock	Russell
Flight ID:	1-52-85	**Max Altitude:**	180,000	153,600	**Take-Off Time:**	10:57		
X-15 (s/n)	56-6670 (52)	**Speed (mph):**	—	3,702	**Landing Time:**	12:16		
Flight Date:	26 Feb 65	**X-15 Flight Time:**	—	00:09:24.7	**B-52 Flight Time:**	01:19		
Pilot (flight #):	McKay (16)							
		XLR99 (s/n):	—	110	**Chase 1:**	T-38A		Knight
Launch Lake:	Delamar	**Powered Time (sec):**	83	83.2 (S.D.)	**Chase 2:**	F-104N	NASA 013	Peterson
Launch Time:	11:45:55.0	**Thrust (pct):**	100, 52	100, 52	**Chase 3:**	F-104		Stroface
					Chase 4:	F-104		Engle
Landing Lake:	Rogers	**Configuration:**	Ventral off; Ball-nose; X-20 IFDS		**Chase 5:**			
Landing Time:	11:55:19.7		Tip pods					

Purpose: (#12) Atmospheric density experiment;
(#17) MIT horizon definition phase I experiment;
(#19) High-altitude sky brightness experiment

Notes: Computer malfunction at launch;
"NO DROP" light in X-15 cockpit changed to "23 SECONDS";
Modified RAS including 13-cycle nortch filter;
Experiment #5 quartz window removed (replaced with steel plate)

Aborts:
1-A-82 26 Jan 65 Inertial system failure
1-A-83 19 Feb 65 #2 APU failure
1-A-84 25 Feb 65 Edwards weather

All aborts used NB-52B 52-008; McKay was the X-15 pilot for all aborts

			Plan	Actual				
Program Flight #:	129				**NASA 1:**	McKay		
		Max Mach:	5.15	5.17	**B-52 - Pilots - LP:**	52-008	Fulton / Bock	Russell
Flight ID:	1-53-86	**Max Altitude:**	104,000	101,900	**Take-Off Time:**	10:16		
X-15 (s/n)	56-6670 (53)	**Speed (mph):**	—	3,580	**Landing Time:**	11:44		
Flight Date:	26 Mar 65	**X-15 Flight Time:**	—	00:11:24.3	**B-52 Flight Time:**	01:28		
Pilot (flight #):	Rushworth (26)							
		XLR99 (s/n):	—	108	**Chase 1:**	T-38A	59-1600	Engle
Launch Lake:	Delamar	**Powered Time (sec):**	75.5	79.6 (S.D.)	**Chase 2:**	F-104N	N812NA	Dana
Launch Time:	11:02:30.0	**Thrust (pct):**	100	100	**Chase 3:**	F-104D	57-1314	Gentry
					Chase 4:	F-104A	56-0817	Knight
Landing Lake:	Rogers	**Configuration:**	Ventral off; Ball-nose; X-20 IFDS		**Chase 5:**			
Landing Time:	11:13:54.3		Tip pods					

Purpose: Honeywell X-20 inertial system checkout; (#23) Infrared scanning radiometer experiment; (#31) Fixed ball nose on tip pod evaluation

Notes: Alpha crosspointer did not work properly

Aborts: — 25 Mar 65 Weather prior to taxi

			Plan	Actual				
Program Flight #:	130				**NASA 1:**	Thompson		
		Max Mach:	5.20	5.48	**B-52 - Pilots - LP:**	52-008	Fulton / Cotton	Butchart
Flight ID:	3-41-64	**Max Altitude:**	78,000	79,700	**Take-Off Time:**	09:05		
X-15 (s/n)	56-6672 (41)	**Speed (mph):**	—	3,657	**Landing Time:**	10:13		
Flight Date:	23 Apr 65	**X-15 Flight Time:**	—	00:07:42.1	**B-52 Flight Time:**	01:08		
Pilot (flight #):	Engle (11)							
		XLR99 (s/n):	—	111	**Chase 1:**	T-38A		Rushworth
Launch Lake:	Hidden Hills	**Powered Time (sec):**	93	91.4 (B.O.)	**Chase 2:**	F-104N	N812NA	McKay
Launch Time:	09:44:58.0	**Thrust (pct):**	100, 57	100, 57	**Chase 3:**	F-104		Knight
					Chase 4:	F-104N	N813NA	Walker
Landing Lake:	Rogers	**Configuration:**	Ventral off; Ball-nose		**Chase 5:**			
Landing Time:	09:52:40.1		Sharp rudder					

Purpose: Heat transfer data with surface distortion panels; Boundary layer noise data; (#3) UV exhaust plume experiment; Martin MA-25S ablator on upper fixed vertical

Notes: Tmin changed from 40% to 50%

Aborts: None

			Plan	Actual				
Program Flight #:	131				**NASA 1:**	Rushworth		
		Max Mach:	4.70	4.80	**B-52 - Pilots - LP:**	52-008	Bock / Townsend	Russell
Flight ID:	2-37-64	**Max Altitude:**	84,000	92,600	**Take-Off Time:**	11:41		
X-15 (s/n)	56-6671 (37 / 6)	**Speed (mph):**	—	3,260	**Landing Time:**	13:00		
Flight Date:	28 Apr 65	**X-15 Flight Time:**	—	00:07:52.6	**B-52 Flight Time:**	01:19		
Pilot (flight #):	McKay (17)							
		XLR99 (s/n):	—	110	**Chase 1:**	YT-38A	58-1197	Sorlie
Launch Lake:	Hidden Hills	**Powered Time (sec):**	83	78.9 (S.D.)	**Chase 2:**	F-104N	N812NA	Thompson
Launch Time:	12:26:32.0	**Thrust (pct):**	100	100	**Chase 3:**	F-104A	56-0763	Engle
					Chase 4:			
Landing Lake:	Rogers	**Configuration:**	Ventral off; Ball-nose		**Chase 5:**			
Landing Time:	12:34:24.6							

Purpose: Stability and control evaluation; Landing gear loads data; Landing dynamics data; (#1) UV stellar photography experiment checkout

Notes: Highest 'q' for damper off flight during program (1200-1500 psf); Inertial altitude rate (H-dot) failed

Aborts: None

			Plan	Actual				
Program Flight #:	132				**NASA 1:**	Rushworth		
		Max Mach:	5.20	5.17	**B-52 - Pilots - LP:**	52-008	Fulton / Jones	Russell
Flight ID:	2-38-66	**Max Altitude:**	96,000	102,100	**Take-Off Time:**	09:07		
X-15 (s/n)	56-6671 (38 / 7)	**Speed (mph):**	—	3,541	**Landing Time:**	10:35		
Flight Date:	18 May 65	**X-15 Flight Time:**	—	00:09:42.0	**B-52 Flight Time:**	01:28		
Pilot (flight #):	McKay (18)							
		XLR99 (s/n):	—	110	**Chase 1:**	T-38A		Sorlie
Launch Lake:	Mud	**Powered Time (sec):**	81.5	78.9 (S.D.)	**Chase 2:**	F-104N	N812NA	Mallick
Launch Time:	09:56:56.0	**Thrust (pct):**	100	100	**Chase 3:**	F-104		Gentry
					Chase 4:	F-104		Engle
Landing Lake:	Rogers	**Configuration:**	Ventral off; Ball-nose		**Rover:**	F-104N	N811NA	Haise
Landing Time:	10:06:38.0							

Purpose: Stability and control evaluation; Landing gear loads data; Landing dynamics data; (#1) UV stellar photography experiment checkout

Notes: Engine shutdown during igniter idle - reset

Aborts: 2-A-65 13 May 65 Cabin pressurization

Abort used NB-52B 52-008; McKay was the X-15 pilot for the abort

Program Flight #:	133			Plan	Actual	**NASA 1:**	Engle		
			Max Mach:	4.90	4.87	**B-52 - Pilots - LP:**	52-008	Fulton / Jones	Butchart
Flight ID:	1-54-88		**Max Altitude:**	180,000	179,800	**Take-Off Time:**	09:22		
X-15 (s/n)	56-6670	(54)	**Speed (mph):**	—	3,418	**Landing Time:**	10:35		
Flight Date:	25 May 65		**X-15 Flight Time:**	—	00:09:02.5	**B-52 Flight Time:**	01:13		
Pilot (flight #):	Thompson	(11)							
			XLR99 (s/n):	—	108	**Chase 1:**	T-38A		Rushworth
Launch Lake:	Mud		**Powered Time (sec):**	82	81.1 (S.D.)	**Chase 2:**	F-104D	57-1315	Peterson
Launch Time:	10:12:07.5		**Thrust (pct):**	100	100	**Chase 3:**	F-104		Stroface
						Chase 4:	F-104		Knight
Landing Lake:	Rogers		**Configuration:**	Ventral off; Ball-nose; X-20 IFDS		**Rover:**	F-104N	N811NA	Walker
Landing Time:	10:21:10.0			Tip pods					

Purpose: Honeywell X-20 inertial system checkout;
Pilot altitude buildup
(#16) Pace transducer experiment;
(#17) MIT horizon definition phase I experiment;

Notes: Squat switch never armed

Aborts:
— 04 May 65 X-20 inertial failure prior to taxi
1-A-87 11 May 65 SAS and APU malfunctions — Abort used NB-52B 52-008; Thompson was the X-15 pilot for the abort

Program Flight #:	134			Plan	Actual	**NASA 1:**	Thompson		
			Max Mach:	5.40	5.17	**B-52 - Pilots - LP:**	52-008	Fulton / Jones	Butchart
Flight ID:	3-42-65		**Max Altitude:**	200,000	209,600	**Take-Off Time:**	08:56		
X-15 (s/n)	56-6672	(42)	**Speed (mph):**	—	3,754	**Landing Time:**	10:24		
Flight Date:	28 May 65		**X-15 Flight Time:**	—	00:09:35.6	**B-52 Flight Time:**	01:28		
Pilot (flight #):	Engle	(12)							
			XLR99 (s/n):	—	107	**Chase 1:**	T-38A		Sorlie
Launch Lake:	Delamar		**Powered Time (sec):**	82	82.5 (S.D.)	**Chase 2:**	F-104N	N812NA	Haise
Launch Time:	09:43:47.0		**Thrust (pct):**	100	100	**Chase 3:**	F-104		Parsons
						Chase 4:	F-104		Knight
Landing Lake:	Rogers		**Configuration:**	Ventral off; Ball-nose		**Chase 5:**			
Landing Time:	09:53:22.6			Sharp rudder					

Purpose: Boundary layer noise data;
(#3) UV exhaust plume experiment;
(#4) LaRC horizon definition experiment;
Pilot buildup

Notes: Good flight
First flight for altitude predictor

Aborts: None

Program Flight #:	135			Plan	Actual	**NASA 1:**	McKay		
			Max Mach:	5.00	4.69	**B-52 - Pilots - LP:**	52-003	Fulton / Cretney	Russell
Flight ID:	3-43-66		**Max Altitude:**	240,000	244,700	**Take-Off Time:**	09:38		
X-15 (s/n)	56-6672	(43)	**Speed (mph):**	—	3,404	**Landing Time:**	11:00		
Flight Date:	16 Jun 65		**X-15 Flight Time:**	—	00:09:46.4	**B-52 Flight Time:**	01:22		
Pilot (flight #):	Engle	(13)							
			XLR99 (s/n):	—	107	**Chase 1:**	T-38A	59-1600	Wood
Launch Lake:	Delamar		**Powered Time (sec):**	79	77.8 (S.D.)	**Chase 2:**	F-104N	N813NA	Mallick
Launch Time:	10:26:14.0		**Thrust (pct):**	100	100	**Chase 3:**	F-104D	57-1315	Sorlie
						Chase 4:	F-104A	56-0817	Twinting
Landing Lake:	Rogers		**Configuration:**	Ventral off; Ball-nose		**Chase 5:**			
Landing Time:	10:36:00.4			Sharp rudder					

Purpose: Boundary layer noise data;
(#3) UV exhaust plume experiment;
Pilot buildup

Notes: Good flight
The highest Mach number was achieved during descent from max altitude

Aborts: None

Program Flight #:	136			Plan	Actual	**NASA 1:**	Rushworth		
			Max Mach:	5.15	5.14	**B-52 - Pilots - LP:**	52-008	Fulton / Cotton	Russell
Flight ID:	1-55-89		**Max Altitude:**	104,000	108,500	**Take-Off Time:**	08:56		
X-15 (s/n)	56-6670	(55)	**Speed (mph):**	—	3,541	**Landing Time:**	10:23		
Flight Date:	17 Jun 65		**X-15 Flight Time:**	—	00:08:54.0	**B-52 Flight Time:**	01:27		
Pilot (flight #):	Thompson	(12)							
			XLR99 (s/n):	—	108	**Chase 1:**	T-38A		Twinting
Launch Lake:	Delamar		**Powered Time (sec):**	81.5	82.2 (S.D.)	**Chase 2:**	F-104N	N813NA	McKay
Launch Time:	09:40:53.0		**Thrust (pct):**	100	100	**Chase 3:**	F-104		Stroface
						Chase 4:	F-104		Engle
Landing Lake:	Rogers		**Configuration:**	Ventral off; Ball-nose; X-20 IFDS		**Rover:**	F-104N	N811NA	Mallick
Landing Time:	09:49:47.0								

Purpose: Honeywell X-20 inertial system checkout;
Cross-track vernier;
GE ablator on forward BCS panels
(#23) Infrared scanning radiometer experiment;

Notes: Two pitch-out SAS tripouts (to ASAS) - reset once

Aborts: None

Program Flight #:	137
Flight ID:	2-39-70
X-15 (s/n)	56-6671 (39 / 8)
Flight Date:	22 Jun 65
Pilot (flight #):	McKay (19)
Launch Lake:	Delamar
Launch Time:	09:43:44.0
Landing Lake:	Rogers
Landing Time:	09:53:31.7

	Plan	Actual
Max Mach:	5.40	5.64
Max Altitude:	160,000	155,900
Speed (mph):	—	3,938
X-15 Flight Time:	—	00:09:47.7
XLR99 (s/n):	—	103
Powered Time (sec):	83	85.3 (B.O.)
Thrust (pct):	100	100
Configuration:	Ventral off; Ball-nose RAS installed	

NASA 1:	Engle		
B-52 - Pilots - LP:	52-008	Fulton / Bock	Butchart
Take-Off Time:	08:57		
Landing Time:	10:15		
B-52 Flight Time:	01:18		
Chase 1:	T-38A		Rushworth
Chase 2:	F-104N	N812NA	Peterson
Chase 3:	F-104		Gentry
Chase 4:	F-104		Knight
Chase 5:			

Purpose: Landing gear loads data;
(#1) UV stellar photography experiment checkout
(#27) Hycon camera experiment

2-A-67	04 Jun 65	Cockpit pressure regulator
2-A-68	08 Jun 65	Helium source pressure
2-A-69	11 Jun 65	Helium source leak

Notes: Good flight

All aborts used NB-52B 52-008; McKay was the X-15 pilot for all aborts

Program Flight #:	138
Flight ID:	3-44-67
X-15 (s/n)	56-6672 (44)
Flight Date:	29 Jun 65
Pilot (flight #):	Engle (14)
Launch Lake:	Delamar
Launch Time:	10:21:18.0
Landing Lake:	Rogers
Landing Time:	10:31:50.3

	Plan	Actual
Max Mach:	5.10	4.94
Max Altitude:	283,000	280,600
Speed (mph):	—	3,432
X-15 Flight Time:	—	00:10:32.3
XLR99 (s/n):	—	107
Powered Time (sec):	82	81.0 (S.D.)
Thrust (pct):	100	100
Configuration:	Ventral off; Ball-nose Sharp rudder	

NASA 1:	Thompson		
B-52 - Pilots - LP:	52-008	Fulton / Andonian	Russell
Take-Off Time:	09:38		
Landing Time:	11:05		
B-52 Flight Time:	01:27		
Chase 1:	T-38A		Wood
Chase 2:	F-104		McKay
Chase 3:	F-104		Gentry
Chase 4:	F-104		Parsons
Chase 5:			

Purpose: Reentry manuever techniques;
Boundary layer noise data;
(#3) UV exhaust plume experiment;
(#4) LaRC horizon definition experiment;

Aborts: None

Notes: Engle's astronaut qualification flight
The highest Mach number was achieved during descent from max altitude

Program Flight #:	139
Flight ID:	2-40-72
X-15 (s/n)	56-6671 (40 / 9)
Flight Date:	08 Jul 65
Pilot (flight #):	McKay (20)
Launch Lake:	Delamar
Launch Time:	09:16:50.0
Landing Lake:	Rogers
Landing Time:	09:26:23.4

	Plan	Actual
Max Mach:	5.20	5.19
Max Altitude:	200,000	212,600
Speed (mph):	—	3,659
X-15 Flight Time:	—	00:09:33.4
XLR99 (s/n):	—	103
Powered Time (sec):	82.5	82.9 (S.D.)
Thrust (pct):	100	100
Configuration:	Ventral off; Ball-nose	

NASA 1:	Rushworth		
B-52 - Pilots - LP:	52-003	Fulton / Cotton	Russell
Take-Off Time:	08:28		
Landing Time:	09:50		
B-52 Flight Time:	01:21		
Chase 1:	T-38A		Adams
Chase 2:	F-104N	N812NA	Peterson
Chase 3:	F-104		Gentry
Chase 4:	F-104		Knight
Chase 5:			

Purpose: Altitude buildup;
Landing dynamics data;
(#1) UV stellar photography experiment;
MA-25S ablator test

Aborts: 2-A-71 02 Jul 65 Inertial platform (loose umbilical)

Notes: ASAS manual engage switch added;
RAS failed to operate

Abort used NB-52A 52-003; McKay was the X-15 pilot

Program Flight #:	140
Flight ID:	3-45-69
X-15 (s/n)	56-6672 (45)
Flight Date:	20 Jul 65
Pilot (flight #):	Rushworth (27)
Launch Lake:	Delamar
Launch Time:	09:59:28.0
Landing Lake:	Rogers
Landing Time:	10:10:02.5

	Plan	Actual
Max Mach:	5.50	5.40
Max Altitude:	92,000	105,400
Speed (mph):	—	3,760
X-15 Flight Time:	—	00:10:34.5
XLR99 (s/n):	—	107
Powered Time (sec):	80	79.5 (S.D.)
Thrust (pct):	100	100
Configuration:	Ventral off; Ball-nose Sharp rudder	

NASA 1:	Thompson		
B-52 - Pilots - LP:	52-008	Jones / Andonian	Russell
Take-Off Time:	09:09		
Landing Time:	10:38		
B-52 Flight Time:	01:29		
Chase 1:	T-38A		Knight
Chase 2:	F-104D	57-1315	Dana
Chase 3:	F-104		Whelan
Chase 4:	F-104		Gentry
Chase 5:			

Purpose: Boundary layer noise data

Aborts:

—	16 Jul 65	Weather prior to taxi
—	15 Jul 65	Weather prior to taxi
3-A-68	13 Jul 65	Cabin pressurization

Notes: Alpha exceeded 20 degrees after launch (subsonic)

Abort used NB-52B 52-008; Rushworth was the X-15 pilot for the abort

Program Flight #:	141		Plan	Actual	NASA 1:	Engle		
Flight ID:	2-41-73	Max Mach:	5.15	5.16	B-52 - Pilots - LP:	52-008	Bock / Andonian	Butchart
X-15 (s/n)	56-6671 (41 / 10)	Max Altitude:	200,000	208,700	Take-Off Time:	11:51		
Flight Date:	03 Aug 65	Speed (mph):	—	3,602	Landing Time:	13:05		
Pilot (flight #):	Rushworth (28)	X-15 Flight Time:	—	00:09:32.0	B-52 Flight Time:	01:14		
Launch Lake:	Delamar	XLR99 (s/n):	—	103	Chase 1:	T-38A	59-1599	Sorlie
Launch Time:	12:39:50.0	Powered Time (sec):	82	82.4 (S.D.)	Chase 2:	F-104D	57-1314	Dana
Landing Lake:	Rogers	Thrust (pct):	100	100	Chase 3:	F-104D	57-1315	Whelen
Landing Time:	12:49:22.0	Configuration:	Ventral off; Ball-nose		Chase 4:	F-104A	56-0755	Stroface
					Chase 5:			

Purpose: Altitude buildup; RAS checkout; Landing dynamics data; (#1) UV stellar photography experiment

Aborts: None

Notes: Right roll out of trim
The highest Mach number was achieved during descent from max altitude

Program Flight #:	142		Plan	Actual	NASA 1:	McKay		
Flight ID:	1-56-93	Max Mach:	5.15	5.15	B-52 - Pilots - LP:	52-008	Fulton / Andonian	Butchart
X-15 (s/n)	56-6670 (56)	Max Altitude:	104,000	103,200	Take-Off Time:	08:51		
Flight Date:	06 Aug 65	Speed (mph):	—	3,534	Landing Time:	10:36		
Pilot (flight #):	Thompson (13)	X-15 Flight Time:	—	00:10:13.0	B-52 Flight Time:	01:45		
Launch Lake:	Delamar	XLR99 (s/n):	—	108	Chase 1:	T-38A		Rushworth
Launch Time:	09:41:40.0	Powered Time (sec):	81	83.0 (S.D.)	Chase 2:	F-104D	57-1314	Haise
Landing Lake:	Rogers	Thrust (pct):	100	100	Chase 3:	F-104		Livingston
Landing Time:	09:51:53.0	Configuration:	Ventral off; Ball-nose; X-20 IFDS		Chase 4:	F-104		Engle
					Chase 5:			

Purpose: Stability and control data; (#23) Infrared scanning radiometer experiment;

Aborts:

—	22 Jul 65	Weather prior to taxi
1-A-90	23 Jul 65	Pressure Suit anomaly
1-A-91	27 Jul 65	X-15 radio antenna damage
1-A-92	28 Jul 65	Pilot error during preflight

Notes: Engine time did not start
No experiment #23 data obtained due to broken wire
All aborts used NB-52A 52-003; Thompson was the X-15 pilot for all aborts

Program Flight #:	143		Plan	Actual	NASA 1:	Rushworth		
Flight ID:	3-46-70	Max Mach:	5.20	5.20	B-52 - Pilots - LP:	52-003	Jones / Andonian	Butchart
X-15 (s/n)	56-6672 (46)	Max Altitude:	266,000	271,000	Take-Off Time:	10:28		
Flight Date:	10 Aug 65	Speed (mph):	—	3,550	Landing Time:	12:00		
Pilot (flight #):	Engle (15)	X-15 Flight Time:	—	00:09:51.8	B-52 Flight Time:	01:32		
Launch Lake:	Delamar	XLR99 (s/n):	—	107	Chase 1:	T-38A	59-1599	Sorlie
Launch Time:	11:24:10.0	Powered Time (sec):	81	82.1 (S.D.)	Chase 2:	F-104D	57-1314	Dana
Landing Lake:	Rogers	Thrust (pct):	100	100	Chase 3:	F-104D	57-1315	Gentry
Landing Time:	11:34:01.8	Configuration:	Ventral off; Ball-nose; Sharp rudder		Chase 4:	F-104A	56-0763	Stroface
					Rover:	F-104N	N811NA	Haise

Purpose: Boundary layer noise data; Reentry maneuver techniques; (#25) Optical background experiment

Aborts:

—	04 Aug 65	Pitch angle sensor failed prior to taxi
—	05 Aug 65	Inertial system failure prior to taxi

Notes: Yaw damper dropped off at launch, and 20 other times during the flight, but the alternate flight profile was not flown
The highest Mach number was achieved during descent from max altitude
Engle's second flight above 50 miles.

Program Flight #:	144		Plan	Actual	NASA 1:	Engle		
Flight ID:	1-57-96	Max Mach:	5.20	5.11	B-52 - Pilots - LP:	52-003	Fulton / Cotton	Russell
X-15 (s/n)	56-6670 (57)	Max Altitude:	222,000	214,100	Take-Off Time:	09:05		
Flight Date:	25 Aug 65	Speed (mph):	—	3,604	Landing Time:	10:38		
Pilot (flight #):	Thompson (14)	X-15 Flight Time:	—	00:08:51.7	B-52 Flight Time:	01:33		
Launch Lake:	Delamar	XLR99 (s/n):	—	108	Chase 1:	T-38A	59-1598	Rushworth
Launch Time:	09:54:46.8	Powered Time (sec):	81	84.5 (S.D.)	Chase 2:	F-104N	N812NA	McKay
Landing Lake:	Rogers	Thrust (pct):	100	100	Chase 3:	F-104D	57-1314	Marrett
Landing Time:	10:03:38.5	Configuration:	Ventral off; Ball-nose; X-20 IFDS; Tip pods		Chase 4:	F-104A	56-0763	Parsons
					Chase 5:			

Purpose: Stability and control data; (#17) MIT horizon definition phase I experiment; (#16) Pace transducer experiment

Aborts:

—	12 Aug 65	Weather prior to taxi
1-A-94	20 Aug 65	Cabin pressure regulator
1-A-95	24 Aug 65	IFDS computer failure

Notes: Poor pitch control during landing due to aft center of gravity location;
Thompson's last X-15 flight
All aborts used NB-52A 52-003; Thompson was the X-15 pilot for all aborts

Program Flight #:	145	
Flight ID:	3-47-71	
X-15 (s/n):	56-6672	(47)
Flight Date:	26 Aug 65	
Pilot (flight #):	Rushworth	(29)
Launch Lake:	Delamar	
Launch Time:	09:51:47.0	
Landing Lake:	Rogers	
Landing Time:	10:02:14.5	

	Plan	Actual
Max Mach:	5.00	4.79
Max Altitude:	240,000	239,600
Speed (mph):	—	3,372
X-15 Flight Time:	—	00:10:27.5
XLR99 (s/n):	—	107
Powered Time (sec):	79	78.6 (S.D.)
Thrust (pct):	100	100
Configuration:	Ventral off; Ball-nose Sharp rudder	

NASA 1:	Engle		
B-52 - Pilots - LP:	52-008	Cotton / Bock	Russell
Take-Off Time:	09:01		
Landing Time:	10:30		
B-52 Flight Time:	01:29		
Chase 1:	T-38A	59-1599	Sorlie
Chase 2:	F-104D	57-1314	Haise
Chase 3:	F-104A	56-0748	Livingston
Chase 4:	F-104A	56-0763	Parsons
Chase 5:			

Purpose: Boundary layer noise data;
(#3) UV exhaust plume experiment

Notes: Experienced limit cycle 4-5 times during flight

Aborts: None

Program Flight #:	146	
Flight ID:	2-42-74	
X-15 (s/n):	56-6671	(42 / 11)
Flight Date:	02 Sep 65	
Pilot (flight #):	McKay	(21)
Launch Lake:	Delamar	
Launch Time:	09:40:26.0	
Landing Lake:	Rogers	
Landing Time:	09:49:38.8	

	Plan	Actual
Max Mach:	5.00	5.16
Max Altitude:	228,000	239,800
Speed (mph):	—	3,570
X-15 Flight Time:	—	00:09:12.8
XLR99 (s/n):	—	104
Powered Time (sec):	82	84.0 (S.D.)
Thrust (pct):	100	100
Configuration:	Ventral off; Ball-nose	

NASA 1:	Engle		
B-52 - Pilots - LP:	52-008	Bock / Jones	Russell
Take-Off Time:	08:52		
Landing Time:	10:15		
B-52 Flight Time:	01:23		
Chase 1:	T-38A		Rushworth
Chase 2:	F-104D	57-1316	Peterson
Chase 3:	F-104		Stroface
Chase 4:	F-104		Knight
Rover:	F-104N	N811NA	Haise

Purpose: Altitude buildup;
RAS checkout;
Landing dynamics data;
(#1) UV stellar photography experiment

Notes: Good flight;
The highest Mach number was achieved during descent from max altitude

The X-15A-2 structure was X-ray inspected at the AFFTC X-ray facility, no flaws were found

Aborts: None

Program Flight #:	147	
Flight ID:	1-58-97	
X-15 (s/n):	56-6670	(58)
Flight Date:	09 Sep 65	
Pilot (flight #):	Rushworth	(30)
Launch Lake:	Delamar	
Launch Time:	09:55:33.0	
Landing Lake:	Rogers	
Landing Time:	10:06:43.2	

	Plan	Actual
Max Mach:	5.15	5.25
Max Altitude:	104,000	97,200
Speed (mph):	—	3,534
X-15 Flight Time:	—	00:11:10.2
XLR99 (s/n):	—	108
Powered Time (sec):	80	82.1 (S.D.)
Thrust (pct):	100	100
Configuration:	Ventral off; Ball-nose; X-20 IFDS	

NASA 1:	Knight / Thompson		
B-52 - Pilots - LP:	52-008	Bock / Fulton	Russell
Take-Off Time:	09:09		
Landing Time:	10:40		
B-52 Flight Time:	01:31		
Chase 1:	T-38A	59-1598	Wood
Chase 2:	F-104N	N812NA	Peterson
Chase 3:	F-104A	56-0748	Livingston
Chase 4:	F-104A	56-0755	Parsons
Rover:	F-104N	N811NA	Haise

Purpose: (#23) Infrared scanning radiometer experiment;
GE ablator on ventral and lower speed brakes

Notes: Alpha indicator failed;
Unexplained buffet during flight

Aborts: None

Program Flight #:	148	
Flight ID:	3-48-72	
X-15 (s/n):	56-6672	(48)
Flight Date:	14 Sep 65	
Pilot (flight #):	McKay	(22)
Launch Lake:	Delamar	
Launch Time:	10:01:42.0	
Landing Lake:	Rogers	
Landing Time:	10:11:40.0	

	Plan	Actual
Max Mach:	5.10	5.03
Max Altitude:	230,000	239,000
Speed (mph):	—	3,519
X-15 Flight Time:	—	00:09:58.0
XLR99 (s/n):	—	107
Powered Time (sec):	80	80.9 (S.D.)
Thrust (pct):	100	100
Configuration:	Ventral off; Ball-nose Sharp rudder	

NASA 1:	Dana		
B-52 - Pilots - LP:	52-008	Bock / Jones	Russell
Take-Off Time:	09:12		
Landing Time:	10:39		
B-52 Flight Time:	01:27		
Chase 1:	T-38A	59-1601	Rushworth
Chase 2:	F-104N	N811NA	Haise
Chase 3:	F-104D	57-1314	Evenson
Chase 4:	F-104A	56-0755	Knight
Chase 5:			

Purpose: Boundary layer noise data;
(#25) Optical background experiment

Notes: Auto-BCS affect adversely by servo transients;
The highest Mach number was achieved during descent from max altitude

Aborts: None

Program Flight #:	149		**Plan**	**Actual**	**NASA 1:**	Knight		
		Max Mach:	5.15	5.18	**B-52 - Pilots - LP:**	52-003	Bock / Jones	Russell
Flight ID:	1-59-98	**Max Altitude:**	104,000	100,300	**Take-Off Time:**	10:08		
X-15 (s/n)	56-6670 (59)	**Speed (mph):**	—	3,550	**Landing Time:**	11:38		
Flight Date:	22 Sep 65	**X-15 Flight Time:**	—	00:10:54.3	**B-52 Flight Time:**	01:30		
Pilot (flight #):	Rushworth (31)							
		XLR99 (s/n):	—	108	**Chase 1:**	T-38A		Sorlie
Launch Lake:	Delamar	**Powered Time (sec):**	80	82.0 (S.D.)	**Chase 2:**	F-104D	57-1314	Dana
Launch Time:	10:59:05.0	**Thrust (pct):**	100	100	**Chase 3:**	F-104		Adams
					Chase 4:	F-104		Engle
Landing Lake:	Rogers	**Configuration:**	Ventral off; Ball-nose; X-20 IFDS		**Rover:**	F-104N	N811NA	McKay
Landing Time:	11:09:59.3		Tip pods					

Purpose: (#23) Infrared scanning radiometer experiment

Aborts: — 17 Sep 65 Weather prior to taxi

Notes: Infrared experiment (#23) failed during flight

Program Flight #:	150		**Plan**	**Actual**	**NASA 1:**	Dana		
		Max Mach:	5.15	5.33	**B-52 - Pilots - LP:**	52-003	Bock / Andonian	Russell
Flight ID:	3-49-73	**Max Altitude:**	260,000	295,600	**Take-Off Time:**	09:24		
X-15 (s/n)	56-6672 (49)	**Speed (mph):**	—	3,732	**Landing Time:**	10:42		
Flight Date:	28 Sep 65	**X-15 Flight Time:**	—	00:11:56.8	**B-52 Flight Time:**	01:18		
Pilot (flight #):	McKay (23)							
		XLR99 (s/n):	—	109	**Chase 1:**	T-38A		Rushworth
Launch Lake:	Delamar	**Powered Time (sec):**	79	80.8 (S.D.)	**Chase 2:**	F-104N	N812NA	Peterson
Launch Time:	10:08:06.0	**Thrust (pct):**	100	100	**Chase 3:**	F-104N	N811NA	Haise
					Chase 4:	F-104		Engle
Landing Lake:	Rogers	**Configuration:**	Ventral off; Ball-nose		**Chase 5:**			
Landing Time:	10:20:02.8		Sharp rudder					

Purpose: Horizontal tail loads data;
Boundary layer noise data;
(#3) UV exhaust plume experiment;
Martin MA-25S ablator on F-3 and F-4 panels

Aborts: None

Notes: Roll-hold drop-out at launch
The highest Mach number was achieved during descent from max altitude;
Overshot altitude by 35,600 feet

Since McKay was a NASA pilot, he did not get astronaut wings for a flight above 50 miles (the NASA standard was 62 miles)

Program Flight #:	151		**Plan**	**Actual**	**NASA 1:**	Rushworth		
		Max Mach:	4.00	4.06	**B-52 - Pilots - LP:**	52-003	Bock / Fulton	Russell
Flight ID:	1-60-99	**Max Altitude:**	74,000	76,600	**Take-Off Time:**	08:55		
X-15 (s/n)	56-6670 (60)	**Speed (mph):**	—	2,718	**Landing Time:**	10:10		
Flight Date:	30 Sep 65	**X-15 Flight Time:**	—	00:08:22.6	**B-52 Flight Time:**	01:15		
Pilot (flight #):	Knight (1)							
		XLR99 (s/n):	—	108	**Chase 1:**	T-38A		Sorlie
Launch Lake:	Hidden Hills	**Powered Time (sec):**	126	127.4 (S.D.)	**Chase 2:**	F-104N	N811NA	Peterson
Launch Time:	09:43:55.0	**Thrust (pct):**	53	94, 53	**Chase 3:**	F-104		Engle
					Chase 4:			
Landing Lake:	Rogers	**Configuration:**	Ventral off; Ball-nose; X-20 IFDS		**Rover:**	F-104D	57-1315	Haise
Landing Time:	09:52:17.6		Tip pods					

Purpose: Pilot familiarization – Knight's first X-15 flight;
(#23) Infrared scanning radiometer experiment

Aborts: — 21 Sep 65 Weather prior to taxi

Notes: Good flight;
Infrared experiment (#23) even though Flight 1-59-98 was supposed to be the last flight (but no data was acquired)

Program Flight #:	152		**Plan**	**Actual**	**NASA 1:**	Rushworth		
		Max Mach:	4.50	4.62	**B-52 - Pilots - LP:**	52-008	Jones / Fulton	Russell
Flight ID:	3-50-74	**Max Altitude:**	91,000	94,400	**Take-Off Time:**	09:01		
X-15 (s/n)	56-6672 (50)	**Speed (mph):**	—	3,108	**Landing Time:**	10:22		
Flight Date:	12 Oct 65	**X-15 Flight Time:**	—	00:07:07.8	**B-52 Flight Time:**	01:20		
Pilot (flight #):	Knight (2)							
		XLR99 (s/n):	—	109	**Chase 1:**	T-38A		Sorlie
Launch Lake:	Hidden Hills	**Powered Time (sec):**	93	86.2 (S.D.)	**Chase 2:**	F-104A	56-0817	Petersen
Launch Time:	09:43:14.0	**Thrust (pct):**	78	93, 78	**Chase 3:**	F-104		Engle
					Chase 4:	F-104N	N811NA	Haise
Landing Lake:	Rogers	**Configuration:**	Ventral off; Ball-nose		**Chase 5:**			
Landing Time:	09:50:21.8		Sharp rudder					

Purpose: Pilot checkout

Aborts: None

Notes: #2 APU shut down 1.5 seconds after launch;
Pitch/roll SAS servos locked up for 5 seconds;
APU restarted 90 seconds after shutdown

Program Flight #:	153			Plan	Actual	NASA 1:	Rushworth		
			Max Mach:	5.15	5.08	B-52 - Pilots - LP:	52-003	Bock / Jones	Peterson
Flight ID:	1-61-101		Max Altitude:	250,000	266,500	Take-Off Time:	11:54		
X-15 (s/n)	56-6670	(61)	Speed (mph):	—	3,554	Landing Time:	13:26		
Flight Date:	14 Oct 65		X-15 Flight Time:	—	00:09:17.7	B-52 Flight Time:	01:32		
Pilot (flight #):	Engle	(16)							
			XLR99 (s/n):	—	108	Chase 1:	T-38A	59-1601	Sorlie
Launch Lake:	Delamar		Powered Time (sec):	83	84.8 (S.D.)	Chase 2:	F-104N	N812NA	McKay
Launch Time:	12:45:57.0		Thrust (pct):	100	100	Chase 3:	F-104A	56-0817	Parsons
						Chase 4:	F-104A	56-0755	Knight
Landing Lake:	Rogers		Configuration:	Ventral off; Ball-nose; X-20 IFDS		Rover:	F-104N	N811NA	Haise
Landing Time:	12:55:14.7			Tip pods					

Purpose: (#16) Pace transducer experiment;
(#17) MIT horizon definition phase I experiment

Notes: Engle's third flight above 50 miles;
Engle's last X-15 flight;
Yaw damper tripped twice - reset
Internal NASA data timer problem
The highest Mach number was achieved during descent from max altitude

Aborts: 1-A-100 08 Oct 65 Leak in ballistic pitch thruster
— 13 Oct 65 Weather prior to taxi

Abort used NB-52A 52-003; Engle was the X-15 pilot for the abort

Program Flight #:	154			Plan	Actual	NASA 1:	Rushworth		
			Max Mach:	5.15	5.06	B-52 - Pilots - LP:	52-003	Fulton / Jones	Russell
Flight ID:	3-51-75		Max Altitude:	260,000	236,900	Take-Off Time:	09:56		
X-15 (s/n)	56-6672	(51)	Speed (mph):	—	3,519	Landing Time:	11:20		
Flight Date:	27 Oct 65		X-15 Flight Time:	—	00:11:53.7	B-52 Flight Time:	01:23		
Pilot (flight #):	McKay	(24)							
			XLR99 (s/n):	—	109	Chase 1:	T-38A	59-1601	Sorlie
Launch Lake:	Delamar		Powered Time (sec):	79	75.6 (S.D.)	Chase 2:	F-104N	N811NA	Peterson
Launch Time:	10:49:29.0		Thrust (pct):	100	100	Chase 3:	F-104A	56-0748	Stroface
						Chase 4:	F-104A	56-0763	Engle
Landing Lake:	Rogers		Configuration:	Ventral off; Ball-nose		Chase 5:			
Landing Time:	11:01:22.7			Sharp rudder					

Purpose: Horizontal tail loads data;
Boundary layer noise data;
(#3) UV exhaust plume experiment

Notes: Roll-hold engaged 8 degrees off heading at launch

Aborts: None

Program Flight #:	155			Plan	Actual	NASA 1:	McKay		
			Max Mach:	2.20	2.31	B-52 - Pilots - LP:	52-003	Bock / Doryland	Russell
Flight ID:	2-43-75		Max Altitude:	70,000	70,600	Take-Off Time:	08:26		
X-15 (s/n)	56-6671	(43 / 12)	Speed (mph):	—	1,500	Landing Time:	09:33		
Flight Date:	03 Nov 65		X-15 Flight Time:	—	00:05:01.6	B-52 Flight Time:	01:07		
Pilot (flight #):	Rushworth	(32)							
			XLR99 (s/n):	—	104	Chase 1:	T-38A	59-1606	Knight
Launch Lake:	Cuddeback		Powered Time (sec):	80	84.1 (S.D.)	Chase 2:	F-104D	57-1315	Haise
Launch Time:	09:09:32.0		Thrust (pct):	58	58	Chase 3:	F-104A	56-0755	Engle
						Chase 4:	JT-38A	59-1599	Sorlie
Landing Lake:	Rogers		Configuration:	Ventral on; Ball-nose		Chase 5:			
Landing Time:	09:14:33.6			Tanks (empty)					

Purpose: Handling qualities with external tanks;
Tank separation characteristics;
Tank trajectory evaluation

Notes: First flight with external tanks (empty);
First, and only, launch from Cuddeback;
LOX chute did not deploy - tank not repairable;
Ventral chute did not deploy;
TM antenna moved to forward fuselage
Tanks dropped at Mach 2.25, 70,300 feet, q=343 psf, 5° alpha

Aborts: None

Program Flight #:	156			Plan	Actual	NASA 1:	Rushworth		
			Max Mach:	4.00	4.22	B-52 - Pilots - LP:	52-008	Bock / Doryland	Russell
Flight ID:	1-62-103		Max Altitude:	74,000	80,200	Take-Off Time:	08:22		
X-15 (s/n)	56-6670	(62)	Speed (mph):	—	2,765	Landing Time:	09:33		
Flight Date:	04 Nov 65		X-15 Flight Time:	—	00:08:45.8	B-52 Flight Time:	01:11		
Pilot (flight #):	Dana	(1)							
			XLR99 (s/n):	—	110	Chase 1:	T-38A		Sorlie
Launch Lake:	Hidden Hills		Powered Time (sec):	123	124.2 (S.D.)	Chase 2:	F-104A	56-0187	Peterson
Launch Time:	09:11:13.0		Thrust (pct):	55	55	Chase 3:	F-104		Knight
						Chase 4:			
Landing Lake:	Rogers		Configuration:	Ventral off; Ball-nose; X-20 IFDS		Rover:	F-104N	N812NA	Haise
Landing Time:	09:19:58.8			Tip pods					

Purpose: Pilot familiarization – Dana's first X-15 flight;

Notes: Two engine restarts required

Aborts: 1-A-102 02 Nov 65 Cockpit pressure regulator

Abort used NB-52B 52-008; Dana was the X-15 pilot for the abort

Program Flight #:	157			Plan	Actual	**NASA 1:**	Dana		
			Max Mach:	5.30	2.21	**B-52 - Pilots - LP:**	52-003	Fulton / Doryland	Butchart
Flight ID:	1-63-104		**Max Altitude:**	199,000	68,400	**Take-Off Time:**	12:34		
X-15 (s/n)	56-6670	(63)	**Speed (mph):**	—	1,434	**Landing Time:**	14:22		
Flight Date:	06 May 66		**X-15 Flight Time:**	—	00:06:02.7	**B-52 Flight Time:**	01:48		
Pilot (flight #):	McKay	(25)							
			XLR99 (s/n):	—	103	**Chase 1:**	T-38A		Knight
Launch Lake:	Delamar		**Powered Time (sec):**	82	35.4 (S.D.)	**Chase 2:**	F-104D	57-1316	Peterson
Launch Time:	13:29:03.0		**Thrust (pct):**	100, 28	100, 28	**Chase 3:**	F-104D		Gentry / Hoag
						Chase 4:	F-104		Stroface
Landing Lake:	Delamar		**Configuration:**	Ventral off; Ball-nose; X-20 IFDS		**Chase 5:**	T-38A		Curtis / Livingston
Landing Time:	13:35:05.7			Tip pods					

Purpose: (#12) Atmospheric density experiment;
(#13) Micrometeorite collection experiment;
(#17) MIT horizon definition phase I experiment;
(#19) High-altitude sky brightness experiment

Aborts: — 22 Apr 66 No C-130 support

Notes: Window shade installed on left canopy window to eliminate sun glare normally associated with afternoon flights
Pump failure required premature shutdown;
Landing at Delamar; aircraft slid off lakebed; no damage;
Canopy jettisoned prior to reaching end of lakebed;
Micrometeorite experiment opened;

Program Flight #:	158			Plan	Actual	**NASA 1:**	McKay		
			Max Mach:	5.38	5.43	**B-52 - Pilots - LP:**	52-003	Fulton / Doryland	Russell
Flight ID:	2-44-79		**Max Altitude:**	100,000	99,000	**Take-Off Time:**	09:33		
X-15 (s/n)	56-6671	(44 / 13)	**Speed (mph):**	—	3,689	**Landing Time:**	11:00		
Flight Date:	18 May 66		**X-15 Flight Time:**	—	00:08:56.8	**B-52 Flight Time:**	01:27		
Pilot (flight #):	Rushworth	(33-11)							
			XLR99 (s/n):	—	106	**Chase 1:**	T-38A		Sorlie
Launch Lake:	Mud		**Powered Time (sec):**	84	81.9 (S.D.)	**Chase 2:**	F-104D	57-1314	Dana / Manke
Launch Time:	10:23:50.0		**Thrust (pct):**	100	100	**Chase 3:**	F-104N	N811NA	Peterson
						Chase 4:	F-104		Gentry
Landing Lake:	Rogers		**Configuration:**	Ventral on; Ball-nose		**Chase 5:**			
Landing Time:	10:32:46.8								

Purpose: Ventral-on stability and control; MA-25S ablator evaluation

Aborts:

—	05 Apr 66	No C-130 support
—	12 Apr 66	High winds at Edwards prior to taxi
2-A-76	13 Apr 66	Inertial system (cross-range)
2-A-77	20 Apr 66	Yaw SAS would not engage
2-A-78	05 May 66	Yaw SAS would not engage

Notes: Good flight;
Stabilizer torque tube enclosures;
Large-scale test of MA-25S/ESA-3560 ablators

All aborts used NB-52A 52-003; Rushworth was the X-15 pilot for all aborts

Program Flight #:	159			Plan	Actual	**NASA 1:**	McKay		
			Max Mach:	6.00	1.70	**B-52 - Pilots - LP:**	52-008	Fulton / Doryland	Russell
Flight ID:	2-45-81		**Max Altitude:**	100,000	44,800	**Take-Off Time:**	10:11		
X-15 (s/n)	56-6671	(45 / 14)	**Speed (mph):**	—	1,061	**Landing Time:**	11:55		
Flight Date:	01 Jul 66		**X-15 Flight Time:**	—	00:04:28.6	**B-52 Flight Time:**	01:44		
Pilot (flight #):	Rushworth	(34)							
			XLR99 (s/n):	—	106	**Chase 1:**	T-38A		Knight
Launch Lake:	Mud		**Powered Time (sec):**	132	33.2 (S.D.)	**Chase 2:**	F-104D	57-1316	Peterson
Launch Time:	11:01:55.0		**Thrust (pct):**	100, 58	100, 58	**Chase 3:**	F-104		Curtis
						Chase 4:	T-38A		Sorlie
Landing Lake:	Mud		**Configuration:**	Ventral on; Ball-nose		**Rover:**	F-104N	N812NA	Dana
Landing Time:	11:06:23.6			Tanks; Alternate pitot					

Purpose: Full external tank checkout;
MA-25S Ablator evaluation;
Alternate pitot-static checkout;
(#27) Maurer camera experiment checkout

Aborts: 2-C-80 27 Jun 66 Sceduled captive with full tanks

Notes: Telemetry indicated no NH3 flow from external tanks caused pilot to throttle back, jettison external tanks, and land at Mud Lake - faulty TM signal;
Rushworth's last X-15 flight (what a way to go out)
X-15 wing impacted camper on the return trip to Edwards.

Captive used NB-52B 52-008; Rushworth was the X-15 pilot

Program Flight #:	160			Plan	Actual	**NASA 1:**	McKay		
			Max Mach:	5.30	5.34	**B-52 - Pilots - LP:**	52-003	Fulton / Bowline	Russell
Flight ID:	1-64-107		**Max Altitude:**	130,000	130,000	**Take-Off Time:**	10:44		
X-15 (s/n)	56-6670	(64)	**Speed (mph):**	—	3,652	**Landing Time:**	12:25		
Flight Date:	12 Jul 66		**X-15 Flight Time:**	—	00:08:38.5	**B-52 Flight Time:**	01:41		
Pilot (flight #):	Knight	(3)							
			XLR99 (s/n):	—	107	**Chase 1:**	T-38A		Curtis
Launch Lake:	Mud		**Powered Time (sec):**	80	83.2 (S.D.)	**Chase 2:**	F-104B	57-1303	Dana
Launch Time:	11:32:13.0		**Thrust (pct):**	100	100	**Chase 3:**	F-104		Hoag
						Chase 4:	F-104		Gentry
Landing Lake:	Rogers		**Configuration:**	Ventral off; Ball-nose; X-20 IFDS		**Chase 5:**			
Landing Time:	11:40:51.5								

Purpose: Pilot checkout;
Electrical loads survey;
Non-glare glass evaluation;
Window shade checkout

Aborts:

1-A-105	02 Jun 66	Inertial System Failure
1-A-106	10 Jun 66	Inertial System Computer failure

Notes: Was originally scheduled as a 200,000-foot flight with Jack McKay as pilot

All aborts used NB-52A 52-003; McKay was the X-15 pilot for all aborts

Program Flight #:	161
Flight ID:	3-52-78
X-15 (s/n)	56-6672 (52)
Flight Date:	18 Jul 66
Pilot (flight #):	Dana (2)
Launch Lake:	Hidden Hills
Launch Time:	11:38:20.0
Landing Lake:	Rogers
Landing Time:	11:45:50.2

	Plan	Actual
Max Mach:	5.15	4.71
Max Altitude:	104,000	96,100
Speed (mph):	—	3,217
X-15 Flight Time:	—	00:07:30.2
XLR99 (s/n):	—	111
Powered Time (sec):	80	95.5 (S.D.)
Thrust (pct):	100	71
Configuration:	Ventral off; Ball-nose; X-20 IFDS Sharp rudder; 3rd skid	

NASA 1:	McKay		
B-52 - Pilots - LP:	52-003	Fulton / Doryland	Russell
Take-Off Time:	10:52		
Landing Time:	12:15		
B-52 Flight Time:	01:23		
Chase 1:	T-38A		Curtis
Chase 2:	F-104A	56-0817	Manke
Chase 3:	F-104A	56-0755	Gentry
Chase 4:			
Rover:	JF-104A	55-2961	Peterson

Purpose: Pilot checkout;
Honeywell X-20 inertial system checkout;
Horizontal tail loads data

Notes: Could not see through the sunshade during 90-degree left bank - replaced for next flight;
First flight with Lear cockpit display

Aborts:

3-A-76	20 Jun 66	Inertial Computer overheat
3-A-77	13 Jul 66	Computer light and TM failure

All aborts used NB-52A 52-003; Dana was the X-15 pilot for all aborts

Program Flight #:	162
Flight ID:	2-46-83
X-15 (s/n)	56-6671 (46 / 15)
Flight Date:	21 Jul 66
Pilot (flight #):	Knight (4)
Launch Lake:	Delamar
Launch Time:	12:01:16.0
Landing Lake:	Rogers
Landing Time:	12:10:07.0

	Plan	Actual
Max Mach:	5.10	5.12
Max Altitude:	180,000	192,300
Speed (mph):	—	3,568
X-15 Flight Time:	—	00:08:51.0
XLR99 (s/n):	—	106
Powered Time (sec):	81	81.3 (S.D.)
Thrust (pct):	100	100
Configuration:	Ventral off; Ball-nose Alternate pitot; PAI on I-panel	

NASA 1:	Dana		
B-52 - Pilots - LP:	52-003	Doryland / Bowline	Russell
Take-Off Time:	11:08		
Landing Time:	12:30		
B-52 Flight Time:	01:21		
Chase 1:	F-104D	57-1314	Manke
Chase 2:	F-104A	56-0748	Sorlie
Chase 3:	F-104A	56-0817	Gentry
Chase 4:			
Rover:	F5D-1	142350 (802)	Peterson

Purpose: Pilot altitude buildup;
Alternate pitot static system checkout;
MA-25S ablator evaluation;
Base drag study;
(#1) UV stellar photography experiment;

Notes: Right roll out of trim

Aborts:

2-A-82	20 Jul 66	Weather at launch lake

Abort used NB-52A 52-003; Knight was the X-15 pilot for the abort

Program Flight #:	163
Flight ID:	1-65-108
X-15 (s/n)	56-6670 (65)
Flight Date:	28 Jul 66
Pilot (flight #):	McKay (26)
Launch Lake:	Delamar
Launch Time:	10:01:03.0
Landing Lake:	Rogers
Landing Time:	10:10:46.0

	Plan	Actual
Max Mach:	5.20	5.19
Max Altitude:	220,000	241,800
Speed (mph):	—	3,702
X-15 Flight Time:	—	00:09:43.0
XLR99 (s/n):	—	107
Powered Time (sec):	83	85.4 (S.D.)
Thrust (pct):	100	100
Configuration:	Ventral off; Ball-nose; X-20 IFDS Tip pods	

NASA 1:	Dana		
B-52 - Pilots - LP:	52-008	Fulton / Bowline	Russell
Take-Off Time:	09:08		
Landing Time:	11:05		
B-52 Flight Time:	01:57		
Chase 1:	T-38A		Curtis
Chase 2:	JF-104A	55-2961	Peterson
Chase 3:	F-104D		Sorlie / Adams
Chase 4:	F-104A	56-0755	Gentry
Chase 5:			

Purpose: (#13) Micrometeorite collection experiment;
(#16) Pace transducer experiment;
(#17) MIT horizon definition phase I experiment;
(#19) High-altitude sky brightness experiment

Notes: Computer malfunction and pitch trip-out during boost; inertials degraded after malfunction;
H-dot failed pre-launch

Aborts:

—	25 Jul 66	IFDS failed preflight

Program Flight #:	164
Flight ID:	2-47-84
X-15 (s/n)	56-6671 (47 / 16)
Flight Date:	03 Aug 66
Pilot (flight #):	Knight (5)
Launch Lake:	Delamar
Launch Time:	08:43:26.0
Landing Lake:	Rogers
Landing Time:	08:52:36.7

	Plan	Actual
Max Mach:	5.02	5.03
Max Altitude:	230,000	249,000
Speed (mph):	—	3,440
X-15 Flight Time:	—	00:09:10.7
XLR99 (s/n):	—	106
Powered Time (sec):	82	81.8 (S.D.)
Thrust (pct):	100	100
Configuration:	Ventral off; Ball-nose Alternate pitot	

NASA 1:	Dana		
B-52 - Pilots - LP:	52-008	Doryland / Bowline	Russell
Take-Off Time:	07:52		
Landing Time:	09:24		
B-52 Flight Time:	01:31		
Chase 1:	T-38A	59-1601	Curtis
Chase 2:	F-104A	56-0755	Manke
Chase 3:	F-104A	56-0748	Parsons
Chase 4:	F-104A	56-0763	Sorlie
Rover:	F-104N	N812NA	Petersen

Purpose: Pilot altitude buildup;
Alternate pitot static system checkout;
Base drag study;
(#1) UV stellar photography experiment

Notes: Inertial altitude read wrong most of the flight;
The highest Mach number was achieved during descent from max altitude

Aborts:

—	03 Aug 66	Weather prior to taxi

Program Flight #:	165		**Plan**	**Actual**	**NASA 1:**	McKay			
		Max Mach:	5.50	5.34	**B-52 - Pilots - LP:**	52-008	Doryland / Bowline	Russell	
Flight ID:	3-53-79	**Max Altitude:**	130,000	132,700	**Take-Off Time:**	09:06			
X-15 (s/n)	56-6672 (53)	**Speed (mph):**	—	3,693	**Landing Time:**	10:45			
Flight Date:	04 Aug 66	**X-15 Flight Time:**	—	00:08:28.0	**B-52 Flight Time:**	01:39			
Pilot (flight #):	Dana (3)								
		XLR99 (s/n):	—	111	**Chase 1:**	T-38A	59-1601	Curtis	
Launch Lake:	Mud	**Powered Time (sec):**	80	78.9 (S.D.)	**Chase 2:**	JF-104A	55-2961	Manke	
Launch Time:	09:55:23.0	**Thrust (pct):**	100	100	**Chase 3:**	F-104D		Parsons / Sorlie	
					Chase 4:	F-104A	56-0817	Gentry	
Landing Lake:	Rogers	**Configuration:**	Ventral off; Ball-nose; X-20 IFDS Sharp rudder; 3rd skid		**Chase 5:**				
Landing Time:	10:03:51.0								

Purpose: Pilot checkout; Lear Panel checkout; Boundary layer noise data; Horizontal tail loads data; (#25) Optical background experiment

Aborts: None

Notes: Tape 'q' read 50 psf higher than the gauge

Program Flight #:	166		**Plan**	**Actual**	**NASA 1:**	Dana			
		Max Mach:	5.15	5.21	**B-52 - Pilots - LP:**	52-003	Doryland / Bowline	Russell	
Flight ID:	1-66-111	**Max Altitude:**	250,000	251,000	**Take-Off Time:**	08:53			
X-15 (s/n)	56-6670 (66)	**Speed (mph):**	—	3,590	**Landing Time:**	10:19			
Flight Date:	11 Aug 66	**X-15 Flight Time:**	—	00:09:22.2	**B-52 Flight Time:**	01:26			
Pilot (flight #):	McKay (27)								
		XLR99 (s/n):	—	107	**Chase 1:**	T-38A	59-1598	Sorlie	
Launch Lake:	Delamar	**Powered Time (sec):**	84	84.8 (S.D)	**Chase 2:**	JF-104A	55-2961	Manke	
Launch Time:	09:44:26.0	**Thrust (pct):**	100	100	**Chase 3:**	F-104D	57-1314	Evenson / Smith	
					Chase 4:	F-104A	56-0755	Gentry	
Landing Lake:	Rogers	**Configuration:**	Ventral off; Ball-nose; X-20 IFDS Tip pods		**Chase 5:**				
Landing Time:	09:53:48.2								

Purpose: (#13) Micrometeorite collection experiment; (#16) Pace transducer experiment; (#17) MIT horizon definition phase II experiment; (#19) High-altitude sky brightness experiment

Aborts:

1-A-109	09 Aug 66	Inertial system failure
1-A-110	10 Aug 66	Launch lake helicopter lost engine

Notes: Highest dynamic pressure (2,202 psf) for any X-15; Computer malfunction and pitch-roll trip-out during boost - reset; The highest Mach number was achieved during descent from max altitude

All aborts used NB-52A 52-003; McKay was the X-15 pilot for all aborts

Program Flight #:	167		**Plan**	**Actual**	**NASA 1:**	McKay			
		Max Mach:	5.02	5.02	**B-52 - Pilots - LP:**	52-003	Doryland / Bowline	Russell	
Flight ID:	2-48-85	**Max Altitude:**	230,000	231,100	**Take-Off Time:**	09:38			
X-15 (s/n)	56-6671 (48 / 17)	**Speed (mph):**	—	3,472	**Landing Time:**	11:04			
Flight Date:	12 Aug 66	**X-15 Flight Time:**	—	00:08:36.6	**B-52 Flight Time:**	01:26			
Pilot (flight #):	Knight (6)								
		XLR99 (s/n):	—	106	**Chase 1:**	T-38A	59-1598	Sorlie	
Launch Lake:	Delamar	**Powered Time (sec):**	82	81.7 (S.D.)	**Chase 2:**	JF-104A	55-2961	Mallick	
Launch Time:	10:25:05.0	**Thrust (pct):**	100	100	**Chase 3:**	F-104D	57-1315	Smith	
					Chase 4:	F-104A	56-0763	Adams	
Landing Lake:	Rogers	**Configuration:**	Ventral off; Ball-nose Alternate pitot		**Chase 5:**	F-104A	56-0748	Gentry	
Landing Time:	10:33:41.6				**Rover:**	F-104N	N812NA	Dana	

Purpose: Alternate pitot static system checkout; Base drag study; (#1) UV stellar photography experiment

Aborts: None

Notes: Good flight; The highest Mach number was achieved during descent from max altitude

Additional Chase:

Rover: F-104N N812NA Dana

Program Flight #:	168		**Plan**	**Actual**	**NASA 1:**	Knight			
		Max Mach:	5.20	5.20	**B-52 - Pilots - LP:**	52-003	Fulton / Bowline	Russell	
Flight ID:	3-54-80	**Max Altitude:**	180,000	178,000	**Take-Off Time:**	09:03			
X-15 (s/n)	56-6672 (54)	**Speed (mph):**	—	3,607	**Landing Time:**	10:45			
Flight Date:	19 Aug 66	**X-15 Flight Time:**	—	00:09:33.1	**B-52 Flight Time:**	01:42			
Pilot (flight #):	Dana (4)								
		XLR99 (s/n):	—	110	**Chase 1:**	T-38A	59-1598	Sorlie	
Launch Lake:	Delamar	**Powered Time (sec):**	80	75.8 (S.D.)	**Chase 2:**	JF-104A	55-2961	Manke	
Launch Time:	10:03:03.0	**Thrust (pct):**	100	100	**Chase 3:**	F-104D		Smith / Evenson	
					Chase 4:	F-104A	56-0755	Adams	
Landing Lake:	Rogers	**Configuration:**	Ventral off; Ball-nose; X-20 IFDS Sharp rudder; 3rd skid		**Chase 5:**	F-104D	57-1315	Gentry	
Landing Time:	10:12:36.1								

Purpose: Altitude buildup; Lear Panel checkout; Boundary layer noise data; Horizontal tail loads data; (#25) Optical background experiment

Aborts: None

Aborts:

Notes: Tape 'q' read 80 psf higher than gauge; Landed with center stick

Program Flight #:	169			**Plan**	**Actual**	**NASA 1:**	Dana		
			Max Mach:	5.15	5.11	**B-52 - Pilots - LP:**	52-003	Doryland / Bowline	Russell
Flight ID:	1-67-112		**Max Altitude:**	250,000	257,500	**Take-Off Time:**	08:56		
X-15 (s/n)	56-6670	(67)	**Speed (mph):**	—	3,543	**Landing Time:**	10:35		
Flight Date:	25 Aug 66		**X-15 Flight Time:**	—	00:10:16.2	**B-52 Flight Time:**	01:39		
Pilot (flight #):	McKay	(28)							
			XLR99 (s/n):	—	107	**Chase 1:**	T-38A	59-1600	Adams
Launch Lake:	Delamar		**Powered Time (sec):**	84.5	83.4 (S.D.)	**Chase 2:**	F-104N	N811NA	Manke
Launch Time:	09:47:09.0		**Thrust (pct):**	100	100	**Chase 3:**	F-104D	57-1315	Smith
						Chase 4:	F-104A	56-0757	Knight
Landing Lake:	Rogers		**Configuration:**	Ventral off; Ball-nose; X-20 IFDS		**Chase 5:**			
Landing Time:	09:57:25.2			Tip pods					

Purpose: (#13) Micrometeorite collection experiment;
(#16) Pace transducer experiment;
(#17) MIT horizon definition phase II experiment

Notes: Telemetry lost after launch;
Inertial malfunction after launch;
The highest Mach number was achieved during descent from max altitude

Aborts: None

Program Flight #:	170			**Plan**	**Actual**	**NASA 1:**	Dana		
			Max Mach:	5.30	5.21	**B-52 - Pilots - LP:**	52-008	Doryland / Cotton	Peterson
Flight ID:	2-49-86		**Max Altitude:**	102,000	100,200	**Take-Off Time:**	09:01		
X-15 (s/n)	56-6671	(49 / 18)	**Speed (mph):**	—	3,543	**Landing Time:**	10:30		
Flight Date:	30 Aug 66		**X-15 Flight Time:**	—	00:08:57.9	**B-52 Flight Time:**	01:29		
Pilot (flight #):	Knight	(7)							
			XLR99 (s/n):	—	106	**Chase 1:**	F-104A	56-0743	Curtis
Launch Lake:	Mud		**Powered Time (sec):**	81.8	80.5 (B.O.)	**Chase 2:**	F-104N	N812NA	Manke
Launch Time:	09:50:53.0		**Thrust (pct):**	100	100	**Chase 3:**	F-104D	57-1316	Hover
						Chase 4:	F-104A	56-0755	Stroface
Landing Lake:	Rogers		**Configuration:**	Ventral on; Ball-nose		**Rover:**	F-104N	N811NA	Thompson
Landing Time:	09:59:50.9			Alternate pitot					

Purpose: Ventral on stability and control data;
MA-25S ablator tests;
Glass fog test
Base drag study;
(#27) Maurer camera experiment

Notes: Pitch and roll SAS drop-out;
First flight with Maurer camera on board;
Ventral chute deployed premature - ventral lost

Aborts: None

Program Flight #:	171			**Plan**	**Actual**	**NASA 1:**	Adams		
			Max Mach:	5.42	2.44	**B-52 - Pilots - LP:**	52-008	Doryland / Cotton	Russell
Flight ID:	1-68-113		**Max Altitude:**	243,000	73,200	**Take-Off Time:**	09:40		
X-15 (s/n)	56-6670	(68)	**Speed (mph):**	—	1,602	**Landing Time:**	11:40		
Flight Date:	08 Sep 66		**X-15 Flight Time:**	—	00:06:26.5	**B-52 Flight Time:**	02:00		
Pilot (flight #):	McKay	(29)							
			XLR99 (s/n):	—	107	**Chase 1:**	T-38A	59-1598	Curtis
Launch Lake:	Smith Ranch		**Powered Time (sec):**	85.5	45.5 (S.D)	**Chase 2:**	F-104N	N811NA	Manke
Launch Time:	10:37:24.0		**Thrust (pct):**	100	100	**Chase 3:**	F-104D	57-1316	Stroface
						Chase 4:	F-104A	56-0755	Gentry
Landing Lake:	Smith Ranch		**Configuration:**	Ventral off; Ball-nose; X-20 IFDS		**Rover:**	JF-104A	55-2961	Peterson
Landing Time:	10:43:50.5								

Purpose: (#17) MIT horizon definition phase II-1 experiment;
Electrical loads survey;
Horizontal stabilizer angle of attack investigation

Notes: Fuel line low indication caused a throttleback,
shutdown, and emergency landing at Smith Ranch Lake;
McKay's last X-15 flight

Aborts: None

Program Flight #:	172			**Plan**	**Actual**	**NASA 1:**	Knight		
			Max Mach:	5.10	5.12	**B-52 - Pilots - LP:**	52-003	Doryland / Cotton	Russell
Flight ID:	3-55-82		**Max Altitude:**	250,000	254,200	**Take-Off Time:**	11:11		
X-15 (s/n)	56-6672	(55)	**Speed (mph):**	—	3,586	**Landing Time:**	13:10		
Flight Date:	14 Sep 66		**X-15 Flight Time:**	—	00:08:58.6	**B-52 Flight Time:**	01:59		
Pilot (flight #):	Dana	(5)							
			XLR99 (s/n):	—	110	**Chase 1:**	T-38A	59-1598	Curtis
Launch Lake:	Delamar		**Powered Time (sec):**	77	79.3 (S.D.)	**Chase 2:**	JF-104A	55-2961	Manke
Launch Time:	12:00:14.0		**Thrust (pct):**	100	100	**Chase 3:**	F-104D	57-1316	Hover
						Chase 4:	F-104A	56-0763	Stroface
Landing Lake:	Rogers		**Configuration:**	Ventral off; Ball-nose; X-20 IFDS		**Rover:**	F-104N	N811NA	Peterson
Landing Time:	12:09:12.6			Tip pods; Sharp rudder; 3rd skid					

Purpose: Altitude buildup;
Lear Panel checkout;
(#3) UV exhaust plume experiment;
(#16) Pace transducer experiment;
(#29) Solar spectrum measurement experiment

Notes: First wing-tip pod flight on X-15-3;
Alert computer would not turn on (too cold);
Third skid did not deploy;
The highest Mach number was achieved during descent from max altitude

Aborts: 3-A-81 13 Sep 66 Blown fuse in new ARC-51 radio

Abort used NB-52A 52-003; Dana was the X-15 pilot for the abort

Program Flight #:	173	
Flight ID:	1-69-116	
X-15 (s/n)	56-6670	(69)
Flight Date:	06 Oct 66	
Pilot (flight #):	Adams	(1)
Launch Lake:	Hidden Hills	
Launch Time:	12:16:09.0	
Landing Lake:	Cuddeback	
Landing Time:	12:24:35.0	

	Plan	Actual
Max Mach:	4.00	3.00
Max Altitude:	74,000	75,400
Speed (mph):	—	1,977
X-15 Flight Time:	—	00:08:26.0
XLR99 (s/n):	—	107
Powered Time (sec):	129	89.9 (S.D.)
Thrust (pct):	90, 50	88, 52, 0
Configuration:	Ventral off; Ball-nose; X-20 IFDS	

NASA 1:	Knight		
B-52 - Pilots - LP:	52-003	Doryland / Cotton	Russell
Take-Off Time:	11:30		
Landing Time:	13:10		
B-52 Flight Time:	01:40		
Chase 1:	T-38A	59-1598	Sorlie
Chase 2:	F-104D	57-1316	Dana
Chase 3:	F-104A	56-0755	Gentry
Chase 4:			
Chase 5:			

Purpose: Pilot familiarization – Adam's first X-15 flight

Aborts:

—	22 Sep 66	Wet lakes uprange
1-A-114	28 Sep 66	Weather in launch area
—	29 Sep 66	Rain at Edwards
1-A-115	04 Oct 66	Cabin source pressure
—	05 Oct 66	Weather in launch area

Notes: Wet lakes forced planned altitude flight with Jack McKay to be changed to a pilot familiarization flight for Mike Adams; Ruptured fuel tank caused premature shutdown and landing at Cuddeback;

All aborts used NB-52A 52-003; Adams was the X-15 pilot for all aborts

---

Program Flight #:	174	
Flight ID:	3-56-83	
X-15 (s/n)	56-6672	(56)
Flight Date:	01 Nov 66	
Pilot (flight #):	Dana	(6)
Launch Lake:	Smith Ranch	
Launch Time:	13:24:47.0	
Landing Lake:	Rogers	
Landing Time:	13:35:30.8	

	Plan	Actual
Max Mach:	5.27	5.46
Max Altitude:	267,000	306,900
Speed (mph):	—	3,750
X-15 Flight Time:	—	00:10:43.8
XLR99 (s/n):	—	110
Powered Time (sec):	81	82.8 (S.D.)
Thrust (pct):	100	100
Configuration:	Ventral off; Ball-nose; X-20 IFDS Tip pods; Sharp rudder; 3rd skid	

NASA 1:	Knight		
B-52 - Pilots - LP:	52-003	Doryland / Reschke	Russell
Take-Off Time:	12:23		
Landing Time:	14:23		
B-52 Flight Time:	01:59		
Chase 1:	T-38A	59-1598	Adams
Chase 2:	F-104N	N812NA	Peterson
Chase 3:	F-104D	57-1316	Stroface
Chase 4:	F-104A	56-0755	Gentry
Rover:	F-104N	N811NA	Manke

Purpose: Precision attitude checkout;
(#13) Micrometeorite collection experiment;
(#19) Sky brightness experiment;
(#25) Optical background experiment

Aborts:

—	31 Oct 66	Malfunction of PAI

Notes: Last X-15 flight above 300,000 feet; Micrometeorite collector did not cycle; The highest Mach number was achieved during descent from max altitude; Overshot altitude by 39,900 feet

Since Dana was a NASA pilot, he did not get astronaut wings for a flight above 50 miles (the NASA standard was 62 miles)

Program Flight #:	175	
Flight ID:	2-50-89	
X-15 (s/n)	56-6671	(50 / 19)
Flight Date:	18 Nov 66	
Pilot (flight #):	Knight	(8)
Launch Lake:	Mud	
Launch Time:	13:24:54.0	
Landing Lake:	Rogers	
Landing Time:	13:33:20.8	

	Plan	Actual
Max Mach:	6.00	6.33
Max Altitude:	100,000	98,900
Speed (mph):	—	4,250
X-15 Flight Time:	—	00:08:26.8
XLR99 (s/n):	—	106
Powered Time (sec):	132	136.4 (S.D.)
Thrust (pct):	100	100
Configuration:	Ventral on; Ball-nose; Eyelid Tanks; Alternate pitot	

NASA 1:	Dana		
B-52 - Pilots - LP:	52-008	Fulton / Cotton	Russell
Take-Off Time:	12:29		
Landing Time:	14:10		
B-52 Flight Time:	01:40		
Chase 1:	T-38A		Adams
Chase 2:	F-104A	56-0802	Peterson
Chase 3:	F-104		Curtis
Chase 4:	F-104N	N812NA	McKay
Chase 5:	F-104		Gentry

Purpose: Full tanks handling qualities;
(#27) Maurer camera experiment

Aborts:

2-A-87	07 Oct 66	Telemetry malfunction
2-A-88	19 Oct 66	MH3 low tank pressure
—	20 Oct 66	Overcast skies at Edwards
—	08 Nov 66	Weather at Edwards

Notes: X-15-3 aborted a flight earlier in the day; Tanks dropped at Mach 2.27, 69,700 feet, q=340 psf, 3.5° alpha; Recovered; Fuel line low light - throttled back, then to 100%; World absolute speed record

2-A-87 used NB-52B 52-008; Knight was the X-15 pilot
2-A-88 used NB-52A 52-003; Knight was the X-15 pilot

Program Flight #:	176	
Flight ID:	3-57-86	
X-15 (s/n)	56-6672	(57)
Flight Date:	29 Nov 66	
Pilot (flight #):	Adams	(2)
Launch Lake:	Hidden Hills	
Launch Time:	11:38:49.0	
Landing Lake:	Rogers	
Landing Time:	11:46:45.2	

	Plan	Actual
Max Mach:	4.50	4.65
Max Altitude:	95,000	92,000
Speed (mph):	—	3,120
X-15 Flight Time:	—	00:07:56.2
XLR99 (s/n):	—	110
Powered Time (sec):	98	97.9 (S.D.)
Thrust (pct):	75	75
Configuration:	Ventral off; Ball-nose; X-20 IFDS Tip pods; Sharp rudder; 3rd skid	

NASA 1:	McKay		
B-52 - Pilots - LP:	52-003	Fulton / Cotton	Russell
Take-Off Time:	10:55		
Landing Time:	12:25		
B-52 Flight Time:	01:30		
Chase 1:	T-38A	59-1600	Knight
Chase 2:	F-104N	N811NA	Manke
Chase 3:	F-104A	56-0763	Gentry
Chase 4:			
Chase 5:			

Purpose: Pilot checkout;
Tip pod accelerometer data;
(#16) Pace transducer experiment;

Aborts:

3-A-84	18 Nov 66	Loss of Hadley transformer (Dana)
3-A-85	23 Nov 66	APU bearing temperatures too high

Notes: No radio from launch to Cuddeback

3-A-84 used NB-52A 52-003; Dana was the X-15 pilot
3-A-85 used NB-52A 52-003; Adams was the X-15 pilot

Program Flight #:	177			Plan	Actual	**NASA 1:**	McKay		
			Max Mach:	5.50	5.59	**B-52 - Pilots - LP:**	52-003	Cotton / Reschke	Russell
Flight ID:	1-70-119		**Max Altitude:**	130,000	133,100	**Take-Off Time:**	08:58		
X-15 (s/n)	56-6670	(70)	**Speed (mph):**	—	3,822	**Landing Time:**	10:15		
Flight Date:	22 Mar 67		**X-15 Flight Time:**	—	00:09:29.5	**B-52 Flight Time:**	01:17		
Pilot (flight #):	Adams	(3)							
			XLR99 (s/n):	—	108	**Chase 1:**	T-38A	59-1601	Gentry
Launch Lake:	Mud		**Powered Time (sec):**	82.5	79.7 (S.D.)	**Chase 2:**	JF-104A	55-2961	Peterson
Launch Time:	09:52:56.0		**Thrust (pct):**	100	100	**Chase 3:**	F-104A	56-0763	Evenson
						Chase 4:	F-104A	56-0755	Knight
Landing Lake:	Rogers		**Configuration:**	Ventral off; Ball-nose; X-20 IFDS		**Chase 5:**	F-4C	63-7651	Hoag
Landing Time:	10:02:25.5			3rd skid; PAI					

Purpose: Electrical loads evaluation;
Third skid checkout;
Sonic boom study at Mach 5.5,

Aborts: 1-A-117 15 Mar 67 Weather
1-A-118 21 Mar 67 Inertial system failure

Notes: Cockpit pressure lost during boost; Intertials failed after shutdown; Roll out of trim

Additional Chase:

Chase 6:	F-104A	56-0817	Cuthill
Rover:	F-104N	N812NA	Manke

All aborts used NB-52A 52-003; Adams was the X-15 pilot for all aborts

Program Flight #:	178			Plan	Actual	**NASA 1:**	Adams		
			Max Mach:	1.65	1.80	**B-52 - Pilots - LP:**	52-008	Cotton / Bowline	Russell
Flight ID:	3-58-87		**Max Altitude:**	71,000	53,400	**Take-Off Time:**	10:17		
X-15 (s/n)	56-6672	(58)	**Speed (mph):**	—	1,163	**Landing Time:**	12:09		
Flight Date:	26 Apr 67		**X-15 Flight Time:**	—	00:05:16.8	**B-52 Flight Time:**	01:52		
Pilot (flight #):	Dana	(7)							
			XLR99 (s/n):	—	103	**Chase 1:**	T-38A	59-1598	Gentry
Launch Lake:	Silver		**Powered Time (sec):**	103	23.2 (S.D.)	**Chase 2:**	JF-104A	55-2961	Manke
Launch Time:	11:18:36.0		**Thrust (pct):**	100	100	**Chase 3:**	F-104A	56-0817	Knight
						Chase 4:			
Landing Lake:	Silver		**Configuration:**	Ventral off; Ball-nose; X-20 IFDS		**Rover:**	F-104N	N811NA	Petersen
Landing Time:	11:23:52.8			Tip pods; Sharp rudder; 3rd skid					

Purpose: Boost guidance checkout;
Cold wall heat transfer panel;
Horizontal tail loads data;
PCM system checkout;
Somic boom study

Aborts: None

Notes: Frozen ball-nose required a 10 minute turn
prior to launch;
Premature shutdown due to fuel line low indication
(frozen pressure sensing line);
First flight with PCM telemetry system;
Cold wall panel

Program Flight #:	179			Plan	Actual	**NASA 1:**	McKay		
			Max Mach:	5.20	5.44	**B-52 - Pilots - LP:**	52-003	Cotton / Bowline	Russell
Flight ID:	1-71-121		**Max Altitude:**	180,000	167,200	**Take-Off Time:**	08:31		
X-15 (s/n)	56-6670	(71)	**Speed (mph):**	—	3,720	**Landing Time:**	10:30		
Flight Date:	28 Apr 67		**X-15 Flight Time:**	—	00:09:15.9	**B-52 Flight Time:**	01:58		
Pilot (flight #):	Adams	(4)							
			XLR99 (s/n):	—	104	**Chase 1:**	T-38A	59-1601	Sorlie
Launch Lake:	Delamar		**Powered Time (sec):**	81	82.0 (S.D.)	**Chase 2:**	F-104N	N812NA	Manke
Launch Time:	09:23:41.0		**Thrust (pct):**	100	100	**Chase 3:**	F-104D	57-1316	Evenson
						Chase 4:	F-104A	56-0763	Cuthill
Landing Lake:	Rogers		**Configuration:**	Ventral off; Ball-nose; X-20 IFDS		**Chase 5:**	JF-104A	55-2961	Jackson
Landing Time:	09:32:56.9			3rd skid; PAI					

Purpose: Third skid checkout;
IRIG timer checkout;
(#17) MIT horizon definition phase II-1 experiment;
(#20) WTR experiment checkout;
Sonic boom study

Aborts: 1-A-120 20 Apr 67 Weather in launch area

Notes: Pitch attitude malfunction;
Inertial velocity erratic

Additional Chase:

Rover:	F-104N	N811NA	Dana

Abort used NB-52A 52-003; Adams was the X-15 pilot for the abort

Program Flight #:	180			Plan	Actual	**NASA 1:**	McKay		
			Max Mach:	4.50	4.75	**B-52 - Pilots - LP:**	52-008	Cotton / Reschke	Russell
Flight ID:	2-51-92		**Max Altitude:**	90,000	97,600	**Take-Off Time:**	11:43		
X-15 (s/n)	56-6671	(51 / 20)	**Speed (mph):**	—	3,193	**Landing Time:**	12:59		
Flight Date:	08 May 67		**X-15 Flight Time:**	—	00:08:26.6	**B-52 Flight Time:**	01:15		
Pilot (flight #):	Knight	(9)							
			XLR99 (s/n):	—	109	**Chase 1:**	T-38A	59-1601	Sorlie
Launch Lake:	Hidden Hills		**Powered Time (sec):**	74	76.9 (S.D.)	**Chase 2:**	F-104D	57-1315	Evenson
Launch Time:	12:27:28.0		**Thrust (pct):**	100	100	**Chase 3:**	F-104N	N811NA	Dana
						Chase 4:	F-104A	56-0763	Adams
Landing Lake:	Rogers		**Configuration:**	Ventral off; Ball-nose; Eyelid		**Chase 5:**			
Landing Time:	12:35:54.6			Alternate pitot; Dummy ramjet					

Purpose: Stability and control data with dummy ramjet;
Canopy eyelid checkout;
Ramjet sepration characteristics;
MA-25S ablator test

Aborts: 2-C-90 22 Dec 66 Scheduled captive with ramjet
2-A-91 05 May 67 Weather in launch area

Notes: Three-axis transients when eyelid opened;
Ramjet chute came off but ramjet was refurbishable;
Left window fogged when eyelid opened in pattern;
20-degree nose cone on dummy ramjet

Captive flight used NB-52A 52-003; Knight was the X-15 pilot
Abort used NB-52B 52-008; Knight was the X-15 pilot

Program Flight #:	181			Plan	Actual	NASA 1:	Adams		
			Max Mach:	4.65	4.80	B-52 - Pilots - LP:	52-003	Reschke / Cotton	Russell
Flight ID:	3-59-89		Max Altitude:	71,000	71,100	Take-Off Time:	09:55		
X-15 (s/n)	56-6672	(59)	Speed (mph):	—	3,177	Landing Time:	11:22		
Flight Date:	17 May 67		X-15 Flight Time:	—	00:06:55.6	B-52 Flight Time:	01:27		
Pilot (flight #):	Dana	(8)							
			XLR99 (s/n):	—	103	Chase 1:	T-38A	59-1601	Sorlie
Launch Lake:	Silver		Powered Time (sec):	103	96.1 (B.O.)	Chase 2:	F-104N	N811NA	Manke
Launch Time:	10:43:45.0		Thrust (pct):	100, 50	100, 50	Chase 3:	F-104D	57-1316	Evenson
						Chase 4:	F-104A	56-0817	Cuthill
Landing Lake:	Rogers		Configuration:	Ventral off; Ball-nose; X-20 IFDS		Rover:	F-104N	N812NA	McKay
Landing Time:	10:50:40.6			Tip pods; Sharp rudder; 3rd skid					

Purpose: Boost guidance checkout; Cold wall heat transfer panel; Horizontal tail loads data; PCM system checkout; Somic boom study

Notes: Cold-wall panel ejected at q=1,500 psf - caused a severe oscillation in upper vertical tail

Aborts: 3-A-88 12 May 67 Ball-nose failure

Abort used NB-52A 52-003; Dana was the X-15 pilot for the abort

Program Flight #:	182			Plan	Actual	NASA 1:	Knight		
			Max Mach:	5.15	5.14	B-52 - Pilots - LP:	52-003	Cotton / Reschke	Russell
Flight ID:	1-72-125		Max Altitude:	220,000	229,300	Take-Off Time:	10:10		
X-15 (s/n)	56-6670	(72)	Speed (mph):	—	3,606	Landing Time:	12:00		
Flight Date:	15 Jun 67		X-15 Flight Time:	—	00:09:11.0	B-52 Flight Time:	01:50		
Pilot (flight #):	Adams	(5)							
			XLR99 (s/n):	—	104	Chase 1:	T-38A	59-1600	Gentry
Launch Lake:	Delamar		Powered Time (sec):	81	81.4 (S.D.)	Chase 2:	F-104N	N812NA	Manke
Launch Time:	11:10:07.0		Thrust (pct):	100	100	Chase 3:	F-104A	56-0817	Davey
						Chase 4:	F-104A	56-0744	Hoag
Landing Lake:	Rogers		Configuration:	Ventral off; Ball-nose; X-20 IFDS		Chase 5:	F-4A	145313	Jackson
Landing Time:	11:19:18.0			3rd skid; PAI					

Purpose: IRIG timer checkout; (#17) MIT horizon definition phase II-1 experiment; (#20) WTR experiment

Notes: Stick kicker inoperative; The highest Mach number was achieved during descent from max altitude

Additional Chase:
Rover: F-104N N811NA Dana

Aborts:
1-A-122 25 May 67 Inertial system failure
1-A-123 01 Jun 67 Inertial system failure
1-A-124 14 Jun 67 X-15 radio failure

All aborts used NB-52A 52-003; Adams was the X-15 pilot for all aborts

Program Flight #:	183			Plan	Actual	NASA 1:	McKay		
			Max Mach:	5.30	5.34	B-52 - Pilots - LP:	52-008	Cotton / Sturmthal	Russell
Flight ID:	3-60-90		Max Altitude:	82,000	82,200	Take-Off Time:	13:55		
X-15 (s/n)	56-6672	(60)	Speed (mph):	—	3,611	Landing Time:	15:38		
Flight Date:	22 Jun 67		X-15 Flight Time:	—	00:07:06.5	B-52 Flight Time:	01:42		
Pilot (flight #):	Dana	(9)							
			XLR99 (s/n):	—	103	Chase 1:	T-38A	59-1598	Knight
Launch Lake:	Hidden Hills		Powered Time (sec):	95	93.2 (B.O.)	Chase 2:	F-104N	N811NA	Manke
Launch Time:	14:55:40.0		Thrust (pct):	100, 50	100	Chase 3:	F-104B	57-1303	Krier
						Chase 4:	F-104A	56-0817	Gentry
Landing Lake:	Rogers		Configuration:	Ventral off; Ball-nose; X-20 IFDS		Chase 5:			
Landing Time:	15:02:46.5			Tip pods; Sharp rudder; 3rd skid					

Purpose: Boost guidance checkout; Cold wall heat transfer panel; Somic boom study

Notes: Cold wall panel ejected at q=1,200 psf - severe oscillations; Window shade would not retract; Buffet at 10 degrees pull-up at Mach 3

Aborts: — 20 Jun 67 PCM failure prio to taxi

Program Flight #:	184			Plan	Actual	NASA 1:	Adams		
			Max Mach:	5.70	4.17	B-52 - Pilots - LP:	52-008	Reschke / Sturmthal	Russell
Flight ID:	1-73-126		Max Altitude:	250,000	173,000	Take-Off Time:	10:22		
X-15 (s/n)	56-6670	(73)	Speed (mph):	—	2,870	Landing Time:	12:00		
Flight Date:	29 Jun 67		X-15 Flight Time:	—	00:10:07.0	B-52 Flight Time:	01:38		
Pilot (flight #):	Knight	(10)							
			XLR99 (s/n):	—	108	Chase 1:	T-38A	59-1598	Cuthill
Launch Lake:	Smith Ranch		Powered Time (sec):	87	67.6 (S.D.)	Chase 2:	F-104N	N812NA	Dana
Launch Time:	11:28:23.0		Thrust (pct):	100	100	Chase 3:	F-104N	N811NA	Jackson
						Chase 4:	F-104A	56-0763	Evenson
Landing Lake:	Mud		Configuration:	Ventral off; Ball-nose; X-20 IFDS		Chase 5:	F-104D	57-1314	Hoag / Davey
Landing Time:	11:38:30.0			3rd skid					

Purpose: Horizontal stabilizer angle of attack data; Yaw ASAS checkout; (#17) MIT horizon definition phase II-1 experiment; (#20) WTR experiment

Notes: Total power failure going through 107,000 feet both APUs shut down (loss of all electrics and hydraulics); One APU restarted; Emergency landing at Mud Lake (should have landed at Grapevine per energy)

Aborts: None

Program Flight #:	185			**Plan**	**Actual**	**NASA 1:**	Knight		
			Max Mach:	5.30	5.44	**B-52 - Pilots - LP:**	52-008	Cotton / Fulton	Russell
Flight ID:	3-61-91		**Max Altitude:**	82,000	84,300	**Take-Off Time:**	09:19		
X-15 (s/n)	56-6672	(61)	**Speed (mph):**	—	3,693	**Landing Time:**	10:42		
Flight Date:	20 Jul 67		**X-15 Flight Time:**	—	00:07:36.5	**B-52 Flight Time:**	01:23		
Pilot (flight #):	Dana	(10)							
			XLR99 (s/n):	—	103	**Chase 1:**	T-38A		Adams
Launch Lake:	Hidden Hills		**Powered Time (sec):**	95	92.1 (B.O.)	**Chase 2:**	F-104N	N812NA	Krier
Launch Time:	10:10:26.0		**Thrust (pct):**	100, 50	100	**Chase 3:**	F-104		Davey
						Chase 4:			
Landing Lake:	Rogers		**Configuration:**	Ventral off; Ball-nose; X-20 IFDS		**Rover:**	F-104N	N811NA	Manke
Landing Time:	10:18:02.5			Tip pods; Sharp rudder; 3rd skid					

Purpose: Boost guidance checkout;
Cold wall heat transfer panel;
Horizontal tail loads data;
PCM system checkout

Notes: Alert computer did not operate;
Cold wall panel ejected at q=1,000 psf

Aborts: None

Program Flight #:	186			**Plan**	**Actual**	**NASA 1:**	Dana		
			Max Mach:	5.10	4.94	**B-52 - Pilots - LP:**	52-008	Cotton / Reschke	Russell
Flight ID:	2-52-96		**Max Altitude:**	90,000	91,000	**Take-Off Time:**	10:00		
X-15 (s/n)	56-6671	(52 / 21)	**Speed (mph):**	—	3,368	**Landing Time:**	11:30		
Flight Date:	21 Aug 67		**X-15 Flight Time:**	—	00:07:39.3	**B-52 Flight Time:**	01:29		
Pilot (flight #):	Knight	(11)							
			XLR99 (s/n):	—	110	**Chase 1:**	T-38A	57-1598	Cuthill
Launch Lake:	Hidden Hills		**Powered Time (sec):**	85	82.2 (B.O.)	**Chase 2:**	F-104D	57-1314	Gentry
Launch Time:	10:58:52.0		**Thrust (pct):**	100	100	**Chase 3:**	F-104A	56-0748	Manke
						Chase 4:	F-104D	57-1332	Davey
Landing Lake:	Rogers		**Configuration:**	Ventral off; Ball-nose; Eyelid		**Chase 5:**	F-104A	56-0755	Adams
Landing Time:	11:06:31.3			Ablator; Dummy ramjet					

Purpose: Stability and control data with dummy ramjet;
MA-25S full ablator test;
(#27) Hycon phase II camera experiment

Aborts:
2-C-93 07 Aug 67 Scheduled captive flight (with ext. tanks)
2-A-94 11 Aug 67 LN2 leak in pylon
2-A-95 16 Aug 67 #2 APU source pressure loss

Notes: First flight with full ablative coating; No tanks;
Forward quarter of window smeared due to ablative;
Ramjet ejected too close to ground - refurbished;
20-degree nose cone on dummy ramjet

Scheduled captive flight used NB-52B 52-008; Knight was X-15 pilot
Both aborts used NB-52B 52-008; Knight was the X-15 pilot for both aborts

Program Flight #:	187			**Plan**	**Actual**	**NASA 1:**	Dana		
			Max Mach:	6.00	4.63	**B-52 - Pilots - LP:**	52-003	Bowline / Reschke	Dustin
Flight ID:	3-62-92		**Max Altitude:**	100,000	84,400	**Take-Off Time:**	12:35		
X-15 (s/n)	56-6672	(62)	**Speed (mph):**	—	3,115	**Landing Time:**	14:01		
Flight Date:	25 Aug 67		**X-15 Flight Time:**	—	00:07:37.0	**B-52 Flight Time:**	01:26		
Pilot (flight #):	Adams	(6)							
			XLR99 (s/n):	—	103	**Chase 1:**	T-38A	59-1598	Gentry
Launch Lake:	Hidden Hills		**Powered Time (sec):**	132	71.3 (S.D.)	**Chase 2:**	F-104A	56-0755	Jackson
Launch Time:	13:29:35.0		**Thrust (pct):**	100	100	**Chase 3:**	F-104		Knight
						Chase 4:			
Landing Lake:	Rogers		**Configuration:**	Ventral off; Ball-nose; X-20 IFDS		**Rover:**	F-104N	N811NA	Krier
Landing Time:	13:37:12.0			Sharp rudder; 3rd skid					

Purpose: Cold wall heat transfer panel;
Horizontal tail loads data;
Boundary layer noise data

Notes: Engine relight required at 16 seconds;
Inertials and Ball-nose failed 10 seconds prior to
touchdown (circuit breaker)

Aborts: None

Program Flight #:	188			**Plan**	**Actual**	**NASA 1:**	Dana		
			Max Mach:	6.50	6.70	**B-52 - Pilots - LP:**	52-008	Cotton / Reschke	Russell
Flight ID:	2-53-97		**Max Altitude:**	100,000	102,100	**Take-Off Time:**	13:31		
X-15 (s/n)	56-6671	(53 / 22)	**Speed (mph):**	—	4,520	**Landing Time:**	15:20		
Flight Date:	03 Oct 67		**X-15 Flight Time:**	—	00:08:12.1	**B-52 Flight Time:**	01:48		
Pilot (flight #):	Knight	(12)							
			XLR99 (s/n):	—	110	**Chase 1:**	T-38A	59-1600	Cuthill
Launch Lake:	Mud		**Powered Time (sec):**	141	140.7 (S.D.)	**Chase 2:**	F-104D	57-1314	Twinting
Launch Time:	14:32:11.0		**Thrust (pct):**	100	100	**Chase 3:**	F-104B	57-1303	Krier
						Chase 4:	F-104A	56-0748	Adams
Landing Lake:	Rogers		**Configuration:**	Ventral off; Ball-nose; Eyelid		**Rover:**	F-104N	N812NA	Jackson
Landing Time:	14:40:23.1			Tanks; Ablator; Dummy ramjet					

Purpose: MA-25S full ablator tests;
Ramjet local flow tests;
Stability and control with ramjet;
Fluidic temperaure probe test

Notes: Fastest flight of X-15 program;
Last flight of X-15A-2 aircraft;
Extensive thermal damage to pylon and ramjet;
Unofficial world's speed record for class
Tanks dropped at Mach 2.4, 72,300 feet, q=287 psf, 4.4° alpha;
Eyelid opened at Mach 1.6;
40-degree nose cone on dummy ramjet

Aborts: None

Program Flight #:	**189**			**Plan**	**Actual**	**NASA 1:**	Adams		
			Max Mach:	5.50	5.53	**B-52 - Pilots - LP:**	52-003	Cotton / Reschke	Dustin
Flight ID:	3-63-94		**Max Altitude:**	130,000	251,100	**Take-Off Time:**	09:12		
X-15 (s/n):	56-6672	(63)	**Speed (mph):**	—	3,897	**Landing Time:**	11:03		
Flight Date:	04 Oct 67		**X-15 Flight Time:**	—	00:10:47.5	**B-52 Flight Time:**	01:51		
Pilot (flight #):	Dana	(11)							
			XLR99 (s/n):	—	103	**Chase 1:**	T-38A		Cuthill
Launch Lake:	Smith Ranch		**Powered Time (sec):**	82.5	84.7 (B.O.)	**Chase 2:**	F-104N	N812NA	Krier
Launch Time:	10:16:35.0		**Thrust (pct):**	100	100	**Chase 3:**	F-104		Gentry
						Chase 4:	JF-104A	55-2961	Manke
Landing Lake:	Rogers		**Configuration:**	Ventral off; Ball-nose; X-20 IFDS		**Chase 5:**			
Landing Time:	10:27:22.5			Tip pods; Sharp rudder; 3rd skid					

Purpose: (#3) UV exhaust plume experiment;
(#13) Micrometeorite collection experiment;
(#14) Ames boost guidance;
(#29) Solar spectrum measurement experiment

Notes: Pilot's oxygen low light in pattern;
Micrometeorite experiment did not retract;
Inertials failed after shutdown;
The highest Mach number was achieved during descent from max altitude

Aborts: 3-A-93 22 Sep 67 Weather at launch lake — Abort used NB-52B 52-008; Dana was the X-15 pilot for the abort

Program Flight #:	**190**			**Plan**	**Actual**	**NASA 1:**	Dana		
			Max Mach:	5.60	5.53	**B-52 - Pilots - LP:**	52-008	Reschke / Miller	Dustin
Flight ID:	3-64-95		**Max Altitude:**	273,000	280,500	**Take-Off Time:**	08:41		
X-15 (s/n):	56-6672	(64)	**Speed (mph):**	—	3,869	**Landing Time:**	10:28		
Flight Date:	17 Oct 67		**X-15 Flight Time:**	—	00:10:06.4	**B-52 Flight Time:**	01:46		
Pilot (flight #):	Knight	(13)							
			XLR99 (s/n):	—	103	**Chase 1:**	T-38A		Cuthill
Launch Lake:	Smith Ranch		**Powered Time (sec):**	84.4	84.2 (B.O.)	**Chase 2:**	F-104		Twinting
Launch Time:	09:38:36.0		**Thrust (pct):**	100	100	**Chase 3:**	F-104		Gentry
						Chase 4:	F-104		Adams
Landing Lake:	Rogers		**Configuration:**	Ventral off; Ball-nose; X-20 IFDS		**Rover:**	F-104N	N812NA	Krier
Landing Time:	09:48:42.4			Tip pods; Sharp rudder; 3rd skid					

Purpose: (#3) UV exhaust plume experiment;
(#13) Micrometeorite collection experiment;
(#14) Ames boost guidance;
(#29) Solar spectrum measurement experiment

Notes: Third skid did not deploy;
The highest Mach number was achieved during descent from max altitude;
Knight's Astronaut qualification flight.

Aborts: None

Program Flight #:	**191**			**Plan**	**Actual**	**NASA 1:**	Knight		
			Max Mach:	5.10	5.20	**B-52 - Pilots - LP:**	52-008	Cotton / Miller	Russell
Flight ID:	3-65-97		**Max Altitude:**	250,000	266,000	**Take-Off Time:**	09:13		
X-15 (s/n):	56-6672	(65)	**Speed (mph):**	—	3,570	**Landing Time:**	11:25		
Flight Date:	15 Nov 67		**X-15 Flight Time:**	—	00:04:50.1	**B-52 Flight Time:**	02:12		
Pilot (flight #):	Adams	(7)							
			XLR99 (s/n):	—	111	**Chase 1:**	T-38A		Cuthill
Launch Lake:	Delamar		**Powered Time (sec):**	79	82.3 (S.D.)	**Chase 2:**	F-104N	N812NA	Jackson
Launch Time:	10:30:07.4		**Thrust (pct):**	100	100	**Chase 3:**	F-104N	N811NA	Dana
						Chase 4:	F-104		Twinting
Landing Lake:	N/A		**Configuration:**	Ventral off; Ball-nose; X-20 IFDS		**Chase 5:**			
Lost Telemetry:	10:34:57.5			Tip pods; Sharp rudder; 3rd skid					

Purpose: (#3) UV exhaust plume experiment;
(#13) Micrometeorite collection experiment;
(#14) Ames boost guidance;
(#29) Solar spectrum measurement experiment;
Saturn insulation

Notes: Inertial malfunction, damper malfunction, lack of proper response to heading error caused uncontrolled gyrations, aircraft broke up and crashed near Red Mountain; only fatality of program;
Adams posthumously awarded Astronaut Wings

Aborts: 3-A-96 31 Oct 67 Engine would not go into igniter idle — Abort used NB-52B 52-008; Adams was the X-15 pilot for the abort

Program Flight #:	**192**			**Plan**	**Actual**	**NASA 1:**	Manke		
			Max Mach:	4.10	4.36	**B-52 - Pilots - LP:**	52-008	Cotton / Stroup	Dustin
Flight ID:	1-74-130		**Max Altitude:**	106,000	104,500	**Take-Off Time:**	10:34		
X-15 (s/n):	56-6670	(74)	**Speed (mph):**	—	2,878	**Landing Time:**	11:55		
Flight Date:	01 Mar 68		**X-15 Flight Time:**	—	00:07:34.7	**B-52 Flight Time:**	01:21		
Pilot (flight #):	Dana	(12)							
			XLR99 (s/n):	—	109	**Chase 1:**	T-38A	59-1601	Twinting
Launch Lake:	Hidden Hills		**Powered Time (sec):**	66	65.6 (S.D.)	**Chase 2:**	F-104N	N812NA	Krier
Launch Time:	11:30:05.0		**Thrust (pct):**	100	100	**Chase 3:**	F-104D	57-1316	Knight
						Chase 4:	F-104A	56-0748	Hoag
Landing Lake:	Rogers		**Configuration:**	Ventral off; Ball-nose; X-20 IFDS		**Chase 5:**	F-104N	N811NA	Jackson
Landing Time:	11:37:39.7			3rd skid					

Purpose: Aircraft systems and yaw ASAS checkout;
(#17) MIT horizon definition phase II-1 experiment;
(#20) WTR experiment

Notes: g-suit grabbed at 1.5-g during pattern;
Saturn ablative evaluation

Aborts:
1-C-127 06 Feb 68 Scheduled captive — Captive flight used NB-52B 52-008; Dana was the X-15 pilot
1-A-128 07 Feb 68 Cabin pressurization and weather
1-A-129 27 Feb 68 SAS failure — Both aborts used NB-52B 52-008; Dana was the X-15 pilot for both aborts

Program Flight #:	193
Flight ID:	1-75-133
X-15 (s/n):	56-6670 (75)
Flight Date:	04 Apr 68
Pilot (flight #):	Dana (13)
Launch Lake:	Delamar
Launch Time:	10:03:46.0
Landing Lake:	Rogers
Landing Time:	10:13:08.8

	Plan	Actual
Max Mach:	5.00	5.27
Max Altitude:	180,000	187,500
Speed (mph):	—	3,610
X-15 Flight Time:	—	00:09:22.8
XLR99 (s/n):	—	109
Powered Time (sec):	79	78.8 (S.D.)
Thrust (pct):	100	100

Configuration: Ventral off; Ball-nose; X-20 IFDS Tip pods; 3rd skid

NASA 1:	Manke		
B-52 - Pilots - LP:	52-008	Cotton / Sturmthal	Russell
Take-Off Time:	08:29		
Landing Time:	10:43		
B-52 Flight Time:	02:13		
Chase 1:	T-38A	59-1598	Cuthill
Chase 2:	F-104N	N812NA	Jackson
Chase 3:	F-104A	56-0748	Smith
Chase 4:	F-104A	56-0817	Hoag
Chase 5:	F-104N	N811NA	Fulton

Purpose: Saturn ablatives on upper speed brakes;
Tip pod camera;
(#20) WTR experiment;
(#31) Fixed alpha nose experiment

Aborts:
1-A-131 28 Mar 68 Radio and source pressure
1-A-132 03 Apr 68 Weather at Delamar

Notes: First flight with second set of wing-tip pods installed;
Emergency retract of WTR experiment

All aborts used NB-52B 52-008; Dana was the X-15 pilot for all aborts

Program Flight #:	194
Flight ID:	1-76-134
X-15 (s/n):	56-6670 (76)
Flight Date:	26 Apr 68
Pilot (flight #):	Knight (14)
Launch Lake:	Delamar
Launch Time:	11:51:49.8
Landing Lake:	Rogers
Landing Time:	12:01:06.9

	Plan	Actual
Max Mach:	5.10	5.05
Max Altitude:	100,000	209,600
Speed (mph):	—	3,545
X-15 Flight Time:	—	00:09:17.1
XLR99 (s/n):	—	108
Powered Time (sec):	80	81.5 (S.D.)
Thrust (pct):	100	100

Configuration: Ventral off; Ball-nose; X-20 IFDS Tip pods; 3rd skid

NASA 1:	Dana		
B-52 - Pilots - LP:	52-008	Sturmthal / Reschke	Dustin
Take-Off Time:	10:49		
Landing Time:	12:45		
B-52 Flight Time:	01:55		
Chase 1:	F5D-1	142350 (802)	Manke
Chase 2:	F-104A	56-0790	Krier
Chase 3:	F-104D	57-1316	Livingston
Chase 4:	F-104D	57-1314	Gentry
Rover:	F-104N	N811NA	Fulton

Purpose: Saturn (2nd stage) ablatives on upper speed brakes;
(#17) MIT horizon definition phase II-2 experiment;
(#31) Fixed alpha nose experiment

Aborts: None

Notes: Low alpha, high-q rotation performed with 10°
speed brakes during boost for Saturn experiment

Program Flight #:	195
Flight ID:	1-77-136
X-15 (s/n):	56-6670 (77)
Flight Date:	12 Jun 68
Pilot (flight #):	Dana (14)
Launch Lake:	Smith Ranch
Launch Time:	08:31:01.0
Landing Lake:	Rogers
Landing Time:	08:42:33.9

	Plan	Actual
Max Mach:	5.40	5.15
Max Altitude:	222,000	220,100
Speed (mph):	—	3,563
X-15 Flight Time:	—	00:11:32.9
XLR99 (s/n):	—	108
Powered Time (sec):	84.6	83.4 (S.D.)
Thrust (pct):	100	100

Configuration: Ventral off; Ball-nose; X-20 IFDS Tip pods; 3rd skid

NASA 1:	Knight		
B-52 - Pilots - LP:	52-008	Reschke / Cotton	Russell
Take-Off Time:	07:19		
Landing Time:	09:24		
B-52 Flight Time:	02:05		
Chase 1:	T-38A	59-1598	Gentry
Chase 2:	F5D-1	142350 (802)	Manke
Chase 3:	F-104N	N811NA	Jackson
Chase 4:	F-104A	56-0755	Hoag
Rover:	F-104N	N812NA	Fulton

Purpose: Saturn ablatives on lower speed brakes;
(#17) MIT horizon definition phase II-2 experiment;
(#20) WTR experiment;
(#31) Fixed alpha nose experiment

Aborts: 1-A-135 23 May 68 Malfunction of second stage ignitor

Notes: Emergency retract of WTR experiment

Abort used NB-52B 52-008; Dana was the X-15 pilot for the abort

Program Flight #:	196
Flight ID:	1-78-138
X-15 (s/n):	56-6670 (78)
Flight Date:	16 Jul 68
Pilot (flight #):	Knight (15)
Launch Lake:	Railroad
Launch Time:	15:23:06.7
Landing Lake:	Rogers
Landing Time:	15:32:49.3

	Plan	Actual
Max Mach:	4.95	4.79
Max Altitude:	250,000	221,500
Speed (mph):	—	3,382
X-15 Flight Time:	—	00:09:42.6
XLR99 (s/n):	—	104
Powered Time (sec):	83	80.5 (S.D.)
Thrust (pct):	100	100

Configuration: Ventral off; Ball-nose; X-20 IFDS Tip pods w/camera; 3rd skid

NASA 1:	Dana		
B-52 - Pilots - LP:	52-003	Sturmthal / Reschke	Russell
Take-Off Time:	14:17		
Landing Time:	16:24		
B-52 Flight Time:	02:07		
Chase 1:	F-104A	56-0743	Gentry
Chase 2:	F5D-1	142350 (802)	Manke
Chase 3:	F-104A	56-0748	Cuthill
Chase 4:	F-104A	56-0763	Davey
Rover:	F-104N	N812NA	Krier

Purpose: Fluidic probe;
(#19) High-altitude sky brightness experiment
(#20) WTR experiment;
(#31) Fixed alpha nose experiment

Aborts: 1-A-137 15 Jul 68 Roll RAS malfunction

Notes: First launch from Railroad Valley;
Hydraulic gauge malfunction during boost;
WTR experiment not extended due to vibrations
The highest Mach number was achieved during descent from max altitude

Abort used NB-52A 52-003; Knight was the X-15 pilot for the abort

Program Flight #:	197	
Flight ID:	1-79-139	
X-15 (s/n)	56-6670	(79)
Flight Date:	21 Aug 68	
Pilot (flight #):	Dana	(15)
Launch Lake:	Railroad	
Launch Time:	09:04:48.0	
Landing Lake:	Rogers	
Landing Time:	09:14:11.3	

	Plan	Actual
Max Mach:	4.95	5.01
Max Altitude:	250,000	267,500
Speed (mph):	—	3,443
X-15 Flight Time:	—	00:09:23.3
XLR99 (s/n):	—	104
Powered Time (sec):	82.5	82.9 (S.D.)
Thrust (pct):	100	100
Configuration:	Ventral off; Ball-nose; X-20 IFDS Tip pods; 3rd skid	

NASA 1:	Manke		
B-52 - Pilots - LP:	52-003	Sturmthal / Fulton	Russell
Take-Off Time:	07:52		
Landing Time:	10:30		
B-52 Flight Time:	02:38		
Chase 1:	T-38A	59-1598	Cuthill
Chase 2:	F-104N	N811NA	Krier
Chase 3:	F-104D	57-1316	Hoag
Chase 4:	F-104A	56-0755	Gentry
Chase 5:	F-104A	56-0763	Shawler

Purpose: Fluidic probe;
(#17) MIT horizon definition phase II-2 experiment;
(#20) WTR experiment;
(#31) Fixed alpha nose experiment

Aborts: None

Notes: WTR retracted on timer due to altitude overshoot;
Last X-15 flight over 50 miles altitude
The highest Mach number was achieved during descent from max altitude

Since Dana was a NASA pilot, he did not get astronaut wings for a flight above 50 miles (the NASA standard was 62 miles)

Program Flight #:	198	
Flight ID:	1-80-140	
X-15 (s/n)	56-6670	(80)
Flight Date:	13 Sep 68	
Pilot (flight #):	Knight	(16)
Launch Lake:	Smith Ranch	
Launch Time:	11:19:23.2	
Landing Lake:	Rogers	
Landing Time:	11:30:18.7	

	Plan	Actual
Max Mach:	5.47	5.37
Max Altitude:	250,000	254,100
Speed (mph):	—	3,723
X-15 Flight Time:	—	00:10:55.5
XLR99 (s/n):	—	103
Powered Time (sec):	88	84.3 (B.O.)
Thrust (pct):	100	100
Configuration:	Ventral off; Ball-nose; X-20 IFDS Tip pods w/braces; 3rd skid	

NASA 1:	Dana		
B-52 - Pilots - LP:	52-003	Sturmthal / Miller	Dustin
Take-Off Time:	10:06		
Landing Time:	12:15		
B-52 Flight Time:	02:09		
Chase 1:	T-38A	59-1598	Twinting
Chase 2:	F-104N	N811NA	Manke
Chase 3:	F-104A	56-0748	Shawler
Chase 4:	F-104A	56-0763	Gentry
Chase 5:	F-104A	56-0790	Krier

Purpose: Fluidic probe;
(#17) MIT horizon definition phase II-2 experiment;
(#20) WTR experiment;
(#31) Fixed alpha nose experiment

Aborts: None

Notes: Emergency retract of WTR experiment;
Knight's last flight in the X-15;
The highest Mach number was achieved during descent from max altitude

Additional Chase:
Rover: F-104A 56-0755 Powell

Program Flight #:	199	
Flight ID:	1-81-141	
X-15 (s/n)	56-6670	(81)
Flight Date:	24 Oct 68	
Pilot (flight #):	Dana	(16)
Launch Lake:	Smith Ranch	
Launch Time:	10:02:47.3	
Landing Lake:	Rogers	
Landing Time:	10:14:15.3	

	Plan	Actual
Max Mach:	5.45	5.38
Max Altitude:	250,000	255,000
Speed (mph):	—	3,716
X-15 Flight Time:	—	00:11:28.0
XLR99 (s/n):	—	103
Powered Time (sec):	84	83.8 (S.D.)
Thrust (pct):	100	100
Configuration:	Ventral off; Ball-nose; X-20 IFDS Tip pods w/braces; 3rd skid	

NASA 1:	Knight		
B-52 - Pilots - LP:	52-003	Sturmthal / Miller	Russell
Take-Off Time:	08:56		
Landing Time:	11:05		
B-52 Flight Time:	02:09		
Chase 1:	T-38A	59-1598	Cuthill
Chase 2:	F-104N	N811NA	Krier
Chase 3:	F-104A	56-0740	Enovoldsen
Chase 4:	F-104A	56-0746	Evenson
Chase 5:	F-104A	56-0817	Hoag

Purpose: Fluidic probe;
(#20) WTR experiment;
(#31) Fixed alpha nose experiment

Aborts: None

Notes: WTR experiment extended but lost power;
No. 2 RCS never turned on

Last flight of the X-15 program

Additional Chase:
Rover: F-104B 57-1303 Manke

Program Flight #:	200	
Flight ID:	Not Flown	
X-15 (s/n)	56-6670	*(82)*
Flight Date:	Not Flown	
Pilot (flight #):	Knight	*(17)*

Configuration: Ventral off; Ball-nose; X-20 IFDS
Tip pods w/braces; 3rd skid
(#24) High-altitude IR background experiment
(#19) High-altitude sky brightness experiment
(#31) Fixed alpha nose experiment

Cancellation:	(1-82-142)	21 Nov 68	Flight cancelled due to NB-52A 52-003 problems. Would have been a Smith Ranch launch. X-15 transferred to the NB-52B 52-008
		27 Nov 68	Flight cancelled due to a helium leak in APU #2
Cancellation:	(1-82-142)	27 Nov 68	Flight cancelled due to hydrogen peroxide leak and other problems. X-15 transferred back to NB-52A 52-003 on 9 December. Launch lake would have been Railroad Valley.
Cancellation:	(1-82-142)	10 Dec 68	Cancelled for weather.
Cancellation:	(1-82-142)	11 Dec 68	Cancelled for weather.
Abort:	1-A-142	12 Dec 68	Last X-15 flight attempt. Aborted due to intertial guidance system failure. Launch lake would have been Railroad Valley.
Cancellation:	(1-82-143)	13 Dec 68	Cancelled for weather.
Cancellation:	(1-82-143)	17 Dec 68	Cancelled due to lack of C-130 support.
Cancellation:	(1-82-143)	18 Dec 68	Cancelled for weather.
Cancellation:	(1-82-143)	19 Dec 68	No microwave available. Flight plan changed to Hidden Hills launch lake.
Cancellation:	(1-82-143)	20 Dec 68	Bill Dana taxied an F-104 for a weather flight, but was recalled by John Manke due to snow at Edwards. Launch lake would have been Hidden Hills.
The End.		20 Dec 68	X-15 demated from NB-52A 52-003 and prepared for indefinite storage. The X-15 program ends.

APPENDIX C

PHYSICAL CHARACTERISTICS OF THE X-15 AIRPLANE

(Source: Edwin J. Saltzman, "Preliminary Full-Scale Power-Off Drag of the X-15 Airplane for Mach Numbers from 0.7 to 3.1," NASA technical memorandum X-430, December 1960; Gene J. Matranga, "Analysis of X-15 Landing Approach and Flare Characteristics Determined from the First 30 Flights," NASA technical note D-1057, July 1961; and Lawrence C. Montoya, "Drag Characteristics Obtained From Several Configurations of the Modified X-15A-2 Airplane Up to Mach 6.7," NASA technical memorandum X-2056, August 1970.) The data given are for the stub (ramjet-ready) ventral on X-15A-2.

			X-15	X-15A-2
Fuselage				
	Length (feet):		50.75	53.16
	Maximum width (feet):		7.33	7.33
	Maximum depth (feet):		4.67	4.67
	Maximum depth over canopy (feet):		4.97	4.97
	Side area, total (square feet):		215.66	221.38
	Fineness ratio:		10.91	11.38
Base area (fuselage, side fairings, verticals; square feet):			31.18	32.19
Wing				
	Airfoil section:		NASA 66005 (modified)	same
	Total area, including 94.98 square feet covered by the fuselage (square feet):		200.00	200.00
	Span (feet):		22.36	22.36
	Mean aerodynamic chord (feet):		10.27	10.27
	Root chord (feet):		14.91	14.91
	Tip chord (feet):		2.98	2.98
	Taper ratio:		0.20	0.20
	Aspect ratio:		2.50	2.50
	Sweep at 25% chord line (degrees):		25.64	25.64
	Incidence (degrees):		0	0
	Dihedral (degrees):		0	0
	Aerodynamic twist (degrees):		0	0

			X-15	X-15A-2
	Flap			
		Type:	Plain	Plain
		Area, each (square feet):	8.30	8.30
		Span, each (feet):	4.50	4.50
		Inboard chord (feet):	2.61	2.61
		Outboard chord (feet):	1.08	1.08
		Deflection (degrees)	–40/–30	–40/–30
		Ratio flap chord to wing chord:	0.22	0.22
		Ratio total flap area to wing area:	0.08	0.08
		Ratio flap span to wing semispan:	0.40	0.40
		Trailing-edge angle (degrees):	5.67	5.67
		Sweepback angle of hinge line (degrees):	0	0
Horizontal stabilizer				
	Airfoil section:		NACA 66005 (modified)	same
	Total area, including 63.29 square feet by the fuselage (square feet):		115.34	115.34
	Span (feet):		18.08	18.08
	Mean aerodynamic chord (feet):		7.05	7.05
	Root chord (feet):		10.22	10.22
	Tip chord (feet):		2.11	2.11
	Taper ratio:		0.21	0.21
	Aspect ratio:		2.83	2.83
	Sweep at 25% chord line (degrees):		45	45
	Dihedral (degrees):		–15	–15
	Ratio horizontal stabilizer area to wing area:		0.58	0.58
	Movable surface area (square feet):		51.77	51.77
	Deflection:			
		Longitudinal (degrees):	+15/–35	+15/–35

		Lateral differential, pilot authority (degrees):	±15	±15
		Lateral differential, auto-pilot authority (degrees):	±30	±30
Dorsal stabilizer				
	Airfoil section:		10-degree single wedge	same
	Total area (square feet):		40.91	40.91
	Span (feet):		4.58	4.58
	Mean aerodynamic chord (feet):		8.95	8.95
	Root chord (feet):		10.21	10.21
	Tip chord, feet		7.56	7.56
	Taper ratio:		0.74	0.74
	Aspect ratio:		0.51	0.51
	Sweep at 25% chord line (degrees):		23.41	23.41
	Ratio dorsal stabilizer to wing area:		0.20	0.20
	Movable surface area (square feet):		26.45	26.45
	Deflection (degrees):		±7.50	±7.50
	Sweepback of hinge line (degrees):		0	0
Ventral stabilizer				
	Airfoil section:		10-degree single wedge	same
	Total area (square feet):		34.41	14.46
	Span (feet):		3.83	3.83
	Mean aerodynamic chord (feet):		9.17	7.38
	Root chord (feet):		10.21	7.38
	Tip chord (feet):		8.00	7.38
	Taper ratio:		0.78	1.00
	Aspect ratio:		0.43	0.43
	Sweep at 25% chord line (degrees):		23.41	0
	Ratio ventral stabilizer to wing area:		0.17	0.08
	Movable surface area (square feet):		19.95	0
	Deflection (degrees):		±7.50	–
	Sweepback of hinge line (degrees):		0	–

Speed brake				
	Area, each (square feet):		5.37	5.37
	Mean span, each (feet):		1.60	1.60
	Chord, each (feet):		3.36	3.36
	Deflection (degrees):		35	35
	Frontal area at maximum deflection (square feet):		13.80	13.80

APPENDIX D

INDEX

Symbols

A

B

C

D

F

G

H

I

J

K

L

N

R

S

T

U

V

W

X